The ELIAS BOOK of BASEBALL RECORDS

MAJOR LEAGUE BASEBALL RECORDS

WORLD SERIES RECORDS

CHAMPIONSHIP SERIES RECORDS

DIVISION SERIES RECORDS

ALL-STAR GAME RECORDS

HALL OF FAME RECORDS

SEYMOUR SIWOFF, Editor and Publisher

500 Fifth Avenue, New York, NY 10110

A STATEMENT FROM THE PUBLISHER

THE ELIAS BOOK OF BASEBALL RECORDS is the most accurate baseball record book ever published. It is produced by the acknowledged authority for sports history, information and statistics.

THE ELIAS BOOK OF BASEBALL RECORDS contains five major sections

- REGULAR-SEASON RECORDS
- WORLD SERIES RECORDS
- CHAMPIONSHIP SERIES RECORDS
- DIVISION SERIES RECORDS
- ALL-STAR GAME RECORDS

Each section lists records in the following order:
- LIFETIME • SEASON • GAME • INNING

If a single-game record was set in a game that extended into extra innings, the record for a nine-inning game is also listed.

The index, and various tables showing annual leaders in major categories, are located at the back of the book.

YEARS: Hyphenated items are inclusive and consecutive.
CLUB, LEAGUE & INDIVIDUAL RECORDS: Generally disregard the following seasons:
　　　1918 - abbreviated due to World War I
　　　1972, 1981, 1994 & 1995 - shortened seasons
　　　1994 - League Championship Series not played
　　　1904 & 1994 - World Series not played

International Standard Book Number: 0-917050-09-6　ISBN13: 978-0-917050-09-1

Library of Congress Control Number: 2007920420

COMMISSIONERS

Kenesaw M. Landis	1920-1944
Albert B. Chandler	1945-1951
Ford C. Frick	1951-1965
William D. Eckert	1965-1968
Bowie K. Kuhn	1969-1984
Peter V. Ueberroth	1984-1989
A. Bartlett Giamatti	1989
Francis T. Vincent	1989-1992
Allan H. Selig	1998-

AMERICAN LEAGUE PRESIDENTS

B. Bancroft Johnson	1901-1927
Ernest S. Barnard	1927-1931
William Harridge	1931-1959
Joseph E. Cronin	1959-1973
Leland S. MacPhail, Jr.	1974-1983
Robert W. Brown	1984-1994
Gene A. Budig	1994-1999

NATIONAL LEAGUE PRESIDENTS

Morgan G. Bulkeley	1876
William A. Hulbert	1877-1882
Arthur H. Soden	1882
Abraham G. Mills	1883-1884
Nicholas E. Young	1885-1902
Harry C. Pulliam	1903-1909
John A. Heydler	1909
Thomas J. Lynch	1910-1913
John K. Tener	1913-1918
John A. Heydler	1918-1934
Ford C. Frick	1934-1951
Warren C. Giles	1951-1969
Charles S. Feeney	1970-1986
A. Bartlett Giamatti	1987-1989
William D. White	1989-1994
Leonard S. Coleman, Jr.	1994-1999

ABBREVIATIONS

LEAGUES

Major leagues
American League
National League
American Association
Union Association
Players League
Federal League

CLUBS

Altoona
Anaheim
Arizona
Atlanta
Baltimore
Boston
Brooklyn
Buffalo
California
Chicago
Cincinnati
Cleveland
Colorado
Columbus
Detroit
Florida
Hartford
Houston
Indianapolis
Kansas City
Los Angeles
Louisville
Milwaukee
Minnesota
Montreal
Newark
New York
Oakland
Philadelphia

Pitt	Pittsburgh
Prov	Providence
Rich	Richmond
Roch	Rochester
StL	St. Louis
StP	St. Paul
SD	San Diego
SF	San Francisco
Sea	Seattle
Syr	Syracuse
TB	Tampa Bay
Tex	Texas
Tol	Toledo
Tor	Toronto
Wash	Washington
Wil	Wilmington
Wor	Worcester

GENERAL

g	games
dec	decisions
dh	doubleheader
1g	first game
2g	second game
inn	inning
n	night game

BATTING

ab	at-bats
r	runs
h	hits
tb	total bases
1b	singles
2b	doubles
3b	triples
hr	home runs
rbi	runs batted in
sh	sacrifice hits
sf	sacrifice flies
bb	walks

hp	hit by pitch
so	strikeouts
sb	stolen bases
cs	caught stealing
lob	left on base
ba	batting average
slg	slugging percentage
pct	percentage
avg	average
DH	designated hitter

FIELDING

tc	total chances
ca	chances accepted, errorless
po	putouts
a	assists
e	errors
dp	double plays
tp	triple plays
pb	passed balls

PITCHING

lhp	left-handed pitcher
rhp	right-handed pitcher
gs	games started
cg	complete games
gf	games finished
sv	saves
sho	shutouts
era	earned run average
ip	innings pitched
er	earned runs
bfp	batters faced
hb	hit batters
wp	wild pitches
bk	balks

NATIONAL LEAGUE CLUB HISTORY

NUMBER	CLUB	YEARS
#1	Chicago	1876-
#2	Boston	1876-1952 to Milwaukee #32
#3	New York (Mutual Club)	1876
#4	Philadelphia (Athletic Club)	1876
#5	Hartford	1876-1877
#6	St. Louis	1876-1877
#7	Cincinnati	1876-1880
#8	Louisville	1876-1877
#9	Indianapolis	1878
#10	Milwaukee	1878
#11	Providence	1878-1885
#12	Buffalo	1879-1885
#13	Cleveland	1879-1884
#14	Syracuse	1879
#15	Troy	1879-1882
#16	Worcester	1880-1882
#17	Detroit	1881-1888
#18	New York	1883-1957 to San Francisco #33
#19	Philadelphia	1883-
#20	St. Louis	1885-1886
#21	Washington	1886-1889
#22	Kansas City	1886
#23	Pittsburgh	1887-
#24	Indianapolis	1887-1889
#25	Cleveland	1889-1899
#26	Brooklyn	1890-1957 to Los Angeles #34
#27	Cincinnati	1890-
#28	St. Louis	1892-
#29	Baltimore	1892-1899
#30	Louisville	1892-1899
#31	Washington	1892-1899
#32	Milwaukee	1953-1965 to Atlanta #37
#33	San Francisco	1958-
#34	Los Angeles	1958-
#35	Houston	1962-
#36	New York	1962-
#37	Atlanta	1966-
#38	Montreal	1969-2004 to Washington #44
#39	San Diego	1969-
#40	Colorado	1993-
#41	Florida	1993-
#42	Arizona	1998-
#43	Milwaukee	1998-
#44	Washington	2005-

AMERICAN LEAGUE CLUB HISTORY

NUMBER	CLUB	YEARS
# 1	Chicago	1901-
# 2	Milwaukee	1901 to St. Louis #9
# 3	Cleveland	1901-
# 4	Detroit	1901-
# 5	Washington	1901-1960 to Minnesota #13
# 6	Boston	1901-
# 7	Baltimore	1901-1902 to New York #10
# 8	Philadelphia	1901-1954 to Kansas City #12
# 9	St. Louis	1902-1953 to Baltimore #11
#10	New York	1903-
#11	Baltimore	1954-
#12	Kansas City	1955-1967 to Oakland #16
#13	Minnesota	1961-
#14	Washington	1961-1971 to Texas #20
#15	Los Angeles	1961-
#16	Oakland	1968-
#17	Kansas City	1969-
#18	Seattle	1969 to Milwaukee #19
#19	Milwaukee	1970-1997 to National League #43
#20	Texas	1972-
#21	Seattle	1977-
#22	Toronto	1977-
#23	Tampa Bay	1998-

INDIVIDUAL BATTING RECORDS

SERVICE (See INDIVIDUAL PITCHING RECORDS for pitchers' service)

Most Seasons, Lifetime
26   Deacon McGuire, AA:Tol. 1884; Clev. 88; Roch. 90; Wash. 91
      NL:Det. 85, 88; Phil. 86-88; Wash. 92-99; Brk. 1899-1901
      AL:Det. 02-03, 12; NY 04-07; Bos. 07-08; Clev. 08, 10

Most Seasons, Consecutive, Lifetime
25   Bobby Wallace, NL:Clev. 1894-98; StL. 1899-1901, 17-18; AL:StL. 1902-16
      Eddie Collins, AL:Phil. 1906-14, 27-30; Chi. 15-26
      Rickey Henderson, AL:Oak.. 1979-84, 89-95, 98; NY 85-89; Tor. 93; Ana. 97; Sea. 2000;
            Bos. 02; NL:SD 96-97, 2001; NY 99-2000; LA 03

Most Seasons, League
25   Eddie Collins, AL:Phil. 1906-14, 27-30; Chi. 15-26
24   Pete Rose, NL:Cin. 1963-78, 84-86; Phil. 79-83; Mtl. 84

Most Seasons, Consecutive, League
25   Eddie Collins, AL:Phil. 1906-14, 27-30; Chi. 15-26
24   Pete Rose, NL:Cin. 1963-78, 84-86; Phil. 79-83; Mtl. 84

Most Leagues, Lifetime
4   By many players. Last:
     Lave Cross, AA 1887-89, 91; Lou. 1887-88; Phil. 1889, 91; PL 1890; Phil. 1890;
           NL 1892-1900; Phil. 1892-97; StL. 1898-1900; Clev. 1899; Brk. 1900;
           AL 1901-07; Phil. 1901-05; Wash. 1906-07

Most Clubs, Lifetime
12   Deacon McGuire, AA:Tol. 1884; Clev. 88; Roch. 90; Wash. 91; NL:Det. 85, 88; Phil. 86-88;
            Wash. 92-99; Brk. 1899-1901; AL:Det. 02-03, 12; NY 04-07; Bos. 07-08; Clev. 08, 10
      Since 1900:
11   Todd Zeile, NL:StL.1989-95; Chi. 95; Phil. 96; LA 97-98; Fla. 98; NY 2000-01, 04;
            Col. 02; Mtl. 03; AL:Balt. 1996; Tex. 98-99; NY 2003

Most Clubs, League
9   Dan Brouthers, NL:Troy 1879-80; Buff. 81-85; Det. 86-88; Bos. 89; Brk. 92-93;Balt. 94-95;
           Lou. 95; Phil. 96; NY 1904
      Since 1900:
8   Juan Beniquez, AL:Bos. 1971-72, 74-75; Tex. 76-78; NY 79; Sea. 80;
           Cal. 81-85; Balt. 86; KC 87; Tor. 87-88
     Ruben Sierra, AL:Tex. 1986-92, 2000-01, 03; Oak. 92-95; NY 95-96, 2003-05;
           Det. 96; Tor. 97; Chi. 98; Sea. 2002; Minn. 2006
     Chris Jones, NL:Cin. 1991; Hou. 92; Col. 93-94; NY 95-96; SD 97; Ari. 98; SF 98, Mil. 2000
     Todd Zeile, NL:StL.1989-95; Chi. 95; Phil. 96; LA 97-98; Fla. 98; NY 2000-01, 04; Col. 02; Mtl. 03
     Lenny Harris, NL:Cin. 1988-89, 95-98; LA 89-93; NY 98, 2000-01; Col. 99;
           Ari. 99-2000; Mil. 02, Chi. 03; Fla. 03-05

Most Clubs, Season
4   By many players; Last:
     Jose Bautista, AL:Balt.-TB-KC; NL:Pitt. 2004

Most Clubs, League, Season
4   Tom Dowse, NL:Lou-Cin.-Phil.-Wash. 1892
     Frank Huelsman, AL:Chi.Det.-StL.-Wash. 1904
     Paul Lehner, AL:Phil.-Chi.-StL.-Clev. 1951
     Ted Gray, AL:Chi.-Clev.-NY-Balt. 1955

Most Clubs, One Day
2   Max Flack, NL:Chi.-StL. May 30, 1922
     Cliff Heathcote, NL:StL.-Chi. May 30, 1922
     (Flack & Heathcote traded for each other between games of doubleheader)
     Joel Youngblood, NL:NY-Mtl. Aug. 4, 1982

One Club, Most Seasons
23   Brooks Robinson, AL:Balt. 1955-77
      Carl Yastrzemski, AL:Bos. 1961-83
22   Cap Anson, NL:Chi. 1876-97
      Mel Ott, NL:NY 1926-47
      Stan Musial, NL:StL. 1941-63 (1945 Military Service)

One Club, Most Seasons, Consecutive
23   Brooks Robinson, AL:Balt. 1955-77
      Carl Yastrzemski, AL:Bos. 1961-83
22   Cap Anson, NL:Chi. 1876-97
      Mel Ott, NL:NY 1926-47
      Stan Musial, NL:StL. 1941-63 (1945 Military Service)

POSITIONS

Most Positions, Lifetime
| 9 | By many players |

Most Positions, League
| 9 | By many players |

Played Nine Positions, Season, Since 1900
9	Sam Mertes, AL:Chi. 1902
	Jack Rothrock, AL:Bos. 1928
	Bert Campaneris, AL:KC 1965
	Cesar Tovar, AL:Minn. 1968
	Shane Halter, AL:Det. 2000
	Scott Sheldon, AL:Tex. 2000
	Jimmy Walsh, NL:Phil. 1911
	Gene Paulette, NL:StL. 1918
	Jose Oquendo, NL:StL. 1988

Played Nine Positions, Game
9	Bert Campaneris, AL:KC Sept. 8, 1965 (13 inn)
	Cesar Tovar, AL:Minn. Sept. 22, 1968
	Scott Sheldon, AL:Tex. Sept. 6, 2000
	Shane Halter, AL:Det. Oct. 1, 2000

Most Games, One Day, One Position
| 3 | Clyde Barnhart, NL:Pitt. Oct. 2, 1920 (3b) |
| | Pat Duncan, NL:Cin. Oct. 2, 1920 (lf) |

BATTING AVERAGE

Most Seasons Leading Major Leagues
| 11 | Ty Cobb, AL:Det. 1907, 09-15, 17-19 |

Most Seasons, Consecutive, Leading Major Leagues
| 7 | Ty Cobb, AL:Det. 1909-15 |

Most Seasons Leading League
12	Ty Cobb, AL:Det. 1907-15, 17-19
8	Honus Wagner, NL:Pitt. 1900, 03-04, 06-09, 11
	Tony Gwynn, NL:SD 1984, 87-89, 94-97

Most Seasons, Consecutive, Leading League
| 9 | Ty Cobb, AL:Det. 1907-15 |
| 6 | Rogers Hornsby, NL:StL. 1920-25 |

Highest Batting Average, Lifetime, Since 1900 (Minimum: 5000 at-bats)
| .367 | Ty Cobb, AL:Det. 1905-26; Phil. 27-28 |
| .359 | Rogers Hornsby, NL:StL. 1915-26, 33; NY 27; Bos. 28; Chi. 29-32 |

Highest Batting Average, Season
.442	Tip O'Neill, AA:StL. 1887
.438	Hugh Duffy, NL:Bos. 1894
	Since 1900:
.424	Rogers Hornsby, NL:StL. 1924
.422	Napoleon Lajoie, AL:Phil. 1901

Most Seasons, .400 or higher Batting Average (Minimum: 400 at-bats or 500 plate appearances)
3	Jesse Burkett, NL:Clev. 1895-96; StL. 99
	Rogers Hornsby, NL:StL. 1922, 24-25
	Ty Cobb, AL:Det. 1911-12, 22

Most Seasons, Consecutive, .400 or higher Batting Average (Minimum: 400 at-bats or 500 plate appearances)
2	Jesse Burkett, NL:Clev. 1895-96
	Rogers Hornsby, NL:StL. 1924-25
	Ty Cobb, AL:Det. 1911-12

Most Seasons, .300 or higher Batting Average (Minimum: 400 at-bats or 500 plate appearances)
| 19 | Ty Cobb, AL:Det. 1907-13, 15-25; Phil. 27 |
| 17 | Stan Musial, NL:StL. 1942-44, 46-58, 62 |

Most Seasons, Consecutive, .300 or higher Batting Average (Minimum: 400 at-bats or 500 plate appearances)
16	Honus Wagner, NL:Lou. 1898-99; Pitt. 1900-13
	Tony Gwynn, NL:SD 1984-99
12	Lou Gehrig, AL:NY 1926-37

Lowest Batting Average, Lifetime (Minimum: 5000 at-bats)
| .218 | George McBride, AL:Mil. 1901, Wash. 08-20, NL:Pitt. 1905; StL. 05-06 |

Lowest Batting Average, League (Minimum: 5000 at-bats)
| .224 | Ed Brinkman, AL:Wash. 1961-70; Det. 71-74; Tex.-NY 75 |
| .232 | Mickey Doolan, NL:Phil. 1905-13; Chi.-NY 16; Brk. 18 |

Lowest Batting Average, Season (Minimum: 400 at-bats or 500 plate appearances)
.166 Jim Canavan, NL:Chi. 1892 (439 at-bats)
    Since 1900:
.179 Rob Deer, AL:Det. 1991 (448 at-bats)
.184 Bill Hallman, NL:Phil. 1901 (445 at-bats)

SLUGGING PERCENTAGE

Most Seasons Leading Major Leagues
12 Babe Ruth, AL:Bos. 1918-19; NY 20-21, 23-24, 26-31

Most Seasons, Consecutive, Leading Major Leagues
6 Babe Ruth, AL:NY 1926-31

Most Seasons Leading League
13 Babe Ruth, AL:Bos. 1918-19; NY 20-24, 26-31
9 Rogers Hornsby, NL:StL. 1917, 20-25; Bos. 28; Chi. 29

Most Seasons, Consecutive, Leading League
7 Babe Ruth, AL:Bos. 1918-19; NY 20-24
6 Dan Brouthers, NL:Buff. 1881-85, Det. 86
  Rogers Hornsby, NL:StL. 1920-25

Highest Slugging Percentage, Lifetime (Minimum: 5000 at-bats)
.690 Babe Ruth, AL:Bos. 1914-19; NY 20-34 NL:Bos. 35

Highest Slugging Percentage, League (Minimum: 5000 at-bats)
.692 Babe Ruth, AL:Bos. 1914-19; NY 20-34
.608 Barry Bonds, NL:Pitt. 1986-92; SF 93-2006

Highest Slugging Percentage, Season (Minimum: 400 at-bats or 500 plate appearances)
.863 Barry Bonds, NL:SF 2001
.849 Babe Ruth, AL:NY 1920

Most Seasons, .700 or higher Slugging Percentage (Minimum: 400 at-bats or 500 plate appearances)
9 Babe Ruth, AL:NY 1920-21, 23-24, 26-28, 30-31
4 Barry Bonds, NL:SF 2001-04

Most Seasons, Consecutive, .700 or higher Slugging Percentage (Minimum: 400 at-bats or 500 plate appearances)
4 Barry Bonds, NL:SF 2001-04
3 Babe Ruth, AL:NY 1926-28

Most Seasons, .600 or higher Slugging Percentage (Minimum: 400 at-bats or 500 plate appearances)
13 Babe Ruth, AL:Bos. 1919; NY 20-24, 26-32
9 Barry Bonds, NL:Pitt. 1992; SF 1993, 96, 98, 2000-04

Most Seasons, Consecutive, .600 or higher Slugging Percentage (Minimum: 400 at-bats or 500 plate appearances)
7 Babe Ruth, AL:NY 1926-32
5 Rogers Hornsby, NL:StL. 1921-25
  Barry Bonds, NL:SF 2000-04

Lowest Slugging Percentage, Lifetime (Minimum: 5000 at-bats)
.264 George McBride, AL:Mil. 1901; Wash. 08-20 NL:Pitt.-StL. 05; StL. 06

Lowest Slugging Percentage, League (Minimum: 5000 at-bats)
.280 Mark Belanger, AL:Balt. 1965-81
.307 Mickey Doolan, NL:Phil. 1905-11; Chi.-NY 16; Brk. 18

Lowest Slugging Percentage, Season (Minimum: 400 at-bats or 500 plate appearances)
.197 Jim Lillie, NL:KC 1886
    Since 1900:
.206 Pete Childs, NL:Phil. 1902
.225 Charlie Moran, AL:Wash.-StL. 1904

PLATE APPEARANCES

Most Plate Appearances, Lifetime
15,890 Pete Rose, NL:Cin. 1963-78, 84-86; Phil. 79-83; Mtl. 84

Most Plate Appearances, League
15,890 Pete Rose, NL:Cin. 1963-78, 84-86; Phil. 79-83; Mtl. 84
13,992 Carl Yastrzemski, AL:Bos. 1961-83

Most Plate Appearances, Season
773 Len Dykstra, NL:Phil. 1993
762 Ichiro Suzuki, AL:Sea. 2004

Most Plate Appearances, Game

8   By many players; Last:
Mike Cameron, NL:Cin. May 19, 1999
Darryl Hamilton, AL:Mil. Aug. 28, 1992
Extra-Inning Game:

12   Felix Millan, NL:NY Sept. 11, 1974 (25 inn)
John Milner, NL:NY Sept. 11, 1974 (25 inn)

11   Rudy Law, AL:Chi. May 8, 1984 (25 inn)
Carlton Fisk, AL:Chi. May 8, 1984 (25 inn)
Harold Baines, AL:Chi. May 8, 1984 (25 inn)

Most Plate Appearances, Inning

3   Larry Murphy, AA:Wash. June 17, 1891 (1st)
Marty Callaghan, NL:Chi. Aug. 25, 1922 (4th)
Billy Cox, NL:Brk. May 21, 1952 (1st)
Pee Wee Reese, NL:Brk. May 21, 1952 (1st)
Duke Snider, NL:Brk. May 21, 1952 (1st)
Gil Hodges, NL:Brk. Aug. 8, 1954 (8th)
Dusty Baker, NL:Atl. Sept. 20, 1972 (2nd)
Luis Quinones, NL:Cin. Aug. 3, 1989 (1st)
Mariano Duncan, NL:Cin. Aug. 3, 1989 (1st)
Stan Javier, NL:SF July 15, 1997 (7th)
Ted Williams, AL:Bos. July 4, 1948 (7th)
Sammy White AL:Bos. June 18, 1953 (7th)
Gene Stephens, AL:Bos. June 18, 1953 (7th)
Tom Umphlett, AL:Bos. June 18, 1953 (7th)
Johnny Lipon, AL:Bos. June 18, 1953 (7th)
George Kell, AL:Bos. June 18, 1953 (7th)
Darryl Hamilton, AL:Tex. Apr. 19, 1996 (8th)
Johnny Damon, AL:Bos. June 27, 2003 (1st)

REACHING BASE SAFELY

Most Times Reaching Base Safely, Lifetime
5929   Pete Rose, NL:Cin. 1963-78, 84-86; Phil. 79-83; Mtl. 84

Most Times Reaching Base Safely, League
5929   Pete Rose, NL:Cin. 1963-78, 84-86; Phil. 79-83; Mtl. 84
5534   Ty Cobb, AL:Det. 1905-26; Phil. 27-28

Most Times Reaching Base Safely, Season
Since 1900:
379   Babe Ruth, AL:NY 1923
376   Barry Bonds, NL:SF 2004

Most Times Reaching Base Safely, Game
8   Piggy Ward, NL:Cin. June 18, 1893
Since 1900:
7   Ben Chapman, AL:NY May 24, 1936
Cliff Heathcote, NL:Chi. Aug. 25, 1922
Cookie Lavagetto, NL:Brk. Sept. 23(1g), 1939
Mel Ott, NL:NY Apr. 30, 1944
Rennie Stennett, NL:Pitt. Sept. 16, 1975
Sean Casey, NL:Cin. May 19, 1999
Extra-Inning Game:
9   Max Carey, NL:Pitt. July 7, 1922 (18 inn)
Johnny Burnett, AL:Clev. July 10, 1932 (18 inn)

Most Times Reaching Base Safely, Inning
3   Ned Williamson, NL:Chi. Sept. 6, 1883 (7th)
Tommy Burns, NL:Chi. Sept. 6, 1883 (7th)
Fred Pfeffer, NL:.Chi. Sept. 6, 1883 (7th)
Herman Long, NL:Bos. June 18, 1894 (1g; 1st)
Bobby Lowe, NL:Bos. June 18, 1894 (1g;1st)
Hugh Duffy, NL:Bos. June 18, 1894 (1g;1st)
Pee Wee Reese, NL:Brk. May 21, 1952 (1st)
Sammy White, AL:Bos. June 18, 1953 (7th)
Gene Stephens, AL:Bos. June 18, 1953 (7th)
Tom Umphlett, AL:Bos. June 18, 1953 (7th)
Johnny Damon, AL:Bos. June 27, 2003 (1st)

GAMES

Most Seasons Leading Major Leagues
8   Cal Ripken, AL:Balt. 1983-84, 87, 91-93, 96-97

Most Seasons, Consecutive, Leading Major Leagues
3   Steve Garvey, NL:LA 1980-82
    Juan Pierre, NL:Fla. 2004-05; Chi. 06
    Cal Ripken, AL:Balt. 1991-93
    Hideki Matsui, AL:NY 2003-05
    Miguel Tejada, AL:Balt. 2004-06

Most Seasons Leading League
9   Cal Ripken, AL:Balt. 1983-84, 87, 89, 91-93, 96-97
6   Ernie Banks, NL:Chi. 1954-55, 57-60
    Steve Garvey, NL:LA 1977-78, 80-82; SD 85

Most Seasons, Consecutive, Leading League
4   Del Pratt, AL:StL. 1913-16
    Brooks Robinson, AL:Balt. 1961-64
    Ernie Banks, NL:Chi. 1957-60
    Dale Murphy, NL:Atl. 1982-85
    Juan Pierre, NL:Fla. 2003-05; Chi. 06

Most Games, Lifetime
3562   Pete Rose, NL:Cin. 1963-78, 84-86 Phil. 79-83; Mtl. 84
3308   Carl Yastrzemski, AL:Bos. 1961-83

Most Games, Consecutive, Lifetime
2632   Cal Ripken, AL:Balt. May 30, 1982-Sept. 19, 1998
1207   Steve Garvey, NL:LA-SD Sept. 2, 1975-July 29(1g), 1983

Most Games, One Club
3308   Carl Yastrzemski, AL:Bos. 1961-83
3076   Hank Aaron, NL:Mil./Atl. 1954-74

Most Games, Season
165   Maury Wills, NL:LA 1962
164   Cesar Tovar, AL:Minn. 1967

Most Seasons, 150 or more Games
17   Pete Rose, NL:Cin. 1963, 65-66, 69-78; Phil. 79-80, 82-83
15   Cal Ripken, AL:Balt. 1982-93, 96-98

Most Seasons, Consecutive, 150 or more Games
13   Willie Mays, NL:NY/SF 1954-66
12   Cal Ripken, AL:Balt. 1982-93

Most Seasons, 100 or more Games, Lifetime
23   Pete Rose, NL:Cin. 1963-78, 84-85; Phil. 79-83; Mtl. 84
22   Carl Yastrzemski, AL:Bos. 1961-80, 82-83

Most Seasons, Consecutive. 100 or more Games
23   Pete Rose, NL:Cin. 1963-78, 84-85; Phil. 79-83; Mtl. 84
20   Carl Yastrzemski AL:Bos. 1961-80

Most Games, One Day, Since 1900
3   Clyde Barnhart, NL:Pitt. Oct. 2, 1920
    Pat Duncan, NL:Cin. Oct. 2, 1920
    Fred Nicholson, NL:Pitt. Oct. 2, 1920
    Morrie Rath, NL:Cin. Oct. 2, 1920
    Jim Tierney, NL:Pitt. Oct. 2, 1920

AT-BATS

Most Seasons Leading Major Leagues
6   Doc Cramer, AL:Phil. 1933-34; Bos. 38, 40; Wash. 41; Det. 42

Most Seasons, Consecutive, Leading Major Leagues
3   Doc Cramer, AL:Bos. 1940-Wash. 41-Det. 42
    Dave Cash, NL:Phil. 1974-76

Most Seasons Leading League
7   Doc Cramer, AL:Phil. 1933-35; Bos. 38, 40; Wash. 41; Det. 42
4   Abner Dalrymple, NL:Chi. 1880, 82, 84-85
    Pete Rose, NL:Cin. 1965, 72-73, 77

Most Seasons, Consecutive, Leading League
3   Sparky Adams, NL:Chi. 1925-27
    Dave Cash, NL:Phil. 1974-76
    Doc Cramer, AL:Phil. 1933-35; Bos. 40; Wash. 41; Det. 42
    Bobby Richardson, AL:NY 1962-64
    Ichiro Suzuki, AL:Sea. 2004-06

Most At-Bats, Lifetime
14,053	Pete Rose, NL:Cin. 1963-78, 84-86; Phil. 79-83; Mtl. 84
11,988	Carl Yastrzemski, AL:Bos. 1961-83

Most At-Bats, Season
705	Willie Wilson, AL:KC 1980
701	Juan Samuel, NL:Phil. 1984

Most Seasons, 600 or more At-Bats
17	Pete Rose, NL:Cin. 1963, 65-66, 68-78; Phil. 79-80, 82
13	Cal Ripken, AL:Balt. 1983-87, 89-93, 96-98

Most Seasons, Consecutive, 600 or more At-Bats
13	Pete Rose, NL:Cin. 1968-78; Phil. 79-80
12	Nellie Fox, AL:Chi. 1951-62

Most At-Bats, Game
8	By many NL players prior to 1900
7	By many players since 1900

Extra-Inning Game:
11	Carson Bigbee, NL:Pitt. Aug. 22, 1917 (22 inn)
	Charlie Pick, NL:Bos. May 1, 1920 (26 inn)
	Tony Boeckel, NL:Bos. May 1, 1920 (26 inn)
	Ralph Garr, NL:Atl. May 4, 1973 (20 inn)
	Dave Schneck, NL:NY Sept. 11, 1974 (25 inn)
	Dave Cash, NL:Mtl. May 21, 1977 (21 inn)
	Johnny Burnett, AL:Clev. July 10, 1932 (18 inn)
	Edward Morgan, AL:Clev. July 10, 1932 (18 inn)
	Irv Hall, AL:Phil. July 21, 1945 (24 inn)
	Bobby Richardson, AL:NY June 24, 1962 (22 inn)
	Cecil Cooper, AL:Mil. May 8 1984 (25 inn)
	Rudy Law, AL:Chi. May 8, 1984 (25 inn)
	Carlton Fisk, AL:Chi. May 8, 1984 (25 inn)
	Julio Cruz, AL:Chi. May 8, 1984 (25 inn)

Most At-Bats, Doubleheader
13	Rabbit Maranville, NL:Pitt. Aug. 8, 1922
	Billy Herman, NL:Chi. Aug. 21, 1935
	Dave Philley, AL:Chi. May 30, 1950

Extra Innings:
14	Joe Christopher, NL:NY May 31, 1964 (32 inn)
	Jim Hickman, NL:NY May 31, 1964 (32 inn)
	Ed Kranepool, NL:NY May 31, 1964 (32 inn)
	Roy McMillan, NL:NY May 31, 1964 (32 inn)
	Frank Thomas, NL:NY May 31, 1964 (32 inn)
	Jesus Alou, NL:SF May 31, 1964 (32 inn)
	Rick Monday, AL:KC June 17, 1967 (28 inn)
	Ramon Webster, AL:KC June 17, 1967 (28 inn)

Most At-Bats, Inning
3	By many players; Last:
	Johnny Damon, AL:Bos. June 27, 2003 (1st)
	Luis Quinones, NL:Cin. Aug. 3, 1989 (1st)

RUNS

Most Seasons Leading Major Leagues
8	Babe Ruth, AL:Bos. 1919; NY 20-21, 23-24, 26-28

Most Seasons, Consecutive, Leading Major Leagues
3	Eddie Collins, AL:Phil. 1912-14
	Babe Ruth, AL:Bos. 1919; NY 20-21, 26-28
	Ted Williams, AL:Bos. 1940-42
	Mickey Mantle, AL:NY 1956-58
	Pete Rose, NL:Cin. 1974-76
	Albert Pujols, NL:StL. 2003-05

Most Seasons Leading League
8	Babe Ruth, AL:Bos. 1919; NY 20-21, 23-24, 26-28
5	George Burns, NL:NY 1914, 16-17, 19-20
	Rogers Hornsby, NL:StL. 1921-22, 24; NY 27; Chi. 29
	Stan Musial, NL:StL. 1946, 48, 51-52, 54

Most Seasons, Consecutive, Leading League
3	King Kelly, NL:Chi. 1884-86
	Chuck Klein, NL:Phil. 1930-32
	Duke Snider, NL:Brk. 1953-55
	Pete Rose, NL:Cin. 1974-76
	Albert Pujols, NL:StL. 2003-05
	Ty Cobb, AL:Det. 1909-11
	Eddie Collins, AL:Phil. 1912-14
	Babe Ruth, AL:Bos. 1919-NY 20-21; 26-28
	Ted Williams, AL:Bos. 1940-42
	Mickey Mantle, AL:NY 1956-58

Most Runs Scored, Lifetime
2295	Rickey Henderson, AL:Oak.. 1979-84, 89-95, 98; NY 85-89; Tor. 93; Ana. 97; Sea. 2000; Bos. 02; NL:SD 96-97, 2001; NY 99-2000; LA 03

Most Runs Scored, League
2245	Ty Cobb, AL:Det. 1905-26; Phil. 27-28
2165	Pete Rose, NL:Cin. 1963-78, 84-86; Phil. 79-83; Mtl. 84

Most Runs Scored, Season
196	Billy Hamilton, NL:Phil. 1894
	Since 1900:
177	Babe Ruth, AL:NY 1921
158	Chuck Klein, NL:Phil. 1930

Most Seasons, 100 or more Runs Scored
15	Hank Aaron, NL:Mil./Atl. 1955-70
13	Lou Gehrig, AL:NY 1926-38

Most Seasons, Consecutive, 100 or more Runs Scored
13	Lou Gehrig, AL:NY 1926-38
	Hank Aaron, NL:Mil./Atl. 1955-67

Most Runs Scored, Game
7	Guy Hecker, AA:Lou. Aug. 15(2g), 1886
6	Jim Whitney, NL:Bos. June 9, 1883
	Cap Anson, NL:Chi. Aug. 24, 1886
	Mike Tiernan, NL:NY June 15, 1887
	King Kelly, NL:Bos. Aug. 27, 1887
	Ezra Sutton, NL:Bos. Aug. 27, 1887
	Jimmy Ryan, NL:Chi. July 25, 1894
	Bobby Lowe, NL:Bos. May 3, 1895
	Ginger Beaumont, NL:Pitt. July 22, 1899
	Mel Ott, NL:NY Aug. 4(2g), 1934; Apr. 30(1g), 1944
	Frank Torre, NL:Mil. Sept. 2(1g), 1957
	Edgardo Alfonzo, NL:NY Aug. 30, 1999
	Shawn Green, NL:LA May 23, 2002
	Johnny Pesky, AL:Bos. May 8, 1946
	Spike Owen, AL:Bos. Aug. 21, 1986
	Joe Randa, AL:KC Sept. 9(1g), 2004

Most Games, Consecutive, Runs Scored
24	Billy Hamilton, NL:Phil. July 6-Aug. 2, 1894 (35 runs)
	Since 1900:
18	Red Rolfe, AL:NY Aug. 9-25, 1939 (30 runs)
	Kenny Lofton, AL:Clev. Aug. 15-Sept. 3, 2000 (26 runs)
17	Ted Kluszewski, NL:Cin. Aug. 27-Sept. 13, 1954 (24 runs)

Most Runs Scored, Inning
3	Tommy Burns, NL:Chi. Sept. 6, 1883 (7th)
	Ned Williamson, NL:Chi. Sept. 6, 1883 (7th)
	Since 1900:
3	Sammy White, AL:Bos. June 18, 1953 (7th)
2	By many NL players

HITS

Most Seasons Leading Major Leagues
7	Ty Cobb, AL:Det. 1907, 09, 11-12, 15, 17, 19
	Pete Rose, NL:Cin. 1965, 68, 70, 72-73, 76; Phil. 81

Most Seasons, Consecutive, Leading Major Leagues
2	Dan Brouthers, NL:Buff. 1882-83
	Jesse Burkett, NL:Clev. 1895-96
	Ty Cobb, AL:Det. 1911-12
	Kirby Puckett, AL:Minn. 1988-89
	Ginger Beaumont, NL:Pitt. 1902-03
	Chuck Klein, NL:Phil. 1932-33
	Stan Musial, NL:StL. 1948-49
	Pete Rose, NL:Cin. 1972-73
	Tony Gwynn, NL:SD 1994-95

Most Seasons Leading League
8	Ty Cobb, AL:Det. 1907-09, 11-12, 15, 17, 19
7	Pete Rose, NL:Cin. 1965, 68, 70, 72-73, 76; Phil. 81
	Tony Gwynn, NL:SD 1984, 86-87, 89, 94-95, 97

Most Seasons, Consecutive, Leading League
3	Ty Cobb, AL:Det. 1907-09
	Tony Oliva, AL:Minn. 1964-66
	Kirby Puckett, AL:Minn. 1987-89
	Ginger Beaumont, NL:Pitt. 1902-04
	Rogers Hornsby, NL:StL. 1920-22
	Frank McCormick, NL:Cin. 1938-40

Most Hits, Lifetime
4256	Pete Rose, NL:Cin. 1963-78, 84-86; Phil. 79-83; Mtl. 84
4191	Ty Cobb, AL:Det. 1905-26; Phil. 27-28

Most Hits, Season
262	Ichiro Suzuki, AL:Sea. 2004
254	Lefty O'Doul, NL:Phil. 1929
	Bill Terry, NL:NY 1930

Most Seasons, 200 or more Hits
10	Pete Rose, NL:Cin. 1965-66, 68-70, 73, 75-77; Phil. 79
9	Ty Cobb, AL:Det. 1907, 09, 11-12, 15-17, 22, 24

Most Seasons, Consecutive, 200 or more Hits
8	Willie Keeler, NL:Balt. 1894-98, Brk. 99-1901
	Since 1900:
7	Wade Boggs, AL:Bos. 1983-89
5	Chuck Klein, NL:Phil. 1929-33

Most Hits, Consecutive, Season
12	Mike Higgins, AL:Bos. June 19-21, 1938 (2-bb)
	Walt Dropo, AL:Det. July 14-15, 1952
10	Ed Delahanty, NL:Phil. July 13-14, 1897 (1-bb)
	Jake Gettman, NL:Wash. Sept. 10-11, 1897
	Ed Konetchy, NL:Brk. June 28-July 1, 1919
	Kiki Cuyler, NL:Pitt. Sept. 18-21, 1925 (1-bb)
	Chick Hafey, NL:StL. July 6-9, 1929 (2-bb)
	Joe Medwick, NL:StL. July 19-21, 1936 (1-bb)
	Buddy Hassett, NL:Bos. June 9(2g)-14, 1940 (1-bb)
	Woody Williams, NL:Cin. Sept. 5-6, 1943 (1-bb)
	Bip Roberts, NL:Cin. Sept. 19-23, 1992
	Matt Diaz, NL:Atl. Aug. 12-14, 2006

Most Hits, Game
7	Wilbert Robinson, NL:Balt. June 10(1g), 1892
	Rennie Stennett, NL:Pitt. Sept. 16, 1975
6	By many AL players; Last:
	Raul Ibanez, AL:Sea. Sept. 22, 2004
	Extra-Inning Game:
9	Johnny Burnett, AL:Clev. July 10, 1932 (18 inn)

Most Hits, Consecutive, Game
7	Wilbert Robinson, NL:Balt. June 10(1g), 1892
	Rennie Stennett, NL:Pitt. Sept. 16, 1975
6	By many AL players
	Extra-Inning Game:
7	Cesar Gutierrez, AL:Det. June 21, 1970 (2g, 12 inn)

Most Hits, First Major League Game
5   Fred Clarke, NL:Lou. June 30, 1894 (1-3b)
    Since 1900:
4   Ray Jansen, AL:StL. Sept. 30, 1910
    Art Shires, AL:Chi. Aug. 20, 1928 (1-3b)
    Russ Van Atta, AL:NY Apr. 25, 1933
    Spook Jacobs, AL:Phil. Apr. 13, 1954
    Ted Cox, AL:Bos. Sept. 18, 1977 (1-2b)
    Kirby Puckett, AL:Minn. May 8, 1984
    Billy Bean, AL:Det. Apr. 25, 1987 (2-2b)
    Casey Stengel, NL:Brk. Sept. 17, 1912
    Ed Freed, NL:Phil. Sept 11, 1942 (2-2b, 1-3b)
    Willie McCovey, NL:SF July 30, 1959 (2-3b)
    Mack Jones, NL:Mil. July 13, 1961 (1-2b)
    Delino DeShields, NL:Mtl. Apr. 9, 1990 (1-2b)
    Derrick Gibson, NL:Col. Sept. 8, 1998 (1-2b)
    Extra-Inning Game:
5   Cecil Travis, AL:Wash. May 16, 1933 (12 inn)

Most Games, 6 or more Hits, Lifetime
2   Cal McVey, NL:Chi. July 22-25, 1876 (cons)
    Ed Delahanty, PL:Clev. June 2, 1890; NL:Phil. June 16, 1894
    Jim Bottomley, NL:StL. Sept. 16, 1924, Aug. 5, 1931
    Jimmie Foxx, AL:Phil. May 30, 1930 (13 inn), July 10, 1932 (18 inn)
    Doc Cramer, AL:Phil. June 20, 1932, July 13(1g), 1935
    Kirby Puckett, AL:Minn. Aug. 30, 1987; May 23, 1991 (11 inn)

Most Games, 5 or more Hits, Lifetime
14   Ty Cobb, AL:Det. 1905-26; Phil. 27-28
10   Willie Keeler, NL:NY 1892-93, 1910; Brk. 93, 99-1902; Balt. 94-98
    Pete Rose, NL:Cin. 1963-78, 84-86; Phil. 79-83; Mtl. 84

Most Games, 5 or more Hits, Season
4   Willie Keeler, NL:Balt. July 17, Aug. 14, Sept. 3, 6, 1897
    Stan Musial, NL:StL. Apr. 30, May 19, June 22, Sept. 22, 1948
    Tony Gwynn, NL:SD Apr. 18, 30, July 27, Aug. 4, 1993
    Ty Cobb, AL:Det. May 7, July 7, 12, 17, 1922
    Ichiro Suzuki, AL:Sea. July 29, Aug. 3(1g), Sept. 4, 21, 2004

Most Games, 1 or more Hits, Season
135   Rogers Hornsby, NL:StL. 1922 (154 g)
    Chuck Klein, NL:Phil. 1930 (156 g)
    Wade Boggs, AL:Bos. 1985 (161 g)
    Derek Jeter, AL:NY 1999 (158 g)
    Ichiro Suzuki, AL:Sea. 2001 (157 g)

Most Games, Consecutive, 1 or more Hits, Lifetime
56   Joe DiMaggio, AL:NY May 15-July 16, 1941
45   Willie Keeler, NL:Balt. Sept 26, 1896-June 18, 1897
    NL Since 1900:
44   Pete Rose, NL:Cin. June 14-July 31, 1978

Most Games, Consecutive, 1 or more Hits, Season
56   Joe DiMaggio, AL:NY May 15-July 16, 1941
44   Willie Keeler, NL:Balt. Apr. 22-June 18, 1897
    Pete Rose, NL:Cin. June 14-July 31, 1978

Most Games, Consecutive, 1 or more Hits, Start of Season
44   Willie Keeler, NL:Balt. Apr. 22-June 18, 1897
    Since 1900:
34   George Sisler, AL:StL. Apr. 14-May 19, 1925
25   Charlie Grimm, NL:Pitt. Apr. 17-May 16, 1923

Most Hits, 2 Consecutive Games
12   Cal McVey, NL:Chi. July 22-25, 1876
    Since 1900:
11   Johnny Burnett, AL:Clev. July 9-10, 1932
10   Roberto Clemente, NL:Pitt. Aug. 22-23, 1970
    Rennie Stennett, NL:Pitt. Sept. 16-17, 1975
    Mike Benjamin, NL:SF June 13-14, 1995

Most Hits, Doubleheader
9   Fred Carroll, AA:Pitt. July 5, 1886
    Wilbert Robinson, NL:Balt. June 10, 1892
    Joe Kelley, NL:Balt. Sept. 3, 1894 (cons)
    Fred Lindstrom, NL:NY June 25, 1928
    Bill Terry, NL:NY June 18, 1929
    Ray Morehart, AL:Chi. Aug. 31, 1926
    George Case, AL:Wash. July 4, 1940
    Lee Thomas, AL:LA Sept. 5, 1961

Most Hits, 3 Consecutive Games
14	Willie Keeler, NL:Balt. Sept. 3-6, 1897
	Mike Benjamin, NL:SF June 11-14, 1995
13	Joe Cronin, AL:Wash. June. 19-22, 1933
	Walt Dropo, AL:Det. July 14-15, 1952
	Tim Salmon, AL:Cal. May 10-13, 1994

Most Hits, Inning
3	Tommy Burns, NL:Chi. Sept. 6, 1883 (7th; hr, 2-2b)
	Fred Pfeffer, NL:Chi. Sept. 6, 1883 (7th; 2b, 2-1b)
	Ned Williamson, NL:Chi. Sept. 6, 1883 (7th; 2b, 2-1b)
	Gene Stephens, AL:Bos. June 18, 1953 (7th; 2b, 2-1b)
	Johnny Damon, AL:Bos. June 27, 2003 (1st; 3b, 2b, 1b)
	NL Since 1900:
2	By many NL players

Fewest Hits, Season (Most at-bats)
0	Bob Buhl, NL:Mil.-Chi. 1962 (70 at-bats)
	Bill Wight, AL:Chi. 1950 (61 at-bats)

Fewest Hits, Game (Most at-bats)
0	Charlie Pick, NL:Bos. May 1, 1920 (11 ab, 26 inn)
	George Kell, AL:Phil. July 21, 1945 (10 ab, 24 inn)
	Danny Thompson, AL:Minn. May 12, 1972 (10 ab, 22 inn)

XTRA-BASE HITS

Most Seasons Leading Major Leagues
7	Stan Musial, NL:StL. 1943-44, 46, 48-50, 53

Most Seasons, Consecutive, Leading Major Leagues
4	Babe Ruth, AL:Bos. 1918-19; NY 20-21

Most Seasons Leading League
7	Honus Wagner, NL:Pitt. 1900, 02-04, 07-09
	Stan Musial, NL:StL. 1943-44, 46, 48-50, 53
	Babe Ruth, AL:Bos. 1918-19; NY 20-21, 23-24, 28

Most Seasons, Consecutive, Leading League
4	Babe Ruth, AL:Bos. 1918-19; NY 20-21
3	Dan Brouthers, NL:Buff. 1885; Det. 86-87
	Honus Wagner, NL:Phil. 1902-04, 07-09
	Rogers Hornsby, NL:StL. 1920-22
	Joe Medwick, NL:StL. 1935-37
	Johnny Mize, NL:StL. 1938-40
	Stan Musial, NL:StL. 1948-50
	Duke Snider, NL:Brk. 1954-56

Most Extra-Base Hits, Lifetime
1477	Hank Aaron, NL:Mil./Atl. 1954-74; AL:Mil. 75-76

Most Extra-Base Hits, League
1429	Hank Aaron, NL:Mil./Atl. 1954-74
1350	Babe Ruth, AL:Bos. 1914-19; NY 20-34

Most Extra-Base Hits, Season
119	Babe Ruth, AL:NY 1921
107	Chuck Klein, NL:Phil. 1930
	Barry Bonds, NL:SF 2001

Most Games, 4 or more Extra-Base Hits, League
5	Lou Gehrig, AL:NY 1926, 28, 30, 32, 34
	Joe DiMaggio, AL:NY 1936-37, 41, 48, 50
4	Willie Stargell, NL:Pitt. 1965, 68, 70, 73

Most Games, 4 or more Extra-Base Hits, Season
2	Henry Larkin, AA:Phil. June 16, July 29, 1885
	George Burns, AL:Clev. June 19(1g), July 23, 1924
	Jimmie Foxx, AL:Phil. Apr. 24, July 2(2g), 1933
	Rafael Palmeiro, AL:Tex. July 15, Sept. 6, 1993
	Albert Belle, AL:Balt. Aug. 29, Sept. 23, 1999
	Shannon Stewart, AL:Tor. June 9, July 18, 2000
	Joe Medwick, NL:StL. May 12, Aug. 4, 1937
	Billy Williams, NL:Chi. Apr. 9, Sept. 5, 1969
	Paul O'Neill, NL:Cin. May 11, Sept. 13, 1991
	Jim Edmonds, NL:StL. Apr. 4, June 28, 2003
	Alfonso Soriano, NL:Wash. Apr. 21, July 22, 2006

Most Extra-Base Hits, Consecutive, Season
7	Elmer Smith, AL:Clev. Sept. 4-5, 1921 (4-hr, 3-2b)
	Earl Sheely, AL:Chi. May 20-21, 1926 (1-hr, 6-2b)
6	Larry Walker, NL:Col. May 21-22, 1996 (1-hr, 3-3b, 2-2b)

Most Extra-Base Hits, Game
5	George Strief, AA:Phil. June 25, 1885 (4-3b, 1-2b)
	George Gore, NL:Chi. July 9, 1885 (2-3b, 3-2b)
	Larry Twitchell, NL:Clev. Aug. 15, 1889 (1-hr, 3-3b, 1-2b)
	Joe Adcock, NL:Mil. July 31, 1954 (4-hr, 1-2b)
	Willie Stargell, NL:Pitt. Aug. 1, 1970 (2-hr, 3-2b)
	Steve Garvey, NL:LA Aug. 28, 1977 (2-hr, 3-2b)
	Shawn Green, NL:LA May 23, 2002 (4-hr, 1-2b)
	Lou Boudreau, AL:Clev. July 14(1g), 1946 (1-hr, 4-2b)

Most Extra-Base Hits, 2 Consecutive Games
7	Ed Delahanty, NL:Phil. July 13-14, 1896 (4-hr, 1-3b, 2-2b)
	Red Schoendienst, NL:StL. June 5-6, 1948 (1 hr, 6-2b)
	Joe Adcock, NL:Mil. July 30-31, 1954 (5-hr, 2-2b)
	Larry Walker, NL:Col. May 21-22, 1996 (2-hr, 3-3b, 2-2b)
	Earl Sheely, AL:Chi. May 20-21, 1926 (1-hr, 6-2b)

Most Extra-Base Hits, Inning
3	Tommy Burns, NL:Chi. Sept. 6, 1883 (7th: 1-hr, 2-2b)
	Since 1900:
2	By many players

TOTAL BASES

Most Seasons Leading Major Leagues
6	Babe Ruth, AL:Bos. 1919; NY 21, 23-24, 26, 28
	Stan Musial, NL:StL. 1943, 46, 48-49, 51-52

Most Seasons, Consecutive, Leading Major Leagues
2	Dan Brouthers, NL:Buff. 1882-83
	Jimmy Ryan, NL:Chi. 1888-89
	Babe Ruth, AL:NY 1923-24
	Jimmie Foxx, AL:Phil. 1932-33
	Stan Musial, NL:StL. 1948-49 & 51-52
	Duke Snider, NL:Brk. 1953-54
	Hank Aaron, NL:Mil. 1959-60
	Frank Howard, AL:Wash. 1968-69
	Jim Rice, AL:Bos. 1978-79
	Mike Schmidt, NL:Phil. 1980-81
	Don Mattingly, AL:NY 1985-86
	Sammy Sosa, NL:Chi. 1998-99
	Albert Pujols, NL:StL. 2003-04

Most Seasons Leading League
8	Hank Aaron, NL:Mil. 1956-57, 59-61, 63; Atl. 67, 69
6	Ty Cobb, AL:Det. 1907-09, 11, 15, 17
	Babe Ruth, AL:Bos. 1919; NY 21, 23-24, 26, 28
	Ted Williams, AL:Bos. 1939, 42, 46-47, 49, 51

Most Seasons, Consecutive, Leading League
4	Honus Wagner, NL:Pitt. 1906-09
	Chuck Klein, NL:Phil. 1930-33
3	Ty Cobb, AL:Det. 1907-09
	Jim Rice, AL:Bos. 1977-79

Most Total Bases, Lifetime
6856	Hank Aaron, NL:Mil./Atl. 1954-74; AL:Mil. 75-76

Most Total Bases, League
6591	Hank Aaron, NL:Mil./Atl. 1954-74
5863	Ty Cobb, AL:Det. 1905-26; Phil. 27-28

Most Total Bases, Season
457	Babe Ruth, AL:NY 1921
450	Rogers Hornsby, NL:StL. 1922

Most Seasons, 400 or more Total Bases
5	Lou Gehrig, AL:NY 1927, 30-31, 34, 36
3	Chuck Klein, NL:Phil. 1929-30, 32

Most Seasons, Consecutive, 400 or more Total Bases
2	Lou Gehrig, AL:NY 1930-31
	Jimmie Foxx, AL:Phil. 1932-33
	Chuck Klein, NL:Phil. 1929-30
	Todd Helton, NL:Col. 2000-01

Most Seasons, 300 or more Total Bases
15	Hank Aaron, NL:Mil. 1955-63; Atl. 69, 71
13	Lou Gehrig, AL:NY 1926-38

Most Seasons, Consecutive, 300 or more Total Bases
13	Lou Gehrig, AL:NY 1926-38
	Willie Mays, NL:NY/SF 1954-66

Most Total Bases, Game
19	Shawn Green, NL:LA May 23, 2002 (4-hr, 1-2b, 1-1b)
16	Ty Cobb, AL Det. May 5, 1925 (3-hr, 1-2b, 2-1b)
	Lou Gehrig, AL:NY June 3, 1932 (4-hr)
	Jimmie Foxx, AL:Phil. July 10, 1932 (18 inn; 3-hr, 1-2b, 2-1b)
	Pat Seerey, AL:Chi. July 18, 1948 (1g; 11 inn; 4-hr)
	Rocky Colavito, AL:Clev. June 10, 1959 (4-hr)
	Fred Lynn, AL:Bos. June 18, 1975 (3-hr, 1-3b, 1-1b)
	Mike Cameron, AL:Sea. May 2, 2002 (4-hr)
	Carlos Delgado, AL:Tor. Sept. 25, 2003 (4-hr)

Most Total Bases, 2 Consecutive Games
25	Ty Cobb, AL:Det. May 5-6, 1925
	Joe Adcock, NL:Mil. July 30-31, 1954
	Shawn Green, NL:LA May 23-24, 2002

Most Total Bases, Doubleheader
22	Nate Colbert, NL:SD Aug. 1, 1972
21	Jimmie Foxx, AL:Phil. July 2, 1933 (19 inn)
	Al Oliver, AL:Tex. Aug. 17, 1980

Most Total Bases, Inning
8	Tommy Burns, NL:Chi. Sept. 6, 1883 (7th)
	Also by many players (2 home runs, inning)

INGLES

Most Seasons Leading Major Leagues
6	Ty Cobb, AL:Det. 1907, 09, 11-12, 15, 17
	Nellie Fox, AL:Chi. 1952, 54-57, 59

Most Seasons, Consecutive, Leading Major Leagues
4	Nellie Fox, AL:Chi. 1954-57

Most Seasons Leading League
8	Nellie Fox, AL:Chi. 1952, 54-60
7	Tony Gwynn, NL:SD 1984, 86-87, 89, 94-95, 97

Most Seasons, Consecutive, Leading League
7	Nellie Fox, AL:Chi. 1954-60
4	Brett Butler, NL:SF 1990; LA 1991-93

Most Singles, Lifetime
3215	Pete Rose, NL:Cin. 1963-78, 84-86; Phil. 79-83; Mtl. 84
3053	Ty Cobb, AL:Det. 1905-26; Phil. 27-28

Most Singles, Season
225	Ichiro Suzuki, AL:Sea. 2004
201	Willie Keeler, NL:Balt. 1898
	NL Since 1900:
198	Lloyd Waner, NL:Pitt. 1927

Most Singles, Game
6	Hick Carpenter, AA:Cin. Sept. 12, 1883
	George Pinkney, AA:Brk. June 25, 1885
	By many players since 1900; Last:
	Raul Ibanez, AL:Sea. Sept. 22, 2004
	Willie Davis, NL:LA May 24, 1973 (19 inn)
	Extra-Inning Game:
7	Johnny Burnett, AL:Clev. July 10, 1932 (18 inn)

Most Singles, Inning
2	By many players

DOUBLES

Most Seasons Leading Major Leagues
7	Tris Speaker, AL:Bos. 1912, 14; Clev. 18, 20-23

Most Seasons, Consecutive, Leading Major Leagues
4	Tris Speaker, AL:Clev. 1920-23

Most Seasons Leading League
8	Honus Wagner, NL:Pitt. 1900-02, 04, 06-09
	Stan Musial, NL:StL. 1943-44, 46, 48-49, 52-54
	Tris Speaker, AL:Bos. 1912, 14; Clev. 16, 18, 20-23

Most Seasons, Consecutive, Leading League
4	Honus Wagner, NL:Pitt. 1906-09
	Tris Speaker, AL:Clev. 1920-23

Most Doubles, Lifetime
793	Tris Speaker,AL:Bos. 1907-15; Clev. 16-26; Wash. 27; Phil. 28
746	Pete Rose, NL:Cin. 1963-78, 84-86; Phil. 79-83; Mtl. 84

Most Doubles, Season
67	Earl Webb, AL:Bos. 1931
64	Joe Medwick, NL:StL. 1936

Most Seasons, 50 or more Doubles
5	Tris Speaker, AL:Bos. 1912; Clev. 20-21, 23, 26
3	Paul Waner, NL:Pitt. 1928, 32, 36
	Stan Musial, NL:StL. 1944, 46, 53

Most Doubles, Game
4	By many players; Last:
	Matt Murton, NL:Chi. Aug. 3(2g), 2006
	Tomas Perez, AL:TB July 29, 2006

Most Doubles, Consecutive, Game
4	Frank Bonner, NL:Balt. Aug. 4, 1894
	Joe Kelley, NL:Balt. Sept 3, 1894
	Dick Bartell, NL:Phil. Apr. 25, 1933
	Ernie Lombardi, NL:Cin. May 8(1g), 1935
	Billy Werber, NL:Cin. May 13, 1940
	Willie Jones, NL:Phil. Apr. 20, 1949
	Billy Williams, NL:Chi. Apr. 9, 1969
	Marcus Giles, NL:Atl. July 27, 2003
	Matt Murton, NL:Chi. Aug. 3(2g), 2006
	Billy Werber, AL:Bos. July 17(1g), 1935
	Mike Kreevich, AL:Chi. Sept. 4, 1937
	Johnny Lindell, AL:NY Aug. 17, 1944
	Lou Boudreau, AL:Clev. July 14(1g), 1946
	Vic Wertz, AL:Clev. Sept. 26, 1956
	Bill Bruton, AL:Det. May 19, 1963
	Dave Duncan, AL:Balt. June 30(2g), 1975
	Sandy Alomar, Jr., AL:Clev. June 6, 1997
	Albert Belle, AL:Balt. Aug. 29 & Sept. 23(2g), 1999

Most Doubles, 2 Consecutive Games
6	Cap Anson, NL:Chi. July 3-4, 1883
	Sam Thompson, NL:Phil. June 29-July 1, 1895
	Red Schoendienst, NL:StL. June 5-6, 1948
	Joe Dugan, AL:Phil. Sept. 24-25, 1920
	Earl Sheely, AL:Chi. May 20-21, 1926
	Hank Majeski, AL:Phil. Aug. 27-27, 1948
	Kirby Puckett, AL:Minn. May 13-14, 1989

Most Doubles, 3 Consecutive Games
8	Red Schoendienst, NL:StL. June 5-6(dh), 1948
7	Joe Dugan, AL:Phil. Sept. 23-25, 1920
	Earl Sheely, AL:Chi. May 20-22, 1926

Most Doubles, Inning
2	By many players.

TRIPLES

Most Seasons Leading Major Leagues
5	Sam Crawford, NL:Cin. 1902; AL:Det. 03, 10, 13-14

Most Seasons, Consecutive, Leading Major Leagues
2	Dave Orr, AA:NY 1885-86
	Sam Crawford, NL:Cin. 1902-AL:Det. 03 & Det. 13-14
	Elmer Flick, AL:Clev. 1906-07
	Earle Combs, AL:NY 1927-28
	George Brett, AL:KC 1975-76
	Lance Johnson, AL:Chi. 1993-94
	Jose Offerman, AL:KC 1998-Bos. 99
	Cristian Guzman, AL:Minn. 2000-01
	Jose Reyes, NL:NY 2005-06

Most Seasons Leading League
6	Sam Crawford, NL:Cin. 1902; AL:Det. 1903, 10, 13-15
5	Sam Crawford, AL:Det. 1903, 10, 13-15
	Willie Wilson, AL:KC 1980, 82, 85, 87-88
	Stan Musial, NL:StL. 1943, 46, 48-49, 51

Most Seasons, Consecutive, Leading League
4	Lance Johnson, AL:Chi. 1991-94
3	Garry Templeton, NL:StL. 1977-79

Most Triples, Lifetime
312   Sam Crawford, NL:Cin. 1899-1902; AL:Det. 03-17

Most Triples, League
297   Ty Cobb, AL:Det. 1905-26; Phil. 27-28
252   Honus Wagner, NL:Lou. 1897-99; Pitt. 1900-17

Most Triples, Season
36   Owen Wilson, NL:Pitt. 1912
26   Joe Jackson, AL:Clev. 1912
         Sam Crawford, AL:Det. 1914

Most Seasons, 20 or more Triples, Lifetime
5   Sam Crawford, NL:Cin. 1902; AL:Det. 03, 12-14

Most Seasons, 20 or more Triples, League
4   Sam Crawford, AL:Det. 1903, 12-14
         Ty Cobb, AL:Det. 1908, 11-12, 17
3   Dan Brouthers, NL:Det. 1887; Brk. 92; Balt. 94
         Roger Connor, NL:NY 1886-87; NY-StL. 94
         Sam Thompson, NL:Det. 1887; Phil. 94-95
         NL Since 1900:
2   By many players

Most Seasons, Consecutive, 20 or more Triples
3   Sam Crawford, AL:Det. 1912-14
2   Roger Connor, NL:NY 1886-87
         George Davis, NL:NY 1893-94
         Sam Thompson, NL:Phil. 1894-95

Most Triples, Game
4   George Strief, AA:Phil. June 25, 1885
         Bill Joyce, NL:NY May 18, 1897
         Since 1900:
3   By many players; Last:
         Rafael Furcal, NL:Atl. Apr. 21, 2002
         Lance Johnson, AL:Chi. Sept. 23, 1995

Most Triples, Consecutive, Game
3   By many players

Most Triples, Inning
2   Harry Wheeler, AA:Cin. June 28, 1882(11th)
         Harry Stovey, AA:Phil. Aug. 18, 1884 (8th)
         Joe Hornung, NL:Bos. May 6, 1882 (8th)
         Heinie Peitz, NL:StL. July 2, 1895 (1st)
         Frank Shugart, NL:Lou. July 30, 1895 (5th)
         Buck Freeman, NL:Bos. July 25, 1900 (1st)
         Bill Dahlen, NL:Brk. Aug. 30, 1900 (8th)
         Curt Walker, NL:Cin. July 22, 1926 (2nd)
         Cory Sullivan, NL:Col. Apr. 9, 2006 (5th)
         Al Zarilla, AL:StL. July 13, 1946 (4th)
         Gil Coan, AL:Wash. Apr. 21, 1951 (6th)

Fewest Triples, Season (most at-bats)
0   Miguel Tejada, AL:Oak. 2002 (662 at-bats)
         Sammy Sosa, NL:Chi. 1998 (643 at-bats)

HOME RUNS

Most Seasons Leading Major Leagues
11   Babe Ruth, AL:Bos. 1918-19; NY 20-21, 23-24, 26-29, 31

Most Seasons, Consecutive, Leading Major Leagues
6   Ralph Kiner, NL:Pitt. 1947-52

Most Seasons Leading League
12   Babe Ruth, AL:Bos. 1918-19; NY 20-21, 23-24, 26-31
8   Mike Schmidt, NL:Phil. 1974-76, 80-81, 83-84, 86

Most Seasons, Consecutive, Leading League
7   Ralph Kiner, NL:Pitt. 1946-52
6   Babe Ruth, AL:NY 1926-31

Most Home Runs, Lifetime
755   Hank Aaron, NL:Mil./Atl. 1954-74; AL:Mil. 75-76

Most Home Runs, League
734   Barry Bonds, NL:Pitt. 1986-92; SF 93-2006
708   Babe Ruth, AL:Bos. 1914-19; NY 20-34

Most Home Runs, Season
73	Barry Bonds, NL:SF 2001
61	Roger Maris, AL:NY 1961

Most Seasons, 50 or more Home Runs
4	Babe Ruth, AL:NY 1920-21, 27-28
	Mark McGwire, AL:Oak. 1996; AL:Oak.-NL:StL. 97; NL:StL. 98-99
	Sammy Sosa, NL:Chi. 1998-2001

Most Seasons, Consecutive, 50 or more Home Runs
4	Mark McGwire, AL:Oak. 1996; AL:Oak.-NL:StL. 97; NL:StL. 98-99
	Sammy Sosa, NL:Chi. 1998-2001
2	Babe Ruth, AL:NY 1920-21; 27-28
	Ken Griffey, Jr. AL:Sea. 1997-98
	Alex Rodriguez, AL:Tex. 2001-02

Most Seasons, 40 or more Home Runs
11	Babe Ruth, AL:NY 1920-21, 23-24, 26-32
8	Hank Aaron, NL:Mil. 1957, 60, 62-63; Atl. 66, 69, 71, 73
	Barry Bonds, NL:SF 1993, 96-97, 2000-04

Most Seasons, Consecutive, 40 or more Home Runs
7	Babe Ruth, AL:NY 1926-32
6	Sammy Sosa, NL:Chi. 1998-2003

Most Seasons, 30 or more Home Runs
15	Hank Aaron, NL:Mil. 1957-63, 65; Atl. 66-67, 69-73
13	Babe Ruth, AL:NY 1920-24, 26-33

Most Seasons, Consecutive, 30 or more Home Runs
13	Barry Bonds, NL:Pitt. 1992; SF 93-2004
12	Jimmie Foxx, AL:Phil. 1929-35; Bos. 36-40

Most Seasons, 20 or more Home Runs
20	Hank Aaron, NL:Mil. 1955-65; Atl. 66-74
16	Babe Ruth, AL:Bos. 1919; NY 20-34
	Ted Williams, AL:Bos. 1939-42, 46-51, 54-58, 60
	Reggie Jackson, AL:Oak. 1968-75; Balt. 76; NY 77-80; Cal. 82, 84-85

Most Seasons, Consecutive, 20 or more Home Runs
20	Hank Aaron, NL:Mil. 1955-65; Atl. 66-74
16	Babe Ruth, AL:Bos. 1919; NY 20-34

Most Home Runs, Consecutive Seasons
135	Mark McGwire, NL:StL. 1998 (70)-99 (65)
114	Babe Ruth, AL:NY 1927 (60)-28 (54)

Most Home Runs, Season, Home
39	Hank Greenberg, AL:Det. 1938
38	Mark McGwire, NL:StL. 1998

Most Home Runs, Season, Road
36	Barry Bonds, NL:SF 2001
32	Babe Ruth, AL:NY 1927
	David Ortiz, AL:Bos. 2006

Most Home Runs, Season, vs. One Club
14	Lou Gehrig, AL:NY vs Clev. 1936
13	Hank Sauer, NL:Chi. vs Pitt. 1954
	Joe Adcock, NL:Mil. vs Brk. 1956

Most Home Runs, Season, vs. One Club, Home
10	Gus Zernial, AL:Chi.-Phil. vs StL. 1951
9	Stan Musial, NL:StL. vs NY 1954

Most Home Runs, Season, vs. One Club, Road
10	Harry Heilmann, AL:Det. vs Phil. 1922
9	Joe Adcock, NL:Mil. vs Brk. 1954
	Willie Mays, NL:NY vs Brk. 1955

Most Home Runs, One Month
20	Sammy Sosa, NL:Chi. June 1998
18	Rudy York, AL:Det. Aug. 1937

Most Home Runs, Game
4	Bobby Lowe, NL:Bos. May 30 (2g), 1894 (cons)
	Ed Delahanty, NL:Phil. July 13, 1896
	Chuck Klein, NL:Phil. July 10, 1936 (10 inn)
	Gil Hodges, NL:Brk. Aug. 31, 1950
	Joe Adcock, NL:Mil. July 31, 1954
	Willie Mays, NL:SF Apr. 30, 1961
	Mike Schmidt, NL:Phil. Apr. 17, 1976 (cons; 10 inn)
	Bob Horner, NL:Atl. July 6, 1986
	Mark Whiten, NL:StL. Sept. 7(2g), 1993
	Shawn Green, NL:LA May 23, 2002
	Lou Gehrig, AL:NY June 3, 1932 (cons)
	Pat Seerey, AL:Chi. July 18, 1948 (11 inn)
	Rocky Colavito, AL:Clev. June 10, 1959 (cons)
	Mike Cameron, AL:Sea. May 2, 2002 (cons)
	Carlos Delgado, AL:Tor. Sept. 25, 2003 (cons)

Most Home Runs, Leadoff Batter, First Inning, Lifetime
81	Rickey Henderson, AL:Oak. 1979-84, 89-95, 98; NY 85-89; Tor. 93; Ana. 97; Sea. 2000; Bos. 02; NL:SD 96-97, 2001; NY 99-2000; LA 03

Most Home Runs, Leadoff Batter, First Inning, League
73	Rickey Henderson, AL:Oak. 1979-84, 89-95, 98; NY 85-89; Tor. 93; Ana. 97; Sea. 2000; Bos. 02
50	Craig Biggio, NL:Hou. 1992-94, 97-99, 2001-06

Most Home Runs, Leadoff Batter, First Inning, Season
13	Alfonso Soriano, AL:NY 2003
11	Bobby Bonds, NL:SF 1973

Most Games, 3 or more Home Runs, Lifetime
6	Johnny Mize, NL:StL.-NY; AL:NY
	Sammy Sosa, NL:Chi.
5	Joe Carter, AL:Clev.; Tor.
	Carlos Delgado, AL:Tor.

Most Games, 3 or more Home Runs, Season
3	Sammy Sosa, NL:Chi. 2001
2	Ted Williams, AL:Bos. 1957
	Doug DeCinces, AL:Balt. 1982
	Joe Carter, AL:Clev. 1989
	Cecil Fielder, AL:Det. 1990
	Geronimo Berroa, AL:Oak. 1996
	Carlos Delgado AL:Tor. 2001

Most Games, 2 or more Home Runs, Lifetime
72	Babe Ruth, AL:Bos. 1914-19; NY 20-34; NL:Bos. 35

Most Games, 2 or more Home Runs, League
71	Babe Ruth, AL:Bos. 1914-19; NY 20-34
69	Barry Bonds, NL:Pitt. 1987-92, SF 93-2004, 06

Most Games, 2 or more Home Runs, Season
11	Hank Greenberg, AL:Det. 1938
	Sammy Sosa, NL:Chi. 1998

Most Games, Switch-Hitting Home Runs, Lifetime
11	Eddie Murray, AL:Balt.1977, 79, 81-82, 85, 87; Clev. 94; NL:LA 90
	Chili Davis NL:SF 1983, 87; AL:Cal. 88-89, 93-94, 96; Minn. 92; KC 97

Most Games, Switch-Hitting Home Runs, League
10	Mickey Mantle, AL:NY 1955-59, 61-62, 64
	Ken Caminiti, NL:Hou. 1994, 99; SD 95-96, 98

Most Games, Switch-Hitting Home Runs, Season
4	Ken Caminiti, NL:SD 1996
3	Tony Clark, AL:Det. 1998

Most Switch-Hitting Home Runs, Inning, Lifetime
1	Carlos Baerga, AL:Clev. Apr. 8, 1993 (7th)
	Mark Bellhorn, NL:Chi. Aug. 29, 2002 (4th)

Most Home Runs, Consecutive At-Bats (*consecutive plate appearances)

4	Bobby Lowe, NL:Bos. May 30 (2g), 1894*
	Bill Nicholson, NL:Chi. July 22-23, 1944
	Ralph Kiner, NL:Pitt. Aug. 15-16, 1947
	Ralph Kiner, NL:Pitt. Sept. 11-13, 1949*
	Stan Musial, NL:StL. July 7-8, 1962
	Art Shamsky, NL:Cin. Aug. 12-14, 1966*
	Deron Johnson, NL:Phil. July 10-11, 1971*
	Johnny Bench, NL:Cin. May 8-9, 1973
	Mike Schmidt, NL:Phil. Apr. 17, 1976*
	Mike Schmidt, NL:Phil. July 6-7, 1979*
	Tuffy Rhodes, NL:Chi. Oct. 3, 1993-Apr. 4, 1994
	Benito Santiago, NL:Phil. Sept. 14-15, 1996
	Barry Bonds, NL:SF May 19-20, 2001
	Shawn Green NL:LA June 14-15, 2002*
	Andruw Jones NL:Atl. Sept. 7-10, 2002
	Albert Pujols, NL:StL. Apr. 16-17, 2006*
	Tilly Walker, AL:Phil. July 1(2g)-2, 1922
	Lou Gehrig, AL:NY June 3, 1932*
	Jimmie Foxx, AL:Phil. June 7-8, 1933*
	Hank Greenberg, AL:Det. Jul 26-27, 1938*
	Ted Williams, AL:Bos. Sept. 17-20-21-22, 1957
	Charlie Maxwell, AL:Det. May 3-3, 1959
	Rocky Colavito, AL:Clev. June 10, 1959*
	Willie Kirkland, AL:Clev. July 9(2g)-13, 1961
	Johnny Blanchard, AL:NY July 21-22-26, 1961*
	Mickey Mantle, AL:NY July 4-6, 1962*
	Bobby Murcer, AL:NY June 24-24, 1970
	Mike Epstein, AL:Oak. June 15-16, 1971*
	Don Baylor, AL:Balt. July 1-2, 1975
	Larry Herndon, AL:Det. May 16-18, 1982*
	Bo Jackson, AL:KC July 17-Aug. 26, 1990*
	Jeff Manto, AL:Balt. June 8-10, 1995
	Bobby Higginson, AL:Det. June 30-July 1, 1997
	Manny Ramirez, AL:Clev. Sept. 15-16, 1998*
	Mike Cameron, AL:Sea. May 2, 2002*
	Troy Glaus, AL:Ana. Sept. 15-16, 2002*
	Carlos Delgado, AL:Tor. Sept. 25, 2003*

Most Consecutive Innings, Home Run, Game

3	George Kelly, NL:NY Sept. 17, 1923 (3rd, 4th, 5th)
	Larry Parrish, NL:Mtl. July 30, 1978 (3rd, 4th, 5th)
	Andres Galarraga, NL:Col. June 25, 1995 (6th, 7th, 8th)
	Sammy Sosa, NL:Chi. Aug. 10, 2002 (3rd, 4th, 5th)
	Shea Hillenbrand, NL:Ari. July 7, 2003 (4th, 5th, 6th)
	Carl Reynolds, AL:Chi. July 2(2g), 1930 (1st, 2nd, 3rd)
	Kevin Mench, AL:Tex. June 30, 2005 (5th, 6th, 7th)

Most Home Runs, 2 Consecutive Innings, Game

3	Nomar Garciaparra, AL:Bos. July 28(1g), 2002 (3rd, 4th)
2	By many NL players

Most Games, Consecutive, 1 or more Home Runs

8	Dale Long, NL:Pitt. May 19-28, 1956
	Don Mattingly, AL:NY July 8-18, 1987
	Ken Griffey, Jr., AL:Sea. July 20-28, 1993

Most Home Runs, 2 Consecutive Games

5	Cap Anson, NL:Chi. Aug. 5-6, 1884
	Ralph Kiner, NL:Pitt. Aug. 15-16, 1947
	Ralph Kiner, NL:Pitt. Sept. 11(2g)-12, 1947
	Don Mueller, NL:NY Sept. 1-2, 1951
	Stan Musial, NL:StL. May 2, 1954 (dh)
	Joe Adcock, NL:Mil. July 30-31, 1954
	Billy Williams, NL:Chi. Sept. 8-10. 1968
	Nate Colbert, NL:SD Aug. 1, 1972 (dh)
	Mike Schmidt, NL:Phil. Apr. 17-18, 1976
	Dave Kingman, NL:Chi. July 27-28, 1979
	Gary Carter, NL:NY Sept. 3-4, 1985
	Barry Larkin, NL:Cin. June 27-28, 1991
	Geoff Jenkins, NL:Mil. Apr. 28-29, 2001
	Barry Bonds, NL:SF May 19-20, 2001
	Shawn Green, NL:LA May 23-24, 2002
	Ty Cobb, AL:Det. May 5-6, 1925
	Tony Lazzeri, AL:NY May 23-24, 1936
	Carl Yastrzemski, AL:Bos. May 19-20, 1976
	Mark McGwire, AL:Oak. June 27-28, 1987
	Joe Carter, AL:Clev. July 18-19, 1989
	Mark McGwire, AL:Oak. June 10-11, 1995
	Albert Belle, AL:Clev. Sept 18-19, 1995
	Matt Williams, AL:Clev. Apr. 25-26, 1997
	Manny Ramirez, AL:Clev. Sept. 15-16, 1998
	Edgar Martinez, AL:Sea. May 17-18, 1999
	Nomar Garciaparra, AL:Bos. July 21-23(1g), 2002
	Alex Rodriguez, AL:Tex. Aug. 17-18, 2002
	Travis Hafner, AL:Clev. July 19-20, 2004

Most Home Runs, Doubleheader

5	Stan Musial, NL:StL. May 2, 1954
	Nate Colbert, NL:SD Aug. 1, 1972
4	Earl Averill, AL:Clev. Sept. 17, 1930
	Jimmie Foxx, AL:Phil. July 2, 1933
	Jim Tabor, AL:Bos. July 4, 1939
	Gus Zernial, AL:Chi. Oct. 1, 1950
	Charlie Maxwell, AL:Det. May 3, 1959
	Roger Maris, AL:NY July 25, 1961
	Rocky Colavito, AL:Det. Aug. 27, 1961
	Harmon Killebrew, AL:Minn. Sept. 21, 1963
	Bobby Murcer, AL:NY June 24, 1970
	Graig Nettles, AL:NY Apr. 14, 1974
	Otto Velez, AL:Tor. May 4, 1980
	Al Oliver, AL:Tex. Aug. 17, 1980

Most Home Runs, 3 Consecutive Games (HR in each game)

7	Shawn Green, NL:LA May 23-25, 2002
6	Tony Lazzeri, AL:NY May 23(dh)-24, 1936
	Gus Zernial, AL:Phil. May 13-16, 1951
	Manny Ramirez, AL:Clev. Sept. 15-17, 1998
	Alex Rodriguez, AL:Tex. Aug. 16-18, 2002
	Jeff DaVanon, AL:Ana. June 1-4, 2003

Most Home Runs, 4 Consecutive Games (HR in each game)

8	Ralph Kiner, NL:Pitt. Sept. 10-12, 1947
7	Tony Lazzeri, AL:NY May 21-24, 1936
	Gus Zernial, AL:Phil. May 13-17, 1951
	Frank Howard, AL:Wash. May 12-16, 1968
	Pitchers' batting:
4	Ken Brett, NL:Phil. June 9-23, 1973

Most Home Runs, 5 Consecutive Games (HR in each game)

8	Frank Howard, AL:Wash. May 12-17; 14-18, 1968
	Barry Bonds, NL:SF May 17-21, 2001
	Barry Bonds, NL:SF May 18-22, 2001

Most Home Runs, 6 Consecutive Games (HR in each game)

10	Frank Howard, AL:Wash. May 12-18, 1968
9	Barry Bonds, NL:SF May 17-22, 2001

Most Home Runs, 7 Consecutive Games (HR in each game)

9	Don Mattingly, AL:NY July 8-17, 1987
8	Barry Bonds, NL:SF Apr. 12-20, 2004

Most Home Runs, 8 Consecutive Games (HR in each game)

10	Don Mattingly, AL:NY July 8-18, 1987
8	Dale Long, NL:Pitt. May 19-28, 1956

Most Home Runs, First Major League Game

2	Charlie Reilly, AA:Colu. Oct. 9, 1889
	Bob Nieman, AL:StL. Sept. 14, 1951
	Bert Campaneris, AL:KC July 23, 1964
	Mark Quinn, AL:KC Sept. 14(2g), 1999
1	By many NL players

Most Home Runs, First Two Major League Games

3	Charlie Reilly, AA:Colu. Oct. 9-10, 1889
	Joe Cunningham, NL:StL. June 30-July 1(2g), 1954
2	Earl Averill, AL:Clev. Apr. 16-17, 1929
	Zeke Bonura, AL:Chi. Apr. 17-18, 1934
	Bob Nieman, AL:StL. Sept. 14, 1951
	Bert Campaneris, AL:KC July 23, 1964
	Joe Lefebvre, AL:NY May 22-23, 1980
	Dave Stapleton, AL:Bos. May 30-31, 1980
	Tim Laudner, AL:Minn. Aug. 28-29, 1981
	Alvin Davis, AL:Sea. Apr. 11-13, 1984
	Sam Horn, AL:Bos. July 25-26, 1987
	Manny Ramirez, AL:Clev. Sept. 2-3, 1993
	Gabe Alvarez, AL:Det. June 22-23, 1998
	Mark Quinn, AL:KC Sept. 14(2g), 1999
	Josh Bard, AL:Clev. Aug. 23-24, 2002
	Kenji Johjima, AL:Sea. Apr. 3-4, 2006
	Kevin Kouzmanoff, AL:Clev. Sept. 2-3, 2006

Most Home Runs, Inning

2	Lou Bierbauer, PL:Brk. July 12, 1890 (3rd)
	Ed Cartwright, AA:StL. Sept. 23, 1890 (3rd)
	Charley Jones, NL:Bos. June 10, 1880 (8th)
	Bobby Lowe, NL:Bos. May 30, 1894 (3rd)
	Jake Stenzel, NL:Pitt. June 6, 1894 (3rd)
	Hack Wilson, NL:NY July 1(2g), 1925 (3rd)
	Hank Leiber, NL:NY Aug. 24, 1935 (2nd)
	Sid Gordon, NL:NY July 31(2g), 1949 (2nd)
	Andy Seminick, NL:Phil. June 2, 1949 (8th)
	Willie McCovey, NL:SF Apr. 12, 1973 (4th)
	John Boccabella, NL:Mtl. July 6. 1973 (6th)
	Lee May, NL:Hou. Apr. 29, 1974 (6th)
	Willie McCovey, NL:SF June 27, 1977 (6th)
	Andre Dawson, NL:Mtl. July 30, 1978 (3rd)
	Ray Knight, NL:Cin. May 13, 1980 (5th)
	Von Hayes, NL:Phil. June 11, 1985 (1st)
	Andre Dawson, NL:Mtl. Sept. 24, 1985 (5th)
	Dale Murphy, NL:Atl. July 27, 1989 (6th)
	Jeff Bagwell, NL:Hou. June 24, 1994 (6th)
	Jeff King, NL:Pitt. Aug. 8, 1995 (2nd)
	Jeff King, NL:Pitt. Apr. 30, 1996 (4th)
	Sammy Sosa, NL:Chi. May 16, 1996 (7th)
	Mike Lansing, NL:Mtl. May 7, 1997 (6th)
	Gary Sheffield, NL:Fla. July 13, 1997 (4th)
	Fernando Tatis, NL:StL. Apr. 23, 1999 (3rd)
	Eric Karros, NL:LA Aug. 22, 2000 (6th)
	Aaron Boone, NL:Cin. Aug. 9, 2002 (1st)
	Mark Bellhorn, NL:Chi. Aug. 29, 2002 (4th)
	Reggie Sanders, NL:Pitt. Aug. 20, 2003 (5th)
	Juan Rivera, NL:Mtl. June 19, 2004 (2nd)
	Ken Williams, AL:StL. Aug. 7, 1922 (6th)
	Bill Regan, AL:Bos. June 16, 1928 (4th)
	Joe DiMaggio, AL:NY June 24, 1936 (5th)
	Al Kaline, AL:Det. Apr. 17, 1955 (6th)
	Jim Lemon, AL:Wash. Sept. 5, 1959 (3rd)
	Joe Pepitone, AL:NY May 23, 1962 (8th)
	Rick Reichardt, AL:Cal. Apr. 30. 1966 (8th)
	Cliff Johnson, AL:NY June 30, 1977 (8th)
	Ellis Burks, AL:Bos. Aug. 27, 1990 (4th)
	Carlos Baerga, AL:Clev. Apr. 8, 1993 (7th)
	Joe Carter, AL:Tor. Oct. 3, 1993 (2nd)
	Dave Nilsson, AL:Mil. May 17, 1996 (6th)
	Mark McGwire, AL:Oak. Sept. 22, 1996 (5th)
	Bret Boone, AL:Sea. May 2, 2002 (1st)
	Mike Cameron, AL:Sea. May 2, 2002 (1st)
	Jared Sandberg, AL:TB June 11, 2002 (5th)
	Nomar Garciaparra, AL:Bos. July 23(1g), 2002 (3rd)
	Carl Everett, AL:Tex. July 26, 2002 (7th)
	Julio Lugo, AL:TB July 22, 2006 (5th)

Most At-Bats, No Home Runs, Season
672 Rabbit Maranville, NL:Pitt. 1922
658 Doc Cramer, AL:Bos. 1938

GRAND SLAM HOME RUNS

Most Grand Slam Home Runs, Lifetime
23 Lou Gehrig, AL:NY 1923-39
18 Willie McCovey, NL:SF 1959-73, 77-80; SD 74-76

Most Grand Slam Home Runs, Season
6 Don Mattingly, AL:NY 1987
   Travis Hafner, AL:Clev. 2006
5 Ernie Banks, NL:Chi. 1955

Most Grand Slam Home Runs, One Month
3 Rudy York, AL:Det. May 16, 22, 30, 1938
   Jim Northrup, AL:Det. June 24 (2), 29, 1968
   Larry Parrish, AL:Tex. July 4, 7, 10, 1982
   Mike Blowers, AL:Sea. Aug. 3, 14, 18, 1995
   Shane Spencer, AL:NY Sept. 18, 24, 27, 1998
   Eric Davis, NL:Cin. May 1, 3, 30, 1987
   Mike Piazza, NL:LA Apr. 9, 10, 24, 1998
   Devon White, NL:Mil. May 10, 15, 20, 2001
   Carlos Beltran, NL:NY July 16, 18, 30, 2006

Most Grand Slam Home Runs, Game
2 Tony Lazzeri, AL:NY May 24, 1936 (2nd, 5th)
   Jim Tabor, AL:Bos. July 4(2g), 1939 (3rd, 6th)
   Rudy York, AL:Bos. July 27, 1946 (2nd, 5th)
   Jim Gentile, AL:Balt. May 9, 1961 (1st, 2nd)
   Jim Northrup, AL:Det. June 24, 1968 (5th, 6th)
   Frank Robinson, AL:Balt. June 26, 1970 (5th, 6th)
   Robin Ventura, AL:Chi. Sept. 4, 1995 (4th, 5th)
   Chris Hoiles, AL:Balt. Aug. 14, 1998 (3rd, 8th)
   Nomar Garciaparra, AL:Bos. May 10, 1999 (1st, 8th)
   Bill Mueller, AL:Bos. July 29, 2003 (7th, 8th)
   Tony Cloninger, NL:Atl. July 3, 1966 (1st, 4th)
   Fernando Tatis, NL:StL. Apr. 23, 1999 (3rd, both)

Most Grand Slam Home Runs, First Major League Game
1 Bill Duggleby, NL:Phil. Apr. 21, 1898 (2nd; first at-bat)
   Bobby Bonds, NL:SF June 25, 1968 (6th)
   Jeremy Hermida, NL:Fla. Aug. 31, 2005 (7th; first at-bat; ph)
   Kevin Kouzmanoff, AL:Clev. Sept. 2, 2006 (1st; first at-bat)

Most Consecutive Games with a Grand Slam Home Run
2 Jimmy Bannon, NL:Bos. Aug. 6-7, 1894
   Jimmy Sheckard, NL:Brk. Sept. 23-24, 1901
   Phil Garner, NL:Pitt. Sept 14-15, 1978
   Fred McGriff, NL:SD Aug. 13-14, 1991
   Eric Davis, NL:Cin. May 4-5, 1996
   Mike Piazza, NL:LA Apr. 9-10, 1998
   Sammy Sosa, NL:Chi. July 27-28, 1998
   Robin Ventura, NL:NY May 20(1g)-20(2g), 1999
   Carlos Beltran, NL:NY July 16-18, 2006
   Babe Ruth, AL:NY Sept. 27-29, 1927
   Babe Ruth, AL:NY Aug. 6-7, 1929
   Bill Dickey, AL:NY Aug. 3-4, 1937
   Jimmie Foxx, AL:Bos. May 20-21, 1940
   Jim Busby, AL:Clev. July 5-6, 1956
   Brooks Robinson, AL:Balt. May 6-9, 1962
   Willie Aikens, AL:Cal. June 13(2g)-14, 1979
   Greg Luzinski, AL:Chi. June 8-9, 1984
   Rob Deer, AL:Mil. Aug. 19-20, 1987
   Mike Blowers, AL:Sea. May 16-17, 1993
   Dan Gladden, AL:Det. Aug. 10-11, 1993
   Ken Griffey, Jr. AL:Sea. Apr. 29-30, 1999
   Albert Belle, AL:Balt. June 14-15, 2000
   David Eckstein, AL:Ana. Apr. 27-28, 2002

RUNS BATTED IN (Since 1920 - Prior seasons not compiled on official scores)

Most Seasons Leading Major Leagues
4 Babe Ruth, AL:NY 1920-21, 23, 26, 28
   Lou Gehrig, AL:NY 1927-28, 31-34
   Hank Aaron, NL:Mil./Atl. 1957, 60, 63, 66

Most Seasons, Consecutive, Leading Major Leagues
3   Cecil Fielder, AL:Det. 1990-92

Most Seasons Leading League
5   Lou Gehrig, AL:NY 1927-28, 30-31, 34
4   Rogers Hornsby, NL:StL. 1920-22, 25
            Hank Aaron, NL:Mil. 1957, 60, 63; Atl. 66
            Mike Schmidt, NL:Phil. 1980-81, 84, 86

Most Seasons, Consecutive, Leading League
3   Rogers Hornsby, NL:StL. 1920-22
            Joe Medwick, NL:StL. 1936-38
            George Foster, NL:Cin. 1976-78
            Cecil Fielder, AL:Det. 1990-92

Most Runs Batted In, Lifetime
2297   Hank Aaron, NL:Mil./Atl. 1954-74; AL:Mil. 75-76

Most Runs Batted In, League
2202   Hank Aaron, NL:Mil./Atl. 1954-74
1996   Lou Gehrig, AL:NY 1923-39

Most Runs Batted In, Season
191   Hack Wilson, NL:Chi. 1930
184   Lou Gehrig, AL:NY 1931

Most Seasons, 150 or more Runs Batted In, League
7   Lou Gehrig, AL:NY 1927, 30-32, 34, 36-37
2   Rogers Hornsby, NL:StL. 1922; Chi. 1929
            Hack Wilson, NL:Chi. 1929-30
            Sammy Sosa, NL:Chi. 1998, 2001

Most Seasons, Consecutive, 150 or more Runs Batted In, League
3   Babe Ruth, AL:NY 1929-31
            Lou Gehrig, AL:NY 1930-32
2   Hack Wilson, NL:Chi. 1929-30

Most Seasons, 100 or more Runs Batted In, League
13   Lou Gehrig, AL:NY 1926-38
            Jimmie Foxx, AL:Phil. 1929-35; Bos. 36-41
12   Barry Bonds, NL:Pitt. 1990-92; SF 93, 95-98, 2000-02, 04

Most Seasons, Consecutive, 100 or more Runs Batted In, League
13   Lou Gehrig, AL:NY 1926-38
            Jimmie Foxx, AL:Phil. 1929-35; Bos. 36-41
9   Sammy Sosa, NL:Chi. 1995-2003

Most Runs Batted In, Game
12   Jim Bottomley, NL:StL. Sept. 16, 1924
            Mark Whiten, NL:StL. Sept. 7(2g), 1993
11   Tony Lazzeri, AL:NY May 24, 1936

Most Runs Batted In, Game, All of Team's Runs
8   George Kelly, NL:NY June 14, 1924
            Bob Johnson, AL:Phil. June 12, 1938
            Extra-Inning Game:
9   Mike Greenwell, AL:Bos. Sept. 2, 1996 (10 inn)

Most Runs Batted In, Two Consecutive Games
15   Tony Lazzeri, AL:NY May 23-24, 1936
14   Sammy Sosa, NL:Chi. Aug. 10-11, 2002

Most Runs Batted In, Doubleheader
13   Nate Colbert, NL:SD Aug. 1, 1972
            Mark Whiten, NL:StL. Sept. 7, 1993
11   Earl Averill, AL:Clev. Sept. 17, 1930
            Jim Tabor, AL:Bos. July 4, 1939
            Boog Powell, AL:Balt. July 6, 1966 (20 inn)

Most Games, Consecutive, Runs Batted In
17   Ray Grimes, NL:Chi. June 27-July 23, 1922
13   Taft Wright, AL:Chi. May 4-20, 1941
            Mike Sweeney, AL:KC June 23-July 4, 1999

Most Runs Batted In, Inning

8	Fernando Tatis, NL:StL. Apr. 23, 1999 (3rd)
6	Bob Johnson, AL:Phil. Aug. 29(1g), 1937 (1st)
	Tom McBride, AL:Bos. Aug. 4, 1945 (2g;4th)
	Joe Astroth, AL:Phil. Sept. 23, 1950 (6th)
	Gil McDougald, AL:NY May 3, 1951 (9th)
	Sam Mele, AL:Chi. June 10, 1952 (4th)
	Jim Lemon, AL;Wash. Sept. 5, 1959 (3rd)
	Carlos Quintana, AL:Bos. July 30, 1991 (3rd)
	Matt Stairs, AL:Oak. July 5, 1996 (1st)
	Matt Williams, AL:Clev. Aug. 27, 1997 (4th)
	Bobby Abreu, AL:NY Sept. 12, 2006 (1st)

SACRIFICE HITS

Most Season Leading Major Leagues

4	Phil Rizzuto, AL:NY 1949-52

Most Seasons, Consecutive, Leading Major Leagues

4	Phil Rizzuto, AL:NY 1949-52

Most Seasons Leading League

6	Mule Haas, AL:Phil. 1930-32; Chi. 33-34, 36
4	Otto Knabe, NL:Phil. 1907-08, 10, 13

Most Seasons, Consecutive, Leading League

5	Mule Haas, AL:Phil. 1930-32; Chi. 33-34
2	By many NL players; Last:
	Jack Wilson, NL:Pitt. 2001-02

Most Sacrifice Hits, League

511	Eddie Collins, AL:Phil. 1906-14, 27-30; Chi. 15-26
392	Jake Daubert, NL:Brk. 1910-18; Cin. 19-24

Most Sacrifice Hits, Season (including Sacrifice Flies)

67	Ray Chapman, AL:Clev. 1917
46	Jimmy Sheckard, NL:Chi. 1909

Most Sacrifice Hits, Season (not including Sacrifice Flies)

46	Bill Bradley, AL:Clev. 1907
43	Kid Gleason, NL:Phil. 1905

Most Sacrifice Hits, Game

4	Cy Seymour, NL:Cin. July 25, 1902
	Jake Daubert, NL:Brk. Aug. 15(2g), 1914
	Kris Benson, NL:Pitt. Apr. 18, 2004
	Cory Sullivan, NL:Col. June 14, 2006
	Red Killefer, AL:Wash. Aug. 27(1g), 1910
	Jack Barry, AL:Bos. Aug. 21, 1916
	Ray Chapman, AL:Clev. Aug. 31, 1919
	Felix Fermin, AL:Clev. Aug. 22, 1989 (10 inn)

Most Sacrifice Hits, Inning

2	Al Benton, AL:Det. Aug. 6, 1941 (3rd)

SACRIFICE FLIES (1908 to 1930, 1939, since 1954)

Most Seasons Leading Major Leagues

3	Ron Santo, NL:Chi. 1963, 67, 69

Most Seasons, Consecutive, Leading Major Leagues

1	By many players

Most Seasons Leading League

4	Brooks Robinson, AL:Balt. 1962, 64, 67-68
3	Ron Santo, NL:Chi. 1963, 67, 69
	Johnny Bench, NL:Cin. 1970, 72-73
	Dante Bichette, NL:Col. 1996, 98-99

Most Seasons, Consecutive, Leading League

2	Gil Hodges, NL:Brk. 1954-55
	Johnny Bench, NL:Cin. 1972-73
	Mike Schmidt, NL:Phil. 1979-80
	Dante Bichette, NL:Col. 1998-99
	Aramis Ramirez, NL:Pitt.-Chi. 2002-03
	Jackie Jensen, AL:Bos. 1954-55
	Minnie Minoso, AL:Chi. 1960-61
	Dave Johnson, AL:Balt. 1966-67
	Brooks Robinson, AL:Balt. 1967-68

Most Sacrifice Flies, Lifetime
128   Eddie Murray, AL:Balt. 1977-88, 96; Clev. 94-96; Ana. 97; NL:LA 89-91, 97; NY 92-93

Most Sacrifice Flies, League
127   Cal Ripken, AL:Balt. 1981-2001
113   Hank Aaron, NL:Mil./Atl. 1954-74

Most Sacrifice Flies, Season
19   Gil Hodges, NL:Brk. 1954
17   Roy White, AL:NY 1971
      Bobby Bonilla, AL:Balt. 1996

Most Sacrifice Flies, Game
3   Harry Steinfeldt, NL:Chi. May 5, 1909
      Ernie Banks, NL:Chi. June 2, 1961
      Vince Coleman, NL:StL. May 1, 1986
      Candy Maldonado, NL:SF Aug. 29, 1987
      Bob Meusel, AL:NY Sept. 15, 1926
      Russ Nixon, AL:Bos. Aug. 31(2g), 1965
      Don Mattingly, AL:NY May 3, 1986
      George Bell, AL:Tor. Aug. 14, 1990
      Chad Kreuter, AL:Det. July 30, 1994
      Juan Gonzalez, AL:Tex. July 3, 1999
      Edgar Martinez, AL:Sea. Aug. 3, 2002

Most Sacrifice Flies, Inning
1   By many players

WALKS (Since 1913)

Most Seasons Leading Major Leagues
11   Babe Ruth, AL:NY 1920-21, 23-24, 26-28, 30-33

Most Seasons, Consecutive, Leading Major Leagues
4   Babe Ruth, AL:NY 1930-33
      Barry Bonds, NL:SF 2001-04

Most Seasons Leading League
11   Babe Ruth, AL:NY 1920-21, 23-24, 26-28, 30-33
      Barry Bonds, NL:Pitt. 1992; SF 94-97, 2000-04, 06

Most Seasons, Consecutive, Leading League
5   Barry Bonds, NL:SF 2000-04
4   Babe Ruth, AL:NY 1930-33
      Ted Williams, AL:Bos. 1946-49

Most Walks, Lifetime
2426   Barry Bonds, NL:Pitt. 1986-92; SF 93-2006
2043   Babe Ruth, AL:Bos. 1914-19; NY 20-34

Most Walks, Season
232   Barry Bonds, NL:SF 2004
170   Babe Ruth, AL:NY 1923

Most Seasons, 100 or more Walks
13   Babe Ruth, AL:Bos. 1919; NY 20-21, 23-24, 26-28, 30-34
      Barry Bonds, NL:Pitt. 1991-92; SF 93, 95-98, 2000-04, 06

Most Seasons, Consecutive, 100 or more Walks
8   Max Bishop, AL:Phil. 1926-33
      Frank Thomas, AL:Chi. 1991-98
      Bobby Abreu, NL:Phil. 1999-2005; NL:Phil.-AL:NY 2006
7   Mel Ott, NL:NY 1936-42
      Jeff Bagwell, NL:Hou. 1996-2002
      Bobby Abreu, NL:Phil. 1998-2005

Most Walks, Game
6   Walter Wilmot, NL:Chi. Aug. 22, 1891 (cons)
      Jeff Bagwell, NL:Hou. Aug. 20, 1999 (16 inn)
      Jimmie Foxx, AL:Bos. June 16, 1938 (cons)
      Andre Thornton, AL:Clev. May 2, 1984 (16 inn)
      NL Since 1900 (nine-inning game):
5   By many NL players; Last:
      Ryan Howard, NL:Phil. July 30(1g), 2006 (cons)

Most Games, 5 or more Walks, League
4   Mel Ott, NL:NY Oct. 5, 1929(2g); Sept. 1(1g), 1933; June 17, 1943; Apr. 30(1g), 1944
2   Max Bishop, AL:Phil. Apr. 29, 1929; May 21(1g), 1930
      Rickey Henderson, AL:Oak. Apr. 8, 1982 (16 inn); Sea. July 30, 2000

Most Games, Consecutive, 1 or more Walks, Lifetime
22	Roy Cullenbine, AL:Det. July 2-22, 1947
20	Barry Bonds, NL:SF Sept. 9, 2002-Apr. 1, 2003

Most Games, Consecutive, 1 or more Walks, Season
22	Roy Cullenbine, AL:Det. July 2-22, 1947
18	Barry Bonds, NL:SF Sept. 9-28, 2002

Most Walks, Consecutive, Season
7	Billy Rogell, AL:Det. Aug. 17-19, 1938
	Jose Canseco, AL:Oak. Aug. 4-5 1992
	Mel Ott, NL:NY June 16-18, 1943
	Eddie Stanky, NL:NY Aug. 29-30, 1950
	Barry Bonds, NL:SF Sept. 24-26, 2004

Most Walks, Inning
2	By many players

INTENTIONAL WALKS (Since 1955)

Most Seasons Leading Major Leagues
9	Barry Bonds, NL:Pitt. 1992; SF 93, 96-98, 2002-04, 06

Most Seasons, Consecutive, Leading Major Leagues
4	Frank Robinson, NL:Cin. 1961-64

Most Seasons Leading League
11	Barry Bonds, NL:Pitt. 1992; SF 93-98, 2002-04, 06
6	Wade Boggs, AL:Bos. 1987-92

Most Seasons, Consecutive, Leading League
7	Barry Bonds, NL:Pitt. 1992; SF 93-98
6	Wade Boggs, AL:Bos. 1987-92

Most Intentional Walks, Lifetime
645	Barry Bonds, NL:Pitt. 1986-92; SF 93-2006
228	George Brett, AL:KC 1973-93

Most Intentional Walks, Season
120	Barry Bonds, NL:SF 2004
33	Ted Williams, AL:Bos. 1957
	John Olerud, AL:Tor. 1993

Most Seasons, 20 or more Intentional Walks
14	Barry Bonds, NL:Pitt. 1989, 91-92; SF 93, 95-98, 2000-04, 06
3	Frank Thomas, AL:Chi. 1993, 95-96
	Ken Griffey, Jr., AL:Sea. 1991, 93, 97

Most Seasons Consecutive, 20 or more Intentional Walks
5	Barry Bonds. NL:SF 2000-04
2	Harmon Killebrew, AL:Minn. 1969-70
	Frank Howard, AL:Wash. 1970-71
	Mo Vaughn, AL:Bos. 1993-94
	Frank Thomas, AL:Chi. 1995-96
	Vladimir Guerrero, AL:LA 2005-06

Most Intentional Walks, Game
4	Barry Bonds, NL:SF May 1, 2004; Sept. 22, 2004
3	By many AL players
	Extra-Inning Game:
5	Andre Dawson, NL:Chi. May 22, 1990 (16 inn)
4	Roger Maris, AL:NY May 22, 1962 (12 inn)
	Manny Ramirez, AL:Bos. June 5, 2001 (18 inn)

Most Intentional Walks, Inning
1	By many players

HIT BY PITCH

Most Seasons Leading Major Leagues
9	Minnie Minoso, AL:Clev.-Chi. 1951; Chi. 53-54, 56-57, 60-61; Clev. 58-59

Most Seasons, Consecutive, Leading Major Leagues
6	Minnie Minoso, AL:Chi. 1956-57, 60-61; Clev. 58-59
	Ron Hunt, NL:SF 1968-70; Mtl. 71-73

Most Seasons Leading League
10	Minnie Minoso, AL:Clev.-Chi. 1951; Chi. 52-54, 56-57, 60-61; Clev. 58-59
7	Ron Hunt, NL:SF 1968-70; Mtl. 71-73; Mtl.-StL. 74

Most Seasons, Consecutive, Leading League
7	Ron Hunt, NL:SF 1968-70; Mtl. 71-73; Mtl.-StL. 74
6	Minnie Minoso, AL:Chi. 1956-57, 60-61; Clev. 58-59

Most Hit By Pitch, Lifetime
287	Hughie Jennings, AA:Lou. 1891; NL:Lou. 92-93; Balt. 93-99; Brk. 99-1900, 03; Phil. 01-02; AL:Det. 1907, 09, 12, 18

Most Hit By Pitch, League
282	Craig Biggio, NL:Hou. 1988-2006
267	Don Baylor, AL:Balt. 1970-75; Oak. 76, 88; Cal. 77-82; NY 83-85; Bos. 86-87; Minn. 87

Most Hit By Pitch, Season
51	Hughie Jennings, NL:Balt. 1896
	Since 1900:
50	Ron Hunt, NL:Mtl. 1971
35	Don Baylor, AL:Bos. 1986

Most Hit By Pitch, Game
3	By many players; Last:
	Nomar Garciaparra, NL:LA July 3, 2006
	Reed Johnson, AL:Tor. Apr. 29, 2006

Most Hit By Pitch, Doubleheader
4	Frank Chance, NL:Chi. May 30, 1904
3	By many AL players

Most Hit By Pitch, Inning
2	Willard Schmidt, NL:Cin. Apr. 26, 1959 (3rd)
	Frank Thomas, NL:NY Apr. 29, 1962 (1g; 4th)
	Andres Galarraga, NL:Col. July 12, 1996 (7th)
	Brady Anderson, AL:Balt. May 23, 1999 (1st)

Most Plate Appearances, Season, No Hit By Pitch
739	Sandy Alomar, AL:Cal. 1971
728	Cesar Izturis, NL:LA 2004

STRIKEOUTS (Since 1910 in NL; Since 1913 in AL)

Most Seasons Leading Major Leagues
4	Babe Ruth, AL:Bos. 1918; NY 23-24, 27
	Rob Deer, AL:Mil. 1987-88; Det. 91; Det.-Bos. 93

Most Seasons, Consecutive, Leading Major Leagues
3	Hack Wilson, NL:Chi. 1928-30
	Mike Schmidt, NL:Phil. 1974-76
	Adam Dunn, NL:Cin. 2004-06

Most Seasons Leading League
6	Vince DiMaggio, NL:Bos. 1937-38; Pitt. 42-44; Phil. 45
5	Jimmie Foxx, AL:Phil. 1939, 33, 35; Bos. 36, 41
	Mickey Mantle, AL:NY 1952, 54, 58-60
	Reggie Jackson, AL:Oak. 1968-71, Cal. 82

Most Seasons, Consecutive, Leading League
4	Hack Wilson, NL:Chi. 1927-30
	Vince DiMaggio, NL:Pitt. 1942-44; Phil. 45
	Juan Samuel, NL:Phil. 1984-87
	Reggie Jackson, AL:Oak. 1968-71

Most Strikeouts, Lifetime
2597	Reggie Jackson, AL:Oak. 1968-75, 87; Balt. 76; NY77-81; Cal. 82-86
1936	Willie Stargell, NL:Pitt. 1962-82

Most Strikeouts, Season
195	Adam Dunn, NL:Cin. 2004
186	Rob Deer, AL:Mil. 1987

Most Seasons, 100 or more Strikeouts, Lifetime
18	Reggie Jackson, AL:Oak. 1968-75; Balt. 76; NY 77-80; Cal. 82-86
13	Willie Stargell, NL:Pitt. 1965-76, 79

Most Seasons, Consecutive, 100 or more Strikeouts, Lifetime
13	Reggie Jackson, AL:Oak. 1968-75; Balt. 76; NY 77-80
12	Willie Stargell, NL:Pitt. 65-76

Most Strikeouts, Consecutive At-Bats, Season
15	Mike Thurman, NL:Mtl. July 24-Sept. 10, 1998
13	Jim Hannan, AL:Wash. July 24-Aug. 13, 1968

Most Strikeouts, Consecutive Plate Appearances, Season

12	Sandy Koufax, NL:Brk. June 24-Sept. 24, 1955	
11	Dean Chance, AL:Cal. July 24-Aug. 13, 1966	
	Non-Pitcher:	
9	Adolfo Phillips, NL:Chi. June 8-11, 1966	
	Eric Davis, NL:Cin. Apr. 24-25, 1987	
	Steve Balboni, AL:KC Aug. 20-22, 1984	
	Reggie Jackson, AL:Oak. July 6-11, 1987	
	Bo Jackson, AL:KC Sept. 16-19, 1988	

Most Strikeouts, Game

5	By many players; Last:
	Alex Rios AL:Tor. July 29, 2006 (cons)
	Clay Hensley, NL:SD May 14, 2006 (cons)
	Extra-Inning Game:
6	Carl Weilman, AL:StL. July 25, 1913 (15 inn, cons)
	Rick Reichardt, AL:Cal. May 31, 1966 (17 inn)
	Billy Cowan, AL:Cal. July 9, 1971 (20 inn)
	Cecil Cooper, AL:Bos. June 14, 1974 (15 inn)
	Sam Horn, AL:Balt. July 17, 1991 (15 inn)
	Alex Gonzalez, AL:Tor. Sept. 9, 1998 (13 inn)
	Don Hoak, NL:Chi. May 2, 1956 (17 inn)
	Geoff Jenkins, NL:Mil. June 8, 2004 (17 inn)

Most Strikeouts, Inning

2	By many players

Most Games, Consecutive, No Strikeouts, Season (non-pitcher)

115	Joe Sewell, AL:Clev. May 17-Sept. 19, 1929
77	Lloyd Waner, NL:Pitt.-Bos.-Cin. Apr. 24-Sept. 16, 1941

GROUNDED INTO DOUBLE PLAYS (Since 1933 in NL; Since 1940 in AL)

Most Seasons Leading Major Leagues

4	Jim Rice, AL:Bos. 1982-85

Most Seasons, Consecutive, Leading Major Leagues

4	Jim Rice, AL:Bos. 1982-85

Most Seasons Leading League

4	Ernie Lombardi, NL:Cin. 1933-34, 38; NY 44
	Jim Rice, AL:Bos. 1982-85

Most Seasons, Consecutive, Leading League

4	Jim Rice, AL:Bos. 1982-85
2	Ernie Lombardi, NL:Cin. 1933-34
	Frank McCormick, NL:Cin. 1940-41
	Joe Torre, NL:Mil. 1964-65
	Willie Montanez, NL:Phil.-SF 1975; SF-Atl. 76
	Ray Knight, NL:Cin. 1980-81

Most Grounded into Double Plays, Lifetime

350	Cal Ripken, AL:Balt. 1981-2001
305	Hank Aaron, NL:Mil./Atl. 1954-74

Most Grounded Into Double Plays, Season

36	Jim Rice, AL Bos. 1984
30	Ernie Lombardi, NL:Cin. 1938
	Brad Ausmus, NL:Hou. 2002

Most Grounded Into Double Plays, Game

4	Goose Goslin, AL:Det. Apr. 28, 1934 (cons)
	Joe Torre, NL:NY July 21, 1975 (cons)

Most Grounded Into Double Plays, 2 Consecutive Games

5	Zeke Bonura, NL:NY July 8-9, 1939
4	By many AL players

Most At-Bats, No Grounded Into Double Plays, Season

646	Augie Galan. NL:Chi. 1935
570	Dick McAuliffe, AL:Det. 1968

STOLEN BASES (Prior to 1898 stolen bases credited on fielder's choice)

Most Seasons Leading Major Leagues

6	Lou Brock, NL:StL. 1966, 68, 71-74
	Rickey Henderson, AL:Oak. 1980, 82-83, 98, NY 88, NY-Oak. 89

Most Seasons, Consecutive, Leading Major Leagues

5	George Case, AL:Wash. 1939-43

Most Seasons Leading League
12	Rickey Henderson, AL:Oak. 1980-84, 90-91, 98; NY 85-86, 88; NY-Oak. 89
10	Max Carey, NL:Pitt. 1913, 15-18, 20, 22-25

Most Seasons, Consecutive, Leading League
9	Luis Aparicio, AL:Chi. 1956-62; Balt. 63-64
6	Maury Wills, NL:LA 1960-65
	Vince Coleman, NL:StL. 1985-90

Most Stolen Bases, Lifetime
1406	Rickey Henderson, AL:Oak. 1979-84, 89-95, 98; NY 85-88; Tor.93; Ana. 97; Sea. 2000; Bos. 02; NL:SD 96-97, 2001; NY 99-2000; LA 03

Most Stolen Bases, League
1270	Rickey Henderson, AL:Oak. 1979-84, 89-95, 98; NY 85-88; Tor. 93; Ana. 97; Sea. 2000; Bos. 02
938	Lou Brock, NL:Chi. 1961-64; StL. 64-79

Most Stolen Bases, Season
156	Harry Stovey, AA:Phil. 1888
	Since 1900:
130	Rickey Henderson, AL:Oak. 1982
118	Lou Brock, NL:StL. 1974

Most Seasons, 100 or more Stolen Bases
3	Rickey Henderson, AL:Oak. 1980, 82-83
	Vince Coleman, NL:StL. 1985-87

Most Seasons, Consecutive, 100 or more Stolen Bases
3	Vince Coleman, NL:StL. 1985-87
2	Rickey Henderson, AL:Oak. 1982-83

Most Seasons, 50 or more Stolen Bases
13	Rickey Henderson, AL:Oak. 1980-84, 90-91, 98; NY 85-86, 88; NY-Oak. 89; Oak.-Tor. 93
12	Lou Brock, NL:StL. 1965-76

Most Seasons, Consecutive, 50 or more Stolen Bases
12	Lou Brock, NL:StL. 1965-76
7	Rickey Henderson, AL:Oak. 1980-84; NY 85-86

Most Stolen Bases, Consecutive, League
50	Vince Coleman, NL:StL. Sept. 18, 1988-July 26, 1989
40	Tim Raines, AL:Chi. July 23, 1993-Aug. 4, 1995

Most Stolen Bases, Consecutive, Season
44	Vince Coleman, NL:StL. Apr. 3-July 26, 1989
39	Ichiro Suzuki, AL:Sea. Apr. 29-Sept. 30, 2006

Most Stolen Bases, Game
7	George Gore, NL:Chi. June 25, 1881
	Billy Hamilton, NL:Phil. Aug. 31(2g), 1894
	Since 1900:
6	Eddie Collins, AL:Phil. Sept. 11, 22(1g), 1912
	Otis Nixon, NL:Atl. June 16, 1991
	Eric Young, NL:Col. June 30, 1996

Most Stolen Bases, Inning
3	By many players; Last:
	Eric Young, NL:Col. June 30, 1996 (3rd)
	Chris Stynes, AL:KC May 12, 1996 (1st)

Most Stolen Home, Lifetime
54	Ty Cobb, AL:Det. 1905-26; Phil. 27-28

Most Stolen Home, League
54	Ty Cobb, AL:Det. 1905-26; Phil. 27-28
33	Max Carey, NL:Pitt. 1910-26, Brk. 26-29

Most Stolen Home, Season
8	Ty Cobb, AL:Det. 1912
7	Pete Reiser, NL:Brk. 1946

Most Stolen Home, Game
2	Honus Wagner, NL:Pitt. June 20, 1901
	Ed Konetchy, NL:StL. Sept. 30, 1907
	Joe Tinker, NL:Chi. June 28, 1910
	Larry Doyle, NL:NY Sept. 18, 1911
	Sherry Magee, NL:Phil. July 20, 1912
	Doc Gautreau, NL:Bos. Sept. 3(1g), 1927
	Joe Jackson, AL:Clev. Aug. 11, 1912
	Guy Zinn, AL:NY Aug. 15, 1912
	Eddie Collins, AL:Phil. Sept. 6, 1913
	Ty Cobb, AL:Det. June 18, 1915
	Bill Barrett, AL:Chi. May 1, 1924
	Vic Power, AL:Clev. Aug. 14, 1958 (10 inn)

Most Stolen Home, Inning
1   By many players

Highest Percentage Successful, Lifetime (Minimum: 300 stolen bases)
.847   Tim Raines, NL:Mtl. 1979-90, 2001; Fla. 02; AL:Chi. 91-95; NY 96-98; Oak. 99; Balt. 01 (808-954)

Highest Percentage Successful, League (Minimum: 300 stolen bases)
.857   Tim Raines, NL:Mtl. 1979-90, 2001; Fla. 2002 (635-741)
.833   Willie Wilson, AL:KC 1976-90, Oak. 1991-92 (660-792)

Highest Percentage Successful, Season (Minimum: 30 stolen bases)
.969   Brady Anderson, AL:Balt. 1994 (31-32; ML record)
           Carlos Beltran, AL:KC 2001 (31-32; ML record)
.970   Dave Roberts, NL:LA 2004 (33-34)
           (.927, NL:LA-AL:Bos. 2004; 38-41)

Most Stolen Bases, None Caught, Season
21   Kevin McReynolds, NL:NY 1988 (ML record)
28   Carlos Beltran NL:Hou. 2004
           (3 CS with AL:KC 2004)
20   Paul Molitor, AL:Tor. 1994

ᴄAUGHT STEALING (Since 1920 in AL; Since 1951 in NL)

Most Seasons Leading Major Leagues
6   Maury Wills, NL:LA 1961-63, 65-66; Mtl.-LA 69

Most Seasons, Consecutive, Leading Major Leagues
3   Maury Wills, NL:LA 1961-63

Most Seasons Leading League
7   Maury Wills, NL:LA 1961-63, 65-66; Pitt. 68; Mtl.-LA 69
           Lou Brock, NL:Chi.-StL. 1964; StL. 67, 71, 73-74, 76-77
6   Minnie Minoso, AL:Chi. 1952-54, 57, 60; Clev. 58

Most Seasons, Consecutive, Leading League
4   Ben Chapman, AL:NY 1931-34
           Rickey Henderson, AL:Oak. 1980-83
           Juan Pierre, NL:Fla. 2003-05; NL:Chi. 06

Most Caught Stealing, Lifetime
335   Rickey Henderson, AL:Oak. 1979-84, 89-95, 98; NY 85-89; Tor. 93; Ana. 97; Sea. 2000;
                             Bos. 02; NL:SD 97, 2001; NY 99-2000; LA 03

Most Caught Stealing, League
307   Lou Brock, NL:Chi. 1961-64;- StL. 64-79
293   Rickey Henderson, AL:Oak. 1979-84, 89-95, 98; NY 85-89; Tor. 93; Ana. 97;
                             Sea. 2000; Bos. 02

Most Caught Stealing, Season
42   Rickey Henderson, AL:Oak. 1982 (172 attempts)
33   Lou Brock, NL:StL. 1974 (151 attempts)
           Omar Moreno, NL:Pitt. 1980 (129 attempts)

Most Caught Stealing, Game
3   By many players
           Extra-Inning Game:
4   Robby Thompson, NL:SF June 27, 1986 (12 inn)

Most Caught Stealing, Inning
2   Don Baylor, AL:Balt. June 15, 1974 (9th)
           Roberto Kelly, AL:NY Apr. 17, 1990 (2nd)
           Jim Morrison, NL:Pitt. June 15, 1987 (8th)
           Paul Noce, NL:Chi. June 26, 1987 (3rd)
           Donell Nixon, NL:SF July 6, 1988 (6th)
           Tony Fernandez, NL:SD June 26, 1992 (5th)
           Eric Young, NL:Col. May 1, 1993 (8th)
           Phil Plantier, NL:SD Sept. 25, 1993 (5th)
           Derek Bell, NL:Hou. June 19, 1995 (4th)
           Larry Walker, NL:Col. Apr. 30, 1998 (8th)

ᴘINCH HITTING

Most Games, Season
95   Lenny Harris, NL:NY 2001
81   Elmer Valo, AL:NY-Wash. 1960

Most At-Bats, Lifetime
804   Lenny Harris, NL:Cin. 1988-89, 94-98; LA 89-93; NY 98, 2000-01; Col. 99; Ari. 2000; Mil. 02; Chi. 03; Fla. 03-05
414   Gates Brown, AL:Det. 1963-75

Most At-Bats, Season
83   Lenny Harris, NL:NY 2001
72   Dave Philley, AL:Balt. 1961

Most Hits, Lifetime
212   Lenny Harris, NL:Cin. 1988-89, 94-98; LA 89-93; NY 98, 2000-01; Col. 99; Ari. 2000; Mil. 02; Chi. 03; Fla. 03-05
107   Gates Brown, AL:Det. 1963-75

Most Hits, Season
28   John Vander Wal, NL:Col. 1995
24   Dave Philley, AL:Balt. 1961

Most Hits, Consecutive At-Bats, League
9   Dave Philley, NL:Phil. Sept. 9, 1958-Apr. 16, 1959

Most Hits, Consecutive At-Bats, Season
8   Dave Philley, NL:Phil. Sept. 9-28, 1958
     Rusty Staub, NL:NY June 11-26(1g), 1983
7   Bill Stein, AL:Tex. Apr. 14-May 25, 1981
     Randy Bush, AL:Minn. July 5-Aug. 19, 1991
     Ross Gload, AL:Chi. July 2-Sept. 3, 2006

Most Home Runs, Lifetime
20   Cliff Johnson, NL:Hou. 1972-77; Chi. 80; AL:NY 1977-79; Clev. 79-80; Oak. 81-82; Tor. 83-86

Most Home Runs, League
18   Jerry Lynch, NL:Pitt. 1954-56, 63-66; Cin. 57-63
16   Gates Brown, AL:Det. 1963-75

Most Home Runs, Season
7   Dave Hansen, NL:LA 2000
     Craig Wilson, NL:Pitt. 2001
5   Joe Cronin, AL:Bos. 1943

Most Home Runs, Consecutive At-Bats, Season
3   Lee Lacy, NL:LA May 2, 6, 17, 1978
     Del Unser, NL:Phil. June 30, July 5, 10, 1979
     Matthew LeCroy, AL:Minn. May 19, June 1, 17, 2004

Most Grand Slam Home Runs, Lifetime
3   Ron Northey, NL:StL. Sept. 3, 1947; May 30, 1948; Chi. Sept. 18, 1950
     Willie McCovey, NL:SF June 12, 1960; Sept. 10, 1965; SD May 30, 1975
     Rich Reese, AL:Minn. Aug. 3, 1969; June 7, 1970; July 9, 1972

Most Grand Slam Home Runs, Season
2   Dave Johnson, NL:Phil. Apr. 30, June 3, 1978
     Mike Ivie, NL:SF May 28, June 30, 1978
     Darryl Strawberry, AL:NY May 2, Aug. 4, 1998
     Ben Broussard, AL:Clev. June 23, Aug. 12, 2004

Most Walks, Season
20   Matt Franco, NL:NY 1999
18   Elmer Valo, AL:Wash. 1960

Most Runs Batted In, Season
25   Joe Cronin, AL:Bos. 1943
     Jerry Lynch, NL:Cin. 1961
     Rusty Staub, NL:NY 1983

ROOKIE BATTING

(No official rookie rule prior to 1957. Qualifiers based on 130 or fewer previous at-bats. Records listed are for a single season.)

Highest Batting Average (Minimum: 350 at-bats)
.408   Joe Jackson, AL:Clev. 1911
.373   George Watkins, NL:StL. 1930

Highest Slugging Percentage (Minimum: 350 at-bats)
.651   Rudy York, AL:Det. 1937
.621   George Watkins, NL:StL. 1930

Most Games
163	Hideki Matsui, AL:NY 2003
162	Dick Allen NL:Phil. 1964
	Johnny Ray, NL:Pitt. 1982
	Jeff Conine, NL:Fla. 1993

Most At-Bats
701	Juan Samuel, NL:Phil. 1984
692	Ichiro Suzuki, AL:Sea. 2001

Most Runs
152	Mike Griffin, AA:Balt. 1887
135	Roy Thomas, NL:Phil. 1899
	Since 1900:
133	Lloyd Waner, NL:Pitt. 1927
132	Joe DiMaggio, AL:NY 1936

Most Hits
242	Ichiro Suzuki, AL:Sea. 2001
223	Lloyd Waner, NL:Pitt. 1927

Most Games, Consecutive, Hits
34	Benito Santiago, NL:SD Aug. 25-Oct. 2, 1987
30	Nomar Garciaparra, AL:Bos. July 26-Aug. 29, 1997

Most Extra-Base Hits
89	Hal Trosky, AL:Clev. 1934
88	Albert Pujols, NL:StL. 2001

Most Total Bases
374	Hal Trosky, AL:Clev. 1934
	Tony Oliva, AL:Minn. 1964
360	Albert Pujols, NL:StL. 2001

Most Singles
198	Lloyd Waner, NL:Pitt. 1927
192	Ichiro Suzuki, AL:Sea. 2001

Most Doubles
52	Johnny Frederick, NL:Brk. 1929
47	Fred Lynn, AL:Bos. 1975

Most Triples
27	Jimmy Williams, NL:Pitt. 1899
	Since 1900:
25	Tommy Long, NL:StL. 1915
19	Joe Cassidy, AL:Wash. 1904
	Frank Baker, AL:Phil. 1909
	Joe Jackson, AL:Clev. 1911

Most Home Runs
49	Mark McGwire, AL:Oak. 1987
38	Wally Berger, NL:Bos. 1930
	Frank Robinson, NL:Cin. 1956

Most Runs Batted In
145	Ted Williams, AL:Bos. 1939
130	Albert Pujols, NL:StL. 2001

Most Sacrifice Hits (Since 1931)
28	Joe Hoover, AL:Det. 1943
	Jackie Robinson, NL:Brk. 1947
	Ozzie Smith, NL:SD 1978

Most Sacrifice Flies (1908 to 1930, 1939, since 1954)
13	Willie Montanez, NL:Phil. 1971
	Gary Gaetti, AL:Minn. 1982

Most Walks (Since 1913)
107	Ted Williams, AL:Bos. 1939
100	Jim Gilliam, NL:Brk. 1953

Most Intentional Walks (Since 1955)
16	Alvin Davis, AL:Sea. 1984
14	Willie Montanez, NL:Phil. 1971

Most Hit By Pitch
29	Tommy Tucker, AA:Balt. 1887
	Since 1900:
21	Bucky Harris, AL:Wash. 1920
	David Eckstein, AL:Ana. 2001
20	Frank Robinson, NL:Cin. 1956

INDIVIDUAL FIELDING

(Career percentage leaders based on 1000-game minimum; pitchers' minimum: 300 total chances)

FIRST BASE

Most Seasons, League

22	Willie McCovey, NL:SF 1959-73, 77-80; SD 74-76
20	Joe Judge, AL:Wash. 1915-32; Bos. 33-34

PERCENTAGE

Most Seasons Leading League

7	Ed Konetchy, NL:StL. 1910-11, 13; Pitt. 14; Bos. 17-18; Brk. 19
	Charlie Grimm, NL:Pitt. 1920, 23-24; Chi. 28, 30-31, 33
	Don Mattingly, AL:NY 1984-87, 92-94

Most Seasons, Consecutive, Leading League

5	Ted Kluszewski, NL:Cin. 1951-55
4	Don Mattingly, AL:NY 1984-87

Highest Percentage, Lifetime

.9967	Travis Lee, NL:Ari. 1998-2000; Phil. 2000-02; AL:TB 2003, 05-06; NY 04

Highest Percentage, League

.9959	Steve Garvey, NL:LA 1975-82; SD 83-87
.9958	Don Mattingly, AL:NY 1982-95

Highest Percentage, Season

1.000	Steve Garvey, NL:SD 1984
.999	Stuffy McInnis, AL:Bos. 1921

Lowest Percentage, Season, Since 1900

.970	John Doyle, NL:NY 1900
.972	Pat Newnam, AL:StL. 1910

GAMES

Most Seasons Leading League

9	Steve Garvey, NL:LA 1975-81; SD 84-85
7	Lou Gehrig, AL:NY 1926-28, 32, 36-38

Most Games, Lifetime

2413	Eddie Murray, AL:Balt. 1977-88, 96; Clev. 94-96; NL:LA 1989-91; NY 92-93

Most Games, League

2247	Jake Beckley, NL:Pitt. 1888-89, 91-96; NY 96-97; Cin. 1897-1903; St.L. 04-07
2227	Mickey Vernon, AL:Wash. 1939-43, 46-48, 50-55; Clev. 49-50, 58; Bos. 56-57

Most Games, Consecutive

885	Lou Gehrig, AL:NY June 2, 1925-Sept. 27, 1930
652	Frank McCormick, NL:Cin. Apr. 19, 1938-May 24, 1942

Most Games, Season

162	Norm Siebern, AL:KC 1962
	Bill Buckner, AL:Bos. 1985
	Carlos Delgado, AL:Tor. 2000
	Bill White, NL:StL. 1963
	Ernie Banks, NL:Chi. 1965
	Steve Garvey, NL:LA 1976, 79-80; SD 85
	Pete Rose, NL:Phil. 1980, 82
	Jeff Bagwell, NL:Hou. 1996
	Eric Karros, NL:LA 1997
	Derrek Lee, NL:Fla. 2002
	Richie Sexson, NL:Mil. 2003

CHANCES ACCEPTED

Most Seasons Leading League

6	Bill Terry, NL:NY 1927-30, 32, 34
4	Wally Pipp, AL:NY 1915, 19-20, 22
	Carlos Delgado, AL:Tor. 2000-03

Most Chances Accepted, Lifetime

25,000	Jake Beckley, NL:Pitt. 1888-89, 91-96; NY 96-97; Cin. 1897-1903; StL. 04-07; PL:Pitt. 1890

Most Chances Accepted, League

23,687	Jake Beckley, NL:Pitt. 1888-89, 91-96; NY 96-97; Cin. 1897-1903; StL. 04-07
21,198	Mickey Vernon, AL:Wash. 1939-43, 46-48, 50-55; Clev. 49-50, 58; Bos. 56-57

Most Chances Accepted, Season

1986	Jiggs Donahue, AL:Chi. 1907
1862	George Kelly, NL:NY 1920

Most Chances Accepted, Game

22	By many players; Last:
	Alvin Davis, AL:Sea. May 28, 1988
	Ernie Banks, NL:Chi. May 9, 1963
	Extra-Inning Game:
43	Walter Holke, NL:Bos. May 1, 1920 (26 inn)
34	Rudy York, AL:Det. July 21, 1945 (24 inn)
	Mike Epstein, AL:Wash. June 12, 1967 (22 inn)
	Rod Carew, AL:Cal. Apr. 13, 1982 (20 inn)

Fewest Chances Accepted, Game (Complete Nine-Inning Game in Field)

0	Guy Hecker, AA:Lou. Oct. 9, 1887
	Al McCauley, AA:Wash. Aug. 6, 1891
	Bud Clancy, AL:Chi. Apr. 27, 1930
	Norm Cash, AL:Det. June 27, 1963
	Gene Tenace, AL:Oak. Sept. 1, 1974
	Mark McGwire, AL:Oak. Sept. 12, 1995
	Scott Cooper, AL:KC May 31, 1997 (8 inn)
	Robb Quinlan, AL:Ana. Aug. 6, 2003 (8 inn)
	Ripper Collins, NL:Chi. June 29, 1937
	Fred McGriff, NL:Chi. Aug. 15, 2002

▪UTOUTS

Most Seasons Leading League

6	Jake Beckley, NL:Pitt. 1892, 94-95; Cin. 1900, 02; StL. 04
	Frank McCormick, NL:Cin. 1939-42, 44-45
	Steve Garvey, NL:LA 1974-78; SD 85
5	Carlos Delgado, AL:Tor. 1999-2003

Most Putouts, Lifetime

23,696	Jake Beckley, NL:Pitt. 1888-89, 91-96; NY 96-97; Cin. 1897-1903; StL. 04-07; PL:Pitt. 1890

Most Putouts, League

22,438	Jake Beckley, NL:Pitt. 1888-89, 91-96; NY 96-97; Cin. 1897-1903; St,L. 04-07
19,754	Mickey Vernon, AL:Wash. 1939-43, 46-48, 50-55; Clev. 49-50, 58; Bos. 56-57

Most Putouts, Season

1846	Jiggs Donahue, AL:Chi. 1907
1759	George Kelly, NL:NY 1920

Most Putouts, Game

22	Tom Jones, AL:StL. May 11, 1906
	Hal Chase, AL:NY Sept. 21(1g), 1906
	Don Mattingly, AL:NY July 20, 1987
	Alvin Davis, AL:Sea. May 28, 1988
	Ernie Banks, NL:Chi. May 9, 1963
	Extra-Inning Game:
42	Walter Holke, NL:Bos. May 1, 1920 (26 inn)
32	Mike Epstein, AL:Wash. June 12, 1967 (22 inn)
	Rod Carew, AL:Cal. Apr. 13, 1982 (20 inn)

Fewest Putouts, Game (Complete Nine-Inning Game in Field)

0	Guy Hecker, AA:Lou. Oct. 9, 1887 (8 inn)
	Al McCauley, AA:Wash. Aug. 6, 1891
	Solly Hofman, NL:Chi. June 24, 1910 (8 inn)
	Ripper Collins, NL:StL. Aug. 21, 1935; Chi. June 29, 1937
	Dolf Camilli, NL:Phil. July 30, 1937
	Earl Torgeson, NL:Bos. May 30(1g), 1947
	Gary Thomasson, NL:SF July 31, 1977 (8 inn)
	Len Matuszek, NL:Phil. June 1, 1984
	Franklin Stubbs, NL:Hou. July 25, 1990
	Fred McGriff, NL:Chi. Aug. 15, 2002
	Bud Clancy, AL:Chi. Apr. 27, 1930
	Rudy York, AL:Det. June 18, 1943
	Norm Cash, AL:Det. June 27, 1963 (8 inn)
	Bill Skowron, AL:Chi. May 15, 1966 (8 inn)
	Frank Robinson, AL:Balt., July 1, 1971
	Gene Tenace, AL:Oak. Sept. 1, 1974
	Greg Brock, AL:Mil. June 28, 1987
	Mark McGwire, AL:Oak. Sept. 12, 1995
	Scott Cooper, AL:KC May 31, 1997 (8 inn)
	Rafael Palmeiro, AL:Balt. June 23, 1997
	John Olerud, AL:Sea. July 17, 2000 (8 inn)
	Robb Quinlan, AL:Ana. Aug. 6, 2003 (8 inn)
	Raul Ibanez, AL:Sea. Apr. 18, 2005 (8 inn)

ASSISTS

Most Seasons Leading League

8	Fred Tenney, NL:Bos. 1899, 1901-07
6	George Sisler, AL:StL. 1919-20, 22, 24-25, 27
	Vic Power, AL:KC 1955, 57; Clev. 59-61; Minn. 62

Most Assists, Lifetime

1865	Eddie Murray, AL:Balt. 1977-88, 96; Clev. 94-96; NL:LA 89-91; NY 92-93

Most Assists, League

1704	Jeff Bagwell, NL:Hou. 1991-2005
1574	Rafael Palmeiro, AL:Tex. 1989-93, 99-2003; Balt. 94-98, 2004-05

Most Assists, Season

184	Bill Buckner, AL:Bos. 1985
180	Mark Grace, NL:Chi. 1990

Most Assists, Game

8	Bob Skinner, NL:Pitt. July 22, 1954 (14 inn)
	Bob Robertson, NL:Pitt. June 21, 1971
	Darrell Evans, NL:SF May 30, 1981 (14 inn)
7	George Stovall, AL:StL. Aug. 7, 1912
	Ferris Fain, AL:Phil. June 9, 1949 (12 inn)
	Don Mattingly, AL:NY May 11, 1984 (17 inn)

Fewest Assists, Game (Most Innings, Complete Game in Field)

0	Ed Konetchy, NL:Pitt. July 17, 1914 (21 inn)
	Fred Merkle, NL:NY July 17, 1914 (21 inn)

Most Assists, Inning

3	By many players; Last:
	John Olerud, AL:Bos. July 5, 2005 (1st)
	Brad Wilkerson, NL:Mtl. May 20, 2004 (9th)

ERRORS

Most Seasons Leading League (Most Errors)

7	Dick Stuart, NL:Pitt. 1958-62; AL:Bos. 63-64
	Mo Vaughn, AL:Bos. 1992-94, 96-97; Ana. 2000; NL:NY 02
6	Mo Vaughn, AL:Bos. 1992-94, 96-97; Ana. 2000
5	Dick Stuart, NL:Pitt. 1958-62
	Willie McCovey, NL:SF 1967-68, 70-71, 77

Most Errors, League, Since 1900

285	Hal Chase, AL:NY 1905-13; Chi. 13-14
252	Fred Tenney, NL:Bos. 1900-07, 11; NY 08-09
	Fred Merkle, NL:NY 1907-16; Brk. 16-17; Cin. 17-20

Most Errors, Season

62	Joe Quinn, UA:StL. 1884
58	Cap Anson, NL:Chi. 1884
	Since 1900:
43	Jack Doyle, NL:NY 1900
41	Jerry Freeman, AL:Wash. 1908

Fewest Errors, Season
>   **Minimum: 1500 total chances**
> 1   Stuffy McInnis, AL:Bos. 1921 (1652 tc)
> 3   Steve Garvey, NL:LA 1976 (1653 tc)
>   **Minimum: 150 games**
> 0   Steve Garvey, NL:SD 1984 (159 g)
> 1   Stuffy McInnis, AL:Bos. 1921 (152 g)

Most Errors, Game
> 5   John Carbine, NL:Lou. Apr. 29, 1876
>   George Zettlein, NL:Phil. June 22, 1876
>   Everett Mills, NL:Hart. Oct. 7, 1876
>   Dude Esterbrook, NL:Buff. July 27, 1880
>   Roger Connor, NL:Troy May 27, 1882
>   Lew Brown, AA:Lou. Sept. 10, 1883
>   Jack Gorman, UA:KC June 28, 1884
>   Joe Quinn, UA:StL. July 4(1g), 1884
>   **Since 1900:**
> 4   Jock Menefee, NL:Chi. Oct. 6, 1901
>   Johnny Lush, NL:Phil. June 11 & Sept. 15(2g), 1904
>   Fred Tenney, NL:Bos. July 12(1g), 1905
>   Todd Zeile, NL:Phil. Aug. 7, 1996
>   Buck Freeman, AL:Bos. Sept. 23(2g), 1901
>   Hal Chase, AL:Chi. July 23, 1913
>   George Sisler, AL:StL. Apr. 14, 1925
>   Jimmy Wasdell, AL:Wash. May 3, 1939
>   Glenn Davis, AL:Balt. Apr. 18, 1991

Most Errors, Inning
> 3   Dolf Camilli, NL:Phil. Aug. 2, 1935 (1st)
>   Al Oliver, NL:Pitt. May 23, 1969 (4th)
>   Jack Clark, NL:StL. May 25, 1987 (3rd)
>   George Metkovich, AL:Bos., Apr. 17, 1945 (7th)
>   Tom McCraw, AL:Chi. May 3, 1968 (3rd)
>   Willie Upshaw, AL:Tor. July 1, 1986 (5th)

Most Errorless Games, Consecutive, Lifetime
> 193   Steve Garvey, NL:SD June 26, 1983-Apr. 14, 1985
> 178   Mike Hegan, AL:Mil. Sept. 24, 1970-Oak. May 20, 1973

Most Errorless Games, Consecutive, Season
> 159   Steve Garvey, NL:SD 1984 (entire season)
> 121   Travis Lee, AL:TB May 9-Sept. 28, 2003

Most Errorless Chances Accepted, Consecutive, Lifetime
> 1700   Stuffy McInnis, AL:Bos.-Clev. May 31(1g), 1921 - June 2, 1922
> 1633   Steve Garvey, NL:SD June 26, 1983-Apr. 15, 1985

Most Errorless Chances Accepted, Consecutive, Season
> 1319   Steve Garvey, NL:SD 1984 (entire season)
> 1300   Stuffy McInnis, AL:Bos. May 31(1g)-Oct. 2, 1921

)OUBLE PLAYS

Most Seasons Leading League
> 6   Keith Hernandez, NL:StL. 1977, 79-81; NY 83-84
>   Todd Helton, NL:Col. 1998-2000, 02-03, 06
> 4   Stuffy McInnis, AL:Phil. 1912, 14; Bos. 19-20
>   Wally Pipp, AL:NY 1915-17, 20
>   Vic Power, AL:KC 1955; Clev. 59-60; Minn. 62
>   Cecil Cooper, AL:Mil. 1980-83
>   Carlos Delgado, AL:Tor. 1999-2001, 03

Most Double Plays, Lifetime
> 2044   Mickey Vernon, AL:Wash. 1939-43, 46-48, 50-55; Clev. 49-50, 58; Bos. 56-57; NL:Mil. 1959

Most Double Plays, League
> 2041   Mickey Vernon, AL:Wash. 1939-43, 46-48, 50-55; Clev. 49-50, 58
> 1708   Charlie Grimm, NL:StL. 1918; Pitt. 19-24; Chi. 25-36

Most Double Plays, Season
> 194   Ferris Fain, AL:Phil. 1949
> 182   Donn Clendenon, NL:Pitt. 1966

Most Double Plays, Unassisted, Season
> 9   Travis Lee, AL:TB 2005
> 8   Bill White, NL:StL. 1961

Most Double Plays, Game

7	Curt Blefary, NL:Hou. May 4, 1969
6	Jimmie Foxx, AL:Phil. Aug. 24, 1935 (15 inn)
	Ferris Fain, AL:Phil. Sept. 1(2g), 1947
	George Vico, AL:Det. May 19, 1948
	Eddie Robinson, AL:Clev. Aug. 5, 1948
	Lee Thomas, AL:LA Aug. 23, 1963
	Bob Oliver, AL:KC May 14, 1971; NY Apr. 29, 1975
	John Mayberry, AL:KC May 16, 1972
	Rod Carew, AL:Minn. Aug. 29(1g), 1977 (10 inn)
	Kent Hrbek, AL:Minn. July 18, 1990
	Mark McGwire, AL:Oak. May 17, 1995
	Jason Giambi, AL:NY June 17(1g), 2003

Most Double Plays, Unassisted, Game

2	By many players; Last:
	Richie Sexson, NL:Mil. Sept. 11, 2002
	Jason Giambi, AL:Oak. Aug. 2, 2000

TRIPLE PLAYS

Unassisted Triple Play

1	George Burns, AL:Bos. (Clev.) Sept. 14, 1923 (2nd)
	Johnny Neun, AL:Det. (Clev.) May 31, 1927 (9th)

SECOND BASE

Most Seasons, Lifetime

22	Joe Morgan, NL:Hou. 1963-71, 80; Cin. 72-79; SF 81-82; Phil. 83; AL:Oak. 1984

Most Seasons, League

22	Eddie Collins, AL:Phil. 1906, 08-14, 27-28; Chi. 15-26
21	Joe Morgan, NL:Hou. 1963-71, 80; Cin. 72-79; SF 81-82; Phil. 83

PERCENTAGE

Most Seasons Leading League

9	Eddie Collins, AL:Phil. 1909-10, 14; Chi. 15-16, 20-22, 24
6	Red Schoendienst, NL:StL. 1946, 49, 53, 55; StL.-NY 56; Mil. 58

Most Seasons, Consecutive, Leading League

3	Claude Ritchey, NL:Pitt. 1905-07
	Bret Boone, NL:Cin. 1995-97
	Nap Lajoie, AL:Clev. 1906-08
	Eddie Collins, AL:Phil. 1914-Chi. 15-16; Chi. 20-22
	Charlie Gehringer, AL:Det. 1935-37

Highest Percentage, Lifetime

.989	Ryne Sandberg, NL:Phil. 1981; Chi. 82-94, 96-97
.987	Roberto Alomar, AL:Tor. 1991-95; Balt. 96-98; Clev. 99-2001; Chi. 03-04

Highest Percentage, Season

.9968	Mark Ellis, AL:Oak. 2006
.9967	Bret Boone, NL:Cin. 1997

Lowest Percentage, Season, Since 1900

.914	Frank Truesdale, NL:StL. 1910
.927	John Farrell, NL:StL. 1903

GAMES

Most Seasons Leading League

8	Nellie Fox, AL:Chi. 1952-59
	Craig Biggio, NL:Hou. 1992-98, 2001

Most Games, Lifetime

2651	Eddie Collins, AL:Phil. 1906, 08-14, 27-28; Chi. 15-26
2427	Joe Morgan, NL:Hou. 1963-71, 80; Cin. 72-79; SF 81-82; Phil. 83

Most Games, Consecutive

798	Nellie Fox, AL:Chi. Aug. 7, 1955-Sept. 3, 1960
443	Dave Cash, NL:Pitt.-Phil. Sept. 20, 1973-Aug. 5, 1976

Most Games, Season

163	Bill Mazeroski, NL:Pitt. 1967
162	Jake Wood, AL:Det. 1961
	Bobby Grich, AL:Balt. 1973

CHANCES ACCEPTED

Most Seasons Leading League
9	Nellie Fox, AL:Chi. 1952-60
8	Bill Mazeroski, NL:Pitt. 1958, 60-64, 66-67

Most Chances Accepted, Lifetime
14,156	Eddie Collins, AL:Phil. 1906, 08-14, 27-28; Chi. 15-26

Most Chances Accepted, League
14,156	Eddie Collins, AL:Phil. 1906, 08-14, 27-28; Chi. 15-26
12,279	Joe Morgan, NL:Hou. 1963-71, 80; Cin. 72-79; SF 81-82; Phil. 83

Most Chances Accepted, Season
1037	Frankie Frisch, NL:StL. 1927
988	Nap Lajoie, AL:Clev. 1908

Most Chances Accepted, Game
18	Cupid Childs, AA:Syr. June 1, 1890
	Terry Harmon, NL:Phil. June 12, 1971
17	Jimmy Dykes, AL:Phil. Aug. 28, 1921
	Nellie Fox, AL:Chi. June 12, 1952
	Extra-Inning Game:
21	Eddie Moore, NL:Bos. May 17, 1927 (22 inn)
20	Willie Randolph, AL:NY Aug. 25, 1976 (19 inn)

Fewest Chances Accepted, Game (Most Innings, Complete Game in Field)
0	Steve Yerkes, AL:Bos. June 11, 1913 (15 inn)
	Ken Boswell, NL:NY Aug. 7, 1972 (13 inn)

PUTOUTS

Most Seasons Leading League
10	Nellie Fox, AL:Chi. 1952-61
7	Fred Pfeffer, NL:Chi. 1884-89, 91
	Billy Herman, NL:Chi. 1933, 35-36, 38-40; Brk. 42

Most Putouts, Lifetime
6526	Eddie Collins, AL:Phil. 1906, 08-14, 27-28; Chi. 15-26

Most Putouts, League
6526	Eddie Collins, AL:Phil. 1906, 08-14, 27-28; Chi. 15-26
5541	Joe Morgan, NL:Hou. 1963-71, 80; Cin. 72-79; SF 81-82; Phil. 83

Most Putouts, Season
484	Bobby Grich, AL:Balt. 1974
466	Billy Herman, NL:Chi. 1933

Most Putouts, Game
12	Lou Bierbauer, AA:Phil. June 22, 1888
	Billy Gardner, AL:Balt. May 21, 1957 (16 inn)
	Bobby Knoop, AL:Cal. Aug. 30, 1966
	Vern Fuller, AL:Clev. Apr. 11, 1969 (16 inn)
	Tomas Perez, AL:Tor. Aug. 20, 1996 (14 inn)
11	Sam Wise, NL:Wash. May 9, 1893
	Bid McPhee, NL:Cin. Apr. 21, 1894
	Nap Lajoie, NL:Phil. Apr. 25, 1899
	Billy Herman, NL:Chi. June 28(1g), 1933
	Gene Baker, NL:Chi. May 27, 1955
	Charlie Neal, NL:LA July 2, 1959
	Julian Javier, NL:StL. June 27, 1964
	Extra-Inning Game:
15	Jake Pitler, NL:Pitt. Aug. 22, 1917 (22 inn)
13	Roy Hughes, AL:Clev. May 10, 1936 (15 inn)

Fewest Putouts, Game (Most Innings, Complete Game in Field)
0	Phil Garner, NL:Pitt. Aug. 10, 1977 (18 inn)
	Steve Yerkes, AL:Bos. June 11, 1913 (15 inn)
	Denny Doyle, AL:Cal. June 14, 1974 (15 inn)
	Damion Easley, AL:Det. July 8, 2000 (15 inn)

ASSISTS

Most Seasons Leading League
9	Bill Mazeroski, NL:Pitt. 1958, 60-64, 66-68
7	Charlie Gehringer, AL:Det. 1927-28, 33-36, 38

Most Assists, Lifetime
7630	Eddie Collins, AL:Phil. 1906, 08-14, 27-28; Chi. 15-26

Most Assists, League

7630	Eddie Collins, AL:Phil. 1906, 08-14, 27-28; Chi. 15-26
6738	Joe Morgan, NL:Hou. 1963-71, 80; Cin. 72-79; SF 81-82; Phil. 83

Most Assists, Season

641	Frankie Frisch, NL:StL. 1927
572	Oscar Melillo, AL:StL. 1930

Most Assists, Game

12	Monte Ward, NL:Brk. June 10(1g), 1892
	Jim Gilliam, NL:Brk. July 21, 1956
	Jack Perconte, NL:LA Sept. 19, 1981
	Ryne Sandberg, NL:Chi. June 12, 1983
	Glenn Hubbard, NL:Atl. Apr. 14, 1985
	Juan Samuel, NL:Phil. Apr. 20, 1985
	Don Money, AL:Mil. June 24, 1977
	Tony Phillips, AL:Oak. July 6, 1986
	Harold Reynolds, AL:Sea. Aug. 27, 1986
	Extra-Inning Game:
15	Lave Cross, NL:Phil. Aug. 5, 1897 (12 inn)
	Since 1900:
13	Morrie Rath, NL:Cin. Aug. 26, 1919 (15 inn)
	Mark Loretta, NL:SD May 7, 2003 (10 inn)
	Bobby Avila, AL:Clev. July 1, 1952 (19 inn)
	Willie Randolph, AL:NY Aug. 25, 1976 (19 inn)

Fewest Assists, Game (Most Innings, Complete Game in Field)

0	Gordon Slade, NL:Cin. July 1(1g), 1934 (18 inn)
	Delino DeShields, NL:LA Aug. 3, 1996 (18 inn)
	Jerry Browne, AL:Clev. Sept. 21, 1989 (17 inn)

Most Assists, Inning

3	By many players

ERRORS

Most Seasons Leading League (Most Errors)

5	Fred Pfeffer, NL:Chi. 1884-88
	Alfonso Soriano, AL:NY 2001-03, Tex. 04-05
	NL Since 1900:
4	Larry Doyle, NL:NY 1908, 10, 17, 19
	Billy Herman, NL:Chi. 1932-33, 37, 39
	Glenn Beckert, NL:Chi. 1966-67, 69-70

Most Errors, Lifetime

828	Fred Pfeffer, NL:Troy 1882; Chi. 83-89, 91, 96-97; Lou. 92-95; NY 96; PL:Chi. 1890

Most Errors, League

754	Fred Pfeffer, NL:Troy 1882; Chi. 83-89, 91, 96-97; Lou. 92-95; NY 96
	Since 1900:
443	Larry Doyle, NL:NY 1907-16, 18-20; Chi. 16-17
435	Eddie Collins, AL:Phil. 1906, 08-14, 27-28; Chi. 15-26

Most Errors, Season

92	Yank Robinson, AA:StL. 1886
88	Pop Smith, NL:Cin. 1880
	Bob Ferguson, NL:Phil. 1883
	Since 1900:
61	Kid Gleason, AL:Det. 1901
	Hobe Ferris, AL:Bos. 1901
55	George Grantham, NL:Chi. 1923

Fewest Errors, Season

	Minimum: 800 total chances
5	Bobby Grich, AL:Balt. 1973 (945 tc) 162 g
	Jose Oquendo, NL:StL. 1989 (851 tc) 156 g
	Minimum: 150 games
3	Jose Oquendo, NL:StL. 1990 (150 g) 678 tc
5	Bobby Grich, AL:Balt. 1973 (162 g) 945 tc

Most Errors, Game

9	Andy Leonard, NL:Bos. June 14, 1876
	Since 1900:
5	Piano Legs Hickman, AL:Wash. Sept. 29, 1905
	Nap Lajoie, AL:Phil. Apr. 22, 1915
4	By many NL players; Last:
	Casey Wise, NL:Chi. May 3, 1957

Fewest Errors, Game (Most Innings, Complete Game in Field)
0	Felix Millan, NL:NY Sept. 11, 1974 (25 inn)
	Ted Sizemore, NL:StL. Sept. 11, 1974 (25 inn)
	Julio Cruz, AL:Chi. May 8, 1984 (25 inn)

Most Errors, Inning
3	Bid McPhee, NL:Cin. Sept. 23(1g), 1894 (6th)
	Claude Ritchey, NL:Pitt. Sept. 22, 1900 (6th)
	Bama Rowell, NL:Bos. Sept. 25, 1941 (3rd)
	Eddie Stanky, NL:Chi. June 20(1g), 1943 (8th)
	George Hausmann, NL:NY Aug. 13(2g), 1944 (4th)
	Kermit Wahl, NL:Cin. Sept. 18(1g), 1945 (11th)
	Davey Lopes, NL:LA June 2, 1973 (1st)
	Ted Sizemore, NL:StL. Apr. 17, 1975 (6th)
	Del Pratt, AL:StL. Sept. 1(2g), 1914 (4th)
	Bill Wambsganss AL:Clev. May 15, 1923 (8th)
	Bobby Doerr, AL:Bos. May 11, 1949 (2nd)
	Tim Cullen, AL:Wash. Aug. 30, 1969 (8th)

Most Errorless Games, Consecutive, Lifetime
123	Ryne Sandberg, NL:Chi. June 21, 1989-May 17, 1990
113	Denny Hocking, AL:Minn. Sept. 16, 1993-Sept. 13, 1999

Most Errorless Games. Consecutive, Season
99	Luis Castillo, AL:Minn. May 30-Oct. 1, 2006
90	Ryne Sandberg, NL:Chi. June 21-Oct. 1, 1989

Most Errorless Chances Accepted, Consecutive, Lifetime
584	Ryne Sandberg, NL:Chi. June 20, 1989-May 18, 1990
506	Damion Easley, AL:Det. Aug. 20, 1999-July 21, 2000

Most Errorless Chances Accepted, Consecutive, Season
479	Manny Trillo, NL:Phil. Apr. 7-July 31, 1982
448	Luis Castillo, AL:Minn. May 29-Oct. 1, 2006

￭OUBLE PLAYS

Most Seasons Leading League
8	Bill Mazeroski, NL:Pitt. 1960-67
5	Nap Lajoie, AL:Clev. 1903, 06-09
	Eddie Collins, AL:Phil. 1909-10, 12; Chi. 16, 19
	Bucky Harris, AL:Wash. 1921-25
	Bobby Doerr, AL:Bos. 1938, 40, 43, 46-47
	Nellie Fox, AL:Chi. 1954, 56-58, 60
	Harold Reynolds, AL:Sea. 1986-88, 91; Balt. 93

Most Double Plays, Lifetime
1706	Bill Mazeroski, NL:Pitt. 1956-72
1568	Nellie Fox, AL:Phil. 1947-49; Chi. 50-63

Most Double Plays, Season
161	Bill Mazeroski, NL:Pitt. 1966
150	Jerry Priddy, AL:Det. 1950

Most Double Plays, Game
6	Bobby Knoop, AL:Cal. May 1(1g), 1966
	Joe Gordon, AL:Clev. Aug. 31(1g), 1949 (14 inn)
	Alfonso Soriano, AL:NY June 17(1g), 2003
	Felix Millan, NL:Atl. Aug. 5, 1971 (17 inn)
	Bill Doran, NL:Hou. May 8, 1988

Most Double Plays, Unassisted, Game
2	Davy Force, NL:Buff. Sept. 15, 1881
	Claude Ritchey, NL:Lou. July 9(1g), 1899
	Mike Edwards, AL:Oak. Aug. 10, 1978
	Luis Alicea, AL:Ana. Aug. 8, 1997

Unassisted Triple Play
1	Mickey Morandini, NL:Phil. (Pitt.) Sept. 20, 1992 (6th)
	Randy Velarde, AL:Oak. (NY) May 29, 2000 (6th)

THIRD BASE

Most Seasons, Lifetime
23 Brooks Robinson, AL:Balt. 1955-77

Most Seasons, League
23 Brooks Robinson, AL:Balt. 1955-77
18 Mike Schmidt, NL:Phil. 1972-89
   Lenny Harris, NL:Cin. 1988-89, 94-98; LA 89-93; NY 98, 2000-01;
    Col. 99; Ari. 2000; Mil. 02; Chi. 03; Fla. 03-05

PERCENTAGE

Most Seasons Leading League
11 Brooks Robinson, AL:Balt. 1960-64, 66-69, 72, 75
6 Ken Reitz, NL:StL. 1973-74, 77-78, 80; Chi. 81

Most Seasons, Consecutive, Leading League
6 Willie Kamm, AL:Chi. 1924-29
4 Willie Jones, NL:Phil. 1953-56

Highest Percentage, Lifetime
.977 Mike Lowell, AL:NY 1998; Bos. 2006; NL:Fla. 1999-2005

Highest Percentage, League
.971 Brooks Robinson, AL:Balt. 1955-77
.970 Ken Reitz, NL:StL. 1972-75, 77-80; SF 76; Chi. 81; Pitt. 82

Highest Percentage, Season
.991 Steve Buechele, AL:Tex. 1991
.987 Vinny Castilla, NL:Col. 2004

Lowest Percentage, Season, Since 1900
.836 Piano Legs Hickman, NL:NY 1900
.860 Hunter Hill, AL:Wash. 1904

GAMES

Most Seasons Leading League
8 Brooks Robinson, AL:Balt. 1960-64, 66, 68, 70
7 Ron Santo, NL:Chi. 1961, 63, 65-69

Most Games Lifetime
2870 Brooks Robinson, AL:Balt. 1955-77
2212 Mike Schmidt, NL:Phil. 1972-89

Most Games, Consecutive
576 Eddie Yost, AL:Wash. July 3, 1951-May 11, 1955
364 Ron Santo, NL:Chi. Apr. 19, 1964-May 31, 1966

Most Games, Season
164 Ron Santo, NL:Chi. 1965
163 Brooks Robinson, AL:Balt. 1961, 64

CHANCES ACCEPTED

Most Seasons Leading League
9 Ron Santo, NL:Chi. 1961-69
8 Frank Baker. AL:Phil. 1909-10, 12-14; NY 17-19
   Brooks Robinson, AL:Balt. 1960, 63-64, 66-69, 74

Most Chances Accepted, Lifetime
8902 Brooks Robinson, AL:Balt. 1955-77
6636 Mike Schmidt, NL:Phil. 1972-89

Most Chances Accepted, Season
603 Harlond Clift, AL:StL. 1937
601 Jimmy Collins, NL:Bos. 1899
   NL Since 1900:
583 Tommy Leach, NL:Pitt. 1904

Most Chances Accepted, Game

13	Willie Kuehne, NL:Pitt. May 24, 1889
	Jerry Denny, NL:NY May 29, 1890
	Bill Shindle, NL:Balt. Sept. 28, 1893
	Bill Joyce, NL:Wash. May 26, 1894
	Art Devlin, NL:NY May 23(1g), 1908
	Tony Cuccinello, NL:Brk. July 12(1g), 1934
	Roy Hughes, NL:Chi. Aug. 29(2g), 1944
	Wid Conroy, AL:Wash. Sept. 25, 1911
	Extra-Inning Game:
16	Jerry Denny, NL:Prov. Aug. 17, 1882 (18 inn)
	Since 1900:
14	Jimmy Collins, AL:Bos. June 21, 1902 (15 inn)
	Ben Dyer, AL:Det. July 16, 1919 (14 inn)
	Don Hoak, NL:Cin. May 4(2g), 1958 (14 inn)

Fewest Chances Accepted, Game (Most Innings, Complete Game in Field)

0	David Wright, NL:NY May 23, 2006 (16 inn)
	Dean Palmer, AL:KC Sept. 24, 1997 (15 inn)

PUTOUTS

Most Seasons Leading League

8	Eddie Yost, AL:Wash. 1948, 50-54, 56; Det. 59
7	Pie Traynor, NL:Pitt. 1923, 25-27, 31, 33-34
	Willie Jones, NL:Phil. 1949-50, 52-56
	Ron Santo, NL:Chi. 1962-67, 69
	Tim Wallach, NL:Mtl. 1982-85, 87-88; LA 94

Most Putouts, Lifetime

2697	Brooks Robinson, AL:Balt. 1955-77
2288	Pie Traynor, NL:Pitt. 1921-35, 37

Most Putouts, Season

252	Jimmy Collins, NL:Bos. 1900
243	Willie Kamm, AL:Chi. 1928

Most Putouts, Game

10	Willie Kuehne, NL:Pitt. May 24, 1889
	Since 1900:
9	Pat Dillard, NL:StL. June 18, 1900
7	Bill Bradley, AL:Clev. Sept. 21(1g), 1901; May 13, 1909
	Harry Riconda, AL:Phil. July 5(2g), 1924
	Ossie Bluege, AL:Wash. June 18, 1927
	Ray Boone, AL:Det. Apr. 24, 1954

Fewest Putouts, Game (Most Innings, Complete Game in Field)

0	Ryne Sandberg, NL:Chi. Aug. 17, 1982 (21 inn)
	Vern Stephens, AL:Bos. July 13, 1951 (19 inn)
	Don Wert, AL:Det. Aug. 23(2g), 1968 (19 inn)
	Jim Gantner, AL:Mil. May 1, 1991 (19 inn)

ASSISTS

Most Seasons Leading League

8	Brooks Robinson, AL:Balt. 1960, 63-64, 66-69, 74
7	Ron Santo, NL:Chi. 1962-68
	Mike Schmidt, NL:Phil. 1974, 76-77, 80-83

Most Assists, Lifetime

6205	Brooks Robinson, AL:Balt. 1955-77
5045	Mike Schmidt, NL:Phil. 1972-89

Most Assists, Season

412	Graig Nettles, AL:Clev. 1971
404	Mike Schmidt, NL:Phil. 1974

Most Assists, Game

11	Deacon White, NL:Buff. May 16, 1884
	Jerry Denny, NL:NY May 29, 1890
	Damon Phillips, NL:Bos. Aug. 29, 1944
	Chris Sabo, NL:Cin. Apr. 7, 1988
	Kevin Young, NL:Pitt. June 25, 1995
	Frank Baker, AL:NY May 24, 1910 (19 inn)
	Ken McMullen, AL:Wash. Sept. 26(1g), 1966
	Mike Ferraro, AL:NY Sept. 14, 1968
	Doug DeCinces, AL:Cal. May 7, 1983 (12 inn)
	Extra-Inning Game:
12	Bobby Byrne, NL:Pitt. June 8(2g), 1910 (11 inn)

Fewest Assists, Game (Most Innings, Complete Game in Field)
0   Sibby Sisti, NL:Bos. July 5, 1940 (20 inn)
       Toby Harrah, AL:, Tex. Sept. 17, 1977 (17 inn)

Most Assists, Inning
3   By many players

ERRORS

Most Seasons Leading League (Most)
5   Pie Traynor, NL:Pitt. 1926, 28, 31-33
       Jim Tabor, AL:Bos. 1939-43

Most Errors, Lifetime
359   Jimmy Austin, AL:NY 1909-10; StL. 11-22, 25-26, 29

Most Errors, League, Since 1900
359   Jimmy Austin, AL:NY 1909-10; StL. 11-22, 25-26, 29
324   Pie Traynor, NL:Pitt. 1921-35, 37

Most Errors, Season
91   Piano Legs Hickman, NL:NY 1900
64   Sammy Strang, AL:Chi. 1902

Fewest Errors, Season
       Minimum: 450 chances
5   Don Money, AL:Mil. 1974 (472 tc) 157 g
9   Robin Ventura, NL:NY 1999 (452 tc) 160 g
       Minimum: 150 games
5   Don Money, AL:Mil. 1974 (157 g) 472 tc
7   Mike Lowell, NL:Fla. 2004 (154 g) 396 tc

Most Errors, Game
6   Jim Donnelly, UA:KC July 16, 1884
       Joe Moffett, AA:Tol. Aug. 2, 1884
       Joe Werrick, AA:Lou. July 28, 1888
       Billy Alvord, AA:Tol. May 22, 1890
       Joe Mulvey, NL:Phil. July 30, 1884
       Since 1900:
5   Dave Brain, NL:Bos. June 11, 1906
4   By many AL players; Last:
       Edgar Martinez, AL:Sea. May 6, 1990

Fewest Errors, Game (Most Innings, Complete Game in Field)
0   Tony Boeckel, NL:Bos. May 1, 1920 (26 inn)
       Jimmy Johnston, NL:Brk. May 1, 1920 (26 inn)
       Vance Law, AL:Chi. May 8, 1984 (25 inn)

Most Errors, Inning
4   Lew Whistler, NL:NY June 19, 1891 (4th)
       Bob Brenly, NL:SF Sept. 14, 1986 (4th)
       Jimmy Burke, AL:Mil. May 27, 1901 (4th)

Most Errorless Games, Consecutive, Lifetime
99   Jeff Cirillo, NL:Col.-Sea. June 20, 2001-Apr. 19, 2002
       John Wehner, NL:Pitt.-Fla.-Pitt. Aug. 2, 1992-Sept. 29, 2000
88   Don Money, AL:Mil. Sept. 28(2g), 1973-July 16, 1974

Most Errorless Games, Consecutive, Season
86   Don Money, AL:Mil. Apr. 5-July 16, 1974
85   Jeff Cirillo, NL:Col. June 20-Oct. 7, 2001

Most Errorless Chances Accepted, Consecutive, Lifetime
272   Vinny Castilla, NL:Col.-Wash. July 4, 2004-April 22, 2005
261   Don Money, AL:Mil. Sept. 28(1g), 1973-July 16, 1974

Most Errorless Chances Accepted, Consecutive, Season
257   Don Money, AL:Mil. Apr. 5-July 16, 1974
230   Vinny Castilla, NL:Col. July 4 - Oct. 3, 2004

DOUBLE PLAYS

Most Seasons Leading League
6   Heinie Groh, NL:Cin. 1915-16;18-20; NY 22
       Ron Santo, NL:Chi. 1961, 64, 66-68, 71
       Mike Schmidt. NL:Phil. 1978-80, 82-83, 87
5   Ken Keltner, AL:Clev. 1939, 41-42, 44, 47
       Frank Malzone, AL:Bos. 1957-61

Most Seasons, Consecutive, Leading League

5	Frank Malzone, AL:Bos. 1957-61
3	Ken Boyer, NL:StL. 1958-60
	Ron Santo, NL:Chi. 1966-68
	Mike Schmidt, NL:Phil. 1978-80
	Jeff Cirillo, NL:Mil. 1998-99; Col. 2000

Most Double Plays, Lifetime

618	Brooks Robinson, AL:Balt. 1955-77
450	Mike Schmidt, NL:Phil. 1972-89

Most Double Plays, Season

54	Graig Nettles, AL:Clev. 1971
45	Darrell Evans, NL:Atl. 1974
	Jeff Cirillo, NL:Mil. 1998

Most Double Plays, Game

4	Pie Traynor, NL:Pitt. July 9(1g), 1925
	Johnny Vergez, NL:Phil. Aug. 15, 1935
	Denny Walling, NL:Hou. May 8, 1988
	Edgardo Alfonzo, NL:NY May 14, 1997
	Shane Andrews, NL:Chi. Sept. 23, 2000
	Andy Carey, AL:NY July 31(2g), 1955
	Felix Torres, AL:LA Aug. 23, 1963
	Ken McMullen, AL:Wash. Aug. 13, 1965
	Jack Howell, AL:Cal. May 17, 1989
	Scott Brosius, AL:NY July 6, 2000

Most Double Plays, Unassisted, Season

4	Joe Dugan, AL:NY 1924
3	Harry Wolverton, NL:Phil. 1902
	Heinie Groh, NL:Cin. 1915

Most Double Plays, Unassisted, Game

1	By many players

HORTSTOP

Most Seasons, Lifetime

20	Bobby Wallace, NL:StL. 1899-1901, 17-18; AL:StL. 1903-16
	Bill Dahlen, NL:Chi. 1891-98; Brk. 1899-1903, 11; NY 04-07; Bos. 08-09
	Luke Appling, AL:Chi. 1930-43, 45-50
	Alan Trammell, AL:Det. 1977-96
	NL Since 1900:
19	Rabbit Maranville, NL:Bos. 1912-20, 29-31; Pitt. 21-23; Chi. 25; Brk. 26; StL. 27-28
	Chris Speier NL:SF 1971-77, 87-89; Mtl. 77-84; StL. 84; Chi. 85-86
	Dave Concepcion NL:Cin. 1970-88
	Ozzie Smith, NL:SD 1978-81, StL. 82-96
	Barry Larkin, NL:Cin. 1986-2004

ERCENTAGE

Most Seasons Leading League

8	Everett Scott, AL:Bos. 1916-21; NY 22-23
	Lou Boudreau, AL:Clev. 1940-44, 46-48
	Luis Aparicio, AL:Chi. 1959-62; Balt. 63-66
	Ozzie Smith, NL:SD 1981; StL. 82, 84-87, 91, 94

Most Seasons, Consecutive, Leading League

8	Everett Scott, AL:Bos. 1916-21; NY 22-23
	Luis Aparicio, AL:Chi. 1959-62; Balt. 63-66
5	Hughie Jennings, NL:Balt. 1894-98
	NL Since 1900:
4	Eddie Miller, NL:Bos. 1940-42; Cin. 43
	Ozzie Smith, NL:StL. 1984-87

Highest Percentage, Lifetime

.984	Omar Vizquel, AL:Sea. 1989-93; Clev. 94-2004; NL:SF 2005-06

Highest Percentage, League

.983	Omar Vizquel, AL:Sea. 1989-93; Clev. 94-2004
.980	Larry Bowa, NL:Phil. 1970-81; Chi. 82-85; NY 85

Highest Percentage, Season

.998	Mike Bordick, AL:Balt. 2002
.994	Rey Ordonez, NL:NY 1999

Lowest Percentage, Season, Since 1900
.861   Bill Keister, AL:Balt. 1901
.891   Otto Kruger, NL:StL. 1902

GAMES

Most Seasons Leading League
12	Cal Ripken, AL:Balt. 1983-84, 87-96
6	Mickey Doolan, NL:Phil. 1906, 09-13
	Arky Vaughan, NL:Pitt. 1933-34, 36, 38-40
	Roy McMillan, NL:Cin. 1952-54, 56-57; Mil. 61

Most Games, Lifetime
2583	Luis Aparicio, AL:Chi. 1956-62, 68-70; Balt. 63-67; Bos. 71-73
2511	Ozzie Smith, NL:SD 1978-81; StL. 82-96

Most Games, Consecutive
2216	Cal Ripken, AL:Balt. July 1, 1982-July 14, 1996
584	Roy McMillan, NL:Cin. Sept. 16, 1951-Aug. 6, 1955

Most Games, Season
165	Maury Wills, NL:LA 1962
163	Tony Fernandez, AL:Tor. 1986

CHANCES ACCEPTED

Most Seasons Leading League
8	Ozzie Smith, NL:SD 1978, 80-81; StL. 83, 85, 87-89
7	Luis Aparicio, AL:Chi. 1956-61, 68

Most Chances Accepted, Lifetime
12,624	Ozzie Smith, NL:SD 1978-81; StL. 82-96
12,564	Luis Aparicio, AL:Chi. 1956-62, 68-70; Balt. 63-67; Bos. 71-73

Most Chances Accepted, Season
984	Dave Bancroft, NL:NY 19223
969	Donie Bush, AL:Det. 1914

Most Chances Accepted, Game
19	Danny Richardson, NL:Wash. June 20(1g), 1892
	Eddie Joost, NL:Cin. May 7, 1941
17	Bobby Wallace, AL:StL. June 10, 1902
	Extra-Inning Game:
21	Eddie Miller, NL:Bos. June 27, 1939 (23 inn)
18	Fred Parent, AL:Bos. July 9, 1902 (17 inn)
	Chico Carrasquel, AL:Chi. July 13, 1951 (19 inn)
	Skeeter Webb, AL:Det. July 21, 1945 (24 inn)
	Pete Runnels, AL:Wash. June 3, 1952 (17 inn)
	Ron Hansen, AL:Chi. Aug. 29(1g), 1965 (14 inn)

Fewest Chances Accepted, Game (Most Innings, Complete Game in Field)
0	Irv Ray, NL:Bos. Aug. 15, 1888 (12 inn)
	Eddie Feinberg, NL:Phil. May 19, 1939 (12 inn)
	Billy Jurges, NL:NY Sept. 22, 1942 (12 inn)
	Andre Rodgers, NL:SF July, 9, 1960 (12 inn)
	Khalil Greene, NL:SD Aug. 1, 2004 (12 inn)
	John Gochnaur, AL:Clev. July 14, 1903 (12 inn)
	Billy Rogell, AL:Det. June 16, 1937 (12 inn)
	Manuel Lee, AL:Tex. Apr. 29, 1994 (12 inn)

PUTOUTS

Most Seasons Leading League
6	Rabbit Maranville, NL:Bos. 1914-17, 19; Pitt. 23
	Cal Ripken, AL:Balt. 1984-85, 88-89, 91-92

Most Putouts, Lifetime
5133	Rabbit Maranville, NL:Bos. 1912-20, 29-31; Pitt. 21-23; Chi. 25; Brk. 26; StL. 27-28
4548	Luis Aparicio, AL:Chi. 1956-62, 68-70; Balt. 63-67; Bos. 71-73

Most Putouts, Season
425	Hughie Jennings, NL:Balt. 1895
	Donie Bush. AL:Det. 1914
	NL Since 1900:
407	Rabbit Maranville, NL:Bos. 1914

Most Putouts, Game

11	Shorty Fuller, NL:NY Aug. 20, 1895
	Hod Ford, NL:Cin. Sept. 18, 1929
	John Cassidy, AL:Wash. Aug. 30(1g), 1904
	Extra-Inning Game:
15	Jake Pitler, NL:Pitt. Aug. 22, 1917 (22 inn)

Fewest Putouts, Game (Most Innings, Complete Game in Field)

0	Jose Offerman, NL:LA July 7, 1993 (20 inn)
	Deivi Cruz, AL:Det. June 5, 2001 (18 inn)

ASSISTS

Most Seasons Leading League

8	Ozzie Smith, NL:SD 1979-81; StL. 82, 85, 87-89
7	Luke Appling, AL:Chi. 1933, 35, 37, 39, 41, 43, 46
	Luis Aparicio, AL:Chi. 1956-61, 68
	Cal Ripken, AL:Balt. 1983-84, 86-87, 89, 91, 93

Most Assists, Lifetime

8375	Ozzie Smith, NL:SD 1978-81; StL. 82-96
8016	Luis Aparicio, AL:Chi. 1956-62, 68-70; Balt. 63-67; Bos. 71-73

Most Assists, Season

621	Ozzie Smith, NL:SD 1980
583	Cal Ripken, AL:Balt. 1984

Most Assists, Game

14	Herman Long, NL:Bos. May 6, 1892 (14 inn)
	Tommy Corcoran, NL:Cin. Aug. 7, 1903
	Bud Harrelson, NL:NY May 24, 1973 (19 inn)
13	Bobby Reeves, AL:Wash. Aug. 7, 1927
	Alex Gonzalez, AL:Tor. Apr. 26, 1996
	Extra-Inning Game:
15	Rick Burleson, AL:Cal. Apr. 13, 1982 (20 inn)

Fewest Assists, Game (Most Innings, Complete Game in Field)

0	Jack Coffey, NL:Bos. July 26, 1909 (17 inn)
	Tony Batista, AL:Balt. Sept. 30, 2001 (15 inn)

Most Assists, Inning

4	Craig Grebeck, AL:Chi. May 2, 1995 (5th)
	Juan Uribe, NL:Col. May 21, 2002 (4th)

ERRORS

Most Seasons Leading League (Most)

6	Dick Groat, NL:Pitt. 1955-56, 59, 61-62; StL. 64
	Rafael Ramirez, NL:Atl. 1981-85; Hou. 89
5	Luke Appling, AL:Chi. 1933, 35, 37, 39, 46

Most Errors, League, Since 1900

689	Donie Bush, AL:Det. 1908-21; Wash. 21-23
676	Honus Wagner, NL:Pitt. 1901-17

Most Errors, Season

115	Bill Schindler, PL:Phil. 1890
106	Joe Sullivan, NL:Wash. 1893
	Since 1900:
95	John Gochnaur, AL:Clev. 1903
81	Rudy Hulswitt, NL:Phil. 1903

Fewest Errors, Season

	Minimum: 700 tc
6	Tony Fernandez, AL:Tor. 1989 (741 tc) 140 g
9	Larry Bowa, NL:Phil. 1972 (715 tc) 150 g
	Minimum: 150 games
3	Cal Ripken, AL:Balt. 1990 (161 g) 680 tc
4	Rey Ordonez, NL:NY 1999 (154 g) 640 tc
	Omar Vizquel, NL:SF 2006 (152 g) 599 tc

Most Errors, Game
7	Jimmy Hallinan, NL:NY July 29, 1876
	Germany Smith, AA:Brk. June 17, 1885
	Since 1900:
5	Charlie Babb, NL:NY Aug. 24(1g), 1903
	Charlie Babb, NL:Brk. June 20, 1904
	Phil Lewis, NL:Brk. July 20, 1905
	Donie Bush, AL:Det. Aug. 25(1g), 1911
	Extra-Inning Game:
6	Bill O'Neill, AL:Bos. May 21, 1904 (13 inn)

Fewest Errors, Game (Most Innings, Complete Game in Field)
0	Rabbit Maranville, NL:Bos. May 1, 1920 (26 inn)
	Robin Yount, AL:Mil. May 8, 1984 (25 inn)

Most Errors, Inning
4	Shorty Fuller, NL:Wash. Aug. 17, 1888 (2nd)
	Len Merullo, NL:Chi. Sept. 13(2g), 1942 (2nd)
	Ray Chapman, AL:Clev. June 20, 1914 (5th)

Most Errorless Games, Consecutive, Lifetime
110	Mike Bordick, AL:Balt. Apr. 11-Sept. 29, 2002
101	Rey Ordonez, NL:NY June 14, 1999-Mar. 29, 2000

Most Errorless Games, Consecutive, Season
110	Mike Bordick, AL:Balt. Apr. 11-Sept. 29, 2002
100	Rey Ordonez, NL:NY June 14-Oct. 4, 1999

Most Errorless Chances Accepted, Consecutive, Lifetime
544	Mike Bordick, AL:Balt.-Tor. Apr. 10, 2002-Apr. 2, 2003
419	Rey Ordonez, NL:NY June 13, 1999-Mar. 29, 2000

Most Errorless Chances Accepted, Consecutive, Season
543	Mike Bordick, AL:Balt.-Tor. Apr. 10-Sept. 29, 2002
412	Rey Ordonez, NL:NY June 13-Oct. 4, 1999

DOUBLE PLAYS

Most Seasons Leading League
8	Cal Ripken, AL:Balt. 1983-85, 89, 91-92, 94-95
5	Mickey Doolan, NL:Phil. 1907, 09-11, 13
	Dick Groat, NL:Pitt. 1958-59, 61-62; StL. 64
	Ozzie Smith, NL:SD 1980; StL. 84, 86-87, 91

Most Double Plays, League
1590	Ozzie Smith, NL:SD 1978-81; StL. 82-96
1565	Cal Ripken, AL:Balt. 1981-96

Most Double Plays, Season
147	Rick Burleson, AL:Bos. 1980
137	Bobby Wine, NL:Mtl. 1970

Most Double Plays, Game
5	By many players; Last:
	Ben Zobrist, AL:TB Sept. 16, 2006
	David Eckstein, NL:StL. Aug. 18, 2005
	Extra-Inning Game:
6	Bert Campaneris, AL:Oak. Sept. 13(1g), 1970 (11 inn)
	Ozzie Smith, NL:SD Aug. 25, 1979 (19 inn)
	Rafael Ramirez, NL:Atl. June 27, 1982 (14 inn)

Most Double Plays, Unassisted, Game
2	Lee Tannehill, AL:Chi. Aug. 4(1g), 1911

TRIPLE PLAYS

Unassisted Triple Play
1	Neal Ball, AL:Clev. (Bos.) July 19, 1909 (2nd)
	Ron Hansen, AL:Wash. (Clev.) July 30, 1968 (1st)
	John Valentin, AL:Bos. (Sea.) July 8, 1994 (6th)
	Ernie Padgett, NL:Bos. (Phil.) Oct. 6, 1923 (4th)
	Glenn Wright, NL:Pitt. (StL.) May 7, 1925 (9th)
	Jimmy Cooney, NL:Chi. (Pitt.) May 30, 1927 (4th)
	Rafael Furcal, NL:Atl. (StL.) Aug. 10, 2003 (5th)

OUTFIELD

Most Seasons, Lifetime
25   Rickey Henderson, AL:Oak.. 1979-84, 89-95, 98; NY 85-89; Tor. 93; Ana. 97; Sea. 2000; Bos. 02; NL:SD 96-97, 2001; NY 99-2000; LA 03

Most Seasons, League
24   Ty Cobb, AL:Det. 1905-26; Phil. 27-28
22   Willie Mays, NL:NY/SF 1951-52, 54-72; NY 72-73

PERCENTAGE

Most Seasons Leading League
5   Amos Strunk, AL:Phil. 1912, 14, 17; Bos. 18; Phil.-Chi. 20
4   Joe Hornung, NL:Bos. 1881-83, 87
    NL Since 1900:
3   Stan Musial, NL:StL. 1949, 54, 61
    Tony Gonzalez, NL:Phil. 1962, 64, 67

Most Seasons, Consecutive, Leading League
3   Joe Hornung, NL:Bos. 1881-83
    Gene Woodling, AL:NY 1951-53
    NL Since 1900:
2   By many players

Highest Percentage, Lifetime
.995   Darryl Hamilton, AL:Mil. 1988-95; Tex. 96; NL:SF 97-98; Col. 98-99; NY 99-2001

Highest Percentage, League
.993   Terry Puhl, NL:Hou. 1977-90
.991   Amos Otis, AL:KC 1970-83

Highest Percentage, Season (Most Chances)
1.000   Curt Flood, NL:StL. 1966 (396 tc)
    Darryl Hamilton, AL:Tex. 1996 (389 tc)

Lowest Percentage, Season
.843   John Manning, NL:Phil. 1884
    Since 1900:
.872   Bill O'Neill, AL:Wash. 1904
.900   Mike Donlin, NL:Cin. 1903

GAMES

Most Seasons Leading League
6   George Burns, NL:NY 1914, 16, 19-20; Cin. 22-23
    Billy Williams, NL:Chi. 1964-68, 70
    Dale Murphy, NL:Atl. 1982-85, 87-88
5   Rocky Colavito, AL:Clev. 1959, 65; Det. 61-63

Most Games, Lifetime
2938   Ty Cobb, AL:Det. 1905-26; Phil. 27-28
2843   Willie Mays, NL:NY/SF 1951-52, 54-72; NY 72-73

Most Games, Consecutive
897   Billy Williams, NL:Chi.Sept. 22, 1963-June 13, 1969
511   Clyde Milan, AL:Wash. Aug. 12, 1910-Oct. 3, 1913

Most Games, Season
164   Billy Williams, NL:Chi. 1965
163   Leon Wagner, AL:Clev. 1964

CHANCES ACCEPTED

Most Seasons Leading League
9   Max Carey, NL:Pitt. 1912-13, 16-18, 21-24
    Richie Ashburn, NL:Phil. 1949-54, 56-58
8   Tris Speaker, AL:Bos. 1909-10, 12-15; Clev. 18-19

Most Chances Accepted, Lifetime
7290   Willie Mays, NL:NY/SF 1951-52, 54-72; NY 72-73
7244   Tris Speaker, AL:Bos. 1907-15; Clev. 16-26; Wash. 27; Phil. 28

Most Chances Accepted, Season
557   Taylor Douthit, NL:StL. 1928
524   Chet Lemon, AL:Chi. 1977

Most Chances Accepted, Game
13	Earl Clark, NL:Bos. May 10, 1929
	Rolando Roomes, NL:Cin. July 28, 1989 (17 inn)
12	By many AL players

Most Chances Accepted, Left Field, Game
11	Joseph Hornung, NL:Bos. Sept. 23, 1881
	Dick Harley, NL:StL. June 30, 1898
	Topsy Hartsel, NL:Chi. Sept. 10, 1901
	Phil Clark, NL:SD May 1, 1993
	Paul Lehner, AL:Phil. June 25(2g), 1950
	Willie Horton, AL:Det. July 18, 1969
	Extra-Inning Game:
12	Tom McBride, AL:Wash. July 2, 1948 (12 inn)
	Rickey Henderson, AL:NY Sept. 11, 1988 (18 inn)
	Darin Erstad, AL:Ana. July 24, 2000 (12 inn)

Most Chances Accepted, Center Field, Game
13	Earl Clark, NL:Bos. May 10, 1929
12	Happy Felsch, AL:Chi. June 23, 1919
	Johnny Mostil, AL:Chi. May 22, 1928
	AL Extra-Inning Game:
13	Oddibe McDowell, AL:Tex. July 20, 1985 (15 inn)

Most Chances Accepted, Right Field, Game
12	Tony Armas, AL:Oak. June 12, 1982
10	Greasy Neale, NL:Cin. July 13, 1920
	Casey Stengel, NL:Phil. July 30, 1920
	Bill Nicholson, NL:Chi. Sept. 17, 1945
	Bake McBride, NL:Phil. Sept. 8, 1978
	Raul Mondesi, NL:LA Sept. 25, 1995
	Jeromy Burnitz, NL:Mil. Sept. 17, 2001
	Extra-Inning Game:
13	Rolando Roomes, NL:Cin. July 28, 1989 (17 inn)

Fewest Chances Accepted, Left Field, Game (Most Innings, Complete Game in Field)
0	Dave Philley, AL:Det. Aug. 3, 1957 (17 inn)
	Joe Delahanty, NL:StL. July 19. 1908 (16 inn)
	Gary Redus, NL:Cin. June 21, 1983 (16 inn)
	Vince Coleman, NL:StL. May 11, 1988 (16 inn)

Fewest Chances Accepted, Center Field, Game (Most Innings, Complete Game in Field)
0	Bill Bruton, AL:Det. June 24, 1962 (22 inn)
	Ernie Orsatti, NL:StL. July 2(1g), 1933 (18 inn)

Fewest Chances Accepted, Right Field, Game (Most Innings, Complete Game in Field)
0	Cap Peterson, AL:Wash. June 12, 1967 (22 inn)
	Lance Richbourg, NL:Bos. May 14, 1927 (18 inn)
	Art Shamsky, NL. Cin. July 19, 1966 (18 inn)

Most Chances Accepted, Inning
3	By many players

PUTOUTS

Most Seasons Leading League
9	Max Carey, NL:Pitt. 1912-13, 16-18, 21-24
	Richie Ashburn, NL:Phil. 1949-54, 56-58
7	Tris Speaker, AL:Bos. 1909-10, 13-15; Clev. 18-19

Most Putouts, Lifetime
7095	Willie Mays, NL:NY/SF 1951-52, 54-72; NY 72-73
6794	Tris Speaker, AL:Bos. 1907-15; Clev. 16-26; Wash. 27; Phil. 28

Most Putouts, Season
547	Taylor Douthit, NL:StL. 1928
512	Chet Lemon, AL:Chi. 1977

Most Putouts, Game
12	Earl Clark, NL:Bos. May 10, 1929
	Lyman Bostock, AL:Minn. May 25(2g), 1977
	Extra-Inning Game:
13	Rolando Roomes, NL:Cin. July 28, 1989 (17 inn)

Most Putouts, Left Field, Game
11	Dick Harley, NL:StL. June 30, 1898
	Topsy Hartsel, NL:Chi. Sept. 10, 1901
	Paul Lehner, AL:Phil. June 25(2g), 1950
	Willie Horton, AL:Det. July 18, 1969
	Extra-Inning Game:
12	Tom McBride, AL:Wash. July 2, 1948 (12 inn)
	Rickey Henderson, AL:NY Sept. 11, 1988 (18 inn)
	Darin Erstad, AL:Ana. July 24, 2000 (12 inn)

Most Putouts, Center Field, Game
12	Earl Clark, NL:Bos. May 10, 1929
	Carden Gillenwater, NL:Bos. Sept. 11, 1946 (17 inn)
	Lloyd Merriman, NL:Cin. Sept. 7, 1951 (18 inn)
	Garry Maddox, NL:Phil. June 10, 1984 (12 inn)
	Lyman Bostock, AL:Minn. May 25(2g), 1977
	Harry Bay, AL:Clev. July 19, 1904 (12 inn)
	Ruppert Jones, AL:Sea. May 16, 1978 (16 inn)
	Rick Manning, AL:Mil. July 11, 1983 (12 inn)
	Gary Pettis, AL:Cal. June 4, 1985 (15 inn)
	Oddibe McDowell, AL:Tex. July 20, 1985 (15 inn)

Most Putouts, Right Field, Game
11	Tony Armas, AL:Oak. June 12, 1982
10	Bill Nicholson, NL:Chi. Sept. 17, 1945
	Raul Mondesi, NL:LA Sept. 25, 1995
	Extra-Inning Game:
13	Rolando Roomes, NL:Cin. July 28, 1989 (17 inn)

Most Putouts, Consecutive, Game
7	Ben Chapman, AL:Bos. June 25, 1937 (rf)
	Brady Clark, NL:Mil. Apr. 24, 2005 (cf)

ASSISTS

Most Seasons Leading League
7	Carl Yastrzemski, AL:Bos. 1962-64, 66, 69, 71, 77
5	Roberto Clemente, NL:Pitt. 1958, 60-61, 66-67

Most Assists, Lifetime
450	Tris Speaker, AL:Bos. 1907-15; Clev. 16-26; Wash. 27; Phil. 28
356	Jimmy Ryan, NL:Chi. 1885-89, 1891-1900
	NL Since 1900:
339	Max Carey, NL:Pitt. 1910-26; Brk. 26-29

Most Assists, Season, Since 1900
44	Chuck Klein, NL:Phil. 1930
35	Sam Mertes, AL:Chi. 1902
	Tris Speaker, AL:Bos. 1909, 12

Most Assists, Game
4	Bill Crowley, NL:Buff. May 24 & Aug. 27, 1880
	Fred Clarke, NL:Pitt. Aug. 23, 1910
	Ducky Holmes, AL:Chi. Aug. 21, 1903
	Lee Magee, AL:NY June 28, 1916
	Happy Felsch, AL:Chi. Aug. 14, 1919
	Bob Meusel, AL:NY Sept. 5(2g), 1921
	Sam Langford, AL:Clev. May 1, 1928
	Extra-Inning Game:
5	Dusty Miller, NL:Cin. May 30(2g), 1895 (11 inn)

Most Assists, Inning
2	By many players

ERRORS

Most Seasons Leading League (Most)
7	Lou Brock, NL:Chi.-StL. 1964; StL. 65-68, 72-73
	Vladimir Guerrero, NL:Mtl. 1997-2002; AL:LA 06
5	Burt Shotton, AL:StL. 1912, 14-16; Wash. 18
	Reggie Jackson, AL:Oak. 1968, 70, 72, 75; Balt. 76

Most Errors, Lifetime, Since 1900
271	Ty Cobb, AL:Det. 1905-26; Phil. 27-28
235	Max Carey, NL:Pitt. 1910-26; Brk. 26-29

Most Errors, Season
52	Ed Beecher, PL:Buff. 1890
47	George Van Haltren, NL:Balt.-Pitt. 1892
	Since 1900:
36	Cy Seymour, NL:Cin. 1903
31	Roy Johnson, AL:Det. 1929

Fewest Errors, Season
	Most total chances
0	Curt Flood, NL:StL. 1966 (396 tc)
	Darryl Hamilton, AL:Tex. 1996 (389 tc)
	Most games
0	Rocky Colavito, AL:Clev. 1965 (162 g)
	Juan Pierre, NL:Chi. 2006 (162 g)

Most Errors, Game
5	Jack Manning, NL:Bos. May 1, 1876
	Pop Snyder, NL:Lou. July 29, 1876
	Jim O'Rourke, NL:Bos. June 21, 1877
	Charlie Bennett, NL:Mil. June 15, 1878
	Mike Dorgan, NL:NY May 24, 1884
	Mike Tiernan, NL:NY May 16, 1887
	Marty Sullivan, NL:Chi. May 18, 1887
	Jim Clinton, AA:Balt. May 3, 1884
	Fred Tenney, UA:Wash. May 29, 1884
	Since 1900:
4	Kip Selbach, AL:Balt. Aug. 19, 1902
	Fred Nicholson, NL:Bos. June 16, 1922

Fewest Errors, Game (Most Innings, Complete Game in Field)
0	Walt Cruise, NL:Bos. May 1, 1920 (26 inn)
	Les Mann, NL:Bos. May 1, 1920 (26 inn)
	Ray Powell, NL:Bos. May 1, 1920 (26 inn)
	Bernie Nies, NL:Brk. May 1, 1920 (26 inn)
	Zack Wheat, NL:Brk. May 1, 1920 (26 inn)
	Harold Baines, AL:Chi. May 8, 1984 (25 inn)
	Rudy Law, AL:Chi. May 8, 1984 (25 inn)

Most Errors, Inning
3	Jim Donahue, AA:KC July 4(2g), 1889 (1st)
	George Gore, NL:Chi. Aug. 8, 1883 (1st)
	Larry Herndon, NL:SF Sept. 6, 1980 (4th)
	Kip Selbach, AL:Wash. June 23, 1904 (8th)
	Harry Bay, AL:Clev. June 29(2g), 1905 (9th)
	Harry Heilmann, AL:Det. May 22, 1914 (1st)
	Herschel Bennett, AL:StL. Apr. 24, 1925 (8th)
	Scott Lusader, AL:Det. Sept. 9, 1989 (1st)

Most Errorless Games, Consecutive, Lifetime
392	Darren Lewis, AL:Oak.-NL:SF Aug. 21, 1990-June 29, 1994

Most Errorless Games, Consecutive, League
369	Darren Lewis, NL:SF July 13, 1991-June 29, 1994
336	Rich Amaral, AL:Sea.-Balt. Apr. 30, 1995-June 14, 2000

Most Errorless Games, Consecutive, Season
162	Rocky Colavito, AL:Clev. 1965 (entire season)
	Juan Pierre, NL:Chi. 2006 (entire season)

Most Errorless Chances Accepted, Consecutive, Lifetime
938	Darren Lewis, AL:Oak. Aug. 21-Oct. 3, 1990; NL:SF July 13, 1991-June 29, 1994

Most Errorless Chances Accepted, Consecutive, League
905	Darren Lewis, NL:SF July 13, 1991-June 29, 1994
723	Darin Erstad, AL:Ana. May 30, 2001-Sept. 22, 2002

Most Errorless Chances Accepted, Consecutive, Season
458	Darin Erstad, AL:Ana. Mar. 31-Sept. 22, 2002
396	Curt Flood, NL:StL. 1966 (entire season)

DOUBLE PLAYS

Most Seasons Leading League
6	Tris Speaker, AL:Bos. 1909, 12, 14-15; Clev. 16, 25
5	Max Carey, NL:Pitt. 1912, 15-16, 18, 21

Most Double Plays, Lifetime
135	Tris Speaker, AL:Bos. 1907-15; Clev. 16-26; Wash. 27; Phil. 28
86	Max Carey, NL:Pitt. 1910-26; Brk. 26-29

Most Double Plays, Season
15	Happy Felsch, AL:Chi. 1919
14	Jimmy Sheckard, NL:Balt. 1899
	NL since 1900:
12	Cy Seymour, NL:Cin. 1905
	Ginger Beaumont, NL:Bos. 1907
	Jimmy Sheckard, NL:Chi. 1911
	Mel Ott, NL:NY 1929

Most Double Plays, Game
3	Candy Nelson, AA:NY June 9, 1887
	Jack McCarthy, NL:Chi. Apr. 26, 1905
	Ira Flagstead, AL:Bos. Apr. 19(2g), 1926

Most Double Plays, Unassisted, Lifetime
6	Tris Speaker, AL:Bos. 1909, 10, 14; Clev. 18

Most Double Plays, Unassisted, League
6	Tris Speaker, AL:Bos. 1909, 10, 14 (2); Clev. 18 (2)
2	By many NL players

Most Double Plays, Unassisted, Season
2	Socks Seybold, AL:Phil. Aug. 15; Sept. 10(1g), 1907
	Tris Speaker, AL:Bos. Apr. 21; Aug. 8, 1914
	Tris Speaker, AL:Clev. Apr. 18, 29, 1918
	Jose Cardenal, AL:Clev. June 8; July 16, 1968
	Adam Comorosky, NL:Pitt. May 31, June 13, 1931

Most Double Plays, Unassisted, Game
1	By many players; Last:
	Jose Guillen, NL:Wash. May 8, 2005
	Mike Cameron, AL:Sea. May 23, 2003

CATCHER

Most Seasons, Lifetime
25	Deacon McGuire, AA:Tol. 1884; Clev. 88; Roch. 90; Wash. 91
	NL:Det. 1885, 88; Phil. 86-88; Wash. 92-99; Brk. 1899-1901
	AL:Det. 1902-03, 12; NY 04-06; Bos. 07; Clev. 10

Most Seasons, League
24	Carlton Fisk, AL:Bos. 1969, 71-80; Chi. 81-93
21	Bob O'Farrell, NL:Chi. 1915-25, 34; StL. 25-28, 33, 35; NY 28-32; Cin. 34

PERCENTAGE

Most Seasons Leading League
6	Gabby Hartnett, NL:Chi. 1928, 30, 34-37
	Jim Sundberg, AL:Tex. 1976-79; Mil. 84; KC 86

Most Seasons, Consecutive, Leading League
4	Gabby Hartnett, NL:Chi. 1934-37
	Jim Sundberg, AL:Tex. 1976-79

Highest Percentage, Lifetime
.995	Dan Wilson, NL:Cin. 1991-92; AL:Sea. 94-2005

Highest Percentage, League
.995	Dan Wilson, AL:Sea. 1994-2005
.994	Brad Ausmus, NL:SD 1993-96; Hou. 97-98, 2001-06

Highest Percentage, Season (Most Chances)
1.000	Charles Johnson, NL:Fla. 1997 (973 tc)
	Chris Hoiles, AL:Balt. 1997 (630 tc)

GAMES

Most Seasons Leading League
8	Yogi Berra, AL:NY 1950-57
6	Gary Carter, NL:Mtl. 1977-82
	Jason Kendall, NL:Pitt. 1997-98, 2000, 02-04

Most Games, Lifetime
2226	Carlton Fisk, AL:Bos. 1969, 71-80; Chi. 81-93
2056	Gary Carter, NL:Mtl. 1974-84, 92; NY 85-89; SF 90; LA 1991

Most Games, Consecutive
312	Frankie Hayes, AL:StL.-Phil.-Clev. Oct. 2, 1943-May 5, 1946
217	Ray Mueller, NL:Cin. July 31, 1943-Oct. 1, 1944

Most Seasons, 100 or more Games

15	Bob Boone, NL:Phil. 1973-74, 76-80; AL:Cal. 82-88; KC 89
13	Bill Dickey, AL:NY 1929-41
	Johnny Bench, NL:Cin. 1968-80

Most Seasons, Consecutive, 100 or more Games

13	Bill Dickey, AL:NY 1929-41
	Johnny Bench, NL:Cin. 1968-80

Most Games, Season

160	Randy Hundley, NL:Chi. 1968
155	Frankie Hayes, AL:Phil. 1944
	Jim Sundberg, AL:Tex. 1975

Most Games, Consecutive, Season

155	Ray Mueller, NL:Cin. 1944
	Frankie Hayes, AL:Phil. 1944

CHANCES ACCEPTED

Most Seasons Leading League

8	Ray Schalk, AL:Chi. 1913-17, 19-20, 22
	Yogi Berra, AL:NY 1950-52, 54-57, 59
	Gary Carter, NL:Mtl. 1977-82; NY 85, 88

Most Chances Accepted, Lifetime

12,988	Gary Carter, NL:Mtl. 1974-84, 92; NY 85-89; SF 90; LA 91
12,417	Carlton Fisk, AL:Bos. 1969, 71-80; Chi. 81-93

Most Chances Accepted, Season

1214	Johnny Edwards, NL:Hou. 1969
1123	Dan Wilson, AL:Sea. 1997

Most Chances Accepted, Game

23	George Bignal, UA:Mil. Oct. 3, 1884
22	Sandy Nava, NL:Prov. June 7, 1884
	Since 1900:
20	Jerry Grote, NL:NY Apr. 22, 1970
	Sandy Martinez, NL:Chi. May 6, 1998
	Ellie Rodriguez, AL:Cal. Aug. 12, 1974
	Rich Gedman, AL:Bos. Apr. 29, 1986
	Bill Haselman, AL:Bos. Sept. 18, 1996
	Dan Wilson, AL:Sea. Aug. 8, 1997
	Extra-Inning Game:
27	Jose Molina, AL:Ana. June 8, 2004 (17 inn)
25	Damian Miller, NL:Chi. May 15, 2003 (17 inn)

Most Chances Accepted, Inning

5	Joe Garagiola, NL:StL. June 17, 1949 (8th)
4	By many players

PUTOUTS

Most Seasons Leading League

9	Ray Schalk, AL:Chi. 1913-20, 22
8	Gary Carter, NL:Mtl. 1977-82, NY 85, 88

Most Putouts, Lifetime

11,785	Gary Carter, NL:Mtl. 1974-84, 92; NY 85-89; SF 90; LA 91
11,369	Carlton Fisk, AL:Bos. 1969, 71-80; Chi. 81-93

Most Putouts, Season

1135	Johnny Edwards, NL:Hou. 1969
1051	Dan Wilson, AL:Sea. 1997

Most Putouts, Game

20	Jerry Grote, NL:NY Apr. 22, 1970
	Sandy Martinez, NL:Chi. May 6, 1998
	Rich Gedman, AL:Bos. Apr. 29, 1986
	Dan Wilson AL:Sea. Aug. 8, 1997
	Extra-Inning Game:
26	Jose Molina, AL:Ana. June 8, 2004 (17 inn)
24	Damian Miller, NL:Chi. May 15, 2003 (17 inn)

Fewest Putouts, Game (Most Innings, Complete Game in Field)

0	Wally Schang, AL:Bos. Sept. 13, 1920 (14 inn)
	Gene Desautels, AL:Clev. Aug. 11(1g), 1942 (14 inn)
	Jimmie Wilson, NL:Phil. Aug. 31(1g), 1927 (13 inn)
	Hal Finney, NL:Pitt. Sept. 22, 1931 (13 inn)

ASSISTS

Most Seasons Leading League

6	Bob Boone, NL:Phil. 1973 AL:Cal. 82-84, 86, 88
	Gabby Hartnett, NL:Chi. 1925, 27-28, 30, 34-35
	Del Crandall, NL:Mil. 1953-54, 57-60
	Jim Sundberg, AL:Tex. 1975-78, 80-81

Most Assists, Lifetime

1835	Deacon McGuire, AA:Tol. 1884; Clev. 88; Roch. 90; Wash. 91
	NL:Det. 85, 88; Phil. 86-88; Wash. 92-99; Brk. 1899-1901
	AL:Det. 02-03, 12; NY 04-06; Bos. 07; Clev. 08, 10

Most Assists, League

1810	Ray Schalk, AL:Chi. 1912-28
1593	Red Dooin, NL:Phil. 1902-14; Cin. 15; NY 15-16

Most Assists, Season

214	Pat Moran, NL:Bos. 1903
212	Oscar Stanage, AL:Det. 1911

Most Assists, Game

9	Mike Hines, NL:Bos. May 1, 1883
	Since 1900:
8	Wally Schang, AL:Bos. May 12, 1920
7	Ed McFarland, NL:Phil. May 7, 1901
	Fred Jacklitsch, NL:Brk. Apr. 21. 1903
	Bill Bergen, NL:Brk. Aug. 23(2g), 1909
	Jimmy Archer, NL:Pitt. May 24, 1918
	Bert Adams, NL:Phil. Aug. 21, 1919
	Benito Santiago, NL:SD May 15, 1989 (11 inn)

Fewest Assists, Game (Most Innings, Complete Game in Field)

0	Bob Swift, AL:Det. July 21, 1945 (24 inn)
	Jimmie Wilson, NL:StL. Aug. 28, 1930 (20 inn)

Most Assists, Inning

3	By many players; Last:
	Brad Ausmus, NL:Hou. May 7, 2006 (8th)
	Bob Boone, AL:Cal. Aug. 29, 1986 (3rd)

ERRORS

Most Seasons Leading League (Most)

7	Ivey Wingo, NL:StL. 1912-13; Cin. 16-18, 20-21
6	Birdie Tebbetts, AL:Det. 1939-40, 42; Det.-Bos. 47; Bos. 48-49

Most Errors, Lifetime, Since 1900

234	Ivey Wingo, NL:StL. 1911-14; Cin. 15-26, 29

Most Errors, League, Since 1900

234	Ivey Wingo, NL:StL. 1911-14; Cin. 15-26, 29
218	Wally Schang, AL:Phil. 1913-17, 30; Bos. 18-20; NY 21-25; StL. 26-29; Det. 31

Most Errors, Season

94	Nat Hicks, NL:NY 1876
	Since 1900:
41	Oscar Stanage, AL:Det. 1911
40	Red Dooin, NL:Phil. 1909

Most Total Chances, No Errors, Season

973	Charles Johnson, NL:Fla. 1997 (123 g)
630	Chris Hoiles, AL:Balt. 1997 (87 g)

Fewest Errors, Season (Minimum: 150 games)

4	Randy Hundley, NL:Chi. 1967 (152 g; 928 tc)
	Jim Sundberg, AL:Tex. 1979 (150 g; 833 tc)

Most Errors, Game

7	Jack Rowe, NL:Buff. May 16, 1883
	Dickie Lowe, NL:Det. June 26, 1884
	Billy Taylor, AA:Balt. May 29(1g), 1886
	Since 1900:
4	Gabby Street, NL:Bos. June 7, 1905
	John Peters, AL:Clev. May 16, 1918
	Lena Styles, AL:Phil. July 29, 1921
	Bill Moore, AL:Bos. Sept. 26(2g), 1927

Fewest Errors, Game (Most Innings, Complete Game in Field)
0	Mike Powers, AL:Phil. Sept. 1, 1906 (24 inn)
	Buddy Rosar, AL:Phil. July 21, 1945 (24 inn)
	Bob Swift, AL:Det. July 21, 1945 (24 inn)
	Jerry Grote, NL:NY Apr. 15, 1968 (24 inn)
	Hal King, NL:Hou. Apr. 15, 1968 (24 inn)

Most Errors, Inning
4	Doggie Miller, NL:StL. May 24, 1895 (2nd)
	Since 1900:
3	Jeff Sweeney, AL:NY July 10, 1912 (1st)
	John Peters, AL:Clev. May 16, 1918 (1st)
	Andy Seminick, NL:Cin. July 16, 1952 (1st)
	Jeff Reed, NL:Mtl. July 28, 1987 (7th)

Most Errorless Games, Consecutive, Lifetime
252	Mike Matheny, NL:StL. Aug. 2, 2002-Aug. 1, 2004
159	Rick Cerone, AL:NY-Bos. July 5, 1987-May 8, 1989

Most Errorless Games, Consecutive, Season
138	Mike Matheny, NL:StL. March 31-Sept. 28, 2003 (entire season)
117	Buddy Rosar, AL:Phil. Apr. 16-Sept. 29(1g), 1946
	A.J. Pierzynski, AL:Chi. Apr. 19-Oct. 2, 2005

Most Errorless Chances Accepted, Consecutive, Lifetime
1565	Mike Matheny, NL:StL. Aug. 1, 2002-Aug. 4, 2004
967	A.J. Pierzienski, AL:Chi. Apr. 18, 2005-May 17, 2006

Most Errorless Chances Accepted, Consecutive, Season
973	Charles Johnson, NL:Fla. Apr. 1, 1997-Sept. 28, 1997 (entire season)
777	A.J. Pierzynski, AL:Chi. Apr. 18-Oct. 2, 2005

PASSED BALLS

Most Seasons Leading League (Most)
9	Ernie Lombardi, NL:Cin. 1932, 35-41; NY 45
5	Mickey Cochrane, AL:Phil. 1925-26, 29, 31-32
	Rick Ferrell, AL:StL. 1931; Wash. 39-40, 44-46

Most Passed Balls, Season
99	Pop Snyder, NL:Bos. 1881
	Mike Hines, NL:Bos. 1883
	Since 1900:
35	Geno Petralli, AL:Tex. 1987
29	Frank Bowerman, NL:NY 1900

Most Total Chances, No Passed Balls, Season
751	Bill Dickey, AL:NY 1931
712	Al Todd, NL:Pitt. 1937

Most Passed Balls. Game
12	Alex Gardner, AA:Wash. May 10, 1884
10	Pat Dealy, NL:Bos. May 3, 1886
	Since 1900:
6	Rube Vickers, NL:Cin. Oct. 4, 1902
	Jerry Goff, NL:Hou. May 12, 1996
	Geno Petralli, AL:Tex. Aug. 30, 1987

Fewest Passed Balls, Game (Most Innings, Complete Game in Field)
0	Carlton Fisk, AL:Chi. May 8. 1984 (25 inn)
	Jerry Grote, NL:NY Apr. 15, 1968 (24 inn)
	Hal King, NL:Hou. Apr. 15, 1968 (24 inn)

Most Passed Balls, Inning
5	Dan Sullivan, AA:StL. Aug. 9, 1885 (3rd)
4	Ray Katt, NL:NY Sept. 10, 1954 (8th)
	Geno Petralli, AL:Tex. Aug. 22, 1987 (7th)

DOUBLE PLAYS

Most Seasons Leading League
6	Gabby Hartnett, NL:Chi. 1925, 27, 30-31, 34-35
	Yogi Berra, AL:NY 1949-52, 54, 56

Most Double Plays, League
217	Ray Schalk, AL:Chi. 1912-28
163	Gabby Hartnett, NL:Chi. 1922-40; NY 41

Most Double Plays, Season
29	Frankie Hayes, AL:Phil.-Clev. 1945	
23	Tom Haller, NL:LA 1968	

Most Double Plays, Game
4	Chris Hoiles, AL:Balt. Apr. 9, 1998
3	Jack O'Neill, NL:Chi. Apr. 26, 1905
	Bob O'Farrell, NL:Chi. July 9(2g), 1919 (11 inn)
	Shanty Hogan, NL:NY Aug. 19, 1931
	Ebba St. Claire, NL:Bos. Aug. 9, 1951
	Ron Hodges, NL:NY Apr. 23, 1978 (12 inn)
	Eddie Taubensee, NL:Cin. Apr. 23, 1999
	Damian Miller, NL:Ari. May 25, 1999
	Brian Schneider, NL:Mtl. June 11, 2004
	Henry Blanco, NL:Chi. July 22, 2006

ASE RUNNERS CAUGHT STEALING

Most Base Runners Caught Stealing, Game
8	Duke Farrell, NL:Wash. May 11, 1897
	Since 1900:
6	Bill Bergen, NL:Brk. Aug. 23(2g), 1909
	Wally Schang, AL:Phil. May 12, 1915

Most Base Runners Caught Stealing, Inning
3	Jocko Milligan, AA:Phil. July 26, 1887 (3rd)
	Les Nunamaker, AL:NY Aug. 3, 1914 (7th)
2	By many NL players

’ITCHER

Most Seasons, Lifetime
27	Nolan Ryan, NL:NY 1966, 68-71; Hou. 80-88; AL:Cal. 1972-79; Tex. 89-93

Most Seasons, Consecutive, Lifetime
26	Nolan Ryan, NL:NY 1968-71; Hou. 80-88; AL:Cal. 1972-79; Tex. 89-93

Most Seasons, League
23	Early Wynn, AL:Wash. 1939, 41-44, 46-48; Clev. 49-57, 63; Chi. 58-62
22	Steve Carlton, NL:StL. 1965-71; Phil. 72-86; SF 86

Most Seasons, Consecutive, League
22	Sam Jones, AL:Clev. 1914-15; Bos. 16-21; NY 22, 26; StL. 27 Wash. 28-31; Chi. 32-35
	Steve Carlton, NL:StL. 1965-71; Phil. 72-86; SF 86

ERCENTAGE

Most Seasons Leading League
4	Claude Passeau, NL:Phil.-Chi. 1939; Chi. 42-43, 45
	Larry Jackson, NL:StL. 1957; Chi. 64-65; Phil. 68
3	Walter Johnson, AL:Wash. 1913, 17, 22

Most Seasons, Consecutive, Leading League
2	By many players

Highest Percentage, Lifetime (Minimum: 300 total chances)
.990	Don Mossi, AL:Clev. 1954-58, Det. 59-63, Chi. 64, KC 65
.990	Woody Fryman, NL:Pitt. 1966-77; Phil. 68-72; Mtl. 75-76, 78-83; Cin. 77; Chi. 78

Highest Percentage, Season, Most total chances:
1.000	Frank Owen, AL:Chi. 1904 (151 tc)
	Randy Jones, NL:SD 1976 (112 tc)

;AMES

Most Seasons Leading Major Leagues
5	Firpo Marberry, AL:Wash. 1924-26, 28, 32

Most Seasons Leading League
6	Joe McGinnity, NL:Brk. 1900; NY 1903-07
	Firpo Marberry, AL:Wash. 1924-26, 28-29, 32

Most Games, Lifetime
1252	Jesse Orosco, NL:NY 1979, 81-87; LA 88, 2001-02; StL. 2000; SD 03;
	AL:Clev. 89-91, Mil. 92-94, Balt. 95-99; NY 03; Minn. 03

Most Games, League

1119	John Franco, NL:Cin. 1984-89; NY 90-2001, 03-04; Hou. 05
869	Dennis Eckersley, AL:Clev. 1975-77; Bos. 78-84, 98; Oak. 87-95

Most Games, Consecutive, Since 1900

13	Mike Marshall, NL:LA June 18-July 3(1g), 1974
	Dale Mohorcic, AL:Tex. Aug. 6-20, 1986

Most Games, Season

106	Mike Marshall, NL:LA 1974
90	Mike Marshall, AL:Minn. 1979

CHANCES ACCEPTED

Most Seasons Leading League

13	Greg Maddux, NL:Chi. 1989-92; Atl. 93-96, 98-2001, 03
8	Bob Lemon, AL:Clev. 1948-54, 56

Most Chances Accepted, Lifetime, Since 1900

1761	Christy Mathewson, NL:NY 1900-16; Cin. 16
1606	Walter Johnson, AL:Wash. 1907-27

Most Chances Accepted, Season

262	Ed Walsh, AL:Chi. 1907
216	John Clarkson, NL:Bos. 1889
	NL Since 1900:
168	Christy Mathewson, NL:NY 1908

Most Chances Accepted, Game

13	Nick Altrock, AL:Chi. Aug. 6, 1904
	Ed Walsh, AL:Chi. Apr. 19, 1907
12	Rip Sewell, NL:Pitt. June 6(2g), 1941
	Extra-Inning Game:
15	Ed Walsh, AL:Chi. July 16, 1907 (13 inn)
13	Leon Cadore, NL:Brk. May 1, 1920 (26 inn)

Fewest Chances Accepted, Game (Most Innings, Complete Game in Field)

0	Milt Watson, NL:Phil. July 17, 1918 (20 inn)
	Red Ruffing, AL:NY July 23(1g), 1932 (15 inn)

Most Chances Accepted, Inning

4	Phil Regan, NL:Chi. June 6, 1969 (6th)
	Fernando Valenzuela, NL:LA Apr. 20, 1983 (3rd)
	Hideo Nomo, NL:LA Sept. 17, 1996 (6th)
3	By many AL players

PUTOUTS

Most Seasons Leading League

8	Greg Maddux, NL:Chi. 1989-92, 2004; Atl. 93, 96, 98
5	Bob Lemon, AL:Clev. 1948-49, 52-54

Most Putouts, Lifetime, Since 1900

510	Greg Maddux, NL:Chi. 1986-92, 2004-06; Atl. 1993-2003; LA 06
387	Jack Morris, AL:Det. 1977-90; Minn. 1991; Tor. 92-93; Clev. 94

Most Putouts, Season

52	Al Spalding, NL:Chi. 1876
	Since 1900:
49	Nick Altrock, AL:Chi. 1904
	Mike Boddicker, AL:Balt. 1984
41	Kevin Brown, NL:LA 1999

Most Putouts, Game

7	Greg Maddux, NL:Chi. Apr. 29, 1990
6	Bert Blyleven, AL:Clev. June 24, 1984
	Eric King, AL:Det. July 8, 1986
	Kirk Saarloos, AL:Oak. Apr. 22, 2005
	Extra-Inning Game:
7	Dick Fowler, AL:Phil. June 9, 1949 (12 inn)

Fewest Putouts, Game (Most Innings, Complete Game in Field)

0	Babe Adams, NL:Pitt. July 17, 1914 (21 inn)
	Rube Marquard, NL:NY July 17, 1914 (21 inn)
	Saul Rogovin, AL:Chi. July 12, 1951 (17 inn)

Most Putouts, Inning

3	By many players; Last:
	Rob Bell, AL:Tex. July 4, 2002 (5th)
	Darren Dreifort, NL:LA Sept. 5, 1999 (4th)

ASSISTS

Most Seasons Leading League

10	Greg Maddux, NL:Chi. 1990; Atl. 92-93, 95-96, 98, 2000-01, 03; Chi.-LA 06
6	Bob Lemon, AL:Clev. 1948-49, 51-53, 56

Most Assists, Lifetime, Since 1900

1489	Christy Mathewson, NL:NY 1900-16; Cin. 16

Most Assists, League, Since 1900

1489	Christy Mathewson, NL:NY 1900-16; Cin. 16
1337	Walter Johnson, AL:Wash. 1907-27

Most Assists, Season

227	Ed Walsh, AL:Chi. 1907
168	John Clarkson, NL:Bos. 1889
	NL Since 1900:
141	Christy Mathewson, NL:NY 1908

Most Assists, Game

11	Al Orth, AL:NY Aug. 12, 1906
	Ed Walsh, AL:Chi. Apr. 19 & Aug. 12, 1907
	George McConnell, AL:NY Sept. 2(2g), 1912
	Mellie Wolfgang, AL:Chi. Aug. 29, 1914
	Rip Sewell, NL:Pitt. June 6(2g), 1941
	Extra-Inning Game:
12	Ed Walsh, AL:Chi. July 16, 1907 (13 inn)
	Nick Altrock, AL:Chi. June 7, 1908 (10 inn)
	Leon Cadore, NL:Brk. May 1, 1920 (26 inn)

Fewest Assists, Game (Most Innings, Complete Game in Field)

0	Milt Watson, NL:Phil. July 17, 1918 (20 inn)
	Red Ruffing, AL:NY July 23(1g), 1932 (15 inn)

Most Assists, Inning

3	By many players

ERRORS

Most Seasons Leading League (Most)

5	Hippo Vaughn, NL:Chi. 1914-15, 17, 19-20
	Warren Spahn, NL:Bos. 1949-50, 52; Mil. 54, 64
4	Allen Sothoron, AL:StL. 1917-20
	Dizzy Trout, AL:Det. 1943-45, 48
	Dean Chance, AL:LA 1963; Minn. 67-68; Det. 71
	Nolan Ryan, AL:Cal. 1975-78

Most Errors, Lifetime, Since 1900

90	Joe McGinnity, NL:Brk. 1900; NY 1902-08; AL:Balt. 1901-02
	Nolan Ryan, NL:NY 1966, 68-71; Hou. 80-88; AL:Cal. 1972-79; Tex. 89-93

Most Errors, League, Since 1900

79	Rube Waddell, AL:Phil. 1902-07; StL. 08-10
75	Joe McGinnity, NL:Brk. 1900; 1902-08

Most Errors, Season

28	Jim Whitney, NL:Bos. 1881
	Since 1900:
17	Doc Newton, NL:Cin.-Brk. 1901
15	Jack Chesbro, AL:NY 1904
	Rube Waddell, AL:Phil. 1905
	Ed Walsh, AL:Chi. 1912

Most Errors, Game

5	Ed Doheny, NL:NY Aug. 15, 1899
	Since 1900:
4	Doc Newton, NL:Cin. Sept. 13(1g), 1900
	Lave Winham, NL:Pitt. Sept. 21(1g), 1903
	Buster Ross, AL:Bos. May 17, 1925

Fewest Errors, Game (Most Innings, Complete Game in Field)

0	Leon Cadore, NL:Brk. May 1, 1920 (26 inn)
	Joe Oeschger, NL:Bos. May 1, 1920 (26 inn)
	Jack Coombs, AL:Phil. Sept. 1, 1906 (24 inn)
	Joe Harris, AL:Bos. Sept. 1, 1906 (24 inn)

Most Errors, Inning

3	Cy Seymour, NL:NY May 21, 1898 (6th)
	Tommy John, AL:NY July 27, 1988 (4th)
	Mike Sirotka, AL:Chi. Apr. 9, 1999 (5th)

Most Errorless Games, Consecutive, Lifetime
667   Dan Plesac, NL:Chi.-Pitt.-Ari.-Phil.; AL:Tor. July 30, 1993-Sept. 28, 2003

Most Errorless Games, Consecutive, League
546   Lee Smith, NL:Chi.-StL. July 5, 1982-Sept. 22, 1992
541   Dan Plesac, AL:Mil.-Tor. July 11, 1987-May 22, 2002

Most Errorless Games, Consecutive, Season
94   Salomon Torres, NL:Pitt. 2006
88   Wilbur Wood, AL:Chi. 1968
             Sean Runyan, AL:Det. 1998

Most Errorless Chances Accepted, Consecutive, Lifetime
273   Claude Passeau, NL:Chi. Sept. 21, 1941-May 20, 1946
231   Rick Langford, AL:Oak. Apr. 13, 1977-Oct. 2, 1980

DOUBLE PLAYS

Most Seasons Leading League
6   Greg Maddux, NL:Chi. 1987, 90-91; Atl. 94, 96; Chi.-LA 2006
4   Willis Hudlin, AL:Clev. 1929-31, 34

Most Double Plays, Lifetime
89   Greg Maddux, NL: Chi. 1986-92, 2004-06; Atl. 1993-2003; LA 06
78   Bob Lemon, AL:Clev. 1941-42, 46-58

Most Double Plays, Season
15   Bob Lemon, AL:Clev. 1953
12   Art Nehf, NL:NY 1920
             Curt Davis, NL:Phil. 1934
             Randy Jones, NL:SD 1976

Most Double Plays, Game
4   Milt Gaston, AL:Chi. May 17, 1932
             Hal Newhouser, AL:Det. May 19, 1948
3   By many NL players; Last:
             Wandy Rodriguez, NL:Hou. June 15, 2005

Most Double Plays, Unassisted, League
2   Tex Carleton, NL:Chi. 1935; Brk. 40
             Claude Passeau, NL:Phil. 1938; Chi. 45

Most Double Plays, Unassisted, Game
1   By many players

INDIVIDUAL PITCHING RECORDS

SERVICE

Most Seasons, Lifetime
27   Nolan Ryan, NL:NY 1966, 68-71; Hou. 80-88; AL:Cal. 72-79; Tex. 89-93

Most Seasons, Consecutive, Lifetime
26   Nolan Ryan, NL:NY 1968-71; Hou. 80-88; AL:Cal. 72-79; Tex. 89-93

Most Seasons, League
23   Early Wynn, AL:Wash. 1939, 41-44, 46-48; Clev. 49-57, 63; Chi. 58-62
22   Steve Carlton, NL:StL. 1965-71; Phil. 72-86; SF 86

Most Seasons, Consecutive, League
22   Sam Jones, AL:Clev. 1914-15; Bos. 16-21; NY 22-26; StL. 27; Wash. 28-31; Chi. 32-35
         Steve Carlton, NL:StL. 1965-71; Phil. 72-86; SF 86

Most Leagues, Lifetime
4   Jerry Bakely, AA:1883, 88, 91; UA:84; NL:89; PL:90
         Cannonball Crane, UA:1884; NL:86, 88-89, 91-93; PL:90; AA:91
         Gus Weyhing, AA:1887-89, 91; PL:1890; NL:1892-1901; AL:1901
         Frank Foreman, UA:1884; AA:85, 89, 91; NL:90-93, 95-96; AL:1901-02

Most Leagues, Season
3   By many players

CLUBS

Most Seasons, One Club
21   Walter Johnson, AL:Wash. 1907-27
         Ted Lyons, AL:Chi. 1923-42, 46
         Phil Niekro, NL:Mil./Atl. 1964-83, 87

Most Seasons, Consecutive, One Club
21   Walter Johnson, AL:Wash. 1907-27
20   Warren Spahn, NL:Bos.-Mil. 1942-64 (1943-45 Military Service)
         Phil Niekro, NL:Mil./Atl. 1964-83

Most Clubs, Lifetime
12   Mike Morgan, AL:Oak. 1978-79; NY 82; Tor. 83; Sea. 85-87; Balt. 88; Minn. 98; Tex. 99
                 NL:LA 89-91; Chi. 92-95, 98; StL. 95-96; Cin. 96-97; Ari. 2000-02

Most Clubs, League
7   Mike Sullivan, NL:Wash. 1889; Chi. 90; NY 91, 96-97; Cin. 92-93; Wash. 94; Clev. 94-95; Bos 99
         Gus Weyhing, NL:Phil. 1892-95; Pitt. 95; Lou. 95-96; Wash. 98-99; StL. 1900; Brk. 1900; Cin. 01
         Mike Maddux, NL:Phil. 1986-89; LA 90; SD 91-92; NY 93-94; Pitt. 95; Mtl. 98; Hou. 2000
         Kent Bottenfield, NL:Mtl. 1992-93; Col.93-94; SF 94; Chi. 96-97; StL. 98-99; Phil. 2000; Hou. 01
         Manny Aybar, NL:StL. 1997-99; Col. 2000; Cin. 00; Fla. 00; Chi. 01; SF 02-03; NY 05
         Shawn Estes, NL:SF 1995-2001; NY 02; Cin. 02; Chi. 03; Col. 04; Ari. 05; SD 06
         Terry Mulholland, NL:SF 1986, 88-89, 95, 97; Phil. 89-93; 96 Chi. 97-99; Atl. 99-2000; Pitt. 01; LA 01-02; Ari. 06
         Rick White, NL:Pitt. 1994-95, 2005; NY 00-01; Col. 02; StL. 02; Hou. 03; Cin. 06; Phil. 06
         Ken Sanders, AL:KC/Oak. 1964, 66, 68, 76; Bos. 66; Mil. 70-72; Minn. 73; Clev. 73-74; Cal. 74; KC 76
         Ken Brett, AL:Bos. 1967-71; Mil. 72; NY 76; Chi. 76-77; Cal. 77-78; Minn. 79; KC 80-81
         Ed Farmer, AL:Clev. 1971-73; Det. 73; Balt. 77; Mil. 78; Tex. 79; Chi. 79-81; Oak. 83
         Greg Cadaret, AL:Oak. 1987-89; NY 89-92; KC 93; Tor. 94; Det. 94; Ana. 97-98; Tex. 98
         Mike Morgan, AL:Oak. 1978-79; NY 82; Tor. 83; Sea. 85-87; Balt. 88; Minn. 98; Tex. 99

Most Clubs, Major Leagues, Season
4   Willis Hudlin, AL:Clev.-Wash.; NL:StL.-NY 1940
         Ted Gray, AL:Chi.-Clev.-NY-Balt. 1955
         Mike Kilkenny, AL:Det.-Oak.-Clev; NL:SD 1972
         Dan Micelli, NL:Col.-Hou.; AL:Clev.-NY 2003

Most Clubs, League, Season
4   Ted Gray, AL:Chi.-Clev.-NY-Balt. 1955
3   By many NL players

GAMES

Most Seasons Leading Major Leagues
5   Firpo Marberry, AL:Wash. 1924-26, 28, 32

Most Seasons, Consecutive, Leading Major Leagues
3   Bill Hutchinson, NL:Chi. 1890-92
         Ace Adams, NL:NY 1942-44
         Steve Kline, NL:Mtl. 1999-2000; StL. 01
         Firpo Marberry, AL:Wash. 1924-26

Most Seasons Leading League
6	Joe McGinnity, NL:Brk. 1900; NY 03-07
	Firpo Marberry, AL:Wash. 1924-26, 28-29, 32

Most Seasons, Consecutive, Leading League
5	Joe McGinnity, NL:NY 1903-07
3	Ed Walsh, AL:Chi. 1910-12
	Firpo Marberry, AL:Wash. 1924-26
	Wilbur Wood, AL:Chi. 1968-70

Most Games, Lifetime
1252	Jesse Orosco, NL:NY 1979, 81-87; LA 88, 2001-02; StL. 2000; SD 03
	AL:Clev. 89-91, Mil. 92-94, Balt. 95-99; NY 03; Minn. 03

Most Games, League
1119	John Franco, NL:Cin. 1984-89; NY 90-2001, 03-04; Hou. 05
869	Dennis Eckersley, AL:Clev. 1975-77; Bos. 78-84, 98; Oak. 87-95

Most Games, Season
106	Mike Marshall, NL:LA 1974 (0 starts)
90	Mike Marshall, AL:Minn. 1979 (1 start)

Most Games, Consecutive
13	Mike Marshall, NL:LA June 18-July 3(1g), 1974
	Dale Mohorcic, AL:Tex. Aug. 6-20, 1986

GAMES STARTED

Most Seasons Leading Major Leagues
6	Robin Roberts, NL:Phil. 1950-55
	Tom Glavine, NL:Atl. 1993, 96, 99-2002

Most Seasons, Consecutive, Leading Major Leagues
6	Robin Roberts, NL:Phil. 1950-55

Most Seasons Leading League
7	Greg Maddux, NL:Chi. 1990-92, 2005; Atl. 93, 2000, 03
5	Bob Feller, AL:Clev. 1940-41, 46-48
	Early Wynn, AL:Wash. 1943; Clev. 51, 54, 57; Chi. 59

Most Seasons, Consecutive, Leading League
6	Robin Roberts, NL:Phil. 1950-55
4	Wilbur Wood, AL:Chi. 1972-75
	Dave Stewart, AL:Oak. 1988-91

Most Games Started, Lifetime
818	Cy Young, NL:Clev. 1890-98; StL. 1899-1900; Bos. 11; AL:Bos. 1901-08; Clev. 09-11

Most Games Started, League
677	Steve Carlton, NL:StL. 1965-71; Phil. 72-86; SF 86
666	Walter Johnson, AL:Wash. 1907-27

Most Games Started, Consecutive, Lifetime
678	Roger Clemens, AL:Bos.-Tor.-NY; NL:Hou. July 26, 1984-Sept. 29, 2006

Most Games Started, Consecutive, League
645	Greg Maddux, NL:Chi.-Atl.-LA Sept. 15, 1987-Sept. 30, 2006
594	Roger Clemens, AL:Bos.-Tor.-NY July 26, 1984-Sept. 27, 2003

Most Games Started, Season
74	Will White, NL:Cin. 1879
	Since 1900:
51	Jack Chesbro, AL:NY 1904
48	Joe McGinnity, NL:NY 1903
	No relief appearances:
49	Wilbur Wood, AL:Chi. 1972
44	Phil Niekro, NL:Atl. 1979

Most Games Started, Incomplete, Season
37	Steve Bedrosian, NL:Atl. 1985 (37 starts)
36	Stan Bahnsen, AL:Chi. 1972 (41 starts)

Most Games Started, No Complete Games, Season
37	Steve Bedrosian, NL:Atl. 1985
35	Wilson Alvarez, AL:Chi. 1996
	Sterling Hitchcock, AL:Sea. 1996
	Rick Helling, AL:Tex. 2000
	Rodrigo Lopez, AL:Balt. 2005
	Barry Zito, AL:Oak. 2005

Most Games Started, Opening Day, Lifetime
16	Tom Seaver, NL:NY 1968-77, 83; Cin. 78-79, 81; AL:Chi. 1985-86

Most Games Started, Opening Day, League

14	Walter Johnson, AL:Wash. 1910, 12-21, -23-24, 26
	Jack Morris, AL:Det. 1980-90; Minn. 91; Tor. 92-93
	Tom Seaver, NL:NY 1968-77, 83; Cin. 78-79, 81
	Steve Carlton, NL:Phil. 72-75; 77-86

Most Games Started, Consecutive, Opening Day, League

14	Jack Morris, AL:Det. 1980-90; Minn. 91; Tor. 92-93
12	Robin Roberts, NL:Phil. 1950-61
	Tom Seaver, NL:NY 1968-77; Cin. 78-79

COMPLETE GAMES

Most Seasons Leading Major Leagues

7	Warren Spahn, NL:Bos. 1951; Mil. 57-60, 62-63

Most Seasons, Consecutive, Leading Major Leagues

5	Robin Roberts, NL:Phil. 1952-56

Most Seasons Leading League

9	Warren Spahn, NL:Bos. 1949, 51; Mil. 57-63
6	Walter Johnson, AL:Wash. 1910-11, 13-16

Most Seasons, Consecutive, Leading League

7	Warren Spahn, NL:Mil. 1957-63
4	Walter Johnson, AL:Wash. 1913-16

Most Complete Games, Lifetime

751	Cy Young, NL:Clev. 1890-98; StL. 1899-1900; Bos. 11; AL:Bos. 1901-08; Clev. 09-11

Most Complete Games, League

552	Pud Galvin, NL:Buff. 1879-85; Pitt. 87-89, 91-92; StL. 92
	Since 1900:
531	Walter Johnson, AL:Wash. 1907-27
437	Grover Alexander, NL:Phil. 1911-17, 30; Chi. 18-26; StL. 26-29

Most Complete Games, Season

74	Will White, NL:Cin. 1879 (74 starts)
	Since 1900:
48	Jack Chesbro, AL:NY 1904 (51 starts)
45	Vic Willis, NL:Bos. 1902 (46 starts)

Most Complete Games, Consecutive, Lifetime

198	Jack Lynch, NL:Buff. 1881; AA:NY 83-87, 90

Most Complete Games, Consecutive, League

197	Jack Lynch, AA:NY 1883-87, 90
187	Jack Taylor, NL:Chi. 1901-03, 06; StL. 04-06
54	Cy Young, AL:Bos. 1903-04
	Earl Moore, AL:Clev. 1902-04

Most Complete Games, Consecutive, Season, Since 1900

39	Jack Taylor, NL:StL. 1904 (two relief appearances during streak)
37	Bill Dinneen, AL:Bos. 1904

SHUTOUTS

Most Seasons Leading Major Leagues

6	Cy Young, NL:Clev. 1892, 95-96; StL. 1900; AL:Bos. 03-04
	Since 1900:
4	Christy Mathewson, NL:NY 1902, 05, 07-08
	Grover Alexander, NL:Phil. 1911, 15-16; Chi. 19
	Walter Johnson, AL:Wash. 1913-14, 18, 24
	Roger Clemens, AL:Bos. 1987-88, 90, 92

Most Seasons, Consecutive, Leading Major Leagues
3   Tommy Bond, NL:Bos. 1877-79
        Amos Rusie, NL:NY 1893-95
        Since 1900:
2   Jack Chesbro, NL:Pitt. 1901-02
        Christy Mathewson, NL:NY 1907-08
        Grover Alexander, NL:Phil. 1915-16
        Whitlow Wyatt, NL:Brk. 1940-41
        Jim Bunning, NL:Phil. 1966-67
        Jason Schmidt, NL:SF 2003-04
        Cy Young, AL:Bos. 1903-04
        Walter Johnson, AL:Wash. 1913-14
        Allie Reynolds, AL:NY 1951-52
        Camilo Pascual, AL:Minn. 1961-62
        Tommy John, AL:Chi. 1966-67
        Roger Clemens, AL:Bos. 1987-88

Most Seasons Leading League
7   Grover Alexander, NL:Phil. 1911, 13, 15-17; Chi. 19
        Walter Johnson, AL:Wash. 1911, 13-15, 18-19, 24

Most Seasons, Consecutive, Leading League
3   Tommy Bond, NL:Bos. 1877-79
        Amos Rusie, NL:NY 1893-95
        Grover Alexander, NL:Phil. 1915-17
        Walter Johnson, AL:Wash. 1913-15
        Roger Clemens, AL:Bos. 1990-92

Most Shutouts, Lifetime
110   Walter Johnson, AL:Wash. 1907-27
90   Grover Alexander, NL:Phil. 1911-17, 30; Chi. 18-26; StL. 26-29

Most Shutouts, Season
16   George Bradley, NL:StL. 1876
        Grover Alexander, NL:Phil. 1916
13   Jack Coombs, AL:Phil. 1910

Most Seasons, 10 or more Shutouts
2   Ed Walsh, AL:Chi. 1906, 08
        Grover Alexander, NL:Phil. 1915-16

Most Shutouts, Consecutive, Season
6   Don Drysdale, NL:LA May 14-18-22-26-31, June 4, 1968
5   Doc White, AL:Chi. Sept. 12-16-19-25-30, 1904

Most Shutouts, Doubleheader
2   Ed Reulbach, NL:Chi. vs Brk. Sept. 26, 1908 (5-0, 3-0)

Most Shutouts, One Month
6   Doc White, AL:Chi. Sept. 1904
        Ed Walsh, AL:Chi. Aug. 1906 & Sept. 1908
5   George Bradley, NL:StL. May 1876
        Tommy Bond, NL:Hart. June 1876
        Pud Galvin, NL:Buff. Aug. 1884
        Ben Sanders, NL:Phil. Sept. 1888
        Don Drysdale, NL:LA May 1968
        Bob Gibson, NL:StL. June 1968
        Orel Hershiser, NL:LA Sept. 1988

Most Shutouts vs. One Club, League
23   Walter Johnson, AL:Wash. vs Phil. 1907-27
20   Grover Alexander, NL:Phil.-Chi.-StL. vs Cin. 1911-30

Most Shutouts vs. One Club, Season
5   Tony Mullane, AA:Cin. vs NY 1887
        Lady Baldwin, NL:Det. vs Phil. 1886
        Grover Alexander, NL:Phil. vs Cin. 1916
        Larry Jaster, NL:StL. vs LA 1966 (cons)
        Tom Hughes, AL:Wash. vs Clev. 1905

Most Clubs Shutout, Season
8   Bob Gibson, NL:StL. 1968
        Nolan Ryan, AL:Cal. 1972

Most Shutouts, Opening Game, Season
7   Walter Johnson, AL:Wash. 1910, 14-15, 17, 19, 24, 26
3   Rip Sewell, NL:Pitt. 1943, 47, 49
        Chris Short, NL:Phil. 1965, 68, 70
        Rick Mahler, NL:Atl. 1982, 86-87

Most Innings, Shutout Game
18	Monte Ward, NL:Prov. Aug. 17, 1882
	Carl Hubbell, NL:NY July 2(1g), 1933
	Ed Summers, AL:Det. July 19, 1909 (tie)
	Walter Johnson, AL:Wash. May 15, 1918

Most Scoreless Innings, Consecutive, Game
21	Joe Oeschger, NL:Bos. May 1, 1920
20	Joe Harris, AL:Bos. Sept. 1, 1906

Most Hits Allowed, Shutout
14	Larry Cheney, NL:Chi. Sept. 14, 1913
	Milt Gaston, AL:Wash. July 10(2g), 1928

Most Walks Allowed, Shutout
11	Lefty Gomez, AL:NY Aug. 1, 1941
9	Vinegar Bend Mizell, NL:StL. Sept. 1(1g), 1958
	A.J. Burnett, NL:Fla. May 12, 2001
	Extra-Inning Game:
10	Jim Maloney, NL:Cin. Aug. 19(1g), 1965 (10 inn)
	J.R. Richard, NL:Hou. July 6, 1976 (10 inn)

Most Scoreless Innings, Consecutive. Season
59.0	Orel Hershiser, NL:LA Aug. 30-Sept. 28, 1988
55.2	Walter Johnson, AL:Wash. Apr. 10-May 14, 1913

Most Shutouts Lost, Lifetime
65	Walter Johnson, AL:Wash. 1907-27
53	Phil Niekro, NL:Mil./Atl. 1964-83, 87

Most Shutouts Lost, Season
14	Jim Devlin, NL:Lou. 1876
	Since 1900:
11	Bugs Raymond, NL:StL. 1908
10	Walter Johnson, AL:Wash. 1909

Most Shutouts Lost, vs. One Club, Season
5	Jim Devlin, NL:Lou. (Hart.) 1876
	Walter Johnson, AL:Wash. (Chi.) 1909
	NL Since 1900:
4	Irv Young, NL:Bos. (Pitt.) 1906
	Lefty Leifield, NL:Pitt. (Chi.) 1906, 10
	Tom Zachary, NL:Brk. (Pitt.) 1935
	Bob Veale, NL:Pitt. (SF) 1968

Most Shutouts Lost, One Month
5	Cherokee Fisher, NL:Cin. May 1876
	Walter Johnson, AL:Wash. July 1909
	NL Since 1900:
4	Irv Young, NL:Bos. July 1907
	George McQuillan, NL:Phil. June 1908
	Pete Schneider, NL:Cin. Aug. 1915
	Jess Petty, NL:Brk. Aug. 1927
	Freddie Fitzsimmons, NL:NY Sept. 1934
	Max Butcher, NL:Phil. Sept. 1938
	Jim McAndrew, NL:NY Aug. 1968
	Ken Reynolds, NL:Phil. July 1972

GAMES FINISHED

Most Seasons Leading Major Leagues
4	Mike Marshall, NL:Mtl. 1972-73, LA 74; AL:Minn. 79
	Dan Quisenberry, AL:KC 1980, 82-83, 85

Most Seasons, Consecutive, Leading Major Leagues
3	Mike Marshall, NL:Mtl. 1972-73; LA 74

Most Seasons Leading League
5	Mike Marshall, NL:Mtl. 1971-73; LA 74; AL:Minn. 79
	Firpo Marberry, AL:Wash. 1924-26, 28-29
4	Ace Adams, NL:NY 1942-45
	Roy Face, NL:Pitt. 1958, 60-62
	Mike Marshall, NL:Mtl. 1971-73; LA 74
	Rod Beck, NL:SF 1993-94, 97; Chi. 98

Most Seasons, Consecutive, Leading League
4	Ace Adams, NL:NY 1942-45
	Mike Marshall, NL:Mtl. 1971-73; LA 74
3	Firpo Marberry, AL:Wash. 1924-26
	Joe Page, AL:NY 1947-49
	Roberto Hernandez, AL:Chi. 1994-96

Most Games Finished, Lifetime
802	Lee Smith, NL:Chi. 1980-87; StL. 90-93; Cin. 96; Mtl. 97
	AL:Bos. 1988-90; NY 93; Balt. 94; Cal. 95-96

Most Games Finished, League
774	John Franco, NL:Cin. 1984-89; NY 90-2001, 03-04; Hou. 05
600	Mariano Rivara, AL:NY 1995-2006

Most Games Finished, Season
84	Mike Marshall, AL:Minn. 1979
83	Mike Marshall, NL:LA 1974

SAVES (Since 1969)

Most Seasons Leading Major Leagues
3	Rollie Fingers, NL:SD 1977-78; AL:Mil. 81
	Bruce Sutter, NL:Chi. 1979; StL. 82, 84
	Mariano Rivera, AL:NY 1999, 2001, 04

Most Seasons, Consecutive, Leading Major Leagues
2	Rollie Fingers, NL:SD 1977-78

Most Seasons Leading League
5	Bruce Sutter, NL:Chi. 1979-80; StL. 81-82, 84
	Dan Quisenberry, AL:KC 1980, 82-85

Most Seasons, Consecutive, Leading League
4	Bruce Sutter, NL:Chi. 1979-80; StL. 81-82
	Dan Quisenberry, AL:KC 1982-85

Most Saves, Lifetime
482	Trevor Hoffman, NL:Fla. 1993; SD 93-2006
413	Mariano Rivera, AL:NY 1995-2006

Most Saves, Season
57	Bobby Thigpen, AL:Chi. 1990
55	John Smoltz, NL:Atl. 2002
	Eric Gagne, NL:LA 2003

Most Saves, Month
15	Lee Smith, NL:StL. June 1993
	Chad Cordero, NL:Wash. June 2005
	John Wetteland, AL:NY June 1996

Most Saves, Consecutive Appearances, Season
24	John Wetteland, AL:NY May 31-July 14, 1996
23	Todd Jones, NL:Fla. July 19-Sept. 13, 2005

NO-HIT GAMES (Minimum: 9 innings pitched; additional listings on pages 361-367)

Most Perfect Games, Lifetime
1	Lee Richmond, NL:Wor. June 12, 1880 (vs Clev.)
	Monte Ward, NL:Prov. June 17, 1880 (vs Buff.)
	Jim Bunning, NL:Phil. June 21, 1964 (vs NY)
	Sandy Koufax, NL:LA Sept. 9, 1965 (vs Chi.)
	Tom Browning, NL:Cin. Sept. 16, 1988 (vs LA)
	Dennis Martinez, NL:Mtl. July 28, 1991 (vs LA)
	Randy Johnson, NL:Ari. May 18, 2004 (vs. Atl.)
	Cy Young, AL:Bos. May 5, 1904 (vs Phil.)
	Addie Joss, AL:Clev. Oct. 2, 1908 (vs Chi.)
	Charlie Robertson, AL:Chi. Apr. 30, 1922 (vs Det.)
	Catfish Hunter, AL:Oak. May 8, 1968 (vs Minn.)
	Len Barker, AL:Clev. May 15, 1981 (vs Tor.)
	Mike Witt, AL:Cal. Sept. 30, 1984 (vs Tex.)
	Kenny Rogers, AL:Tex. July 28, 1994 (vs Cal.)
	David Wells, AL:NY May 17, 1998 (vs Minn.)
	David Cone, AL:NY July 18, 1999 (vs. Mtl.)

Most No-Hit Games, Lifetime
7	Nolan Ryan, AL:Cal. 1973, 74, 75; Tex. 90, 91; NL:Hou. 1981

Most No-Hit Games, League
6	Nolan Ryan, AL:Cal. 1973, 74, 75; Tex. 90, 91
4	Sandy Koufax, NL:LA 1962, 63, 64, 65

Most No-Hit Games, Season
2	Johnny Vander Meer, NL:Cin. June 11 (Bos.); June 15 (Brk.), 1938
	Allie Reynolds, AL:NY July 12 (Clev.); Sept. 28 (Bos.), 1951
	Virgil Trucks, AL:Det. May 15 (Wash.); Aug. 25 (NY), 1952
	Nolan Ryan, AL:Cal. May 15 (KC); July 15 (Det.), 1973

Most No-Hit Games, Consecutive
2	Johnny Vander Meer, NL:Cin. June 11 (Bos.)-June 15 (Brk.), 1938

Most Innings, No-Hit Game
10	Sam Kimber, AA:Brk. (Tol.) Oct. 4, 1884 (0-0)
	Hooks Wiltse, NL:NY (Phil.) July 4, 1908 (1-0)
	Fred Toney, NL:Cin. (Chi.) May 2, 1917 (1-0)
	Jim Maloney, NL:Cin. (Chi.) Aug. 19, 1965 (1-0)

ONE-HIT GAMES

Most One-Hit Games, Lifetime
12	Bob Feller, AL:Clev. 1936-41, 45-56
	Nolan Ryan, NL:NY 1966, 68-71; Hou. 80-88; AL:Cal. 1972-79; Tex. 89-93

Most One-Hit Games, League
12	Bob Feller, AL:Clev. 1936-41, 45-56
7	Hoss Radbourn, NL:Prov. 1881-85; Bos. 86-89; Cin. 91
	NL Since 1900:
6	Steve Carlton, NL:StL. 1965-71; Phil. 72-86; SF 86

Most One-Hit Games, Season
4	Hugh Daily, UA:Chi. 1884
	Grover Alexander, NL:Phil. 1915
3	Addie Joss, AL:Clev. 1907
	Dave Stieb, AL:Tor. 1988

Most One-Hit Games, Consecutive, Season
2	Hugh Daily, UA:Chi. July 7-10, 1884
	Toad Ramsey, AA:Lou. July 29-31, 1886
	Charlie Buffinton, NL:Phil. Aug. 6-9, 1887
	Rube Marquard, NL:NY Aug. 28-Sept. 1, 1911
	Lon Warneke, NL:Chi. Apr. 17-22, 1934
	Mort Cooper, NL:StL. May 31-June 4, 1943
	Whitey Ford, AL:NY Sept. 2-7, 1955
	Sam McDowell, AL:Clev. Apr. 25-May 1, 1966
	Dave Stieb, AL:Tor. Sept. 24-30, 1988

Most Innings, One-Hit Game
12.2	Harvey Haddix, NL:Pitt. (Mil.) May 26, 1959
10.0	Doc White, AL:Chi. (Clev.) Sept. 6, 1903
	Bobo Newsom, AL:StL. (Bos.) Sept. 18, 1934
	Bert Blyleven, AL:Tex. (Oak.) June 21, 1976

EARNED RUN AVERAGE (Since 1912 in NL; Since 1913 in AL - Prior seasons not compiled on official scores)

Most Seasons Leading Major Leagues
5	Pedro Martinez, NL:Mtl. 1997; AL:Bos. 1999-2000, 02-03

Most Seasons, Consecutive, Leading Major Leagues
3	Lefty Grove, AL:Phil. 1929-31
	Greg Maddux, NL:Atl. 1993-95

Most Seasons Leading League
9	Lefty Grove, AL:Phil. 1926, 29-32; Bos. 35-36, 38-39
5	Grover Alexander, NL:Phil. 1915-17; Chi. 19-20
	Sandy Koufax, NL:LA 1962-66

Most Seasons, Consecutive, Leading League
5	Sandy Koufax, NL:LA 1962-66
4	Lefty Grove, AL:Phil. 1929-32

Lowest Earned Run Average, Lifetime (Minimum: 2000 innings)
2.19	Eddie Cicotte, AL:Chi. 1913-20 (excluding AL:Det.-Bos.-Chi. 1905-12)
2.33	Hippo Vaughn, NL:Chi. 1913-21

Lowest Earned Run Average, Season (Qualifiers)
1.00	Dutch Leonard, AL:Bos. 1914
1.12	Bob Gibson, NL:StL. 1968

WINNING PERCENTAGE

Most Seasons Leading Major Leagues
5	Lefty Grove, AL:Phil. 1929-31, 33; Bos. 38

Most Seasons, Consecutive, Leading Major Leagues
3	Lefty Grove, AL:Phil. 1929-31

Most Seasons Leading League
5	Lefty Grove, AL:Phil. 1929-31, 33; Bos. 38
3	Sam Leever, NL:Pitt. 1901, 03, 05
	Ed Reulbach, NL:Chi. 1906-08

Most Seasons, Consecutive, Leading League
3	Ed Reulbach, NL:Chi. 1906-08
	Lefty Grove, AL:Phil. 1929-31

Highest Winning Percentage, Lifetime (Minimum: 200 wins)
.691	Pedro Martinez, NL:LA 1992-93; Mtl. 94-97; NY 2005-06; AL:Bos. 1998-2004 (206-92)

Highest Winning Percentage, League (Minimum: 200 wins)
.690	Whitey Ford, AL:NY 1950, 53-67 (236-106)
.665	Christy Mathewson, NL:NY 1900-16; Cin. 16 (373-188)

Lowest Winning Percentage, Lifetime (Minimum: 100 wins)
.380	Si Johnson, NL:Cin. 1928-36; StL. 36-38; Phil. 40-43, 46; Bos. 46-47 (101-165)
.406	Sid Hudson, AL:Wash. 1940-42, 46-52; Bos. 52-54 (104-152)

Highest Winning Percentage, Season (Minimum: 15 decisions)
.947	Roy Face, NL:Pitt. 1959 (18-1)
.938	Johnny Allen, AL:Clev. 1937 (15-1)

GAMES WON

Most Seasons Leading Major Leagues
4	Cy Young, NL:Clev. 1892, 95; AL:Bos. 1901-02
	Joe McGinnity, NL:Balt. 1899; Brk. 1900; NY 03, 06
	Grover Alexander, NL:Phil. 1911, 15-17
	Robin Roberts, NL:Phil. 1952-55
	Warren Spahn, NL:Mil. 1953, 57-58, 60
	Tom Glavine, NL:Atl. 1991, 93, 98, 2000
	Roger Clemens, AL:Bos. 1986-87; Tor. 97-98

Most Seasons, Consecutive, Leading Major Leagues
4	Robin Roberts, NL:Phil. 1952-55

Most Seasons Leading League
8	Warren Spahn, NL:Bos. 1949-50; Mil. 53, 57-61
6	Walter Johnson, AL:Wash. 1913-16, 18, 24
	Bob Feller, AL:Clev. 1939-41, 46-47, 51

Most Seasons, Consecutive, Leading League
5	Warren Spahn, NL:Mil. 1957-61
4	Walter Johnson, AL:Wash. 1913-16

Most Games Won, Lifetime
511	Cy Young, NL:Clev. 1890-98; StL. 1899-1900; Bos. 11; AL:Bos. 1901-08; Clev. 09-11

Most Games Won, League
417	Walter Johnson, AL:Wash. 1907-27
373	Christy Mathewson, NL:NY 1900-16; Cin. 16
	Grover Alexander, NL:Phil. 1911-17, 30; Chi. 18-26; StL. 26-29

Most Games Won, Season
60	Hoss Radbourn, NL:Prov. 1884
	Since 1900:
41	Jack Chesbro, AL:NY 1904
37	Christy Mathewson, NL:NY 1908

Most Games Won, No Losses, Season
12	Tom Zachary, AL:NY 1929
10	Howie Krist, NL:StL. 1941

Most Seasons, 30 or more Games Won, Lifetime
7	Kid Nichols, NL:Bos. 1891-94, 96-98

Most Seasons, 30 or more Games Won, League
7	Kid Nichols, NL:Bos. 1891-94, 96-98
	Since 1900:
4	Christy Mathewson, NL:NY 1903-05, 08
2	Cy Young, AL:Bos. 1901-02
	Walter Johnson, AL:Wash. 1912-13

Most Seasons, Consecutive, 30 or more Games Won
6	Tim Keefe, AA:NY 1883-84; NL:NY 85-88
5	Amos Rusie, NL:NY 1880-94
	Since 1900:
3	Christy Mathewson, NL:NY 1903-05
	Grover Alexander, NL:Phil. 1915-17
2	Cy Young, AL:Bos. 1901-02
	Walter Johnson, AL:Wash. 1912-13

Most Seasons, 20 or more Games Won, Lifetime
16	Cy Young, NL:Clev. 1891-98; StL. 1899-1900; AL:Bos. 1901-04, 07-08

Most Seasons, 20 or more Games Won, League
13	Christy Mathewson, NL:NY 1901, 03-14
	Warren Spahn, NL:Bos. 1947, 49-51; Mil. 53-54, 56-61, 63
12	Walter Johnson, AL:Wash. 1910-19, 24-25

Most Seasons, Consecutive, 20 or more Games Won, Lifetime
14	Cy Young, NL:Clev. 1891-98; StL. 1899-1900; AL:Bos. 01-04

Most Seasons, Consecutive, 20 or more Games Won, League
12	Christy Mathewson, NL:NY 1903-14
10	Walter Johnson, AL:Wash. 1910-19

Most Games Won, Consecutive, Lifetime
24	Carl Hubbell, NL:NY July 17, 1936-May 27, 1937
20	Roger Clemens, AL:Tor. -NY June 3, 1998-June 1, 1999

Most Games Won, Consecutive, Season
19	Tim Keefe, NL:NY June 23-Aug. 10, 1888
	Rube Marquard, NL:NY Apr. 11-July 3(1g), 1912
16	Walter Johnson, AL:Wash. July 3(2g)-Aug. 23(1g), 1912
	Smoky Joe Wood, AL:Bos. July 8-Sept. 15(2g), 1912
	Lefty Grove, AL:Phil. June 8-Aug. 19, 1931
	Schoolboy Rowe, AL:Det. June 15-Aug. 25, 1934
	Roger Clemens, AL:NY May 26-Sept. 19, 2001

Most Games Won, Consecutive, Start of Season
19	Rube Marquard, NL:NY Apr. 11-July 3(1g), 1912
15	Johnny Allen, AL:Clev. Apr. 23-Sept. 30(1g), 1937
	Dave McNally, AL:Balt. Apr. 12-July 30, 1969

Most Games Won, Consecutive, End of Season
17	Pat Luby, NL:Chi. Aug. 6(2g)-Oct. 3, 1890
	Since 1900:
16	Carl Hubbell, NL:NY July 17-Sept. 23, 1936
15	General Crowder, AL:Wash. Aug. 2-Sept. 25, 1932
	Roger Clemens, AL:Tor. June 3-Sept. 21, 1998

Most Games Won, Consecutive, Start of Career
12	Hooks Wiltse, NL:NY May 29-Sept. 15, 1904
	Butch Metzger, NL:SF-SD Sept. 21, 1974-Aug. 8, 1976
11	Joe Boehling, AL:Wash. May 31-July 23, 1913
	Jesse Crain, AL:Minn. Sept. 1, 2004-July 1, 2005

Most Games Won, vs. One Club
70	Grover Alexander, NL:Phil.-Chi.-StL. (vs Cin.) 1911-30
66	Walter Johnson, AL:Wash. (vs Det.) 1907-27

Most Games Won, vs. One Club, Season
12	Hoss Radbourn, NL:Prov. (vs Clev.) 1884
	Since 1900:
9	Ed Reulbach, NL:Chi. (vs Brk.) 1908
	Frank Smith, AL:Chi. (vs Wash.) 1904
	Ed Walsh, AL:Chi. (vs NY & Bos.) 1908
	Walter Johnson, AL:Wash. (vs Chi.) 1912

Most Games Won, Consecutive, vs. One Club
24	Christy Mathewson, NL:NY (vs StL.) June 16, 1904-Sept. 15, 1908
	Carl Mays, AL:Bos.-NY (vs Phil.) Aug. 30, 1918-July 24, 1923

GAMES LOST

Most Seasons Leading Major Leagues
3   Pedro Ramos, AL:Wash. 1958-59; Minn. 61

Most Seasons, Consecutive, Leading Major Leagues
2   Jim Devlin, NL:Lou. 1876-77
         Red Ruffing, AL:Bos. 1928-29
         Pedro Ramos, AL:Wash. 1958-59
         Roger Craig, NL:NY 1962-63

Most Seasons Leading League
4   Bobo Newsom, AL:StL. 1934; StL.-Wash. 35; Det. 41; Phil. 45
         Pedro Ramos, AL:Wash. 1958-60; Minn. 61
         Phil Niekro, NL:Atl. 1977-80

Most Seasons, Consecutive, Leading League
4   Pedro Ramos, AL:Wash. 1958-60; Minn. 61
         Phil Niekro, NL:Atl. 1977-80

Most Games Lost, Lifetime
315   Cy Young, NL:Clev. 1890-98; StL. 1899-1900; Bos. 11; AL:Bos. 1901-08; Clev. 09-11

Most Games Lost, League
279   Walter Johnson, AL:Wash. 1907-27
261   Pud Galvin, NL:Buff. 1879-85; Pitt. 87-89, 91-92; StL. 92
         NL Since 1900:
251   Eppa Rixey, NL:Phil. 1912-17, 19-20, Cin. 21-33

Most Games Lost, Season
48   John Coleman, NL:Phil. 1883
         Since 1900:
29   Vic Willis, NL:Bos. 1905
26   Jack Townsend, AL:Wash. 1904
         Bob Groom, AL:Wash. 1909

Most Games Lost, No Wins, Season
13   Terry Felton, AL:Minn. 1982
12   Russ Miller, NL:Phil. 1928

Most Games Lost, Consecutive, Lifetime
27   Anthony Young, NL:NY May 6, 1992-July 24, 1993
19   Jack Nabors, AL:Phil. Apr. 28-Sept. 28, 1916

Most Games Lost, Consecutive, Season
19   Jack Nabors, AL:Phil. Apr. 28-Sept. 28, 1916
18   Cliff Curtis, NL:Bos. June 13(1g)-Sept. 20(1g), 1910
         Roger Craig, NL:NY May 4-Aug. 4, 1963

Most Games Lost, Consecutive, Start of Season
14   Joe Harris, AL:Bos. May 10-July 25, 1906
         Matt Keough, AL:Oak. Apr. 15-Aug. 8, 1979
13   Anthony Young, NL:NY Apr. 9-July 24, 1993

Most Games Lost, Consecutive, End of Season
19   Jack Nabors, AL:Phil. Apr. 28-Sept 28, 1916
18   Cliff Curtis, NL:Bos. June 13(1g) Sept 28(1g), 1910

Most Games Lost, Consecutive, Start of Career
16   Terry Felton, AL:Minn. Apr. 18, 1980-Sept 12, 1982
12   Stump Weidman, NL:Buff.-Det. Aug. 27, 1880-Sept. 5, 1881
         NL Since 1900:
9   Ron Kline, NL:Pitt. Apr. 21, 1952-Apr. 23, 1955
         Jim Brewer, NL:Chi. July 20, 1960-Aug. 17, 1961
         Frank LaCorte, NL:Atl. Sept. 8, 1975-Aug. 8, 1976

Most Games Lost, vs. One Club, Season
7   By many pitchers. Last:
         Cal McLish, NL:Cin. (vs Pitt.) 1960
         Camilo Pascual, AL:Wash. (vs NY) 1956

Most Games Lost, Consecutive, vs. One Club
14   Fred Beebe, NL:StL. (vs NY) July 15, 1906-Sept. 22, 1909
         Eppa Rixey, NL:Phil.-Cin. (vs Bos.) Oct. 3, 1916-May 21, 1921
         George Smith, NL:Phil. (vs Brk.) Sept. 3, 1920-June 25, 1922
         Bob Rush, NL:Chi. (vs Phil.) June 14, 1951-June 17, 1955
         Herm Wehmeier, NL:Cin.-Phil. (vs StL.) July 3, 1949-May 9, 1956
         Joe Bush, AL:Phil. (vs Bos.) June 2, 1914-July 5, 1917
         Slim Harriss, AL:Phil. (vs NY) July 2, 1920-May 30, 1924
         Danny MacFayden, AL:Bos. (vs Wash.) Aug. 7, 1929-June 2, 1932

INNINGS PITCHED

Most Seasons Leading Major Leagues
5   Robin Roberts, NL:Phil. 1951-55

Most Seasons, Consecutive, Leading Major Leagues
5   Robin Roberts, NL:Phil. 1951-55

Most Seasons Leading League
7   Grover Alexander, NL:Phil. 1911-12, 14-17; Chi. 20
5   Walter Johnson, AL:Wash. 1910, 13-16
         Bob Feller, AL:Clev. 1939-41, 46-47

Most Seasons, Consecutive, Leading League
5   Robin Roberts, NL:Phil. 1951-55
         Greg Maddux, NL:Chi. 1991-92; Atl. 93-95
4   Walter Johnson, AL:Wash. 1913-16

Most Innings, Lifetime
7356   Cy Young, NL:Clev. 1890-98; StL. 1899-1900; Bos. 11; AL:Bos. 1901-08; Clev. 09-11

Most Innings, League
5916   Walter Johnson, AL:Wash. 1907-27
5246   Warren Spahn, NL:Bos./Mil. 1942, 46-64; NY 65-SF 65

Most Innings, Season
683   Will White, NL:Cin. 1879
         Since 1900:
464   Ed Walsh, AL:Chi. 1908
434   Joe McGinnity, NL:NY 1903

Most Seasons, 300 or more Innings, Lifetime
16   Cy Young, NL:Clev. 1891-98; StL. 1899-1900; AL:Bos. 1901-05, 07

Most Seasons, Consecutive, 300 or more Innings, Lifetime
15   Cy Young, NL:Clev. 1891-98; StL. 1899-1900; AL:Bos. 1901-05

Most Seasons, 300 or more Innings, League
12   Kid Nichols, NL:Bos. 1890-99, 1901, 04
         Since 1900:
11   Christy Mathewson, NL:NY 1901, 03-05, 07-08, 10-14
9   Walter Johnson, AL:Wash. 1910-18

Most Seasons, Consecutive, 300 or more Innings, League
10   Kid Nichols, NL:Bos. 1890-99
         Cy Young, NL:Clev. 1891-98; StL. 1899-1900
         Since 1900:
9   Walter Johnson, AL:Wash. 1910-18
7   Grover Alexander, NL:Phil. 1911-17

Most Seasons, 200 or more Innings, Lifetime
20   Don Sutton, NL:LA 1966-80, Hou. 82; AL:Mil. 1982-84, Oak. 85, Cal. 85-86

Most Seasons, Consecutive, 200 or more Innings, Lifetime
19   Cy Young, NL:Clev. 1891-98; StL. 1899-1900; AL:Bos. 1901-08, Clev. 09

Most Seasons, 200 or more Innings, League
18   Walter Johnson, AL:Wash. 1908-19, 21-26
         Greg Maddux, NL:Chi. 1988-91, 2004-05; Atl. 1993-2001, 03; Chi.-LA 2006

Most Seasons, Consecutive, 200 or more Innings, League
17   Warren Spahn, NL:Bos. 1947-52; Mil. 53-63
13   Eddie Plank, AL:Phil. 1901-13
         Red Ruffing, AL:Bos. 1928-30; NY 30-40

Most Innings, Game
26   Leon Cadore, NL:Brk. May 1, 1920
         Joe Oeschger, NL:Bos. May 1, 1920
24   Jack Coombs, AL:Phil. Sept. 1, 1906
         Joe Harris, AL:Bos. Sept. 1, 1906

BATTERS FACED

Most Seasons Leading League
7   Steve Carlton, NL:Phil. 1972-74, 80-83
5   Walter Johnson, AL:Wash. 1910, 13-16

Most Seasons, Consecutive, Leading League
4   Walter Johnson, AL:Wash. 1913-16
      Bob Lemon, AL:Clev. 1950-53
      Grover Alexander, NL:Phil. 1914-17
      Robin Roberts, NL:Phil. 1952-55
      Steve Carlton, NL:Phil. 1980-83
      Greg Maddux, NL:Chi. 1991-92; Atl. 93-94

Most Batters Faced, Lifetime
30,418   Cy Young, NL:Clev. 1890-98; StL. 1899-1900; AL:Bos. 1901-08, 11; Clev. 09-11

Most Batters Faced, League
23,433   Walter Johnson, AL:Wash. 1907-27
21,555   Warren Spahn, NL:Bos./Mil. 1942, 46-64; NY 65; SF 65

Most Batters Faced, Season
1807   Joe McGinnity, NL:NY 1903
1745   Ed Walsh, AL:Chi. 1908

Most Batters Faced, Game
67   George Derby, NL:Buff. July 3, 1883
      Since 1900:
57   Roy Patterson, AL:Chi. May 5, 1901
53   Bill Phillips, NL:Cin. June 24(2g), 1901
      Extra-Inning Game:
96   Leon Cadore, NL:Brk. May 1, 1920 (26 inn)
86   Jack Coombs, AL:Phil. Sept. 1, 1906 (24 inn)
      Joe Harris, AL:Bos. Sept. 1, 1906 (24 inn)

Most Batters Faced, Inning
22   Tony Mullane, NL:Balt. June 18(1g), 1894 (1st)
      Since 1900:
16   Doc Adkins, AL:Bos. July 8, 1902 (6th)
      Lefty O'Doul, AL:Bos. July 7(1g), 1923 (6th)
      Howard Ehmke, AL:Bos. Sept. 28, 1923 (6th)
      Hal Kelleher, NL:Phil. May 5, 1938 (8th)

Most Batters Retired, Consecutive, Season
41   Jim Barr, NL:SF Aug. 23-29, 1972
38   David Wells, AL:NY May 12-23, 1998

Most Batters Retired, Consecutive, Extra-Inning Game:
36   Harvey Haddix, NL:Pitt. (vs Mil.) May 26, 1959
28   Walter Johnson, AL:Wash. (vs NY) May 11, 1919

AT-BATS

Most Seasons Leading League
6   Grover Alexander, NL:Phil. 1911, 14-17; Chi. 20
      Steve Carlton, NL:Phil. 1972-73, 80-83
4   Ed Walsh, AL:Chi. 1908, 10-12
      Walter Johnson, AL:Wash. 1913-16
      Bob Lemon, AL:Clev. 1948, 50, 52-53

Most Seasons, Consecutive, Leading League
4   Walter Johnson, AL:Wash. 1913-16
      Grover Alexander, NL:Phil. 1914-17
      Robin Roberts, NL:Phil. 1952-55
      Steve Carlton, NL:Phil. 1980-83

Most At-Bats, Lifetime
29,209   Cy Young, NL:Clev. 1890-98; StL. 1899-1900; AL:Bos. 1901-08, 11; Clev. 09-11

Most At-Bats, League
21,663   Walter Johnson, AL:Wash. 1907-27
19,788   Warren Spahn, NL:Bos./Mil. 1942, 46-64; NY 65; SF 65

Most At-Bats, Season, Since 1900
1680   Ed Walsh, AL:Chi. 1908
1658   Joe McGinnity, NL:NY 1903

Most At-Bats, Game
66   George Derby, NL:Buff. July 3, 1883
      Since 1900:
53   Roy Patterson, AL:Chi. May 5, 1901
49   Doc Parker, NL:Cin. June 21, 1901
      Bill Phillips, NL:Cin. June 24(2g), 1901
      Extra-Inning Game:
86   Leon Cadore, NL:Brk. May 1, 1920 (26 inn)
82   Joe Harris, AL:Bos. Sept. 1, 1906 (24 inn)

Most At-Bats, Inning
14   Howard Ehmke, AL:Bos. Sept. 28, 1923 (6th)
            Hal Kelleher, NL:Phil. May 5, 1938 (8th)

UNS (Since 1900)

Most Seasons Leading Major Leagues
3   Phil Niekro, NL:Atl. 1977-79

Most Seasons, Consecutive, Leading Major Leagues
3   Phil Niekro, NL:Atl. 1977-79

Most Seasons Leading League
3   Burleigh Grimes, NL:Brk. 1923-24; Pitt. 28
            Hugh Mulcahy, NL:Phil. 1938-40
            Robin Roberts. NL:Phil. 1955-57
            Phil Niekro, NL:Atl. 1977-79
            Rick Mahler, NL:Atl. 1986, 88; Cin. 89
            George Mullin, AL:Det. 1905-07
            Wilbur Wood, AL:Chi. 1972-73, 75

Most Seasons, Consecutive, Leading League
3   George Mullin, AL:Det. 1905-07
            Hugh Mulcahy, NL:Phil. 1938-40
            Robin Roberts. NL:Phil. 1955-57
            Phil Niekro, NL:Atl. 1977-79

Most Runs, Lifetime
2337   Phil Niekro, NL:Mil./Atl. 1964-83, 87; AL:NY 1984-85; Clev. 86-87; Tor. 87

Most Runs, League
2117   Red Ruffing, AL:Bos. 1924-30; NY 30-42, 45-46; Chi. 47
2037   Burleigh Grimes, NL:Pitt. 1916-17, 28-29, 34; Brk. 18-26; NY 27;
            Bos. 30; StL. 30-31, 34; Chi. 32-33

Most Runs, Season
544   John Coleman, NL:Phil. 1883
            Since 1900:
224   Bill Carrick, NL:NY 1900
219   Joe McGinnity, AL:Balt. 1901

Most Runs, Game
24   Al Travers, AL:Det. May 18, 1912
21   Doc Parker, NL:Cin. June 21, 1901

Most Runs, Inning
13   Lefty O'Doul, AL:Bos. July 7(1g), 1923 (6th)
12   Hal Kelleher, NL:Phil. May 5, 1938 (8th)

ARNED RUNS (Since 1912 in NL; Since 1913 in AL – Prior seasons not compiled on official scores)

Most Seasons Leading Major Leagues
3   Burleigh Grimes, NL:Brk. 1922, 24-25
            Wilbur Wood, AL:Chi. 1972-73, 75

Most Seasons, Consecutive, Leading Major Leagues
2   Elmer Myers, AL:Phil. 1916-17
            Bump Hadley, AL:Chi.-StL. 1932-33
            Wilbur Wood, AL:Chi. 1972-73
            Burleigh Grimes, NL:Brk. 1924-25
            Robin Roberts, NL:Phil. 1955-56
            Sammy Ellis, NL:Cin. 1965-66

Most Seasons Leading League
3   Bobo Newsom, AL:StL. 1938; Wash. 42; Phil. 45
            Wilbur Wood, AL:Chi. 1972-73, 75
            Burleigh Grimes, NL:Brk. 1922, 24-25
            Murry Dickson, NL:StL. 1948; Pitt. 51-52
            Robin Roberts, NL:Phil. 1955-57
            Jack Fisher, NL:NY 1964-65, 67

Most Seasons, Consecutive, Leading League
3   Robin Roberts, NL:Phil. 1955-57
2   Elmer Myers, AL:Phil. 1916-17
            Red Ruffing, AL:Bos. 1928-29
            Bump Hadley, AL:Chi.-StL. 1932-33
            Wilbur Wood, AL:Chi. 1972-73

Most Earned Runs, Lifetime
2012   Phil Niekro, NL:Mil./Atl. 1964-83, 87; AL:NY 1984-85; Clev. 86-87; Tor. 87

Most Earned Runs, League
1833   Red Ruffing, AL:Bos. 1924-30; NY 30-42, 45-46; Chi. 47
1798   Warren Spahn, NL:Bos./Mil. 1942, 46-64; NY 65; SF 65

Most Earned Runs, Season
186   Bobo Newsom, AL:StL. 1938
155   Guy Bush, NL:Chi. 1930

HITS

Most Seasons Leading Major Leagues
5   Robin Roberts, NL:Phil. 1952-56

Most Seasons, Consecutive, Leading Major Leagues
5   Robin Roberts, NL:Phil. 1952-56

Most Seasons Leading League
5   Robin Roberts, NL:Phil. 1952-56
4   Jim Kaat, AL:Minn. 1965-67; Chi. 75

Most Seasons, Consecutive Leading League
5   Robin Roberts, NL:Phil. 1952-56
3   Wes Ferrell, AL:Bos. 1935-36; Bos.-Wash. 37
     Jim Kaat, AL:Minn. 1965-67

Most Hits, Lifetime
7078   Cy Young, NL:Clev. 1890-98; StL. 1899-1900; AL:Bos. 1901-08, 11; Clev. 09-11

Most Hits, League
5490   Pud Galvin, NL:Buff. 1879-85; Pitt. 87-89, 91-92; StL. 92
        Since 1900:
4920   Walter Johnson, AL:Wash. 1907-27
4868   Grover Alexander, NL:Phil. 1911-17, 30; Chi. 18-26; StL. 26-29

Most Hits, Season
809   John Coleman, NL:Phil. 1883
       Since 1900:
415   Bill Carrick, NL:NY 1900
401   Joe McGinnity, AL:Balt. 1901

Most Hits, Game
36   Jack Wadsworth, NL:Lou. Aug. 17, 1894
      Since 1900:
26   Doc Parker, NL:Cin. June 21, 1901
      Al Travers, AL:Det. May 18, 1912
      Hod Lisenbee, AL:Phil. Sept. 11, 1936
      Extra-Inning Game:
29   Ed Rommel, AL:Phil. July 10, 1932 (last 17 inn of 18 inn game)

Most Hits, Inning
13   Stump Weidman, NL:Det. Sept. 6, 1883 (7th)
      Since 1900:
12   Doc Adkins, AL:Bos. July 8, 1902 (6th)
11   Reggie Grabowski, NL:Phil. Aug. 4(2g), 1934 (9th)

Most Hits, Consecutive, Game
10   Bill Reidy, AL:Mil. June 2, 1901
      Heinie Meine, NL:Pitt. June 23, 1930

Most Hits, Consecutive, Inning
10   Bill Reidy, AL:Mil. June 2, 1901 (9th)
      Heinie Meine, NL:Pitt. June 23, 1930 (6th)

Fewest Hits, 2 Consecutive Complete Games
0   Johnny Vander Meer, NL:Cin. June 11-15, 1938
1   Howard Ehmke, AL:Bos. Sept. 7-11, 1923

Fewest Hits, 3 Consecutive Complete Games
3   Johnny Vander Meer, NL:Cin. June 5-15, 1938
5   By many players

Most Hitless Innings, Consecutive, Season
24   Cy Young, AL:Bos. Apr. 25-May 11, 1904
21   Johnny Vander Meer, NL:Cin. June 11-19, 1938

Most Extra-Base Hits, Game
16   George Derby, NL:Buff. July 3, 1883
11   Earl Whitehill, AL:Wash. July 10, 1935

INGLES

Most Singles, Game
28	Jack Wadsworth, NL:Lou. Aug. 17, 1894
23	Bock Baker, AL:Clev. Apr. 28, 1901

Most Singles, Inning
10	Reggie Grabowski, NL:Phil. Aug. 4(2g), 1934 (9th)
	Elden Auker, AL:Det. Sept. 29(2g), 1935 (2nd)

DOUBLES

Most Doubles, Game
14	George Derby, NL:Buff. July 3, 1883
10	Earl Whitehill, AL:Wash. July 10, 1935

Most Doubles, Inning
6	Lefty Grove, AL:Bos. June 9, 1934 (8th)
	Mike Mussina, AL:NY July 31, 2002 (2nd)
	Dustin Hermanson, NL:Mtl. July 22, 1999 (2nd)

TRIPLES

Most Triples, Game
7	Tom Parrott, NL:Cin. Aug. 1, 1894
	Tony Kaufmann, NL:Chi. Apr. 22, 1925
6	Al Travers, AL:Det. May 18, 1912

Most Triples, Inning
4	Firpo Marberry, AL:Det. May 6, 1934 (4th)
3	By many NL players

HOME RUNS

Most Home Runs, Lifetime
505	Robin Roberts, NL:Phil. 1948-61; Hou. 65-66; Chi. 66; AL:Balt. 1962-65

Most Home Runs, League
434	Warren Spahn, NL:Bos./Mil. 1942, 46-64; NY 65; SF 65
422	Frank Tanana, AL:Cal. 1973-80; Bos. 81; Tex. 82-85; Det. 85-92; NY 93

Most Home Runs, Season
50	Bert Blyleven, AL:Minn. 1986
48	Jose Lima, NL:Hou. 2000

Fewest Home Runs, Season (Most Innings), Since 1900
0	Walter Johnson, AL:Wash. 1916 (371 inn)
	Vic Willis, NL:Pitt. 1906 (322 inn)

Most Home Runs, vs. One Club, Season
15	Jim Perry, AL:Clev. (vs. NY) 1960
13	Warren Hacker, NL:Chi. (vs. Brk.) 1956
	Warren Spahn, NL:Mil. (vs. Chi.) 1958
	Greg Maddux, NL:Chi. (vs. Cin.) 2004

Most Home Runs, Game
7	Charlie Sweeney, NL:StL. June 12, 1886
	Since 1900:
6	Larry Benton, NL:NY May 12, 1930
	Sloppy Thurston, NL:Brk. Aug. 13(1g), 1932
	Bill Kerksieck, NL:Phil. Aug. 13(1g), 1939
	Tommy Thomas, AL:StL. June 27, 1936
	George Caster, AL:Phil. Sept. 24(1g), 1940
	Tim Wakefield, AL:Bos. Aug. 8, 2004
	R.A. Dickey, AL:Tex. Apr. 6, 2006

Most Home Runs, Inning
4	Henry Lampe, NL:Bos. June 6, 1894 (3rd)
	Larry Benton, NL:NY May 12, 1930 (7th)
	Bill Kerksieck, NL:Phil. Aug. 13(1g), 1939 (4th)
	Charlie Bicknell, NL:Phil. June 6(1g), 1948 (6th)
	Ben Wade, NL:Brk. May 28, 1954 (8th)
	Mario Soto, NL:Cin. Apr. 29, 1986 (4th)
	John Smoltz, NL:Atl. June 19, 1994 (1st)
	Jose Lima, NL:Hou. Apr. 27, 2000 (1st)
	Andy Benes, NL:StL. July 23, 2000 (2nd)
	Phil Norton, NL:Chi. Aug. 8, 2000 (4th)
	Steve Trachsel, NL:NY May 17, 2001 (3rd)
	Alan Embree, NL:Atl. May 20, 2001 (7th)
	Jeff Austin, NL:Cin. May 22, 2003 (1st)
	Jose Acevedo, NL:Cin. Sept. 8, 2004 (1st)
	Brandon Claussen, NL:Cin. Apr. 22, 2006 (4th)
	George Caster, AL:Phil. Sept. 24(1g), 1940 (6th)
	Cal McLish, AL:Clev. May 22, 1957 (6th)
	Paul Foytack, AL:LA July 31(2g), 1963 (6th)
	Catfish Hunter, AL:NY June 17, 1977 (1st)
	Mike Caldwell, AL:Mil. May 31, 1980 (4th)
	Scott Sanderson, AL:NY May 2, 1992 (5th)
	Brian Anderson, AL:Cal. Sept. 5, 1995 (2nd)
	Dave Telgheder, AL:Oak. Sept. 21, 1996 (3rd)
	Dave Burba, AL:Clev. June 29, 2001 (4th)
	Pat Mahomes, AL:Tex. Aug. 17, 2001 (6th)
	Travis Harper, AL:TB June 21, 2005 (8th)
	Randy Johnson, AL:NY Aug. 21, 2005 (4th)

Most Home Runs, Consecutive, Inning
4	Paul Foytack, AL:LA (Clev.) July 31(2g), 1963 (6th)
3	By many NL players; Last:
	Brandon Claussen, NL:Cin. Apr. 22, 2006 (4th)

GRAND SLAM HOME RUNS

Most Grand Slam Home Runs, Lifetime
10	Nolan Ryan, NL:NY 1970; Hou. 84, 85, 88; AL:Cal. 1972, 73, 77; Tex. 90, 93
	Mike Jackson, AL:Sea. 1988, 91, 96; Clev. 99; Chi. 2004; NL:SF 93-94

Most Grand Slam Home Runs, League
9	Ned Garver, AL:StL. 1949, 50, 51, 52; Det. 54, 55; KC 59
	Jerry Reuss, NL:StL. 1971; Hou. 72, 73; Pitt. 74, 76; LA 79, 80

Most Grand Slam Home Runs, Season
4	Ray Narleski, AL:Det. 1959
	Mike Schooler, AL:Sea. 1992
	Tug McGraw, NL:Phil. 1979
	Chan Ho Park, NL:LA 1999
	Matt Clement, NL:SD 2000

Most Grand Slam Home Runs, Game
2	Bill Phillips, NL:Pitt. (Chi.) Aug. 16, 1890 (Tommy Burns, Malachi Kittredge)
	Charlie Petty, NL:Wash. (Bos.) May 28, 1894 (Bobby Lowe, Henry Staley)
	Archie Stimmel, NL:Cin. (Brk.) Sept. 23, 1901 (Joe Kelley, Jimmy Sheckard)
	Jock Menefee, NL:Chi. (Bos.) Aug. 12(2g), 1903 (Joe Stanley, Pat Moran)
	Jack Scott, NL:Bos. (Phil.) Apr. 28, 1921 (Ralph Miller, Lee Meadows)
	June Green, NL:Phil. (StL.) July 6(2g), 1929 (Jim Bottomley, Chick Hafey)
	Luke Hamlin, NL:Brk. (NY) July 4(2g), 1938 (Dick Bartell, Gus Mancuso)
	Chan Ho Park, NL:LA (StL.) Apr. 23, 1999 (Fernando Tatis 2)
	Tex Shirley, AL:StL. (Bos.) July 27, 1946 (Rudy York 2)
	Jack Morris, AL:Det. (Bos.) Aug. 7(1g), 1984 (Bill Buckner, Tony Armas)
	Eric Plunk, AL:Oak. (Cal.) July 31, 1986 (Brian Downing, Bob Boone)

Most Games, Consecutive, Grand Slam Home Runs, Season
2	By many players, last:
	Joey Devine, NL:Atl. Aug. 20-23, 2005
	D.J. Carrasco, AL:KC Aug. 11-17, 2005

Most Grand Slam Home Runs, Inning
2	Bill Phillips, NL:Pitt. (Chi.) Aug. 16, 1890 (5th)
	Chan Ho Park, NL:LA (StL.) Apr. 23, 1999 (3rd)

Most Consecutive Innings Allowing a Grand Slam Home Run, Game
2	Jock Menefee, NL:Chi. (Bos.) Aug. 12, 1903 (3rd, 4th)
	Jack Morris, AL:Det. (Bos.) Aug. 7, 1984 (1st, 2nd)
	Eric Plunk, AL:Oak. (Cal.) July 31, 1986 (3rd, 4th)

WALKS

Most Seasons Leading Major Leagues
7   Nolan Ryan, AL:Cal. 1972-74, 76-78; NL:Hou. 82

Most Seasons, Consecutive, Leading Major Leagues
5   Amos Rusie, NL:NY 1890-94
           Since 1900:
3   Togie Pittinger, NL:Bos. 1902-04
           Tommy Byrne, AL:NY 1949-50; NY-StL. 51
           Nolan Ryan, AL:Cal. 1972-74; 76-78
           Randy Johnson, AL:Sea. 1990-92

Most Seasons Leading League
8   Nolan Ryan, AL:Cal. 1972-74, 76-78; NL:Hou. 80, 82
6   Nolan Ryan, AL:Cal. 1972-74; 76-78
5   Amos Rusie, NL:NY 1890-94
           NL Since 1900:
4   Jimmy Ring, NL:Phil. 1922-25
           Kirby Higbe, NL:Chi.-Phil. 1939; Phil. 40; Brk. 41; Brk.-Pitt. 47
           Sam Jones, NL:Chi. 1955-56; StL. 58; SF 59
           Bob Veale, NL:Pitt. 1964-65, 67-68

Most Seasons, Consecutive, Leading League
5   Amos Rusie, NL:NY 1890-94
           Since 1900:
4   George Mullin, AL:Det. 1903-06
           Jimmy Ring, NL:Phil. 1922-25

Most Walks, Lifetime
2795   Nolan Ryan NL:NY 1966, 68-71; Hou. 80-88; AL:Cal. 1972-79; Tex. 89-93

Most Walks, League
1775   Early Wynn, AL:Wash. 1939, 41-44, 46-48; Clev. 49-57, 63; Chi. 58-62
1717   Steve Carlton, NL:StL. 1965-71; Phil. 72-86; SF 86

Most Walks, Season
276   Amos Rusie, NL:NY 1890
           Since 1900:
208   Bob Feller, AL:Clev. 1938
185   Sam Jones, NL:Chi. 1955

Most Intentional Walks, Season
24   Gene Garber, AL:KC-NL:Phil. 1974
23   Mike Garman, NL:StL. 1975
           Dale Murray, NL:Cin.-NY 1978
           Kent Tekulve, NL:Pitt. 1982
19   John Hiller, AL:Det. 1974

Most Walks, Game
16   Bill George, NL:NY May 30(1g), 1887
           George Van Haltren, NL:Chi. June 27, 1887
           Henry Gruber, PL:Clev. Apr. 19, 1890
           Bruno Haas, AL:Phil. June 23, 1915
           Tommy Byrne, AL:StL. Aug. 22, 1951 (13 inn)
           NL Since 1900:
14   Henry Mathewson, NL:NY Oct. 5, 1906

Most Walks, Inning
8   Dolly Gray, AL:Wash. Aug. 28(1g), 1909 (2nd)
7   Tony Mullane, NL:Balt. June 18(1g), 1894 (1st)
           Bob Ewing, NL:Cin. Apr. 19, 1902 (4th)

Most Walks, Consecutive, Inning
7   Dolly Gray, AL:Wash. Aug. 28(1g), 1909 (2nd)
6   Brickyard Kennedy, NL:Brk. Aug. 31, 1900 (2nd)

Fewest Walks, Game (Most Innings)
0   Babe Adams, NL:Pitt. July 17, 1914 (21 inn)
           Cy Young, AL:Bos. July 4(2g), 1905 (20 inn)

Most Innings, Consecutive, No Walks (since 1889)
84.1   Bill Fischer, AL:KC Aug. 3-Sept. 30, 1962
72.1   Greg Maddux, NL:Atl. June 20-Aug. 12, 2001

Most Innings, Consecutive, No Walks, Start Of Season
52.0   Grover Alexander, NL:Chi. Apr. 18-May 17, 1923

HIT BATTERS

Most Seasons Leading Major Leagues
6   Howard Ehmke, AL:Det. 1920-22; Bos. 23, 25; Phil. 27

Most Seasons, Consecutive, Leading Major Leagues
5   Tommy Byrne, AL:NY 1948-50; NY-StL. 51; StL. 52

Most Seasons Leading League
6   Howard Ehmke, AL:Det. 1920-22; Bos. 23, 25; Phil. 27
5   Don Drysdale, NL:LA 1958-61, 65

Most Seasons, Consecutive, Leading League
5   Tommy Byrne, AL:NY 1948-50; NY-StL. 51; StL. 52
4   Don Drysdale, NL:LA 1958-61

Most Hit Batters, Lifetime
206   Walter Johnson, AL:Wash. 1907-27
154   Don Drysdale, NL:Brk./LA 1956-69

Most Hit Batters, Season
41   Joe McGinnity, NL:Brk. 1900
31   Chick Fraser, AL:Phil. 1901

Most Hit Batters, Game
6   Ed Knouff, AA:Balt. Apr. 25, 1887
      John Grimes, NL:StL. July 31(1g), 1897
      Since 1900:
4   By many players; Last:
      Livan Hernandez, NL:Wash. July 20, 2005
      Orlando Hernandez, AL:Chi. June 3, 2005

Most Hit Batters, Inning
3   Pat Luby, NL:Chi. Sept. 5, 1890 (6th)
      Pink Hawley, NL:StL. July 4(1g), 1894 (cons; 1st)
      Pink Hawley, NL:Pitt. May 9, 1896 (7th)
      Walter Thornton, NL:Chi. May 18, 1898 (cons; 4th)
      Deacon Phillippe, NL:Pitt. Sept. 25, 1905 (1st)
      Ray Boggs, NL:Bos. Sept. 17, 1928 (9th)
      Raul Sanchez, NL:Cin. May 15(1g), 1960 (8th)
      Dock Ellis, NL:Pitt. May 1, 1974 (cons; 1st)
      Mark Gardner, NL:Mtl. Aug. 15, 1992 (1st)
      Tom Candiotti, NL:LA Sept. 13, 1997 (1st)
      C.J. Nitkowski, NL:Hou. Aug. 3, 1998 (cons; 8th)
      Brian Lawrence, NL:SD Apr. 22, 2003 (4th)
      Kaz Ishii, NL:LA July 23, 2003 (4th)
      Matt Clement, NL:Chi. May 28(1g), 2004 (5th)
      Jeff Weaver, NL:LA Aug. 21, 2004 (cons; 1st)
      Bert Gallia, AL:Wash. June 20(2g), 1913 (1st)
      Harry Harper, AL:NY Aug. 25, 1921 (8th)
      Tom Morgan, AL:NY June 30, 1954 (3rd)
      Wilbur Wood, AL:Chi. Sept. 10, 1977 (cons; 1st)
      Bud Black, AL:Clev. July 8(2g), 1988 (4th)
      Bert Blyleven, AL:Minn. Sept. 28, 1988 (2nd)
      Steve Sparks, AL:Ana. May 22, 1999 (cons; 3rd)

Fewest Hit Batters, Season (Most Innings)
0   General Crowder, AL:Wash. 1932 (327 inn)
      Sandy Koufax, NL:LA 1966 (323 inn)

Fewest Hit Batters, Game (Most Innings)
0   Leon Cadore, NL:Brk. May 1, 1920 (26 inn)
      Joe Oeschger, NL:Bos. May 1, 1920 (26 inn)
      Ted Lyons, AL:Chi. May 24, 1929 (21 inn)

STRIKEOUTS

Most Seasons Leading Major Leagues
9   Randy Johnson, AL:Sea. 1993-95; AL:Sea.-NL:Hou. 98; NL:Ari. 1999-2002, 04

Most Seasons, Consecutive, Leading Major Leagues
5   Rube Waddell, AL:Phil. 1903-07
      Randy Johnson, AL:Sea.NL:Hou. 1998; NL:Ari. 1999-2002

Most Seasons Leading League
12   Walter Johnson, AL:Wash. 1910, 12-19, 21, 23-24
7   Dazzy Vance, NL:Brk. 1922-28

Most Seasons, Consecutive, Leading League
8	Walter Johnson, AL:Wash. 1912-19
7	Dazzy Vance, NL:Brk. 1922-28

Most Strikeouts, Lifetime
5714	Nolan Ryan, NL:NY 1966, 68-71; Hou. 80-88; AL:Cal. 1972-79; Tex. 89-93

Most Strikeouts, League
4099	Roger Clemens, AL:Bos. 1984-96; Tor. 97-98; NY 99-2003
4000	Steve Carlton, NL:StL. 1965-71; Phil. 72-86; SF 86

Most Strikeouts, Season
505	Matt Kilroy, AA:Balt. 1886 (50-foot distance)
	Since 1900:
383	Nolan Ryan, AL:Cal. 1973
382	Sandy Koufax, NL:LA 1965

Most Seasons, 300 or more Strikeouts, Lifetime
6	Nolan Ryan, AL:Cal. 1972-74, 76-77; Tex. 89
	Randy Johnson, AL:Sea. 1993; AL:Sea.-NL:Hou. 1998; NL:Ari. 1999-2002
4	Randy Johnson, NL:Ari. 1999-2002

Most Seasons, Consecutive, 300 or more Strikeouts, Lifetime
5	Randy Johnson, AL:Sea.-NL:Hou. 1998; NL:Ari. 99-2002
4	Randy Johnson, NL:Ari. 1999-2002
3	Nolan Ryan, AL:Cal. 1972-74

Most Seasons, 200 or more Strikeouts, Lifetime
15	Nolan Ryan, AL:Cal. 1972-74, 76-79; Tex. 89-91; NL:Hou. 80, 82, 85, 87-88

Most Seasons, 200 or more Strikeouts, League
11	Roger Clemens, AL:Bos. 1986-92, 96; Tor. 97-98; NY 2001
10	Tom Seaver, NL:NY 1968-76, 78

Most Seasons, Consecutive, 200 or more Strikeouts, League
9	Tom Seaver, NL:NY 1968-76
7	Walter Johnson, AL:Wash. 1910-16
	Roger Clemens, AL:Bos. 1986-92

Most Strikeouts, Game
20	Roger Clemens, AL:Bos. Apr. 29, 1986
	Roger Clemens, AL:Bos. Sept. 18, 1996
	Kerry Wood, NL:Chi. May 6, 1998
	Randy Johnson, NL:Ari. May 8, 2001 (first 9 inn of 11-inn game)
	Extra-Inning Game:
21	Tom Cheney, AL:Wash. Sept. 12, 1962 (16 inn)

Most Strikeouts, Consecutive, Game
10	Tom Seaver, NL:NY Apr. 22, 1970
8	Nolan Ryan, AL:Cal. July 9, 1972; Aug. 7, 1973
	Ron Davis, AL:NY May 4, 1981
	Roger Clemens, AL:Bos. Apr. 29, 1986
	Blake Stein, AL:KC June 17, 2001

Most Strikeouts, Consecutive, Start of Game
9	Mickey Welch, NL:NY Aug. 28, 1884 (50-foot distance)
	Since 1900:
8	Jim Deshaies, NL:Hou. Sept. 23, 1986
7	Joe Cowley, AL:Chi. May 28, 1986

Most Games, 10 or more Strikeouts, Lifetime
215	Nolan Ryan, NL:NY 1966, 68-71; Hou. 80-88; AL:Cal. 72-79; Tex. 89-93

Most Games, 10 or more Strikeouts, League
148	Nolan Ryan, AL:Cal. 72-79; Tex. 89-93
110	Randy Johnson, NL:Mtl. 1988-89; Hou. 98; Ari. 1999-2004

Most Games, 10 or more Strikeouts, Season
23	Nolan Ryan, AL:Cal. 1973
	Randy Johnson, NL:Ari. 1999-2001

Most Strikeouts, 2 Consecutive Games
34	Dupee Shaw, UA:Bos. July 19 (18)-21 (16), 1884 (50-foot distance)
33	Kerry Wood, NL:Chi. May 6 (20)-11 (13), 1998
32	Luis Tiant, AL:Clev. June 29 (13)-July 3 (19), 1968
	Nolan Ryan, AL:Cal. Aug. 7 (13)-12 (19), 1974
	Randy Johnson, AL:Sea. Aug. 8 (19)-15 (13), 1997
	Pedro Martinez, AL:Bos. Sept. 4 (15)-10 (17), 1999
	Pedro Martinez, AL:Bos. May 6 (17)-12 (15), 2000

Most Strikeouts, 3 Consecutive Games

48	Dupee Shaw, UA:Bos. July 16 (14)-19 (18)-21 (16), 1884 (50-foot distance)
47	Nolan Ryan, AL:Cal. Aug. 12 (19)-16 (9)-20 (19), 1974
43	Dwight Gooden, NL:NY Sept. 7 (11)-12 (16)-17 (16), 1984
	Randy Johnson, NL:Ari. June 25 (14)-30 (17)-July 5 (12), 1999
	Randy Johnson, NL:Ari. Apr. 28 (12)-May 3 (11)-8 (20), 2001
	Randy Johnson, NL:Ari. May 3 (11)-May 8 (20)-13 (12), 2001

Most Strikeouts, Inning

4	Bobby Mathews, AA:Phil. Sept. 30, 1885 (7th)
	Cannonball Crane, NL:NY Oct. 4, 1888 (5th,cons)
	Hooks Wiltse, NL:NY May 15, 1906 (5th,cons)
	Jim Davis, NL:Chi. May 27(1g), 1956 (6th,cons)
	Joe Nuxhall, NL:Cin. Aug. 11(1g), 1959 (6th)
	Pete Richert, NL:LA Apr. 12, 1962 (3rd,cons)
	Don Drysdale, NL:LA Apr. 17, 1965 (2nd,cons)
	Bob Gibson, NL:StL. June 7, 1966 (4th)
	Bill Bonham, NL:Chi. July 31(1g), 1974 (2nd)
	Phil Niekro, NL:Atl. July 29, 1977 (6th)
	Mario Soto, NL:Cin. May 17, 1984 (3rd,cons)
	Mike Scott, NL:Hou. Sept. 3, 1986 (5th)
	Paul Assenmacher, NL:Atl. Aug. 22, 1989 (5th)
	Tim Birtsas, NL:Cin. June 4, 1990 (7th)
	Mark Wohlers, NL:Atl. June 17, 1995 (9th,cons)
	Bruce Ruffin, NL:Col. July 25, 1996 (9th)
	Derek Wallace, NL:NY Sept. 13, 1996 (9th)
	Kirt Ojala, NL:Fla. Sept. 16, 1998 (4th,cons)
	Archie Corbin, NL:Fla. Apr. 28, 1999 (7th)
	Jerry Spradlin, NL:SF July 22, 1999 (7th)
	Steve Kline, NL:Mtl. Aug 17, 1999 (7th,cons)
	Frankie Rodriguez, NL:Cin. July 22, 2001 (7th)
	A.J. Burnett, NL:Fla. July 5, 2002 (1st)
	Kerry Wood, NL:Chi. Sept. 2(1g), 2002 (4th,cons)
	Darren Dreifort, NL:LA May 22, 2003 (2nd)
	Octavio Dotel, NL:Hou. June 11, 2003 (8th,cons)
	Brad Lidge, NL:Hou. June 13, 2004 (7th)
	Mike Stanton, NL:NY Aug. 3, 2004 (8th)
	Jon Rauch, NL:Wash. Apr. 26, 2006 (8th)
	Brad Penny, NL:LA Sept. 23, 2006 (2nd)
	Walter Johnson, AL:Wash. Apr. 15, 1911 (5th)
	Guy Morton, AL:Clev. June 11, 1916 (6th,cons)
	Ryne Duren, AL:LA May 18, 1961 (7th)
	Lee Stange, AL:Clev. Sept. 2, 1964 (7th)
	Mike Cuellar, AL:Balt. May 29, 1970 (4th,cons)
	Mike Paxton, AL:Clev. July 21, 1978 (5th,cons)
	Bobby Witt, AL:Tex. Aug. 2, 1987 (2nd,cons)
	Charlie Hough, AL:Tex. July 4, 1988 (1st)
	Matt Young, AL:Sea. Sept. 9, 1990 (1st)
	Paul Shuey, AL:Clev. May 14, 1994 (9th)
	Kevin Appier, AL:KC Sept. 3, 1996 (4th)
	Wilson Alvarez, AL:Chi. July 21, 1997 (7th,cons)
	Blake Stein, AL:Oak. July 27, 1998 (4th)
	Chuck Finley, AL:Ana. May 12, 1999 (3rd)
	Tim Wakefield, AL:Bos. Aug 10, 1999 (9th)
	Chuck Finley, AL:Ana. Aug. 15, 1999 (1st,cons)
	Chuck Finley, AL:Clev. Apr. 16, 2000 (3rd)
	Erik Hiljus, AL:Oak. June 30, 2001 (7th)
	Kazuhiro Sasaki, AL:Sea. Apr. 4, 2003 (9th,cons)

SACRIFICE HITS

Most Seasons Leading League

3	Eppa Rixey, NL:Phil. 1920; Cin. 21, 28
	Tom Glavine, NL:Atl. 1990, 99; NY 2005
	Earl Whitehill, AL:Det. 1931; Wash. 34-35

Most Sacrifices, Season

Including sacrifice flies:

54	Stan Coveleski, AL:Clev. 1921
	Ed Rommel, AL:Phil. 1923
49	Eppa Rixey, NL:Phil. 1920
	Jack Scott, NL:Phil. 1927

Excluding sacrifice flies:

35	Ed Brandt, NL:Bos. 1933
28	Earl Whitehill, AL:Det. 1931

ACRIFICE FLIES (Since 1955)

Most Seasons Leading Major Leagues
3   Charlie Hough, AL:Tex. 1987; Chi. 91; NL:Fla. 94

Most Seasons, Consecutive, Leading Major Leagues
2   Jamie Navarro, AL:Mil. 1992-93

Most Seasons Leading League
4   Charlie Hough, AL:Tex. 1987, 90; Chi. 91; NL:Fla. 94
3   Rick Reuschel, NL:Chi. 1976, 80; SF 88
     Charlie Hough, AL:Tex. 1987, 90; Chi. 91
     Jamie Navarro, AL:Mil. 1992-93; Chi. 97

Most Seasons, Consecutive, Leading League
2   Ferguson Jenkins. NL:Chi. 1973-AL:Tex. 74
     Jack Morris, AL:Det. 1980-81
     Charlie Hough, AL:Tex. 1990-Chi. 91
     Jaime Navarro, AL:Mil. 1992-93

Most Sacrifice Flies, Lifetime
146   Nolan Ryan, NL:NY 1966, 68-71; Hou. 80-88; AL:Cal. 72-79; Tex. 89-93

Most Sacrifice Flies, League
118   Rick Reuschel, NL:Chi. 1972-81, 83-84; Pitt. 85-87; SF 87-91
114   Jack Morris, AL:Det. 1977-90; Minn. 91; Tor. 92-93; Clev. 94

Most Sacrifice Flies, Season
17   Larry Gura, AL:KC 1983
     Jaime Navarro, AL:Mil. 1993
15   Randy Lerch, NL:Phil. 1979

VILD PITCHES

Most Seasons Leading Major Leagues
6   Larry Cheney, NL:Chi. 1912-14; Brk. 16-18

Most Seasons, Consecutive, Leading Major Leagues
3   Larry Cheney, NL:Chi. 1912-14; Brk. 16-18

Most Seasons Leading League
6   Nolan Ryan, AL:Cal. 1972, 77-78; Tex. 89; NL:Hou. 81, 86
     Larry Cheney, NL:Chi. 1912-14; Brk. 16-18
     Jack Morris, AL:Det. 1983-85, 87; Minn. 91; Clev. 94

Most Seasons, Consecutive, Leading League
3   Larry Cheney, NL:Chi. 1912-14; Brk. 16-18
     John Smoltz, NL:Atl. 1990-92
     Jack Morris, AL:Det. 1983-85

Most Wild Pitches, Lifetime
278   Nolan Ryan, NL:NY 1966, 68-71; Hou. 80-88; AL:Cal. 72-79; Tex. 89-93

Most Wild Pitches, League
206   Jack Morris, AL:Det. 1977-90; Minn. 91; Tor. 92-93; Clev. 94
200   Phil Niekro, NL:Mil./Atl. 1964-83, 87

Most Wild Pitches, Season
64   Bill Stemmeyer, NL:Bos. 1886
     Since 1900:
30   Red Ames, NL:NY 1905
26   Juan Guzman, AL:Tor. 1993

Most Wild Pitches, Game
10   Johnny Ryan, NL:Lou. July 22, 1876
     Since 1900:
6   J.R. Richard, NL:Hou. Apr. 10, 1979
     Phil Niekro, NL:Atl. Aug. 4(2g), 1979
     Bill Gullickson, NL:Mtl. Apr. 10, 1982
5   Charlie Wheatley, AL:Det. Sept. 27, 1912
     Jack Morris, AL:Det. Aug. 3, 1987 (10 inn)

Most Wild Pitches, Inning
4   Walter Johnson, AL:Wash. Sept. 21, 1914 (4th)
     Kevin Gregg, AL:Ana. July 25, 2004 (8th)
     Phil Niekro, NL:Atl. Aug. 4(2g), 1979 (5th)
     Ryan Madson, NL:Phil. July 25, 2006 (3rd)

Fewest Wild Pitches, Season (Most Innings)
0   Joe McGinnity, NL:NY 1906 (340 inn)
     General Crowder, AL:Wash. 1932 (327 inn)

Fewest Wild Pitches, Game (Most Innings)
0	Leon Cadore, NL:Brk. May 1, 1920 (26 inn)
	Jack Coombs, AL:Phil. Sept. 1, 1906 (24 inn)
	Joe Harris, AL:Bos. Sept. 1, 1906 (24 inn)

BALKS

Most Balks, Season
16	Dave Stewart, AL:Oak. 1988
11	Steve Carlton, NL:Phil. 1979

Most Balks, Game
5	Bob Shaw, NL:Mil. May 4, 1963
4	Vic Raschi, AL:NY May 3, 1950
	Bobby Witt, AL:Tex. Apr. 12, 1988
	Rick Honeycutt, AL:Oak. Apr. 13, 1988
	Gene Walter, AL:Sea. July 18, 1988
	John Dopson, AL:Bos. June 13, 1989

Most Balks, Inning
3	Milt Shoffner, AL:Clev. May 12, 1930 (3rd)
	Don Heinkel, AL:Det. May 3, 1988 (6th)
	Jim Owens, NL:Cin. Apr. 24, 1963 (2nd)
	Bob Shaw, NL:Mil. May 4, 1963 (3rd)
	Jim Gott, NL:Pitt. Aug. 6, 1988 (8th)

RELIEF PITCHING

Highest Percentage, Games Won, Lifetime (Minimum: 50 wins)
.708	Hugh Casey, NL:Chi. 1935; Brk. 39-42, 46-48; Pitt. 49; AL:NY 49 (51-21)

Highest Percentage, Games Won, League (Minimum: 50 wins)
.704	Hugh Casey, NL:Chi. 1935; Brk. 39-42, 46-48; Pitt. 49 (50-21)
.680	Eddie Rommel, AL:Phil. 1920-32 (51-24)

Most Games, Lifetime
1248	Jesse Orosco, NL:NY 1979, 81-87; LA 88, 2001-02; StL. 2000; SD 03
	AL:Clev. 89-91; Mil. 92-94; Balt. 95-99; NY 03; Minn. 03

Most Games, League
1119	John Franco, NL:Cin. 1984-89; NY 90-2001, 03-04; Hou. 05
807	Sparky Lyle, AL:Bos. 1967-71; NY 72-78; Tex. 79-80; Chi. 82

Most Games, Consecutive, Lifetime
1199	Jesse Orosco, NL:NY-LA-StL.-SD; AL:Clev.-Mil.-Balt.-NY-Minn. July 20, 1982-Sept. 27, 2003

Most Games, Consecutive, League
1119	John Franco, NL:Cin. 1984-89; NY 90-2001, 03-04; Hou. 05
807	Sparky Lyle, AL:Bos.-NY-Tex.-Chi. July 4, 1967-Sept. 27(2g) 1982

Most Games, Season
106	Mike Marshall, NL:LA 1974
89	Mike Marshall, AL:Minn. 1979
	Mark Eichhorn, AL:Tor. 1987

Most Games Won, Lifetime
124	Hoyt Wilhelm, NL:NY 1952-56; StL. 57; Atl. 69-71; Chi. 70; LA 71-72
	AL:Clev. 57-58; Balt. 58-62; Chi. 63-68; Cal. 69

Most Games Won, League
96	Roy Face, NL:Pitt. 1953, 55-68; Mtl. 69
87	Sparky Lyle, AL:Bos. 1967-71; NY 72-78; Tex. 79-80; Chi. 82

Most Games Won, Consecutive
22	Roy Face, NL:Pitt. June 7, 1958-Aug 30, 1959
19	Rube Waddell, AL:Phil.-StL. July 21, 1902-June 11, 1908

Most Games Won, Consecutive, Start of Career
12	Butch Metzger, NL:SF-SD Sept. 21, 1974-Aug. 8, 1976
	(ML record)
19	Rube Waddell, AL:Phil.-StL. July 21, 1902-June 11, 1908
	(0-3 in NL prior to AL career)

Most Games Won, Season
18	Roy Face, NL:Pitt. 1959 (1 lost)
17	John Hiller, AL:Det. 1974 (14 lost)
	Bill Campbell, AL:Minn. 1976 (5 lost)

Most Games Lost, Lifetime
108	Gene Garber, NL:Pitt. 1969-72; Phil. 74-78; Atl. 78-87; AL:KC 1973-74, 87-88

Most Games Lost, League

98	Gene Garber, NL:Pitt. 1969-72; Phil. 74-78; Atl. 78-87
67	Hoyt Wilhelm, AL:Clev. 1957-58; Balt. 58-62; Chi. 63-68; Cal. 69
	Sparky Lyle, AL:Bos. 1967-71; NY 72-78; Tex. 79-80; Chi. 82

Most Games Lost, Consecutive

14	Skip Lockwood, NL:NY June 16, 1978-May 16, 1979
11	Tom Murphy, AL:Mil.-Bos. May 17, 1975-June 10, 1976
	Mike Henneman, AL:Det.-Tex. May 28, 1994-July 4, 1996
	Heathcliff Slocumb, AL:Bos.-Sea. May 3, 1997-Apr. 14, 1998

Most Games Lost, Season

16	Gene Garber, NL:Atl. 1979 (6 won)
14	Darold Knowles, AL:Wash. 1970 (2 won)
	John Hiller, AL:Det. 1974 (17 won)
	Mike Marshall, AL:Minn. 1979 (10 won)

Most Innings, Lifetime

1871.0	Hoyt Wilhelm, NL:NY 1952-56; StL. 57; Atl. 69-71; Chi. 70; LA 71-72
	AL:Clev. 57-58; Balt. 58-62; Chi. 63-68; Cal. 69

Most Innings, League

1436.2	Kent Tekulve, NL:Pitt. 1974-85; Phil. 85-88; Cin. 89
1265.0	Sparky Lyle, AL:Bos. 1967-71; NY 72-78; Tex. 79-80; Chi. 82

Most Innings, Season

208.0	Mike Marshall, NL:LA 1974
168.1	Bob Stanley, AL:Bos. 1982

Most Innings, Game

18.1	Zip Zabel, NL:Chi. June 17, 1915
17.0	Eddie Rommel, AL:Phil. July 10, 1932

Most Strikeouts, Consecutive, Game

8	Ron Davis, AL:NY May 4, 1981
7	Randy Johnson, NL:Ari. July 18, 2001

)OUBLEHEADERS (Complete Games)

Most Doubleheaders, Lifetime

5	Joe McGinnity, AL:Balt. 1901; NL:NY 1903

Most Doubleheaders, League

3	Joe McGinnity, NL:NY 1903
2	Joe McGinnity, AL:Balt. 1901
	Ed Walsh, AL:Chi. 1905, 08
	Mule Watson, AL:Phil. 1918

Most Doubleheaders, Season

3	Joe McGinnity, NL:NY 1903
2	Joe McGinnity, AL:Balt. 1901
	Mule Watson, AL:Phil. 1918

Most Doubleheaders Won, League

3	Joe McGinnity, NL:NY 1903
1	By many players

Most Doubleheaders Won, Season

3	Joe McGinnity, NL:NY 1903
1	By many players; Last:
	Dutch Levsen, AL:Clev. 1926

Fewest Runs, Doubleheader

0	Ed Reulbach, NL:Chi. Sept. 26, 1908
1	Ed Walsh, AL:Chi. Sept. 29, 1908
	Carl Mays, AL:Bos. Aug. 30, 1918

Fewest Hits, Doubleheader

3	Tim Keefe, AA:NY July 4, 1883
6	Fred Toney, NL:Cin. July 1, 1917
	Hi Bell, NL:StL. July 19, 1924
7	Frank Owen, AL:Chi. July 1, 1905
	Ed Walsh, AL:Chi. Sept. 29, 1908

Fewest Walks, Doubleheader

0	Guy Hecker, AA:Lou. July 4, 1884
1	Ed Walsh, AL:Chi. Sept. 29, 1908
	Grover Alexander, NL:Phil. Sept. 23, 1916 & Sept. 3, 1917

PITCHING – ROOKIE SEASON

(No official rookie rule prior to 1957. Qualifiers based on less than 45 previous innings pitched.)

Most Games
88	Sean Runyan, AL:Det. 1998	
86	Oscar Villarreal, NL:Ari. 2003	

Most Complete Games
66	Jim Devlin, NL:Lou. 1876
	Matt Kilroy, NL:Balt. 1886
	Since 1900:
41	Irv Young, NL:Bos. 1905
35	Roscoe Miller, AL:Det. 1901

Most Shutouts
16	George Bradley, NL:StL. 1876
	Since 1900:
8	Russ Ford, AL:NY 1910
	Reb Russell, AL:Chi. 1913
	Fernando Valenzuela, NL:LA 1981

Most Shutouts, Consecutive, Start of Career
2	Al Spalding, NL:Chi. Apr. 25-27, 1876
	Jim Hughes NL:Balt. Apr. 18-22, 1898
	Al Worthington, NL:NY July 6-11, 1953
	Karl Spooner, NL:Brk. Sept. 22-26, 1954
	Slow Joe Doyle, AL:NY Aug. 25-30, 1906
	Johnny Marcum, AL:Phil. Sept. 7-11, 1933
	Boo Ferriss, AL:Bos. Apr. 29-May 6, 1945
	Tom Phoebus, AL:Balt. Sept. 15-20, 1966

Most Games Won
47	Al Spalding, NL:Chi. 1876 (13 lost)
	Since 1900:
28	Grover Alexander, NL:Phil. 1911 (13 lost)
26	Russ Ford, AL:NY 1910 (6 lost)

Most Games Won, Consecutive
17	Pat Luby, NL:Chi. Aug. 6-Oct. 3, 1890
	Since 1900:
12	Hooks Wiltse, NL:NY May 29-Sept. 15, 1904
	Atley Donald, AL:NY May 9-July 25, 1939

Most Games Lost
48	John Coleman, NL:Phil. 1883 (48 lost)
	Since 1900:
26	Bob Groom, AL:Wash. 1909 (26 lost)
25	Harry McIntire, NL:Brk. 1905 (25 lost)

Most Games Lost, Consecutive
16	Dory Dean, NL:Cin. July 11-Sept. 12, 1876
	Since 1900:
15	Bob Groom, AL:Wash. July 6-Sept. 25, 1909
14	Anthony Young, NL:NY May 6-Sept. 29, 1992

Most Saves, Season
37	Kazuhiro Sasaki, AL:Sea. 2000
36	Todd Worrell, NL:StL. 1986

Most Innings
591	Lee Richmond, NL:Wor. 1880
	Since 1900:
378	Irv Young, NL:Bos. 1905
332	Roscoe Miller, AL:Det. 1901

Fewest Hits, First Game (9 or more innings)
0	Bumpus Jones, NL:Cin. Oct. 15, 1892
	Since 1900:
1	Addie Joss, AL:Clev. Apr. 26, 1902
	Mike Fornieles, AL:Wash. Sept. 2(2g), 1952
	Billy Rohr, AL:Bos. Apr. 14, 1967
	Juan Marichal, NL:SF July 19, 1960
	Jimmy Jones, NL:SD Sept. 21, 1986

Most Scoreless Innings, Consecutive, Start of Career
25	George McQuillan, NL:Phil. May 8, Sept. 22-29, 1907
22	Boo Ferris, AL:Bos. Apr. 29-May 13, 1945

Most Sacrifice Flies (1908 to 1930, 1939, since 1954)
14	Rich DeLucia, AL:Sea. 1991
12	George O'Donnell, NL:Pitt. 1954

Most Intentional Walks (Since 1955)
20	Ron Willis, NL:StL. 1967
16	Ken Sanders, AL:Bos.-KC 1966

Most Strikeouts
276	Dwight Gooden, NL:NY 1984
245	Herb Score, AL:Clev. 1955

Most Strikeouts, First Game
15	Karl Spooner, NL:Brk. Sept. 22, 1954
	J.R. Richard, NL:Hou. Sept. 5(2g), 1971
12	Elmer Myers, AL:Phil. Oct. 6(2g), 1915
	Steve Woodard, AL:Mil. July 28(1g), 1997

Most Strikeouts, Consecutive, First Game
7	Sammy Stewart, AL:Balt. Sept. 1, 1978 (2-4 inn)
6	Karl Spooner, NL:Brk. Sept. 22, 1954 (7-8 inn)
	Pete Richert, NL:LA Apr. 12, 1962 (2-4 inn)

Most Wild Pitches, First Game
5	Jake Seymour, AA:Pitt. Sept. 23, 1882
	Mike Corcoran, NL:Chi. July 15, 1884
	George Winkelman, NL:Wash. Aug. 2, 1886

CLUB BATTING - SEASON

	AL:1901-1960 NL:1900-1961 8 clubs 154 games		AL:1961-1968 NL:1962-1968 10 clubs 162 games		AL:1969- NL:1969- 12-16 clubs 162 games	
Highest Batting Average						
AL:	.316	Det. 1921	.267	NY 1962	.293	Clev. 1996
NL:	.319	NY 1930	.279	Pitt. 1966	.294	Col. 2000
Lowest Batting Average						
AL:	.211	Chi. 1910	.214	NY 1968	.229	Mil. 1971
NL:	.213	Brk. 1908	.219	NY 1963	.225	SD 1969
Highest Slugging Percentage						
AL:	.489	NY 1927	.442	NY 1961	.491	Bos. 2003
NL:	.481	Chi. 1930	.441	SF 1962	.483	Col. 2001
Lowest Slugging Percentage						
AL:	.261	Chi. 1910	.311	Chi. 1968	.318	Cal. 1976
NL:	.274	Bos. 1909	.301	Hou. 1963	.327	StL. 1986
Most At-Bats						
AL:	5646	Clev. 1936	5705	NY 1964	5781	Bos. 1997
NL:	5667	Phil. 1930	5767	Cin. 1968	5734	StL. 1979
Fewest At-Bats						
AL:	4822	Chi. 1913	5275	Balt. 1968	5185	Mil. 1971
NL:	4725	Phil. 1907	5303	Hou. 1964	5330	Pitt. 2002
Most Runs						
AL:	1067	NY 1931	841	Det. 1961	1009	Clev. 1999
NL:	1004	StL. 1930	878	SF 1962	968	Col. 2000
Fewest Runs						
AL:	380	Wash. 1909	463	Chi. 1968	511	Cal. 1971
NL:	372	StL. 1908	464	Hou. 1963	468	SD 1969
Most Hits						
AL:	1724	Det. 1921	1509	NY 1962	1684	Bos. 1997
NL:	1783	Phil. 1930	1586	Pitt. 1966	1664	Col. 2000
Fewest Hits						
AL:	1058	Chi. 1910	1137	NY 1968	1188	Mil. 1971
NL:	1044	Brk. 1908	1168	NY 1963	1203	SD 1969
Most Total Bases						
AL:	2703	NY 1936	2455	NY 1961	2832	Bos. 2003
NL:	2684	Chi. 1930	2483	Cin. 1965	2748	Col. 2001
Fewest Total Bases						
AL:	1310	Chi. 1910	1681	Chi. 1968	1694	Cal. 1969
NL:	1358	Brk. 1908	1618	Hou. 1963	1756	StL. 1986
Most Extra-Base Hits						
AL:	580	NY 1936	494	Minn. 1964	649	Bos. 2003
NL:	566	StL. 1930	512	Cin. 1965	598	Col. 2001
Fewest Extra-Base Hits						
AL:	171	StL. 1909	273	Chi. 1968	268	Cal. 1969
NL:	182	Bos. 1909	271	Hou. 1963	282	Atl. 1976
Most Singles						
AL:	1298	Det. 1921	1075	Chi. 1961	1202	Tex. 1980
NL:	1297	Pitt. 1922	1239	Pitt. 1967	1168	StL. 1971
Fewest Singles						
AL:	837	Wash. 1959	811	Balt. 1968	850	Balt. 2002
NL:	846	Brk. 1908	865	NY 1965	863	Chi. 2002

	AL:1901-1960 NL:1900-1961 8 clubs 154 games		AL:1961-1968 NL:1962-1968 10 clubs 162 games		AL:1969- NL:1969- 12-16 clubs 162 games

Most Doubles

AL:	356	Clev. 1930	257	Clev. 1961 Bos. 1962 Minn. 1965	373	Bos. 1997, 2004
NL:	373	StL. 1930	281	Cin. 1968	342	StL. 2003

Fewest Doubles

AL:	115	Chi. 1910	154	NY 1968	151	Cal. 1969
NL:	110	Brk. 1908	156	NY 1963	170	Atl. 1976

Most Triples

AL:	113	Bos. 1903	59	KC 1965	79	KC 1979
NL:	129	Pitt. 1912	66	StL. 1963 Pitt. 1966	70	Pitt. 1970

Fewest Triples

AL:	19	Balt. 1958	17	NY 1967 Bos. 1968	11	Balt. 1998
NL:	19	Bos. 1942	23	NY 1967	12	Cin. 2006

Most Home Runs

AL:	193	NY 1960	240	NY 1961	264	Sea. 1997
NL:	221	NY 1947 Cin. 1956	207	Atl. 1966	249	Hou. 2000

Fewest Home Runs

AL:	3	Chi. 1908	69	KC 1967	55	Cal. 1975
NL:	9	Pitt. 1917	62	Hou. 1963	49	Hou. 1979

Most Grand Slam Home Runs

AL:	10	Det. 1938	8	Minn. 1961 Bos. 1964	14	Oak. 2000 Clev. 2006
NL:	9	Chi. 1929	8	Mil. 1962	12	Atl. 1997 StL. 2000

Most Home Runs, Pinch-Hitters

AL:	7	NY 1953-54, 60 Clev. & Det. 1958	10	NY 1961	11	Balt. 1982
NL:	12	Cin. 1957	9	Cin. 1962 NY 1962, 66	14	Ari. 2001 SF 2001

Most Grand Slam Home Runs, Pinch-Hitters

AL:	2	Phil. 1931; Det. 1952 NY 1953; Bos. 1960	2	Chi.& NY 1961	3	Balt. 1982
NL:	2	NY 1934; Phil. 1945	1	By many clubs	3	By many clubs

Most Runs Batted In (Since 1920)

AL:	995	NY 1936	791	NY 1962	960	Clev. 1999
NL:	942	StL. 1930	807	SF 1962	909	Col. 1996

Fewest Runs Batted In (Since 1920)

AL:	440	Phil. 1945	431	Chi. 1968	477	Cal. 1971
NL:	354	Phil. 1942	420	Hou. 1963	431	SD 1969

Most Sacrifice Hits

AL:	207	Chi. 1906	109	Chi. 1966	142	Minn. 1979
NL:	231	Chi. 1906	120	LA 1964	133	SD 1975

Fewest Sacrifice Hits

AL:	41	Bos. 1957	35	Bos. 1964	9	Tex. 2005
NL:	32	NY 1957	46	NY 1963	29	SD 2001

Most Sacrifice Flies (1908 to 1930, 1939, since 1954)

AL:	59	Clev. 1954-55 Chi. 1960	59	Minn. 1965	77	Oak. 1984
NL:	66	StL. 1954	53	LA 1963	75	Col. 2000

	AL:1901-1960 NL:1900-1961 8 clubs 154 games		AL:1961-1968 NL:1962-1968 10 clubs 162 games		AL:1969- NL:1969- 12-16 clubs 162 games

Fewest Sacrifice Flies (1908 to 1930, 1939, since 1954)

AL:	27	Balt. 1955	23	Cal. 1967	25	TB 2001
NL:	26	StL. 1959	26	NY 1964	19	SD 1971

Most Walks

AL:	835	Bos. 1949	681	LA 1961	775	Sea. 2000
NL:	732	Brk. 1947	615	NY 1962	729	SF 1970

Fewest Walks

AL:	283	Wash. 1904	397	Chi. 1968	363	Det. 2002
NL:	282	StL. 1908	345	StL. 1966	388	Col. 1993

Most Intentional Walks (Since 1955)

AL:	66	NY 1957	79	Minn. 1965	78	Minn. 1969
NL:	91	Brk. 1956	101	Phil. 1967	153	SF 2004

Fewest Intentional Walks (Since 1955)

AL:	20	Wash. 1959	10	KC 1961	17	Chi. 2002
NL:	21	LA 1958	29	NY 1962	20	Pitt. 1998

Most Hit By Pitch

AL:	82	Wash. 1910	61	Det. 1968	92	Tor. 1996
NL:	92	NY 1903	53	Phil. 1962	100	Hou. 1997

Fewest Hit By Pitch

AL:	5	Phil. 1937	15	Wash. 1962	11	Clev. 1976
NL:	9	Phil. 1939	17	Pitt. 1962	9	SD 1989

Most Strikeouts

AL:	883	Wash. 1960	1125	Wash. 1965	1268	Det. 1996
NL:	1054	Phil. 1960	1203	NY 1968	1399	Mil. 2001

Fewest Strikeouts

AL:	326	Phil. 1927	612	Chi. 1961	589	Tex. 1980
NL:	308	Cin. 1921	782	Atl. 1968	649	StL. 1975

Most Stolen Bases

AL:	291	Wash. 1913	153	Chi. 1966	341	Oak. 1976
NL:	347	NY 1911	198	LA 1962	314	StL. 1985

Fewest Stolen Bases

AL:	13	Wash. 1957	18	Bos. 1964	25	Clev. 1970
NL:	17	StL. 1949	22	SF 1967	23	Pitt. 1973

Most Caught Stealing

AL:	118	Chi. 1923	82	Chi. 1967	123	Oak. 1976
NL:	149	Chi. 1924	77	LA 1965	120	Pitt. 1977

Fewest Caught Stealing

AL:	11	KC 1960	11	Clev. 1961	12	Bos. 2005
NL:	8	Mil. 1958	27	Mil. 1962 SF 1965	16	Chi. 1970

Most Grounded into Double Plays

AL:	170	Phil. 1950	157	Bos. 1965	174	Bos. 1990
NL:	166	StL. 1958	149	SF 1965	158	Mil. 2003

Fewest Grounded into Double Plays

AL:	93	StL. 1944 NY 1952	79	KC 1967	81	Det. 1985
NL:	75	StL. 1945	79	LA 1965	76	Hou. 1983

Most Left on Base

AL:	1334	StL. 1941	1246	Chi. 1964	1312	Det. 1993
NL:	1278	Brk. 1947	1218	NY 1962	1328	Cin. 1976

Fewest Left on Base

AL:	925	KC 1957	995	KC 1966	975	Cal. 1992
NL:	964	Chi. 1924	1019	SF 1966	978	Col. 1993

ATTING AVERAGE

Most Seasons Leading League
23 **NL:**StL. 1915, 20-21, 34, 38-39, 42-44,
46, 49, 52, 54, 56-57, 63, 71, 75, 79-
80, 85, 92, 2004
AL: Bos. 1903, 38-39, 41-42, 44, 46, 49-50, 64,
67, 75, 79, 81, 84-85, 87-90, 97, 2003, 05

Most Seasons, Consecutive, Leading League
8 **NL:**Col. 1995-2002
5 **AL:**Phil. 1910-14

Most Players, .300 or Higher, Season
(Minimum: 300 at-bats)
8 **NL:**Phil. 1894
StL. 1930
7 **AL:**Phil. 1927

LUGGING PERCENTAGE

Most Seasons Leading League
30 **AL:**Balt./NY 1901, 20-21, 23-24, 26-28, 30-
31, 36-39, 43-45, 47-48, 51, 53-58,60-
62, 86
23 **NL:**NY/SF 1889, 91, 1904-05, 08, 10-11, 19,
23-24, 27-28, 35, 45, 47-48, 52, 61-63,
89, 93, 2002

Most Seasons, Consecutive, Leading League
6 **AL:**NY 1953-58
5 **NL:**Col. 1995-99

LATE APPEARANCES

Most Batters, Game
71 **NL:**Chi. (Lou.) June 29, 1897
Since 1900:
66 **NL:**Phil. (Chi.) Aug. 25, 1922
65 **AL:**Mil. (Tor.) Aug. 28, 1992
Extra-Inning Game
104 **AL:**Chi. (Mil.) May 8, 1984 (25 inn)
103 **NL:**NY(StL.) Sept. 11, 1974 (25 inn)

Most Batters, Both Clubs, Game
125 **NL:**Phil. (66) Chi. (59) Aug. 25, 1922
110 **AL:**TB (61) Tor. (49) June 24, 2004
Extra-Inning Game:
202 **NL:**NY (103) StL. (99) Sept. 11, 1974 (25 inn)
198 **AL:**Chi. (104) Mil. (94) May 8, 1984 (25 inn)

Most Batters, Inning
23 **NL:**Chi. (Det.) Sept. 6, 1883 (7th)
Since 1900:
23 **AL:**Bos. (Det.) June 18, 1953 (7th)
21 **NL:**Brk. (Cin.) May 21, 1952 (1st)

Most Batters, 3 Appearances, Inning
5 **NL:**Chi. (Det.) Sept. 6, 1883 (7th)
AL: Bos. (Det.) June 18, 1953 (7th)
NL Since 1900:
3 **NL:**Brk. (Cin.) May 21, 1952 (1st)

Most Batters on Base, Inning
20 **AL:**Bos. (Det.) June 18, 1953 (7th)
19 **NL:**Bos. (Balt.) June 18, 1894 (1g; 1st)
Brk. (Cin.) May 21, 1952 (1st)

Most Batters, Consecutive, On Base, Inning
19 **NL:**Brk. (Cin.) May 21, 1952 (1st)
13 **AL:**KC (Chi.) Apr. 21, 1956 (2nd)
KC (Det.) Sept. 9(1g), 2004 (3rd)

Most Batters, On Base 3 Times, Inning
3 **NL:**Chi. (Det.) Sept. 6, 1883 (7th)
Bos. (Balt.) June 18, 1894 (1g; 1st)
AL: Bos. (Det.) June 18, 1953 (7th)
NL Since 1900:
1 **NL:**Brk. (Cin.) May 21, 1952 (1st)

AT-BATS

Most At-Bats, Game
66 **NL:**Chi. (Buff.) July 3, 1883
Since 1900:
58 **NL:**NY (Phil.) Sept. 2, 1925
NY (Phil.) July 11, 1931
57 **AL:**Mil. (Tor.) Aug. 28, 1992
Extra-Inning Game
95 **AL:**Chi. (Mil.) May 8, 1984 (25 inn)
89 **NL:**NY (StL.) Sept. 11, 1974 (25 inn)

Most At-Bats, Both Clubs, Game
106 **NL:**Chi. (64) Lou (42) July 22, 1876
Since 1900:
99 **NL:**NY (56) Cin. (43) June 9, 1901
NY (58) Phil. (41) July 11, 1931
96 **AL:**Clev. (51) Phil. (45) Apr. 29, 1952
Extra-Inning Game:
175 **NL:**NY (89) StL. (86) Sept. 11, 1974 (25 inn)
AL: Chi. (95) Mil. (80) May 8, 1984 (25 inn)

Fewest At-Bats, Game
9 innings:
22 **NL:**Atl. (Cin.) Apr. 11, 1980
23 **AL:**Chi. (StL.) May 6, 1917
Clev. (Chi.) May 9, 1961
Det. (Balt.) May 6, 1968
8 innings:
19 **AL:**Balt. (KC) Sept. 12, 1964
21 **NL:**Pitt. (StL.) Sept. 8, 1908
Atl. (Pitt.) Sept. 6, 1986

Fewest At-Bats, Both Clubs, Game
9 innings:
46 **AL:**Balt. (19) KC (27) Sept. 12, 1964
48 **NL:**Bos. (25) Phil. (23) Apr. 22, 1910
Brk. (24) Cin. (24) July 22, 1911
Cin. (26) Atl. (22) Apr. 11, 1980

RUNS

Most Seasons Leading League
27 **AL:**NY 1921, 26-28, 30-33, 36-39, 42-43, 45,
47, 53-54, 56-58, 60, 62, 85, 98, 2002, 06
21 **NL:**Chi. 1876, 78, 80-86, 88, 1906, 11, 13,
18, 29, 31, 35, 37, 67, 84, 89
NY/SF 1889, 1904-05, 08, 10, 12 14, 16-
17, 19-21, 23-24, 27, 47-48, 58, 61-62, 70

Most Seasons, Consecutive, Leading League
7 **NL:**Chi. 1880-86
Since 1900:
5 **NL:**Brk. 1949-53
4 **AL:**Det. 1907-10
NY 1930-33, 36-39
Bos. 1948-51

Most Games, Consecutive, Scoring Runs
308 **AL:**NY Aug. 3, 1931-Aug. 2, 1933
208 **NL:**Cin. Apr. 3, 2000-May 23, 2001

Most Runs, Game
36 **NL:**Chi. (Lou.) June 29, 1897
Since 1900:
29 **AL:**Bos. (StL.) June 8, 1950
Chi. (KC) Apr. 23, 1955
28 **NL:**StL. (Phil.) July 6, 1929

Most Runs, Both Clubs, Game
49 **NL:**Chi. (26) Phil. (23) Aug. 25, 1922
36 **AL:**Bos. (22) Phil. (14) June 29, 1950

Most Runs, 2 Consecutive Games
53 **NL:**Chi. July 22-25, 1876
Since 1900:
49 **AL:**Bos. June 7-8, 1950
45 **NL:**Pitt. June 20-22, 1925

Most Runs, 3 Consecutive Games
71 **NL:**Chi. July 20-25, 1876
56 **AL:**Bos. June 7-9, 1950
NL Since 1900:
54 **NL:**Pitt. June 19-22, 1925

Most Runs, 4 Consecutive Games
88 **NL:**Chi. July 20-27, 1876
65 **AL:**Bos. June 5-8, 1950
Since 1900:
59 **NL:**Chi. June 1-5, 1930

Most Runs, Inning
18 **NL:**Chi. (Det.) Sept. 6, 1883 (7th)
Since 1900:
17 **AL:**Bos. (Det.) June 18, 1953 (7th)
15 **NL:**Brk. (Cin.) May 21, 1952 (1st)

Most Runs, Both Clubs, Inning
19 **AA:**Wash. (14) Balt. (5) June 17, 1891 (1st)
AL: Clev. (13) Bos. (6) Apr. 10, 1977 (8th)
18 **NL:**Chi. (18) Det. (0) Sept. 6, 1883 (7th)
Since 1900:
17 **NL:**Bos. (10) NY (7) June 20, 1912 (9th)

Most Runs, Extra Inning
12 **AL:**Tex. (Oak.) July 3, 1983 (15th)
10 **NL:**KC (Det.) July 21, 1886 (11th)
Bos. (NY) June 17, 1887 (10th)
Cin. (Brk.) May 15, 1919 (13th)

Most Runs, Both Clubs, Extra Inning
12 **AL:**Minn. (11) Oak. (1) June 21, 1969 (10th)
Tex. (12) Oak. (0) July 3, 1983 (15th)
11 **NL:**NY (8) Pitt. (3) June 15, 1929 (14th)
NY (6) Brk. (5) Apr. 24, 1955 (10th)
NY (6) Chi. (5) June 30, 1979 (11th)
Pitt. (6) Chi. (5) Apr. 21, 1991 (11th)

Most Runs, 1st Inning
16 **NL:**Bos. (Balt.) June 18(1g), 1894
Since 1900:
15 **NL:**Brk. (Cin.) May 21, 1952
14 **AL:**Clev. (Phil.) June 18(2g), 1950
Bos. (Fla.) June 27, 2003

Most Runs, 2nd Inning
13 **NL:**Chi. (Cin.) Aug. 7, 1877
NY (Clev.) July 19(1g), 1890
Atl. (Hou.) Sept. 20, 1972
SD (Pitt.) May 31, 1994
AL:KC (Chi.) Apr. 21, 1956
NY (TB) Apr. 18, 2005

Most Runs, 3rd Inning
14 **NL:**Clev. (Wash.) Aug. 7, 1889
Since 1900:
13 **NL:**SF (StL.) May 7, 1966
12 **AL:**NY (Wash.) Sept. 11(1g), 1949

Most Runs, 4th Inning
15 **NL:**Hart. (NY) May 13, 1876
Since 1900:
14 **NL:**Chi. (Phil.) Aug. 25, 1922
13 **AL:**Chi. (Wash.) Sept. 26(1g), 1943

Most Runs, 5th Inning
14 **AL:**NY (Wash.) July 6, 1920
13 **NL:**Chi. (Pitt.) Aug. 16, 1890
NL Since 1900:
12 **NL:**NY (Bos.) Sept. 3, 1926
Cin. (Atl.) Apr. 25, 1977
Mtl. (Chi.) Sept. 24, 1985

Most Runs, 6th Inning
14 **PL:**Phil. (Buff.) June 26, 1890
13 **AL:**Clev. (Bos.) July 7(1g), 1923
Det. (NY) June 17, 1925
NL: Mtl. (SF) May 7, 1997

Most Runs, 7th Inning
18 **NL:**Chi. (Det.) Sept. 6, 1883
Since 1900:
17 **AL:**Bos. (Det.) June 18, 1953
13 **NL:**SF (SD) July 15, 1997

Most Runs, 8th Inning
16 **AL:**Tex. (Balt.) Apr. 19, 1996
13 **NL:**Brk. (Cin.) Aug. 8, 1954

Most Runs, 9th Inning
14 **NL:**Balt. (Bos.) Apr. 24, 1894
Since 1900:
13 **AL:**Cal. (Tex.) Sept. 14, 1978
Det. (Tex.) Aug. 8, 2001
12 **NL:**SF (Cin.) Aug. 23, 1961
SD (Col.) Sept. 12, 2004

Most Runs, 10th Inning
11 **AL:**Minn. (Oak.) June 21, 1969
10 **NL:**Bos. (NY) June 17(1g), 1887
NL Since 1900:
9 **NL:**Cin. (Phil.) Aug. 24(1g), 1947
SD (Phil.) May 28, 1995

Most Runs, 11th Inning
10 **NL:**KC (Det.) July 21, 1886
Since 1900:
9 **NL:**SD (Col.) June 28(2g), 1994
8 **AL:**Phil. (Det.) May 1, 1951
Tex. (Sea.) Sept. 23, 1991
Sea. (KC) Sept. 8, 2002

Most Runs, 12th Inning
11 **AL:**NY (Det.) July 26(1g), 1928
9 **NL:**Chi. (Pitt.) July 23, 1923

Most Runs, 13th Inning
10 **NL:**Cin. (Brk.) May 15, 1919
9 **AL:**Clev. (Det.) Aug. 5(1g), 1933

Most Runs, 14th Inning
8 **NL:**NY (Pitt.) June 15, 1929
7 **AL:**Clev. (StL.) June 3, 1935
Det. (Mil.) May 27, 1991

Most Runs, 15th Inning
12 **AL:**Tex. (Oak.) July 3, 1983
7 **NL:**StL. (Bos.) Sept. 28, 1928

Most Runs, 16th Inning
8 **AL:**Chi. (Wash.) May 20, 1920
5 **NL:**Cin. (NY) Aug. 20, 1973
Hou. (Cin.) Apr. 8, 1988

Most Runs, 17th Inning
7 **NL:**NY (Pitt.) July 16, 1920
6 **AL:**NY (Det.) July 20, 1941

Most Runs, 18th Inning
5 **NL:**Chi. (Bos.) May 14, 1927
4 **AL:**Minn. (Sea.) July 19, 1969

Most Runs, 19th Inning
5 **NL:**NY (Atl.) July 4, 1985
4 **AL:**Clev. (Det.) Apr. 27, 1984

Most Runs, 20th Inning
4 **NL:**Brk. (Bos.) July 5, 1940
3 **AL:**Bos. (Sea.) July 27, 1969
   Wash. (Clev.) Sept. 14(2g), 1971

Most Runs, 21st Inning
4 **AL:**Chi. (Clev.) May 26, 1973
3 **NL:**SD (Mtl.) May 21, 1977

Most Runs, 22nd Inning
2 **AL:**NY (Det.) June 24, 1962
1 **NL:**Brk. (Pitt.) Aug. 22, 1917
   Chi. (Bos.) May 17, 1927
   Hou. (LA) June 3, 1989
   LA (Mtl.) Aug. 23, 1989

Most Runs, 23rd Inning
2 **NL:**SF (NY) May 31(2g), 1964
0 **AL:**Bos. (Phil.) Sept. 1, 1906
   Phil. (Bos.) Sept. 1, 1906
   Det. (Phil.) July 21, 1945
   Phil. (Det.) July 21, 1945
   Chi. (Mil.) May 8, 1984
   Mil. (Chi.) May 8, 1984

Most Runs, 24th Inning
3 **AL:**Phil. (Bos.) Sept. 1, 1906
1 **NL:**Hou. (NY) Apr. 15, 1968

Most Runs, 25th Inning
1 **NL:**StL. (NY) Sept. 11, 1974
   AL: Chi. (Mil.) May 8, 1984

Most Runs 26th Inning
0 **NL:**Bos. (Brk.) May 1, 1920
   Brk. (Bos.) May 1, 1920
   AL: No games

Most Runs, Both Clubs, 1st Inning
19 **AA:**Wash. (14) Balt. (5) June 17, 1891
16 **NL:**Bos. (16) Balt. (0) June 18(1g), 1894
   AL: Oak. (13) Cal. (3) July 5, 1996
   NL Since 1900:
15 **NL:**Brk. (15) Cin. (0) May 21, 1952

Most Runs, Both Clubs, 2nd Inning
14 **NL:**Buff. (8) Wor. (6) Apr 4(2g), 1882
   Clev. (10) Bos. (4) May 20, 1891
   Bos. (9) Pitt. (5) Aug. 19(1g), 1893
   Balt. (10) Chi. (4) Sept. 4, 1893
   AL: Phil. (10) Det. (4) Sept. 23, 1913
   NY (11) Det. (3) Aug. 28(2g), 1936
   Chi. (8) Clev. (6) Sept. 2, 2001
   NL Since 1900:
13 **NL:**Chi. (10) Phil. (3) Aug. 25, 1922
   Brk. (11) NY (2) Apr. 29, 1930
   Atl. (13) Hou. (0) Sept. 20, 1972
   SD (13) Pitt. (0) May 31, 1994

Most Runs, Both Clubs, 3rd Inning
15 **NL:**NY (13) Phil. (2) Sept. 8, 1883
   Since 1900:
13 **AL:**Clev. (8) StL. (5) July 6, 1917
   Phil. (7) Bos. (6) July 4(2g), 1939
   Bos. (8) Det. (5) July 2, 1995
   NL: Brk. (9) Cin. (4) Aug. 22, 1929
   SF (13) StL. (0) May 7, 1966
   StL. (7) Atl. (6) Aug. 21, 1973
   ML:AL Clev. (10) NL:Ari. (3) June 17, 2005

Most Runs, Both Clubs, 4th Inning
15 **NL:**Hart. (15) NY (0) May 13, 1876
   Chi. (14) Phil. (1) Aug. 25, 1922
14 **AL:**Chi. (12) Det. (2) June 10, 1952

Most Runs, Both Clubs, 5th Inning
18 **AL:**Tex. (10) Det. (8) May 8, 2004
16 **NL:**Brk. (11) NY (5) June 3, 1890
   NL Since 1900:
15 **NL:**Brk. (10) Cin. (5) June 12, 1949
   Phil. (9) Pitt. (6) Apr. 16, 1953

Most Runs, Both Clubs, 6th Inning
15 **AL:**Phil. (10) NY (5) Sept. 5(1g), 1912
   Det. (10) Minn. (5) June 13, 1967
   NL:NY (10) Cin. (5) June 12, 1979

Most Runs, Both Clubs, 7th Inning
18 **NL:**Chi. (18) Det. (0) Sept. 6, 1883
   Since 1900:
17 **AL:**Bos. (17) Det. (0) June 18, 1953
13 **NL:**Chi. (12) Cin. (1) May 28, 1925
   StL. (7) NY (6) June 26, 1940
   Phil. (10) Chi. (3) July 22(2g), 1945
   SF (13) SD (0) July 15, 1997

Most Runs, Both Clubs, 8th Inning
19 **NL:**Clev. (13) Bos. (6) Apr. 10, 1977
14 **NL:**NY (11) Pitt. (3) May 25, 1954
   Brk. (13) Cin. (1) Aug. 8, 1954
   Atl. (9) SD (5) Apr. 27(1g), 1975
   Col. (8) LA (6) June 29, 1996

Most Runs, Both Clubs, 9th Inning
17 **NL:**Bos. (10) NY (7) June 20, 1912
15 **AL:**Tor. (11) Sea. (4) July 20, 1984

Most Runs, Both Clubs, 10th Inning
12 **AL:**Minn. (11) Oak. (1) June 21, 1969
11 **NL:**NY (6) Brk. (5) Apr. 24, 1955

Most Runs, Both Clubs, 11th Inning
11 **AL:**Sea. (6) Bos. (5) May 16, 1969
   NL:NY (6) Chi. (5) June 30, 1979
   Pitt. (6) Chi. (5) Apr. 21, 1991

Most Runs, Both Clubs, 12th Inning
11 **AL:**NY (8) Det. (3) May 14, 1923
   NY (11) Det. (0) May 26(1g), 1928
9 **NL:**Chi. (9) Pitt. (0) July 23, 1923
   NY (8) Brk. (1) May 30(2g), 1940
   Hou. (8) Cin. (1) June 2, 1966
   SD (5) Hou. (4) July 5, 1969

Most Runs, Both Clubs, 13th Inning
10 **NL:**Cin. (10) Brk. (0) May 15, 1919
9 **AL:**Clev. (9) Det. (0) Aug. 5(1g), 1933

Most Runs, Both Clubs, 14th Inning
11 **NL:**NY (8) Pitt. (3) June 15, 1929
8 **AL:**Det. (7) Mil. (1) May 27, 1991

Most Runs, Both Clubs, 15th Inning
12 **AL:**Tex. (12) Oak. (0) July 3, 1983
7 **NL:**StL. (7) Bos. (0) Sept. 28, 1928
   SF (4) LA (3) May 2, 1995

Most Runs, Both Clubs, 16th Inning
8 **AL:**Chi. (8) Wash. (0) May 20, 1920
5 **NL:**NY (4) Lou. (1) July 10, 1876
   Cin. (4) Brk. (1) July 29, 1914
   Cin. (5) NY (0) Aug. 20, 1973
   Hou. (5) Cin. (0) Apr. 8, 1988
   Ari. (3) LA (2) Apr. 13, 1999

Most Runs, Both Clubs, 17th Inning
7 **NL:**NY (7) Pitt. (0) July 16, 1920
6 **AL:**NY (3) Bos. (3) Sept. 5(1g), 1927
   NY (6) Det. (0) July 20, 1941

Most Runs, Both Clubs, 18th Inning
5 **NL:**Chi. (5) Bos. (0) May 14, 1927
   AL: Oak. (3) Minn. (2) Aug. 8, 2004

Most Runs, Both Clubs, 19th Inning
7 **NL:**NY (5) Atl. (2) July 4, 1985
5 **AL:**Chi. (3) Bos. (2) July 13, 1951

Most Runs, Both Clubs, 20th Inning
4 **AL:**Bos. (3) Sea. (1) July 27, 1969
   Wash. (3) Clev. (1) Sept. 14(2g), 1971
   NL: Brk. (4) Bos. (0) July 5, 1940

Most Runs, Both Clubs, 21st Inning
6 **AL:**Mil. (3) Chi. (3) May 8, 1984
3 **NL:**SD (3) Mtl. (0) May 21, 1977

Most Runs, 2 Consecutive Innings, Game
21 **NL:**Pitt. (Bos.) June 6, 1894 (3-4)
Since 1900:
19 **AL:**Bos. (Phil.) May 2, 1901 (2-3)
Bos. (Det.) June 18, 1953 (6-7)
Mil. (Cal.) July 8, 1990 (4-5)
18 **NL:**Mtl. (SF) May 7, 1997 (5-6)

Most Runs, None Out, Inning
13 **NL:**Chi. (Det.) Sept. 6, 1883 (7th)
Since 1900:
12 **NL:**Brk. (Phil.) May 24, 1953 (8th)
11 **AL:**Det. (NY) June 17, 1925 (6th)

Most Runs, Two Out, Inning
13 **AL:**Clev. (Bos.) July 7, 1923 (6th)
KC (Chi.) Apr. 21, 1956 (2nd)
12 **NL:**Brk. (Cin.) May 21, 1952 (1st)
Brk. (Cin.) Aug. 8, 1954 (8th)

Most Runs, 2 Out, 0 On Base, Inning
12 **NL:**Brk. (Cin.) Aug. 8, 1954 (8th)
10 **AL:**Chi. (Det.) Sept. 2, 1959 (5th)

Most Runs, None Out, 1st Inning
10 **AL:**Bos. (Fla.) June 27, 2003
9 **NL:**Phil. (NY) Aug. 13, 1948

Most Innings Scored, Consecutive, Season
17 **AL:**Bos. Sept. 15-17, 1903 (3 g)
14 **NL:**Pitt. July 31-Aug. 2, 1894 (3 g)
NY July 18-20, 1949 (3 g)
Col. May 4-7, 1999 (3 g)

Scoring Each Inning, Game
9 **AA:** Colu. (Pitt.) June 14, 1883
KC (Brk.) May 20, 1889
NL: Clev. (Bos.) Aug. 15, 1889
Wash. (Bos.) June 22, 1894
Clev. (Phil.) July 12, 1894
Chi. (Lou.) June 29, 1897
NY (Phil.) June 1, 1923
StL. (Chi.) Sept. 13, 1964
Col. (Chi.) May 5, 1999
AL:none

Scoring Each Inning, Game
(Did not bat in 9th)
8 **NL:**By many clubs
AL: Bos. (Clev.) Sept. 16, 1903
Clev. (Bos.) July 7, 1923
NY (StL.) July 26, 1939
Chi. (Bos.) May 11, 1949
KC (Oak.) Sept. 14, 1998
NY (Tor.) Apr. 29, 2006

Most Innings Scored, Both Clubs, Game
15 **NL:**Phil. (8) Det. (7) July 1, 1887
Wash. (9) Bos. (6) June 22, 1894
AA:KC (9) Brk. (6) May 20, 1889
PL:NY (8) Chi. (7) May 23, 1890
Since 1900:
14 **NL:**NY (9) Phil. (5) June 1, 1923
StL. (8) Phil. (6) July 5, 1923
Pitt. (8) Chi. (6) July 6, 1975
LA (8) Chi. (6) May 5, 1976
Col. (8) LA (6) June 30, 1996
Col. (8) SD (6) Sept. 24, 2001
AL: Balt. (8) Phil. (6) May 7, 1901
StL. (7) Det. (7) Apr. 23, 1927
Det. (7) Chi. (7) July 2, 1940
Chi. (7) Det. (7) May 28, 1995
ML: Sea. (7) SF (7) June 12, 1999
Extra-Inning Game:
15 **NL:**Pitt. (8) NY (7) June 15, 1929 (14 inn)
Phil. (8) Pitt. (7) July 23, 1930 (13 inn)
Chi. (8) Brk. (7) July 22, 1935 (11 inn)
NY (8) Atl. (7) July 4, 1985 (19 inn)
Hou. (8) Chi. (7) Sept. 28, 1995 (11 inn)
AL: Phil. (8) Clev. (7) July 10, 1932 (18 inn)

Most Runs Overcome to Win Game
12 **AL:**Det. (Chi.) June 18, 1911
Phil. (Clev.) June 15, 1925
Clev. (Sea.) Aug. 5, 2001 (11 inn)
11 **NL:**StL. (NY) June 15(1g), 1952
Phil. (Chi.) Apr. 17, 1976 (10 inn)
Hou. (StL.) July 18, 1994

Most Runs, Opening Game, Season
21 **AL:**Clev. (StL.) Apr. 14, 1925
19 **NL:**Phil. (Bos.) Apr. 19, 1900 (10 inn)

Most Runs, Both Clubs, Opening Game
36 **NL:**Phil. (19) Bos. (17) Apr. 19, 1900 (10 inn)
35 **AL:**Clev. (21) StL. (14) Apr. 14, 1925

Most Players, 100 or more Runs, Season
7 **NL:**Bos. 1894
Since 1900:
6 **AL:**NY 1931
NL: Brk. 1953

Most Players Scoring a Run, Game
15 **NL:**Atl. (Fla.) Oct. 3, 1999
14 **AL:**Oak. (Tex.) Sept. 30, 2000

Most Players, 2 or more Runs, Game
10 **NL:**Chi. (Lou.) June 29, 1897
Since 1900:
9 **NL:**StL. (Chi.) Apr. 16, 1912
Chi. (Phil.) Aug. 25, 1922
StL. (Phil.) July 6(2g), 1929
Chi. (Col.) Aug. 18, 1995
AL: Bos. (Phil.) May 2, 1901
Clev. (Bos.) July 7(1g), 1923
NY (Chi.) July 26, 1931
NY (Phil.) May 24, 1936
Bos. (Phil.) June 29, 1950
Cal. (Tor.) Aug. 25, 1979
Minn. (Det.) June 4, 1994

Most Players, 3 or more Runs, Game
9 **NL:**Chi. (Buff.) July 3, 1883
Since 1900:
7 **AL:**Bos. (StL.) June 8, 1950
6 **NL:**NY (Phil.) Sept. 2(2g), 1925

Most Players, 4 or more Runs, Game
6 **NL:**Chi. (Clev.) July 24, 1882
Chi. (Lou.) June 29, 1897
Since 1900:
4 **NL:**StL. (Phil.) July 6(2g), 1929
AL: Bos. (StL.) June 8, 1950

Most Players, 5 or more Runs, Game
3 **NL:**Chi. (Clev.) July 24, 1882
    Bos. (Phil.) June 20, 1883
    Bos. (Pitt.) Aug. 27, 1887
    NY (Brk.) Apr. 30(1g), 1944
    Chi. (Bos.) July 3, 1945
  AL: Clev. (Balt.) Sept. 2, 1902
    Chi. (KC) Apr. 23, 1955

Most Players, 6 or more Runs, Game
2 **NL:**Bos. (Pitt.) Aug. 27, 1887
1 **AL:**Bos. (Chi.) May 8, 1946
    Bos. (Clev.) Aug. 21, 1986
    KC (Det.) Sept. 9(1g), 2004

Most Runs, Two Players, Game
12 **NL:**Bos. (Pitt.) Aug. 27, 1887
   Since 1900:
11 **NL:**NY (Brk.) Apr. 30(1g), 1944
10 **AL:**Clev. (Balt.) Sept. 2, 1902
    Chi. (KC) Apr. 23, 1955
    KC (Det.) Sept. 9(1g), 2004

Most Players, 2 or more Runs, Inning
7 **NL:**Chi. (Det.) Sept. 6, 1883 (7th)
  Since 1900:
6 **NL:**Brk. (Cin.) May 21, 1952 (1st)
    Cin. (Hou.) Aug. 3, 1989 (1st)
5 **AL:**NY (Wash.) July 6, 1920 (5th)
    NY (Bos.) June 21, 1945 (5th)
    Bos. (Phil.) July 4, 1948 (7th)
    Clev. (Phil.) June 18, 1950 (1st)
    Bos. (Det.) June 18, 1953 (7th)
    Mil. (Cal.) July 8, 1990 (5th)
    Ana. (Chi.) May 12, 1997 (7th)
    Bos. (Fla.) June 27, 2003 (1st)

ITS

Most Seasons Leading League
26 **NL:**StL. 1901, 20-21, 26, 34, 38-40, 42-47,
    49, 54, 56-57, 63-64, 75, 79-80, 83,
    92, 2004
23 **AL:**Bos. 1903, 39-42, 45-46, 49-50, 54, 67,
    70, 75, 81, 84-85, 87-90, 97, 2003, 05

Most Seasons, Consecutive, Leading League
8 **NL:**Col. 1995-2002
4 **AL:**Bos. 1939-42, 1987-90

Most Players, 200 or more Hits, Season
4 **NL:**Phil. 1929
  AL: Det. 1937

Most Hits, Game
36 **NL:**Phil. (Lou.) Aug. 17, 1894
   Since 1900:
31 **NL:**NY (Cin.) June 9, 1901
   AL: Mil. (Tor.) Aug. 28, 1992
   Extra-Inning Game:
33 **AL:**Clev. (Phil.) July 10, 1932 (18 inn)

Most Hits, Consecutive, Game
12 **NL:**StL. (Bos.) Sept. 17, 1920
    Brk. (Pitt.) June 23, 1930
10 **AL:**Bos. (Mil.) June 2, 1901
    Det. (Balt.) Sept. 20, 1983
    Tor. (Minn.) Sept. 4, 1992
    Bos. (Fla.) June 27, 2003
    KC (Det.) Sept. 9(1g), 2004

Most Hits, Both Clubs, Game
51 **NL:**Phil. (26) Chi. (25) Aug. 25, 1922
45 **AL:**Phil. (27) Bos. (18) July 8, 1902
    Det. (28) NY (17) Sept. 29, 1928
   Extra-Inning Game:
58 **AL:**Clev. (33) Phil. (25) July 10, 1932 (18 inn)
52 **NL:**NY (28) Pitt. (24) June 15, 1929 (14 inn)

Most Hits, 2 Consecutive Games
55 **NL:**Phil. Aug. 16-17, 1894
   Since 1900:
51 **AL:**Bos. June 7-8, 1950
49 **NL:**Pitt. Aug. 7-8, 1922

Fewest Hits, Game, 10 or more innings:
0 **NL:**See No-Hit Games
1 **AL:**Clev. (Chi.) Sept. 6, 1903 (10 inn)
    Bos. (StL.) Sept. 18, 1934 (10 inn)
    LA (NY) May 22, 1962 (12 inn)
    Oak. (Tex.) June 21, 1976 (10 inn)

Fewest Hits, Both Clubs, Game
1 **NL:**Chi. (0) LA (1) Sept. 9, 1965
2 **AL:**Clev. (1) StL. (1) Apr. 23, 1952
    Chi. (1) Balt. (1) June 21, 1956
    Balt. (1) KC (1) Sept. 12, 1964
    Det. (0) Balt. (2) Apr. 30, 1967

Fewest Hits, 2 Consecutive Games
2 **AA:**Balt. July 28-29, 1886
  NL:NY June 17-18, 1884
    Cin. July 5-6, 1900
    Bos. Sept. 28-30, 1916
    NY Sept. 10-11, 1965
    LA Sept. 26-27, 1981
    SF Sept. 24-25, 1986
  AL:NY Sept. 25-26, 1907
    StL. Sept. 25-27, 1910
    Chi. Aug. 10-11, 1917
    Mil. June 18-19, 1974
    Clev. Apr. 12-12, 1992
    Det. May 3-4, 1996

Fewest Hits, Doubleheader
2 **AL:**Clev. (Bos.) Apr. 12, 1992
3 **NL:**Brk. (StL.) Sept. 21, 1934
    NY (Phil.) June 21, 1964

Most Hits, No Runs, Game
14 **NL:**NY (Chi.) Sept. 14, 1913
   AL: Clev. (Wash.) July 10, 1928
   Extra-Inning Game:
15 **NL:**Bos. (Pitt.) July 10, 1901 (12 inn)
    Bos. (Pitt.) Aug. 1, 1918 (21 inn)
  AL: Bos. (Wash.) July 3, 1913 (15 inn)

Most Players, 1 or more Hits, Game
15 **NL:**Atl. (Fla.) Oct. 3, 1999
    StL.(NY) Sept. 28(2g), 1979 (11 inn)
14 **AL:**Clev. (StL.) Aug. 12, 1948

Most Players, 1 or more Hits, Both Clubs, Game
24 **NL:**StL.(15) NY (9) Sept. 28(2g), 1979 (11 inn)
    SF (13) LA (11) Sept. 19, 1998
23 **AL:**Minn. (12) Clev. (11) July 13, 1996

Most Players, 2 or more Hits, Game
10 **AA:**Brk. (Phil.) June 25, 1885
  NL: Pitt. (Phil.) Aug. 7, 1922
    NY (Phil.) Sept. 2, 1925
9 **AL:**By many, Last:
    Balt. (Clev.) Apr. 19, 2006

Most Players, 3 or more Hits, Game
8 **NL:**Chi. (Det.) Sept. 6, 1883
   Since 1900:
7 **NL:**Cin. (Pitt.) May 13, 1902
    Pitt. (Phil.) June 12, 1928
    NY (Atl.) July 4, 1985 (19 inn)
    Cin. (Hou.) Aug. 3, 1989
    Cin. (Col.) May 19, 1999
  AL:NY (Phil.) June 28, 1939
    Chi. (KC) Apr. 23, 1955
    Oak. (Tex.) July 1, 1979 (15 inn)

Most Players, 4 or more Hits, Game
7 **NL:**Chi. (Clev.) July 24, 1882
   Since 1900:
5 **NL:**SF (LA) May 13, 1958
4 **AL:**Det. (NY) Sept. 29, 1928
   Chi. (Phil.) Sept. 11, 1936
   Bos. (StL.) June 8, 1950
   Oak. (Tex.) July 1, 1979 (15 inn)
   Mil. (Tor.) Aug. 28, 1992
   Minn. (Clev.) June 4, 2002
   Bos. (TB) Sept. 20, 2005

Most Players, 5 or more Hits, Game
4 **NL:**Phil. (Lou.) Aug. 17, 1894
   Since 1900:
3 **NL:**NY (Cin.) June 9, 1901
   NY (Phil.) June 1, 1923
   AL: Det. (Wash.) July 30, 1917
   Clev. (Phil.) July 10, 1932 (18 inn)
   Wash. (Clev.) May 16, 1933 (12 inn)
   Chi. (Phil.) Sept. 11, 1936

Most Players, 6 or more Hits, Game
2 **AA:**Cin. (Pitt.) Sept. 12, 1883
   NL: Balt. (StL.) Sept. 3, 1897
   Since 1900:
1 By many clubs

Most Hits, Inning
18 **NL:**Chi. (Det.) Sept. 6, 1883, (7th)
    Since 1900:
16 **NL:**Cin. (Hou.) Aug. 3, 1989 (1st)
14 **AL:**Bos. (Det.) June 18, 1953 (7th)

Most Hits, Consecutive, Inning
10 **AL:**Bos. (Mil.) June 2, 1901 (9th)
    Det. (Balt.) Sept. 20, 1983 (1st; bb)
    Tor. (Minn.) Sept. 4, 1992 (2nd)
    Bos. (Fla.) June 27, 2003 (1st; bb)
    KC (Det.) Sept. 9(1g), 2004 (3rd; 3 bb)
    NL: StL. (Bos.) Sept. 17, 1920 (4th)
    StL. (Phil.) June 12, 1922 (6th)
    Chi. (Bos.) Sept. 7, 1929 1g (4th)
    Brk. (Pitt.) June 23, 1930 (6th)
    Phil. (Mil.) Sept. 22, 1999 (8th; sh, 2 hbp)

Most Hits, Consecutive, No Outs, 1st Inning
8 **NL:**Chi. (Pitt.) Apr. 21, 1973
   Phil. (Chi.) Aug. 5, 1975
   Pitt. (Atl.) Aug. 26, 1975
   AL: Oak. (Chi.) Sept. 27, 1981
   NY (Balt.) Sept. 25, 1990

Most Players, 2 or more Hits, Inning
7 **NL:**Cin. (Hou.) Aug. 3, 1989 (1st)
5 **AL:**Phil. (Bos.) July 8, 1902 (4th)
   NY (Phil.) Sept. 10, 1921 (9th)

EXTRA-BASE HITS

Most Seasons Leading League
29 **AL:**Bos. 1903, 12-14, 40-42, 44, 46, 49-50,
    54-57, 65, 67, 69-72, 75-79, 89, 2003-04
21 **NL:**StL. 1920-23, 26-28, 30, 34, 36-40, 42-
    44, 46, 49, 52, 80

Most Seasons, Consecutive, Leading League
5 **NL:**Chi. 1882-86
   StL. 1936-40
   Col. 1995-99
   AL:NY 1958-62
   Bos. 1975-79

Most Extra-Base Hits, Game
17 **AL:**Bos. (StL.) June 8, 1950
16 **NL:**Chi. (Buff.) July 3, 1883
    NL Since 1900:
15 **NL:**Phil. (Chi.) June 23, 1986
    Cin. (Col.) May 19, 1999

Most Extra-Base Hits, Both Clubs, Game
24 **NL:**StL. (13) Chi. (11) July 12, 1931
    AL: Clev. (15) Minn. (9) July 13, 1996

Fewest Extra-Base Hits, Game (Most Innings)
0 **NL:**Brk. (Bos.) May 1, 1920 (26 inn)
   AL: Det. (NY) Aug. 23, 1968 (19 inn)

**Fewest Extra-Base Hits, Both Clubs, Game
(Most Innings)**
0 **AL:**Chi. (NY) Aug. 21, 1933 (18 inn)
   NL: Bos. (Chi.) Sept. 21, 1901 (17 inn)

Most Extra-Base Hits, Inning
8 **NL:**Chi. (Det.) Sept. 6, 1883 (7th)
   Since 1900:
7 **AL:**StL. (Wash.) Aug. 7, 1922 (6th)
   Bos. (Phil.) Sept. 24, 1940 (6th)
   NY (StL.) May 3, 1951 (9th)
   Sea. (Bos.) Sept. 3, 1982 (6th)
   Tex. (NY) July 31, 2002 (2nd)
   NL: Bos. (StL.) Aug. 25, 1936 (1st)
   Phil. (Cin.) June 2, 1949 (8th)
   Phil. (Cin.) July 6, 1986 (3rd)

TOTAL BASES

Most Seasons, Leading League
28 **AL:**NY 1921, 23-24, 26-28, 30-31, 36-39,
    43-45, 47, 51, 53-62, 93
20 **NL:**Chi. 1876, 78, 80-82, 84-85, 88, 90,
    1906, 16, 30-31, 37, 58, 61, 83, 88-89, 200

Most Seasons, Consecutive, Leading League
10 **AL:**NY 1953-62
7 **NL:**Brk. 1949-55

Most Total Bases, Game
60 **AL:**Bos. (StL.) June 8, 1950
58 **NL:**Mtl. (Atl.) July 30, 1978

Most Total Bases, Both Clubs, Game
81 **NL:**Cin. (55) Col. (26) May 19, 1999
77 **AL:**NY (50) Phil. (27) June 3, 1932
    NY (47) TB (30) June 21, 2005
    Extra-Inning Game:
97 **NL:**Chi. (49) Phil. (48) May 17, 1979 (10 inn)
85 **AL:**Clev. (45) Phil. (40) July 10, 1932 (18 inn)

Fewest Total Bases, Game (Most Innings)
0 **AA:**Tol. (Brk.) Oct. 4, 1884 (10 inn)
   NL: Phil. (NY) July 4, 1908 1g (10 inn)
   Chi. (Cin.) May 2, 1917 (10 inn)
   Chi. (Cin.) Aug. 19, 1965 (10 inn)
   Hou. (Pitt.) July 12, 1997 (10 inn)
   AL: By many (9 inn)

Fewest Total Bases, Both Clubs, Game
2 **NL:**Chi. (0) LA (2) Sept. 9, 1965
   AL: Det. (0) Balt. (2) Apr. 30, 1967

Most Total Bases, 2 Consecutive Games
102 **AL:**Bos. June 7-8, 1950
89 **NL:**Pitt. June 20-22, 1925

Most Total Bases, Inning
29 **NL:**Chi. (Det.) Sept. 6, 1883 (7th)
    Since 1900:
27 **NL:**SF (Cin.) Aug. 23, 1961 (9th)
    AL:NY (TB) June 21, 2005 (8th)

SINGLES

Most Seasons Leading League
27 **NL:**StL. 1900-01, 20, 23, 39, 41-43, 45, 49, 54,
    56-57, 61-64, 71, 75, 77, 79, 85, 87-89, 92, 9
25 **AL:**Wash./Minn. 1918, 24, 26, 29, 32-33, 35,
    37-39, 41-42, 44-45, 69, 71, 73-77, 89, 92,
    96, 2006

Most Seasons, Consecutive, Leading League
   5 **AL:**Minn. 1973-77
      NL: Col. 1998-2002

Most Singles, Game
  28 **NL:**Phil. (Lou.) Aug. 17, 1894
      Bos. (Balt.) Apr. 20, 1896
      Since 1900:
  26 **AL:**Mil. (Tor.) Aug. 28, 1992
  23 **NL:**NY (Chi.) Sept. 21, 1931
      Hou. (Atl.) May 30, 1976

Most Singles, Both Clubs, Game
  37 **NL:**Balt. (21) Wash. (16) Aug. 8, 1896
      Since 1900:
  36 **NL:**NY (22) Cin. (14) June 9, 1901
      AL: Chi. (21) Bos. (15) Aug. 15, 1922

Most Singles, Inning
  12 **NL:**Cin. (Hou.) Aug. 3, 1989 (1st)
  11 **AL:**Bos. (Det.) June 18, 1953 (7th)

Most Singles, Consecutive, Inning
  10 **NL:**StL. (Bos.) Sept. 17, 1920 (4th)
   8 **AL:**Wash. (Clev.) May 7, 1951 (4th)
      Oak. (Chi.) Sept. 27, 1981 (1st)
      Balt. (Tex.) May 18, 1990 (1st)

OUBLES

Most Seasons Leading League
  40 **AL:**Bos. 1912, 14, 41-42, 44, 46, 48-50, 52,
      54-59, 62-64, 67, 70-72, 74-75, 79, 83,
      85-86, 88-89, 91, 93, 95, 97-98, 2002-05
  28 **NL:**StL. 1920-24, 28-31, 33-34, 36-39, 42,
      44, 46, 49, 52-54, 56, 63, 69, 79-80,
      2003

Most Seasons, Consecutive, Leading League
   8 **AL:**Clev. 1916-23
   5 **NL:**StL. 1920-24

Most Doubles, Game
  14 **NL:**Chi. (Buff.) July 3, 1883
      Since 1900:
  13 **NL:**StL. (Chi.) July 12, 1931
  12 **AL:**Bos. (Det.) July 29, 1990
      Clev. (Minn.) July 13, 1996

Most Doubles, Both Clubs, Game
  23 **NL:**StL. (13) Chi. (10) July 12(2g), 1931
  19 **AL:**KC (11) NY (8) Aug. 11, 2003

Most Doubles, Inning
   7 **NL:**Bos. (StL.) Aug. 25, 1936 (1st)
   6 **AL:**Wash. (Bos.) June 9, 1934 (8th)
      Tex. (NY) July 31, 2002 (2nd)

Most Doubles, Consecutive, Inning
   5 **AL:**Wash. (Bos.) June 9, 1934 (8th)
   4 **NL:**By many

Most Players, 2 or more Doubles, Inning
   3 **NL:**Bos. (StL.) Aug. 25, 1936 (1st)
   2 **AL:**NY (Bos.) July 3, 1932 (6th)
      Tor. (Balt.) June 26, 1978 (2nd)

RIPLES

Most Seasons Leading League
  46 **NL:**Pitt. 1893, 97, 99-1900, 1902-04, 08-
      09, 11-12, 16, 21-25, 28-30, 32-37, 43-
      44, 50, 55-56, 58, 61-62, 64, 66-67,
      69-72, 78, 89, 92, 97, 2004
  24 **AL:**Wash./Minn. 1923-24, 26, 31-37, 39,
      45-46, 48, 53-54, 56, 60, 68, 70, 81,
      96, 2000, 03

Most Seasons, Consecutive, Leading League
   7 **AL:**Wash. 1931-37
   6 **NL:**Pitt. 1932-37

Most Triples, Game
   8 **NL:**Pitt. (StL.) May 30(2g), 1925
   6 **AL:**Chi. (Mil.) Sept. 15, 1901
      Phil. (Det.) May 18, 1912
      Chi. (NY) Sept. 17, 1920
      Det. (NY) June 17, 1922

Most Triples, Both Clubs, Game
   9 **NL:**Wash. (6) Lou. (3), Aug. 24, 1893
      Pitt. (7) Cin. (2), Aug. 1, 1894
      Pitt. (6) Chi. (3) July 4, 1904
      Pitt. (8) StL. (1) May 30, 1925
      AL: Det. (6) NY (3) June 17, 1922

Fewest Triples, Game, (Most Innings)
   0 **NL:**Brk. (Bos.) May 1, 1920 (26 inn)
      AL: Mil. (Chi.) May 8, 1984 (25 inn)
      Chi. (Mil.) May 8, 1984 (25 inn)

Fewest Triples, Both Clubs, Game, (Most Innings)
   0 **NL:**StL. (NY) Sept. 11, 1974 (25 inn)
      AL: Mil. (Chi.) May 8, 1984 (25 inn)

Most Triples, Inning
   5 **AL:**Chi. (Mil.) Sept. 15, 1901 (8th)
   4 **NL:**Bos. (Troy) May 6, 1882 (8th)
      Balt. (StL.) July 27, 1892 (7th)
      StL. (Chi.) July 2, 1895 (1st)
      Chi. (StL.) Apr. 17, 1899 (4th)
      Brk. (Pitt.) Aug. 23, 1902 (3rd)
      Cin. (Bos.) July 22, 1926 (2nd)
      NY (Pitt.) July 17, 1936 (1st)

Most Triples, Consecutive, Inning
   4 **AL:**Bos. (Det.) May 6, 1934 (4th)
   3 **NL:**By many; Last:
      Mtl. (SD) May 6, 1981 (9th)

HOME RUNS

Most Seasons Leading League
  35 **AL:**NY 1915-17, 19-21, 23-31, 33, 36-47, 51,
      55-56, 58, 60-61, 2004
  29 **NL:**NY/SF 1904-05, 07, 09, 12, 17, 24-25,
      27-28, 31, 33-35, 37-39, 42-43, 45-48,
      54, 62-64, 72, 2001

Most Seasons, Consecutive, Leading League
  12 **AL:**NY 1936-47
   7 **NL:**Brk. 1949-55

Most Home Runs, At Home, Season
  153 **AL:**Tex. 2005
  149 **NL:**Col. 1996

Most Home Runs, Away, Season
  138 **NL:**SF 2001
  136 **AL:**Balt. 1996

Most Home Runs vs. One Club, Season
  48 **AL:**NY (KC) 1956
  44 **NL:**Cin. (Brk.) 1956

Most Home Runs, One Month
  58 **AL:**Balt. May 1987
      Sea. May 1999
  55 **NL:**NY July 1947
      StL. Apr. 2000
      Atl. May 2003

Most Home Runs, Game
  10 **AL:**Tor. (Balt.) Sept. 14, 1987
   9 **NL:**Cin. (Phil.) Sept. 4, 1999

Most Home Runs, Both Clubs, Game
12 **AL:**Det. (7) Chi. (5) May 28, 1995
     Det. (6) Chi. (6) July 2, 2002
11 **NL:**Chi. (7) NY (4) June 11, 1967
     Pitt. (6) Cin. (5) Aug. 12, 1966 (13 inn)
     Chi. (6) Cin. (5) July 28, 1977 (13 inn)
     Chi. (6) Phil. (5) May 17, 1979 (10 inn)

Fewest Home Runs, Both Clubs, Game (Most Innings)
0 **NL:**Bos. (Brk.) May 1, 1920 (26 inn)
   AL: Bos. (Phil.) Sept. 1, 1906 (24 inn)
     Det. (Phil.) July 21, 1945 (24 inn)

Most Home Runs, Opening Game
6 **NL:**NY (Mtl.) Apr. 4, 1988
5 **AL:**NY (Phil.) Apr. 12, 1932
     Bos. (Wash.) Apr. 12, 1965
     Mil. (Bos.) Apr. 10, 1980
     Clev. (Tex.) Apr. 27, 1995
     Minn. (KC) Apr. 1, 2002

Most Home Runs, Both Clubs, Opening Game
8 **NL:**SD (5) Col. (3) Apr. 4, 2005
7 **AL:**NY (5) Phil. (2) Apr. 12, 1932
     Bos. (5) Wash. (2) Apr. 12, 1965
     Mil. (5) Bos. (2) Apr. 10, 1980
     Mil. (4) Cal. (3) Apr. 2, 1996

Most Home Runs, Only Runs, Game
6 **AL:**Oak. (Minn.) Aug. 3, 1991
5 **NL:**NY (Chi.) June 16, 1930
     StL. (Brk.) Sept. 1, 1953
     Cin. (Mil.) Apr. 16, 1955
     Chi. (Pitt.) Apr. 21, 1964
     Pitt. (LA) May 7, 1973
     Col. (SF) May 9, 1994
     Atl. (Col.) Apr. 19, 1998 (1g)

Most Home Runs, Both Clubs, Only Runs, Game
5 **NL:**SF (3) Mil. (2) Aug. 30, 1962
     Mtl. (3) SD (2) May 16, 1986
     Col. (4) Mtl. (1) July 9, 1995
   ML:AL:Balt. (3) NL:Atl. (2) June 5, 1998
4 **AL:**Clev. (4) NY (0) Aug. 2, 1956
     NY (4) Balt. (0) May 13(1g), 1973
     Balt. (3) Det. (1) Apr. 24, 1977
     Tor. (4) Det. (0) May 23, 1983
     Det. (4) NY (0) June 14, 1985
     Det. (3) Cal. (1) July 31, 1991
     Minn. (3) KC (1) June 18, 1992
     KC (3) Chi. (1) Apr. 11, 1999

Most Games, Consecutive, 1 or more HRs, Season
27 **AL:**Tex. Aug. 11-Sept. 9, 2002 (55 hr)
25 **NL:**Atl. Apr. 18-May 13, 1998 (45 hr)

Most Games, Consecutive, 1 or more HRs, Start of Season
14 **AL:**Clev. Mar. 31-Apr. 17, 2002 (21 hr)
13 **NL:**Chi. Apr. 13-May 2, 1954 (28 hr)

Most Home Runs, 2-Game Span, Season
14 **NL:**Cin. Sept. 4-5, 1999
13 **AL:**NY June 28 (dh), 1939
     Ana. June 3-4, 2003

Most Home Runs, 3-Game Span, Season
16 **AL:**Bos. June 17-19, 1977
15 **NL:**LA June 29-July 1, 1996
     Cin. Sept 3-5, Sept. 4-6, 1999
     Chi. Aug. 10-12, 2002

Most Home Runs, 4-Game Span, Season
18 **AL:**Bos. June 16-19, 1977
     Oak. June 25-29, 1996
   NL: Hou. Aug 13-16, 2000

Most Home Runs, 5-Game Span, Season
21 **AL:**Bos. June 14-19, 1977
   NL: Cin. Sept. 4-7, 1999

Most Home Runs, 6-Game Span, Season
24 **AL:**Bos. June 17-22, 1977
23 **NL:**Atl. July 9-18, 2006

Most Home Runs, 7-Game Span, Season
26 **AL:**Bos. June 16-22, 1977
24 **NL:**NY July 5-11, 1954
     Cin. Sept. 1-7, 1999
     Atl. July 8-18, 9-19, 14-21, 2006

Most Home Runs, 8-Game Span, Season
29 **AL:**Bos. June 14-22, 1977
27 **NL:**Atl. July 19-21, 2006

Most Home Runs, 9-Game Span, Season
30 **AL:**Bos. June 14-22, 16-24, 1977
   NL: Atl. July 14-24, 2006

Most Home Runs, 10-Game Span, Season
33 **AL:**Bos. June 14-24, 1977
   NL: Atl. July 9-24, 2006

Most Home Runs, 15-Game Span, Season
39 **NL:**Mil. June 8-24, 1961
     Atl. July 2-21, 6-26, 7-27, 2006
38 **AL:**Minn. Apr. 28-May 14, May 1-16, 1964
     Bos. June 8-24, 1977
     Balt. May 5-19, 7-22, & 8-23, 1987
     Oak. June 14-29, June 17-July 2, 1996
     Sea. May 11-28, 1999
     Chi. July 17-Aug. 1, 2003
     Bos. July 22-Aug 7, July 23-Aug 8, 2003
     NY July 3-21, July 4-22, 2005

Most Home Runs, 20-Game Span, Season
51 **AL:**Sea. Apr. 28-May 19, 1999
49 **NL:**Atl. July 1-26, 2-27, 2006

Most Home Runs, 25-Game Span, Season
59 **AL:**Oak. June 25-July 23, 1996
     Sea. Apr. 23-May 19, Apr. 28-May 25, & Apr. 29-May 26, 1999
58 **NL:**Atl. May 15-June 12, May 16-June 13, 200

Most Games, Consecutive, 2 or more HRs
9 **AL:**Clev. May 13-21, 1962
     Balt. May 8-16, 1987
     Balt. Aug. 3-11, 1996
8 **NL:**Mil. July 19-26, 1956
     Chi. June 25-July 1, 1961
     Mil. Aug. 8-15, 1965
     Pitt. May 23-31, 2006
     Cin. June 25-July 3, 2006

Most Home Runs, Inning
5 **NL:**NY (Cin.) June 6, 1939 (4th)
     Phil. (Cin.) June 2, 1949 (8th)
     SF (Cin.) Aug. 23, 1961 (9th)
     Mil. (Cin.) Apr. 22, 2006 (4th)
   AL: Minn. (KC) June 9, 1966 (7th)

Most Home Runs, Consecutive, Inning
4 **NL:**Mil. (Cin.) June 8, 1961 (7th)
     LA (SD) Sept. 18, 2006 (9th)
   AL: Clev. (LA) July 31, 1963 (6th)
     Minn. (KC) May 2, 1964 (11th)

Most Home Runs, Both Clubs, Inning
5 **AL:**StL. (3) Phil. (2) June 8, 1928 (9th)
   Det. (4) NY (1) June 23, 1950 (4th)
   Minn. (5) KC (0) June 9, 1966 (7th)
   Balt. (4) Bos. (1) May 17, 1967 (7th)
   Minn. (4) Oak. (1) May 16, 1983 (9th)
   Clev. (3) Tex. (2) June 29, 1984 (5th)
   Balt. (3) Bos. (2) Sept. 10, 1985 (8th)
   Clev. (3) Mil. (2) Apr. 25, 1997 (4th)
   Det. (3) Balt. (2) Apr. 7, 2000 (5th)
   Sea. (3) KC (2) Aug. 27, 2004 (5th)
  NL:NY (5) Cin. (0) June 6, 1939 (4th)
   Phil. (5) Cin. (0) June 2, 1949 (8th)
   NY (3) Bos. (2) July 6, 1951 (3rd)
   Cin. (3) Brk. (2) June 11, 1954 (7th)
   SF (5) Cin. (0) Aug. 23, 1961 (9th)
   Phil. (3) Chi. (2) Apr. 17, 1964 (5th)
   Chi. (3) Atl. (2) July 3, 1967 (1st)
   Pitt. (3) Atl. (2) Aug. 1, 1970 (7th)
   Cin. (3) Chi. (2) July 28, 1977 (1st)
   SF (3) Atl. (2) May 25, 1979 (4th)
   Cin. (4) Atl. (1) June 19, 1994 (1st)
   SF (3) Pitt. (2) July 27(2g), 1997 (9th)
   Col. (3) StL. (2) July 31, 1999 (3rd)
   Atl. (4) SF (1) May 20, 2001 (7th)
   Mil. (5) Cin. (0) Apr. 22, 2006 (4th)

Most Home Runs, None on Base, Game
7 **AL:**Bos. (Tor.) July 4, 1977
6 **NL:**NY (Phil.) Aug. 13, 1939
   NY (Cin.) June 24, 1950
   Atl. (Chi.) Aug. 3, 1967
   Chi. (SD) Aug. 19, 1970
   Atl. (Cin.) May 31, 1996
  Extra-Inning Game:
7 **NL:**Atl. May 28, 2006 (11 inn)

**Most Home Runs, None on Base,
Both Clubs, Game**
10 **AL:**Det. (5) Chi. (5) May 28, 1995
8 **NL:**Col. (4) Mtl. (4) Aug. 14, 1999

Most Home Runs, None on Base, Inning
4 **NL:**NY (Phil.) Aug. 13, 1939 (4th)
   Atl. (SF) May 20, 2001 (7th)
   LA (SD) Sept. 18, 2006 (9th)
  AL: Clev. (LA) July 31, 1963 (6th)
   Minn. (KC) May 2, 1964 (11th)
   Minn. (KC) June 9, 1966 (7th)
   Bos. (NY) June 17, 1977 (1st)
   Bos. (Tor.) July 4, 1977 (8th)
   Bos. (Mil.) May 31, 1980 (4th)
   Minn. (NY) May 2, 1992 (5th)
   Balt. (Cal.) Sept 5, 1995 (2nd)
   Sea. (Oak.) Sept. 21, 1996 (3rd)

Most Home Runs, Two Out, Inning
5 **NL:**NY (Cin.) June 6, 1939 (4th)
4 **AL:**Bos. (Det.) July 18, 1998 (4th)
   Tex. (NL:Hou.) May 21, 2005 (2nd)

Most Players, 50 or more Home Runs, Season
2 **AL:**NY 1961
1 **NL:**By many clubs

Most Players, 40 or more Home Runs, Season
3 **NL:**Atl. 1973
   Col. 1996, 97
2 **AL:**NY 1927, 30-31, 61
   Det. 1961
   Bos. 1969, 2004-05
   Sea. 1996-99
   Tor. 1999-2000
   Tex. 2001-02
   Chi. 2006

Most Players, 30 or more Home Runs, Season
4 **NL:**LA 1977, 97
   Col. 1995-97, 99
   Atl. 1998
   Chi. 2004
  AL: Ana. & Tor. 2000
   Chi. 2006

Most Players, 20 or more Home Runs, Season
7 **AL:**Balt. 1996
   Tor. 2000
   Tex. 2005
6 **NL:**Mil. 1965
   Atl. 2003

Most Players, Home Runs, Game
8 **NL:**Cin. (Phil.) Sept. 4, 1999
7 **AL:**Balt. (Bos.) May 17, 1967
   Oak. (Cal.) June 27, 1996
   Det. (Tor.) June 20, 2000
   Tex. (NL:Hou.) May 21, 2005

Most Players, Home Runs, Both Clubs, Game
9 **NL:**NY (5) Brk. (4) Sept. 2, 1939
   NY (6) Pitt. (3) July 11, 1954
   Chi. (5) Pitt. (4) Apr. 21, 1964
   Cin. (6) Atl. (3) Apr. 21, 1970
   LA (5) Atl. (4) Apr. 24, 1977
   Cin. (5) Chi. (4) July 28, 1977 (13 inn)
   Chi. (6) Mil. (3) Sept. 12, 1998
   Chi. (5) Col. (4) June 22, 1999
   Cin. (8) Phil. (1) Sept. 4, 1999
  AL:NY (5) Det. (4) June 23, 1950
   Minn. (5) Bos. (4) May 25, 1965
   Balt. (7) Bos. (2) May 17, 1967
   Cal. (5) Clev. (4) Aug. 30, 1970
   Bos. (5) Mil. (4) May 22(1g), 1977
   Cal. (5) Oak. (4) Apr. 23, 1985
   Balt. (5) Cal. (4) July 1, 1994
   Det. (5) Balt. (4) Apr. 7, 2000
   Det. (7) Tor. (2) June 20, 2000
   Det. (5) Chi. (4) July 2, 2002
  ML:NL:Col. (5) AL:Sea. (4) June 9, 1999
   AL:Tex. (7) NL:Hou. (2) May 21, 2005
   AL:Det. (6) NL:Chi. (3) June 18, 2006

Most Players, 3 or more Home Runs, Game
2 **NL:**Mil. (Ari.) Sept. 25, 2001
1 **AL:**By many clubs

Most Players, 2 or more Home Runs, Game
3 **NL:**Pitt. (StL.) Aug. 16, 1947
   Chi. (StL.) Apr. 16, 1955 (14 inn)
   NY (Pitt.) July 8, 1956
   Cin. (Mil.) Aug. 18, 1956
   Phil. (NY) Sept. 8, 1998
   Col. (Mtl.) Aug. 14, 1999
   Hou. (Mil.) Sept. 9, 2000
   SF (Col.) July 2, 2002
  AL: Bos. (StL.) June 8, 1950
   NY (Bos.) May 30, 1961
   Tor. (Balt.) Sept. 14, 1987
   Tor. (Cal.) July 14, 1990
   Det. (Chi.) May 28, 1995
   Sea. (Mil.) July 31, 1996
   Ana. (TB) Apr. 21, 2000
   Minn. (Mil.) July 12, 2001
   Bos. (NY) July 4, 2003

**Most Players, 2 or more Home Runs, Both
Clubs, Game**
4 **NL:**Pitt. (3) StL. (1) Aug. 16, 1947
   Col. (3) Mtl. (1) Aug. 14, 1999
  AL: Det. (3) Chi. (1) May 28, 1995

Most Players, 2 or more Home Runs, Inning
2 **AL:**Sea. (Chi.) May 2, 2002
   (1st: Boone, Cameron)
1 **NL:**By many teams

GRAND SLAM HOME RUNS

Most Grand Slam HRs, Game
2   By many clubs; Last:
    NL:NY (Chi.) July 16, 2006
    AL: Balt. (Det.) June 4, 2005

Most Grand Slam HRs, Both Clubs, Game
3   **AL:**Balt. (2) Tex. (1) Aug. 6, 1986
    NL: Chi. (2) Hou. (1) June 3, 1987

Most Grand Slam HRs, 2 Consecutive Games
3   **NL:**Brk. Sept. 23(2g)-24, 1901
    Pitt. June 20-22(2g), 1925
    LA May 20-21, 2000
    NY July 16-18, 2006
    AL: Mil. Apr. 10-12(2g), 1980
    Chi. May 18-19, 1996
    Sea. Aug. 7-8(1g), 2000

Most Games, Consecutive, Grand Slam HR
3   **NL:**Clev. June 15-17(2g), 1895
    AL: Mil. Apr. 7- 9, 1978
    Det. Aug. 10-12, 1993
    Chi. June 23-25, 2006
    NL Since 1900:
2   By many clubs

Most Grand Slam HRs, Inning
2   **NL:**Chi. (Pitt.) Aug. 16, 1890
    (5th: Burns, Kittredge)
    Hou. (NY) July 30, 1969
    (9th: Menke, Wynn)
    StL. (LA) Apr. 23, 1999
    (3rd: Tatis 2)
    NY (Chi.) July 16, 2006
    (6th: Floyd, Beltran)
    AL: Minn. (Clev.) July 18, 1962
    (1st: Allison, Killebrew)
    Mil. (Bos.) Apr. 12, 1980
    (2nd: Cooper, Money)
    Balt. (Tex.) Aug. 6, 1986
    (4th: Sheets, Dwyer)

Grand Slam HRs, Both Clubs, Inning
2   **NL:**Chi. (NY) May 18, 1950 (6th)
    Atl. (Cin.) Sept. 12(1g), 1974 (2nd)
    Chi. (Pitt.) Sept. 9, 1992 (6th)
    Atl. (LA) May 13, 2005 (8th)
    StL. (NY) Aug. 22, 2006 (5th)
    AL: Bos. (Wash.) June 18, 1961 (9th)
    Clev. (Tex.) Apr. 14, 1980 (1st)
    ML:AL:Ana. (NL:Ari.) June 9, 1998 (3rd)

RUNS BATTED IN (Since 1920)

Most Runs Batted In, Game
29 **AL:**Bos. (StL.) June 8, 1950
26 **NL:**NY (Brk.) Apr. 30, 1944
    Chi. (Col.) Aug. 18, 1995

Most Runs Batted In, Both Clubs, Game
43 **NL:**Chi. (24) Phil. (19) Aug. 25, 1922
35 **AL:**Bos. (21) Phil. (14) June 29, 1950
    Extra-Inning Game:
45 **NL:**Phil. (23) Chi. (22) May 17, 1979 (10 inn)

Fewest RBIs, Both Clubs, Game (Most Innings)
0   **NL:**NY (Hou.) Apr. 15, 1968 (24 inn)
    AL: Wash. (Det.) July 16, 1909 (18 inn)
    Wash. (Chi.) May 15, 1918 (18 inn)

Most Runs Batted In, 2 Consecutive Game
49 **AL:**Bos. June 7-8, 1950
39 **NL:**Pitt. June 20-22, 1925

Most Runs Batted In, Inning
17 **AL:**Bos. (Det.) June 18, 1953 (7th)
15 **NL:**Brk. (Cin.) May 21, 1952 (1st)

Most Players, 100 or more RBIs, Season
5   **AL:**NY 1936
4   **NL:**Pitt. 1925
    Chi. 1929
    Phil. 1929
    Col. 1996-97, 99
    Ari. 1999
    Atl. 2003

SACRIFICE HITS

Most Sacrifice Hits, Season (Includes sac flies)
310 **AL:**Bos. 1917
270 **NL:**Chi. 1908

Most Sacrifice Hits, Game
8   **AL:**NY (Bos.) May 4, 1918
    Chi. (Det.) July 11, 1927
    StL. (Clev.) July 23, 1928
    Tex. (Chi.) Aug. 1, 1977
    NL: Cin. (Phil.) May 6, 1926

Most Sacrifice Hits, Both Clubs, Game
11 **AL:**Wash. (7) Bos. (4) Sept. 1, 1926
9   **NL:**NY (5) Chi. (4) Aug. 29, 1921
    Cin. (8) Phil. (1) May 6, 1926
    SF (6) SD (3) May 23, 1970 (15 inn)

Most Sacrifice Hits, Inning
3   **AL:**Clev. (StL.) July 10, 1949 (5th)
    Det. (Balt.) July 12, 1970 (2nd)
    Oak. (KC) June 26(1g), 1977 (5th)
    Clev. (Chi.) June 8, 1980 (6th)
    Sea. (Cal.) Apr. 29, 1984 (6th)
    Cal. (Det.) June 5, 1977 (8th)
    Minn. (Mil.) July 26, 1991 (8th)
    NL: Chi. (Mil.) Aug. 1962 (6th)
    Phil. (LA) Sept. 23, 1967 (7th)
    LA (SF) May 23, 1972 (6th)
    Hou. (SD) Apr. 29, 1975 (7th)
    Hou. (Atl.) July 6, 1975 (9th)
    Pitt. (StL.) Sept. 20, 1988 (8th)
    Hou. (AL:Tex.) June 26, 2005 (7th)

SACRIFICE FLIES (1908 to 1930, 1939, since 195

Most Seasons Leading League
10 **NL:**Pitt. 1962, 65, 70, 82, 87-92
7   **AL:**NY 1962, 74-75, 85, 95-97
    Bos. 1959, 72, 75, 87-88, 2003, 05

Most Seasons, Consecutive, Leading League
6   **NL:**Pitt. 1987-92
3   **AL:**Balt. 1967-69
    Mil. 1990-92
    NY 1995-97

Most Sacrifice Flies, Game
5   **AL:**Sea. (Oak.) Aug. 7, 1988
    NL: Col. (Pitt.) June 7, 2006

Most Sacrifice Flies, Both Clubs, Game
5   By many; Last:
    AL: Bos. (4) Oak. (1) July 25, 2006
    NL: Col. (5) Pitt. (0) June 7, 2006

Most Sacrifice Flies, Inning
3   **AL:**Chi. (Clev.) July 1(1g), 1962 (5th)
    NY (Det.) June 29, 2000 (4th)
    NY (Ana.) Aug. 19, 2000 (3rd)
    NL:NY (AL:NY) June 24, 2005 (2nd)

WALKS

Most Seasons Leading League
27 **AL:**NY 1902-03, 10, 13-14, 26-28, 30-34,
36-39, 43, 45, 53, 94-95, 97-98, 2002-04
21 **NL:**NY/SF 1904-08, 20-21, 23, 50-51, 64,
68-71, 81-82, 96, 98, 2000, 04

Most Seasons, Consecutive, Leading League
7 **AL:**Clev. 1917-23
6 **NL:**Brk. 1952-57

Most Walks, Game
19 **AA:**Lou. (Clev.) Sept. 21, 1887
18 **AL:**Det. (Phil.) May 9, 1916
Clev. (Bos.) May 20, 1948
17 **NL:**Chi. (NY) May 30, 1887
Brk. (Phil.) Aug. 27, 1903
NY (Brk.) Apr. 30, 1944
Extra-Inning Game
20 **AL:**Bos. (Det.) Sept. 17, 1920 (12 inn)
18 **NL:**Phil. (AL:Balt.) July 2, 2004 (16 inn)

Most Walks, Both Clubs, Game
30 **AL:**Det. (18) Phil. (12) May 9, 1916
Wash. (19) Clev. (11) Sept. 14, 1971
(20 inn)
26 **NL:**Hou. (13) SF (13) May 4(2g), 1975

Fewest Walks, Game (Most Innings)
0 **NL:**LA (Mtl.) Aug. 23, 1989 (22 inn)
AL: Phil. (Bos.) July 4, 1905 (20 inn)

Fewest Walks, Both Clubs, Game (Most Innings)
0 **AL:**Wash. (Det.) July 22, 1904 (13 inn)
Bos. (Phil.) Sept. 9, 1907 (13 inn)
NL: Chi. (LA) July 27, 1980 (12 inn)

Most Walks, Doubleheader
25 **NL:**NY (Brk.) Apr. 30, 1944
23 **AL:**Clev. (Phil.) June 18, 1950

Most Walks, Both Clubs, Doubleheader
42 **NL:**Hou. (21) SF (21) May 4, 1975
32 **AL:**Balt. (18) Chi. (14) May 28, 1954
Det. (20) KC (12) Aug. 1, 1962
Tex. (17) Chi. (15) May 24, 1995

Fewest Walks, Doubleheader (Most Innings)
0 **NL:**StL. (NY) July 2, 1933 (27 inn)
AL: Det. (Phil.) Aug. 28, 1908 (20 inn)

Fewest Walks, Both Clubs, Doubleheader
1 **NL:**Brk. (0) Cin. (1) Aug. 6, 1905
Pitt. (0) Cin. (1) Sept. 7, 1924
StL. (0) Brk. (1) Sept. 22, 1929
2 **AL:**Det. (0) Phil. (2) Aug. 28, 1908 (20 inn)
Chi. (1) Phil. (1) July 12, 1912
Chi. (0) Clev. (2) Sept. 6, 1930

Most Walks, 2 Consecutive Games
29 **AL:**Det. May 9-10, 1916
25 **NL:**NY Apr. 30 (dh), 1944
Hou. Apr. 28-29, 2000

Most Walks, No Runs, Game
11 **AL:**StL. (NY) Aug. 1, 1941
Wash. (NY) May 21, 1970
10 **NL:**Chi. (Cin.) Aug. 19(1g), 1965 (10 inn)
NY (Hou.) July 6, 1976 (10 inn)
Mtl. (NY) Apr. 24, 1982
SF (Ari.) May 29, 2001 (18 inn)
Ari. (SD) Sept. 2, 2001 (13 inn)

Most Walks, Inning
11 **AL:**NY (Wash.) Sept. 11(1g), 1949 (3rd)
9 **NL:**Cin. (Chi.) Apr. 24, 1957 (5th)

Most Walks, Consecutive, Inning
7 **AL:**Chi. (Wash.) Aug. 28, 1909 (2nd)
NL: Atl. (Pitt.) May 25, 1983 (3rd)

INTENTIONAL WALKS (Since 1955)

Most Seasons, Leading League
11 **NL:**SF 1964, 70-71, 86, 93, 97, 2001-04, 06
9 **AL:**NY 1955, 57-58, 61-62, 64, 78, 88, 99

Most Seasons, Consecutive, Leading League
4 **NL:**SF 2001-04
3 **AL:**Chi. 1994-96

Most Intentional Walks, Game
6 **NL:**SF (StL.) July 19, 1975
5 **AL:**Cal. (NY) May 10, 1967
Wash. (Clev.) Sept. 2, 1970
NY (Cal.) Aug. 29, 1978
Oak. (Clev.) July 16, 1991
Extra-Inning Game
7 **NL:**NY (Chi.) May 2, 1956 (17 inn)
Hou. (Phil.) July 15, 1984 (16 inn)
Chi. (Cin.) May 22, 1990 (16 inn)
6 **AL:**KC (Tex.) June 6, 1991 (19 inn)

Most Intentional Walks, Both Clubs, Game
7 **NL:**NY (4) Pitt. (3) June 27, 1979
6 **AL:**Cal. (5) NY (1) May 10, 1967
Extra-Inning Game
11 **NL:**NY (7) Chi. (4) May 2, 1956 (17 inn)
7 **AL:**By many; Last:
Sea. (6) NY (1) May 15, 2004 (13 inn)

Most Intentional Walks, Inning
3 By many clubs

HIT BY PITCH

Most Hit By Pitch, Game
6 **AA:**Brk. (Balt.) Apr. 25, 1887
NL: Lou. (StL.) July 31 (1g), 1897
AL:NY (Wash.) June 20, 1913
NL Since 1900:
5 Atl. (Cin.) July 2, 1969
Hou. (LA) Apr. 19, 2000

Most Hit By Pitch, Both Clubs, Game
9 **NL:**Det. (5) Ind. (4) Apr. 30, 1887
Since 1900:
7 **AL:**Det. (4) Wash. (3) Aug. 24, 1914
Minn. (4) KC (3) Apr. 13, 1971
KC (5) Tex. (2) Sept. 3, 1989
Oak. (5) Ana. (2) June 7, 2001
6 **NL:**Brk. (4) NY (2) July 17, 1900
Mtl. (4) Fla. (2) July 29, 1994
Fla. (4) Phil. (2) May 16, 1995 (10 inn)
Pitt. (4) Fla. (2) May 22, 1999
Pitt. (4) Hou. (2) Sept. 16, 2000 (10 inn)

Most Hit By Pitch, Inning
    4 **NL:**Bos. (Pitt.) Aug. 19(1g), 1893 (2nd)
    Since 1900:
    3 **NL:**NY (Pitt.) Sept. 25, 1905 (1st)
       Chi. (Bos.) Sept. 17, 1928 (9th)
       Phil. (Cin.) May 15(1g), 1960 (8th)
       Atl. (Cin.) July 2, 1969 (2nd)
       Cin. (Pitt.) May 1, 1974 (1st)
       StL. (Mtl.) Aug. 15, 1992 (1st)
       SD (Col.) June 28, 1994 (11th)
       Hou. (LA) Sept. 13, 1997 (1st)
       Fla. (Hou.) Aug. 3, 1998 (8th)
       Atl. (SD) Aug. 16, 2000 (8th)
       StL. (SD) Sept. 26, 2000 (8th)
       Chi. (SD) Apr. 22, 2003 (4th)
       Col. (LA) July 23, 2003 (4th)
       Pitt. (Chi.) May 28(1g), 2004 (5th)
       Mil. (Col.) June 22, 2004 (7th)
       LA (Atl.) Aug. 21, 2004 (1st)
       Mil. (SF) July 31, 2005 (6th)
    AL:NY (Wash.) June 20(2g), 1913 (1st)
       Clev. (NY) Aug. 25, 1921 (8th)
       Bos. (NY) June 20, 1954 (3rd)
       Balt. (Cal.) Aug. 9, 1968 (7th)
       Cal. (Chi.) Sept. 10, 1977 (1st)
       Cal. (Clev.) July 8, 1988 (4th)
       Oak. (Minn.) Sept. 28, 1988 (2nd)
       Oak. (Sea.) Sept. 22, 1996 (5th)
       Tor. (Chi.) July 15(2g), 1998 (7th)
       TB (Ana.) May 22, 1999 (3rd)
       Bos. (KC) Apr. 30, 2003 (9th)
       Ana. (Balt.) May 14, 2004 (2nd)
       Chi. (Clev.) Apr. 5, 2006 (6th)

STRIKEOUTS

Most Strikeouts, Game
    20 **AL:**Sea. (Bos.) Apr. 29, 1986
        Det. (Bos.) Sept. 18, 1996
        NL: Hou. (Chi.) May 6, 1998
        Extra-Inning Game:
    26 **ML:**Mil. (Ana.) June 8, 2004 (17 inn)
        AL: Cal. (Oak.) July 9, 1971 (20 inn)
    24 **NL:**Mil. (Chi.) May 15, 2003 (17 inn)

Most Strikeouts, Both Clubs, Game
    31 **AL:**Tex. (18) Sea. (13) July 13, 1997
    30 **NL:**Hou. (20) Chi. (10) May 6, 1998
        Extra-Inning Game:
    43 **AL:**Cal. (26) Oak. (17) July 9, 1971 (20 inn)
    40 **NL:**SF (20) SD (20) June 19, 2001 (15 inn)

Most Strikeouts, 2 Consecutive Games
    37 **NL:**Chi. May 30-31, 2003
    36 **AL:**Sea. Apr. 29-30, 1986

Most Strikeouts, Doubleheader
    27 **NL:**NY (Ari.) Apr. 27, 2003
    25 **AL:**LA (Clev.) July 31, 1963
        Including Extra-Inning Game:
    31 **NL:**Pitt. (Phil.) Sept. 22, 1958 (23 inn)
        NY (Phil.) Oct. 2, 1965 (27 inn)
    27 **AL:**Clev. (Bos.) Aug. 25, 1963 (24 inn)

Most Strikeouts, Both Clubs, Doubleheader
    44 **AL:**Det. (24) Balt. (20) Sept. 8, 1980
    41 **NL:**Phil. (26) NY (15) Sept. 9, 1970
        SD (26) NY (15) May 29, 1971
        Chi. (21) NY (20) Sept. 15, 1971
        Including Extra-Inning Game:
    51 **NL:**NY (30) Phil. (21) Sept. 26, 1975 (24 inn)
    48 **AL:**KC (24) Det. (24) June 17, 1967 (28 inn)

Most Strikeouts, Start of Game
    9 **NL:**Clev. (NY) Aug. 28, 1884
    Since 1900:
    8 **NL:**LA (Hou.) Sept. 23, 1986
    7 **AL:**Tex. (Chi.) May 28, 1986

Most Strikeouts, Consecutive, Game
    10 **NL:**SD (NY) Apr. 22, 1970
    8 **AL:**Bos. (Cal.) July 9, 1972
        Mil. (Cal.) Aug. 7, 1973
        Cal. (NY) May 4, 1981
        Sea. (Bos.) Apr. 29, 1986
        NY (Hou.) June 11, 2003

Fewest Strikeouts, Game (Most Innings)
    0 **NL:**NY (Cin.) June 26, 1893 (17 inn)
       Cin. (NY) Aug. 27, 1920 (17 inn)
    AL: Clev. (NY) June 7, 1936 (16 inn)

Fewest Strikeouts, Both Clubs, Game (Most Inning
    0 **AL:**Chi. (StL.) July 7, 1931 (12 inn)
       NL: Bos. (NY) Apr. 19, 1928 (10 inn)

Fewest Strikeouts, Doubleheader (Most Innings)
    0 **NL:**Pitt. (Phil.) July 12, 1924 (21 inn)
       AL: Bos. (StL.) July 28, 1917 (20 inn)

Fewest Strikeouts, Both Clubs, Doubleheader
    1 **AL:**Bos. (0) Clev. (1) Aug. 28, 1926
    2 **NL:**NY (0) Brk. (2) Aug. 13, 1932
       StL. (0) Pitt. (2) Sept. 6, 1948

Most Strikeouts, Inning
    4 **AA:**Pitt. (Phil.) Sept. 30, 1885 (7th)
       NL: Chi. (NY) Oct. 4, 1888 (5th)
       Cin. (NY) May 15, 1906 (5th)
       StL. (Chi.) May 27(1g), 1956 (6th)
       Mil. (Cin.) Aug. 11(1g), 1959 (6th)
       Cin. (LA) Apr. 12, 1962 (3rd)
       Phil. (LA) Apr. 17, 1965 (2nd)
       Pitt. (StL.) June 7, 1966 (4th)
       Mtl. (Chi.) July 31(1g), 1974 (2nd,cons)
       Pitt. (Atl.) July 29, 1977 (6th)
       Chi. (Cin.) May 17, 1984 (3rd,cons)
       Chi. (Hou.) Sept. 3, 1986 (5th)
       StL. (Atl.) Aug. 22, 1989 (5th)
       SF (Cin.) June 4, 1990 (7th)
       Chi. (Atl.) June 7, 1995 (9th, cons)
       SD (Col.) Sept. 19, 1995 (6th)
       Atl. (NY) Sept. 13, 1996 (9th)
       Chi. (Col.) July 25, 1996 (9th)
       Mtl. (Fla.) Sept. 16, 1998 (4th, cons)
       Chi. (Fla.) Apr. 28, 1999 (7th)
       SD (SF) July 22, 1999 (7th)
       SF (Mtl.) Aug. 17, 1999 (7th, cons)
       Mil. (Mtl.) May 5, 2000 (9th)
       Fla. (Cin.) July 22, 2001 (7th)
       NY (Fla.) July 5, 2002 (1st)
       Mil. (Chi.) Sept. 2(2g), 2002 (4th, cons
       Col. (LA) May 22, 2003 (2nd)
       Mil. (Hou.) June 13, 2004 (7th)
       Mil. (NY) Aug. 3, 2004 (8th)
       Cin. (Wash.) Apr. 26, 2006 (8th)
       Ari (LA) Sept. 23, 2006 (2nd)
    4 **AL:**Bos. (Wash.) Apr. 15, 1911 (5th)
       Phil. (Clev.) June 11, 1916 (6th)
       Chi. (LA) May 18, 1961 (7th)
       Wash. (Clev.) Sept. 2, 1964 (7th)
       Cal. (Balt.) May 29, 1970 (4th)
       Sea. (Clev.) July 21, 1978 (5th, cons)
       Balt. (Tex.) Aug. 2, 1987 (2nd, cons)
       NY (Tex.) July 4, 1988 (1st)
       Bos. (Det.) Aug. 13, 1988 (6th)
       Bos. (Sea.) Sept. 9, 1990 (1st)
       Cal. (Clev.) Apr. 11, 1994 (9th)
       Det. (Clev.) May 14, 1994 (9th)
       Tor. (KC) Sept. 3, 1996 (4th, cons)
       Det. (Chi.) July 21, 1997 (7th, cons)
       TB (Oak.) July 27, 1998 (4th)
       NY (Ana.) May 12, 1999 (3rd)
       KC (Bos.) Aug. 10, 1999 (9th)
       Det. (Ana.) Aug. 15, 1999 (1st, cons)
       Tex. (Clev.) Apr. 16, 2000 (3rd)
       Tex. (Oak.) June 30, 2001 (7th)
       Tex. (Sea.) Apr. 4, 2003 (9th, cons)
       NY (Hou.) June 11, 2003 (8th, cons)

GROUNDED INTO DOUBLE PLAYS

Most Grounded Into Double Plays, Game
```
 7  NL:SF (Hou.) May 4, 1969
 6  AL:Wash. (Clev.) Aug. 5, 1948
    Bos. (Cal.) May 1, 1966
    Balt. (KC) May 6, 1972
    Clev. (NY) Apr. 29, 1975
    Tor. (Minn.) Aug. 29(1g), 1977 (10 inn)
    Bos. (Det.) Apr. 13, 1984
    Mil. (Chi.) May 8, 1984 (25 inn)
    Bos. (Chi.) Apr. 27, 1989 (16 inn)
    Bos. (Minn.) July 18, 1990
    Det. (Tor.) Apr. 16, 1996
    TB (NY) June 17(1g), 2003
```

Most Grounded Into Double Plays, Both Clubs, Game
```
 9  AL:Bos. (6) Cal. (3) May 1, 1966
    Bos. (6) Minn. (3) July 18, 1990
 8  NL:Bos. (5) Chi. (3) Sept. 18, 1928
    Extra-Inning Game:
10  NL:NY (6) SF (4) Aug. 21, 2004 (12 inn)
```

STOLEN BASES

Most Seasons Leading League
```
29  AL:Chi. 1901-04, 17, 19, 23-24, 28-29, 39,
    41-43, 46-47, 49, 51-61, 66
25  NL:Brk./LA 1890-92, 1900, 03, 38, 42, 46-
    53, 55, 58-65, 70
```

Most Seasons, Consecutive, Leading League
```
11  AL:Chi. 1951-61
 8  NL:Brk. 1946-53
    LA 1958-65
```

Most Stolen Bases, Game
```
19  AA:Phil. (Syr.) Apr. 22, 1890
17  NL:NY (Pitt.) May 23, 1890
    Since 1900:
15  AL:NY (StL.) Sept. 28, 1911
11  NL:StL. (Pitt.) Aug. 13, 1916 (2g; 5 inn)
```

Most Stolen Bases, Both Clubs, Game
```
21  AA:Phil. (19) Syr. (2) Apr. 22, 1890
20  NL:NY (17) Pitt. (3) May 23, 1890
    Since 1900:
15  AL:StL. (8) Det. (7) Oct. 1, 1916
14  NL:NY (9) Bos. (5) June 20, 1912
```

Most Triple Steals, Game
```
 2  AL:Phil. (Clev.) July 25, 1930
 1  NL:By many clubs
```

Fewest Stolen Bases, Game (Most Innings)
```
 0  NL:Bos. (Brk.) May 1, 1920 (26 inn)
    AL:Det. (Phil.) July 21, 1945 (24 inn)
    Phil. (Det.) July 21, 1945 (24 inn)
```

Fewest Stolen Bases, Both Clubs, Game (Most Innings)
```
 0  AL:Det. (Phil.) July 21, 1945 (24 inn)
    NL:NY (SF) May 31(2g), 1964 (23 inn)
```

Most Stolen Bases, Inning
```
 8  AL:Wash. (Clev.) July 19, 1915 (1st)
    NL:Phil. (NY) July 7(1g), 1919 (9th)
```

Most Stealing Home, Season
```
16  NL:Chi. 1911
15  AL:Chi. 1906
```

Most Stealing Home, Game
```
 3  AL:Chi. (StL.) July 2, 1909
    NL:Chi. (Bos.) Aug. 23, 1909
    NY (Pitt.) Sept. 18, 1911
```

Most Stealing Home, Inning
```
 2  By many; Last:
    AL:Oak. (KC) May 28, 1980 (1st)
    NL:StL. (Brk.) Sept. 19, 1925 (7th)
```

CAUGHT STEALING

Most Caught Stealing, Game
```
 8  NL:Balt. (Wash.) May 11, 1897
    Since 1900:
 6  NL:StL. (Brk.) Aug. 23, 1909
    AL:StL. (Phil.) May 12, 1915
    Chi. (Phil.) June 18, 1915
```

Most Caught Stealing, Inning
```
 3  AA:Cin. (Phil.) July 26, 1887 (3rd)
    AL:Det. (NY) Aug. 3, 1914 (2nd)
 2  NL:By many clubs
```

LEFT ON BASE

Most Left on Base, Game
```
20  AL:NY (Bos.) Sept. 21, 1956
18  NL:By many clubs; Last:
    Atl. (LA) June 23, 1986
    Extra-Inning Game:
27  NL:Atl. (Phil.) May 4, 1973 (20 inn)
25  AL:Wash. (Clev.) Sept. 14, 1971 (20 inn)
    KC (Tex.) June 6, 1991 (18 inn)
```

Most Left on Base, Both Clubs, Game
```
30  NL:Brk. (16) Pitt. (14) June 30, 1893
    NY (17) Phil. (13) July 18, 1943
    Atl. (18) Phil. (12) Aug. 30(1g), 1982
    AL:NY (15) Chi. (15) Aug. 27, 1935
    LA (15) Wash. (15) July 21, 1961
    Extra-Inning Game:
45  NL:NY (25) StL. (20) Sept. 11, 1974 (25 inn)
    AL:KC (25) Tex. (20) June 6, 1991 (18 inn)
```

Most Left on Base, No Runs, Game
```
16  NL:StL. (Phil.) May 24, 1994
    AL:Sea. (Tor.) May 7, 1998
    Extra-Inning Game:
19  NL:Ari. (SD) Sept. 2, 2001 (13 inn)
```

Fewest Left on Base, Both Clubs, Game
```
 1  NL:LA (0) Chi. (1) Sept. 9, 1965
 2  AL:Many games
```

Fewest Left on Base, 2 Consecutive Games
```
 1  AL:Clev. June 23-24, 1976
    Det. May 3-4, 1996
    TB May 12-13, 2006
    NL:Pitt. Aug. 3-4, 1999
```

Most Left on Base, Doubleheader
```
30  AL:Phil. (StL.) June 22, 1949
29  NL:StL. (Phil.) Sept. 15, 1928
    Phil. (Mil.) May 15, 1955
    Extra Innings
33  NL:Fla. (Pitt.) Aug. 18, 1995 (22 inn)
    AL:NY (Det.) July 20, 1998 (26 inn)
```

Most Left on Base, Both Clubs, Doubleheader
```
49  NL:Brk. (25) Pitt. (24) July 24, 1926
    AL:NY (27) Chi. (22) Aug. 27, 1935
```

Fewest Left on Base, Doubleheader
```
 3  AL:Wash. (NY) Aug. 6, 1963
    Balt. (NY) Sept. 14, 1982
    Chi. (Sea.) Sept. 27, 1982
    NL:SF (Hou.) Sept. 24, 1978
    NY (Mtl.) Sept. 21, 1982
    Pitt. (NY) Sept. 19, 2004
```

Fewest Left on Base, Both Clubs, Doubleheader
```
10  NL:StL. (6) Bos. (4) July 19, 1924
13  AL:Chi. (9) Phil. (4) July 18, 1918
```

PINCH-HITTERS

Most Pinch-Hitters, Game
9 **NL:**LA (StL.) Sept. 22, 1959
Mtl. (Pitt.) Sept. 5(2g), 1975
LA (StL.) Sept. 1, 1982 (13 inn)
LA (NY) Sept. 8, 1985 (14 inn)
SF (LA) Sept. 28, 1986 (16 inn)
Atl. (Mtl.) Sept. 21, 1993
StL. (Cin.) Sept. 25, 1997 (14 inn)
8 **AL:**Balt. (Chi.) May 28, 1954
Balt. (NY) Sept. 25, 1984
Minn. (Sea.) Sept. 13, 1986
Extra-Inning Game:
10 **AL:**Oak. (Chi.) Sept. 19, 1972 (15 inn)

Most Pinch-Hitters, Both Clubs, Game
13 **NL:**LA (7) SD (6) Sept. 25, 1986
Atl. (9) Mtl. (5) Sept. 21, 1993
10 **AL:**Balt. (6) NY (4) Apr. 26, 1959
Extra-Inning Game:
14 **NL:**NY (7) Chi. (7) May 2, 1956 (17 inn)
LA (9) StL. (5) Sept. 1, 1982 (13 inn)
LA (7) Atl. (7) Sept. 18, 1986 (12 inn)
SF (9) LA (5) Sept. 28, 1986 (16 inn)
AL: Oak. (10) Chi. (4) Sept. 19, 1972 (15 inn)

Most Pinch-Hitters, Doubleheader
10 **AL:**NY (Bos.) Sept. 6, 1954
Balt. (Wash.) Apr. 19, 1959
NL: StL. (Chi.) May 11, 1958
StL. (Pitt.) July 13, 1958
Extra-Innings:
15 **NL:**Mtl. (Pitt.) Sept. 5, 1975 (19 inn)

Most Pinch-Hitters, Both Clubs, Doubleheader
15 **NL:**Mil. (8) SF (7) Aug. 30, 1964
14 **AL:**NY (10) Bos. (4) Sept. 6. 1954
Extra innings:
19 **NL:**Mtl. (15) Pitt. (4) Sept. 5, 1975 (19 inn)
17 **AL:**NY (9) Wash. (8) Aug. 14, 1960 (24 inn)

Most Pinch-Hitters, Inning
6 **NL:**SF (Pitt.) May 5, 1958 (9th)
SD (SF) Sept. 16, 1986 (9th)
Atl. (Mtl.) Sept. 21, 1993 (7th)
LA (Col.) Sept. 14, 2002 (6th)
AL: Det. (NY) Sept. 5, 1971 (7th)

Most Pinch-Hitters, Both Clubs, Inning
8 **AL:**Chi. (5) Balt. (3) May 18, 1957 (7th)
NL: Phil. (5) StL. (3) Apr. 30, 1961 (8th)
NY (5) SF (3) Sept. 16, 1966 (9th)

Most Pinch-Hits, Game
6 **NL:**Brk. (Phil.) Sept. 9, 1926
4 **AL:**Clev. (Chi.) Apr. 22, 1930
Phil. (Det.) Sept. 18, 1940
Det. (Chi.) Apr. 22, 1953
KC (Det.) Sept. 1, 1958
NY (Clev.) Aug. 26, 1960 (11 inn)
Clev. (Bos.) Sept. 21, 1967
Oak. (Det.) Aug. 30, 1970
Chi. (Oak.) Sept. 7, 1970
Tex. (KC) June 8, 1995 (10 inn)
Bos. (NY) Sept. 8, 1995

Most Pinch-Hits, Inning
4 **NL:**Chi. (Brk.) May 21(2g), 1927 (9th)
Phil. (Pitt.) Sept. 12, 1974 (8th)
AL: Phil. (Det.) Sept. 18, 1940 (9th)
Tex. (KC) June 8, 1995 (8th)
Bos. (NY) Sept. 8, 1995 (8th)

Most Pinch-Hit Home Runs, Game
2 **NL:**Phil. (StL.) June 2, 1928
StL. (Brk.) July 21, 1930
StL. (Cin.) May 12, 1951
Chi. (Phil.) June 9, 1954
NY (StL.) June 20, 1954
SF (Mil.) June 4, 1958
Phil. (Pitt.) Aug. 13, 1958
NY (Phil.) Aug. 15, 1962 (13 inn)
LA (Chi.) Aug. 8, 1963 (10 inn)
NY (Phil.) Sept. 17, 1963
NY (SF) Aug. 4, 1966
Mtl. (Atl.) July 13(1g), 1973
Chi. (Pitt.) Sept. 10, 1974
LA (StL.) July 23, 1975
Chi. (Hou.) Aug. 23, 1975
LA (Chi.) Aug. 27, 1982
SF (SD) Sept. 28, 1987
NY (SF) May 4, 1991 (12 inn)
Col. (LA) May 6, 1995
Cin. (Atl.) June 22, 1995
Hou. (Chi.) Sept. 28, 1995 (11 inn)
Atl. (StL.) July 22, 1996
NY (StL.) May 11, 1997
Chi. (StL.) July 13, 1997
Chi. (Mil.) Sept. 12, 1998
Atl. (Mil.) May 25, 1999
SD (Col.) July 2, 1999
Ari. (LA) Apr. 12, 2001
SF (Mtl.) Aug. 23, 2001
Mil. (Chi.) June 25, 2003 (10 inn)
Fla. (Cin.) June 22, 2006 (10 inn)
Cin. (Hou.) Sept. 18, 2006
AL: Clev. (Phil.) May 26, 1937
NY (KC) July 23, 1955
Clev. (Minn.) Aug. 15, 1965, (11 inn)
Balt. (Bos.) Aug. 26, 1966 (12 inn)
Det. (Bos.) Aug. 11, 1968 (14 inn)
Sea. (NY) Aug. 2, 1969
Minn. (Det.) July 31, 1970
Minn. (Cal.) July 28(2g), 1974
Sea. (NY) Apr. 27, 1979
Chi. (Oak.) July 6(2g), 1980
Minn. (Oak.) May 16, 1983
Balt. (Tex.) May 5, 1984
Balt. (Clev.) Aug. 12, 1985
Tor. (Det.) June 14, 1986
Tex. (Bos.) Sept. 1, 1986
Cal. (Chi.) June 28, 1987
Bos. (Chi.) Sept. 19, 1997 (10 inn)
Bos. (Mil.) June 7, 2003
Tor. (Tex.) Sept. 11, 2004

Most Pinch-Hit Home Runs, Both Clubs, Game
3 **NL:**Phil. (2) StL. (1) June 2, 1928
StL. (2) Brk. (1) July 21, 1930
Col. (2) LA (1) May 6, 1995
SD (2) Col. (1) July 2, 1999
2 **AL:**Many games. Last:
Tor. (2) Tex. (0) Sept. 11, 2004

Most Pinch-Hit Home Runs, 2 Cons. Games
3 **NL:**Mtl. July 13-13, 1973
SF Sept. 27-28, 1987
Chi. Sept. 11-12, 1998
AL: By many clubs

Most Pinch-Hit Home Runs, Inning
2 **NL:**NY (StL.) June 20, 1954 (6th)
SF (Mil.) June 4, 1958 (10th)
LA (Chi.) Aug. 8, 1963 (5th)
LA (StL.) July 23, 1975 (9th)
NY (SF) May 4, 1991 (9th)
Cin. (Atl.) June 22, 1995 (8th)
NY (StL.) May 11, 1997 (9th)
Atl. (Mil.) May 25, 1999 (9th)
SD (Col.) July 2, 1999 (9th)
SF (Mtl.) Aug. 23, 2001 (9th)
Fla. (AL:Balt.) June 22, 2006 (9th)
AL:NY (KC) July 23, 1955 (9th)
Balt. (Bos.) Aug. 26, 1966 (9th)
Sea. (NY) Apr. 27, 1979 (8th)
Minn. (Oak.) May 16, 1983 (9th)
Balt. (Clev.) Aug. 12, 1985 (9th)
Tex. (Bos.) Sept. 1, 1986 (9th)
Bos. (Chi.) Sept. 19, 1997 (9th)
Tor. (Tex.) Sept. 11, 2004 (8th)

Most Grand Slam HRs, Game
1 By many

Most Grand Slam HRs, Both Clubs, Game
2 **NL:**Bos. (1) NY (1) May 26, 1929
1 **AL:**By many

Most Walks, Inning
3 **NL:**Pitt. (Phil.) June 3, 1911 (9th)
Brk. (NY) Apr. 22, 1922 (7th)
Bos. (Brk.) June 2, 1932 (9th)
Chi. (Phil.) July 29, 1947 (7th)
StL. (NY) May 6, 1994 (9th)
NY (Col.) May 18, 1997 (8th)
Phil. (Pitt.) July 18, 1997 (6th)
AL: Balt. (Wash.) Apr. 22, 1955 (7th)
Wash. (Bos.) May 14, 1961 (9th)
Sea. (Bos.) June 3, 1995 (9th)
Tex. (Ari.) July 15, 1999 (9th)

Most Strikeouts, Game
5 **AL:**Det. (NY) Sept. 8, 1979
NL: Chi. (Cin.) May 22, 1990 (16 inn)
Cin. (SF) Sept. 20, 2000

Most Strikeouts, Both Clubs, Game
5 **AL:**NY (4) Bos. (1) July 4, 1955
Wash. (4) Clev. (1) May 1, 1957
Det. (4) Clev. (1) Aug. 4, 1967
Det. (5) NY (0) Sept. 8, 1979
NL:LA (3) Cin. (2) Sept. 16. 1990
NY (3) SF (2) Aug. 19, 1996
Phil. (3) Cin. (2) Apr. 26, 1997
Hou. (4) NY (1) Aug. 30, 1999
Cin. (5) SF (0) Sept. 20, 2000
Chi. (3) Hou. (2) July 20, 2002
Extra-Inning Game:
7 **NL:**Chi. (5) Cin. (2) May 22, 1990 (16 inn)

Most Strikeouts, Inning
3 By many; Last:
NL:LA (Col.) Sept. 14, 2002 (6th)
AL:KC (Det.) July 9, 1995 (7th)

PINCH-RUNNERS

Most Pinch-Runners, Game
5 **AL:**Bos. (Balt.) Oct. 3, 2004
4 **NL:**By many clubs
Extra-Inning Game:
5 **NL:**Chi. (Hou.) Sept. 2, 1986 (18 inn)

Most Pinch-Runners, Inning
4 **AL:**Chi. (Minn.) Sept. 16, 1967 (9th)
Oak. (Chi.) Sept. 24, 1975 (8th)
Tex. (Cal.) Sept. 10, 1987 (9th)
Ana. (Tex.) Sept. 23, 2000 (7th)
NY (TB) Sept. 13, 2005 (6th)
NL:SD (Cin.) Aug. 10, 1978 (7th)

Most Runs, Inning
3 **AL:**Chi. (Minn.) Sept. 16, 1967 (9th)
Chi. (Oak.) May 19, 1968 (5th)
Oak. (Cal.) May 7, 1975 (7th)
Minn. (Balt.) June 19, 1991 (9th)
Tex. (Balt.) Apr. 19, 1996 (8th)
NY (TB) Sept. 13, 2005 (6th)
Tex. (LA) Oct. 2, 2005 (3rd)
2 **NL:**By many; Last:
SF (Col.) Sept. 20, 2006 (8th)

CLUB FIELDING – SEASON

	AL:1901-1960 NL:1900-1961 8 clubs 154 games		AL:1961-1968 NL:1962-1968 10 clubs 162 games		AL:1969- NL:1969- 12-16 clubs 162 games	
Highest Fielding Average						
AL:	.983	Clev. 1949	.985	Balt. 1964	.989	Bos. 2006
NL:	.983	Cin. 1958	.982	Phil. 1966	.989	NY 1999
Lowest Fielding Average						
AL:	.928	Det. 1901	.969	LA 1961	.970	Oak. 1977
NL:	.936	Phil. 1904	.967	NY 1963	.969	Chi. 1974
Most Total Chances						
AL:	6895	Chi. 1907	6557	Chi. 1967	6653	Cal. 1983
NL:	6682	NY 1920	6601	Pitt. 1968	6661	Chi. 1977
Fewest Total Chances						
AL:	5596	Clev. 1945	5930	Det. 1962	5830	Minn. 2002
NL:	5655	Phil. 1955	5964	Cin. 1966	5907	Phil. 2000
Most Chances Accepted						
AL:	6655	Chi. 1907	6419	Chi. 1967	6499	Cal. 1983
NL:	6472	NY 1920	6462	Pitt. 1968	6508	Chi. 1977
Fewest Chances Accepted						
AL:	5470	Clev. 1945	5774	Det. 1962	5706	Chi. 1977
NL:	5545	Phil. 1955	5842	Cin. 1966	5804	Chi. 2001
Most Putouts						
AL:	4396	Clev. 1910	4520	NY 1964	4493	Minn. 1969
NL:	4359	Phil. 1913	4471	Cin. 1968	4480	Pitt. 1979
Fewest Putouts						
AL:	3907	Clev. 1945	4245	KC 1961	4188	Det. 1975
NL:	3887	Phil. 1907	4280	Phil. 1962	4223	Atl. 1979
Most Assists						
AL:	2446	Chi. 1907	1975	NY 1968	2077	Cal. 1983
NL:	2293	StL. 1917	2068	Chi. 1964	2104	Chi. 1977
Fewest Assists						
AL:	1493	NY 1948	1443	Det. 1962	1422	Minn. 2002
NL:	1437	Phil. 1957	1534	Cin. 1966	1462	NY 1989
Most Errors						
AL:	425	Det. 1901	192	LA 1961	191	Tex. 1975
NL:	408	Brk. 1905	210	NY 1962-63	199	Chi. 1974
Fewest Errors						
AL:	103	Clev. 1949	95	Balt. 1964	65	Sea. 2003
NL:	100	Cin. 1958	113	Phil. 1966	68	NY 1999
Most Double Plays						
AL:	217	Phil. 1949	186	Cal. 1966	206	Bos. & Tor. 1980
NL:	198	LA 1958	215	Pitt. 1966	202	Col. 1997
Fewest Double Plays						
AL:	74	Bos. 1913	114	Det. 1962	109	Tor. 1992
NL:	94	Pitt. 1935	100	Hou. 1963	104	LA 1997
Most Triple Plays						
AL:	3	Det. 1911 Bos. 1924	2	Wash. 1968	3	Bos. 1979 Oak. 1979
NL:	2	By many	3	Phil. 1964 Chi. 1965	2	Hou. 1971, 78, 91 NY 1982 Mtl. 1993 Cin. 1995
Most Passed Balls						
AL:	49	Balt. 1959	45	Chi. 1965	73	Tex. 1987
NL:	42	Bos. 1905	42	Atl. 1967	38	Atl. 1976
Fewest Passed Balls						
AL:	0	NY 1931	5	Minn. 1966	2	Tex. 1999
NL:	2	Bos. 1943	4	Chi. 1967	2	NY 1980 SD 1992 Pitt. 2004

VERAGE

Most Seasons Leading League
21 **NL:**Bos./Mil./Atl. 1878-79, 82, 84, 91, 97,
99-1900, 02, 15-16, 24, 32-33, 54, 61-63,
69, 98, 2005
19 **AL:**StL./Balt. 1902, 63-64, 66, 69, 74-78,
80, 82, 84, 89, 91, 94-95, 98-99

Most Seasons, Consecutive, Leading League
6 **AL:**Bos. 1916-21
NL: StL. 1984-89

HANCES ACCEPTED

Most Chances Accepted, Game
55 **NL:**Pitt. (NY) June 7, 1911
54 **AL:**StL. (Phil.) Aug. 16, 1919
Extra-Inning game:
119 **NL:**Bos. (Brk.) May 1, 1920 (26 inn)
110 **AL:**Det. (Phil.) July 21, 1945 (24 inn)

UTOUTS

Most Players, 1 or more Putouts, 9-Inning Game
15 **AL:**Bos. (Balt.) Oct. 3, 2004
14 **NL:**By many clubs; Last:
NY (Atl.) Sept. 29, 2002

Most Players, 1 or more Putouts, Both Clubs, 9-Inning Game
25 Many games; Last:
AL: Bos. (15) Balt. (10) Oct. 3, 2004
NL:SD (14) SF (11) Sept. 26, 1997

SSISTS

Most Assists, Game
28 **NL:**Pitt. (NY) June 7, 1911
27 **AL:**StL. (Phil.) Aug. 16, 1919
Extra-Inning game:
42 **AL:**Minn. (Clev.) Aug. 31, 1993 (22 inn)
41 **NL:**Bos. (Brk.) May 1, 1920 (26 inn)

Fewest Assists, Game (9+ fielding innings)
0 **AL:**StL. (Clev.) Aug. 8(2g), 1943
Clev. (NY) July 4(1g), 1945
NY (Clev.) Sept. 11, 1995
NL:NY (Phil.) June 25, 1989
Cin. (Col.) Aug. 20, 1997

Most Assists, Both Clubs, Game
44 **AL:**Clev. (22) StL. (22) May 27, 1909
43 **NL:**Brk. (24) NY (19) Apr. 21, 1903
Extra inning game:
72 **NL:**Bos. (41) Brk. (31) May 1, 1920 (26 inn)
AL: Det. (38) Phil. (34) July 21,
1945 (24 inn)

Fewest Assists, Both Clubs, Game
5 **AL:**Balt. (3) Clev. (2) Aug. 31, 1955
Bos. (4) NY (1) Aug. 9, 1992
Det. (4) Oak. (1) June 12, 1991
6 **NL:**Chi. (5) Phil. (1) May 2, 1957
Phil. (3) SF (3) May 13, 1959
Atl. (3) Hou. (3) Sept. 19, 1989
LA (3) SF (3) Sept. 27, 1989
Atl. (3) Mtl. (3) May 28, 1990
Mtl. (3) NY (3) Sept. 10, 1991
Cin. (5) Chi. (1) Aug. 26, 1998
Cin. (5) SF (1) Sept. 6, 2006

Most Assists, Infield, Game
22 **AL:**Sea. (NY) May 28, 1988
21 **NL:**NY (Pitt.) July 13, 1919
Phil. (Bos.) May 30(2g), 1931
Brk. (Pitt.) Aug. 18(2g), 1935
StL. (NY) June 27, 1993
Phil. (Mtl.) Apr. 17, 1996

Fewest Assists, Infield, Game (9+ innings)
0 By many clubs; Last:
NL: Fla. (Mtl.) July 21, 2002
AL: Tor. (Bos.) July 12, 1997

Most Assists, Infield, Both Clubs, Game
38 **NL:**Brk. (20) Cin. (18) June 10, 1917
35 **AL:**Det. (19) Clev. (16) Apr. 18, 1924
Chi. (18) Bos. (17) Sept. 17(2g), 1945
Det. (18) TB (17) Aug. 1, 1998

Fewest Assists, Infield, Both Clubs, Game
2 **AL:**Wash. (0) Phil. (2) May 5, 1910
NL: Phil. (0) Chi. (2) May 2, 1957

Most Assists, Outfield, Game
5 **NL:**Pitt. (Phil.) Aug. 23, 1910
AL:NY (Bos.) Sept. 5(2g), 1921
Clev. (StL.) May 1, 1928

Most Assists, Inning
10 **AL:**Clev. (Phil.) Aug. 17, 1921
Bos. (NY) May 10, 1952
8 **NL:**Bos. (Phil.) May 1, 1911
Cin. (StL.) June 3, 1992
Phil. (AL:Chi.) Aug. 30, 2004

Most Players, 1 or more Assists, 9-Inning Game
12 **NL:**Chi. (Pitt.) Sept. 28, 2003
11 **AL:**Wash. (Phil.) Oct. 3, 1920
Bos. (Phil.) May 1, 1929
Wash. (Balt.) Apr. 29(1g), 1956
Chi. (KC) Sept. 22(2g), 1970

ERRORS – MOST

Most Seasons Leading League
18 **AL:**Phil./KC/Oak. 1915-16, 18-21, 36-41,
64, 77-79, 82, 84
NL: Phil. 1883, 1904, 14, 19, 21, 30-36,
38, 42-43, 45, 48, 59

Most Seasons, Consecutive, Leading League
7 **NL:**Phil. 1930-36
6 **NL:**Phil. 1936-41
StL. 1948-53

Most Errors, Game
24 **NL:**Bos. (StL.) June 14, 1876
Since 1900:
12 **AL:**Det. (Chi.) May 1, 1901
Chi. (Det.) May 6, 1903
11 **NL:**StL. (Pitt.) Apr. 19, 1902
Bos. (StL.) June 11, 1906
StL. (Cin.) July 3(2g), 1909

Most Errors, Both Clubs, Game
40 **NL:**Bos. (24) StL. (16) June 14, 1876
Since 1900:
18 **AL:**Chi. (12) Det. (6) May 6, 1903
15 **NL:**StL. (11) Pitt. (4) Apr. 19, 1902
Bos. (10) Chi. (5) Oct. 3, 1904

Most Errors, Inning, Since 1900
7 **AL:**Clev. (Chi.) Sept. 20, 1905 (8th)
6 **NL:**Pitt. (NY) Aug. 20, 1903 (1g; 1st)

ERRORS – FEWEST

Most Seasons Leading League
25 **NL:**Cin. 1896, 1919, 27, 30, 40-41, 43,
57-58, 60, 64-65, 67, 71-73, 75-77, 80-
81, 83, 90, 95, 97
19 **AL:**StL./Balt. 1938, 43, 60, 63-64, 66, 69,
75-78, 80, 82, 89, 91, 94-95, 98-99

Most Seasons, Consecutive, Leading League
6 **AL:**Phil. 1909-14
Bos. 1916-21
4 **NL:**Chi. 1905-08

Most Errorless Games, Season
112 **AL:**Sea. 2003
105 **NL:**StL. 2003

Most Errorless Games, Consecutive, Season
17 **AL:**Bos. June 11(2g)-30, 2006
16 **NL:**StL. July 30-Aug. 16, 1992

Fewest Errors, Game (Most Innings)
0 **AL:**Chi. (Wash.) June 12, 1967 (22 inn)
Wash. (Chi.) June 12, 1967 (22 inn)
NL: Bos. (Pitt.) Aug. 1, 1918 (21 inn)
SF (Cin.) Sept. 1, 1967 (21 inn)
SD (Mtl.) May 21, 1977 (21 inn)

Fewest Errors, Both Clubs, Game (Most Innings)
0 **AL:**Chi. (Wash.) June 12, 1967 (22 inn)
NL: Chi. (Phil.) July 17, 1918 (21 inn)

DOUBLE PLAYS

Most Seasons Leading League
21 **NL:**Pitt. 1904, 06, 11, 25, 38, 49, 55, 59-
67, 70, 72, 94, 2002, 04
15 **AL:**NY 1941-42, 46, 52, 54-58, 61, 65, 72,
84, 89

Most Seasons, Consecutive, Leading League
9 **NL:**Pitt. 1959-67
5 **AL:**NY 1954-58

Most Double Plays, Game
7 **AL:**NY (Phil.) Aug. 14, 1942
NL: Hou. (SF) May 4, 1969
Atl. (Cin.) June 27, 1982 (14 inn)
StL. (Pitt.) June 16, 1994 (10 inn)

Most Double Plays, Both Clubs, Game
10 **AL:**Minn. (6) Bos. (4) July 18, 1990
9 **NL:**Chi. (5) Cin. (4) July 3, 1929
LA (5) Pitt. (4) Apr. 15, 1961
Extra-Inning Game:
10 **NL:**Bos. (5) Cin. (5) June 7, 1925 (12 inn)
Cin. (6) NY (4) May 1, 1955 (16 inn)
SF (6) NY (4) Aug. 21, 2004 (12 inn)

Most Double Plays, Unassisted, Game
2 By many

Most Double Plays, Unassisted, Both Clubs, Game
2 By many

Most Double Plays, Doubleheader
9 **AL:**Phil. (Clev.) Sept. 14, 1931
Bos. (StL.) June 25, 1950
NL: StL. (Cin.) June 11, 1944
Including Extra-Inning Game:
10 **AL:**Wash. (Chi.) Aug. 18, 1943 (23 inn)

Most Double Plays, Both Clubs, Doubleheader
13 **NL:**NY (7) Phil. (6) Sept. 28, 1939
Pitt. (8) StL. (5) Sept. 6, 1948
12 **AL:**Phil. (9) Clev. (3) Sept. 14, 1931
Bos. (7) Chi. (5) Sept. 15, 1947
NY (7) KC (5) July 31, 1955
Cal. (8) Bos. (4) May 1, 1966
Cal. (7) Balt. (5) May 19, 1988 (19 inn)

Most Games, Consecutive, Double Plays
25 **AL:**Bos. May 7-June 4, 1951 (38)
Clev. Aug. 21-Sept. 12, 1953 (38)
23 **NL:**Brk. Aug. 7-27, 1952 (36)

Most Double Plays, 2 Consecutive Games
10 **NL:**NY Aug. 12-13(1g) 1932
AL: Det. May 18-19, 1948
Clev. May 3-5, 1970
KC May 5-6, 1972

Most Double Plays, 3 Consecutive Games
13 **NL:**SF Apr. 24-26, 1987
12 **AL:**Bos. June 25-27, 1950
NY Apr. 19-21, 1952
Chi. Sept 2-3, 1973

Most Double Plays, 4 Consecutive Games
15 **NL:**SF Apr. 24-27, 1987
14 **AL:**Chi. July 12-14, 1951
NY Apr. 18-21, 1952
Clev. Sept. 10-13, 2005

Most Double Plays, 5 Consecutive Games
16 **AL:**NY Apr. 19-23, 1952
Clev. Sept. 11-16, 2005
NL:SF Apr. 22-27, 1987

TRIPLE PLAYS

Most Seasons, Consecutive, Triple Plays
4 **NL:**Pitt. 1968-71
3 **AL:**Det. 1910-12
StL. 1915-17
NY 1916-18
Wash. 1921-23
Bos. 1922-24, 65-67
Balt. 1977-79
Minn. 1982-84

Most Triple Plays, Season
3 **AL:**Det. 1911
Bos. 1924, 79
Oak. 1979
NL: Phil. 1964
Chi. 1965

Most Triple Plays, Game
2 **AL:**Minn. (Bos.) July 17, 1990 (4th, 8th)
1 **NL:**By many

Most Triple Plays, Both Clubs, Game
2 **AL:**Minn. (2) Bos. (0) July 17, 1990

Most Games, Consecutive, Triple Plays
2 **AL:**Det. June 6-7, 1908
1 **NL:**By many clubs

ASSED BALLS

Most Seasons Leading League (Most)
Since 1903:
22 **NL:** Bos.-Mil./Atl. 1904-05, 07, 24, 26, 28-30, 42, 65-67, 69-72, 74-79
Since 1912:
16 **AL:** Bos. 1917, 19, 24, 31, 50, 54, 94, 96-2000, 03-06

Most Seasons, Consecutive, Leading League (Most)
7 **AL:** Tex. 1984-90
6 **NL:** Atl. 1974-79

Most Seasons Leading League (Fewest)
Since 1912:
18 **AL:** NY 1914, 29, 31, 36-37, 42, 44, 51-52, 55, 58, 62-63, 67-68, 74, 88-89
Since 1903:
15 **NL:** Bos.-Mil./Atl. 1913, 15-16, 20, 35, 37-38, 43, 45, 49, 57-59, 62, 83

Most Seasons, Consecutive, Leading League (Fewest)
5 **NL:** SF 1960-64
3 **AL:** Clev. 1939-41

Most Passed Balls, Game
12 **AA:** Wash. (NY) May 10, 1884
10 **NL:** Bos. (Wash.) May 3, 1886
Since 1900:
6 **NL:** Cin. (Pitt.) Oct. 4, 1902
Hou. (Mtl.) May 12, 1996
AL: Tex. (Det.) Aug. 30, 1987

Fewest Passed Balls, Game (Most Innings)
0 **NL:** Bos. (Brk.) May 1, 1920 (26 inn)
Brk. (Bos.) May 1, 1920 (26 inn)
AL: Chi. (Mil.) May 8, 1984 (25 inn)

Most Passed Balls, Both Clubs, Game
14 **AA:** Wash. (12) NY (2) May 10, 1884
11 **NL:** Troy (7) Clev. (4) June 16, 1880
Since 1900:
6 **NL:** Cin. (6) Pitt. (0) Oct. 4, 1902
Hou. (6) Mtl. (0) May 12, 1996
AL: Tex. (6) Det. (0) Aug. 30, 1987

Fewest Passed Balls, Both Clubs, Game
(Most Innings)
0 **NL:** Bos.-Brk. May 1, 1920 (26 inn)
AL: Bos.-Phil. Sept. 1, 1906 (24 inn)
Det.-Phil. July 21, 1945 (24 inn)

CLUB PITCHING – SEASON

	AL:1901-1960 NL:1900-1961 8 clubs 154 games		AL:1961-1968 NL:1962-1968 10 clubs 162 games		AL:1969- NL:1969- 12-16 clubs 162 games

Lowest Earned Run Average (Since 1912 in NL, 1913 in AL)

AL:	2.16	Chi. 1917	2.45	Chi. 1967	2.83	Balt. 1969
NL:	2.12	Brk. 1916	2.49	StL. 1968	2.91	NY 1988

Highest Earned Run Average (Since 1912 in NL, 1913 in AL)

AL:	6.24	StL. 1936	4.79	KC 1962	6.38	Det. 1996
NL:	6.70	Phil. 1930	5.04	NY 1962	6.01	Col. 1999

Most No-Hit Games

AL:	2	Bos. 1904, 16 Clev. 1908; StL. 1917 NY 1951; Det. 1952	2	Bos. 1962	2	Cal. 1973
NL:	2	Cin. 1938; Brk. 1956 Mil. 1960	1	By many	2	Chi. 1972

Most No-Hit Games Against

AL:	2	Chi. 1917 Phil. 1923	2	Det. 1967	2	Det. 1973 Cal. 1977
NL:	2	Phil. 1960	2	Chi. 1965	2	Cin. 1971 Col. 1996 SD 2001

Most Complete Games

AL:	148	Bos. 1904	62	Det. 1961	94	Oak. 1980
NL:	146	StL. 1904	77	SF 1968	75	Chi. 1971

Fewest Complete Games

AL:	26	KC 1957	18	KC 1964-65	1	TB 2001, 05 NY 2004 Minn. 2006
NL:	27	Chi. 1958	24	Cin. 1968	1	Col. 2002 Hou. 2003 LA & Wash. 2006

Most Shutouts Participating

AL:	47	Chi. 1910	44	LA 1964	38	Cal. 1972
NL:	46	Brk. 1907; StL. 1908	47	NY 1968	42	NY 1969

Fewest Shutouts Participating

AL:	7	NY 1926, 30; Chi. 1930	12	Chi. 1961	4	Tex. 2001
NL:	6	Phil. 1930	10	NY 1962	5	Col. & SF 1999; Hou. 2000

Most Shutouts

AL:	32	Chi. 1906	28	Cal. 1964	23	Mil. 1971 Oak. 1972
NL:	33	Chi. 1907, 09	30	StL. 1968	28	NY 1969

Most Times Shut Out

AL:	30	Wash. 1909	23	Chi. 1968	27	Tex. 1972
NL:	33	StL. 1908	30	NY 1963	24	Atl. 1978

Fewest Shutouts

AL:	1	Chi. 1924 Wash. 1956	3	Chi. 1961	1	Sea. 1977; Balt. 1996, Oak. 1997; Ana. & KC 2001
NL:	1	Bos. 1928	4	Chi. & NY 1962 Mil. 1965	0	Col. 1993

Fewest Times Shut Out

AL:	0	NY 1932 (156g)	3	Minn. 1965	1	Mil. 1979, 82; Tor. 1993 Clev. 1996 Tex. 2001
NL:	1	Brk. 1953 (155g)	6	By many	0	Cin. 2000

Most 1-0 Games Won

AL:	11	Wash. 1914	10	LA 1964	8	Balt. 1974
NL:	10	Pitt. 1908	8	StL. 1968	9	NY 1969 Hou. 1976

Most 1-0 Games Lost

AL:	9	NY 1914	9	Chi. 1968	7	Tex. 1976
NL:	10	Pitt. 1914 Chi. 1916	10	Phil. 1967	7	NY 1973 LA 1976, 89 StL. 1991

	AL:1901-1960 NL:1900-1961 8 clubs 154 games		AL:1961-1968 NL:1962-1968 10 clubs 162 games		AL:1969- NL:1969- 12-16 clubs 162 games

Most 1-Hit Games

AL:	3	By many	5	Balt. 1964	3	By many clubs
NL:	4	Chi. 1906, 09 Phil. 1907, 11, 15	3	LA, Mil. Pitt. 1965	4	Phil. 1979 Cin. 1999

Most 1-Hit Games Against

AL:	5	StL. 1910 Clev. 1915	4	Wash. 1963, 65	3	By many
NL:	3	By many	4	NY 1965	4	Stl. 1991

Most Games Decided By One Run

AL:	65	Phil. 1908; StL. 1916	74	Chi. 1968	70	KC 1993
NL:	69	Cin. 1946	68	LA 1968	75	Hou. 1971

Fewest Games Decided By One Run

AL:	22	StL. 1936	39	Bos. 1962; Minn. 1963 Det. 1967	30	Det. 1993 Sea. 1998
NL:	28	Brk. 1949	40	Phil. 1962	28	Mtl. 2001

Most 1-Run Games Won

AL:	38	Clev. 1917 NY 1943	38	Chi. 1967	40	Balt. 1970, 74
NL:	41	Cin. 1940	37	Phil. 1968	42	SF 1978

Fewest 1-Run Games Won

AL:	10	StL. 1937 Clev. 1948	13	Minn. 1963	10	Sea. 1998
NL:	7	Bos. 1935	17	NY 1964	13	Pitt. 1996 Mil. & Mtl. 2001

Most 1-Run Games Lost

AL:	40	Phil. 1908	44	Chi. 1968	36	Clev. 2005
NL:	41	Cin. 1916, 46	39	NY 1962	43	Hou. 1971

Fewest 1-Run Games Lost

AL:	11	Wash. 1925 StL. 1936 Bos. 1950	17	KC 1961 NY 1963 Det. 1966	10	Bos. 1986 NY 1998 Tor. 2006
NL:	12	Pitt. 1908, Brk. 1949	14	Phil. 1962	12	SF 2003

Most Saves (Since 1969)

AL:	-	-	-	-	68	Chi. 1990
NL:	-	-	-	-	61	Mtl. 1993

Fewest Saves (Since 1969)

AL:	-	-	-	-	11	Tor. 1979
NL:	-	-	-	-	13	Chi. 1971

Most Innings

AL:	1465	Clev. 1910	1507	NY 1964	1498	Minn. 1969
NL:	1455	Phil. 1913	1490	Cin. 1968	1493	Pitt. 1979

Fewest Innings

AL:	1302	Clev. 1945	1415	KC 1961; NY 1966	1396	Det. 1975
NL:	1299	Phil. 1907	1427	Phil. 1962 NY 1963, 66	1408	Atl. 1979

Most Batters Faced

AL:	6382	StL. 1936	6428	KC 1964	6713	Det. 1996
NL:	6549	Phil. 1930	6380	LA 1962	6574	Col. 1999

Fewest Batters Faced

AL:	5559	Clev. 1945	5864	Balt. 1968	5799	Balt. 1971
NL:	5684	Brk. 1956	5941	LA 1966	5877	NY 1988

Most At-Bats

AL:	5653	StL. 1936	5666	Clev. 1964	5770	Oak. 1997
NL:	5763	Phil. 1930	5664	LA 1962	5741	Chi. 1974

Fewest At-Bats

AL:	4933	Clev. 1945	5237	Balt. 1968	5268	Balt. & Mil. 1971
NL:	5062	Phil. 1947	5363	Phil. 1963	5297	StL. 1978

Most Runs

AL:	1064	StL. 1936	863	KC 1961	1103	Det. 1996
NL:	1199	Phil. 1930	948	NY 1962	1028	Col. 1999

Fewest Runs

AL:	408	Phil. 1909	491	Chi. 1967	517	Balt. 1969
NL:	381	Chi. 1906	472	StL. 1968	532	NY 1988

	AL:1901-1960 NL:1900-1961 8 clubs 154 games		AL:1961-1968 NL:1962-1968 10 clubs 162 games		AL:1969- NL:1969- 12-16 clubs 162 games	
Most Earned Runs (Since 1912 in NL, 1913 in AL)						
AL:	935	StL. 1936	764	KC 1962	1015	Det. 1996
NL:	1024	Phil. 1930	801	NY 1962	955	Col. 1999
Fewest Earned Runs (Since 1912 in NL, 1913 in AL)						
AL:	342	Chi. 1917	406	Chi. 1967	463	Balt. 1969
NL:	332	Phil. 1915	409	StL. 1968	465	NY 1988
Most Hits						
AL:	1776	StL. 1936	1519	KC 1961	1734	Oak. 1997
NL:	1994	Phil. 1930	1577	NY 1962	1700	Col. 1999
Fewest Hits						
AL:	1069	Phil. 1909	1087	Clev. 1968	1194	Balt. 1969
NL:	1018	Chi. 1906	1223	LA 1965	1203	Hou. 1986
Most Home Runs						
AL:	187	KC 1956	220	KC 1964	241	Det. 1996
NL:	185	StL. 1955	192	NY 1962	239	Col. 2001
Fewest Home Runs						
AL:	6	Bos. 1913	87	Chi. 1967	80	Balt. 1976
						Clev. 1976
NL:	5	Cin. 1909	65	LA 1968	68	SF 1976
Most Grand Slam Home Runs						
AL:	9	Chi. 1934	8	Clev. 1963	14	Det. 1996
		StL. 1938, 50				
NL:	8	Phil. 1933	6	Chi. 1962	12	Mtl. 2000
		Pitt. 1951		LA 1962		
		Chi. 1961		Phil. 1962		
				Mil. 1965		
Most Sacrifice Hits						
AL:	147	KC 1954	106	Chi. 1961	92	KC 1970
						Oak. 1978
						Tor. 1980
NL:	133	Brk. 1946	99	Hou. 1964	112	SD 1975
Fewest Sacrifice Hits						
AL:	46	NY 1958	51	Balt. 1968	20	Balt. 2002
NL:	44	Mil. 1958	53	Phil. 1966	45	Ari. 2002
Most Sacrifice Flies (1908 to 1930, 1939, since 1954)						
AL:	63	Balt. & KC 1955	64	KC 1961	80	Oak. 1997
NL:	79	Pitt. 1954	58	Hou. 1963	78	Col. 1993
Fewest Sacrifice Flies (1908 to 1930, 1939, since 1954)						
AL:	27	KC 1958	17	Det. 1968	27	Cal. 1969
NL:	24	Brk. 1955	17	SF 1963	19	LA 2003
Most Walks						
AL:	827	Phil. 1915	713	LA 1961	784	Det. 1996
NL:	701	StL. 1911	600	Chi. 1962	737	Col. 1999
Fewest Walks						
AL:	233	Bos. 1904	392	Minn. 1966	356	Minn. 2006
NL:	258	Cin. 1933	344	SF 1968	383	StL. 1993
Most Intentional Walks (Since 1955)						
AL:	59	Clev. 1957	78	Oak. 1968	94	Sea. 1980
NL:	85	Chi. 1956	101	LA 1967	116	SD 1974
Fewest Intentional Walks (Since 1955)						
AL:	18	Det. 1959	21	Bos. & KC 1961	12	Minn. 2000
NL:	33	Brk. 1957	19	Hou. 1962	9	LA 1974
Most Hit Batters						
AL:	81	Phil. 1911	66	Chi. 1968	95	TB 2003
NL:	68	Brk. 1903	61	Phil. 1966	92	Wash. 2006
Fewest Hit Batters						
AL:	5	StL. 1945	12	Chi. 1961	10	Balt. 1983
NL:	9	Chi. 1944	17	Chi. 1964	11	Pitt. 1984

	AL:1901-1960 NL:1900-1961 8 clubs 154 games		AL:1961-1968 NL:1962-1968 10 clubs 162 games		AL:1969- NL:1969- 12-16 clubs 162 games	
Most Strikeouts						
AL:	896	Det. 1946	1189	Clev. 1967	1266	NY 2001
NL:	1122	LA 1960	1123	Cin. 1964	1404	Chi. 2003
Fewest Strikeouts						
AL:	310	Bos. 1925	666	Wash. 1961	575	Mil. 1980
NL:	310	Cin. 1933	717	NY 1964	652	SD 1976
Most Wild Pitches						
AL:	67	Phil. 1936	73	Minn. 1964 Bos. 1968	94	Tex. 1986
NL:	70	LA 1958	83	Cin. 1965 Atl. 1966	96	Cin. 2000
Fewest Wild Pitches						
AL:	10	StL. 1930 Clev. 1943	27	Clev. 1962 NY 1962, 68	15	Bos. 1977
NL:	9	Cin. 1944	30	StL. 1964, 68 Phil. 1968	22	NY 2002
Most Balks						
AL:	14	NY 1950	12	Bos. 1965 Balt. 1968	76	Oak. 1988
NL:	14	Phil. 1950	20	NY 1963	41	Mtl. 1988
Most Pitchers, 20 or more Games Won						
AL:	4	Chi. 1920	2	NY 1963	4	Balt. 1971
NL:	3	Pitt. 1902 Chi. 1903 NY 1904-05, 13, 20 Cin. 1923	2	Cin. 1962, 65 LA 1965 SF 1966	2	LA & Chi. 1969 StL. 1985 Atl. & SF 1993 Hou. 1999 Ari. 2001-02
Most Pitchers, 20 or more Games Lost						
AL:	3	Wash. 1904 StL. 1905 Phil. 1916	1	Minn. 1961 KC 1963 NY 1966	2	Chi. 1973
NL:	4	Bos. 1905-06	2	NY 1962, 65	1	SD 1969, 72, 74 Phil. 1973 Chi. & Mtl. 1974 NY 1977 Atl. 1977, 79

EARNED RUN AVERAGE (since 1912 in NL, 1913 in AL)

Seasons Leading League
Lowest:
26 **AL:** NY 1919-21, 23, 27, 32, 34-39, 42-43,
47, 52-53, 55, 57-58, 60, 76, 78, 81, 97-98
NL: Brk./LA 1899, 1916, 20, 27-28, 30, 41, 55
57, 60, 63-66, 72-75, 77-78, 82-83, 2003
Highest:
33 **NL:** Phil. 1914, 18-34, 36-42, 45-46, 56, 61,
81, 88-89, 92
18 **AL:** StL./Balt. 1927, 30, 33, 35-39, 46-49,
51, 83, 91
Phil./KC/Oak. 1915-17, 19, 40-41, 43,
50, 54-55, 59, 61-62, 64, 67, 84, 93, 97

Seasons, Consecutive, Leading League
Lowest:
6 **AL:** NY 1934-39
NL: Atl. 1997-2002
Highest:
17 **NL:** Phil. 1918-34
5 **AL:** StL. 1935-39

COMPLETE GAMES

Seasons Leading League
Most:
30 **NL:** Bos./Mil./Atl. 1877, 85, 90-91, 93,
1905-06, 13-14, 16-18, 37-38, 47-51,
55-61, 63, 91, 94-95
17 **AL:** NY: 1914-15, 21-23, 32, 34, 37-39,
42-43, 63, 75, 83, 98, 2001
Fewest:
21 **NL:** Cin. 1893, 95-97, 1934, 36, 38, 48, 54-55,
60, 66-68, 71-72, 75, 78, 87, 91, 2001, 05
18 **AL:** Phil./KC/Oak. 1902, 13, 25, 38-39,
45-46, 50, 55-57, 64-66, 78, 85, 92, 97

Seasons, Consecutive, Leading League
Most:
7 **NL:** Mil. 1955-61
LA 1984-90
4 **AL:** Clev. 1951-54
Fewest:
7 **NL:** StL. 1916-22
6 **AL:** NY 1903-08

Most Incomplete Games, Consecutive
194 **AL:** TB Apr. 14, 2001-May 19, 2002
170 **NL:** Pitt. June 18, 2002-June 28, 2003

Most Incomplete Games, Consecutive, Season
160 **AL:** TB. Apr. 4-Sept. 30, 2005
148 **NL:** Chi. Apr. 3-Sept. 15, 2006

SHUTOUTS

Seasons Leading League
Most:
24 **NL:** Brk./LA 1928, 30, 40, 47, 49, 56-57, 63-66,
70-72, 75, 77, 80-82, 84, 89, 91, 2002-03
23 **AL:** NY 1920, 24, 27, 32, 34, 37-39, 42, 50-53,
58-60, 80-81, 83, 93, 96, 98, 2005
Fewest:
21 **NL:** Phil. 1883, 93, 1920-23, 30-31, 38-42,
45, 56, 60, 68, 74, 76, 84, 92
AL: Phil./KC/Oak. 1915, 17, 19-22, 36, 40-43,
50, 54-55, 60, 62, 65, 79, 93, 97-98
Mil./StL/Balt. 1901, 05, 10, 15, 27, 31,
35-40, 47, 49, 51-52, 90-91, 96, 2002-03

Seasons, Consecutive, Leading League
Most:
7 **NL:** Chi. 1904-10
5 **AL:** Det. 1943-47
Fewest:
5 **NL:** Phil. 1938-42
4 **AL:** Phil. 1919-22, 40-43

Won, Consecutive, Season
6 **NL:** Pitt. June 2-8, 1903
5 **AL:** Balt. Sept. 2-6, 1974
Balt. Sept. 26-Oct. 1, 1995

Lost, Consecutive, Season
4 **NL:** Bos. May 19-23, 1906
Cin. July 30-Aug. 3, 1908
Cin. July 31-Aug. 3, 1931
Hou. June 20-23, 1963
Hou. Sept. 9-11, 1966
Chi. June 16-20, 1968
Atl. May 8-12, 1985
Chi. Apr. 27-May 1, 1992
AL: Bos. Aug. 2-6, 1906 (includes tie game
Phil. Sept. 23-25, 1906
StL. Aug. 25-30, 1913
Wash. Sept. 19-22, 1958
Wash. Sept. 1-5, 1964

Won, vs. Opponent Season
10 **NL:** Pitt. (Bos.) 1906
8 **AL:** Chi. (Bos.) 1906
Clev. (Wash.) 1956
Oak. (Clev.) 1968

1-0 Games Won, Consecutive, Season
3 **AL:** Chi. Apr. 25-27, 1909
NL: StL. Aug. 31-Sept. 1, 1917

1-0 Games Lost, Consecutive, Season
3 **NL:** Brk. Sept. 7-8, 1908
Pitt. Aug. 31-Sept. 1, 1917
Phil. May 11-13, 1960
AL: StL. Apr. 25-27, 1909
Wash. May 7-10, 1909

Runs Scored, Shutout Game
28 **NL:** Prov. (Phil.) Aug. 21, 1883
Since 1900:
22 **NL:** Pitt. (Chi.) Sept. 16, 1975
AL: Clev. (NY) Aug. 31, 2004

Runs Scored, Doubleheader Shutouts
26 **AL:** Det. (StL.) Sept. 22, 1936 (12, 14)
19 **NL:** NY (Cin.) July 31, 1949 (10, 9)

Innings, Consecutive
56 **NL:** Pitt. June 1-9, 1903
54 **AL:** Balt. Sept. 1-7, 1974

Innings, Consecutive, No Runs Scored
48 **AL:** Phil. Sept. 22-26, 1906
NL: Chi. June 15-21, 1968

SAVES (Since 1969)

Seasons Leading League
Most:
11 **NL:** Cin. 1969-70, 72, 74-76, 90, 92, 96-97, 9
10 **AL:** NY 1978, 80, 85-87, 96, 99, 2001, 03-04
Fewest:
8 **AL:** KC 1970, 90, 97, 99-2001, 04-05
6 **NL:** StL. 1970, 72, 78-80, 83
LA 1982, 86-87, 90, 92, 94
Chi. 1971, 81, 96, 99, 2002, 06

Seasons, Consecutive, Leading League
Most:
3 **NL:** Cin. 1974-76
   AL: NY 1985-87
     Bos. 1998-2000
Fewest:
4 **AL:** Cal. 1972-75
3 **NL:** StL. 1978-80
   Atl. 1987-89

NNINGS

Seasons Leading League:
20 **NL:** Brk./LA 1892, 1910, 16, 19-20, 39-41, 46, 48-49, 51-52, 59, 62, 64, 73, 76, 82, 93
18 **AL:** Chi. 1901, 05, 09, 12, 17, 22-23, 39-41, 51, 59, 63, 65-67, 93, 2005

Seasons, Consecutive, Leading League
3 **NL:** Brk. 1939-41
     StL. 1943-45
   AL: Chi. 1939-41, 65-67

One Day
32 **NL:** SF (NY) May 31, 1964 (dh)
29 **AL:** Bos. (Phil.) July 4, 1905 (dh)
     Bos. (NY) Aug. 29, 1967 (dh)
     Wash. (Clev.) Sept. 14, 1971 (dh)

RUNS

Seasons Leading League
Most:
32 **NL:** Phil. 1883-84, 1904, 14, 19-33, 35-39, 41-42, 45-46, 56, 58, 89, 92
22 **AL:** Phil./KC/Oak. 1915-17, 19-22, 33, 40-41, 43, 54-55, 59, 61-62, 64, 67, 82, 84, 93, 97
Fewest:
27 **NL:** Bos./Mil./Atl. 1877-79, 89-91, 97-99, 1916, 37, 47-48, 53, 56, 58, 92-2002
24 **AL:** NY 1919-20, 22-23, 27, 34-39, 41-43, 46-47, 52-53, 57, 76-78, 81, 98

Seasons, Consecutive, Leading League
Most:
15 **NL:** Phil. 1919-33
6 **AL:** StL. 1946-51
Fewest:
11 **NL:** Atl. 1992-2002
6 **AL:** NY 1934-39
   Chi. 1962-67

EARNED RUNS (Since 1912 in NL, 1913 in AL)

Seasons Leading League
Most:
33 **NL:** Phil. 1914, 18-34, 36-39, 41-42, 45-46, 56, 61, 79, 81, 88-89, 92
18 **AL:** StL./Balt. 1925, 27, 30, 32-33, 35-40, 46-49, 51, 88, 91
Fewest:
27 **AL:** NY 1919-21, 23, 27, 32, 34-39, 41-43, 46-47, 52-53, 55, 57-58, 76, 78, 81, 97-98
24 **NL:** Brk./LA 1920, 27-28, 30, 55, 57, 60, 63-66, 72-75, 77-78, 83, 85, 87, 89, 91, 96, 2003

Seasons, Consecutive, Leading League
Most:
17 **NL:** Phil. 1918-34
6 **AL:** StL. 1935-40
Fewest:
6 **AL:** NY 1934-39
     Balt. 1968-73
   NL: Atl. 1997-2002

HITS

Seasons Leading League
Most:
29 **NL:** Phil. 1904, 14, 19, 21-33, 35-38, 41, 45-46, 56, 58, 60, 68-69, 89
17 **AL:** StL. 1913, 17, 31-33, 36-41, 46-51
Fewest:
27 **AL:** NY 1919-23, 27, 34-37, 39, 41-42, 46-47, 49, 52-53, 55, 57-58, 63, 76, 78, 81, 96, 98
25 **NL:** Brk./LA 1902, 16, 27-28, 30, 41, 46-49, 56-57, 60, 62, 64-66, 72-75, 80, 85, 2000, 03

Seasons, Consecutive, Leading League
Most:
13 **NL:** Phil. 1921-33
6 **AL:** StL. 1936-41, 46-51
Fewest:
8 **NL:** Chi. 1903-10
4 **AL:** NY 1934-37

HOME RUNS

Seasons Leading League
Most:
22 **NL:** Bos./Mil./Atl. 1878, 93-94, 96, 98-1900, 02-03, 05-08, 10-11, 45, 64, 70-72, 77-78
19 **AL:** Phil./KC/Oak. 1920-23, 32, 36, 38-42, 52, 54-57, 62, 64, 91
Fewest:
25 **NL:** Pitt. 1888, 85-86, 98, 1902-05, 13, 15-18, 20-21, 35, 40, 46, 58, 60-61, 65, 69, 75, 2004
23 **AL:** Clev. 1903-04, 11, 14, 18, 20-21, 23, 25, 27, 32-34, 36-37, 39-40, 45, 51, 53, 76, 78, 94

Seasons, Consecutive, Leading League
Most:
8 **AL:** StL. 1924-31
5 **NL:** Phil. 1927-31
     NY 1940-44
Fewest:
6 **AL:** Balt. 1956-61
5 **NL:** Cin. 1921-25
     Mil. 1953-57

WALKS

Seasons Leading League
Most:
22 **AL:** Phil./KC/Oak. 1913, 15-19, 24, 33-36, 42, 55, 62, 64, 66, 79, 82-83, 93-94, 97
20 **NL:** Chi. 1880, 88, 94, 1914, 25-27, 31, 54-58, 60, 62, 80, 87, 92, 2003, 06
Fewest:
25 **AL:** Chi. 1906-09, 11, 13, 15-19, 25, 30, 39-41, 51, 55-57, 63-65, 82-83
20 **NL:** Pitt. 1887, 89, 1900-02, 06-07, 09-10, 19-20, 35-36, 42, 59-61, 80, 90-91

Seasons, Consecutive, Leading League
Most:
5 **AL:** Phil. 1915-19
NL: Chi. 1954-58
Fewest:
6 **NL:** Cin. 1922-27
5 **AL:** Chi. 1915-19

INTENTIONAL WALKS (Since 1955)

Seasons Leading League
Most:
14 **AL:** Det. 1956, 74, 85-86, 88-96, 98
8 **NL:** SD 1969, 72, 74, 76-77, 80, 93-94
Fewest:
13 **AL:** Minn. 1965-66, 73-75, 92-94, 96, 2000-02, 04
12 **NL:** Brk./LA 1955-57, 69, 71, 73-78, 2000

Seasons, Consecutive, Leading League
Most:
9 **AL:** Det. 1988-96
3 **NL:** Pitt. 1957-59
Fewest:
6 **NL:** LA 1973-78
3 **AL:** NY 1956-58
KC 1969-71
Minn. 1973-75;92-94;2000-02

STRIKEOUTS

Seasons Leading League
Most:
33 **NL:** Brk./LA 1920, 22-29, 36, 40, 45-46, 48-63, 66, 74, 84, 97
18 **AL:** NY 1921, 23-24, 31-36, 47, 49-51, 57, 58, 81, 84, 2001
Fewest:
21 **NL:** Bos./Mil./Atl. 1907-09, 11, 20, 23, 25, 28, 35-40, 42, 47, 56, 61, 68, 72, 87
14 **AL:** Phil./KC/Oak. 1918, 23, 33, 39, 41, 47, 51-52, 54-57, 60, 84

Seasons, Consecutive, Leading League
Most:
16 **NL:** Brk./LA 1948-63
9 **AL:** Phil. 1902-10
Fewest:
6 **NL:** Bos. 1935-40
4 **AL:** Phil./KC 1954-57
Wash. 1961-64
Mil. 1977-80

WILD PITCHES

Most Wild Pitches, Game
10 **NL:** Lou. July 22, 1876
Since 1900:
6 **NL:** Hou. (LA) Apr. 10, 1979
Atl. (Hou.) Aug. 4(2g), 1979
Mtl. (Phil.) Apr. 10, 1982
AL: Cal. (Minn.) Apr. 13, 1991

Most Wild Pitches, Inning
4 **AL:** Wash. (Chi.) Sept. 21, 1914 (4th)
Ana. (Sea.) July 25, 2004 (8th)
NL: Atl. (Hou.) Aug. 4(2g), 1979 (5th)
Phil. (Ari.) July 25, 2006 (3rd)

BALKS

Most Balks, Game
6 **NL:** Mil. (Chi.) May 4, 1963
5 **AL:** Mil. (NY) Apr. 10, 1988
Oak. (Sea.) Apr. 13, 1988

Most Balks, Both Clubs, Game
7 **NL:** Pitt. (4) Cin. (3) Apr. 13, 1963
Mil. (6) Chi. (1) May 4, 1963
6 **AL:** Mil. (5) NY (1) Apr. 10, 1988
Chi. (4) Cal. (2) Apr. 12, 1988

Fewest Balks, Both Clubs, Game (Most Innings)
0 **NL:** Bos. (Brk.) May 1, 1920 (26 inn)
AL: Chi. (Mil.) May 8, 1984 (25 inn)

Most Balks, Inning
3 **AL:** Clev. (Phil.) May 12, 1930 (3rd)
Det. (Oak.) May 3, 1988 (6th)
NL: Cin. (LA) Apr. 24, 1963 (2nd)
Mil. (Chi.) May 4, 1963 (3rd)
Pitt. (NY) Aug. 6, 1988 (8th)

CLUB GENERAL – SEASON

	AL:1901-1960 NL:1900-1961 8 clubs 154 games		AL:1961-1968 NL:1962-1968 10 clubs 162 games		AL:1969- NL:1969- 12-16 clubs 162 games	
Most Games Played						
AL:	162	Det. 1904	164	By many	163	By many
NL:	160	Cin. 1915	165	LA & SF 1962	164	Pitt. & StL. 1989
Fewest Games Played						
AL:	147	Clev. 1945	159	Wash. 1966	158	Balt. 1971
NL:	149	Phil. 1907, 34	160	Cin. 1966	160	By many
Highest Percentage Games Won						
AL:	.721	Clev. 1954 (111-43)	.673	NY 1961 (109-53)	.716	Sea. 2001 (116-46)
NL:	.763	Chi. 1906 (116-36)	.627	StL. 1967 (101-60)	.667	Cin. 1975 (108-54) NY 1986 (108-54)
Lowest Percentage Games Won						
AL:	.235	Phil. 1916 (36-117)	.346	Wash. 1963 (56-106)	.265	Det. 2003 (43-119)
NL:	.248	Bos. 1935 (38-115)	.250	NY 1962 (40-120)	.315	Ari. 2004 (51-111)
Lowest Percentage Games Won, First Place						
AL:	.575	Det. 1945 (88-65)	.568	Bos. 1967 (92-70)	.519	KC 1984 (84-78)
NL:	.564	LA 1959 (88-68)	.574	StL. 1964 (93-69)	.506	SD 2005 (82-80)
Highest Percentage Games Won, Last Place						
AL:	.431	Chi. 1924 (66-87)	.440	NY 1966 (70-89)	.500	Cal. 1991 (81-81)
NL:	.454	NY 1915 (69-83)	.444	Hou. 1968 (72-90)	.500	Wash. 2005 (81-81)
Most Games Won						
AL:	111	Clev. 1954	109	NY 1961	116	Sea. 2001
NL:	116	Chi. 1906	103	SF 1962	108	Cin. 1975; NY 1986
Fewest Games Won						
AL:	36	Phil. 1916	56	Wash. 1963	43	Det. 2003
NL:	38	Bos. 1935	40	NY 1962	51	Ari. 2004
Most Games Won, Home						
AL:	62	NY 1932	65	NY 1961	62	NY 1998
NL:	60	StL. 1942 Brk. 1953	61	SF 1962	64	Cin. 1975
Fewest Games Won, Home						
AL:	18	StL. 1939	26	KC 1964	23	Det. 2003
NL:	20	Phil. 1923	22	NY 1962	24	Mtl. 1969
Most Games Won, Away						
AL:	54	NY 1939	51	Det. 1961 Minn. 1965	59	Sea. 2001
NL:	60	Chi. 1906	52	StL. 1967	53	Cin. 1972, 76; NY 1986 Atl. 1993; SF 1993
Fewest Games Won, Away						
AL:	13	Phil. 1916	24	Cal. 1961	20	Balt. 1988; Det. 2003 TB 2006
NL:	13	Bos. 1935	17	NY 1963	21	Atl. 1977
Most Games Lost						
AL:	117	Phil. 1916	106	Wash. 1963	119	Det. 2003
NL:	115	Bos. 1935	120	NY 1962	111	Ari. 2004
Fewest Games Lost						
AL:	43	Clev. 1954	53	NY 1961	46	Sea. 2001
NL:	36	Chi. 1906	60	StL. 1967	54	Cin. 1975; NY 1986
Most Games Lost, Home						
AL:	59	StL. 1939	55	KC 1964	58	Det. 2003
NL:	55	Phil. 1923, 40, 45 Bos. 1923	58	NY 1962	57	Mtl. 1969
Fewest Games Lost, Home						
AL:	15	NY 1932	16	NY 1961	19	NY 1998
NL:	17	StL. 1942 Brk. 1953	21	SF 1962	17	Cin. 1975
Most Games Lost, Away						
AL:	64	Phil. 1916	57	Wash. 1963	61	Balt. 1988; Det. 2003 TB 2006
NL:	65	Bos. 1935	64	NY 1963	60	Atl. 1977

	AL:1901-1960 NL:1900-1961 8 clubs 154 games		AL:1961-1968 NL:1962-1968 10 clubs 162 games		AL:1969- NL:1969- 12-16 clubs 162 games	
Fewest Games Lost, Away						
AL:	20	NY 1939	30	Det. 1961 Minn. 1965	22	Sea. 2001
NL:	15	Chi. 1906	28	StL. 1967	25	Cin. 1972
Most Games Tied						
AL:	10	Det. 1904	2	By many	3	Chi. 1974
NL:	9	StL. 1911	2	By many	3	Chi. 1981
Most Night Games						
AL:	87	Balt. 1960	107	Cal. 1964, 68	134	Sea. 1982
NL:	105	LA 1961	118	Hou. 1964	134	Hou. 1984
Fewest Night Games (Since 1935)						
AL:	2	Det. 1939	66	Minn. 1961 Bos. & NY 1962	62	Clev. 1973
NL:	0	NY 1935-39	43	Chi. 1962-65	46	Chi. 1969
Most Night Games Won						
AL:	47	Balt. 1960	64	Det. 1968	80	Balt. 1980
NL:	61	LA 1961	70	StL. 1967	77	Atl. 1993
Fewest Night Games Won						
AL:	1	By many	25	Bos. 1966	29	Chi. 1970
NL:	1	By many	11	Chi. 1962	17	Chi. 1980
Most Night Games Lost						
AL:	48	KC 1956	68	Wash. 1963	83	Sea. 1980
NL:	67	Phil. 1961	68	Hou. 1964	83	Atl. 1977
Fewest Night Games Lost						
AL:	1	By many	26	Det. & NY 1962	32	Oak. 1971
NL:	0	By many	26	Chi. 1963, 65	21	Chi. 1969
Most Extra-Inning Games						
AL:	31	Bos. 1943	26	NY 1964	26	Tex. 1976
NL:	27	Bos. 1943	27	LA 1967	27	Hou. 1990
Fewest Extra-Inning Games						
AL:	3	StL. 1936	9	KC 1961-62 Minn. & NY 1966 Det. 1967	5	Chi. 2002
NL:	5	Chi. & Cin. 1948	7	Mil. 1964	6	Atl. 1998
Most Extra-Inning Games Won						
AL:	18	Clev. 1949	16	Clev. 1967	16	Balt. 1970
NL:	19	Pitt. 1959	15	StL. 1968	18	Mtl. 1988
Fewest Extra-Inning Games Won						
AL:	1	By many	3	KC 1962, 65	1	Chi. 1978 Minn. 1982 Tex. 1985
NL:	1	By many	2	Pitt. 1964 NY 1968	0	Mtl. 1969
Most Extra-Inning Games Lost						
AL:	18	StL. 1943	16	Bos. 1966	15	Clev. 1977, 89 Chi. 1988
NL:	17	Phil. 1924 Cin. 1942	17	LA 1967	17	NY 1978 Pitt. 1984
Fewest Extra-Inning Games Lost						
AL:	0	Phil. 1928	2	NY 1961	1	Oak. 1975 Tor. 2006
NL:	0	Cin. 1948	2	Cin.& Mil. 1964 Phil. 1968	1	Pitt. 1969 NY 1984 Mtl. 1987 SD 2001 SF 2002
Most Extra-Inning Games Tied						
AL:	6	Det. 1904 Bos. 1907	1	By many	1	By many
NL:	6	Phil. 1913	1	By many	2	Chi. 1981

	AL:1901-1960 NL:1900-1961 8 clubs 154 games		AL:1961-1968 NL:1962-1968 10 clubs 162 games		AL:1969- NL:1969- 12-16 clubs 162 games
Most Doubleheaders					
AL:	44	Chi. 1943; Wash. 1945	34	Chi. 1961	22	NY 1972
NL:	46	Bos. 1945	30	NY 1962	22	NY 1969
Fewest Doubleheaders					
AL:	8	Det. 1910	14	Bos. & Minn. 1968	0	By many
NL:	6	LA 1961	8	LA 1966; StL. 1968	0	By many
Most Doubleheaders Won					
AL:	14	Clev. 1943; NY 43, 47 Wash. 1945 Bos. 1946	15	Chi. 1961	10	NY 1972
NL:	20	Chi. 1945	8	Cin.& Mil. 1964	11	NY 1969
Fewest Doubleheaders Won					
AL:	0	By many	1	Minn. 1964, 68 Cal. & Wash. 1968	0	By many
NL:	1	By many	0	SF 1963	0	By many
Most Doubleheaders Lost					
AL:	19	StL. 1937	12	Cal. 1961, 65	13	Chi. 1970
NL:	18	Chi. 1950 Bos. 1935	15	NY 1962	11	NY 1974
Fewest Doubleheaders Lost					
AL:	0	By many	1	By many	0	By many
NL:	0	By many	0	Cin. 1967	0	By many
Most Doubleheaders Split					
AL:	19	By many	17	KC 1965, 67 Bos. 1966	14	Oak. 1969
NL:	25	Phil. 1944	13	NY 1967	12	Chi. 1973
Most Players					
AL:	56	Phil. 1915	52	KC 1961	59	Clev. 2002
NL:	53	Brk. 1944	54	NY 1967	59	SD 2002
Fewest Players					
AL:	18	Bos. 1904	30	NY 1963 Bos. 1965	30	Balt. 1969
NL:	20	Chi. 1905	30	LA 1962	29	Cin. 1975-76
Most Pitchers					
AL:	27	Phil. 1915 KC 1955	24	KC 1965	32	Clev. 2000
NL:	24	Cin. 1912 Brk. 1944 Phil. 1946	27	NY 1967	37	SD 2002
Fewest Pitchers					
AL:	5	Bos. 1904	12	Bos.& Chi. 1965 Minn. 1967	11	Balt. 1972, 74 Oak. 1974 Bos. 1976
NL:	5	Bos. 1901	12	LA 1962, 65 SF 1962, 68 Cin. 1963	11	Phil. 1976 Atl. 1980
Most Starting Pitchers					
AL:	24	Phil. 1915	17	Wash. 1963 Cal. 1967	18	Clev. 1993
NL:	19	Brk. 1944 Phil. 1946	20	NY 1967	18	Pitt. 1996
Most Appearances by Relief Pitchers					
AL:	263	NY 1960	378	KC 1965	494	Tex. 2003
NL:	293	Chi. 1958	321	Cin. 1968	542	Chi. 2006
Fewest Appearances by Relief Pitchers					
AL:	9	Bos. 1904	168	Balt. 1961	139	Bos. 1974
NL:	8	StL. 1904	167	SF 1968	170	LA 1975
Most Pinch Hitters					
AL:	309	Wash. 1960	277	Wash. 1962	326	Mil. 1970
NL:	300	Cin. 1958	363	NY 1965	353	LA 1992
Most Managers					
AL:	4	Bos. 1907	3	Det. 1966 Chi. 1968	4	Tex. 1977
NL:	4	Chi. 1961	3	Chi. 1962	4	StL. 1980

GAMES

Same Clubs, Consecutive
12 **NL:** Bos. vs Phil. Sept. 2-8, 1903
11 **AL:** Det. vs StL. Sept. 8-14, 1904

One Day
3 **NL:** Brk. vs Pitt. Sept. 1, 1890
Balt. vs Lou. Sept. 7, 1896
Cin. vs Pitt. Oct. 2, 1920
2 **AL:** By many clubs

TIME

Shortest Game (9 innings)
0:51 **NL:** NY 6 Phil. 1 Sept. 28(1g), 1919
0:55 **AL:** StL. 6 NY 2 Sept. 26(2g), 1926

Shortest Doubleheader (18 innings)
2:07 **AL:** NY vs StL. Sept. 26, 1926
2:20 **NL:** Chi. vs Brk. Aug. 14, 1919

Longest Game
4:45 **AL:** NY 14 Bos. 11 Aug 18(2g) 2006
4:27 **NL:** LA 11 SF 10 Oct. 5, 2001
Extra Innings:
8:06 **AL:** Chi. 7 Mil. 6 May 8, 1984 (25 inn)
7:23 **NL:** SF 8 NY 6 May 31(2g), 1964 (23 inn)

Longest Doubleheader
7:39 **AL:** Tex. vs Chi. May 24, 1995
6:46 **NL:** Brk. vs NY Aug. 7, 1952
Extra Innings:
9:52 **NL:** SF vs NY May 31, 1964 (32 inn)
9:05 **AL:** KC vs Det. June 17, 1967 (28 inn)

INNINGS

Most Innings, Game
26 **NL:** Brk. (1) Bos. (1) May 1, 1920
25 **AL:** Chi. (7) Mil. (6) May 8, 1984

Most Innings, 2 Consecutive Games
45 **NL:** Bos. May 1-3, 1920
37 **AL:** Mil. May 12-13, 1972
Minn. May 12-13, 1972

Most Innings, 3 Consecutive Games
58 **NL:** Brk. May 1-3, 1920
46 **AL:** Mil. May 10-13, 12-14, 1972
Minn. May 10-13, 12-14, 1972

Most Innings, 2 Consecutive Games, Same Clubs
40 **NL:** Bos. vs Chi. May 14-17, 1927
37 **AL:** Mil. vs Minn. May 12-13, 1972

Most Innings, Opening-Day Game
15 **AL:** Wash. (1) Phil. (0) Apr. 13, 1926
Det. (4) Clev. (2) Apr. 19, 1960
14 **NL:** Phil. (5) Brk. (5) Apr. 17, 1923
Pitt. (4) Mil. (3) Apr. 15, 1958
Pitt. (6) StL. (2) Apr. 8, 1969
Cin. (2) LA (1) Apr. 7, 1975
NY (1) Phil. (0) Mar. 31, 1998

Most Innings, Shutout
24 **NL:** Hou. (1) NY (0) Apr. 15, 1968
20 **AL:** Oak. (1) Cal. (0) July 9, 1971

Most Innings, 0-0 Game
19 **NL:** Brk. vs Cin. Sept. 11, 1946
18 **AL:** Det. vs Wash. July 16, 1909

Most Innings, 1-0 Game
24 **NL:** Hou. vs NY Apr. 15, 1968
20 **AL:** Oak. vs Cal. July 9, 1971

Most Innings, Tie Game
26 **NL:** Brk. vs Bos. May 1, 1920 (1-1)
24 **AL:** Det. vs Phil. July 21, 1945 (1-1)

FIRST PLACE

Most Seasons
44 **AL:** NY 1921-23, 26-28, 32, 36-39, 41-43,
47, 49-53, 55-58, 60-64, 76-78, 80-81,
94, 96, 98-2006
28 **NL:** Bos./Mil./Atl. 1877-78, 83, 91-93, 97-98,
1914, 48, 57-58, 69, 82, 91-93, 95-2005

Most Seasons, Consecutive
11 **NL:** Atl. 1995-2005
9 **AL:** NY 1998-2006

Fewest Decisions to Clinch
136 **AL:** NY 1941 (Sept. 4)
137 **NL:** NY 1904 (Sept. 22)

Earliest Date To Clinch
Sept. 4 **AL:** NY 1941 (136 dec)
Sept. 7 **NL:** Cin. 1945 (142 dec)

Days In First Place
Most:
182 **AL:** Sea. 2001 162g (entire season)
(not including Sept. 11-16, 2001)
Chi. 2005 162g (entire season)
NL: SF 2003 161g (entire season)
Fewest (by team finishing in 1st place):
3 **NL:** NY 1951 154g (before playoff)
4 **AL:** Minn. 2006 162g

Largest Gain, Standings, From Previous Season
9 **NL:** Brk. 1899 (10th to 1st)
Since 1900:
8 **AL:** Bos. 1967 (9th to 1st)
NL: NY 1969 (9th to 1st)

LAST PLACE

Most Seasons
29 **AL:** Phil./KC/Oak. 1915-21, 35-36, 38, 40-
43, 45-46, 50, 54, 56, 60-61, 64-65, 6
77, 79, 93, 97-98
27 **NL:** Phil. 1883, 1904, 19-21, 23, 26-28, 30,
36, 38-42, 44-45, 47, 58-61, 72, 96-97
2000

Most Seasons, Consecutive
7 **AL:** Phil. 1915-21
5 **NL:** Phil. 1938-42

GAMES AHEAD

Most, End of Season
30.0 **AL:** Clev. 1995
27.5 **NL:** Pitt. 1902

Most, 1st-Place Finisher, Through July 4
14.5 **NL:** NY 1912
13.0 **AL:** Clev. 1999

GAMES BEHIND

Most, End Of Season
80.0 **NL:** Clev. 1899
Since 1900:
66.5 **NL:** Bos. 1906
64.5 **AL:** StL. 1939

Fewest, End Of Season, Last Place Club
10.0 **AL:** Cal. 1987
AL: Tex. 1987
9.0 **NL:** Wash. 2005

Most, 1st-Place Finisher, Through July 4
15.0 **NL:**Bos. 1914 (8th place)
9.0 **AL:**NY 1978 (2nd place)
Minn. 2006 (3rd place)

ˈERCENTAGE

One Month (Minimum: 15 decisions)
Highest:
.947 **UA:**StL. May 1884 (18-1)
.944 **NL:**Prov. Aug. 1884 (17-1)
Since 1900:
.900 **AL:**Det. Apr. 1984 (18-2)
.897 **NL:**Chi. Aug. 1906 (26-3)
Lowest:
.036 **NL:**Pitt. Aug. 1890 (1-27)
Clev. Sept. 1899 (1-27)
Since 1900:
.043 **AL:**Balt. Apr. 1988 (1-22)
.120 **NL:**Phil. May 1928 (3-22)

ˈLAYOFF WINNERS

One-Game Playoff:
AL: Clev. (Bos.) 1948
NY (Bos.) 1978
Sea. (Cal.) 1995
NL: Hou. (LA) 1980
Chi. (SF) 1998
NY (Cin.) 1999

Best-Of-Three Series:
NL: StL. (Brk.) 1946 (2-0)
NY (Brk.) 1951 (2-1)
LA (Mil.) 1959 (2-0)
SF (LA) 1962 (2-1)
AL:none

ˈAMES WON

Opening Games Won, Consecutive Seasons
10 **NL:**Bos. 1887-96
Since 1900:
9 **AL:**StL. 1937-45
NL:NY 1975-83
Cin. 1983-91

Most Seasons, 100 or more Games Won
18 **AL:**NY 1927-28, 32, 36-37, 39, 41-42,
54, 61, 63, 77-78, 80, 98, 2002-04
8 **NL:**Bos./Atl. 1892, 98, 1993, 97-99, 2002-03
StL. 1931, 42-44, 67, 85, 2004-05

Most Seasons, Consecutive, 100 or more Wins
3 **AL:**Phil. 1929-31
Balt. 1969-71
NY 2002-04
NL: StL. 1942-44
Atl. 1997-99

Most Wins, 2 Consecutive Seasons
223 **NL:**Chi. 1906-07
217 **AL:**Balt. 1969-70

Most Wins, 3 Consecutive Seasons
322 **NL:**Chi. 1906-08
318 **AL:**Balt. 1969-71

Most Wins, Consecutive, Season
26 **NL:**NY Sept. 7-30, 1916 (+1 tie)
20 **AL:**Oak. Aug. 13-Sept. 4, 2002

Most Wins, Consecutive, Season (no ties)
21 **NL:**Chi. June 2-July 8, 1880
Chi. Sept. 4-27, 1935
20 **AL:**Oak. Aug. 13-Sept. 4, 2002

Most Wins, Consecutive, Start of Season
20 **UA:**StL. Apr. 20-May 22, 1884
13 **NL:**Atl. Apr. 6-21, 1982
AL: Mil. Apr. 6-20, 1987

Most Wins, vs. One Opponent, Season
21 **NL:**Chi. (Bos.) 1909 (lost 1)
Pitt. (Cin.) 1937 (lost 1)
Chi. (Cin.) 1945 (lost 1)
AL:NY (StL.) 1927 (lost 1)

Most Wins, Consecutive, vs. One Opponent
27 **NL:**Pro. (Det.) June 24, 1883-Sept. 18, 1884
23 **AL:**Balt. (KC) May 10, 1969-Aug. 2, 1970
NL Since 1900:
20 **NL:**StL. (Phil.) July 15, 1927-July 20, 1928
Pitt. (Cin.) May 31, 1937-Apr. 24, 1938

Most Wins, Consecutive Seasons, vs. One Opponent
40 **NL:**Pitt. (StL.) 1907-08
37 **AL:**Phil. (StL.) 1910-11
Chi. (Phil.) 1915-16
NY (Phil.) 1919-20
NY (StL.) 1926-27

Most Wins, vs. Pennant Winner, Season
16 **NL:**StL. (Chi.) 1945 (lost 6)
14 **AL:**Phil. (Det.) 1909 (lost 8)
Minn. (Oak.) 1973 (lost 4)

Most Home Wins, vs. One Club, Season
16 **NL:**Brk. (Pitt.) 1890 (lost 2)
Phil. (Pitt.) 1890 (lost 1)
Since 1900:
13 **NL:**NY (Phil.) 1904 (lost 2)
12 **AL:**Chi. (StL.) 1915 (lost 0)

Most Home Wins, Consecutive, vs. One Club
32 **NL:**Balt. (Lou.) June 7, 1894-July 11, 1899
Since 1900:
27 **AL:**Clev. (StL./Balt.) Aug. 13, 1952-
Aug. 15, 1954
25 **NL:**StL. (Cin.) Apr. 27, 1929-May 31, 1931

Most Away Wins, Consecutive, vs. One Club
19 **NL:**Brk. (Cin.) June 22, 1947-May 22, 1949
18 **AL:**Bos. (NY) Oct. 3, 1911-June 2, 1913

Most Away Wins, vs. One Club, Season, No Losses:
11 **NL:**Pitt. (StL.) 1908
Chi. (Bos.) 1909
Brk. (Phil.) 1945
AL: Chi. (Phil.) 1915
NY (StL.) 1927, 39
Clev. (Bos.) 1954

Most Home Wins, Consecutive, Season
27 **AA:**StL. Apr. 26-July 16, 1885
26 **NL:**NY Sept. 7-30, 1916 (includes tie)
24 **AL:**Bos. June 25-Aug. 13, 1988

Most Away Wins, Consecutive, Season
17 **NL:**NY May 9-29, 1916
AL: Det. Apr. 3-May 24, 1984

Most Wins, One Month
29 **NL:**NY Sept. 1916 (lost 5)
28 **AL:**NY Aug. 1938 (lost 4)

Most Wins, One Day
3 **NL:**Brk. (Pitt.) Sept. 1, 1890
Balt. (Lou.) Sept. 7, 1896
2 **AL:**By many clubs

Most Wins, 2 Consecutive Days
5 **NL:**Balt. Sept. 7-8, 1896
4 **AL:**By many clubs

Most Days, 2 Wins, vs. One Club, Season
7 **AL:**Chi. (Phil.) 1943
NL: Chi. (Cin.) 1945

GAMES LOST

Opening Games Lost, Consecutive Seasons
9 **NL:** NY 1893-1901
   Atl. 1972-80
8 **AL:** Wash. 1963-70

Most Seasons, 100 or more Games Lost
16 **AL:** Phil./KC/Oak. 1915-16, 19-21, 36, 40, 43, 46, 50, 54, 56, 61, 64-65, 79
14 **NL:** Phil. 1904, 21, 23, 27-28, 30, 36, 38-42, 45, 61

Most Seasons, Consecutive, 100 or more Games Lost
5 **NL:** Phil. 1938-42
4 **AL:** Wash. 1961-64

Most Losses, 2 Consecutive Seasons
231 **NL:** NY 1962-63 (162 g)
226 **AL:** Phil. 1915-16
220 **NL:** Phil. 1941-42(154 g)

Most Losses, 3 Consecutive Seasons
340 **NL:** NY 1962-64 (162 g)
324 **AL:** Phil. 1915-17
323 **NL:** Phil. 1940-42 (154 g)

Most Losses, Consecutive, Season
26 **AA:** Lou. May 22-June 22, 1889
24 **NL:** Clev. Aug. 26-Sept. 16, 1899
   Since 1900:
23 **NL:** Phil. July 29-Aug. 20, 1961
21 **AL:** Balt. Apr. 4-28, 1988

Most Losses, Consecutive, Start of Season
21 **AL:** Balt. Apr. 4-28, 1988
14 **NL:** Chi. Apr. 1-20, 1997

Most Home Losses, Consecutive, Season
20 **AL:** StL. June 3-July 7, 1953
15 **NL:** NY Aug. 1-Sept. 3, 2002

Most Away Losses, Consecutive, Season
41 **NL:** Pitt. July 18-Sept. 12, 1890
22 **AL:** Phil. July 11(2g)-Aug. 24(1g), 1943
   NL Since 1900:
22 **NL:** NY June 16-July 28, 1963

Most Losses, One Month
29 **AL:** Wash. July 1909 (won 5)
27 **NL:** Pitt. Aug. 1890 (won 1)
   Clev. Sept. 1899 (won 1)
   StL. Sept. 1908 (won 7)
   Brk. Sept. 1908 (won 6)
   Phil. Sept. 1939 (won 6)

Most Losses, One Day
3 **NL:** Pitt. (Brk.) Sept. 1, 1890
   Lou. (Balt.) Sept. 7, 1896
2 **AL:** By many clubs

Most Losses, 2 Consecutive Days
5 **NL:** Pitt. Aug. 30-Sept. 1, 1890
   Lou. Sept. 7-8, 1896
4 **AL:** By many clubs

NO-HIT GAMES

Most No-Hit Games, vs. One Club, Season
2 **AL:** StL. (Chi.) 1917
   NL: Mil. (Phil.) 1960

EXTRA-INNING GAMES

Most Consecutive Extra-Inning Games, Season
5 **AL:** Det. Sept. 9-13, 1908
4 **NL:** Pitt. Aug. 18-22, 1917
   Brk. Sept. 20-23, 1924
   Cin. Aug. 21-23, 1926
   Pitt. May 8-15, 1938
   Cin. Sept. 5-7, 1939
   SF July 7-10, 1987
   Mil. Sept. 15-19, 1999

Most Consecutive Extra-Inning Games, Same Clubs, Season
4 **AL:** Chi. vs Det. Sept. 9-12, 1908
   Clev. vs StL. May 1-5, 1910
   Bos. vs StL. May 31-June 2, 1943
   Tex. vs Sea. Sept. 16-19, 2002
3 **NL:** Brk. vs Pitt. Aug. 20-22, 1917
   Cin. vs Bos. June 4-7, 1925
   Bos. vs Cin. Aug. 21-22, 1926
   Bos. vs Phil. July 2-3, 1928
   NY vs Chi. Sept. 13-15, 1932
   Pitt. vs Cin. Sept. 6-7, 1939
   Chi. vs Pitt. Aug. 18-20, 1961
   Mtl. vs NY June 17-19, 1975
   Cin. vs NY May 5-7, 1980
   Atl. vs LA Aug. 5-7, 1982
   Mil. vs Chi. Sept. 17-19, 1999
   NY vs Hou. July 31-Aug. 2, 2001

DOUBLEHEADERS

Most Consecutive Doubleheaders, Season
9 **NL:** Bos. Sept. 4-15, 1928
8 **AL:** Wash. July 27-Aug. 5, 1909

Most Doubleheaders Won, Consecutive, Season
5 **AL:** NY Aug. 30-Sept. 4, 1906
4 **NL:** Brk. Sept. 1-4, 1924
   NY Sept. 10-14, 1928

Most Doubleheaders Lost, Consecutive, Season
5 **NL:** Bos. Sept. 8-14, 1928
4 **AL:** Bos. June 29-July 5, 1921

Most Doubleheaders, Consecutive, Same Clubs, Season
5 **AL:** Phil. vs Wash. Aug. 5-10, 1901
4 **NL:** NY vs Bos. Sept. 10-14, 1928

PERSONNEL

Most Players, Game
27 **AL:** KC (Cal.) Sept. 10, 1969
26 **NL:** LA (Cin.) Oct. 6, 1985
   Extra-Inning Game:
30 **AL:** Oak. (Chi.) Sept. 19, 1972 (15 inn)
28 **NL:** LA (SD) Sept. 13, 1982 (16 inn)
   Doubleheader:
42 **AL:** Tex. (Balt.) Sept. 7, 1989
   AL: Minn. (Chi.) Oct. 3, 1991 (22 inn)
41 **NL:** SD (SF) May 30, 1977
   Doubleheader, Extra Innings
43 **NL:** LA (SD) Sept. 21, 1988 (19 inn)

Most Players, Both Clubs, Game
46 **AL:** NY (24) Bos. (22) Oct. 2, 2005
45 **NL:** Chi. (24) Mtl. (21) Sept. 5, 1978
Atl. (24) NY (21) Sept. 29, 2002
Extra-Inning Game:
54 **AL:** Sea. (29) Tex. (25) Sept. 25 1992(16 inn)
53 **NL:** Chi. (27) Hou. (26) Sept. 2, 1986 (18 inn)
Doubleheader:
74 **NL:** SD (41) SF (33) May 30, 1977
71 **AL:** Tex. (42) Balt. (29) Sept. 7, 1989
Doubleheader, Extra Innings:
83 **AL:** Minn. (42) Chi. (41) Oct. 3, 1991 (22 inn)
78 **NL:** Hou. (39) NY (39) Sept. 15, 1998 (21 inn)

Most Pitchers, Game
10 **AL:** Balt. (NY) Sept. 12, 2004
9 **NL:** Mtl. (Chi.) Sept. 10, 1996
StL. (LA) Sept. 8, 2001
StL. (Cin.) Oct. 2, 2005
Hou. (Phil.) Sept. 25, 2006
Col. (LA) Sept. 28, 2006
Extra-Inning Game:
11 **AL:** Sea. (Tex.) Sept. 25, 1992 (16 inn)
10 **NL:** Chi. (Pitt.) Apr. 20, 1986 (17 inn)
Hou. (Chi.) Sept. 28, 1995 (11 inn)
Col. (Atl.) Aug. 22, 2000 (12 inn)
Atl. (Phil.) Sept. 27, 2003 (10 inn)
Phil. (NY) Sept. 11, 2004 (13 inn)
Chi. (Hou.) Aug. 15, 2006 (18 inn)
Ari. (Col.) Sept. 16, 2006 (16 inn)
Col. (Chi.) Sept. 30, 2006 (14 inn)
Chi. (Col.) Sept. 30, 2006 (14 inn)
Doubleheader:
13 **NL:** Mil. (Phil.) May 12, 1963 (23 inn)
Col. (SD) June 28 1994 (20 inn)
SD (SF) May 30, 1977
12 **AL:** Clev. (Det.) Sept. 7, 1959
Cal. (Det.) Sept. 30, 1967
Doubleheader, Extra Innings:
13 **AL:** Balt. (Tex.) Aug. 13, 1991 (21 inn)

Most Pitchers, Both Clubs, Game
16 **NL:** Hou. (8) SF (8) Sept. 28, 2002
Hou (9) Phil. (7) Sept. 25, 2006
Col. (9) LA (7) Sept. 28, 2006
15 **AL:** Det. (8) Minn. (7) Oct. 1, 2000
Balt. (10) NY (5) Sept. 12, 2004
Extra-Inning Game:
20 **NL:** Col. (10) Chi. (10) Sept. 30, 2006 (14 inn)
18 **AL:** Sea. (9) Oak. (9) Sept. 20, 1997 (15 inn)
Det. (10) Chi. (8) Sept. 14, 1998 (12 inn)
Doubleheader:
22 **NL:** Mil. (11) NY (11) July 26, 1964
StL. (11) Phil. (11) June 20, 1989
Chi. (11) Pitt. (11) Sept. 27, 1996 (19 inn)
Chi. (12) Pitt. (10) Sept. 19, 2003
AL: Wash. (12) Clev. (10) Sept. 14, 1971 (29 inn)
Chi. (12) Minn. (10) Oct. 3, 1991 (22 inn)
Det. (12) NY (10) July 20, 1998 (26 inn)

Most Pitchers, Combination Shutout Win
7 **AL:** Tex. (Ana.) Sept. 18, 2004
6 By many NL clubs; last time:
NL: SF (SD) Aug. 14, 2006
Extra-Inning Game:
8 **AL:** Bos. (Balt.) Oct. 3, 1999 (10 inn)
7 **NL:** Atl. (StL.) May 16, 1997 (13 inn)
Ari. (SF) May 29, 2001 (18 inn)

Most Pitchers, Inning
6 **AL:** Oak. (Clev.) Sept. 3, 1983 (9th)
5 **NL:** By many; Last:
Col. (Atl.) Sept. 23, 2006 (8th)

Most Pitchers, Both Clubs, Inning
8 **NL:** LA (5) NY (3) Aug. 26, 1987 (8th)
LA (4) StL.(4) May 14, 1995 (8th)
AL: NY (4) Mil. (4) May 25, 1992 (8th)
Minn. (4) NY (4) Aug. 8, 1993 (8th)
Clev. (5) Minn. (3) May 10, 2000 (7th)
Tex. (4) Oak. (4) July 26, 2002 (7th)
Bos. (4) Tex (4) Aug. 10, 2005 (8th)

LEAGUE RECORDS – SEASON

BATTING

	AL:1901-1960 NL:1900-1961 8 clubs 154 games		AL:1961-1968 NL:1962-1968 10 clubs 162 games		AL:1969- NL:1969- 12-16 clubs 162 games	
Highest Batting Average						
AL	.292	1921	.256	1961	.277	1996
NL	.303	1930	.261	1962	.268	1999
Lowest Batting Average						
AL	.239	1908	.230	1968	.239	1972
NL	.239	1908	.243	1968	.246	1989
Highest Slugging Percentage						
AL	.421	1936	.395	1961	.445	1996
NL	.448	1930	.393	1962	.432	2000
Lowest Slugging Percentage						
AL	.304	1908	.339	1968	.343	1972
NL	.306	1908	.341	1968	.361	1976
Most Tie Games						
AL	19	1910	4	1961, 64	3	1974, 80
NL	16	1913	4	1965	4	1981
Fewest Tie Games						
AL	0	1930	0	1963, 65	0	Many seasons
NL	0	1925, 54, 58	1	1963, 66-67	0	Many seasons
Most Extra-Inning Games						
AL	91	1943	91	1965	117	1991
NL	82	1920, 57	93	1967	135	1998, 2000
Most At-Bats						
AL	43,747	1936	55,239	1962	79,090	1996
NL	43,891	1936	55,449	1962	89,011	1999
Fewest At-Bats						
AL	39,914	1913	53,709	1968	64,642	1971
NL	39,326	1907	54,803	1963	65,156	1978
Most Runs						
AL	7,009	1936	7,342	1961	12,208	1996
NL	7,025	1930	7,278	1962	12,976	2000
Fewest Runs						
AL	4,267	1909	5,532	1968	7,472	1971
NL	4,136	1908	5,577	1968	7,522	1988
Most Hits						
AL	12,657	1936	14,068	1962	21,922	1996
NL	13,260	1930	14,453	1962	23,880	1999
Fewest Hits						
AL	9,703	1908	12,359	1968	15,957	1971
NL	9,566	1907	13,351	1968	16,215	1989
Most Total Bases						
AL	18,427	1936	21,762	1962	35,195	1996
NL	19,572	1930	21,781	1962	38,305	2000
Fewest Total Bases						
AL	12,337	1908	18,221	1968	23,537	1971
NL	12,142	1907	18,737	1968	23,767	1976
Most Extra-Base Hits						
AL	3,706	1936	4,190	1962	7,377	2000
NL	3,903	1930	3,977	1962	8,235	2006
Fewest Extra-Base Hits						
AL	1,879	1909	3,316	1968	4,177	1976
NL	1,793	1907	3,245	1968	4,264	1976
Most Singles						
AL	9,214	1921	9,878	1962	15,072	1980
NL	9,476	1922	10,476	1962	15,856	1999
Fewest Singles						
AL	7,573	1959	9,043	1968	11,696	1971
NL	7,466	1956	9,796	1963	11,536	1989

	AL:1901-1960 NL:1900-1961 8 clubs 154 games		AL:1961-1968 NL:1962-1968 10 clubs 162 games		AL:1969- NL:1969- 12-16 clubs 162 games	
Most Doubles						
AL	2,400	1936	2,238	1962	4,301	2006
NL	2,386	1930	2,161	1964	4,834	2006
Fewest Doubles						
AL	1,271	1909	1,874	1968	2,385	1969
NL	1,148	1907	1,984	1963	2,455	1969
Most Triples						
AL	694	1921	408	1966	644	1977
NL	684	1911, 12	453	1962	561	2006
Fewest Triples						
AL	267	1959	333	1964	351	1971
NL	323	1942	359	1968	386	1973
Most Home Runs						
AL	1,091	1959	1,552	1962	2,742	1996
NL	1,263	1955	1,449	1962	3,005	2000
ML	2,294	1956	3,001	1962	5,693	2000
Fewest Home Runs						
AL	104	1907	1,104	1968	1,122	1976
NL	126	1906	891	1968	1,113	1976
ML	242	1907	1,995	1968	2,235	1976
Most Clubs, 100 or more Home Runs						
AL	8	1958, 60	10	1964	14	Many seasons; Last: 2006
NL	8	1956, 58-59, 61	10	1962	16	1998-2006
ML	16	1958	19	1962	30	1998-2006
Fewest Clubs, 100 or more Home Runs						
AL	0	many. Last: 1945	6	1968	5	1976
NL	0	many. Last: 1943	4	1968	5	1976
ML	0	many. Last: 1924	10	1968	10	1976
Most Grand Slam Home Runs						
AL	37	1938	48	1961	89	2000
NL	35	1950	37	1962	87	2000
ML	68	1950	77	1961	176	2000
Fewest Grand Slam Home Runs						
AL	1	1907, 09, 15	20	1967	23	1976
NL	1	1920	16	1968	21	1976, 82
ML	3	1907	38	1968	44	1976
Most Home Runs, Pinch-hitters						
AL	27	1953, 58	51	1961	53	1980
NL	42	1958, 59	45	1962	98	2006
ML	69	1958	84	1962	133	2004
Most Grand Slam Home Runs, Pinch-hitters						
AL	5	1953	7	1961	7	2004
NL	4	1959	3	1963, 67	9	1978, 95
ML	8	1953	7	1961	13	1978, 2004
Most Runs Batted In						
AL	6,520	1936	6,841	1961	11,583	1996
NL	6,582	1930	6,760	1962	12,321	1999
Most Sacrifice Hits						
AL	1,731	1917	779	1965	1,016	1978
NL	1,655	1908	794	1968	1,190	2004, 06
Fewest Sacrifice Hits						
AL	531	1958	673	1964	461	2006
NL	511	1957	655	1962	809	1984
Most Sacrifice Flies (1908 to 1930, 1939, since 1954)						
AL	370	1954	448	1961	765	1979
NL	425	1954	410	1962	809	2000
Fewest Sacrifice Flies (1908 to 1930, 1939, since 1954)						
AL	312	1959	348	1967	484	1969
NL	304	1959	363	1966	430	1969

REGULAR SEASON – LEAGUE BATTING

	AL:1901-1960 NL:1900-1961 8 clubs 154 games		AL:1961-1968 NL:1962-1968 10 clubs 162 games		AL:1969- NL:1969- 12-16 clubs 162 games	
Most Walks						
AL	5,627	1949	5,902	1961	8,592	1996
NL	4,545	1950	5,264	1962	9,735	2000
Fewest Walks						
AL	2,611	1904	4,881	1968	6,127	1976
NL	2,906	1921	4,275	1968	5,793	1988
Most Intentional Walks (since 1955)						
AL	353	1957	534	1965	734	1993
NL	506	1956	804	1967	964	2002
Fewest Intentional Walks (since 1955)						
AL	257	1959	290	1961	420	1998
NL	389	1957	451	1962	626	1991
Most Hit By Pitch						
AL	464	1911	426	1968	921	2001
NL	513	1900	404	1965	1,030	2006
Fewest Hit By Pitch						
AL	132	1947	316	1965	372	1982
NL	156	1943	327	1964	249	1984
Most Strikeouts						
AL	6,082	1959	9,956	1964	14,617	1997
NL	6,825	1960	9,649	1965	17,908	2001
Fewest Strikeouts						
AL	3,245	1924	8,330	1961	9,143	1976
NL	3,359	1926	9,032	1962	9,602	1976
Most Stolen Bases						
AL	1,809	1912	811	1968	1,734	1987
NL	1,692	1911	788	1962	1,959	1999
Fewest Stolen Bases						
AL	278	1950	540	1964	863	1970
NL	337	1954	636	1964	817	1969
Most Grounded into Double Plays						
AL	1,181	1950	1,256	1961	1,969	1980
NL	1,105	1933	1,251	1962	2,085	2002
Fewest Grounded into Double Plays						
AL	890	1945	1,060	1967	1,442	1976
NL	820	1945	1,120	1963	1,198	1991
Most Left on Base						
AL	9,628	1936	11,683	1961	16,711	1996
NL	9,424	1945	11,414	1962	18,939	2000
Fewest Left on Base						
AL	8,618	1958	10,667	1966	13,507	1976
NL	8,254	1920	10,994	1966	13,295	1988

IELDING

	AL:1901-1960 NL:1900-1961 8 clubs 154 games		AL:1961-1968 NL:1962-1968 10 clubs 162 games		AL:1969- NL:1969- 12-16 clubs 162 games	
Highest Fielding Average						
AL	.979	1958	.980	1964	.984	2006
NL	.977	1956	.978	1968	.983	2005
Lowest Fielding Average						
AL	.937	1901	.976	1961	.975	1975
NL	.949	1903	.975	1962	.976	1974
Most Total Chances						
AL	53,194	1910	62,296	1968	88,541	1980
NL	52,196	1917	63,636	1968	99,083	1998
Fewest Total Chances						
AL	47,293	1958	62,042	1966	74,387	1971
NL	47,539	1955	62,857	1962	74,562	1991
Most Chances Accepted						
AL	50,870	1910	60,997	1964	86,621	1980
NL	50,419	1920	62,247	1968	97,233	1998
Fewest Chances Accepted						
AL	46,086	1938	60,550	1961	72,875	1971
NL	46,404	1955	61,302	1962	72,495	1990
Most Putouts						
AL	33,830	1916	43,847	1964	61,146	1991
NL	33,724	1917	44,042	1968	69,720	1998
Fewest Putouts						
AL	32,235	1938	43,281	1961	51,821	1975
NL	32,296	1906	43,470	1962	52,000	1978
Most Assists						
AL	17,167	1910	17,269	1961	25,626	1980
NL	16,759	1920	18,205	1968	27,513	1998
Fewest Assists						
AL	13,219	1958	17,048	1963	21,001	1971
NL	13,345	1956	17,681	1963	20,351	1990
Most Errors						
AL	2,889	1901	1,506	1961	1,989	1977
NL	2,590	1904	1,586	1964	1,915	1999
Fewest Errors						
AL	1,002	1958	1,261	1964	1,377	2006
NL	1,082	1956	1,389	1968	1,401	1992
Most Passed Balls						
AL	178	1914	211	1965	267	1987
NL	202	1905	216	1962	217	1969
Fewest Passed Balls						
AL	53	1949	147	1963, 66	127	1976
NL	65	1936	148	1968	122	1980
Most Double Plays						
AL	1,487	1949	1,585	1961	2,368	1980
NL	1,337	1951	1,596	1962	2,484	2002
Fewest Double Plays						
AL	818	1912	1,388	1967-68	1,821	1976
NL	1,007	1920	1,431	1963	1,527	1991
Most Triple Plays						
AL	7	1922, 36	5	1968	10	1979
NL	7	1905, 10, 29	5	1964-65	5	1991
Fewest Triple Plays						
AL	0	1904, 33, 42, 56	0	1961-62	0	1974, 75, 87, 93, 98, 2003, 05
NL	0	1928, 38, 41, 43, 45-46, 59, 61	1	1963	0	1974, 84, 2001, 06

PITCHING

	AL:1901-1960 NL:1900-1961 8 clubs 154 games		AL:1961-1968 NL:1962-1968 10 clubs 162 games		AL:1969- NL:1969- 12-16 clubs 162 games	
Lowest Earned Run Average						
AL	2.73	1914	2.98	1968	3.06	1972
NL	2.62	1916	2.99	1968	3.45	1988
Highest Earned Run Average						
AL	5.04	1936	4.02	1961	4.99	1996
NL	4.97	1930	3.94	1962	4.63	2000
Most Complete Games						
AL	1,100	1904	426	1968	650	1974
NL	1,089	1904	471	1968	546	1971
Fewest Complete Games						
AL	312	1960	323	1965	66	2006
NL	328	1961	402	1966	71	2004
Most Saves (since 1969)						
AL	–	–	–	–	637	1990
NL	–	–	–	–	697	2004
Fewest Saves (since 1969)						
AL	–	–	–	–	260	1974
NL	–	–	–	–	257	1974
Most Shutouts						
AL	146	1909	154	1968	193	1972
NL	164	1908	185	1968	166	1969
Fewest Shutouts						
AL	41	1930	100	1961	79	1996
NL	49	1925	95	1962	93	1999
Most No-Hit Games (9 or more innings)						
AL	5	1917	4	1962	5	1990
NL	3	1960	3	1963-64, 68	5	1969
ML	6	1917	5	1962, 68	7	1990
Fewest No-Hit Games (9 or more innings)						
AL	0	Many seasons Last: 1960	0	1961, 63-64	0	Many seasons Last: 2006
NL	0	Many seasons Last: 1959	0	1966	0	Many seasons Last: 2005
ML	0	Many seasons Last: 1959	1	1961, 66	0	1982, 85, 89, 2000, 05
Most One-Hit Games						
AL	12	1910, 15	11	1968	13	1979, 88
NL	12	1906, 11	15	1965	12	1971
Fewest One-Hit Games						
AL	0	1922, 26-27, 30	2	1962	3	1998, 2005
NL	0	1924, 29, 32, 52	3	1962	2	1976, 96
Most 1-0 Games Won						
AL	41	1908	38	1968	42	1971
NL	43	1907	44	1968	45	2001
Fewest 1-0 Games Won						
AL	4	1930, 36	16	1961	10	1998
NL	5	1932, 56	13	1962	12	1997
Most Games Won By One Run						
AL	217	1943	281	1967-68	368	1978
NL	223	1946	294	1968	417	1998
Fewest Games Won By One Run						
AL	157	1938	242	1963	213	1993
NL	170	1949	245	1968	286	1990
Most Earned Runs						
AL	6,120	1936	6,451	1961	11,241	1996
NL	6,046	1930	6,345	1962	11,884	2000
Fewest Earned Runs						
AL	3,414	1914	4,817	1968	6,650	1971
NL	3,258	1916	4,870	1968	6,695	1988

	AL:1901-1960 NL:1900-1961 8 clubs 154 games		AL:1961-1968 NL:1962-1968 10 clubs 162 games		AL:1969- NL:1969- 12-16 clubs 162 games
Most Wild Pitches					
AL	325	1936	513	1966	785	1997
NL	356	1961	550	1965	884	1999
Fewest Wild Pitches					
AL	166	1931	404	1962	491	1976
NL	174	1943	478	1967	443	1980
Most Balks					
AL	46	1950	51	1966	558	1988
NL	76	1950	147	1963	366	1988
Fewest Balks					
AL	18	1933, 41	29	1964	43	1973
NL	13	1936, 46, 56	25	1965	52	1971, 73
Most Pitchers 40 or more Games Won					
AL	1	1904, 08	0	1961-68	0	1969 to date
NL	0	1900-61	0	1962-68	0	1969 to date
Most Pitchers 30 or more Games Won					
AL	2	1912	1	1968	0	1969 to date
NL	2	1903-04	0	1962-68	0	1969 to date
Most Pitchers 20 or more Games Won					
AL	10	1907, 20	5	1963	12	1973
NL	9	1901, 03, 04	7	1965	9	1969
Fewest Pitchers 20 or more Games Won					
AL	0	1955, 60	2	1961, 64-66	0	1982, 95, 2006
NL	0	1931	2	1967	0	1983, 87, 95, 2006
Most Pitchers 20 or more Games Lost					
AL	7	1904	1	1962, 64, 67	2	1973-74
NL	8	1905	4	1962	3	1974
Fewest Pitchers 20 or more Games Lost					
AL	0	17 seasons Last: 1960	0	1962, 64-65, 67-68	0	Many seasons Last: 2006
NL	0	22 seasons Last: 1961	0	1967-68	0	Many seasons Last: 2006

GENERAL

	AL:1901-1960 NL:1900-1961 8 clubs 154 games		AL:1961-1968 NL:1962-1968 10 clubs 162 games		AL:1969- NL:1969- 12-16 clubs 162 games	
Most Players						
AL	323	1955	369	1962	623	2004
NL	333	1946	373	1967	699	2000, 06
Fewest Players						
AL	166	1904	351	1968	416	1976
NL	188	1905	336	1968	420	1979
Most Pitchers						
AL	133	1946	170	1962	315	2006
NL	149	1946	167	1967	360	2006
Most Pinch-Hitters						
AL	1,950	1960	2,403	1967	2,993	1970
NL	1,911	1960	2,448	1965	4,322	2006
ML	3,861	1960	4,723	1967	5,804	1970
Most Batters, .300 Batting Average (Minimum: 300 at-bats)						
AL	34	1921, 24	11	1962	37	1996
NL	45	1930	17	1962	38	2000
Fewest Batters, .300 Batting Average (Minimum: 300 at-bats)						
AL	3	1905	1	1968	6	1971-72
NL	4	1907, 09	5	1968	9	1982
Most Players 150 or more Games						
AL	19	1904, 21, 36	30	1962	46	1998
NL	23	1953	34	1965	42	1998, 2002
Most Players 600 or more At-Bats						
AL	15	1936	17	1962	24	2005
NL	13	1929	19	1962	16	1979, 96
Most Players 100 or more Runs						
AL	24	1936	6	1961	29	1999
NL	19	1929	10	1962	31	1999
Most Players 200 or more Hits						
AL	9	1936-37	1	1962, 64	6	1986
NL	12	1929-30	5	1963-64	6	1970
Most Players 300 or more Total Bases						
AL	12	1930, 37	7	1961	22	2000
NL	14	1930	9	1963, 65	20	1999, 2001
Most Players 40 or more Doubles						
AL	12	1937	3	1962, 65	15	2000, 06
NL	13	1929	3	1968	16	2006
Most Players 20 or more Triples						
AL	4	1912	0	1961-68	1	1979, 85, 2000
NL	3	1911-12	0	1962-68	1	1996
Most Players 50 or more Home Runs						
AL	2	1938	2	1961	2	1996, 2002
NL	2	1947	1	1965	3	1998, 2001
Most Players 40 or more Home Runs						
AL	3	1936	6	1961	8	1996, 98
NL	6	1954-55	2	1961-63, 66	9	2000
Most Players 30 or more Home Runs						
AL	6	1937-38, 40, 58-59	9	1964	23	2000
NL	9	1953, 56	10	1965	25	2001
Most Players 20 or more Home Runs						
AL	18	1959	25	1964	51	1987
NL	23	1956	25	1962	54	1999
Most Players 100 or more Runs Batted In						
AL	18	1936	8	1962	31	1999-2000
NL	17	1930	10	1962	27	1999
Most Players 100 or more Walks						
AL	8	1949	5	1961-62	10	2000
NL	4	1949, 51	1	1962-63	9	2004

	AL:1901-1960 NL:1900-1961 8 clubs 154 games		AL:1961-1968 NL:1962-1968 10 clubs 162 games		AL:1969- NL:1969- 12-16 clubs 162 games	
Most Players 100 or more Strikeouts						
AL	3	1958-60	15	1967	38	1997
NL	4	1960	17	1965	42	2001
Most Managers						
AL	12	1933, 46	15	1966	20	1986
NL	12	1902, 48	12	1965-68	19	2002-04
ML	21	1902, 33	27	1966	38	2002

MISCELLANEOUS SERVICE

Oldest Player
AL: Satchel Paige, KC Sept. 25, 1965 (59 years, 78 days)
NL: Jim O'Rourke, NY Sept. 22, 1904 (52 years, 29 days)

Youngest Player
AA: Fred Chapman, Phil. July 22, 1887 (14 years, 140 days)
NL: Joe Nuxhall, Cin. June 10, 1944 (15 years, 316 days)
AL: Carl Scheib, Phil. Sept. 6, 1943 (16 years, 248 days)

Oldest Manager
AL: Connie Mack, Phil. Oct. 1, 1950, (87 years, 282 days)
NL: Casey Stengel, NY July 24, 1965 (74 years, 359 days)

Youngest Manager
AL: Roger Peckinpaugh, NY Sept. 16, 1914 (23 years, 223 days)
NL: George Davis, NY Apr. 18, 1895 (24 years, 238 days)

Oldest Batting Leader
NL: Barry Bonds, SF 2004 (40 years, 71 days)
AL: Ted Williams, Bos. 1958 (40 years, 28 days)

Youngest Batting Leader
AL: Al Kaline, Det. 1955 (20 years, 280 days)
NL: Pete Reiser, Brk. 1941 (22 years, 195 days)

Oldest Home Run Leader
NL: Cy Williams, Phil. 1927 (39 years, 286 days)
AL: Darrell Evans, Det. 1985 (38 years, 133 days)

Youngest Home Run Leader
AL: Tony Conigliaro, Bos. 1965 (20 years, 270 days)
NL: Sam Crawford, Cin. 1901 (21 years, 171 days)

CLUB SEASON RECORDS PRIOR TO 1900

(The following exceed or equal Major League records listed in preceding sections)

BATTING

Highest Batting Average
.343 **NL:**Phil. 1894

Lowest Batting Average
.208 **NL:**Wash. 1888

Most Runs Scored
1,220 **NL:**Bos. 1894

Most Singles
1,338 **NL:**Phil. 1894

Most Triples
153 **NL:**Balt. 1894

Most Hit By Pitch
121 **NL:**Balt. 1896

Most Stolen Bases
638 **AA:**Phil. 1887
426 **NL:**NY 1893

FIELDING

Most Errors
867 **NL:**Wash. 1886

Most Triple Plays
3 **AA:**Cin. 1882
Roch. 1890
NL:NY 1885

Most Passed Balls
167 **NL:**Bos. 1883

PITCHING

Fewest Shutouts Won
0 **NL:**Brk., StL., Wash. 1898
Clev. 1899

Most No-Hit Games
2 **AA:**Lou. 1882
Colu. 1884
Phil. 1888

Most No-Hit Games Against
2 **AA:**Pitt. 1884
NL: Prov. 1885
Bos. 1898

GENERAL

Highest Pct. Games Won, First Place
.850 **UA:**StL. 1884 (91-16)
.798 **NL:**Chi. 1880 (67-17)

Lowest Pct. Games Won, Last Place
.130 **NL:**Clev. 1899 (20-134)

Fewest Games Won
20 **NL:**Clev. 1899

Fewest Games Won, Away
11 **NL:**Clev. 1899

Most Games Lost
134 **NL:**Clev. 1899

Most Games Lost, Away
101 **NL:**Clev. 1899

MANAGERS

Most, Season
7 **AA:**Lou. 1889
4 **NL:**Wash. 1892, 98
StL. 1895, 96, 97

MANAGERS

Most Seasons, Lifetime
53 Connie Mack, NL:Pitt. (3) 1894-96; AL:Phil. (50) 1901-50

Most Seasons, League
50 Connie Mack, AL:Phil. 1901-50
32 John McGraw, NL:Balt. 1899; NY 1902-32

Most Seasons, One Club
50 Connie Mack, AL:Phil. 1901-50
31 John McGraw, NL:NY 1902-32

Most Clubs, Lifetime
7 Frank Bancroft, NL:Wor. 1880; Det. 81-82; Clev. 83; Prov. 84-85; Ind. 89; Cin. 1902; AA:Phil. 1887
   Since 1900:
6 Jimmy Dykes, AL:Chi. 1934-46; Phil. 51-53; Balt. 54; Det. 59-60; Clev. 60-61; NL:Cin. 1958
   Dick Williams, AL:Bos. 1967-69; Oak. 71-73; Cal. 74-76; Sea. 86-88; NL:Mtl. 1977-81; SD 82-85
   John McNamara, AL:Oak. 1969-70; Cal. 83-84; Bos. 85-88; Clev. 90-91; NL:SD 1974-77; Cin. 79-82

Most Clubs, League
6 Frank Bancroft, NL:Wor. 1880; Det. 81-82; Clev. 83; Prov. 84-85; Ind. 89; Cin. 1902
5 Jimmy Dykes, AL:Chi. 1934-46; Phil. 51-53; Balt. 54; Det. 59-60; Clev. 60-61
   Billy Martin, AL:Minn. 1969; Det. 71-73; Tex. 73-75; NY 75-78, 79, 83, 85; Oak. 80-82
   NL since 1900:
4 Bill McKechnie, NL:Pitt. 1922-26; StL. 28-29; Bos. 30-37; Cin. 38-46
   Rogers Hornsby, NL:StL. 1925-26; Bos. 28; Chi. 30-32; Cin. 52-53
   Leo Durocher, NL:Brk. 1939-46, 48; NY 48-55; Chi. 66-72; Hou. 72-73

Most Clubs, Season
2 Joe Battin, AA:Pitt.-UA:Pitt. 1884
   Bill Watkins, NL:Det.-AA: Colu. 1888
   Gus Schmelz, NL:Clev.-AA: Colu. 1890
   John McGraw, AL:Balt.-NL:NY 1902
   Rogers Hornsby, AL:StL.-NL:Cin. 1952
   Bill Virdon, AL:NY-NL:Hou. 1975
   Pat Corrales, NL:Phil.-AL:Clev. 1983
   Buck Rodgers, NL:Mtl.-AL:Cal. 1991
   Also following item

Most Clubs, League, Season
2 Ted Sullivan UA:StL.-KC 1884
   Billy Barnie, AA:Balt.-Phil. 1891
   Leo Durocher. NL:Brk.-NY 1948; Chi.-Hou. 1972
   Jimmy Dykes, AL:Det.-Clev. 1960
   Joe Gordon, AL:Clev.-Det. 1960
   (Dykes & Gordon switched teams Aug. 3, 1960)
   Billy Martin, AL:Det.-Tex. 1973; Tex.-NY 1975
   Bob Lemon, AL:Chi.-NY 1978
   Tony LaRussa, AL:Chi.-Oak. 1986

Most Different Terms, Same Club
5 Billy Martin, AL:NY 1975-78; 1979; 1983; 1985; 1988
4 Danny Murtaugh, NL:Pitt. 1957-64; 1967; 1970-71; 1973-76

Most Seasons, Manager, League Champion
10 John McGraw, NL:NY 1904-05, 11-13, 17, 21-24
   Casey Stengel, AL:NY 1949-53, 55-58, 60

Most Seasons, Consecutive, Manager, League Champion
5 Casey Stengel, AL:NY 1949-53
4 John McGraw, NL:NY 1921-24

AMERICAN LEAGUE WORLD SERIES

TEAM	No	Series W	L	All Games G	W	L	Home Games G	W	L	Road Games G	W	L
New York Yankees	39	26	13	219	130	88	106	65	40	113	65	48
Phil./Oak. Athletics	14	9	5	75	41	34	37	22	15	38	19	19
Boston Red Sox	10	6	4	64	37	26	33	20	12	31	17	14
Detroit Tigers	10	4	6	61	27	33	30	13	17	31	14	16
St. Louis/Baltimore	7	3	4	39	21	18	20	11	9	19	10	9
Washington/Minnesota	6	3	3	40	19	21	22	17	5	18	2	16
Chicago White Sox	5	3	2	30	17	13	15	8	7	15	9	6
Cleveland Indians	5	2	3	30	14	16	15	9	6	15	5	10
Kansas City Royals	2	1	1	13	6	7	7	4	3	6	2	4
Toronto Blue Jays	2	2	0	12	8	4	6	4	2	6	4	2
Anaheim Angels	1	1	0	7	4	3	4	3	1	3	1	2
Milwaukee Brewers	1	0	1	7	3	4	3	2	1	4	1	3
TOTALS	102	60	42	597	327	267	298	178	118	299	149	149

NATIONAL LEAGUE WORLD SERIES

TEAM	No	Series W	L	All Games G	W	L	Home Games G	W	L	Road Games G	W	L
Brk./LA Dodgers	18	6	12	105	45	60	51	30	21	54	15	39
St. Louis Cardinals	17	10	7	105	52	53	52	27	25	53	25	28
NY/SF Giants	17	5	12	100	45	53	50	25	25	50	20	28
Chicago Cubs	10	2	8	53	19	33	27	7	19	26	12	14
Bos./Mil./Atl. Braves	9	3	6	53	24	29	26	14	12	27	10	17
Cincinnati Reds	9	5	4	51	26	25	26	12	14	25	14	11
Pittsburgh Pirates	7	5	2	47	23	24	23	12	11	24	11	13
Philadelphia Phillies	5	1	4	26	8	18	14	5	9	12	3	9
New York Mets	4	2	2	24	12	12	13	8	5	11	4	7
Florida Marlins	2	2	0	13	8	5	7	4	3	6	4	2
San Diego Padres	2	0	2	9	1	8	4	1	3	5	0	5
Arizona Diamondbacks	1	1	0	7	4	3	4	4	0	3	0	3
Houston Astros	1	0	1	4	0	4	2	0	2	2	0	2
TOTALS	102	42	60	597	267	327	299	149	149	298	118	178

TIE GAMES

1907 Oct. 8	Detroit AL at Chicago NL	3-3	12 innings
1912 Oct. 9	New York NL at Boston AL	6-6	11 innings
1922 Oct. 5	New York NL at New York AL	3-3	10 innings

WORLD SERIES RECORDS

OTE: Individual and Club records are listed under appropriate headings according to the duration of each annual Series,
       immediately preceding records for lifetime, game and inning. Players' complete names are found in the annual rosters.
       8-Game Series records that tied or exceeded those shown are included under 7-Game Series

ATTING – INDIVIDUAL

	4 Games		5 Games		6 Games		7 Games
ighest Batting Average (Minimum: 3.1 PA per game)							
.750	Hatcher, NL:Cin. 1990	.529	Casey, AL:Det. 2006	.500	Robertson, NL:NY 1917	.500	Martin, NL:StL 1931
					Martin, AL:NY 1953		Lindell, AL:NY 1947
					Molitor, AL:Tor. 1993		Garner, NL:Pitt. 1979
ighest Slugging Percentage (Minimum: 3.1 PA per game)							
.727	Gehrig, AL:NY 1928	1.071	Clendenon, NL:NY 1969	1.250	Jackson, AL:NY 1977	1.294	Bonds, NL:SF 2002
ost At-Bats							
21	Damon, AL:Bos. 2004	23	Janvrin, AL:Bos. 1916	29	Duncan, NL:Phil. 1993	36	Collins, AL:Bos. 1903 (8g)
	Podsednik, AL:Chi. 2005		Moore, NL:NY 1937			33	Harris, AL:Wash. 1924
			Richardson, AL:NY 1961				Rice, AL:Wash. 1925
							Moreno, NL:Pitt. 1979
							White, NL:Fla. 1997
ost Runs							
9	Ruth, AL:NY 1928	6	Baker, AL:Phil. 1910	10	Jackson, AL:NY 1977	8	By many players
	Gehrig, AL:NY 1932		Murphy, AL:Phil. 1910		Molitor, AL:Tor. 1993		
			Hooper, AL:Bos. 1916				
			Simmons, AL:Phil. 1929				
			May, NL:Cin. 1970				
			Powell, AL:Balt 1970				
			Whitaker, AL:Det. 1984				
			Jeter, AL:NY 2000				
ost Hits							
10	Ruth, AL:NY 1928	9	Baker, AL:Phil. 1910, 13	12	Martin, AL:NY 1953	13	Richardson, AL:NY 1964
			Collins, AL:Phil. 1910		Alomar, AL:Tor. 1993		Brock, NL:StL. 1968
			Groh, NL:NY 1922		Molitor, AL:Tor. 1993		Barrett, AL:Bos. 1986
			Moore, NL:NY 1937		Grissom, NL:Atl. 1996		
			Richardson, AL:NY 1961				
			Blair, AL:Balt 1970				
			B. Robinson, AL:Balt 1970				
			Trammell, AL:Det. 1984				
			Jeter, AL:NY 2000				
			O'Neill, AL:NY 2000				
ost Extra-Base Hits							
6	Ruth, AL:NY 1928	5	Dempsey, AL:Balt. 1983	6	Jackson, AL:NY 1977	7	Stargell, NL:Pitt. 1979
			Jeter, AL:NY 2000		Molitor & White, AL:Tor. 1993		
ost Total Bases							
22	Ruth, AL:NY 1928	19	Jeter, AL:NY 2000	25	Jackson, AL:NY 1977	25	Stargell, NL:Pitt. 1979
ost Singles							
9	Munson, AL:NY 1976	8	Chance, NL:Chi. 1908	10	Rolfe, AL:NY 1936	12	Rice, AL:Wash. 1925
			Baker, AL:Phil. 1913		Irvin, NL:NY 1951		
			Groh, NL:NY 1922				
			Moore, NL:NY 1937				
			Richardson, AL:NY 1961				
			Blair, AL:Balt 1970				
			Garvey, NL:LA 1974				
ost Doubles							
4	Hatcher, NL:Cin. 1990	4	Collins, AL:Phil. 1910	5	Hafey, NL:StL. 1930	6	Fox, AL:Det. 1934
	Boone, NL:Atl. 1999		Dempsey, AL:Balt 1983				
ost Triples							
2	Gehrig, AL:NY 1927	2	Collins, AL:Phil. 1913	2	Rohe, AL:Chi. 1906	4	Leach, NL:Pitt. 1903 (8g)
	Davis, NL:LA 1963		Brown, AL:NY 1949		Meusel, AL:NY 1923	3	Johnson, AL:NY 1947
	R. Henderson, AL:Oak. 1989		O'Neill, AL:NY 2000		Martin, AL:NY 1953		Lemke, NL:Atl. 1991
	Podsednik, AL:Chi. 2005				Molitor, AL:Tor. 1993		
					White, AL:Tor. 1993		

WORLD SERIES - INDIVIDUAL BATTING

4 Games	5 Games	6 Games	7 Games
Most Home Runs			
4 Gehrig, AL:NY 1928	3 Clendenon, NL:NY 1969	5 Jackson, AL:NY 1977	4 Ruth, AL:NY 1926 Snider, NL:Brk. 1952, 55 Bauer, AL:NY 1958 Tenace, AL:Oak. 1972 Bonds, NL:SF 2002
Most Runs Batted In			
9 Gehrig, AL:NY 1928	8 Murphy, AL:Phil. 1910 May, NL:Cin. 1970	10 Kluszewski, AL:Chi. 1959	12 Richardson, AL:NY 1960
Most Sacrifice Hits			
3 By many players	4 Lewis, AL:Bos. 1916	3 Sheckard, NL:Chi. 1906 Steinfeldt, NL:Chi. 1906 Tinker, NL:Chi. 1906 Barry, AL:Phil. 1911 Lee, NL:Chi. 1935	5 Clarke, NL:Pitt. 1909 Daubert, NL:Cin. 1919 (8g)
Most Sacrifice Flies (1908 to 1930, 1939, since 1954)			
2 Westrum, NL:NY 1954 Matheny, NL:StL. 2004	2 Nettles, NL:SD 1984 Brosius, AL:NY 2000	3 Carter, AL:Tor. 1993	2 Campanella, NL:Brk. 1956 B. Robinson, AL:Balt. 1971 Stargell, NL:Pitt. 1979 Ramirez, AL:Clev. 1997 Williams, NL:Ari. 2001 Sanders, NL:SF 2002
Most Walks			
7 Thompson, NL:NY 1954	7 Sheckard, NL:Chi. 1910 Cochrane, AL:Phil. 1929 Gordon, AL:NY 1941	9 Randolph, AL:NY 1981	13 Bonds, NL:SF 2002
Most Intentional Walks (Since 1955)			
3 Williams, AL:NY 1999	3 Posada, AL:NY 2000	3 Milbourne, AL:NY 1981	7 Bonds, NL:SF 2002
Most Strikeouts			
7 Meusel, AL:NY 1927 Caminiti, NL:SD 1998 Ensberg, NL:Hou. 2005	9 Martinez, NL:SD 1984	12 Wilson, AL:KC 1980	11 Mathews, NL:Mil. 1958 Garrett, NL:NY 1973 Gonzalez, NL:Ari. 2001 Miller, NL:Ari. 2001
Most Stolen Bases			
3 R. Henderson, AL:Oak. 1989-90 Jeter, AL:NY 1999	6 Slagle, NL:Chi. 1907	6 Lofton, AL:Clev. 1995	7 Brock, NL:StL. 1967-68
Most Caught Stealing			
2 Aparicio, AL:Balt. 1966 Foster, NL:Cin. 1976	5 Schulte, NL:Chi. 1910	3 Devore, NL:NY 1911	4 Neale, NL:Cin. 1919 (8g) 3 Brock, NL:StL. 1968

ERVICE

Most Series, Lifetime
14 Yogi Berra, AL:NY 1947, 49-53, 55-58, 60-63

Most Series, Consecutive
5 By many. See rosters AL:NY 1949-53; 60-64

LUBS

Most Series, One Club, Lifetime
14 Yogi Berra, AL:NY 1947, 49-53, 55-58, 60-63

Most Series, Winning Club
10 Yogi Berra, AL:NY 1947, 49-53, 56, 58, 61-62

Most Series, Losing Club
6 Pee Wee Reese, NL:Brk. 1941, 47, 49, 52-53, 56
Elston Howard, AL:NY 1955, 57, 60, 63-64; Bos. 67

Most Positions Played, Lifetime
4 Fred Snodgrass, NL:NY 1911-13 (cf, lf, rf, 1b)
Babe Ruth, AL:Bos. 1915-16, 18 (p, lf); NY 21-23, 26-28, 32 (lf, rf, 1b)
Jackie Robinson, NL:Brk. 1947, 49, 52-53, 55-56 (1b, 2b, lf, 3b)
Tony Kubek, AL:NY 1957-58, 60-63 (lf, 3b, cf, ss)
Elston Howard, AL:NY 1955-58, 60-64 (lf, rf, 1b, c); Bos. 67 (c)
Pete Rose, NL:Cin. 1970, 72, 75-76 (rf, lf, 3b); Phil. 80, 83 (1b)

ATTING AVERAGE

Highest Batting Average (Minimum: 75 at-bats)
.391 Lou Brock, NL:StL. 1964, 67-68

Most Series, .300 or Higher Batting Average
6 Babe Ruth, AL:NY 1921, 23, 26-28, 32

Most Series Leading Club (Playing all games)
3 Frank Baker, AL:Phil. 1911, 13-14
Pee Wee Reese, NL:Brk. 1947, 49, 52
Duke Snider, NL:Brk. 1952, 55-56
Gil Hodges, NL:Brk. 1953, 56; LA 59
Steve Garvey, NL:LA 1974, 77, 81

LUGGING PERCENTAGE

Highest Slugging Percentage (Minimum: 75 at-bats)
.755 Reggie Jackson, AL:Oak. 1973-74; NY 77-78, 81

AMES

Most Games, Lifetime
75 Yogi Berra, AL:NY 1947, 49-53, 55-58, 60-63

Most Games, One Club
75 Yogi Berra, AL:NY 1947, 49-53, 55-58, 60-63

Most Games, Consecutive
30 Bobby Richardson, AL:NY 1960-64

T-BATS

Most At-Bats, Lifetime
259 Yogi Berra, AL:NY 1947, 49-53, 55-58, 60-63

Most At-Bats, Game
6 Pat Dougherty, AL:Bos. Oct. 7, 1903
Jimmy Collins, AL:Bos. Oct. 7, 1903
Jimmy Sheckard, NL:Chi. Oct. 10, 1908
Heinie Groh, NL:Cin. Oct. 9, 1919
George Burns, NL:NY Oct. 7, 1921
Mark Koenig, AL:NY Oct. 6, 1926
Frankie Crosetti, AL:NY Oct. 2, 1932
Bill Dickey, AL:NY Oct. 2, 1932
Joe Sewell, AL:NY Oct. 2, 1932
Red Rolfe, AL:NY Oct. 6, 1936
Joe DiMaggio, AL:NY Oct. 6, 1936
Jimmy Brown, NL:StL. Oct. 4, 1942
Red Schoendienst, NL:StL. Oct. 10, 1946
Enos Slaughter, NL:StL. Oct. 10, 1946
Pee Wee Reese, NL:Brk. Oct. 5, 1956
Tony Kubek, AL:NY Oct. 6, 1960
Bill Skowron, AL:NY Oct. 6, 1960
Clete Boyer, AL:NY Oct. 12, 1960
Bobby Richardson, AL:NY Oct. 9, 1961
Tony Kubek, AL:NY Oct. 9, 1961
Paul Molitor, AL:Mil. Oct. 12, 1982
Robin Yount, AL:Mil. Oct. 12, 1982
Jim Rice, AL:Bos. Oct. 19, 1986
Rickey Henderson, AL:Oak. Oct. 28, 1989
Roberto Alomar, AL:Tor. Oct. 20, 1993
Joe Carter, AL:Tor. Oct. 20, 1993
Tony Fernandez, AL:Tor. Oct. 20, 1993
Mariano Duncan, NL:Phil. Oct. 20, 1993
Tony Womack, NL:Ari. Nov. 3, 2001
Darin Erstad, AL:Ana. Oct. 22, 2002
Garret Anderson, AL:Ana. Oct. 22, 2002
Kenny Lofton, NL:SF Oct. 24, 2002
Rich Aurilia, NL:SF Oct. 24, 2002
Johnny Damon, AL:Bos. Oct. 23, 2004
Extra-Inning Game:
8 Scott Podsednik, AL:Chi. Oct. 25, 2005 (14 inn)

Most Plate Appearances, No At-Bats, Game
5 Fred Clarke, NL:Pitt. Oct. 16, 1909

Most At-Bats, Inning
2 By many players

RUNS

Most Runs, Lifetime
42 Mickey Mantle, AL:NY 1951-53, 55-58, 60-64

Most Runs, Game
4 Babe Ruth, AL:NY Oct. 6, 1926
Earle Combs, AL:NY Oct. 2, 1932
Frankie Crosetti, AL:NY Oct. 2, 1936
Enos Slaughter, NL:StL. Oct. 10, 1946
Reggie Jackson, AL:NY Oct. 18, 1977
Kirby Puckett, AL:Minn. Oct. 24, 1987
Carney Lansford, AL:Oak. Oct. 27, 1989
Len Dykstra, NL:Phil. Oct. 20, 1993
Jeff Kent, NL:SF Oct. 24, 2002

Most Runs, Inning
2 Frankie Frisch, NL:NY Oct. 7, 1921 (7th)
Al Simmons, AL:Phil. Oct. 12, 1929 (7th)
Jimmie Foxx, AL:Phil. Oct. 12, 1929 (7th)
Dick McAuliffe, AL:Det. Oct. 9, 1968 (3rd)
Mickey Stanley, AL:Det. Oct. 9, 1968 (3rd)
Al Kaline, AL:Det. Oct. 9, 1968 (3rd)
Greg Colbrunn, NL:Ari. Nov. 3, 2001 (3rd)

Most Games, Consecutive, Runs
9 Babe Ruth, AL:NY 1927-28, 32
Frank Baker, AL:Phil. 1910-11

HITS

Most Hits, Lifetime
71 Yogi Berra, AL:NY 1947, 49-53, 55-58, 60-63

Most Hits, Game
　5　Paul Molitor, AL:Mil. Oct. 12, 1982

Most Games, 4 or more Hits
　2　Robin Yount, AL:Mil. Oct. 12 & 17, 1982

Most Games, 4 or more Hits, One Series
　2　Robin Yount, AL:Mil. Oct. 12 & 17, 1982

Most Hits, 2 Consecutive Games
　7　Frank Isbell, AL:Chi. Oct. 13-14, 1906
　　Freddie Lindstrom, NL:NY Oct. 7-8, 1924
　　Monte Irvin, NL:NY Oct. 4-5, 1951
　　Thurman Munson, AL:NY Oct. 19-21, 1976
　　Paul Molitor, AL:Mil. Oct. 12-13, 1982
　　Billy Hatcher, NL:Cin. Oct. 16-17, 1990

Most Hits, Inning
　2　Ross Youngs, NL:NY Oct. 7, 1921 (7th)
　　Al Simmons, AL:Phil. Oct. 12, 1929 (7th)
　　Jimmie Foxx, AL:Phil. Oct. 12, 1929 (7th)
　　Jimmy Dykes, AL:Phil. Oct. 12, 1929 (7th)
　　Joe Moore, NL:NY Oct. 4, 1933 (6th)
　　Dizzy Dean, NL:StL. Oct. 9, 1934 (3rd)
　　Joe DiMaggio, AL:NY Oct. 6, 1936 (9th)
　　Hank Leiber, NL:NY Oct. 9, 1937 (2nd)
　　Stan Musial, NL:StL. Oct. 4, 1942 (4th)
　　Elston Howard, AL:NY Oct. 6, 1960 (6th)
　　Bobby Richardson, AL:NY Oct. 6, 1960 (6th)
　　Bob Cerv, AL:NY Oct. 8, 1960 (1st)
　　Frank Quilici, AL:Minn. Oct. 6, 1965 (3rd)
　　Al Kaline, AL:Det. Oct. 9, 1968 (3rd)
　　Norm Cash, AL:Det. Oct. 9, 1968 (3rd)
　　Merv Rettenmund, AL:Balt. Oct. 11, 1971 (5th)
　　Gary Gaetti, AL:Minn. Oct. 17, 1987 (4th)
　　Matt Williams, NL:Ari. Nov. 3, 2001 (3rd)

Most Hits, Consecutive At-Bats
　7　Thurman Munson, AL:NY 1976-77
　　Billy Hatcher, NL:Cin. 1990

Most Hits, Consecutive At-Bats, One Series
　7　Billy Hatcher, NL:Cin. 1990

Most Games, Consecutive, Hits
　17　Hank Bauer, AL:NY 1956-58

Hitless At-Bats
　Most At-Bats, No Hits, Lifetime
　22　George Earnshaw, AL:Phil. 1929-31
　Consecutive At-Bats, No Hits
　31　Marv Owen, AL:Det. 1934-35
　One Series, Most At-Bats, No Hits:
　22　Dal Maxvill, NL:StL. 1968
　Game, Most At-Bats, No Hits:
　　6　Travis Jackson, NL:NY Oct. 10, 1924 (12 inn)
　　　Hughie Critz, NL:NY Oct. 6, 1933 (11 inn)
　　　Felix Millan, NL:NY Oct. 14, 1973 (12 inn)
　　　Mickey Rivers, AL:NY Oct. 11, 1977 (12 inn)
　　　Ron Gant, NL:Atl. Oct. 22, 1991 (12 inn)
　　　Devon White, NL:Fla. Oct. 26, 1997 (11 inn)
　　　Craig Counsell, NL:Ari. Nov. 1, 2001 (12 inn)
　　　Brad Ausmus, NL:Hou. Oct. 25, 2005 (14 inn)
　　　Willy Taveras, NL:Hou. Oct. 25, 2005 (14 inn)

XTRA-BASE HITS

Most Extra-Base Hits, Lifetime
　26　Mickey Mantle, AL:NY 1951-53, 55-58, 60-64

Most Extra-Base Hits, Game
　4　Frank Isbell, AL:Chi. Oct. 13, 1906 (4-2b)

Most Extra-Base Hits, Inning
　2　Ross Youngs, NL:NY Oct. 7, 1921 (7th; 2b, 3b)
　　Matt Williams, NL:Ari. Nov. 3, 2001 (3rd; 2-2b)

TOTAL BASES

Most Total Bases, Lifetime
123 Mickey Mantle, AL:NY 1951-53, 55-58, 60-64

Most Total Bases, Game
12 Babe Ruth, AL:NY Oct. 6, 1926
Babe Ruth, AL:NY Oct. 9, 1928
Reggie Jackson, AL:NY Oct. 18, 1977

Most Total Bases, Inning
5 Ross Youngs, NL:NY Oct. 7, 1921 (7th)
Al Simmons, AL:Phil. Oct. 12, 1929 (7th)

SINGLES

Most Singles, Lifetime
49 Yogi Berra, AL:NY 1947, 49-53, 55-58, 60-63

Most Singles, Game
5 Paul Molitor, AL:Mil. Oct. 12, 1982

Most Singles, Inning
2 Jimmie Foxx, AL:Phil. Oct. 12, 1929 (7th)
Joe Moore, NL:NY Oct. 4, 1933 (6th)
Joe DiMaggio, AL:NY Oct. 6, 1936 (9th)
Hank Leiber, NL:NY Oct. 9, 1937 (2nd)
Bob Cerv, AL:NY Oct. 8, 1960 (1st)
Al Kaline, AL:Det. Oct. 9, 1968 (3rd)
Norm Cash, AL:Det. Oct. 9, 1968 (3rd)
Merv Rettenmund, AL:Balt. Oct. 11, 1971 (5th)

DOUBLES

Most Doubles, Lifetime
10 Frankie Frisch, NL:NY 1921-24; StL. 28, 30-31, 34
Yogi Berra, AL:NY 1947, 49-53, 55-58, 60-63

Most Doubles, Game
4 Frank Isbell, AL:Chi. Oct. 13, 1906

Most Doubles, Inning
2 Matt Williams, NL:Ari. Nov. 3, 2001 (3rd)

TRIPLES

Most Triples, Lifetime
4 Tommy Leach, NL:Pitt. 1903, 09
Tris Speaker, AL:Bos. 1912, 15; Clev. 20
Billy Johnson, AL:NY 1943, 47, 49-50

Most Triples, Game
2 Tommy Leach, NL:Pitt. Oct. 1, 1903
Patsy Dougherty, AL:Bos. Oct. 7, 1903
Dutch Ruether, NL:Cin. Oct. 1, 1919
Bobby Richardson, AL:NY Oct. 12, 1960
Tommy Davis, NL:LA Oct. 3, 1963
Mark Lemke, NL:Atl. Oct. 24, 1991

Most Triples, Inning
1 By many players

HOME RUNS

Most Home Runs, Lifetime
18 Mickey Mantle, AL:NY 1951-53, 55-58, 60-64

Most Home Runs, Game
3 Babe Ruth, AL:NY Oct. 6, 1926
Babe Ruth, AL:NY Oct. 9, 1928
Reggie Jackson, AL:NY Oct. 18, 1977

Most Home Runs, Game, Rookie
2 Charlie Keller, AL:NY Oct. 7, 1939
Tony Kubek, AL:NY Oct. 5, 1957
Willie McGee, NL:StL. Oct. 15, 1982
Andruw Jones, NL:Atl. Oct. 20, 1996

Most Games, Consecutive, Home Runs
4   Lou Gehrig, AL:NY Oct. 5, 7(2), 9, 1928; Sept. 28, 1932
    Reggie Jackson, AL:NY Oct. 15, 16, 18 (3), 1977; Oct. 10, 1978

Most Home Runs, First Game
2   Ted Kluszewski, AL:Chi. Oct. 1, 1959
    Gene Tenace, AL:Oak. Oct. 14, 1972
    Willie Aikens, AL:KC Oct. 14, 1980
    Andruw Jones, NL:Atl. Oct. 20, 1996
    Greg Vaughn, NL:SD Oct. 17, 1998
    Troy Glaus, AL:Ana. Oct. 19, 2002

Most Games, 2 or more Home Runs
4   Babe Ruth, AL:NY Oct. 11, 1923; Oct. 6, 1926; Oct. 9, 1928; Oct. 1, 1932

Most Games, One Series, 2 or more Home Runs
2   Willie Aikens, AL:KC Oct. 14, 18, 1980

Most Home Runs, Consecutive At-Bats
4   Reggie Jackson, AL:NY Oct. 16-18, 1977

Most Home Runs, Inning
1   By many players

Most Consecutive Innings, Home Run, Game
2   Babe Ruth, AL:NY Oct. 11, 1923 (4th-5th)
    Babe Ruth, AL:NY Oct. 9, 1928 (7th-8th)
    Ted Kluszewski, AL:Chi. Oct. 1, 1959 (3rd-4th)
    Reggie Jackson, AL:NY Oct. 18, 1977 (4th-5th)
    Willie Aikens, AL:KC Oct. 18, 1980 (1st-2nd)
    Dave Henderson, AL:Oak. Oct. 27, 1989 (4th-5th)
    Chris Sabo, NL:Cin. Oct. 19, 1990 (2nd-3rd)
    Andruw Jones, NL:Atl. Oct. 20, 1996 (2nd-3rd)
    Scott Brosius, AL:NY Oct. 20, 1998 (7th-8th)
    Jeff Kent, NL:SF Oct. 24, 2002 (6th-7th)

Home Run, First Career At-Bat *(* = NOT first plate appearance)*

Chick Fewster, AL:NY Oct. 11, 1921*	Amos Otis, AL:KC Oct. 14, 1980
Joe Harris, AL:Wash. Oct. 7, 1925	Bob Watson, AL:NY Oct. 20, 1981
George Watkins, NL:StL. Oct. 2, 1930	Jim Dwyer, AL:Balt. Oct. 11, 1983
Mel Ott, NL:NY Oct. 3, 1933	Jose Canseco, AL:Oak. Oct. 15, 1988*
George Selkirk, AL:NY Sept. 30, 1936	Mickey Hatcher, NL:LA Oct. 15, 1988
Dusty Rhodes, NL:NY Sept. 29, 1954	Bill Bathe, NL:SF Oct. 27, 1989
Elston Howard, AL:NY Sept. 28, 1955	Eric Davis, NL:Cin. Oct. 16, 1990
Roger Maris, AL:NY Oct. 5, 1960	Ed Sprague, AL:Tor. Oct. 18, 1992
Don Mincher, AL:Minn. Oct. 6, 1965	Fred McGriff, NL:Atl. Oct. 21, 1995
Brooks Robinson, AL:Balt. Oct. 5, 1966	Andruw Jones, NL:Atl. Oct. 20, 1996
Jose Santiago, AL:Bos. Oct. 4, 1967	Barry Bonds, NL:SF Oct. 19, 2002
Mickey Lolich, AL:Det. Oct. 3, 1968	Troy Glaus, AL:Ana. Oct. 19, 2002
Don Buford, AL:Balt. Oct. 11, 1969	David Ortiz, AL:Bos. Oct. 23, 2004
Gene Tenace, AL:Oak. Oct. 14, 1972	Mike Lamb, NL:Hou. Oct. 22, 2005
Jim Mason, AL:NY Oct. 19, 1976	Geoff Blum, AL:Chi. Oct. 25, 2005
Doug DeCinces, AL:Balt. Oct. 10, 1979	

Home Run, Each of First Two Career At-Bats
2   Gene Tenace, AL:Oak. Oct. 14, 1972
    Andruw Jones, NL:Atl. Oct. 20, 1996

Home Run, Leading Off First Inning

Patsy Dougherty, AL:Bos. Oct. 2, 1903	Tommie Agee, NL:NY Oct. 14, 1969
Davy Jones, AL:Det. Oct. 13, 1909	Pete Rose, NL:Cin. Oct. 20, 1972
Phil Rizzuto, AL:NY Oct. 5, 1942	Wayne Garrett, NL:NY Oct. 16, 1973
Dale Mitchell, AL:Clev. Oct. 10, 1948	Davey Lopes, NL:LA Oct. 17, 1978
Gene Woodling, AL:NY Oct. 4, 1953	Len Dykstra, NL:NY Oct. 21, 1986
Al Smith, AL:Clev. Sept. 30, 1954	Rickey Henderson, AL:Oak. Oct. 28, 1989
Bill Bruton, NL:Mil. Oct. 2, 1958	Derek Jeter, AL:NY Oct. 25, 2000
Lou Brock, NL:StL. Oct. 6, 1968	Johnny Damon, AL:Bos. Oct. 27, 2004
Don Buford, AL:Balt. Oct. 11, 1969	

Grand Slam Home Runs

Elmer Smith (rf) AL:Clev. (Brk.) Oct. 10, 1920 (1st: Burleigh Grimes)
Tony Lazzeri (2b) AL:NY (NY) Oct. 2, 1936 (3rd: Dick Coffman)
Gil McDougald (2b) AL:NY (NY) Oct. 9, 1951 (3rd: Larry Jansen)
Mickey Mantle (cf) AL:NY (Brk.) Oct. 4, 1953 (3rd: Russ Meyer)
Yogi Berra (c) AL:NY (Brk.) Oct. 5, 1956 (2nd: Don Newcombe)
Bill Skowron (1b) AL:NY (Brk.) Oct. 10, 1956 (7th: Roger Craig)
Bobby Richardson (2b) AL:NY (Pitt.) Oct. 8, 1960 (1st: Clem Labine)
Chuck Hiller (2b) NL:SF (NY) Oct. 8, 1962 (7th: Marshall Bridges)
Ken Boyer (3b) NL:StL. (NY) Oct. 11, 1964 (6th: Al Downing)
Joe Pepitone (1b) AL:NY (StL.) Oct. 14, 1964 (8th: Gordie Richardson)
Jim Northrup (cf) AL:Det. (StL.) Oct. 9, 1968 (3rd: Larry Jaster)
Dave McNally (p) AL:Balt. (Cin.) Oct. 13, 1970 (6th: Wayne Granger)
Dan Gladden (lf) AL:Minn. (StL.) Oct. 17, 1987 (4th: Bob Forsch)
Kent Hrbek (1b) AL:Minn. (StL.) Oct. 24, 1987 (6th: Ken Dayley)
Jose Canseco (rf) AL:Oak. (LA) Oct. 15, 1988 (2nd: Tim Belcher)
Lonnie Smith (dh) NL:Atl. (Tor.) Oct. 22, 1992 (5th: Jack Morris)
Tino Martinez (1b) AL:NY (SD) Oct. 17, 1998 (7th: Mark Langston)
Paul Konerko, (1b) AL:Chi. (Hou.) Oct. 23, 2005 (7th: Chad Qualls)

RUNS BATTED IN

Most Runs Batted In, Lifetime
40 Mickey Mantle, AL:NY 1951-53, 55-58, 60-64

Most Runs Batted In, Game
6 Bobby Richardson, AL:NY Oct. 8, 1960

Most Runs Batted In, Inning
4 By many players

SACRIFICE HITS

Most Sacrifice Hits, Lifetime
8 Eddie Collins, AL:Phil. 1910-11, 13-14; Chi. 17, 19

Most Sacrifice Hits, Game
3 Joe Tinker, NL:Chi. Oct. 12, 1906
   Craig Counsell, NL:Ari. Oct. 31, 2001 (10 inn)

Most Sacrifice Hits, Inning
1 By many players

SACRIFICE FLIES (1908 to 1930, 1939, since 1954)

Most Sacrifice Flies, Lifetime
4 Joe Carter, AL:Tor. 1992-93

Most Sacrifice Flies, Game
2 Wes Westrum, NL:NY Oct. 2, 1954
   Manny Ramirez, AL:Clev. Oct. 25, 1997
   Mike Matheny, NL:StL. Oct. 23, 2004

Most Sacrifice Flies, Inning
1 By many players

Most Runs Batted In, Sacrifice Fly
2 Tommy Herr, NL:StL. Oct. 16, 1982 (2nd)

WALKS

Most Walks, Lifetime
43 Mickey Mantle, AL:NY 1951-53, 55-58, 60-64

Most Walks, Consecutive
5 Lou Gehrig, AL:NY Oct. 7-9, 1928

Most Walks, Game
4 Fred Clarke, NL:Pitt. Oct. 16, 1909
   Dick Hoblitzell, AL:Bos. Oct. 9, 1916 (14 inn)
   Ross Youngs, NL:NY Oct. 10, 1924 (12 inn)
   Babe Ruth, AL:NY Oct. 10, 1926
   Jackie Robinson, NL:Brk. Oct. 5, 1952 (11 inn)
   Doug DeCinces, AL:Balt. Oct. 13, 1979

Most Walks, Inning
2 Lefty Gomez, AL:NY Oct. 6, 1937 (6th)
   Dick McAuliffe, AL:Det. Oct. 9, 1968 (3rd)

Most Intentional Walks. Lifetime
   7 Bernie Williams, AL:NY 1996, 98-2000
      Barry Bonds, NL:SF 2002

IT BY PITCH

Most Hit By Pitch, Lifetime
   3 Honus Wagner, NL:Pitt. 1903, 09
      Frank Chance, NL:Chi. 1906-07
      Fred Snodgrass, NL:NY 1911-12
      Max Carey, NL:Pitt. 1925
      Yogi Berra, AL:NY 1953, 55
      Elston Howard, AL:NY 1960, 62, 64
      Frank Robinson, NL:Cin. 1961; AL:Balt. 71
      Bert Campaneris, AL:Oak. 1973-74
      Reggie Jackson, AL:NY 1977-78
      Derek Jeter, AL:NY 1996, 2001, 03

Most Hit By Pitch, Game
   2 Max Carey, NL:Pitt. Oct. 7, 1925
      Yogi Berra, AL:NY Oct. 2, 1953
      Frank Robinson, NL:Cin. Oct. 8, 1961
      Todd Pratt, NL:NY Oct. 21, 2000 (12 inn)
      Jeff Bagwell, NL:Hou. Oct. 22, 2005

Most Hit By Pitch, Inning
   1 By many players

TRIKEOUTS

Most Strikeouts, Lifetime
  54 Mickey Mantle, AL:NY 1951-53, 55-58, 60-64

Most Strikeouts, Consecutive Plate Appearances
   8 Vida Blue, AL:Oak. Oct. 14, 1973-Oct. 17, 1974
      David Justice, AL:NY Oct. 27-31, 2001

Most Strikeouts, Game
   5 George Pipgras, AL:NY Oct. 1, 1932

Most Strikeouts, Inning
   2 Edgar Renteria, NL:Fla. Oct. 23, 1997 (6th)

ROUNDED INTO DOUBLE PLAYS

Most Grounded Into Double Plays, Lifetime
   8 George Kelly, NL:NY 1921-24

Most Grounded Into Double Plays, Game
   3 Willie Mays, NL:NY Oct. 8, 1951

TOLEN BASES

Most Stolen Bases, Lifetime
  14 Eddie Collins, AL:Phil. 1910-11, 13-14; Chi. 17, 19
      Lou Brock, NL:StL. 1964, 67-68

Most Stolen Bases, Game
   3 Honus Wagner, NL:Pitt. Oct. 11, 1909
      Willie Davis, NL:LA Oct. 11, 1965
      Lou Brock, NL:StL. Oct. 12, 1967
      Lou Brock, NL:StL. Oct. 5, 1968

Most Stolen Bases, Inning
   2 George Browne, NL:NY Oct. 12, 1905 (9th)
      Jimmy Slagle, NL:Chi. Oct. 8, 1907 (10th)
      Ty Cobb, AL:Det. Oct. 12, 1908 (9th)
      Honus Wagner, NL:Pitt. Oct. 13, 1909 (7th)
      Eddie Collins, AL:Chi. Oct. 7, 1917 (6th)
      Babe Ruth, AL:NY Oct. 6, 1921 (5th)
      Lou Brock, NL:StL. Oct. 12, 1967 (5th)
      Davey Lopes, NL:LA Oct. 15, 1974 (1st)
      Roberto Alomar, AL:Tor. Oct. 19, 1993 (6th)
      Kenny Lofton, AL:Clev. Oct. 21, 1995 (1st)
      Omar Vizquel, AL:Clev. Oct. 26, 1997 (5th)

Most Steals of Home, Lifetime
   2 Bob Meusel, AL:NY 1921, 28

Most Steals of Home, Game
1 Bill Dahlen, NL:NY Oct. 12, 1905 (5th)
   George Davis, AL:Chi. Oct. 13, 1906 (3rd)
   Jimmy Slagle, NL:Chi. Oct. 11, 1907 (7th)
   Ty Cobb, AL:Det. Oct. 9, 1909 (3rd)
   Buck Herzog, NL:NY Oct. 14, 1912 (1st)
   Butch Schmidt, NL:Bos. Oct. 9, 1914 (8th)
   Mike McNally, AL:NY Oct. 5, 1921 (5th)
   Bob Meusel, AL:NY Oct. 6, 1921 (8th)
   Bob Meusel, AL:NY Oct. 7, 1928 (6th)
   Hank Greenberg, AL:Det. Oct. 6, 1934 (8th)
   Monte Irvin, NL:NY Oct. 4, 1951 (1st)
   Jackie Robinson, NL:Brk. Sept. 28, 1955 (8th)
   Tim McCarver, NL:StL. Oct. 15, 1964 (4th)
   Brad Fullmer, AL:Ana. Oct. 20, 2002 (1st)

CAUGHT STEALING

Most Caught Stealing, Game
2 Frank Schulte, NL:Chi. Oct. 17, 23, 1910
   Fred Luderus, NL:Phil. Oct. 8, 1915
   Jimmy Johnston, NL:Brk. Oct. 9, 1916
   Mickey Livingston, NL:Chi. Oct. 3, 1945
   Billy Martin, AL:NY Sept. 28, 1955

Most Caught Stealing, Inning
1 By many players

PINCH-HITTING

Most Games, Lifetime
12 Luis Polonia, AL:Oak. 1988, NY 2000; NL:Atl. 1995-96

Most Games, One Series
6 Luis Polonia, NL:Atl. 1996

Most At-Bats, Lifetime
11 Luis Polonia, AL:Oak. 1988, NY 2000; NL:Atl. 1995-96

Most Hits, Lifetime
3 Ken O'Dea, NL:Chi. 1935; StL. 42, 44
   Bobby Brown, AL:NY 1947
   Johnny Mize, AL:NY 1949, 52
   Dusty Rhodes, NL:NY 1954
   Carl Furillo, NL:Brk. 1947; LA 59
   Bob Cerv, AL:NY 1955-56, 60
   Johnny Blanchard, AL:NY 1960-61, 64
   Carl Warwick, NL:StL. 1964
   Gonzalo Marquez, AL:Oak. 1972
   Ken Boswell, NL:NY 1973

Most Hits, One Series
3 Bobby Brown, AL:NY 1947
   Dusty Rhodes, NL:NY 1954
   Carl Warwick. NL:StL. 1964
   Gonzalo Marquez, AL:Oak. 1972
   Ken Boswell, NL:NY 1973

Most Total Bases, One Series
8 Chuck Essegian, NL:LA 1959
   Bernie Carbo, AL:Bos. 1975

Most Home Runs, Lifetime
2 Chuck Essegian, NL:LA 1959
   Bernie Carbo, AL:Bos. 1975

Most Runs Batted In, One Series
6 Dusty Rhodes, NL:NY 1954

Most Runs Batted In, Game
3 Dusty Rhodes, NL:NY Sept. 29, 1954
   Hank Majeski, AL:Clev. Oct. 2, 1954
   Bernie Carbo, AL:Bos. Oct. 21, 1975
   Bill Bathe, NL:SF Oct. 27, 1989

Most Walks, One Series
3 Bennie Tate, AL:Wash. 1924

Most Strikeouts, One Series
3 Gabby Hartnett, NL:Chi. 1929
   Rollie Hemsley, NL:Chi. 1932
   Otto Velez, AL:NY 1976
   Luis Polonia, NL:Atl. 1996
   Ruben Sierra, AL:NY 2003

NCH-RUNNING

Most Games, Lifetime
9 Allan Lewis, AL:Oak. 1972-73

Most Games, One Series
6 Allan Lewis, AL:Oak. 1972

ISCELLANY

Awarded First Base on Interference
1 Roger Peckinpaugh, AL:Wash. Oct. 15, 1925 (1st)
   Bud Metheny, AL:NY Oct. 6, 1943 (6th)
   Ken Boyer, NL:StL. Oct. 12, 1964 (1st)
   Pete Rose, NL:Cin. Oct. 10, 1970 (5th)
   George Hendrick, NL:StL. Oct. 15, 1982 (9th)

FIELDING — FIRST BASEMEN

4 Games	5 Games	6 Games	7 Games
Highest Average 1.000 (Most Chances)			
55 Schmidt, NL:Bos. 1914	73 Hoblitzell, AL:Bos. 1916	72 McInnis, AL:Bos. 1918	93 Pipp, AL:NY 1921 (8g)
			Kelly, NL:NY 1921 (8g)
			80 Bottomley, NL:StL. 1926
Chances Accepted			
55 Schmidt, NL:Bos. 1914	73 Hoblitzell, AL:Bos. 1916	87 Donahue, AL:Chi. 1906	93 Pipp, AL:NY 1921 (8g)
			Kelly, NL:NY 1921 (8g)
			81 Cooper, AL:Mil. 1982
Putouts			
52 Schmidt, NL:Bos. 1914	69 Hoblitzell, AL:Bos. 1916	79 Donahue, AL:Chi. 1906	92 Pipp, AL:NY 1921 (8g)
			79 Bottomley, NL:StL. 1926
Assists			
6 Wertz, AL:Clev. 1954	5 Rossman, AL:Det. 1908	9 Merkle, NL:Chi. 1918	10 Cooper, AL:Mil. 1982
Pepitone, AL:NY 1963	Camilli, NL:Brk. 1941		
	Sanders, NL:StL. 1943		
	Skowron, AL:NY 1961		
Errors			
2 McGwire, AL:Oak. 1990	3 Chance, NL:Chi. 1908	3 Greenberg, AL:Det. 1935	5 Abstein, NL:Pitt. 1909
Hunter, NL:Atl. 1999	Davis, AL:Phil. 1910		
Double Plays			
7 Pepitone, AL:NY 1963	7 Pipp, AL:NY 1922	8 Robinson, AL:Clev. 1948	11 Hodges, NL:Brk. 1955
		Rose, NL:Phil. 1980	
Double Plays Started			
2 Hunter, NL:Atl. 1999	2 May, NL:Cin. 1970	2 Garvey, NL:LA 1977	3 Hodges, NL:Brk. 1955
	Garvey, NL:SD 1984	McGriff, NL:Atl. 1996	

IELDING – FIRST BASEMEN

Most Series
8 Bill Skowron, AL:NY 1955-58, 60-62; NL:LA 63

Games
38 Gil Hodges, NL:Brk. 1949, 52-53, 55-56; LA 59

Chances Accepted
Lifetime:
351 Gil Hodges, NL:Brk. 1949, 52-53, 55-56; LA 59
Game:
20 Fred McGriff, NL:Atl. Oct. 21, 1995
Extra-Inning Game:
23 Dick Hoblitzell, AL:Bos. Oct. 16, 1916 (14 inn)
Inning:
4 Bill Abstein, NL:Pitt. Oct. 12, 1909 (7th)
Wally Pipp, AL:NY Oct. 7, 1922 (5th)
George Kelly, NL:NY Oct. 11, 1923 (7th)
Steve Garvey, NL:LA Oct. 12, 1977 (4th)

Putouts
Lifetime:
326 Gil Hodges, NL:Brk. 1949, 52-53, 55-56; LA 59
Game:
19 George Kelly, NL:NY Oct. 15, 1923
Fred McGriff, NL:Atl. Oct. 21, 1995
Extra-Inning Game:
22 Dick Hoblitzell, AL:Bos. Oct. 16, 1916 (14 inn)
Inning:
3 By many players

Assists
Lifetime:
29 Bill Skowron, AL:NY 1955-58, 60-62; NL:LA 63
Game:
4 Marv Owen, AL:Det. Oct. 6, 1935
Don Mincher, AL:Minn. Oct. 7, 1965
Inning:
2 By many players

Errors
Lifetime:
8 Fred Merkle, NL:NY 1911-13; Brk. 16; Chi. 18
Game:
2 By many players
Inning:
2 Claude Rossman, AL:Det. Oct. 12, 1908 (4th)
Hank Greenberg, AL:Det. Oct. 3, 1935 (5th)
Johnny McCarthy, NL:NY Oct. 8, 1937 (5th)
Frank Torre, NL:Mil. Oct. 9, 1958 (2nd)
Brian Hunter, NL:Atl. Oct. 23, 1999 (8th)

Double Plays
Lifetime:
31 Gil Hodges, NL:Brk. 1949, 52-53, 55-56; LA 59
Game:
4 Stuffy McInnis, AL:Phil. Oct. 9, 1914
Joe Collins, AL:NY Oct. 8, 1951
Gene Tenace, AL:Oak. Oct. 17, 1973
Pete Rose, NL:Phil. Oct. 15, 1980
Game, started:
2 Brian Hunter, NL:Atl. Oct. 26, 1999
Game, unassisted:
1 George Grantham, NL:Pitt. Oct. 7, 1925
Joe Judge, AL:Wash. Oct. 13, 1925
Jimmie Foxx, AL:Phil. Oct. 8, 1930
Jim Bottomley, NL:StL. Oct. 1, 1931
Lou Gehrig, AL:NY Oct. 10, 1937
Ripper Collins, NL:Chi. Oct. 5, 1938
Joe Collins, AL:NY Oct. 7, 1956
Gordy Coleman, NL:Cin. Oct. 8, 1961
Tony Perez, NL:Cin. Oct. 11, 1975
Steve Garvey, NL:SD Oct. 9, 1984
Fred McGriff, NL:Atl. Oct. 24, 1996
Jim Thome, AL:Clev. Oct. 22, 1997
Tino Martinez, AL:NY Oct. 17, 1998
Brian Hunter, NL:Atl. Oct. 26, 1999

FIELDING – SECOND BASEMEN

4 Games	5 Games	6 Games	7 Games
Highest Average 1.000 (Most Chances)			
26 Randolph, AL:Oak. 1990	43 Gordon, AL:NY 1943	39 Gehringer, AL:Det. 1935	49 Doerr, AL:Bos. 1946
Chances Accepted			
28 Lazzeri, AL:NY 1927	43 Gordon, AL:NY 1943	40 Lopes, NL:LA 1981	54 Harris, AL:Wash. 1924
Putouts			
14 Randolph, AL:Oak. 1990	20 Gordon, AL:NY 1943	26 Lopes, NL:LA 1981	26 Harris, AL:Wash. 1924
Assists			
18 Lazzeri, AL:NY 1927	23 Gordon, AL:NY 1943	27 Ward, AL:NY 1923	33 Ward AL:NY 1921 (8g)
			Gantner, AL:Mil. 1982
Errors			
2 Lazzeri, AL:NY 1928	4 Murphy, AL:Phil. 1905	6 Lopes, NL:LA 1981	5 Gantner, AL:Mil. 1982
Gordon, AL:NY 1938			
Herman, NL:Chi. 1938			
Morgan, NL:Cin. 1976			
Double Plays			
6 Herman, NL:Chi. 1932	6 Green, AL:Oak. 1974	7 Frisch, NL:NY 1923	9 Garner, NL:Pitt. 1979
		Gordon, AL:Clev. 1948	
		Neal, NL:LA 1959	
		Baerga, AL:Clev. 1995	
		Castillo, NL:Fla. 2003	
Double Plays Started			
5 Herman, NL:Chi. 1932	4 Gordon, AL:NY 1941	4 Castillo, NL:Fla. 2003	5 Herr, NL:StL. 1985
	Green, AL:Oak. 1974		

IELDING – SECOND BASEMEN

Most Series
7 Frankie Frisch, NL:NY 1922-24; StL. 28, 30-31, 34

Games
42 Frankie Frisch, NL:NY 1922-24; StL. 28, 30-31, 34

Chances Accepted
Lifetime:
241 Frankie Frisch, NL:NY 1922-24; StL. 28, 30-31, 34
Game:
13 Claude Ritchey, NL:Pitt. Oct. 10, 1903
Bucky Harris, AL:Wash. Oct. 11, 1925
Davey Lopes, NL:LA Oct. 16, 1974
Extra-inning game:
14 Hughie Critz, NL:NY Oct. 6, 1933 (11 inn)
Inning:
4 Phil Garner, NL:Pitt. Oct. 11, 1979 (8th)

Putouts
Lifetime:
105 Frankie Frisch, NL:NY 1922-24; StL. 28, 30-31, 34
Game:
8 Bucky Harris, AL:Wash. Oct. 8, 1924
Davey Lopes, NL:LA Oct. 16, 1974
Extra-Inning Game:
9 Hughie Critz, NL:NY Oct. 6, 1933 (11 inn)
Inning:
3 Larry Doyle, NL:NY Oct. 9, 1913 (7th)
Bill Wambsganss, AL:Clev. Oct. 10, 1920 (5th)
Johnny Rawlings, NL:NY Oct. 11, 1921 (9th)
Frankie Frisch, NL:StL. Oct. 7, 1931 (7th)
Davey Lopes, NL:LA Oct. 16, 1974 (6th)
Davey Lopes, NL:LA Oct. 21, 1981 (4th)
Lou Whitaker, AL:Det. Oct. 14, 1984 (8th)

Assists
Lifetime:
136 Frankie Frisch, NL:NY 1922-24; StL. 28, 30-31, 34
Game:
8 Claude Ritchey, NL:Pitt. Oct. 10, 1903
Germany Schaefer, AL:Det. Oct. 12, 1907
Hal Janvrin, AL:Bos. Oct. 7, 1916
Eddie Collins, AL:Chi. Oct. 15, 1917
Bucky Harris, AL:Wash. Oct. 7, 1924
Joe Gordon, AL:NY Oct. 5, 1943
Bobby Doerr, AL:Bos. Oct. 9, 1946
Mark Lemke, NL:Atl. Oct. 21, 1995
Inning:
3 Eddie Collins, AL:Phil. Oct. 12, 1914 (4th)
Pete Kilduff, NL:Brk. Oct. 10, 1920 (3rd)
Aaron Ward, AL:NY Oct. 12, 1921 (6th)
Joe Gordon, AL:NY Oct. 11, 1943 (8th)
Jackie Robinson, NL:Brk. Oct. 8, 1949 (7th)
Gil McDougald, AL:NY Oct. 2, 1958 (2nd)
Phil Garner, NL:Pitt. Oct. 13, 1979 (9th)
Frank White, AL:KC Oct. 19, 1980 (8th)
Marty Barrett, AL:Bos. Oct. 23, 1986 (1st)

Errors
Lifetime:
8 Larry Doyle, NL:NY 1911-13
Eddie Collins, AL:Phil. 1910-11, 13-14; Chi. 17, 19
Game:
3 Danny Murphy, AL:Phil. Oct. 12, 1905
Buddy Myer, AL:Wash. Oct. 3, 1933
Davey Lopes, NL:LA Oct. 25, 1981
Inning:
2 Danny Murphy, AL:Phil. Oct. 12, 1905 (5th)
Mike Andrews, AL:Oak. Oct. 14, 1973 (12th)
Davey Lopes, NL:LA Oct. 25, 1981 (4th)

Double Plays
Lifetime:
24 Frankie Frisch, NL:NY 1922-24; StL. 28, 30-31, 34
Game:
3 By many players
Game, started:
3 Dick Green, AL:Oak. Oct. 15, 1974
Game, Unassisted:
1 Hobe Ferris, AL:Bos. Oct. 2, 1903
Larry Doyle, NL:NY Oct. 9, 1913
Buck Herzog, NL:NY Oct. 7, 1917
Frank White, AL:KC Oct. 17, 1980
Mark Lemke, NL:Atl. Oct. 27, 1991

Triple Plays
1 Bill Wambsganss, AL:Clev. Oct. 10, 1920
(Unassisted, 5th)

FIELDING – THIRD BASEMEN

4 Games	5 Games	6 Games	7 Games
Highest Average 1.000 (Most Chances)			
25 Baker, AL:Phil. 1914	20 Groh, NL:NY 1922	26 Nettles, AL:NY 1978	29 Menke, NL:Cin. 1972
Chances Accepted			
25 Baker, AL:Phil. 1914	25 Gardner, AL:Bos. 1916	27 Thomson, NL:NY 1951	37 Frisch, NL:NY 1921 (8g)
			34 Higgins, AL:Det. 1940
Putouts			
10 Baker, AL:Phil. 1914	10 Steinfeldt, NL:Chi. 1907	14 Rolfe, AL:NY 1936	13 Kurowski, NL:StL. 1946
Assists			
15 Baker, AL:Phil. 1914	18 Gardner, AL:Bos. 1916	20 Nettles, AL:NY 1977	30 Higgins, AL:Det. 1940
Errors			
3 Mueller, AL:Bos. 2004	4 Steinfeldt, NL:Chi. 1910	3 Rohe, AL:Chi. 1906	4 Leach, NL:Pitt. 1903 (8g)
		Herzog, NL:NY 1911	Gardner, AL:Bos. 1912 (8g)
		Jackson, NL:NY 1936	Martin, NL:StL. 1934
		Elliott, NL:Bos. 1948	McDougald, AL:NY 1952
		Boone, AL:NY 2003	
Double Plays			
3 Nettles, AL:NY 1976	2 Jackson, NL:NY 1933	4 Nettles, AL:NY 1978	4 Davenport, NL:SF 1962
Mueller, AL:Bos. 2004	B. Robinson, AL:Balt. 1970		Madlock, NL:Pitt. 1979
	Rolen, NL:StL. 2006		
Double Plays Started			
2 Rolfe, AL:NY 1939	2 Jackson, NL:NY 1933	3 Nettles, AL:NY 1978	4 Davenport, NL:SF 1962
Nettles, AL:NY 1976	B. Robinson, AL:Balt. 1970	Madlock, NL:Pitt. 1979	
Brosius, AL:NY 1999	Rolen, NL:StL. 2006		
Mueller, AL:Bos. 2004			

IELDING – THIRD BASEMEN

Most Series
6 Red Rolfe, AL:NY 1936-39, 41-42

Games
31 Gil McDougald, AL:NY 1951-53, 55, 60

Chances Accepted
Lifetime:
96 Graig Nettles, AL:NY 1976-78, 81; NL:SD 84
Game:
10 Larry Gardner, AL:Bos. Oct. 9, 1916 (14 inn)
Pinky Higgins, AL:Det. Oct. 5, 1940
Chris Sabo, NL:Cin. Oct. 19, 1990
Inning:
4 Eddie Mathews, NL:Mil. Oct. 5, 1957 (3rd)

Putouts
Lifetime:
37 Frank Baker, AL:Phil. 1910-11, 13-14; NY 21
Game:
4 Art Devlin, NL:NY Oct. 13, 1905
Bill Coughlin, AL:Det. Oct. 10, 1907
Bobby Byrne, NL:Pitt. Oct. 9, 1909
Tommy Leach, NL:Pitt. Oct. 16, 1909
Buck Herzog, NL:NY Oct. 17, 1911
Frank Baker, AL:Phil. Oct. 24, 1911
Frank Baker; AL:Phil. Oct. 12, 1914
Heinie Zimmerman, NL:NY Oct. 7, 1917
Jimmy Dykes, AL:Phil. Oct. 2, 1930
Bob Elliott, NL:Bos. Oct. 11, 1948
Willie Jones, NL:Phil. Oct. 4, 1950
Bill Mueller, AL:Bos. Oct. 24, 2004
Inning:
3 Freddie Lindstrom, NL:NY Oct. 6, 1924 (9th)

Assists
Lifetime:
68 Graig Nettles, AL:NY 1976-78, 81; NL:SD 84
Game:
9 Pinky Higgins, AL:Det. Oct. 5, 1940
Inning:
3 Ossie Bluege, AL:Wash. Oct. 13, 1925 (3rd)
Jose Pagan, NL:Pitt. Oct. 14, 1971 (9th)
Sal Bando, AL:Oak. Oct. 16, 1974 (6th)
Wade Boggs, AL:Bos. Oct. 19, 1986 (3rd)
Terry Pendleton, NL:Atl. Oct. 27, 1991 (7th)

Errors
Lifetime:
8 Larry Gardner, AL:Bos. 1912, 15-16; Clev. 20
Game:
3 Pepper Martin, NL:StL. Oct. 6, 1934
Buck Herzog, NL:NY Oct. 17, 1911 (11 inn)
Bill Mueller, AL:Bos. Oct. 24, 2004
Inning:
2 Harry Steinfeldt, NL:Chi. Oct. 18, 1910 (3rd)
Larry Gardner, AL:Bos. Oct. 16, 1912 (2nd)
Doug DeCinces, AL:Balt. Oct. 10, 1979 (6th)

Double Plays
Lifetime:
8 Graig Nettles, AL:NY 1976-78, 81; NL:SD 84
Game:
2 By many players
Game, started:
2 Fred McMullin, AL:Chi. Oct. 13, 1917
Ossie Bluege, AL:Wash. Oct. 5, 1924
Whitey Kurowski, NL:StL. Oct. 13, 1946
Clete Boyer, AL:NY Oct. 12, 1960
Dalton Jones, AL:Bos. Oct. 4, 1967
Graig Nettles, AL:NY Oct. 19, 1976
Bobby Bonilla, NL:Fla. Oct. 19, 1997 `
Game, unassisted:
None

Triple Plays
None

FIELDING – SHORTSTOPS

4 Games	5 Games	6 Games	7 Games
Highest Average 1.000 (Most Chances)			
27 Wills, NL:LA 1966	29 Dahlen, NL:NY 1905 Scott, AL:NY 1922 Marion, NL:StL. 1942 Harrelson, NL:NY 1969	36 Scott, AL:Bos. 1918	42 Gelbert, NL:StL. 1931
Chances Accepted			
27 Wills, NL:LA 1966	38 Tinker, NL:Chi. 1907	37 Rizzuto, AL:NY 1951	51 Risberg, AL:Chi. 1919 (8g) 42 Gelbert, NL:StL. 1931
Putouts			
16 Crosetti, AL:NY 1938	15 Tinker, NL:Chi. 1907 Rizzuto, AL:NY 1942	16 Jurges, NL:Chi. 1935	24 Wagner, AL:Bos. 1912 (8g) 22 O. Smith, NL:StL. 1982
Assists			
21 Barry, AL:Phil. 1914	25 Scott, AL:Bos. 1916	26 Russell, NL:LA 1981	32 Foli, NL:Pitt. 1979
Errors			
4 Crosetti, AL:NY 1932	4 Olson, NL:Brk. 1916 English, NL:Chi. 1929	4 Fletcher, NL:NY 1911 Weaver, AL:Chi. 1917	8 Peckinpaugh, AL:Wash. 192
Double Plays			
5 Jurges, NL:Chi. 1932 Kubek, AL:NY 1963 Everett, NL:Hou. 2005	6 Scott, AL:NY 1922 Rizzuto, AL:NY 1941	8 Rizzuto, AL:NY 1951	7 Reese, NL:Brk. 1955-56 Foli, NL:Pitt. 1979 Renteria, NL:Fla. 1997
Double Plays Started			
3 Koenig, AL:NY 1928 Uribe, AL:Chi. 2005	4 Tinker, NL:Chi. 1907	7 Bowa, NL:Phil. 1980	4 Reese, NL:Brk. 1947 McDougald, AL:NY 1957 Linz, AL:NY 1964 Wills, NL:LA 1965 Foli, NL:Pitt. 1979 Eckstein, AL:Ana. 2002

⬛ELDING – SHORTSTOPS

Most Series
9 Phil Rizzuto, AL:NY 1941-42, 47, 49-53, 55

Games
52 Phil Rizzuto, AL:NY 1941-42, 47, 49-53, 55

Chances Accepted
Lifetime:
250 Phil Rizzuto, AL:NY 1941-42, 47, 49-53, 55
Game:
13 Buck Weaver, AL:Chi. Oct. 7, 1917
Inning:
4 Charley Gelbert, NL:StL. Oct. 6, 1931 (3rd)
Alvin Dark, NL:NY Oct. 6, 1951 (3rd)

Putouts
Lifetime:
107 Phil Rizzuto, AL:NY 1941-42, 47, 49-53, 55
Game:
7 Buck Weaver, AL:Chi. Oct. 7, 1917
Phil Rizzuto, AL:NY Oct. 5, 1942
Inning:
3 Freddy Parent, AL:Bos. Oct. 1, 1903 (4th)
Art Fletcher, NL:NY Oct. 25, 1911 (9th)
Phil Rizzuto, AL:NY Oct. 5, 1947 (4th)
Mickey Stanley, AL:Det. Oct. 10, 1968 (6th)

Assists
Lifetime:
143 Phil Rizzuto, AL:NY 1941-42, 47, 49-53, 55
Game:
9 Roger Peckinpaugh, AL:NY Oct. 5, 1921
Extra-Inning Game:
10 Johnny Logan, NL:Mil. Oct. 6, 1957 (10 inn)
Inning:
3 Everett Scott, AL:Bos. Sept. 6, 1918 (6th)
Everett Scott, AL:Bos. Sept. 10, 1918 (3rd)
Joe Sewell, AL:Clev. Oct. 9, 1920 (6th)
Dave Bancroft, NL:NY Oct. 8, 1922 (3rd)
Ossie Bluege, AL:Wash. Oct. 7, 1924 (6th)
Glenn Wright, NL:Pitt. Oct. 8, 1927 (2nd)
Blondy Ryan, NL:NY Oct. 7. 1933 (3rd)
Phil Rizzuto, AL:NY Oct. 3, 1942 (2nd)
Ernie Bowman, NL:SF Oct. 8, 1962 (9th)
Bud Harrelson, NL:NY Oct. 14, 1969 (5th)
Mark Belanger, AL:Balt. Oct. 16, 1971 (7th)
Bud Harrelson, NL:NY Oct. 13, 1973 (7th)
Tim Foli, NL:Pitt. Oct. 12, 1979 (2nd)
Omar Vizquel, AL:Clev. Oct. 18, 1997 (5th)

Errors
Lifetime:
12 Art Fletcher, NL:NY 1911-13, 17
Game:
3 Jack Barry, AL:Phil. Oct. 26, 1911
Art Fletcher, NL:NY Oct. 9, 1912 (12 inn)
Buck Weaver, AL:Chi. Oct. 13, 1917
Inning:
2 Honus Wagner, NL:Pitt. Oct. 7, 1903 (6th)
Ivy Olson, NL:Brk. Oct. 12, 1916 (3rd)
Roger Peckinpaugh, AL:Wash. Oct. 8, 1925 (8th)
Woody English, NL:Chi. Oct. 8, 1929 (9th)
Dick Bartell, NL:NY Oct. 9, 1937 (3rd)
Pee Wee Reese, NL:Brk. Oct. 2, 1941 (8th)

Double Plays
Lifetime:
32 Phil Rizzuto, AL:NY 1941-42, 47, 49-53, 55
Game:
4 Phil Rizzuto, AL:NY, Oct. 8, 1951
Game, started:
3 Phil Rizzuto, AL:NY Oct. 10, 1951
Maury Wills, NL:LA Oct. 11, 1965
Larry Bowa, NL:Phil. Oct. 15, 1980
Game, unassisted:
1 Joe Tinker, NL:Chi. Oct. 10, 1907
Joe Tinker, NL:Chi. Oct. 11, 1907
Charlie Gelbert, NL:StL. Oct. 2, 1930
Eddie Kasko, NL:Cin. Oct. 7, 1961
Greg Gagne, AL:Minn. Oct. 26, 1991

Triple Plays
None

FIELDING — OUTFIELDERS

4 Games	*5 Games*	*6 Games*	*7 Games*
Highest Average 1.000 (Most Chances)			
16 Combs, AL:NY 1927	20 DiMaggio, AL:NY 1942	25 Rivers, AL:NY 1977	24 Murray, NL:NY 1912 (8g)
			Evans, AL:Bos. 1975
			Geronimo, NL:Cin. 1975
			Lynn, AL:Bos. 1975
			McGee, NL:StL. 1982
Chances Accepted			
16 Combs, AL:NY 1927	20 DiMaggio, AL:NY 1942	25 Rivers, AL:NY 1977	33 Roush, NL:Cin. 1919 (8g)
			26 Pafko, NL:Chi. 1945
			Gladden, AL:Minn. 1991
Putouts			
16 Combs, AL:NY 1927	20 DiMaggio, AL:NY 1942	24 Rivers, AL:NY 1977	30 Roush, NL:Cin. 1919 (8g)
			25 Gladden, AL:Minn. 1991
Assists			
2 By many players	2 By many players	2 By many players	4 Rice, AL:Wash. 1924
Errors			
3 Davis, NL:LA 1966	2 By many players	3 Murray, NL:NY 1911	4 Speaker, AL:Bos. 1912 (8g)
		J. Collins, AL:Chi. 1917	Devore, NL:NY 1912 (8g)
			Felsch, AL:Chi. 1919 (8g)
			Roush, NL:Cin. 1919 (8g)
			2 Crawford, AL:Det. 1909
			Wheat, NL:Brk. 1920
			Orsatti, NL:StL. 1934
			Goslin, AL:Det. 1934
			Mantle, AL:NY 1964
			Northrup, AL:Det. 1968
Double Plays			
1 Ramirez, AL:Bos. 2004	2 Murphy, AL:Phil. 1910	1 By many players	2 Speaker, AL:Bos. 1912 (8g)
			Roush, NL:Cin. 1919 (8g)
			Howard, AL:NY 1958
Double Plays Started			
1 Ramirez, AL:Bos. 2004	2 Murphy, AL:Phil. 1910	1 By many players	2 See preceding record

FIELDING – OUTFIELDERS

Most Series
12 Mickey Mantle, AL:NY 1951-53, 55-58, 60-64

Games
63 Mickey Mantle, AL:NY 1951-53, 55-58, 60-64

Chances Accepted
Lifetime:
150 Joe DiMaggio, AL:NY 1936-39, 41-42, 47, 49-51
Game, Left-fielder:
8 George Foster, NL:Cin. Oct. 21, 1976
Game, Center-fielder:
8 Edd Roush, NL:Cin. Oct. 1, 1919
Hank Leiber, NL:NY Oct. 2, 1936
Juan Pierre, NL:Fla. Oct. 22, 2003
Extra-Inning Game:
9 Edd Roush, NL:Cin. Oct. 7, 1919 (10 inn)
Mickey Rivers, AL:NY Oct. 11, 1977 (12 inn)
Amos Otis, AL:KC Oct. 17, 1980 (10 inn)
Game, Right-fielder:
7 Red Murray, NL:NY Oct. 14, 1912
Bing Miller, AL:Phil. Oct. 5, 1930
Ray Blades, NL:StL. Oct. 5, 1930
Tony Oliva, AL:Minn. Oct. 6, 1965
Al Kaline, AL:Det. Oct. 9, 1968
Frank Robinson, AL:Balt. Oct. 14, 1969
Inning:
3 By many players

Putouts
Lifetime:
150 Joe DiMaggio, AL:NY 1936-39, 41-42, 47, 49-51
Game, Left-fielder:
8 George Foster, NL:Cin. Oct. 21, 1976
Game, Center-fielder:
8 Edd Roush, NL:Cin. Oct. 1, 1919
Juan Pierre, NL:Fla. Oct. 22, 2003
Extra-Inning Game:
9 Amos Otis, AL:KC Oct. 17, 1980 (10 inn)
Game, Right-fielder:
7 Red Murray, NL:NY Oct. 14, 1912
Bing Miller, AL:Phil. Oct. 5, 1930
Ray Blades, NL:StL. Oct. 5, 1930
Tony Oliva, AL:Minn. Oct. 6, 1965
Al Kaline, AL:Det. Oct. 9, 1968
Frank Robinson, AL:Balt. Oct. 14, 1969
Inning, Left-fielder:
3 By many players; Last:
Deion Sanders, NL:Atl. Oct. 22, 1992 (5th)
Inning, Center-fielder:
3 By many players; Last:
Curtis Granderson, AL:Det. Oct. 24, 2006 (3rd)
Inning, Right-fielder:
3 By many players; Last:
David Justice, NL:Atl. Oct. 22, 1995 (5th)

Assists
Lifetime:
5 Harry Hooper, AL:Bos. 1912, 15-16, 18
Ross Youngs, NL:NY 1921-24
Game:
2 By many players
Inning:
1 By many players

Errors
Lifetime:
4 Ross Youngs, NL:NY 1921-24
Game:
3 Willie Davis, NL:LA Oct. 6, 1966
Inning:
3 Willie Davis, NL:LA Oct. 6, 1966 (5th)

Double Plays
Lifetime:
2 By many players
Game:
2 Edd Roush, NL:Cin. Oct. 7, 1919 (10 inn)
Game, started:
2 Edd Roush, NL:Cin. Oct. 7, 1919 (10 inn)
Game, unassisted:
1 Tris Speaker, AL:Bos. Oct. 15, 1912

Triple Plays
None

FIELDING – CATCHERS

4 Games	5 Games	6 Games	7 Games
Highest Average 1.000 (Most Chances)			
43 Roseboro, NL:LA 1963	61 Cochrane, AL:Phil. 1929	56 Campanella, NL:Brk. 1953	72 Grote, NL:NY 1973
Chances Accepted			
43 Roseboro, NL:LA 1963	61 Cochrane, AL:Phil. 1929	56 Campanella, NL:Brk. 1953	73 Posada, AL:NY 2001
Putouts			
43 Roseboro, NL:LA 1963	59 Cochrane, AL:Phil. 1929	55 W. Cooper, NL:StL. 1944	69 Posada, AL:NY 2001
Assists			
7 Munson, AL:NY 1976	9 Kling, NL:Chi. 1907	12 Meyers, NL:NY 1911	15 Schalk, AL:Chi. 1919 (8g)
	Schmidt, AL:Det. 1907		11 Schmidt, AL:Det. 1909
	Burns, NL:Phil. 1915		
Errors			
3 Oliver, NL:Cin. 1990	2 Schmidt, AL:Det. 1907	2 Schalk, AL:Chi. 1917	5 Schmidt, AL:Det. 1909
	W. Cooper, NL:StL. 1943		
	Ferguson, NL:LA 1974		
Double Plays			
2 Hartnett, NL:Chi. 1932	2 Burns, NL:Phil. 1915	3 Kling, NL:Chi. 1906	3 Schmidt, AL:Det. 1909
	Mancuso, NL:NY 1933		Schang, AL:NY 1921 (8g)
			Bench, NL:Cin. 1975
Double Plays Started			
1 By many players	1 By many players	2 Posada, AL:NY 2003	3 Schang, AL:NY 1921 (8g)
			2 Schmidt, AL:Det. 1909
			Crandall, NL:Mil. 1957-58
			Battey, AL:Minn. 1965
Passed Balls			
2 Schang, AL:Phil. 1914	2 Meyers, NL:Brk. 1916	2 Kling, NL:Chi. 1906	3 Burgess, NL:Pitt. 1960
		Killefer, AL:Chi. 1918	Howard, AL:NY 1964

ELDING – CATCHERS

Most Series
12 Yogi Berra, AL:NY 1947, 49-53, 55-58, 60, 62

Games
63 Yogi Berra, AL:NY 1947, 49-53, 55-58, 60, 62

Chances Accepted
Lifetime:
457 Yogi Berra, AL:NY 1947, 49-53, 55-58, 60, 62
Game:
18 Johnny Roseboro, NL:LA Oct. 2, 1963
Tim McCarver, NL:StL. Oct. 2, 1968
Inning:
4 Boss Schmidt, AL:Det. Oct. 14, 1908 (8th)
Ira Thomas, AL:Phil. Oct. 14, 1911 (6th)
Steve O'Neill, AL:Clev. Oct. 6, 1920 (3rd)
Jimmie Wilson, NL:StL. Oct. 1, 1931 (3rd)
Roy Campanella, NL:Brk. Sept. 29, 1955 (2nd)
Tim McCarver, NL:StL. Oct. 9, 1967 (9th)

Putouts
Lifetime:
421 Yogi Berra, AL:NY 1947, 49-53, 55-58, 60, 62
Game:
18 Johnny Roseboro, NL:LA Oct. 2, 1963
Inning:
3 By many players

Assists
Lifetime:
36 Yogi Berra, AL:NY 1947, 49-53, 55-58, 60, 62
Game:
4 Roger Bresnahan, NL:NY Oct. 12, 1905
Johnny Kling, NL:Chi. Oct. 9, 1907
Boss Schmidt, AL:Det. Oct. 11, 1907
Boss Schmidt, AL:Det. Oct. 14, 1908
Bill Rariden, NL:NY Oct. 10, 1917
Sam Agnew, AL:Bos. Sept. 6, 1918
Bill DeLancey, NL:StL. Oct. 8, 1934
Extra-Inning Game:
6 Jack Lapp, AL:Phil. Oct. 17, 1911 (11 inn)
Inning:
2 By many players

Errors
Lifetime:
7 Boss Schmidt, AL:Det. 1907-09
Game:
2 Lou Criger, AL:Bos. Oct. 1, 1903
Billy Sullivan, Sr. AL:Chi. Oct. 10, 1906
Boss Schmidt, AL:Det. Oct. 8, 1907 (13 inn)
Jimmie Wilson, NL:StL. Oct. 7, 1928
Joe Ferguson, NL:LA Oct. 15, 1974
Carlton Fisk, AL:Bos. Oct. 14, 1975 (10 inn)
Inning:
2 Lou Criger, AL:Bos. Oct. 1, 1903 (1st)
Jimmie Wilson, NL:StL. Oct. 7, 1928 (6th)

Passed Balls
Lifetime:
4 Wally Schang, AL:Phil.1913-14; Bos.18; NY 21-23
Elston Howard, AL:NY 1955-58, 60-64; Bos. 67
Game:
2 Johnny Kling, NL:Chi. Oct. 9, 1906
Bill Killefer, NL:Chi. Sept. 9, 1918
Paul Richards, AL:Det. Oct. 3, 1945
Bruce Edwards, NL:Brk. Oct. 4, 1947
Smoky Burgess, NL:Pitt. Oct. 6, 1960
Elston Howard, AL:NY Oct. 7, 1964
Inning:
1 By many players

Double Plays
Lifetime:
6 Yogi Berra, AL:NY 1947, 49-53, 55-58, 60, 62
Johnny Bench, NL:Cin. 1970, 72, 75
Game:
2 By many players
Game, started:
2 Boss Schmidt, AL:Det. Oct. 14, 1909
Wally Schang, AL:NY Oct. 11, 1921
Game, unassisted:
None

Triple Plays
None

FIELDING – PITCHERS

4 Games	5 Games	6 Games	7 Games
Highest Average 1.000 (Most Chances)			
6 Tyler, NL:Bos. 1914	8 Marquard, NL:NY 1913	17 Altrock, AL:Chi. 1906	13 Mathewson, NL:NY 1912 (8g
Ruffing, AL:NY 1938	Shore, AL:Bos. 1916	Vaughn, NL:Chi. 1918	12 Mullin, AL:Det. 1909
	Smith, NL:Brk. 1916		
Chances Accepted			
6 Tyler, NL:Bos. 1914	10 Mathewson, NL:NY 1905	17 Altrock, AL:Chi. 1906	13 Mathewson, NL:NY 1912 (8g
Ruffing, AL:NY 1938	Brown, NL:Chi. 1910	Vaughn, NL:Chi. 1918	12 Mullin, AL:Det. 1909
Putouts			
3 Ford, AL:NY 1963	5 Morris, AL:Det. 1984	6 Altrock, AL:Chi. 1906	5 Kaat, AL:Minn. 1965
Stewart, AL:Oak. 1989		Vaughn, NL:Chi. 1918	
Assists			
5 Bush, AL:Phil. 1914	10 Brown, NL:Chi. 1910	12 Brown, NL:Chi. 1906	12 Mullin, AL:Det. 1909
Tyler, NL:Bos. 1914			Mathewson, NL:NY 1912 (8g
James, NL:Bos. 1914			
Moore, AL:NY 1927			
Pearson, AL:NY 1939			
Errors			
1 By many players	2 Coombs, AL:Phil. 1910	2 Potter, AL:StL. 1944	2 Phillippe, NL:Pitt. 1909
	Lanier, NL:StL. 1942		Cicotte, AL:Chi. 1919 (8g)
	Verlander, AL:Det. 2006		Reynolds, AL:NY 1952
Double Plays			
2 Bender, AL:Phil. 1914	2 Bush, AL:NY 1922	2 Faber, AL:Chi. 1917	2 Johnson, AL:Wash. 1924
		Reynolds, AL:NY 1951	Stafford, AL:NY 1960
		Gura, AL:KC 1980	
Double Plays Started			
2 Bender, AL:Phil. 1914	2 Bush, AL:NY 1922	2 Faber, AL:Chi. 1917	2 Stafford, AL:NY 1960
		Reynolds, AL:NY 1951	

IELDING — PITCHERS

Most Series
11 Whitey Ford, AL:NY 1950, 53, 55-58, 60-64

Games:
22 Whitey Ford, AL:NY 1950, 53, 55-58, 60-64

Chances Accepted
Lifetime:
40 Christy Mathewson, NL:NY 1905, 11-13
Game:
11 Nick Altrock, AL:Chi. Oct. 12, 1906
Inning:
3 By many players

Putouts
Lifetime:
11 Whitey Ford, AL:NY 1950, 53, 55-58, 60-64
Game:
5 Jim Kaat, AL:Minn. Oct. 7, 1965
Inning:
2 Johnny Beazley, NL:StL. Oct. 5, 1942 (8th)
Bob Turley, AL:NY Oct. 9, 1957 (7th)
Whitey Ford, AL:NY Oct. 8, 1960 (9th)
Bob Purkey, NL:Cin. Oct. 7, 1961 (9th)
John Denny, NL:Phil. Oct. 15, 1983 (5th)
Dave Stewart, AL:Oak. Oct. 16, 1990 (3rd)
Jeff Nelson, AL:NY Oct. 23, 1996 (7th)

Assists
Lifetime:
35 Christy Mathewson, NL:NY 1905, 11-13
Game:
8 Nick Altrock, AL:Chi. Oct. 12, 1906
Lon Warneke, NL:Chi. Oct. 2, 1935
Inning:
3 Eddie Plank, AL:Phil. Oct. 13, 1905 (8th)
Ed Reulbach, NL:Chi. Oct. 10, 1908 (6th)
Rube Marquard, NL:NY Oct. 7, 1913 (4th)
Lon Warneke, NL:Chi. Oct. 2, 1935 (3rd)
Johnny Murphy, AL:NY Oct. 8, 1939 (8th)
Bob Rush, NL:Mil. Oct. 4, 1958 (3rd)
Ray Washburn, NL:Cin. Oct. 15, 1970 (7th)

Errors
Lifetime:
3 Deacon Phillippe, NL:Pitt. 1903, 09
Eddie Cicotte, AL:Chi. 1917, 19
Max Lanier, NL:StL. 1942-44
Dave Stewart, NL:LA 1981; AL:Oak. 1989-90
Game:
2 Deacon Phillippe, NL:Pitt. Oct. 12, 1909
Jack Coombs, AL:Phil. Oct. 18, 1910
Eddie Cicotte, AL:Chi. Oct. 4, 1919
Max Lanier, NL:StL. Sept. 30, 1942
Nels Potter, AL:StL. Oct. 5, 1944 (11 inn)
Inning:
2 Jack Coombs, AL:Phil. Oct. 18, 1910 (5th)
Eddie Cicotte, AL:Chi. Oct. 4, 1919 (5th)
Max Lanier, NL:StL. Sept. 30, 1942 (9th)
Nels Potter, AL:StL. Oct. 5, 1944 (3rd)

Double Plays
Lifetime:
3 Chief Bender, AL:Phil. 1905, 10-11, 13-14
Joe Bush, AL:Phil.1913-14; Bos.18; NY 22-23
Allie Reynolds, AL:NY 1947, 49-53
Game:
2 Chief Bender, AL:Phil. Oct. 9, 1914
Joe Bush, AL:NY Oct. 8, 1922
Allie Reynolds, AL:NY Oct. 8, 1951
Larry Gura, AL:KC Oct. 19, 1980
Game, started:
2 Chief Bender, AL:Phil. Oct. 9, 1914
Joe Bush, AL:NY Oct. 8, 1922
Allie Reynolds, AL:NY Oct. 8, 1951
Game, unassisted:
None

Triple Plays
None

INDIVIDUAL PITCHING

4 Games	5 Games	6 Games	7 Games
Earned Run Average 0.00 (Most Innings)			
11.0 James, NL:Bos. 1914	27.0 Mathewson, NL:NY 1905	14.0 Benton, NL:NY 1917	27.0 Hoyt, AL:NY 1921 (8g)
			18.0 Ford, AL:NY 1960
Games			
4 Nelson, AL:NY 1999	5 Marshall, NL:LA 1974	6 Quisenberry, AL:KC 1980	7 Knowles, AL:Oak. 1973
Foulke, AL:Bos. 2004			
Cotts, AL:Chi. 2005			
Jenks, AL:Chi. 2005			
Games Started			
2 By many players; Last:	3 Mathewson, NL:NY 1905	3 By many players; Last:	5 Phillippe, NL:Pitt. 1903 (8g)
Brown, NL:SD 1998	Coombs, AL:Phil. 1910	Wynn, AL:Chi. 1959	3 By many players; Last:
			Schilling, NL:Ari. 2001
Complete Games			
2 Rudolph, NL:Bos. 1914	3 Mathewson, NL:NY 1905	3 Bender, AL:Phil. 1911	5 Phillippe, NL:Pitt. 1903 (8g)
Hoyt, AL:NY 1928	Coombs, AL:Phil. 1910	Vaughn, NL:Chi. 1918	3 Adams, NL:Pitt. 1909
Ruffing, AL:NY 1938			Mullin, AL:Det. 1909
Koufax, NL:LA 1963			Coveleski, AL:Clev. 1920
			Johnson, AL:Wash. 1925
			Newsom, AL:Det. 1940
			Burdette, NL:Mil. 1957
			Gibson, NL:StL. 1967-68
			Lolich, AL:Det. 1968
Shutouts			
1 By many pitchers	3 Mathewson, NL:NY 1905	1 By many pitchers	2 Dineen, AL:Bos. 1903 (8g)
			Burdette, NL:Mil. 1957
			Ford, AL:NY 1960
			Koufax, NL:LA 1965
Games Finished			
4 Foulke, AL:Bos. 2004	5 Marshall, NL:LA 1974	6 Quisenberry, AL:KC 1980	6 Casey, NL:Brk. 1947
Saves (Since 1969)			
3 Rivera, AL:NY 1998	2 Fingers, AL:Oak. 1974	4 Wetteland, AL:NY 1996	3 Tekulve, NL:Pitt. 1979
	T. Martinez, AL:Balt. 1983		Percival, AL:Ana. 2002
	Hernandez, AL:Det. 1984		
	Rivera, AL:NY 2000		
Won			
2 Rudolph, NL:Bos. 1914	3 Mathewson, NL:NY 1905	3 Faber, AL:Chi. 1917	3 Phillippe, NL:Pitt. 1903 (8g)
James, NL:Bos. 1914	Coombs, AL:Phil. 1910		Dinneen, AL:Bos. 1903 (8g)
Hoyt, AL:NY 1928			Adams, NL:Pitt. 1909
Ruffing, AL:NY 1938			Wood, AL:Bos. 1912 (8g)
Koufax, NL:LA 1963			Coveleski, AL:Clev. 1920
Stewart, AL:Oak. 1989			Brecheen, NL:StL. 1946
Moore, AL:Oak. 1989			Burdette, NL:Mil. 1957
Rijo, NL:Cin. 1990			Gibson, NL:StL. 1967
			Lolich, AL:Det. 1968
			Johnson, NL:Ari. 2001
Lost			
2 Sherdel, NL:StL. 1928	2 By many players; Last:	3 Frazier, AL:NY 1981	3 Williams, AL:Chi. 1919 (8g)
Lee, NL:Chi. 1938	Verlander, AL:Det. 2006		2 By many players; Last:
Walters, NL:Cin. 1939	Hudson, NL:Phil. 1983		Washburn, AL:Ana. 2002
Lemon, AL:Clev. 1954			Hernandez, NL:SF 2002
Ford, AL:NY 1963			
Drysdale, NL:LA 1966			
Garrelts, NL:SF 1989			
Stewart, AL:Oak. 1990			
Lidge, NL:Hou. 2005			

	4 Games	5 Games	6 Games	7 Games
...nings	18.0 Rudolph, NL:Bos. 1914 Hoyt, AL:NY 1928 Ruffing, AL:NY 1938 Koufax, NL:LA 1963	27.0 Mathewson, NL:NY 1905 Coombs, AL:Phil. 1910	27.0 Mathewson, NL:NY 1911 Faber, AL:Chi. 1917 Vaughn, NL:Chi. 1918	44.0 Phillippe, NL:Pitt. 1903 (8g) 32.0 Mullin, AL:Det. 1909
...ns	11 Alexander, NL:StL. 1928 Lemon, AL:Clev. 1954	16 Brown, NL:Chi. 1910	10 Sallee, NL:NY 1917 Ruffing, AL:NY 1936 Gullett, AL:NY 1977 Sutton, NL:LA 1978 Morris, AL:Tor. 1992	19 Phillippe, NL:Pitt. 1903 (8g) 17 Burdette, NL:Mil. 1958
...ts	17 Ruffing, AL:NY 1938	23 Coombs, AL:Phil. 1910 Brown, NL:Chi. 1910	25 Mathewson, NL:NY 1911	38 Phillippe, NL:Pitt. 1903 (8g) 30 Johnson, AL:Wash. 1924
...me Runs	4 Sherdel, NL:StL. 1928 Root, NL:Chi. 1932 Thompson, NL:Cin. 1939 Garrelts, NL:SF 1989	4 Nolan, NL:Cin. 1970 Hudson, NL:Phil. 1983	4 Reynolds, AL:NY 1953	5 Burdette, NL:Mil. 1958 Hughes, NL:StL. 1967
...alks	8 Lemon, AL:Clev. 1954	14 Coombs, AL:Phil. 1910	11 Tyler, NL:Chi. 1918 Gomez, AL:NY 1936 Reynolds, AL:NY 1951	13 Nehf, NL:NY 1921 (8g) 11 Johnson, AL:Wash. 1924 Bevens, AL:NY 1947
...ost Intentional Walks (since 1955)	2 Brown, NL:SD 1998	3 Brosnan, NL:Cin. 1961	2 By many players	4 Lackey, AL:Ana. 2002
...rikeouts	23 Koufax, NL:LA 1963	18 Mathewson, NL:NY 1905	20 Bender, AL:Phil. 1911	35 Gibson, NL:StL. 1968

SERVICE

Most Series, Lifetime
11 Whitey Ford, AL:NY 1950, 53, 55-58, 60-64

Most Series, Relief Pitcher, Lifetime
6 Johnny Murphy, AL:NY 1936-39, 41, 43
Mariano Rivera, AL:NY 1996, 98-2001, 03

GAMES

Most Games, Lifetime
22 Whitey Ford, AL:NY 1950, 53, 55-58, 60-64

Most Games, Relief Pitcher, Lifetime
20 Mike Stanton, NL:Atl. 1991-92; AL:NY 98-2001
Mariano Rivera, AL:NY 1996, 98-2001, 03

Most Games, Consecutive
7 Darold Knowles, AL:Oak. 1973
Jeff Nelson, AL:NY 1998-2000

GAMES STARTED

Most Games Started, Lifetime
22 Whitey Ford, AL:NY 1950, 53, 55-58, 60-64

Most Games Started, Consecutive
22 Whitey Ford, AL:NY 1950, 53, 55-58, 60-64

Most Opening Games Started, Lifetime
8 Whitey Ford, AL:NY 1955-58, 61-64

COMPLETE GAMES

Most Complete Games, Lifetime
10 Christy Mathewson, NL:NY 1905, 11-13

Most Complete Games, Consecutive
9 Chief Bender, AL:Phil. 1905, 10-11, 13

GAMES FINISHED

Most Games Finished, Lifetime
15 Mariano Rivera, AL:NY 1996, 98-2001, 03

SAVES (since 1969)

Most Saves, Lifetime
9 Mariano Rivera, AL:NY 1996, 98-2001, 03

SHUTOUTS

Most Shutouts
4 Christy Mathewson, NL:NY 1905, 13

Most Shutouts, Consecutive
3 Christy Mathewson, NL:NY 1905
Whitey Ford, AL:NY 1960-61

Most Consecutive Scoreless Innings
Complete game:
10 Christy Mathewson, NL:NY Oct. 8, 1913
Clem Labine, NL:Brk. Oct. 9, 1956
Jack Morris, AL:Minn. Oct. 27, 1991
Game, consecutive:
13 Babe Ruth, AL:Bos. Oct. 9, 1916
Consecutive:
33 Whitey Ford, AL:NY 1960-62

GAMES WON

Most Won, Lifetime
10 Whitey Ford, AL:NY 1950, 53, 55-58, 60-64

Most Won, Consecutive
7 Bob Gibson, NL:StL. 1964, 67-68

GAMES LOST

Most Lost, Lifetime
8 Whitey Ford, AL:NY 1950, 53, 55-58, 60-64

Most Lost Consecutive
5 Joe Bush, AL:Phil. 1914; Bos. 18; NY 22-23

INNINGS PITCHED

Most Innings, Lifetime
146 Whitey Ford, AL:NY 1950, 53, 55-58, 60-64

Most Innings, Game
14 Babe Ruth, AL:Bos. Oct. 9, 1916

RUNS

Most Runs, Lifetime
51 Whitey Ford, AL:NY 1950, 53, 55-58, 60-64

Most Runs, Game
10 Brickyard Kennedy, NL:Pitt. Oct. 7, 1903

Most Runs, Inning
7 Hooks Wiltse, NL:NY Oct. 26, 1911 (7th)
Carl Hubbell, NL:NY Oct. 6, 1937 (6th)

EARNED RUNS

Most Earned Runs, Lifetime
44 Whitey Ford, AL:NY 1950, 53, 59-58, 60-64

Earned Runs, Game
8 Grover Alexander, NL:StL. Oct. 5, 1928
Guy Bush, NL:Chi. Sept. 28, 1932
Jay Witasick, AL:NY Nov. 3, 2001

Earned Runs, Inning
6 Bill Donovan, AL:Det. Oct. 11, 1908 (8th)
Hooks Wiltse, NL:NY Oct. 26, 1911 (7th)
Charlie Root, NL:Chi. Oct. 12, 1929 (7th)
General Crowder, AL:Wash. Oct. 4, 1933 (6th)
Harry Gumbert, NL:NY Oct. 2, 1936 (9th)
Hank Borowy, AL:NY Oct. 4, 1942 (4th)
Danny Cox, NL:StL. Oct. 18, 1987 (4th)
Jay Witasick, AL:NY Nov. 3, 2001 (3rd)

HITS

Most Hits, Lifetime
132 Whitey Ford, AL:NY 1950, 53, 55-58, 60-64

Most Hits, Game
15 Walter Johnson, AL:Wash. Oct. 15, 1925

Most Hits, Inning
8 Jay Witasick, AL:NY Nov. 3, 2001 (3rd)

Most Hits, Consecutive, Inning
6 Ed Summers, AL:Det. Oct. 10, 1908 (9th)

Most Hitless Innings, Consecutive
11.1 Don Larsen, AL:NY 1956-57

HOME RUNS

Most Home Runs, Lifetime
9 Catfish Hunter, AL:Oak. 1972-74; NY 76-78

Most Home Runs, Game
4 Charlie Root, NL:Chi. Oct. 1, 1932
   Junior Thompson, NL:Cin. Oct. 7, 1939
   Dick Hughes, NL:StL. Oct. 11, 1967

Most Home Runs, Inning
3 Dick Hughes, NL:StL. Oct. 11, 1967 (4th)

Most Home Runs, Consecutive, Inning
2 By many pitchers, Last:
   Kevin Appier, AL:Ana. Oct. 20, 2002 (2nd)

Most Grand Slam Home Runs, Lifetime
1 By many pitchers. See Batter's record.

WALKS

Most Walks, Lifetime
34 Whitey Ford, AL:NY 1950, 53, 55-58, 60-64

Most Walks, Game
10 Bill Bevens, AL:NY Oct. 3, 1947

Most Walks, Inning
4 Wild Bill Donovan, AL:Det. Oct. 16, 1909 (2nd)
   Art Reinhart, NL:StL. Oct. 6, 1926 (5th)
   Paul Derringer, NL:StL. Oct. 9, 1931 (5th)
   Guy Bush, NL:Chi. Sept. 28, 1932 (6th)
   Don Gullett, NL:Cin. Oct. 22, 1975 (3rd)
   Bobby Castillo, NL:LA Oct. 20, 1981 (4th)
   Tom Glavine, NL:Atl. Oct. 24, 1991 (6th)
   Todd Stottlemyre, AL:Tor. Oct. 20, 1993 (1st)
   Al Leiter, NL:Fla. Oct. 21, 1997 (4th)
   Jarrod Washburn, AL:Ana. Oct. 24, 2002 (1st)
   Tim Wakefield, AL:Bos. Oct. 23, 2004 (4th)
   Consecutive:
3 By many players; Last:
   Tim Wakefield, AL:Bos. Oct. 23, 2004 (4th)

Most Intentional Walks, Lifetime (since 1955)
4 By many pitchers

HIT BATTERS

Most Hit Batters, Lifetime
4 Wild Bill Donovan, AL:Det. 1907, 09
   Eddie Plank, AL:Phil. 1905, 11, 13-14

Most Hit Batters, Game
3 Bruce Kison, NL:Pitt. Oct. 13, 1971

Most Hit Batters, Inning
2 Ed Willett, AL:Det. Oct. 11, 1909 (2nd)
   Wayne Granger, NL:StL. Oct. 9, 1968 (8th)

STRIKEOUTS

Most Strikeouts, Lifetime
94 Whitey Ford, AL:NY 1950, 53, 55-58, 60-64

Most Strikeouts, Game
17 Bob Gibson, NL:StL. Oct. 2, 1968
    Relief pitcher:
11 Moe Drabowsky, AL:Balt. Oct. 5, 1966

Most Strikeouts, Inning
4 Orval Overall, NL:Chi. Oct. 14, 1908 (1st)

Most Strikeouts, Consecutive Batters Faced
6 Hod Eller, NL:Cin. Oct. 6, 1919
   Moe Drabowsky, AL:Balt. Oct. 5, 1966
   Todd Worrell, NL:StL. Oct. 24, 1985

Most Strikeouts, Consecutive, Start of Game:
5 Mort Cooper, NL:StL. Oct. 11, 1943
   Sandy Koufax, NL:LA, Oct. 2, 1963

WILD PITCHES

Most Wild Pitches, Lifetime
5 Hal Schumacher, NL:NY 1933, 36-37
   Jack Morris, AL:Det. 1984; Minn. 91; Tor. 92

Most Wild Pitches, Game
2 Jeff Tesreau, NL:NY Oct. 15, 1912
   Jeff Pfeffer, NL:Brk. Oct. 12, 1916
   Bob Shawkey, AL:NY Oct. 5, 1922
   Vic Aldridge, NL:Pitt. Oct. 15, 1925
   Johnny Miljus, NL:Pitt. Oct. 8, 1927
   Tex Carleton, NL:Chi. Oct. 9, 1938
   Jim Bouton, AL:NY Oct. 5, 1963
   John Stuper, NL:StL. Oct. 13, 1982
   Doc Medich, AL:Mil. Oct. 19, 1982
   Jack Morris, AL:Det. Oct. 13, 1984
   Ron Darling, NL:NY Oct. 18, 1986
   Mike Moore, AL:Oak. Oct. 15, 1989
   Jack Morris, AL:Minn. Oct. 23, 1991
   John Smoltz, NL:Atl. Oct. 18, 1992
   Glendon Rusch, NL:NY Oct. 21, 2000
   Justin Verlander, AL:Det. Oct. 27, 2006

Most Wild Pitches, Inning
2 Bob Shawkey, AL:NY Oct. 5, 1922 (5th)
   Vic Aldridge, NL:Pitt. Oct. 15, 1925 (1st)
   Johnny Miljus, NL:Pitt. Oct. 8, 1927 (9th)
   Tex Carleton, NL:Chi. Oct. 9, 1938 (8th)
   Doc Medich, AL:Mil. Oct. 19, 1982 (6th)
   Justin Verlander, AL:Det. Oct. 27, 2006 (1st)

BALKS

1912	Oct.	14	AL:Bos	O'Brien, Buck
1919	Oct.	2	NL:Cin.	Sallee, Slim
1925	Oct.	8	NL:Pitt.	Aldridge, Vic
1926	Oct.	6	NL:StL.	Bell, Hi
1935	Oct.	5	NL:Chi.	Carleton, Tex
1947	Sept.	30	AL:NY	Shea, Spec
1948	Oct.	10	AL:Clev.	Paige, Satchel
1948	Oct.	11	AL:Clev.	Lemon, Bob
1952	Oct.	6	NL:Brk.	Loes, Billy
1953	Oct.	2	AL:NY	Raschi, Vic
1965	Oct.	7	NL:LA	Perranoski, Ron
1967	Oct.	4	AL:Bos.	Wyatt, Whitlow
1975	Oct.	11	AL:Bos.	Tiant, Luis
1979	Oct.	12	AL:Balt.	McGregor, Scott
1982	Oct.	19	AL:Mil.	Sutton, Don
1983	Oct.	15	AL:Balt.	Stewart, Sammy
1984	Oct.	10	AL:Det.	Petry, Dan
1985	Oct.	22	NL:StL.	Horton, Ricky
1987	Oct.	20	AL:Minn.	Straker, Les
1987	Oct.	22	AL:Minn.	Atherton, Keith
1988	Oct.	15	AL:Oak.	Stewart, Dave
1988	Oct.	18	NL:LA	Leary, Tim
1989	Oct.	27	NL:SF	Brantley, Jeff
1991	Oct.	20	NL:Atl.	Glavine, Tom
1993	Oct.	17	AL:Tor.	Stewart, Dave
1995	Oct.	25	NL:Atl.	Avery, Steve
1996	Oct.	23	AL:NY	Weathers, David

CLUB BATTING – SERIES

BATTING AVERAGE

	4 Games	5 Games	6 Games	7 Games
Highest Batting Average, Winning Club	.317 NL:Cin. (Oak.) 1990	.316 AL:Phil. (Chi.) 1910	.311 AL:Tor. (Phil.) 1993	.323 NL:Pitt. (Balt.) 1979
Highest Batting Average, Losing Club	.253 NL:Chi. (NY) 1932	.265 NL:SD (Det.) 1984	.300 NL:Brk. (NY) 1953	.338 AL:NY (Pitt.) 1960
Highest Batting Average, Both Clubs	.283 AL:NY (Chi.) 1932	.272 AL:Phil. (Chi.) 1910	.292 AL:Tor. (Phil.) 1993	.300 AL:NY (Pitt.) 1960
Lowest Batting Average, Winning Club	.200 AL:Balt. (LA) 1966	.209 NL:NY (Phil.) 1905	.186 AL:Bos. (Chi.) 1918	.199 AL:NY (SF) 1962
Lowest Batting Average, Losing Club	.142 NL:LA (Balt.) 1966	.146 AL:Balt. (NY) 1969	.175 NL:NY (Phil.) 1911	.183 AL:NY (Ari.) 2001
Lowest Batting Average, Both Clubs	.171 NL:LA (Balt.) 1966	.184 AL:Balt. (NY) 1969	.197 AL:Chi. (Chi.) 1906	.209 AL:Oak. (Cin.) 1972

SLUGGING PERCENTAGE

	4 Games	5 Games	6 Games	7 Games
Highest Slugging Percentage, Winning Club	.582 AL:Oak. (SF) 1989	.509 AL:Balt. (Cin.) 1970	.510 AL:Tor. (Phil.) 1993	.465 AL:Ana. (SF) 2002
Highest Slugging Percentage, Losing Club	.397 NL:Chi. (NY) 1932	.361 NL:SD (Det.) 1984	.484 NL:Brk. (NY) 1953	.528 AL:NY (Pitt.) 1960
Highest Slugging Percentage, Both Clubs	.468 AL:Oak. (SF) 1989	.433 AL:Balt. (Cin.) 1970	.483 NL:Brk. (NY) 1953	.481 AL:Ana. (SF) 2002
Lowest Slugging Percentage, Winning Club	.304 AL:NY (Phil.) 1950	.255 NL:NY (Phil.) 1905	.233 AL:Bos. (Chi.) 1918	.276 AL:NY (SF) 1962
Lowest Slugging Percentage, Losing Club	.192 NL:LA (Balt.) 1966	.194 AL:Phil. (NY) 1905	.243 NL:NY (Phil.) 1911	.237 NL:Brk. (Clev.) 1920
Lowest Slugging Percentage, Both Clubs	.267 AL:Balt. (LA) 1966	.224 NL:NY (Phil.) 1905	.241 NL:Chi. (Bos.) 1918	.285 AL:Clev. (Brk.) 1920

AT-BATS

	4 Games	5 Games	6 Games	7 Games
Most At-Bats	154 AL:Chi. (Hou.) 2005	179 AL:NY (NY) 2000	222 AL:NY (LA) 1978	282 AL:Bos. (Pitt.) 1903 (8g)
				269 AL:NY (Pitt.) 1960
Most At-Bats, Both Clubs	297 AL:Chi. (Hou.) 2005	354 AL:NY (NY) 2000	421 AL:NY (LA) 1978	552 AL:Bos. (Pitt.) 1903 (8g)
				512 NL:StL. (Det.) 1934
Fewest At-Bats	117 NL:LA (NY) 1963	142 AL:Oak. (LA) 1974	172 AL:Bos. (Chi.) 1918	215 NL:Brk. (Clev.) 1920
				NL:Brk. (NY) 1956
				AL:Minn. (LA) 1965
Fewest At-Bats, Both Clubs	240 AL:Balt. (LA) 1966	300 AL:Oak. (LA) 1974	348 NL:Chi. (Bos.) 1918	432 AL:Clev. (Brk.) 1920

RUNS

	4 Games	5 Games	6 Games	7 Games
Most Runs	37 AL:NY (Chi.) 1932	35 AL:Phil. (Chi.) 1910	45 AL:Tor. (Phil.) 1993	55 AL:NY (Pitt.) 1960
Most Runs, Losing Club	19 NL:Chi. (NY) 1932	20 NL:Cin. (Balt.) 1970	36 NL:Phil. (Tor.) 1993	55 AL:NY (Pitt.) 1960
Most Runs, Both Clubs	56 AL:NY (Chi.) 1932	53 AL:Balt. (Cin.) 1970	81 AL:Tor. (Phil.) 1993	85 AL:Ana. (SF) 2002
Fewest Runs	2 NL:LA (Balt.) 1966	3 AL:Phil. (NY) 1905	9 AL:Bos. (Chi.) 1918	8 NL:Brk. (Clev.) 1920
Fewest Runs, Both Clubs	15 AL:Balt. (LA) 1966	18 NL:NY (Phil.) 1905	19 NL:Chi. (Bos.) 1918	29 AL:Clev. (Brk.) 1920

HITS

	4 Games	5 Games	6 Games	7 Games
Most Hits	45 AL:NY (Chi.) 1932 NL:Cin. (Oak.) 1990	56 AL:Phil. (Chi.) 1910	68 AL:NY (LA) 1978	91 AL:NY (Pitt.) 1960
Most Hits, Both Clubs	82 AL:NY (Chi.) 1932	91 AL:Phil. (Chi.) 1910 AL:Phil. (Chi.) 1929	122 AL:Tor. (Phil.) 1993	151 AL:NY (Pitt.) 1960
Fewest Hits	17 NL:LA (Balt.) 1966	23 AL:Balt. (NY) 1969	32 AL:Bos. (Chi.) 1918	40 NL:StL (KC) 1985
Fewest Hits, Both Clubs	41 AL:Balt. (LA) 1966	57 NL:NY (Phil.) 1905	69 NL:Chi. (Bos.) 1918	92 AL:Oak. (Cin.) 1972

EXTRA-BASE HITS

	4 Games	5 Games	6 Games	7 Games
Most Extra-Base Hits	20 AL:Oak. (SF) 1989	21 AL:Phil. (Chi.) 1910	24 AL:Tor. (Phil.) 1993	27 AL:NY (Pitt.) 1960
Most Extra-Base Hits, Both Clubs	29 AL:Oak. (SF) 1989 AL:Chi. (Hou.) 2005	33 AL:Phil. (Chi.) 1910	41 NL:Brk. (NY) 1953	45 AL:Ana. (SF) 2002
Fewest Extra-Base Hits	4 NL:Cin. (NY) 1939 NL:LA (Balt.) 1966	3 AL:Det. (Chi.) 1907	5 AL:Bos. (Chi.) 1918	6 NL:Brk. (Clev.) 1920
Fewest Extra-Base Hits, Both Club	12 AL:Balt. (LA) 1966	10 NL:Chi. (Det.) 1907	11 NL:Chi. (Bos.) 1918	19 AL:Clev. (Brk.) 1920

TOTAL BASES

	4 Games	5 Games	6 Games	7 Games
Most Total Bases	85 AL:Oak. (SF) 1989	87 AL:Balt. (Cin.) 1970	105 AL:Tor. (Phil.) 1993	142 AL:NY (Pitt.) 1960
Most Total Bases, Both Clubs	133 AL:NY (Chi.) 1932	145 AL:Balt. (Cin.) 1970	200 NL:Brk. (NY) 1953	231 AL:Ana. (SF) 2002
Fewest Total Bases	23 NL:LA (Balt.) 1966	30 AL:Phil. (NY) 1905	40 AL:Bos. (Chi.) 1918	51 NL:Brk. (Clev.) 1920
Fewest Total Bases, Both Clubs	64 AL:Balt. (LA) 1966	69 NL:NY (Phil.) 1905	84 NL:Chi. (Bos.) 1918	123 AL:Clev. (Brk.) 1920

SINGLES

	4 Games	5 Games	6 Games	7 Games
Most Singles	32 AL:NY (SD) 1998	46 NL:NY (NY) 1922	57 AL:NY (LA) 1978	64 AL:NY (Pitt.) 1960
Most Singles, Both Clubs	55 AL:NY (Chi.) 1932	71 NL:Chi. (Phil.) 1929	95 AL:NY (LA) 1978	109 AL:NY (Pitt.) 1960
Fewest Singles	13 AL:Phil. (Bos.) 1914 NL:LA (Balt.) 1966	19 NL:Brk. (NY) 1941 AL:Balt. (NY) 1969 AL:Det. (StL.) 2006	17 AL:Phil. (StL) 1930	27 AL:Minn. (LA) 1965 NL:StL. (KC) 1985
Fewest Singles, Both Clubs	29 AL:Balt. (LA) 1966	40 NL:NY (Balt.) 1969	42 NL:StL (Phil.) 1930	66 NL:StL. (Bos.) 1967

DOUBLES

4 Games	5 Games	6 Games	7 Games
Most Doubles			
11 AL:Bos. (StL) 2004	19 AL:Phil. (Chi.) 1910	15 AL:Phil. (NY) 1911	19 NL:StL. (Bos.) 1946
Most Doubles, Both Clubs			
19 AL:Bos. (StL) 2004	30 AL:Phil. (Chi.) 1910	26 AL:Phil. (NY) 1911	29 AL:Det. (Pitt.) 1909
Fewest Doubles			
3 By many clubs	1 AL:Det. (Chi.) 1907 AL:Balt. (NY) 1969	2 AL:Bos. (Chi.) 1918 NL:NY (NY) 1923	3 AL:Balt. (Pitt.) 1971
Fewest Doubles, Both Clubs			
6 NL:LA (NY) 1963 AL:Balt. (LA) 1966	6 NL:Phil. (Bos.) 1915	7 NL:Chi. (Bos.) 1918	11 AL:Bos. (Pitt.) 1903 (8g) NL:StL. (Det.) 1968

TRIPLES

Most Triples			
3 NL:Cin. (NY) 1976 AL:Oak. (SF) 1989	6 AL:Bos. (Brk.) 1916	5 AL:Tor. (Phil.) 1993	16 AL:Bos. (Pitt.) 1903 (8g) 5 NL:StL. (Det.) 1934 AL:NY (Brk.) 1947
Most Triples, Both Clubs			
4 NL:Cin. (NY) 1976 AL:Oak. (SF) 1989	11 AL:Bos. (Brk.) 1916	7 AL:NY (NY) 1923 AL:Tor. (Phil.) 1993	25 AL:Bos. (Pitt.) 1903 (8g) 8 AL:Minn. (Atl.) 1991
Fewest Triples			
0 By many	0 By many	0 By many	0 By many
Fewest Triples, Both Clubs			
1 NL:StL. (NY) 1928 AL:Clev. (NY) 1954 AL:Balt. (LA) 1966 AL:NY (SD) 1998 AL:NY (Atl.) 1999	0 NL:NY (Phil.) 1905 NL:NY (Wash.) 1933 NL:NY (Balt.) 1969 NL:SD (Det.) 1984	0 AL:Clev. (Bos.) 1948 AL:NY (LA) 1978 AL:Tor. (Atl.) 1992	0 NL:StL. (Phil.) 1931 AL:NY (Ari.) 2001

HOME RUNS

Most Home Runs			
9 AL:NY (StL.) 1928 AL:Oak. (SF) 1989	10 AL:Balt. (Cin.) 1970	9 AL:NY (Brk.) 1953 NL:LA (NY) 1977	14 NL:SF (Ana.) 2002
Most Home Runs, Both Clubs			
13 AL:Oak. (SF) 1989	15 AL:Balt. (Cin.) 1970	17 AL:NY (Brk.) 1953 NL:LA (NY) 1977	21 AL:Ana. (SF) 2002
Fewest Home Runs			
0 By many	0 By many	0 By many	0 NL:Cin. (Chi.) 1919 (8g) NL:Brk. (Clev.) 1920
Fewest Home Runs, Both Clubs			
1 NL:Bos. (Phil.) 1914	0 NL:NY (Phil.) 1905 NL:Chi. (Det.) 1907	0 AL:Chi. (Chi.) 1906 AL:Bos. (Chi.) 1918	1 AL:Chi. (Cin.) 1919 (8g)

RUNS BATTED IN

Most Runs Batted In			
36 AL:NY (Chi.) 1932	32 AL:Balt. (Cin.) 1970	45 AL:Tor. (Phil.) 1993	54 AL:NY (Pitt.) 1960
Most Runs Batted In, Both Clubs			
52 AL:NY (Chi.) 1932	52 AL:Balt. (Cin.) 1970	80 AL:Tor. (Phil.) 1993	80 AL:NY (Pitt.) 1960 AL:Ana. (SF) 2002
Fewest Runs Batted In			
2 NL:LA (Balt.) 1966	2 AL:Phil. (NY) 1905	6 AL:Bos. (Chi.) 1918	8 NL:Brk. (Clev.) 1920
Fewest Runs Batted In, Both Clubs			
12 NL:LA (Balt.) 1966	15 AL:Phil. (NY) 1905	16 AL:Bos. (Chi.) 1918	25 NL:Brk. (Clev.) 1920

ACRIFICE HITS

4 Games	5 Games	6 Games	7 Games
ost Sacrifice Hits			
6 By many	12 AL:Bos. (Brk.) 1916	13 NL:Chi. (Chi.) 1906	13 NL:Cin. (Chi.) 1919 (8g)
			12 NL:Pitt. (Det.) 1909
			NL:StL. (NY) 1926
ost Sacrifice Hits, Both Clubs			
12 AL:NY (Pitt.) 1927	18 AL:Bos. (Brk.) 1916	19 NL:Chi. (Chi.) 1906	22 NL:StL. (NY) 1926
west Sacrifice Hits			
0 By many	0 By many	0 NL:NY (NY) 1923	0 NL:StL. (Bos.) 1967
		AL:NY (NY) 1951	
		NL:LA (NY) 1977	
		AL:Tor. (Phil.) 1993	
		AL:Clev. (Atl.) 1995	
west Sacrifice Hits, Both Clubs			
0 NL:Cin. (NY) 1976	0 AL:NY (Brk.) 1941	1 AL:Tor. (Phil.) 1993	2 NL:StL. (Mil.) 1982
AL:Oak. (SF) 1989	AL:Balt. (Phil.) 1983		

ACRIFICE FLIES (1908 to 1930, 1939, since 1954)

ost Sacrifice Flies			
3 NL:StL. (Bos.) 2004	3 AL:Balt. (Phil.) 1983	7 AL:Tor. (Phil.) 1993	5 NL:Pitt. (Balt.) 1979
	NL:SD (Det.) 1984		
	AL:NY (NY) 2000		
ost Sacrifice Flies, Both Clubs			
3 NL:Cin. (NY) 1976	5 NL:SD (Det.) 1984	8 AL:Tor. (Phil.) 1993	7 AL:Ana. (SF) 2002
AL:NY (SD) 1998			
NL:StL. (Bos.) 2004			
west Sacrifice Flies			
0 By many	0 By many	0 By many	0 By many
west Sacrifice Flies, Both Clubs			
0 AL:Balt. (LA) 1966	0 NL:StL. (Det.) 2006	0 AL:NY (LA) 1978	0 AL:Minn. (LA) 1965
AL:NY (Atl.) 1999			AL:KC (StL.) 1985

VALKS

ost Walks			
24 AL:Bos. (StL.) 2004	25 AL:NY (NY) 2000	34 NL:Phil. (Tor.) 1993	40 AL:Clev. (Fla.) 1997
ost Walks, Both Clubs			
36 AL:Bos. (StL.) 2004	37 AL:NY (Brk.) 1941	59 NL:Phil. (Tor.) 1993	76 AL:Clev. (Fla.) 1997
west Walks			
4 NL:Pitt. (NY) 1927	5 AL:Phil. (NY) 1905	4 AL:Phil. (NY) 1911	9 NL:StL. (Phil.) 1931
west Walks, Both Clubs			
15 AL:NY (Cin.) 1939	15 NL:NY (Phil.) 1913	17 AL:Chi. (NY) 1917	27 AL:Bos. (Pitt.) 1903 (8g)
ost Intentional Walks			
4 NL:NY (Clev.) 1954	7 AL:NY (NY) 2000	7 AL:NY (LA) 1981	9 NL:SF (Ana.) 2002

HIT BY PITCH

4 Games	5 Games	6 Games	7 Games
Most Hit By Pitch			
5 NL:Hou. (Chi.) 2005	4 NL:Chi. (Det.) 1907	4 AL:NY (Brk.) 1953	6 NL:Pitt. (Det.) 1909
			NL:Ari. (NY) 2001
Most Hit By Pitch, Both Clubs			
8 NL:Hou. (Chi.) 2005	6 AL:NY (NY) 2000	6 AL:NY (Brk.) 1953	10 NL:Pitt. (Det.) 1909
Fewest Hit By Pitch			
0 By many	0 By many	0 By many	0 By many
Fewest Hit By Pitch, Both Clubs			
0 NL:LA (Balt.) 1966	0 AL:Wash. (NY) 1933	0 AL:StL. (StL.) 1944	0 AL:Clev. (Brk.) 1920
AL:NY (Atl.) 1999	AL:NY (StL.) 1942-43		AL:Det. (Cin.) 1940
	AL:Balt. (Cin.) 1970		AL:NY (Brk.) 1956
			AL:NY (Mil.) 1958

STRIKEOUTS

4 Games	5 Games	6 Games	7 Games
Most Strikeouts			
37 AL:NY (LA) 1963	50 NL:Chi. (Phil.) 1929	50 NL:Phil. (Tor.) 1993	70 NL:Ari. (NY) 2001
Most Strikeouts, Both Clubs			
66 AL:Chi. (Hou.) 2005	88 AL:NY (NY) 2000	97 NL:Fla. (NY) 2003	133 AL:NY (Ari.) 2001
Fewest Strikeouts			
7 NL:Pitt. (NY) 1927	15 NL:NY (NY) 1922	14 NL:Chi. (Bos.) 1918	20 NL:Brk. (Clev.) 1920
Fewest Strikeouts, Both Clubs			
32 AL:NY (Pitt.) 1927	35 NL:NY(Phil.) 1913	35 AL:Bos. (Chi.) 1918	41 AL:Clev. (Brk.) 1920
NL:Cin. (NY) 1976	AL:NY (NY) 1922		

STOLEN BASES

4 Games	5 Games	6 Games	7 Games
Most Stolen Bases			
9 NL:Bos. (Phil.) 1914	18 NL:Chi. (Det.) 1907	15 NL:Atl. (Tor.) 1992	18 NL:Pitt. (Det.) 1909
Most Stolen Bases, Both Clubs			
11 NL:Bos. (Phil.) 1914	26 NL:Chi. (Det.) 1907	20 NL:Atl. (Tor.) 1992	24 NL:Pitt. (Det.) 1909
Fewest Stolen Bases			
0 By many	0 By many	0 By many	0 By many
Fewest Stolen Bases, Both Clubs			
1 NL:Cin. (NY) 1939	1 NL:Chi. (Phil.) 1929	0 NL:StL. (StL.) 1944	1 NL:Cin. (Det.) 1940
NL:NY (Clev.) 1954	AL:Wash. (NY) 1933		
NL:LA (Balt.) 1966	NL:NY (NY) 1937		
NL:StL. (Bos.) 2004	AL:NY (Cin.) 1961		
	NL:Cin. (Balt.) 1970		
	AL:NY (NY) 2000		

CAUGHT STEALING

4 Games	5 Games	6 Games	7 Games
Most Caught Stealing			
5 NL:Cin. (NY) 1976	8 NL:Chi. (Phil.) 1910	10 NL:NY (Phil.) 1911	10 NL:Cin. (Chi.) 1919 (8g)
			8 NL:StL. (Det.) 1968
Most Caught Stealing, Both Clubs			
7 NL:Cin. (NY) 1976	15 NL:Chi. (Phil.) 1910	16 NL:NY (Phil.) 1911	15 AL:Chi. (Cin.) 1919 (8g)
			AL:NY (NY) 1921 (8g)
			10 NL:Pitt. (Det.) 1909
			AL:Det. (StL.) 1968
Fewest Caught Stealing (Most Attempts)			
0 AL:Oak. (Cin.) 1990 (7)	0 AL:NY (StL.) 1942 (3)	0 AL:Tor. (Atl.) 1992 (5)	0 AL:Minn. (StL.) 1987 (6)
	AL:Oak. (LA) 1988 (3)		AL:Ana. (SF) 2002 (6)
Fewest Caught Stealing, Both Clubs (Most Attempts)			
0 AL:NY (Pitt.) 1927 (2)	0 AL:NY (Brk.) 1949 (3)	0 NL:Bos. (Clev.) 1948 (3)	0 AL:NY (StL.) 1964 (5)

EFT ON BASE

4 Games	5 Games	6 Games	7 Games
ost Left on Base			
41 AL:Bos. (StL.) 2004	52 AL:NY (NY) 2000	55 AL:NY (LA) 1981	72 NL:NY (Oak.) 1973
ost Left on Base, Both Clubs			
65 AL:Clev. (NY) 1954	88 AL:NY (NY) 2000	101 AL:NY (LA) 1981	130 NL:NY (Oak.) 1973
AL:Bos. (StL.) 2004			
ewest Left on Base			
16 NY (Cin.) 1939	23 NL:Phil. (Bos.) 1915	29 AL:Phil. (NY) 1911	36 AL:Minn. (LA 1965
	NL:Phil. (Balt.) 1983		
ewest Left on Base, Both Clubs			
39 NL:Cin. (NY) 1939	51 NL:Phil. (Balt.) 1983	61 NL:NY (Phil.) 1911	82 AL:Clev. (Brk.) 1920
			NL:Brk. (NY) 1956
			AL:NY (SF) 1962

INCH-HITTING

ost Pinch-Hitters			
16 AL:Clev. (NY) 1954	15 NL:Cin. (NY) 1961	14 NL:LA (NY) 1981	23 AL:Balt. (Pitt.) 1979
ost Pinch-Hitters, Both Clubs			
19 AL:Clev. (NY) 1954	23 AL:Balt. (Phil.) 1983	24 NL:LA (NY) 1981	37 AL:Minn. (Atl.) 1991
ewest Pinch-Hitters			
0 AL:NY (Cin.) 1939	0 AL:Phil. (Chi.) 1910	0 AL:Phil. (NY) 1911	1 NL:Pitt. (Bos.) 1903 (8g)
AL:Balt. (LA) 1966	AL:Phil. (NY) 1913		
NL:Cin. (NY) 1976			
ewest Pinch-Hitters, Both Clubs			
3 NL:Cin. (NY) 1939	2 NL:NY (Phil.) 1905	6 NL:NY (Phil.) 1911	5 AL:Bos. (Pitt.) 1903 (8g)
		AL:Chi. (Chi.) 1906	AL:NY (NY) 1921 (8g)

INCH-RUNNING

ost Pinch-Runners			
4 NL:Phil. (NY) 1950	5 NL:NY (Phil.) 1913	5 AL:NY (LA) 1981	8 AL:Oak. (Cin.) 1972
ost Pinch-Runners, Both Clubs			
6 NL:Phil. (NY) 1950	6 AL:Oak. (LA) 1974	7 AL:NY (LA) 1981	10 AL:Oak. (Cin.) 1972
	AL:Balt. (Phil.) 1983		
ewest Pinch-Runners			
0 By many	0 By many	0 By many	0 By many
ewest Pinch-Runners, Both Clubs			
0 AL:NY (Chi.) 1938	0 NL:NY (Phil.) 1905	0 AL:Chi. (NY) 1917	0 AL:Bos. (Pitt.) 1903 (8g)
NL:LA (NY) 1963	AL:Phil. (Chi.) 1929	AL:Phil. (StL.) 1930	AL:NY (Brk.) 1956
NL:Cin. (NY) 1976	AL:NY (NY) 1937	AL:Det. (Chi.) 1935	NL:Cin. (Bos.) 1975
AL:Oak. (SF) 1989	AL:Balt. (Cin.) 1970	AL:NY (Brk.) 1953	

AT-BATS

Most At-Bats, Game
46 NL:Ari. (NY) Nov. 3, 2001
  Extra-Inning Game:
54 NL:NY (Oak.) Oct. 14, 1973 (12 inn)
  Fewest, 9-Inning Game:
23 NL:Cin. (Chi.) Oct. 2, 1919

Most At-Bats, Both Clubs, Game
  Most, 9 innings:
85 AL:Tor. (Phil.) Oct. 20, 1993
  Extra-Inning Game:
101 NL:NY (Oak.) Oct. 14, 1973 (12 inn)
  Fewest, 9-Inning Game:
53 NL:Brk. (Clev.) Oct. 7, 1920
  AL:NY (NY) Oct. 6, 1921
  AL:NY (Brk.) Oct. 8, 1956
  NL:LA (NY) Oct. 5, 1963

Most At-Bats, Inning
13 AL:Phil. (Chi.) Oct. 12, 1929 (7th)

Most At-Bats, Both Clubs, Inning
17 AL:Phil. (Chi.) Oct. 12, 1929 (7th)

RUNS

Most Runs, Game
18 AL:NY (NY) Oct. 2, 1936

Most Earned Runs, Game
17 AL:NY (NY) Oct. 2, 1936

Most Runs, Both Clubs, Game
29 AL:Tor. (Phil.) Oct. 20, 1993

Most Runs, Inning
10 AL:Phil. (Chi.) Oct. 12, 1929 (7th)
  AL:Det. (StL.) Oct. 9, 1968 (3rd)

Most Runs, Both Clubs, Inning
11 AL:Phil. (Chi.) Oct. 12, 1929 (7th)
  NL:Brk. (NY) Oct. 5, 1956 (2nd)
  NL:Fla. (Clev.) Oct. 21, 1997 (9th)

Most Innings Scoring a Run, Game
6 AL:NY (StL.) Oct. 6, 1926
  AL:NY (Brk.) Oct. 1, 1947
  AL:NY (Pitt.) Oct. 6, 1960
  NL:Phil. (Tor.) Oct. 20, 1993
  NL:Fla. (Clev.) Oct. 21, 1997

Most Innings Scoring a Run, Both Clubs, Game
10 NL:Phil. (Tor.) Oct. 20, 1993
  NL:Fla. (Clev.) Oct. 21, 1997

Most Earned Runs, Both Clubs, Game
29 AL:Tor. (Phil.) Oct. 20, 1993

Most Runs, Each Inning, Club

7	1st:	NL:Mil. (NY) Oct. 2, 1958
6	2nd:	AL:NY (NY) Oct. 13, 1923
		NL:NY (NY) Oct. 9, 1937
		NL:Brk. (NY) Oct. 2, 1947
		NL:Brk. (NY) Oct. 5, 1956
10	3rd:	AL:Det. (StL.) Oct. 9, 1968
7	4th:	AL:Minn. (StL.) Oct. 17, 1987
6	5th:	AL:Balt. (Pitt.) Oct. 11, 1971
		AL:KC (StL.) Oct. 27, 1985
7	6th:	AL:NY (NY) Oct. 6, 1937
		AL:NY (Pitt.) Oct. 6, 1960
10	7th:	AL:Phil. (Chi.) Oct. 12, 1929
6	8th:	NL:Chi. (Det.) Oct. 11, 1908
		AL:Balt. (Pitt.) Oct. 13, 1979
		AL:Tor. (Phil.) Oct. 20, 1993
7	9th:	AL:NY (NY) Oct. 6, 1936
		NL:Fla. (Clev.) Oct. 21, 1997
3	10th:	NL:NY (Phil.) Oct. 8, 1913
		AL:NY (Cin.) Oct. 8, 1939
		NL:NY (Clev.) Sept. 29, 1954
		NL:Mil. (NY) Oct. 6, 1957
		NL:StL. (NY) Oct. 12, 1964
		NL:NY (Bos.) Oct. 25, 1986
2	11th:	AL:Phil. (NY) Oct. 17, 1911
		AL:Tor. (Atl.) Oct. 24, 1992
4	12th:	NL:NY (Oak.) Oct. 14, 1973
0	13th:	No runs scored
2	14th:	AL:Chi. (Hou.) Oct. 25, 2005

HITS

Most Hits, Game
22 NL:Ari. (NY) Nov. 3, 2001

Most Hits, Both Clubs, Game
32 AL:NY (Pitt.) Oct. 6, 1960
  AL:Tor. (Phil.) Oct. 20, 1993

Most Hits, Inning
10 AL:Phil. (Chi.) Oct. 12, 1929 (7th)

Most Hits, Both Clubs, Inning
12 AL:Phil. (Chi.) Oct. 12, 1929 (7th)

Most Hits, Consecutive, Inning
6 NL:Chi. (Det.) Oct. 10, 1908 (9th)

Most Hitless Innings, Consecutive
11 NL:Cin. (NY) Oct. 4-5, 1939
  Complete game:
9 NL:Brk. (NY) Oct. 8, 1956

EXTRA-BASE HITS

Most Extra-Base Hits, Game
9 NL:Pitt. (Wash.) Oct. 15, 1925

Most Extra-Base Hits, Both Clubs, Game
13 NL:Phil. (Tor.) Oct. 20, 1993

Most Extra-Base Hits, Inning
4 AL:Chi. (LA) Oct. 1, 1959 (3rd)
  AL:NY (Cin.) Oct. 9, 1961 (1st)
  AL:KC (Phil.) Oct. 18, 1980 (1st)

TOTAL BASES

Most Total Bases, Game
34 NL:Atl. (Minn.) Oct. 24, 1991

Most Total Bases, Both Clubs, Game
53 NL:Phil. (Tor.) Oct. 20, 1993

Most Total Bases, Inning
17 AL:Phil. (Chi.) Oct. 12, 1929 (7th)

Most Total Bases, Both Clubs, Inning
21 AL:Phil. (Chi.) Oct. 12, 1929 (7th)

SINGLES

Most Singles, Game
16 AL:NY (LA) Oct. 15, 1978
NL:Ari. (NY) Nov. 3, 2001

Most Singles, Both Clubs, Game
24 AL:NY (LA) Oct. 15, 1978

Most Singles, Inning
7 AL:Phil. (Chi.) Oct. 12, 1929 (7th)
NL:NY (Wash.) Oct. 4, 1933 (6th)
NL:NY (NY) Oct. 9, 1937 (2nd)
NL:Brk. (NY) Oct. 8, 1949 (6th)

Most Singles, Both Clubs, Inning
8 AL:Phil. (Chi.) Oct. 12, 1929 (7th)
NL:NY (Wash.) Oct. 4, 1933 (6th)
NL:NY (NY) Oct. 9, 1937 (2nd)
NL:Brk. (NY) Oct. 8, 1949 (6th)

DOUBLES

Most Doubles, Game
8 AL:Chi. (Chi.) Oct. 13, 1906
NL:Pitt. (Wash.) Oct. 15, 1925

Most Doubles, Both Clubs, Game
11 AL:Chi. (Chi.) Oct. 13, 1906

Most Doubles, Inning
3 AL:Chi. (Chi.) Oct. 13, 1906 (4th)
AL:Phil. (Chi.) Oct. 18, 1910 (7th)
AL:Phil. (NY) Oct. 24, 1911 (4th)
NL:Pitt. (Wash.) Oct. 15, 1925 (8th)
NL:StL. (Det.) Oct. 9, 1934 (3rd)
NL:Brk. (NY) Oct. 2, 1947 (2nd)
NL:Brk. (NY) Oct. 5, 1947 (3rd)
AL:NY (Brk.) Oct. 8, 1949 (4th)
AL:Chi. (LA) Oct. 1, 1959 (3rd)
NL:Cin. (Balt.) Oct. 15, 1970 (1st)
NL:StL. (KC) Oct. 20, 1985 (9th)
NL:Ari. (NY) Nov. 3, 2001 (3rd)

TRIPLES

Most Triples, Game
5 AL:Bos. (Pitt.) Oct. 7, 10, 1903

Most Triples, Both Clubs, Game
7 AL:Bos. (Pitt.) Oct. 10, 1903

Most Triples, Inning
2 AL:Bos. (Pitt.) Oct. 1, 1903 (7th)
AL:Bos. (Pitt.) Oct. 7, 1903 (6th)
AL:Bos. (Pitt.) Oct. 10, 1903 (1st, 4th)
AL:Bos. (NY) Oct. 12, 1912 (3rd)
AL:Phil. (NY) Oct. 7, 1913 (4th)
AL:Bos. (Chi.) Sept. 6, 1918 (9th)
AL:NY (Brk.) Oct. 1, 1947 (3rd)
AL:NY (Brk.) Sept 30, 1953 (1st)
AL:Det. (StL.) Oct. 7, 1968 (4th)

HOME RUNS

Most Home Runs, Game
5 AL:NY (StL.) Oct. 9, 1928
AL:Oak. (SF) Oct. 27, 1989

Most Home Runs, Both Clubs, Game
7 AL:Oak. (SF) Oct. 27, 1989

Most Home Runs, Inning
3 AL:Bos. (StL.) Oct. 11, 1967 (4th)

Most Home Runs, Both Clubs, Inning
3 NL:NY (NY) Oct. 11, 1921 (2nd)
AL:Bos. (StL.) Oct. 11, 1967 (4th)
AL:Ana. (SF) Oct. 19, 2002 (2nd)
AL:Ana. (SF) Oct. 20, 2002 (2nd)

Most Home Runs, Consecutive, Inning
2 AL:Wash. (Pitt.) Oct. 11, 1925 (3rd)
AL:NY (StL.) Oct. 9, 1928 (4th)
AL:NY (Chi.) Oct. 1, 1932 (5th)
AL:NY (StL.) Oct. 14, 1964 (6th)
AL:Balt. (LA) Oct. 5, 1966 (1st)
AL:Bos. (StL.) Oct. 11, 1967 (4th)
NL:Cin. (Bos.) Oct. 14, 1975 (6th)
AL:NY (LA) Oct. 16, 1977 (8th)
NL:LA (NY) Oct. 25, 1981 (7th)
AL:Bos. (NY) Oct. 27, 1986 (2nd)
NL:Fla. (Clev.) Oct. 18, 1997 (4th)
NL:SD (NY) Oct. 17, 1998 (5th)
NL:SF (Ana.) Oct. 20, 2002 (2nd)

Most Consecutive Games with a Home Run
9 AL:NY 1932-37
AL:NY 1952-53
Games, One Series
7 AL:Wash. (Pitt.) 1925
AL:NY (Brk.) 1952

RUNS BATTED IN

Most Runs Batted In, Game
18 AL:NY (NY) Oct. 2, 1936

Most Runs Batted In, Both Clubs, Game
29 AL:Tor. (Phil.) Oct. 20, 1993

Most Runs Batted In, Inning
10 AL:Phil. (Chi.) Oct. 12, 1929 (7th)
AL:Det. (StL.) Oct. 9, 1968 (3rd)

Most Runs Batted In, Both Clubs, Inning
11 AL:Phil. (Chi.) Oct. 12, 1929 (7th)
NL:Brk. (NY) Oct. 5, 1956 (2nd)

SACRIFICE HITS

Most Sacrifice Hits, Game
5 NL:Chi. (Chi.) Oct. 12, 1906
NL:Chi. (Det.) Oct. 10, 1908
NL:Pitt. (Det.) Oct. 16, 1909

Most Sacrifice Hits, Both Clubs, Game
7 NL:Chi. (Det.) Oct. 10, 1908

Most Sacrifice Hits, Inning
2 By many clubs

Most Sacrifice Hits, Consecutive, Inning
2 By many clubs

SACRIFICE FLIES (1908 to 1930, 1939, since 1954)

Most Sacrifice Flies, Game
3 AL:Tor. (Phil.) Oct. 19, 1993

Most Sacrifice Flies, Both Clubs, Game
3 AL:Tor. (Phil.) Oct. 19, 1993
   AL:Tor. (Phil.) Oct. 23, 1993
   AL:Clev. (Fla.) Oct. 25, 1997
   AL:Ana. (SF) Oct. 24, 2002

Most Sacrifice Flies, Inning
2 AL:Balt. (Pitt.) Oct. 13, 1971 (1st)

Most Sacrifice Flies, Both Clubs, Inning
2 AL:Balt. (Pitt.) Oct. 13, 1971 (1st)
   AL:Det. (SD) Oct. 10, 1984 (1st)
   AL:Clev. (Fla.) Oct. 25, 1997 (5th)

Most Sacrifice Flies, Consecutive, Inning
2 AL:Balt. (Pitt.) Oct. 13, 1971 (1st)

WALKS

Most Walks, Game
11 NL:Brk. (NY) Oct. 5, 1956
    AL:NY (Mil.) Oct. 5, 1957
    AL:Det. (SD) Oct. 12, 1984
    Extra-Inning Game:
12 NL:Hou. (Chi.) Oct. 25, 2005 (14 inn)

Most Walks, Both Clubs, Game
19 AL:NY (Mil.) Oct. 5, 1957
    Extra-Inning Game:
21 NL:Hou. (Chi.) Oct. 25, 2005 (14 inn)

Most Walks, Inning
5 AL:NY (StL.) Oct. 6, 1926 (5th)

Most Walks, Both Clubs, Inning
6 AL:NY (NY) Oct. 7, 1921 (3rd)
   AL:NY (StL.) Oct. 6, 1926 (5th)
   NL:LA (NY) Oct. 28, 1981 (6th)
   NL:Phil. (Tor.) Oct. 20, 1993 (1st)
   NL:StL. (Bos.) Oct. 23, 2004 (4th)

Fewest Walks, Both Clubs, Game
0 AL:Phil. (NY) Oct. 16, 1911
   NL:NY (Chi.) Oct. 10, 1917
   NL:NY (NY) Oct. 9, 1921
   AL:Bos. (StL.) Oct. 7, 1967
   NL:Phil. (Balt.) Oct. 11, 1983

HIT BY PITCH

Most Hit By Pitch, Game
3 AL:Det. (StL.) Oct. 9, 1968
   AL:Balt. (Pitt.) Oct. 13, 1971
   NL:Hou. (Chi.) Oct. 22, 2005

Most Hit By Pitch, Both Clubs, Game
3 NL:Phil. (Bos.) Oct. 13, 1915
   NL:Cin. (Chi.) Oct. 9, 1919
   NL:Pitt. (Wash.) Oct. 7, 1925
   AL:Det. (StL.) Oct. 9, 1968
   AL:Balt. (Pitt.) Oct. 13, 1971
   NL:NY (Oak.) Oct. 14, 1973 (12 inn)
   AL:Minn. (StL.) Oct. 21, 1987
   NL:Hou. (Chi.) Oct. 22, 2005
   AL:Det. (StL.) Oct. 22, 2006

Most Hit By Pitch, Inning
2 NL:Pitt. (Det.) Oct. 11, 1909 (2nd)
   AL:Det. (StL.) Oct. 9, 1968 (8th)
   NL:Pitt. (Balt.) Oct. 17, 1979 (9th)
   NL:Hou. (Chi.) Oct. 22, 2005 (7th)

STRIKEOUTS

Most Strikeouts, Game
17 AL:Det. (StL.) Oct. 2, 1968

Most Strikeouts, Both Clubs, Game
25 AL:NY (LA) Oct. 2, 1963
    AL:Oak. (NY) Oct. 14, 1973 (12 inn)
    AL:NY (NY) Oct. 24, 2000
    AL:Chi. (Hou.) Oct. 25, 2005 (14 inn)

Most Strikeouts, Inning
4 AL:Det. (Chi.) Oct. 14, 1908 (1st)

Most Strikeouts, Both Clubs, Inning
6 NL:Cin. (Oak.) Oct. 18, 1972 (5th)
   AL:KC (StL.) Oct. 24, 1985 (7th)
   AL:NY (NY) Oct. 24, 2000 (2nd)

Most Strikeouts, Consecutive, Game
6 AL:Chi. (Cin.) Oct. 6, 1919
   AL:KC (StL.) Oct. 24, 1985
   NL:LA (Balt.) Oct. 5, 1966

Fewest Strikeouts, Both Clubs, Game
0 NL:Pitt. (NY) Oct. 13, 1960

STOLEN BASES

Most Stolen Bases, Game
6 NL:Chi. (Chi.) Oct. 10, 1906
   Extra-Inning Game:
7 NL:Chi. (Det.) Oct. 8, 1907 (13 inn)

Most Stolen Bases, Both Clubs, Game
7 NL:Chi. (Det.) Oct. 12, 1907
   Extra-Inning Game:
11 NL:Chi. (Det.) Oct. 8, 1907 (13 inn)

Most Stolen Bases, Inning
3 NL:Pitt. (Bos.) Oct. 1, 1903 (1st)
   NL:NY (Phil.) Oct. 12, 1905 (9th)
   NL:Chi. (Det.) Oct. 8, 1907 (10th)
   NL:Chi. (Det.) Oct. 11, 1908 (8th)
   AL:Det. (Chi.) Oct. 12, 1908 (9th)
   NL:NY (Bos.) Oct. 14, 1912 (1st)

CAUGHT STEALING

Most Caught Stealing, Game
3 By many clubs; Last:
   NL:LA (Oak.) Oct. 19, 1988
   Extra-Inning Game:
5 NL:NY (Phil.) Oct. 17, 1911 (11 inn)

Most Caught Stealing, Both Clubs, Game
5 AL:Phil. (Chi.) Oct. 17, 1910
   Extra-Inning Game
6 NL:NY (Phil.) Oct. 17, 1911 (11 inn)

Most Caught Stealing Inning
2 NL:NY (Phil.) Oct. 12, 1905 (7th)
   NL:NY (Phil.) Oct. 17, 1911 (10th)
   NL:NY (Bos.) Oct. 9, 1912 (11th)
   AL:Bos. (Phil.) Oct. 9, 1915 (1st)
   AL:Bos. (Brk.) Oct. 12, 1916 (3rd)
   AL:Chi. (Cin.) Oct. 3, 1919 (6th)
   NL:Brk. (NY) Oct. 6, 1947 (1st)
   AL:NY (Brk.) Oct. 2, 1952 (1st)
   NL:StL. (Det.) Oct. 10, 1968 (6th)

EFT ON BASE

Most Left on Base, Game
15 NL:NY (Oak.) Oct. 14, 1973 (12 inn)
NL:Phil. (KC) Oct. 17, 1980 (10 inn)
AL:NY (NY) Oct. 21, 2000 (12 inn)
AL:Ana. (SF) Oct. 22, 2002
AL:Chi. (Hou.) Oct. 25, 2005 (14 inn)
NL:Hou. (Chi.) Oct. 25, 2005 (14 inn)

Most Left on Base, Both Clubs, Game
24 AL:Det. (SD) Oct. 12, 1984
Extra-Inning Game:
30 AL:Chi. (Hou.) Oct. 25, 2005 (14 inn)

Fewest Left on Base, Game
0 NL:Brk. (NY) Oct. 8, 1956
NL:LA (NY) Oct. 6, 1963

Fewest Left on Base, Both Clubs, Game
3 NL:Brk. (NY) Oct. 8, 1956

INCH-HITTING

Most Pinch-Hitters, Game
6 NL:LA (Chi.) Oct. 6, 1959
Extra-Inning Game:
8 AL:Minn. (Atl.) Oct. 22, 1991 (12 inn)

Most Pinch-Hitters, Both Clubs, Game
8 AL:Balt. (Phil.) Oct. 15, 1983
AL:Oak. (NY) Oct. 14, 1973
Extra-Inning Game:
12 AL:Minn. (Atl.) Oct. 22, 1991 (12 inn)

Most Pinch-Hitters, Inning
4 NL:NY (Oak.) Oct. 13, 1973 (9th)
AL:Balt. (Phil.) Oct. 15, 1983 (6th)
AL:KC (StL.) Oct. 26, 1985 (9th)
AL:Minn. (StL.) Oct. 22, 1987 (9th)
NL:SD (NY) Oct. 18, 1998 (8th)
NL:Atl. (NY) Oct. 23, 1999 (8th)
NL:NY (NY) Oct. 25, 2000 (7th)

Most Pinch-Hits, Series
6 AL:NY (Brk.) 1947 (7g)
AL:NY (Pitt.) 1960 (7g)
AL:Oak. (Cin.) 1972 (7g)
AL:Balt. (Pitt.) 1979 (7g)

Most Pinch-Hits, Both Clubs, Series
11 AL:NY (Brk.) 1947 (7g)

Most Pinch-Hits, Game
3 AL:Oak. (Cin.) Oct. 19, 1972
AL:Balt. (Pitt.) Oct. 13, 1979
NL:SD (NY) Oct. 18, 1998

Most Pinch-Hits, Both Clubs, Game
3 By many

Most Pinch-Hits, Inning
3 AL:Oak. (Cin.) Oct. 19, 1972 (9th)
NL:SD (NY) Oct. 18, 1998 (8th)

Most Pinch-Hit Home Runs
6 AL:NY 1947, 52, 55, 60-61, 99

Most Pinch-Hit Home Runs, One Series
2 NL:LA (Chi.) 1959
AL:Bos. (Cin.) 1975

Most Pinch-Hit HRs, Both Clubs, One Series
2 AL:Clev. (NY) 1954
NL:LA (Chi.) 1959
AL:Bos. (Cin.) 1975

Most Pinch-Hit Walks, Inning
2 AL:NY (NY) Oct. 15, 1923 (8th)
AL:Balt. (Pitt.) Oct. 11, 1979 (7th)
AL:Balt. (Phil.) Oct. 15, 1983 (6th)
AL:NY (Atl.) Oct. 23, 1999 (8th)

Most Pinch-Hit Strikeouts, Game
4 AL:StL. (StL.) Oct. 8, 1944
AL:StL. (StL.) Oct. 9, 1944

Most Pinch-Hit Strikeouts, Inning
3 AL:StL. (StL.) Oct. 8, 1944 (9th)

PINCH-RUNNERS

Most Pinch-Runners, Game
2 By many

Most Pinch-Runners, Both Clubs, Game
4 NL:StL. (KC) Oct. 26, 1985

Most Pinch-Runners, Inning
2 NL:NY (NY) Oct. 10, 1923 (3rd)
AL:NY (NY) Oct. 15, 1923 (8th)
NL:Brk. (NY) Oct. 3, 1947 (9th)
NL:Bos. (Clev.) Oct. 6, 1948 (8th)
NL:Phil. (NY) Oct. 7, 1950 (9th)
NL:LA (Chi.) Oct. 6, 1959 (7th)
AL:Oak. (Cin.) Oct. 19, 1972 (9th)
NL:StL. (KC) Oct. 26, 1985 (8th)
AL:KC (StL.) Oct. 26, 1985 (9th)
NL:Ari. (NY) Nov. 4, 2001 (9th)
AL:Bos. (StL.) Oct. 27, 2004 (8th)

Most Pinch-Runners, Both Clubs, Inning
2 By many; Last:
AL:Bos. (StL.) Oct. 27, 2004 (8th)
AL:Chi. (Hou.) Oct. 25, 2005 (8th)

CLUB FIELDING

AVERAGE

	4 Games		5 Games		6 Games		7 Games
Highest Average (Most Chances)							
1.000	AL:Balt. (LA) 1966 (141 tc)	1.000	AL:NY (NY) 1937 (179 tc)	.996	AL:Bos. (Chi.) 1918	.993	NL:Cin. (Bos.) 1975
Highest Average, Both Clubs							
.986	AL:NY (LA) 1963	.986	AL:NY (Brk.) 1941	.992	NL:LA (NY) 1977	.990	NL:StL. (KC) 1985
Lowest Average							
.946	AL:Bos. (StL.) 2004	.942	NL:Brk. (Bos.) 1916	.938	NL:NY (Phil.) 1911	.934	AL:Det. (Pitt.) 1909
Lowest Average, Both Clubs							
.954	AL:NY (Chi.) 1932	.946	NL:Chi. (Phil.) 1910	.947	NL:NY (Phil.) 1911	.941	AL:Det. (Pitt.) 1909

CHANCES ACCEPTED

	4 Games		5 Games		6 Games		7 Games
Most Chances Accepted							
179	NL:Bos. (Phil.) 1914	237	AL:Bos. (Brk.) 1916	271	AL:Chi. (Chi.) 1906	329	NL:NY (Bos.) 1912 (8g) AL:Chi. (Cin.) 1919 (8g)
						300	AL:Wash. (NY) 1924
Most Chances Accepted, Both Clubs							
356	NL:Bos. (Phil.) 1914	449	AL:Bos. (Brk.) 1916	514	AL:Chi. (Chi.) 1906	649	NL:NY (Bos.) 1912 (8g)
						594	AL:Wash. (NY) 1924
Fewest Chances Accepted							
136	AL:NY (StL.) 1928 NL:Atl. (NY) 1999	166	NL:SD (Det.) 1984	197	AL:Phil. (StL.) 1930	234	NL:StL. (Det.) 1968
Fewest Chances Accepted, Both Clubs							
274	AL:NY (StL.) 1928	348	NL:LA (Oak.) 1988	404	AL:Phil. (StL.) 1930	489	AL:Ana. (SF) 2002

PUTOUTS

	4 Games		5 Games		6 Games		7 Games
Most Putouts							
123	AL:Chi. (Hou.) 2005	147	NL:Bos. (Brk.) 1916	168	AL:NY (LA) 1977 AL:NY (Fla.) 2003	222	AL:Bos. (NY) 1912 (8g)
						202	AL:Minn. (Atl.) 1991
Most Putouts, Both Clubs							
241	AL:Chi. (Hou.) 2005	289	AL:Bos. (Brk.) 1916	333	AL:NY (LA) 1977	443	AL:Bos. (NY) 1912 (8g)
						401	NL:NY (Wash.) 1924
Fewest Putouts							
102	NL:StL. (NY) 1928 NL:Chi. (NY) 1932 NL:Chi. (NY) 1938 AL:NY (LA) 1963 AL:LA (Balt.) 1966 NL:SF (Oak.) 1989 NL:SD (NY) 1998 NL:StL. (Bos.) 2004	126	NL:LA (Oak.) 1974 NL:SD (Det.) 1984 AL:Det. (StL.) 2006	153	NL:NY (Chi.) 1917 AL:StL. (Phil.) 1930 AL:NY (LA) 1981	177	NL:Brk. (Clev.) 1920 NL:StL. (Minn.) 1987
Fewest Putouts, Both Clubs							
210	NL:StL. (NY) 1928 NL:Chi. (NY) 1932, 38 AL:NY (LA) 1963 NL:LA (Balt.) 1966 NL:SF (Oak.) 1989 AL:NY (SD) 1998 NL:StL. (Bos.) 2004	258	NL:LA (Oak.) 1974 NL:SD (Det.) 1984 NL:StL. (Det.) 2006	309	NL:NY (Chi.) 1917 NL:StL. (Phil.) 1930 AL:NY (LA) 1981	357	NL:StL. (Minn.) 1987

ASSISTS

	4 Games		5 Games		6 Games		7 Games

Most Assists

	4 Games		5 Games		6 Games		7 Games
67	NL:Phil. (Bos.) 1914	90	NL:Bos. (Brk.) 1916	99	AL:Chi. (Chi.) 1906	115	AL:Chi. (Cin.) 1919 (8g)
						99	AL:Wash. (NY) 1924

Most Assists, Both Clubs

129	AL:Phil. (Bos.) 1914	160	AL:Bos. (Brk.) 1916	183	AL:Chi. (Chi.) 1906	211	AL:Chi. (Cin.) 1919 (8g)
						193	AL:Wash. (NY) 1924

Fewest Assists

28	AL:NY (StL.) 1928	36	NL:LA (Oak.) 1988	41	AL:Phil. (StL.) 1930	48	NL:StL. (Det.) 1968

Fewest Assists, Both Clubs

64	AL:NY (StL.) 1928	76	NL:StL. (Det.) 2006	96	AL:Phil. (StL.) 1930	120	NL:StL. (Det.) 1968

ERRORS

Most Errors

8	AL:NY (Chi.) 1932	13	NL:Brk. (Bos.) 1916	16	NL:NY (Phil.) 1911	19	AL:Det. (Pitt.) 1909
	AL:Bos. (StL.) 2004						

Most Errors, Both Clubs

14	AL:NY (Chi.) 1932	23	NL:Chi. (Phil.) 1910	27	NL:NY (Phil.) 1911	34	AL:Det. (Pitt.) 1909

Fewest Errors

0	AL:Balt. (LA) 1966	0	AL:NY (NY) 1937	1	By many clubs	2	By many clubs

Fewest Errors, Both Clubs

4	AL:NY (LA) 1963	5	AL:Oak. (LA) 1988	4	NL:LA (NY) 1977	5	NL:StL. (KC) 1985

Most Errorless Games

4	AL:Balt. (LA) 1966	5	AL:NY (NY) 1937	5	AL:Bos. (Chi.) 1918	5	NL:NY (NY) 1921 (8g)
					NL:StL. (StL.) 1944		AL:Phil. (StL.) 1931
					AL:NY (Brk.) 1953		AL:NY (Brk.) 1955
					NL:LA (NY) 1977		NL:Brk. (NY) 1956
							NL:StL. (Det.) 1968
							NL:Cin. (Bos.) 1975
							AL:KC (StL.) 1985
							NL:StL. (KC) 1985
							AL:Bos. (NY) 1986
							AL:Clev. (Fla.) 1997

Most Errorless Games, Both Clubs

3	AL:Balt. (LA) 1966	2	AL:NY (NY) 1937	3	AL:NY (LA) 1977	4	AL:KC (StL.) 1985
	NL:Cin. (NY) 1976		NL:LA (Oak.) 1988		AL:Tor. (Atl.) 1992		
			AL:NY (NY) 2000				

DOUBLE PLAYS

Most Double Plays

7	NL:Chi. (NY) 1932	7	AL:NY (NY) 1922	10	AL:NY (NY) 1951	12	NL:Brk. (NY) 1955
	AL:NY (LA) 1963		AL:NY (Brk.) 1941				
			NL:Cin. (NY) 1961				

Most Double Plays, Both Clubs

10	NL:Cin. (NY) 1976	12	AL:NY (Brk.) 1941	16	NL:Phil. (KC) 1980	19	NL:Brk. (NY) 1955
	AL:Chi. (Hou.) 2005						

Fewest Double Plays

1	AL:NY (Chi.) 1932	0	NL:NY (Balt.) 1969	2	AL:Chi. (Chi.) 1906	2	NL:StL. (Det.) 1934
	NL:Cin. (NY) 1939				NL:NY (Phil.) 1911		AL:Balt. (Pitt.) 1971
	NL:Phil. (NY) 1950				AL:Phil. (NY) 1911		NL:StL. (Minn.) 1987
	NL:LA (NY) 1963				AL:Phil. (StL.) 1930		
	AL:Oak. (SF) 1989				AL:NY (NY) 1936		
					AL:Chi. (LA) 1959		
					AL:NY (LA) 1977, 81		
					NL:Atl. (Clev.) 1995		

Fewest Double Plays, Both Clubs

4	NL:NY (Clev.) 1954	4	NL:NY (Balt.) 1969	4	AL:Phil. (NY) 1911	6	NL:StL. (Minn.) 1987
	AL:Oak. (SF) 1989		AL:NY (NY) 2000				

TRIPLE PLAYS

4 Games	5 Games	6 Games	7 Games
Most Triple Plays			
none	none	none	1 AL:Clev. (Brk.) 1920

PASSED BALLS

4 Games	5 Games	6 Games	7 Games
Most Passed Balls			
2 AL:Phil. (Bos.) 1914	2 NL:Brk. (Bos.) 1916	2 NL:Chi. (Chi.) 1906 NL:Chi. (Bos.) 1918 NL:LA (NY) 1978	3 NL:Pitt. (NY) 1960 AL:NY (StL.) 1964
Most Passed Balls, Both Clubs			
2 AL:Phil. (Bos.) 1914	3 NL:Brk. (Bos.) 1916	3 NL:Chi. (Chi.) 1906 NL:Chi. (Bos.) 1918	4 NL:Brk. (NY) 1947

HANCES ACCEPTED

Chances Accepted, Game
48 AL:Chi. (Chi.) Oct. 12, 1906
AL:Chi. (NY) Oct. 7, 1917
AL:Bos. (Chi.) Sept. 9, 1918
Extra-Inning Game:
74 AL:Bos. (Brk.) Oct. 9, 1916 (14 inn)

Chances Accepted, Both Clubs, Game
91 AL:Chi. (Chi.) Oct. 12, 1906
Extra-Inning Game:
137 AL:Bos. (Brk.) Oct. 9, 1916 (14 inn)

UTOUTS

Putouts, Game
42 AL:Bos. (Brk.) Oct. 9, 1916 (14 inn)
AL:Chi. (Hou.) Oct. 25, 2005 (14 inn)
NL:Hou. (Chi.) Oct. 25, 2005 (14 inn)

Putouts, Both Clubs, Game
84 AL:Chi. (Hou.) Oct. 25, 2005 (14 inn)

SSISTS

Assists, Game
21 AL:Chi. (Chi.) Oct. 12, 1906
AL:Chi. (NY) Oct. 7, 1917
AL:Bos. (Chi.) Sept. 9, 1918
Extra-Inning Game:
32 AL:Bos. (Brk.) Oct. 9, 1916 (14 inn)

Assists, Both Clubs, Game
37 AL:Chi. (Chi.) Oct. 12, 1906
Extra-Inning Game:
55 NL:Brk. (Bos.) Oct. 9, 1916 (14 inn)

RRORS

Errors, Game
6 AL:Chi. (Chi.) Oct. 13, 1906
NL:Pitt. (Det.) Oct. 12, 1909
AL:Chi. (NY) Oct. 13, 1917
NL:LA (Balt.) Oct. 6, 1966

Errors, Both Clubs, Game
9 AL:Chi. (NY) Oct. 13, 1917

Errors, Inning
3 By many clubs; Last:
AL:Det. (StL.) Oct. 21, 2006 (6th)

OUBLE PLAYS

Double Plays, Game
5 AL:Phil. (Bos.) Oct. 9, 1914

Double Plays, Both Clubs, Game
6 AL:Phil. (Bos.) Oct. 9, 1914
AL:NY (Brk.) Sept. 29, 1955
NL:Phil. (KC) Oct. 15, 1980
AL:Ana. (SF) Oct. 23, 2002
NL:Hou. (Chi.) Oct. 25, 2005

RIPLE PLAYS

Triple Plays
1 AL:Clev. (Brk.) Oct. 10, 1920 (5th)

PASSED BALLS

Passed Balls, Game
2 NL:Chi. (Chi.) Oct. 9, 1906
NL:Chi. (Bos.) Sept. 9, 1918
AL:Det. (Chi.) Oct. 3, 1945
NL:Brk. (NY) Oct. 4, 1947
NL:Pitt. (NY) Oct. 6, 1960
AL:NY (StL.) Oct. 7, 1964
NL:LA (NY) Oct. 5, 1978

Passed Balls, Inning
1 By many clubs

CLUB PITCHING

	4 Games	5 Games	6 Games	7 Games
Most Complete Games	4 AL:NY (StL.) 1928	5 AL:Phil. (NY) 1905, 13 AL:Phil. (Chi.) 1910 AL:Bos. (Phil.) 1915	5 AL:Phil. (NY) 1911 AL:Bos. (Chi.) 1918 AL:Det. (Chi.) 1935	7 AL:Bos. (Pitt.) 1903 (8g) 5 AL:Clev. (Brk.) 1920 AL:NY (Brk.) 1956
Most Complete Games, Both Clubs	5 AL:Bos. (Phil.) 1914	9 AL:Phil. (NY) 1905 AL:Bos. (Phil.) 1915	9 AL:Bos. (Chi.) 1918	13 AL:Bos. (Pitt.) 1903 (8g) 8 1909, 20, 25, 34, 40, 56
Fewest Complete Games	0 By many clubs	0 By many clubs	0 By many clubs	0 By many clubs
Fewest Complete Games, Both Clubs	0 AL:NY (SD) 1998 AL:NY (Atl.) 1999 AL:Bos. (StL.) 2004 AL:Chi. (Hou.) 2005	0 AL:Oak. (LA) 1974 AL:NY (NY) 2000 NL:StL. (Det.) 2006	0 AL:Chi. (LA) 1959 AL:KC (Phil.) 1980 AL:NY (Atl.) 1996	0 AL:Oak. (Cin.) 1972 AL:Oak. (NY) 1973 AL:Minn. (StL.) 1987 AL:Clev. (Fla.) 1997 AL:Ana. (SF) 2002
Most Saves (since 1969)	3 AL:NY (SD) 1998 AL:Chi. (Hou.) 2005	3 AL:Oak. (LA) 1974	4 AL:NY (Atl.) 1996	4 AL:Oak. (NY) 1973
Most Saves, Both Clubs (since 1969)	3 AL:NY (SD) 1998 AL:Chi. (Hou.) 2005	4 AL:Oak. (LA) 1974	4 NL:Phil. (KC) 1980 AL:Tor. (Atl.) 1992 NL:Atl. (Clev.) 1995 AL:NY (Atl.) 1996	7 AL:Oak. (NY) 1973
Fewest Saves (since 1969)	0 AL:NY (Cin.) 1976 NL:SF (Oak.) 1989 AL:Oak. (Cin.) 1990 NL:SD (NY) 1998 NL:Atl. (NY) 1999 NL:StL. (Bos.) 2004	0 AL:Balt. (NY) 1969 NL:Cin. (Balt.) 1970 AL:Oak. (LA) 1988	0 NL:LA(NY) 1977 AL:NY (LA) 1977-78 NL:Atl. (NY) 1996	0 AL:Bos. (Cin.) 1975 AL:Balt. (Pitt.) 1979 AL:KC (StL.) 1985 NL:Atl. (Minn.) 1991 NL:Ari. (NY) 2001
Fewest Saves, Both Clubs (since 1969)	1 NL:SF (Oak.) 1989 AL:Oak. (Cin.) 1990 AL:Bos. (StL.) 2004	1 AL:Oak. (LA) 1988	0 AL:NY (LA) 1977	1 NL:Ari. (NY) 2001
Most Shutouts	3 AL:Balt. (LA) 1966	4 NL:NY (Phil.) 1905	2 NL:NY (Chi.) 1917 AL:Chi. (LA) 1959	3 NL:LA (Minn.) 1965
Most Shutouts, Both Clubs	3 AL:Balt. (LA) 1966	5 NL:NY (Phil.) 1905	2 By many clubs	3 AL:Clev. (Brk.) 1920 AL:NY (Brk.) 1956 AL:NY (Mil.) 1958 AL:Minn. (LA) 1965
Most Shutouts, Consecutive	3 AL:Balt. (LA) 1966	3 NL:NY (Phil.) 1905	2 NL:NY (Chi.) 1917	2 NL:Cin. (Chi.) 1919 (8g) AL:Clev. (Brk.) 1920 NL:NY (NY) 1921 (8g)
Most Shutouts, Consecutive, Both Clubs	3 AL:Balt. (LA) 1966	5 NL:NY (Phil.) 1905	2 NL:Chi. (Chi.) 1906 NL:NY (Chi.) 1917	3 NL:Cin. (Chi.) 1919 (8g) AL:NY (Brk.) 1956 AL:NY (Mil.) 1958
Fewest Shutouts	0 By many clubs	0 By many clubs	0 By many clubs	0 By many clubs
Fewest Shutouts, Both Clubs	0 1927, 28, 32, 38, 54, 76, 99	0 1910, 15, 16, 29, 37, 41, 70, 74, 84, 2000	0 By many clubs	0 1912, 24, 47, 64, 87, 97, 2002
Most Shutout Innings, Consecutive	33 AL:Balt. (LA) 1966	28 NL:NY (Phil.) 1905	24 NL:NY (Chi.) 1917	26 NL:Cin. (Chi.) 1919 (8g) 22 NL:Pitt. (Balt.) 1971

4 Games	5 Games	6 Games	7 Games
ost Wild Pitches			
3 NL:Pitt. (NY) 1927	5 AL:Det. (StL.) 2006	4 NL:Chi. (Chi.) 1906	5 NL:Pitt. (NY) 1960
AL:Clev. (NY) 1954			AL:Minn. (Atl.) 1991
ost Wild Pitches, Both Clubs			
4 AL:Clev. (NY) 1954	7 NL:StL. (Det.) 2006	6 AL:Chi. (Chi.) 1906	8 AL:NY (Brk.) 1947

CLUB GENERAL

	4 Games	5 Games	6 Games	7 Games
Most Players, Club				
	25 AL:Oak. (Cin.) 1990 NL:Atl. (NY) 1999 NL:StL. (Bos.) 2004	25 NL:Brk. (NY) 1949 NL:NY (NY) 2000	25 NL:LA (NY) 1977 AL:NY (Atl.) 1996	26 AL:Det. (Chi.) 1945 AL:Bos. (StL.) 1946
Most Players, Both Clubs				
	48 AL:NY (Atl.) 1999 AL:Chi. (Hou.) 2005	47 AL:NY (NY) 2000 NL:StL. (Det.) 2006	49 AL:NY (Atl.) 1996	51 AL:Det. (Chi.) 1945
Fewest Players				
	13 NL:LA (NY) 1963 AL:Balt. (LA) 1966	12 NL:NY (Phil.) 1905 AL:Phil. (Chi.) 1910 AL:Phil. (NY) 1913	14 NL:Chi. (Chi.) 1906 AL:Phil. (NY) 1911	13 AL:Bos. (Pitt.) 1903 (8g) NL:NY (NY) 1921 (8g)
Fewest Players, Both Clubs				
	31 AL:Phil. (Bos.) 1914	25 AL:Phil. (NY) 1905	29 NL:NY (Phil.) 1911	27 AL:Bos. (Pitt.) 1903 (8g)
Most Pitchers				
	11 NL:StL. (Bos.) 2004 AL:Chi. (Hou.) 2005 NL:Hou. (Chi.) 2005	11 AL:Det. (StL.) 2006	10 By many teams	11 AL:Bos. (StL.) 1946 AL:Clev. (Fla.) 1997 NL:SF (Ana.) 2002
Most Pitchers, Both Clubs				
	22 AL:Chi. (Hou.) 2005	21 NL:StL. (Det.) 2006	20 AL:Tor. (Phil.) 1993 AL:NY (Atl.) 1996	21 NL:Fla. (Clev.) 1997 AL:Ana. (SF) 2002
Fewest Pitchers				
	3 NL:Bos. (Phil.) 1914 AL:NY (StL.) 1928	2 AL:Phil. (Chi.) 1910	3 AL:Phil. (NY) 1911	3 AL:Bos. (Pitt.) 1903 (8g)
Fewest Pitchers, Both Clubs				
	9 NL:Bos. (Phil.) 1914 AL:NY (StL.) 1928	6 AL:Phil. (NY) 1905	8 AL:Chi. (Chi.) 1906 AL:Phil. (NY) 1911 AL:Bos. (Chi.) 1918	8 AL:Bos. (Pitt.) 1903 (8g)
Most Extra-Inning Games				
	1 NL:Bos. (Phil.) 1914 AL:NY (Cin.) 1939 AL:NY (Phil.) 1950 NL:NY (Clev.) 1954 AL:Oak. (Cin.) 1990 AL:NY (Atl.) 1999 AL:Chi. (Hou.) 2005	2 NL:NY (Wash.) 1933	2 AL:Phil. (NY) 1911	3 AL:Minn. (Atl.) 1991
Most 1-Run Decisions				
	3 AL:NY (Phil.) 1950	4 AL:Bos. (Phil.) 1915 AL:Oak. (LA) 1974	5 NL:Atl. (Clev.) 1995	6 AL:Oak. (Cin.) 1972
Most 1-Run Decisions, Consecutive				
	3 AL:NY (Phil.) 1950	4 AL:Bos. (Phil.) 1915	3 NL:LA (NY) 1981 AL:Tor. (Atl.) 1992 AL:Clev. (Atl.) 1995	5 AL:Oak. (Cin.) 1972
Most 1-Run Decisions Won				
	3 AL:NY (Phil.) 1950	4 AL:Bos. (Phil.) 1915	4 AL:Bos. (Chi.) 1918 AL:Tor. (Atl.) 1992	4 AL:Oak. (Cin.) 1972
Most 1-Run Decisions Won, Consecutive				
	3 AL:NY (Phil.) 1950	4 AL:Bos. (Phil.) 1915	3 NL:LA (NY) 1981 AL:Tor. (Atl.) 1992	3 AL:NY (Ari.) 2001
Most 1-0 Games Won (See Table)				
	2 AL:Balt. (LA) 1966	1 By many clubs	1 By many clubs	1 By many clubs

PERSONNEL

Most Players, Game
21 AL:NY (Brk.) Oct. 5, 1947
NL:Cin. (NY) Oct. 9, 1961
Extra-Inning Game:
23 AL:Minn. (Atl.) Oct. 22, 1991 (12 inn)

Most Players, Both Clubs, Game
38 AL:NY (Brk.) Oct. 5, 1947
Extra-Inning Game:
43 AL:Chi. (Hou.) Oct. 25, 2005 (14 inn)

Most Pitchers, Game
Winning Club:
6 NL:Cin. (Oak.) Oct. 20, 1972
Extra-Inning Game:
9 AL:Chi. (Hou.) Oct. 25, 2005 (14 inn)
Losing Club:
8 NL:Cin. (NY) Oct. 9, 1961
NL:StL. (Bos.) Oct. 11, 1967
NL:Cin. (Bos.) Oct. 21, 1975 (12 inn)
NL:Hou. (Chi.) Oct. 25, 2005 (14 inn)

Most Pitchers, Both Clubs, Game
11 NL:StL. (Bos.) Oct. 11, 1967
NL:SF (Oak.) Oct. 28, 1989
NL:Phil. (Tor.) Oct. 20, 1993
AL:Clev. (Fla.) Oct. 21, 1997
NL:SF (Ana.) Oct. 20, 2002
NL:StL. (Bos.) Oct. 23, 2004
Extra-Inning Game:
17 AL:Chi. (Hou.) Oct. 25, 2005 (14 inn)

Most Pitchers, Inning
5 AL:Balt. (Pitt.) Oct. 17, 1979 (9th)
NL:StL. (KC) Oct. 27, 1985 (5th)

DATES

Earliest Date, First Game
Sept. 5, 1918 AL:Bos. at Chi.

Earliest Date, Last Game
Sept. 11, 1918 AL:Bos. at Chi.

Latest Date, First Game
Oct. 27, 2001 AL:NY at Ari.

Latest Date, Final Game
Nov. 4, 2001 AL:NY at Ari.

ATTENDANCE

Game, Largest
92,706 AL:Chi. at LA Oct. 6, 1959

Game, Smallest
6,210 NL:Chi. at Det. Oct. 14, 1908

TIME

Longest Game
4:14 AL:Tor. at Phil. Oct. 20, 1993
Extra-Inning Game:
5:41 AL:Chi. (Hou.) Oct. 25, 2005 (14 inn)

Shortest Game
1:25 NL:Chi. at Det. Oct. 14, 1908

SCORELESS INNINGS

Most, Consecutive, By Pitchers, Spanning Series:
39 AL:Balt. (LA) 1966 (33); (NY) 1969 (6)

LOW-HIT GAMES (Pitching)

No Hits

1956	Oct. 8	AL:NY Don Larsen

1 Hit

1906	Oct. 10	NL:Chi. Ed Reulbach
1945	Oct. 5	NL:Chi. Claude Passeau
1947	Oct. 3	AL:NY Bill Bevens (Lost)
1967	Oct. 5	AL:Bos. Jim Lonborg
1995	Oct. 28	NL:Atl. Tom Glavine & Mark Wohlers

2 Hits

1906	Oct. 11	AL:Chi. Ed Walsh
1906	Oct. 12	NL:Chi. Three Finger Brown
1913	Oct. 11	AL:Phil. Eddie Plank
1914	Oct. 10	NL:Bos. Bill James
1921	Oct. 6	AL:NY Waite Hoyt
1931	Oct. 5	NL:StL. Burleigh Grimes
1931	Oct. 6	AL:Phil. George Earnshaw
1939	Oct. 5	AL:NY Monte Pearson
1944	Oct. 4	NL:StL. Mort Cooper & Blix Donnelly (Lost)
1948	Oct. 6	AL:Clev. Bob Feller (Lost)
1949	Oct. 5	AL:NY Allie Reynolds
1950	Oct. 4	AL:NY Vic Raschi
1958	Oct. 5	NL:Mil. Warren Spahn
1961	Oct. 4	AL:NY Whitey Ford
1963	Oct. 6	AL:NY Whitey Ford & Hal Reniff (Lost)
1969	Oct. 12	NL:NY Jerry Koosman & Ron Taylor
1971	Oct. 14	NL:Pitt. Nelson Briles
1990	Oct. 20	NL:Cin. Jose Rijo & Randy Myers
1995	Oct. 21	NL:Atl. Greg Maddux
1999	Oct. 23	AL:NY Orlando Hernandez, Jeff Nelson, Mike Stanton & Mariano Rivera
2006	Oct. 21	NL:StL Anthony Reyes & Braden Looper

HIGH-HIT GAMES (Batting)

22 Hits

2001	Nov. 3	NL:Ari. vs. NY

20 Hits

1921	Oct. 7	NL:NY vs NY
1946	Oct. 10	NL:StL. vs Bos.

19 Hits

1932	Oct. 2	AL:NY vs Chi.
1960	Oct. 6	AL:NY vs Pitt.

18 Hits

1978	Oct. 15	AL:NY vs LA
1986	Oct. 19	AL:Bos. vs NY
1993	Oct. 20	AL:Tor. vs Phil.

17 Hits

1934	Oct. 9	NL:StL. vs Det.
1936	Oct. 2	AL:NY vs NY
1936	Oct. 6	AL:NY vs NY
1960	Oct. 12	AL:NY vs Pitt.
1979	Oct. 13	NL:Pitt. vs Balt.
1982	Oct. 12	AL:Mil. vs StL.
1991	Oct. 24	NL:Atl. vs Minn.

16 Hits

1912	Oct. 15	NL:NY vs Bos.
1919	Oct. 9	NL:Cin. vs Chi.
1960	Oct. 8	AL:NY vs Pitt.
1997	Oct. 21	NL:Fla. vs Clev.
1998	Oct. 18	AL:NY vs SD
2002	Oct. 20	AL:Ana. vs SF
2002	Oct. 22	AL:Ana. vs SF
2002	Oct. 24	NL:SF vs Ana.

XTRA-INNING GAMES

14 AL:Bos. 2 Brk. 1 Oct. 9, 1916
    AL:Chi. 7 Hou. 5 Oct. 25, 2005
12 NL:Chi. 3 Det. 3 Oct. 8, 1907
    NL:Bos. 5 Phil. 4, Oct. 12, 1914
    NL:NY 4 Wash. 3, Oct. 4, 1924
    AL:Wash. 4 NY 3, Oct. 10, 1924
    AL:Det. 3 StL. 2 Oct. 4 1934
    NL:Chi. 8 Det. 7, Oct. 8, 1945
    NL:NY 10 Oak. 7, Oct. 14, 1973
    AL:Bos. 7 Cin. 6 Oct. 21, 1975
    AL:NY 4 LA 3 Oct. 11, 1977
    NL:Atl. 5 Minn. 4, Oct. 22, 1991
    AL:NY 4 NY 3, Oct. 21, 2000
    AL:NY 3 Ari. 2, Nov. 1, 2001
    NL:Fla. 4 NY 3, Oct. 22, 2003
11 AL:Phil. 3 NY 2, Oct. 17, 1911
    NL:NY 6 Bos. 6, Oct. 9, 1912
    NL:NY 2 Wash. 1, Oct. 6, 1933
    AL:Det. 6 Chi. 5, Oct. 4, 1935
    NL:StL. 3 StL. 2, Oct. 5, 1944
    NL:Brk. 6 NY 5, Oct. 5, 1952
    AL:Oak. 3 NY 2, Oct. 16, 1973
    AL:Minn. 4 Atl. 3, Oct. 26, 1991
    AL:Tor. 4 Atl. 3, Oct. 24, 1992
    AL:Clev. 7 Atl. 6, Oct. 24, 1995
    NL:Fla. 3 Clev. 2 Oct. 26, 1997
10 NL:Chi. 4 Phil. 3, Oct. 22, 1910
    NL:NY 4 Phil. 3, Oct. 25, 1911
    AL:Bos. 3 NY 2, Oct. 16, 1912
    NL:NY 3 Phil. 0, Oct. 8, 1913
    AL:Chi. 5 Cin. 4, Oct. 7, 1919
    NL:NY 3 NY 3, Oct. 5, 1922
    AL:NY 3 StL. 2 Oct. 7, 1926
    NL:NY 4 Wash. 3, Oct. 7, 1933
    NL:NY 5 NY 4 Oct. 5, 1936
    AL:NY 7 Cin. 4, Oct. 8, 1939
    AL:Bos. 3 StL. 2, Oct. 6, 1946
    AL:NY 2 Phil. 1, Oct. 5, 1950
    NL:NY 5 Clev. 2, Sept. 29, 1954
    NL:Brk. 1 NY 0, Oct. 9, 1956
    NL:Mil. 7 NY 5, Oct. 6, 1957
    NL:Mil. 4 NY 3, Oct. 1, 1958
    AL:NY 4 Mil. 3, Oct. 8, 1958
    NL:StL. 5 NY 2, Oct. 12, 1964
    NL:NY 2 Balt. 1, Oct. 15, 1969
    AL:Balt. 3 Pitt. 2, Oct. 16, 1971
    NL:Cin. 6 Bos. 5, Oct. 14, 1975
    AL:NY 4 LA 3, Oct. 14, 1978
    AL:KC 4 Phil. 3, Oct. 17, 1980
    NL:NY 6 Bos. 5, Oct. 25, 1986
    NL:Cin. 5 Oak. 4, Oct. 17, 1990
    AL:Minn. 1 Atl. 0, Oct. 27, 1991
    AL:NY 8 Atl. 6, Oct. 23, 1996
    AL:NY 6 Atl. 5 Oct. 26, 1999
    AL:NY 4 Ari. 3 Oct. 31, 2001

WORLD SERIES – CLUB BATTING

AMERICAN LEAGUE	BA	SLG	G	AB	R	ER	H	TB	1B	2B	3B	HR	RBI	SH	SF	BB	HB	SO	SB	LOB
New York Yankees	.250	.386	219	7345	957	855	1834	2832	1308	264	52	210	905	108	20	769	48	1241	74	1519
Philadelphia/Oakland	.228	.338	75	2457	267	211	559	830	393	107	13	46	244	65	4	223	13	461	41	490
Boston Red Sox	.242	.363	64	2130	228	183	516	774	369	71	41	35	207	57	7	198	17	326	19	466
Detroit Tigers	.230	.324	61	2039	221	191	468	660	347	80	11	35	206	34	3	213	20	315	36	444
Washington/Minnesota	.238	.366	40	1340	145	128	319	491	228	46	9	36	140	24	2	128	6	229	23	279
St. Louis/Baltimore	.212	.329	39	1261	135	127	267	415	189	41	4	33	122	24	7	125	6	240	5	238
Chicago White Sox	.246	.343	30	1000	106	88	246	343	181	45	8	12	93	8	7	79	11	156	24	201
Cleveland Indians	.227	.341	30	987	110	94	224	337	158	40	5	21	101	21	3	114	2	158	17	212
Kansas City Royals	.289	.422	13	443	51	49	128	187	93	21	5	10	48	14	3	54	1	105	13	110
Toronto Blue Jays	.271	.438	12	402	62	60	109	176	71	21	4	12	62	5	3	43	4	63	12	77
Anaheim Angels	.310	.465	7	245	41	37	76	114	53	15	5	7	38	2	8	23	2	38	6	54
Milwaukee Brewers	.269	.399	7	238	33	26	64	95	45	12	2	5	29	2	1	19	1	28	1	44

NATIONAL LEAGUE	BA	SLG	G	AB	R	ER	H	TB	1B	2B	3B	HR	RBI	SH	SF	BB	HB	SO	SB	LOB
Brooklyn/Los Angeles	.232	.350	105	3420	347	310	794	1197	572	120	23	79	327	54	11	321	17	584	57	689
St. Louis Cardinals	.241	.344	105	3500	378	310	842	1205	600	169	25	48	348	70	9	261	10	569	64	695
New York/San Francisco	.246	.342	100	3326	351	287	818	1138	625	117	25	51	322	70	7	271	20	503	60	658
Boston/Milwaukee/Atlanta	.235	.353	53	1760	188	174	414	622	296	68	10	40	182	35	12	189	9	316	41	367
Chicago Cubs	.242	.325	53	1753	178	134	425	569	322	75	15	13	154	63	0	139	9	301	53	345
Cincinnati Reds	.243	.358	51	1690	192	166	411	605	289	77	18	27	187	29	9	148	13	225	40	332
Pittsburgh Pirates	.254	.359	47	1576	175	135	400	565	289	76	16	19	162	39	5	109	6	226	42	337
Philadelphia Phillies	.237	.342	26	848	87	78	201	290	147	34	5	15	82	14	6	73	6	145	14	167
New York Mets	.247	.362	24	835	87	74	206	302	154	29	2	21	73	15	4	73	8	162	8	192
Florida Marlins	.254	.369	13	453	54	46	115	167	84	20	1	10	51	6	4	50	2	96	6	105
San Diego Padres	.253	.367	9	300	28	26	76	110	55	14	1	6	25	1	5	23	0	55	3	61
Arizona Diamondbacks	.264	.394	7	246	37	30	65	97	45	14	0	6	36	5	2	17	6	70	2	49
Houston Astros	.203	.336	4	143	14	12	29	48	36	8	1	3	14	5	1	17	5	36	5	34

AMERICAN LEAGUE

	PCT	G	TC	CA	PO	A	E	DP	TP	PB
New York Yankees	.980	219	8340	8177	5863	2314	163	193	0	15
Philadelphia/Oakland	.972	75	2870	2791	2016	775	79	56	0	5
Boston Red Sox	.972	64	2561	2490	1731	759	71	48	0	6
Detroit Tigers	.962	61	2423	2332	1633	699	91	42	0	0
Washington/Minnesota	.976	40	1563	1526	1081	445	37	35	0	2
St. Louis/Baltimore	.972	39	1472	1431	1039	392	41	27	0	0
Chicago White Sox	.964	30	1263	1217	810	407	46	24	0	4
Cleveland Indians	.975	30	1164	1135	797	338	29	35	1	1
Kansas City Royals	.980	13	504	494	342	152	10	11	0	1
Toronto Blue Jays	.974	12	427	416	324	92	11	10	0	0
Anaheim Angels	.980	7	244	239	183	56	5	6	0	1
Milwaukee Brewers	.960	7	272	261	180	81	11	3	0	0

NATIONAL LEAGUE

	PCT	G	TC	CA	PO	A	E	DP	TP	PB
Brooklyn/Los Angeles	.975	105	3975	3875	2759	1116	100	89	0	9
St. Louis Cardinals	.977	105	3888	3799	2777	1022	89	82	0	5
New York/San Francisco	.967	100	4007	3873	2676	1197	134	76	0	8
Boston/Milwaukee/Atlanta	.980	53	2092	2050	1436	614	42	50	0	1
Chicago Cubs	.969	53	2133	2066	1420	646	67	48	0	6
Cincinnati Reds	.976	51	1946	1899	1367	532	47	47	0	2
Pittsburgh Pirates	.966	47	1834	1772	1235	537	62	39	0	5
Philadelphia Phillies	.985	26	955	941	688	253	14	20	0	1
New York Mets	.976	24	905	883	659	224	22	10	0	1
Florida Marlins	.980	13	509	499	360	139	10	17	0	0
San Diego Padres	.978	9	316	309	228	81	7	10	0	1
Arizona Diamondbacks	.988	7	259	256	195	61	3	6	0	0
Houston Astros	.988	4	173	171	118	53	2	6	0	0

AMERICAN LEAGUE	ERA	OBA	G	CG	SV	SHO	AB	IP	H	TB	2B	3B	HR	RBI	R	ER	BB	HP	SO	WP	BK
New York Yankees	3.05	.240	219	79	15	16	7275	1954.1	1746	2538	291	45	137	728	769	663	620	39	1245	25	3
Philadelphia/Oakland	2.56	.228	75	34	11	3	2473	672.1	563	790	105	16	30	210	235	191	208	16	448	17	1
Boston Red Sox	2.75	.235	64	30	3	7	2109	577.0	495	712	85	27	26	195	214	176	172	16	307	9	3
Detroit Tigers	3.16	.255	61	34	3	2	2060	544.2	525	733	99	17	25	216	244	191	156	15	323	13	1
Washington/Minnesota	3.07	.263	40	12	3	3	1374	360.1	361	511	54	9	26	138	147	123	105	11	207	10	2
St. Louis/Baltimore	2.52	.235	39	15	5	4	1295	346.1	304	454	57	6	27	112	117	97	111	5	240	8	2
Chicago White Sox	2.83	.238	30	13	5	3	980	270.0	233	330	35	13	12	94	105	85	78	14	140	6	0
Cleveland Indians	3.18	.241	30	10	3	3	975	266.0	235	341	36	2	22	101	106	94	104	3	145	6	2
Kansas City Royals	2.92	.237	13	3	1	1	417	114.0	99	139	23	1	5	39	40	37	33	2	59	7	0
Toronto Blue Jays	4.25	.248	12	0	5	0	412	108.0	102	149	13	2	10	54	56	51	54	2	98	5	1
Anaheim Angels	5.75	.359	7	0	3	0	235	61.0	66	117	7	1	14	42	44	39	30	1	50	1	0
Milwaukee Brewers	4.80	.273	7	1	2	1	245	60.0	67	101	16	3	4	34	39	32	20	0	26	3	1

NATIONAL LEAGUE	ERA	OBA	G	CG	SV	SHO	AB	IP	H	TB	2B	3B	HR	RBI	R	ER	BB	HP	SO	WP	BK
Brooklyn/Los Angeles	3.52	.239	105	32	4	9	3416	919.2	818	1263	119	28	90	379	407	360	365	21	610	22	3
St. Louis Cardinals	3.37	.240	105	36	8	11	3482	925.2	834	1269	145	22	82	374	403	347	363	25	632	22	2
New York/San Francisco	3.36	.308	100	40	4	11	3361	892.1	821	1195	133	29	61	362	401	333	294	15	482	24	1
Boston/Milwaukee/Atlanta	2.90	.218	53	16	4	7	1750	478.2	382	601	62	8	47	169	176	154	171	4	322	10	2
Chicago Cubs	3.59	.243	53	23	0	8	1764	473.1	428	594	75	11	23	207	225	189	177	19	246	12	1
Cincinnati Reds	3.34	.236	51	13	8	3	1687	455.2	398	608	56	11	44	179	190	169	173	6	259	8	1
Pittsburgh Pirates	4.08	.259	47	17	4	2	1597	412.1	413	620	60	24	33	202	221	187	127	17	224	14	1
Philadelphia Phillies	4.04	.265	26	6	5	1	871	229.1	231	361	35	10	25	105	109	103	85	6	153	6	0
New York Mets	2.70	.230	24	2	8	0	825	219.2	190	280	32	8	14	73	76	66	96	8	183	6	0
Florida Marlins	4.43	.278	13	1	4	1	454	120.0	126	191	22	2	13	63	65	59	62	3	100	2	0
San Diego Padres	5.21	.279	9	0	1	0	297	76.0	83	131	6	0	13	48	49	44	44	3	56	3	0
Arizona Diamondbacks	1.94	.183	7	1	0	1	229	65.0	42	66	6	0	6	14	14	14	16	1	63	4	0
Houston Astros	4.58	.286	4	0	0	0	154	39.1	44	75	9	2	6	20	20	20	15	3	30	0	0

	AB	R	H	TB	1B	2B	3B	HR	RBI	SH	SF	BB	HP	SO	SB	LOB	BA	SLG
03 (8)																		
AL:Bos.	282	39	71	113	49	4	16	2	35	6	-	13	2	27	5	55	.252	.401
NL:Pitt.	270	24	64	92	47	7	9	1	23	3	-	14	1	45	7	51	.237	.341
05 (5)																		
NL:NY	153	15	32	39	25	7	0	0	13	5	-	15	2	26	11	31	.209	.255
AL:Phil.	155	3	25	30	20	5	0	0	2	3	-	5	1	25	2	26	.161	.194
06 (6)																		
AL:Chi.	187	22	37	53	24	10	3	0	19	6	-	18	3	35	6	33	.198	.283
NL:Chi.	184	18	36	45	27	9	0	0	11	13	-	18	2	27	8	37	.196	.245
07 (5)																		
NL:Chi.	167	19	43	51	36	6	1	0	16	9	-	12	4	25	18	35	.257	.305
AL:Det.	172	6	36	41	33	1	2	0	6	3	-	9	1	21	7	35	.209	.238
08 (5)																		
NL:Chi.	164	24	48	59	41	4	2	1	21	9	-	13	0	26	13	30	.293	.360
AL:Det.	158	15	32	37	27	5	0	0	14	5	-	12	2	26	5	27	.203	.234
09 (7)																		
NL:Pitt.	223	34	49	70	34	12	1	2	26	12	-	20	6	34	18	44	.220	.320
AL:Det.	233	28	55	77	37	16	0	2	25	4	-	20	4	22	6	50	.236	.330
10 (5)																		
AL:Phil.	177	35	56	80	35	19	1	1	29	7	-	17	2	24	7	36	.316	.452
NL:Chi.	158	15	35	48	23	11	1	0	13	7	-	18	0	31	3	31	.222	.304
11 (6)																		
AL:Phil.	205	27	50	74	32	15	0	3	21	9	-	4	0	31	4	29	.244	.361
NL:NY	189	13	33	46	21	11	1	0	10	6	-	14	3	44	4	32	.175	.243
12 (8)																		
AL:Bos.	273	25	60	89	39	14	6	1	21	8	-	19	1	36	6	55	.220	.326
NL:NY	274	31	74	99	55	14	4	1	25	7	-	22	3	39	12	53	.270	.361
13 (5)																		
AL:Phil.	174	23	46	64	36	4	4	2	21	7	-	7	0	16	5	30	.264	.368
NL:NY	164	15	33	41	28	3	1	1	15	2	-	8	3	19	5	24	.201	.250
14 (4)																		
NL:Bos.	135	16	33	46	24	6	2	1	14	3	-	15	1	18	9	27	.244	.341
AL:Phil.	128	6	22	31	13	9	0	0	5	3	-	13	0	28	2	21	.172	.242
15 (5)																		
AL:Bos.	159	12	42	57	35	2	2	3	11	7	-	11	1	25	1	35	.264	.358
NL:Phil.	148	10	27	36	21	4	1	1	9	5	-	10	2	25	2	23	.182	.243
16 (5)																		
AL:Bos.	164	21	39	64	24	7	6	2	18	12	-	18	0	25	1	31	.238	.390
NL:Brk.	170	13	34	49	26	2	5	1	11	6	-	14	2	19	1	32	.200	.288
17 (6)																		
AL:Chi.	197	21	54	63	47	6	0	1	18	3	-	11	0	28	6	37	.274	.320
NL:NY	199	17	51	70	40	5	4	2	16	3	-	6	2	27	4	37	.256	.352
18 (6)																		
AL:Bos.	172	9	32	40	27	2	3	0	6	8	-	16	1	21	3	32	.186	.233
NL:Chi.	176	10	37	44	31	5	1	0	10	4	-	18	2	14	3	31	.210	.250
19 (8)																		
NL:Cin.	251	35	64	88	47	10	7	0	34	13	-	25	5	22	7	46	.255	.351
AL:Chi.	263	20	59	78	45	10	3	1	17	7	-	15	3	30	5	52	.224	.297
20 (7)																		
AL:Clev.	217	21	53	72	40	9	2	2	18	3	-	21	0	21	2	43	.244	.332
NL:Brk.	215	8	44	51	38	5	1	0	8	5	-	10	0	20	1	39	.205	.237
21 (8)																		
NL:NY	264	29	71	98	52	13	4	2	28	6	-	22	1	38	7	54	.269	.371
AL:NY	241	22	50	65	40	7	1	2	20	9	-	27	1	44	6	43	.207	.270
22 (5)																		
NL:NY	162	18	50	57	46	2	1	1	18	6	-	12	0	15	1	32	.309	.352
AL:NY	158	11	32	46	23	6	1	2	11	6	-	8	2	20	2	25	.203	.291
23 (6)																		
AL:NY	205	30	60	91	43	8	4	5	29	6	-	20	1	22	1	43	.293	.444
NL:NY	201	17	47	70	37	2	3	5	17	0	-	12	1	18	1	35	.234	.348
24 (7)																		
AL:Wash.	248	26	61	85	47	9	0	5	23	6	-	29	0	34	5	57	.246	.343
NL:NY	253	27	66	91	51	9	2	4	22	7	-	25	2	40	3	59	.261	.360

	AB	R	H	TB	1B	2B	3B	HR	RBI	SH	SF	BB	HP	SO	SB	LOB	BA	SLG
1925 (7)																		
NL:Pitt.	230	25	61	89	43	12	2	4	25	8	-	17	4	32	7	54	.265	.387
AL:Wash.	225	26	59	91	43	8	0	8	25	10	-	17	2	31	2	46	.262	.404
1926 (7)																		
NL:StL.	239	31	65	91	48	12	1	4	30	12	-	11	1	30	2	43	.272	.381
AL:NY	223	21	54	78	39	10	1	4	19	10	-	31	1	31	1	55	.242	.350
1927 (4)																		
AL:NY	136	23	38	54	28	6	2	2	20	6	-	13	1	25	2	29	.279	.397
NL:Pitt.	130	10	29	37	22	6	1	0	10	6	-	4	1	7	0	23	.223	.285
1928 (4)																		
AL:NY	134	27	37	71	21	7	0	9	25	5	-	13	1	12	4	24	.276	.530
NL:StL.	131	10	27	37	20	5	1	1	9	2	-	11	1	29	3	27	.206	.282
1929 (5)																		
AL:Phil.	171	26	48	71	37	5	0	6	26	7	-	13	1	27	0	35	.281	.415
NL:Chi.	173	17	43	56	34	6	2	1	15	2	-	13	0	50	1	36	.249	.324
1930 (6)																		
AL:Phil.	178	21	35	67	17	10	2	6	21	7	-	24	1	32	0	36	.197	.376
NL:StL.	190	12	38	56	25	10	1	2	11	4	-	11	0	33	1	37	.200	.295
1931 (7)																		
NL:StL.	229	19	54	71	41	11	0	2	17	4	-	9	0	41	8	40	.236	.310
AL:Phil.	227	22	50	64	42	5	0	3	20	4	-	28	1	46	0	52	.220	.282
1932 (5)																		
AL:NY	144	37	45	75	31	6	0	8	36	1	-	23	4	26	0	33	.313	.521
NL:Chi.	146	19	37	58	24	8	2	3	16	1	-	11	0	24	2	31	.253	.397
1933 (5)																		
NL:NY	176	16	47	61	39	5	0	3	16	6	-	11	0	21	0	39	.267	.347
AL:Wash.	173	11	37	47	31	4	0	2	11	3	-	13	0	24	1	37	.214	.272
1934 (7)																		
NL:StL.	262	34	73	103	52	14	5	2	32	4	-	11	1	31	2	49	.279	.393
AL:Det.	250	23	56	76	41	12	1	2	20	6	-	25	2	43	4	64	.224	.304
1935 (6)																		
AL:Det.	206	21	51	67	38	11	1	1	18	3	-	25	2	27	1	51	.248	.325
NL:Chi.	202	18	48	73	35	6	2	5	17	7	-	11	1	29	1	38	.238	.361
1936 (6)																		
AL:NY	215	43	65	96	49	8	1	7	41	3	-	26	1	35	1	43	.302	.447
NL:NY	203	23	50	71	37	9	0	4	20	7	-	21	0	33	0	46	.246	.350
1937 (5)																		
AL:NY	169	28	42	68	28	6	4	4	25	2	-	21	1	21	0	36	.249	.402
NL:NY	169	12	40	49	33	6	0	1	12	0	-	11	0	21	1	36	.237	.290
1938 (4)																		
AL:NY	135	22	37	60	25	6	1	5	21	1	-	11	1	16	3	24	.274	.444
NL:Chi.	136	9	33	45	26	4	1	2	8	1	-	6	0	26	0	26	.243	.331
1939 (4)																		
AL:NY	131	20	27	54	15	4	1	7	18	2	-	9	0	20	0	16	.206	.412
NL:Cin.	133	8	27	32	23	3	1	0	8	2	-	6	1	22	1	23	.203	.316
1940 (7)																		
NL:Cin.	232	22	58	78	42	14	0	2	21	4	-	15	0	30	1	49	.250	.336
AL:Det.	228	28	56	83	40	9	3	4	24	3	-	30	0	30	0	50	.246	.364
1941 (5)																		
AL:NY	166	17	41	54	33	5	1	2	16	0	-	23	2	18	2	42	.247	.325
NL:Brk.	159	11	29	43	19	7	2	1	11	0	-	14	0	21	0	27	.182	.270
1942 (5)																		
NL:StL.	163	23	39	53	31	4	2	2	23	7	-	17	0	19	0	32	.239	.325
AL:NY	178	18	44	59	35	6	0	3	14	1	-	8	0	22	3	34	.247	.331
1943 (5)																		
AL:NY	159	17	35	50	26	5	2	2	14	4	-	12	0	30	2	30	.220	.314
NL:StL.	165	9	37	48	30	5	0	2	8	5	-	11	0	26	1	37	.224	.291
1944 (6)																		
NL:StL.	204	16	49	69	36	9	1	3	15	7	-	19	0	43	0	51	.240	.338
AL:StL.	197	12	36	50	25	9	1	1	9	1	-	23	0	49	0	44	.183	.254
1945 (7)																		
AL:Det.	242	32	54	70	42	10	0	2	32	3	-	33	2	22	3	53	.223	.289
NL:Chi.	247	29	65	90	45	16	3	1	27	10	-	19	0	48	2	50	.263	.364

	AB	R	H	TB	1B	2B	3B	HR	RBI	SH	SF	BB	HP	SO	SB	LOB	BA	SLG
'46 (7)																		
NL:StL.	232	28	60	86	38	19	2	1	27	8	-	19	2	30	3	50	.259	.371
AL:Bos.	233	20	56	77	44	7	1	4	18	3	-	22	1	28	2	53	.240	.330
'47 (7)																		
AL:NY	238	38	67	100	47	11	5	4	36	3	-	38	2	37	2	63	.282	.420
NL:Brk.	226	29	52	70	37	13	1	1	26	3	-	30	1	32	7	46	.230	.310
'48 (6)																		
AL:Clev.	191	17	38	57	27	7	0	4	16	3	-	12	1	26	2	34	.199	.298
NL:Bos.	187	17	43	61	33	6	0	4	16	7	-	16	0	19	1	34	.230	.326
'49 (5)																		
AL:NY	164	21	37	57	23	10	2	2	20	3	-	18	0	27	2	32	.226	.348
NL:Brk.	162	14	34	55	22	7	1	4	14	2	-	15	1	38	1	31	.210	.340
'50 (4)																		
AL:NY	135	11	30	41	24	3	1	2	10	2	-	13	1	12	1	33	.222	.304
NL:Phil.	128	5	26	34	19	6	1	0	3	6	-	7	1	24	1	26	.203	.266
'51 (6)																		
AL:NY	199	29	49	75	35	7	2	5	25	0	-	26	1	23	0	41	.246	.377
NL:NY	194	18	46	61	36	7	1	2	15	2	-	25	1	22	2	45	.237	.314
'52 (7)																		
AL:NY	232	26	50	89	33	5	2	10	24	2	-	31	1	32	1	48	.216	.384
NL:Brk.	233	20	50	75	37	7	0	6	18	6	-	24	1	49	5	52	.215	.322
'53 (6)																		
AL:NY	201	33	56	97	37	6	4	9	32	4	-	25	4	43	2	47	.279	.483
NL:Brk.	213	27	64	103	42	13	1	8	26	2	-	15	2	30	2	49	.300	.484
'54 (4)																		
NL:NY	130	21	33	42	28	3	0	2	20	6	2	17	0	24	1	28	.254	.323
AL:Clev.	137	9	26	42	17	5	1	3	9	3	0	16	1	23	0	37	.190	.307
'55 (7)																		
NL:Brk.	223	31	58	95	40	8	1	9	30	6	2	33	2	38	2	55	.260	.426
AL:NY	222	26	55	87	41	4	2	8	25	1	0	22	2	39	3	41	.248	.392
'56 (7)																		
AL:NY	229	33	58	100	40	6	0	12	33	4	2	21	0	43	2	40	.253	.437
NL:Brk.	215	25	42	61	30	8	1	3	24	2	3	32	0	47	1	42	.199	.284
'57 (7)																		
NL:Mil.	225	23	47	79	32	6	1	8	22	6	0	22	3	40	1	46	.209	.351
AL:NY	230	25	57	87	42	7	1	7	25	3	1	22	0	34	1	45	.248	.378
'58 (7)																		
AL:NY	233	29	49	86	33	5	1	10	29	2	2	21	0	42	1	40	.210	.369
NL:Mil.	240	25	60	81	46	10	1	3	24	4	3	27	0	56	1	58	.250	.338
'59 (6)																		
NL:LA	203	21	53	79	42	3	1	7	19	4	0	12	0	27	5	42	.261	.389
AL:Chi.	199	23	52	74	38	10	0	4	19	3	1	20	2	33	2	43	.261	.372
'60 (7)																		
NL:Pitt.	234	27	60	83	45	11	0	4	26	3	0	12	3	26	2	42	.256	.355
AL:NY	269	55	91	142	64	13	4	10	54	2	1	18	2	40	0	51	.338	.528
'61 (5)																		
AL:NY	165	27	42	73	26	8	1	7	26	3	1	24	0	25	1	34	.255	.442
NL:Cin.	170	13	35	52	24	8	0	3	11	0	0	8	3	27	0	33	.206	.306
'62 (7)																		
AL:NY	221	20	44	61	34	6	1	3	17	1	1	21	2	39	4	43	.199	.276
NL:SF	226	21	51	80	34	10	2	5	19	4	0	12	1	39	1	39	.226	.354
'63 (4)																		
NL:LA	117	12	25	41	17	3	2	3	12	2	1	11	0	25	2	17	.214	.373
AL:NY	129	4	22	31	17	3	0	2	4	1	0	5	1	37	0	24	.171	.240
'64 (7)																		
NL:StL.	240	32	61	90	45	8	3	5	29	4	2	18	0	30	3	47	.254	.375
AL:NY	239	33	60	101	39	21	0	10	33	1	2	25	2	54	2	47	.251	.423
'65 (7)																		
NL:LA	234	24	64	91	48	10	1	5	21	6	0	13	3	31	9	52	.274	.389
AL:Minn.	215	20	42	71	27	7	2	6	19	2	0	19	0	54	2	36	.195	.330
'66 (4)																		
AL:Balt.	120	13	24	41	16	3	1	4	10	2	0	11	0	17	0	18	.200	.342
NL:LA	120	2	17	23	13	3	0	1	2	1	0	13	0	28	1	24	.142	.192

	AB	R	H	TB	1B	2B	3B	HR	RBI	SH	SF	BB	HP	SO	SB	LOB	BA	SLG
1967 (7)																		
NL:StL.	229	25	51	81	33	11	2	5	24	0	2	17	0	30	7	40	.223	.354
AL:Bos.	222	21	48	80	33	6	1	8	19	4	2	17	2	49	1	43	.216	.360
1968 (7)																		
AL:Det.	231	34	56	90	41	4	3	8	33	2	1	27	3	59	0	44	.242	.390
NL:StL.	239	27	61	95	44	7	3	7	27	1	0	21	1	40	11	49	.255	.397
1969 (5)																		
NL:NY	159	15	35	61	21	8	0	6	13	2	1	15	1	35	1	34	.220	.384
AL:Balt.	157	9	23	33	19	1	0	3	9	0	1	15	0	28	1	29	.146	.210
1970 (5)																		
AL:Balt.	171	33	50	87	33	7	0	10	32	2	0	20	0	33	0	31	.292	.509
NL:Cin.	164	20	35	58	23	6	1	5	20	2	1	15	0	23	1	28	.213	.354
1971 (7)																		
NL:Pitt.	238	23	56	84	40	9	2	5	21	4	0	26	1	47	5	63	.235	.353
AL:Balt.	219	24	45	65	36	3	1	5	22	2	3	20	4	35	1	39	.205	.297
1972 (7)																		
AL:Oak.	220	16	46	65	37	4	0	5	16	6	0	21	1	37	1	45	.209	.295
NL:Cin.	220	21	46	65	34	8	1	3	21	5	3	27	1	46	12	49	.209	.295
1973 (7)																		
AL:Oak.	241	21	51	75	34	12	3	2	20	2	1	28	2	62	3	58	.212	.311
NL:NY	261	24	66	89	53	7	2	4	16	4	0	26	3	36	0	72	.253	.341
1974 (5)																		
AL:Oak.	142	16	30	46	22	4	0	4	14	7	1	16	2	42	3	26	.211	.324
NL:LA	158	11	36	54	27	4	1	4	10	3	1	16	1	32	3	36	.228	.342
1975 (7)																		
NL:Cin.	244	29	59	95	40	9	3	7	29	2	2	25	2	30	9	50	.242	.389
AL:Bos.	239	30	60	89	45	7	2	6	30	4	3	30	1	40	0	52	.251	.372
1976 (4)																		
NL:Cin.	134	22	42	70	25	10	3	4	21	0	2	12	0	16	7	22	.313	.522
AL:NY	135	8	30	38	25	3	1	1	8	0	1	12	1	16	1	33	.222	.281
1977 (6)																		
AL:NY	205	26	50	84	32	10	0	8	25	4	1	11	2	37	1	32	.244	.410
NL:LA	208	28	48	86	31	5	3	9	28	0	2	16	1	36	2	31	.231	.413
1978 (6)																		
AL:NY	222	36	68	85	57	8	0	3	34	1	0	16	2	40	5	47	.306	.383
NL:LA	199	23	52	78	38	8	0	6	22	1	0	20	0	31	5	38	.261	.392
1979 (7)																		
NL:Pitt.	251	32	81	110	59	18	1	3	32	3	5	16	3	35	0	60	.323	.438
AL:Balt.	233	26	54	78	39	10	1	4	23	1	0	26	1	41	2	49	.232	.335
1980 (6)																		
NL:Phil.	201	27	59	81	43	13	0	3	26	2	4	15	2	17	3	41	.294	.403
AL:KC	207	23	60	97	41	9	2	8	22	2	3	26	0	49	6	54	.290	.469
1981 (6)																		
NL:LA	198	27	51	77	38	6	1	6	26	4	2	20	2	44	6	46	.258	.389
AL:NY	193	22	46	74	31	8	1	6	22	5	2	33	0	24	4	55	.238	.383
1982 (7)																		
NL:StL.	245	39	67	101	44	16	3	4	34	1	1	20	0	26	7	49	.273	.412
AL:Mil.	238	33	64	95	45	12	2	5	29	1	1	19	1	28	1	44	.269	.399
1983 (5)																		
AL:Balt.	164	18	35	61	21	8	0	6	17	0	3	10	1	37	1	28	.213	.372
NL:Phil.	159	9	31	49	22	4	1	4	9	0	1	7	0	29	1	23	.195	.308
1984 (5)																		
AL:Det.	158	23	40	65	29	4	0	7	22	2	2	24	2	27	7	39	.253	.411
NL:SD	166	15	44	60	34	7	0	3	14	1	3	11	0	26	2	34	.265	.361
1985 (7)																		
AL:KC	236	28	68	90	52	12	2	2	26	3	0	28	1	56	7	56	.288	.381
NL:StL.	216	13	40	58	27	10	1	2	13	3	0	18	0	42	2	38	.185	.269
1986 (7)																		
NL:NY	240	32	65	92	52	6	0	7	29	6	2	21	1	43	7	50	.271	.383
AL:Bos.	248	27	69	99	51	11	2	5	26	4	2	28	3	53	0	69	.278	.398
1987 (7)																		
AL:Minn.	238	38	64	101	44	10	3	7	38	1	0	29	3	36	6	56	.269	.424
NL:StL.	232	26	60	74	50	8	0	2	25	2	1	13	1	44	12	43	.259	.319

	AB	R	H	TB	1B	2B	3B	HR	RBI	SH	SF	BB	HP	SO	SB	LOB	BA	SLG
88 (5)																		
NL:LA	167	21	41	66	27	8	1	5	19	1	0	13	1	36	4	30	.246	.395
AL:Oak.	158	11	28	37	23	3	0	2	11	1	1	17	1	41	3	34	.177	.234
89 (4)																		
AL:Oak.	146	32	44	85	24	8	3	9	30	0	0	18	1	22	4	31	.301	.582
NL:SF	134	14	28	46	19	4	1	4	14	0	1	8	0	27	2	21	.209	.343
90 (4)																		
NL:Cin.	142	22	45	67	31	9	2	3	22	1	1	15	1	9	2	32	.317	.472
AL:Oak.	135	8	28	41	21	4	0	3	8	2	1	12	0	28	7	31	.207	.304
91 (7)																		
AL:Minn.	241	24	56	96	36	8	4	8	24	2	2	21	1	48	7	47	.232	.398
NL:Atl.	249	29	63	105	41	10	4	8	29	4	3	26	1	39	5	52	.253	.422
92 (6)																		
AL:Tor.	196	17	45	71	31	8	0	6	17	2	1	18	1	33	5	38	.230	.362
NL:Atl.	200	20	44	59	35	6	0	3	19	2	2	20	1	48	15	40	.220	.295
93 (6)																		
AL:Tor.	206	45	64	105	40	13	5	6	45	0	7	25	3	30	7	39	.311	.510
NL:Phil.	212	36	58	90	42	7	2	7	35	1	1	34	1	50	7	54	.274	.425
95 (6)																		
NL:Atl.	193	23	47	81	29	10	0	8	23	5	1	25	2	34	5	44	.244	.420
AL:Clev.	195	19	35	59	22	7	1	5	17	0	0	25	0	37	8	39	.179	303
96 (6)																		
AL:NY	199	18	43	57	48	6	1	2	16	2	0	26	1	43	4	48	.216	.286
NL:Atl.	201	26	51	74	37	9	1	4	26	4	3	23	1	36	3	41	.254	.368
97 (7)																		
NL:Fla.	250	37	68	106	47	12	1	8	34	1	2	36	1	48	4	62	.272	.424
AL:Clev.	247	44	72	107	52	12	1	7	42	5	3	40	0	51	5	59	.291	.433
98 (4)																		
AL:NY	139	26	43	66	32	5	0	6	25	1	1	20	1	29	1	34	.309	.475
NL:SD	134	13	32	50	21	7	1	3	11	0	2	12	0	29	1	27	.239	.373
99 (4)																		
AL:NY	137	21	37	57	27	5	0	5	20	3	0	13	0	31	5	27	.270	.416
NL:Atl.	130	9	26	36	19	5	1	1	9	0	0	15	0	26	1	25	.200	.277
00 (5)																		
AL:NY	179	19	47	73	32	8	3	4	18	1	3	25	3	40	1	52	.263	.408
NL:NY	175	16	40	60	28	8	0	4	15	3	1	11	3	48	0	36	.229	.343
01 (7)																		
NL:Ari.	246	37	65	97	45	14	0	6	36	5	2	17	6	70	2	49	.264	.394
AL:NY	229	14	42	66	30	6	0	6	14	1	0	16	1	63	1	38	.183	.288
02 (7)																		
AL:Ana.	245	41	76	114	53	15	1	7	38	2	3	23	2	38	6	54	.310	.465
NL:SF	235	44	66	117	44	7	1	14	42	4	4	30	1	50	5	47	.281	.498
03 (6)																		
NL:Fla.	203	17	47	61	37	8	0	2	17	5	2	14	1	48	2	43	.232	.300
AL:NY	207	21	54	84	37	10	1	6	21	2	2	22	3	49	2	47	.261	.406
04 (4)																		
AL:Bos.	138	24	39	66	22	11	2	4	24	1	0	24	4	20	0	41	.283	.478
NL:StL.	126	12	24	38	14	8	0	2	8	2	3	12	1	32	1	24	.190	.302
05 (4)																		
AL:Chi.	154	20	44	75	27	9	2	6	20	2	0	15	3	30	5	36	.286	.487
NL:Hou.	143	14	29	48	17	8	1	3	14	5	1	17	5	36	5	34	.203	.336
06 (5)																		
NL:StL.	158	22	36	54	22	12	0	2	16	4	0	23	2	34	1	39	.228	.342
AL:Det.	161	11	32	54	19	8	1	4	11	3	0	8	2	37	1	31	.199	.335

WORLD SERIES CLUB PITCHING & FIELDING

[PL=Players Used   PI=Pitchers Used]

	Fielding:										Pitching:					
	PL	TC	CA	PO	A	E	DP	TP	PB	AVG	PI	IP	ER	ERA	CG	SHO
1903 (8)																
AL:Bos.	13	329	315	213	102	14	6	0	2	.957	3	71.0	16	2.03	7	2
NL:Pitt.	14	324	306	210	96	18	5	0	0	.944	5	70.0	29	3.73	6	0
1905 (5)																
NL:NY	12	219	213	135	78	6	3	0	0	.973	3	45.0	0	0.00	4	3
AL:Phil.	13	194	185	129	56	9	3	0	0	.954	3	43.0	4	0.83	5	1
1906 (6)																
AL:Chi.	16	275	261	162	99	14	2	0	1	.949	4	54.0	10	1.67	4	1
NL:Chi.	14	250	243	159	84	7	4	0	3	.972	4	53.0	19	3.22	4	1
1907 (5)																
NL:Chi.	15	219	209	144	65	10	6	0	1	.954	4	48.0	4	0.75	4	1
AL:Det.	14	217	208	138	70	9	2	0	0	.959	4	46.0	11	2.15	4	0
1908 (5)																
NL:Chi.	13	214	209	135	74	5	4	0	1	.977	4	45.0	13	2.60	3	2
AL:Det.	16	204	194	131	63	10	5	0	1	.951	5	44.0	18	3.68	3	0
1909 (7)																
NL:Pitt.	17	285	270	182	88	15	3	0	0	.947	6	61.0	18	2.65	4	1
AL:Det.	16	289	270	183	87	19	4	0	1	.934	5	61.0	20	2.95	4	1
1910 (5)																
AL:Phil.	12	206	195	136	59	11	6	0	0	.947	2	45.2	14	2.75	5	0
NL:Chi.	18	221	209	132	77	12	3	0	0	.946	7	44.0	23	4.70	1	0
1911 (6)																
AL:Phil.	14	250	239	167	72	11	2	0	0	.956	3	55.2	8	1.29	5	0
NL:NY	15	257	241	162	79	16	2	0	1	.938	5	54.0	17	2.83	2	0
1912 (8)																
AL:Bos.	17	337	323	222	101	14	5	0	0	.958	5	74.0	22	2.67	3	0
NL:NY	17	346	329	221	108	17	4	0	0	.951	5	73.2	15	1.83	6	0
1913 (5)																
AL:Phil.	12	197	192	138	54	5	6	0	0	.975	3	46.0	11	2.15	5	0
NL:NY	20	209	202	135	67	7	1	0	1	.967	5	45.0	19	3.80	3	1
1914 (4)																
NL:Bos.	15	183	179	117	62	4	4	0	0	.978	3	39.0	5	1.15	3	1
AL:Phil.	16	180	177	111	66	3	4	0	1	.983	6	37.0	15	3.55	2	0
1915 (5)																
AL:Bos.	17	194	190	132	58	4	2	0	0	.979	3	44.0	9	1.84	5	0
NL:Phil.	16	188	185	131	54	3	3	0	0	.984	4	43.2	10	2.06	4	0
1916 (5)																
AL:Bos.	20	243	237	147	90	6	5	0	1	.975	5	49.0	8	1.46	3	0
NL:Brk.	20	225	212	142	70	13	2	0	2	.942	7	47.1	16	3.04	1	0
1917 (6)																
AL:Chi.	16	250	238	156	82	12	7	0	1	.952	5	52.0	16	2.38	4	0
NL:NY	17	236	225	153	72	11	3	0	1	.953	6	51.0	17	3.00	3	2
1918 (6)																
AL:Bos.	15	247	246	159	88	1	4	0	1	.996	4	53.0	10	1.70	5	1
NL:Chi.	17	237	232	156	76	5	7	0	2	.979	4	52.0	6	1.04	4	1
1919 (8)																
NL:Cin.	17	324	312	216	96	12	7	0	0	.963	6	72.0	13	1.62	5	2
AL:Chi.	19	341	329	213	116	12	9	0	1	.965	7	71.0	28	3.54	5	1
1920 (7)																
AL:Clev.	20	283	271	182	89	12	8	1	0	.958	5	61.0	6	0.88	5	2
NL:Brk.	21	274	268	177	91	6	5	0	2	.978	7	59.0	16	2.44	3	1
1921 (8)																
NL:NY	13	319	314	212	102	5	5	0	2	.984	4	71.0	20	2.53	5	1
AL:NY	19	322	316	210	106	6	8	0	0	.981	8	70.0	24	3.08	6	2
1922 (5)																
NL:NY	16	214	208	138	70	6	4	0	0	.972	5	46.0	8	1.56	4	1
AL:NY	17	193	192	129	62	1	7	0	1	.995	5	43.0	16	3.35	2	0
1923 (6)																
AL:NY	17	242	239	162	77	3	6	0	0	.988	5	54.0	17	2.83	2	0
NL:NY	22	245	239	159	80	6	8	0	0	.976	8	53.0	25	4.24	1	1

	Fielding:										Pitching:					
	PL	TC	CA	PO	A	E	DP	TP	PB	AVG	PI	IP	ER	ERA	CG	SHO
1924 (7)																
AL:Wash.	21	312	300	201	99	12	10	0	1	.962	8	67.0	16	2.16	3	0
NL:NY	21	300	294	200	94	6	4	0	0	.980	9	66.2	23	3.07	2	0
1925 (7)																
NL:Pitt.	18	278	271	182	89	7	4	0	0	.975	7	61.0	25	3.69	4	0
AL:Wash.	21	264	255	180	75	9	8	0	1	.966	6	60.0	19	2.85	4	1
1926 (7)																
NL:StL.	19	292	287	189	98	5	6	0	0	.983	8	63.0	19	2.71	4	1
AL:NY	19	278	271	189	82	7	3	0	1	.975	7	63.0	22	3.14	3	0
1927 (4)																
AL:NY	15	155	152	108	44	3	4	0	0	.981	4	36.0	8	2.00	3	0
NL:Pitt.	21	156	150	104	46	6	2	0	0	.962	7	34.2	20	5.19	0	0
1928 (4)																
AL:NY	16	142	136	108	28	6	3	0	0	.958	3	36.0	9	2.25	4	0
NL:StL.	20	143	138	102	36	5	3	0	0	.965	6	34.0	23	6.08	0	0
1929 (5)																
AL:Phil.	17	179	175	135	40	4	2	0	0	.978	6	45.0	13	2.60	2	0
NL:Chi.	19	182	175	131	44	7	4	0	0	.962	6	43.2	21	4.33	2	0
1930 (6)																
AL:Phil.	15	200	197	156	41	3	2	0	0	.985	5	52.0	10	1.73	4	1
NL:StL.	21	212	207	153	54	5	4	0	1	.976	7	51.0	21	5.40	4	1
1931 (7)																
NL:StL.	21	263	259	186	73	4	7	0	0	.985	6	62.0	16	2.32	3	1
AL:Phil.	20	254	252	183	69	2	4	0	0	.992	6	61.0	18	2.66	4	1
1932 (4)																
AL:NY	16	157	149	108	41	8	1	0	0	.949	6	36.0	13	3.25	2	0
NL:Chi.	22	148	142	102	40	6	7	0	0	.959	8	34.0	35	9.26	1	0
1933 (5)																
NL:NY	15	212	208	141	67	4	5	0	0	.981	5	47.0	8	1.53	3	0
AL:Wash.	19	202	201	138	65	4	4	0	0	.981	7	46.0	14	2.73	1	1
1934 (7)																
NL:StL.	20	284	269	196	73	15	2	0	0	.947	8	65.1	17	2.34	4	1
AL:Det.	17	277	265	195	70	12	6	0	0	.957	6	65.0	27	3.74	4	0
1935 (6)																
AL:Det.	15	146	137	165	72	9	7	0	1	.963	5	55.0	14	2.29	5	0
NL:Chi.	18	244	238	164	74	6	5	0	0	.975	7	54.2	18	2.96	2	1
1936 (6)																
AL:NY	16	225	219	162	57	6	2	0	0	.973	6	54.0	20	3.33	3	0
NL:NY	22	228	221	159	62	7	7	0	0	.969	8	53.0	40	6.79	3	0
1937 (5)																
AL:NY	17	179	179	132	47	0	2	0	0	1.000	7	44.0	12	2.45	3	0
NL:NY	20	184	175	129	46	9	5	0	0	.951	7	43.0	23	4.81	1	0
1938 (4)																
AL:NY	14	153	147	108	39	6	4	0	0	.961	4	36.0	7	1.75	3	0
NL:Chi.	20	140	137	102	35	3	3	0	0	.979	8	34.0	19	5.03	0	0
1939 (4)																
AL:NY	15	163	161	111	50	2	5	0	0	.988	7	37.0	5	1.21	2	1
NL:Cin.	18	144	140	106	34	4	1	0	0	.972	5	35.1	17	4.34	2	0
1940 (7)																
NL:Cin.	23	257	249	183	66	8	9	0	1	.969	9	61.0	25	3.68	4	1
AL:Det.	20	264	260	180	80	4	4	0	0	.985	8	60.0	20	3.00	4	1
1941 (5)																
AL:NY	18	192	190	135	55	2	7	0	0	.990	7	45.0	9	1.80	3	0
NL:Brk.	20	196	192	132	60	4	5	0	0	.980	7	44.0	13	2.65	2	0
1942 (5)																
NL:StL.	18	190	180	135	45	10	3	0	0	.947	6	45.0	13	2.60	3	1
AL:NY	20	182	177	132	45	5	2	0	0	.973	7	44.0	22	4.50	2	0
1943 (5)																
AL:NY	16	203	198	135	63	5	3	0	0	.975	5	45.0	7	1.40	3	1
NL:StL.	20	192	182	129	53	10	4	0	0	.948	6	43.0	12	2.51	2	0
1944 (6)																
NL:StL.	20	225	224	165	59	1	3	0	1	.996	8	55.0	12	1.96	2	1
AL:StL.	22	233	223	163	60	10	4	0	0	.957	7	54.1	9	1.49	3	0

	Fielding:										Pitching:					
	PL	TC	CA	PO	A	E	DP	TP	PB	AVG	PI	IP	ER	ERA	CG	SHO
1945 (7)																
AL:Det.	26	287	282	197	85	5	4	0	2	.983	9	65.2	28	3.83	4	0
NL:Chi.	25	279	273	195	78	6	5	0	1	.978	8	65.0	30	4.15	2	2
1946 (7)																
NL:StL.	19	258	254	186	68	4	7	0	1	.984	7	62.0	16	2.32	4	1
AL:Bos.	26	269	259	183	76	10	5	0	0	.963	11	61.0	20	2.95	2	1
1947 (7)																
AL:NY	24	259	255	185	70	4	4	0	2	.985	9	61.2	28	4.09	3	0
NL:Brk.	24	259	251	180	71	8	8	0	2	.969	8	60.0	37	5.55	0	0
1948 (6)																
AL:Clev.	23	234	231	159	72	3	9	0	0	.987	8	53.0	16	2.72	4	1
NL:Bos.	20	216	210	156	54	6	3	0	0	.972	6	52.0	15	2.60	2	1
1949 (5)																
AL:NY	20	182	179	135	44	3	5	0	0	.984	5	45.0	14	2.80	2	1
NL:Brk.	25	177	172	132	40	5	1	0	0	.972	9	44.0	21	4.29	2	1
1950 (4)																
AL:NY	18	154	152	111	41	2	4	0	0	.987	5	37.0	3	0.73	2	1
NL:Phil.	20	146	142	107	35	4	1	0	0	.973	5	35.2	9	2.27	1	0
1951 (6)																
AL:NY	21	230	226	159	67	4	10	0	1	.982	8	53.0	11	1.87	3	0
NL:NY	24	231	221	156	65	10	4	0	0	.957	9	52.0	27	4.67	1	0
1952 (7)																
AL:NY	19	268	258	192	66	10	7	0	1	.963	8	64.0	20	2.81	2	1
NL:Brk.	19	267	263	192	71	4	4	0	0	.985	6	64.0	25	3.52	3	0
1953 (6)																
AL:NY	20	217	216	156	60	1	5	0	0	.995	9	52.0	26	4.50	2	0
NL:Brk.	23	223	216	154	62	7	3	0	0	.969	10	51.1	28	4.94	2	0
1954 (4)																
NL:NY	15	157	150	111	39	7	2	0	0	.955	6	37.0	6	1.46	1	0
AL:Clev.	24	150	146	106	40	4	2	0	0	.973	7	35.1	19	4.84	1	0
1955 (7)																
NL:Brk.	22	270	264	180	84	6	12	0	0	.978	10	60.0	25	3.75	2	1
AL:NY	24	254	252	180	72	2	7	0	0	.992	9	60.0	28	4.20	2	0
1956 (7)																
AL:NY	22	257	251	185	66	6	7	0	0	.977	8	61.2	17	2.48	5	2
NL:Brk.	21	254	252	183	69	2	8	0	0	.992	8	61.0	32	4.72	3	1
1957 (7)																
NL:Mil.	23	282	279	186	93	3	10	0	1	.989	8	62.0	24	3.48	4	2
AL:NY	23	265	259	187	72	6	5	0	0	.977	9	62.1	20	2.89	2	0
1958 (7)																
AL:NY	22	259	256	191	65	3	5	0	1	.988	9	63.2	24	3.39	1	2
NL:Mil.	19	274	267	189	78	7	5	0	0	.974	6	63.0	26	3.71	3	1
1959 (6)																
NL:LA	24	232	228	159	69	4	7	0	0	.983	9	53.0	19	3.23	0	0
AL:Chi.	21	222	218	156	62	4	2	0	1	.982	7	52.0	20	3.46	0	2
1960 (7)																
NL:Pitt.	25	257	253	186	67	4	7	0	3	.984	10	62.0	49	7.11	0	0
AL:NY	25	284	276	183	93	8	9	0	0	.972	10	61.0	24	3.54	2	2
1961 (5)																
AL:NY	18	190	185	135	50	5	1	0	1	.974	6	45.0	8	1.60	1	2
NL:Cin.	24	178	174	132	42	4	7	0	1	.978	9	44.0	24	4.91	2	0
1962 (7)																
AL:NY	18	255	250	183	67	5	5	0	0	.980	6	61.0	20	2.95	4	1
NL:SF	21	258	250	183	67	8	9	0	1	.969	7	61.0	18	2.66	2	1
1963 (4)																
NL:LA	13	142	139	108	31	3	1	0	0	.979	4	36.0	4	1.00	3	1
AL:NY	20	153	152	102	50	1	7	0	0	.993	7	34.0	11	2.91	0	0
1964 (7)																
NL:StL	21	257	253	189	64	4	6	0	0	.984	8	63.0	30	4.29	2	0
AL:NY	21	277	268	186	82	9	6	0	3	.986	9	62.0	26	3.77	2	0
1965 (7)																
NL:LA	20	258	252	180	72	6	7	0	0	.977	7	60.0	14	2.10	4	3
AL:Minn.	21	243	238	180	58	5	3	0	0	.979	9	60.0	21	3.15	3	0

	Fielding:										Pitching:					
	PL	TC	CA	PO	A	E	DP	TP	PB	AVG	PI	IP	ER	ERA	CG	SHO
1966 (4)																
AL:Balt.	13	141	141	108	33	0	4	0	0	1.000	4	36.0	2	0.50	3	3
NL:LA	23	152	146	102	44	6	4	0	0	.961	8	34.0	10	2.65	1	0
1967 (7)																
NL:StL.	23	253	249	183	66	4	3	0	0	.984	10	61.0	18	2.66	4	1
AL:Bos.	25	253	249	183	66	4	4	0	1	.984	10	61.0	23	3.39	2	1
1968 (7)																
AL:Det.	24	269	258	186	72	11	4	0	0	.959	9	62.0	24	3.48	4	0
NL:StL.	25	236	234	186	48	2	7	0	0	.992	10	62.0	32	4.65	3	1
1969 (5)																
NL:NY	21	179	177	135	42	2	0	0	0	.989	6	45.0	9	1.80	2	1
AL:Balt.	21	184	180	129	51	4	4	0	0	.978	7	43.0	13	2.72	2	0
1970 (5)																
AL:Balt.	21	183	178	135	43	5	3	0	0	.973	9	45.0	17	3.40	2	0
NL:Cin.	24	182	179	129	50	3	4	0	0	.984	9	43.0	32	6.70	0	0
1971 (7)																
NL:Pitt.	25	258	255	185	70	3	7	0	1	.988	10	61.2	24	3.50	3	1
AL:Balt.	21	261	252	183	69	9	2	0	0	.966	10	61.0	18	2.66	1	0
1972 (7)																
AL:Oak.	23	260	251	186	65	9	4	0	0	.965	8	62.	21	3.05	0	0
NL:Cin.	22	280	275	187	88	5	4	0	0	.982	8	62.1	15	2.17	0	1
1973 (7)																
AL:Oak.	24	286	277	198	79	9	8	0	1	.969	8	66.0	17	2.32	0	0
NL:NY	22	275	265	195	70	10	3	0	1	.964	7	65.0	16	2.22	0	1
1974 (5)																
AL:Oak.	20	188	183	132	51	5	6	0	0	.973	5	44.0	10	2.05	0	0
NL:LA	19	182	176	126	50	6	5	0	0	.967	6	42.0	13	2.79	0	0
1975 (7)																
NL:Cin.	22	273	271	195	76	2	8	0	0	.993	9	65.0	28	3.88	0	0
AL:Bos.	23	274	268	196	72	6	6	0	0	.978	10	65.1	28	3.86	2	1
1976 (7)																
NL:Cin.	16	147	142	108	34	5	4	0	0	.966	7	36.0	8	2.00	0	0
AL:NY	21	146	144	104	40	2	6	0	0	.986	7	34.2	21	5.45	1	0
1977 (6)																
AL:NY	20	239	236	168	68	3	2	0	1	.987	7	56.0	25	4.02	3	0
NL:LA	25	235	234	165	69	1	4	0	0	.996	9	55.0	25	4.09	2	0
1978 (6)																
AL:NY	24	214	212	159	54	2	9	0	0	.991	8	53.0	22	3.74	2	0
NL:LA	23	229	222	158	64	7	2	0	2	.969	8	52.2	32	5.47	0	0
1979 (7)																
NL:Pitt.	24	274	265	186	79	9	11	0	0	.967	9	62.0	22	3.19	0	1
AL:Balt.	25	280	271	186	85	9	5	0	0	.968	8	62.0	30	4.35	2	0
1980 (6)																
NL:Phil.	22	231	229	161	68	2	8	0	0	.991	10	53.2	22	3.69	0	0
AL:KC	21	235	228	156	72	7	8	0	0	.970	7	52.0	24	4.15	0	0
1981 (6)																
NL:LA	24	230	221	156	65	9	6	0	0	.961	10	52.0	19	3.29	2	0
AL:NY	24	212	208	153	55	4	2	0	1	.981	9	51.0	24	4.24	0	1
1982 (7)																
NL:StL	22	264	257	183	74	7	9	0	0	.973	8	61.0	23	3.39	1	0
AL:Mil	21	272	261	180	81	11	3	0	0	.960	9	60.0	32	4.80	1	1
1983 (5)																
AL:Balt.	23	189	185	135	50	4	5	0	0	.979	7	45.0	8	1.60	2	1
NL:Phil.	23	177	174	132	42	3	3	0	0	.983	8	44.0	17	3.48	0	0
1984 (5)																
AL:Det.	22	188	184	132	52	4	2	0	0	.979	7	44.0	15	3.07	2	0
NL:SD	24	170	166	126	40	4	5	0	0	.976	10	42.0	22	4.71	0	0
1985 (7)																
AL:KC	22	269	266	186	80	3	3	0	1	.989	6	62.0	13	1.89	3	1
NL:StL.	24	246	244	184	60	2	9	0	1	.992	9	61.1	27	3.96	1	1
1986 (7)																
NL:NY	22	257	252	189	63	5	4	0	0	.980	8	63.0	23	3.29	0	0
AL:Bos.	21	271	267	188	79	4	7	0	1	.985	8	62.2	30	4.31	1	1

		Fielding:										Pitching:					
	PL	TC	CA	PO	A	E	DP	TP	PB	AVG		PI	IP	ER	ERA	CG	SHO
1987 (7)																	
AL:Minn.	24	256	253	180	73	3	4	0	0	.998		9	60.0	25	3.75	0	0
NL:StL.	24	252	246	177	69	6	2	0	1	.976		9	59.0	37	5.64	0	0
1988 (5)																	
NL:LA	22	172	169	133	36	3	3	0	1	.983		7	44.1	10	2.03	2	1
AL:Oak.	24	176	174	131	43	2	2	0	1	.989		10	43.2	19	3.92	0	0
1989 (4)																	
AL:Oak.	19	144	143	108	35	1	1	0	1	.993		6	36.0	14	3.50	1	1
NL:SF	24	146	142	102	40	4	3	0	0	.973		9	34.0	31	8.21	0	0
1990 (4)																	
NL:Cin.	21	157	153	111	42	4	2	0	0	.975		8	37.0	7	1.70	0	1
AL:Oak.	25	157	152	106	46	5	5	0	0	.968		10	35.1	15	3.82	1	0
1991 (7)																	
AL:Minn.	25	280	276	202	74	4	6	0	1	.986		9	67.1	28	3.74	1	1
NL:Atl.	25	288	282	196	86	6	9	0	0	.979		10	65.1	21	2.89	1	0
1992 (6)																	
AL:Tor.	23	216	212	165	47	4	5	0	0	.981		10	55.0	17	2.78	0	0
NL:Atl.	22	233	231	163	68	2	7	0	0	.991		8	54.1	16	2.65	2	0
1993 (6)																	
AL:Tor.	23	211	204	159	45	7	5	0	0	.967		10	53.0	34	5.77	0	0
NL:Phil.	23	213	211	157	54	2	5	0	1	.991		10	52.1	44	7.57	1	1
1995 (6)																	
NL:Atl.	23	238	232	162	73	6	2	0	0	.975		10	54.0	16	2.67	1	1
AL:Clev.	23	237	231	159	69	6	8	0	1	.975		9	53.0	21	3.57	0	0
1996 (6)																	
AL:NY	25	233	228	165	63	5	7	0	0	.979		10	55.0	24	3.93	0	1
NL:Atl.	24	239	235	162	73	4	6	0	0	.983		10	54.0	14	2.33	0	1
1997 (7)																	
NL:Fla.	25	282	274	192	82	8	9	0	0	.972		10	64.0	39	5.48	0	0
AL:Clev.	23	260	255	191	64	5	8	0	0	.981		11	63.2	32	4.52	0	0
1998 (4)																	
AL:NY	19	146	144	108	36	2	4	0	0	.986		9	36.0	11	2.75	0	1
NL:SD	23	146	143	102	41	3	5	0	1	.979		10	34.0	22	5.82	0	0
1999 (4)																	
AL:NY	20	160	159	111	48	1	5	0	0	.994		9	37.0	9	2.19	0	0
NL:Atl.	23	140	136	105	31	4	4	0	0	.971		9	35.0	17	4.37	0	0
2000 (5)																	
AL:NY	22	189	187	141	46	2	1	0	1	.989		8	47.0	14	2.68	0	0
NL:NY	25	192	187	140	47	5	3	0	0	.974		10	46.2	18	3.47	0	0
2001 (7)																	
NL:Ari.	25	259	256	195	61	3	6	0	0	.988		10	65.0	14	1.94	1	0
AL:NY	25	273	265	190	75	8	7	0	0	.971		10	63.1	30	4.26	0	0
2002 (7)																	
AL:Ana.	22	244	239	183	56	5	6	0	1	.980		10	61.0	39	5.75	0	0
NL:SF	21	255	250	180	70	5	7	0	1	.980		11	60.0	37	5.55	0	0
2003 (6)																	
NL:Fla.	20	227	225	168	57	2	8	0	0	.991		9	56.0	20	3.21	1	1
AL:NY	23	236	231	165	66	5	6	0	1	.979		9	55.0	13	2.13	0	0
2004 (4)																	
AL:Bos.	21	148	140	108	32	8	5	0	1	.946		8	36.0	10	2.50	0	1
NL:StL.	25	140	139	102	37	1	3	0	0	.993		11	34.0	23	6.09	0	0
2005 (4)																	
AL:Chi.	24	175	172	123	49	3	4	0	0	.983		11	41.0	12	2.63	0	1
NL:Hou.	24	173	171	118	53	2	6	0	0	.988		10	39.1	20	4.58	0	0
2006 (5)																	
NL:StL.	23	179	175	132	43	4	3	0	0	.978		10	44.0	10	2.05	0	1
AL:Det.	24	185	177	126	51	8	4	0	0	.957		11	42.0	14	3.00	0	0

BATTING AVERAGE LEADERS

(Playing all games)

Year	Player	AB	H	AVG
1903				
AL	Chick Stahl, Bos.	33	10	.303
NL	Jimmy Sebring, Pitt.	30	11	.367
1905				
AL	Topsy Hartsel, Phil.	17	5	.294
NL	Mike Donlin NY	19	6	.316
1906				
AL	George Rohe, Chi.	21	7	.333
AL	Jiggs Donahue, Chi.	18	6	.333
NL	Solly Hofman, Chi.	23	7	.304
1907				
AL	Claude Rossman, Det.	20	8	.400
NL	Harry Steinfeldt, Chi.	17	8	.471
1908				
AL	Ty Cobb, Det.	19	7	.368
NL	Frank Chance, Chi.	19	8	.421
1909				
AL	Jim Delahanty, Det.	26	9	.346
NL	Honus Wagner, Pitt.	24	8	.333
1910				
AL	Eddie Collins, Phil.	21	9	.429
NL	Frank Chance, Chi.	17	6	.353
NL	Wildfire Schulte, Chi.	17	6	.353
1911				
AL	Frank Baker, Phil.	24	9	.375
NL	Larry Doyle, NY	23	7	.304
1912				
AL	Tris Speaker, Bos.	30	9	.300
NL	Buck Herzog, NY	30	12	.400
1913				
AL	Frank Baker, Phil.	20	9	.450
NL	Larry McLean, NY	12	6	.500
1914				
AL	Frank Baker, Phil.	16	4	.250
NL	Hank Gowdy, Bos.	11	6	.545
1915				
AL	Duffy Lewis, Bos.	18	8	.444
NL	Fred Luderus, Phil.	16	7	.438
1916				
AL	Duffy Lewis, Bos.	17	6	.353
NL	Ivy Olson, Brk.	16	4	.250
1917				
AL	Eddie Collins, Chi.	22	9	.409
NL	Dave Robertson, NY	22	11	.500
1918				
AL	Stuffy McInnis, Bos.	20	5	.250
AL	George Whiteman, Bos.	20	5	.250
NL	Charlie Pick, Chi.	18	7	.389
1919				
AL	Joe Jackson, Chi.	32	12	.375
NL	Greasy Neale, Cin.	28	10	.357
1920				
AL	Steve O'Neill, Clev.	21	7	.333
NL	Zack Wheat, Brk.	27	9	.333
1921				
AL	Wally Schang, NY	21	6	.286
NL	Irish Meusel, NY	29	10	.345
1922				
AL	Bob Meusel, NY	20	6	.300
NL	Heinie Groh, NY	19	9	.474

Year	Player	AB	H	AVG
1923				
AL	Aaron Ward, NY	24	10	.417
NL	Casey Stengel, NY	12	5	.417
1924				
AL	Joe Judge, Wash.	26	10	.385
NL	Frankie Frisch, NY	30	10	.333
NL	Freddie Lindstrom. NY	30	10	.333
1925				
AL	Bucky Harris, Wash.	25	11	.440
NL	Max Carey, Pitt.	24	11	.458
1926				
AL	Earle Combs, NY	28	10	.357
NL	Tommy Thevenow, StL.	24	10	.417
1927				
AL	Mark Koenig, NY	18	9	.500
NL	Lloyd Waner, Pitt.	15	6	.400
1928				
AL	Babe Ruth, NY	16	10	.625
NL	Rabbit Maranville, StL.	13	4	.308
1929				
AL	Jimmy Dykes, Phil.	19	8	.421
NL	Hack Wilson, Chi.	17	8	.471
1930				
AL	Al Simmons, Phil.	22	8	.364
NL	Charlie Gelbert, StL.	17	6	.353
1931				
AL	Jimmie Foxx, Phil.	23	8	.348
NL	Pepper Martin, StL.	24	12	.500
1932				
AL	Lou Gehrig, NY	17	9	.529
NL	Riggs Stephenson, Chi.	18	8	.444
1933				
AL	Fred Schulte, Wash.	21	7	.333
NL	Mel Ott, NY	18	7	.389
1934				
AL	Charlie Gehringer, Det.	29	11	.379
NL	Joe Medwick, StL.	29	11	.379
1935				
AL	Pete Fox, Det.	26	10	.385
NL	Hank Gowdy, Bos.	11	6	.545
1936				
AL	Jake Powell, NY	22	10	.455
NL	Dick Bartell, NY	21	8	.381
1937				
AL	Tony Lazzeri, NY	15	6	.400
NL	Joe Moore, NY	23	9	.391
1938				
AL	Bill Dickey, NY	15	6	.400
AL	Joe Gordon, NY	15	6	.400
NL	Stan Hack, Chi.	17	8	.471
1939				
AL	Charlie Keller, NY	16	7	.438
NL	Frank McCormick, Cin.	15	6	.400
1940				
AL	Bruce Campbell, Det.	25	9	.360
NL	Bill Werber, Cin.	27	10	.370
1941				
AL	Joe Gordon, NY	14	7	.500
NL	Joe Medwick, Brk.	17	4	.235
1942				
AL	Phil Rizzuto, NY	21	8	.381
NL	Jimmy Brown, StL.	20	6	.300
1943				
AL	Billy Johnson, NY	20	6	.300
NL	Marty Marion, StL.	14	5	.357

YEAR	PLAYER	AB	H	AVG	YEAR	PLAYER	AB	H	AVG
1944					1965				
AL	George McQuinn, StL.	16	7	.438	AL	Zoilo Versalles, Minn.	28	8	.286
NL	Emil Verban, StL.	17	7	.412	AL	Harmon Killebrew, Minn.	21	6	.286
1945					NL	Ron Fairly, LA	29	11	.379
AL	Doc Cramer, Det.	29	11	.379	1966				
NL	Phil Cavarretta, Chi.	26	11	.423	AL	Boog Powell, Balt.	14	5	.357
1946					NL	Lou Johnson, LA	15	4	.267
AL	Rudy York, Bos.	23	6	.261	1967				
NL	Harry Walker, StL.	17	7	.412	AL	Carl Yastrzemski, Bos.	25	10	.400
1947					NL	Lou Brock, StL.	29	12	.414
AL	Tommy Henrich, NY	31	10	.323	1968				
NL	Pee Wee Reese, Brk.	23	7	.304	AL	Norm Cash, Det.	26	10	.385
1948					NL	Lou Brock, StL.	28	13	.464
AL	Larry Doby, Clev.	22	7	.318	1969				
NL	Bob Elliott, Bos.	21	7	.333	AL	Boog Powell, Balt.	19	5	.263
1949					NL	Al Weis, NY	11	5	.455
AL	Tommy Henrich, NY	19	5	.263	1970				
NL	Pee Wee Reese, Brk.	19	6	.316	AL	Paul Blair, Balt.	19	9	.474
1950					NL	Lee May, Cin.	18	7	.389
AL	Gene Woodling, NY	14	6	.429	1971				
NL	Granny Hamner, Phil.	14	6	.429	AL	Brooks Robinson, Balt.	22	7	.318
1951					NL	Roberto Clemente, Pitt.	29	12	.414
AL	Phil Rizzuto, NY	25	8	.320	1972				
NL	Monte Irvin, NY	24	11	.458	AL	Gene Tenace, Oak	23	8	.348
1952					NL	Tony Perez, Cin.	23	10	.435
AL	Gene Woodling, NY	23	8	.348	1973				
NL	Pee Wee Reese, Brk.	29	10	.345	AL	Joe Rudi, Oak.	27	9	.333
NL	Duke Snider, Brk.	29	10	.345	NL	Rusty Staub, NY	26	11	.423
1953					1974				
AL	Billy Martin, NY	24	12	.500	AL	Bert Campaneris, Oak.	17	6	.353
NL	Gil Hodges, Brk.	22	8	.364	NL	Steve Garvey, LA	21	8	.381
1954					1975				
AL	Vic Wertz, Clev.	16	8	.500	AL	Carl Yastrzemski, Bos.	29	9	.310
NL	Alvin Dark, NY	17	7	.412	NL	Pete Rose, Cin.	27	10	.370
1955					1976				
AL	Yogi Berra, NY	24	10	.417	AL	Thurman Munson, NY	17	9	.529
NL	Duke Snider, Brk.	25	8	.320	NL	Johnny Bench, Cin.	15	8	.533
1956					1977				
AL	Yogi Berra, NY	25	9	.360	AL	Reggie Jackson, NY	20	9	.450
NL	Gil Hodges, Brk.	23	7	.304	NL	Steve Garvey, LA	24	9	.375
NL	Duke Snider, Brk.	23	7	.304	1978				
1957					AL	Brian Doyle, NY	16	7	.438
AL	Jerry Coleman, NY	22	8	.364	NL	Bill Russell, LA	26	11	.423
NL	Hank Aaron, Mil.	28	11	.393	1979				
1958					AL	Kiko Garcia, Balt.	20	8	.400
AL	Hank Bauer, NY	31	10	.323	NL	Phil Garner, Pitt.	24	12	.500
NL	Bill Bruton, Mil.	17	7	.412	1980				
1959					AL	Amos Otis, KC	23	11	.478
AL	Ted Kluszewski, Chi.	23	9	.391	NL	Bob Boone, Phil.	17	7	.412
NL	Gil Hodges, LA	23	9	.391	1981				
1960					AL	Lou Piniella, NY	16	7	.438
AL	Mickey Mantle, NY	25	10	.400	NL	Steve Garvey, LA	24	10	.417
NL	Bill Mazeroski, Pitt.	25	8	.320	1982				
1961					AL	Robin Yount, Mil.	29	12	.414
AL	Bobby Richardson, NY	23	9	.319	NL	George Hendrick, StL.	28	9	.321
NL	Wally Post, Cin.	18	6	.333	NL	Lonnie Smith, StL.	28	9	.321
1962					1983				
AL	Tom Tresh, NY	28	9	.321	AL	John Shelby, Balt	9	4	.444
NL	Jose Pagan, SF	19	7	.368	NL	Bo Diaz, Phil.	15	5	.333
1963					1984				
AL	Elston Howard, NY	15	5	.333	AL	Alan Trammell, Det.	20	9	.450
NL	Tommy Davis, LA	15	6	.400	NL	Kurt Bevacqua, SD	17	7	.412
1964					1985				
AL	Bobby Richardson, NY	32	13	.406	AL	George Brett, KC	27	10	.370
NL	Tim McCarver, StL.	23	11	.478	NL	Tito Landrum, StL.	25	9	.360

AR	PLAYER	AB	H	AVG
86				
AL	Marty Barrett, Bos.	30	13	.433
NL	Ray Knight, NY	23	9	.391
87				
AL	Kirby Puckett, Minn.	28	10	.357
NL	Tony Pena, StL.	22	9	.409
88				
AL	Dave Henderson, Oak.	20	6	.300
NL	Mickey Hatcher, LA	19	7	.368
89				
AL	Rickey Henderson, Oak.	19	9	.474
NL	Kevin Mitchell, SF	17	5	.294
90				
AL	Rickey Henderson, Oak.	15	5	.333
NL	Billy Hatcher, Cin.	12	9	.750
91				
AL	Brian Harper, Minn.	21	8	.381
NL	Rafael Belliard, Atl.	16	6	.375
92				
AL	Pat Borders, Tor.	20	9	.450
NL	Otis Nixon, Atl.	27	8	.296
93				
AL	Paul Molitor, Tor.	24	12	.500
NL	Len Dykstra, Phil.	23	8	.348
NL	John Kruk, Phil.	23	8	.348
95				
AL	Albert Belle, Clev.	17	4	.235
NL	Marquis Grissom, Atl.	25	9	.360
96				
NL	Marquis Grissom, Atl.	27	12	.444
AL	Cecil Fielder, NY	23	9	.391
97				
AL	Matt Williams, Clev.	26	10	.385
NL	Darren Daulton, Fla.	18	7	.389
98				
AL	Ricky Ledee, NY	10	6	.600
NL	Tony Gwynn, SD	16	8	.500
99				
AL	Scott Brosius, NY	16	6	.375
NL	Bret Boone, Atl.	13	7	.538
00				
AL	Paul O'Neill, NY	19	9	.474
NL	Todd Zeile, NY	20	8	.400
01				
AL	Alfonso Soriano, NY	25	6	.240
NL	Steve Finley, Ari.	19	7	.368
02				
AL	Troy Glaus, Ana.	26	10	.385
NL	Barry Bonds, SF	17	8	.471
03				
AL	Bernie Williams, NY	25	10	.400
NL	Jeff Conine, Fla.	21	7	.333
NL	Juan Pierre, Fla.	21	7	.333
04				
AL	Bill Mueller, Bos.	14	6	.429
NL	Larry Walker, StL.	14	5	.357
05				
AL	Carl Everett, Chi.	9	4	.444
NL	Lance Berkman, Hou.	13	5	.385
06				
AL	Sean Casey, Det.	17	9	.529
NL	Scott Rolen, StL.	19	8	.421

HITTING SAFELY, EACH GAME

YEAR	PLAYER	AB	H	AVG
1907 - (5 games)				
NL	Wildfire Schulte, Chi.	20	5	.250
1908 - (5 games)				
NL	Wildfire Schulte, Chi.	18	7	.389
1910 - (5 games)				
AL	Eddie Collins, Phil.	21	9	.429
AL	Danny Murphy, Phil.	20	7	.350
1914 - (4 games)				
NL	Johnny Evers, Bos.	16	7	.438
NL	Butch Schmidt, Bos.	17	5	.294
1915 - (5 games)				
AL	Duffy Lewis, Bos	18	8	.444
AL	Harry Hooper, Bos.	20	7	.350
1916 - (5 games)				
AL	Harry Hooper, Bos.	21	7	.333
1917 - (6 games)				
NL	Dave Robertson, NY	22	11	.500
1922 - (5 games)				
AL	Bob Meusel, N. Y.	20	6	.300
AL	Wally Pipp, NY	21	6	.286
NL	Heinie Groh, NY	19	9	.474
NL	Irish Meusel, NY	20	5	.250
1923 - (6 games)				
AL	Aaron Ward, NY	24	10	.417
AL	Babe Ruth, NY	19	7	.368
AL	Wally Schang, NY	22	7	.318
1924 - (7 games)				
AL	Bucky Harris, Wash.	33	11	.333
NL	George Kelly, NY	31	9	.290
1925 - (7 games)				
AL	Joe Harris, Wash.	25	11	.440
1926 - (7 games)				
AL	Earle Combs, NY	28	10	.357
NL	Jim Bottomley, StL.	29	10	.345
1927 - (4 games)				
AL	Mark Koenig, NY	18	9	.500
NL	Lloyd Waner, Pitt.	15	6	.400
NL	Clyde Barnhart, Pitt.	16	5	.313
1928 - (4 games)				
AL	Babe Ruth, NY	16	10	.625
AL	Lou Gehrig, NY	11	6	.545
1929 - (5 games)				
AL	Bing Miller, Phil.	19	7	.368
NL	Riggs Stephenson, Chi.	19	6	.316
1930 - (6 games)				
AL	Jimmie Foxx, Phil.	21	7	.333
1932 - (4 games)				
AL	Lou Gehrig, NY	17	9	.529
AL	Bill Dickey, NY	16	7	.438
AL	Babe Ruth, NY	15	5	.333
NL	Riggs Stephenson, Chi.	18	8	.444
NL	Gabby Hartnett, Chi.	16	5	.313
1933 - (5 games)				
NL	Kiddo Davis, NY	19	7	.368
1934 - (7 games)				
AL	Charlie Gehringer, Det.	29	11	.379
NL	Pepper Martin, StL.	31	11	.355
1935 - (6 games)				
AL	Pete Fox, Det.	26	10	.385
1936 - (6 games)				
AL	George Selkirk, NY	24	8	.333
NL	Dick Bartell, NY	21	8	.381

YEAR	PLAYER	AB	H	AVG
1937 - (5 games)				
AL	Tony Lazzeri, NY	15	6	.400
NL	Joe Moore, NY	23	9	.391
1938 - (4 games)				
AL	Joe Gordon, NY	15	6	.400
AL	Lou Gehrig, NY	14	4	.286
NL	Stan Hack, Chi.	17	8	.471
NL	Phil Cavarretta, Chi.	13	6	.462
1939 - (4 games)				
AL	Charlie Keller, NY	16	7	.438
AL	Joe DiMaggio, NY	16	5	.313
AL	Bill Dickey, NY	15	4	.267
1941 - (5 games)				
AL	Joe Gordon, NY	14	7	.500
AL	Johnny Sturm, NY	21	6	.286
1943 - (5 games)				
NL	Walker Cooper, StL.	17	5	.294
1944 - (6 games)				
NL	Ray Sanders, StL.	21	6	.286
1947 - (7 games)				
AL	Tommy Henrich, NY	31	10	.323
1950 - (4 games)				
AL	Gene Woodling, NY	14	6	.429
1951 - (6 games)				
AL	Phil Rizzuto, NY	25	8	.320
NL	Alvin Dark, NY	24	10	.417
1953 - (6 games)				
AL	Billy Martin, NY	24	12	.500
1954 - (4 games)				
AL	Vic Wertz, Clev.	16	8	.500
NL	Alvin Dark, NY	17	7	.412
NL	Hank Thompson, NY	11	4	.364
1955 - (7 games)				
AL	Yogi Berra, NY	24	10	.417
1956 - (7 games)				
AL	Billy Martin, NY	27	8	.296
AL	Hank Bauer, NY	32	9	.281
1957 - (7 games)				
AL	Hank Bauer, NY	31	8	.258
NL	Hank Aaron, Mil.	28	11	.393
1960 - (7 games)				
NL	Roberto Clemente, Pitt.	29	9	.310
1961 - (5 games)				
AL	Bobby Richardson, NY	23	9	.391
1964 - (7 games)				
AL	Bobby Richardson, NY	32	13	.406
NL	Tim McCarver, StL.	23	11	.478
1965 - (7 games)				
NL	Ron Fairly, LA	29	11	.379
1966 - (4 games)				
AL	Boog Powell, Balt.	14	5	.357
1968 - (7 games)				
NL	Lou Brock, StL.	28	13	.464
1970 - (5 games)				
AL	Brooks Robinson, Balt.	21	9	.429
NL	Lee May, Cin.	18	7	.389
1971 - (7 games)				
NL	Roberto Clemente, Pitt.	29	12	.414
1972 - (7 games)				
NL	Tony Perez, Cin.	23	10	.435
1974 - (5 games)				
NL	Steve Garvey, LA	21	8	.381
1975 - (7 games)				
AL	Denny Doyle, Bos.	30	8	.267

YEAR	PLAYER	AB	H	AVG
1976 - (4 games)				
AL	Thurman Munson, NY	17	9	.529
AL	Chris Chambliss, NY	16	5	.313
NL	Johnny Bench, Cin.	15	8	.533
NL	George Foster, Cin.	14	6	.429
NL	Dave Concepcion, Cin.	14	5	.357
NL	Joe Morgan, Cin.	15	5	.333
1977 - (6 games)				
AL	Thurman Munson, NY	25	8	.320
1978 - (6 games)				
AL	Bucky Dent, NY	24	10	.417
AL	Reggie Jackson, NY	23	9	.391
AL	Roy White, NY	24	8	.333
AL	Lou Piniella, NY	25	7	.350
NL	Bill Russell, LA	26	11	.423
1979 - (7 games)				
NL	Phil Garner, Pitt.	24	12	.500
1980 - (6 games)				
AL	George Brett, KC	24	9	.375
NL	Mike Schmidt, Phil.	21	8	.381
NL	Larry Bowa, Phil.	24	9	.375
1981 - (6 games)				
NL	Steve Garvey, LA	24	10	.417
1984 - (5 games)				
NL	Kurt Bevacqua, SD	17	7	.412
1985 - (7 games)				
AL	Willie Wilson, KC	30	11	.367
NL	Tito Landrum, StL.	25	9	.360
1986 - (7 games)				
AL	Marty Barrett, Bos.	30	13	.433
1987 - (7 games)				
AL	Dan Gladden, Minn.	31	9	.290
1988 - (5 games)				
NL	Mickey Hatcher, LA	19	6	.368
NL	Steve Sax, LA	20	6	.300
1989 - (4 games)				
AL	Rickey Henderson, Oak.	19	9	.474
AL	Carney Lansford, Oak.	16	7	.438
AL	Terry Steinbach, Oak.	16	4	.250
NL	Kevin Mitchell, SF	17	5	.294
1990 - (4 games)				
NL	Chris Sabo, Cin.	16	9	.563
NL	Joe Oliver, Cin.	18	6	.333
1992 - (6 games)				
AL	Pat Borders, Tor.	20	9	.450
1993 - (6 games)				
AL	Paul Molitor, Tor.	24	12	.500
AL	Roberto Alomar, Tor.	25	12	.480
1995 - (6 games)				
NL	Marquis Grissom, Atl.	25	9	.350
1996 - (6 games)				
NL	Marquis Grissom, Atl.	27	12	.444
1998 - (4 games)				
AL	Scott Brosius, NY	17	8	.471
AL	Chuck Knoblauch, NY	16	6	.375
AL	Derek Jeter, NY	17	6	.353
NL	Tony Gwynn, SD	16	8	.500
1999 - (4 games)				
AL	Derek Jeter, NY	17	6	.353
NL	Bret Boone, Atl.	13	7	.538
2000 - (5 games)				
AL	Derek Jeter, NY	22	9	.409
NL	Jay Payton, NY	21	7	.333
NL	Mike Piazza, NY	22	6	.273

YEAR	PLAYER	AB	H	AVG
2002 - (7 games)				
AL	Garret Anderson, Ana.	32	9	.281
NL	J.T. Snow, SF	27	11	.407
2003 - (6 games)				
AL	Bernie Williams, NY	25	10	.400
2004 - (4 games)				
AL	Bill Mueller, Bos.	14	6	.429
AL	Manny Ramirez, Bos.	17	7	.412
AL	Johnny Damon, Bos.	21	6	.286
2005 - (4 games)				
AL	Jermaine Dye, Chi.	16	7	.438
AL	Joe Crede, Chi.	17	5	.294
AL	Aaron Rowand, Chi.	17	5	.294
AL	Scott Podsednik, Chi.	21	6	.286
AL	A.J. Pierzynski, Chi.	15	4	.267
2006 - (5 games)				
NL	Scott Rolen, StL.	19	8	.421
NL	Yadier Molina, StL.	17	7	.412

1903 [3]
AL: BOSTON - 2
    Patsy Dougherty - lf (2)
NL: PITTSBURGH - 1
    Jimmy Sebring - rf

1904 No Series

1905 [0]
AL: PHILADELPHIA - 0
NL: NEW YORK - 0

1906 [0]
AL: CHICAGO - 0
NL: CHICAGO - 0

1907 [0]
AL: DETROIT - 0
NL: CHICAGO - 0

1908 [1]
AL: DETROIT - 0
NL: CHICAGO - 1
    Joe Tinker - ss

1909 [4]
AL: DETROIT - 2
    Sam Crawford - cf
    Davy Jones - lf
NL: PITTSBURGH - 2
    Fred Clarke - lf (2)

1910 [1]
AL: PHILADELPHIA - 1
    Danny Murphy - rf
NL: CHICAGO - 0

1911 [3]
AL: PHILADELPHIA - 3
    Frank Baker - 3b (2)
    Rube Oldring - cf
NL: NEW YORK - 0

1912 [2]
AL: BOSTON - 1
    Larry Gardner - 3b
NL: NEW YORK - 1
    Larry Doyle - 2b

1913 [3]
AL: PHILADELPHIA - 2
    Frank Baker - 3b
    Wally Schang - c
NL: NEW YORK - 1
    Fred Merkle - 1b

1914 [1]
AL: PHILADELPHIA - 0
NL: BOSTON - 1
    Hank Gowdy - c

1915 [4]
AL: BOSTON - 3
    Harry Hooper - rf (2)
    Duffy Lewis - lf
NL: PHILADELPHIA - 1
    Fred Luderus - 1b

1916 [3]
AL: BOSTON - 2
    Larry Gardner - 3b (2)
NL: BROOKLYN - 1
    Hy Myers - cf

1917 [3]
AL: CHICAGO - 1
    Happy Felsch - cf
NL: NEW YORK - 2
    Benny Kauff - cf (2)

1918 [0]
AL: BOSTON - 0
NL: CHICAGO - 0

1919 [1]
AL: CHICAGO - 1
    Joe Jackson - lf
NL: CINCINNATI - 0

1920 [2]
AL: CLEVELAND - 2
    Jim Bagby - p
    Elmer Smith - rf
NL: BROOKLYN - 0

1921 [4]
AL: NEW YORK - 2
    Chick Fewster - lf
    Babe Ruth - lf
NL: NEW YORK - 2
    Irish Meusel - lf
    Frank Snyder - c

1922 [3]
AL: NEW YORK - 2
    Aaron Ward - 2b (2)
NL: NEW YORK - 1
    Irish Meusel - lf

1923 [10]
AL: NEW YORK - 5
    Babe Ruth - rf (3)
    Joe Dugan - 3b
    Aaron Ward - 2b
NL: NEW YORK - 5
    Casey Stengel - cf (2)
    Irish Meusel - lf
    Frank Snyder - c
    Ross Youngs - rf

1924 [9]
AL: WASHINGTON - 5
    Goose Goslin - lf (3)
    Bucky Harris - 2b (2)
NL: NEW YORK - 4
    Jack Bentley - p
    George Kelly - cf
    Rosy Ryan - p
    Bill Terry - 1b

1925 [12]
AL: WASHINGTON - 8
    Goose Goslin - lf (3)
    Joe Harris - rf (3)
    Joe Judge - 1b
    Roger Peckinpaugh - ss
NL: PITTSBURGH - 4
    Kiki Cuyler - rf
    Eddie Moore - 2b
    Pie Traynor - 3b
    Glenn Wright - ss

1926 [8]
AL: NEW YORK - 4
    Babe Ruth - lf (3), rf (1)
NL: ST. LOUIS - 4
    Les Bell - 3b
    Jesse Haines - p
    Billy Southworth - rf
    Tommy Thevenow - ss

1927 [2]
AL: NEW YORK - 2
    Babe Ruth - rf (2)
NL: PITTSBURGH - 0

1928 [10]
AL: NEW YORK - 9
    Lou Gehrig - 1b (4)
    Babe Ruth - lf (3)
    Cedric Durst - cf
    Bob Meusel - lf
NL: ST. LOUIS - 1
    Jim Bottomley - 1b

1929 [7]
AL: PHILADELPHIA - 6
    Jimmie Foxx - 1b (2)
    Mule Haas - cf (2)
    Al Simmons - lf (2)
NL: CHICAGO - 1
    Charlie Grimm - 1b

1930 [8]
AL: PHILADELPHIA - 6
    Mickey Cochrane - c (2)
    Al Simmons - lf (1), cf (1)
    Jimmy Dykes - 3b
    Jimmie Foxx - 1b
NL: ST. LOUIS - 2
    Taylor Douthit - cf
    George Watkins - rf

1931 [5]
AL: PHILADELPHIA - 3
    Al Simmons - lf (2)
    Jimmie Foxx - 1b
NL: ST. LOUIS - 2
    Pepper Martin - cf
    George Watkins - rf

1932 [11]
AL: NEW YORK - 8
    Lou Gehrig - 1b (3)
    Tony Lazzeri - 2b (2)
    Babe Ruth - lf (2)
    Earle Combs - cf
NL: CHICAGO - 3
    Kiki Cuyler - rf
    Frank Demaree - cf
    Gabby Hartnett - c

1933 [5]
AL: WASHINGTON - 2
    Goose Goslin - rf
    Fred Schulte - cf
NL: NEW YORK - 3
    Mel Ott - rf (2)
    Bill Terry - 1b

1934 [4]
AL: DETROIT - 2
    Charlie Gehringer - 2b
    Hank Greenberg - 1b
NL: ST. LOUIS - 2
    Bill DeLancey - c
    Joe Medwick - lf

1935 [6]
AL: DETROIT - 1
    Hank Greenberg - 1b
NL: CHICAGO - 5
    Frank Demaree - rf (2)
    Gabby Hartnett - c
    Billy Herman - 2b
    Chuck Klein - cf

1936 [11]
AL: NEW YORK - 7
Lou Gehrig - 1b (2)
George Selkirk - rf (2)
Bill Dickey - c
Tony Lazzeri - 2b
Jake Powell - lf
NL: NEW YORK - 4
Dick Bartell - ss
Joe Moore - lf
Mel Ott - rf
Jimmy Ripple - cf

1937 [5]
AL: NEW YORK - 4
Joe DiMaggio - cf
Lou Gehrig - 1b
Myril Hoag - lf
Tony Lazzeri - 2b
NL: NEW YORK - 1
Mel Ott - 3b

1938 [7]
AL: NEW YORK - 5
Frankie Crosetti - ss
Bill Dickey - c
Joe DiMaggio - cf
Joe Gordon - 2b
Tommy Henrich - rf
NL: CHICAGO - 2
Joe Marty - cf
Ken O'Dea - c

1939 [7]
AL: NEW YORK - 7
Charlie Keller - rf (3)
Bill Dickey - c (2)
Babe Dahlgren - 1b
Joe DiMaggio - cf
NL: CINCINNATI - 0

1940 [6]
AL: DETROIT - 4
Bruce Campbell - rf
Hank Greenberg - lf
Pinky Higgins - 3b
Rudy York - 1b
NL: CINCINNATI - 2
Jimmy Ripple - lf
Bucky Walters - p

1941 [3]
AL: NEW YORK - 2
Joe Gordon - 2b
Tommy Henrich - rf
NL: BROOKLYN - 1
Pete Reiser - cf

1942 [5]
AL: NEW YORK - 3
Charlie Keller - lf (2)
Phil Rizzuto - ss
NL: ST. LOUIS - 2
Whitey Kurowski - 3b
Enos Slaughter - rf

1943 [4]
AL: NEW YORK - 2
Bill Dickey - c
Joe Gordon - 2b
NL: ST. LOUIS - 2
Marty Marion - ss
Ray Sanders - 1b

1944 [4]
AL: ST. LOUIS - 1
George McQuinn - 1b
NL: ST. LOUIS - 3
Danny Litwhiler - lf
Stan Musial - rf
Ray Sanders - 1b

1945 [3]
AL: DETROIT - 2
Hank Greenberg - lf (2)
NL: CHICAGO - 1
Phil Cavarretta - 1b

1946 [5]
AL: BOSTON - 4
Rudy York - 1b (2)
Leon Culberson - rf
Bobby Doerr - 2b
NL: ST. LOUIS - 1
Enos Slaughter - rf

1947 [5]
AL: NEW YORK - 4
Joe DiMaggio - cf (2)
Yogi Berra - ph
Tommy Henrich - rf
NL: BROOKLYN - 1
Dixie Walker - rf

1948 [8]
AL: CLEVELAND - 4
Larry Doby - cf
Joe Gordon - 2b
Jim Hegan - c
Dale Mitchell - lf
NL: BOSTON - 4
Bob Elliott - 3b (2)
Marv Rickert - lf
Bill Salkeld - c

1949 [6]
AL: NEW YORK - 2
Joe DiMaggio - cf
Tommy Henrich - 1b
NL: BROOKLYN - 4
Roy Campanella - c
Gil Hodges - 1b
Luis Olmo - lf
Pee Wee Reese - ss

1950 [2]
AL: NEW YORK - 2
Yogi Berra - c
Joe DiMaggio - cf
NL: PHILADELPHIA - 0

1951 [7]
AL: NEW YORK - 5
Joe Collins - 1b
Joe DiMaggio - cf
Gil McDougald - 2b
Phil Rizzuto - ss
Gene Woodling - lf
NL: NEW YORK - 2
Alvin Dark - ss
Whitey Lockman - 1b

1952 [16]
AL: NEW YORK - 10
Johnny Mize - 1b (2), ph (1)
Yogi Berra - c (2)
Mickey Mantle - cf (2)
Billy Martin - 2b
Gil McDougald - 3b
Gene Woodling - lf
NL: BROOKLYN - 6
Duke Snider - cf (4)
Pee Wee Reese - ss
Jackie Robinson - 2b

1953 [17]
AL: NEW YORK - 9
Mickey Mantle - cf (2)
Billy Martin - 2b (2)
Gil McDougald - 3b (2)
Yogi Berra - c
Joe Collins - 1b
Gene Woodling - lf
NL: BROOKLYN - 8
Jim Gilliam - 2b (2)
Roy Campanella - c
Billy Cox - 3b
Carl Furillo - rf
Gil Hodges - 1b
George Shuba - ph
Duke Snider - cf

1954 [5]
AL: CLEVELAND - 3
Hank Majeski - ph
Al Smith - lf
Vic Wertz - 1b
NL: NEW YORK - 2
Dusty Rhodes - ph (1), lf (1)

1955 [17]
AL: NEW YORK - 8
Joe Collins - 1b (2)
Yogi Berra - c
Bob Cerv - ph
Elston Howard - lf
Mickey Mantle - cf
Gil McDougald - 3b
Bill Skowron - 1b
NL: BROOKLYN - 9
Duke Snider - cf (4)
Roy Campanella - c (2)
Sandy Amoros - lf
Carl Furillo - rf
Gil Hodges - 1b

1956 [15]
AL: NEW YORK - 12
Yogi Berra - c (3)
Mickey Mantle - cf (3)
Billy Martin - 2b (2)
Hank Bauer - rf
Elston Howard - lf
Bill Skowron - 1b
Enos Slaughter - lf
NL: BROOKLYN - 3
Gil Hodges - 1b
Jackie Robinson - 3b
Duke Snider - cf

1957 [15]
- AL: NEW YORK - 7
  - Hank Bauer - rf (2)
  - Tony Kubek - lf (2)
  - Yogi Berra - c
  - Elston Howard - 1b
  - Mickey Mantle - cf
- NL: MILWAUKEE - 8
  - Hank Aaron - cf (3)
  - Frank Torre - 1b (2)
  - Del Crandall - c
  - Johnny Logan - ss
  - Eddie Mathews - 3b

1958 [13]
- AL: NEW YORK - 10
  - Hank Bauer - rf (4)
  - Mickey Mantle - cf (2)
  - Gil McDougald - 2b (2)
  - Bill Skowron - 1b (2)
- NL: MILWAUKEE - 3
  - Bill Bruton - cf
  - Lew Burdette - p
  - Del Crandall - c

1959 [11]
- AL: CHICAGO - 4
  - Ted Kluszewski - 1b (3)
  - Sherm Lollar - c
- NL: LOS ANGELES - 7
  - Chuck Essegian - ph (2)
  - Charlie Neal - 2b (2)
  - Gil Hodges - 1b
  - Wally Moon - lf
  - Duke Snider - cf

1960 [14]
- AL: NEW YORK - 10
  - Mickey Mantle - cf (3)
  - Roger Maris - rf (2)
  - Bill Skowron - 1b (2)
  - Yogi Berra - lf
  - Elston Howard - ph
  - Bobby Richardson - 2b
- NL: PITTSBURGH - 4
  - Bill Mazeroski - 2b (2)
  - Rocky Nelson - 1b
  - Hal W. Smith - c

1961 [10]
- AL: NEW YORK - 7
  - Johnny Blanchard -ph (1),rf (1)
  - Yogi Berra - lf
  - Elston Howard - c
  - Hector Lopez - lf
  - Roger Maris - rf
  - Bill Skowron - 1b
- NL: CINCINNATI - 3
  - Gordy Coleman - 1b
  - Wally Post - lf
  - Frank Robinson - rf

1962 [8]
- AL: NEW YORK - 3
  - Clete Boyer - 3b
  - Roger Maris - rf
  - Tom Tresh - lf
- NL: SAN FRANCISCO - 5
  - Ed Bailey - c
  - Tom Haller - c
  - Chuck Hiller - 2b
  - Willie McCovey - 1b
  - Jose Pagan - ss

1963 [5]
- AL: NEW YORK - 2
  - Mickey Mantle - cf
  - Tom Tresh - lf
- NL: LOS ANGELES - 3
  - Frank Howard - rf
  - Johnny Roseboro - c
  - Bill Skowron - 1b

1964 [15]
- AL: NEW YORK - 10
  - Mickey Mantle - rf (3)
  - Phil Linz - ss (2)
  - Tom Tresh - lf (2)
  - Clete Boyer - 3b
  - Roger Maris - cf
  - Joe Pepitone - 1b
- NL: ST. LOUIS - 5
  - Ken Boyer - 3b (2)
  - Lou Brock - lf
  - Tim McCarver - c
  - Mike Shannon - rf

1965 [11]
- AL: MINNESOTA - 6
  - Bob Allison - lf
  - Mudcat Grant - p
  - Harmon Killebrew - 3b
  - Don Mincher - 1b
  - Tony Oliva - rf
  - Zoilo Versalles - ss
- NL: LOS ANGELES - 5
  - Ron Fairly - rf (2)
  - Lou Johnson - lf (2)
  - Wes Parker - 1b

1966 [5]
- AL: BALTIMORE - 4
  - Frank Robinson - rf (2)
  - Paul Blair - cf
  - Brooks Robinson - 3b
- NL: LOS ANGELES - 1
  - Jim Lefebvre - 2b

1967 [13]
- AL: BOSTON - 8
  - Carl Yastrzemski - lf (3)
  - Rico Petrocelli - ss (2)
  - Reggie Smith - cf (2)
  - Jose Santiago - p
- NL: ST. LOUIS - 5
  - Lou Brock - lf
  - Bob Gibson - p
  - Julian Javier - 2b
  - Roger Maris - rf
  - Mike Shannon - 3b

1968 [15]
- AL: DETROIT - 8
  - AL Kaline - rf (2)
  - Jim Northrup - cf (2)
  - Norm Cash - 1b
  - Willie Horton - lf
  - Mickey Lolich - p
  - Dick McAuliffe - 2b
- NL: ST. LOUIS - 7
  - Lou Brock - lf (2)
  - Orlando Cepeda - 1b (2)
  - Bob Gibson - p
  - Tim McCarver - c
  - Mike Shannon - 3b

1969 [9]
- AL: BALTIMORE - 3
  - Don Buford - lf
  - Dave McNally - p
  - Frank Robinson - rf
- NL: NEW YORK - 6
  - Donn Clendenon - 1b (3)
  - Tommie Agee - cf
  - Ed Kranepool - 1b
  - AL Weis - 2b

1970 [15]
- AL: BALTIMORE - 10
  - Boog Powell - 1b (2)
  - Brooks Robinson - 3b (2)
  - Frank Robinson - rf (2)
  - Don Buford - lf
  - Ellie Hendricks - c
  - Dave McNally - p
  - Merv Rettenmund - lf
- NL: CINCINNATI - 5
  - Lee May - 1b (2)
  - Johnny Bench - c
  - Pete Rose - rf
  - Bobby Tolan - cf

1971 [10]
- AL: BALTIMORE - 5
  - Don Buford - lf (2)
  - Frank Robinson - rf (2)
  - Merv Rettenmund - cf
- NL: PITTSBURGH - 5
  - Roberto Clemente - rf (2)
  - Bob Robertson - 1b (2)
  - Richie Hebner - 3b

1972 [8]
- AL: OAKLAND - 5
  - Gene Tenace - c (4)
  - Joe Rudi - lf
- NL: CINCINNATI - 3
  - Johnny Bench - c
  - Denis Menke - 3b
  - Pete Rose - lf

1973 [6]
- AL: OAKLAND - 2
  - Bert Campaneris - ss
  - Reggie Jackson - cf
- NL: NEW YORK - 4
  - Wayne Garrett - 3b (2)
  - Cleon Jones - lf
  - Rusty Staub - rf

1974 [8]
- AL: OAKLAND - 4
  - Ray Fosse - c
  - Ken Holtzman - p
  - Reggie Jackson - 1b
  - Joe Rudi - 1b
- NL: LOS ANGELES - 4
  - Bill Buckner - lf
  - Willie Crawford - rf
  - Joe Ferguson - rf
  - Jimmy Wynn - cf

1975 [13]
AL: BOSTON - 6
  Bernie Carbo - ph (2)
  Carlton Fisk - c (2)
  Dwight Evans - rf
  Fred Lynn - cf
NL: CINCINNATI - 7
  Tony Perez - 1b (3)
  Cesar Geronimo - cf (2)
  Johnny Bench - c
  Dave Concepcion - ss

1976 [5]
AL: NEW YORK - 1
  Jim Mason - ss
NL: CINCINNATI - 4
  Johnny Bench - c (2)
  Dan Driessen - dh
  Joe Morgan - 2b

1977 [17]
AL: NEW YORK - 8
  Reggie Jackson - rf (5)
  Chris Chambliss - 1b
  Thurman Munson - c
  Willie Randolph - 2b
NL: LOS ANGELES - 9
  Reggie Smith - rf (3)
  Steve Yeager - c (2)
  Dusty Baker - lf
  Ron Cey - 3b
  Steve Garvey - 1b
  Davey Lopes - 2b

1978 [9]
AL: NEW YORK - 3
  Reggie Jackson - dh (2)
  Roy White - lf
NL: LOS ANGELES - 6
  Davey Lopes - 2b (3)
  Dusty Baker - lf
  Ron Cey - 3b
  Reggie Smith - rf

1979 [7]
AL: BALTIMORE - 4
  Benny Ayala - lf
  Rich Dauer - 2b
  Doug DeCinces - 3b
  Eddie Murray - 1b
NL: PITTSBURGH - 3
  Willie Stargell - 1b (3)

1980 [11]
AL: KANSAS CITY - 8
  Willie Aikens - 1b (4)
  Amos Otis - cf (3)
  George Brett - 3b
NL: PHILADELPHIA - 3
  Mike Schmidt - 3b (2)
  Bake McBride - rf

1981 [12]
AL: NEW YORK - 6
  Willie Randolph - 2b (2)
  Bob Watson - 1b (2)
  Rick Cerone - c
  Reggie Jackson - rf
NL: LOS ANGELES - 6
  Pedro Guerrero - rf (2)
  Steve Yeager - c (2)
  Ron Cey - 3b
  Jay Johnstone - ph

1982 [9]
AL: MILWAUKEE - 5
  Ted Simmons - c (2)
  Cecil Cooper - 1b
  Ben Oglivie - lf
  Robin Yount - ss
NL: ST. LOUIS - 4
  Willie McGee - cf (2)
  Keith Hernandez - 1b
  Darrell Porter - c

1983 [10]
AL: BALTIMORE - 6
  Eddie Murray - 1b (2)
  Rick Dempsey - c
  Jim Dwyer - rf
  Dan Ford - rf
  John Lowenstein - lf
NL: PHILADELPHIA - 4
  Joe Morgan - 2b (2)
  Garry Maddox - cf
  Gary Matthews - lf

1984 [10]
AL: DETROIT - 7
  Kirk Gibson - rf (2)
  Alan Trammell - ss (2)
  Marty Castillo - 3b
  Larry Herndon - lf
  Lance Parrish - c
NL: SAN DIEGO - 3
  Kurt Bevacqua - dh (2)
  Terry Kennedy - c

1985 [4]
AL: KANSAS CITY - 2
  Darryl Motley - rf
  Frank White - 2b
NL: ST. LOUIS - 2
  Tito Landrum - lf
  Willie McGee - cf

1986 [12]
AL: BOSTON - 5
  Dwight Evans - rf (2)
  Dave Henderson - cf (2)
  Rich Gedman - c
NL: NEW YORK - 7
  Gary Carter - c (2)
  Len Dykstra - cf (2)
  Ray Knight - 3b
  Darryl Strawberry - rf
  Tim Teufel - 2b

1987 [9]
AL: MINNESOTA - 7
  Don Baylor - dh
  Gary Gaetti - 3b
  Greg Gagne - ss
  Dan Gladden - lf
  Kent Hrbek - 1b
  Tim Laudner - c
  Steve Lombardozzi - 2b
NL: ST. LOUIS - 2
  Tommy Herr - 2b
  Tom Lawless - 3b

1988 [7]
AL: OAKLAND - 2
  Jose Canseco - rf
  Mark McGwire - 1b
NL: LOS ANGELES - 5
  Mickey Hatcher - lf (2)
  Mike Davis - dh
  Kirk Gibson - ph
  Mike Marshall - rf

1989 [13]
AL: OAKLAND - 9
  Dave Henderson - cf (2)
  Jose Canseco - rf
  Rickey Henderson - lf
  Carney Lansford - 3b
  Dave Parker - dh
  Tony Phillips - 2b
  Terry Steinbach - c
  Walt Weiss - ss
NL: SAN FRANCISCO - 4
  Bill Bathe - ph
  Greg Litton - 2b
  Kevin Mitchell - lf
  Matt Williams - ss

1990 [6]
AL: OAKLAND - 3
  Harold Baines - dh
  Jose Canseco - rf
  Rickey Henderson - lf
NL: CINCINNATI - 3
  Chris Sabo - 3b (2)
  Eric Davis - lf

1991 [16]
AL: MINNESOTA - 8
  Chili Davis - dh (1), ph (1)
  Kirby Puckett - cf (2)
  Greg Gagne - ss
  Kent Hrbek - 1b
  Scott Leius - 3b
  Mike Pagliarulo - 3b
NL: ATLANTA - 8
  Lonnie Smith - lf (3)
  David Justice - rf (2)
  Terry Pendleton - 3b (2)
  Brian Hunter - 1b

1992 [9]
AL: TORONTO - 6
  Joe Carter - 1b (1), rf (1)
  Pat Borders - c
  Kelly Gruber - 3b
  Candy Maldonado - lf
  Ed Sprague - ph
NL: ATLANTA - 3
  Damon Berryhill - c
  David Justice - rf
  Lonnie Smith - dh

1993 [13]
AL: TORONTO - 6
  Joe Carter - rf (2)
  Paul Molitor - 1b (1), dh (1)
  John Olerud - 1b
  Devon White - cf
NL: PHILADELPHIA - 7
  Len Dykstra - cf (4)
  Darren Daulton - c
  Jim Eisenreich - rf
  Milt Thompson - lf

1994 No Series

1995 [13]
AL: CLEVELAND - 5
    Albert Belle - 1f (2)
    Eddie Murray - 1b
    Manny Ramirez - rf
    Jim Thome - 3b
NL: ATLANTA - 8
    Ryan Klesko - dh (3)
    Fred McGriff - 1b (2)
    David Justice - rf
    Javier Lopez - c
    Luis Polonia - lf

1996 [6]
AL: NEW YORK - 2
    Jim Leyritz - c
    Bernie Williams - cf
NL: ATLANTA - 4
    Andruw Jones - lf (2)
    Fred McGriff - 1b (2)

1997 [15]
AL: CLEVELAND - 7
    Sandy Alomar, Jr. - c (2)
    Manny Ramirez - rf (2)
    Jim Thome - 1b (2)
    Matt Williams - 3b
NL: FLORIDA - 8
    Moises Alou - lf (3)
    Bobby Bonilla - 3b
    Darren Daulton - 1b
    Jim Eisenreich - dh
    Charles Johnson - c
    Gary Sheffield - rf

1998 [9]
AL: NEW YORK - 6
    Scott Brosius - 3b (2)
    Chuck Knoblauch - 2b
    Tino Martinez - 1b
    Jorge Posada - c
    Bernie Williams - cf
NL: SAN DIEGO - 3
    Greg Vaughn - lf (2)
    Tony Gwynn - rf

1999 [6]
AL: NEW YORK - 5
    Chad Curtis - lf (2)
    Chuck Knoblauch - 2b
    Jim Leyritz - ph/dh
    Tino Martinez - 1b
NL: ATLANTA - 1
    Chipper Jones - 3b

2000 [8]
AL: NEW YORK - 4
    Derek Jeter - ss (2)
    Scott Brosius - 3b
    Bernie Williams - cf
NL: NEW YORK - 4
    Mike Piazza - c (2)
    Jay Payton - cf
    Robin Ventura - 3b

2001 [12]
AL: NEW YORK - 6
    Scott Brosius - 3b
    Derek Jeter - ss
    Tino Martinez - 1b
    Jorge Posada - c
    Alfonso Soriano - 2b
    Shane Spencer - lf
NL: ARIZONA - 6
    Rod Barajas - c
    Craig Counsell - 2b
    Steve Finley - cf
    Luis Gonzalez - lf
    Mark Grace - 1b
    Matt Williams - 3b

2002 [21]
AL: ANAHEIM - 7
    Troy Glaus - 3b (3)
    Tim Salmon - rf (2)
    Darin Erstad - cf
    Scott Spiezio - 1b
NL: SAN FRANCISCO - 14
    Barry Bonds - lf (4)
    Jeff Kent - 2b (3)
    Rich Aurilia - ss (2)
    Reggie Sanders - rf (2)
    David Bell - 3b
    Shawon Dunston - dh
    J.T. Snow - 1b

2003 [8]
AL: NEW YORK - 6
    Bernie Williams - cf (2)
    Aaron Boone - 3b
    Jason Giambi - ph
    Hideki Matsui - lf
    Alfonso Soriano - 2b
NL: FLORIDA - 2
    Miguel Cabrera - rf
    Alex Gonzalez - ss

2004 [6]
AL: BOSTON - 4
    Mark Bellhorn - 2b
    Johnny Damon - cf
    David Ortiz - dh
    Manny Ramirez - lf
NL: ST. LOUIS - 2
    Larry Walker - rf (2)

2005 [9]
AL: CHICAGO - 6
    Joe Crede - 3b (2)
    Geoff Blum - 2b
    Jermaine Dye - rf
    Paul Konerko - 1b
    Scott Podsednik - lf
NL: HOUSTON - 3
    Morgan Ensberg - 3b
    Mike Lamb - 1b
    Jason Lane - rf

2006 [6]
AL: DETROIT - 4
    Sean Casey - 1b (2)
    Craig Monroe - lf (2)
NL: ST. LOUIS - 2
    Albert Pujols - 1b
    Scott Rolen - 3b

0

05	Oct. 13	NL:	NY vs Phil. (Joe McGinnity)
06	Oct. 12	NL:	Chi. vs Chi. (Three Finger Brown)
14	Oct. 10	NL:	Bos. vs Phil. (Bill James)
18	Sept. 5	AL:	Bos. vs Chi. (Babe Ruth)
20	Oct. 11	AL:	Clev. vs Brk. (Duster Mails)
21	Oct. 13	NL:	NY vs NY (Art Nehf)
23	Oct. 12	NL:	NY vs NY (Art Nehf)
48	Oct. 6	NL:	Bos. vs Clev. (Johnny Sain)
49	Oct. 5	AL:	NY vs Brk. (Allie Reynolds)
49	Oct. 6	NL:	Brk. vs NY (Preacher Roe)
50	Oct. 4	AL:	NY vs Phil. (Vic Raschi)
56	Oct. 9	NL:	Brk. vs NY (Clem Labine, 10 inn)
57	Oct. 7	NL:	Mil. vs NY (Lew Burdette)
59	Oct. 6	AL:	Chi. vs LA (Bob Shaw, Billy Pierce & Dick Donovan)
62	Oct. 16	AL:	NY vs SF (Ralph Terry)
63	Oct. 5	NL:	LA vs NY (Don Drysdale)
66	Oct. 8	AL:	Balt. vs LA (Wally Bunker)
66	Oct. 9	AL:	Balt. vs LA (Dave McNally)
72	Oct. 18	NL:	Cin. vs Oak. (Jack Billingham & Clay Carroll)
86	Oct. 18	AL:	Bos. vs NY (Bruce Hurst & Calvin Schiraldi)
91	Oct. 27	AL:	Minn. vs Atl. (Jack Morris)
95	Oct. 28	NL:	Atl. vs Clev. (Tom Glavine & Mark Wohlers)
96	Oct. 24	AL:	NY vs Atl. (Andy Pettitte & John Wetteland)
05	Oct. 26	AL:	Chi. vs Hou. (Freddy Garcia, Cliff Politte, Neal Cotts & Bobby Jenks)

0

05	Oct. 14	NL:	NY vs Phil. (Christy Mathewson)
07	Oct. 12	NL:	Chi. vs Det. (Three Finger Brown)
08	Oct. 14	NL:	Chi. vs Det. (Orval Overall)
17	Oct. 10	NL:	NY vs Chi. (Rube Benton)
19	Oct. 4	NL:	Cin. vs Chi. (Jimmy Ring)
30	Oct. 6	AL:	Phil. vs StL. (George Earnshaw & Lefty Grove)
31	Oct. 2	NL:	StL. vs Phil. (Bill Hallahan)
42	Oct. 3	NL:	StL. vs NY (Ernie White)
43	Oct. 11	AL:	NY vs StL. (Spud Chandler)
44	Oct. 8	NL:	StL. vs StL. (Mort Cooper)

1948	Oct. 8	AL:	Clev. vs Bos. (Gene Bearden)
1952	Oct. 4	AL:	NY vs Brk. (Allie Reynolds)
1955	Oct. 4	NL:	Brk. vs NY (Johnny Podres)
1956	Oct. 8	AL:	NY vs Brk. (Don Larsen)
1961	Oct. 4	AL:	NY vs Cin. (Whitey Ford)
1962	Oct. 5	NL:	SF vs NY (Jack Sanford)
1965	Oct. 14	NL:	LA vs Minn. (Sandy Koufax)
1973	Oct. 18	NL:	NY vs Oak. (Jerry Koosman & Tug McGraw)
1993	Oct. 21	NL:	Phil. vs Tor. (Curt Schilling)
2003	Oct. 25	NL:	Fla. vs. NY (Josh Beckett)

3-0

1903	Oct. 2	AL:	Bos. vs Pitt. (Bill Dinneen)
1903	Oct. 13	AL:	Bos. vs Pitt. (Bill Dinneen)
1905	Oct. 9	NL:	NY vs Phil. (Christy Mathewson)
1905	Oct. 10	AL:	Phil. vs NY (Chief Bender)
1906	Oct. 11	AL:	Chi. vs Chi. (Ed Walsh)
1908	Oct. 13	NL:	Chi. vs Det. (Three Finger Brown)
1913	Oct. 8	NL:	NY vs Phil. (Christy Mathewson, 10 inn)
1918	Sept. 10	NL:	Chi. vs Bos. (Hippo Vaughn)
1919	Oct. 3	AL:	Chi. vs Cin. (Dickie Kerr)
1920	Oct. 6	NL:	Brk. vs Clev. (Burleigh Grimes)
1920	Oct. 12	AL:	Clev. vs Brk. (Stan Coveleski)
1921	Oct. 5	AL:	NY vs NY (Carl Mays)
1921	Oct. 6	AL:	NY vs NY (Waite Hoyt)
1922	Oct. 6	NL:	NY vs NY (Jack Scott)
1931	Oct. 6	AL:	Phil. vs StL. (George Earnshaw)
1935	Oct. 2	NL:	Chi. vs Det. (Lon Warneke)
1945	Oct. 5	NL:	Chi. vs Det. (Claude Passeau)
1946	Oct. 7	NL:	StL. vs Bos. (Harry Brecheen)
1958	Oct. 5	NL:	Mil. vs NY (Warren Spahn)
1981	Oct. 21	AL:	NY vs LA (Tommy John & Rich Gossage)
1985	Oct. 23	NL:	StL. vs KC (John Tudor)
1998	Oct. 21	AL:	NY vs SD (Andy Pettitte, Jeff Nelson & Mariano Rivera)
2004	Oct. 27	AL:	Bos. vs. StL. (Derek Lowe, Bronson Arroyo, Alan Embree & Keith Foulke)

4-0

1925	Oct. 11	AL:	Wash. vs Pitt. (Walter Johnson)
1926	Oct. 5	NL:	StL. vs NY (Jesse Haines)
1933	Oct. 5	AL:	Wash. vs NY (Earl Whitehill)
1939	Oct. 5	AL:	NY vs Cin. (Monte Pearson)
1940	Oct. 7	NL:	Cin. vs Det. (Bucky Walters)
1946	Oct. 9	AL:	Bos. vs StL. (Boo Ferriss)
1958	Oct. 4	AL:	NY vs Mil. (Don Larsen & Ryne Duren)
1965	Oct. 9	NL:	LA vs Minn. (Claude Osteen)
1968	Oct. 2	NL:	StL. vs Det. (Bob Gibson)
1971	Oct. 14	NL:	Pitt. vs Balt. (Nelson Briles)
1979	Oct. 16	NL:	Pitt. vs Balt. (John Candelaria & Kent Tekulve)
1996	Oct. 21	NL:	Atl. vs NY (Greg Maddux)
2001	Oct. 28	NL:	Ari. vs NY (Randy Johnson)

5-0

1909	Oct. 12	AL:	Det. vs Pitt. (George Mullin)
1917	Oct. 11	NL:	NY vs Chi. (Ferdie Schupp)
1919	Oct. 6	NL:	Cin. vs Chi. (Hod Eller)
1930	Oct. 4	NL:	StL. vs Phil. (Bill Hallahan)
1957	Oct. 10	NL:	Mil. vs NY (Lew Burdette)
1967	Oct. 5	AL:	Bos. vs StL. (Jim Lonborg)
1969	Oct. 14	NL:	NY vs Balt. (Gary Gentry & Nolan Ryan)
1983	Oct. 16	AL:	Balt. vs Phil. (Scott McGregor)
1989	Oct. 14	AL:	Oak. vs SF (Dave Stewart)
2006	Oct. 24	NL:	StL. vs Det. (Chris Carpenter & Braden Looper)

6-0

1966	Oct. 6	AL:	Balt. vs LA (Jim Palmer)
1967	Oct. 8	NL:	StL. vs Bos. (Bob Gibson)
1975	Oct. 11	AL:	Bos. vs Cin. (Luis Tiant)
1988	Oct. 16	NL:	LA vs Oak. (Orel Hershiser)

7-0

1958	Oct. 6	AL:	NY vs Mil. (Bob Turley)
1961	Oct. 8	AL:	NY vs Cin. (Whitey Ford & Jim Coates)
1965	Oct. 11	NL:	LA vs Minn. (Sandy Koufax)
1990	Oct. 16	NL:	Cin. vs Oak. (Jose Rijo, Rob Dibble & Randy Myers)

8-0

1909	Oct. 16	NL:	Pitt. vs Det. (Babe Adams)
1940	Oct. 6	AL:	Det. vs Cin. (Bobo Newsom)

9-0

1905	Oct. 12	NL:	NY vs Phil. (Christy Mathewson)
1945	Oct. 3	NL:	Chi. vs Det. (Hank Borowy)
1956	Oct. 10	AL:	NY vs Brk. (Johnny Kucks)

10-0

1960	Oct. 8	AL:	NY vs Pitt. (Whitey Ford)
1982	Oct. 12	AL:	Mil. vs StL. (Mike Caldwell)

11-0

1934	Oct. 9	NL:	StL. vs Det. (Dizzy Dean)
1959	Oct. 1	AL:	Chi. vs LA (Early Wynn & Gerry Staley)
1985	Oct. 27	AL:	KC vs StL. (Bret Saberhagen)

12-0

1960	Oct. 12	AL:	NY vs Pitt. (Whitey Ford)

PITCHER, CLUB, YEAR		W	L
Adams, Babe NL:Pitt. 1909		3	0
Aguilera, Rick	NL:NY 1986 (1-0)		
	AL:Minn. 1991 (1-1)	2	1
Aldridge, Vic NL:Pitt. 1925, 27		2	1
Alexander, Doyle AL:NY 1976		0	1
Alexander, Grover	NL:Phil. 1915 (1-1)		
	NL:StL. 1926, 28 (2-1)	3	2
Altrock, Nick AL:Chi. 1906		1	1
Ames, Red NL:NY 1911		0	1
Anderson, Brian NL:Ari. 2001		0	1
Anderson, Fred NL:NY 1917		0	1
Andujar, Joaquin AL:StL. 1982, 85		2	1
Antonelli, Johnny NL:NY 1954		1	0
Arroyo, Luis AL:NY 1961		1	0
Ashby, Andy NL:SD 1998		0	1
Astacio, Ezequiel NL:Hou. 2005		0	1
Auker, Elden AL:Det. 1934		1	1
Avery, Steve NL:Atl. 1992, 95-96		1	2
Bagby, Jim AL:Clev. 1920		1	1
Bair, Doug NL:StL. 1982		0	1
Barnes, Jesse NL:NY 1921		2	0
Barnes, Virgil NL:NY 1924		0	1
Barney, Rex NL:Brk. 1947, 49		0	2
Bearden, Gene AL:Clev. 1948		1	0
Beattie, Jim AL:NY 1978		1	0
Beazley, Johnny NL:StL. 1942		2	0
Beckett, Josh NL:Fla. 2003		1	1
Bedient, Hugh AL:Bos. 1912		1	0
Belcher, Tim NL:LA 1988		1	0
Bell, Gary AL:Bos. 1967		0	1
Bender, Chief AL:Phil. 1905, 10-11, 13-14		6	4
Bentley, Jack NL:NY 1923-24		1	3
Benton, Rube NL:NY 1917		1	1
Berenguer, Juan AL:Minn. 1987		0	1
Bessent, Don NL:Brk. 1956		1	0
Bevens, Bill AL:NY 1947		0	1
Bickford, Vern NL:Bos. 1948		0	1
Billingham, Jack NL:Cin. 1972, 76		2	0
Black, Bud AL:KC 1985		0	1
Black, Joe NL:Brk. 1952		1	2
Blake, Sheriff NL:Chi. 1929		0	1
Blass, Steve NL:Pitt. 1971		2	0
Blue, Vida AL:Oak. 1972-74		0	3
Blyleven, Bert	NL:Pitt. 1979 (1-0)		
	AL:Minn. 1987 (1-1)	2	1
Boddicker, Mike AL:Balt. 1983		1	0
Bonham, Ernie AL:NY 1941-43		1	2
Borbon, Pedro, Sr. NL:Cin. 1972		0	1
Borowy, Hank	AL:NY 1943 (1-0)		
	NL:Chi. 1945 (2-2)	3	2
Bouton, Jim AL:NY 1963-64		2	1
Boyd, Oil Can AL:Bos. 1986		0	1
Branca, Ralph NL:Brk. 1947, 49		1	2
Brazle, Al NL:StL. 1943, 46		0	2
Brecheen, Harry NL:StL. 1943-44, 46		4	1
Bridges, Tommy AL:Det. 1934-35, 40		4	1
Briles, Nelson	NL:StL. 1967-68 (1-1)		
	NL:Pitt. 1971 (1-0)	2	1
Brown, Kevin	NL:Fla. 1997 (0-2)		
	NL:SD 1998 (0-1)	0	3
Brown, Three Finger NL:Chi. 1906-08, 10		5	4
Browning, Tom NL:Cin. 1990		1	0
Bryant, Clay NL:Chi. 1935		0	1
Buhl, Bob NL:Mil. 1957		0	1
Bunker, Wally AL:Balt. 1966		1	0
Burdette, Lew NL:Mil. 1957-58		4	2
Burton, Jim AL:Bos. 1975		0	1
Bush, Guy NL:Chi. 1929, 32		1	1
Bush, Joe	AL:Phil. 1913-14 (0-2)		
	AL:Bos. 1918 (0-1)		
	AL:NY 1922-23 (2-2)	2	5
Byrne, Tommy AL:NY 1955		1	1

PITCHER, CLUB, YEAR		W	L
Cadore, Leon NL:Brk. 1920		0	1
Caldwell, Mike AL:Mil. 1982		2	0
Caldwell, Ray AL:Clev. 1920		0	1
Camnitz, Howie, NL:Pitt. 1909		0	1
Candelaria, John, NL:Pitt. 1979		1	1
Carlton, Tex, NL:Chi. 1935		0	1
Carlton, Steve	NL:StL. 1965 (0-1)		
	NL:Phil. 1980, 83 (2-1)	2	2
Carpenter, Chris, NL:StL. 2006		1	0
Carroll, Clay, NL:Cin. 1970, 72, 75		2	1
Casey, Hugh NL:Brk. 1941, 47		2	2
Castillo, Tony AL:Tor. 1993		1	0
Chalmers, George NL:Phil. 1915		0	1
Chandler, Spud AL:NY 1941-43		2	2
Christenson, Larry NL:Phil. 1980		0	1
Cicotte, Eddie AL:Chi. 1917, 19		2	3
Clancy, Jim NL:Atl. 1991		1	0
Clemens, Roger AL:NY 1999-2001		3	0
Cleveland, Reggie AL:Bos. 1975		0	1
Cloninger, Tony NL:Cin. 1970		0	1
Coakley, Andy AL:Phil. 1905		0	1
Coates, Jim AL:NY 1962		0	1
Cone, David AL:NY 1996, 99		2	0
Contreras, Jose	AL:NY 2003 (0-1)		
	AL:Chi. 2005 (1-0)	1	1
Cook, Dennis NL:Fla. 1997		1	0
Coombs, Jack	AL:Phil. 1910-11 (4-0)		
	NL:Brk. 1916 (1-0)	5	0
Cooper, Mort NL:StL. 1942-44		2	3
Cotts, Neal AL:Chi. 2005		1	0
Coveleski, Stan	AL:Clev. 1920 (3-0)		
	AL:Wash. 1925 (0-2)	3	2
Cox, Danny NL:StL. 1987		1	0
Craig, Roger	NL:Brk/LA 1955-56, 59 (1-2)		
	NL:StL. 1964 (1-0)	2	2
Crandall, Doc NL:NY 1911		1	0
Crawford, Steve AL:Bos. 1986		1	0
Crowder, General	AL:Wash. 1933 (0-1)		
	AL:Det. 1934-35 (1-1)	1	2
Cuellar, Mike AL:Balt. 1969-71		2	2
Daley, Bud AL:NY 1961		1	0
Darcy, Pat NL:Cin. 1975		0	1
Darling, Ron NL:NY 1986		1	1
Davis, Curt NL:Brk. 1941		0	1
Davis, Storm	AL:Balt. 1983 (1-0)		
	AL:Oak. 1988 (0-2)	1	2
Dayley, Ken NL:StL. 1985		1	0
Dean, Dizzy	NL:StL. 1934 (2-1)		
	NL:Chi. 1938 (0-1)	2	2
Dean, Paul NL:StL. 1934		2	0
Demaree, Al NL:NY 1913		0	1
Denny, John NL:Phil. 1983		1	1
Derringer, Paul	NL:StL. 1931 (0-2)		
	NL:Cin. 1939-40 (2-2)	2	4
Dibble, Rob NL:Cin. 1990		1	0
Dickson, Murry NL:StL. 1946		0	1
Dinneen, Bill AL:Bos. 1903		3	1
Ditmar, Art AL:NY 1960		0	2
Dobson, Joe AL:Bos. 1946		1	0
Donald, Atley AL:NY 1942		0	1
Donnelly, Blix NL:StL. 1944		1	0
Donnelly, Brendan AL:Ana. 2002		1	0
Donovan, Dick AL:Chi. 1959		0	1
Donovan, Wild Bill AL:Det. 1907-09		1	4
Douglas, Phil	NL:Chi. 1918 (0-1)		
	NL:NY 1921 (2-1)	2	2
Downing, Al	AL:NY 1963-64 (0-2)		
	NL:LA 1974 (0-1)	0	3
Drabowsky, Moe AL:Balt. 1966		1	0
Drago, Dick AL:Bos. 1975		0	1
Drysdale, Don NL:LA 1959, 63, 65-66		3	3
Duren, Ryne AL:NY 1958		1	1

PITCHER, CLUB, YEAR		W	L
Earnshaw, George AL:Phil. 1929-31		4	3
Eastwick, Rawly NL:Cin. 1975		2	0
Eckersley, Dennis AL:Oak. 1988, 90		0	2
Ehmke, Howard AL:Phil. 1929		1	0
Eller, Hod NL:Cin. 1919		2	0
Ellis, Dock	NL:Pitt. 1971 (0-1)		
	AL:NY 1976 (0-1)	0	2
Erskine, Carl NL:Brk. 1952-53, 56		2	2
Faber, Red AL:Chi. 1917		3	1
Feller, Bob AL:Clev. 1948		0	2
Ferguson, Alex AL:Wash. 1925		1	1
Ferrick, Tom AL:NY 1950		1	0
Ferriss, Boo AL:Bos. 1946		1	0
Figueroa, Ed AL:NY 1976, 78		0	2
Fingers, Rollie AL:Oak. 1972-74		2	2
Fisher Ray, NL:Cin. 1919		0	1
Fitzsimmons, Freddie NL:NY 1933, 36		0	3
Flanagan, Mike AL:Balt. 1979		1	1
Ford, Whitey AL:NY 1950, 53, 55-58, 60-64		10	8
Forsch, Bob, NL:StL. 1982, 85, 87		1	3
Foster, Rube AL:Bos. 1915		2	0
Foulke, Keith AL:Bos. 2004		1	0
Franco, John NL:NY 2000		1	0
Frazier, George AL:NY 1981		0	3
French, Larry NL:Chi. 1935		0	2
Friend, Bob NL:Pitt. 1960		0	2
Gale, Rich AL:KC 1980		0	1
Galehouse, Denny AL:StL. 1944		1	1
Garcia, Freddy AL:Chi. 2005		1	0
Garcia, Mike AL:Clev. 1954		0	1
Garrelts, Scott NL:SF 1989		0	2
Gentry, Gary NL:NY 1969		1	0
Gibson, Bob NL:StL. 1964, 67-68		7	2
Glavine, Tom NL:Atl. 1991-92, 95-96		4	3
Gomez, Lefty AL:NY 1932, 36-38		6	0
Gomez, Ruben NL:NY 1954		1	0
Gooden, Dwight NL:NY 1986		0	2
Gossage, Goose AL:NY 1978		1	0
Grant, Mudcat AL:Minn. 1965		2	1
Gregg, Hal NL:Brk. 1947		0	1
Grim, Bob AL:NY 1955, 57		0	2
Grimes, Burleigh	NL:Brk. 1920 (1-2)		
	NL:StL. 1930-31 (2-2)	3	4
Grimsley, Ross NL:Cin. 1972		2	1
Grissom, Marv NL:NY 1954		1	0
Gromek, Steve AL:Clev. 1948		1	0
Grove, Lefty AL:Phil. 1930-31		4	2
Guidry, Ron AL:NY 1977-78, 81		3	1
Gullett, Don	NL:Cin. 1975-76 (2-1)		
	AL:NY 1977 (0-1)	2	2
Guthrie, Mark AL:Minn. 1991		0	1
Guzman, Juan AL:Tor. 1993		0	1
Haddix, Harvey NL:Pitt. 1960		2	0
Hadley, Bump AL:NY 1936-37, 39		2	1
Haines, Jesse NL:StL. 1926, 28, 30		3	1
Hall, Dick AL:Balt. 1969		0	1
Hallahan, Bill NL:StL. 1930-31		3	1
Hampton, Mike NL:NY 2000		0	1
Harris, Mickey AL:Bos. 1946		0	2
Hawkins, Andy NL:SD 1984		1	1
Hearn, Jim NL:NY 1951		1	0
Hentgen, Pat AL:Tor. 1993		1	0
Hernandez, Livan	NL:Fla. 1997 (2-0)		
	NL:SF 2002 (0-2)	2	2
Hernandez, Orlando AL:NY 1998-2000		2	1
Hershiser, Orel	NL:LA 1988 (2-0)		
	AL:Clev. 1995, 97 (1-3)	3	3
Hill, Ken AL:Clev. 1995		0	1
Hitchcock, Sterling AL:NY 2001		1	0
Hoerner, Joe NL:StL. 1968		0	1
Hoffman, Trevor NL:SD 1998		0	1
Holtzman, Ken AL:Oak. 1972-74		4	1

PITCHER, CLUB, YEAR		W	L
Honeycutt, Rick AL:Oak. 1988		1	0
Hooton, Burt NL:LA 1977-78		3	3
Howe, Steve NL:LA 1981		1	0
Howell, Jay NL:LA 1988		0	1
Hoyt, Waite	AL:NY 1921-22, 26-28 (6-3)		
	AL:Phil. 1931 (0-1)	6	4
Hubbell, Carl NL:NY 1933, 36-37		4	2
Hudson, Charles NL:Phil. 1983		0	2
Hughes, Dick NL:StL. 1967		0	1
Hughes, Long Tom AL:Bos. 1903		0	1
Hughson, Tex AL:Bos. 1946		0	1
Hunter, Catfish	AL:Oak. 1972-74 (4-0)		
	AL:NY 1976-78 (1-3)	5	3
Hurst, Bruce AL:Bos. 1986		2	0
Jackson, Danny	AL:KC 1985 (1-1)		
	NL:Phil. 1993 (0-1)	1	2
Jackson, Grant NL:Pitt. 1979		1	0
Jakucki, Sig AL:StL. 1944		0	1
James, Bill NL:Bos. 1914		2	0
Jansen, Larry NL:NY 1951		0	2
Jay, Joey NL:Cin. 1961		1	1
John, Tommy	NL:LA 1977-78 (1-1)		
	AL:NY 1981 (1-0)	2	1
Johnson, Bob NL:Pitt. 1971		0	1
Johnson, Earl AL:Bos. 1946		1	0
Johnson, Ernie NL:Mil. 1957		0	1
Johnson, Randy NL:Ari. 2001		3	0
Johnson, Syl NL:StL. 1931		0	1
Johnson, Walter AL:Wash. 1924-25		3	3
Jones, Bobby J. NL:NY 2000		0	1
Jones, Sam	AL:Bos. 1918 (0-1)		
	AL:NY 1923 (0-1)	0	2
Kaat, Jim AL:Minn. 1965		1	2
Kennedy, Brickyard NL:Pitt. 1903		0	1
Kerr, Dickie AL:Chi. 1919		2	0
Key, Jimmy	AL:Tor. 1992 (2-0)		
	AL:NY 1996 (1-1)	3	1
Kim, Byung-Hyun NL:Ari. 2001		0	1
Kison, Bruce NL:Pitt. 1971, 79		1	1
Klinger, Bob AL:Bos. 1946		0	1
Konstanty, Jim NL:Phil. 1950		0	1
Koosman, Jerry NL:NY 1969, 73		3	0
Koslo, Dave NL:NY 1951		1	1
Koufax, Sandy NL:LA 1959, 63, 65-66		4	3
Kramer, Jack AL:StL. 1944		1	0
Kremer, Ray NL:Pitt. 1925, 27		2	2
Kucks, Johnny AL:NY 1956		1	0
Labine, Clem NL:Brk. 1953, 55-56		2	2
Lackey, John AL:Ana. 2002		1	0
Lamabe, Jack NL:StL. 1967		0	1
Lanier, Max NL:StL. 1942-44		2	1
Larsen, Don	AL:NY 1955-58 (3-2)		
	NL:SF 1962 (1-0)	4	2
Law, Vern NL:Pitt. 1960		2	0
Lee, Bill NL:Chi. 1938		0	2
Leever, Sam NL:Pitt. 1903		0	2
Leibrandt, Charlie	AL:KC 1985 (0-1)		
	NL:Atl. 1991-92 (0-3)	0	4
Leifield, Lefty NL:Pitt. 1909		0	1
Leiter, Al	AL:Tor. 1998 (1-0)		
	NL:NY 2000 (0-1)	1	1
Lemon, Bob AL:Clev. 1948, 54		2	2
Leonard, Dennis AL:KC 1980		1	1
Leonard, Dutch AL:Bos. 1915-16		2	0
Liddle, Don NL:NY 1954		1	0
Lidge, Brad NL:Hou. 2005		0	2
Lindblad, Paul AL:Oak. 1973		1	0
Lloyd, Graeme AL:NY 1996		1	0
Loes, Billy NL:Brk. 1952-53, 55		1	2
Lolich, Mickey AL:Det. 1968		3	0
Lollar, Tim NL:SD 1984		0	1
Lombardi, Vic NL:Brk. 1947		0	1

PITCHER, CLUB, YEAR	W	L
Lonborg, Jim AL:Bos. 1967	2	1
Looper, Braden NL:Fla. 2003	1	0
Lopat, Ed AL:NY 1949, 51-53	4	1
Lopez, Albie NL:Ari. 2001	0	1
Lopez, Aurelio AL:Det. 1984	1	0
Lowe, Derek AL:Bos. 2004	1	0
Luque, Dolf NL:NY 1933	1	0
Lyle, Sparky AL:NY 1977	1	0
Maddox, Nick NL:Pitt. 1909	1	0
Maddux, Greg NL:Atl. 1995-96, 99	2	3
Maglie, Sal NL:NY 1951 (0-1)		
NL:Brk. 1956 (1-1)	1	2
Magrane, Joe NL:StL. 1987	0	1
Mails, Duster AL:Clev. 1920	1	0
Malone, Pat NL:Chi. 1929 (0-2)		
AL:NY 1936 (0-1)	0	3
Marberry, Firpo AL:Wash. 1924	0	1
Marquard, Rube NL:NY 1911-13 (2-2)		
NL:Brk. 1916, 20 (0-3)	2	5
Marquis, Jason NL:StL. 2004	0	1
Marshall, Mike NL:LA 1974	0	1
Marte, Damaso AL:Chi. 2005	1	0
Martinez, Dennis AL:Clev. 1995	0	1
Martinez, Pedro AL:Bos. 2004	1	0
Mathewson, Christy NL:NY 1905, 11-13	5	5
Matlack, Jon NL:NY 1973	1	2
May, Jakie NL:Chi. 1932	0	1
Mayer, Erskine NL:Phil. 1915	0	1
Mays, Carl AL:Bos. 1916, 18 (2-1)		
AL:NY 1921-22 (1-3)	3	4
McClure, Bob AL:Mil. 1982	0	2
McDonald, Jim AL:NY 1953	1	0
McDowell, Roger NL:NY 1986	1	0
McGinnity, Joe NL:NY 1905	1	1
McGraw, Tug NL:NY 1973 (1-0)		
NL:Phil. 1980 (1-1)	2	1
McGregor, Scott AL:Balt. 1979, 83	2	2
McIntire, Harry NL:Chi. 1910	0	1
McLain, Denny AL, Det. 1968	1	2
McNally, Dave AL:Balt. 1966, 69-71	4	2
McQuillan, Hugh NL:NY 1922-24	2	1
Meadow, Lee NL:Pitt. 1925, 27	0	2
Melton, Cliff NL:NY 1937	0	2
Mendoza, Ramiro AL:NY 1998	1	0
Merritt, Jim NL:Cin. 1970	0	1
Mesa, Jose AL:Clev. 1995	1	0
Messersmith, Andy NL:LA 1974	0	2
Meyer, Russ NL:Phil. 1950	0	1
Mikkelsen, Pete AL:NY 1964	0	1
Miljus, Johnny NL:Pitt. 1927	0	1
Miller, Bob J. NL:Phil. 1950	0	1
Miller, Bob L. NL:Pitt. 1971	0	1
Millwood, Kevin NL:Atl. 1999	0	1
Mizell, Vinegar Bend NL:Pitt. 1960	0	1
Mogridge, George AL:Wash. 1924	1	0
Moore, Mike AL:Oak. 1989-90	2	1
Moore, Wilcy AL:NY 1927, 32	2	0
Morgan, Tom AL:NY 1956	0	1
Morris, Jack AL:Det. 1984 (2-0)		
AL:Minn. 1991 (2-0)		
AL:Tor. 1992 (0-2)	4	2
Morris, Matt NL:StL. 2004	0	1
Mulholland, Terry NL:Phil. 1993	1	0
Mullin, George AL:Det. 1907-09	3	3
Muncrief, Bob AL:StL. 1944	0	1
Munger, George NL:StL. 1946	1	0
Murphy, Johnny AL:NY 1939, 41	2	0
Mussina, Mike AL:NY 2003	1	0
Nagy, Charles AL:Clev. 1997	0	1
Nehf, Art NL:NY 1921-24	4	4
Nelson, Jeff AL:NY 2000	1	0
Newcombe, Don NL:Brk. 1949, 55-56	0	4

PITCHER, CLUB, YEAR	W	L
Newhouser, Hal AL:Det. 1945	2	1
Newsom, Bobo AL:Det. 1940 (2-1)		
AL:NY 1947 (0-1)	2	2
Nipper, Al AL:Bos. 1986	0	1
Nolan, Gary NL:Cin. 1970, 72, 76	1	2
Norman, Fred NL:Cin. 1975	0	1
O'Brien, Buck AL:Bos. 1912	0	2
O'Dell, Billy NL:SF 1962	0	1
Odom, Blue Moon AL:Oak. 1972, 74	1	1
Ogea, Chad AL:Clev. 1997	2	0
Ojeda, Bob NL:NY 1986	1	0
Ortiz, Ramon AL:Ana. 2002	1	0
Osteen, Claude NL:LA 1965-66	1	2
O'Toole, Jim NL:Cin. 1961	0	2
Overall, Orval NL:Chi. 1907-08, 10	3	1
Overmire, Stubby AL:Det. 1945	0	1
Page, Joe AL:NY 1947, 49	2	1
Palmer, Jim AL:Balt. 1969-71, 79, 83	4	2
Parker, Harry NL:NY 1973	0	1
Pascual, Camilo NL:Minn. 1965	0	1
Passeau, Claude NL:Chi. 1945	1	0
Pearson, Monte AL:NY 1936-39	4	0
Pena, Alejandro NL:LA 1988 (1-0)		
NL:Atl. 1991, 95 (0-2)	1	2
Pennock, Herb AL:NY 1923, 26-27	5	0
Penny, Brad NL:Fla. 2003	2	0
Petry, Dan AL:Det. 1984	0	1
Pettitte, Andy AL:NY 1996, 98, 2001, 03	3	4
Pfeffer, Jeff NL:Brk. 1916	0	1
Pfiester, Jack NL:Chi. 1906-08	1	3
Phillippe, Deacon NL:Pitt. 1903	3	2
Phoebus, Tom AL:Balt. 1970	1	0
Pierce, Bill NL:SF 1962	1	1
Pipgras, George AL:NY 1927-28, 32	3	0
Plank, Eddie AL:Phil. 1905, 11, 13-14	2	5
Plunk, Eric AL:Clev. 1997	0	1
Podres, Johnny NL:Brk/LA 1953, 55, 59, 63	4	1
Pollet, Howie NL:StL. 1946	0	1
Poole, Jim AL:Clev. 1995	0	1
Potter, Nels AL:StL. 1944	0	1
Powell, Jay NL:Fla. 1997	1	0
Prim, Ray NL:Chi. 1945	0	1
Purkey, Bob NL:Cin. 1961	0	1
Quinn, Jack AL:NY 1921	0	1
Quisenberry, Dan AL:KC 1980, 85	2	2
Raschi, Vic AL:NY 1949-53	5	3
Rau, Doug NL:LA 1977	0	1
Reardon, Jeff NL:Atl. 1992	0	1
Redman, Mark NL:Fla. 2003	0	1
Reinhart, Art NL:StL. 1926	0	1
Remlinger, Mike NL:Atl. 1999	0	1
Reulbach, Ed NL:Chi. 1906-07	2	0
Reuschel, Rick NL:SF 1989	0	1
Reuss, Jerry NL:LA 1981	1	1
Reyes, Anthony NL:StL. 2006	1	0
Reynolds, Allie AL:NY 1947, 49-53	7	2
Rhem, Flint NL:StL. 1930	0	1
Rhoden, Rick NL:LA 1977	0	1
Rijo, Jose NL:Cin. 1990	2	0
Ring, Jimmy NL:Cin. 1919	1	1
Rivera, Mariano, AL:NY 1999, 2001	2	1
Rixey, Eppa NL:Phil. 1915	0	1
Roberts, Robin, NL:Phil. 1950	0	1
Robertson, Nate, AL:Det. 2006	0	1
Robinson, Don, NL:Pitt. 1979 (1-0)		
NL:SF 1989 (0-1)	1	1
Rodriguez, Felix NL:SF 2002	0	1
Rodriguez, Francisco AL:Ana. 2002	1	1
Rodriguez, Wandy NL:Hou. 2005	0	1
Roe, Preacher NL:Brk. 1949, 52-53	2	1
Rogers, Kenny AL:Det. 2006	1	0
Rommel, Eddie AL:Phil. 1929	1	0

PITCHER, CLUB, YEAR	W	L
Root, Charlie NL:Chi. 1929, 32, 35	0	3
Rowe, Schoolboy AL:Det. 1934-35, 40	2	5
Rudolph, Dick NL:Bos. 1914	2	0
Ruether, Dutch NL:Cin. 1919 (1-0)		
AL:NY 1926 (0-1)	1	1
Ruffing, Red AL:NY 1932, 36-39, 41-42	7	2
Rush, Bob NL:Mil. 1958	0	1
Russell, Jack AL:Wash. 1933	0	1
Russo, Marius AL:NY 1941, 43	2	0
Ruth, Babe AL:Bos. 1916, 18	3	0
Ryan, Rosy NL:NY 1922-23	2	0
Saberhagen, Bret AL:KC 1985	2	0
Sadecki, Ray NL:StL. 1964	1	0
Sain, Johnny NL:Bos. 1948 (1-1)		
AL:NY 1952-53 (1-1)	2	2
Sallee, Slim NL:NY 1917 (0-2)		
NL:Cin. 1919 (1-1)	1	3
Sanford, Jack NL:SF 1962	1	2
Santiago, Jose AL:Bos. 1967	0	2
Saunders, Tony NL:Fla. 1997	0	1
Schatzeder, Dan AL:Minn. 1987	1	0
Schilling, Curt NL:Phil. 1993 (1-1)		
NL:Ari. 2001 (1-0)		
AL:Bos. 2004 (1-0)	3	1
Schiraldi, Calvin AL:Bos. 1986	0	2
Schmidt, Jason NL:SF 2002	1	0
Schultz, Barney NL:StL. 1964	0	1
Schumacher, Hal NL:NY 1933, 36-37	2	2
Schupp, Ferdie NL:NY 1917	1	0
Scott, Jack NL:NY 1922-23	1	1
Seaver, Tom NL:NY 1969, 73	1	2
Shantz, Bobby AL:NY 1957	0	1
Shaw, Bob AL:Chi. 1959	1	1
Shawkey, Bob AL:Phil. 1914 (0-1)		
AL:NY 1921, 23, 26 (1-2)	1	3
Shea, Spec AL:NY 1947	2	0
Sherdel, Bill NL:StL. 1926, 28	0	4
Sherry, Larry NL:LA 1959	2	0
Shocker, Urban AL:NY 1926	0	1
Shore, Ernie AL:Bos. 1915-16	3	1
Show, Eric NL:SD 1984	0	1
Siever, Ed AL:Det. 1907	0	1
Simmons, Curt NL:StL. 1964	0	1
Slaton, Jim AL:Mil. 1982	1	0
Smith, Sherry NL:Brk. 1916, 20	1	2
Smoltz, John NL:Atl. 1992, 96, 99	2	2
Spahn, Warren NL:Bos/Mil. 1948, 57-58	4	3
Spooner, Karl NL:Brk. 1955	0	1
Stafford, Bill AL:NY 1962	1	0
Staley, Gerry AL:Chi. 1959	0	1
Stanhouse, Don AL:Balt. 1979	0	1
Stanton, Mike NL Atl. 1991 (1-0)		
AL:NY 2000 (2-0)	3	0
Stewart, Dave AL:Oak. 1988-90 (2-3)		
AL:Tor. 1993 (0-1)	2	4
Stewart, Lefty AL:Wash. 1933	0	1
Stoddard, Tim AL:Balt. 1979	1	0
Stottlemyre, Mel AL:NY 1964	1	1
Stuper, John NL:StL. 1982	1	0
Sturdivant, Tom AL:NY 1956	1	0
Summers, Ed AL:Det. 1908-09	0	4
Suppan, Jeff NL:StL. 2004	0	1
Sutter, Bruce NL:StL. 1982	1	0
Sutton, Don NL:LA 1974, 77-78 (2-2)		
AL:Mil. 1982 (0-1)	2	3
Tapani, Kevin AL:Minn. 1991	1	1
Tavarez, Julian NL:StL. 2004	0	1
Tekulve, Kent NL:Pitt. 1979	0	1
Terry, Ralph AL:NY 1960-62	2	4
Tesreau, Jeff NL:NY 1912-13	1	3
Thompson, Junior NL:Cin. 1939-40	0	2
Thurmond, Mark NL:SD 1984	0	1

PITCHER, CLUB, YEAR	W	L
Tiant, Luis AL:Bos. 1975	2	0
Torrez, Mike AL:NY 1977	2	0
Trout, Dizzy AL:Det. 1940, 45	1	2
Trucks, Virgil AL:Det. 1945	1	0
Tudor, John NL:StL. 1985, 87	3	2
Turley, Bob AL:NY 1955, 58, 60	4	3
Turner, Jim NL:Cin. 1940	0	1
Tyler, Lefty NL:Chi. 1918	1	1
Valenzuela, Fernando NL:LA 1981	1	0
Vaughn, Hippo NL:Chi. 1918	1	2
Verlander, Justin, AL:Det. 2006	0	2
Viola, Frank AL:Minn. 1987	2	1
Voiselle, Bill NL:Bos. 1948	0	1
Vuckovich, Pete AL:Mil. 1982	0	1
Wainwright, Adam, NL:StL. 2006	1	0
Walberg, Rube AL:Phil. 1929-30	1	1
Walk, Bob NL:Phil. 1980	1	0
Walker, Bill NL:StL. 1934	0	2
Wall, Donne NL:SD 1998	0	1
Walsh, Ed AL:Chi. 1906	2	0
Walters, Bucky NL:Cin. 1939-40	2	2
Ward, Duane AL:Tor. 1992-93	3	0
Warneke, Lon NL:Chi. 1932, 35	2	1
Washburn, Jarrod AL:Ana. 2002	0	2
Washburn, Ray NL:StL. 1968	1	1
Watt, Eddie AL:Balt. 1969-71	0	3
Weaver, Jeff AL:NY. 2003 (0-1)		
NL:StL. 2006 (1-1)	1	2
Weaver, Monte AL:Wash. 1933	0	1
Welch, Bob NL:LA 1978	0	1
Wells, David AL:NY 1998, 2003	1	1
Wendell, Turk NL:NY 2000	0	1
White, Doc AL:Chi. 1906	1	1
White, Ernie NL:StL. 1942	1	0
Whitehill, Earl AL:Wash. 1933	1	0
Wilcox, Milt NL:Cin. 1970 (0-1)		
AL:Det. 1984 (1-0)	1	1
Wilks, Ted NL:StL. 1944	0	1
Williams, Lefty AL:Chi. 1919	0	3
Williams, Mitch NL:Phil. 1993	0	2
Willis, Vic NL:Pitt. 1909	0	1
Willoughby, Jim AL:Bos. 1975	0	1
Wilson, Earl AL:Det. 1968	0	1
Wise, Rick AL:Bos. 1975	1	0
Wood, Smoky Joe AL:Bos. 1912	3	1
Worrell, Tim NL:SF 2002	1	1
Worrell, Todd NL:StL. 1985	0	1
Wright, Jaret NL:Clev. 1997	1	0
Wyatt, John AL:Bos. 1967	1	0
Wyatt, Whitlow NL:Brk. 1941	1	1
Wynn, Early AL:Clev. 1954 (0-1)		
AL:Chi. 1959 (1-1)	1	2
Wyse, Hank NL:Chi. 1945	0	1
Yde, Emil NL:Pitt. 1925	0	1
Young, Cy AL:Bos. 1903	2	1
Zachary, Tom AL:Wash 1924 (2-0)		
AL:NY 1928 (1-0)	3	0
Zachry, Pat NL:Cin. 1976	1	0
Zerbe, Chad NL:SF 2002	1	0
Zumaya, Joel AL:Det. 2006	0	1

AMERICAN LEAGUE WORLD SERIES MANAGERS

	SERIES			GAMES		YEARS	
	No.	Won	Lost	Won	Lost	Won	Lost
Altobelli, Joe Balt.	1	1	0	4	1	1983	
*Anderson, Sparky Det.	1	1	0	4	1	1984	
Baker, Del Det.	1	0	1	3	4		1940
Barrow, Ed Bos.	1	1	0	4	2	1918	
Bauer, Hank Balt.	1	1	0	4	0	1966	
*Berra, Yogi NY	1	0	1	3	4		1964
Boudreau, Lou Clev.	1	1	0	4	2	1948	
Carrigan, Bill Bos.	2	2	0	8	2	1915-16	
Cochrane, Mickey Det.	2	1	1	7	6	1935	1934
Collins, Jimmy Bos.	1	1	0	5	3	1903	
Cronin, Joe Wash.	1	0	1	1	4		1933
Bos.	1	0	1	3	4		1946
Totals	(2)	(0)	(2)	(4)	(8)		
*Dark, Alvin Oak.	1	1	0	4	1	1974	
Francona, Terry, Bos.	1	1	0	4	0	2004	
Frey, Jim KC	1	0	1	2	4		1980
Gaston, Cito Tor.	2	2	0	8	4	1992-93	
Gleason, Kid Chi.	1	0	1	3	5		1919
Guillen, Ozzie Chi.	1	1	0	4	0	2005	
Hargrove, Mike Clev.	2	0	2	5	8		1995, 97
Harris, Bucky Wash.	2	1	1	7	7	1924	1925
NY	1	1	0	4	3	1947	
Totals	(3)	(2)	(1)	(11)	(10)		
Houk, Ralph NY	3	2	1	8	8	1961-62	1963
Howser, Dick KC	1	1	0	4	3	1985	
Huggins, Miller NY	6	3	3	18	15	1923, 27-28	1921-22, 26
Jennings, Hughie Det.	3	0	3	4	12		1907-09
Johnson, Darrell Bos.	1	0	1	3	4		1975
Jones, Fielder Chi.	1	1	0	4	2	1906	
Kelly, Tom Minn.	2	2	0	8	6	1987, 91	
Kuenn, Harvey Mil.	1	0	1	3	4		1982
*LaRussa, Tony Oak.	3	1	2	5	8	1989	1988, 90
Lemon, Bob NY	2	1	1	6	6	1978	1981
*Leyland, Jim Det.	1	0	1	1	4		2006
Lopez, Al Clev.	1	0	1	0	4		1954
Chi.	1	0	1	2	4		1959
Totals	(2)	(0)	(2)	(2)	(8)		
Mack, Connie Phil.	8	5	3	24	19	1910-11, 13, 29-30	1905, 14, 31
Martin, Billy NY	2	1	1	4	6	1977	1976
*McCarthy Joe NY	8	7	1	29	9	1932, 36-39, 41, 43	1942
McNamara John Bos.	1	0	1	3	4		1986
Mele, Sam Minn.	1	0	1	3	4		1965
O'Neill, Steve Det.	1	1	0	4	3	1945	
Rowland, Pants Chi.	1	1	0	4	2	1917	
Scioscia, Mike Ana.	1	1	0	4	3	2002	
Sewell, Luke StL.	1	0	1	2	4		1944
Smith, Mayo Det.	1	1	0	4	3	1968	
Speaker, Tris Clev.	1	1	0	5	2	1920	
Stahl, Jake Bos.	1	1	0	4	3	1912	
Stengel, Casey NY	10	7	3	37	26	1949-53, 56, 58	1955, 57, 60
Torre, Joe NY	6	4	2	21	11	1996, 98-2000	2001, 03
Weaver, Earl Balt.	4	1	3	11	13	1970	1969, 71, 79
*Williams, Dick Bos.	1	0	1	3	4		1967
Oak.	2	2	0	8	6	1972-73	
A.L. Totals	(3)	(2)	(1)	(11)	(10)		

* Also managed in the World Series for the National League (see next page)

NATIONAL LEAGUE WORLD SERIES MANAGERS

	SERIES			GAMES		YEARS	
	No.	Won	Lost	Won	Lost	Won	Lost
Alston, Walter Brk./LA	7	4	3	20	20	1955, 59, 63, 65	1956, 66, 74
*Anderson, Sparky Cin.	4	2	2	12	11	1975-76	1970, 72
Baker, Dusty SF	1	0	1	3	4		2002
*Berra, Yogi NY	1	0	1	3	4		1973
Bochy, Bruce SD	1	0	1	0	4		1998
Brenly, Bob Ari.	1	1	0	4	3	2001	
Bush, Donie Pitt.	1	0	1	0	4		1927
Chance, Frank Chi.	4	2	2	11	9	1907-08	1906, 10
Clarke, Fred Pitt.	2	1	1	7	8	1909	1903
Cox, Bobby Atl.	5	1	4	11	18	1995	1991-92, 96, 99
Craig, Roger SF	1	0	1	0	4		1989
*Dark, Alvin SF	1	0	1	3	4		1962
Dressen, Chuck Brk.	2	0	2	5	8		1952-53
Durocher, Leo Brk.	1	0	1	1	4		1941
NY	2	1	1	6	4	1954	1951
Totals	(3)	(1)	(2)	(7)	(8)		
Dyer, Eddie StL.	1	1	0	4	3	1946	
Fregosi, Jim Phil.	1	0	1	2	4		1993
Frisch, Frankie StL.	1	1	0	4	3	1934	
Garner, Phil Hou.	1	0	1	0	4		2005
Green, Dallas Phil.	1	1	0	4	2	1980	
Grimm, Charlie Chi.	3	0	3	5	12		1932, 35, 45
Haney, Fred Mil.	2	1	1	7	7	1957	1958
Hartnett, Gabby Chi.	1	0	1	0	4		1938
Herzog, Whitey StL.	3	1	2	10	11	1982	1985, 87
Hodges, Gil NY	1	1	0	4	1	1969	
Hornsby, Rogers StL.	1	1	0	4	3	1926	
Hutchinson, Fred Cin.	1	0	1	1	4		1961
Johnson, Davey NY	1	1	0	4	3	1986	
Keane, Johnny StL.	1	1	0	4	3	1964	
*LaRussa, Tony, StL.	2	1	1	4	5	2006	2004
Lasorda, Tommy LA	4	2	2	12	11	1981, 88	1977-78
*Leyland, Jim Fla.	1	1	0	4	3	1997	
*McCarthy, Joe Chi.	1	0	1	1	4		1929
McGraw, John NY	9	3	6	26	28	1905, 21-22	1911-13, 17, 23-24
McKeon, Jack Fla.	1	1	0	4	2	2003	
McKechnie, Bill Pitt.	1	1	0	4	3	1925	
Cin.	2	1	1	4	7	1940	1939
StL.	1	0	1	0	4		1928
Totals	(4)	(2)	(2)	(8)	(14)		
Mitchell, Fred Chi.	1	0	1	2	4		1918
Moran, Pat Phil.	1	0	1	1	4		1915
Cin.	1	1	0	5	3	1919	
Totals	(2)	(1)	(1)	(6)	(7)		
Murtaugh, Danny Pitt.	2	2	0	8	6	1960, 71	
Owens, Paul Phil.	1	0	1	1	4		1983
Piniella, Lou Cin.	1	1	0	4	0	1990	
Robinson, Wilbert Brk.	2	0	2	3	9		1916, 20
Sawyer, Eddie Phil.	1	0	1	0	4		1950
Schoendienst, Red StL.	2	1	1	7	7	1967	1968
Shotton, Burt Brk.	2	0	2	4	8		1947, 49
Southworth, Billy StL.	3	2	1	9	7	1942, 44	1943
Bos.	1	0	1	2	4		1948
Totals	(4)	(2)	(2)	(11)	(11)		
Stallings, George Bos.	1	1	0	4	0	1914	
Street, Gabby StL.	2	1	1	6	7	1931	1930
Tanner, Chuck Pitt.	1	1	0	4	3	1979	
Terry, Bill NY	3	1	2	7	9	1933	1936-37
Valentine, Bobby NY	1	0	1	1	4		2000
*Williams, Dick SD	1	0	1	1	4		1984

* Also managed in the World Series for the American League (see previous page)

World Series Umpires

Ashford, Emmett 1970
Ballanfant, Lee 1940, 46, 51, 55
Barlick, Al 1946, 50, 51, 54, 58, 62, 67
Barnett, Larry 1975, 81, 84, 90
Barr, George 1937, 42, 48-49
Basil, Steve. 1937, 40
Bell, Wally 2006
Berry, Charlie 1946, 50, 54, 58, 62
Boggess, Dusty 1940, 52, 56, 60
Boyer, Jim 1947
Bremigan, Nick 1980
Brennan, Bill 1911
Brinkman, Joe 1978, 86, 95
Burkhart, Ken 1962, 64, 70
Byron, Bill 1914
Cederstrom, Gary 2005
Chill, Ollie 1921
Chylak, Nestor 1957, 60, 66, 71, 77
Clark, Al 1983, 89
Coble, Drew 1991
Colosi, Nick 1975, 81
Conlan, Jocko 1945, 50, 54, 57, 61
Connolly, Tom 1903, 08, 10-11, 13, 16, 20, 24
Cooney, Terry 1981
Cousins, Derryl 1988, 99, 2005
Crawford, Jerry 1988, 92, 98, 2000, 02
Crawford, Shag 1961, 63, 69
Dale, Jerry 1977
Darling, Gary 2003
Dascoli, Frank 1953, 55, 59
Davidson, Satch 1975, 82
Davidson, Bob 1992
Davis, Gerry 1996, 99, 2004
Deegan, Bill 1976
DeMuth, Dana 1993, 98, 2001
Denkinger, Don 1974, 80, 85, 91
DiMuro, Lou 1969, 76
Dinneen, Bill 1911, 14, 16, 20, 26, 29, 32
Dixon, Hal 1959
Donatelli, Augie 1955, 57, 61, 67, 73
Drummond, Cal 1966
Dunn, Tom 1944
Egan, Rip 1913
Engel, Bob 1972, 79, 85
Evans, Jim 1977, 82, 86, 96
Evans, Billy 1909, 12, 15, 17, 19, 23
Flaherty, Red 1955, 58, 65, 70
Ford, Dale 1986, 97
Frantz, Art 1975
Froemming, Bruce 1976, 84, 88, 95
Garcia, Rich 1981, 84, 89, 98
Geisel, Harry 1930, 34, 36
Goetz, Larry 1941, 47, 52
Goetz, Russ 1973, 79
Gore, Artie 1951, 53
Gorman, Brian 2004
Gorman, Tom 1956, 58, 63, 68, 74
Gregg, Eric 1989
Grieve, Bill 1941, 48, 53
Haller, Bill 1968, 72, 78, 82
Hart, Bob 1923
Harvey, Doug 1968, 74, 81, 84, 88
Hendry, Ted 1990
Hernandez, Angel 2002, 05
Hildebrand, George 1914, 18, 22, 26
Hirschbeck, John 1995, 2006
Hirschbeck, Mark 1998, 2001
Honochick, Jim 1952, 55, 60, 62, 68, 72
Hubbard, Cal 1938, 42, 46, 49
Hurley, Ed 1949, 53, 59, 65
Jackowski, Bill 1958, 60, 66
Johnson, Mark 1993
Johnstone, Jim 1906, 09
Jorda, Lou 1945, 49
Joyce, Jim 1999, 2001
Kaiser, Ken 1987, 97
Kellogg, Jeff 2000, 03
Kibler, John 1971, 78, 82, 86
Kinnamon, Bill 1968
Klem, Bill 1908-09, 11-15, 17-18, 20, 22, 24, 26, 29, 31-32, 34, 40
Kolls, Lou 1938
Kosc, Greg 1987, 97
Kunkel, Bill 1974, 80
Landes, Stan 1960, 62, 68
Layne, Jerry 2005
Luciano, Ron 1974
Magerkurth, George 1932, 36, 42, 47

Maloney, George 1975
Marsh, Randy 1990, 97, 99, 2003, 06
Marquez, Alfonso 2006
McClelland, Tim 1993, 2000, 02, 06
McCormick, Barry 1922, 25
McCoy, Larry 1977, 88
McGowan, Bill 1928, 31, 35, 39, 41, 44, 47, 50
McKean, Jim 1979, 85, 95
McKinley, Bill 1950, 52, 57, 64
McSherry, John 1977, 87
Meriwether, Chuck 2004
Merrill, Durwood 1988
Montague, Ed 1986, 91, 97, 2000, 04
Moran, Charlie 1927, 29, 33, 38
Moriarty, George 1921, 25, 30, 33, 35
Morrison, Dan 1992
Nallin, Dick 1919, 23, 27, 31
Napp, Larry 1954, 56, 63, 69
Nelson, Jeff 2005
Neudecker, Jerry 1973, 79
O'Day, Hank 1903, 05, 07-08, 10, 16, 18, 20, 23, 26
Odom, Jim 1971
O'Loughlin, Silk 1906, 09, 12, 15, 17
Olsen, Andy 1974
Ormsby, Red 1927, 33, 37, 40
Owens, Brick 1918, 22, 25, 28, 34
Palermo, Steve 1983
Paparella, Joe 1948, 51, 57, 63
Passarella, Art 1945, 49, 52
Pelekoudas, Chris 1966, 72
Pfirman, Cy 1928, 33, 36
Phillips, Dave 1976, 82, 87, 93
Pinelli, Babe 1939, 41, 47-48, 52, 56
Pipgras, George 1944
Pryor, Paul 1967, 73, 80
Pulli, Frank 1978, 83, 90, 95
Quick, Jim 1985, 90
Quigley, Ernie 1916, 19, 21, 24, 27, 35
Rapuano, Ed 2001, 03
Reardon, Beans 1930, 34, 39, 43, 49
Reed, Rick 1991
Reilly, Mike 1984, 92, 2002
Reliford, Charlie 2000, 04
Rennert, Dutch 1980, 83, 89
Rice, John 1959, 63, 66, 71
Rigler, Cy 1910, 12-13, 15, 17, 19, 21, 25, 28, 30
Rippley, Steve 1996, 99, 2001
Roe, Rocky 1990, 99
Rommel, Ed 1943, 47
Rue, Joe 1943
Runge, Ed 1956, 61, 67
Runge, Paul 1979, 84, 89, 93
Scott, Dale 1998, 2001, 04
Sears, Ziggy 1938, 44
Secory, Frank 1957, 59, 64, 69
Sheridan, Jack 1905, 07-08, 10
Shulock, John 1985, 92
Smith, Vinnie 1964
Smith, Al 1964
Soar, Hank 1953, 56, 62, 64, 69
Springstead, Marty 1973, 78, 83
Stark, Dolly 1931, 35
Steiner, Mel 1966, 72
Stello, Dick 1975, 81
Stevens, Johnny 1951, 54, 60, 67
Stewart, Bob 1961, 65, 70
Stewart, Bill 1937, 43, 48, 53
Sudol, Ed 1965, 71, 77
Summers, Bill 1936, 39, 42, 45, 48, 51, 55, 59
Tata, Terry 1979, 87, 91, 96
Tschida, Tim 1998, 2002
Umont, Frank 1958, 61, 67, 72
Van Graflan, Roy 1929, 32
Vargo, Ed 1965, 71, 78, 83
Venzon, Tony 1963, 65, 70
Voltaggio, Vic 1989
Warneke, Lon 1954
Welke, Tim 1996, 2000, 03
Wendelstedt, Harry 1973, 80, 86, 91, 95
West, Joe 1992, 97, 2005
Weyer, Lee 1969, 76, 82, 87
Williams, Charlie 1993
Williams, Billy 1970, 76, 85
Winters, Mike 2002, 06
Young, Larry 1996, 2003

1903 – BOSTON RED SOX A.L. (5) vs. PITTSBURGH PIRATES N.L. (3)
(Huntington Grounds / Exposition Park)

Oct. 1	at Bos.	Pittsburgh (Phillippe)	7	Boston (Young)	3
Oct. 2	at Bos.	Boston (Dinneen)	3	Pittsburgh (Leever)	0
Oct. 3	at Bos.	Pittsburgh (Phillippe)	4	Boston (Hughes)	2
Oct. 6	at Pitt.	Pittsburgh (Phillippe)	5	Boston (Dinneen)	4
Oct. 7	at Pitt.	Boston (Young)	11	Pittsburgh (Kennedy)	2
Oct. 8	at Pitt.	Boston (Dinneen)	6	Pittsburgh (Leever)	3
Oct. 10	at Pitt.	Boston (Young)	7	Pittsburgh (Phillippe)	3
Oct. 13	at Bos.	Boston (Dinneen)	3	Pittsburgh (Phillippe)	0

POSTPONED: (Rain) Oct. 5, 12(Cold) Oct. 9

MANAGERS: Jimmy Collins, Red Sox; Fred Clarke, Pirates

Red Sox — Lou Criger, Duke Farrell, catchers; Bill Dinneen, Long Tom Hughes, Cy Young, pitchers; Jimmy Collins, Hobe Ferris, Candy LaChance, Freddy Parent, infielders; Patsy Dougherty, Buck Freeman, Jack O'Brien, Chick Stahl, outfielders.

Pirates — Ed Phelps, Harry Smith, catchers; Brickyard Kennedy, Sam Leever, Deacon Phillippe, Gus Thompson, Bucky Veil, pitchers; Kitty Bransfield, Tommy Leach, Claude Ritchey, Honus Wagner, infielders; Ginger Beaumont, Fred Clarke, Jimmy Sebring, outfielders.

1904 – NO WORLD SERIES PLAYED

1905 – NEW YORK GIANTS N.L. (4) vs. PHILADELPHIA ATHLETICS A.L. (1)
(Polo Grounds / Columbia Park)

Oct. 9	at Phil.	New York (Mathewson)	3	Philadelphia (Plank)	0
Oct. 10	at NY	Philadelphia (Bender)	3	New York (McGinnity)	0
Oct. 12	at Phil.	New York (Mathewson)	9	Philadelphia (Coakley)	0
Oct. 13	at NY	New York (McGinnity)	1	Philadelphia (Plank)	0
Oct. 14	at NY	New York (Mathewson)	2	Philadelphia (Bender)	0

MANAGERS: John McGraw, Giants; Connie Mack, Athletics

Giants — Frank Bowerman, Roger Bresnahan, Boileryard Clarke, catchers; Leon Ames, Claude Elliott, Christy Mathewson, Joe McGinnity, Dummy Taylor, Hooks Wiltse, pitchers; Bill Dahlen, Art Devlin, Billy Gilbert, Dan McGann, Sammy Strang, infielders; George Browne, Mike Donlin, Sam Mertes, outfielders.

Athletics — Mike Powers, Ossee Schreckengost, catchers; Chief Bender, Andy Coakley, Jimmy Dygert, Weldon Henley, Eddie Plank, Rube Waddell, pitchers; Lave Cross, Monte Cross, Harry Davis, John Knight, Danny Murphy, infielders; Harry Barton, Topsy Hartsel, Danny Hoffman, Bris Lord, Socks Seybold, outfielders.

1906 – CHICAGO WHITE SOX A.L. (4) vs. CHICAGO CUBS N.L. (2)
(South Side Park / West Side Park)

Oct. 9	at Cubs	White Sox (Altrock)	2	Cubs (Brown)	1
Oct. 10	at White Sox	Cubs (Reulbach)	7	White Sox (White)	1
Oct. 11	at Cubs	White Sox (Walsh)	3	Cubs (Pfiester)	0
Oct. 12	at White Sox	Cubs (Brown)	1	White Sox (Altrock)	0
Oct. 13	at Cubs	White Sox (Walsh)	8	Cubs (Pfiester)	6
Oct. 14	at White Sox	White Sox (White)	8	Cubs (Brown)	3

MANAGERS: Fielder Jones, White Sox; Frank Chance, Cubs

White Sox — Hub Hart, Ed McFarland, Billy Sullivan, Sr., Babe Towne, catchers; Nick Altrock, Lou Fiene, Frank Owen, Roy Patterson, Frank Smith, Ed Walsh, Doc White, pitchers; George Davis, Jiggs Donahue, Gus Dundon, Frank Isbell, Bill O'Neill, George Rohe, Lee Tannehill, infielders; Patsy Dougherty, Ed Hahn, Fielder Jones, outfielders.

Cubs — Johnny Kling, Pat Moran, Tom Walsh, catchers; Three Finger Brown, Jack Harper, Carl Lundgren, Orval Overall, Jack Pfiester, Ed Reulbach, Jack Taylor, pitchers; Frank Chance, Johnny Evers, Barry McCormick, Harry Steinfeldt, Joe Tinker, infielders; Doc Gessler, Solly Hofman, Wildfire Schulte, Jimmy Sheckard, Jimmy Slagle, outfielders.

1907 – CHICAGO CUBS N.L. (4) vs. DETROIT TIGERS A.L. (0) 1 tie
(West Side Park / Bennett Park)

Oct. 8	at Chi.	Chicago (tie)	3	Detroit (tie)	3	(12 Innings, tie)
Oct. 9	at Chi.	Chicago (Pfiester)	3	Detroit (Mullin)	1	
Oct. 10	at Chi.	Chicago (Reulbach)	5	Detroit (Siever)	1	
Oct. 11	at Det.	Chicago (Overall)	6	Detroit (Donovan)	1	
Oct. 12	at Det.	Chicago (Brown)	2	Detroit (Mullin)	0	

MANAGERS: Frank Chance, Cubs; Hughie Jennings, Tigers

Cubs – Johnny Kling, Pat Moran, Tom Walsh, catchers; Three Finger Brown, Chick Fraser, Carl Lundgren, Orval Overall, Jack Pfiester, Ed Reulbach, pitchers; Frank Chance, Johnny Evers, Del Howard, Harry Steinfeldt, Joe Tinker, Heinie Zimmerman, infielders; Kid Durbin, Solly Hofman, Wildfire Schulte, Jimmy Sheckard, Jimmy Slagle, outfielders.

Tigers – Jimmy Archer, Fred Payne, Boss Schmidt, catchers; Wild Bill Donovan, Ed Killian, George Mullin, Ed Siever, Ed Willett, pitchers; Bill Coughlin, Red Downs, Bobby Lowe, Charley O'Leary, Claude Rossman, Germany Schaefer, infielders; Ty Cobb, Sam Crawford, Davy Jones, Matty McIntyre, outfielders.

1908 – CHICAGO CUBS N.L. (4) vs. DETROIT TIGERS A.L. (1)
(West Side Park / Bennett Park)

Oct. 10	at Det.	Chicago (Brown)	10	Detroit (Summers)	6
Oct. 11	at Chi.	Chicago (Overall)	6	Detroit (Donovan)	1
Oct. 12	at Chi.	Detroit (Mullin)	8	Chicago (Pfiester)	3
Oct. 13	at Det.	Chicago (Brown)	3	Detroit (Summers)	0
Oct. 14	at Det.	Chicago (Overall)	2	Detroit (Donovan)	0

MANAGERS: Frank Chance, Cubs; Hughie Jennings, Tigers

Cubs – Johnny Kling, Doc Marshall, Pat Moran, catchers; Three Finger Brown, Chick Fraser, Rube Kroh, Carl Lundgren, Orval Overall, Jack Pfiester, Ed Reulbach, pitchers; Frank Chance, Johnny Evers, Del Howard, Harry Steinfeldt, Joe Tinker, Heinie Zimmerman, infielders; Kid Durbin, Solly Hofman, Wildfire Schulte, Jimmy Sheckard, Jimmy Slagle, outfielders.

Tigers – Boss Schmidt, Ira Thomas, catchers; Wild Bill Donovan, Ed Killian, George Mullin, George Suggs, Ed Summers, Ed Willett, George Winter, pitchers; Bill Coughlin, Red Downs, Red Killefer, Charley O'Leary, Claude Rossman, Germany Schaefer, infielders; Ty Cobb, Sam Crawford, Davy Jones, Matty McIntyre, outfielders.

1909 – PITTSBURGH PIRATES N.L. (4) vs. DETROIT TIGERS A.L. (3)
(Forbes Field / Bennett Park)

Oct. 8	at Pitt.	Pittsburgh (Adams)	4	Detroit (Mullin)	1
Oct. 9	at Pitt.	Detroit (Donovan)	7	Pittsburgh (Camnitz)	2
Oct. 11	at Det.	Pittsburgh (Maddox)	8	Detroit (Summers)	6
Oct. 12	at Det.	Detroit (Mullin)	5	Pittsburgh (Leifield)	0
Oct. 13	at Pitt.	Pittsburgh (Adams)	8	Detroit (Summers)	4
Oct. 14	at Det.	Detroit (Mullin)	5	Pittsburgh (Willis)	4
Oct. 16	at Det.	Pittsburgh (Adams)	8	Detroit (Donovan)	0

MANAGERS: Fred Clarke, Pirates; Hughie Jennings, Tigers

Pirates – George Gibson, Paddy O'Connor, Mike Simon, catchers; Babe Adams, Chick Brandom, Howie Camnitz, Sam Frock, Sam Leever, Lefty Leifield, Nick Maddox, Gene Moore, Deacon Phillippe, Bill Powell, Vic Willis, pitchers; Ed Abbaticchio, Bill Abstein, Bobby Byrne, Dots Miller, Honus Wagner, infielders; Fred Clarke, Ham Hyatt, Tommy Leach, Owen Wilson, outfielders.

Tigers – Heinie Beckendorf, Boss Schmidt, Oscar Stanage, catchers; Wild Bill Donovan, Ed Killian, George Mullin, George Speer, Ed Summers, Ed Willett, Ralph Works, pitchers; Donie Bush, Jim Delahanty, Tom Jones, George Moriarty, Charley O'Leary, infielders; Ty Cobb, Sam Crawford, Davy Jones, Matty McIntyre, outfielders.

1910 – PHILADELPHIA ATHLETICS A.L. (4) vs. CHICAGO CUBS N.L. (1)
(Shibe Park / West Side Park)

Oct. 17	at Phil.	Philadelphia (Bender)	4	Chicago (Overall)	1	
Oct. 18	at Phil.	Philadelphia (Coombs)	9	Chicago (Brown)	3	
Oct. 20	at Chi.	Philadelphia (Coombs)	12	Chicago (McIntyre)	5	
Oct. 22	at Chi.	Chicago (Brown)	4	Philadelphia (Bender)	3	(10 innings)
Oct. 23	at Chi.	Philadelphia (Coombs)	7	Chicago (Brown)	2	

MANAGERS: Connie Mack, Athletics; Frank Chance, Cubs

Athletics — Pat Donahue, Jack Lapp, Paddy Livingston, Ira Thomas, catchers; Tommy Atkins, Chief Bender, Jack Coombs, Jimmy Dygert, Harry Krause, Cy Morgan, Eddie Plank, pitchers; Frank Baker, Jack Barry, Eddie Collins, Harry Davis, Claud Derrick, Ben Houser, Stuffy McInnis, infielders; Topsy Hartsel, Bristol Lord, Danny Murphy, Rube Oldring, Amos Strunk, outfielders.

Cubs — Jimmy Archer, Johnny Kling, Tom Needham, catchers; Three Finger Brown, King Cole, Bill Foxen, Harry McIntyre, Orval Overall, Big Jeff Pfeffer, Jack Pfiester, Ed Reulbach, Lew Richie, Orlie Weaver, pitchers; Frank Chance, Johnny Evers, Harry Steinfeldt, Joe Tinker, Heinie Zimmerman, infielders; Ginger Beaumont, Solly Hofman, John Kane, Wildfire Schulte, Jimmy Sheckard, outfielders.

1911 – PHILADELPHIA ATHLETICS A.L. (4) vs. NEW YORK GIANTS N.L. (2)
(Shibe Park / Polo Grounds)

Oct. 14	at NY	New York (Mathewson)	2	Philadelphia (Bender)	1	
Oct. 16	at Phil.	Philadelphia (Plank)	3	New York (Marquard)	1	
Oct. 17	at NY	Philadelphia (Coombs)	3	New York (Mathewson)	2	(11 innings)
Oct. 24	at Phil.	Philadelphia (Bender)	4	New York (Mathewson)	2	
Oct. 25	at NY	New York (Crandall)	4	Philadelphia (Plank)	3	(10 innings)
Oct. 26	at Phil.	Philadelphia (Bender)	13	New York (Ames)	2	

POSTPONED: (Rain) Oct. 18, 19, 20, 21, 23

MANAGERS: Connie Mack, Athletics; John McGraw, Giants

Athletics — Jack Lapp, Paddy Livingston, Ira Thomas, catchers; Chief Bender, Jack Coombs, Dave Danforth, Harry Krause, Doc Martin, Cy Morgan, Eddie Plank, pitchers; Frank Baker, Jack Barry, Eddie Collins, Harry Davis, Claud Derrick, Stuffy McInnis, infielders; Topsy Hartsel, Bristol Lord, Danny Murphy, Rube Oldring, Amos Strunk, outfielders.

Giants — Grover Hartley, Chief Meyers, Art Wilson, catchers; Leon Ames, Doc Crandall, Louis Drucke, Rube Marquard, Christy Mathewson, Hooks Wiltse, pitchers; Art Devlin, Larry Doyle, Art Fletcher, Buck Herzog, Fred Merkle, Gene Paulette, infielders; Beals Becker, Josh Devore, Red Murray, Fred Snodgrass, outfielders.

1912 – BOSTON RED SOX A.L. (4) vs. NEW YORK GIANTS N.L. (3) 1 tie
(Fenway Park / Polo Grounds)

Oct. 8	at NY	Boston (Wood)	4	New York (Tesreau)	3	
Oct. 9	at Bos.	Boston (tie)	6	New York (tie)	6	(11 innings, tie)
Oct. 10	at Bos.	New York (Marquard)	2	Boston (O'Brien)	1	
Oct. 11	at NY	Boston (Wood)	3	New York (Tesreau)	1	
Oct. 12	at Bos.	Boston (Bedient)	2	New York (Mathewson)	1	
Oct. 14	at NY	New York (Marquard)	5	Boston (O'Brien)	2	
Oct. 15	at Bos.	New York (Tesreau)	11	Boston (Wood)	4	
Oct. 16	at Bos.	Boston (Wood)	3	New York (Mathewson)	2	(10 innings)

MANAGERS: Jake Stahl, Red Sox; John McGraw, Giants

Red Sox — Hick Cady, Bill Carrigan, Les Nunamaker, Pinch Thomas, catchers; Hugh Bedient, Ray Collins, Charley Hall, Buck O'Brien, Larry Pape, Smoky Joe Wood, pitchers; Neal Ball, Hugh Bradley, Clyde Engle, Larry Gardner, Marty Krug, Jake Stahl, Heinie Wagner, Steve Yerkes, infielders; Olaf Henriksen, Harry Hooper, Duffy Lewis, Tris Speaker, outfielders.

Giants — Grover Hartley, Chief Meyers, Art Wilson, catchers; Red Ames, Doc Crandall, Rube Marquard, Christy Mathewson, Jeff Tesreau, Hooks Wiltse, pitchers; Larry Doyle, Art Fletcher, Heinie Groh, Buck Herzog, Fred Merkle, Tillie Shafer, infielders; Beals Becker, George Burns, Josh Devore, Red Murray, Moose McCormick, Fred Snodgrass, outfielders.

1913 – PHILADELPHIA ATHLETICS A.L. (4) vs. NEW YORK GIANTS N.L. (1)

(Shibe Park / Polo Grounds)

Oct. 7	at NY	Philadelphia (Bender)	6	New York (Marquard)	4	
Oct. 8	at Phil.	New York (Mathewson)	3	Philadelphia (Plank)	0	(10 innings)
Oct. 9	at NY	Philadelphia (Bush)	8	New York (Tesreau)	2	
Oct. 10	at Phil.	Philadelphia (Bender)	6	New York (Demaree)	5	
Oct. 11	at NY	Philadelphia (Plank)	3	New York (Mathewson)	1	

MANAGERS: Connie Mack, Athletics; John McGraw, Giants

Athletics – Jack Lapp, Wally Schang, Ira Thomas, catchers; Chief Bender, Boardwalk Brown, Joe Bush, Jack Coombs, Byron Houck, Herb Pennock, Eddie Plank, Bob Shawkey, John Wyckoff, pitchers; Frank Baker, Jack Barry, Eddie Collins, Harry Davis, Doc Lavan, Stuffy McInnis, Bill Orr, infielders; Tom Daley, Danny Murphy, Eddie Murphy, Rube Oldring, Amos Strunk, James Walsh, outfielders.

Giants – Grover Hartley, Chief Meyers, Larry McLean, Art Wilson, catchers; Doc Crandall, Al Demaree, Art Fromme, Rube Marquard, Christy Mathewson, Jeff Tesreau, Hooks Wiltse, pitchers; Larry Doyle, Art Fletcher, Eddie Grant, Buck Herzog, Fred Merkle, Tillie Shafer, infielders; George Burns, Claude Cooper, Moose McCormick, Red Murray, Fred Snodgrass, Jim Thorpe, outfielders.

1914 – BOSTON BRAVES N.L. (4) vs. PHILADELPHIA ATHLETICS A.L. (0)

(Fenway Park / Shibe Park)

Oct. 9	at Phil.	Boston (Rudolph)	7	Philadelphia (Bender)	1	
Oct. 10	at Phil.	Boston (James)	1	Philadelphia (Plank)	0	
Oct. 12	at Bos.	Boston (James)	5	Philadelphia (Bush)	4	(12 innings)
Oct. 13	at Bos.	Boston (Rudolph)	3	Philadelphia (Shawkey)	1	

MANAGERS: George Stallings, Braves; Connie Mack, Athletics

Braves – Hank Gowdy, Bert Whaling, catchers; Gene Cocreham, Ensign Cottrell, Dick Crutcher, George Davis, Otto Hess, Bill H. James, Dick Rudolph, Paul Strand, Lefty Tyler, pitchers; Charlie Deal, Oscar Dugey, Johnny Evers, Rabbit Maranville, Bill Martin, Butch Schmidt, Red Smith, infielders; Ted Cather, Joe Connolly, Josh Devore, Larry Gilbert, Les Mann, Herbie Moran, Possum Whitted, outfielders.

Athletics – Jack Lapp, Wickey McAvoy, Wally Schang, Ira Thomas, catchers; Chief Bender, Rube Bressler, Joe Bush, Jack Coombs, Chick Davies, Herb Pennock, Eddie Plank, Bob Shawkey, John Wyckoff, pitchers; Frank Baker, Jack Barry, Eddie Collins, Harry Davis, Larry Kopf, Stuffy McInnis, infielders; Eddie Murphy, Rube Oldring, Amos Strunk, Shag Thompson, Jimmy Walsh, outfielders.

1915 – BOSTON RED SOX A.L. (4) vs. PHILADELPHIA PHILLIES N.L. (1)

(Braves Field / Baker Bowl)

Oct. 8	at Phil.	Philadelphia (Alexander)	3	Boston (Shore)	1
Oct. 9	at Phil.	Boston (Foster)	2	Philadelphia (Mayer)	1
Oct. 11	at Bos.	Boston (Leonard)	2	Philadelphia (Alexander)	1
Oct. 12	at Bos.	Boston (Shore)	2	Philadelphia (Chalmers)	1
Oct. 13	at Phil.	Boston (Foster)	5	Philadelphia (Rixey)	4

MANAGERS: Bill Carrigan, Red Sox; Pat Moran, Phillies

Red Sox – Hick Cady, Bill Carrigan, Pinch Thomas, catchers; Ray Collins, Rube Foster, Vean Gregg, Dutch Leonard, Carl Mays, Babe Ruth, Ernie Shore, Smoky Joe Wood, pitchers; Jack Barry, Del Gainer, Larry Gardner, Dick Hoblitzell, Hal Janvrin, Mike McNally, Everett Scott, Heinie Wagner, infielders; Olaf Henriksen, Harry Hooper, Duffy Lewis, Tris Speaker, outfielders.

Phillies – Bert Adams, Ed Burns, Bill Killefer, catchers; Grover Alexander, Stan Baumgartner, George Chalmers, Al Demaree, Erskine Mayer, George McQuillan, Eppa Rixey, Ben Tincup, pitchers; Dave Bancroft, Bobby Byrne, Oscar Dugey, Fred Luderus, Bert Niehoff, Milt Stock, infielders; Beals Becker, Gavvy Cravath, Dode Paskert, Bud Weiser, Possum Whitted, outfielders.

1916 - BOSTON RED SOX A.L. (4) vs. BROOKLYN DODGERS N.L. (1)
(Braves Field / Ebbets Field)

Oct. 7	at Bos.	Boston (Shore)	6	Brooklyn (Marquard)	5	
Oct. 9	at Bos.	Boston (Ruth)	2	Brooklyn (Smith)	1	(14 innings)
Oct. 10	at Brk.	Brooklyn (Coombs)	4	Boston (Mays)	3	
Oct. 11	at Brk.	Boston (Leonard)	6	Brooklyn (Marquard)	2	
Oct. 12	at Bos.	Boston (Shore)	4	Brooklyn (Pfeffer)	1	

MANAGERS: Bill Carrigan, Red Sox; Wilbert Robinson, Dodgers

Red Sox — Sam Agnew, Hick Cady, Bill Carrigan, Pinch Thomas, catchers; Rube Foster, Vean Gregg, Sam Jones, Dutch Leonard, Carl Mays, Babe Ruth, Ernie Shore, John Wyckoff, pitchers; Jack Barry, Del Gainer, Larry Gardner, Dick Hoblitzell, Hal Janvrin, Mike McNally, Everett Scott, Heinie Wagner, infielders; Olaf Henriksen, Harry Hooper, Duffy Lewis, Chick Shorten, Tilly Walker, Jimmy Walsh, outfielders.

Dodgers — Chief Meyers, Otto Miller, catchers; Ed Appleton, Larry Cheney, Jack Coombs, Wheezer Dell, Duster Mails, Rube Marquard, Jeff Pfeffer, Nap Rucker, Sherry Smith, pitchers; George Cutshaw, Jake Daubert, Gus Getz, Fred Merkle, Mike Mowrey, Ivy Olson, Ollie O'Mara, infielders; Jimmy Johnston, Hy Myers, Casey Stengel, Zack Wheat, outfielders.

1917 - CHICAGO WHITE SOX A.L. (4) vs. NEW YORK GIANTS N.L. (2)
(Comiskey Park / Polo Grounds)

Oct. 6	at Chi.	Chicago (Cicotte)	2	New York (Sallee)	1
Oct. 7	at Chi.	Chicago (Faber)	7	New York (Anderson)	2
Oct. 10	at NY	New York (Benton)	2	Chicago (Cicotte)	0
Oct. 11	at NY	New York (Schupp)	5	Chicago (Faber)	0
Oct. 13	at Chi.	Chicago (Faber)	8	New York (Sallee)	5
Oct. 15	at NY	Chicago (Faber)	4	New York (Benton)	2

MANAGERS: Pants Rowland, White Sox; John McGraw, Giants

White Sox — Joe Jenkins, Byrd Lynn, Ray Schalk, catchers; Joe Benz, Eddie Cicotte, Dave Danforth, Red Faber, Reb Russell, Jim Scott, Lefty Williams, Red Wolfgang, pitchers; Bobby Byrne, Eddie Collins, Chick Gandil, Ziggy Hasbrook, Ted Jourdan, Fred McMullin, Swede Risberg, Buck Weaver, infielders; Shano Collins, Happy Felsch, Joe Jackson, Nemo Leibold, Eddie Murphy, outfielders.

Giants — George Gibson, Lew McCarty, Jack Onslow, Bill Rariden, catchers; Fred Anderson, Rube Benton, Al Demaree, Pol Perritt, Slim Sallee, Ferdie Schupp, Jeff Tesreau, pitchers; Al Baird, Art Fletcher, Buck Herzog, Walter Holke, Hans Lobert, Jimmy Smith, Heinie Zimmerman, infielders; George Burns, Benny Kauff, Red Murray, Dave Robertson, Jim Thorpe, Joe Wilhoit, outfielders.

1918 - BOSTON RED SOX A.L. (4) vs. CHICAGO CUBS N.L. (2)
(Fenway Park / Comiskey Park)

Sept. 5	at Chi.	Boston (Ruth)	1	Chicago (Vaughn)	0
Sept. 6	at Chi.	Chicago (Tyler)	3	Boston (Bush)	1
Sept. 7	at Chi.	Boston (Mays)	2	Chicago (Vaughn)	1
Sept. 9	at Bos.	Boston (Ruth)	3	Chicago (Douglas)	2
Sept. 10	at Bos.	Chicago (Vaughn)	3	Boston (Jones)	0
Sept. 11	at Bos.	Boston (Mays)	2	Chicago (Tyler)	1

POSTPONED: (Rain) Sept. 4

MANAGERS: Ed Barrow, Red Sox; Fred Mitchell, Cubs

Red Sox — Sam Agnew, Wally Mayer, Wally Schang, catchers; Joe Bush, Jean Dubuc, Sam Jones, Walt Kinney, Carl Mays, Bill Pertica, Babe Ruth, pitchers; George Cochran, Jack Coffey, Stuffy McInnis, Everett Scott, Dave Shean, Fred Thomas, Heinie Wagner, infielders; Harry Hooper, Hack Miller, Amos Strunk, George Whiteman, outfielders.

Cubs — Tommy Clarke, Bill Killefer, Bob O'Farrell, catchers; Paul Carter, Phil Douglas, Claude Hendrix, Speed Martin, Lefty Tyler, Hippo Vaughn, Roy Walker, pitchers; Charlie Deal, Charlie Hollocher, Otto Knabe, Bill McCabe, Fred Merkle, Charlie Pick, Chuck Wortman, Rollie Zeider, infielders; Turner Barber, Max Flack, Les Mann, Dode Paskert, outfielders.

1919 – CINCINNATI REDS N.L. (5) vs. CHICAGO WHITE SOX A.L. (3)
(Redland Field / Comiskey Park)

Oct. 1	at Cin.	Cincinnati (Ruether)	9	Chicago (Cicotte)	1	
Oct. 2	at Cin.	Cincinnati (Sallee)	4	Chicago (Williams)	2	
Oct. 3	at Chi.	Chicago (Kerr)	3	Cincinnati (Fisher)	0	
Oct. 4	at Chi.	Cincinnati (Ring)	2	Chicago (Cicotte)	0	
Oct. 6	at Chi.	Cincinnati (Eller)	5	Chicago (Williams)	0	
Oct. 7	at Cin.	Chicago (Kerr)	5	Cincinnati (Ring)	4	(10 Innings)
Oct. 8	at Cin.	Chicago (Cicotte)	4	Cincinnati (Sallee)	1	
Oct. 9	at Chi.	Cincinnati (Eller)	10	Chicago (Williams)	5	

MANAGERS: Pat Moran, Reds; Kid Gleason, White Sox

Reds – Nick Allen, Bill Rariden, Ivy Wingo, catchers; Hod Eller, Ray Fisher, Ed Gerner, Dolf Luque, Roy Mitchell, Jimmy Ring, Dutch Ruether, Slim Sallee, pitchers; Jake Daubert, Heinie Groh, Larry Kopf, Morrie Rath, Hank Schreiber, Jimmy Smith, infielders; Rube Bressler, Pat Duncan, Sherry Magee, Greasy Neale, Edd Roush, Charlie See, outfielders.

White Sox – Joe Jenkins, Byrd Lynn, Ray Schalk, catchers; Eddie Cicotte, Red Faber, Bill James, Dickie Kerr, Grover Lowdermilk, Erskine Mayer, John Sullivan, Roy Wilkinson, Lefty Williams, pitchers; Eddie Collins, Chick Gandil, Hervey McClellan, Fred McMullin, Swede Risberg, Buck Weaver, infielders; Shano Collins, Happy Felsch, Joe Jackson, Nemo Leibold, Eddie Murphy, outfielders.

1920 – CLEVELAND INDIANS A.L. (5) vs. BROOKLYN DODGERS N.L. (2)
(League Park / Ebbets Field)

Oct. 5	at Brk.	Cleveland (Coveleski)	3	Brooklyn (Marquard)	1
Oct. 6	at Brk.	Brooklyn (Grimes)	3	Cleveland (Bagby)	0
Oct. 7	at Brk.	Brooklyn (Smith)	2	Cleveland (Caldwell)	1
Oct. 9	at Clev.	Cleveland (Coveleski)	5	Brooklyn (Cadore)	1
Oct. 10	at Clev.	Cleveland (Bagby)	8	Brooklyn (Grimes)	1
Oct. 11	at Clev.	Cleveland (Mails)	1	Brooklyn (Smith)	0
Oct. 12	at Clev.	Cleveland (Coveleski)	3	Brooklyn (Grimes)	0

MANAGERS: Tris Speaker, Indians; Wilbert Robinson, Dodgers

Indians – Les Nunamaker, Steve O'Neill, Pinch Thomas, catchers; Jim Bagby, Ray Caldwell, Bob Clark, Stan Coveleski, George Ellison, Duster Mails, Guy Morton, George Uhle, pitchers; Tioga George Burns, Larry Gardner, Doc Johnston, Harry Lunte, Joe Sewell, Bill Wambsganss, infielders; Joe Evans, Jack Graney, Charlie Jamieson, Elmer Smith, Tris Speaker, Smoky Joe Wood, outfielders.

Dodgers – Rowdy Elliott, Ernie Krueger, Otto Miller, Zack Taylor, catchers; Leon Cadore, Burleigh Grimes, Al Mamaux, Rube Marquard, Johnny Miljus, Clarence Mitchell, George Mohart, Jeff Pfeffer, Sherry Smith, pitchers; Jimmy Johnston, Pete Kilduff, Ed Konetchy, Bill McCabe, Ivy Olson, Ray Schmandt, Jack Sheehan, Chuck Ward, infielders; Tommy Griffith, Bill Lamar, Hy Myers, Bernie Neis, Zack Wheat, outfielders.

1921 – NEW YORK GIANTS N.L. (5) vs. NEW YORK YANKEES A.L. (3)
(Polo Grounds / Polo Grounds)

Oct. 5	at Giants	Yankees (Mays)	3	Giants (Douglas)	0
Oct. 6	at Yankees	Yankees (Hoyt)	3	Giants (Nehf)	0
Oct. 7	at Giants	Giants (Barnes)	13	Yankees (Quinn)	5
Oct. 9	at Yankees	Giants (Douglas)	4	Yankees (Mays)	2
Oct. 10	at Giants	Yankees (Hoyt)	3	Giants (Nehf)	1
Oct. 11	at Yankees	Giants (Barnes)	8	Yankees (Shawkey)	5
Oct. 12	at Giants	Giants (Douglas)	2	Yankees (Mays)	1
Oct. 13	at Yankees	Giants (Nehf)	1	Yankees (Hoyt)	0

MANAGERS: John McGraw, Giants; Miller Huggins, Yankees

Giants – Alex Gaston, Earl Smith, Frank Snyder, catchers; Jesse Barnes, Red Causey, Phil Douglas, Art Nehf, Rosy Ryan, Slim Sallee, Red Shea, Fred Toney, pitchers; Dave Bancroft, Frankie Frisch, Mike Gonzalez, George Kelly, Wally Kopf, Johnny Rawlings, infielders; Eddie Brown, George Burns, Bill Cunningham, Irish Meusel, Casey Stengel, Ross Youngs, outfielders.

Yankees – Al DeVormer, Wally Schang, catchers; Rip Collins, Alex Ferguson, Harry Harper, Waite Hoyt, Carl Mays, Bill Piercy, Jack Quinn, Tom Rogers, Bob Shawkey, pitchers; Frank Baker, Mike McNally, Johnny Mitchell, Roger Peckinpaugh, Wally Pipp, Aaron Ward, infielders; Chick Fewster, Chicken Hawks, Bob Meusel, Elmer Miller, Braggo Roth, Babe Ruth, outfielders.

1922 – NEW YORK GIANTS N.L. (4) vs. NEW YORK YANKEES A.L. (0) 1 tie
(Polo Grounds / Polo Grounds)

Oct. 4	at Giants	Giants (Ryan)	3	Yankees (Bush)	2	
Oct. 5	at Yankees	Giants (tie)	3	Yankees (tie)	3	(10 Innings, tie)
Oct. 6	at Giants	Giants (Scott)	3	Yankees (Hoyt)	0	
Oct. 7	at Yankees	Giants (McQuillan)	4	Yankees (Mays)	3	
Oct. 8	at Giants	Giants (Nehf)	5	Yankees (Bush)	3	

MANAGERS: John McGraw, Giants; Miller Huggins, Yankees

Giants – Alex Gaston, Earl Smith, Frank Snyder, catchers; Jesse Barnes, Virgil Barnes, Clint Blume, Carmen Hill, Claude Jonnard, Hugh McQuillan, Art Nehf, Rosy Ryan, Jack Scott, pitchers; Dave Bancroft, Frankie Frisch, Heinie Groh, George Kelly, Johnny Rawlings, infielders; Bill Cunningham, Lee King, Irish Meusel, Dave Robertson, Casey Stengel, Ross Youngs, outfielders.

Yankees – Al DeVormer, Fred Hofmann, Wally Schang, catchers; Joe Bush, Waite Hoyt, Sam Jones, Carl Mays, George Murray, Lefty O'Doul, Bob Shawkey, pitchers; Frank Baker, Joe Dugan, Mike McNally, Wally Pipp, Everett Scott, Aaron Ward, infielders; Norm McMillan, Bob Meusel, Babe Ruth, Camp Skinner, Elmer Smith, Whitey Witt, outfielders.

1923 – NEW YORK YANKEES A.L. (4) vs. NEW YORK GIANTS N.L. (2)
(Yankee Stadium / Polo Grounds)

Oct. 10	at Yankees	Giants (Ryan)	5	Yankees (Bush)	4
Oct. 11	at Giants	Yankees (Pennock)	4	Giants (McQuillan)	2
Oct. 12	at Yankees	Giants (Nehf)	1	Yankees (Jones)	0
Oct. 13	at Giants	Yankees (Shawkey)	8	Giants (Scott)	4
Oct. 14	at Yankees	Yankees (Bush)	8	Giants (Bentley)	1
Oct. 15	at Giants	Yankees (Pennock)	6	Giants (Nehf)	4

MANAGERS: Miller Huggins, Yankees; John McGraw, Giants

Yankees – Benny Bengough, Fred Hofmann, Wally Schang, catchers; Joe Bush, Waite Hoyt, Sam Jones, Carl Mays, Herb Pennock, George Pipgras, Oscar Roettger, Bob Shawkey, pitchers; Joe Dugan, Mike Gazella, Ernie Johnson, Mike McNally, Wally Pipp, Everett Scott, Aaron Ward, infielders; Hinkey Haines, Harvey Hendrick, Bob Meusel, Babe Ruth, Elmer Smith, Whitey Witt, outfielders.

Giants – Alex Gaston, Hank Gowdy, Frank Snyder, catchers; Virgil Barnes, Jack Bentley, Dinty Gearin, Claude Jonnard, Hugh McQuillan, Art Nehf, Rosy Ryan, Jack Scott, Mule Watson, pitchers; Dave Bancroft, Frankie Frisch, Heinie Groh, Travis Jackson, George Kelly, Freddie Maguire, infielders; Bill Cunningham, Irish Meusel, Jimmy O'Connell, Ralph Shinners, Casey Stengel, Ross Youngs, outfielders.

1924 – WASHINGTON SENATORS A.L. (4) vs. NEW YORK GIANTS N.L. (3)
(Griffith Stadium / Polo Grounds)

Oct. 4	at Wash.	New York (Nehf)	4	Washington (Johnson)	3	(12 innings)
Oct. 5	at Wash.	Washington (Zachary)	4	New York (Bentley)	3	
Oct. 6	at NY	New York (McQuillan)	6	Washington (Marberry)	4	
Oct. 7	at NY	Washington (Mogridge)	7	New York (Barnes)	4	
Oct. 8	at NY	New York (Bentley)	6	Washington (Johnson)	2	
Oct. 9	at Wash.	Washington (Zachary)	2	New York (Nehf)	1	
Oct. 10	at Wash.	Washington (Johnson)	4	New York (Bentley)	3	(12 innings)

MANAGERS: Bucky Harris, Senators; John McGraw, Giants

Senators – Pinky Hargrave, Muddy Ruel, Bennie Tate, catchers; Walter Johnson, Firpo Marberry, Joe Martina, George Mogridge, Curly Ogden, Allan Russell, Byron Speece, Tom Zachary, Paul Zahniser, pitchers; Ossie Bluege, Bucky Harris, Joe Judge, Ralph Miller, Roger Peckinpaugh, Mule Shirley, Tommy Taylor, infielders; Showboat Fisher, Goose Goslin, Nemo Leibold, Earl McNeely, Sam Rice, outfielders.

Giants – Hank Gowdy, Frank Snyder, catchers; Harry Baldwin, Virgil Barnes, Jack Bentley, Wayland Dean, Walter Huntzinger, Claude Jonnard, Ernie Maun, Hugh McQuillan, Art Nehf, Rosy Ryan, Mule Watson, pitchers; Frankie Frisch, Heinie Groh, Travis Jackson, George Kelly, Fred Lindstrom, Bill Terry, infielders; Irish Meusel, Jimmy O'Connell, Billy Southworth, Hack Wilson, Ross Youngs, outfielders.

1925 – PITTSBURGH PIRATES N.L. (4) vs. WASHINGTON SENATORS A.L. (3)

(Forbes Field / Griffith Stadium)

Oct. 7	at Pitt.	Washington (Johnson)	4	Pittsburgh (Meadows)	1
Oct. 8	at Pitt.	Pittsburgh (Aldridge)	3	Washington (Coveleski)	2
Oct. 10	at Wash.	Washington (Ferguson)	4	Pittsburgh (Kremer)	3
Oct. 11	at Wash.	Washington (Johnson)	4	Pittsburgh (Yde)	0
Oct. 12	at Wash.	Pittsburgh (Aldridge)	6	Washington (Coveleski)	3
Oct. 13	at Pitt.	Pittsburgh (Kremer)	3	Washington (Ferguson)	2
Oct. 15	at Pitt.	Pittsburgh (Kremer)	9	Washington (Johnson)	7

POSTPONED: (Rain) Oct. 14

MANAGERS: Bill McKechnie, Pirates; Bucky Harris, Senators

Pirates — Johnny Gooch, Earl Smith, Roy Spencer, catchers; Babe Adams, Vic Aldridge, Bud Culloton, Remy Kremer, Lee Meadows, Johnny Morrison, Red Oldham, Tom Sheehan, Emil Yde, pitchers; Jewel Ens, George Grantham, Stuffy McInnis, Eddie Moore, Johnny Rawlings, Fresco Thompson, Pie Traynor, Glenn Wright, infielders; Clyde Barnhart, Carson Bigbee, Max Carey, Kiki Cuyler, Mule Haas, outfielders.

Senators — Muddy Ruel, Hank Severeid, Bennie Tate, catchers; Win Ballou, Stan Coveleski, Alex Ferguson, Walter Johnson, Firpo Marberry, Dutch Ruether, Allan Russell, Tom Zachary, pitchers; Spencer Adams, Ossie Bluege, Bucky Harris, Joe Judge, Buddy Myer, Roger Peckinpaugh, Everett Scott, infielders; Goose Goslin, Joe Harris, Tex Jeanes, Nemo Leibold, Earl McNeely, Sam Rice, Bobby Veach, outfielders.

1926 – ST. LOUIS CARDINALS N.L. (4) vs. NEW YORK YANKEES A.L. (3)

(Sportsmans Park / Yankee Stadium)

Oct. 2	at NY	New York (Pennock)	2	St. Louis (Sherdel)	1	
Oct. 3	at NY	St. Louis (Alexander)	6	New York (Shocker)	2	
Oct. 5	at StL.	St. Louis (Haines)	4	New York (Ruether)	0	
Oct. 6	at StL.	New York (Hoyt)	10	St. Louis (Reinhart)	5	
Oct. 7	at StL.	New York (Pennock)	3	St. Louis (Sherdel)	2	(10 innings)
Oct. 9	at NY	St. Louis (Alexander)	10	New York (Shawkey)	2	
Oct. 10	at NY	St. Louis (Haines)	3	New York (Hoyt)	2	

MANAGERS: Rogers Hornsby, Cardinals; Miller Huggins, Yankees

Cardinals — Bob O'Farrell, Ernie Vick, catchers; Grover Alexander, Herman Bell, Ed Clough, Jesse Haines, Bill Hallahan, Syl Johnson, Vic Keen, Art Reinhart, Flint Rhem, Bill Sherdel, Allen Sothoron, pitchers; Les Bell, Jim Bottomley, Jake Flowers, Rogers Hornsby, Tommy Thevenow, Specs Toporcer, infielders; Ray Blades, Taylor Douthit, Chick Hafey, Roscoe Holm, Billy Southworth, outfielders.

Yankees — Benny Bengough, Pat Collins, Hank Severeid, catchers; Walter Beall, Garland Braxton, Waite Hoyt, Sam Jones, Herb McQuaid, Herb Pennock, Dutch Ruether, Bob Shawkey, Urban Shocker, Myles Thomas, pitchers; Spencer Adams, Joe Dugan, Michael Gazella, Lou Gehrig, Mark Koenig, Tony Lazzeri, Aaron Ward, infielders; Roy Carlyle, Earle Combs, Bob Meusel, Ben Paschal, Babe Ruth, outfielders.

1927 – NEW YORK YANKEES A.L. (4) vs. PITTSBURGH PIRATES N.L. (0)

(Yankee Stadium / Forbes Field)

Oct. 5	at Pitt.	New York (Hoyt)	5	Pittsburgh (Kremer)	4
Oct. 6	at Pitt.	New York (Pipgras)	6	Pittsburgh (Aldridge)	2
Oct. 7	at NY	New York (Pennock)	8	Pittsburgh (Meadows)	1
Oct. 8	at NY	New York (Moore)	4	Pittsburgh (Miljus)	3

MANAGERS: Miller Huggins, Yankees; Donie Bush, Pirates

Yankees — Benny Bengough, Pat Collins, Johnny Grabowski, catchers; Joe Giard, Waite Hoyt, Wilcy Moore, Herb Pennock, George Pipgras, Dutch Ruether, Bob Shawkey, Urban Shocker, Myles Thomas, pitchers; Joe Dugan, Mike Gazella, Lou Gehrig, Mark Koenig, Tony Lazzeri, Ray Morehart, Julie Wera, infielders; Earle Combs, Cedric Durst, Bob Meusel, Ben Paschal, Babe Ruth, outfielders.

Pirates — Johnny Gooch, Earl Smith, Roy Spencer, catchers; Vic Aldridge, Mike Cvengros, Joe Dawson, Carmen Hill, Remy Kremer, Lee Meadows, Johnny Miljus, Emil Yde, pitchers; Joe Cronin, George Grantham, Heinie Groh, Joe Harris, Hal Rhyne, Pie Traynor, Glenn Wright, infielders; Clyde Barnhart, Fred Brickell, Kiki Cuyler, Lloyd Waner, Paul Waner, outfielders.

1928 - NEW YORK YANKEES A.L. (4) vs. ST. LOUIS CARDINALS N.L. (0)
(Yankee Stadium / Sportsmans Park)

Oct. 4	at NY	New York (Hoyt)	4	St. Louis (Sherdel)	1	
Oct. 5	at NY	New York (Pipgras)	9	St. Louis (Alexander)	3	
Oct. 7	at StL.	New York (Zachary)	7	St. Louis (Haines)	3	
Oct. 9	at StL.	New York (Hoyt)	7	St. Louis (Sherdel)	3	

MANAGERS: Miller Huggins, Yankees; Bill McKechnie, Cardinals

Yankees — Benny Bengough, Pat Collins, Bill Dickey, Johnny Grabowski, catchers; Fred Heimach, Waite Hoyt, Herb Pennock, George Pipgras, Rosy Ryan, Myles Thomas, Tom Zachary, pitchers; Joe Dugan, Leo Durocher, Mike Gazella, Lou Gehrig, Mark Koenig, Tony Lazzeri, Gene Robertson, infielders; Earle Combs, Cedric Durst, Bob Meusel, Ben Paschal, Babe Ruth, outfielders.

Cardinals — Earl Smith, Jimmie Wilson, catchers; Grover Alexander, Fred Frankhouse, Hal Haid, Jesse Haines, Syl Johnson, Clarence Mitchell, Art Reinhart, Flint Rhem, Bill Sherdel, pitchers; Jim Bottomley, Frankie Frisch, Andy High, Wattie Holm, Rabbit Maranville, Tommy Thevenow, infielders; Ray Blades, Taylor Douthit, Chick Hafey, George Harper, Pepper Martin, Ernie Orsatti, Wally Roettger, Howie Williamson, outfielders.

1929 - PHILADELPHIA ATHLETICS A.L. (4) vs. CHICAGO CUBS N.L. (1)
(Shibe Park / Wrigley Field)

Oct. 8	at Chi.	Philadelphia (Ehmke)	3	Chicago (Root)	1
Oct. 9	at Chi.	Philadelphia (Earnshaw)	9	Chicago (Malone)	3
Oct. 11	at Phil.	Chicago (Bush)	3	Philadelphia (Earnshaw)	1
Oct. 12	at Phil.	Philadelphia (Rommel)	10	Chicago (Blake)	8
Oct. 14	at Phil.	Philadelphia (Walberg)	3	Chicago (Malone)	2

MANAGERS: Connie Mack, Athletics; Joe McCarthy, Cubs

Athletics — Mickey Cochrane, Cy Perkins, catchers; Bill Breckinridge, George Earnshaw, Howard Ehmke, Lefty Grove, Jack Quinn, Ed Rommel, Bill Shores, Rube Walberg, Carroll Yerkes, pitchers; Max Bishop, Joe Boley, George Burns, Eddie Collins, Jim Cronin, Jimmy Dykes, Jimmie Foxx, Sammy Hale, infielders; Walter French, Mule Haas, Bevo LeBourveau, Bing Miller, Al Simmons, Homer Summa, outfielders.

Cubs — Mike Gonzalez, Gabby Hartnett, Johnny Schulte, Zack Taylor, catchers; Sheriff Blake, Guy Bush, Hal Carlson, Mike Cvengros, Henry Grampp, Pat Malone, Art Nehf, Ken Penner, Charlie Root, pitchers; Clyde Beck, Footsie Blair, Woody English, Charlie Grimm, Rogers Hornsby, Norm McMillan, Chick Tolson, infielders; Kiki Cuyler, Cliff Heathcote, Johnny Moore, Riggs Stephenson, Hack Wilson, outfielders.

1930 - PHILADELPHIA ATHLETICS A.L. (4) vs. ST. LOUIS CARDINALS N.L. (2)
(Shibe Park / Sportsmans Park)

Oct. 1	at Phil.	Philadelphia (Grove)	5	St. Louis (Grimes)	2
Oct. 2	at Phil.	Philadelphia (Earnshaw)	6	St. Louis (Rhem)	1
Oct. 4	at StL.	St. Louis (Hallahan)	5	Philadelphia (Walberg)	0
Oct. 5	at StL.	St. Louis (Haines)	3	Philadelphia (Grove)	1
Oct. 6	at StL.	Philadelphia (Grove)	2	St. Louis (Grimes)	0
Oct. 8	at Phil.	Philadelphia (Earnshaw)	7	St. Louis (Hallahan)	1

MANAGERS: Connie Mack, Athletics; Gabby Street, Cardinals

Athletics — Mickey Cochrane, Cy Perkins, Wally Schang, catchers; George Earnshaw, Lefty Grove, Lee Roy Mahaffey, Jack Quinn, Ed Rommel, Bill Shores, Rube Walberg, pitchers; Max Bishop, Joe Boley, Eddie Collins, Jimmy Dykes, Jimmie Foxx, Pinky Higgins, Eric McNair, Dib Williams, infielders; Mule Haas, Bing Miller, Jimmy Moore, Al Simmons, Homer Summa, outfielders.

Cardinals — Gus Mancuso, Jimmie Wilson, catchers; Hi Bell, Al Grabowski, Burleigh Grimes, Jesse Haines, Bill Hallahan, Syl Johnson, Jim Lindsey, Flint Rhem, pitchers; Sparky Adams, Jim Bottomley, Frankie Frisch, Charley Gelbert, Andy High, infielders; Ray Blades, Taylor Douthit, Showboat Fisher, Chick Hafey, Ernie Orsatti, George Puccinelli, George Watkins, outfielders.

1931- ST. LOUIS CARDINALS N.L. (4) vs. PHILADELPHIA ATHLETICS A.L. (3)

(Sportsmans Park / Shibe Park)

Oct. 1	at StL.	Philadelphia (Grove)	6	St. Louis (Derringer)	2
Oct. 2	at StL.	St. Louis (Hallahan)	2	Philadelphia (Earnshaw)	0
Oct. 5	at Phil.	St. Louis (Grimes)	5	Philadelphia (Grove)	2
Oct. 6	at Phil.	Philadelphia (Earnshaw)	3	St. Louis (Johnson)	0
Oct. 7	at Phil.	St. Louis (Hallahan)	5	Philadelphia (Hoyt)	1
Oct. 9	at StL.	Philadelphia (Grove)	8	St. Louis (Derringer)	1
Oct. 10	at StL.	St. Louis (Grimes)	4	Philadelphia (Earnshaw)	2

POSTPONED: (Rain) Oct. 4

MANAGERS: Gabby Street, Cardinals; Connie Mack, Athletics

Cardinals — Mike Gonzalez, Gus Mancuso, Jimmie Wilson, catchers; Paul Derringer, Burleigh Grimes, Jesse Haines, Bill Hallahan, Syl Johnson, Tony Kaufman, Jim Lindsey, Flint Rhem, Allyn Stout, pitchers; Sparky Adams, Jim Bottomley, Ripper Collins, Jake Flowers, Frankie Frisch, Charley Gelbert, Andy High, infielders; Ray Blades, Chick Hafey, Pepper Martin, Ernie Orsatti, Wally Roettger, George Watkins, outfielders.

Athletics — Mickey Cochrane, Johnnie Heving, Joe Palmisano, catchers; George Earnshaw, Lefty Grove, Waite Hoyt, Lew Krausse, Lee Roy Mahaffey, Hank McDonald, Jim Peterson, Ed Rommel, Rube Walberg, pitchers; Max Bishop, Joe Boley, Jimmy Dykes, Jimmie Foxx, Eric McNair, Philip Todt, Dib Williams, infielders; Doc Cramer, Mule Haas, Bing Miller, Jimmy Moore, Al Simmons, outfielders.

1932 – NEW YORK YANKEES A.L. (4) vs. CHICAGO CUBS N.L. (0)

(Yankee Stadium / Wrigley Field)

Sept. 28	at NY	New York (Ruffing)	12	Chicago (Bush)	6
Sept. 29	at NY	New York (Gomez)	5	Chicago (Warneke)	2
Oct. 1	at Chi.	New York (Pipgras)	7	Chicago (Root)	5
Oct. 2	at Chi.	New York (Moore)	13	Chicago (May)	6

MANAGERS: Joe McCarthy, Yankees; Charlie Grimm, Cubs

Yankees — Bill Dickey, Arndt Jorgens, catchers; Johnny Allen, Jumbo Brown, Charlie Devens, Lefty Gomez, Danny MacFayden, Wilcy Moore, Herb Pennock, George Pipgras, Red Ruffing, Ed Wells, pitchers; Frankie Crosetti, Doc Farrell, Lou Gehrig, Lyn Lary, Tony Lazzeri, Joe Sewell, infielders; Sammy Byrd, Ben Chapman, Earle Combs, Myril Hoag, Babe Ruth, outfielders.

Cubs — Gabby Hartnett, Rollie Hemsley, Zack Taylor, catchers; Guy Bush, Burleigh Grimes, LeRoy Herrmann, Pat Malone, Frank May, Charlie Root, Bob Smith, Bud Tinning, Lon Warneke, pitchers; Woody English, Charlie Grimm, Stan Hack, Billy Herman, Billy Jurges, Mark Koenig, infielders; Kiki Cuyler, Frank Demaree, Marv Gudat, Johnny Moore, Riggs Stephenson, outfielders.

1933 – NEW YORK GIANTS N.L. (4) vs. WASHINGTON SENATORS A.L. (1)

(Polo Grounds / Griffith Stadium)

Oct. 3	at NY	New York (Hubbell)	4	Washington (Stewart)	2	
Oct. 4	at NY	New York (Schumacher)	6	Washington (Crowder)	1	
Oct. 5	at Wash.	Washington (Whitehill)	4	New York (Fitzsimmons)	0	
Oct. 6	at Wash.	New York (Hubbell)	2	Washington (Weaver)	1	(11 innings)
Oct. 7	at Wash.	New York (Luque)	4	Washington (Russell)	3	(10 innings)

MANAGERS: Bill Terry, Giants; Joe Cronin, Senators

Giants — Harry Danning, Gus Mancuso, Paul Richards, catchers; Hi Bell, Watty Clark, Freddie Fitzsimmons, Carl Hubbell, Dolf Luque, Roy Parmelee, Jack Salveson, Hal Schumacher, Glenn Spencer, pitchers; Hughie Critz, Chuck Dressen, Travis Jackson, Bernie James, Blondy Ryan, Bill Terry, Johnny Vergez, infielders; Kiddo Davis, Joe Moore, Lefty O'Doul, Mel Ott, Homer Peel, outfielders.

Senators — Moe Berg, Cliff Bolton, Luke Sewell, catchers; Bobby Burke, Ed Chapman, General Crowder, Alex McColl, Jack Russell, Lefty Stewart, Tommy Thomas, Monte Weaver, Earl Whitehill, pitchers; Ossie Bluege, Bob Boken, Joe Cronin, John Kerr, Joe Kuhel, Buddy Myer, infielders. Goose Goslin, Dave Harris, Heinie Manush, Sam Rice, Fred Schulte, outfielders.

1934 - ST. LOUIS CARDINALS N.L. (4) vs. DETROIT TIGERS A.L. (3)
(Sportsmans Park / Navin Field)

Oct. 3	at Det.	St. Louis (Dizzy Dean)	8	Detroit (Crowder)	3	
Oct. 4	at Det.	Detroit (Rowe)	3	St. Louis (Walker)	2	(12 innings)
Oct. 5	at StL.	St. Louis (Daffy Dean)	4	Detroit (Bridges)	1	
Oct. 6	at StL.	Detroit (Auker)	10	St. Louis (Walker)	4	
Oct. 7	at StL.	Detroit (Bridges)	3	St. Louis (Dizzy Dean)	1	
Oct. 8	at Det.	St. Louis (Daffy Dean)	4	Detroit (Rowe)	3	
Oct. 9	at Det.	St. Louis (Dizzy Dean)	11	Detroit (Auker)	0	

MANAGERS: Frankie Frisch, Cardinals; Mickey Cochrane, Tigers

Cardinals — Spud Davis, Bill DeLancey, Francis Healy, catchers; Tex Carleton, Dizzy Dean, Daffy Dean, Jesse Haines, Bill Hallahan, Jim Mooney, Dazzy Vance, Bill Walker, pitchers; Ripper Collins, Pat Crawford, Leo Durocher, Frankie Frisch, Pepper Martin, Burgess Whitehead, infielders; Chick Fullis, Joe Medwick, Ernie Orsatti, Jack Rothrock, outfielders.

Tigers — Mickey Cochrane, Ray Hayworth, catchers; Elden Auker, Tommy Bridges, General Crowder, Carl Fischer, Luke Hamlin, Chief Hogsett, Firpo Marberry, Schoolboy Rowe, Vic Sorrell, pitchers; Flea Clifton, Charlie Gehringer, Hank Greenberg, Marv Owen, Billy Rogell, Heinie Schuble, infielders; Frank Doljack, Pete Fox, Goose Goslin, Gee Walker, Jo-Jo White, outfielders.

1935 - DETROIT TIGERS A.L. (4) vs. CHICAGO CUBS N.L. (2)
(Navin Field / Wrigley Field)

Oct. 2	at Det.	Chicago (Warneke)	3	Detroit (Rowe)	0	
Oct. 3	at Det.	Detroit (Bridges)	8	Chicago (Root)	3	
Oct. 4	at Chi.	Detroit (Rowe)	6	Chicago (French)	5	(11 innings)
Oct. 5	at Chi.	Detroit (Crowder)	2	Chicago (Carleton)	1	
Oct. 6	at Chi.	Chicago (Warneke)	3	Detroit (Rowe)	1	
Oct. 7	at Det.	Detroit (Bridges)	4	Chicago (French)	3	

MANAGERS: Mickey Cochrane, Tigers; Charlie Grimm, Cubs

Tigers — Mickey Cochrane, Ray Hayworth, Frank Reiber, catchers; Elden Auker, Tommy Bridges, General Crowder, Chief Hogsett, Roxie Lawson, Schoolboy Rowe, Vic Sorrell, Joe Sullivan, pitchers; Flea Clifton, Charlie Gehringer, Hank Greenberg, Marv Owen, Billy Rogell, Heinie Schuble, infielders; Pete Fox, Goose Goslin, Hugh Shelley, Gee Walker, Jo-Jo White, outfielders.

Cubs — Gabby Hartnett, Ken O'Dea, Walter Stephenson, catchers; Tex Carleton, Hugh Casey, Larry French, Roy Henshaw, Fabian Kowalik, Bill Lee, Charlie Root, Clyde Shoun, Lon Warneke, pitchers; Phil Cavarretta, Woody English, Charlie Grimm, Stan Hack, Billy Herman, Bill Jurges, infielders; Frank Demaree, Augie Galan, Chuck Klein, Freddie Lindstrom, Tuck Stainback, outfielders.

1936 - NEW YORK YANKEES A.L. (4) vs. NEW YORK GIANTS N.L. (2)
(Yankee Stadium / Polo Grounds)

Sept. 30	at Giants	Giants (Hubbell)	6	Yankees (Ruffing)	1	
Oct. 2	at Giants	Yankees (Gomez)	18	Giants (Schumacher)	4	
Oct. 3	at Yankees	Yankees (Hadley)	2	Giants (Fitzsimmons)	1	
Oct. 4	at Yankees	Yankees (Pearson)	5	Giants (Hubbell)	2	
Oct. 5	at Yankees	Giants (Schumacher)	5	Yankees (Malone)	4	(10 innings)
Oct. 6	at Giants	Yankees (Gomez)	13	Giants (Fitzsimmons)	5	
POSTPONED: (Rain) Oct. 1						

MANAGERS: Joe McCarthy, Yankees; Bill Terry, Giants

Yankees — Bill Dickey, Joe Glenn, Arndt Jorgens, catchers; Johnny Broaca, Jumbo Brown, Lefty Gomez, Bump Hadley, Pat Malone, Johnny Murphy, Monte Pearson, Red Ruffing, Kemp Wicker, pitchers; Frankie Crosetti, Lou Gehrig, Don Heffner, Tony Lazzeri, Red Rolfe, Jack Saltzgaver, infielders; Joe DiMaggio, Roy Johnson, Jake Powell, Bob Seeds, George Selkirk, outfielders.

Giants — Harry Danning, Gus Mancuso, Roy Spencer, catchers; Slick Castleman, Dick Coffman, Freddie Fitzsimmons, Frank Gabler, Harry Gumbert, Carl Hubbell, Hal Schumacher, Al Smith, pitchers; Dick Bartell, Travis Jackson, Mark Koenig, Sam Leslie, Eddie Mayo, Bill Terry, Burgess Whitehead, infielders; Kiddo Davis, Hank Leiber, Joe Moore, Mel Ott, Jimmy Ripple, outfielders.

1937 – NEW YORK YANKEES A.L. (4) vs. NEW YORK GIANTS N.L. (1)

(Yankee Stadium / Polo Grounds)

Oct. 6	at Yankees	Yankees (Gomez)	8	Giants (Hubbell)	1	
Oct. 7	at Yankees	Yankees (Ruffing)	8	Giants (Melton)	1	
Oct. 8	at Giants	Yankees (Pearson)	5	Giants (Schumacher)	1	
Oct. 9	at Giants	Giants (Hubbell)	7	Yankees (Hadley)	3	
Oct. 10	at Giants	Yankees (Gomez)	4	Giants (Melton)	2	

MANAGERS: Joe McCarthy, Yankees; Bill Terry, Giants

Yankees — Bill Dickey, Joe Glenn, Arndt Jorgens, catchers; Ivy Andrews, Spud Chandler, Lefty Gomez, Bump Hadley, Frank Makosky, Pat Malone, Johnny Murphy, Monte Pearson, Red Ruffing, Kemp Wicker, pitchers; Frankie Crosetti, Lou Gehrig, Don Heffner, Tony Lazzeri, Red Rolfe, Jack Saltzgaver, infielders; Joe DiMaggio, Tommy Henrich, Myril Hoag, Jake Powell, George Selkirk, outfielders.

Giants — Harry Danning, Ed Madjeski, Gus Mancuso, catchers; Tom Baker, Don Brennan, Slick Castleman, Dick Coffman, Harry Gumbert, Carl Hubbell, Cliff Melton, Hal Schumacher, Al Smith, pitchers; Dick Bartell, Lou Chiozza, Mickey Haslin, Sam Leslie, Johnny McCarthy, Mel Ott, Blondy Ryan, Burgess Whitehead, infielders; Wally Berger, Hank Leiber, Joe Moore, Jimmy Ripple, outfielders.

1938 – NEW YORK YANKEES A.L. (4) vs. CHICAGO CUBS N.L. (0)

(Yankee Stadium / Wrigley Field)

Oct. 5	at Chi.	New York (Ruffing)	3	Chicago (Lee)	1
Oct. 6	at Chi.	New York (Gomez)	6	Chicago (Dean)	3
Oct. 8	at NY	New York (Pearson)	5	Chicago (Bryant)	2
Oct. 9	at NY	New York (Ruffing)	8	Chicago (Lee)	3

MANAGERS: Joe McCarthy, Yankees; Gabby Hartnett, Cubs

Yankees — Bill Dickey, Joe Glenn, Arndt Jorgens, catchers; Ivy Andrews, Spud Chandler, Wes Ferrell, Lefty Gomez, Bump Hadley, Johnny Murphy, Monte Pearson, Red Ruffing, Steve Sundra, pitchers; Frankie Crosetti, Babe Dahlgren, Lou Gehrig, Joe Gordon, Billy Knickerbocker, Red Rolfe, infielders; Joe DiMaggio, Tommy Henrich, Myril Hoag, Jake Powell, George Selkirk, outfielders.

Cubs — Bob Garbark, Gabby Hartnett, Ken O'Dea, catchers; Clay Bryant, Tex Carleton, Dizzy Dean, Larry French, Bill Lee, Vance Page, Charlie Root, Jack Russell, pitchers; Phil Cavarretta, Ripper Collins, Stan Hack, Billy Herman, Billy Jurges, Tony Lazzeri, infielders; Jim Asbell, Frank Demaree, Augie Galan, Joe Marty, Carl Reynolds, outfielders.

1939 – NEW YORK YANKEES A.L. (4) vs. CINCINNATI REDS N.L. (0)

(Yankee Stadium / Crosley Field)

Oct. 4	at NY	New York (Ruffing)	2	Cincinnati (Derringer)	1	
Oct. 5	at NY	New York (Pearson)	4	Cincinnati (Walters)	0	
Oct. 7	at Cin.	New York (Hadley)	7	Cincinnati (Thompson)	3	
Oct. 8	at Cin.	New York (Murphy)	7	Cincinnati (Walters)	4	(10 innings)

MANAGERS: Joe McCarthy, Yankees; Bill McKechnie, Reds

Yankees — Bill Dickey, Arndt Jorgens, Buddy Rosar, catchers; Spud Chandler, Atley Donald, Lefty Gomez, Bump Hadley, Oral Hildebrand, Johnny Murphy, Monte Pearson, Red Ruffing, Marius Russo, Steve Sundra, pitchers; Frankie Crosetti, Babe Dahlgren, Lou Gehrig, Joe Gordon, Billy Knickerbocker, Red Rolfe, infielders; Joe DiMaggio, Tommy Henrich, Charlie Keller, Jake Powell, George Selkirk, outfielders.

Reds — Willard Hershberger, Ernie Lombardi, catchers; Paul Derringer, Lee Grissom, Hank Johnson, Whitey Moore, Johnny Niggeling, Milt Shoffner, Junior Thompson, Johnny Vander Meer, Bucky Walters, pitchers; Lonny Frey, Eddie Joost, Frank McCormick, Billy Myers, Lew Riggs, Les Scarsella, Bill Werber, infielders; Wally Berger, Tony Bongiovanni, Frenchy Bordagaray, Harry Craft, Lee Gamble, Ival Goodman, Al Simmons, outfielders.

1940 – CINCINNATI REDS N.L. (4) vs. DETROIT TIGERS A.L. (3)
(Crosley Field / Briggs Stadium)

Oct. 2	at Cin.	Detroit (Newsom)	7	Cincinnati (Derringer)	2
Oct. 3	at Cin.	Cincinnati (Walters)	5	Detroit (Rowe)	3
Oct. 4	at Det.	Detroit (Bridges)	7	Cincinnati (Turner)	4
Oct. 5	at Det.	Cincinnati (Derringer)	5	Detroit (Trout)	2
Oct. 6	at Det.	Detroit (Newsom)	8	Cincinnati (Thompson)	0
Oct. 7	at Cin.	Cincinnati (Walters)	4	Detroit (Rowe)	0
Oct. 8	at Cin.	Cincinnati (Derringer)	2	Detroit (Newsom)	1

MANAGERS: Bill McKechnie, Reds; Del Baker, Tigers

Reds – Bill Baker, Ernie Lombardi, Jimmie Wilson, catchers; Joe Beggs, Paul Derringer, Witt Guise, Johnny Hutchings, Whitey Moore, Elmer Riddle, Milt Shoffner, Junior Thompson, Jim Turner, Johnny Vander Meer, Bucky Walters, pitchers; Lonny Frey, Eddie Joost, Frank McCormick, Billy Myers, Lew Riggs, Bill Werber, infielders; Morris Arnovich, Harry Craft, Ival Goodman, Myron McCormick, Jimmy Ripple, outfielders.

Tigers – Billy Sullivan, Jr., Birdie Tebbetts, catchers; Al Benton, Tommy Bridges, Johnny Gorsica, Fred Hutchinson, Archie McKain, Hal Newhouser, Bobo Newsom, Schoolboy Rowe, Tom Seats, Clay Smith, Dizzy Trout, pitchers; Dick Bartell, Frank Croucher, Charlie Gehringer, Pinky Higgins, Dutch Meyer, Rudy York, infielders; Earl Averill, Bruce Campbell, Pete Fox, Hank Greenberg, Barney McCosky, Tuck Stainback, outfielders.

1941 – NEW YORK YANKEES A.L. (4) vs. BROOKLYN DODGERS N.L. (1)
(Yankee Stadium / Ebbets Field)

Oct. 1	at NY	New York (Ruffing)	3	Brooklyn (Davis)	2
Oct. 2	at NY	Brooklyn (Wyatt)	3	New York (Chandler)	2
Oct. 4	at Brk.	New York (Russo)	2	Brooklyn (Casey)	1
Oct. 5	at Brk.	New York (Murphy)	7	Brooklyn (Casey)	4
Oct. 6	at Brk.	New York (Bonham)	3	Brooklyn (Wyatt)	1

POSTPONED: (Rain) Oct. 3

MANAGERS: Joe McCarthy, Yankees; Leo Durocher, Dodgers

Yankees – Bill Dickey, Buddy Rosar, Ken Silvestri, catchers; Ernie Bonham, Norm Branch, Marv Breuer, Spud Chandler, Atley Donald, Lefty Gomez, Johnny Murphy, Steve Peek, Red Ruffing, Marius Russo, Charley Stanceu, pitchers; Frankie Crosetti, Joe Gordon, Jerry Priddy, Phil Rizzuto, Red Rolfe, Johnny Sturm, infielders; Frenchy Bordagaray, Joe DiMaggio, Tommy Henrich, Charlie Keller, George Selkirk, outfielders.

Dodgers – Herman Franks, Mickey Owen, catchers; Ed Albosta, Johnny Allen, Hugh Casey, Curt Davis, Tom Drake, Freddie Fitzsimmons, Larry French, Luke Hamlin, Kirby Higbe, Newt Kimball, Whit Wyatt, pitchers; Dolph Camilli, Pete Coscarart, Leo Durocher, Billy Herman, Cookie Lavagetto, Pee Wee Reese, Lew Riggs, infielders; Augie Galan, Joe Medwick, Pete Reiser, Dixie Walker, Jimmy Wasdell, outfielders.

1942 – ST. LOUIS CARDINALS N.L. (4) vs. NEW YORK YANKEES A.L. (1)
(Sportsmans Park / Yankee Stadium)

Sept. 30	at StL.	New York (Ruffing)	7	St. Louis (M. Cooper)	4
Oct. 1	at StL.	St. Louis (Beazley)	4	New York (Bonham)	3
Oct. 3	at NY	St. Louis (White)	2	New York (Chandler)	0
Oct. 4	at NY	St. Louis (Lanier)	9	New York (Donald)	6
Oct. 5	at NY	St. Louis (Beazley)	4	New York (Ruffing)	2

MANAGERS: Billy Southworth, Cardinals; Joe McCarthy, Yankees

Cardinals – Walker Cooper, Sam Narron, Ken O'Dea, catchers; Johnny Beazley, Mort Cooper, Murry Dickson, Harry Gumbert, Howie Krist, Max Lanier, Whitey Moore, Howie Pollet, Ernie White, pitchers; Jimmy Brown, Creepy Crespi, Johnny Hopp, Whitey Kurowski, Marty Marion, Ray Sanders, infielders; Terry Moore, Stan Musial, Enos Slaughter, Coaker Triplett, Harry Walker, outfielders.

Yankees – Bill Dickey, Rollie Hemsley, Buddy Rosar, catchers; Ernie Bonham, Hank Borowy, Marv Breuer, Spud Chandler, Atley Donald, Lefty Gomez, Johnny Lindell, Johnny Murphy, Red Ruffing, Marius Russo, Jim Turner, pitchers; Frankie Crosetti, Joe Gordon, Buddy Hassett, Gerry Priddy, Phil Rizzuto, Red Rolfe, infielders; Roy Cullenbine, Joe DiMaggio, Charlie Keller, George Selkirk, Tuck Stainback, outfielders.

1943 – NEW YORK YANKEES A.L. (4) vs. ST. LOUIS CARDINALS N.L. (1)
(Yankee Stadium / Sportsmans Park)

Oct. 5	at NY	New York (Chandler)	4	St. Louis (Lanier)	2
Oct. 6	at NY	St. Louis (M. Cooper)	4	New York (Bonham)	3
Oct. 7	at NY	New York (Borowy)	6	St. Louis (Brazle)	2
Oct. 10	at StL.	New York (Russo)	2	St. Louis (Brecheen)	1
Oct. 11	at StL.	New York (Chandler)	2	St. Louis (M. Cooper)	0

MANAGERS: Joe McCarthy, Yankees; Billy Southworth, Cardinals

Yankees – Bill Dickey, Rollie Hemsley, Ken Sears, catchers; Ernie Bonham, Hank Borowy, Marv Breuer, Tommy Byrne, Spud Chandler, Atley Donald, Johnny Murphy, Marius Russo, Jim Turner, Butch Wensloff, Bill Zuber, pitchers; Frankie Crosetti, Nick Etten, Joe Gordon, Oscar Grimes, Billy Johnson, Snuffy Stirnweiss, infielders; Charlie Keller, Johnny Lindell, Bud Metheny, Tuck Stainback, Roy Weatherly, outfielders.

Cardinals – Walker Cooper, Sam Narron, Ken O'Dea, catchers; Al Brazle, Harry Brecheen, Mort Cooper, Murry Dickson, Harry Gumbert, Howie Krist, Max Lanier, George Munger, Ernie White, pitchers; George Fallon, Debs Garms, Lou Klein, Whitey Kurowski, Marty Marion, Ray Sanders, infielders; Frank Demaree, Johnny Hopp, Danny Litwhiler, Stan Musial, Harry Walker, outfielders.

1944 – ST. LOUIS CARDINALS N.L. (4) vs. ST. LOUIS BROWNS A.L. (2)
(Sportsmans Park / Sportsmans Park)

Oct. 4	at Cardinals	Browns (Galehouse)	2	Cardinals (M. Cooper)	1	
Oct. 5	at Cardinals	Cardinals (Donnelly)	3	Browns (Muncrief)	2	(11 innings)
Oct. 6	at Browns	Browns (Kramer)	6	Cardinals (Wilks)	2	
Oct. 7	at Browns	Cardinals (Brecheen)	5	Browns (Jakucki)	1	
Oct. 8	at Browns	Cardinals (M. Cooper)	2	Browns (Galehouse)	0	
Oct. 9	at Cardinals	Cardinals (Lanier)	3	Browns (Potter)	1	

MANAGERS: Billy Southworth, Cardinals; Luke Sewell, Browns

Cardinals – Walker Cooper, Bob Keely, Ken O'Dea, catchers; Harry Brecheen, Bud Byerly, Mort Cooper, Blix Donnelly, Al Jurisich, Max Lanier, Freddy Schmidt, Ted Wilks, pitchers; George Fallon, Whitey Kurowski, Marty Marion, Ray Sanders, Emil Verban, infielders; Augie Bergamo, Debs Garms, Johnny Hopp, Danny Litwhiler, Pepper Martin, Stan Musial, outfielders.

Browns – Red Hayworth, Frank Mancuso, Tom Turner, catchers; George Caster, Denny Galehouse, Al Hollingsworth, Willis Hudlin, Sig Jakucki, Jack Kramer, Bob Muncrief, Nels Potter, Tex Shirley, Sam Zoldak, pitchers; Floyd Baker, Mark Christman, Ellis Clary, Don Gutteridge, George McQuinn, Vern Stephens, infielders; Milt Byrnes, Mike Chartak, Mike Kreevich, Chet Laabs, Gene Moore, Al Zarilla, outfielders.

1945 – DETROIT TIGERS A.L. (4) vs. CHICAGO CUBS N.L. (3)
(Briggs Stadium / Wrigley Field)

Oct. 3	at Det.	Chicago (Borowy)	9	Detroit (Newhouser)	0	
Oct. 4	at Det.	Detroit (Trucks)	4	Chicago (Wyse)	1	
Oct. 5	at Det.	Chicago (Passeau)	3	Detroit (Overmire)	0	
Oct. 6	at Chi.	Detroit (Trout)	4	Chicago (Prim)	1	
Oct. 7	at Chi.	Detroit (Newhouser)	8	Chicago (Borowy)	4	
Oct. 8	at Chi.	Chicago (Borowy)	8	Detroit (Trout)	7	(12 innings)
Oct. 10	at Chi.	Detroit (Newhouser)	9	Chicago (Borowy)	3	

MANAGERS: Steve O'Neill, Tigers; Charlie Grimm, Cubs

Tigers – Hack Miller, Paul Richards, Bob Swift, catchers; Al Benton, Tommy Bridges, George Caster, Zeb Eaton, Art Houtteman, Les Mueller, Hal Newhouser, Stubby Overmire, Billy Pierce, Jim Tobin, Dizzy Trout, Virgil Trucks, Walter Wilson, pitchers; Red Borom, Joe Hoover, Bob Meier, Eddie Mayo, John McHale, Jimmy Outlaw, Skeeter Webb, Rudy York, infielders; Doc Cramer, Roy Cullenbine, Hank Greenberg, Chuck Hostetler, Ed Mierkowicz, Hub Walker, outfielders.

Cubs – Paul Gillespie, Mickey Livingston, Clyde McCullough, Len Rice, Dewey Williams, catchers; Hi Bithorn, Hank Borowy, Bob Chipman, Paul Derringer, Paul Erickson, Ed Hanyzewski, Claude Passeau, Ray Prim, Walter Signer, Ray Starr, Hy Vandenburg, Lon Warneke, Hank Wyse, pitchers; Heinz Becker, Sy Block, Phil Cavarretta, Stan Hack, Roy Hughes, Don Johnson, Lennie Merullo, Bill Schuster, infielders; Peanuts Lowrey, Bill Nicholson, Andy Pafko, Ed Sauer, Frank Secory, outfielders.

1946 – ST. LOUIS CARDINALS N.L. (4) vs. BOSTON RED SOX A.L. (3)

(Sportsmans Park / Fenway Park)

Oct. 6	at StL.	Boston (Johnson)	3	St. Louis (Pollet)	2	(10 innings)
Oct. 7	at StL.	St. Louis (Brecheen)	3	Boston (Harris)	0	
Oct. 9	at Bos.	Boston (Ferriss)	4	St. Louis (Dickson)	0	
Oct. 10	at Bos.	St. Louis (Munger)	12	Boston (Hughson)	3	
Oct. 11	at Bos.	Boston (Dobson)	6	St. Louis (Brazle)	3	
Oct. 13	at StL.	St. Louis (Brecheen)	4	Boston (Harris)	1	
Oct. 15	at StL.	St. Louis (Brecheen)	4	Boston (Klinger)	3	

MANAGERS: Eddie Dyer, Cardinals; Joe Cronin, Red Sox

Cardinals – Joe Garagiola, Clyde Kluttz, Del Rice, catchers; Red Barrett, Johnny Beazley, Al Brazle, Harry Brecheen, Ken Burkhart, Murry Dickson, Johnny Grodzicki, Howie Krist, George Munger, Howie Pollet, Freddy Schmidt, Ted Wilks, pitchers; Jeff Cross, Nippy Jones, Whitey Kurowski, Marty Marion, Stan Musial, Red Schoendienst, infielders; Buster Adams, Erv Dusak, Bill Endicott, Terry Moore, Walter Sessi, Dick Sisler, Enos Slaughter, Harry Walker, outfielders.

Red Sox – Ed McGah, Roy Partee, Hal Wagner, catchers; Jim Bagby, Mace Brown, Joe Dobson, Clem Dreisewerd, Boo Ferriss, Mickey Harris, Tex Hughson, Earl Johnson, Bob Klinger, Mike Ryba, Charlie Wagner, Bill Zuber, pitchers; Paul Campbell, Bobby Doerr, Don Gutteridge, Pinky Higgins, Eddie Pellagrini, Johnny Pesky, Rip Russell, Rudy York, infielders; Leon Culberson, Dom DiMaggio, Johnny Lazor, Tom McBride, George Metkovich, Wally Moses, Ted Williams, outfielders.

1947 – NEW YORK YANKEES A.L. (4) vs. BROOKLYN DODGERS N.L. (3)

(Yankee Stadium / Ebbets Field)

Sept. 30	at NY	New York (Shea)	5	Brooklyn (Branca)	3
Oct. 1	at NY	New York (Reynolds)	10	Brooklyn (Lombardi)	3
Oct. 2	at Brk.	Brooklyn (Casey)	9	New York (Newsom)	8
Oct. 3	at Brk.	Brooklyn (Casey)	3	New York (Bevens)	2
Oct. 4	at Brk	New York (Shea)	2	Brooklyn (Barney)	1
Oct. 5	at NY	Brooklyn (Branca)	8	New York (Page)	6
Oct. 6	at NY	New York (Page)	5	Brooklyn (Gregg)	2

MANAGERS: Bucky Harris, Yankees; Burt Shotton, Dodgers

Yankees – Yogi Berra, Ralph Houk, Sherm Lollar, Aaron Robinson, catchers; Bill Bevens, Spud Chandler, Karl Drews, Randy Gumpert, Don Johnson, Bobo Newsom, Joe Page, Vic Raschi, Allie Reynolds, Spec Shea, Butch Wensloff, pitchers; Bobby Brown, Lonny Frey, Billy Johnson, George McQuinn, Jack Phillips, Phil Rizzuto, Snuffy Stirnweiss, infielders; Allie Clark, Joe DiMaggio, Tommy Henrich, Charlie Keller, Johnny Lindell, outfielders.

Dodgers – Bobby Bragan, Bruce Edwards, Gil Hodges, catchers; Dan Bankhead, Rex Barney, Hank Behrman, Ralph Branca, Hugh Casey, Hal Gregg, Joe Hatten, Clyde King, Vic Lombardi, Harry Taylor, pitchers; Tommy Brown, Spider Jorgensen, Cookie Lavagetto, Eddie Miksis, Pee Wee Reese, Jackie Robinson, Stan Rojek, Eddie Stanky, Arky Vaughan, infielders; Carl Furillo, Al Gionfriddo, Gene Hermanski, Pete Reiser, Dixie Walker, outfielders.

1948 – CLEVELAND INDIANS A.L. (4) vs. BOSTON BRAVES N.L. (2)

(Cleveland Stadium / Braves Field)

Oct. 6	at Bos.	Boston (Sain)	1	Cleveland (Feller)	0
Oct. 7	at Bos.	Cleveland (Lemon)	4	Boston (Spahn)	1
Oct. 8	at Clev.	Cleveland (Bearden)	2	Boston (Bickford)	0
Oct. 9	at Clev.	Cleveland (Gromek)	2	Boston (Sain)	1
Oct. 10	at Clev.	Boston (Spahn)	11	Cleveland (Feller)	5
Oct. 11	at Bos.	Cleveland (Lemon)	4	Boston (Voiselle)	3

MANAGERS: Lou Boudreau, Indians; Billy Southworth, Braves

Indians – Jim Hegan, Joe Tipton, catchers; Gene Bearden, Russ Christopher, Bob Feller, Steve Gromek, Eddie Klieman, Bob Lemon, Bob Muncrief, Satchel Paige, Sam Zoldak, pitchers; Johnny Berardino, Ray Boone, Lou Boudreau, Joe Gordon, Ken Keltner, Eddie Robinson, Al Rosen, infielders; Allie Clark, Larry Doby, Walt Judnich, Bob Kennedy, Dale Mitchell, Hal Peck, Thurman Tucker, outfielders.

Braves – Phil Masi, Bill Salkeld, catchers; Red Barrett, Vern Bickford, Bobby Hogue, Al Lyons, Nels Potter, Johnny Sain, Clyde Shoun, Warren Spahn, Bill Voiselle, Ernie White, pitchers; Alvin Dark, Bob Elliott, Frank McCormick, Connie Ryan, Ray Sanders, Sibby Sisti, Eddie Stanky, Bobby Sturgeon, Earl Torgeson, infielders; Clint Conatser, Tommy Holmes, Mike McCormick, Marv Rickert, outfielders.

1949 – NEW YORK YANKEES A.L. (4) vs. BROOKLYN DODGERS N.L. (1)
(Yankee Stadium / Ebbets Field)

Oct. 5	at NY	New York (Reynolds)	1	Brooklyn (Newcombe)	0	
Oct. 6	at NY	Brooklyn (Roe)	1	New York (Raschi)	0	
Oct. 7	at Brk.	New York (Page)	4	Brooklyn (Branca)	3	
Oct. 8	at Brk.	New York (Lopat)	6	Brooklyn (Newcombe)	4	
Oct. 9	at Brk.	New York (Raschi)	10	Brooklyn (Barney)	6	

MANAGERS: Casey Stengel, Yankees; Burt Shotton, Dodgers

Yankees – Yogi Berra, Gus Niarhos, Charlie Silvera, catchers; Ralph Buxton, Tommy Byrne, Ed Lopat, Cuddles Marshall, Joe Page, Duane Pillette, Vic Raschi, Allie Reynolds, Fred Sanford, pitchers; Bobby Brown, Jerry Coleman, Tommy Henrich, Billy Johnson, Johnny Mize, Phil Rizzuto, Snuffy Stirnweiss, infielders; Hank Bauer, Joe DiMaggio, Charlie Keller, Johnny Lindell, Cliff Mapes, Gene Woodling, outfielders.

Dodgers – Roy Campanella, Bruce Edwards, catchers; Jack Banta, Rex Barney, Ralph Branca, Carl Erskine, Joe Hatten, Paul Minner, Don Newcombe, Erv Palica, Preacher Roe, pitchers; Billy Cox, Gil Hodges, Spider Jorgensen, Eddie Miksis, Pee Wee Reese, Jackie Robinson, infielders; Tommy Brown, Carl Furillo, Gene Hermanski, Mike McCormick, Luis Olmo, Marv Rackley, Duke Snider, Dick Whitman, outfielders.

1950 – NEW YORK YANKEES A.L. (4) vs. PHILADELPHIA PHILLIES N.L. (0)
(Yankee Stadium / Shibe Park)

Oct. 4	at Phil.	New York (Raschi)	1	Philadelphia (Konstanty)	0	
Oct. 5	at Phil.	New York (Reynolds)	2	Philadelphia (Roberts)	1	(10 innings)
Oct. 6	at NY	New York (Ferrick)	3	Philadelphia (Meyer)	2	
Oct. 7	at NY	New York (Ford)	5	Philadelphia (Miller)	2	

MANAGERS: Casey Stengel, Yankees; Eddie Sawyer, Phillies

Yankees – Yogi Berra, Ralph Houk, Charlie Silvera, catchers; Tommy Byrne, Tom Ferrick, Whitey Ford, Ed Lopat, Joe Ostrowski, Joe Page, Vic Raschi, Allie Reynolds, Fred Sanford, pitchers; Bobby Brown, Jerry Coleman, Joe Collins, Johnny Hopp, Billy Johnson, Billy Martin, Johnny Mize, Phil Rizzuto, infielders; Hank Bauer, Joe DiMaggio, Jackie Jensen, Cliff Mapes, Gene Woodling, outfielders.

Phillies – Stan Lopata, Andy Seminick, Ken Silvestri, catchers; Milo Candini, Bubba Church, Blix Donnelly, Ken Heintzelman, Ken Johnson, Jim Konstanty, Russ Meyer, Bob Miller, Robin Roberts, Jocko Thompson, pitchers; Jimmy Bloodworth, Ralph Caballero, Mike Goliat, Granny Hamner, Willie Jones, Eddie Waitkus, infielders; Richie Ashburn, Del Ennis, Stan Hollmig, Jackie Mayo, Dick Sisler, Dick Whitman, outfielders.

1951 – NEW YORK YANKEES A.L. (4) vs. NEW YORK GIANTS N.L. (2)
(Yankee Stadium / Polo Grounds)

Oct. 4	at Yankees	Giants (Koslo)	5	Yankees (Reynolds)	1
Oct. 5	at Yankees	Yankees (Lopat)	3	Giants (Jansen)	1
Oct. 6	at Giants	Giants (Hearn)	6	Yankees (Raschi)	2
Oct. 8	at Giants	Yankees (Reynolds)	6	Giants (Maglie)	2
Oct. 9	at Giants	Yankees (Lopat)	13	Giants (Jansen)	1
Oct. 10	at Yankees	Yankees (Raschi)	4	Giants (Koslo)	3

POSTPONED: (Rain) Oct. 7

MANAGERS: Casey Stengel, Yankees; Leo Durocher, Giants

Yankees – Yogi Berra, Ralph Houk, Charlie Silvera, catchers; Bobby Hogue, Bob Kuzava, Ed Lopat, Tom Morgan, Joe Ostrowski, Stubby Overmire, Vic Raschi, Allie Reynolds, Johnny Sain, Art Schallock, Spec Shea, pitchers; Bobby Brown, Jerry Coleman, Joe Collins, Johnny Hopp, Billy Martin, Gil McDougald, Johnny Mize, Phil Rizzuto, infielders; Hank Bauer, Joe DiMaggio, Mickey Mantle, Gene Woodling, outfielders.

Giants – Ray Noble, Wes Westrum, Sal Yvars, catchers; Al Corwin, Jim Hearn, Larry Jansen, Sheldon Jones, Monte Kennedy, Alex Konikowski, Dave Koslo, Sal Maglie, George Spencer, pitchers; Alvin Dark, Whitey Lockman, Jack Lohrke, Bill Rigney, Hank Schenz, Eddie Stanky, Hank Thompson, Bobby Thomson, Davey Williams, infielders; Clint Hartung, Monte Irvin, Willie Mays, Don Mueller, outfielders.

1952 – NEW YORK YANKEES A.L. (4) vs. BROOKLYN DODGERS N.L. (3)
(Yankee Stadium / Ebbets Field)

Oct. 1	at Brk.	Brooklyn (Black)	4	New York (Reynolds)	2	
Oct. 2	at Brk.	New York (Raschi)	7	Brooklyn (Erskine)	1	
Oct. 3	at NY	Brooklyn (Roe)	5	New York (Lopat)	3	
Oct. 4	at NY	New York (Reynolds)	2	Brooklyn (Black)	0	
Oct. 5	at NY	Brooklyn (Erskine)	6	New York (Sain)	5	(11 innings)
Oct. 6	at Brk.	New York (Raschi)	3	Brooklyn (Loes)	2	
Oct. 7	at Brk.	New York (Reynolds)	4	Brooklyn (Black)	2	

MANAGERS: Casey Stengel, Yankees; Chuck Dressen, Dodgers

Yankees — Yogi Berra, Ralph Houk, Charlie Silvera, catchers; Ewell Blackwell, Tom Gorman, Bob Kuzava, Ed Lopat, Jim McDonald, Bill Miller, Joe Ostrowski, Vic Raschi, Allie Reynolds, Johnny Sain, Ray Scarborough, pitchers; Loren Babe, Jim Brideweser, Joe Collins, Billy Martin, Gil McDougald, Johnny Mize, Phil Rizzuto, infielders; Hank Bauer, Mickey Mantle, Irv Noren, Gene Woodling, outfielders.

Dodgers — Roy Campanella, Rube Walker, catchers; Joe Black, Ralph Branca, Carl Erskine, Clyde King, Clem Labine, Joe Landrum, Ken Lehman, Billy Loes, Ray Moore, Preacher Roe, Johnny Rutherford, Ben Wade, pitchers; Rocky Bridges, Billy Cox, Gil Hodges, Bobby Morgan, Rocky Nelson, Pee Wee Reese, Jackie Robinson, infielders; Sandy Amoros, Carl Furillo, Tommy Holmes, Andy Pafko, George Shuba, Duke Snider, outfielders.

1953 – NEW YORK YANKEES A.L. (4) vs. BROOKLYN DODGERS N.L. (2)
(Yankee Stadium / Ebbets Field)

Sept. 30	at NY	New York (Sain)	9	Brooklyn (Labine)	5
Oct. 1	at NY	New York (Lopat)	4	Brooklyn (Roe)	2
Oct. 2	at Brk.	Brooklyn (Erskine)	3	New York (Raschi)	2
Oct. 3	at Brk.	Brooklyn (Loes)	7	New York (Ford)	3
Oct. 4	at Brk.	New York (McDonald)	11	Brooklyn (Podres)	7
Oct. 5	at NY	New York (Reynolds)	4	Brooklyn (Labine)	3

MANAGERS: Casey Stengel, Yankees; Chuck Dressen, Dodgers

Yankees — Yogi Berra, Charlie Silvera, Gus Triandos, catchers; Whitey Ford, Tom Gorman, Steve Kraly, Bob Kuzava, Ed Lopat, Jim McDonald, Bill Miller, Vic Raschi, Allie Reynolds, Johnny Sain, Art Schallock, pitchers; Don Bollweg, Andy Carey, Jerry Coleman, Joe Collins, Billy Martin, Gil McDougald, Willie Miranda, Johnny Mize, Phil Rizzuto, infielders; Hank Bauer, Mickey Mantle, Irv Noren, Bill Renna, Gene Woodling, outfielders.

Dodgers — Roy Campanella, Rube Walker, catchers; Joe Black, Carl Erskine, Jim Hughes, Clem Labine, Billy Loes, Russ Meyer, Bob Milliken, Erv Palica, Johnny Podres, Preacher Roe, Ben Wade, pitchers; Wayne Belardi, Billy Cox, Jim Gilliam, Gil Hodges, Bobby Morgan, Pee Wee Reese, infielders; Bill Antonello, Carl Furillo, Jackie Robinson, George Shuba, Duke Snider, Don Thompson, Dick Williams, outfielders.

1954 – NEW YORK GIANTS N.L. (4) vs. CLEVELAND INDIANS A.L. (0)
(Polo Grounds / Cleveland Stadium)

Sept. 29	at NY	New York (Grissom)	5	Cleveland (Lemon)	2	(10 innings)
Sept. 30	at NY	New York (Antonelli)	3	Cleveland (Wynn)	1	
Oct. 1	at Clev.	New York (Gomez)	6	Cleveland (Garcia)	2	
Oct. 2	at Clev.	New York (Liddle)	7	Cleveland (Lemon)	4	

MANAGERS: Leo Durocher, Giants; Al Lopez, Indians

Giants — Ray Katt, Wes Westrum, catchers; Johnny Antonelli, Al Corwin, Paul Giel, Ruben Gomez, Marv Grissom, Jim Hearn, Alex Konikowski, Don Liddle, Sal Maglie, Windy McCall, Hoyt Wilhelm, Al Worthington, pitchers; Joey Amalfitano, Foster Castleman, Alvin Dark, Billy Gardner, Bobby Hofman, Whitey Lockman, Hank Thompson, Davey Williams, infielders; Monte Irvin, Willie Mays, Don Mueller, Dusty Rhodes, Bill Taylor, outfielders.

Indians — Mickey Grasso, Jim Hegan, Hal Naragon, catchers; Bob Feller, Mike Garcia, Bob Hooper, Art Houtteman, Bob Lemon, Don Mossi, Ray Narleski, Hal Newhouser, Early Wynn, pitchers; Bobby Avila, Sam Dente, Bill Glynn, Hank Majeski, Rudy Regalado, Al Rosen, George Strickland, Vic Wertz, infielders; Larry Doby, Dale Mitchell, Dave Philley, David Pope, Al Smith, Wally Westlake, outfielders.

1955 – BROOKLYN DODGERS N.L. (4) vs. NEW YORK YANKEES A.L. (3)

(Ebbets Field / Yankee Stadium)

Sept. 28	at NY	New York (Ford)	6	Brooklyn (Newcombe)	5	
Sept. 29	at NY	New York (Byrne)	4	Brooklyn (Loes)	2	
Sept. 30	at Brk.	Brooklyn (Podres)	8	New York (Turley)	3	
Oct. 1	at Brk.	Brooklyn (Labine)	8	New York (Larsen)	5	
Oct. 2	at Brk.	Brooklyn (Craig)	5	New York (Grim)	3	
Oct. 3	at NY	New York (Ford)	5	Brooklyn (Spooner)	1	
Oct. 4	at NY	Brooklyn (Podres)	2	New York (Byrne)	0	

MANAGERS: Walter Alston, Dodgers; Casey Stengel, Yankees

Dodgers – Roy Campanella, Dixie Howell, Rube Walker, catchers; Don Bessent, Roger Craig, Carl Erskine, Sandy Koufax, Clem Labine, Billy Loes, Russ Meyer, Don Newcombe, Johnny Podres, Ed Roebuck, Karl Spooner, pitchers; Jim Gilliam, Don Hoak, Gil Hodges, Frank Kellert, Jackie Robinson, Pee Wee Reese, Don Zimmer, infielders; Sandy Amoros, Carl Furillo, George Shuba, Duke Snider, outfielders.

Yankees – Yogi Berra, Charlie Silvera, catchers; Tommy Byrne, Rip Coleman, Whitey Ford, Bob Grim, Johnny Kucks, Don Larsen, Tom Morgan, Tom Sturdivant, Bob Turley, Bob Wiesler, pitchers; Andy Carey, Tommy Carroll, Jerry Coleman, Joe Collins, Frank Leja, Gil McDougald, Billy Martin, Phil Rizzuto, Eddie Robinson, Bill Skowron, infielders; Hank Bauer, Bob Cerv, Elston Howard, Mickey Mantle, Irv Noren, outfielders.

1956 – NEW YORK YANKEES A.L. (4) vs. BROOKLYN DODGERS N.L. (3)

(Yankee Stadium / Ebbets Field)

Oct. 3	at Brk.	Brooklyn (Maglie)	6	New York (Ford)	3	
Oct. 5	at Brk.	Brooklyn (Bessent)	13	New York (Morgan)	8	
Oct. 6	at NY	New York (Ford)	5	Brooklyn (Craig)	3	
Oct. 7	at NY	New York (Sturdivant)	6	Brooklyn (Erskine)	2	
Oct. 8	at NY	New York (Larsen)	2	Brooklyn (Maglie)	0	
Oct. 9	at Brk.	Brooklyn (Labine)	1	New York (Turley)	0	(10 innings)
Oct. 10	at Brk.	New York (Kucks)	9	Brooklyn (Newcombe)	0	

POSTPONED: (Rain) Oct. 4

MANAGERS: Casey Stengel, Yankees; Walter Alston, Dodgers

Yankees – Yogi Berra, Charlie Silvera, catchers; Tommy Byrne, Rip Coleman, Whitey Ford, Bob Grim, Johnny Kucks, Don Larsen, Mickey McDermott, Tom Morgan, Tom Sturdivant, Bob Turley, pitchers; Andy Carey, Tommy Carroll, Jerry Coleman, Joe Collins, Billy Hunter, Billy Martin, Gil McDougald, Bill Skowron, infielders; Hank Bauer, Bob Cerv, Elston Howard, Mickey Mantle, Norm Siebern, Enos Slaughter, Ted Wilson, outfielders.

Dodgers – Roy Campanella, Dixie Howell, Rube Walker, catchers; Don Bessent, Roger Craig, Don Drysdale, Carl Erskine, Sandy Koufax, Clem Labine, Ken Lehman, Sal Maglie, Don Newcombe, Ed Roebuck, pitchers; Chico Fernandez, Jim Gilliam, Gil Hodges, Randy Jackson, Charlie Neal, Pee Wee Reese, Jackie Robinson, infielders; Sandy Amoros, Gino Cimoli, Carl Furillo, Dale Mitchell, Duke Snider, outfielders.

1957 – MILWAUKEE BRAVES N.L. (4) vs. NEW YORK YANKEES A.L. (3)

(County Stadium / Yankee Stadium)

Oct. 2	at NY	New York (Ford)	3	Milwaukee (Spahn)	1	
Oct. 3	at NY	Milwaukee (Burdette)	4	New York (Shantz)	2	
Oct. 5	at Mil.	New York (Larsen)	12	Milwaukee (Buhl)	3	
Oct. 6	at Mil.	Milwaukee (Spahn)	7	New York (Grim)	5	(10 innings)
Oct. 7	at Mil.	Milwaukee (Burdette)	1	New York (Ford)	0	
Oct. 9	at NY	New York (Turley)	3	Milwaukee (Johnson)	2	
Oct. 10	at NY	Milwaukee (Burdette)	5	New York (Larsen)	0	

MANAGERS: Fred Haney, Braves; Casey Stengel, Yankees

Braves – Del Crandall, Del Rice, Carl Sawatski, catchers; Bob Buhl, Lew Burdette, Gene Conley, Ernie Johnson, Dave Jolly, Don McMahon, Taylor Phillips, Juan Pizarro, Warren Spahn, Bob Trowbridge, pitchers; Joe Adcock, Nippy Jones, Johnny Logan, Felix Mantilla, Eddie Mathews, Mel Roach, Red Schoendienst, Frank Torre, infielders; Hank Aaron, Wes Covington, John DeMerit, Bob Hazle, Andy Pafko, outfielders.

Yankees – Yogi Berra, Darrell Johnson, catchers; Tommy Byrne, Al Cicotte, Art Ditmar, Whitey Ford, Bob Grim, Johnny Kucks, Don Larsen, Bobby Shantz, Tom Sturdivant, Bob Turley, pitchers; Andy Carey, Jerry Coleman, Joe Collins, Tony Kubek, Jerry Lumpe, Gil McDougald, Bobby Richardson, Bill Skowron, infielders; Hank Bauer, Elston Howard, Mickey Mantle, Harry Simpson, Enos Slaughter, outfielders.

1958 – NEW YORK YANKEES A.L. (4) vs. MILWAUKEE BRAVES N.L. (3)
(Yankee Stadium / County Stadium)

Oct. 1	at Mil.	Milwaukee (Spahn)	4	New York (Duren)	3	(10 innings)
Oct. 2	at Mil.	Milwaukee (Burdette)	13	New York (Turley)	5	
Oct. 4	at NY	New York (Larsen)	4	Milwaukee (Rush)	0	
Oct. 5	at NY	Milwaukee (Spahn)	3	New York (Ford)	0	
Oct. 6	at NY	New York (Turley)	7	Milwaukee (Burdette)	0	
Oct. 8	at Mil.	New York (Duren)	4	Milwaukee (Spahn)	3	(10 innings)
Oct. 9	at Mil.	New York (Turley)	6	Milwaukee (Burdette)	2	

MANAGERS: Casey Stengel, Yankees; Fred Haney, Braves

Yankees – Yogi Berra, Elston Howard, Darrell Johnson, catchers; Murry Dickson, Art Ditmar, Ryne Duren, Whitey Ford, Johnny Kucks, Don Larsen, Duke Maas, Zack Monroe, Bobby Shantz, Tom Sturdivant, Bob Turley, pitchers; Andy Carey, Tony Kubek, Jerry Lumpe, Gil McDougald, Bobby Richardson, Bill Skowron, Marv Throneberry, infielders; Hank Bauer, Mickey Mantle, Norm Siebern, Enos Slaughter, outfielders.
Braves – Del Crandall, Del Rice, catchers; Bob Buhl, Lew Burdette, Gene Conley, Ernie Johnson, Don McMahon, Juan Pizarro, Humberto Robinson, Bob Rush, Warren Spahn, Bob Trowbridge, Carl Willey, pitchers; Joe Adcock, Harry Hanebrink, Johnny Logan, Felix Mantilla, Eddie Mathews, Red Schoendienst, Frank Torre, Casey Wise, infielders; Hank Aaron, Bill Bruton, Wes Covington, Andy Pafko, outfielders.

1959 – LOS ANGELES DODGERS N.L. (4) vs. CHICAGO WHITE SOX A.L. (2)
(Memorial Coliseum / Comiskey Park)

Oct. 1	at Chi.	Chicago (Wynn)	11	Los Angeles (Craig)	0
Oct. 2	at Chi.	Los Angeles (Podres)	4	Chicago (Shaw)	3
Oct. 4	at LA	Los Angeles (Drysdale)	3	Chicago (Donovan)	1
Oct. 5	at LA	Los Angeles (Sherry)	5	Chicago (Staley)	4
Oct. 6	at LA	Chicago (Shaw)	1	Los Angeles (Koufax)	0
Oct. 8	at Chi.	Los Angeles (Sherry)	9	Chicago (Wynn)	3

MANAGERS: Walter Alston, Dodgers; Al Lopez, White Sox

Dodgers – Joe Pignatano, Johnny Roseboro, catchers; Chuck Churn, Roger Craig, Don Drysdale, Johnny Klippstein, Sandy Koufax, Clem Labine, Danny McDevitt, Johnny Podres, Larry Sherry, Stan Williams, pitchers; Jim Gilliam, Gil Hodges, Charlie Neal, Maury Wills, Don Zimmer, infielders; Don Demeter, Chuck Essegian, Ron Fairly, Carl Furillo, Norm Larker, Wally Moon, Rip Repulski, Duke Snider, outfielders.
White Sox – Earl Battey, Sherm Lollar, Johnny Romano, catchers; Rudy Arias, Dick Donovan, Barry Latman, Turk Lown, Ken McBride, Ray Moore, Billy Pierce, Bob Shaw, Gerry Staley, Early Wynn, pitchers; Luis Aparicio, Norm Cash, Sammy Esposito, Nellie Fox, Billy Goodman, Ted Kluszewski, Bubba Phillips, Earl Torgeson, infielders; Jim Landis, Jim McAnany, Jim Rivera, Al Smith, outfielders.

1960 – PITTSBURGH PIRATES N.L. (4) vs. NEW YORK YANKEES A.L. (3)
(Forbes Field / Yankee Stadium)

Oct. 5	at Pitt.	Pittsburgh (Law)	6	New York (Ditmar)	4
Oct. 6	at Pitt.	New York (Turley)	16	Pittsburgh (Friend)	3
Oct. 8	at NY	New York (Ford)	10	Pittsburgh (Mizell)	0
Oct. 9	at NY	Pittsburgh (Law)	3	New York (Terry)	2
Oct. 10	at NY	Pittsburgh (Haddix)	5	New York (Ditmar)	2
Oct. 12	at Pitt.	New York (Ford)	12	Pittsburgh (Friend)	0
Oct. 13	at Pitt.	Pittsburgh (Haddix)	10	New York (Terry)	9

MANAGERS: Danny Murtaugh, Pirates; Casey Stengel, Yankees

Pirates – Smoky Burgess, Bob Oldis, Hal W. Smith, catchers; Tom Cheney, Roy Face, Bob Friend, Joe Gibbon, Fred Green, Harvey Haddix, Clem Labine, Vern Law, Vinegar Bend Mizell, George Witt, pitchers; Gene Baker, Dick Groat, Don Hoak, Bill Mazeroski, Rocky Nelson, Dick Schofield, Dick Stuart, infielders; Joe Christopher, Gino Cimoli, Roberto Clemente, Bob Skinner, Bill Virdon, outfielders.
Yankees – Yogi Berra, Johnny Blanchard, Elston Howard, catchers; Luis Arroyo, Jim Coates, Art Ditmar, Ryne Duren, Whitey Ford, Eli Grba, Duke Maas, Bobby Shantz, Bill Stafford, Ralph Terry, Bob Turley, pitchers; Clete Boyer, Joe DeMaestri, Tony Kubek, Dale Long, Gil McDougald, Bobby Richardson, Bill Skowron, infielders; Bob Cerv, Hector Lopez, Mickey Mantle, Roger Maris, outfielders.

1961 - NEW YORK YANKEES A.L. (4) vs. CINCINNATI REDS N.L. (1)

(Yankee Stadium / Crosley Field)

Oct. 4	at NY	New York (Ford)	2	Cincinnati (O'Toole)	0
Oct. 5	at NY	Cincinnati (Jay)	6	New York (Terry)	2
Oct. 7	at Cin.	New York (Arroyo)	3	Cincinnati (Purkey)	2
Oct. 8	at Cin.	New York (Ford)	7	Cincinnati (O'Toole)	0
Oct. 9	at Cin.	New York (Daley)	13	Cincinnati (Jay)	5

MANAGERS: Ralph Houk, Yankees; Fred Hutchinson, Reds

Yankees — Johnny Blanchard, Elston Howard, catchers; Luis Arroyo, Tex Clevenger, Jim Coates, Bud Daley,
Al Downing, Whitey Ford, Hal Reniff, Rollie Sheldon, Bill Stafford, Ralph Terry, Bob Turley, pitchers;
Clete Boyer, Joe DeMaestri, Billy Gardner, Bob Hale, Tony Kubek, Bobby Richardson, Bill Skowron, infielders;
Yogi Berra, Hector Lopez, Mickey Mantle, Roger Maris, Jack Reed, outfielders.

Reds — Johnny Edwards, Darrell Johnson, Jerry Zimmerman, catchers; Jim Brosnan, Bill Henry, Jay Hook, Ken Hunt,
Joey Jay, Ken Johnson, Jim Maloney, Jim O'Toole, Bob Purkey, pitchers; Don Blasingame, Leo Cardenas,
Elio Chacon, Gordy Coleman, Gene Freese, Dick Gernert, Eddie Kasko, infielders; Gus Bell, Jerry Lynch,
Vada Pinson, Wally Post, Frank Robinson, outfielders.

1962 - NEW YORK YANKEES A.L. (4) vs. SAN FRANCISCO GIANTS N.L. (3)

(Yankee Stadium / Candlestick Park)

Oct. 4	at SF	New York (Ford)	6	San Francisco (O'Dell)	2
Oct. 5	at SF	San Francisco (Sanford)	2	New York (Terry)	0
Oct. 7	at NY	New York (Stafford)	3	San Francisco (Pierce)	2
Oct. 8	at NY	San Francisco (Larsen)	7	New York (Coates)	3
Oct. 10	at NY	New York (Terry)	5	San Francisco (Sanford)	3
Oct. 15	at SF	San Francisco (Pierce)	5	New York (Ford)	2
Oct. 16	at SF	New York (Terry)	1	San Francisco (Sanford)	0

POSTPONED: (Rain) Oct. 9, 12, 13, 14

MANAGERS: Ralph Houk, Yankees; Alvin Dark, Giants

Yankees — Johnny Blanchard, Elston Howard, catchers; Luis Arroyo, Jim Bouton, Marshall Bridges, Tex Clevenger,
Jim Coates, Bud Daley, Whitey Ford, Rollie Sheldon, Bill Stafford, Ralph Terry, Bob Turley, pitchers;
Clete Boyer, Tony Kubek, Phil Linz, Dale Long, Bobby Richardson, Bill Skowron, infielders; Yogi Berra,
Hector Lopez, Mickey Mantle, Roger Maris, Jack Reed, Tom Tresh, outfielders.

Giants — Ed Bailey, Tom Haller, John Orsino, catchers; Bobby Bolin, Jim Duffalo, Bob Garibaldi, Don Larsen,
Juan Marichal, Mike McCormick, Stu Miller, Billy O'Dell, Billy Pierce, Jack Sanford, pitchers; Ernie Bowman,
Orlando Cepeda, Jim Davenport, Chuck Hiller, Willie McCovey, Jose Pagan, infielders; Felipe Alou, Matty Alou,
Carl Boles, Harvey Kuenn, Willie Mays, Bob Nieman, outfielders.

1963 - LOS ANGELES DODGERS N.L. (4) vs. NEW YORK YANKEES A.L. (0)

(Dodger Stadium / Yankee Stadium)

Oct. 2	at NY	Los Angeles (Koufax)	5	New York (Ford)	2
Oct. 3	at NY	Los Angeles (Podres)	4	New York (Downing)	1
Oct. 5	at LA	Los Angeles (Drysdale)	1	New York (Bouton)	0
Oct. 6	at LA	Los Angeles (Koufax)	2	New York (Ford)	1

MANAGERS: Walter Alston, Dodgers; Ralph Houk, Yankees

Dodgers — Doug Camilli, Johnny Roseboro, catchers; Dick Calmus, Don Drysdale, Sandy Koufax, Bob Miller,
Ron Perranoski, Johnny Podres, Pete Richert, Ken Rowe, Larry Sherry, pitchers; Marv Breeding, Ron Fairly,
Jim Gilliam, Ken McMullen, Bill Skowron, Dick Tracewski, Maury Wills, infielders; Tommy Davis, Willie Davis,
Al Ferrara, Frank Howard, Wally Moon, Lee Walls, outfielders.

Yankees — Yogi Berra, Elston Howard, catchers; Jim Bouton, Marshall Bridges, Al Downing, Whitey Ford,
Steve Hamilton, Bill Kunkel, Tom Metcalf, Hal Reniff, Bill Stafford, Ralph Terry, Stan Williams, pitchers;
Clete Boyer, Harry Bright, Tony Kubek, Phil Linz, Joe Pepitone, Bobby Richardson, infielders;
Johnny Blanchard, Hector Lopez, Mickey Mantle, Roger Maris, Jack Reed, Tom Tresh, outfielders.

1964 - ST. LOUIS CARDINALS N.L. (4) vs. NEW YORK YANKEES A.L. (3)
(Busch Stadium / Yankee Stadium)

Oct. 7	at StL.	St. Louis (Sadecki)	9	New York (Ford)	5	
Oct. 8	at StL.	New York (Stottlemyre)	8	St. Louis (Gibson)	3	
Oct. 10	at NY	New York (Bouton)	2	St. Louis (Schultz)	1	
Oct. 11	at NY	St. Louis (Craig)	4	New York (Downing)	3	
Oct. 12	at NY	St. Louis (Gibson)	5	New York (Mikkelsen)	2	(10 innings)
Oct. 14	at StL.	New York (Bouton)	8	St. Louis (Simmons)	3	
Oct. 15	at StL.	St. Louis (Gibson)	7	New York (Stottlemyre)	5	

MANAGERS: Johnny Keane, Cardinals; Yogi Berra, Yankees

Cardinals — Tim McCarver, Bob Uecker, catchers; Roger Craig, Mike Cuellar, Bob Gibson, Bob Humphreys, Gordie Richardson, Ray Sadecki, Barney Schultz, Curt Simmons, Ron Taylor, Ray Washburn, pitchers; Ken Boyer, Jerry Buchek, Dick Groat, Julian Javier, Dal Maxvill, Ed Spiezio, Bill White, infielders; Lou Brock, Curt Flood, Charlie James, Mike Shannon, Bob Skinner, Carl Warwick, outfielders.

Yankees — Johnny Blanchard, Elston Howard, catchers: Jim Bouton, Al Downing, Whitey Ford, Steve Hamilton, Pete Mikkelsen, Hal Reniff, Rollie Sheldon, Bill Stafford, Mel Stottlemyre, Ralph Terry, Stan Williams, pitchers. Clete Boyer, Pedro Gonzalez, Mike Hegan, Phil Linz, Joe Pepitone, Bobby Richardson, Chet Trail, infielders: Hector Lopez, Mickey Mantle, Roger Maris, Archie Moore, Tom Tresh, outfielders.

1965 - LOS ANGELES DODGERS N.L. (4) vs. MINNESOTA TWINS A.L. (3)
(Dodger Stadium / Metropolitan Stadium)

Oct. 6	at Minn.	Minnesota (Grant)	8	Los Angeles (Drysdale)	2
Oct. 7	at Minn.	Minnesota (Kaat)	5	Los Angeles (Koufax)	1
Oct. 9	at LA	Los Angeles (Osteen)	4	Minnesota (Pascual)	0
Oct. 10	at LA	Los Angeles (Drysdale)	7	Minnesota (Grant)	2
Oct. 11	at LA	Los Angeles (Koufax)	7	Minnesota (Kaat)	0
Oct. 13	at Minn.	Minnesota (Grant)	5	Los Angeles (Osteen)	1
Oct. 14	at Minn.	Los Angeles (Koufax)	2	Minnesota (Kaat)	0

MANAGERS: Walter Alston, Dodgers; Sam Mele, Twins

Dodgers — Johnny Roseboro, Jeff Torborg, catchers: Jim Brewer, Don Drysdale, Mike Kekich, Sandy Koufax, Bob Miller, Claude Osteen, Ron Perranoski, Johnny Podres, John Purdin, Howie Reed, Nick Willhite, pitchers; Ron Fairly, Jim Gilliam, John Kennedy, Jim Lefebvre, Don LeJohn, Wes Parker, Dick Tracewski, Maury Wills, infielders; Willie Crawford, Willie Davis, Lou Johnson, Wally Moon, outfielders.

Twins — Earl Battey, John Sevcik, Jerry Zimmerman, catchers: Dave Boswell, Mudcat Grant, Jim Kaat, Johnny Klippstein, Jim Merritt, Mel Nelson, Camilo Pascual, Jim Perry, Bill Pleis, Dick Stigman, Al Worthington, pitchers; Harmon Killebrew, Jerry Kindall, Don Mincher, Frank Quilici, Rich Rollins, Zoilo Versalles, infielders: Bob Allison, Jimmie Hall, Joe Nossek, Tony Oliva, Sandy Valdespino, outfielders.

1966 - BALTIMORE ORIOLES A.L. (4) vs. LOS ANGELES DODGERS N.L. (0)
(Memorial Stadium / Dodger Stadium)

Oct. 5	at LA	Baltimore (Drabowsky)	5	Los Angeles (Drysdale)	2
Oct. 6	at LA	Baltimore (Palmer)	6	Los Angeles (Koufax)	0
Oct. 8	at Balt.	Baltimore (Bunker)	1	Los Angeles (Osteen)	0
Oct. 9	at Balt.	Baltimore (McNally)	1	Los Angeles (Drysdale)	0

MANAGERS: Hank Bauer, Orioles; Walter Alston, Dodgers

Orioles — Andy Etchebarren, Larry Haney, Vic Roznovsky, catchers; Frank Bertaina, Gene Brabender, Wally Bunker, Moe Drabowsky, Eddie Fisher, Dick Hall, Dave McNally, John Miller, Stu Miller, Jim Palmer, Eddie Watt, pitchers; Luis Aparicio, Woody Held, Dave Johnson, Bob Johnson, Boog Powell, Brooks Robinson, Infielders; Paul Blair, Curt Blefary, Sam Bowens, Frank Robinson, Russ Snyder, outfielders.

Dodgers — Johnny Roseboro, Jeff Torborg, catchers; Jim Brewer, Don Drysdale, Sandy Koufax, Bob Miller, Joe Moeller, Claude Osteen, Ron Perranoski, Phil Regan, Don Sutton, pitchers; Jim Gilliam, John Kennedy, Jim Lefebvre, Nate Oliver, Wes Parker, Dick Stuart, Maury Wills, infielders; Jim Barbieri, Wes Covington, Tommy Davis, Willie Davis, Ron Fairly, Al Ferrara, Lou Johnson, outfielders.

1967 – ST. LOUIS CARDINALS N.L. (4) vs. BOSTON RED SOX A.L. (3)
(Busch Memorial Stadium / Fenway Park)

Oct. 4	at Bos.	St. Louis (Gibson)	2	Boston (Santiago)	1	
Oct. 5	at Bos.	Boston (Lonborg)	5	St. Louis (Hughes)	0	
Oct. 7	at StL.	St. Louis (Briles)	5	Boston (Bell)	2	
Oct. 8	at StL.	St. Louis (Gibson)	6	Boston (Santiago)	0	
Oct. 9	at StL.	Boston (Lonborg)	3	St. Louis (Carlton)	1	
Oct. 11	at Bos.	Boston (Wyatt)	8	St. Louis (Lamabe)	4	
Oct. 12	at Bos.	St. Louis (Gibson)	7	Boston (Lonborg)	2	

MANAGERS: Red Schoendienst, Cardinals; Dick Williams, Red Sox

Cardinals – Tim McCarver, Dave Ricketts, catchers; Nelson Briles, Steve Carlton, Bob Gibson, Joe Hoerner, Dick Hughes, Al Jackson, Larry Jaster, Jack Lamabe, Ray Washburn, Ron Willis, Hal Woodeshick, pitchers; Eddie Bressoud, Orlando Cepeda, Phil Gagliano, Julian Javier, Dal Maxvill, Mike Shannon, Ed Spiezio, infielders; Lou Brock, Curt Flood, Alex Johnson, Roger Maris, Bobby Tolan, outfielders.

Red Sox – Russ Gibson, Elston Howard, Mike Ryan, catchers; Gary Bell, Ken Brett, Jim Lonborg, Dave Morehead, Dan Osinski, Jose Santiago, Lee Stange, Jerry Stephenson, Gary Waslewski, John Wyatt, pitchers; Jerry Adair, Mike Andrews, Joe Foy, Dalton Jones, Rico Petrocelli, George Scott, infielders; Ken Harrelson, Norm Siebern, Reggie Smith, Jose Tartabull, George Thomas, Carl Yastrzemski, outfielders.

1968 – DETROIT TIGERS A.L. (4) vs. ST. LOUIS CARDINALS N.L. (3)
(Tiger Stadium / Busch Memorial Stadium)

Oct. 2	at StL.	St. Louis (Gibson)	4	Detroit (McLain)	0
Oct. 3	at StL.	Detroit (Lolich)	8	St. Louis (Briles)	1
Oct. 5	at Det.	St. Louis (Washburn)	7	Detroit (Wilson)	3
Oct. 6	at Det.	St. Louis (Gibson)	10	Detroit (McLain)	1
Oct. 7	at Det.	Detroit (Lolich)	5	St. Louis (Hoerner)	3
Oct. 9	at StL.	Detroit (McLain)	13	St. Louis (Washburn)	1
Oct. 10	at StL.	Detroit (Lolich)	4	St. Louis (Gibson)	1

MANAGERS: Mayo Smith, Tigers; Red Schoendienst, Cardinals

Tigers – Bill Freehan, Jim Price, catchers; Pat Dobson, John Hiller, Fred Lasher, Mickey Lolich, Dennis McLain, Don McMahon, Daryl Patterson, Joe Sparma, Jon Warden, Earl Wilson, pitchers; Norm Cash, Tommy Matchick, Eddie Mathews, Dick McAuliffe, Ray Oyler, Mickey Stanley, Dick Tracewski, Don Wert, infielders; Gates Brown, Wayne Comer, Willie Horton, Al Kaline, Jim Northrup, outfielders.

Cardinals – Johnny Edwards, Tim McCarver, Dave Ricketts, catchers; Nelson Briles, Steve Carlton, Bob Gibson, Wayne Granger, Joe Hoerner, Dick Hughes, Larry Jaster, Mel Nelson, Ray Washburn, Ron Willis, pitchers; Orlando Cepeda, Phil Gagliano, Julian Javier, Dal Maxvill, Dick Schofield, Mike Shannon, Ed Spiezio, infielders; Lou Brock, Ron Davis, Curt Flood, Roger Maris, Bobby Tolan, outfielders.

1969 – NEW YORK METS N.L. (4) vs. BALTIMORE ORIOLES A.L. (1)
(Shea Stadium / Memorial Stadium)

Oct. 11	at Balt.	Baltimore (Cuellar)	4	New York (Seaver)	1	
Oct. 12	at Balt.	New York (Koosman)	2	Baltimore (McNally)	1	
Oct. 14	at NY	New York (Gentry)	5	Baltimore (Palmer)	0	
Oct. 15	at NY	New York (Seaver)	2	Baltimore (Hall)	1	(10 innings)
Oct. 16	at NY	New York (Koosman)	5	Baltimore (Watt)	3	

MANAGERS: Gil Hodges, Mets; Earl Weaver, Orioles

Mets – Duffy Dyer, Jerry Grote, J.C. Martin, catchers; Don Cardwell, Jack DiLauro, Gary Gentry, Cal Koonce, Jerry Koosman, Jim McAndrew, Tug McGraw, Nolan Ryan, Tom Seaver, Ron Taylor, pitchers; Ken Boswell, Ed Charles, Donn Clendenon, Wayne Garrett, Buddy Harrelson, Ed Kranepool, Al Weis, infielders; Tommie Agee, Rod Gaspar, Cleon Jones, Art Shamsky, Ron Swoboda, outfielders.

Orioles – Clay Dalrymple, Andy Etchebarren, Elrod Hendricks, Dick Hall, Jim Hardin, catchers; Mike Cuellar, Dave Leonhard, Marcelino Lopez, Dave McNally, Jim Palmer, Tom Phoebus, Pete Richert, Eddie Watt, pitchers; Mark Belanger, Bobby Floyd, Dave Johnson, Boog Powell, Brooks Robinson, Chico Salmon, infielders; Paul Blair, Don Buford, Dave May, Curt Motton, Merv Rettenmund, Frank Robinson, outfielders.

1970 – BALTIMORE ORIOLES A.L. (4) vs. CINCINNATI REDS N.L. (1)
(Memorial Stadium / Riverfront Stadium)

Oct. 10	at Cin.	Baltimore (Palmer)	4	Cincinnati (Nolan)	3	
Oct. 11	at Cin.	Baltimore (Phoebus)	6	Cincinnati (Wilcox)	5	
Oct. 13	at Balt.	Baltimore (McNally)	9	Cincinnati (Cloninger)	3	
Oct. 14	at Balt.	Cincinnati (Carroll)	6	Baltimore (Watt)	5	
Oct. 15	at Balt.	Baltimore (Cuellar)	9	Cincinnati (Merritt)	3	

MANAGERS: Earl Weaver, Orioles; Sparky Anderson, Reds

Orioles – Andy Etchebarren, Elrod Hendricks, catchers; Mike Cuellar, Moe Drabowsky, Dick Hall, Jim Hardin, Dave Leonhard, Marcelino Lopez, Dave McNally, Jim Palmer, Tom Phoebus, Pete Richert, Eddie Watt, pitchers; Mark Belanger, Bobby Grich, Dave Johnson, Boog Powell, Brooks Robinson, Chico Salmon, infielders; Paul Blair, Don Buford, Terry Crowley, Curt Motton, Merv Rettenmund, Frank Robinson, outfielders.

Reds – Johnny Bench, Pat Corrales, catchers; Mel Behney, Clay Carroll, Tony Cloninger, Wayne Granger, Don Gullett, Jim McGlothlin, Jim Merritt, Gary Nolan, Ray Washburn, Milt Wilcox, pitchers; Darrel Chaney, Dave Concepcion, Tommy Helms, Lee May, Tony Perez, Jim Stewart, Woody Woodward, infielders; Angel Bravo, Bernie Carbo, Ty Cline, Hal McRae, Pete Rose, Bobby Tolan, outfielders.

1971 – PITTSBURGH PIRATES N.L. (4) vs. BALTIMORE ORIOLES A.L. (3)
(Three Rivers Stadium / Memorial Stadium)

Oct. 9	at Balt.	Baltimore (McNally)	5	Pittsburgh (Ellis)	3	
Oct. 11	at Balt.	Baltimore (Palmer)	11	Pittsburgh (Johnson)	3	
Oct. 12	at Pitt.	Pittsburgh (Blass)	5	Baltimore (Cuellar)	1	
Oct. 13n	at Pitt.	Pittsburgh (Kison)	4	Baltimore (Watt)	3	
Oct. 14	at Pitt.	Pittsburgh (Briles)	4	Baltimore (McNally)	0	
Oct. 16	at Balt.	Baltimore (McNally)	3	Pittsburgh (Miller)	2	(10 innings)
Oct. 17	at Balt.	Pittsburgh (Blass)	2	Baltimore (Cuellar)	1	

POSTPONED: (Rain) Oct. 10

MANAGERS: Danny Murtaugh, Pirates; Earl Weaver, Orioles

Pirates – Milt May, Charlie Sands, Manny Sanguillen, catchers; Steve Blass, Nelson Briles, Dock Ellis, Dave Giusti, Bob Johnson, Bruce Kison, Bob Miller, Bob Moose, Bob Veale, Luke Walker, pitchers; Gene Alley, Dave Cash, Richie Hebner, Jackie Hernandez, Bill Mazeroski, Jose Pagan, Bob Robertson, infielders; Roberto Clemente, Gene Clines, Vic Davalillo, Al Oliver, Willie Stargell, outfielders.

Orioles – Clay Dalrymple, Andy Etchebarren, Elrod Hendricks, catchers; Mike Cuellar, Pat Dobson, Tom Dukes, Dick Hall, Grant Jackson, Dave Leonhard, Dave McNally, Jim Palmer, Pete Richert, Eddie Watt, pitchers; Mark Belanger, Jerry DaVanon, Dave Johnson, Boog Powell, Brooks Robinson, Chico Salmon, infielders; Paul Blair, Don Buford, Curt Motton, Merv Rettenmund, Frank Robinson, Tom Shopay, outfielders.

1972 – OAKLAND ATHLETICS A.L. (4) vs. CINCINNATI REDS N.L. (3)
(Oakland Coliseum / Riverfront Stadium)

Oct. 14	at Cin.	Oakland (Holtzman)	3	Cincinnati (Nolan)	2
Oct. 15	at Cin.	Oakland (Hunter)	2	Cincinnati (Grimsley)	1
Oct. 18n	at Oak.	Cincinnati (Billingham)	1	Oakland (Odom)	0
Oct. 19n	at Oak.	Oakland (Fingers)	3	Cincinnati (Carroll)	2
Oct. 20	at Oak.	Cincinnati (Grimsley)	5	Oakland (Fingers)	4
Oct. 21	at Cin.	Cincinnati (Grimsley)	8	Oakland (Blue)	1
Oct. 22	at Cin.	Oakland (Hunter)	3	Cincinnati (Borbon)	2

POSTPONED: (Rain) Oct. 17

MANAGERS: Dick Williams, Athletics; Sparky Anderson, Reds

Athletics – Dave Duncan, Gene Tenace, catchers; Vida Blue, Rollie Fingers, Dave Hamilton, Ken Holtzman, Joel Horlen, Catfish Hunter, Bob Locker, Blue Moon Odom, pitchers; Sal Bando, Bert Campaneris, Tim Cullen, Mike Epstein, Dick Green, Mike Hegan, Ted Kubiak, Gonzalo Marquez, Dal Maxvill, Don Mincher, infielders; Matty Alou, George Hendrick, Allan Lewis, Angel Mangual, Joe Rudi, outfielders.

Reds – Johnny Bench, Bill Plummer, catchers; Jack Billingham, Pedro Borbon, Sr., Clay Carroll, Ross Grimsley, Don Gullett, Tom Hall, Jim McGlothlin, Gary Nolan, Wayne Simpson, Ed Sprague, pitchers; Darrell Chaney, Dave Concepcion, Julian Javier, Denis Menke, Joe Morgan, Tony Perez, infielders; George Foster, Cesar Geronimo, Joe Hague, Hal McRae, Pete Rose, Bobby Tolan, Ted Uhlaender, outfielders.

1973 - OAKLAND ATHLETICS A.L. (4) vs. NEW YORK METS N.L. (3)

(Oakland Coliseum / Shea Stadium)

Oct. 13	at Oak.	Oakland (Holtzman)	2	New York (Matlack)	1	
Oct. 14	at Oak.	New York (McGraw)	10	Oakland (Fingers)	7	(12 innings)
Oct. 16n	at NY	Oakland (Lindblad)	3	New York (Parker)	2	(11 innings)
Oct. 17n	at NY	New York (Matlack)	6	Oakland (Holtzman)	1	
Oct. 18n	at NY	New York (Koosman)	2	Oakland (Blue)	0	
Oct. 20	at Oak.	Oakland (Hunter)	3	New York (Seaver)	1	
Oct. 21	at Oak.	Oakland (Holtzman)	5	New York (Matlack)	2	

MANAGERS: Dick Williams, Athletics; Yogi Berra, Mets

Athletics — Ray Fosse, catcher; Vida Blue, Rollie Fingers, Ken Holtzman, Catfish Hunter, Darold Knowles, Paul Lindblad, Blue Moon Odom, Horacio Pina, pitchers; Mike Andrews, Sal Bando, Pat Bourque, Bert Campaneris, Vic Davalillo, Dick Green, Deron Johnson, Ted Kubiak, Gene Tenace infielders; Jesus Alou, Billy Conigliaro, Reggie Jackson, Allan Lewis, Angel Mangual, Joe Rudi, outfielders.

Mets — Duffy Dyer, Jerry Grote, Ron Hodges, catchers; Buzz Capra, Jerry Koosman, Jon Matlack, Jim McAndrew, Tug McGraw, Harry Parker, Ray Sadecki, Tom Seaver, George Stone, pitchers; Jim Beauchamp, Ken Boswell, Wayne Garrett, Bud Harrelson, Ed Kranepool, Teddy Martinez, Felix Millan, infielders; Don Hahn, Cleon Jones, Willie Mays, John Milner, Rusty Staub, George Theodore, outfielders.

1974 - OAKLAND ATHLETICS A.L. (4) vs. LOS ANGELES DODGERS N.L. (1)

(Oakland Coliseum / Dodger Stadium)

Oct. 12	at LA	Oakland (Fingers)	3	Los Angeles (Messersmith)	2
Oct. 13	at LA	Los Angeles (Sutton)	3	Oakland (Blue)	2
Oct. 15n	at Oak.	Oakland (Hunter)	3	Los Angeles (Downing)	2
Oct. 16n	at Oak.	Oakland (Holtzman)	5	Los Angeles (Messersmith)	2
Oct. 17n	at Oak.	Oakland (Odom)	3	Los Angeles (Marshall)	2

MANAGERS: Alvin Dark, Athletics; Walter Alston, Dodgers

Athletics — Ray Fosse, Larry Haney, catchers; Glenn Abbott, Vida Blue, Rollie Fingers, Dave Hamilton, Ken Holtzman, Catfish Hunter, Darold Knowles, Paul Lindblad, Blue Moon Odom, pitchers; Sal Bando, Bert Campaneris, Dick Green, Jim Holt, Ted Kubiak, Dal Maxvill, Gene Tenace, infielders; Jesus Alou, Reggie Jackson, Angel Mangual, Billy North, Joe Rudi, Claudell Washington, Herb Washington, outfielders.

Dodgers — Steve Yeager, catcher; Jim Brewer, Al Downing, Charlie Hough, Mike Marshall, Andy Messersmith, Doug Rau, Eddie Solomon, Don Sutton, Geoff Zahn, pitchers; Rick Auerbach, Ron Cey, Steve Garvey, Gail Hopkins, Lee Lacy, Davey Lopes, Ken McMullen, Bill Russell, infielders; Bill Buckner, Willie Crawford, Joe Ferguson, Von Joshua, Manny Mota, Tom Paciorek, Jimmy Wynn, outfielders.

1975 - CINCINNATI REDS N.L. (4) vs. BOSTON RED SOX A.L. (3)

(Riverfront Stadium / Fenway Park)

Oct. 11	at Bos.	Boston (Tiant)	6	Cincinnati (Gullett)	0	
Oct. 12	at Bos.	Cincinnati (Eastwick)	3	Boston (Drago)	2	
Oct. 14n	at Cin.	Cincinnati (Eastwick)	6	Boston (Willoughby)	5	(10 innings)
Oct. 15n	at Cin.	Boston (Tiant)	5	Cincinnati (Norman)	4	
Oct. 16n	at Cin.	Cincinnati (Gullett)	6	Boston (Cleveland)	2	
Oct. 21n	at Bos.	Boston (Wise)	7	Cincinnati (Darcy)	6	(12 innings)
Oct. 22n	at Bos.	Cincinnati (Carroll)	4	Boston (Burton)	3	

POSTPONED: (Rain) Oct. 18, 19, 20

MANAGERS: Sparky Anderson, Reds; Darrell Johnson, Red Sox

Reds — Johnny Bench, Bill Plummer, catchers; Jack Billingham, Pedro Borbon, Sr., Clay Carroll, Pat Darcy, Rawly Eastwick, Don Gullett, Clay Kirby, Will McEnaney, Gary Nolan, Fred Norman, pitchers; Darrel Chaney, Dave Concepcion, Dan Driessen, Doug Flynn, Joe Morgan, Tony Perez, Pete Rose, infielders; Ed Armbrister, Terry Crowley, George Foster, Cesar Geronimo, Ken Griffey, Sr., Merv Rettenmund, outfielders.

Red Sox — Tim Blackwell, Carlton Fisk, Bob Montgomery, catchers; Jim Burton, Reggie Cleveland, Dick Drago, Bill Lee, Roger Moret, Dick Pole, Diego Segui, Luis Tiant, Jim Willoughby, Rick Wise, pitchers: Rick Burleson, Cecil Cooper, Denny Doyle, Doug Griffin, Bob Heise, Rico Petrocelli, Carl Yastrzemski, infielders; Juan Beniquez, Bernie Carbo, Dwight Evans, Fred Lynn, Rick Miller, outfielders.

1976 - CINCINNATI REDS N.L. (4) vs. NEW YORK YANKEES A.L. (0)
(Riverfront Stadium / Yankee Stadium)

Oct. 16	at Cin.	Cincinnati (Gullett)	5	New York (Alexander)	1	
Oct. 17n	at Cin.	Cincinnati (Billingham)	4	New York (Hunter)	3	
Oct. 19n	at NY	Cincinnati (Zachry)	6	New York (Ellis)	2	
Oct. 21n	at NY	Cincinnati (Nolan)	7	New York (Figueroa)	2	

POSTPONED: (Rain) Oct. 20

MANAGERS: Sparky Anderson, Reds; Billy Martin, Yankees

Reds — Johnny Bench, Bill Plummer, catchers; Santo Alcala, Jack Billingham, Pedro Borbon, Sr., Rawly Eastwick, Don Gullett, Will McEnaney, Gary Nolan, Fred Norman, Manny Sarmiento, Pat Zachry, pitchers; Bob Bailey, Dave Concepcion, Dan Driessen, Doug Flynn, Joe Morgan, Tony Perez, Pete Rose, infielders; Ed Armbrister, George Foster, Cesar Geronimo, Ken Griffey, Sr., Mike Lum, Joel Youngblood, outfielders.

Yankees — Fran Healy, Elrod Hendricks, Thurman Munson, catchers; Doyle Alexander, Dock Ellis, Ed Figueroa, Ron Guidry, Ken Holtzman, Catfish Hunter, Grant Jackson, Sparky Lyle, Dick Tidrow, pitchers; Sandy Alomar, Sr. Chris Chambliss, Jim Mason, Graig Nettles, Willie Randolph, Fred Stanley, infielders; Oscar Gamble, Elliott Maddox, Carlos May, Lou Piniella, Mickey Rivers, Otto Velez, Roy White, outfielders.

1977 - NEW YORK YANKEES A.L. (4) vs. LOS ANGELES DODGERS N.L. (2)
(Yankee Stadium / Dodger Stadium)

Oct. 11n	at NY	New York (Lyle)	4	Los Angeles (Rhoden)	3	(12 innings)
Oct. 12n	at NY	Los Angeles (Hooton)	6	New York (Hunter)	1	
Oct. 14n	at LA	New York (Torrez)	5	Los Angeles (John)	3	
Oct. 15	at LA	New York (Guidry)	4	Los Angeles (Rau)	2	
Oct. 16	at LA	Los Angeles (Sutton)	10	New York (Gullett)	4	
Oct. 18n	at NY	New York (Torrez)	8	Los Angeles (Hooton)	4	

MANAGERS: Billy Martin, Yankees; Tommy Lasorda, Dodgers

Yankees — Fran Healy, Cliff Johnson, Thurman Munson, catchers: Ken Clay, Ed Figueroa, Ron Guidry, Don Gullett, Ken Holtzman, Catfish Hunter, Sparky Lyle, Dick Tidrow, Mike Torrez, pitchers; Chris Chambliss, Bucky Dent, Mickey Klutts, Graig Nettles, Willie Randolph, Fred Stanley, George Zeber, infielders; Paul Blair, Reggie Jackson, Lou Piniella, Mickey Rivers, Roy White, outfielders.

Dodgers — Jerry Grote, Johnny Oates, Steve Yeager, catchers; Mike Garman, Burt Hooton, Charlie Hough, Tommy John, Doug Rau, Lance Rautzhan, Rick Rhoden, Elias Sosa, Don Sutton, pitchers; Ron Cey, Steve Garvey, Ed Goodson, Rafael Landestoy, Davey Lopes, Bill Russell, infielders; Dusty Baker, Glenn Burke, Vic Davalillo, Lee Lacy, Rick Monday, Manny Mota, Reggie Smith, outfielders.

1978 - NEW YORK YANKEES A.L. (4) vs LOS ANGELES DODGERS N.L. (2)
(Yankee Stadium / Dodger Stadium)

Oct. 10n	at LA	Los Angeles (John)	11	New York Figueroa)	5	
Oct. 11n	at LA	Los Angeles (Hooton)	4	New York (Hunter)	3	
Oct. 13n	at NY	New York (Guidry)	5	Los Angeles (Sutton)	1	
Oct. 14	at NY	New York (Gossage)	4	Los Angeles (Welch)	3	(10 innings)
Oct. 15	at NY	New York (Beattie)	12	Los Angeles (Hooton)	2	
Oct. 17n	at LA	New York (Hunter)	7	Los Angeles (Sutton)	2	

MANAGERS: Bob Lemon, Yankees; Tommy Lasorda, Dodgers

Yankees — Mike Heath, Cliff Johnson, Thurman Munson, catchers: Jim Beattie, Ken Clay, Ed Figueroa, Rich Gossage, Ron Guidry, Catfish Hunter, Paul Lindblad, Sparky Lyle, Dick Tidrow pitchers; Chris Chambliss, Bucky Dent, Brian Doyle, Graig Nettles, Jim Spencer, Fred Stanley, infielders; Paul Blair, Reggie Jackson, Jay Johnstone, Lou Piniella, Mickey Rivers, Gary Thomasson, Roy White, outfielders.

Dodgers — Joe Ferguson, Jerry Grote, Johnny Oates, Steve Yeager. catchers; Terry Forster, Burt Hooton, Charlie Hough, Tommy John, Doug Rau, Lance Rautzhan, Rick Rhoden, Don Sutton, Bob Welch, pitchers; Ron Cey, Steve Garvey, Davey Lopes, Teddy Martinez, Bill Russell, infielders; Dusty Baker, Vic Davalillo, Lee Lacy, Rick Monday, Manny Mota, Billy North, Reggie Smith, outfielders.

1979 - PITTSBURGH PIRATES N.L. (4) vs. BALTIMORE ORIOLES A.L. (3)

(Three Rivers Stadium / Memorial Stadium)

Oct. 10n	at Balt.	Baltimore (Flanagan)	5	Pittsburgh (Kison)	4
Oct. 11n	at Balt.	Pittsburgh (D. Robinson)	3	Baltimore (Stanhouse)	2
Oct. 12n	at Pitt.	Baltimore (McGregor)	8	Pittsburgh (Candelaria)	4
Oct. 13	at Pitt.	Baltimore (Stoddard)	9	Pittsburgh (Tekulve)	6
Oct. 14	at Pitt.	Pittsburgh (Blyleven)	7	Baltimore (Flanagan)	1
Oct. 16n	at Balt.	Pittsburgh (Candelaria)	4	Baltimore (Palmer)	0
Oct. 17n	at Balt.	Pittsburgh (Jackson)	4	Baltimore (McGregor)	1

POSTPONED: (Rain) Oct. 9

MANAGERS: Chuck Tanner, Pirates; Earl Weaver, Orioles

Pirates — Steve Nicosia, Ed Ott, Manny Sanguillen, catchers; Jim Bibby, Bert Blyleven, John Candelaria, Grant Jackson, Bruce Kison, Dave Roberts, Don Robinson, Enrique Romo, Jim Rooker, Kent Tekulve, pitchers; Tim Foli, Phil Garner, Bill Madlock, Willie Stargell, Rennie Stennett, infielders; Matt Alexander, Mike Easler, Lee Lacy, John Milner, Omar Moreno, Dave Parker, Bill Robinson, outfielders.

Orioles — Rick Dempsey, Dave Skaggs, catchers; Mike Flanagan, Dennis Martinez, Tippy Martinez, Scott McGregor, Jim Palmer, Don Stanhouse, Sammy Stewart, Tim Stoddard, Steve Stone, pitchers; Mark Belanger, Terry Crowley, Rich Dauer, Doug DeCinces, Kiko Garcia, Lee May, Eddie Murray, Billy Smith, infielders; Benny Ayala, Al Bumbry, Pat Kelly, John Lowenstein, Gary Roenicke, Ken Singleton, outfielders.

1980 - PHILADELPHIA PHILLIES N.L. (4) vs. KANSAS CITY ROYALS A.L. (2)

(Veterans Stadium / Royals Stadium)

Oct. 14n	at Phil.	Philadelphia (Walk)	7	Kansas City (Leonard)	6	
Oct. 15n	at Phil.	Philadelphia (Carlton)	6	Kansas City (Quisenberry)	4	
Oct. 17n	at KC	Kansas City (Quisenberry)	4	Philadelphia (McGraw)	3	(10 innings)
Oct. 18	at KC	Kansas City (Leonard)	5	Philadelphia (Christenson)	3	
Oct. 19	at KC	Philadelphia (McGraw)	4	Kansas City (Quisenberry)	3	
Oct. 21n	at Phil.	Philadelphia (Carlton)	4	Kansas City (Gale)	1	

MANAGERS: Dallas Green, Phillies; Jim Frey, Royals

Phillies — Bob Boone, Keith Moreland, catchers; Warren Brusstar, Marty Bystrom, Steve Carlton, Larry Christenson, Tug McGraw, Dickie Noles, Ron Reed, Dick Ruthven, Kevin Saucier, Bob Walk, pitchers; Ramon Aviles, Larry Bowa, Pete Rose, Mike Schmidt, Manny Trillo, John Vukovich, infielders; Greg Gross, Greg Luzinski, Garry Maddox, Bake McBride, Lonnie Smith, Del Unser, George Vukovich, outfielders.

Royals — Darrell Porter, Jamie Quirk, John Wathan, catchers; Ken Brett, Rich Gale, Larry Gura, Dennis Leonard, Renie Martin, Marty Pattin, Dan Quisenberry, Paul Splittorff, Jeff Twitty, pitchers; Willie Aikens, George Brett, Dave Chalk, Onix Concepcion, Pete LaCock, Rance Mulliniks, U.L. Washington, Frank White, infielders; Jose Cardenal, Clint Hurdle, Hal McRae, Amos Otis, Willie Wilson, outfielders.

1981 - LOS ANGELES DODGERS N.L. (4) vs. NEW YORK YANKEES A.L. (2)

(Dodger Stadium / Yankee Stadium)

Oct. 20n	at NY	New York (Guidry)	5	Los Angeles (Reuss)	3
Oct. 21n	at NY	New York (John)	3	Los Angeles (Hooton)	0
Oct. 23n	at LA	Los Angeles (Valenzuela)	5	New York (Frazier)	4
Oct. 24	at LA	Los Angeles (Howe)	8	New York (Frazier)	7
Oct. 25	at LA	Los Angeles (Reuss)	2	New York (Guidry)	1
Oct. 28n	at NY	Los Angeles (Hooton)	9	New York (Frazier)	2

POSTPONED: (Rain) Oct. 27

MANAGERS: Tommy Lasorda, Dodgers; Bob Lemon, Yankees

Dodgers — Mike Scioscia, Steve Yeager, catchers; Bobby Castillo, Terry Forster, Dave Goltz, Burt Hooton, Steve Howe, Tom Niedenfuer, Alejandro Pena, Jerry Reuss, Dave Stewart, Fernando Valenzuela, Bob Welch, pitchers; Ron Cey, Steve Garvey, Davey Lopes, Bill Russell, Steve Sax, Derrel Thomas, infielders; Dusty Baker, Pedro Guerrero, Jay Johnstone, Ken Landreaux, Rick Monday, Reggie Smith, outfielders.

Yankees — Rick Cerone, Barry Foote, catchers; Ron Davis, George Frazier, Rich Gossage, Ron Guidry, Tommy John, Dave LaRoche, Rudy May, Rick Reuschel, Dave Righetti, pitchers; Larry Milbourne, Graig Nettles, Willie Randolph, Dave Revering, Andre Robertson, Aurelio Rodriguez, Bob Watson, infielders; Bobby Brown, Oscar Gamble, Reggie Jackson, Jerry Mumphrey, Bobby Murcer, Lou Piniella, Dave Winfield, outfielders.

1982 – ST. LOUIS CARDINALS N.L. (4) vs. MILWAUKEE BREWERS A.L. (3)

(Busch Stadium / County Stadium)

Oct. 12n	at StL.	Milwaukee (Caldwell)	10	St. Louis (Forsch)	0
Oct. 13n	at StL.	St. Louis (Sutter)	5	Milwaukee (McClure)	4
Oct. 15n	at Mil.	St. Louis (Andujar)	6	Milwaukee (Vuckovich)	2
Oct. 16	at Mil.	Milwaukee (Slaton)	7	St. Louis (Bair)	5
Oct. 17	at Mil.	Milwaukee (Caldwell)	6	St. Louis (Forsch)	4
Oct. 19n	at StL.	St. Louis (Stuper)	13	Milwaukee (Sutton)	1
Oct. 20n	at StL.	St. Louis (Andujar)	6	Milwaukee (McClure)	3

MANAGERS: Whitey Herzog, Cardinals; Harvey Kuenn, Brewers

Cardinals – Glenn Brummer, Darrell Porter, Gene Tenace, catchers; Joaquin Andujar, Doug Bair, Bob Forsch, Jim Kaat, Jeff Lahti, Dave LaPoint, John Martin, Steve Mura, John Stuper, Bruce Sutter, pitchers; Julio Gonzalez, Keith Hernandez, Tommy Herr, Ken Oberkfell, Mike Ramsey, Ozzie Smith, infielders; Steve Braun, David Green, George Hendrick, Dane Iorg, Willie McGee, Lonnie Smith, outfielders.
Brewers – Ted Simmons, Ned Yost, catchers; Dwight Bernard, Pete Ladd, Bob McClure, Doc Medich, Mike Caldwell, Rollie Fingers, Moose Haas, Jim Slaton, Don Sutton, Pete Vuckovich, pitchers; Roy Howell, Paul Molitor, Cecil Cooper, Jim Gantner, Don Money, Rob Picciolo, Ed Romero, Robin Yount, infielders; Mark Brouhard, Marshall Edwards, Charlie Moore, Ben Oglivie, Gorman Thomas, outfielders.

1983 – BALTIMORE ORIOLES A.L. (4) vs. PHILADELPHIA PHILLIES N.L. (1)

(Memorial Stadium / Veterans Stadium)

Oct. 11n	at Balt.	Philadelphia (Denny)	2	Baltimore (McGregor)	1
Oct. 12n	at Balt.	Baltimore (Boddicker)	4	Philadelphia (Hudson)	1
Oct. 14n	at Phil.	Baltimore (Palmer)	3	Philadelphia (Carlton)	2
Oct. 15	at Phil.	Baltimore (Davis)	5	Philadelphia (Denny)	4
Oct. 16	at Phil.	Baltimore (McGregor)	5	Philadelphia (Hudson)	0

MANAGERS: Joe Altobelli, Orioles; Paul Owens, Phillies

Orioles – Rick Dempsey, Joe Nolan, catchers; Mike Boddicker, Storm Davis, Mike Flanagan, Dennis Martinez, Tippy Martinez, Scott McGregor, Jim Palmer, Sammy Stewart, Tim Stoddard, pitchers; Todd Cruz, Rich Dauer, Eddie Murray, Cal Ripken, Lenn Sakata, infielders; Benny Ayala, Al Bumbry, Jim Dwyer, Dan Ford, Tito Landrum, John Lowenstein, Gary Roenicke, John Shelby, Ken Singleton, outfielders.
Phillies – Bo Diaz, Ozzie Virgil, catchers; Larry Andersen, Marty Bystrom, Steve Carlton, John Denny, Kevin Gross, Willie Hernandez, Al Holland, Charles Hudson, Tug McGraw, Ron Reed, pitchers; Ivan DeJesus, Kiko Garcia, Joe Morgan, Tony Perez, Pete Rose, Juan Samuel, Mike Schmidt, infielders; Bob Dernier, Greg Gross, Von Hayes, Joe Lefebvre, Sixto Lezcano, Garry Maddox, Gary Matthews, outfielders.

1984 – DETROIT TIGERS A.L. (4) vs. SAN DIEGO PADRES N.L. (1)

(Tiger Stadium / Jack Murphy Stadium)

Oct. 9n	at SD	Detroit (Morris)	3	San Diego (Thurmond)	2
Oct. 10n	at SD	San Diego (Hawkins)	5	Detroit (Petry)	3
Oct. 12n	at Det.	Detroit (Wilcox)	5	San Diego (Lollar)	2
Oct. 13	at Det.	Detroit (Morris)	4	San Diego (Show)	2
Oct. 14	at Det.	Detroit (Lopez)	8	San Diego (Hawkins)	4

MANAGERS: Sparky Anderson, Tigers; Dick Williams, Padres

Tigers – Marty Castillo, Lance Parrish, catcher; Doug Bair, Juan Berenguer, Willie Hernandez, Aurelio Lopez, Jack Morris, Dan Petry, Dave Rozema, Bill Scherrer, Milt Wilcox, pitchers; Doug Baker, Dave Bergman, Tom Brookens, Darrell Evans, Howard Johnson, Alan Trammell, Lou Whitaker, infielders; Barbaro Garbey, Kirk Gibson, Johnny Grubb, Larry Herndon, Ruppert Jones, Rusty Kuntz, Chet Lemon, outfielders.
Padres – Bruce Bochy, Terry Kennedy, catchers; Greg Booker, Dave Dravecky, Rich Gossage, Greg Harris, Andy Hawkins, Craig Lefferts, Tim Lollar, Eric Show, Mark Thurmond, Ed Whitson, pitchers; Kurt Bevacqua, Tim Flannery, Steve Garvey, Graig Nettles, Mario Ramirez, Luis Salazar, Garry Templeton, Alan Wiggins, infielders; Bobby Brown, Tony Gwynn, Carmelo Martinez, Ron Roenicke, Champ Summers, outfielders.

1985 – KANSAS CITY ROYALS A.L. (4) vs. ST. LOUIS CARDINALS N.L. (3)

(Royals Stadium / Busch Stadium)

Oct. 19n	at KC	St. Louis (Tudor)	3	Kansas City (Jackson)	1
Oct. 20n	at KC	St. Louis (Daley)	4	Kansas City (Leibrandt)	2
Oct. 22n	at StL.	Kansas City (Saberhagen)	6	St. Louis (Andujar)	1
Oct. 23n	at StL.	St. Louis (Tudor)	3	Kansas City (Black)	0
Oct. 24n	at StL.	Kansas City (Jackson)	6	St. Louis (Forsch)	1
Oct. 26n	at KC	Kansas City (Quisenberry)	2	St. Louis (Worrell)	1
Oct. 27n	at KC	Kansas City (Saberhagen)	11	St. Louis (Tudor)	0

MANAGERS: Dick Howser, Royals; Whitey Herzog, Cardinals

Royals – Jamie Quirk, Jim Sundberg, John Wathan, catchers; Joe Beckwith, Bud Black, Steve Farr, Mark Gubicza, Danny Jackson, Charlie Leibrandt, Dan Quisenberry, Bret Saberhagen, pitchers; Steve Balboni, Buddy Biancalana, George Brett, Onix Concepcion, Greg Pryor, Frank White, infielders; Dane Iorg, Lynn Jones, Hal McRae, Darryl Motley, Jorge Orta, Pat Sheridan, Lonnie Smith, Willie Wilson, outfielders.

Cardinals – Tom Nieto, Darrell Porter, catchers; Joaquin Andujar, Bill Campbell, Danny Cox, Ken Dayley, Bob Forsch, Rick Horton, Jeff Lahti, John Tudor, Todd Worrell, pitchers; Jack Clark, Ivan DeJesus, Tommy Herr, Mike Jorgensen, Tom Lawless, Terry Pendleton, Ozzie Smith, infielders; Steve Braun, Cesar Cedeno, Vince Coleman, Brian Harper, Terry Landrum, Willie McGee, Andy Van Slyke, outfielders.

1986 – NEW YORK METS N.L. (4) vs. BOSTON RED SOX A.L. (3)

(Shea Stadium / Fenway Park)

Oct. 18n	at NY	Boston (Hurst)	1	New York (Darling)	0	
Oct. 19n	at NY	Boston (Crawford)	9	New York (Gooden)	3	
Oct. 21n	at Bos.	New York (Ojeda)	7	Boston (Boyd)	1	
Oct. 22n	at Bos.	New York (Darling)	6	Boston (Nipper)	2	
Oct. 23n	at Bos.	Boston (Hurst)	4	New York (Gooden)	2	
Oct. 25n	at NY	New York (Aguilera)	6	Boston (Schiraldi)	5	(10 innings)
Oct. 27n	at NY	New York (McDowell)	8	Boston (Schiraldi)	5	

POSTPONED: (Rain) Oct. 26

MANAGERS: Davey Johnson, Mets; John McNamara, Red Sox

Mets – Gary Carter, Ed Hearn, catchers; Rick Aguilera, Ron Darling, Sid Fernandez, Dwight Gooden, Roger McDowell, Randy Niemann, Bob Ojeda, Jesse Orosco, Doug Sisk, pitchers; Wally Backman, Kevin Elster, Keith Hernandez, Howard Johnson, Ray Knight, Lee Mazzilli, Kevin Mitchell, Rafael Santana, Tim Teufel, infielders; Len Dykstra, Danny Heep, Darryl Strawberry, Mookie Wilson, outfielders.

Red Sox – Rich Gedman, Marc Sullivan, catchers; Oil Can Boyd, Roger Clemens, Steve Crawford, Bruce Hurst, Tim Lollar, Al Nipper, Joe Sambito, Calvin Schiraldi, Bob Stanley, Sammy Stewart, pitchers; Marty Barrett, Wade Boggs, Bill Buckner, Spike Owen, Ed Romero, Dave Stapleton, infielders; Tony Armas, Don Baylor, Dwight Evans, Mike Greenwell, Dave Henderson, Jim Rice, outfielders.

1987 – MINNESOTA TWINS A.L. (4) vs. ST. LOUIS CARDINALS N.L. (3)

(Metrodome / Busch Stadium)

Oct. 17n	at Minn.	Minnesota (Viola)	10	St. Louis (Magrane)	1
Oct. 18n	at Minn.	Minnesota (Blyleven)	8	St. Louis (Cox)	4
Oct. 20n	at StL.	St. Louis (Tudor)	3	Minnesota (Berenguer)	1
Oct. 21n	at StL.	St. Louis (Forsch)	7	Minnesota (Viola)	2
Oct. 22n	at StL.	St. Louis (Cox)	4	Minnesota (Blyleven)	2
Oct. 24	at Minn.	Minnesota (Schatzeder)	11	St. Louis (Tudor)	5
Oct. 25n	at Minn.	Minnesota (Viola)	4	St. Louis (Cox)	2

MANAGERS: Tom Kelly, Twins; Whitey Herzog, Cardinals

Twins – Sal Butera, Tim Laudner, catchers; Keith Atherton, Juan Berenguer, Bert Blyleven, George Frazier, Joe Niekro, Jeff Reardon, Dan Schatzeder, Les Straker, Frank Viola, pitchers; Don Baylor, Gary Gaetti, Greg Gagne, Kent Hrbek, Gene Larkin, Steve Lombardozzi, Al Newman, Roy Smalley, infielders; Tom Brunansky, Randy Bush, Mark Davidson, Dan Gladden, Kirby Puckett, outfielders.

Cardinals – Steve Lake, Tom Pagnozzi, Tony Pena, catchers; Danny Cox, Bill Dawley, Ken Dayley, Bob Forsch, Ricky Horton, Joe Magrane, Greg Mathews, John Tudor, Lee Tunnell, Todd Worrell, pitchers; Dan Driessen, Tommy Herr, Tom Lawless, Jim Lindeman, Jose Oquendo, Terry Pendleton, Ozzie Smith, infielders; Vince Coleman, Curt Ford, Lance Johnson, Willie McGee, John Morris, outfielders.

1988 - LOS ANGELES DODGERS N.L. (4) vs. OAKLAND ATHLETICS A.L. (1)
(Dodger Stadium / Oakland Coliseum)

Oct. 15n	at LA	Los Angeles (Pena)	5	Oakland (Eckersley)	4
Oct. 16n	at LA	Los Angeles (Hershiser)	6	Oakland (Davis)	0
Oct. 18n	at Oak.	Oakland (Honeycutt)	2	Los Angeles (J. Howell)	1
Oct. 19n	at Oak.	Los Angeles (Belcher)	4	Oakland (Stewart)	3
Oct. 20n	at Oak.	Los Angeles (Hershiser)	5	Oakland (Davis)	2

MANAGERS: Tommy Lasorda, Dodgers; Tony LaRussa, Athletics.

Dodgers — Rick Dempsey, Mike Scioscia, catchers; Tim Belcher, Orel Hershiser, Brian Holton, Ricky Horton, Jay Howell, Tim Leary, Jesse Orosco, Alejandro Pena, John Tudor, pitchers; Dave Anderson, Alfredo Griffin, Jeff Hamilton, Danny Heep, Steve Sax, Mike Sharperson, Franklin Stubbs, Tracy Woodson, infielders; Mike Davis, Kirk Gibson, Jose Gonzalez, Mickey Hatcher, Mike Marshall, John Shelby, outfielders.

Athletics — Ron Hassey, Terry Steinbach, catchers; Todd Burns, Greg Cadaret, Storm Davis, Dennis Eckersley, Rick Honeycutt, Gene Nelson, Eric Plunk, Dave Stewart, Bob Welch, Curt Young, pitchers; Mike Gallego, Glenn Hubbard, Carney Lansford, Mark McGwire, Tony Phillips, Walt Weiss, infielders; Don Baylor, Jose Canseco, Dave Henderson, Stan Javier, Doug Jennings, Dave Parker, Luis Polonia, outfielders.

1989 - OAKLAND ATHLETICS A.L. (4) vs. SAN FRANCISCO GIANTS N.L. (0)
(Oakland Coliseum / Candlestick Park)

Oct. 14n	at Oak.	Oakland (Stewart)	5	San Francisco (Garrelts)	0
Oct. 15n	at Oak.	Oakland (Moore)	5	San Francisco (Reuschel)	1
Oct. 27n	at SF	Oakland (Stewart)	13	San Francisco (Garrelts)	7
Oct. 28n	at SF	Oakland (Moore)	9	San Francisco (Robinson)	6

POSTPONED: *(Earthquake) Oct. 17 through Oct. 26*

MANAGERS: Tony LaRussa, Athletics; Roger Craig, Giants

Athletics — Ron Hassey, Terry Steinbach, catchers; Todd Burns, Storm Davis, Dennis Eckersley, Rick Honeycutt, Mike Moore, Gene Nelson, Dave Stewart, Bob Welch, Curt Young, Matt Young, pitchers; Lance Blankenship, Mike Gallego, Carney Lansford, Mark McGwire, Ken Phelps, Tony Phillips, Walt Weiss, infielders; Jose Canseco, Dave Henderson, Rickey Henderson, Stan Javier, Dave Parker, outfielders.

Giants — Bill Bathe, Terry Kennedy, Kirt Manwaring, catchers; Steve Bedrosian, Jeff Brantley, Kelly Downs, Scott Garrelts, Atlee Hammaker, Mike LaCoss, Craig Lefferts, Rick Reuschel, Don Robinson, pitchers; Will Clark, Greg Litton, Ken Oberkfell, Ernest Riles, Rob Thompson, Jose Uribe, Matt Williams, infielders; Brett Butler, Candy Maldonado, Kevin Mitchell, Donell Nixon, Pat Sheridan, outfielders.

1990 - CINCINNATI REDS N.L. (4) vs. OAKLAND ATHLETICS A.L. (0)
(Riverfront Stadium / Oakland Coliseum)

Oct. 16n	at Cin.	Cincinnati (Rijo)	7	Oakland (Stewart)	0	
Oct. 17n	at Cin.	Cincinnati (Dibble)	5	Oakland (Eckersley)	4	(10 innings)
Oct. 19n	at Oak.	Cincinnati (Browning)	8	Oakland (Moore)	3	
Oct. 20n	at Oak.	Cincinnati (Rijo)	2	Oakland (Stewart)	1	

MANAGERS: Lou Piniella, Reds; Tony LaRussa, Athletics

Reds — Joe Oliver, Jeff Reed, catchers; Jack Armstrong, Tom Browning, Norm Charlton, Rob Dibble, Danny Jackson, Rick Mahler, Randy Myers, Jose Rijo, Scott Scudder, pitchers; Billy Bates, Todd Benzinger, Mariano Duncan, Barry Larkin, Terry Lee, Hal Morris, Ron Oester, Luis Quinones, Chris Sabo, infielders; Glenn Braggs, Eric Davis, Billy Hatcher, Paul O'Neill, Herm Winningham, outfielders.

Athletics — Ron Hassey, Jamie Quirk, Terry Steinbach, catchers; Todd Burns, Dennis Eckersley, Rick Honeycutt, Joe Klink, Mike Moore, Gene Nelson, Scott Sanderson, Dave Stewart, Bob Welch, Curt Young, pitchers; Lance Blankenship, Mike Bordick, Mike Gallego, Carney Lansford, Mark McGwire, Willie Randolph, infielders; Harold Baines, Jose Canseco, Dave Henderson, Rickey Henderson, Doug Jennings, Willie McGee, outfielders.

1991 – MINNESOTA TWINS A.L. (4) vs. ATLANTA BRAVES N.L. (3)

(Metrodome / Atlanta-Fulton County Stadium)

Oct. 19n	at Minn.	Minnesota (Morris)	5	Atlanta (Leibrandt)	2	
Oct. 20n	at Minn.	Minnesota (Tapani)	3	Atlanta (Glavine)	2	
Oct. 22n	at Atl.	Atlanta (Clancy)	5	Minnesota (Aguilera)	4	(12 innings)
Oct. 23n	at Atl.	Atlanta (Stanton)	3	Minnesota (Guthrie)	2	
Oct. 24n	at Atl.	Atlanta (Glavine)	14	Minnesota (Tapani)	5	
Oct. 26n	at Minn.	Minnesota (Aguilera)	4	Atlanta (Leibrandt)	3	(11 innings)
Oct. 27n	at Minn.	Minnesota (Morris)	1	Atlanta (Pena)	0	(10 innings)

MANAGERS: Tom Kelly, Twins; Bobby Cox, Braves

Twins – Brian Harper, Junior Ortiz, catchers; Rick Aguilera, Steve Bedrosian, Scott Erickson, Mark Guthrie, Terry Leach, Jack Morris, Kevin Tapani, David West, Carl Willis, pitchers; Greg Gagne, Kent Hrbek, Chuck Knoblauch, Scott Leius, Al Newman, Mike Pagliarulo, Paul Sorrento, infielders; Jarvis Brown, Randy Bush, Chili Davis, Dan Gladden, Gene Larkin, Shane Mack, Kirby Puckett, outfielders.

Braves – Francisco Cabrera, Greg Olson, Jerry Willard, catchers; Steve Avery, Jim Clancy, Tom Glavine, Charlie Leibrandt, Kent Mercker, Alejandro Pena, John Smoltz, Mike Stanton, Randy St. Claire, Mark Wohlers, pitchers; Rafael Belliard, Jeff Blauser, Sid Bream, Brian Hunter, Mark Lemke, Terry Pendleton, Jeff Treadway, infielders; Ron Gant, Tommy Gregg, David Justice, Keith Mitchell, Lonnie Smith, outfielders.

1992 – TORONTO BLUE JAYS A.L. (4) vs. ATLANTA BRAVES N.L. (2)

(SkyDome / Atlanta-Fulton County Stadium)

Oct. 17n	at Atl.	Atlanta (Glavine)	3	Toronto (Morris)	1	
Oct. 18n	at Atl.	Toronto (D. Ward)	5	Atlanta (Reardon)	4	
Oct. 20n	at Tor.	Toronto (D. Ward)	3	Atlanta (Avery)	2	
Oct. 21n	at Tor.	Toronto (Key)	2	Atlanta (Glavine)	1	
Oct. 22n	at Tor.	Atlanta (Smoltz)	7	Toronto (Morris)	2	
Oct. 24n	at Atl.	Toronto (Key)	4	Atlanta (Leibrandt)	3	(11 innings)

MANAGERS: Cito Gaston, Blue Jays; Bobby Cox, Braves

Blue Jays – Pat Borders, Randy Knorr, Ed Sprague, catchers; David Cone, Mark Eichhorn, Juan Guzman, Tom Henke, Jimmy Key, Jack Morris, Todd Stottlemyre, Mike Timlin, Duane Ward, David Wells, pitchers; Roberto Alomar, Alfredo Griffin, Kelly Gruber, Manuel Lee, Rance Mulliniks, John Olerud, Pat Tabler, infielders; Derek Bell, Joe Carter, Candy Maldonado, Devon White, Dave Winfield, outfielders.

Braves – Damon Berryhill, Francisco Cabrera, Javier Lopez, catchers; Steve Avery, Tom Glavine, Charlie Leibrandt, Kent Mercker, David Nied, Jeff Reardon, Pete Smith, John Smoltz, Mike Stanton, Mark Wohlers, pitchers; Rafael Belliard, Jeff Blauser, Sid Bream, Brian Hunter, Mark Lemke, Terry Pendleton, Jeff Treadway, infielders; Ron Gant, David Justice, Otis Nixon, Deion Sanders, Lonnie Smith, outfielders.

1993 – TORONTO BLUE JAYS A.L. (4) vs. PHILADELPHIA PHILLIES N.L. (2)

(SkyDome / Veterans Stadium)

Oct. 16n	at Tor.	Toronto (Leiter)	8	Philadelphia (Schilling)	5	
Oct. 17n	at Tor.	Philadelphia (Mulholland)	6	Toronto (Stewart)	4	
Oct. 19n	at Phil.	Toronto (Hentgen)	10	Philadelphia (Jackson)	3	
Oct. 20n	at Phil.	Toronto (Castillo)	15	Philadelphia (Williams)	14	
Oct. 21n	at Phil.	Philadelphia (Schilling)	2	Toronto (Guzman)	0	
Oct. 23n	at Tor.	Toronto (D. Ward)	8	Philadelphia (Williams)	6	

MANAGERS: Cito Gaston, Blue Jays; Jim Fregosi, Phillies

Blue Jays – Pat Borders, Randy Knorr, catchers; Tony Castillo, Danny Cox, Mark Eichhorn, Juan Guzman, Pat Hentgen, Al Leiter, Dave Stewart, Todd Stottlemyre, Mike Timlin, Duane Ward, pitchers; Roberto Alomar, Tony Fernandez, Alfredo Griffin, Paul Molitor, John Olerud, Dick Schofield, Ed Sprague, infielders; Rob Butler, William Canate, Joe Carter, Darnell Coles, Rickey Henderson, Devon White, outfielders.

Phillies – Darren Daulton, Todd Pratt, catchers; Larry Andersen, Tommy Greene, Danny Jackson, Roger Mason, Terry Mulholland, Ben Rivera, Curt Schilling, Bobby Thigpen, David West, Mitch Williams, pitchers; Kim Batiste, Mariano Duncan, Dave Hollins, Ricky Jordan, John Kruk, Mickey Morandini, Kevin Stocker, infielders; Wes Chamberlain, Len Dykstra, Jim Eisenreich, Pete Incaviglia, Tony Longmire, Milt Thompson, outfielders.

1994 - NO WORLD SERIES PLAYED

1995 - ATLANTA BRAVES N.L. (4) vs CLEVELAND INDIANS A.L. (2)
(Atlanta-Fulton County Stadium / Jacobs Field)

Oct. 21n	at Atl.	Atlanta (Maddux)	3	Cleveland (Hershiser)	2	
Oct. 22n	at Atl.	Atlanta (Glavine)	4	Cleveland (Martinez)	3	
Oct. 24n	at Clev.	Cleveland (Mesa)	7	Atlanta (Pena)	6	(11 innings)
Oct. 25n	at Clev.	Atlanta (Avery)	5	Cleveland (Hill)	2	
Oct. 26n	at Clev.	Cleveland (Hershiser)	5	Atlanta (Maddux)	4	
Oct. 28n	at Atl.	Atlanta (Glavine)	1	Cleveland (Poole)	0	

MANAGERS: Bobby Cox, Braves; Mike Hargrove, Indians

Braves — Javier Lopez, Charlie O'Brien, Eduardo Perez, catchers; Steve Avery, Pedro Borbon, Jr., Brad Clontz, Tom Glavine, Greg Maddux, Greg McMichael, Kent Mercker, Alejandro Pena, John Smoltz, Mark Wohlers, pitchers; Rafael Belliard, Jeff Blauser, Chipper Jones, Mark Lemke, Fred McGriff, Mike Mordecai, infielders; Mike Devereaux, Marquis Grissom, David Justice, Ryan Klesko, Luis Polonia, Dwight Smith, outfielders.

Indians — Sandy Alomar, Jr., Tony Pena, catchers; Paul Assenmacher, Alan Embree, Orel Hershiser, Ken Hill, Dennis Martinez, Jose Mesa, Charles Nagy, Chad Ogea, Eric Plunk, Jim Poole, Julian Tavarez, pitchers; Carlos Baerga, Alvaro Espinoza, Eddie Murray, Herbert Perry, Paul Sorrento, Jim Thome, Omar Vizquel, infielders; Ruben Amaro, Jr., Albert Belle, Wayne Kirby, Kenny Lofton, Manny Ramirez, outfielders

1996 - NEW YORK YANKEES A.L. (4) vs ATLANTA BRAVES N.L. (2)
(Yankee Stadium / Atlanta-Fulton County Stadium)

Oct. 20n	at NY	Atlanta (Smoltz)	12	New York (Pettitte)	1	
Oct. 21n	at NY	Atlanta (Maddux)	4	New York (Key)	0	
Oct. 22n	at Atl.	New York (Cone)	5	Atlanta (Glavine)	2	
Oct. 23n	at Atl.	New York (Lloyd)	8	Atlanta (Avery)	6	(10 innings)
Oct. 24n	at Atl.	New York (Pettitte)	1	Atlanta (Smoltz)	0	
Oct. 26n	at NY	New York (Key)	3	Atlanta (Maddux)	2	

POSTPONED: (Rain) Oct. 19

MANAGERS: Joe Torre, Yankees; Bobby Cox, Braves

Yankees — Joe Girardi, Jim Leyritz, catchers; Brian Boehringer, David Cone, Jimmy Key, Graeme Lloyd, Jeff Nelson, Andy Pettitte, Mariano Rivera, Kenny Rogers, David Weathers, John Wetteland, pitchers; Wade Boggs, Mariano Duncan, Cecil Fielder, Andy Fox, Charlie Hayes, Derek Jeter, Tino Martinez, Luis Sojo, infielders; Mike Aldrete, Paul O'Neill, Tim Raines, Darryl Strawberry, Bernie Williams, outfielders.

Braves — Joe Ayrault, Javier Lopez, Eduardo Perez, catchers; Steve Avery, Mike Bielecki, Brad Clontz, Tom Glavine, Greg Maddux, Greg McMichael, Denny Neagle, John Smoltz, Terrell Wade, Mark Wohlers, pitchers; Rafael Belliard, Jeff Blauser, Chipper Jones, Mark Lemke, Fred McGriff, Mike Mordecai, Terry Pendleton, infielders; Jermaine Dye, Marquis Grissom, Andruw Jones, Ryan Klesko, Luis Polonia, outfielders.

1997 - FLORIDA MARLINS N.L. (4) vs CLEVELAND INDIANS A.L. (3)
(Pro Player Stadium / Jacobs Field)

Oct. 18n	at Fla.	Florida (Hernandez)	7	Cleveland (Hershiser)	4	
Oct. 19n	at Fla.	Cleveland (Ogea)	6	Florida (Brown)	1	
Oct. 21n	at Clev.	Florida (Cook)	14	Cleveland (Plunk)	11	
Oct. 22n	at Clev.	Cleveland (Wright)	10	Florida (Saunders)	3	
Oct. 23n	at Clev.	Florida (Hernandez)	8	Cleveland (Hershiser)	7	
Oct. 25n	at Fla.	Cleveland (Ogea)	4	Florida (Brown)	1	
Oct. 26n	at Fla.	Florida (Powell)	3	Cleveland (Nagy)	2	(11 innings)

MANAGERS: Jim Leyland, Marlins; Mike Hargrove, Indians

Marlins — Charles Johnson, Gregg Zaun, catchers; Antonio Alfonseca, Kevin Brown, Dennis Cook, Felix Heredia, Livan Hernandez, Al Leiter, Robb Nen, Jay Powell, Tony Saunders, Ed Vosberg, pitchers; Kurt Abbott, Alex Arias, Bobby Bonilla, Jeff Conine, Darren Daulton, Cliff Floyd, Edgar Renteria, infielders; Moises Alou, John Cangelosi, Craig Counsell, Jim Eisenreich, Gary Sheffield, Devon White, outfielders.

Indians — Sandy Alomar, Jr., Pat Borders, catchers; Brian Anderson, Paul Assenmacher, Orel Hershiser, Mike Jackson, Jeff Juden, Jose Mesa, Alvin Morman, Charles Nagy, Chad Ogea, Eric Plunk, Jaret Wright, pitchers; Jeff Branson, Tony Fernandez, Jeff Manto, Bip Roberts, Kevin Seitzer, Jim Thome, Omar Vizquel, Matt Williams, infielders; Brian Giles, Marquis Grissom, David Justice, Manny Ramirez, outfielders.

1998 - NEW YORK YANKEES A.L. (4) vs SAN DIEGO PADRES N.L. (0)
(Yankee Stadium / Qualcomm Stadium)

Oct. 17n	at NY	New York (Wells)	9	San Diego (Wall)	6
Oct. 18n	at NY	New York (Hernandez)	9	San Diego (Ashby)	3
Oct. 20n	at SD	New York (Mendoza)	5	San Diego (Hoffman)	4
Oct. 21n	at SD	New York (Pettitte)	3	San Diego (Brown)	0

MANAGERS: Joe Torre, Yankees; Bruce Bochy, Padres

Yankees — Joe Girardi, Jorge Posada, catchers; David Cone, Orlando Hernandez, Hideki Irabu, Graeme Lloyd, Ramiro Mendoza, Jeff Nelson, Andy Pettitte, Mariano Rivera, Mike Stanton, David Wells, pitchers; Scott Brosius, Homer Bush, Derek Jeter, Chuck Knoblauch, Tino Martinez, Luis Sojo, infielders; Chad Curtis, Chili Davis, Ricky Ledee, Paul O'Neill, Tim Raines, Shane Spencer, Bernie Williams, outfielders.

Padres — Carlos Hernandez, Jim Leyritz, Greg Myers, catchers; Andy Ashby, Brian Boehringer, Kevin Brown, Joey Hamilton, Sterling Hitchcock, Trevor Hoffman, Mark Langston, Dan Miceli, Randy Myers, Donne Wall, pitchers; George Arias, Ken Caminiti, Chris Gomez, Wally Joyner, Andy Sheets, Quilvio Veras, infielders; Steve Finley, Tony Gwynn, Ruben Rivera, Mark Sweeney, John Vander Wal, Greg Vaughn, outfielders.

1999 - NEW YORK YANKEES A.L. (4) vs ATLANTA BRAVES N.L. (0)
(Yankee Stadium / Turner Field)

Oct. 23n	at Atl.	New York (Hernandez)	4	Atlanta (Maddux)	1	
Oct. 24n	at Atl.	New York (Cone)	7	Atlanta (Millwood)	2	
Oct. 26n	at NY	New York (Rivera)	6	Atlanta (Remlinger)	5	(10 innings)
Oct. 27n	at NY	New York (Clemens)	4	Atlanta (Smoltz)	1	

MANAGERS: Joe Torre, Yankees; Bobby Cox, Braves

Yankees — Joe Girardi, Jorge Posada, catchers; Roger Clemens, David Cone, Jason Grimsley, Orlando Hernandez, Ramiro Mendoza, Jeff Nelson, Andy Pettitte, Mariano Rivera, Mike Stanton, Allen Watson, pitchers; Clay Bellinger, Scott Brosius, Derek Jeter, Chuck Knoblauch, Jim Leyritz, Tino Martinez, Luis Sojo, infielders; Chad Curtis, Chili Davis, Ricky Ledee, Paul O'Neill, Darryl Strawberry, Bernie Williams, outfielders.

Braves — Jorge Fabregas, Greg Myers, Eddie Perez, catchers; Tom Glavine, Greg Maddux, Kevin McGlinchy, Kevin Millwood, Terry Mulholland, Mike Remlinger, John Rocker, John Smoltz, Russ Springer, pitchers; Howard Battle, Bret Boone, Ozzie Guillen, Jose Hernandez, Brian Hunter, Chipper Jones, Ryan Klesko, Keith Lockhart, Walt Weiss, infielders; Andruw Jones, Brian Jordan, Otis Nixon, Gerald Williams, outfielders.

2000 - NEW YORK YANKEES A.L. (4) vs NEW YORK METS N.L. (1)
(Yankee Stadium / Shea Stadium)

Oct. 21n	at Yankees	Yankees (Stanton)	4	Mets (Wendell)	3	(12 innings)
Oct. 22n	at Yankees	Yankees (Clemens)	6	Mets (Hampton)	5	
Oct. 24n	at Mets	Mets (J. Franco)	4	Yankees (Hernandez)	2	
Oct. 25n	at Mets	Yankees (Nelson)	3	Mets (Jones)	2	
Oct. 26n	at Mets	Yankees (Stanton)	4	Mets (Leiter)	2	

MANAGERS: Joe Torre, Yankees; Bobby Valentine, Mets

Yankees — Jorge Posada, Chris Turner, catchers; Roger Clemens, David Cone, Dwight Gooden, Jason Grimsley, Orlando Hernandez, Denny Neagle, Jeff Nelson, Andy Pettitte, Mariano Rivera, Mike Stanton, pitchers; Clay Bellinger, Scott Brosius, Derek Jeter, Chuck Knoblauch, Tino Martinez, Luis Sojo, Jose Vizcaino, infielders; Jose Canseco, Glenallen Hill, David Justice, Paul O'Neill, Luis Polonia, Bernie Williams, outfielders.

Mets — Mike Piazza, Todd Pratt, catchers; Armando Benitez, Dennis Cook, John Franco, Mike Hampton, Bobby J. Jones, Al Leiter, Rick Reed, Glendon Rusch, Turk Wendell, Rick White, pitchers; Kurt Abbott, Edgardo Alfonzo, Mike Bordick, Matt Franco, Lenny Harris, Robin Ventura, Todd Zeile, infielders; Benny Agbayani, Darryl Hamilton, Joe McEwing, Jay Payton, Timo Perez, Bubba Trammell, outfielders.

001 - ARIZONA DIAMONDBACKS N.L. (4) vs NEW YORK YANKEES A.L. (3)
(Bank One Ballpark / Yankee Stadium)

Oct. 27n	at Ari.	Arizona (Schilling)	9	New York (Mussina)	1	
Oct. 28n	at Ari.	Arizona (Johnson)	4	New York (Pettitte)	0	
Oct. 30n	at NY	New York (Clemens)	2	Arizona (Anderson)	1	
Oct. 31n	at NY	New York (Rivera)	4	Arizona (Kim)	3	(10 innings)
Nov. 1n	at NY	New York (Hitchcock)	3	Arizona (Lopez)	2	(12 innings)
Nov. 3n	at Ari.	Arizona (Johnson)	15	New York (Pettitte)	2	
Nov. 4n	at Ari.	Arizona (Johnson)	3	New York (Rivera)	2	

MANAGERS: Bob Brenly, Diamondbacks; Joe Torre, Yankees

Diamondbacks – Rod Barajas, Damian Miller, catchers; Brian Anderson, Miguel Batista, Troy Brohawn, Randy Johnson, Byung-Hyun Kim, Albie Lopez, Mike Morgan, Curt Schilling, Greg Swindell, Bobby Witt, pitchers; Jay Bell, Greg Colbrunn, Craig Counsell, Erubiel Durazo, Mark Grace, Matt Williams, Tony Womack, infielders; Danny Bautista, Midre Cummings, David Dellucci, Steve Finley, Luis Gonzalez, Reggie Sanders, outfielders.

Yankees – Todd Greene, Jorge Posada, catchers; Randy Choate, Roger Clemens, Orlando Hernandez, Sterling Hitchcock, Ramiro Mendoza, Mike Mussina, Andy Pettitte, Mariano Rivera, Mike Stanton, Jay Witasick, pitchers; Scott Brosius, Derek Jeter, Tino Martinez, Luis Sojo, Alfonso Soriano, Randy Velarde, Enrique Wilson, infielders; Clay Bellinger, David Justice, Chuck Knoblauch, Paul O'Neill, Shane Spencer, Bernie Williams, outfielders.

2002 - ANAHEIM ANGELS A.L. (4) vs SAN FRANCISCO GIANTS N.L. (3)
(Edison International Field of Anaheim / Pacific Bell Park)

Oct. 19n	at Ana.	San Francisco (Schmidt)	4	Anaheim (Washburn)	3
Oct. 20n	at Ana.	Anaheim (Rodriguez)	11	San Francisco (Rodriguez)	10
Oct. 22n	at SF	Anaheim (Ortiz)	10	San Francisco (Hernandez)	4
Oct. 23n	at SF	San Francisco (Worrell)	4	Anaheim (Rodriguez)	3
Oct. 24n	at SF	San Francisco (Zerbe)	16	Anaheim (Washburn)	4
Oct. 26n	at Ana.	Anaheim (Donnelly)	6	San Francisco (Worrell)	5
Oct. 27n	at Ana.	Anaheim (Lackey)	4	San Francisco (Hernandez)	1

MANAGERS: Mike Scioscia, Angels; Dusty Baker, Giants

Angels – Bengie Molina, Jose Molina, catchers; Kevin Appier, Brendan Donnelly, John Lackey, Ramon Ortiz, Troy Percival, Francisco Rodriguez, Scott Schoeneweis, Scot Shields, Jarrod Washburn, Ben Weber, pitchers; David Eckstein, Chone Figgins, Brad Fullmer, Benji Gil, Troy Glaus, Adam Kennedy, Scott Spiezio, Shawn Wooten, infielders; Garret Anderson, Darin Erstad, Alex Ochoa, Orlando Palmeiro, Tim Salmon, outfielders.

Giants – Benito Santiago, Yorvit Torrealba, catchers; Scott Eyre, Aaron Fultz, Livan Hernandez, Robb Nen, Russ Ortiz, Felix Rodriguez, Kirk Rueter, Jason Schmidt, Jay Witasick, Tim Worrell, Chad Zerbe, pitchers; Rich Aurilia, David Bell, Pedro Feliz, Jeff Kent, Ramon Martinez, J.T. Snow, infielders; Barry Bonds, Shawon Dunston, Tom Goodwin, Kenny Lofton, Reggie Sanders, Tsuyoshi Shinjo, outfielders.

2003 - FLORIDA MARLINS N.L. (4) vs NEW YORK YANKEES A.L. (2)
(Pro Player Stadium / Yankee Stadium)

Oct. 18n	at NY	Florida (Penny)	3	New York (Wells)	2	
Oct. 19n	at NY	New York (Pettitte)	6	Florida (Redman)	1	
Oct. 21n	at Fla.	New York (Mussina)	6	Florida (Beckett)	1	
Oct. 22n	at Fla.	Florida (Looper)	4	New York (Weaver)	3	(12 innings)
Oct. 23n	at Fla.	Florida (Penny)	6	New York (Contreras)	4	
Oct. 25n	at NY	Florida (Beckett)	2	New York (Pettitte)	0	

MANAGERS: Jack McKeon, Marlins; Joe Torre, Yankees

Marlins – Mike Redmond, Ivan Rodriguez, catchers; Josh Beckett, Nate Bump, Chad Fox, Rick Helling, Braden Looper, Carl Pavano, Brad Penny, Mark Redman, Michael Tejera, Ugueth Urbina, Dontrelle Willis, pitchers; Luis Castillo, Alex Gonzalez, Lenny Harris, Derrek Lee, Mike Lowell, Mike Mordecai, infielders; Brian Banks, Miguel Cabrera, Jeff Conine, Juan Encarnacion, Todd Hollandsworth, Juan Pierre, outfielders.

Yankees – John Flaherty, Jorge Posada, catchers; Roger Clemens, Jose Contreras, Chris Hammond, Felix Heredia, Mike Mussina, Jeff Nelson, Andy Pettitte, Mariano Rivera, Jeff Weaver, David Wells, Gabe White, pitchers; Aaron Boone, Jason Giambi, Derek Jeter, Nick Johnson, Alfonso Soriano, Enrique Wilson, infielders; David Dellucci, Karim Garcia, Hideki Matsui, Juan Rivera, Ruben Sierra, Bernie Williams, outfielders.

2004 - BOSTON RED SOX A.L. (4) vs ST. LOUIS CARDINALS N.L. (0)
(Fenway Park / Busch Stadium)

Oct. 23n	at Bos.	Boston (Foulke)	11	St. Louis (Tavarez)	9
Oct. 24n	at Bos.	Boston (Schilling)	6	St. Louis (Morris)	2
Oct. 26n	at StL.	Boston (Martinez)	4	St. Louis (Suppan)	1
Oct. 27n	at StL.	Boston (Lowe)	3	St. Louis (Marquis)	0

MANAGERS: Terry Francona, Red Sox; Tony LaRussa, Cardinals

Red Sox – Doug Mirabelli, Jason Varitek, catchers; Bronson Arroyo, Alan Embree, Keith Foulke, Curtis Leskanic, Derek Lowe, Pedro Martinez, Mike Myers, Curt Schilling, Mike Timlin, Tim Wakefield, pitchers; Mark Bellhorn, Orlando Cabrera, Doug Mientkiewicz, Kevin Millar, Bill Mueller, David Ortiz, Pokey Reese, Kevin Youkilis, infielders; Johnny Damon, Gabe Kapler, Trot Nixon, Manny Ramirez, Dave Roberts, outfielders.

Cardinals – Mike Matheny, Yadier Molina, catchers; Kiko Calero, Cal Eldred, Dan Haren, Jason Isringhausen, Ray King, Jason Marquis, Matt Morris, Al Reyes, Jeff Suppan, Julian Tavarez, Woody Williams, pitchers; Marlon Anderson, Hector Luna, Albert Pujols, Edgar Renteria, Scott Rolen, Tony Womack, infielders; Roger Cedeno, Jim Edmonds, John Mabry, Reggie Sanders, So Taguchi, Larry Walker, outfielders.

2005 - CHICAGO WHITE SOX A.L. (4) vs HOUSTON ASTROS N.L. (0)
(U.S. Cellular Field / Minute Maid Park)

Oct. 22n	at Chi.	Chicago (Contreras)	5	Houston (Rodriguez)	3	
Oct. 23n	at Chi.	Chicago (Cotts)	7	Houston (Lidge)	6	
Oct. 25n	at Hou.	Chicago (Marte)	7	Houston (Astacio)	5	(14 innings)
Oct. 26n	at Hou.	Chicago (Garcia)	1	Houston (Lidge)	0	

MANAGERS: Ozzie Guillen, White Sox; Phil Garner, Astros

White Sox — A.J. Pierzynski, Chris Widger, catchers; Mark Buehrle, Jose Contreras, Neal Cotts, Freddy Garcia, Jon Garland, Dustin Hermanson, Orlando Hernandez, Bobby Jenks, Damaso Marte, Cliff Politte, Luis Vizcaino, pitchers; Geoff Blum, Joe Crede, Willie Harris, Tadahito Iguchi, Paul Konerko, Juan Uribe, Pablo Ozuna, infielders; Jermaine Dye, Carl Everett, Timo Perez, Scott Podsednik, Aaron Rowand, outfielders.

Astros — Brad Ausmus, Raul Chavez, catchers; Ezequiel Astacio, Brandon Backe, Roger Clemens, Mike Gallo, Brad Lidge, Roy Oswalt, Andy Pettitte, Chad Qualls, Wandy Rodriguez, Russ Springer, Dan Wheeler, pitchers; Jeff Bagwell, Lance Berkman, Craig Biggio, Eric Bruntlett, Morgan Ensberg, Adam Everett, Mike Lamb, Jose Vizcaino, infielders; Chris Burke, Jason Lane, Orlando Palmeiro, Willy Taveras, outfielders.

2006 - ST. LOUIS CARDINALS N.L. (4) vs DETROIT TIGERS A.L. (1)
(Busch Stadium / Comerica Park)

Oct. 21n	at Det.	St. Louis (Reyes)	7	Detroit (Verlander)	2
Oct. 22n	at Det.	Detroit (Rogers)	3	St. Louis (Weaver)	1
Oct. 24n	at StL.	St. Louis (Carpenter)	5	Detroit (Robertson)	0
Oct. 26n	at StL.	St. Louis (Wainwright)	5	Detroit (Zumaya)	4
Oct. 27n	at StL.	St. Louis (Weaver)	4	Detroit (Verlander)	2
POSTPONED: (Rain) Oct. 25					

MANAGERS: Tony LaRussa, Cardinals; Jim Leyland, Tigers

Cardinals — Gary Bennett, Yadier Molina, catchers; Chris Carpenter, Randy Flores, Josh Hancock, Tyler Johnson, Josh Kinney, Braden Looper, Anthony Reyes, Jeff Suppan, Brad Thompson, Adam Wainwright, Jeff Weaver, pitchers; Ronnie Belliard, David Eckstein, Aaron Miles, Albert Pujols, Scott Rolen, Scott Spiezio, infielders; Chris Duncan, Jim Edmonds, Juan Encarnacion, John Rodriguez, So Taguchi, Preston Wilson, outfielders.

Tigers — Ivan Rodriguez, Vance Wilson, catchers; Jeremy Bonderman, Jason Grilli, Todd Jones, Wil Ledezma, Zach Miner, Nate Robertson, Fernando Rodney, Kenny Rogers, Justin Verlander, Jamie Walker, Joel Zumaya, pitchers; Sean Casey, Carlos Guillen, Omar Infante, Brandon Inge, Neifi Perez, Placido Polanco, Ramon Santiago, infielders; Alexis Gomez, Curtis Granderson, Craig Monroe, Magglio Ordonez, Marcus Thames, outfielders.

AMERICAN LEAGUE CHAMPIONSHIP SERIES

	SERIES			GAMES				
	No.	W	L	No.	W	L	WON	LOST
New York	12	10	2	61	39	22	1976-78, 81, 96, 98-2001, 03	1980, 2004
Oakland	11	6	5	46	23	23	1972-74, 88-90	1971, 75, 81, 92, 2006
Baltimore	9	5	4	37	21	16	1969-71, 79, 83	1973-74, 96, 97
Boston	7	3	4	37	15	22	1975, 86, 2004	1988, 90, 99, 2003
Kansas City	6	2	4	27	12	15	1980, 85	1976-78, 84
Toronto	5	2	3	29	13	16	1992-93	1985, 89, 91
Cal./Ana./LA	5	1	4	26	11	15	2002	1979, 82, 86, 2005
Minnesota	5	2	3	21	9	12	1987, 91	1969-70, 2002
Cleveland	3	2	1	18	10	8	1995, 97	1998
Seattle	3	0	3	17	5	12		1995, 2000-01
Chicago	3	1	2	15	7	8	2005	1983, 93
Detroit	4	2	2	17	10	7	1984, 2006	1972, 87
Milwaukee	1	1	0	5	3	2	1982	

NATIONAL LEAGUE CHAMPIONSHIP SERIES

	SERIES			GAMES				
	No.	W	L	No.	W	L	WON	LOST
Atlanta	11	5	6	60	27	33	1991-92, 95-96, 99	1969, 82, 93, 97-98, 2001
St. Louis	9	5	4	53	26	27	1982, 85, 87, 2004, 06	1996, 2000, 02, 05
Pittsburgh	9	2	7	42	17	25	1971, 79	1970, 72, 74-75, 90-92
Cincinnati	8	5	3	32	18	14	1970, 72, 75-76, 90	1973, 79, 95
Los Angeles	7	5	2	34	19	15	1974, 77-78, 81, 88	1983, 85
New York	7	4	3	39	22	17	1969, 73, 86, 2000	1988, 99, 2006
Philadelphia	6	3	3	26	12	14	1980, 83, 93	1976-78
Houston	4	1	3	24	11	13	2005	1980, 86, 2004
San Francisco	4	2	2	21	12	9	1989, 2002	1971, 87
Chicago	3	0	3	17	6	11		1984, 89, 2003
Florida	2	2	0	13	8	5	1997, 2003	
San Diego	2	2	0	11	7	4	1984, 98	
Arizona	1	1	0	5	4	1	2001	
Montreal	1	0	1	5	2	3		1981

(Note: 1994 Championship Series Not Played)

EAGUE CHAMPIONSHIP SERIES - YEARLY RESULTS

=Wild Card, since 1995)

American League

National League

1969

Baltimore 3, Minnesota 0

10/4	at Balt.	Balt.	4	Minn.	3 (12 inn)
10/5	at Balt.	Balt.	1	Minn.	0 (11 inn)
10/6	at Minn.	Balt.	11	Minn.	2

New York 3, Atlanta 0

10/4	at Atl.	NY	9	Atl.	5
10/5	at Atl.	NY	11	Atl.	6
10/6	at NY	NY	7	Atl.	4

1970

Baltimore 3, Minnesota 0

10/3	at Minn.	Balt.	10	Minn.	6
10/4	at Minn.	Balt.	11	Minn.	3
10/5	at Balt.	Balt.	6	Minn.	1

Cincinnati 3, Pittsburgh 0

10/3	at Pitt.	Cin.	3	Pitt.	0 (10 inn)
10/4	at Pitt.	Cin.	3	Pitt.	1
10/5	at Cin.	Cin.	3	Pitt.	2

1971

Baltimore 3, Oakland 0

10/3	at Balt.	Balt.	5	Oak.	3
10/4	at Balt.	Balt.	5	Oak.	1
10/5	at Oak.	Balt.	5	Oak.	3

Pittsburgh 3, San Francisco 1

10/2	at SF	SF	5	Pitt.	4
10/3	at SF	Pitt.	9	SF	4
10/5	at Pitt.	Pitt.	2	SF	1
10/6	at Pitt.	Pitt.	9	SF	5

1972

Oakland 3, Detroit 2

10/7	at Oak.	Oak.	3	Det.	2 (11 inn)
10/8	at Oak.	Oak.	5	Det.	0
10/10	at Det.	Det.	3	Oak.	0
10/11	at Det.	Det.	4	Oak.	3 (10 inn)
10/12	at Det.	Oak.	2	Det.	1

Cincinnati 3, Pittsburgh 2

10/7	at Pitt.	Pitt.	5	Cin.	1
10/8	at Pitt.	Cin.	5	Pitt.	3
10/9	at Cin.	Pitt.	3	Cin.	2
10/10	at Cin.	Cin.	7	Pitt.	1
10/11	at Cin.	Cin.	4	Pitt.	3

1973

Oakland 3, Baltimore 2

10/6	at Balt.	Balt.	6	Oak.	0
10/7	at Balt.	Oak.	6	Balt.	3
10/9	at Oak.	Oak.	2	Balt.	1 (11 inn)
10/10	at Oak.	Balt.	5	Oak.	4
10/11	at Oak.	Oak.	3	Balt.	0

New York 3, Cincinnati 2

10/6	at Cin.	Cin.	2	NY	1
10/7	at Cin.	NY	5	Cin.	0
10/8	at NY	NY	9	Cin.	2
10/9	at NY	Cin.	2	NY	1 (12 inn)
10/10	at NY	NY	7	Cin.	2

1974

Oakland 3, Baltimore 1

10/5	at Oak.	Balt.	6	Oak.	3
10/6	at Oak.	Oak.	5	Balt.	0
10/8	at Balt.	Oak.	1	Balt.	0
10/9	at Balt.	Oak.	2	Balt.	1

Los Angeles 3, Pittsburgh 1

10/5	at Pitt.	LA	3	Pitt.	0
10/6	at Pitt.	LA	5	Pitt.	2
10/8	at LA	Pitt.	7	LA	0
10/9	at LA	LA	12	Pitt.	1

American League

(*=Wild Card, since 1995)

National League

1975

Boston 3, Oakland 0

10/4	at Bos.	Bos.	7	Oak.	1
10/5	at Bos.	Bos.	6	Oak.	3
10/7	at Oak.	Bos.	5	Oak.	3

Cincinnati 3, Pittsburgh 0

10/4	at Cin.	Cin.	8	Pitt.	3	
10/5	at Cin.	Cin.	6	Pitt.	1	
10/7	at Pitt.	Cin.	5	Pitt.	3	(10 inn)

1976

New York 3, Kansas City 2

10/9	at KC	NY	4	KC	1
10/10	at KC	KC	7	NY	3
10/12	at NY	NY	5	KC	3
10/13	at NY	KC	7	NY	4
10/14	at NY	NY	7	KC	6

Cincinnati 3, Philadelphia 0

10/9	at Phil.	Cin.	6	Phil.	3
10/10	at Phil.	Cin.	6	Phil.	2
10/12	at Cin.	Cin.	7	Phil.	6

1977

New York 3, Kansas City 2

10/5	at NY	KC	7	NY	2
10/6	at NY	NY	6	KC	2
10/7	at KC	KC	6	NY	2
10/8	at KC	NY	6	KC	4
10/9	at KC	NY	5	KC	3

Los Angeles 3, Philadelphia 1

10/4	at LA	Phil.	7	LA	5
10/5	at LA	LA	7	Phil.	1
10/7	at Phil.	LA	6	Phil.	5
10/8	at Phil.	LA	4	Phil.	1

1978

New York 3, Kansas City 1

10/3	at KC	NY	7	KC	1
10/4	at KC	KC	10	NY	4
10/6	at NY	NY	6	KC	5
10/7	at NY	NY	2	KC	1

Los Angeles 3, Philadelphia 1

10/4	at Phil.	LA	9	Phil.	5	
10/5	at Phil.	LA	4	Phil.	0	
10/6	at LA	Phil.	9	LA	4	
10/7	at LA	LA	4	Phil.	3	(10 inn)

1979

Baltimore 3, California 1

10/3	at Balt.	Balt.	6	Cal.	3	(10 inn)
10/4	at Balt.	Balt.	9	Cal.	8	
10/5	at Cal.	Cal.	4	Balt.	3	
10/6	at Cal.	Balt.	8	Cal.	0	

Pittsburgh 3, Cincinnati 0

10/2	at Cin.	Pitt.	5	Cin.	2	(11 inn)
10/3	at Cin.	Pitt.	3	Cin.	2	(10 inn)
10/5	at Pitt.	Pitt.	7	Cin.	1	

1980

Kansas City 3, New York 0

10/8	at KC	KC	7	NY	2
10/9	at KC	KC	3	NY	2
10/10	at NY	KC	4	NY	2

Philadelphia 3, Houston 2

10/7	at Phil.	Phil.	3	Hou.	1	
10/8	at Phil.	Hou.	7	Phil.	4	(10 inn)
10/10	at Hou.	Hou.	1	Phil.	0	(11 inn)
10/11	at Hou.	Phil.	5	Hou.	3	(10 inn)
10/12	at Hou.	Phil.	8	Hou.	7	(10 inn)

American League

(=Wild Card, since 1995)*

National League

1981

New York 3, Oakland 0

10/13	at NY	NY	3	Oak.	1
10/14	at NY	NY	13	Oak.	3
10/15	at Oak.	NY	4	Oak.	0

Los Angeles 3, Montreal 2

10/13	at LA	LA	5	Mtl.	1
10/14	at LA	Mtl.	3	LA	0
10/16	at Mtl.	Mtl.	4	LA	1
10/17	at Mtl.	LA	7	Mtl.	1
10/19	at Mtl.	LA	2	Mtl.	1

1982

Milwaukee 3, California 2

10/5	at Cal.	Cal.	8	Mil.	3
10/6	at Cal.	Cal.	4	Mil.	2
10/8	at Mil.	Mil.	5	Cal.	3
10/9	at Mil.	Mil.	9	Cal.	5
10/10	at Mil.	Mil.	4	Cal.	3

St. Louis 3, Atlanta 0

10/7	at StL.	StL.	7	Atl.	0
10/9	at StL.	StL.	4	Atl.	3
10/10	at Atl.	StL.	6	Atl.	2

1983

Baltimore 3, Chicago 1

10/5	at Balt.	Chi.	2	Balt.	1
10/6	at Balt.	Balt.	4	Chi.	0
10/7	at Chi.	Balt.	11	Chi.	1
10/8	at Chi.	Balt.	3	Chi.	0 (10 inn)

Philadelphia 3, Los Angeles 1

10/4	at LA	Phil.	1	LA	0
10/5	at LA	LA	4	Phil.	1
10/7	at Phil.	Phil.	7	LA	2
10/8	at Phil.	Phil.	7	LA	2

1984

Detroit 3, Kansas City 0

10/2	at KC	Det.	8	KC	1
10/3	at KC	Det.	5	KC	3 (11 inn)
10/5	at Det.	Det.	1	KC	0

San Diego 3, Chicago 2

10/2	at Chi.	Chi.	13	SD	0
10/3	at Chi.	Chi.	4	SD	2
10/4	at SD	SD	7	Chi.	1
10/6	at SD	SD	7	Chi.	5
10/7	at SD	SD	6	Chi.	3

1985

Kansas City 4, Toronto 3

10/8	at Tor.	Tor.	6	KC	1
10/9	at Tor.	Tor.	6	KC	5 (10 inn)
10/11	at KC	KC	6	Tor.	5
10/12	at KC	Tor.	3	KC	1
10/13	at KC	KC	2	Tor.	0
10/15	at Tor.	KC	5	Tor.	3
10/16	at Tor.	KC	6	Tor.	2

St. Louis 4, Los Angeles 2

10/9	at LA	LA	4	StL.	1
10/10	at LA	LA	8	StL.	2
10/12	at StL.	StL.	4	LA	2
10/13	at StL.	StL.	12	LA	2
10/14	at StL.	StL.	3	LA	2
10/16	at LA	StL.	7	LA	5

1986

Boston 4, California 3

10/7	at Bos.	Cal.	8	Bos.	1
10/8	at Bos.	Bos.	9	Cal.	2
10/10	at Cal.	Cal.	5	Bos.	3
10/11	at Cal.	Cal.	4	Bos.	3 (11 inn)
10/12	at Cal.	Bos.	7	Cal.	6 (11 inn)
10/14	at Bos.	Bos.	10	Cal.	4
10/15	at Bos.	Bos.	8	Cal.	1

New York 4, Houston 2

10/8	at Hou.	Hou.	1	NY	0
10/9	at Hou.	NY	5	Hou.	1
10/11	at NY	NY	6	Hou.	5
10/12	at NY	Hou.	3	NY	1
10/14	at NY	NY	2	Hou.	1 (12 inn)
10/15	at Hou.	NY	7	Hou.	6 (16 inn)

American League

(*=Wild Card, since 1995)

National League

1987

Minnesota 4, Detroit 1

10/7	at Minn.	Minn. 8	Det.	5
10/8	at Minn.	Minn. 6	Det.	3
10/10	at Det.	Det. 7	Minn.	6
10/11	at Det.	Minn. 5	Det.	3
10/12	at Det.	Minn. 9	Det.	5

St. Louis 4, San Francisco 3

10/6	at StL.	StL.	5	SF	3
10/7	at StL.	SF	5	StL.	0
10/9	at SF	StL.	6	SF	5
10/10	at SF	SF	4	StL.	2
10/11	at SF	SF	6	StL.	3
10/13	at StL.	StL.	1	SF	0
10/14	at StL.	StL.	6	SF	0

1988

Oakland 4, Boston 0

10/5	at Bos.	Oak. 2	Bos.	1
10/6	at Bos.	Oak. 4	Bos.	3
10/8	at Oak.	Oak. 10	Bos.	6
10/9	at Oak.	Oak. 4	Bos.	1

Los Angeles 4, New York 3

10/4	at LA	NY	3	LA	2	
10/5	at LA	LA	6	NY	3	
10/8	at NY	NY	8	LA	4	
10/9	at NY	LA	5	NY	4	(12 inn)
10/10	at NY	LA	7	NY	4	
10/11	at LA	NY	5	LA	1	
10/12	at LA	LA	6	NY	0	

1989

Oakland 4, Toronto 1

10/3	at Oak.	Oak. 7	Tor.	3
10/4	at Oak.	Oak. 6	Tor.	3
10/6	at Tor.	Tor. 7	Oak.	3
10/7	at Tor.	Oak. 6	Tor.	5
10/8	at Tor.	Oak. 4	Tor.	3

San Francisco 4, Chicago 1

10/4	at Chi.	SF	11	Chi.	3
10/5	at Chi.	Chi.	9	SF	5
10/7	at SF	SF	5	Chi.	4
10/8	at SF	SF	6	Chi.	4
10/9	at SF	SF	3	Chi.	2

1990

Oakland 4, Boston 0

10/6	at Bos.	Oak. 9	Bos.	1
10/7	at Bos.	Oak. 4	Bos.	1
10/9	at Oak.	Oak. 4	Bos.	1
10/10	at Oak.	Oak. 3	Bos.	1

Cincinnati 4, Pittsburgh 2

10/4	at Cin.	Pitt.	4	Cin.	3
10/5	at Cin.	Cin.	2	Pitt.	1
10/8	at Pitt.	Cin.	6	Pitt.	3
10/9	at Pitt.	Cin.	5	Pitt.	3
10/10	at Pitt.	Pitt.	3	Cin.	2
10/12	at Cin.	Cin.	2	Pitt.	1

1991

Minnesota 4, Toronto 1

10/8	at Minn.	Minn. 5	Tor.	4	
10/9	at Minn.	Tor. 5	Minn.	2	
10/11	at Tor.	Minn. 3	Tor.	2	(10 inn)
10/12	at Tor.	Minn. 9	Tor.	3	
10/13	at Tor.	Minn. 8	Tor.	5	

Atlanta 4, Pittsburgh 3

10/9	at Pitt.	Pitt.	5	Atl.	1	
10/10	at Pitt.	Atl.	1	Pitt.	0	
10/12	at Atl.	Atl.	10	Pitt.	3	
10/13	at Atl.	Pitt.	3	Atl.	2	(10 inn)
10/14	at Atl.	Pitt.	1	Atl.	0	
10/16	at Pitt.	Atl.	1	Pitt.	0	
10/17	at Pitt.	Atl.	4	Pitt.	0	

American League

(=Wild Card, since 1995)*

National League

1992

Toronto 4, Oakland 2

10/7	at Tor.	Oak.	4	Tor.	3	
10/8	at Tor.	Tor.	3	Oak.	1	
10/10	at Oak.	Tor.	7	Oak.	5	
10/11	at Oak.	Tor.	7	Oak.	6	(11 inn)
10/12	at Oak.	Oak.	6	Tor.	2	
10/14	at Tor.	Tor.	9	Oak.	2	

Atlanta 4, Pittsburgh 3

10/6	at Atl.	Atl.	5	Pitt.	1	
10/7	at Atl.	Atl.	13	Pitt.	5	
10/9	at Pitt.	Pitt.	3	Atl.	2	
10/10	at Pitt.	Atl.	6	Pitt.	4	
10/11	at Pitt.	Pitt.	7	Atl.	1	
10/13	at Atl.	Pitt.	13	Atl.	4	
10/14	at Atl.	Atl.	3	Pitt.	2	

1993

Toronto 4, Chicago 2

10/5	at Chi.	Tor.	7	Chi.	3	
10/6	at Chi.	Tor.	3	Chi.	1	
10/8	at Tor.	Chi.	6	Tor.	1	
10/9	at Tor.	Chi.	7	Tor.	4	
10/10	at Tor.	Tor.	5	Chi.	3	
10/12	at Chi.	Tor.	6	Chi.	3	

Philadelphia 4, Atlanta 2

10/6	at Phil.	Phil.	4	Atl.	3	(10 inn)
10/7	at Phil.	Atl.	14	Phil.	3	
10/9	at Atl.	Atl.	9	Phil.	4	
10/10	at Atl.	Phil.	2	Atl.	1	
10/11	at Atl.	Phil.	4	Atl.	3	(10 inn)
10/13	at Phil.	Phil.	6	Atl.	3	

1995

Cleveland 4, Seattle 2

10/10	at Sea.	Sea.	3	Clev.	2	
10/11	at Sea.	Clev.	5	Sea.	2	
10/13	at Clev.	Sea.	5	Clev.	2	(11 inn)
10/14	at Clev.	Clev.	7	Sea.	0	
10/15	at Clev.	Clev.	3	Sea.	2	
10/17	at Sea.	Clev.	4	Sea.	0	

Atlanta 4, Cincinnati 0

10/10	at Cin.	Atl.	2	Cin.	1	(11 inn)
10/11	at Cin.	Atl.	6	Cin.	2	(10 inn)
10/13	at Atl.	Atl.	5	Cin.	2	
10/14	at Atl.	Atl.	6	Cin.	0	

1996

New York 4, Baltimore* 1

10/9	at NY	NY	5	Balt.	4	(11 inn)
10/10	at NY	Balt.	5	NY	3	
10/11	at Balt.	NY	5	Balt.	2	
10/12	at Balt.	NY	8	Balt.	4	
10/13	at Balt.	NY	6	Balt.	4	

Atlanta 4, St. Louis 3

10/9	at Atl.	Atl.	4	StL.	2	
10/10	at Atl.	StL.	8	Atl.	3	
10/12	at StL.	StL.	3	Atl.	2	
10/13	at StL.	StL.	4	Atl.	3	
10/14	at StL.	Atl.	14	StL.	0	
10/16	at Atl.	Atl.	3	StL.	1	
10/17	at Atl.	Atl.	15	StL.	0	

1997

Cleveland 4, Baltimore 2

10/8	at Balt.	Balt.	3	Clev.	0	
10/9	at Balt.	Clev.	5	Balt.	4	
10/11	at Clev.	Clev.	2	Balt.	1	(12 inn)
10/12	at Clev.	Clev.	8	Balt.	7	
10/13	at Clev.	Balt.	4	Clev.	2	
10/15	at Balt.	Clev.	1	Balt.	0	(11 inn)

Florida* 4, Atlanta 2

10/7	at Atl.	Fla.	5	Atl.	3	
10/8	at Atl.	Atl.	7	Fla.	1	
10/10	at Fla.	Fla.	5	Atl.	2	
10/11	at Fla.	Atl.	4	Fla.	0	
10/12	at Fla.	Fla.	2	Atl.	1	
10/14	at Atl.	Fla.	7	Atl.	4	

American League

(*=Wild Card, since 1995)

National League

1998

New York 4, Cleveland 2

10/6	at NY	NY	7	Clev.	2	
10/7	at NY	Clev.	4	NY	1	(12 inn)
10/9	at Clev.	Clev.	6	NY	1	
10/10	at Clev.	NY	4	Clev.	0	
10/11	at Clev.	NY	5	Clev.	3	
10/13	at NY	NY	9	Clev.	5	

San Diego 4, Atlanta 2

10/7	at Atl.	SD	3	Atl.	2	(10 inn)
10/8	at Atl.	SD	3	Atl.	0	
10/10	at SD	SD	4	Atl.	1	
10/11	at SD	Atl.	8	SD	3	
10/12	at SD	Atl.	7	SD	6	
10/14	at Atl.	SD	5	Atl.	0	

1999

New York 4, Boston* 1

10/13	at NY	NY	4	Bos.	3	(10 inn)
10/14	at NY	NY	3	Bos.	2	
10/16	at Bos.	Bos.	13	NY	1	
10/17	at Bos.	NY	9	Bos.	2	
10/18	at Bos.	NY	6	Bos.	1	

Atlanta 4, New York* 2

10/12	at Atl.	Atl.	4	NY	2	
10/13	at Atl.	Atl.	4	NY	3	
10/15	at NY	Atl.	1	NY	0	
10/16	at NY	NY	3	Atl.	2	
10/17	at NY	NY	4	Atl.	3	(15 inn)
10/19	at Atl.	Atl.	10	NY	9	(11 inn)

2000

New York 4, Seattle* 2

10/10	at NY	Sea.	2	NY	0
10/11	at NY	NY	7	Sea.	1
10/13	at Sea.	NY	8	Sea.	2
10/14	at Sea.	NY	5	Sea.	0
10/15	at Sea.	Sea.	6	NY	2
10/17	at NY	NY	9	Sea.	7

New York* 4, St. Louis 1

10/11	at StL.	NY	6	StL.	2
10/12	at StL.	NY	6	StL.	5
10/14	at NY	StL.	8	NY	2
10/15	at NY	NY	10	StL.	6
10/16	at NY	NY	7	StL.	0

2001

New York 4, Seattle 1

10/17	at Sea.	NY	4	Sea.	2
10/18	at Sea.	NY	3	Sea.	2
10/20	at NY	Sea.	14	NY	3
10/21	at NY	NY	3	Sea.	1
10/22	at NY	NY	12	Sea.	3

Arizona 4, Atlanta 1

10/16	at Ari.	Ari.	2	Atl.	0
10/17	at Ari.	Atl.	8	Ari.	1
10/19	at Atl.	Ari.	5	Atl.	1
10/20	at Atl.	Ari.	11	Atl.	4
10/21	at Atl.	Ari.	3	Atl.	2

2002

Anaheim* 4, Minnesota 1

10/8	at Minn.	Minn.	2	Ana.	1
10/9	at Minn.	Ana.	6	Minn.	3
10/11	at Ana.	Ana.	2	Minn.	1
10/12	at Ana.	Ana.	7	Minn.	1
10/13	at Ana.	Ana.	13	Minn.	5

San Francisco* 4, St. Louis 1

10/9	at StL.	SF	9	StL.	6
10/10	at StL.	SF	4	StL.	1
10/12	at SF	StL.	5	SF	4
10/13	at SF	SF	4	StL.	3
10/14	at SF	SF	2	StL.	1

American League
(*=Wild Card, since 1995)

National League

2003

New York 4, Boston* 3

10/8	at NY	Bos.	5	NY	2	
10/9	at NY	NY	6	Bos.	2	
10/11	at Bos.	NY	4	Bos.	3	
10/13	at Bos.	Bos.	3	NY	2	
10/14	at Bos.	NY	4	Bos.	2	
10/15	at NY	Bos.	9	NY	6	
10/16	at NY	NY	6	Bos.	5	(11 inn)

Florida* 4, Chicago 3

10/7	at Chi.	Fla.	9	Chi.	8	(11 inn)
10/8	at Chi.	Chi.	12	Fla.	3	
10/10	at Fla.	Chi.	5	Fla.	4	(11 inn)
10/11	at Fla.	Chi.	8	Fla.	3	
10/12	at Fla.	Fla.	4	Chi.	0	
10/14	at Chi.	Fla.	8	Chi.	3	
10/15	at Chi.	Fla.	9	Chi.	6	

2004

Boston* 4, New York 3

10/12	at NY	NY	10	Bos.	7	
10/13	at NY	NY	3	Bos.	1	
10/16	at Bos.	NY	19	Bos.	8	
10/17	at Bos.	Bos.	6	NY	4	(12 inn)
10/18	at Bos.	Bos.	5	NY	4	(14 inn)
10/19	at NY	Bos.	4	NY	2	
10/20	at NY	Bos.	10	NY	3	

St. Louis 4, Houston* 3

10/13	at StL.	StL.	10	Hou.	7	
10/14	at StL.	StL.	6	Hou.	4	
10/16	at Hou.	Hou.	5	StL.	2	
10/17	at Hou.	Hou.	6	StL.	5	
10/18	at Hou.	Hou.	3	StL.	0	
10/20	at StL.	StL.	6	Hou.	4	(12 inn)
10/21	at StL.	StL.	5	Hou.	2	

2005

Chicago 4, Los Angeles 1

10/11	at Chi.	LA	3	Chi.	2
10/12	at Chi.	Chi.	2	LA	1
10/14	at LA	Chi.	5	LA	2
10/15	at LA	Chi.	8	LA	2
10/16	at LA	Chi.	6	LA	3

Houston* 4, St. Louis 2

10/12	at StL.	StL.	5	Hou.	3
10/13	at StL.	Hou.	4	StL.	1
10/15	at Hou.	Hou.	4	StL.	3
10/16	at Hou.	Hou.	2	StL.	1
10/17	at Hou.	StL.	5	Hou.	4
10/19	at StL.	Hou.	5	StL.	1

2006

Detroit* 4, Oakland 0

10/10	at Oak.	Det.	5	Oak.	1
10/11	at Oak.	Det.	8	Oak.	5
10/13	at Det.	Det.	3	Oak.	0
10/14	at Det.	Det.	6	Oak.	3

St. Louis 4, New York 3

10/12	at NY	NY	2	StL.	0
10/13	at NY	StL.	9	NY	6
10/14	at StL.	StL.	5	NY	0
10/15	at StL.	NY	12	StL.	5
10/17	at StL.	StL.	4	NY	2
10/18	at NY	NY	4	StL.	2
10/19	at NY	StL.	3	NY	1

AMERICAN LEAGUE CLUB CHAMPIONSHIP SERIES RECORDS

(Winning club first. IB = innings batted)

YEAR G	IB	AB	R	ER	H	TB	1B	2B	3B	HR	RBI	SH	SF	BB	HP	SO	SB	CS	GDP	BA	SLG	LOB	PO	A	E	DP	ERA	CG	SHO
1969 3																													
Balt	31.1	123	16	14	36	58	23	8	1	4	15	2	0	13	0	14	0	4	3	.293	.472	28	96	31	1	2	1.13	2	1
Minn	32.	110	5	4	17	25	12	3	1	1	5	0	1	12	0	27	2	0	2	.155	.227	22	94	34	5	3	4.02	0	0
1970 3																													
Balt	26	109	27	22	36	61	23	7	0	6	24	2	2	12	1	19	1	0	4	.330	.560	20	81	29	0	3	3.33	2	0
Minn	27	101	10	10	24	39	16	4	1	3	10	1	0	9	0	22	0	0	3	.238	.386	20	78	28	6	5	7.62	0	0
1971 3																													
Balt	25	95	15	15	26	47	14	7	1	4	14	0	1	13	0	22	0	0	3	.274	.495	19	81	30	1	3	2.33	2	0
Oak	27	96	7	7	22	41	10	8	1	3	7	2	0	5	0	16	0	1	3	.229	.427	15	75	15	0	4	5.40	1	0
1972 5																													
Oak	46.1	170	13	11	38	49	29	8	0	1	10	4	1	12	3	35	7	2	2	.224	.288	38	138	60	3	5	1.76	1	1
Det	46	162	10	9	32	52	21	6	1	4	10	3	0	13	0	25	0	2	5	.198	.321	30	139	48	7	4	2.14	1	1
1973 5																													
Oak	45	160	15	14	32	54	21	5	1	5	15	4	1	17	2	39	3	1	2	.200	.338	34	138	47	4	4	2.74	2	1
Balt	46	171	15	14	36	52	26	7	0	3	15	0	0	16	2	25	1	4	2	.211	.304	36	135	52	2	2	2.80	2	1
1974 4																													
Oak	35	120	11	7	22	37	14	4	1	3	11	2	1	22	0	16	3	3	3	.183	.308	30	108	43	2	4	1.75	2	2
Balt	36	124	7	7	22	32	18	1	0	3	7	2	0	5	0	20	0	3	3	.177	.258	16	105	50	4	4	1.80	1	0
1975 3																													
Bos	25	98	18	12	31	45	21	8	0	2	14	5	1	3	0	12	3	0	3	.316	.459	14	81	33	4	3	1.67	1	0
Oak	27	98	7	5	19	28	12	6	0	1	7	0	0	9	1	14	0	0	2	.194	.286	19	75	40	6	4	4.32	0	0
1976 5																													
NY	43	174	23	21	55	84	36	13	2	4	21	2	1	16	0	15	4	3	4	.316	.483	41	132	60	6	3	4.70	1	0
KC	44	162	24	23	40	60	28	6	4	2	24	0	4	11	1	18	5	5	2	.247	.370	22	129	51	4	5	4.40	0	0
1977 5																													
NY	44	175	21	16	46	64	32	12	0	2	17	1	2	9	0	16	2	0	1	.263	.366	34	132	51	2	2	4.50	1	0
KC	44	163	22	22	42	66	27	9	3	3	21	2	2	15	0	22	5	4	2	.258	.405	28	132	54	5	2	3.27	1	0
1978 4																													
NY	34	140	19	18	42	62	33	3	1	5	18	0	0	7	0	18	0	1	3	.300	.443	27	105	35	1	2	3.86	1	0
KC	35	133	17	15	35	59	22	6	3	4	16	1	2	14	0	21	6	3	0	.263	.444	28	102	36	4	4	4.76	1	0
1979 4																													
Balt	35.2	133	26	23	37	53	28	5	1	3	25	1	3	18	1	24	5	1	4	.278	.398	23	109	52	5	5	2.97	1	1
Cal	36.1	137	15	12	32	48	22	7	1	3	14	0	2	7	0	13	2	1	4	.234	.350	22	107	37	2	7	5.80	0	0
1980 3																													
KC	25	97	14	12	28	45	18	6	1	3	14	0	0	9	1	15	3	5	2	.289	.464	18	81	29	1	3	1.67	1	0
NY	27.	102	6	5	26	44	15	7	1	3	5	1	0	6	0	16	0	0	2	.255	.431	22	75	42	1	2	4.32	1	0

AMERICAN LEAGUE CLUB CHAMPIONSHIP SERIES RECORDS

YEAR	G	IB	AB	R	ER	H	TB	1B	2B	3B	HR	RBI	SH	SF	BB	HP	SO	SB	CS	GDP	BA	SLG	LOB	PO	A	E	DP	ERA	CG	SHO
1981	3																													
NY		25	107	20	19	36	49	29	4	0	3	20	2	1	13	0	10	2	1	1	.336	.458	30	81	30	1	6	1.33	0	1
Oak		27.	99	4	4	22	28	17	4	1	0	4	0	0	6	0	23	2	0	6	.222	.283	20	75	33	4	1	6.84	0	0
1982	5																													
Mil		42	151	23	20	33	52	24	4	0	5	20	2	3	15	2	28	2	2	2	.219	.344	24	129	45	8	6	4.19	1	0
Cal		43	157	23	20	40	62	27	8	1	4	23	5	2	16	1	34	1	2	4	.255	.395	29	126	47	4	3	4.29	2	0
1983	4																													
Balt		36	129	19	16	28	46	16	9	0	3	17	1	3	16	2	24	2	0	5	.217	.357	24	111	49	2	4	0.49	1	2
Chi		37.	133	3	2	28	32	24	4	0	0	2	1	0	12	3	26	4	1	2	.211	.241	35	108	51	3	5	4.00	1	0
1984	3																													
Det		28.	107	14	11	25	43	16	4	1	4	14	2	1	8	0	17	4	0	2	.234	.402	20	87	27	1	0	1.24	0	1
KC		29.	106	4	4	18	21	16	1	1	0	4	0	0	6	0	21	0	1	0	.170	.198	21	84	26	7	2	3.54	1	0
1985	7																													
KC		62.	227	26	26	51	83	34	9	1	7	26	4	2	22	1	51	2	4	2	.225	.366	44	188	87	6	7	3.16	1	1
Tor		62.2	242	25	22	65	90	44	19	0	2	23	0	2	16	3	37	2	2	4	.269	.372	50	186	61	4	4	3.77	0	0
1986	7																													
Bos		64.	254	41	28	69	102	50	11	2	6	35	3	2	19	3	31	2	0	7	.272	.402	48	196	73	7	5	3.58	1	0
Cal		65.1	256	30	26	71	103	53	11	0	7	29	4	2	20	4	44	1	4	5	.277	.402	60	192	78	8	7	3.94	1	0
1987	5																													
Minn		43.	171	34	32	46	85	24	8	1	8	33	0	1	10	0	25	4	3	1	.269	.497	37	132	41	3	3	4.50	0	0
Det		44.	167	23	22	40	65	29	4	0	7	21	2	2	18	1	35	5	0	3	.240	.389	37	129	56	5	1	6.70	0	0
1988	4																													
Oak		34.	137	20	20	41	70	26	9	1	7	20	3	2	20	1	32	1	3	2	.299	.511	26	108	30	3	5	2.00	0	0
Bos		36.	126	11	8	26	36	20	5	0	2	10	0	2	15	0	24	0	0	3	.206	.286	30	102	34	1	2	5.29	0	0
1989	5																													
Oak		43.	158	26	24	43	75	26	9	1	7	23	3	3	20	4	32	9	3	2	.272	.475	29	132	45	3	4	3.89	0	0
Tor		44.	165	21	19	40	54	32	5	0	3	19	4	2	15	0	24	1	0	3	.242	.327	30	129	40	2	5	5.02	0	0
1990	4																													
Oak		34.	127	20	17	38	42	34	4	0	0	18	3	3	19	4	21	8	4	2	.299	.331	35	108	43	1	3	1.00	0	0
Bos		36.	126	4	4	23	31	17	5	0	1	4	2	2	6	0	16	7	1	3	.183	.246	23	102	47	5	6	4.50	0	0
1991	5																													
Minn		45.	181	27	23	50	70	37	9	1	3	25	1	2	15	1	37	8	4	4	.276	.387	38	138	51	4	3	3.33	0	0
Tor		46.	173	19	17	43	52	36	6	0	1	18	3	1	15	0	30	7	1	3	.249	.301	35	135	49	7	6	4.60	0	0
1992	6																													
Tor		54.	210	31	27	59	99	40	8	1	10	30	1	4	23	0	29	7	5	4	.281	.471	45	165	60	8	7	3.44	1	0
Oak		55.	207	24	21	52	71	42	5	1	4	23	3	2	24	1	33	16	2	5	.251	.343	48	162	55	7	5	4.50	1	0
1993	6																													
Tor		53.	216	26	21	65	85	52	8	3	2	24	1	1	21	2	36	7	2	5	.301	.394	56	162	57	2	7	3.67	0	0
Chi		54.	194	23	22	46	68	35	5	1	5	22	5	1	32	3	43	3	2	4	.237	.351	50	159	56	7	5	3.57	1	0

AMERICAN LEAGUE CLUB CHAMPIONSHIP SERIES RECORDS

YEAR	G	IB	AB	R	ER	H	TB	1B	2B	3B	HR	RBI	SH	SF	BB	HP	SO	SB	CS	GDP	BA	SLG	LOB	PO	A	E	DP	ERA	CG	SHO
1995	**6**																													
Clev		54	206	23	20	53	86	37	6	3	7	21	1	2	25	1	37	9	1	6	.257	.417	50	165	66	7	4	1.64	0	2
Sea		55	201	12	10	37	60	24	8	0	5	10	1	0	15	3	46	9	2	2	.184	.299	43	162	59	6	7	3.33	0	0
1996	**5**																													
NY		46	183	27	21	50	91	30	9	1	10	24	0	0	20	2	37	3	0	6	.273	.497	40	141	44	1	2	3.64	0	0
Balt		47	176	19	19	39	70	26	4	0	9	19	0	3	15	0	33	0	0	1	.222	.398	34	138	58	4	7	4.11	0	0
1997	**6**																													
Clev		58	207	18	17	40	63	27	8	0	5	15	2	0	23	4	62	5	0	3	.193	.304	44	174	61	5	11	2.95	0	1
Balt		58	218	19	19	54	86	36	11	0	7	19	1	0	23	1	47	3	1	10	.248	.394	50	174	60	5	4	2.64	0	1
1998	**6**																													
NY		55	197	27	22	43	65	30	8	1	4	25	3	3	35	2	42	9	2	7	.218	.330	48	168	54	2	5	3.21	0	1
Clev		56	205	20	20	45	77	32	3	1	9	19	0	1	16	5	51	6	1	5	.220	.376	39	165	77	7	7	3.60	1	0
1999	**5**																													
NY		45	176	23	18	42	72	29	4	1	8	21	2	0	18	1	44	3	1	0	.239	.409	42	135	38	5	7	3.80	0	0
Bos		45	184	21	19	54	86	34	13	2	5	19	1	0	15	1	38	4	1	6	.293	.467	45	132	40	10	0	3.68	0	0
2000	**6**																													
NY		52	204	31	31	57	85	41	10	0	6	31	1	3	25	3	41	4	2	4	.279	.417	49	159	54	1	5	3.06	1	1
Sea		53	191	18	18	41	68	24	12	0	5	18	2	1	21	0	48	3	2	2	.215	.356	38	156	58	3	4	5.37	0	1
2001	**5**																													
NY		43.1	159	25	21	42	70	28	7	0	7	24	4	1	23	2	31	3	3	4	.264	.440	34	135	47	4	4	3.80	0	0
Sea		45	171	22	19	36	59	25	4	2	5	20	1	0	18	1	35	3	0	3	.211	.345	34	130	45	1	5	4.36	0	0
2002	**5**																													
Ana		42	171	29	28	49	82	34	5	2	8	26	2	0	9	2	26	3	1	2	.287	.480	29	132	38	2	4	2.45	0	0
Minn		44	160	12	12	37	46	28	9	0	0	11	2	2	7	1	38	1	1	4	.231	.287	28	126	43	4	4	6.00	0	0
2003	**7**																													
NY		63	238	30	28	54	90	34	12	0	8	29	0	1	21	4	49	5	1	4	.227	.378	45	192	73	5	12	3.94	0	0
Bos.		64	250	29	28	68	117	45	9	2	12	26	0	0	17	3	60	2	5	9	.272	.468	49	189	67	3	5	4.00	0	0
2004	**7**																													
Bos.		69.2	271	41	40	75	119	52	12	1	10	40	1	2	28	1	53	4	2	8	.277	.439	53	207	66	1	4	5.87	0	0
NY		69	277	45	45	78	130	46	21	2	9	44	3	1	33	7	51	3	0	3	.282	.469	69	209	74	4	9	5.17	0	0
2005	**5**																													
Chi.		44.2	165	23	17	41	68	25	10	1	5	23	3	2	16	4	36	5	4	2	.248	.412	33	135	66	3	4	2.20	4	0
LA		45	154	11	11	27	41	19	5	0	3	11	3	1	4	1	22	2	0	4	.175	.266	17	134	47	7	5	3.43	0	0
2006	**4**																													
Det.		34.2	137	22	22	39	67	25	7	0	7	22	1	2	19	0	25	2	0	3	.285	.489	33	108	37	1	7	2.25	0	1
Oak.		36	131	9	9	29	48	18	7	0	4	9	0	0	14	1	28	0	0	7	.221	.366	29	104	44	3	4	5.71	0	0

NATIONAL LEAGUE CLUB CHAMPIONSHIP SERIES RECORDS

(Winning club first   IB = innings batted)

YEAR	Club	G	IB	AB	R	ER	H	TB	1B	2B	3B	HR	RBI	SH	SF	BB	HP	SO	SB	CS	GDP	BA	SLG	LOB	PO	A	E	DP	ERA	CG	SHO
1969	NY	3	26.	113	27	20	37	65	22	8	1	6	24	1	0	10	0	25	5	1	2	.327	.575	19	81	23	2	2	5.00	0	0
	Atl		27.	106	15	15	27	51	13	9	0	5	15	0	1	11	1	20	1	0	2	.255	.481	23	78	37	6	4	6.92	0	0
1970	Cin	3	27.	100	9	8	22	36	15	3	1	3	8	0	0	8	0	12	1	1	2	.220	.360	18	84	39	1	1	0.96	0	1
	Pitt		28.	102	3	3	23	29	17	6	0	0	3	2	0	12	0	19	1	2	1	.225	.284	29	81	37	2	3	2.67	0	0
1971	Pitt	4	34.	144	24	23	39	67	27	4	0	8	23	1	0	5	2	33	2	1	0	.271	.465	26	105	32	3	3	3.34	0	0
	SF		35.	132	15	13	31	51	21	5	0	5	14	4	0	16	1	28	2	0	3	.235	.386	33	102	37	4	1	6.09	2	0
1972	Cin	5	43.2	166	19	16	42	67	27	9	2	4	16	3	1	10	0	28	4	1	0	.253	.404	30	132	53	4	3	3.07	1	0
	Pitt		44.	158	15	15	30	47	20	6	1	3	14	2	0	9	2	27	0	1	2	.190	.297	24	131	38	4	3	3.30	0	0
1973	NY	5	46	168	23	23	37	51	29	5	0	3	22	3	1	19	0	28	0	0	3	.220	.304	30	142	44	4	3	1.33	3	1
	Cin		47.1	167	8	7	31	52	20	6	0	5	8	3	0	13	1	42	0	1	3	.186	.311	35	138	59	2	3	4.50	0	0
1974	LA	4	35	138	20	19	37	56	25	8	1	3	19	1	0	30	0	16	5	0	2	.268	.406	44	108	46	7	8	2.00	1	1
	Pitt		36	129	10	8	25	35	21	1	0	3	10	2	0	8	2	17	0	0	5	.194	.271	24	105	38	4	2	4.89	0	1
1975	Cin	3	26	102	19	19	29	45	21	4	0	4	18	0	0	9	0	28	11	0	2	.284	.441	17	84	31	1	2	2.25	1	0
	Pitt		28	101	7	7	20	26	16	3	0	1	7	0	0	10	1	18	0	0	2	.198	.257	21	78	20	2	3	6.58	0	0
1976	Cin	3	26.1	99	19	15	25	45	14	5	3	3	17	3	2	15	0	16	5	1	1	.253	.455	20	81	32	2	2	3.33	0	0
	Phil		27	100	11	10	27	40	17	8	1	1	11	2	2	12	0	9	0	1	2	.270	.400	25	79	34	2	3	5.13	0	0
1977	LA	4	35	133	22	21	35	52	25	6	1	3	20	2	0	14	1	22	3	1	2	.263	.391	22	108	44	5	3	2.25	0	0
	Phil		36	138	14	9	31	40	26	3	0	2	12	2	1	11	3	21	1	0	3	.225	.290	32	105	49	3	3	5.40	0	0
1978	LA	4	36.2	147	21	19	42	80	23	8	3	8	21	2	3	9	1	22	2	1	4	.286	.544	28	111	50	3	4	3.41	1	1
	Phil		37	140	17	14	35	57	25	3	2	5	16	2	0	9	0	21	0	1	4	.250	.407	24	110	46	4	4	4.66	1	0
1979	Pitt	3	29	105	15	14	28	47	19	3	2	4	14	5	3	13	0	13	4	0	2	.267	.448	24	90	34	0	2	1.50	1	0
	Cin		30.	107	5	5	23	35	16	4	1	2	5	7	1	11	1	26	4	0	2	.215	.327	25	87	39	1	2	4.34	0	0
1980	Phil	5	49	190	20	19	55	68	45	7	3	0	19	5	3	13	1	37	7	3	7	.289	.358	43	148	71	6	7	3.28	0	0
	Hou		49.1	172	19	18	40	57	28	7	5	0	18	7	1	31	2	19	4	3	4	.233	.331	45	147	52	3	4	3.49	2	1
1981	LA	5	44	163	15	14	38	55	30	3	1	4	15	4	0	12	0	23	5	0	5	.233	.337	33	132	53	2	5	1.84	0	0
	Mtl		44	158	10	9	34	44	26	6	2	0	8	3	0	12	0	25	2	1	8	.215	.278	31	132	52	4	8	2.86	2	1
1982	StL	3	25.1	103	17	17	34	45	27	4	2	1	16	5	3	12	3	16	1	0	3	.330	.437	31	81	35	2	3	1.33	1	1
	Atl		27	89	5	4	15	16	14	1	0	0	3	2	1	6	1	15	1	2	0	.169	.180	12	76	39	1	0	6.04	0	0

NATIONAL LEAGUE CLUB CHAMPIONSHIP SERIES RECORDS

(Winning club first. IB = innings batted)

YEAR / G	IB	AB	R	ER	H	TB	1B	2B	3B	HR	RBI	SH	SF	BB	HP	SO	SB	CS	GDP	BA	SLG	LOB	PO	A	E	DP	ERA	CG	SHO
1983 4																													
Phil.	34	130	16	15	34	53	25	4	0	5	15	3	1	15	0	22	2	1	3	.262	.408	31	105	36	5	0	1.03	1	1
LA	35	129	8	4	27	40	19	5	1	2	7	2	0	11	2	31	3	3	0	.209	.310	31	102	38	1	3	3.97	0	0
1984 5																													
SD	42.1	155	22	20	41	54	33	5	1	2	20	2	4	14	2	22	2	2	6	.265	.348	27	129	43	1	4	5.23	0	0
Chi.	43	162	26	25	42	80	22	11	0	9	25	1	2	20	2	28	6	3	3	.259	.494	32	127	48	3	6	4.25	0	1
1985 6																													
StL	51.1	201	29	22	56	77	42	10	1	3	26	2	1	30	0	34	6	6	3	.279	.383	51	156	54	4	4	3.46	0	0
LA	52	197	23	20	46	75	28	12	1	5	23	1	1	19	0	31	4	1	3	.234	.381	40	154	71	6	3	3.51	1	0
1986 6																													
NY	62.2	227	21	20	43	60	34	4	2	3	19	1	3	14	0	57	4	0	3	.189	.264	36	189	94	1	6	2.29	1	0
Hou.	63	225	17	16	49	70	38	6	0	5	17	2	0	17	1	40	8	4	4	.218	.311	39	188	66	7	3	2.87	2	1
1987 7																													
StL	60	215	23	22	56	74	46	4	4	2	22	5	4	16	0	42	4	4	7	.260	.344	37	183	67	3	5	2.95	2	2
SF	61	226	23	20	54	90	37	7	1	9	20	3	1	17	2	51	5	4	5	.239	.398	43	180	77	6	10	3.30	2	1
1988 7																													
LA	64	243	31	28	52	70	41	7	1	3	30	1	2	25	2	54	9	1	2	.214	.288	50	195	61	4	9	3.32	1	1
NY	65	240	27	24	58	87	40	12	1	5	27	3	1	28	4	42	6	2	8	.242	.363	54	192	62	8	2	3.94	1	0
1989 5																													
SF	42	165	30	26	44	78	28	6	2	8	29	2	1	17	1	29	2	1	1	.267	.473	30	132	49	5	7	4.09	0	0
Chi.	44	175	22	20	53	77	38	9	3	3	21	3	2	16	1	27	3	0	4	.303	.440	43	126	40	3	1	5.57	0	0
1990 6																													
Cin.	52	192	20	19	49	70	36	9	0	4	20	3	1	10	1	37	6	3	4	.255	.365	33	159	45	2	3	2.38	0	0
Pitt.	53	186	15	14	36	58	22	9	2	3	14	0	1	27	1	49	6	2	2	.194	.312	41	156	71	5	4	3.29	0	0
1991 7																													
Atl.	63	229	19	18	53	80	37	10	1	5	19	5	1	22	2	42	10	4	2	.231	.349	51	189	62	4	6	1.57	1	3
Pitt.	63	228	12	11	51	70	38	10	0	3	11	4	1	22	0	57	6	2	4	.224	.307	54	189	75	6	3	2.57	1	1
1992 7																													
Atl.	60.2	234	34	30	57	90	38	11	2	6	32	2	2	29	0	51	5	0	3	.244	.385	51	183	73	2	3	4.72	0	0
Pitt.	61	231	35	32	59	100	31	20	3	5	32	3	3	29	2	42	1	2	3	.255	.433	50	182	63	5	6	4.45	3	0
1993 6																													
Phil.	54.1	207	23	19	47	87	25	11	4	7	22	3	2	26	0	51	2	0	1	.227	.420	52	165	47	7	2	4.75	0	0
Atl.	55	215	33	29	59	88	40	14	0	5	32	5	2	22	1	54	0	3	2	.274	.409	47	163	55	5	1	3.15	0	0
1995 4																													
Atl.	37	149	19	19	42	62	31	6	1	4	17	1	0	16	0	22	2	1	3	.282	.416	36	117	54	3	8	1.15	1	0
Cin.	39	134	5	5	28	35	22	5	1	0	4	1	1	12	2	31	4	3	8	.209	.261	28	111	43	2	4	4.62	0	0
1996 7																													
Atl.	60	249	44	44	77	118	55	11	3	8	43	2	3	25	3	51	4	1	3	.309	.474	58	183	55	4	6	1.92	0	2
StL	61	221	18	13	45	65	35	4	2	4	15	1	1	11	1	53	1	1	5	.204	.294	34	180	62	6	5	6.60	0	0

NATIONAL LEAGUE CLUB CHAMPIONSHIP SERIES RECORDS

(Winning club first. IB = innings batted)

YEAR	G	IB	AB	R	ER	H	TB	1B	2B	3B	HR	RBI	SH	SF	BB	HP	SO	SB	CS	GDP	BA	SLG	LOB	PO	A	E	DP	ERA	CG	SHO
1997	**6**																													
Fla.		52	181	20	15	36	47	27	8	0	1	20	5	0	23	3	52	2	1	4	.199	.260	36	159	57	3	4	3.57	2	0
Atl.		53	194	21	21	49	76	36	5	2	6	21	5	3	16	2	49	1	1	3	.253	.392	40	156	57	4	7	2.60	1	1
1998	**6**																													
SD		54	208	24	21	53	75	41	7	0	5	20	2	0	27	1	48	2	1	6	.255	.361	52	165	60	1	6	2.78	1	2
Atl.		55	200	18	17	47	65	38	4	1	4	17	2	1	26	0	54	3	1	4	.235	.325	46	162	74	8	6	3.50	0	0
1999	**6**																													
Atl.		60	206	24	23	46	72	31	9	1	5	22	7	1	31	4	47	14	3	5	.223	.350	47	181	55	7	4	2.69	0	1
NY		61	225	21	18	49	70	36	9	0	4	21	3	2	14	0	49	7	3	3	.218	.311	42	178	82	8	9	3.49	0	0
2000	**5**																													
NY		43	164	31	28	43	69	26	12	1	4	27	3	3	27	3	24	2	1	3	.262	.421	40	135	39	4	1	3.60	1	1
StL		45	177	21	18	47	64	34	11	0	2	18	4	2	11	1	39	3	0	0	.266	.362	39	129	49	7	3	5.86	0	0
2001	**5**																													
Ari.		44	172	22	13	40	52	32	6	0	2	19	2	0	18	1	32	3	1	5	.233	.302	39	135	43	3	3	3.00	2	1
Atl.		45	169	15	15	35	56	24	6	0	5	14	0	0	11	0	39	0	1	3	.207	.331	30	132	53	7	5	2.66	0	0
2002	**5**																													
SF		43.2	158	23	23	39	67	27	3	2	7	23	8	2	21	3	36	1	0	3	.247	.424	38	135	49	1	4	3.20	0	0
StL		45	171	16	16	44	73	29	8	0	7	16	5	2	10	2	23	1	1	3	.257	.427	39	131	40	1	4	4.74	0	0
2003	**7**																													
Fla.		66	256	40	35	68	116	43	12	3	10	39	3	2	28	2	45	4	3	4	.266	.453	53	198	70	3	4	5.59	1	0
Chi.		66	252	42	41	65	122	38	10	4	13	41	7	1	23	2	57	1	0	4	.258	.484	45	198	82	4	6	4.36	0	0
2004	**7**																													
StL		62.1	235	34	34	60	107	36	12	1	11	33	6	1	17	2	56	2	0	2	.255	.455	40	190	66	1	5	4.26	0	0
Hou.		63.1	233	31	30	53	105	29	10	0	14	30	1	1	25	5	42	6	4	3	.227	.451	44	187	71	2	2	4.91	0	1
2005	**6**																													
Hou.		52	198	22	17	55	81	41	7	2	5	19	8	2	15	1	33	4	1	2	.278	.409	46	159	77	3	4	2.72	1	0
StL		53	187	16	16	39	54	30	6	0	3	16	3	4	16	3	42	5	0	4	.209	.289	38	156	73	5	3	2.94	0	0
2006	**7**																													
StL		61	226	28	27	56	98	36	7	4	9	27	4	0	29	3	33	4	1	6	.248	.434	51	183	73	4	4	3.84	0	0
NY		61	234	27	26	54	92	33	12	1	8	27	2	0	24	3	36	5	0	3	.231	.393	53	183	77	4	10	3.98	0	1

CHAMPIONSHIP SERIES – INDIVIDUAL BATTING

	3 Games	4 Games	5 Games	6 Games	7 Games
Batting Average (Minimum: 3.1 PA per game)					
AL:	.583 B. Robinson Balt. 1970	.529 Polanco Det. 2006	.611 Lynn Cal. 1982	.458 Lofton Clev. 1995	.455 Boone Cal. 1986
NL:	.778 Johnstone Phil. 1976	.467 Baker LA 1978 Schmidt Phil. 1983	.650 Clark SF 1989	.500 Perez Atl. 1999	.542 Lopez Atl. 1996
Slugging Percentage (Minimum: 3.1 PA per game)					
AL:	1.000 Buford Balt. 1970	1.056 Brett KC 1978	1.000 Brunansky Minn. 1987 Henderson Oak. 1989	.826 Thome Clev. 1998	.826 Brett KC 1985
NL:	1.182 Stargell Pitt. 1979	1.250 Robertson Pitt. 1971	1.200 Clark SF 1989	.900 Perez Atl. 1999	1.000 Lopez Atl. 1996 Pujols StL. 2004
Plate Appearances					
AL:	17 Blair & Buford Balt. 1969	20 Bumbry Balt. 1979	25 Offerman Bos. 1999 Valentin Bos. 1999	30 Knoblauch NY 1998	38 Jeter NY 2004
NL:	16 Agee NY 1969	20 Lopes LA 1974	25 Rose & Schmidt Phil. 1980 Cabell Hou. 1980 Sandberg Chi. 1989	31 Williams Atl. 1999	36 Pierre Fla. 2003
At-Bats					
AL:	15 Belanger Balt. 1969 Blair Balt. 1969 Law Chi. 1983	18 Brett KC 1978 Munson NY 1978 Bradley Oak. 2006	24 Puckett Minn. 1987 Jeter NY 1996 Offerman Bos. 1999	27 Carter & White Tor. 1993 Raines Chi. 1993 Lofton Clev. 1998	36 Williams NY 2004
NL:	15 Oberkfell StL. 1982	19 Cash Pitt. 1971 Maddox Phil. 1978 Grissom Atl. 1995	24 Schmidt Phil. 1980	28 Williams Atl. 1999	35 Grissom Atl. 1996
Runs					
AL:	5 Belanger Balt. 1970	7 Brett KC 1978	8 R. Henderson Oak. 1989	7 Winfield Tor. 1992 Molitor Tor. 1993	9 Matsui NY 2004
NL:	4 By many players	6 Garvey LA 1978	8 Clark SF 1989 Perez NY 2000	6 McGee StL. 1985 McGriff Atl. 1993 Sheffield Fla. 1997	12 Beltran Hou. 2004
Hits					
AL:	7 B. Robinson Balt. 1969-70	9 Bradley Oak. 2006 Polanco Det. 2006	11 Chambliss NY 1976 Lynn Cal. 1982 Offerman Bos. 1999	12 Raines Chi. & White Tor. 1993	14 Matsui NY 2004
NL:	7 Shamsky NY 1969 Johnstone Phil. 1976	8 Cash Pitt. 1971	13 Clark SF 1989	10 O. Smith StL. 1985 McGriff Atl. 1993 Perez Atl. 1999	14 Pujols StL. 2004
Extra-Base Hits					
AL:	4 Watson NY 1980	5 Brett KC 1978	6 Brunansky Minn. 1987	5 Buhner Sea. 1995	9 Matsui NY 2004
NL:	5 Aaron Atl. 1969	6 Garvey LA 1978	6 Clark SF 1989	5 Herr StL. 1985	7 Lopez Atl. 1996

CHAMPIONSHIP SERIES – INDIVIDUAL BATTING

	3 Games	4 Games	5 Games	6 Games	7 Games
Total Bases					
AL:	11 By many players	19 Brett KC 1978	20 Chambliss NY 1976	19 Thome Clev. 1998	28 Matsui NY 2004
NL:	16 H. Aaron Atl. 1969	22 Garvey LA 1978	24 Clark SF 1989	18 Madlock LA 1985 Perez Atl. 1999	28 Pujols StL. 2004
Singles					
AL:	6 B. Robinson Balt. 1969	8 Polanco Det. 2006	10 Offerman Bos. 1999	10 Raines Chi. 1993 Vizquel Clev. 1998	9 Barrett Bos. 1986 Boone Cal. 1986 Cabrera Bos. 2004
NL:	7 Shamsky NY 1969	7 Russell LA 1974	8 Puhl Hou. 1980 Rose Phil. 1980 Walton Chi. 1989	8 Biggio Hou. 2005	9 Bell Pitt. 1991 C. Jones Atl. 1996 Lemke Atl. 1996 Lofton Chi. 2003
Doubles					
AL:	3 Watson NY 1980	3 Carew Cal. 1979	4 Alou Oak. 1972 Brunansky Minn. 1987	3 Giles Clev. 1997 Olerud & McLemore Sea. 2000	6 Matsui NY 2004
NL:	3 Morgan Cin. 1975 Porter StL. 1982	4 McGriff Atl. 1995	4 Rose Cin. 1972	4 Herr StL. 1985 Alfonzo NY 1999	5 Lopez Atl. 1996
Triples					
AL:	1 By many players	1 By many players	2 Brett KC 1977	2 Lofton Clev. 1995	1 By many players
NL:	2 McGee StL. 1982	1 By many players	1 By many players	2 Duncan Phil. 1993	2 Pierre Fla. 2003 Spiezio StL. 2006
Home Runs					
AL:	2 By many players	3 Brett KC 1978 Canseco Oak. 1988	3 Strawberry NY 1996 Zeile Balt. 1996 Williams NY 2001 Kennedy Ana. 2002	4 Thome Clev. 1998	3 Brett KC 1985 Giambi NY 2003 Nixon Bos. 2003 Ortiz Bos. 2004
NL:	3 H. Aaron Atl. 1969	4 Robertson Pitt. 1971 Garvey LA 1978	3 Staub NY 1973	3 Madlock LA 1985	4 Leonard SF 1987 Beltran Hou. 2004 Pujols StL. 2004
Runs Batted In					
AL:	9 Nettles NY 1981	6 Jackson NY 1978 Ordonez Det. 2006	10 Baylor Cal. 1982	8 Thome Clev. 1998 Justice NY 2000	11 Ortiz Bos. 2004
NL:	7 H. Aaron Atl. 1969	8 Baker 1977 Matthews Phil. 1983	9 Williams SF 1989	7 Madlock LA 1985	10 Rodriguez Fla. 2003
Walks					
AL:	6 Killebrew Minn. 1969	5 By many players	7 Whitaker Det. 1987 R. Henderson Oak. 1989	10 Thomas Chi. 1993	7 Brett KC 1985 Posada NY 2004
NL:	6 Morgan Cin. 1976	9 Wynn LA 1974	10 Bonds SF 2002	9 C. Jones Atl. 1999	8 Beltran Hou. 2004

CHAMPIONSHIP SERIES – INDIVIDUAL BATTING

Intentional Walks

	3 Games	4 Games	5 Games	6 Games	7 Games
AL:	1 By many players	2 Rudi Oak. 1974 Murray Balt. 1979 Baines Oak. 1990	2 By many players	2 By many players	3 Brett KC 1985
NL:	2 Morgan Cin. 1976 Hernandez StL 1982	3 McCovey SF 1971 Cey LA 1974	4 Cruz Hou. 1980	5 Guerrero LA 1985	4 Pujols StL 2006

Hit By Pitch

	3 Games	4 Games	5 Games	6 Games	7 Games
AL:	1 By many players	1 By many players	2 Gladden Minn. 1987 Sheridan Det. 1987	2 Cora Sea. 1995 Grich Cal. 1986	4 Cairo NY 2004
NL:	1 By many players	1 By many players	1 By many players	2 Eckstein StL 2005	2 Dykstra NY 1986 Blauser Atl. 1996 Ensberg Hou. 2004 Kent Hou. 2004 Eckstein StL 2006

Strikeouts

	3 Games	4 Games	5 Games	6 Games	7 Games
AL:	7 Cardenas Minn. 1969	7 D. Henderson Oak. 1988	8 Gibson Det. 1987 Davis Minn. 1991 Koskie Minn. 2002	10 Palmeiro Balt. 1997 Vizquel Clev. 1997	11 Soriano NY 2003 Bellhorn Bos. 2004
NL:	7 Geronimo Cin. 1975	10 R. Sanders Cin. 1995	9 Edmonds StL 2000	12 Strawberry NY 1986	12 Shelby LA 1988

Stolen Bases

	3 Games	4 Games	5 Games	6 Games	7 Games
AL:	2 By many players	4 Otis KC 1978	8 R. Henderson Oak. 1989	7 Wilson Oak. 1992	2 Soriano NY 2003 Damon Bos. 2004
NL:	4 Morgan Cin. 1975	3 Lopes LA 1974	5 Lopes LA 1981	3 Hatcher Hou. 1986 Larkin Cin. 1990 C. Jones & Williams Atl. 1999	7 Gant Atl. 1991

Caught Stealing

	3 Games	4 Games	5 Games	6 Games	7 Games
AL:	3 McRae KC 1980	2 By many players	3 Patek KC 1976	4 White Tor. 1992	2 Pettis Cal. 1986 Nixon Bos. 2003
NL:	1 By many players	2 Marshall LA 1983	2 Rose Phil. 1980	3 McGee StL 1985 Bass Hou. 1986	3 Pierre Fla. 2003

Grounded into Double Plays

	3 Games	4 Games	5 Games	6 Games	7 Games
AL:	2 Thompson Minn. 1970	2 Anderson Cal. 1979 Singleton Balt. 1983 Benzinger Bos. 1988 Pena Bos. 1990 Guillen Det. 2006 Kotsay Oak. 2006	3 Taylor Det. 1972	3 Sorrento Clev. 1995	3 DeCinces Cal. 1986 Mueller Bos. 2004
NL:	2 Jones NY 1969 Royster Atl. 1982	2 Bowa Phil. 1977 Boone Cin. 1995 Devereaux Atl. 1995	4 Guerrero LA 1981	3 Gomez SD 1998	3 Herr StL 1987

Most Series
11 Reggie Jackson, AL:Oak. 1971-75,
   NY 77-78, 80-81,Cal. 82, 86
10 Tom Glavine NL:Atl. 1991-93, 95-99, 2001
   NY 2006

Most Games
46 David Justice, NL:Atl.; AL:Clev.-NY
45 Reggie Jackson, AL:Oak.-NY-Cal.
38 Terry Pendleton, NL:StL.-Atl.

Highest Batting Average (50 or more at-bats)
.468 Will Clark, NL:SF-StL. (62ab-29h)
.392 Devon White, AL:Cal.-Tor. (74ab-29h)

Highest Slugging Percentage (50 or more at-bats)
.806 Will Clark, NL:SF-StL. (62ab-50tb)
.728 George Brett, AL:KC (103ab-75tb)

Most Plate Appearances
195 David Justice, NL:Atl.; AL:Clev.-NY
194 Derek Jeter, AL:NY
154 Chipper Jones, NL:Atl.

Most Plate Appearances, Game
6 By many players
Extra-Inning Game:
8 Mookie Wilson NL:NY Oct. 15, 1986 (16 inn)
   Chipper Jones, NL:Atl. Oct. 17 1999 (15 inn)
   Brian Jordan, NL:Atl. Oct. 17, 1999 (15 inn)
   Gerald Williams, NL:Atl. Oct. 17, 1999 (15inn)
   Derek Jeter, AL:NY Oct. 18, 2004 (14 inn)

Most Plate Appearances, Inning
2 By many players

Most At-Bats
168 Derek Jeter, AL:NY
135 Terry Pendleton, NL:StL.-Atl.

Most At-Bats, Game
6 Paul Blair, AL:Balt. Oct. 6, 1969
   Dan Gladden, AL:Minn. Oct. 12 1987
   Kirby Puckett, AL:Minn. Oct. 12, 1987
   Rickey Henderson, AL:Tor. Oct. 5, 1993
   Jose Offerman, AL:Bos. Oct. 16, 1999
   John Valentin, AL:Bos. Oct. 16, 1999
   Todd Walker AL:Bos. Oct. 15, 2003
   Hideki Matsui, AL:NY Oct. 16, 2004
   Bernie Williams, AL:NY Oct. 16, 2004
   Ruben Sierra, AL:NY Oct. 16, 2004
   Johnny Damon, AL:Bos. Oct. 20, 2004
   Marquis Grissom, NL:Atl. Oct. 14, 17 1996
   Fred McGriff, NL:Atl. Oct. 14, 1996
   Jermaine Dye, NL:Atl. Oct. 14, 1996
   Tony Womack, NL:Ari. Oct. 20, 2001
   Craig Counsell, NL:Ari. Oct. 20, 2001
   Paul Lo Duca, NL:NY Oct. 15, 2006
   Jose Reyes, NL:NY Oct. 15, 2006
Extra-Inning Game:
7 Mookie Wilson NL:NY Oct. 15, 1986 (16 inn)
   Keith Hernandez NL:NY Oct. 15, 1986 (16 inn)
   Bill Doran NL:Hou. Oct. 15, 1986 (16 inn)
   Billy Hatcher NL:Hou. Oct. 15, 1986 (16 inn)
   Glenn Davis NL:Hou. Oct. 15, 1986 (16 inn)
   Brian Jordan NL:Atl. Oct. 17, 1999 (15 inn)
   Robin Ventura NL:NY Oct. 17, 1999 (15 inn)
   Gerald Williams NL:Atl. Oct.17, 1999 (15 inn)
   Derek Jeter, NY:AL Oct. 18, 2004 (14 inn)
   Hideki Matsui, NY:AL Oct. 18, 2004 (14 inn)
   Bernie Williams, NY:AL Oct. 18, 2004 (14 inn)
   Tony Clark, NY:AL Oct. 18, 2004 (14 inn)

Most At-Bats, Inning
2 By many players

Most Runs
31 Bernie Williams, AL:NY
20 Chipper Jones, NL:Atl.
   Albert Pujols, NL:StL
   Carlos Beltran, NL:Hou.-NY

Most Runs, Game
5 Alex Rodriguez, AL:NY Oct. 16, 2004
   Hideki Matsui, AL:NY Oct. 16, 2004
4 Bob Robertson, NL:Pitt. Oct. 3, 1971
   Steve Garvey, NL:LA Oct. 9, 1974
   Will Clark, NL:SF Oct. 4, 1989
   Javier Lopez, NL:Atl. Oct. 14, 1996
   Fred McGriff, NL:Atl. Oct. 17, 1996
   Carlos Beltran, NL:NY Oct. 15, 2006

Most Runs, Inning
2 Jack Clark, NL:StL. Oct. 13, 1985 (2nd)
   Cesar Cedeno, NL:StL. Oct. 13, 1985 (2nd)
   Chone Figgins, AL:Ana. Oct. 13, 2002 (7th)
   Scott Spiezio, AL:Ana. Oct. 13, 2002 (7th)

Most Hits
52 Bernie Williams, AL:NY
45 Pete Rose, NL:Cin.-Phil.

Most Hits, Game
5 Paul Blair, AL:Balt. Oct. 6, 1969
   Hideki Matsui, AL:NY Oct. 16, 2004
4 Bob Robertson, NL:Pitt. Oct. 3, 1971
   Ron Cey, NL:LA Oct. 6, 1974
   Steve Garvey, NL:LA Oct. 9, 1974
   Dusty Baker, NL:LA Oct. 7, 1978 (10 inn)
   Terry Puhl, NL:Hou. Oct. 12, 1980 (10 inn)
   Steve Garvey, NL:SD Oct. 6, 1984
   Tito Landrum, NL:StL. Oct. 13, 1985
   Kevin McReynolds, NL:NY Oct. 11, 1988
   Will Clark, NL:SF Oct. 4, 1989
   Otis Nixon, NL:Atl. Oct. 10, 1992
   Chipper Jones, NL:Atl. Oct. 9, 1996
   Mark Lemke, NL:Atl. Oct. 14, 1996
   Javier Lopez, NL:Atl. Oct. 14, 1996
   Keith Lockhart, NL:Atl. Oct. 14, 1997
   Kenny Lofton, NL:Chi. Oct. 8, 2003

Most Hits, Inning
2 Graig Nettles, AL:NY Oct. 14, 1981 (4th)
   Rickey Henderson, AL:Oak. Oct. 6, 1990 (9th)
   Adam Kennedy AL:Ana. Oct. 13, 2002 (7th)
   Scott Spiezio, AL:Ana. Oct. 13, 2002 (7th)
   Jack Clark, NL:StL. Oct. 13, 1985 (2nd)
   Tito Landrum, NL:StL. Oct. 13, 1985 (2nd)
   Jerome Walton, NL:Chi. Oct. 5, 1989 (1st)
   Barry Bonds, NL:Pitt. Oct. 13, 1992 (2nd)
   Lloyd McClendon, NL:Pitt. Oct. 13, 1992 (2nd)
   Juan Pierre, NL:Fla. Oct. 14, 2003 (8th)

Most Extra-Base Hits
19 Bernie Williams, AL:NY
12 Steve Garvey, NL:LA-SD
   Will Clark, NL:SF-StL.
   Javy Lopez, NL:Atl.
   Albert Pujols, NL:StL.
   Jim Edmonds, NL:StL.

Most Extra-Base Hits, Game
4 Bob Robertson, NL:Pitt. Oct. 3, 1971
   Hideki Matsui, AL:NY Oct. 16, 2004

Most Extra-Base Hits, Inning
1 By many players

Most Total Bases
89 Bernie Williams, AL:NY
63 Pete Rose, NL:Cin.-Phil.

Most Total Bases Game
14 Bob Robertson, NL:Pitt. Oct. 3, 1971
13 Adam Kennedy, AL:Ana. Oct. 13, 2002
   Hideki Matsui, AL:NY Oct. 16, 2004

Most Total Bases Inning
5 Barry Bonds, NL:Pitt. Oct. 13, 1992 (2nd)
Adam Kennedy, AL:Ana. Oct. 13, 2002 (7th)

Most Singles
34 Pete Rose, NL:Cin.-Phil.
33 Bernie WIlliams, AL:NY

Most Singles, Game
4 Brooks Robinson, AL:Balt. Oct. 4, 1969 (12 inn)
Chris Chambliss, AL:NY Oct. 4, 1978
Kelly Gruber, AL:Tor. Oct. 7, 1989
Jerry Browne, AL:Oak. Oct. 12, 1992
Terry Puhl, NL:Hou. Oct. 12, 1980 (10 inn)
Tito Landrum, NL:StL. Oct. 13, 1985
Chipper Jones, NL:Atl. Oct. 9, 1996
Keith Lockhart, NL:Atl. Oct. 14, 1997
Kenny Lofton, NL:Chi. Oct. 8, 2003

Most Singles, Inning
2 Graig Nettles, AL:NY Oct. 14, 1981 (4th)
Rickey Henderson, AL:Oak. Oct. 6, 1990 (9th)
Scott Spiezio, AL:Ana. Oct. 13, 2002 (7th)
Jack Clark, NL:StL. Oct. 13, 1985 (2nd)
Tito Landrum, NL:StL. Oct. 13, 1985 (2nd)
Jerome Walton, NL:Chi. Oct. 5, 1989 (1st)
Lloyd McClendon, NL:Pitt. Oct. 13, 1992 (2nd)

Most Doubles
10 Bernie WIlliams, AL:NY
7 Pete Rose, NL:Cin.-Phil.
Richie Hebner, NL:Pitt.-Phil
Mike Schmidt, NL:Phil.
Ron Cey, NL:LA-Chi.
Javier Lopez, NL:Atl.
Fred McGriff, NL:Atl.
Will Clark, NL:SF-StL.
Chipper Jones, NL:Atl.

Most Doubles, Game
2 By many players
Extra-Inning Game:
3 Fred McGriff, NL:Atl. Oct. 11, 1995 (10 inn)

Most Doubles, Inning
1 By many players

Most Triples
4 George Brett, AL:KC
3 Willie McGee, NL:StL.
Mariano Duncan, NL:LA-Phil.
Keith Lockhart, NL:Atl.

Most Triples, Game
2 Mariano Duncan, NL:Phil. Oct. 9, 1993
1 By many AL players

Most Triples, Inning
1 By many players

Most Home Runs
9 George Brett, AL:KC
Bernie Williams, AL:NY
8 Steve Garvey, NL:LA-SD
Albert Pujols, NL:StL.

Most Home Runs, Game
3 Bob Robertson, NL:Pitt. Oct. 3, 1971
George Brett, AL:KC Oct. 6, 1978
Adam Kennedy, AL:Ana. Oct. 13, 2002

Most Games, Consecutive, Home Runs
4 Gary Matthews, NL:Phil.-Chi. Oct. 5, 7-8, 1983-Oct. 2, 1984
Jeffrey Leonard, NL:SF Oct. 6-7, 9-10, 1987
Carlos Beltran, NL:Hou. Oct. 13-14, 16-17, 2004
3 Bernie Williams, AL:NY Oct. 20-22, 2001

Most Grand Slam Home Runs, Game
1 Mike Cuellar, AL:Balt. Oct. 3, 1970
Don Baylor, AL:Cal. Oct. 9, 1982
Jim Thome, AL:Clev. Oct. 13, 1998
Ricky Ledee, AL:NY Oct. 17, 1999
Johnny Damon, AL:Bos. Oct. 20, 2004
Ron Cey, NL:LA Oct. 4, 1977
Dusty Baker, NL:LA Oct. 5, 1977
Will Clark, NL:SF Oct. 4, 1989
Ron Gant, NL:Atl. Oct. 7, 1992
Gary Gaetti, NL:StL. Oct. 10, 1996
Andres Galarraga, NL:Atl. Oct. 11, 1998
Aramis Ramirez, NL:Chi. Oct. 11, 2003

Most Runs Batted In
33 Bernie Williams, AL:NY
21 Steve Garvey, NL:LA-SD

Most Runs Batted In, Game
6 Will Clark, NL:SF Oct. 4, 1989
Aramis Ramirez, NL:Chi. Oct. 11, 2003
Johnny Damon, AL:Bos. Oct. 20, 2004

Most Runs Batted In, Inning
4 Mike Cuellar, AL:Balt. Oct. 3, 1970 (4th)
Don Baylor, AL:Cal. Oct. 9, 1982 (8th)
Jim Thome, AL:Clev. Oct. 13, 1998 (5th)
Ricky Ledee, AL:NY Oct. 17, 1999 (9th)
Johnny Damon, AL:Bos. Oct. 20, 2004 (2nd)
Ron Cey, NL:LA Oct. 4, 1977 (7th)
Dusty Baker, NL:LA Oct. 5, 1977 (4th)
Will Clark, NL:SF Oct. 4, 1989 (4th)
Ron Gant, NL:Atl. Oct. 7, 1992 (5th)
Gary Gaetti, NL:StL. Oct. 10, 1996 (7th)
Andres Galarraga, NL:Atl. Oct. 11, 1998 (7th)
Aramis Ramirez, NL:Chi. Oct. 11, 2003 (1st)

Most Sacrifice Hits
6 Greg Maddux, NL:Chi.-Atl.
5 Derek Jeter, AL:NY

Most Sacrifice Hits, Game
2 Dock Ellis, NL:Pitt. Oct. 3, 1970 (10 inn)
Gaylord Perry, NL:SF Oct. 2, 1971
Jim Bibby, NL:Pitt. Oct. 3, 1979 (10 inn)
Manny Trillo, NL:Phil. Oct. 8, 1980 (10 inn)
Joaquin Andujar, NL:StL. Oct. 10, 1982
Greg Mathews, NL:StL. Oct. 6, 1987
Tim Wakefield, NL:Pitt. Oct. 13, 1992
Otis Nixon, NL:Atl. Oct. 10, 1993
Greg Maddux, NL:Atl. Oct. 13, 1993
Tommy Greene, NL:Phil. Oct. 13, 1993
Mark Prior, NL:Chi. Oct. 8 2003
Edgar Renteria, NL:StL. Oct. 21, 2004
Chris Carpenter, NL:StL. Oct. 12, 2005
Jeff Suppan, StL. Oct. 14, 2006
Freddie Patek, AL:KC Oct. 7, 1977
Mike Gallego, AL:Oak. Oct. 8, 1989
Joey Cora, AL:Chi. Oct. 8, 1993

Most Sacrifice Flies
3 Robin Ventura, AL:Chi.; NL:NY
2 By many AL & NL players

Most Sacrifice Flies, Game
1 By many players

Most Walks
26 Jorge Posada, AL:NY
24 Chipper Jones, NL:Atl.
Barry Bonds, NL:Pitt.-SF

Most Walks, Game
4 Ruppert Jones AL:Cal. Oct. 11, 1986 (11 inn)
Frank Thomas, AL:Chi. Oct. 5, 1993
Darren Daulton, NL:Phil. Oct. 10, 1993
Ken Caminiti, NL:SD Oct. 8, 1998

Most Walks, Inning
1 By many players

Most Intentional Walks
- 6 Keith Hernandez, NL:StL.-NY.
- 4 Eddie Murray, AL:Balt.-Clev.
  Jorge Posada, AL:NY

Most Intentional Walks, Game
- 2 By many players
  Extra-Inning Game:
- 3 Jose Cruz, NL:Hou. Oct. 10, 1980 (11 inn)

Most Intentional Walks, Inning
- 1 By many players

Most Hit By Pitch
- 5 David Eckstein, AL:Ana.-NL:StL.
- 4 Richie Hebner, NL:Pitt.-Phil.-Chi.
  Miguel Cairo, AL:NY

Most Hit By Pitch, Game
- 2 Dan Gladden, AL:Minn. Oct. 11, 1987
  Pat Sheridan, AL:Det. Oct. 12, 1987
- 1 By many NL players

Most Strikeouts
- 41 Reggie Jackson, AL:Oak.-NY-Cal.
- 32 Reggie Sanders, NL:Cin.-Ari.-SF-StL.

Most Strikeouts, Game
- 4 Dave Boswell, AL:Minn. Oct. 5, 1969 (11 inn)
  Marquis Grissom, AL:Clev. Oct. 11, 1997 (12 inn)
  Rafael Palmeiro, AL:Balt. Oct. 11, 1997 (12 inn)
  Marquis Grissom, AL:Clev. Oct. 15, 1997 (11 inn)
  Corey Koskie, AL:Minn. Oct. 11, 2002
  Alfonso Soriano, AL:NY Oct. 16, 2003 (11 inn)
  Johnny Damon, AL:Bos. Oct. 12, 2004
  Mark Bellhorn, AL:Bos. Oct. 16, 2004
  Tony Clark, AL:NY Oct. 18, 2004 (14 inn)
  John Kruk, NL:Phil. Oct. 10, 1993
  Reggie Sanders, NL:Cin. Oct. 11, 1995 (11 inn)
  Bobby Bonilla, AL:Balt. Oct. 10, 1996
  Gerald Williams, NL:Atl. Oct. 10, 1998

Most Strikeouts, Inning
- 2 Ron Karkovice, AL:Chi. Oct. 8, 1993 (3rd)

Most Stolen Bases
- 17 Rickey Henderson, AL:Oak.-Tor.; NL:NY
- 16 Rickey Henderson, AL:Oak.-Tor.
- 9 Davey Lopes, NL:LA-Chi.-Hou.

Most Stolen Bases, Game
- 4 Rickey Henderson, AL:Oak. Oct. 4, 1989
- 3 Joe Morgan, NL:Cin. Oct. 4, 1975
  Ken Griffey, Sr. NL:Cin. Oct. 5, 1975
  Steve Sax, NL:LA Oct. 9, 1988 (12 inn)
  Ron Gant, NL:Atl. Oct. 10, 1991
  Edgar Renteria, NL:StL. Oct. 12, 2000

Most Stolen Bases, Inning
- 2 Bert Campaneris, AL:Oak. Oct. 8, 1972 (1st)
  Reggie Jackson, AL:Oak. Oct. 12, 1972 (2nd)
  Juan Beniquez, AL:Bos. Oct. 4, 1975 (7th)
  Randy Bush, AL:Minn. Oct. 8, 1987 (4th)
  Rickey Henderson, AL:Oak. Oct. 4, 1989 (4th)
  Rickey Henderson, AL:Oak. Oct. 4, 1989 (7th)
  Willie Wilson, AL:Oak. Oct. 8, 1992 (5th)
  Joe Morgan, NL:Cin. Oct. 4, 1975 (3rd)
  Ken Griffey, Sr. NL:Cin. Oct. 5, 1975 (6th)
  Steve Sax, NL:LA Oct. 9, 1988 (3rd)
  Barry Bonds, NL:Pitt. Oct. 10, 1991 (2nd)
  Ron Gant, NL:Atl. Oct. 10, 1991 (3rd)
  Roger Cedeno, NL:NY Oct. 16, 1999 (8th)

Most Times Stealing Home
- 1 Reggie Jackson, AL:Oak. Oct. 12, 1972
  Marquis Grissom, AL:Clev. Oct. 11, 1997
  Scott Spiezio, AL:Ana. Oct. 9, 2002
  Jeff Branson, NL:Cin. Oct. 11, 1995

Most Caught Stealing
- 6 Hal McRae, AL:KC
  Devon White, AL:Cal.-Tor.
- 4 Vince Coleman, NL:StL.
  Willie McGee, NL:StL.

Most Caught Stealing, Game
- 2 Brooks Robinson, AL:Balt. Oct. 4, 1969 (12 inn)
  Trot Nixon, AL:Bos. Oct. 13, 2003
- 1 By many NL players
  NL Extra-Inning Game:
- 2 Kevin Bass NL:Hou. Oct. 15, 1986 (16 inn)

Most Caught Stealing, Inning
- 1 By many players

Most Grounded into Double Plays
- 6 Manny Ramirez, AL:Clev.-Bos.
- 5 Pedro Guerrero, NL:LA

Most Grounded into Double Plays, Game
- 3 Tony Taylor, AL:Det. Oct. 10, 1972
- 2 Cleon Jones, NL:NY Oct. 4, 1969
  Garry Maddox, NL:Phil. Oct. 12, 1980 (10 inn)
  Pedro Guerrero, NL:LA Oct. 16, 1981
  Jerry Royster, NL:Atl. Oct. 10, 1982
  Bret Boone, NL:Cin. Oct. 10, 1995 (11 inn)
  Chris Gomez, NL:SD Oct. 7, 1998 (10 inn)
  Gerald Williams, NL:Atl. Oct. 13, 1999
  Damian Miller, NL:Ari. Oct. 20, 2001

Most Bases on Interference
- 1 Richie Hebner, NL:Pitt. Oct. 8, 1974
  Mike Scioscia, NL:LA Oct. 14, 1985

CHAMPIONSHIP SERIES FIELDING RECORDS
FIRST BASEMEN – FIELDING

	3 Games	4 Games	5 Games	6 Games	7 Games
Highest Percentage 1.000 (Most Chances)					
AL:	34 Powell Balt. 1969	40 McGwire Oak. 1990	58 Konerko Chi. 2005	57 Palmeiro Balt. 1997	64 Johnson NY 2003
NL:	36 Hernandez StL. 1982	49 Garvey LA 1978	60 Rose Phil. 1980	79 Hernandez NY 1986	72 Lee Fla. 2003
Games					
AL:	3 By many players	4 By many players	5 By many players	6 By many players	7 By many players
NL:	3 By many players	4 By many players	5 By many players	6 By many players	7 By many players
Total Chances					
AL:	34 Powell Balt. 1969 Watson NY 1980	49 Murray Balt. 1979	58 Konerko Chi. 2005	58 Olerud Tor. 1993	81 Balboni KC 1985
NL:	36 Hernandez StL. 1982	49 Garvey LA 1978	60 Rose Phil. 1980	79 Hernandez NY 1986	72 Lee Fla. 2003
Chances Accepted					
AL:	34 Powell Balt. 1969	47 Murray Balt. 1979	58 Konerko Chi. 2005	57 Olerud Tor. 1993 Palmeiro Balt. 1997	79 Balboni KC 1985
NL:	36 Hernandez StL. 1982	49 Garvey LA 1978	60 Rose Phil. 1980	79 Hernandez NY 1986	72 Lee Fla. 2003
Putouts					
AL:	34 Powell Balt. 1969	44 Murray Balt. 1979	57 Konerko Chi. 2005	55 Palmeiro Balt. 1997	72 Balboni KC 1985
NL:	35 Hernandez StL. 1982	44 Garvey LA 1978	53 Rose Phil. 1980	67 Hernandez NY 1986	66 Lee Fla. 2003
Assists					
AL:	5 Reese Minn. 1969	3 Murray Balt. 1979, 83 Paciorek Chi. 1983	8 Hrbek Minn. 1991	9 Olerud Tor. 1993	8 Millar Bos. 2003
NL:	5 Perez Cin. 1975 Chambliss Atl. 1982	3 Garvey LA 1978	7 Rose Phil. 1980 Franco Atl. 2001	12 Hernandez NY 1986	8 Pujols StL. 2004
Errors					
AL:	1 By many players	2 Murray Balt. 1979	2 Mayberry KC 1977 Cooper Mil. 1982	2 Sorrento Clev. 1995	2 Balboni KC 1985
NL:	2 Cepeda Atl. 1969	1 By many players	2 Clark StL. 2000	4 Galarraga Atl. 1998	2 Hatcher LA 1988 Redus Pitt. 1991
Double Plays					
AL:	5 Watson NY 1981	6 Carew Cal. 1979	6 Palmeiro Balt. 1996 Martinez NY 1999	8 Thome Clev. 1997	9 Johnson NY 2003
NL:	3 Hernandez StL. 1982	8 McGriff Atl. 1995	6 Cromartie Mtl. 1981 Durham Chi. 1984 Clark SF 1989	6 Galarraga Atl. 1998	10 Clark SF 1987

IRST BASEMEN

Most Series
7 Tino Martinez, AL:Sea. 1995; NY 96, 98-2001;
NL:StL. 02
John Olerud, AL:Tor. 1991-93; Sea. 2000-01;
NY 04; NL:NY 99
6 Tino Martinez, AL:Sea. 1995; NY 96, 98-2001
John Olerud, AL:Tor. 1991-93; Sea. 2000-01; NY 04
5 Bob Robertson, NL:Pitt. 1970-72, 74-75
Tony Perez, NL:Cin. 1970,72-73, 75-76
Steve Garvey, NL:LA 1974, 77-78, 81 SD 84

Most Games
38 John Olerud, AL:Tor.-Sea.-NY; NL:NY
33 Tino Martinez, AL:Sea.-NY
23 Fred McGriff, NL:Atl.

Highest Percentage (Most Chances)
1.000 Albert Pujols, NL:StL. (207 tc)
Boog Powell, AL:Balt. (118 tc)

Most Total Chances
346 John Olerud, AL:Tor.-Sea.-NY; NL:NY
285 Tino Martinez, AL:Sea.-NY
222 Steve Garvey, NL:LA-SD

Most Total Chances, Game
18 Steve Garvey, NL:LA Oct. 6, 1978
16 Steve Balboni, AL:KC Oct. 12, 1985
George Hendrick, AL:Cal. Oct. 11, 1986 (11 inn)
John Olerud, AL:Tor. Oct. 11, 1991 (10 inn)
Herbert Perry, AL:Clev. Oct. 13, 1995 (11 inn)
Kevin Millar, AL:Bos. Oct. 9, 2003
Kevin Millar, AL:Bos. Oct. 14, 2003
Extra-Inning Game:
27 Keith Hernandez, NL:NY Oct. 15, 1986 (16 inn)

Most Total Chances, Inning
4 Dick Allen, NL:Phil. Oct. 10, 1976 (6th)
Enos Cabell, NL:LA Oct. 9, 1985 (4th)
Mark McGwire, AL:Oak. Oct. 4, 1989 (3rd)
Will Clark, NL:StL. Oct. 12, 2000 (9th)
Mike Lamb, NL:Hou. Oct. 17, 2005 (7th)

Most Chances Accepted
343 John Olerud, AL:Tor.-Sea.-NY; NL:NY
283 Tino Martinez, AL:Sea.-NY
221 Steve Garvey, NL:LA-SD

Most Chances Accepted, Game
18 Steve Garvey, NL:LA Oct. 6, 1978
16 Steve Balboni, AL:KC Oct. 12, 1985
George Hendrick, AL:Cal. Oct. 11, 1986 (11 inn)
John Olerud, AL:Tor. Oct. 11, 1991 (10 inn)
Herbert Perry, AL:Clev. Oct. 13, 1995 (11 inn)
Kevin Millar, AL:Bos. Oct. 9, 2003
Extra-Inning Game:
27 Keith Hernandez, NL:NY Oct. 15, 1986 (16 inn)

Most Chances Accepted, Inning
4 Enos Cabell, NL:LA Oct. 9, 1985 (4th)

Most Putouts
313 John Olerud, AL:Tor.-Sea.-NY; NL:NY
256 Tino Martinez, AL:Sea.-NY
208 Steve Garvey, NL:LA-SD

Most Putouts, Game
17 Andres Galarraga, NL:Atl. Oct. 14, 1998
Albert Pujols, NL:StL. Oct. 12, 2005
15 Chris Chambliss, AL:NY Oct. 14, 1976
Mark McGwire, AL:Oak. Oct. 4, 1989
Extra-Inning Game:
21 Glenn Davis, NL:Hou. Oct. 15, 1986 (16 inn)
16 John Olerud, AL:Tor. Oct. 11, 1991 (10 inn)
Herbert Perry, AL:Clev. Oct. 13, 1995 (11 inn)

Most Assists
33 Tino Martinez, AL:Sea.-NY; NL:StL.
27 Tino Martinez, AL:Sea.-NY
17 Keith Hernandez, NL:StL.-NY
Will Clark, NL:SF-StL.

Most Assists, Game
5 Tino Martinez, NL:StL. Oct. 12, 2002
4 Steve Balboni, AL:KC Oct. 12, 1985
Kevin Millar, AL:Bos. Oct. 9, 2003
Extra-Inning Game:
7 Keith Hernandez, NL:NY Oct. 15, 1986 (16 inn)

Most Assists, Inning
2 By many players

Most Errors
4 Andres Galarraga, NL:Atl.
3 Cecil Cooper, AL:Bos.-Mil.
Eddie Murray, AL:Balt.
Steve Balboni, AL:KC

Most Errors, Game
2 Paul Sorrento, AL:Clev. Oct. 15, 1995
Andres Galarraga, NL:Atl. Oct. 7, 1998 (10 inn)
Ryan Klesko, NL:Atl. Oct. 17, 1999 (15 inn)

Most Errors, Inning
2 Paul Sorrento, AL:Clev. Oct. 15, 1995 (7th)
Andres Galarraga, NL:Atl. Oct. 7, 1998 (10th)
Ryan Klesko, NL:Atl. Oct. 17, 1999 (6th)

Most Double Plays
31 John Olerud, AL:Tor.-Sea.-NY; NL:NY
27 Tino Martinez, AL:Sea.-NY
21 Steve Garvey, NL:LA-SD

Most Double Plays, Game
4 Will Clark, NL:SF Oct. 10, 1987
3 Rich Reese, AL:Minn. Oct. 3, 1970
Mike Epstein, AL:Oak. Oct. 10, 1972
Gene Tenace, AL:Oak. Oct. 5, 1975
Eddie Murray, AL:Balt. Oct. 6, 1979
Bobby Grich, AL:Cal. Oct. 14, 1986
Jim Thome, AL:Clev. Oct. 9, 1998
Tino Martinez, AL:NY Oct. 17, 1999
Sean Casey, AL:Det. Oct. 10, 2006
Extra-Inning Game:
5 Fred McGriff, NL:Atl. Oct. 10, 1995 (11 inn)

Double Plays, Unassisted
1 Tino Martinez, AL:NY Oct. 11 1996 (5th)
Tino Martinez, AL:NY Oct. 22, 2001 (4th)
Kevin Millar, AL:Bos. Oct. 13, 2003 (1st)
John Olerud, AL:NY Oct. 16, 2004 (4th)
John Mabry, NL:StL. Oct. 14, 1996 (2nd)
Will Clark, NL:StL. Oct. Oct. 14, 2000 (4th)

SECOND BASEMEN – FIELDING

		3 Games	4 Games	5 Games	6 Games	7 Games
Highest Percentage 1.000 (Most Chances)						
	AL:	25 Randolph NY 1981	23 Cruz Chi. 1983	30 Iguchi Chi. 2005	34 Baerga Clev. 1995	40 Barrett Bos. 1986
	NL:	23 Helms Cin. 1970 / Morgan Cin. 1979	29 Lemke Atl. 1995	40 Morgan Cin. 1973	38 Lind Pitt. 1990	46 Valentin NY 2006
Games						
	AL:	3 By many players	4 By many players	5 By many players	6 By many players	7 By many players
	NL:	3 By many players	4 By many players	5 By many players		7 By many players
Total Chances						
	AL:	25 Randolph NY 1981	26 Grich Balt. 1974	42 Alomar Balt. 1996	41 Cora Chi. 1993	40 Barrett Bos. 1986
	NL:	23 Helms Cin. 1970	29 Lemke Atl. 1995	44 Trillo Phil. 1980	38 Lind Pitt. 1990	46 Valentin NY 2006
Chances Accepted						
	AL:	25 Randolph NY 1981	25 Grich Balt. 1974	40 Alomar Balt. 1996	38 Cora Chi. 1993	40 Barrett Bos. 1986
	NL:	23 Helms Cin. 1970	29 Lemke Atl. 1995	43 Trillo Phil. 1980	38 Lind Pitt. 1990	46 Valentin NY 2006
Putouts						
	AL:	12 Randolph NY 1981	13 Grich Balt. 1974 / Jimenez Oak. 2006	16 Grich Balt. 1973 / Alomar Balt. 1996 / Offerman Bos. 1999	18 Cora Chi. 1993	19 Barrett Bos. 1986
	NL:	12 Morgan Cin. 1979	13 Lemke Atl. 1995	18 Trillo Phil. 1980	19 Lind Pitt. 1990	20 Grudzielanek Chi. 2003
Assists						
	AL:	13 Randolph NY 1981	14 Cruz Chi. 1983	25 Alomar Balt. 1996	22 Baerga Clev. 1995	28 White KC 1985
	NL:	12 Helms Cin. 1970	18 Lopes LA 1974	28 Morgan Cin. 1973	21 Sax LA 1985	31 Valentin NY 2006
Errors						
	AL:	1 By many players	2 Green Oak. 1974 / Jimenez Oak. 2006	2 Green Oak. 1973 / Alomar Balt. 1996 / Offerman Bos. 1999	3 Cora Chi. 1993	2 Grich Cal. 1986
	NL:	1 By many players	2 Sizemore Phil. 1977 / Lopes LA 1978	2 Giles Atl. 2001	1 Duncan Cin. 1990 & Phil. 1993 / Counsell Fla. 1997 / Alfonzo NY 1999	2 Backman NY 1988 / Lind Pitt. 1992 / Grudzielanek Chi. 2003 / Belliard StL. 2006
Double Plays						
	AL:	4 Randolph NY 1981	6 Polanco Det. 2006	7 Alomar Balt. 1996	5 Alomar Tor. 1993 / Roberts Clev. 1997 / Knoblauch NY 1998	9 Soriano NY 2003
	NL:	3 Cash Pitt. 1970	5 Lemke Atl. 1995 / Herr StL. 1982	7 Scott Mtl. 1981	6 Alfonzo NY 1999	9 Valentin NY 2006

ECOND BASEMEN

Most Series
7 Joe Morgan, NL:Cin. 1972-73, 75-76, 79; Hou. 80; Phil. 83
6 Frank White, AL:KC 1976-78, 80, 84-85

Most Games
31 Mark Lemke, NL:Atl.
28 Roberto Alomar, AL:Tor.-Balt.

Highest Percentage (Most Chances)
1.000 Joe Morgan, NL:Cin.-Hou.-Phil. (148 tc)
       Willie Randolph, AL:NY-Oak. (93 tc)

Most Total Chances
158 Roberto Alomar, AL:Tor.-Balt.
148 Joe Morgan, NL:Cin.-Hou.-Phil.

Most Total Chances, Game
13 Bobby Grich, AL:Balt. Oct. 6, 1974
    Manny Trillo, NL:Phil. Oct. 7, 1980
    Roberto Alomar, AL:Tor. Oct. 11, 1992 (11 inn)

Most Total Chances, Inning
4 Dick Green, AL:Oak. Oct. 9, 1973 (7th)
   Rodney Scott, NL:Mtl. Oct. 16, 1981 (2nd)

Most Chances Accepted
154 Roberto Alomar, AL:Tor.-Balt.
148 Joe Morgan, NL:Cin.-Hou.-Phil.

Most Chances Accepted, Game
13 Manny Trillo, NL:Phil. Oct. 7, 1980
12 Bobby Grich, AL:Balt. Oct. 6, 1974
    Willie Randolph, AL:NY Oct. 13, 1981
    Extra-Inning Game:
13 Roberto Alomar, AL:Tor. Oct. 11, 1992 (11 inn)

Most Chances Accepted, Inning
3 By many players

Most Putouts
69 Roberto Alomar, AL:Tor.-Balt.
62 Joe Morgan, NL:Cin.-Hou.-Phil.

Most Putouts, Game
7 Bobby Grich, AL:Balt. Oct. 6 1974
6 Dave Cash, NL:Phil. Oct. 12, 1976
   Davey Lopes, NL:LA Oct. 13, 1981
   Jose Lind, NL:Pitt. Oct. 12, 1990
   Extra-Inning Game:
8 Roberto Alomar, AL:Tor. Oct. 11, 1992
7 Steve Sax, NL:LA Oct. 9, 1988 (12 inn)

Most Putouts, Inning
3 Dick Green, AL:Oak. Oct. 8, 1974 (7th)
   Joe Morgan, NL:Cin. Oct. 10, 1976 (8th)
   Ryne Sandberg, NL:Chi. Oct. 4, 1984 (5th)

Most Assists
86 Joe Morgan, NL:Cin.-Hou.-Phil.
85 Roberto Alomar, AL:Tor.-Balt.

Most Assists, Game
9 Joey Cora, AL:Chi. Oct. 6, 1993
   Jose Valentin, NL:NY Oct. 13, 2006
   Extra-Inning Game:
9 Wally Backman, NL:NY Oct. 14, 1986 (12 inn)

Most Assists, Inning
3 Tony Phillips, AL:Oak. Oct. 4, 1989 (5th)
   Joey Cora, AL:Chi. Oct. 6, 1993 (6th)
   Mark Lemke, NL:Atl. Oct. 13, 1993 (1st)
   Edgardo Alfonzo, NL:NY Oct. 11, 2000 (1st)
   Jose Valentin, NL:NY Oct. 13, 2006 (9th)

Most Errors
4 Dick Green, AL:Oak.
   Bobby Grich, AL:Balt.-Cal.
   Joey Cora, AL:Chi.-Sea.
   Roberto Alomar, AL:Tor.-Balt.
   Davey Lopes, NL:LA

Most Errors, Game
2 Dick Green, AL:Oak. Oct. 9, 1973 (11 inn)
   Dick Green, AL:Oak. Oct. 8, 1974
   Lance Blankenship, AL:Oak. Oct. 10, 1992
1 By many NL players

Most Errors, Inning
1 By many players

Most Double Plays
20 Roberto Alomar, AL:Tor.-Balt.
14 Joe Morgan, NL:Cin.-Hou.-Phil.
    Mark Lemke, NL:Atl.

Most Double Plays, Game
4 Davey Lopes, NL:LA Oct. 13, 1981
3 Rob Wilfong, AL:Cal. Oct. 14, 1986
   Bip Roberts, AL:Clev. Oct. 11, 1997 (12 inn)
   Alfonso Soriano, AL:NY Oct. 13, 2003
   Placido Polanco, AL:Det. Oct. 10, 2006

Double Plays, Unassisted
1 Joe Morgan, NL:Cin. Oct. 10, 1976 (8th)

THIRD BASEMEN – FIELDING

	3 Games	4 Games	5 Games	6 Games	7 Games
Highest Percentage 1.000 (Most Chances)					
AL:	16 B. Robinson Balt. 1969	19 Cruz Balt. 1983	22 Bando Oak. 1972	15 Ripken Balt. 1997	17 Mueller Bos. 2004
NL:	8 Madlock Pitt. 1979	19 Schmidt Phil. 1977	17 Williams SF 1989	21 Ventura NY 1999	23 Rolen StL 2004
Games					
AL:	3 By many players	4 By many players	5 By many players	6 By many players	7 By many players
NL:	3 By many players	4 By many players	5 By many players	6 By many players	7 By many players
Total Chances					
AL:	16 B. Robinson Balt. 1969	19 Cruz Balt. 1983	24 DeCinces Cal. 1982	26 Williams Clev. 1997	26 DeCinces Cal. 1986
NL:	14 Schmidt Phil. 1976	23 Schmidt Phil. 1978	22 Cey LA 1981	25 Pendleton StL. 1985 / Knight NY 1986	31 King Pitt. 1992
Chances Accepted					
AL:	16 B. Robinson Balt. 1969	19 Cruz Balt. 1983	22 Bando Oak. 1972	24 Williams Clev. 1997	24 DeCinces Cal. 1986
NL:	13 Schmidt Phil. 1976	21 Cey LA 1977 / Schmidt Phil. 1978	21 Cey LA 1981	24 Pendleton StL. 1985 / Knight NY 1986	30 King Pitt. 1992
Putouts					
AL:	6 By many players	7 Lansford Oak. 1988	9 Decinces Cal. 1982	6 Ventura Chi. 1993 / Williams Clev. 1997	7 Brett KC 1985 / Boggs Bos. 1986 / Mueller Bos. 2004
NL:	5 Perez Cin. 1970	7 Cey LA 1977	5 By many players	7 Sabo Cin. 1990 / Pendleton Atl. 1993	11 King Pitt. 1992
Assists					
AL:	10 B. Robinson Balt. 1969 / Bando Oak. 1975	13 Robinson Balt. 1974 / Cruz Balt. 1983	16 Bando Oak. 1972	18 Williams Clev. 1997	18 DeCinces Cal. 1986
NL:	9 Schmidt Phil. 1976	18 Schmidt Phil. 1978	17 Schmidt Phil. 1980	19 Knight NY 1986	19 King Pitt. 1992
Errors					
AL:	1 By many players	1 By many players	3 Brett KC 1976 / DeCinces Cal. 1982 / Gruber Tor. 1991	2 Williams Clev. 1997	2 By many players
NL:	1 By many players	2 Cey LA 1974 / Schmidt Phil. 1978	3 Williams Ari. 2001	2 C. Jones Atl. 1999 / Luna StL. 2005	2 Hamilton LA 1988 / Rolen StL. 2006
Double Plays					
AL:	2 Bando Oak. 1971 / Nettles NY 1981	3 Lansford Cal. 1979	3 DeCinces Cal. 1982	3 Ripken Balt. 1997 / Williams Clev. 1997	3 DeCinces Cal. 1986
NL:	2 Schmidt Phil. 1976	2 Jones Atl. 1995	3 Parrish Mtl. 1981	4 Ventura NY 1999	5 King Pitt. 1992

HIRD BASEMEN

Most Series
6 Graig Nettles, AL:NY 1976-78, 80-81; NL:SD 84
George Brett, AL:KC 1976-78, 80, 84-85
Terry Pendleton, NL:StL. 1985, 87; Atl. 91-93, 96
Chipper Jones, NL:Atl. 1995-99, 2001

Most Games
34 Terry Pendleton, NL:StL.-Atl.
Chipper Jones, NL:Atl.
27 George Brett, AL:KC

Highest Percentage (Minimum: 40 chances)
.989 Terry Pendleton, NL:StL.-Atl. (90 tc)
.986 Sal Bando, AL:Oak. (73 tc)

Most Total Chances
91 Mike Schmidt, NL:Phil.
79 George Brett, AL:KC

Most Total Chances, Game
10 Ron Cey, NL:LA Oct. 16, 1981
9 Todd Cruz, AL:Balt. Oct. 5, 1983
Wade Boggs, AL:Bos. Oct. 10, 1990

Most Total Chances, Inning
3 By many players

Most Chances Accepted
89 Terry Pendleton, NL:StL.-Atl.
72 Sal Bando, AL:Oak.

Most Chances Accepted, Game
10 Ron Cey, NL:LA Oct. 16, 1981
9 Todd Cruz, AL:Balt. Oct. 5, 1983
Wade Boggs, AL:Bos. Oct. 10, 1990

Most Chances Accepted, Inning
3 Denis Menke, NL:Cin. Oct. 11, 1972 (9th)
Ron Cey, NL:LA Oct. 4, 1977 (4th)
Ron Cey, NL:LA Oct. 16, 1981 (8th)
Jeff King, NL:Pitt. Oct. 6, 1992 (1st)
Gary Gaetti, NL:StL. Oct. 17, 1996 (1st)
Miguel Cairo, NL:StL. Oct. 14, 2002 (6th)
Todd Cruz, AL:Balt. Oct. 5, 1983 (5th)
David Wright, NL:NY Oct. 12, 2006 (3rd)

Most Putouts
25 Sal Bando, AL:Oak.
Terry Pendleton, NL:StL.-Atl.

Most Putouts, Game
4 Carney Lansford, AL:Cal. Oct. 6, 1979
Wade Boggs, AL:Bos. Oct. 10, 1990
3 By many NL players

Most Putouts, Inning
2 By many players

Most Assists
66 Mike Schmidt, NL:Phil.
49 Brooks Robinson, AL:Balt.
George Brett, AL:KC

Most Assists, Game
8 Ron Cey, NL:LA Oct. 16, 1981
6 Sal Bando, AL:Oak. Oct. 8, 1972
Todd Cruz, AL:Balt. Oct. 5, 1983
Tom Brookens, AL:Det. Oct. 11, 1987
Wade Boggs, AL:NY Oct. 13, 1996
Cal Ripken, AL:Balt. Oct. 8, 1997
Eric Chavez, AL:Oak. Oct. 10, 2006
Extra-Inning Game:
7 Aurelio Rodriguez, AL:Det. Oct. 11, 1972 (11 inn)

Most Assists, Inning
3 Ron Cey, NL:LA Oct. 4, 1977 (4th)
Ron Cey, NL:LA Oct. 16, 1981 (8th)
Todd Cruz, AL:Balt. Oct. 5, 1983 (5th)

Most Errors
8 George Brett, AL:KC
5 Mike Schmidt, NL:Phil.

Most Errors, Game
2 Ron Cey, NL:LA Oct. 5, 1974
Fernando Tatis, NL:StL. Oct. 15, 2000
George Brett, AL:KC Oct. 9, 1976
Doug DeCinces, AL:Cal. Oct. 9, 1982
Darrell Evans, AL:Det. Oct. 11, 1987
Kelly Gruber, AL:Tor. Oct. 8, 1991

Most Errors, Inning
2 George Brett, AL:KC Oct. 9, 1976 (1st)
Fernando Tatis, NL:StL. Oct. 15, 2000 (6th)

Most Double Plays
8 Terry Pendleton, NL:StL.-Atl.
7 Doug DeCinces, AL:Balt.-Cal.
Carney Lansford, AL:Cal.-Oak.

Most Double Plays, Game
2 Mike Schmidt, NL:Phil. Oct. 9, 1976
Mike Schmidt, NL:Phil. Oct. 11, 1980 (10 inn)
Larry Parrish, NL:Mtl. Oct. 16, 1981
Jeff King, NL:Pitt. Oct. 9-10, 1992
Robin Ventura, NL:NY Oct. 17, 1999 (15 inn)
Doug DeCinces, AL:Cal. Oct. 14, 1986

Double Plays, Unassisted
1 Mike Schmidt, NL:Phil. Oct. 9, 1976 (5th)
Jeff King, NL:Pitt. Oct. 14, 1992 (6th)

SHORTSTOP – FIELDING

	3 Games	4 Games	5 Games	6 Games	7 Games
Highest Percentage 1.000 (Most Chances)					
AL:	21 Dent NY 1980	20 Campaneris Oak. 1974	31 Patek KC 1976	31 Vizquel Clev. 1997	44 Jeter NY 2003
NL:	17 Concepcion Cin. 1979	29 Russell LA 1974	26 Harrelson NY 1973	31 Santana NY 1986 / Ordonez NY 1999	40 Eckstein StL 2006
Games					
AL:	3 By many players	4 By many players	5 By many players	6 By many players	7 By many players
NL:	3 By many players	4 By many players	5 By many players	6 By many players	7 By many players
Total Chances					
AL:	26 Cardenas Minn. 1969	24 Garcia Balt. 1979	34 Uribe Chi. 2005	38 Vizquel Clev. 1998	45 Jeter NY 2004
NL:	18 Ramirez, Atl. 1982	29 Russell LA 1974	33 Speier Mtl. 1981	37 Larkin Cin. 1990	40 Eckstein StL 2006
Chances Accepted					
AL:	25 Cardenas Minn. 1969	22 Garcia Balt. 1979	33 Uribe Chi. 2005	37 Vizquel Clev. 1998	44 Jeter NY 2003
NL:	17 Concepcion Cin. 1979	29 Russell LA 1974	31 Speier Mtl. 1981	36 Larkin Cin. 1990	40 Eckstein StL 2006
Putouts					
AL:	13 Cardenas Minn. 1969	9 Patek KC 1978	13 Patek KC 1976	16 Vizquel Clev. 1997	23 Jeter NY 2004
NL:	16 By many players	13 Russell LA 1974	19 Templeton SD 1984	21 Larkin Cin. 1990	19 Renteria StL 2004 / Eckstein StL 2006
Assists					
AL:	14 Belanger Balt. 1970	17 Campaneris Oak. 1974	26 Uribe Chi. 2005	26 Vizquel Clev. 1998	25 Jeter NY 2003
NL:	14 Concepcion Cin. 1979	17 Bowa Phil. 1977	16 Chaney Cin. 1972 / Speier Mtl. 1981	24 Ordonez NY 1999	26 Gonzalez Fla. 2003
Errors					
AL:	2 Cardenas Minn. 1970	2 Patek KC 1978 / Garcia Balt. 1979	4 Garciaparra Bos. 1999	3 Lee Tor. 1992	5 Owen Bos. 1986
NL:	1 By many players	2 Russell LA 1977 / Delesus Phil. 1983	3 Chaney Cin. 1972	2 Reynolds Hou. 1986	2 Elster NY 1988 / Blauser Atl. 1992
Double Plays					
AL:	3 By many players	3 Ripken Balt. 1983 / Weiss Oak. 1988 / Rivera Bos. 1990 / Santiago Det. 2006 / Guillen Det. 2006	5 Ripken Balt. 1996 / Jeter NY 1999	8 Vizquel Clev. 1997	9 Jeter NY 2003
NL:	3 Garrido Atl. 1969 / Alley Pitt. 1970	6 Russell LA 1974	6 Bowa Chi. 1984 / Speier Mtl. 1981	4 By many players	7 Uribe SF 1987 / Griffin LA 1988

HORTSTOPS

Most Series
7 Derek Jeter, AL:NY 1996, 98-2001, 03-04
6 Jeff Blauser, NL:Atl. 1991-93, 95-97

Most Games
41 Derek Jeter, AL:NY
29 Jeff Blauser, NL:Atl.

Highest Percentage (Minimum: 40 chances)
1.000 Mike Bordick, AL:Balt.; NL:NY (60 tc)
.990 Mark Belanger, AL:Balt.
.989 Larry Bowa, NL:Phil.-Chi.

Most Total Chances
192 Derek Jeter, AL:NY
109 Bill Russell, NL:LA

Most Total Chances, Game
13 Bill Russell, NL:LA Oct. 8, 1974
11 Kiko Garcia, AL:Balt. Oct. 4, 1979
   Omar Vizquel, AL:Clev. Oct. 9, 1998
   Extra-Inning Game:
12 Leo Cardenas, AL:Minn. Oct. 5, 1969 (11 inn)

Most Total Chances, Inning
3 By many players

Most Chances Accepted
188 Derek Jeter, AL:NY
106 Bill Russell, NL:LA

Most Chances Accepted, Game
13 Bill Russell, NL:LA Oct. 8, 1974
11 Leo Cardenas, AL:Minn. Oct. 5, 1969 (11 inn)
   Kiko Garcia, AL:Balt. Oct. 4, 1979
   Omar Vizquel, AL:Clev. Oct. 9, 1998

Most Chances Accepted, Inning
3 By many players

Most Putouts
82 Derek Jeter, AL:NY
41 Bill Russell, NL:LA
   Edgar Renteria, NL:Fla.-StL.

Most Putouts, Game
7 Garry Templeton, NL:SD Oct. 4, 1984
6 By many AL players

Most Putouts, Inning
3 Mark Belanger, AL:Balt. Oct. 5, 1974 (3rd)
   Freddie Patek, AL:KC Oct. 5, 1977 (2nd)
   Omar Vizquel, AL:Clev. Oct. 15, 1995 (8th)
   Derek Jeter, AL:NY Oct. 19, 2004 (9th)
   Chris Speier, NL:Mtl. Oct. 14, 1981 (5th)

Most Assists
106 Derek Jeter, AL:NY
70 Larry Bowa, NL:Phil.-Chi.

Most Assists, Game
9 Bill Russell, NL:LA Oct. 5, 1978
   Kiko Garcia, AL:Balt. Oct. 4, 1979

Most Assists, Inning
3 Mark Belanger, AL:Balt. Oct. 7, 1973 (7th)
   Walt Weiss, AL:Oak. Oct. 8, 1989 (1st)
   Manuel Lee, AL:Tor. Oct. 13, 1991 (5th)
   Omar Vizquel, AL:Clev. Oct. 10, 1995 (2nd)
   Dave Concepcion, NL:Cin. Oct. 3, 1979 (4th)
   Barry Larkin, NL:Cin. Oct. 10, 1990 (6th)
   Jeff Blauser, NL:Atl. Oct. 13, 1993 (7th)
   Alex Gonzalez, NL:Chi. Oct. 12, 2003 (3rd)

Most Errors
5 Spike Owen, AL:Bos.
   Nomar Garciaparra, AL:Bos.
   Jeff Blauser, NL:Atl.

Most Errors, Game
2 Leo Cardenas, AL:Minn. Oct. 4, 1970
   Manuel Lee, AL:Tor. Oct. 11, 1992 (11 inn)
   Nomar Garciaparra, AL:Bos. Oct. 13, 1999 (10 inn)
   Gene Alley, NL:Pitt. Oct. 10, 1972
   Bill Russell, NL:LA Oct. 4, 1977
   Kevin Elster, NL:NY Oct. 9, 1988 (12 inn)
   Rey Sanchez, NL:Atl. Oct. 20, 2001

Most Errors, Inning
2 Gene Alley, NL:Pitt. Oct. 10, 1972 (4th)
   Kevin Elster, NL:NY Oct. 9, 1988 (5th)
1 By many AL players

Most Double Plays
30 Derek Jeter, AL:NY
18 Bill Russell, NL:LA

Most Double Plays, Game
3 Bill Rssell, NL:LA Oct. 8, 1974
   Bill Russell, NL:LA Oct. 5, 1983
   Jose Uribe, NL:SF Oct. 10, 1987
   Ozzie Smith, NL:StL. Oct. 14, 1987
   Jeff Blauser, NL:Atl. Oct. 10, 1995 (11 inn)
   Jose Reyes, NL:NY Oct. 15, 2006
   Bert Campaneris, AL:Oak. Oct. 5, 1975
   Omar Vizquel, AL:Clev. Oct. 11, 1997 (12 inn)
   Omar Vizquel, AL:Clev. Oct. 13, 1997
   Omar Vizquel, AL:Clev. Oct. 9, 1998
   Derek Jeter, AL:NY Oct. 11, 2003
   Carlos Guillen, AL:Det. Oct. 10, 2006

Double Plays, Unassisted
1 Bill Russell, NL:LA Oct. 8, 1974 (6th)
   Alfredo Griffin, NL:LA Oct. 5, 1988 (1st)
   Walt Weiss, NL:Atl. Oct. 19, 1999 (6th)
   Robin Yount, AL:Mil. Oct. 5, 1982 (4th)
   Buddy Biancalana, AL:KC Oct. 12, 1985 (6th)
   Tony Fernandez, AL:Tor. Oct. 4, 1989 (1st)
   Omar Vizquel, AL:Clev. Oct. 15, 1995 (8th)

OUTFIELDERS – FIELDING

	3 Games	4 Games	5 Games	6 Games	7 Games
Highest Percentage 1.000 (Most Chances)					
AL:	12 Oliva Minn. 1970	16 Miller Cal. 1979	22 D. Henderson Oak. 1989	16 Wilson Oak. 1992 Cameron Sea. 2000	22 Williams NY 2004
NL:	14 Parker Pitt. 1975	13 Stargell Pitt. 1974	23 Maddox Phil. 1980	17 McGee StL. 1985 Wilson NY 1986 A. Jones & Jordan Atl. 1999	27 Lofton Chi. 2003
Games					
AL:	3 By many players	4 By many players	5 By many players	6 By many players	7 By many players
NL:	3 By many players	4 By many players	5 By many players	6 By many players	7 By many players
Total Chances					
AL:	14 Lynn Bos. 1975	16 Miller Cal. 1979	22 D. Henderson Oak. 1989	18 R. Henderson Oak. 1992	29 Pettis Cal. 1986
NL:	14 Parker Pitt. 1975	17 Maddox Phil. 1978	23 Maddox Phil. 1980	17 By many players	27 Lofton Chi. 2003
Chances Accepted					
AL:	13 Lynn Bos. 1975	16 Miller Cal. 1979	22 D. Henderson Oak. 1989	16 Wilson Tor. & White Tor. 1992 Cameron Sea. 2000	28 Pettis Cal. 1986
NL:	14 Parker Pitt. 1975	16 Maddox Phil. 1978	23 Maddox Phil. 1980	18 McGee StL. 1985	27 Lofton Chi. 2003
Putouts					
AL:	12 Lynn Bos. 1975	14 North Oak. 1974 Miller Cal. 1979 Canseco Oak. 1990	22 D. Henderson Oak. 1989	16 Wilson Oak. & White Tor. 1992 Cameron Sea. 2000	28 Pettis Cal. 1986
NL:	13 Parker Pitt. 1975 Geronimo Cin. 1975	16 Maddox Phil. 1978	23 Maddox Phil. 1980	18 McGee StL. 1985	26 Lofton Chi. 2003
Assists					
AL:	2 By many players	2 Miller Cal. 1979	1 By many players	2 Raines Chi. 1993	3 Smith KC 1985
NL:	2 Foster Cin. 1979	2 McBride Phil. 1977	3 McBride Phil. 1980	3 Mora NY 1999	3 Justice Atl. 1992
Errors					
AL:	2 Oliva Minn. 1969 Washington Oak. 1975	2 D. Henderson Oak. 1988	2 Gamble NY 1976 Oglivie Mil. 1982	3 R. Henderson Oak. 1992	2 Barfield Tor. 1985 Smith KC 1985
NL:	1 By many players	1 By many players	1 By many players	2 Lofton Atl. 1997	1 By many players
Double Plays					
AL:	1 By many players	2 Miller Cal. 1979	1 O'Neill NY 1996 Guerrero LA 2005 Anderson LA 2005	1 Carter & Maldonado Tor. 1992	0
NL:	1 Parker Pitt. 1975	1 McBride Phil. 1977	2 McBride Phil. 1980	1 By many players	1 By many players

UTFIELDERS

Most Series
- 10 Reggie Jackson, AL:Oak. 1971-75; NY 77-78, 80-81; Cal. 82
- 5 Cesar Geronimo, NL:Cin. 1972-73, 75-76, 79
  Garry Maddox, NL:Phil. 1976-78, 80, 83
  Ron Gant, NL:Atl. 1991-93; Cin. 95; StL. 96
  Andruw Jones, NL:Atl. 1996-99, 2001
  Reggie Sanders, NL:Cin. 1995; Ari. 2001; SF 02; StL. 04-05
  Jim Edmonds, NL:StL. 2000, 02, 04-06

Most Games
- 41 Bernie Williams, AL:NY
- 31 Ron Gant, NL:Atl.-Cin.-StL.

Highest Percentage (Minimum: 30 chances)
- 1.000 Paul O'Neill, NL:Cin. (64 tc)
  Andruw Jones, NL:Atl. (63 tc)
  Paul O'Neill, AL:NY (53 tc)

Most Total Chances
- 106 Bernie Williams, AL:NY
- 83 Jim Edmonds, NL:StL.

Most Total Chances, Game
- 9 Jesse Barfield, AL:Tor. Oct. 11, 1985
  Gary Pettis, AL:Cal. Oct. 10, 1986
  Darin Erstad, AL:Ana. Oct. 13, 2002
- 8 Al Oliver, NL:Pitt. Oct. 7, 1972
  Don Hahn, NL:NY Oct. 8, 1973
  Brian Jordan, NL:Atl. Oct. 21, 2001

Most Total Chances, Inning
- 3 By many players

Most Chances Accepted
- 105 Bernie Williams, AL:NY
- 80 Jim Edmonds, NL:StL.

Most Chances Accepted, Game
- 9 Jesse Barfield, AL:Tor. Oct. 11, 1985
  Gary Pettis, AL:Cal. Oct. 10, 1986
  Darin Erstad, AL:Ana. Oct. 13, 2002
- 8 Al Oliver, NL:Pitt. Oct. 7, 1972
  Don Hahn, NL:NY Oct. 8, 1973
  Brian Jordan, NL:Atl. Oct. 21, 2001

Most Chances Accepted, Inning
- 3 By many players

Most Putouts
- 103 Bernie Williams, AL:NY
- 79 Jim Edmonds, NL:StL.

Most Putouts, Game
- 9 Jesse Barfield, AL:Tor. Oct. 11, 1985
  Gary Pettis, AL:Cal. Oct. 10, 1986
  Darin Erstad, AL:Ana. Oct. 13, 2002
- 8 Al Oliver, NL:Pitt. Oct. 7, 1972
  Don Hahn, NL:NY Oct. 8, 1973
  Brian Jordan, NL:Atl. Oct. 21, 2001

Most Putouts, Inning
- 3 By many players

Most Assists
- 6 Lonnie Smith, NL:Phil.-StL.-Atl.; AL:KC
- 5 Bake McBride, NL:Phil.
- 4 Reggie Jackson, AL:Oak.-NY-Cal.

Most Assists, Game
- 2 Tony Oliva, AL:Minn. Oct. 4, 1970
  Rickey Henderson, NL:NY Oct. 15, 1999
  George Foster, NL:Cin. Oct. 3, 1979 (10 inn)
  Bake McBride, NL:Phil. Oct. 11, 1980 (10 inn)
  Wes Chamberlain, NL:Phil. Oct. 11, 1993 (10 inn)

Most Assists, Inning
- 1 By many players

Most Errors
- 7 Rickey Henderson, AL:Oak.-Tor.; NL:NY
- 6 Rickey Henderson, AL:Oak.-Tor.
- 3 Jim Edmonds, NL:StL.

Most Errors, Game
- 2 Tony Oliva, AL:Minn. Oct. 6, 1969
  Ben Oglivie, AL:Mil. Oct. 10, 1982
  Albert Belle, AL:Chi. Oct. 15, 1995
- 1 By many NL players

Most Errors, Inning
- 2 Albert Belle, AL:Clev. Oct. 15, 1995 (5th)
- 1 By many NL players

Most Double Plays
- 3 Bake McBride, NL:Phil.
- 2 Rick Miller, AL:Cal.

Most Double Plays, Game
- 1 By many players
  Extra-Inning Game:
- 2 Bake McBride, NL:Phil. Oct. 11, 1980 (10 inn)

Double Plays, Unassisted
- 0 Not Accomplished

CATCHERS – FIELDING

	3 Games	4 Games	5 Games	6 Games	7 Games
Highest Percentage 1.000 (Most Chances)					
AL:	25 Cerone NY 1981	39 Gedman Bos. 1988	39 Simmons Mil. 1982	54 Posada NY 2000	66 Posada NY 2003
NL:	28 Ott Pitt. 1979	36 Dietz SF 1971	42 Matheny StL. 2002	60 Ashby Hou. 1986	63 Olson Atl. 1991
Games					
AL:	3 By many players	4 By many players	5 By many players	6 By many players	7 By many players
NL:	3 By many players	4 By many players	5 By many players	6 By many players	7 By many players
Total Chances					
AL:	25 Cerone NY 1981	39 Gedman Bos. 1988	46 Varitek Bos. 1999	54 Posada NY 2000	66 Posada NY 2003
NL:	31 Sanguillen Pitt. 1975	36 Dietz SF 1971	44 Grote NY 1973	60 Ashby Hou. 1986	63 Olson Atl. 1991
Chances Accepted					
AL:	25 Cerone NY 1981	39 Gedman Bos. 1988	45 Varitek Bos. 1999	54 Posada NY 2000	66 Posada NY 2003
NL:	30 Sanguillen Pitt. 1975	36 Dietz SF 1971	43 Grote NY 1973	60 Ashby Hou. 1986	63 Olson Atl. 1991
Putouts					
AL:	23 Cerone NY 1981	34 Gedman Bos. 1988	44 Varitek Bos. 1999	51 Posada NY 2000	60 Posada NY 2003
NL:	29 Sanguillen Pitt. 1975	34 Dietz SF 1971	42 Grote NY 1973	59 Ashby Hou. 1986	62 Olson Atl. 1991
Assists					
AL:	4 Mitterwald Minn. 1969 4 Cerone NY 1980	5 Gedman Bos. 1988	7 B. Molina LA 2005	7 Steinbach Oak. 1992	6 Posada NY 2003
NL:	4 Bench Cin. 1975-76	2 By many players	4 Kennedy SD 1984 Matheny StL. 2002	7 Ausmus Hou. 2005	5 By many players
Errors					
AL:	3 Slaught KC 1984	1 Dempsey Balt. 1983 Pena Bos. 1990	2 Munson NY 1976 Borders Tor. 1991 Pierzynski Minn. 2002	2 Webster Balt. 1997 Alomar Clev. 1998	1 Sundberg KC 1985
NL:	1 Sanguillen Pitt. 1970, 75	2 Sanguillen Pitt. 1974	1 By many players	3 Piazza NY 1999	1 Rodriguez Fla. 2003 Lo Duca NY 2006
Passed Balls					
AL:	1 Cerone NY 1981	1 By many players	2 Borders Tor. 1991 Pierzynski Chi. 2005	3 Borders Tor. 1992	3 Varitek Bos. 2004
NL:	2 Sanguillen Pitt. 1975	1 By many players	1 By many players	2 Ashby Hou. 1986 Daulton Phil. 1993	2 Slaught Pitt. 1992 Bako Chi. 2003
Double Plays					
AL:	2 Mitterwald Minn. 1970	1 By many players	2 Fosse Oak. 1973	1 Borders Tor. 1992-93 Alomar Clev. 1997 Posada NY 2000	3 Posada NY 2003
NL:	1 By many players	1 By many players	2 Kennedy SF 1989	2 Lopez Atl. 1997 Piazza NY 1999	2 Olson Atl. 1991

ATCHERS

Most Series
6 Bob Boone, NL:Phil. 1976-78, 80; AL:Cal. 82, 86
Johnny Bench, NL:Cin. 1970, 72-73, 75-76, 79
Steve Yeager, NL:LA 1974,77-78, 81, 83, 85
Javy Lopez, NL:Atl. 1992, 95-98, 2001
Jorge Posada, AL:NY 1998-2001, 03-04

Most Games
33 Jorge Posada, AL:NY
27 Javy Lopez, NL:Atl.

Highest Percentage (Most Chances)
1.000 Gary Carter, NL:Mtl.-NY (136 tc)
Rich Gedman, AL:Bos. (88 tc)

Most Total Chances
275 Jorge Posada, AL:NY
195 Javy Lopez, NL:Atl.

Most Total Chances, Game
16 Rick Dempsey, AL:Balt. Oct. 6, 1983
Chris Hoiles, AL:Balt. Oct. 11, 1997 (12 inn)
Jorge Posada, AL:NY Oct. 18, 2004 (14 inn)
Charles Johnson, NL:Fla. Oct. 12, 1997
Extra-Inning Game:
18 Mike Piazza, NL:NY Oct. 17, 1999 (15 inn)

Most Total Chances, Inning
4 Pat Borders, AL:Tor. Oct. 8, 1991 (3rd)
Jorge Posada, AL:NY Oct. 16, 1999 (5th)
3 By many NL players

Most Chances Accepted
274 Jorge Posada, AL:NY
193 Javy Lopez, NL:Atl.

Most Chances Accepted, Game
16 Rick Dempsey, AL:Balt. Oct. 6, 1983
Chris Hoiles, AL:Balt. Oct. 11, 1997 (12 inn)
Jorge Posada, AL:NY Oct. 18, 2004 (14 inn)
Charles Johnson, NL:Fla. Oct. 12, 1997
Extra-Inning Game:
18 Mike Piazza, NL:NY Oct. 17, 1999 (15 inn)

Most Chances Accepted, Inning
4 Pat Borders, AL:Tor. Oct. 8, 1991 (3rd)
3 By many NL players

Most Putouts
255 Jorge Posada, AL:NY
183 Javy Lopez, NL:Atl.

Most Putouts, Game
15 Rick Dempsey, AL:Balt. Oct. 6, 1983
Chris Hoiles, AL:Balt. Oct. 11, 1997 (12 inn)
Jorge Posada, AL:NY Oct. 14, 2000
Jason Varitek, AL:Bos. Oct. 18, 2004 (14 inn)
Charles Johnson, NL:Fla. Oct. 12, 1997
Extra-Inning Game:
16 Mike Piazza, NL:NY Oct. 17, 1999 (15 inn)

Most Putouts, Inning
3 By many players

Most Assists
19 Jorge Posada, AL:NY
18 Johnny Bench, NL:Cin.

Most Assists, Game
4 Bengie Molina, AL:LA Oct. 16, 2005
3 Johnny Bench, NL:Cin. Oct. 3, 1970 (10 inn)
Johnny Bench, NL:Cin. Oct. 5, 1975
Gary Carter, NL:NY Oct. 15, 1986 (16 inn)
Mike Matheny, NL:StL. Oct. 12, 2002
Brad Ausmus, NL:Hou. Oct. 17, 2005

Most Assists, Inning
3 Bengie Molina, AL:LA Oct. 16, 2005 (9th)
2 Johnny Bench, NL:Cin. Oct. 7, 1973 (8th)
Mike Scioscia, NL:LA Oct. 10, 1985 (1st)
Gary Carter, NL:NY Oct. 15, 1986 (12th)
Raul Chavez, NL:Hou. Oct. 20, 2004 (10th)

Most Errors
5 Manny Sanguillen, NL:Pitt.
3 Don Slaught, AL:KC
Pat Borders, AL:Tor.
Sandy Alomar, Jr. AL:Clev.

Most Errors, Game
2 Manny Sanguillen, NL:Pitt. Oct. 6, 1974
Mike Piazza, NL:NY Oct. 19, 1999 (11 inn)
Thurman Munson, AL:NY Oct. 10, 1976
Don Slaught, AL:KC Oct. 5, 1984
Sandy Alomar, Jr. AL:Clev. Oct. 10, 1998

Most Errors, Inning
1 By many players

Most Passed Balls
5 Pat Borders, AL:Tor.
Jason Varitek, AL:Bos.
4 Manny Sanguillen, NL:Pitt.

Most Passed Balls, Game
2 Manny Sanguillen, NL:Pitt. Oct. 4, 1975
Alan Ashby, NL:Hou. Oct. 11, 1986
Don Slaught, NL:Pitt. Oct. 13, 1992
Pat Borders, AL:Tor. Oct. 13, 1991
Pat Borders, AL:Tor. Oct. 14, 1992
Extra-Inning Game:
3 Jason Varitek, AL:Bos. Oct. 18, 2004 (14 inn)

Most Passed Balls, Inning
3 Jason Varitek, AL:Bos. Oct. 18, 2004 (13th)
1 By many NL players

Most Double Plays
5 Jorge Posada, AL:NY
3 Manny Sanguillen, NL:Pitt.
Terry Kennedy, NL:SD-SF

Most Double Plays, Game
1 By many players

Double Plays, Unassisted
0 Not accomplished

PITCHERS – FIELDING

	3 Games	4 Games	5 Games	6 Games	7 Games
Highest Percentage 1.000 (Most Chances)					
AL:	5 By many players	5 By many players	5 John Cal. 1982 Flanagan Tor. 1989 Rivera NY 2001	5 Erickson Balt. 1997	10 Leibrandt KC 1985
NL:	5 Gullett Cin. 1975	6 Marichal SF 1971 Carlton Phil. 1983	5 Blass Pitt. 1972 Ryan Hou. 1980 Kile StL 2000 Glavine Atl. 2001 Rueter SF 2002	9 Oswalt Hou. 2005	9 Cox StL. 1987
Games					
AL:	3 By many players	4 Eckersley Oak. 1988 Kennedy Oak. 2006	5 Acker Tor. 1989	5 Assenmacher Clev. 1997 Jackson Clev. 1997 Shuey Clev. 1998	6 Embree Bos. 2004 Gordon NY 2004
NL:	3 By many players	4 Giusti Pitt. 1971 Wohlers Atl. 1995	5 McGraw Phil. 1980	6 Rocker Atl. 1998-99	6 Petkovsek StL. 1996 Isringhausen StL. 2004
Total Chances					
AL:	5 By many players	5 By many players	6 Contreras Chi. 2005	5 Erickson Balt. 1997	10 Leibrandt KC 1985
NL:	5 Gullett Cin. 1975	6 Marichal SF 1971 Carlton Phil. 1983	6 Maddux Atl. 2001	10 Maddux Atl. 1993	9 Cox StL. 1987
Chances Accepted					
AL:	5 By many players	5 By many players	5 John Cal. 1982 Flanagan Tor. 1989 Morris Minn. 1991 Rivera NY 2001 Contreras Chi. 2005	5 Erickson Balt. 1997	10 Leibrandt KC 1985
NL:	5 Gullett Cin. 1975	6 Marichal SF 1971 Carlton Phil. 1983	5 Blass Pitt. 1972 Ryan Hou. 1980 Kile StL 2000 Glavine Atl. 2001 Maddux Atl. 2001 Rueter SF 2002	9 Maddux Atl. 1993 Oswalt Hou. 2005	9 Cox StL. 1987
Putouts					
AL:	2 By many players	3 Hunter Oak. 1974	4 Rivera NY 2001	4 Tomko Sea. 2000	4 Lowe Bos. 2004
NL:	4 Gullett Cin. 1975	2 By many players	2 By many players	4 Maddux Atl. 1993 Ashby SD 1998 Oswalt Hou. 2005	4 Cox StL. 1987

PITCHING FIELDING

	3 Games	4 Games	5 Games	6 Games	7 Games
Most Assists					
AL:	4 By many players	5 Cuellar Balt. 1974	4 Contreras Chi. 2005	5 Erickson Balt. 1997	7 Leibrandt KC 1985
NL:	3 By many players	5 Carlton Phil. 1983	4 Kile StL. 2000	8 Carpenter StL. 2005	5 Cox StL. 1987
Errors					
AL:	1 Saberhagen KC 1984	1 Clemens Bos. 1988 Gray & Boddicker Bos. 1990	1 By many players	1 By many players	0
NL:	1 Walker Pitt. 1970	1 By many players	1 By many players	2 Andujar StL. 1985	1 Reuschel SF 1987 Munro Hou. 2004
Double Plays					
AL:	1 By many players	1 Loaiza Oak. 2006 Harden Oak. 2006 Rodney Det. 2006	2 Flanagan Tor. 1989	2 Nelson Sea. 1995	1 By many players
NL:	1 Jarvis & Upshaw Atl. 1969	1 By many players	2 Maddux Atl. 2001	2 Mahomes NY 1999	2 Cox StL. 1987

PITCHERS

Most Series
10 Tom Glavine, NL:Atl. 1991-93, 95-99, 2001
NY 2006
7 Roger Clemens, AL:Bos. 1986, 88, 90;
NY 99-2001, 03
Jeff Nelson, AL:Sea. 1995, 2001;
NY:1996, 98-2000, 03
Mariano Rivera, AL:NY 1996, 98-2001, 03-04

Most Games
25 Mariano Rivera, AL:NY
18 Mark Wohlers, NL:Atl.

Highest Percentage (Most Chances)
1.000 Tom Glavine, NL:Atl.-NY (29 tc)
Mariano Rivera, AL:NY (22 tc)

Most Total Chances
39 Greg Maddux, NL:Chi.-Atl.
22 Mariano Rivera, AL:NY

Most Total Chances, Game
8 Charlie Leibrandt, AL:KC Oct. 12, 1985
6 Juan Marichal, NL:SF Oct. 5, 1971

Most Total Chances, Inning
3 Pat Zachry, NL:Cin. Oct. 10, 1976 (4th)
John Smoltz, NL:Atl. Oct. 7, 1998 (1st)
Bud Black, AL:KC Oct. 9, 1985 (7th)
Mariano Rivera, AL:NY Oct. 17, 2001 (9th)

Most Chances Accepted
36 Greg Maddux, NL:Chi.-Atl.
22 Mariano Rivera, AL:NY

Most Chances Accepted, Game
8 Charlie Leibrandt, AL:KC Oct. 12, 1985
6 Juan Marichal, NL:SF Oct. 5, 1971

Most Chances Accepted, Inning
3 Pat Zachry, NL:Cin. Oct. 10, 1976 (4th)
Bud Black, AL:KC Oct. 9, 1985 (7th)
Mariano Rivera, AL:NY Oct. 17, 2001 (9th)

Most Putouts
12 Mariano Rivera, AL:NY
11 Greg Maddux, NL:Chi.-Atl.

Most Putouts, Game
4 Don Gullett, NL:Cin. Oct. 4, 1975
3 Tommy John, AL:Cal. Oct. 5, 1982
Charlie Leibrandt, AL:KC Oct. 12, 1985
Charles Nagy, AL:Clev. Oct. 7, 1998 (12 inn)
Derek Lowe, AL:Bos. Oct. 20, 2004

Most Putouts, Inning
2 Don Gullett, NL:Cin. Oct. 4, 1975 (3rd)
Dwight Gooden, NL:NY Oct. 8, 1986 (3rd)
Roger McDowell, NL:NY Oct. 15, 1986 (10th)
Mike Torrez, AL:NY Oct. 7, 1977 (2nd)
Charlie Leibrandt, AL:KC Oct. 12, 1985 (5th)
Bret Saberhagen, AL:KC Oct. 16, 1985 (3rd)
Mike Witt, AL:Cal. Oct. 12, 1986 (1st)
Andy Pettitte, AL:NY Oct. 13, 1996 (2nd)
Mariano Rivera, AL:NY Oct. 17, 2001 (9th)
Derek Lowe, AL:Bos. Oct. 20, 2004 (4th)

Most Assists
25 Greg Maddux, NL:Chi.-Atl.
12 Mike Cuellar, AL:Balt.

Most Assists, Game
5 Charlie Leibrandt, AL:KC Oct. 12, 1985
4 Juan Marichal, NL:SF Oct. 5, 1971
Greg Maddux, NL:Atl. Oct. 7, 1997
Tom Glavine, NL:Atl. Oct. 14, 1997
Andy Ashby, NL:SD Oct. 7, 1998 (10 inn)
Greg Maddux, NL:Atl. Oct. 12, 1999
Kenny Rogers, NL:NY Oct. 13, 1999
Chris Carpenter, NL:StL. Oct. 12, 2005
Chris Carpenter, NL:StL. Oct. 17, 2005

Most Assists, Inning
3 Pat Zachry, NL:Cin. Oct. 10, 1976 (4th)
2 By many AL players

Most Errors
3 Greg Maddux, NL:Chi.-Atl.
2 Bret Saberhagen, AL:KC-Bos.

Most Errors, Game
1 By many players

Most Errors, Inning
1 By players

Most Double Plays
3 Greg Maddux, NL:Chi.-Atl.
2 Mike Flanagan, AL:Tor.
Jeff Nelson, AL:Sea.
Mariano Rivera, AL:NY

Most Double Plays, Game
2 Danny Cox, NL:StL. Oct. 14, 1987
Greg Maddux, NL:Atl. Oct. 16, 2001
Mike Flanagan, AL:Tor. Oct. 7, 1989
Jeff Nelson, AL:Sea. Oct. 14, 1995

Double Plays, Unassisted
Not accomplished

	3 Games	4 Games	5 Games	6 Games	7 Games
Games					
AL:	3 Perranoski Minn. 1969; Todd Oak. 1975; Hernandez Det. 1984	4 Eckersley Oak. 1988; Kennedy Oak. 2006	5 Acker Tor. 1989	5 Assenmacher Clev. 1997; Jackson Clev. 1997; Shuey Clev. 1998; Paniagua Sea. 2000	6 Embree Bos. 2004; Gordon NY 2004
NL:	3 By many players	4 Giusti Pitt. 1971; Wohlers Atl. 1995	5 McGraw Phil. 1980	6 Rocker Atl. 1998-99	6 Petkovsek StL. 1996; Isringhausen StL. 2004
Games Started					
AL:	2 Holtzman Oak. 1975	2 By many players	2 By many players	2 By many players	3 Stieb Tor. 1985; Clemens Bos. 1986
NL:	1 By many players	2 By many players	2 By many players	2 By many players	3 Hershiser LA 1988; Drabek Pitt.; Smoltz Atl. 1992
Complete Games					
AL:	1 By many players	1 By many players	1 By many players	1 By many players	1 By many players
NL:	1 By many players	1 By many players	1 By many players	2 Scott Hou. 1986	2 Cox StL. 1987; Wakefield Pitt. 1992
Games Finished					
AL:	3 Perranoski Minn. 1969	4 Eckersley Oak. 1988	4 Lyle NY 1977; Reardon Minn. 1987; Eckersley Oak. 1989; Rivera NY 2001	4 Henke Tor. 1992; Hernandez Chi. 1993; Ward Tor. 1993	4 Quisenberry KC 1985; Schiraldi Bos. 1986; Rivera NY 2003
NL:	2 By many players	4 Giusti Pitt. 1971	4 Borbon Cin. 1973; Bedrosian SF 1989	4 Orosco NY 1986; Wohlers Atl. 1993; Lidge Hou. 2005	5 Isringhausen StL. 2004
Saves					
AL:	2 Drago Bos. 1975	4 Eckersley Oak. 1988	3 Eckersley Oak. 1989; Aguilera Minn. 1991	3 Henke Tor. 1992	3 Williamson Bos. 2003
NL:	2 Gullett Cin. 1970	3 Giusti Pitt. 1971	3 Bedrosian SF 1989; Nen SF 2002	3 Myers Cin. 1990; Lidge Hou. 2005	3 Pena Atl. 1991; Isringhausen StL. 2004
Most Decisions					
AL:	2 Holtzman Oak. 1975	2 By many players	2 By many players	2 By many players	3 Leibrandt KC 1985; Wakefield Bos. 2003
NL:	1 By many players	2 By many players	2 By many players	3 Orosco NY 1986	3 Drabek Pitt. 1992; Tavarez StL. 2004

CHAMPIONSHIP SERIES PITCHING RECORDS

		3 Games	4 Games	5 Games	6 Games	7 Games
Most Won	AL:	1 By many players	2 Nelson Oak. 1988 Stewart Oak. 1990	2 By many players	2 By many players	2 Henke Tor. 1985 Wakefield Bos. 2003
	NL:	1 By many players	2 Sutton LA 1974 Carlton Phil. 1983	2 Hooton LA 1981 Lefferts SD 1984 Hampton NY 2000 Johnson Ari. 2001 Worrell SF 2002	3 Orosco NY 1986	2 Myers NY 1988 Belcher LA 1988 Avery Atl. 1991 Smoltz NL Atl. 1991-92, 96 Wakefield Pitt. 1992 Tavarez StL 2004
Most Lost	AL:	2 Holtzman Oak. 1975	2 Leonard KC 1978 Hurst Bos. 1988	2 Fryman Det. 1972 Alexander Det. 1987 Stieb Tor. 1989 Sele Sea. 2001 Escobar LA 2005	2 Moore Oak. 1992 Fernandez & McDowell Chi. 1993 Benitez Balt. 1997 Ogea Clev. 1997 Neagle NY 2000	2 Leibrandt KC 1985 McCaskill Cal. 1986 Mussina NY 2003 Lowe Bos. 2003
	NL:	1 By many players	2 Reuss Pitt. 1974; LA 83	2 Gullickson Mtl. 1981 Kile StL. 2000 Maddux Atl. 2001 Morris StL. 2002	2 Niedenfuer LA 1985 Smith Pitt. 1990 Maddux Atl. 1997 Glavine Atl. 1998 Rogers NY 1999 Mulder StL. 2005	3 Drabek Pitt. 1992
Innings	AL:	11.0 McNally Balt. 1969 Holtzman Oak. 1975	16.0 Stewart Oak. 1990	19.0 Lolich Det. 1972	16.2 Stewart Oak. 1992	22.2 Clemens Bos. 1986
	NL:	9.2 Ellis Pitt. 1970	17.0 Sutton LA 1974	17.0 Burris Mtl. 1981	18.0 Scott Hou. 1986	24.2 Hershiser LA 1988
Runs	AL:	9 Perry Minn. 1970	10 Frost Cal. 1979	10 Alexander Det. 1987	10 McDowell Chi. 1993	13 McCaskill Cal. 1986 Drabek Pitt. 1992
	NL:	9 Niekro Atl. 1969	11 Perry SF 1971	12 Maddux Chi. 1989	10 Andujar StL. 1985 Greene Phil. 1993	11 Glavine Atl. 1992 Stottlemyre StL. 1996
Earned Runs	AL:	8 Perry Minn. 1970	9 Frost Cal. 1979	10 Alexander Det. 1987	10 McDowell Chi. 1993	11 Clemens Bos. 1986
	NL:	6 Jarvis Atl. 1969 Koosman NY 1969	10 Perry SF 1971	11 Maddux Chi. 1989	10 Greene Phil. 1993	11 Stottlemyre StL. 1996
Hits	AL:	12 Holtzman Oak. 1975	13 Leonard KC 1978	18 Gura KC 1976	18 McDowell Chi. 1993	22 Clemens Bos. 1986
	NL:	10 Jarvis Atl. 1969	19 Perry SF 1971 Perez Atl. 1982	16 Ryan Hou. 1980 Garrelts SF 1989 Morris StL. 2002	17 Hershiser LA 1985	19 Andy Benes StL. 1996

CHAMPIONSHIP SERIES PITCHING RECORDS

	3 Games	4 Games	5 Games	6 Games	7 Games
Home Runs					
AL:	4 Hunter Oak. 1971	3 Hunter Oak. 1974 & NY 1978 Boddicker Bos. 1988	4 McNally 1973 Pettitte NY 1996	4 Pettitte NY 1998	5 Mussina NY 2003
NL:	3 Jarvis Atl. 1969	4 Blass Pitt. 1971	5 Show SD 1984	3 Greene Phil. 1993	4 Wakefield Pitt. 1992 Zambrano Chi. 2003
Walks					
AL:	7 Boswell Minn. 1969	13 Cuellar Balt. 1974	8 Palmer Balt. 1973 Abbott Sea. 2001	9 Morris Tor. 1992 Guzman Tor. 1993	10 Stieb Tor. 1985
NL:	5 Norman Cin. 1974 Carlton Phil. 1978	8 Reuss Pitt. 1974 Carlton Phil. 1977	8 Carlton Phil. 1980 Sutcliffe Chi. 1984	11 Glavine Atl. 1997	10 Smoltz Atl. 1992
Intentional Walks					
AL:	2 Segui Oak. 1971	2 Gardner Bos. 1988	3 Henneman Det. 1987	3 Fernandez Chi. 1993	2 Stieb Tor. 1985 Schiraldi Bos. 1986
NL:	2 By many players	4 Giusti Pitt. 1974	3 McGraw Phil. 1980 Christenson Phil. 1980	3 Welch LA 1985 Lopez Hou. 1986 Avery Atl. 1993 Glavine Atl. 1997	2 Tudor StL 1987 Gooden NY 1988 Glavine Atl. 1991 Smoltz Atl. 1992 Farnsworth Chi. 2003 Isringhausen StL 2004
Hit Batters					
AL:	1 By many players	2 By many players	3 Tanana Det. 1987	3 Key Balt. 1997	3 Martinez Bos. 2004
NL:	1 By many players	2 John LA 1977	3 Morris StL. 2002	2 Leiter NY 1999 Oswalt Hou. 2005	2 Hershiser LA 1988 Glavine Atl. 1992
Strikeouts					
AL:	12 Palmer Balt. 1970	14 Boddicker Balt. 1983	15 Palmer Balt. 1973	25 Mussina Balt. 1997	18 Stieb Tor. 1985
NL:	14 Candelaria Pitt. 1975	13 Sutton LA 1974 Carlton Phil. 1983 Schourek Cin. 1995	19 Johnson Ari. 2001	19 Scott Hou. 1986	20 Gooden NY 1988
Wild Pitches					
AL:	1 By many players	2 Haren Oak. 2006	3 John Cal. 1982	3 Guzman Tor. 1993	2 Black KC 1985 Contreras NY 2003
NL:	2 McGraw Phil. 1976 Eastwick Cin. 1976 Andujar StL. 1982	2 Marichal SF 1971 Carlton Phil. 1983 Pena LA 1983	4 Ankiel StL. 2000	2 Worrell StL. 1985 Calhoun Hou. 1986 Avery Atl. 1993 Hitchcock SD 1998 Mulder StL. 2005 Tavarez StL. 2005	2 Gooden NY 1988 Hershiser LA 1988 Pena Atl. 1991 Smoltz Atl. 1996 Morris StL. 2004

INDIVIDUAL PITCHING

Most Series
- 10 Tom Glavine, NL:Atl. 1991-93, 95-99, 2001
      NY 2006
- 7 Roger Clemens, AL:Bos. 1986, 88, 90;
      NY 99-2001, 03
     Jeff Nelson, AL:Sea. 1995, 2001;
      NY 96, 98-2000, 03
     Mariano Rivera, AL:NY 1996, 98-2001, 03-04

Lowest Earned Run Average (Minimum: 30 IP)
- 0.93 Mariano Rivera, AL:NY (38.2 inn)
- 1.69 Jeff Suppan, NL:StL. (32 inn)

Most Games
- 25 Mariano Rivera, AL:NY
- 18 Mark Wohlers, NL:Atl.

Most Games Started
- 17 Tom Glavine, NL:Atl.-NY
- 11 Roger Clemens, AL:Bos.-NY

Most Complete Games
- 5 Jim Palmer, AL:Balt.
- 2 Kevin Brown, NL:Fla.-SD
     Danny Cox, NL:StL.
     Doug Drabek, NL:Pitt.
     Orel Hershiser, NL:LA
     Tommy John, NL:LA
     Mike Scott, NL:Hou.
     Don Sutton, NL:LA
     Tim Wakefield, NL:Pitt.

Most Games Finished
- 21 Mariano Rivera, AL:NY
- 14 Mark Wohlers, NL:Atl.

Most Saves
- 11 Dennis Eckersley, AL:Oak.; NL:StL.
- 10 Dennis Eckersley, AL:Oak.
     Mariano Rivera, AL:NY
- 5 Tug McGraw, NL:NY-Phil.
     Robb Nen, NL:Fla.-SF
     Brad Lidge, NL:Hou.
     Jason Isringhausen, NL:StL.

Shutouts
- 1 By many players

Most Games Won
- 8 Dave Stewart, AL:Oak.-Tor.
- 6 John Smoltz, NL:Atl.
     Tom Glavine, NL:Atl.-NY

Most Games Lost
- 10 Tom Glavine, NL:Atl.-NY
- 4 Doyle Alexander, AL:Balt.-Tor.-Det.

Most Innings
- 103.1 Tom Glavine, NL:Atl.-NY
- 75.1 Dave Stewart, AL:Oak.-Tor.

Most Innings, Game
- 11.0 Dave McNally, AL:Balt. Oct. 5, 1969
      Ken Holtzman, AL:Oak. Oct. 9, 1973
- 10.0 Joe Niekro, NL:Hou. Oct. 10, 1980
      Dwight Gooden, NL:NY Oct. 14, 1986

Most Runs
- 50 Greg Maddux, NL:Chi.-Atl.
- 29 Roger Clemens, AL:Bos.-NY

Most Runs, Game
- 9 Phil Niekro, NL:Atl. Oct. 4, 1969
- 8 Jim Perry, AL:Minn. Oct. 3, 1970
     Roger Clemens, AL:Bos. Oct. 7, 1986
     Hideki Irabu, AL:NY Oct. 16, 1999

Most Runs, Inning
- 8 Tom Glavine, NL:Atl. Oct. 13, 1992 (2nd)
- 6 Jim Perry, AL:Minn. Oct. 3, 1970 (4th)
     Scott Erickson, AL:Balt. Oct. 13, 1996 (3rd)

Most Earned Runs
- 37 Tom Glavine, NL:Atl.-NY
- 27 Roger Clemens, AL:Bos.-NY

Most Earned Runs, Game
- 8 Greg Maddux, NL:Chi. Oct. 4, 1989
- 7 Jim Perry, AL:Minn. Oct. 3, 1970
     Roger Clemens, AL:Bos. Oct. 7, 1986
     Jack McDowell, AL:Chi. Oct. 5, 1993
     Hideki Irabu, AL:NY Oct. 16, 1999
     Esteban Loaiza, AL:Oak. Oct. 11, 2006

Most Earned Runs, Inning
- 7 Tom Glavine, NL:Atl. Oct. 13, 1992 (2nd)
- 6 Jim Perry, AL:Minn. Oct. 3, 1970 (4th)

Most Hits
- 102 Tom Glavine, NL:Atl.-NY
- 63 Andy Pettitte, AL:NY

Most Hits, Game
- 13 Jack McDowell, AL:Chi. Oct. 5, 1993
     Hideki Irabu, AL:NY Oct. 16, 1999
- 11 Kevin Brown, NL:Fla. Oct. 14, 1997

Fewest Hits, Complete Game
- 1 Roger Clemens, AL:NY Oct. 14, 2000
- 2 Ross Grimsley, NL:Cin. Oct. 10, 1972
     Jon Matlack, NL:NY Oct. 7, 1973
     Dave Dravecky, NL:SF Oct. 7, 1987
     Josh Beckett, NL:Fla. Oct. 12, 2003

Most Hits, Inning
- 6 Jim Perry, AL:Minn. Oct. 3, 1970 (4th)
     Kirk McCaskill, AL:Cal. Oct. 14, 1986 (3rd)
     Greg Harris, NL:SD Oct. 2, 1984 (5th)
     Tom Glavine, NL:Atl. Oct. 13, 1992 (2nd)
     Todd Stottlemyre, NL:StL. Oct. 14, 1996 (1st)
     Matt Morris, NL:StL. Oct. 9, 2002 (2nd)

Most Home Runs
- 12 Catfish Hunter, AL:Oak-NY
- 9 Tom Glavine, NL:Atl.-NY

Most Home Runs, Game
- 4 Catfish Hunter, AL:Oak. Oct. 4, 1971
     Dave McNally, AL:Balt. Oct. 7, 1973
     Andy Pettitte, AL:NY Oct. 9, 1998
- 3 Pat Jarvis, NL:Atl. Oct. 6, 1969
     Eric Show, NL:SD Oct. 2, 1984
     Danny Cox, NL:StL. Oct. 10, 1987
     Carlos Zambrano, NL:Chi. Oct. 7, 2003
     Oliver Perez, NL:NY Oct. 15, 2006

Most Home Runs, Inning
- 3 Scott Erickson, AL:Balt. Oct. 13 1996 (3rd)
     Jaret Wright, AL:Clev. Oct. 12, 1997 (3rd)
     Andy Pettitte, AL:NY Oct. 9, 1998 (5th)
     Carlos Zambrano, NL:Chi. Oct. 7, 2003 (3rd)

Most Grand Slam Home Runs
- 2 Greg Maddux, NL:Atl.
- 1 Jim Perry, AL:Minn.
     Moose Haas, AL:Mil.
     David Cone, AL:NY
     Rod Beck, AL:Bos.
     Javier Vazquez, AL:NY

Most Walks
- 42 Tom Glavine, NL:Atl.-NY
- 26 Orlando Hernandez, AL:NY

Most Walks, Game
- 9 Mike Cuellar, AL:Balt. Oct. 9, 1974
- 8 Fernando Valenzuela, NL:LA Oct. 14, 1985

Most Walks, Inning
4 Mike Cuellar, AL:Balt. Oct. 9, 1974 (5th)
Burt Hooton, NL:LA Oct. 7, 1977 (2nd)
Bob Welch, NL:LA Oct. 12, 1985 (1st)

Most Walks, Consecutive
4 Mike Cuellar, AL:Balt. Oct. 9, 1974
Burt Hooton, NL:LA Oct. 7, 1977

Most Intentional Walks
8 Tom Glavine, NL:Atl.-NY
3 Mike Henneman, AL:Det.
Alex Fernandez, AL:Chi.

Most Intentional Walks, Game
3 Dave Giusti, NL:Pitt. Oct. 5, 1974
Tug McGraw, NL:Phil. Oct. 10, 1980
Bob Welch, NL:LA Oct. 12, 1985
Steve Avery, NL:Atl. Oct. 6, 1993
Tom Glavine, NL:Atl. Oct. 14, 1997
2 Diego Segui, AL:Oak. Oct. 5, 1971
Mark Littell, AL:KC Oct. 5, 1977
Dave Stieb, AL:Tor. Oct. 12, 1985
Calvin Schiraldi, AL:Bos. Oct. 11, 1986 (11 inn)
Mike Henneman, AL:Det. Oct. 10, 1987
Wes Gardner, AL:Bos. Oct. 8, 1988
Alex Fernandez, AL:Chi. Oct. 6, 1993
Danny Cox, AL:Tor. Oct. 8, 1993

Most Intentional Walks, Inning
2 Tom Seaver, NL:NY Oct. 4, 1969 (3rd)
Dave Giusti, NL:Pitt. Oct. 5, 1974 (9th)
Lance Rautzhan, NL:LA Oct. 6, 1978 (7th)
Tug McGraw, NL:Phil. Oct. 10, 1980 (11th)
Joe Beckwith, NL:LA Oct. 8, 1983 (5th)
Bob Welch, NL:LA Oct. 12, 1985 (1st)
Dwight Gooden, NL:NY Oct. 12, 1988 (2nd)
Rick Sutcliffe, NL:Chi. Oct. 7, 1989 (1st)
Steve Avery, NL:Atl. Oct. 6, 1993 (6th)
Mike Jackson, NL:Cin. Oct. 14, 1995 (7th)
John Smoltz, NL:Atl. Oct. 10, 1997 (6th)
Kenny Rogers, NL:NY Oct. 19, 1999 (11th)
Jason Isringhausen, NL:StL. Oct. 10, 2002 (9th)
Kyle Farnsworth, NL:Chi. Oct. 14, 2003 (8th)
1 By many AL players

Most Hit Batters
5 Tom Glavine, NL:Atl.
Greg Maddux, NL:Chi.-Atl.
4 Frank Tanana, AL:Cal.-Det.
Mike Boddicker, AL:Balt.-Bos.
David Wells, AL:Balt-NY
Jeff Nelson, AL:NY
Pedro Martinez, AL:Bos.

Most Hit Batters, Game
3 Frank Tanana, AL:Det. Oct. 11, 1987
Jimmy Key, AL:Balt. Oct. 9, 1997
Matt Morris, NL:StL. Oct. 14, 2002

Most Hit Batters, Inning
3 Jimmy Key, AL:Balt. Oct. 9, 1997 (1st)
2 Al Leiter, NL:NY Oct. 19, 1999 (1st)

Most Strikeouts
89 John Smoltz, NL:Atl.
66 Mike Mussina, AL:Balt.-NY

Most Strikeouts, Game
15 Livan Hernandez, NL:Fla. Oct. 12, 1997
Mike Mussina, AL:Balt. Oct. 11, 1997 (12 inn)
Roger Clemens, AL:NY Oct. 14, 2000

Most Strikeouts, Inning
3 By many players

Most Strikeouts, Consecutive
5 Curt Schilling, NL:Phil. Oct. 6, 1993
Mark Wohlers, NL:Atl. Oct. 7-10, 1993
Mike Mussina, AL:Balt. Oct. 11, 1997
Mike Mussina, AL:NY Oct 12, 2004

Most Strikeouts, 2 Consecutive Innings
6 Jim Palmer, AL:Balt. Oct. 6, 1973
5 By many NL players

Most Wild Pitches
4 Orel Hershiser, NL:LA; AL:Clev.
Roger Clemens, AL:Bos.-NY; NL:Hou.
Rick Ankiel, NL:StL.
Alejandro Pena, NL:LA-Atl.
Juan Guzman, AL:Tor.
Tommy John, AL:NY-Cal.

Most Wild Pitches, Game
3 Tommy John, AL:Cal. Oct. 9, 1982
Juan Guzman, AL:Tor. Oct. 5, 1993
2 By many NL players

Most Wild Pitches, Inning
2 Chris Zachary, AL:Det. Oct. 8, 1972 (5th)
Tommy John, AL:Cal. Oct. 9, 1982 (4th)
David West, AL:Minn. Oct. 11, 1991 (5th)
Juan Guzman, AL:Tor. Oct. 5, 1993 (1st)
Mariano Rivera, AL:NY Oct. 17, 2001 (9th)
Jeff Calhoun, NL:Hou. Oct. 15, 1986 (16th)
Sterling Hitchcock, NL:SD Oct. 14, 1998 (2nd)
Rick Ankiel, NL:StL. Oct. 12, 2000 (1st)
Rick Ankiel, NL:StL. Oct. 16, 2000 (7th)

Most Balks
1 By many

Most Balks, Game
1 By many

Shutouts

American League: *(* = Winning Pitcher)*

1-0	1969 Oct. 5	Dave McNally, Balt. (vs Minn.)
5-0	1972 Oct. 8	Blue Moon Odom, Oak. (vs Det.)
3-0	1972 Oct. 10	Joe Coleman, Det. (vs Oak.)
6-0	1973 Oct. 6	Jim Palmer, Balt. (vs Oak.)
3-0	1973 Oct. 11	Catfish Hunter, Oak. (vs Balt.)
5-0	1974 Oct. 6	Ken Holtzman, Oak. (vs Balt.)
1-0	1974 Oct. 8	Vida Blue, Oak. (at Balt.)
8-0	1979 Oct. 6	Scott McGregor, Balt. (at Cal.)
4-0	1981 Oct. 15	Dave Righetti*, Ron Davis, Rich Gossage, NY (at Oak.)
4-0	1983 Oct. 6	Mike Boddicker, Balt. (vs Chi.)
3-0	1983 Oct. 8	Storm Davis, Tippy Martinez*, Balt. (at Chi.)
1-0	1984 Oct. 5	Milt Wilcox*, Willie Hernandez, Det. (vs KC)
2-0	1985 Oct. 13	Danny Jackson, KC (vs Tor.)
7-0	1995 Oct. 14	Ken Hill*, Jim Poole, Chad Ogea Alan Embree, Clev. (vs Sea.)
4-0	1995 Oct. 17	Dennis Martinez*, Julian Tavarez, Jose Mesa, Clev. (at Sea.)
3-0	1997 Oct. 8	Scott Erickson*, Randy Myers, Balt. (vs Clev.)
1-0	1997 Oct. 15	Charles Nagy, Paul Assenmacher, Mike Jackson, Brian Anderson*, Jose Mesa, Clev. (at Balt.)
4-0	1998 Oct. 10	Orlando Hernandez*, Mike Stanton, Mariano Rivera, NY (at Clev.)
2-0	2000 Oct. 10	Freddy Garcia*, Jose Paniagua, Arthur Rhodes, Kazuhiro Sasaki, Sea. (at NY)
5-0	2000 Oct. 14	Roger Clemens, NY (at Sea.)
3-0	2006 Oct. 13	Kenny Rogers*, Fernando Rodney, Todd Jones, Det. (vs. Oak)

National League: *(* = Winning Pitcher)*

3-0	1970 Oct. 3	Gary Nolan*, Clay Carroll, Cin. (at Pitt.)
5-0	1973 Oct. 7	Jon Matlack, NY (at Cin.)
3-0	1974 Oct. 5	Don Sutton, LA (at Pitt.)
7-0	1974 Oct. 8	Bruce Kison*, Ramon Hernande Pitt. (at LA)
4-0	1978 Oct. 5	Tommy John, LA (at Phil.)
1-0	1980 Oct. 10	Joe Niekro, Dave Smith*, Hou. (vs Phil.)
3-0	1981 Oct. 14	Ray Burris, Mtl. (at LA)
7-0	1982 Oct. 7	Bob Forsch, StL. (vs Atl.)
1-0	1983 Oct. 4	Steve Carlton*, Al Holland, Phil. (at LA)
13-0	1984 Oct. 2	Rick Sutcliffe*, Warren Brusstar, Chi. (vs SD)
1-0	1986 Oct. 8	Mike Scott, Hou. (vs NY)
5-0	1987 Oct. 7	Dave Dravecky, SF (at StL.)
1-0	1987 Oct. 13	John Tudor*, Todd Worrell, Ken Dayley, StL. (vs SF)
6-0	1987 Oct. 14	Danny Cox, StL. (vs SF)
6-0	1988 Oct. 12	Orel Hershiser, LA (vs NY)
1-0	1991 Oct. 10	Steve Avery*, Alejandro Pena, Atl. (at Pitt.)
1-0	1991 Oct. 14	Zane Smith*, Roger Mason, Pitt. (at Atl.)
1-0	1991 Oct. 16	Steve Avery*, Alejandro Pena, Atl. (at Pitt.)
4-0	1991 Oct. 17	John Smoltz, Atl. (at Pitt.)
6-0	1995 Oct. 14	Steve Avery*, Greg McMichael, Alejandro Pena, Mark Wohlers, Atl. (vs Cin.)
14-0	1996 Oct. 14	John Smoltz*, Mike Bielecki, Terrell Wade, Brad Clontz, Atl. (at St
15-0	1996 Oct. 17	Tom Glavine*, Mike Bielecki, Steve Avery, Atl. (vs StL.)
4-0	1997 Oct. 11	Denny Neagle, Atl. (at Fla.)
3-0	1998 Oct. 8	Kevin Brown, SD (at Atl.)
5-0	1998 Oct. 14	Sterling Hitchcock*, Brian Boehringer, Mark Langston, Joey Hamilton, Trevor Hoffman, SD (at Atl.)
1-0	1999 Oct. 15	Tom Glavine*, Mike Remlinger, John Rocker, Atl. (at NY)
7-0	2000 Oct. 16	Mike Hampton, NY (vs StL.)
2-0	2001 Oct. 16	Randy Johnson, Ari. (vs Atl.)
4-0	2003 Oct. 12	Josh Beckett, Fla. (vs Chi.)
3-0	2004 Oct. 18	Brandon Backe, Brad Lidge*, Ho (vs. StL.)
2-0	2006 Oct. 12	Tom Glavine*, Guillermo Mota, Billy Wagner, NY (Vs. StL.)
5-0	2006 Oct. 14	Jeff Suppan*, Josh Kinney StL. (vs. NY)

	3 Games	4 Games	5 Games	6 Games	7 Games
Batting Average					
AL:	.336 New York 1981	.300 New York 1978	.316 New York 1976	.301 Toronto 1993	.282 New York 2004
NL:	.330 St Louis 1982	.286 Los Angeles 1978	.303 Chicago 1989	.279 St Louis 1985.	.309 Atlanta 1996
Batting Average Both Clubs					
AL:	.286 Balt. .330 Minn. .238 1970	.282 NY .300 KC .263 1978	.283 NY .316 KC .247 1976	.271 Tor. .301 Chi. .237 1993	.279 Bos. .277 NY. .282 2004
NL:	.292 NY .327 Atl. .255 1969	.268 LA. .286 Phil. .250 1978	.285 Chi. .303 SF .267 1989	.256 StL .279 LA .234 1985	.262 Fla. .266 Chi. .258 2003
Slugging Percentage					
AL:	.560 Baltimore 1970	.511 Oakland 1988	.497 NY 1996	.471 Toronto 1992	.469 New York 2004
NL:	.575 New York 1969	.544 Los Angeles 1978	.494 Chicago 1984	.420 Philadelphia 1993	.484 Chicago 2003
Slugging Percentage Both Clubs					
AL:	.476 Balt. .560 & Minn. .386 1970	.443 KC .444 NY .443 1978	.448 NY .497 Balt. .398 1996	.408 Tor. .471 Oak. .343 1992	.454 Bos. .439 NY .469 2004
NL:	.530 NY .575 Atl. .481 1969	.477 LA .544 Phil. .407 1978	.456 SF .473 Chi. .440 1989	.415 Phil. .420 Atl. .409 1993	.469 Fla. .453 Chi. .484 2003
At-Bats					
AL:	123 Baltimore 1969	140 New York 1978	184 Boston 1999	218 Baltimore 1997	277 New York 2004
NL:	113 New York 1969	149 Atlanta 1995	190 Philadelphia 1980	227 New York 1986	256 Florida 2003
At-Bats, Both Clubs					
AL:	233 Balt. 123 Minn. 110 1969	273 NY 140 KC 133 1978	360 NY 176 Bos. 184 1999	425 Balt. 218 Clev. 207 1997	548 Bos. 271 NY 277 2004
NL:	219 NY 113 Atl. 106 1969	287 LA 147 Phil. 140 1978	362 Phil. 190 Hou. 172 1980	452 NY 227 Hou. 225 1986	508 Fla. 256 Chi. 252 2003
Runs					
AL:	27 Baltimore 1970	26 Baltimore 1979	34 Minnesota 1987	31 Tor. 1992 & NY 2000	45 New York 2004
NL:	27 New York 1969	24 Pittsburgh 1971	31 New York 2000	33 Atlanta 1993	44 Atlanta 1996
Runs, Both Clubs					
AL:	37 Balt. 27 Minn. 10 1970	41 Balt. 26 Cal. 15 1979	57 Minn. 34 Det. 23 1987	55 Tor. 31 Oak. 24 1992	86 Bos. 41 NY 45 2004
NL:	42 NY 27 Atl. 15 1969	39 Pitt. 24 SF 15 1971	52 SF 30 Chi. 22 1989 NY 31 StL. 21 2000	56 Atl. 33 Phil. 23 1993	82 Fla. 40 Chi. 42 2003
Hits					
AL:	36 Balt. 1969-70; NY 1981	42 New York 1978	55 New York 1976	65 Toronto 1993	78 New York 2004
NL:	37 New York 1969	42 Los Angeles 1978 Atlanta 1995	55 Philadelphia 1980	59 Atlanta 1993	77 Atlanta 1996
Hits, Both Clubs					
AL:	60 Balt. 36 Minn. 24 1970	77 NY 42 KC 35 1978	96 NY 42 Bos. 54 1999	111 Tor. 59 Oak. 52 1992 Tor. 65 Chi. 46 1993	153 Bos. 75 NY 78 2004
NL:	64 NY 37 Atl. 27 1969	77 LA 42 Phil. 35 1978	97 Chi. 53 SF 44 1989	106 Atl. 59 Phil. 47 1993	133 Fla. 68 Chi. 65 2003
Extra-Base Hits					
AL:	13 Baltimore 1969-70	15 Oakland 1988	22 Minnesota 1987	19 Toronto 1992	32 New York 2004
NL:	15 New York 1969	19 Los Angeles 1978	20 Chicago 1984	22 Philadelphia 1993	28 Pittsburgh 1992

CHAMPIONSHIP SERIES – CLUB BATTING

	3 Games	4 Games	5 Games	6 Games	7 Games
Extra-Base Hits, Both Clubs					
AL:	24 Balt. 12 Oak. 12 1971	25 Det. 14 Oak. 11 2006	33 Minn. 22 Det. 11 1987 NY 20 Balt. 13 1996 Bos. 20 NY 13 1999	33 Sea. 17 NY 16 2000	55 Bos. 23 NY 32 2004
NL:	29 NY 15 Atl. 14 1969	29 LA 19 Phil. 10 1978	31 SF 16 Chi. 15 1989	41 Phil. 22 Atl. 19 1993	52 Chi. 27 Fla. 25 2003
Total Bases					
AL:	61 Baltimore 1970	70 Oakland 1988	91 New York 1996	99 Toronto 1992	130 New York 2004
NL:	65 New York 1969	80 Los Angeles 1978	80 Chicago 1984	88 Atlanta 1993	122 Chicago 2003
Total Bases, Both Clubs					
AL:	100 Balt. 61 Minn. 39 1970	121 NY 62 KC 59 1978	161 NY 91 Balt. 70 1996	170 Tor. 99 Oak. 71 1992	249 Bos. 119 NY 130 2004
NL:	116 NY 65 Atl. 51 1969	137 LA 80 Phil. 57 1978	155 SF 78 Chi. 77 1989	175 Atl. 88 Phil. 87 1993	238 Fla. 116 Chi. 122 2003
Singles					
AL:	29 New York 1981	34 Oakland 1990	37 Minnesota 1991	52 Toronto 1993	53 California 1986
NL:	27 St Louis 1982	31 Atlanta 1995	45 Philadelphia 1980	42 St Louis 1985	55 Atlanta 1996
Singles, Both Clubs					
AL:	46 NY 29 Oak. 17 1981	55 NY 33 KC 22 1978	73 Minn. 37 Tor. 36 1991	87 Tor. 52 Chi. 35 1993	103 Cal. 53 Bos. 50 1986
NL:	41 StL. 27 Atl. 14 1982	53 Atl. 31 Cin. 22 1995	73 Phil. 45 Hou. 28 1980	79 SD 41 Atl. 38 1998	90 Atl. 55 StL. 35 1996
Doubles					
AL:	8 By many clubs	9 Baltimore 1983	13 NY 1976 Minn. 1987 Boston 1999	12 Seattle 2000	21 New York 2004
NL:	9 Atlanta 1969	8 Los Angeles 1974, 78	12 New York 2000	14 Atlanta 1993	20 Pittsburgh 1992
Doubles, Both Clubs					
AL:	15 Oak. 8 Balt. 7 1971	14 Det. 7 Oak. 7 2006	21 NY 12 KC 9 1977	22 Sea. 12 NY 10 2000	33 Bos. 12 NY 21 2004
NL:	17 Atl. 9 NY 8 1969	11 LA 8 Phil. 3 1978 Atl. 6 Cin. 5 1995	23 NY 12 StL 11 2000	25 Atl. 14 Phil. 11 1993	31 Pitt. 20 Atl. 11 1992
Triples					
AL:	1 By many clubs	3 Kansas City 1978	4 Kansas City 1976	3 Toronto 1993 Cleveland 1995	2 Boston 1986 & 2003 New York 2004
NL:	3 Cincinnati 1976	3 Los Angeles 1978	5 Houston 1980	4 Philadelphia 1993	4 St Louis 1987 Chicago 2003 St. Louis 2006
Triples, Both Clubs					
AL:	2 Balt. 1 Minn. 1 1969 Balt. 1 Oak. 1 1971 KC 1 NY 1 1980	4 KC 3 NY 1 1978	6 KC 4 NY 2 1976	4 Tor. 3 Chi. 1 1993	3 Bos. 1 NY 2 2004
NL:	4 Cin. 3 Phil. 1 1976	5 LA 3 Phil. 2 1978	6 Hou. 5 Phil. 1 1980	4 Phil. 4 Atl. 0 1993	7 Chi. 4 Fla. 3 2003

		3 Games	4 Games	5 Games	6 Games	7 Games
Home Runs						
	AL:	6 Baltimore 1970	7 Oakland 1988 Detroit 2006	10 New York 1996	10 Toronto 1992	12 Boston 2003
	NL:	6 New York 1969	8 By many clubs	9 Chicago 1984	7 Philadelphia 1993	14 Houston 2004
Home Runs, Both Clubs						
	AL:	9 Balt. 6 Minn. 3 1970	11 Det. 7 Oak. 4 2006	19 NY 10 Balt. 9 1996	14 Tor. 10 Oak. 4 1992	20 NY 8 Bos. 12 2003
	NL:	11 NY 6 Atl. 5 1969	13 Pitt. 8 SF 5 1971 LA 8 Phil. 5 1978	14 SF 7 StL. 7 2002	12 Phil. 7 Atl. 5 1993	25 StL. 11 Hou. 14 2004
Runs Batted In						
	AL:	24 Baltimore 1970	25 Baltimore 1979	33 Minnesota 1987	31 New York 2000	44 New York 2004
	NL:	24 New York 1969	23 Pittsburgh 1971	29 San Francisco 1989	32 Atlanta 1993	43 Atlanta 1996
Runs Batted In, Both Clubs						
	AL:	34 Balt. 24 Minn. 10 1970	39 Balt. 25 Cal. 14 1979	54 Minn. 33 Det. 21 1987	53 Tor. 30 Oak. 23 1992	84 Bos. 40 NY 44 2004
	NL:	39 NY 24 Atl. 15 1969	37 Pitt. 23 SF 14 1971 LA 21 Phil. 16 1978	50 SF 29 Chi. 21 1989	54 Atl. 32 Phil. 22 1993	80 Chi. 41 Fla. 39 2003
Sacrifice Hits						
	AL:	5 Boston 1975	4 Oakland 1990	5 California 1982	5 Chicago 1993	4 KC 1985 Cal. 1986
	NL:	5 Pitt. 1979; StL. 1982	4 San Francisco 1971	8 San Francisco 2002	8 Houston 2005	7 Chicago 2003
Sacrifice Hits, Both Clubs						
	AL:	5 Bos. 5 Oak. 0 1975	5 Oak. 4 Bos. 1 1990	7 Oak. 4 Det. 3 1972 Cal. 5 Mil. 2 1982	6 Chi. 5 Tor. 1 1993	7 Cal. 4 Bos. 3 1986
	NL:	7 StL. 5 Atl. 2 1982	5 SF 4 Pitt. 1 1971 Phil. 3 LA 2 1983	13 SF 8 StL. 5 2002	11 Hou. 8 StL. 3 2005	10 Fla. 3 Chi. 7 2003
Sacrifice Flies						
	AL:	2 Baltimore 1970	3 Baltimore 1979 Oakland 1990	4 Kansas City 1976	4 Toronto 1992	2 KC & Tor. 1985 Bos. & Cal. 1986 Boston 2004
	NL:	3 By many clubs	1 Philadelphia 1978 83 Cincinnati 1995	4 San Diego 1984	4 St. Louis 2005	4 St Louis 1987
Sacrifice Flies, Both Clubs						
	AL:	2 Balt. 2 Minn. 0 1970	5 Balt. 3 Cal. 2 1979 Oak. 3 Bos. 2 1990	5 KC 4 NY 1 1976 Mil. 3 Cal. 2 1982 Tor. 3 Oak. 2 1989	6 Tor. 4 Oak. 2 1992	4 KC 2 Tor. 2 1985
	NL:	5 Cin. 3 Phil. 2 1976	1 Phil. 1 LA 0 1978, 83 Cin. 1 Atl. 0 1995	6 SD 4 Chi. 2 1984	6 StL. 4 Hou. 2 2005	5 StL. 4 SF 1 1987 Pitt. 3 Atl. 2 1992

CHAMPIONSHIP SERIES – CLUB BATTING

		3 Games	4 Games	5 Games	6 Games	7 Games
Walks						
	AL:	13 Balt. 1969 71; NY 81	22 Oakland 1974	23 New York 2001	35 New York 1998	33 New York 2004
	NL:	15 Cincinnati 1976	30 Los Angeles 1974	31 Houston 1980	31 Atlanta 1999	29 Atl. & Pitt. 1992 / St. Louis 2006
Walks, Both Clubs						
	AL:	25 Balt. 13 Minn. 12 1969	33 Det. 19 Oak. 14 2006	41 NY 23 Sea. 18 2001	53 Chi. 32 Tor. 21 1993	61 Bos. 28 NY 33 2004
	NL:	27 Cin. 15 Phil. 12 1976	38 LA 30 Pitt. 8 1974	44 Hou. 31 Phil. 13 1980	53 SD 27 Atl. 26 1998	58 Atl. 29 Pitt. 29 1992
Intentional Walks						
	AL:	2 By many clubs	3 By many clubs	3 Oak. 1973 Minn. 1987 / New York 1999	4 Chi. & Tor. 1993	4 KC 1985 Cal. 1986
	NL:	4 By many clubs	8 Los Angeles 1984	9 Houston 1980	10 Atlanta 1999	5 St. Louis 2006
Hit By Pitch						
	AL:	2 New York 1981	4 Oakland 1990	5 Minnesota 1987	5 Cleveland 1998	7 New York 2004
	NL:	1 By many clubs	3 Philadelphia 1977	3 New York 2000 / San Francisco 2002	4 Atlanta 1999	5 Houston 2004
Hit By Pitch, Both Clubs						
	AL:	2 NY 2 Oak. 0 1981	5 Oak. 3 Balt. 2 1983	8 Minn. 5 Det. 3 1987	7 NY 2 Clev. 5 1998	8 Bos. 1 NY 7 2004
	NL:	1 Atl. 1 NY 0 1969 / Pitt. 1 Cin. 0 1975	3 Pitt. 2 SF 1 1971 / Phil. 3 LA 0 1977	5 SF 3 StL 2 2002	5 Fla. 3 Atl. 2 1997	7 StL 2 Hou. 5 2004
Strikeouts						
	AL:	27 Minnesota 1969	35 Oakland 1988	44 New York 1999	62 Cleveland 1997	60 Boston 2003
	NL:	28 Cincinnati 1975	33 Pittsburgh 1971	42 Cincinnati 1973	57 New York 1986	57 Pittsburgh 1991 / Chicago 2003
Strikeouts, Both Clubs						
	AL:	41 Minn. 27 Balt. 14 1969 / Minn. 22 Balt. 19 1970	58 Oak. 35 Bos. 23 1988	82 NY 44 Bos. 38 1999	109 Clev. 62 Balt. 47 1997	109 NY 49 Bos. 60 2003
	NL:	46 Cin. 28 Pitt. 18 1975	61 Pitt. 33 SF 28 1971	71 Atl. 39 Ari. 32 2001	105 Atl. 54 Phil. 51 1993	104 StL 53 Atl. 51 1996
Stolen Bases						
	AL:	4 Detroit 1984	9 Oakland 1990	13 Oakland 1989	16 Oakland 1992	5 New York 2003
	NL:	11 Cincinnati 1975	5 Los Angeles 1974	7 Philadelphia 1980	14 Atlanta 1999	10 Atlanta 1991
Stolen Bases, Both Clubs						
	AL:	4 NY 2 Oak. 2 1981 / Det. 4 KC 0 1984	10 Oak. 9 Bos. 1 1990	24 Oak. 13 Tor. 11 1989	23 Oak. 16 Tor. 7 1992	7 NY 5 Bos. 2 2003 / Bos. 4 NY 3 2004
	NL:	11 Cin. 11 Pitt. 0 1975	6 LA 5 Pitt. 1 1974 / Cin. 4 Atl. 2 1995	11 Phil. 7 Hou. 4 1980	21 Atl. 14 NY 7 1999	16 Atl. 10 Pitt. 6 1991

Caught Stealing

	3 Games	4 Games	5 Games	6 Games	7 Games
AL:	5 Kansas City 1980	3 By many clubs	5 Kansas City 1976	5 Toronto 1992	5 Boston 2003
NL:	2 By many clubs	3 Los Angeles 1983 Cincinnati 1995	3 Philadelphia 1980 Chicago 1984	6 St. Louis 1985	4 StL. & SF 1987 Atlanta 1991 Houston 2004

Caught Stealing, Both Clubs

	3 Games	4 Games	5 Games	6 Games	7 Games
AL:	5 KC 5 NY 0 1980	6 Oak. 3 Balt. 3 1974	8 KC 5 NY 3 1976	7 Tor. 5 Oak. 2 1992	6 KC 4 Tor. 2 1985 NY 1 Bos. 5 2003
NL:	3 Pitt. 2 Cin. 1 1970	4 Cin. 3 Atl. 1 1995	5 Chi. 3 SD 2 1984	7 StL 6 LA 1 1985	8 SF 4 StL. 4 1987

Grounded into Double Plays

	3 Games	4 Games	5 Games	6 Games	7 Games
AL:	6 Oakland 1981	7 Oakland 2006	6 New York 1996 Boston 1999	10 Baltimore 1997	9 Boston 2003
NL:	3 Atlanta 1982	8 Cincinnati 1995	7 Los Angeles 1981	6 San Diego 1998	8 St. Louis 1987

Grounded into Double Plays, Both Clubs

	3 Games	4 Games	5 Games	6 Games	7 Games
AL:	7 Balt. 4 Minn. 3 1970 Oak. 6 NY 1 1981	10 Oak. 7 Det. 3 2006	7 Det. 5 Oak. 2 1972 Minn. 4 Tor. 3 1991 NY 6 Balt. 1 1996 NY 4 Sea. 3 2001	13 Balt. 10 Clev. 3 1997	13 NY 4 Bos. 9 2003
NL:	4 NY 2 Atl. 2 1969 Cin. 2 Pitt. 2 1975 Pitt. 2 Cin. 2 1979	11 Cin. 8 Atl. 3 1995	11 LA 7 Mtl. 4 1981	10 SD 6 Atl. 4 1998	13 StL. 8 SF 5 1987

Left on Base

	3 Games	4 Games	5 Games	6 Games	7 Games
AL:	30 New York 1981	35 Chicago 1983 Oakland 1990	45 Boston 1999	56 Toronto 1993	69 New York 2004
NL:	31 St. Louis 1982	44 Los Angeles 1974	45 Houston 1980	52 Philadelphia 1993 San Diego 1998	58 Atlanta 1996

Left on Base, Both Clubs

	3 Games	4 Games	5 Games	6 Games	7 Games
AL:	50 Balt. 28 Minn. 22 1969 NY 30 Oak. 20 1981	62 Det. 33 Oak. 29 2006	87 Bos. 45 NY 42 1999	106 Tor. 56 Chi. 50 1993	122 Bos. 53 NY 69 2004
NL:	49 Cin. 25 Pitt. 24 1979	68 LA 44 Pitt. 24 1974	88 Hou. 45 Phil. 43 1980	99 Phil. 52 Atl. 47 1993	105 Pitt. 54 Atl. 51 1991

BATTING

Highest Batting Average, Game
.468   Atlanta NL Oct. 14, 1996
.468   New York AL Oct. 16, 2004

Highest Slugging Percentage, Game
.936   New York AL Oct. 16, 2004
.895   Chicago NL Oct. 2, 1984

Most Plate Appearances, Game
53   New York AL Oct. 16, 2004
52   Atlanta NL Oct. 14, 1996
   Extra-Inning Game:
67   Atlanta NL Oct. 17, 1999 (15 inn)
64   New York AL Oct. 18, 2004 (14 inn)

Most Plate Appearances, Both Clubs, Game
97   NY (53) Bos. (44) AL Oct. 16, 2004
90   Ari. (50) Atl. (40) NL Oct. 20, 2001
   Extra-Inning Game:
126   NY (59) Atl. (67) NL Oct. 17, 1999 (15 inn)
122   NY (64) Bos. (58) AL Oct. 16, 2004 (14 inn)

Most Plate Appearances, Inning
15   Anaheim AL Oct. 13, 2002 (7th)
14   St. Louis NL Oct. 13, 1985 (2nd)

Most At-Bats, Game
47   Atlanta NL Oct. 14, 1996
      New York AL Oct. 16, 2004
   Extra-Inning Game:
56   Houston NL Oct. 15, 1986 (16 inn)
53   New York AL Oct. 18, 2004 (14 inn)

Most At-Bats, Both Clubs, Game
87   NY (47) Bos. (40) AL Oct. 16, 2004
80   Atl. (47) StL. (33) NL Oct. 14, 1996
      Ari. (42) Atl. (38) NL Oct. 20, 2001
   Extra-Inning Game:
110   Hou. (56) NY (54) NL Oct. 15, 1986 (16 inn)
103   NY (53) Bos. (50) AL Oct. 18, 2004 (14 inn)

Most At-Bats, Inning
13   Anaheim AL Oct. 13, 2002 (7th)
12   St. Louis NL Oct. 13, 1985 (2nd)

Most Runs, Game
19   New York AL Oct. 16, 2004
15   Atlanta NL Oct. 17, 1996

Most Runs, Both Clubs, Game
27   NY (19) Bos. (8) AL Oct. 16, 2004
18   Atl. (13) Pitt. (5) NL Oct. 7, 1992
   Extra-Inning Game:
19   Atl. (10) NY (9) NL Oct. 19, 1999 (11 inn)

Most Runs, Inning
10   Anaheim AL Oct. 13, 2002 (7th)
9   St. Louis NL Oct. 13, 1985 (2nd)

Most Earned Runs, Game
19   New York AL Oct. 16, 2004
15   Atlanta NL Oct. 17, 1996

Most Earned Runs, Both Clubs, Game
26   NY (19) Bos. (7) AL Oct. 16, 2004
17   Atl. (13) Pitt. (4) NL Oct. 7, 1992
      Hou. (10) StL. (7) NL Oct. 13, 2004
   Extra-Inning Game:
18   Atl. (10) NY (8) NL Oct. 19, 1999 (11 inn)

Most Earned Runs, Inning
10   Anaheim AL Oct. 13, 2002 (7th)
7   Pittsburgh NL Oct. 13, 1992 (2nd)

Most Innings Scoring, Game
6   New York NL Oct. 5, 1969
      Los Angeles NL Oct. 9, 1974
      Atlanta NL Oct. 14, 1996
      Detroit AL Oct. 2, 1984
      Toronto AL Oct. 10, 1992
      Boston AL Oct. 16, 1999
      New York AL Oct. 16, 2004

Most Innings Scoring, Consecutive, Game
5   New York NL Oct. 5, 1969
      Seattle AL Oct. 20, 2001

Most Innings Scoreless, Consecutive, Series
30   Baltimore AL Oct. 5-9, 1974
26   Atlanta NL Oct. 13-16, 1991

Most Hits, Game
22   Atlanta NL Oct. 14, 1996
      New York AL Oct. 16, 2004

Most Hits, Both Clubs, Game
37   NY (22) Bos. (15) AL Oct. 16, 2004
29   Atl. (22) StL. (7) Oct. 14, 1996

Fewest Hits, Game
1   Oakland AL Oct. 9, 1974
      Seattle AL Oct. 14, 2000
      Pittsburgh NL Oct. 12, 1990
      St. Louis NL Oct. 18, 2004

Most Hits, Inning
10   Anaheim AL Oct. 13, 2002 (7th)
8   St. Louis NL Oct. 13, 1985 (2nd)
      Pittsburgh NL Oct. 13, 1992 (2nd)

Most Total Bases, Game
44   New York AL Oct. 16, 2004
34   Chicago NL Oct. 2, 1984
      Atlanta NL Oct. 14, 1996

Most Total Bases, Both Clubs, Game
70   NY (44) Bos. (26) AL Oct. 16, 2004
50   NY (28) StL. (22) NL Oct. 15, 2006
   Extra-Inning Game:
60   Fla. (32) Chi. (28) NL Oct. 7, 2003 (11 inn)

Fewest Total Bases, Game
1   St. Louis NL Oct. 18, 2004
2   Baltimore AL Oct. 8, 1974
      Oakland AL Oct. 9, 1974
      Kansas City AL Oct. 12, 1985
      Seattle AL Oct. 14, 2000
      Oakland AL Oct. 13, 2006

Most Total Bases, Inning
16   Baltimore AL Oct. 3, 1970 (4th)
      Pittsburgh NL Oct. 13, 1992 (2nd)

Most Extra-Base Hits, Game
13   New York AL Oct. 16, 2004
8   Cincinnati NL Oct. 9, 1976
      Chicago NL Oct. 2, 1984
   Extra-Inning Game:
9   Chicago NL Oct. 7, 2003 (11 inn)

Most Extra-Base Hits, Both Clubs, Game
20   NY (13) Bos. (7) AL Oct. 16, 2004
12   Phil. (7) Atl. (5) NL Oct. 9, 1993
   NL Extra-Inning Game:
17   Fla. (9) Chi. (8) NL Oct. 7, 2003 (11 inn)

Most Extra-Base Hits, Inning
5   New York NL Oct. 15, 2000 (1st)
4   Baltimore AL Oct. 12, 1997 (3rd)
      Seattle AL Oct. 20, 2001 (6th)

Most Singles, Game
15   New York AL Oct. 14, 1981
      Atlanta NL Oct. 14, 1996

Most Singles, Both Clubs, Game
    25 KC (13) NY (12) AL Oct. 4, 1978
    22 Atl. (15) StL. (7) NL Oct. 14, 1996

Most Singles, Inning
    9 Anaheim AL Oct. 13, 2002 (7th)
    8 St. Louis NL Oct. 13, 1985 (2nd)

Most Doubles, Game
    8 New York AL Oct. 16, 2004
    6 Philadelphia NL Oct. 12, 1976
       Atlanta NL Oct. 17, 1999 (15 inn)
       New York NL Oct. 15, 2000

Most Doubles, Both Clubs, Game
    13 NY (8) Bos. (5) AL Oct. 16, 2004
    8 LA (5) StL. (3) NL Oct. 12, 1985
       Phil. (5) Atl. (3) NL Oct. 6, 1993 (10 inn)
       Atl. (5) Phil. (3) NL Oct. 9, 1993
       NY (6) StL (2) NL Oct. 15, 2000

Most Doubles, Inning
    5 New York NL Oct. 15, 2000 (1st)
    3 Oakland AL Oct. 10, 1973 (2nd)
       Boston AL Oct. 4, 1975 (7th)
       Minnesota AL Oct. 8, 1987 (2nd)
       New York AL Oct. 16, 2003 (8th)

Most Triples, Game
    3 Philadelphia NL Oct. 9, 1993
    2 Kansas City AL Oct. 13, 1976
       Kansas City AL Oct. 8, 1977
       Seattle AL Oct. 20, 2001

Most Triples, Both Clubs, Game
    3 LA (2) Phil. (1) NL Oct. 4, 1978
       Phil. (3) Atl. (0) NL Oct. 9, 1993
    2 Balt. (1) Minn. (1) AL Oct. 6, 1969
       KC (1) NY (1) AL Oct. 9, 1976
       KC (2) NY (0) AL Oct. 13, 1976
       KC (2) NY (0) AL Oct. 8, 1977
       Det. (1) KC (1) AL Oct. 2, 1984
       Chi. (1) Tor. (1) AL Oct. 9, 1993
       Sea. (2) NY (0) AL Oct. 20, 2001
    Extra-Inning Game:
    4 Fla. (2) Chi. (2) NL Oct. 7, 2003 (11 inn)

Most Triples, Inning
    2 Kansas City AL Oct. 8, 1977 (3rd)
       Philadelphia NL Oct. 9, 1993 (4th)
       Chicago NL Oct. 7, 2003 (1st)

Most Home Runs, Game
    5 Chicago NL Oct. 2, 1984
    4 Baltimore AL Oct. 4, 1971
       Oakland AL Oct. 7, 1973
       Oakland AL Oct. 9, 1988
       New York AL Oct. 12, 1996
       Cleveland AL Oct. 9, 1998
       Anaheim AL Oct. 13, 2002
       New York AL Oct. 16, 2004
       Boston AL Oct. 20, 2004

Most Home Runs, Both Clubs, Game
    7 Fla. (4) Chi. (3) NL Oct. 7, 2003 (11 inn)
       NY (4) StL. (3) NL Oct. 15, 2006
    6 Balt. (3) NY (3) AL Oct. 13, 1996
       NY (3) Bos. (3) AL Oct. 16, 2003 (11 inn)
       NY (4) Bos. (2) AL Oct. 16, 2004

Most Home Runs, Inning
    3 Baltimore AL Oct. 3, 1970 (4th)
       New York AL Oct. 13, 1996 (3rd)
       Baltimore AL Oct. 12, 1997 (3rd)
       Cleveland AL Oct. 9, 1998 (5th)
       Florida NL Oct. 7, 2003 (3rd)

Most Grand Slam Home Runs, Game
    1 By many clubs (see individual batting)

Most Runs Batted In, Game
    18 New York AL Oct. 16, 2004
    14 Atlanta NL Oct. 7, 1993
        Atlanta NL Oct. 14, 1996
        Atlanta NL Oct. 17, 1996

Most Runs Batted In, Both Clubs, Game
    25 NY (18) Bos. (7) AL Oct. 16, 2004
    17 NY (11) Atl. (6) NL Oct. 5, 1969
        Atl. (13) Pitt. (4) NL Oct. 7, 1992
        Atl. (14) Phil. (3) NL Oct. 7, 1993
        NY (12) StL. (5) NL Oct. 15, 2006
    Extra-Inning Game:
    18 Atl. (9) NY (9) NL Oct. 19, 1999 (11 inn)

Most Runs Batted In, Inning
    9 Anaheim AL Oct. 13, 2002 (7th)
    8 St. Louis NL Oct. 13, 1985 (2nd)
       Florida NL Oct. 14, 2003 (8th)

Most Sacrifice Hits, Game
    3 Pittsburgh NL Oct. 3, 1979 (10 inn)
       Philadelphia NL Oct. 8, 1980 (10 inn)
       Los Angeles NL Oct. 17, 1981
       Atlanta NL Oct. 19, 1999 (11 inn)
       St. Louis NL Oct. 10, 1982
       San Francisco NL Oct. 12, 2002
       Florida NL Oct. 10, 2003 (11 inn)
       St. Louis NL Oct. 21, 2004
       Houston NL Oct. 19, 2005
       California AL Oct. 10, 1982
       California AL Oct. 12, 1986 (11 inn)

Most Sacrifice Hits, Both Clubs, Game
    4 LA (3) Mtl. (1) NL Oct. 17, 1981
       StL. (2) Atl. (2) NL Oct. 9, 1982
       Atl. (2) Phil. (2) NL Oct. 13, 1993
    3 Cal. (3) Mil. (0) AL Oct. 10, 1982
       Bos. (2) Cal. (1) AL Oct. 11, 1986 (11 inn)
       Cal. (3) Bos. (0) AL Oct. 12, 1986 (11 inn)
       Oak. (2) Bos. (1) AL Oct. 6, 1990
       NY (2) Bos. (1) Oct. 17, 2004 (12 inn)
    Extra-Inning Game:
    5 Phil. (3) Hou. (2) NL Oct. 8, 1980 (10 inn)
       Chi. (2) Fla. (3) Oct. 10, 2003 (11 inn)

Most Sacrifice Hits, Inning
    2 Philadelphia NL Oct. 10, 1976 (4th)
    1 By many AL clubs

Most Sacrifice Flies, Game
    3 St. Louis NL Oct. 7, 1982
    2 By many AL clubs

Most Sacrifice Flies, Both Clubs, Game
    3 StL. (3) Atl. (0) NL Oct. 7, 1982
       StL. (2) SF (1) NL Oct. 11, 1987
       NY (2) Atl. (1) NL Oct. 19, 1999 (11 inn)
       Chi. (2) LA (1) AL Oct. 16, 2005

Most Sacrifice Flies, Inning
    2 Milwaukee AL Oct. 8, 1982 (4th)
       Baltimore AL Oct. 7, 1983 (9th)
       Detroit AL Oct. 7, 1987 (8th)
       San Diego NL Oct. 7, 1984 (6th)

Most Walks, Game
    11 Oakland AL Oct. 9, 1974
        New York AL Oct. 11, 1998
        Los Angeles NL Oct. 9, 1974

Most Walks, Both Clubs, Game
    15 NY (10) Sea. (5) AL Oct. 21, 2001
        Bos. (8) NY (7) AL Oct. 17, 2004 (12 inn)
        NY (8) Bos. (7) AL Oct. 18, 2004 (14 inn)
    13 LA (5) StL. (8) NL Oct. 12, 1985
        LA (6) NY (7) NL Oct. 8, 1988
        Pitt. (8) Atl. (5) NL Oct. 7, 1992
    Extra-Inning Game:
    15 Atl. (10) NY (5) NL Oct. 17, 1999 (15 inn)

Most Walks, Inning
4 Oakland AL Oct. 9, 1974 (5th)
   Philadelphia NL Oct. 7, 1977 (2nd)
   St. Louis NL Oct. 12, 1985 (1st)
   San Francisco NL Oct. 9, 1989 (8th)

Most Walks, Consecutive, Inning
4 Oakland AL Oct. 9, 1974 (5th)
   Philadelphia NL Oct. 7, 1977 (2nd)

Most Intentional Walks, Game
5 Houston NL Oct. 10, 1980 (11 inn)
   St. Louis NL Oct. 12, 1985
   Atlanta NL Oct. 17, 1999 (15 inn)
3 New York AL Oct. 17, 1999

Most Intentional Walks, Both Clubs, Game
6 StL. (5) LA (1) NL Oct. 12, 1985
3 NY (3) Bos. (0) AL Oct. 17, 1999
   NY (2) Sea. (1) AL Oct. 17, 2000
   Extra-Inning Game:
7 Hou. (5) Phil. (2) NL Oct. 10, 1980 (11 inn)

Most Intentional Walks, Inning
2 By many clubs

Most Hit By Pitch, Game
3 Minnesota AL Oct. 11, 1987
   Cleveland AL Oct. 9, 1997
   San Francisco NL Oct. 14, 2002
   Extra-Inning Game:
3 Atlanta NL Oct. 19, 1999 (11 inn)

Most Hit By Pitch, Both Clubs, Game
4 Det. (2) Minn. (2) AL Oct. 12, 1987
   NY (2) Clev. (2) AL Oct. 11, 1998
3 Atl. (2) Fla. (1) NL Oct. 7, 1997
   Atl. (3) NY (0) NL Oct. 19, 1999 (11 inn)

Most Hit By Pitch, Inning
3 Cleveland AL Oct. 9, 1997 (1st)
2 Atlanta NL Oct. 19, 1999 (1st)

Most Strikeouts, Game
15 Philadelphia NL Oct. 10, 1993
    Atlanta NL Oct. 12, 1997
    Seattle AL Oct. 14, 2000
    Extra-Inning Game:
21 Cleveland AL Oct. 11, 1997 (12 inn)
19 Atlanta NL Oct. 17, 1999 (15 inn)

Most Strikeouts, Both Clubs, Game
25 Atl. (15) Fla. (10) NL Oct. 12, 1997
22 NY (13) Sea. (9) AL Oct. 10, 2000
    NY (12) Bos. (10) AL Oct. 13, 2003
    Extra-Inning Game:
33 Clev. (21) Balt. (12) AL Oct. 11, 1997 (12 inn)
32 Atl. (19) NY (13) NL Oct. 17, 1999 (15 inn)

Fewest Strikeouts, Game
0 Pittsburgh NL Oct. 6, 1974
1 Baltimore AL Oct. 11, 1973
   New York AL Oct. 13, 1976
   Kansas City AL Oct. 4, 1978
   Toronto AL Oct. 12, 1985
   Boston AL Oct. 10, 1990

Most Strikeouts, Consecutive, Game
6 Oakland AL Oct. 11, 2006
5 Atlanta NL Oct. 6, 1993
   Arizona NL Oct. 20, 2001

Most Stolen Bases, Game
7 Cincinnati NL Oct. 5, 1975
6 Oakland AL Oct. 4, 1989 & Oct. 8, 1992

Most Stolen Bases, Both Clubs, Game
8 Oak. (6) Tor. (2) AL Oct. 4, 1989
   Oak. (6) Tor. (2) AL Oct. 8, 1992
7 Cin. (7) Pitt. (0) NL Oct. 5, 1975
   Extra-Inning Game:
8 Atl. (6) NY (2) NL Oct. 19, 1999 (11 inn)

Most Stolen Bases, Inning
3 Oakland AL Oct. 12, 1972 (2nd)
   Oakland AL Oct. 4, 1989 (7th)
   Oakland AL Oct. 8, 1992 (5th)
   New York NL Oct. 16, 1999 (8th)

Most Caught Stealing, Game
2 By many clubs

Most Caught Stealing, Both Clubs, Game
3 Balt. (2) Oak. (1) AL Oct. 10, 1973
   KC (2) NY (1) AL Oct. 12, 1976
   Mil. (2) Cal. (1) AL Oct. 9, 1982
   Chi. (2) SD (1) NL Oct. 7, 1984
   StL. (2) LA (1) NL Oct. 12, 1985
   SF (2) StL. (1) NL Oct. 7, 1987

Most Caught Stealing, Inning
2 St. Louis NL Oct. 10, 1985 (1st)
   St. Louis NL Oct. 12, 1985 (2nd)
1 By many AL clubs

Most Grounded into Double Plays, Game
4 Oakland AL Oct. 10, 2006
3 By many NL clubs
   Extra Innings:
5 Cincinnati NL Oct. 10, 1995 (11 inn)

Most Grounded into Double Plays, Both Clubs, Game
4 By many AL & NL clubs
   Extra Innings:
5 Cin. (5) Atl. (0) NL Oct. 10, 1995 (11 inn)

Most Left on Base, Game
15 Philadelphia NL Oct. 10, 1993
    New York AL Oct. 15, 2000
    Extra-Inning Game:
19 Atlanta NL Oct. 17, 1999 (15 inn)
18 New York AL Oct. 18, 2004 (14 inn)

Most Left on Base, Both Clubs, Game
26 Phil. (15) Atl. (11) NL Oct. 10, 1993
25 Chi. (13) Tor. (12) AL Oct. 5, 1993
    Tor. (14) Oak. (11) AL Oct. 11, 1992 (11 in)
    Extra-Inning Game:
31 Atl. (19) NY (12) Oct. 17, 1999 (15 inn)
30 NY (18) Bos. (12) Oct. 18, 2004 (14 inn)

Fewest Left on Base, Game
0 Atlanta NL:Oct. 16, 1999
1 Baltimore AL Oct. 11, 1996
   Los Angeles AL Oct. 14, 2005

PITCHING

Most Wild Pitches, Game
3 California AL Oct. 9, 1982
   Oakland AL Oct. 10, 1992
   Toronto AL Oct. 5, 1993
   Oakland AL Oct. 14, 2006
   St. Louis NL Oct. 19, 2005

Most Wild Pitches, Both Clubs, Game
4 Oak. (3) Det. (1) AL Oct. 14, 2006
3 StL. (2) NY (1) NL Oct. 12, 2000
   StL. (3) Hou. (0) NL Oct. 19, 2005

Most Wild Pitches, Inning
2 Detroit AL Oct. 8, 1972 (5th)
   California AL Oct. 9, 1982 (4th)
   Toronto AL Oct. 5, 1993 (1st)
   New York AL Oct. 17, 2001 (9th)
   Boston AL Oct. 15, 2003 (7th)
   San Diego NL Oct. 14, 1998 (2nd)
   St. Louis NL Oct. 12, 2000 (1st)

CLUB FIELDING

	3 Games	4 Games	5 Games	6 Games	7 Games
Highest Percentage (1,000 Most Chances)					
AL:	1.000 (110) Baltimore 1970	.993 Oakland 1990	.995 New York 1996	.9953 New York 2000	.996 Boston 2004
NL:	1.000 (124) Pittsburgh 1979	.993 Los Angeles 1983	.995 San Francisco 2002	.9964 New York 1986	.996 St. Louis 2004
Highest Percentage, Both Clubs					
AL:	.995 Oak. 1.000 Balt. .991 1971	.987 Det. .993 Oak. .980 2006	.987 NY .995 Balt. .980 1996	.990 NY .995 Sea. .986 2000	.991 Bos. .997 NY .986 2004
NL:	.996 Pitt. 1.000 Cin. .992 1979	.996 LA .993 Phil. .966 1983	.994 SF .995 StL .994 2002	.985 NY .996 Hou. .973 1986	.994 StL .996 Hou. .992 2004
Total Chances					
AL:	133 Minnesota 1969	166 Baltimore 1979	204 Chicago 2005	249 Cleveland 1998	287 New York 2004
NL:	127 Cincinnati 1979	174 Atlanta 1995	225 Philadelphia 1980	284 New York 1986	284 Chicago 2003
Total Chances, Both Clubs					
AL:	261 Minn. 133 Balt. 128 1969	323 Balt. 162 Chi. 161 1983	395 Oak. 201 Det. 194 1972	479 Clev. 240 Balt. 239 1997	561 NY 287 Bos. 274 2004
NL:	244 Cin. 124 Pitt. 120 1970	330 Atl. 174 Cin. 156 1995	427 Phil. 225 Hou. 202 1980	545 NY 284 Hou. 261 1986	555 Fla. 271 Chi. 284 2003
Chances Accepted					
AL:	128 Minnesota 1969	161 Baltimore 1979	201 Chicago 2005	242 Cleveland 1998	283 New York 2004
NL:	126 Cincinnati 1979	171 Atlanta 1995	219 Philadelphia 1980	283 New York 1986	280 Chicago 2003
Chances Accepted, Both Clubs					
AL:	255 Minn. 128 Balt. 127 1969	318 Balt. 160 Chi. 158 1983	385 Oak. 198 Det. 187 1972	469 Clev. 235 Balt. 234 1997	556 NY 283 Bos. 273 2004
NL:	241 Cin. 123 Pitt. 118 1970	325 Atl. 171 Cin. 154 1995	418 Phil. 219 Hou. 199 1980	537 NY 283 Hou. 254 1986	548 Fla. 268 Chi. 280 2003
Putouts					
AL:	96 Baltimore 1969	111 Baltimore 1983	141 New York 1996	174 Baltimore 1997 / Cleveland 1997	209 New York 2004
NL:	90 Pittsburgh 1979 / Atlanta 1982	117 Atlanta 1995	148 Philadelphia 1980	189 New York 1986	198 Chicago & Florida 2003
Putouts, Both Clubs					
AL:	190 Balt. 96 Minn. 94 1969	219 Balt. 111 Chi. 108 1983	279 NY 141 Balt. 138 1996	348 Balt. 174 Clev. 174 1997	416 NY 209 Bos. 207 2004
NL:	177 Pitt. 90 Cin. 87 1979	228 Atl. 117 Cin. 111 1995	295 Phil. 148 Hou. 147 1980	377 NY 189 Hou. 188 1986	396 Fla. 198 Chi. 198 2003
Assists					
AL:	41 New York 1980	52 Baltimore 1979	66 Chicago 2005	77 Cleveland 1998	87 Kansas City 1985
NL:	39 Cincinnati 1979 / Atlanta 1982	54 Atlanta 1995	71 Philadelphia 1980	94 New York 1986	82 Chicago 2003
Assists, Both Clubs					
AL:	73 Oak. 40 Bos. 33 1975	100 Chi. 51 Balt. 49 1983	113 Chi. 66 LA 47 2005	131 Clev. 77 NY 54 1998	151 Cal. 78 Bos. 73 1986
NL:	76 Cin. 39 Pitt. 37 1970	97 Atl. 54 Cin. 43 1995	123 Phil. 71 Hou. 52 1980	160 NY 94 Hou. 66 1986	152 Fla. 70 Chi. 82 2003

CHAMPIONSHIP SERIES – CLUB FIELDING

	3 Games	4 Games	5 Games	6 Games	7 Games
Errors					
AL:	7 Kansas City 1984	5 Baltimore 1979 Boston 1990	10 Boston 1999	8 Toronto 1992	8 California 1986
NL:	6 Atlanta 1969	7 Los Angeles 1974	7 St. Louis 2000 Atlanta 2001	8 Atlanta 1998 New York 1999	8 New York 1988
Errors, Both Clubs					
AL:	10 Oak. 6 Bos. 4 1975	7 Balt. 5 Cal. 2 1979	15 Bos. 10 NY 5 1999	15 Tor. 8 Oak. 7 1992	15 Cal. 8 Bos. 7 1986
NL:	8 Atl. 6 NY 2 1969	11 LA 7 Pitt. 4 1974	11 StL. 7 NY 4 2000	15 NY 8 Atl. 7 1999	13 NY 8 LA 5 1988
Passed Balls					
AL:	1 New York 1981	1 By many clubs	2 Toronto 1991 Chicago 2005	3 Toronto 1992	3 Boston 2003-04
NL:	2 Pittsburgh 1975	1 By many clubs	2 Chicago 1989	2 Houston 1986 Philadelphia 1993	2 Pittsburgh 1992 Chicago 2003
Passed Balls, Both Clubs					
AL:	1 By many clubs	2 NY 1 KC 1 1978 Bos. 1 Oak. 1 1988	2 Tor. 1 Oak. 1 1989 Tor. 2 Minn. 0 1991 Chi. 2 LA 0 2005	3 Tor. 3 Oak. 0 1992	4 Bos. 3 NY 1 2004
NL:	2 NY 1 Atl. 1 1969 Pitt. 2 Cin. 0 1975 Pitt. 2 Atl. 1 1992	2 Pitt. 1 SF 1 1971	3 Chi. 2 SF 1 1989	2 Hou. 2 NY 0 1986 Phil. 2 Atl. 0 1993	3 Pitt. 2 Atl. 1 1992
Double Plays					
AL:	6 New York 1981	7 California 1979 Detroit 2006	7 Baltimore 1996 New York 1999	11 Cleveland 1997	12 New York 2003
NL:	4 Atlanta 1969	8 Los Angeles 1974 Atlanta 1995	8 Montreal 1981	9 New York 1999	10 San Francisco 1987 New York 2006
Double Plays, Both Clubs					
AL:	8 Minn. 5 Balt. 3 1970	12 Cal. 7 Balt. 5 1979	9 Oak. 5 Det. 4 1972 Balt. 6 Cal. 3 1982 Tor. 5 Oak. 4 1989 Balt. 7 NY 2 1996 Sea. 5 NY 4 2001 LA 5 Chi. 4 2005	15 Clev. 11 Balt. 4 1997	17 NY 12 Bos. 5 2003
NL:	6 Atl. 4 NY 2 1969 Cin. 3 Phil. 3 1976	12 Atl. 8 Cin. 4 1995	13 Pitt. 8 LA 5 1981	13 NY 9 Atl. 4 1999	15 SF 10 StL. 5 1987

IELDING

Most Total Chances, Game
48 Atlanta NL Oct. 4, 1969
   Los Angeles NL Oct. 5, 1978
46 Boston AL Oct. 7, 1975
   Extra-Inning Game:
79 New York NL Oct. 15, 1986 (16 inn)
57 New York AL Oct. 18, 2004 (14 inn)

Most Total Chances, Inning
10 New York AL Oct. 10, 1976 (7th)
   Houston NL Oct. 17, 2005 (7th)

Most Chances Accepted, Game
48 Los Angeles NL Oct. 5, 1978
45 Boston AL Oct. 7, 1975
   Extra-Inning Game:
79 New York NL Oct. 15, 1986 (16 inn)
56 New York AL Oct. 18, 2004 (14 inn)

Most Chances Accepted, Inning
8 New York AL Oct. 10, 1976 (7th)
   Los Angeles NL Oct. 7, 1978 (5th)
   Los Angeles NL Oct. 9, 1985 (4th)
   San Francisco NL Oct. 14, 1987 (1st)
   Atlanta NL Oct. 13, 1992 (2nd)
   New York NL Oct. 13, 1999 (2nd)
   Houston NL Oct. 17, 2005 (7th)
   New York NL Oct. 13, 2006 (9th)

Most Assists, Game
21 Los Angeles NL Oct. 5, 1978
   Atlanta NL Oct. 3, 1995
19 Boston AL Oct. 9, 2003
   Extra-Inning Game:
31 New York NL Oct. 15, 1986 (16 inn)

Most Assists, Both Clubs, Game
33 Bos. (18) Oak. (15) AL Oct. 7, 1975
30 LA (21) Phil. (9) NL Oct. 5, 1978
   Extra-Inning Game:
56 NY (31) Hou. (25) NL Oct. 15, 1986 (16 inn)

Most Assists, Inning
5 New York AL Oct. 10, 1976 (7th)
   Los Angeles NL Oct. 7, 1978 (5th)
   Los Angeles NL Oct. 9, 1985 (4th)
   San Francisco NL Oct. 14, 1987 (1st)
   Atlanta NL Oct. 13, 1992 (2nd)
   New York NL Oct. 13, 1999 (2nd)
   Houston NL Oct. 17, 2005 (7th)
   New York NL Oct. 13, 2006 (9th)

Most Errors, Game
5 Los Angeles NL Oct. 8, 1974
   New York AL Oct. 10, 1976

Most Errors, Both Clubs, Game
7 Oak. (4) Bos. (3) AL Oct. 4, 1975
5 LA (5) Pitt. (0) NL Oct. 8, 1974

Most Errors, Inning
3 Oakland AL Oct. 4, 1975 (1st)
   California AL Oct. 8, 1986 (7th)
   Atlanta NL Oct. 20, 2001 (3rd)

Most Double Plays, Game
4 Oakland AL Oct. 5, 1975
   Detroit AL Oct. 10, 2006
   Los Angeles NL Oct. 13, 1981
   San Francisco NL Oct. 10, 1987
   Extra Innings:
5 Atlanta NL Oct. 13, 1995 (11 inn)

Most Double Plays, Both Clubs, Game
6 Oak. (4) Bos. (2) AL Oct. 5, 1975
5 Pitt. (3) Cin. (2) NL Oct. 5, 1975
   Extra-Inning Game:
6 Atl. (5) Cin. (1) Oct. 10, 1995 (11 inn)

Most Passed Balls, Game
2 Pittsburgh NL Oct. 4, 1975
   Houston NL Oct. 11, 1986
   Pittsburgh NL Oct. 13, 1992
   Toronto AL Oct. 13, 1991
   Toronto AL Oct. 14, 1992
   Extra-Inning Game:
3 Boston AL Oct. 18, 2004 (14 inn)

Most Passed Balls, Both Clubs, Game
2 NY (1) Atl. (1) NL Oct. 4, 1969
   Pitt. (1) LA (1) NL Oct. 8, 1974
   Pitt. (2) Cin. (0) NL Oct. 4, 1975
   Hou. (2) NY (0) NL Oct. 11, 1986
   Pitt. (2) Atl. (0) NL Oct. 13, 1992
   Tor. (2) Minn. (0) AL Oct. 13, 1991
   Tor. (2) Oak. (0) AL Oct. 14, 1992
   Extra-Inning Game:
3 Bos. (3) NY (0) AL Oct. 18, 2004 (14 inn)

Most Passed Balls, Inning
3 Boston AL Oct. 18, 2004 (13th)
1 By many NL clubs

CLUB PITCHING

	3 Games	4 Games	5 Games	6 Games	7 Games
Earned Run Average, Lowest					
AL:	1.13 Baltimore 1969	0.49 Baltimore 1983	1.76 Oakland 1972	1.64 Cleveland 1995	3.16 Kansas City 1985
NL:	0.96 Cincinnati 1970	1.03 Philadelphia 1983	1.33 New York 1973	2.29 New York 1986	1.57 Atlanta 1991
Earned Run Average, Lowest, Both Clubs					
AL:	2.37 Det 1.24 KC 3.54 1984	1.77 Oak. 1.75 Balt. 1.80 1974	1.95 Oak. 1.76 Det. 2.14 1972	2.47 Clev. 1.64 Sea. 3.33 1995	3.47 Bos. 3.58 Cal. 3.49 1986
NL:	1.80 Cin. 0.96 Pitt. 2.67 1970	2.47 Phil. 1.03 LA 3.97 1983	2.35 LA 1.84 Mtl. 2.86 1981	2.58 NY 2.29 Hou. 2.87 1986	2.07 Atl. 1.57 Pitt. 2.57 1991
Earned Run Average, Highest					
AL:	7.62 Minnesota 1970	5.80 California 1979	6.70 Detroit 1987	5.37 Seattle 2000	5.87 Boston 2004
NL:	6.92 Atlanta 1969	6.09 San Francisco 1971	5.86 St. Louis 2000	4.75 Philadelphia 1993	6.60 St. Louis 1996
Earned Run Average, Highest, Both Clubs					
AL:	5.43 Minn. 7.62 Balt. 3.33 1970	4.38 Cal. 5.80 Balt. 2.97 1979	5.59 Det. 6.70 Minn. 4.50 1987	4.20 NY 3.06 Sea. 5.37 2000	5.52 NY 5.17 Bos. 5.87 2004
NL:	5.94 Atl. 6.92 NY 5.00 1969	4.70 SF 6.09 Pitt. 3.34 1971	4.81 Chi. 5.57 SF 4.09 1989	3.95 Phil. 4.75 Atl. 3.15 1993	4.98 Fla. 5.59 Chi. 4.36 2003
Complete Games					
AL:	2 Baltimore 1969-71	2 Oakland 1974	4 Chicago AL 2005	1 By many clubs	1 Kansas City 1985 Bos. & Cal. 1986
NL:	1 By many clubs	2 By many clubs Florida 1997	3 New York 1973	2 Houston 1986 Florida 1997	3 Pittsburgh 1992
Complete Games, Both Clubs					
AL:	3 Balt. 2 Oak. 1 1971	3 Balt. 2 Oak. 1 1974	4 Balt. 2 Oak. 2 1973 Chi. 4 LA 0 2005	2 Tor. 1 Oak. 1 1992	2 Cal. 1 Bos. 1 1986
NL:	1 Cin. 1 Pitt. 0 1975 Pitt. 1 Cin. 0 1977 StL. 1 Atl. 0 1982	2 SF 2 Pitt. 0 1971 LA 2 Phil. 0 1977 LA 1 Phil. 1 1978	3 NY 3 Cin. 0 1973 Fla. 2 Atl. 1 1997	3 Hou. 2 NY 1 1986 Fla. 2 Atl. 1 1997	4 SF 3 StL. 2 1987
Saves					
AL:	2 Boston 1975	4 Oakland 1988	3 Mil. 1982; Minn. 1987 & 1991 Oakland 1989; New York 1999	3 Toronto 1992	3 Boston 2003
NL:	3 Cincinnati 1970	3 Pittsburgh 1971	3 San Francisco 1989, 2002	4 Cincinnati 1990	3 St. Louis 1987, 2004 Los Angeles 1988 Atlanta 1991
Saves, Both Clubs					
AL:	2 Bos. 2 Oak. 0 1975	4 Oak. 4 Bos. 0 1988	4 Minn. 3 Tor. 1 1991	4 Tor. 3 Oak. 1 1992	5 NY 2 Bos. 3 2003
NL:	3 Cin. 3 Pitt. 0 1970	3 Pitt. 3 SF 0 1971	4 SF 3 StL. 1 2002	6 Cin. 4 Pitt. 2 1990	5 Atl. 3 Pitt. 2 1991 StL. 3 Hou. 2 2004
Shutouts					
AL:	1 Balt. 1969; NY 1981; Det. 1984	2 Oak. 1974; Balt. 1983	1 By many clubs	2 Cleveland 1995	5 Kansas City 1985
NL:	1 Cin. 1970; StL. 1982	1 LA 1974 78; Phil. 1983	1 By many clubs	2 San Diego 1998	3 Atlanta 1991, 1997

CLUB PITCHING

	3 Games	4 Games	5 Games	6 Games	7 Games
Shutouts, Both Clubs					
AL:	1 Balt. 1 Minn. 0 1969 Oak. 0 1981 Det. 1 KC 0 1984	2 Oak. 2 Balt. 0 1974 Balt. 2 Chi. 0 1983	2 Oak. 1 Det. 1 1972 Oak. 1 Balt. 1 1973	2 Clev. 2 Sea. 0 1995 Balt. 1 Clev. 1 1997 NY 1 Sea. 1 2000	1 KC 1 Tor. 0 1985
NL:	1 Cin. 1 Pitt. 0 1970 StL. 1 Atl. 0 1982	2 LA 1 Pitt. 1 1974 Hou. 1 Phil. 0 1980	1 By many clubs	2 SD 2 Atl. 0 1998	4 Atl. 3 Pitt. 1 1991
Total Batters Faced					
AL:	138 Minnesota 1969	159 Oakland 2006	205 Baltimore 1996	243 Cleveland 1997	321 Boston 2004
NL:	126 Cincinnati 1979	169 Pitt. 1974 Phil. 1993	212 Philadelphia 1980	249 New York 1999	291 Chicago 2003
Total Batters Faced, Both Clubs					
AL:	261 Minn. 138 Balt. 123 1969	305 Oak. 159 Det. 146 2006	399 Balt. 205 NY 194 1996	479 Clev. 243 Balt. 236 1997	624 Bos. 321 NY 303 2004
NL:	246 Cin. 126 Pitt. 120 1979	316 Cin. 166 Atl. 150 1995	422 Phil. 212 Hou. 210 1980	493 NY 249 Atl. 244 1999	576 Fla. 285 Chi. 291 2003
Innings					
AL:	32.0 Baltimore 1969	37.0 Baltimore 1983	47.0 New York 1996	58.0 Baltimore 1997 Cleveland 1997	69.2 New York 2004
NL:	30.0 Pittsburgh 1979	39.0 Atlanta 1995	49.1 Philadelphia 1980	63.0 New York 1986	66.0 Chicago & Florida 2003
Innings, Both Clubs					
AL:	63.1 Balt. 32.0 Minn. 31.1 1969	73.0 Balt. 37.0 Chi. 36.0 1983	93.0 NY 47.0 Balt. 46.0 1996	116.0 Balt. 58 Clev. 58 1997	138.2 NY 69.2 Bos. 69.0 2004
NL:	59.0 Pitt. 30.0 Cin. 29.0 1979	76.0 Atl. 39.0 Cin. 37.0 1995	98.1 Phil. 49.1 Hou. 49.0 1980	125.2 NY 63.0 Hou. 62.2 1986	132.0 Chi. 66.0 Fla. 66.0 2003
Earned Runs, Most					
AL:	22 Minnesota 1970	23 California 1979	32 Detroit 1987	31 Seattle 2000	45 Boston 2004
NL:	20 Atlanta 1969	23 San Francisco 1971	28 St. Louis 2000	29 Philadelphia 1993	44 St. Louis 1996
Earned Runs, Most, Both Clubs					
AL:	32 Minn. 22 Balt. 10 1970	35 Cal. 23 Balt. 12 1979	44 NY 23 KC 21 1976	49 Sea. 31 NY 18 2000	85 Bos. 45 NY 40 2004
NL:	35 Atl. 20 NY 15 1969	36 SF 23 Pitt. 13 1971	46 Chi. 26 SF 20 1989 StL. 28 NY 18 2000	48 Phil. 29 Atl. 19 1993	73 Fla. 41 Chi. 32 2003
Earned Runs, Fewest					
AL:	4 Balt. 1969; NY 1981; Det. 1984	2 Baltimore 1983	9 Oakland 1972	10 Cleveland 1995	22 Kansas City 1985
NL:	3 Cincinnati 1970	4 Philadelphia 1983	7 New York 1973	14 Cincinnati 1990	11 Atlanta 1991
Earned Runs, Fewest, Both Clubs					
AL:	15 Det. 4 KC 11 1984	14 Oak. 7 Balt. 7 1974	20 Oak. 9 Det. 11 1972	30 Clev. 10 Sea. 20 1995	48 KC 22 Tor. 26 1985
NL:	11 Cin. 3 Pitt. 8 1970	19 Phil. 4 LA 15 1983	23 LA 9 Mtl. 14 1981	33 Cin. 14 Pitt. 19 1990 Hou. 16 StL. 17 2005	29 Atl. 11 Pitt. 18 1991

CLUB PITCHING

	3 Games	4 Games	5 Games	6 Games	7 Games
Wild Pitches					
AL:	2 By many clubs	3 California 1979 Oakland 2006	4 Minnesota 1991 Anaheim 2002	5 Toronto 1993	3 Kansas City 1985 New York 2003-04
NL:	2 By many clubs	4 Los Angeles 1983	5 St. Louis 2000	4 San Diego 1998 St. Louis 2005	4 Atlanta 1996 Florida 2003 New York 2006
Wild Pitches, Both Clubs					
AL:	3 Balt. 2 Minn. 1 1969	5 Oak. 3 Det. 2 2006	7 Ana. 4 Minn. 3 2002	7 Tor. 5 Chi. 2 1993	4 KC 3 Tor. 1 1985 NY 3 Bos. 1 2004
NL:	4 Cin. 2 Phil. 2 1976 Atl. 2 StL. 2 1982	6 LA 4 Phil. 2 1983	7 StL. 5 NY 2 2000	4 LA 2 StL. 2 1985 SD 4 Atl. 0 1998 StL 4 Hou. 0 2005	7 Fla. 4 Chi. 3 2003
Balks					
AL:	1 Kansas City 1980	2 Baltimore 1983	1 See individuals	1 Toronto 1993	1 California 1986 Boston 2004
NL:	2 Pittsburgh 1975	1 See individuals	1 See individuals	1 Atlanta 1998	2 New York 1988
Balks, Both Clubs					
AL:	1 KC 1 NY 0 1980	2 Balt. 2 Chi. 0 1983 Bos. 1 Oak. 1 1988	1 Det. 1 Oak. 0 1972 KC 1 NY 0 1977 NY 1 Balt. 0 1996	1 Tor. 1 Chi. 0 1993	1 Cal. 1 Bos. 0 1986 Bos. 1 NY 0 2004
NL:	2 Pitt. 2 Cin. 0 1975	2 LA 1 Phil. 1 1977	1 Chi. 1 SF 0 1989	1 Atl. 1 SD 0 1998	2 NY 2 LA 0 1988

CLUB MISCELLANEOUS

	3 Games	4 Games	5 Games	6 Games	7 Games
Players					
AL:	24 Minnesota 1970 Oakland 1981	23 California 1979 Chicago 1983 Boston 1990 Detroit 2006	25 Oakland 1972 Seattle 2001 Los Angeles 2005	25 Oakland 1992 Cleveland 1995, 98 Seattle 1995, 2000	25 Boston 2004
NL:	24 Pittsburgh 1975	24 Cincinnati 1995	25 St. Louis 2000	25 Los Angeles 1985 Atlanta 1993 New York & Atlanta 1999	25 Pittsburgh 1991-92 Atlanta 1992 St. Louis 1996, 2004, 06 Florida 2003
Players, Both Clubs					
AL:	46 Oak. 24 NY 22 1981	45 Chi. 23 Balt. 22 1983	49 Oak. 25 Det. 24 1972	50 Clev. 25 Sea. 25 1995	48 Bos. 25 NY 23 2004
NL:	42 Pitt. 24 Cin. 18 1975	46 Cin. 24 Atl. 22 1995	49 StL. 25 NY 24 2000	50 Atl. (25) NY (25) 1999	50 Pitt. 25 Atl. 25 1992

CLUB MISCELLANEOUS

Pitchers

	3 Games	4 Games	5 Games	6 Games	7 Games
AL:	9 Minnesota 1969-70	10 Boston 1990 Detroit 2006	11 Seattle 2001 Minnesota 2002	11 Oakland 1992 Cleveland 1997-98	11 Boston 2004 New York 2004
NL:	10 Pittsburgh 1975	9 San Francisco 1971 Los Angeles 1977, 78 Cincinnati 1995	11 Atlanta 2001	11 New York 1999	11 Pittsburgh 1991 Florida 2003 St. Louis 2004, 06 New York 2006

Pitchers, Both Clubs

	3 Games	4 Games	5 Games	6 Games	7 Games
AL:	16 Minn. 9 Balt. 7 1969	19 Det. 10 Oak. 9 2006	20 NY 10 Bos. 10 1999 Sea. 11 NY 9 2001 Ana. 11 Minn. 9 2002	20 Oak. 11 Tor. 9 1992 Clev. 10 Sea. 10 1995 Clev. 11 Balt. 9 1997 Clev. 11 NY 9 1998 NY 10 Sea. 10 2000	22 Bos. 11 NY 11 2004
NL:	17 Pitt. 10 Cin. 7 1975 Cin. 9 Pitt. 8 1979	17 LA 9 Phil. 8 1978 Cin. 9 Atl. 8 1995	20 NY 10 StL. 10 2000 Atl. 11 Ari. 9 2001 SF 10 StL. 10 2002	20 NY 11 Atl. 9 1999	22 StL. 11 NY 11 2006

Pinch-Hitters

	3 Games	4 Games	5 Games	6 Games	7 Games
AL:	10 Minnesota 1970	8 Baltimore 1983	14 Oakland 1972	10 Seattle 1995	13 Toronto 1985
NL:	9 Pittsburgh 1975	13 Cincinnati 1995	18 St. Louis 2000	20 New York 1999	17 St. Louis 2006

Pinch-Hitters, Both Clubs

	3 Games	4 Games	5 Games	6 Games	7 Games
AL:	13 Oak. 8 NY 5 1981	13 Balt. 8 Chi. 5 1983	22 Oak. 14 Det. 8 1972	14 Balt. 8 Clev. 6 1997	21 Tor. 13 KC 8 1985
NL:	12 Pitt. 9 Cin. 3 1975	21 Cin. 13 Atl. 8 1995	28 StL. 18 NY 10 2000	32 NY 20 Atl. 12 1999	28 StL. 17 NY 11 2006

Pinch-Runners

	3 Games	4 Games	5 Games	6 Games	7 Games
AL:	4 Kansas City 1984	5 Oakland 1974 1990	5 Anaheim 2002	4 Oakland 1992 Cleveland 1995; New York 2000	4 Boston 2003-04
NL:	3 New York 1969	1 By many clubs	4 Houston 1980 New York 2000	5 Atlanta 1998	2 SF 1987; NY 1988 LA 1988; Atl. 1996

Pinch-Runners, Both Clubs

	3 Games	4 Games	5 Games	6 Games	7 Games
AL:	5 KC 4 Det. 1 1984	8 Oak. 5 Balt. 3 1974	6 NY 3 Bos. 3 1999	7 Oak. 4 Tor. 3 1992	7 Bos. 4 NY 3 2003
NL:	3 NY 3 Atl. 0 1969 Pitt. 2 Cin. 1 1970	2 LA 1 Pitt. 1 1974 Atl. 1 Cin. 1 1995	7 Hou. 4 Phil. 3 1980 NY 4 StL. 3 2000	5 Atl. 5 SD 0 1998	4 LA 2 NY 2 1988

Extra-Inning Games

	3 Games	4 Games	5 Games	6 Games	7 Games
AL:	2 Balt. & Minn. 1969	1 Balt. & Chi. 1983	2 Det. & Oak. 1972	2 Balt. & Clev. 1997	2 Bos. & Cal. 1986 Bos. & NY 2004
NL:	2 Cin. & Pitt. 1979	2 Atl. & Cin. 1995	4 Hou. & Phil. 1980	2 NY & Hou. 1986 Atl. & Phil. 1993 Atl. & NY 1999	2 Florida & Chicago 2003

PERSONNEL

Most Players, Game
21 St. Louis NL Oct. 16, 2000
20 Oakland AL Oct. 10, 1972
      Oakland AL Oct. 11, 1972 (10 inn)
      Extra-Inning Game:
23 New York NL Oct. 17, 1999 (15 inn)

Most Players, Both Clubs, Game
39 SD (20) Atl. (19) NL Oct. 12, 1998
37 Balt. (19) Clev. (18) AL Oct. 11, 1997 (12 inn)
      Minn. (19) Ana. (18) AL Oct. 13, 2002
      Extra-Inning Game:
45 NY (23) Atl. (22) NL Oct. 17, 1999 (15 inn)

Most Pitchers, Game
7 Minnesota AL Oct. 6, 1969
    Cleveland AL Oct. 11, 1997 (12 inn)
    Cleveland AL Oct. 7 1998 (12 inn)
    Boston AL Oct. 12, 2004
    New York AL Oct. 18, 2004 (14 inn)
    Boston AL Oct. 18, 2004 (14 inn)
    San Francisco NL Oct. 14, 1987
    Pittsburgh NL Oct. 7, 1992
    Atlanta NL Oct. 19, 2001
    New York NL Oct. 13, 2006
    Extra-Inning Game:
9 New York NL Oct. 17, 1999 (15 inn)

Most Pitchers, Both Clubs, Game
13 NY (7) StL. (6) NL Oct. 13, 2006
11 Balt. (6) NY(5) AL Oct. 12, 1996
      Clev. (6) Balt. (5) AL Oct. 12, 1997
      Minn. (6) Ana. (5) AL Oct. 13, 2002
      Bos. (6) NY (5) AL Oct. 15, 2003
      Bos. (7) NY (4) AL Oct. 12, 2004
      Extra-Inning Game:
15 NY (9) Atl. (6) NL Oct. 17, 1999 (15 inn)
14 NY (7) Bos. (7) AL Oct. 18, 2004 (14 inn)

Most Pitchers, Inning
5 Kansas City AL Oct. 12, 1976 (6th)
    New York AL Oct. 18, 1999 (8th)
    Minnesota AL Oct. 12, 2002 (8th)
4 Los Angeles NL Oct. 8, 1988 (8th)
    St. Louis NL Oct. 13, 1996 (6th)
    New York NL Oct. 17, 1999 (7th)

Most Pinch-Hitters, Game
6 Oakland AL Oct. 10, 1972
    Los Angeles NL Oct. 9, 1988 (12 inn)
    Atlanta NL Oct. 19, 1999 (11 inn)
    St. Louis NL Oct. 15, 2006

Most Pinch-Hitters, Both Clubs, Game
7 Oak. (6) Det. (1) AL Oct. 10, 1972
    Chi. (4) SF (3) NL Oct. 4, 1989
    StL. (6) NY (1) NL Oct. 15, 2006
    Extra-Inning Game:
11 Atl. (6) NY (5) NL Oct. 19, 1999 (11 inn)

Most Pinch-Hitters, Inning
4 Philadelphia NL Oct. 5, 1983 (9th)
    Atlanta NL Oct. 7, 1998 (8th)
    Baltimore AL Oct. 7, 1983 (9th)

Most Pinch-Runners, Game
2 By many clubs
    Extra-Inning Game:
3 Kansas City AL Oct. 3, 1984 (11 inn)

Most Pinch-Runners, Both Clubs, Game
3 Phil. (2) Hou. (1) NL Oct. 12, 1980 (10 inn)
Atl. (2) NY (1) NL Oct. 17, 1999 (15 inn)
NY (2) StL. (1) NL Oct. 11, 2000
By many AL clubs
Extra-Inning Game:
4 Bos. (2) Cal. (2) AL Oct. 12, 1986 (11 inn)

Most Pinch-Runners, Inning
2 Oakland AL Oct. 7, 1972 (11th)
Baltimore AL Oct. 9, 1974 (9th)
Boston AL Oct. 14, 1999 (8th)
New York AL Oct. 13, 2000 (9th)
Anaheim AL Oct. 13, 2002 (7th)
Boston AL Oct. 18, 2004 (8th)
New York NL Oct. 11, 2000 (9th)

NNINGS – TIME

Most Innings, Game
NL: 16 NY 7 at Hou. 6 Oct. 15, 1986
AL: 14 NY 4 at Bos. 5 Oct. 18, 2004

Longest Game, Time
AL: 4:20 NY at Bos. Oct. 16, 2004
NL: 3:59 NY at StL. Oct. 12, 2000
Extra-Inning Game:
AL: 5:49 NY at Bos. Oct. 18, 2004 (14 inn)
NL: 5:46 Atl. at NY Oct. 17, 1999 (15 inn)

Shortest Game, Time
AL: 1:57 Oak. at Balt. Oct. 8, 1974
NL: 1:57 Cin. at Pitt. Oct. 7, 1972

AMERICAN LEAGUE DIVISION SERIES

(=Wild Card, since 1995)*

	SERIES			GAMES			WON	LOST
	No.	W	L	No.	W	L		
New York	13	8	5	56	32	24	1981, 96, 98-2001, 03-04	1995, 97, 2002, 05-06
Cleveland	6	3	3	26	14	12	1995, 97-98	1996, 99, 2001
Boston	6	3	3	23	10	13	1999, 2003-04	1995, 98, 2005
Oakland	6	2	4	26	14	12	1981, 2006	2000-03
Seattle	4	3	1	17	10	7	1995, 2000-01	1997
Minnesota	4	1	3	16	5	11	2002	2003-04, 06
Anaheim/Los Angeles	3	2	1	12	6	6	2002, 05	2004
Texas	3	0	3	10	1	9		1996, 98-99
Baltimore	2	2	0	8	6	2	1996-97	
Chicago	2	1	1	6	3	3	2005	2000
Detroit	1	1	0	4	3	1	2006	
Milwaukee	1	0	1	5	2	3		1981
Kansas City	1	0	1	3	0	3		1981

1981

New York 3, Milwaukee 2

10/7	at Mil.	NY	5	Mil.	3
10/8	at Mil.	NY	3	Mil.	0
10/9	at NY	Mil.	5	NY	3
10/10	at NY	Mil.	2	NY	1
10/11	at NY	NY	7	Mil.	3

Oakland 3, Kansas City 0

10/6	at KC	Oak.	4	KC	0
10/7	at KC	Oak.	2	KC	1
10/9	at Oak.	Oak.	4	KC	1

1995

Cleveland 3, Boston 0

10/3	at Clev.	Clev.	5	Bos.	4	(13 inn)
10/4	at Clev.	Clev.	4	Bos.	0	
10/6	at Bos.	Clev.	8	Bos.	2	

Seattle 3, New York* 2

10/3	at NY	NY	9	Sea.	6	
10/4	at NY	NY	7	Sea.	5	(15 inn)
10/6	at Sea.	Sea.	7	NY	4	
10/7	at Sea.	Sea.	11	NY	8	
10/8	at Sea.	Sea.	6	NY	5	(11 inn)

1996

New York 3, Texas 1

10/1	at NY	Tex.	6	NY	2	
10/2	at NY	NY	5	Tex.	4	(12 inn)
10/4	at Tex.	NY	3	Tex.	2	
10/5	at Tex.	NY	6	Tex.	4	

Baltimore* 3, Cleveland 1

10/1	at Balt.	Balt.	10	Clev.	4	
10/2	at Balt.	Balt.	7	Clev.	4	
10/4	at Clev.	Clev.	9	Balt.	4	
10/5	at Clev.	Balt.	4	Clev.	3	(12 inn)

1997

Cleveland 3, New York* 2

9/30	at NY	NY	8	Clev.	6
10/2	at NY	Clev.	7	NY	5
10/4	at Clev.	NY	6	Clev.	1
10/5	at Clev.	Clev.	3	NY	2
10/6	at Clev.	Clev.	4	NY	3

Baltimore 3, Seattle 1

10/1	at Sea.	Balt.	9	Sea.	3
10/2	at Sea.	Balt.	9	Sea.	3
10/4	at Balt.	Sea.	4	Balt.	2
10/5	at Balt.	Balt.	3	Sea.	1

1998

New York 3, Texas 0

9/29	at NY	NY	2	Tex.	0
9/30	at NY	NY	3	Tex.	1
10/2	at Tex.	NY	4	Tex.	0

Cleveland 3, Boston* 1

9/29	at Clev.	Bos.	11	Clev.	3
9/30	at Clev.	Clev.	9	Bos.	5
10/2	at Bos.	Clev.	4	Bos.	3
10/3	at Bos.	Clev.	2	Bos.	1

1999

New York 3, Texas 0

10/5	at NY	NY	8	Tex.	0
10/7	at NY	NY	3	Tex.	1
10/9	at Tex.	NY	3	Tex.	0

Boston* 3, Cleveland 2

10/6	at Clev.	Clev.	3	Bos.	2
10/7	at Clev.	Clev.	11	Bos.	1
10/9	at Bos.	Bos.	9	Clev.	3
10/10	at Bos.	Bos.	23	Clev.	7
10/11	at Clev.	Bos.	12	Clev.	8

*=Wild Card, since 1995)

2000

New York 3, Oakland 2

10/3	at Oak.	Oak.	5	NY	3
10/4	at Oak.	NY	4	Oak.	0
10/6	at NY	NY	4	Oak.	2
10/7	at NY	Oak.	11	NY	1
10/8	at Oak.	NY	7	Oak.	5

Seattle* 3, Chicago 0

10/3	at Chi.	Sea.	7	Chi.	4 (10 inn)
10/4	at Chi.	Sea.	5	Chi.	2
10/6	at Sea.	Sea.	2	Chi.	1

2001

New York 3, Oakland* 2

10/10	at NY	Oak.	5	NY	3
10/11	at NY	Oak.	2	NY	0
10/13	at Oak.	NY	1	Oak.	0
10/14	at Oak.	NY	9	Oak.	2
10/15	at NY	NY	5	Oak.	3

Seattle 3, Cleveland 2

10/9	at Sea.	Clev.	5	Sea.	0
10/11	at Sea.	Sea.	5	Clev.	1
10/13	at Clev.	Clev.	17	Sea.	2
10/14	at Clev.	Sea.	6	Clev.	2
10/15	at Sea.	Sea.	3	Clev.	1

2002

Anaheim* 3, New York 1

10/1	at NY	NY	8	Ana.	5
10/2	at NY	Ana.	8	NY	6
10/4	at Ana.	Ana.	9	NY	6
10/5	at Ana.	Ana.	9	NY	5

Minnesota 3, Oakland 2

10/1	at Oak.	Minn.	7	Oak.	5
10/2	at Oak.	Oak.	9	Minn.	1
10/4	at Minn.	Oak.	6	Minn.	3
10/5	at Minn.	Minn.	11	Oak.	2
10/6	at Oak.	Minn.	5	Oak.	4

2003

New York 3, Minnesota 1

9/30	at NY	Minn.	3	NY	1
10/2	at NY	NY	4	Minn.	1
10/4	at Minn.	NY	3	Minn.	1
10/5	at Minn.	NY	8	Minn.	1

Boston* 3, Oakland 2

10/1	at Oak.	Oak.	5	Bos.	4 (12 inn)
10/2	at Oak.	Oak.	5	Bos.	1
10/4	at Bos.	Bos.	3	Oak.	1 (11 inn)
10/5	at Bos.	Bos.	5	Oak.	4
10/6	at Oak.	Bos.	4	Oak.	3

2004

Boston* 3, Anaheim 0

10/5	at Ana.	Bos.	9	Ana.	3
10/6	at Ana.	Bos.	8	Ana.	3
10/8	at Bos.	Bos.	8	Ana.	6 (10 inn)

New York 3, Minnesota 1

10/5	at NY	Minn.	2	NY	0
10/6	at NY	NY	7	Minn.	6 (12 inn)
10/8	at Minn.	NY	8	Minn.	4
10/9	at Minn.	NY	6	Minn.	5 (11 inn)

2005

Chicago 3, Boston* 0

10/4	at Chi.	Chi.	14	Bos.	2
10/5	at Chi.	Chi.	5	Bos.	4
10/7	at Bos.	Chi.	5	Bos.	3

Los Angeles 3, New York 2

10/4	at LA	NY	4	LA	2
10/5	at LA	LA	5	NY	3
10/7	at NY	LA	11	NY	7
10/9	at NY	NY	3	LA	2
10/10	at LA	LA	5	NY	3

2006

Detroit* 3, New York 1

10/3	at NY	NY	8	Det.	4
10/5	at NY	Det.	4	NY	3
10/6	at Det.	Det.	6	NY	0
10/7	at Det.	Det.	8	NY	3

Oakland 3, Minnesota 0

10/3	at Minn.	Oak.	3	Minn.	2
10/4	at Minn.	Oak.	5	Minn.	2
10/6	at Oak.	Oak.	8	Minn.	3

NATIONAL LEAGUE DIVISION SERIES

(=Wild Card, since 1995)*

	SERIES			GAMES				
	No.	**W**	**L**	**No.**	**W**	**L**	**WON**	**LOST**
Atlanta	11	6	5	42	25	17	1995-99, 2001	2000, 02-05
St. Louis	7	6	1	25	20	5	1996, 2000, 02, 04-06	2001
Houston	7	2	5	28	10	18	2004-05	1981, 97-99, 2001
Los Angeles	5	1	4	18	4	14	1981	1995-96, 2004, 06
San Francisco	4	1	3	16	5	11	2002	1997, 2000, 03
San Diego	4	1	3	14	4	10	1998	1996, 2005-06
New York	3	3	0	11	9	2	1999-2000, 06	
Arizona	3	1	2	12	4	8	2001	1999, 2002
Chicago	2	1	1	8	3	5	2003	1998
Florida	2	2	0	7	6	1	1997, 2003	
Montreal	1	1	0	5	3	2	1981	
Philadelphia	1	0	1	5	2	3		1981
Colorado	1	0	1	4	1	3		1995
Cincinnati	1	1	0	3	3	0	1995	

1981

Los Angeles 3, Houston 2

10/6	at Hou.	Hou.	3	LA	1	
10/7	at Hou.	Hou.	1	LA	0	(11 inn)
10/9	at LA	LA	6	Hou.	1	
10/10	at LA	LA	2	Hou.	1	
10/11	at LA	LA	4	Hou.	0	

Montreal 3, Philadelphia 2

10/7	at Mtl.	Mtl.	3	Phil.	1	
10/8	at Mtl.	Mtl.	3	Phil.	1	
10/9	at Phil.	Phil.	6	Mtl.	2	
10/10	at Phil.	Phil.	6	Mtl.	5	(10 inn)
10/11	at Phil.	Mtl.	3	Phil.	0	

1995

Atlanta 3, Colorado* 1

10/3	at Col.	Atl.	5	Col.	4	
10/4	at Col.	Atl.	7	Col.	4	
10/6	at Atl.	Col.	7	Atl.	5	(10 inn)
10/7	at Atl.	Atl.	10	Col.	4	

Cincinnati 3, Los Angeles 0

10/3	at LA	Cin.	7	LA	2
10/4	at LA	Cin.	5	LA	4
10/6	at Cin.	Cin.	10	LA	1

1996

Atlanta 3, Los Angeles* 0

10/2	at LA	Atl.	2	LA	1	(10 inn)
10/3	at LA	Atl.	3	LA	2	
10/5	at Atl.	Atl.	5	LA	2	

St. Louis 3, San Diego 0

10/1	at StL.	StL.	3	SD	1
10/3	at StL.	StL.	5	SD	4
10/5	at SD	StL.	7	SD	5

1997

Florida* 3, San Francisco 0

9/30	at Fla.	Fla.	2	SF	1
10/1	at Fla.	Fla.	7	SF	6
10/3	at SF	Fla.	6	SF	2

Atlanta 3, Houston 0

9/30	at Atl.	Atl.	2	Hou.	1
10/1	at Atl.	Atl.	13	Hou.	3
10/3	at Hou.	Atl.	4	Hou.	1

1998

San Diego 3, Houston 1

9/29	at Hou.	SD	2	Hou.	1
10/1	at Hou.	Hou.	5	SD	4
10/3	at SD	SD	2	Hou.	1
10/4	at SD	SD	6	Hou.	1

Atlanta 3, Chicago* 0

9/30	at Atl.	Atl.	7	Chi.	1	
10/1	at Atl.	Atl.	2	Chi.	1	(10 inn)
10/3	at Chi.	Atl.	6	Chi.	2	

1999

Atlanta 3, Houston 1

10/5	at Atl.	Hou.	6	Atl.	1	
10/6	at Atl.	Atl.	5	Hou.	1	
10/8	at Hou.	Atl.	5	Hou.	3	(12 inn)
10/9	at Hou.	Atl.	7	Hou.	5	

New York* 3, Arizona 1

10/5	at Ari.	NY	8	Ari.	4	
10/6	at Ari.	Ari.	7	NY	1	
10/8	at NY	NY	9	Ari.	2	
10/9	at NY	NY	4	Ari.	3	(10 inn)

2000

New York* 3, San Francisco 1

10/4	at SF	SF	5	NY	1	
10/5	at SF	NY	5	SF	4	(10 inn)
10/7	at NY	NY	3	SF	2	(13 inn)
10/8	at NY	NY	4	SF	0	

St. Louis 3, Atlanta 0

10/3	at StL.	StL.	7	Atl.	5
10/5	at StL.	StL.	10	Atl.	4
10/7	at Atl.	StL.	7	Atl.	1

=Wild Card, since 1995)

2001

Arizona 3, St. Louis* 2

10/9	at Ari.	Ari.	1	StL.	0
10/10	at Ari.	StL.	4	Ari.	1
10/12	at StL.	Ari.	5	StL.	3
10/13	at StL.	StL.	4	Ari.	1
10/14	at Ari.	Ari.	2	StL.	1

Atlanta 3, Houston 0

10/9	at Hou.	Atl.	7	Hou.	4
10/10	at Hou.	Atl.	1	Hou.	0
10/12	at Atl.	Atl.	6	Hou.	2

2002

San Francisco* 3, Atlanta 2

10/2	at Atl.	SF	8	Atl.	5
10/3	at Atl.	Atl.	7	SF	3
10/5	at SF	Atl.	10	SF	2
10/6	at SF	SF	8	Atl.	3
10/7	at Atl.	SF	3	Atl.	1

St. Louis 3, Arizona 0

10/1	at Ari.	StL.	12	Ari.	2
10/3	at Ari.	StL.	2	Ari.	1
10/5	at StL.	StL.	6	Ari.	3

2003

Florida* 3, San Francisco 1

9/30	at SF	SF	2	Fla.	0	
10/1	at SF	Fla.	9	SF	5	
10/3	at Fla.	Fla.	4	SF	3	(11 inn)
10/4	at Fla.	Fla.	7	SF	6	

Chicago 3, Atlanta 2

9/30	at Atl.	Chi.	4	Atl.	2
10/1	at Atl.	Atl.	5	Chi.	3
10/3	at Chi.	Chi.	3	Atl.	1
10/4	at Chi.	Atl.	6	Chi.	4
10/5	at Atl.	Chi.	5	Atl.	1

2004

St. Louis 3, Los Angeles 1

10/5	at StL.	StL.	8	LA	3
10/7	at StL.	StL.	8	LA	3
10/9	at LA	LA	4	StL.	0
10/10	at LA	StL.	6	LA	2

Houston* 3, Atlanta 2

10/6	at Atl.	Hou.	9	Atl.	3	
10/7	at Atl.	Atl.	4	Hou.	2	(11 inn)
10/9	at Hou.	Hou.	8	Atl.	5	
10/10	at Hou.	Atl.	6	Hou.	5	
10/11	at Atl.	Hou.	12	Atl.	3	

2005

Houston* 3, Atlanta 1

10/5	at Atl.	Hou.	10	Atl.	5	
10/6	at Atl.	Atl.	7	Hou.	1	
10/8	at Hou.	Hou.	7	Atl.	3	
10/9	at Hou.	Hou.	7	Atl.	6	(18 inn)

St. Louis 3, San Diego 0

10/4	at StL.	StL.	8	SD	5
10/6	at StL.	StL.	6	SD	2
10/8	at SD	StL.	7	SD	4

2006

St. Louis 3, San Diego 1

10/3	at SD	StL.	5	SD	1
10/5	at SD	StL.	2	SD	0
10/7	at StL.	SD	3	StL.	1
10/8	at StL.	StL.	6	SD	2

New York 3, Los Angeles* 0

10/4	at NY	NY	6	LA	5
10/5	at NY	NY	4	LA	1
10/7	at LA	NY	9	LA	5

INDIVIDUAL BATTING

Most Series, Lifetime
12 Mariano Rivera, AL:NY 1995-2006
    Bernie Williams, AL:NY 1995-2006
11 Chipper Jones, NL:Atl. 1995-2005

Most Games, Lifetime
48 Bernie Williams, AL:NY
42 Chipper Jones, NL:Atl.

Highest Batting Average, Lifetime (min: 30 AB)
.441 Cal Ripken, AL:Balt. (34ab-15h)
.404 Fernando Vina, NL:StL. (47ab-19h)

Highest Batting Average, Series (min: 3.1 PA/G)
.615 Jeff Kent NL:LA 2006 (13ab-8h)
.600 Luis Alicea, AL:Bos. 1995 (10ab-6h)
      Ichiro Suzuki, AL:Sea. 2001 (20ab-12h)

Highest Slugging Percentage, Lifetime (min: 30 AB)
.839 Carlos Beltran, NL:Hou.-NY (31ab-26tb)
.789 A.J. Pierzynski, AL:Minn.-Chi. (38ab-30tb)

Highest Slugging Percentage, Series (min: 3.1 PA/G)
1.375 Juan Gonzalez, AL:Tex. 1996 (16ab-22tb)
1.286 Jim Edmonds, NL:StL. 2000 (14ab-18tb)

Most Plate Appearances, Lifetime
215 Bernie Williams, AL:NY
189 Chipper Jones, NL:Atl.

Most Plate Appearances, Series
28 Bernie Williams, AL:NY 1995
26 Rafael Furcal, NL:Atl. 2004

Most Plate Appearances, Game
7 Jose Offerman, AL:Bos. Oct. 10, 1999
6 Marquis Grissom, NL:Atl. Oct. 4, 1995
   Eli Marrero, NL:StL. Oct. 1, 2002
   Fernando Vina, NL:StL. Oct. 1, 2002
   Craig Biggio, NL:Hou. Oct. 5, 2005
Extra-Inning Game:
9 Rafael Furcal, NL:Atl. Oct. 9, 2005 (18 inn)
   Marcus Giles, NL:Atl. Oct. 9, 2005 (18 inn)
   Chipper Jones, NL:Atl. Oct. 9, 2005 (18 inn)
   Andruw Jones, NL:Atl. Oct. 9, 2005 (18 inn)
   Jeff Francoeur, NL:Atl. Oct. 9, 2005 (18 inn)

Most Plate Appearances, Inning
2 By many players

Most At-Bats, Lifetime
183 Bernie Williams, AL:NY
151 Chipper Jones, NL:Atl.

Most At-Bats, Series
24 Jay Buhner, AL:Sea. 1995
    Don Mattingly, AL:NY 1995
    Rafael Furcal, NL:Atl. 2002
    Marcus Giles, NL:Atl. 2004

Most At-Bats, Game
6 By many players
Extra-Inning Game:
8 Brian McCann, NL:Atl. Oct. 9, 2005 (18 inn)
7 By many AL players

Most At-Bats, Inning
2 By many players

Most Runs, Lifetime
36 Bernie Williams, AL:NY
30 Chipper Jones, NL:Atl.

Most Runs, Series
9 Ken Griffey, Jr. AL:Sea. 1995
   Carlos Beltran, NL:Hou. 2004

Most Runs, Game
5 Jason Varitek, AL:Bos. Oct. 10, 1999
3 By many NL players

Most Runs, Inning
2 Shawn Wooten, AL:Ana. Oct. 5, 2002 (5th)
1 By many NL players

Most Hits, Lifetime
67 Derek Jeter, AL:NY
41 Chipper Jones, NL:Atl.

Most Hits, Series
12 Edgar Martinez, AL:Sea. 1995
    Ichiro Suzuki, AL:Sea. 2001
11 Marquis Grissom, NL:Atl. 1995

Most Hits, Game
5 Marquis Grissom, NL:Atl. Oct. 7, 1995
   Mike Stanley, AL:Bos. Oct. 10, 1999
   Derek Jeter, AL:NY Oct. 3, 2006

Most Hits, Inning
2 Chuck Knoblauch, AL:NY Oct. 8, 2000 (1st)
   Doug Mientkiewicz, AL:Minn. Oct. 5, 2002 (4th)
   Shawn Wooten, AL:Ana. Oct. 5, 2002 (5th)
   Benji Gil, AL:Ana. Oct. 5, 2002 (5th)
1 By many NL players

Most Extra-Base Hits, Lifetime
24 Bernie Williams, AL:NY
14 Chipper Jones, NL:Atl.
    Jim Edmonds, NL:StL.

Most Extra-Base Hits, Series
6 Jim Edmonds, NL:StL. 2000
   Carlos Beltran, NL:Hou. 2004
5 By many AL players

Most Extra-Base Hits, Game
3 Eric Karros, NL:LA Oct. 4, 1995
   Jim Edmonds, NL:StL. Oct. 5, 2000
   Craig Biggio, NL:Hou. Oct. 8, 2005
   Mo Vaughn, AL:Bos. Sept. 29, 1998
   John Valentin, AL:Bos. Oct. 10, 1999
   Jason Varitek, AL:Bos. Oct. 10, 1999
   Juan Gonzalez, AL:Clev. Oct. 13, 2001
   Troy Glaus, AL:Ana. Oct. 5, 2004
   David Ortiz, AL:Bos. Oct. 8, 2004 (10 inn)
   Derek Jeter, AL:NY Oct. 5, 2006

Most Extra-Base Hits, Inning
1 By many players

Most Total Bases, Lifetime
105 Derek Jeter, AL:NY
73 Chipper Jones, NL:Atl.

Most Total Bases, Series
24 Ken Griffey, Jr. AL:Sea. 1995
    Carlos Beltran, NL:Hou. 2004

Most Total Bases, Game
11 John Valentin, AL:Bos. Oct. 10, 1999
10 Eric Karros, NL:LA Oct. 4, 1995
    Carlos Beltran, NL:Hou. Oct. 11, 2004

Most Total Bases, Inning
5 Shawn Wooten, AL:Ana. Oct. 5, 2002 (5th)
4 By many NL players

Most Singles, Lifetime
48 Derek Jeter, AL:NY
27 Chipper Jones, NL:Atl.

Most Singles, Series
11 Ichiro Suzuki, AL:Sea. 2001
9   Fernando Vina, NL:StL. 2002
    Moises Alou, NL:Chi. 2003

Most Singles, Game
4 Chad Fonville, NL:LA Oct. 4, 1995
   Marquis Grissom, NL:Atl. Oct. 7, 1995
   Fernando Vina, NL:StL. Oct. 3, 2002
   Johnny Damon, AL:Oak. Oct. 10, 2001
   Jason Giambi, AL:Oak. Oct. 15, 2001

Most Singles, Inning
2 Chuck Knoblauch, AL:NY Oct. 8, 2000 (1st)
   Doug Mientkiewicz, AL:Minn. Oct. 5, 2002 (4th)
   Benji Gil AL:Ana. Oct. 5, 2002 (5th)
1 By many NL players

Most Doubles, Lifetime
16 Bernie Williams, AL:NY
7 Edgardo Alfonzo, NL:NY-SF
   Craig Biggio, NL:Hou.
   Jim Edmonds, NL:StL.
   Andruw Jones, NL:Atl.
   Jeff Kent, NL:SF-Hou.-LA

Most Doubles, Series
4 Don Mattingly, AL:NY 1995
   David Justice, AL:Clev. 1998
   Roberto Alomar, AL:Clev. 1999
   Torii Hunter, AL:Minn. 2002
   Derek Jeter, AL:NY 2006
   Jim Edmonds, NL:StL. 2000
   Edgardo Alfonzo, NL:SF 2003
   Craig Biggio, NL:Hou. 2005

Most Doubles, Game
3 Jim Edmonds, NL:StL. Oct. 5, 2000
   Craig Biggio, NL:Hou. Oct. 8, 2005
2 By many AL players

Most Doubles, Inning
1 By many players

Most Triples, Lifetime
2 David Justice, AL:NY-Oak.
   Omar Vizquel, AL:Clev.
   Rafael Furcal, NL:Atl.
   Tony Womack, NL:Ari.-StL.

Most Triples, Series
1 By many players

Most Triples, Game
1 By many NL players

Most Home Runs, Lifetime
9 Chipper Jones, NL:Atl.
   Derek Jeter, AL:NY

Most Home Runs, Series
5 Ken Griffey, Jr. AL:Sea. 1995
   Juan Gonzalez, AL:Tex. 1996
4 Carlos Beltran, NL:Hou. 2004

Most Home Runs, Game
2 Ken Griffey, Jr. AL:Sea. Oct. 3, 1995
   Bernie Williams, AL:NY, Oct. 6, 1995
   Edgar Martinez, AL:Sea. Oct. 7, 1995
   B.J. Surhoff, AL:Balt. Oct. 1, 1996
   Juan Gonzalez, AL:Tex. Oct. 2, 1996 (12 inn)
   Bernie Williams, AL:NY Oct. 5, 1996
   Mo Vaughn, AL:Bos. Sept. 29, 1998
   Manny Ramirez, AL:Clev. Oct. 2, 1998
   John Valentin, AL:Bos. Oct. 10, 1999
   Jim Thome, AL:Clev. Oct. 11, 1999
   Troy O'Leary, AL:Bos. Oct. 11, 1999
   Terrence Long, AL:Oak. Oct. 10, 2001
   Troy Glaus, AL:Ana. Oct. 1, 2002
   Todd Walker, AL:Bos. Oct. 1, 2003 (12 inn)
   A.J. Pierzynski, AL:Chi. Oct. 4, 2005
   Manny Ramirez, AL:Bos. Oct. 7, 2005
   Frank Thomas, AL:Oak. Oct. 3, 2006
   Chipper Jones, NL:Atl. Oct. 3, 1995
   Marquis Grissom, NL:Atl. Oct. 4, 1995
   Eric Karros, NL:LA Oct. 4, 1995
   Fred McGriff, NL:Atl. Oct. 7, 1995
   Ken Caminiti, NL:SD Oct. 5, 1996
   Jeff Kent, NL:SF Oct. 3, 1997
   Edgardo Alfonzo, NL:NY Oct. 5, 1999
   Chipper Jones, NL:Atl. Oct. 4, 2003
   Eric Karros, NL:Chi. Oct. 4, 2003
   Larry Walker, NL:StL. Oct. 5, 2004
   Shawn Green, NL:LA Oct. 9, 2004
   Carlos Beltran, NL:Hou. Oct. 11, 2004

Most Consecutive Games, Home Run
4 Juan Gonzalez, AL:Tex. Oct. 1-5, 1996
3 Jim Leyritz, NL:SD Oct. 1-4, 1998
   Vinny Castilla, NL:Col.-Hou. Oct. 6, 1995-Oct. 9, 2001

Most Home Runs, Inning
1 By many players

Most Grand Slam Home Runs, Lifetime
1 Darren Lewis, NL:Cin. Oct. 6, 1995 (6th)
   Devon White, NL:Fla. Oct. 3, 1997 (6th)
   Ryan Klesko, NL:Atl. Sept. 30, 1998 (7th)
   Eddie Perez, NL:Atl. Oct. 3, 1998 (8th)
   Edgardo Alfonzo, NL:NY Oct. 5, 1999 (9th)
   Reggie Sanders, NL:StL. Oct. 4, 2005 (5th)
   Adam LaRoche, NL:Atl. Oct. 9, 2005 (3rd)
   Lance Berkman, NL:Hou. Oct. 9, 2005 (8th)
   Edgar Martinez, AL:Sea. Oct. 7, 1995 (8th)
   Bobby Bonilla, AL:Balt. Oct. 1, 1996 (6th)
   Albert Belle, AL:Clev. Oct. 4, 1996 (7th)
   Paul O'Neill, AL:NY Oct. 4, 1997 (4th)
   Jim Thome, AL:Clev. Oct. 7, 1999 (4th)
   Troy O'Leary, AL:Bos. Oct. 11, 1999 (3rd)
   Vladimir Guerrero, AL:Ana. Oct. 8, 2004 (7th)

Most Runs Batted In, Lifetime
33 Bernie Williams, AL:NY
26 Chipper Jones, NL:Atl.

Most Runs Batted In, Series
12 John Valentin, AL:Bos. 1999
10 Reggie Sanders, NL:StL. 2005

Most Runs Batted In, Game
7 Edgar Martinez, AL:Sea. Oct. 7, 1995
   Mo Vaughn, AL:Bos. Sept. 29, 1998
   John Valentin, AL:Bos. Oct. 10, 1999
   Troy O'Leary, AL:Bos. Oct. 11, 1999
6 Reggie Sanders, NL: StL. Oct. 4, 2005

Most Runs Batted In, Inning
4 Darren Lewis, NL:Cin. Oct. 6, 1995 (6th)
   Devon White, NL:Fla. Oct. 3, 1997 (6th)
   Ryan Klesko, NL:Atl. Sept. 30, 1998 (7th)
   Eddie Perez, NL:Atl. Oct. 3, 1998 (8th)
   Edgardo Alfonzo, NL:NY Oct. 5, 1999 (9th)
   Reggie Sanders, NL:StL. Oct. 4, 2005 (5th)
   Adam LaRoche, NL:Atl. Oct. 9, 2005 (3rd)
   Lance Berkman, NL:Hou. Oct. 9, 2005 (8th)
   Edgar Martinez, AL:Sea. Oct. 7, 1995 (8th)
   Bobby Bonilla, AL:Balt. Oct. 1, 1996 (6th)
   Albert Belle, AL:Clev. Oct. 4, 1996 (7th)
   Paul O'Neill, AL:NY Oct. 4, 1997 (4th)
   Jim Thome, AL:Clev. Oct. 7, 1999 (4th)
   Troy O'Leary, AL:Bos. Oct. 11, 1999 (3rd)
   Vladimir Guerrero, AL:Ana. Oct. 8, 2004 (7th)

Most Sacrifice Hits, Lifetime
4 Omar Vizquel, AL:Clev.
   Steve Finley, AL:LA
   John Smoltz, NL:Atl.

Most Sacrifice Hits, Series
4 Steve Finley, AL:LA 2005
3 Placido Polanco, NL:StL. 2001

Most Sacrifice Hits, Game
3 Placido Polanco, NL:StL. Oct. 13, 2001
2 Stan Javier, AL:Sea. Oct. 15, 2001

Most Sacrifice Hits, Inning
1 By many players

Most Sacrifice Flies, Lifetime
4 Bernie Williams, AL:NY
3 Barry Bonds, NL:SF

Most Sacrifice Flies, Series
2 Cecil Cooper, AL:Mil. 1981
    Luis Sojo, AL:Sea. 1995
    Nomar Garciaparra, AL:Bos. 1998
    Trot Nixon, AL:Bos. 1999
    Adam Kennedy, AL:Ana. 2002
    Manny Ramirez, AL:Bos. 2004
1 By many NL players

Most Sacrifice Flies, Game
1 By many players

Most Walks, Lifetime
36 Chipper Jones, NL:Atl.
26 Bernie Williams, AL:NY

Most Walks, Series
8 Barry Bonds, NL:SF 2003
7 Bernie Williams, AL:NY 1995
    Jose Offerman, AL:Bos. 1999
    Jason Giambi, AL:Oak. 2000

Most Walks, Game
3 Willie Aikens, AL:KC Oct. 7, 1981
    Edgar Martinez, AL:Sea. Oct. 6, 1995
    Randy Velarde, AL:NY Oct. 7, 1995
    Travis Fryman, AL:Clev. Oct. 7, 1999
    Jason Giambi, AL:Oak. Oct. 7, 2000
    David Ortiz, AL:Bos. Oct. 6, 2004
    Alex Rodriguez, AL:NY Oct. 5, 2005
    Jorge Posada, AL:NY Oct. 9, 2005
    Chris Speier, NL:Mtl. Oct. 7, 1981
    Bill Russell, NL:LA Oct. 7, 1981 (11 inn)
    Chipper Jones, NL:Atl. Oct. 1, 1997
    Andruw Jones, NL:Atl. Oct. 3, 1998
    Richard Hidalgo, NL:Atl. Oct. 9, 2001
    Gary Sheffield, NL:Atl. Oct. 5, 2002
    Gary Sheffield, NL:Atl. Oct. 7, 2002
    Barry Bonds, NL:SF Sept. 30, 2003
    Scott Rolen, NL:StL. Oct. 10, 2004
    Lance Berkman, NL:Hou. Oct. 5, 2005
    Chipper Jones, NL:Atl. Oct. 9, 2005 (18 inn)
    Carlos Beltran, NL:NY Oct. 4, 2006
    Extra-Inning Game:
4 Bernie Williams, AL:NY Oct. 8, 1995 (11 inn)

Most Walks, Inning
1 By many players

Most Intentional Walks, Lifetime
10 Barry Bonds, NL:SF
4 Nomar Garciaparra, AL:Bos.
    David Ortiz, AL:Bos.

Most Intentional Walks, Series
6 Barry Bonds, NL:SF 2003
3 David Ortiz, AL:Bos. 2004

Most Intentional Walks, Game
2 Edgar Martinez, AL:Sea. Oct. 6, 1995
    Nomar Garciaparra, AL:Bos. Oct. 11, 1999
    David Ortiz, AL:Bos. Oct. 6, 2004
    Barry Bonds, NL:SF Sept. 30, 2003
    Barry Bonds, NL:SF Oct. 3, 2003
    Mike Lamb, NL:Hou. Oct. 8, 2005
    Albert Pujols, NL:StL. Oct. 8, 2005

Most Intentional Walks, Inning
1 By many players

Most Hit By Pitch, Lifetime
4 Manny Ramirez, AL:Clev.
3 Larry Walker, NL:Col.-StL.

Most Hit By Pitch, Series
2 Manny Ramirez, AL:Clev. 1998
    Tino Martinez, AL:NY 2001
    Raul Mondesi, AL:NY 2002
    Lew Ford, AL:Minn. 2004
    Corey Koskie, AL:Minn. 2004
    Scott Podsednik, AL:Chi. 2005
    Alex Rodriguez, AL:NY 2005
    Jason Giambi, AL:NY 2006
    Craig Biggio, NL:Hou. 1998
    Mike Bordick, NL:NY 2000
    Derrek Lee, NL:Fla. 2003
    Xavier Nady NL:SD 2005

Most Hit By Pitch, Game
2 Manny Ramirez, AL:Clev. Sept. 30, 1998
    Jason Giambi, AL:NY Oct. 3, 2006
    Derrek Lee, NL:Fla. Oct. 4, 2003
    Xavier Nady NL:SD Oct. 6, 2005

Most Hit By Pitch, Inning
1 By many players

Most Strikeouts, Lifetime
34 Jim Thome, AL:Clev.
30 Chipper Jones, NL:Atl.

Most Strikeouts, Series
11 Bret Boone, AL:Sea. 2001
9 Warren Cromartie, NL:Mtl. 1981
    Reggie Sanders, NL:Cin. 1995
    Jim Edmonds, NL:StL. 2004

Most Strikeouts, Game
5 Reggie Sanders, NL:Cin. Oct. 6, 1995
4 Rafael Palmeiro, AL:Balt. Oct. 5, 1996 (12 in
    Bobby Bonilla, AL:Balt. Oct. 5, 1996 (in
    Pete Incaviglia, AL:Balt. Oct. 5, 1996 (12 in
    Dan Wilson, AL:Sea. Oct. 2, 1997
    Brady Anderson, AL:Balt. Oct. 5, 1997
    Ben Grieve, AL:Oak. Oct. 8, 2000
    Bret Boone, AL:Sea. Oct. 13, 2001
    Derek Jeter, AL:NY Oct. 9, 2004 (11 inn)

Most Strikeouts, Inning
1 By many players

Most Stolen Bases, Lifetime
13 Kenny Lofton, AL:Clev.; NL:Atl.-SF-Chi.
11 Rafael Furcal, NL:Atl.-LA
10 Omar Vizquel, AL:Clev.

Most Stolen Bases, Series
6 Rickey Henderson, NL:NY 1999
5 Kenny Lofton, AL:Clev. 1996

Most Stolen Bases, Game
3 Kenny Lofton, AL:Clev. Oct. 4, 1996
    Rickey Henderson, NL:NY Oct. 6, 1999

Most Stolen Bases, Inning
2 Barry Larkin, NL:Cin. Oct. 3, 1995 (9th)
    Reggie Sanders, NL:Cin. Oct. 4, 1995 (9th)
    Barry Larkin, NL:Cin. Oct. 6, 1995 (1st)
    Rafael Furcal, NL:Atl. Oct. 9, 2005 (11th)
    Kenny Lofton, AL:Clev. Oct. 2, 1996 (6th)

Most Caught Stealing, Lifetime
3 Marquis Grissom, NL:Atl.-SF; AL:Clev.
    Bernie Williams, AL:NY
    Alex Rodriguez, AL:Sea.-NY
2 By many NL players

Most Caught Stealing, Series
2 Cesar Cedeno, NL:Hou. 1981
  Jerry White, NL:Mtl. 1981
  Luis Alicea, NL:StL. 1996
  Sammy Sosa, NL:Chi. 1998
  Omar Vizquel, AL:Clev. 1996
  Ichiro Suzuki, AL:Sea. 2001
  Michael Cuddyer, AL:Minn. 2004
  Adam Kennedy, AL:LA 2005
  Scott Podsednik, AL:Chi. 2005

Most Caught Stealing, Game
1 By many players

Most Grounded Into Double Plays, Lifetime
11 Bernie Williams, AL:NY
7 Chipper Jones, NL:Atl.

Most Grounded Into Double Plays, Series
4 Bernie Williams, AL:NY 2004
2 By many NL players

Most Grounded Into Double Plays, Game
2 Chipper Jones, NL:Atl. Oct. 3, 1995
  Lance Berkman, NL:Hou. Oct. 10, 2001
  Jeff Kent, NL:Hou. Oct. 10, 2004
  Paul O'Neill, AL:NY Oct. 4, 1996
  Sandy Alomar, Jr. AL:Clev. Oct. 30, 1998
  Roberto Alomar, AL:Clev. Oct. 15, 2001
  Darin Erstad, AL:Ana. Oct. 5, 2002
  Bernie Williams, AL:NY Oct. 8, 2004
  Placido Polanco, AL:Det. Oct. 3, 2006

‌NDIVIDUAL FIELDING

‌AMES

Most Games, First Base, Lifetime
37 Tino Martinez, AL:Sea.-NY; NL:StL.
34 Tino Martinez, AL:Sea.-NY
19 Jeff Bagwell, NL:Hou.

Most Games, Second Base, Lifetime
21 Jeff Kent, AL:Clev.; NL:SF-Hou.-LA
20 Jeff Kent, NL:SF-Hou.-LA
18 Roberto Alomar, AL:Balt.-Clev.

Most Games, Third Base, Lifetime
32 Chipper Jones, NL:Atl.
23 Eric Chavez, AL:Oak.

Most Games, Shortstop, Lifetime
45 Derek Jeter, AL:NY
25 Rafael Furcal, NL:Atl.-LA

Most Games, Outfield, Lifetime
45 Bernie Williams, AL:NY
38 Andruw Jones, NL:Atl.

Most Games, Catcher, Lifetime
35 Jorge Posada, AL:NY
21 Javy Lopez, NL:Atl.

Most Games, Pitcher, Lifetime
28 Mariano Rivera, AL:NY
15 John Smoltz, NL:Atl.

‌RRORS

Most Errors, First Base, Lifetime
3 Paul Sorrento, AL:Clev.-Sea
  Jeff Bagwell, NL:Hou.

Most Errors, Second Base, Lifetime
3 Jerry Manuel, NL:Mtl.
  Eric Young, NL:Col.
2 Jim Gantner, AL:Mil.
  Chuck Knoblauch, AL:NY
  Randy Velarde, AL:NY-Oak.
  Todd Walker, AL:Bos.
  Mark Ellis, AL:Oak.
  Alfonso Soriano, AL:NY
  Robinson Cano, AL:NY

Most Errors, Third Base, Lifetime
4 Ken Caminiti, NL:SD-Hou.-Atl.
  Chipper Jones, NL:Atl.
  Todd Zeile, AL:Balt.-Tex.

Most Errors, Shortstop, Lifetime
6 Derek Jeter, AL:NY
5 Edgar Renteria, NL:Fla.-StL.

Most Errors, Outfield, Lifetime
3 Kenny Lofton, AL:Clev.
2 Ryan Klesko, NL:Atl.
  Tony Womack, NL:Ari.
  Marquis Grissom, NL:Atl.-SF

Most Errors, Catcher, Lifetime
4 Sandy Alomar, Jr. AL:Clev.
2 Javy Lopez, NL:Atl.

Most Errors, Pitcher, Lifetime
2 LaTroy Hawkins, AL:Minn.
1 By many NL pitchers

Most Errors, Game
2 Eric Young, NL:Col. Oct. 4, 1995 (2b)
  Ken Caminiti, NL:SD Oct. 5, 1996 (3b)
  Edgar Renteria, NL:Fla. Oct. 3, 1997 (ss)
  Julio Lugo, NL:Hou. Oct. 10, 2001 (ss)
  Eric Chavez, AL:Oak. Oct. 4, 2003 (3b)

Most Errors, Inning
2 Eric Chavez, AL:Oak. Oct. 4, 2003 (3b; 2nd)
1 By many NL players

INDIVIDUAL PITCHING

Most Series
12 Mariano Rivera, AL:NY 1995-2006
10 John Smoltz, NL:Atl. 1995-99, 2001-05
   Greg Maddux, NL:Atl. 1995-2003; LA 06

Lowest ERA, Lifetime (Minimum: 20 innings)
0.42 Mariano Rivera, AL:NY (43 inn)
0.72 Curt Schilling, NL:Ari. (25 inn)

Most Games, Lifetime
28 Mariano Rivera, AL:NY
15 John Smoltz, NL:Atl.

Most Games, Series
5 Kevin Gryboski, NL:Atl. 2003
  Kevin Gryboski, NL:Atl. 2004
  Scott Williamson, AL:Bos. 2003

Most Games Started, Lifetime
12 Andy Pettitte, AL:NY-NL:Hou.
11 Andy Pettitte, AL:NY
   Greg Maddux, NL:Atl.-LA

Most Games Started, Series
2 By many pitchers

Most Complete Games, Lifetime
2 Curt Schilling, NL:Ari.
1 By many AL pitchers

Most Complete Games, Series
2 Curt Schilling, NL:Ari. 2001
1 By many AL pitchers

Most Games Finished, Lifetime
23 Mariano Rivera, AL:NY
8 John Smoltz, NL:Atl.
   Trevor Hoffman, NL:SD

Most Games Finished, Series
4 Trevor Hoffman, NL:SD 1998
   Steve Kline, NL:StL. 2001
3 By many AL pitchers

Most Saves, Lifetime
15 Mariano Rivera, AL:NY
5 Mark Wohlers, NL:Atl.

Most Saves, Series
3 Rich Gossage, AL:NY 1981
   Mike Jackson, AL:Clev. 1998
   Mariano Rivera, AL:NY 2000
   Dennis Eckersley, NL:StL. 1996
   Mark Wohlers, NL:Atl. 1996

Most Shutouts, Lifetime
1 Mike Norris, AL:Oak. Oct. 6, 1981
   Jerry Reuss, NL:LA Oct. 11, 1981
   Steve Rogers, NL:Mtl. Oct. 11, 1981
   Bobby J. Jones, NL:NY Oct. 8, 2000
   Curt Schilling, NL:Ari. Oct. 9, 2001
   Jason Schmidt, NL:SF Sept. 30, 2003
   Jose Lima, NL:LA Oct. 9, 2004

Most Games Won, Lifetime
7 John Smoltz, NL:Atl.
4 Andy Pettitte, AL:NY
   David Wells, AL:Balt.-NY
   Pedro Martinez, AL:Bos.
   Mike Mussina, AL:Balt.-NY
   Barry Zito, AL:Oak.

Most Games Won, Series
2 By many pitchers

Most Games Lost, Lifetime
8 Randy Johnson, AL:Sea.-NY; NL:Hou.-Ari.
5 Randy Johnson, NL:Hou.-Ari.
4 Tim Wakefield, AL:Bos.
   Mike Mussina, AL:NY

Most Games Lost, Series
2 By many pitchers

Most Innings Pitched, Lifetime
74.0 Andy Pettitte, AL:NY-NL:Hou.
70.0 Greg Maddux, NL:Atl.-LA
67.0 Andy Pettitte, AL:NY

Most Innings Pitched, Series
18.0 Jerry Reuss, NL:LA 1981
      Curt Schilling, NL:Ari. 2001
15.2 David Cone, AL:NY 1995

Most Innings Pitched, Game
9.0 By many pitchers

Most Runs, Lifetime
41 Randy Johnson, AL:Sea.-NY; NL:Hou.-Ari.
32 Andy Pettitte, AL:NY
    Greg Maddux, NL:Atl.-LA

Most Runs, Series
13 Tom Glavine, NL:Atl. 2002
11 Andy Pettitte, AL:NY 1997
    Bret Saberhagen, AL:Bos. 1999
    Tim Hudson, AL:Oak. 2002

Most Runs, Game
8 Steve Reed, AL:Clev. Oct. 10, 1999
   Charles Nagy, AL:Clev. Oct. 11, 1999
   Paul Abbott, AL:Sea. Oct. 13, 2001
   David Wells, AL:NY Oct. 5, 2002
   Matt Clement, AL:Bos. Oct. 4, 2005
   Jake Peavy, NL:SD Oct. 4, 2005

Most Runs, Inning
7 David Wells, AL:NY Oct. 5, 2002 (5th)
6 Greg Maddux, NL:Atl. Oct. 3, 2001 (1st)

Most Earned Runs, Lifetime
39 Randy Johnson, AL:Sea.-NY; NL:Hou.-Ari.
32 Andy Pettitte, AL:NY
29 Tom Glavine, NL:Atl.

Most Earned Runs, Series
13 Tom Glavine, NL:Atl. 2002
11 Andy Pettitte, AL:NY 1997
    Bret Saberhagen, AL:Bos. 1999

Most Earned Runs, Game
8 Steve Reed, AL:Clev. Oct. 10, 1999
   Paul Abbott, AL:Sea. Oct. 13, 2001
   David Wells, AL:NY Oct. 5, 2002
   Matt Clement, AL:Bos. Oct. 4, 2005
   Jake Peavy, NL:SD Oct. 4, 2005

Most Earned Runs, Inning
7 David Wells, AL:NY Oct. 5, 2002 (5th)
5 Odalis Perez, NL:LA Oct. 5, 2004 (3rd)
   Russ Ortiz, NL:Atl. Oct. 10, 2004 (2nd)

Most Hits, Lifetime
77 Greg Maddux, NL:Atl.-LA
72 Andy Pettitte, AL:NY

Most Hits, Series
19 Greg Maddux, NL:Atl. 1995
15 David Cone, AL:NY 1995
    Charles Nagy, AL:Clev. 1996
    David Wells, AL:Balt. 1996
    Andy Pettitte, AL:NY 1997
    Andy Pettitte, AL:NY 2000

Most Hits, Game
12 Nate Roberston, AL:Det. Oct. 3, 2006
11 Carlos Zambrano, NL:Chi. Oct. 1, 2003
    Jake Peavy, NL:SD Oct. 3, 2006

Most Hits, Inning
7 David Wells, AL:NY Oct. 5, 2002 (5th)
5 Greg Maddux, NL:Atl. Oct. 3, 2000 (1st)
   Randy Johnson, NL:Ari. Oct. 1, 2002 (4th)
   Russ Ortiz, NL:Atl. Oct. 10, 2004 (2nd)
   Greg Maddux, NL:LA Oct. 7, 2006 (1st)

Most Home Runs, Lifetime
13 Randy Johnson, AL:Sea.-NY; NL:Hou.-Ari.
9 Andy Pettitte, AL:NY
8 John Smoltz, NL:Atl.

Most Home Runs, Series
5 Jaret Wright, NL:Atl. 2004
4 David Cone, AL:NY 1995
   Charles Nagy, AL:Clev. 1996
   Rick Reed, AL:Minn. 2002

Most Home Runs, Game
4 Rick Reed, AL:Minn. Oct. 4, 2002
3 Ismael Valdes, NL:LA Oct. 3, 1996
   Odalis Perez, NL:LA Oct. 5, 2004
   Jaret Wright, NL:Atl. Oct. 6, 2004
   Jason Marquis, NL:StL. Oct. 7, 2004

Most Home Runs, Inning
2 By many pitchers

Most Grand Slam Home Runs, Lifetime
1. Mark Guthrie, NL:LA Oct. 6, 1995
   Wilson Alvarez, NL:SF Oct. 3, 1997
   Matt Karchner, NL:Chi. Sept. 30, 1998
   Rod Beck, NL:Chi. Oct. 3, 1998
   Bobby Chouinard, NL:Ari. Oct. 5, 1999
   Jake Peavy, NL:SD Oct. 4, 2005
   Brandon Backe, NL:Hou. Oct. 9, 2005
   Kyle Farnsworth, NL:Atl. Oct. 9, 2005
   John Wetteland, AL:NY Oct. 7, 1995
   Paul Shuey, NL:Clev. Oct. 1, 1996
   Armando Benitez, AL:Balt. Oct. 4, 1996
   Chad Ogea, AL:Clev. Oct. 4, 1997
   John Wasdin, AL:Bos. Oct. 7, 1998
   Charles Nagy, AL:Clev. Oct. 11, 1999
   Mike Timlin, AL:Bos. Oct. 8, 2004

Most Walks, Lifetime
30. Roger Clemens, AL:Bos.-NY; NL:Hou.
25. Tom Glavine, NL:Atl.-NY
19. Roger Clemens, AL:Bos.-NY

Most Walks, Series
9. David Cone, AL:NY 1995
   Andy Benes, AL:Sea. 1995
8. Steve Carlton, NL:Phil. 1981
   Mike Hampton, NL:Hou. 1997
   Russ Ortiz, NL:SF 2002
   Roger Clemens, NL:Hou. 2004

Most Walks, Game
8. Mike Hampton, NL:Hou. Oct. 1, 1997
6. David Cone, AL:NY Oct. 3, 1995
   Andy Benes, AL:Sea. Oct. 8, 1995
   Andy Pettitte, AL:NY Oct. 2, 1996
   Charles Nagy, AL:Clev. Oct. 4, 1997
   Orlando Hernandez, AL:NY Oct. 5, 1999

Most Walks, Inning
4. Andy Benes, AL:Sea. Oct. 8, 1995 (6th)
   Mike Hampton, NL:Hou. Oct. 1, 1997 (5th)
   Rick Ankiel, NL:StL. Oct. 3, 2000 (3rd)

Most Intentional Walks, Lifetime
7. Greg Maddux, NL:Atl.-LA
3. Derek Lowe, AL:Bos.

Most Intentional Walks, Series
3. Tom Glavine, NL:Atl. 2002
2. Aaron Sele, AL:Tex. 1999
   Chad Bradford, AL:Oak. 2003
   Derek Lowe, AL:Bos. 2003
   Brendan Donnelly, AL:Ana. 2004
   Joe Nathan, AL:Minn. 2004

Most Intentional Walks, Game
2. Steve Carlton, NL:Phil. Oct. 7, 1981
   Greg Maddux, NL:Atl. Oct. 5, 1999
   Jose Lima, NL:Hou. Oct. 6, 1999
   Greg Maddux, NL:Atl. Oct. 3, 2000
   Andy Ashby, NL:Atl. Oct. 5, 2000
   Tom Glavine, NL:Atl. Oct. 6, 2002
   Jake Peavy, NL:SD Oct. 4, 2005
   Jorge Sosa, NL:Atl. Oct. 8, 2005
   Aaron Sele, AL:Tex. Oct. 6, 2004
   Brendan Donnelly, AL:Ana. Oct. 6, 2004

Most Intentional Walks, Inning
2. Aaron Sele, AL:Tex. Oct. 5, 1999 (5th)
   Brendan Donnelly, AL:Ana. Oct. 6, 2004 (9th)
   Jake Peavy, NL:SD Oct. 4, 2005 (3rd)

Most Hit Batters, Lifetime
6. Tim Wakefield, AL:Bos.
3. Kevin Brown, NL:SD
   Greg Maddux, NL:Atl.-LA

Most Hit Batters, Series
3. Kevin Brown, NL:SD 1998
2. Steve Reed, AL:Clev. 1999
   Dwight Gooden, AL:NY 2000
   Roger Clemens, AL:NY 2001
   Barry Zito, AL:Oak. 2001
   Mark Mulder, AL:Oak. 2001
   Tim Wakefield, AL:Bos. 2003
   Felix Heredia, AL:NY 2004
   Javier Vazquez, AL:NY 2004
   Matt Clement, AL:Bos. 2005
   Tim Wakefield, AL:Bos. 2005
   Nate Robertson, AL:Det. 2006

Most Hit Batters, Game
2. Kevin Brown, NL:SD Oct. 3, 1998
   Jeff Weaver, NL:LA Oct. 7, 2004
   Mark Mulder, NL:StL. Oct. 6, 2005
   Steve Reed, AL:Clev. Oct. 10, 1999
   Dwight Gooden, AL:NY Oct. 7, 2000
   Barry Zito, AL:Oak. Oct. 13, 2001
   Mark Mulder, AL:Oak. Oct. 15, 2001
   Tim Wakefield, AL:Bos. Oct. 2, 2003
   Felix Heredia, AL:NY Oct. 8, 2004
   Javier Vazquez, AL:NY Oct. 9, 2004
   Matt Clement, AL:Bos. Oct. 4, 2005
   Tim Wakefield, AL:Bos. Oct. 7, 2005
   Nate Robertson, AL:Det. Oct. 3, 2006

Most Hit Batters, Inning
2. Jeff Weaver, NL:LA Oct. 7, 2004 (5th)
   Felix Heredia, AL:NY Oct. 8, 2004 (9th)
   Tim Wakefield, AL:Bos. Oct. 7, 2005 (1st)

Most Strikeouts, Lifetime
81. Randy Johnson, AL:Sea.-NY; NL:Hou.-Ari.
53. John Smoltz, NL:Atl.
    Mike Mussina, AL:Balt.-NY

Most Strikeouts, Series
21. Kevin Brown, NL:SD 1998
16. Randy Johnson, AL:Sea. 1995
    Randy Johnson, AL:Sea. 1997
    Mike Mussina, AL:Balt. 1997

Most Strikeouts, Game
16. Kevin Brown, NL:SD, Sept. 29, 1998
13. Randy Johnson, AL:Sea. Oct. 5, 1997

Most Strikeouts, Inning
3. By many pitchers

Most Wild Pitches, Lifetime
5. Roger Clemens, AL:Bos.-NY; NL:Hou.
   Rick Ankiel, NL:StL.
3. David Cone, AL:NY
   Francisco Rodriguez, AL:Ana.

Most Wild Pitches, Series
5. Rick Ankiel, NL:StL. 2000
2. David Cone, AL:NY 1995
   Steve Karsay, AL:Clev. 1999
   Francisco Rodriguez, AL:Ana. 2004
   Kelvim Escobar, AL:LA 2005
   John Lackey, AL:LA 2005

Most Wild Pitches, Game
5. Rick Ankiel, NL:StL. Oct. 3, 2000
2. David Cone, AL:NY Oct. 8, 1995 (11 inn)
   Steve Karsay, AL:Clev. Oct. 19, 1999
   Francisco Rodriguez, AL:Ana. Oct. 6, 2004
   Kelvim Escobar, AL:LA Oct. 9, 2005

Most Wild Pitches, Inning
5. Rick Ankiel, NL:StL. Oct. 3, 2000 (3rd)
2. Kelvim Escobar, AL:LA Oct. 9, 2005 (8th)

Most Balks, Lifetime
1. Kevin Tapani, NL:Chi. Oct. 1, 1998 (5th)
   Kevin Millwood, NL:Atl. Oct. 7, 2000 (5th)
   Andy Benes, NL:StL. Oct. 5, 2002 (1st)
   Brett Tomko, NL:LA Oct. 7, 2006 (8th)

CLUB BATTING

Most At-Bats, Series
200 Seattle, AL 1995
180 Atlanta, NL 2004
St. Louis, NL 2004

Most At-Bats, Game
48 Boston, AL Oct. 10, 1999
42 Florida, NL Oct. 1, 2003
Los Angeles, NL Oct. 7, 2006
Extra-Inning Game:
62 Atlanta, NL Oct. 9, 2005 (18 inn)
56 Seattle, AL Oct. 4, 1995 (15 inn)

Most At-Bats, Inning
13 Anaheim, AL Oct. 5, 2002 (5th)
9 Atlanta, NL Oct. 9, 1999 (6th)
San Diego, NL Oct. 4, 2005 (9th)

Most Runs, Series
47 Boston, AL 1999
36 Houston, NL 2004

Most Runs, Game
23 Boston, AL Oct. 10, 1999
13 Atlanta, NL Oct. 1, 1997

Most Runs, Both Clubs, Game
30 Bos. (23) Clev. (7) AL Oct. 10, 1999
16 Atl. (13) Hou. (3) NL Oct. 1, 1997

Most Runs, Inning
8 Anaheim, AL Oct. 5, 2002 (5th)
6 New York, NL Oct. 8, 1999 (6th)
St. Louis, NL Oct. 3, 2000 (1st)
St. Louis, NL Oct. 1, 2002 (7th)

Most Hits, Series
63 Seattle, AL 1995
58 Houston, NL 2004

Most Hits, Game
24 Boston, AL Oct. 10, 1999
17 Houston, NL Oct. 11, 2004

Most Hits, Both Clubs, Game
32 Bos. (24) Clev. (8), AL Oct. 10, 1999
30 LA (16) NY (14), NL Oct. 7, 2006

Most Hits, Inning
10 Anaheim, AL Oct. 5, 2002 (5th)
7 Atlanta, NL Oct. 9, 1999 (6th)

Most Total Bases, Series
105 Boston, AL 1999
103 Houston, NL:2004

Most Total Bases, Game
45 Boston, AL Oct. 10, 1999
30 Houston, NL Oct. 11, 2004

Most Total Bases, Both Clubs, Game
57 Bos. (45) Clev. (12) AL Oct. 10, 1999
45 Hou. (30) Atl. (15) NL Oct. 11, 2004
Atl. (25) Hou. (20) NL Oct. 9, 2005 (18 inn)

Most Total Bases, Inning
14 New York, AL Sept. 30, 1997 (6th)
Anaheim, AL Oct. 5, 2002 (5th)
11 Atlanta, NL Oct. 3, 2002 (2nd)
St. Louis, NL Oct. 5, 2004 (3rd)
Houston, NL Oct. 6, 2004 (3rd)

Most Extra-Base Hits, Series
28 Boston, AL 1999
23 Houston, NL 2004

Most Extra-Base Hits, Game
12 Boston, AL Oct. 10, 1999
8 Houston, NL Oct. 8, 2005
Atlanta, NL:Oct. 9, 2005 (18 inn)

Most Extra-Base Hits, Inning
4 New York, AL Oct. 5, 2003
3 By many NL teams

Most Singles, Series
45 Seattle, AL 1995
39 Atlanta, NL 1999

Most Singles, Game
14 Los Angeles, NL Oct. 7, 2006
12 Seattle, AL Oct. 7, 1995
Boston, AL Oct. 10, 1999
Anaheim, AL Oct. 2, 2002
Anaheim, AL Oct. 5, 2002
Los Angeles, AL: Oct. 7, 2005

Most Singles, Both Clubs, Game
25 LA (14) NY (11) NL Oct. 7, 2006
22 Ana. (12) NY (10) AL Oct. 2, 2002

Most Singles, Inning
8 Anaheim, AL Oct. 5, 2002 (5th)
7 Atlanta, NL Oct. 9, 1996 (6th)

Most Doubles, Series
17 Boston, AL 1999
12 Houston, NL 2004-05

Most Doubles, Game
7 Boston, AL Oct. 10, 1999
Houston, NL Oct. 8, 2005

Most Doubles, Both Clubs, Game
9 Clev. (5) Sea. (4) AL Oct. 13, 2001
Hou. (7) Atl. (2) NL Oct. 8, 2005

Most Doubles, Inning
3 Cincinnati, NL Oct. 3, 1995 (5th)
Cleveland, AL Oct. 13, 2001 (8th)

Most Triples, Series
3 Los Angeles, AL 2005
2 Atlanta, NL 2002
San Diego, NL 2006

Most Triples, Game
2 Chicago, AL Oct. 3, 2000 (10 inn)
Los Angeles, AL Oct. 7, 2005
San Diego, NL Oct. 3, 2006

Most Triples, Both Teams, Game
2 Mtl. (1) Phil. (1) NL Oct. 7, 1981
SD (2) StL. (0) NL Oct. 3, 2006
Chi. (2) Sea. (0) AL Oct. 3, 2000 (10 inn)
LA (2) NY (0) AL Oct. 7, 2005

Most Triples, Inning
1 By many teams

Most Home Runs, Series
11 New York, AL 1995
Seattle, AL 1995
Houston, NL 2004

Most Home Runs, Game
5 St. Louis, NL Oct. 5, 2004
Chicago, AL Oct. 4, 2005

Most Home Runs, Both Clubs, Game
6 NY (4) Sea. (2) AL Oct. 4, 1995 (15 inn)
Bos. (3) Clev. (3) AL Oct. 11, 1999
NY (4) Ana. (2) AL Oct. 1, 2002
Ana. (4) NY (2) AL Oct. 2, 2002
StL. (5) LA (1) NL Oct. 5, 2004

Most Home Runs, Inning
- 3 New York, AL Sept. 30, 1997 (6th)
- 2 Atlanta, NL Oct. 3, 1996 (7th)
- Atlanta, NL Oct. 2, 2002 (8th)
- Atlanta, NL Oct. 3, 2002 (2nd)
- St. Louis, NL Oct. 5, 2004 (3rd)
- Houston, NL Oct. 6, 2004 (3rd)
- Los Angeles, NL Oct. 7, 2004 (4th)
- Atlanta, NL Oct. 11, 2004 (5th)
- New York, NL Oct. 4, 2006 (4th)

Most Grand Slam Home Runs, Series
- 2 Atlanta, NL 1998
- 1 By many AL clubs

Most Grand Slam Home Runs, Game
- 1 Cincinnati, NL Oct. 6, 1995
- Florida, NL Oct. 3, 1997
- Atlanta, NL Sept. 30, 1998
- Atlanta, NL Oct. 3, 1998
- New York, NL Oct. 5, 1999
- St. Louis, NL Oct. 4, 2005
- Atlanta, NL Oct. 9, 2005
- Houston, NL Oct. 9, 2005
- Seattle, AL Oct. 7, 1995
- Baltimore, AL Oct. 1, 1996
- Cleveland, AL Oct. 4, 1996
- New York, AL Oct. 4, 1997
- Cleveland, AL Oct. 7, 1999
- Boston, AL Oct. 11, 1999
- Anaheim, AL Oct. 8, 2004

Most Runs Batted In, Series
- 47 Boston, AL 1999
- 36 Houston, NL 2004

Most Runs Batted In, Game
- 23 Boston, AL Oct. 10, 1999
- 12 Houston, NL Oct. 11, 2004

Most Runs Batted In, Both Clubs, Game
- 30 Bos. (23) Clev. (7) AL Oct. 10, 1999
- 15 Hou. (12) Atl. (3) NL Oct. 11, 2004

Most Runs Batted In, Inning
- 8 Anaheim, AL Oct. 5, 2002 (5th)
- 6 New York, NL Oct. 8, 1999 (6th)

Most Sacrifice Hits, Series
- 8 St. Louis, NL 2001
- 5 Los Angeles, AL 2005

Most Sacrifice Hits, Game
- 4 Houston, NL Oct. 5, 2005
- 3 Oakland, AL Oct. 7, 1981
- Seattle, AL Oct. 6, 2000

Most Sacrifice Hits, Both Clubs, Game
- 4 Oak. (3) KC (1) AL Oct. 7, 1981
- NY (2) Tex. (2) AL Oct. 2, 1996 (12 inn)
- Sea. (3) Chi. (1) AL Oct. 6, 2000
- Hou. (4) Atl. (0) NL Oct. 5, 2005
- **Extra-Inning Game:**
- 5 Chi. (3) Atl. (2) NL Oct. 1, 1998 (10 inn)

Most Sacrifice Hits, Inning
- 2 Los Angeles, AL Oct. 5, 2005 (7th)
- Chicago, AL Oct. 5, 2005 (9th)
- 1 By many NL teams

Most Sacrifice Flies, Series
- 4 Cleveland, AL 1999
- Minnesota, AL 2004
- 3 Atlanta, NL 1999
- Houston, NL 2004

Most Sacrifice Flies, Game
- 2 Atlanta, NL Oct. 6, 1999
- San Francisco, NL Oct. 4, 2003
- Houston, NL Oct. 8, 2005
- Cleveland, AL Oct. 10, 1999
- New York, AL Oct. 8, 2000
- Oakland, AL Oct. 8, 2000
- Oakland, AL Oct. 10, 2001
- New York, AL Oct. 4, 2002
- Minnesota, AL Oct. 9, 2004

Most Sacrifice Flies, Both Clubs, Game
- 4 NY (2) Oak. (2) AL Oct. 8, 2000
- 2 Atl. (2) Hou. (0) NL Oct. 6, 1999
- StL. (1) Ari. (1) NL Oct. 1, 2002
- SF (2) Fla. (0) NL Oct. 4, 2003
- Hou. (2) Atl. (0) NL Oct. 8, 2005
- Atl. (1) Hou. (1) NL Oct. 9, 2005 (18 inn)
- StL. (1) SD (1) NL Oct. 3, 2006

Most Sacrifice Flies, Inning
- 2 New York, AL Oct. 8, 2000 (1st)
- Oakland, AL Oct. 8, 2000 (4th)
- 1 By many NL teams

Most Walks, Series
- 32 New York, AL 1995
- 22 Atlanta, NL 2002

Most Walks, Game
- 10 Atlanta, NL Oct. 1, 1997
- 9 Cleveland, AL Oct. 7, 1999
- Cleveland, AL Oct. 9, 1999
- **Extra-Inning Game:**
- 10 New York, AL Oct. 8, 1995 (11 inn)
- Oakland, AL Oct. 1, 2003 (12 inn)

Most Walks, Both Clubs, Game
- 16 Atl. (10) Hou. (6) NL Oct. 1, 1997
- 14 Tex. (7) NY (7) AL Oct. 5, 1999
- Clev. (9) Bos. (5) AL Oct. 10, 1999
- **Extra-Inning Game:**
- 17 Bos. (7) Oak. (10) AL Oct. 1, 2003 (12 inn)
- Atl. (11) Hou. (6) NL Oct. 9, 2005 (18 inn)

Most Walks, Inning
- 5 Florida, NL Oct. 1, 1997 (4th)
- Cleveland, AL Oct. 10, 1999 (5th)

Most Intentional Walks, Series
- 8 San Francisco, NL 2003
- Houston, NL 2005
- 6 Boston, AL 2004

Most Intentional Walks, Game
- 3 Montreal, NL Oct. 7, 1981
- Houston, NL Oct. 5, 1999
- St. Louis, NL Oct. 3, 2000
- San Francisco, NL Oct. 6, 2002
- Houston, NL Oct. 5, 2005
- Houston, NL Oct. 8, 2005
- Boston, AL Oct. 11, 1999
- Boston, AL Oct. 1, 2003 (12 inn)
- Boston, AL Oct. 6, 2004
- **Extra-Inning NL Game:**
- 4 San Francisco, NL Oct. 3, 2003 (11 inn)

Most Intentional Walks, Both Clubs, Game
- 4 Mtl. (3) Phil. (1) NL Oct. 7, 1981
- **Since 1995:**
- 3 Col. (2) Atl. (1) NL Oct. 3, 1995
- Hou. (3) Atl. (0) NL Oct. 5, 1999
- StL. (3) Atl. (0) NL Oct. 3, 2000
- SF (2) Atl. (1) NL Oct. 2, 2002
- SF (3) Atl. (0) NL Oct. 6, 2002
- Hou. (3) Atl. (0) NL Oct. 5, 2005
- Hou. (3) Atl. (0) NL Oct. 8, 2005
- Bos. (3) Clev. (0) AL Oct. 11, 1999
- Bos. (3) Ana. (0) Oct. 6, 2004
- **Extra-Inning Game:**
- 5 SF (4) Fla. (1) NL Oct. 3, 2003 (11 inn)
- 4 Bos. (3) Oak. (1) AL Oct. 1, 2003 (11 inn)

Most Intentional Walks, Inning
2 Baltimore, AL Oct. 2, 1996 (8th)
   New York, AL Oct. 5, 1999 (5th)
   New York, AL Oct. 4, 2003 (7th)
   Boston, AL Oct. 6, 2004 (9th)
   St. Louis, NL Oct. 4, 2005 (3rd)
   Atlanta, NL Oct. 5, 2005 (8th)

Most Hit By Pitch, Series
5 Houston, NL 1998
   Chicago, AL 2005

Most Hit By Pitch, Game
3 Cleveland, AL Sept. 30. 1998
   Chicago, AL Oct. 4, 2005
   San Diego, NL Oct. 6, 2005

Most Hit By Pitch, Both Clubs, Game
3 Balt. (2) Clev. (1) AL Oct. 1, 1996
   Clev. (3) Balt. (0) AL Sept. 30, 1998
   NY (2) Oak. (1) AL Oct. 15, 2001
   Ana. (2) NY (1) AL Oct. 4, 2002
   Chi. (3) Bos. (0) AL Oct. 4, 2005
   Hou. (2) SD (1) NL Oct. 3, 1998
   SF (1) Fla. (2) NL Oct. 4, 2003
   Hou. (2) Atl. (1) NL Oct. 5, 2005
   SD (3) StL. (0) NL Oct. 6, 2005

Most Hit By Pitch, Inning
2 St. Louis NL Oct. 7, 2004 (5th)
   Minnesota, AL Oct. 8, 2004 (9th)
   Chicago, AL Oct. 4, 2005 (1st)

Most Strikeouts, Series
49 Houston, NL 1998
48 Seattle, AL 2001

Most Strikeouts, Game
17 Houston, NL Sept. 29, 1998
14 Milwaukee, AL Oct. 8, 1981
    AL since 1995:
13 Baltimore, AL Oct. 5, 1997
    Cleveland, AL Oct. 9, 2001
    Seattle, AL Oct. 15, 2001
    Extra-Inning Game:
23 Baltimore, AL Oct. 5, 1996 (12 inn)
18 Atlanta, NL Oct. 8, 1999 (12 inn)

Most Strikeouts, Both Clubs, Game
28 Hou. (17) SD (11) NL Sept. 29, 1998
25 Clev. (13) Sea. (12) AL Oct. 9, 2001
    Extra-Inning Game:
33 Balt. (23) Clev. (10) AL Oct. 5, 1996 (12 inn)
30 Atl. (18) Hou. (12) NL Oct. 8, 1999 (12 inn)
    Atl. (16) Hou. (14) NL Oct. 9, 2005 (18 inn)

Most Strikeouts, Inning
3 By many clubs

Most Stolen Bases, Series
11 Cleveland, AL 1996
9 Cincinnati, NL 1995

Most Stolen Bases, Game
5 Cleveland, AL Oct. 4, 1996
4 Montreal, NL Oct. 7, 1981
   Cincinnati, NL Oct. 4, 1995
   New York, NL Oct. 6, 1999
   Atlanta, NL Oct. 10, 2004

Most Stolen Bases, Both Clubs, Game
6 Clev. (5) Balt. (1) AL Oct. 4, 1996
4 Mtl. (4) Phil. (0) NL Oct. 7, 1981
   Cin. (4) LA (0) NL Oct. 4, 1995
   StL. (2) SD (2) NL Oct. 1, 1996
   NY (4) Ari. (0) NL Oct. 6, 1999
   StL. (3) Ari. (1) NL Oct. 7, 2000
   Atl. (4) Hou. (0) NL Oct. 10, 2004
   Extra-Inning Game:
5 Atl. (3) Hou. (2) NL Oct. 9, 2005 (18 inn)

Most Stolen Bases, Inning
3 Cincinnati, NL Oct. 4, 1995 (9th)
2 Seattle, AL Oct. 6, 1995 (7th)
   Cleveland, AL Oct. 2, 1996 (6th)
   Cleveland, AL Oct. 4, 1996 (1st)
   Cleveland, AL Oct. 4, 1996 (8th)
   Oakland, AL Oct. 3, 2000 (7th)
   Chicago, AL Oct. 4, 2000 (3rd)
   Chicago, AL Oct. 7, 2005 (6th)

Most Caught Stealing, Series
5 Montreal, NL 1981
4 New York, AL 2001
   Minnesota, AL 2004
   Los Angeles, AL 2005
   NL since 1995:
3 By many teams

Most Caught Stealing, Game
2 In many games
   Extra-Inning Game:
3 Atlanta, NL Oct. 2, 1996 (10 inn)
   Minnesota, AL Oct. 9, 2004 (11 inn)

Most Caught Stealing, Both Clubs, Game
2 By many teams
   Extra-Inning Game:
4 Atl. (3) LA (1) NL Oct. 2, 1996 (10 inn)
3 Clev. (2) Balt. (1) AL Oct. 5, 1996 (12 inn)
   Minn. (3) NY (0) Oct. 9, 2004 (11 inn)

Most Caught Stealing, Inning
2 Oakland, AL Oct. 9, 1981 (3rd)
   New York, AL Oct. 15, 2001 (4th)
1 By many NL teams

Most Grounded Into Double Plays, Series
7 Chicago, NL 2003
   Houston, NL 2005
   San Diego, NL 2005
   St. Louis, NL 2006
   New York, AL 2004

Most Grounded Into Double Plays, Game
4 Colorado, NL Oct. 3, 1995
   San Deigo, NL Oct. 6, 2005
   New York, AL Oct. 1, 2002

Most Grounded Into Double Plays, Both Clubs, Game
6 Col. (4) Atl. (2) NL Oct. 3, 1995
   NY (4) Ana. (2) AL Oct. 1, 2002

CLUB FIELDING

Most Errors, Series
7 Colorado, NL 1995
   San Francisco, NL 2003
6 Cleveland, AL 1995
   Oakland, AL 2001
   New York, AL 2005

Most Errors, Game
4 Montreal, NL Oct. 9, 1981
   Colorado, NL Oct. 3, 1995
   Atlanta, NL Oct. 3, 2003
3 by many AL teams
   Extra-Inning AL Game:
4 Oakland, AL Oct. 4, 2003 (11 inn)

Most Errors, Both Clubs, Game
5 Hou. (3) LA (2) NL Oct. 11, 1981
   Col. (4) Atl. (1) NL Oct. 3, 1995
4 Mil. (3) NY (1) AL Oct. 7, 1981
   Bos. (2) Clev. (2) AL Oct. 3, 1995 (13 inn)
   Oak. (3) NY (1) AL Oct. 15, 2001
   Minn. (3) Oak. (1) AL Oct. 6, 2006
   Extra-Inning Game:
6 Oak. (4) Bos. (2) AL Oct. 4, 2003 (11 inn)

Most Errors, Inning
3 Kansas City, AL Oct. 9, 1981 (3rd)
   Oakland, AL Oct. 4, 2003 (2nd)
   NL Since 1995:
2 By many clubs

Most Double Plays, Series
9 Minnesota, AL 2004
8 Atlanta, NL 2003
   San Diego, NL 2006

Most Double Plays, Game
5 Minnesota, AL Oct. 5, 2004
4 Atlanta, NL Oct. 3, 1995
   Houston, NL Oct. 10, 2001
   St. Louis, NL Oct. 6, 2005

Most Double Plays, Both Clubs, Game
7 Hou. (4) Atl. (3) NL Oct. 10, 2001
6 Ana. (4) NY (2) AL Oct. 1, 2002
   Minn. (5) NY (1) Oct. 5, 2004

CLUB PITCHING

Most Earned Runs, Series
46 Cleveland, AL 1999
36 Atlanta, NL 2004

Most Earned Runs, Game
23 Cleveland, AL Oct. 10, 1999
12 Atlanta, NL Oct. 11, 2004

Most Earned Runs, Both Clubs, Game
30 Clev. (23) Bos. (7) AL Oct. 10, 1999
15 Atl. (12) Hou. (3) NL Oct. 11, 2004
    Atl. (10) Hou. (5) NL Oct. 5, 2005

Most Consecutive Scoreless Innings, Series
20 Detroit, AL 2006
18 New York, NL 2000

Most Wild Pitches, Series
5 St. Louis, NL 2000
4 Oakland, AL 2002
   Anaheim, AL 2004
   Los Angeles, AL 2005

Most Wild Pitches, Game
5 St. Louis, NL Oct. 3, 2000
3 Anaheim, AL Oct. 6, 2004

Most Wild Pitches, Both Clubs, Game
5 StL. (5) Atl. (0) NL Oct. 3, 2000
3 Ana. (3) Bos. (0) AL Oct. 6, 2004
   LA (3) NY (0) AL Oct. 9, 2005

Most Wild Pitches, Inning
5 St. Louis, NL Oct. 3, 2000 (3rd)
2 New York, AL Oct. 9, 2005 (8th)

Most Balks, Game
1 Chicago, NL Oct. 1, 1998 (5th)
   Atlanta, NL Oct. 7, 2000 (5th)
   St. Louis, NL Oct. 5, 2002 (1st)
   Los Angeles, NL Oct. 7, 2006 (8th)

CLUB MISCELLANEOUS

Most Players, Game
20 Colorado, NL Oct. 3, 1995
    New York, AL Oct. 2, 1996 (12 inn)
    Texas, AL Oct. 5, 1996
    Extra-Inning Game:
23 Houston, NL Oct. 9, 2005 (18 inn)

Most Players, Both Clubs, Game
39 Tex. (20) NY (19) AL Oct. 5, 1996
37 Col. (20) Atl. (17) NL Oct. 3, 1995
    Fla. (19) SF (18) NL Oct. 1, 2003
    NY (19) LA (18) NL Oct. 7, 2006
    Extra-Inning Game:
42 Hou. (23) Atl. (19) NL Oct. 9, 2005 (18 inn)

Most Pitchers, Game
8 Texas, AL Oct. 5, 1996
   San Francisco, NL Oct. 5, 2002
   Houston, NL Oct. 9, 2005 (18 inn)

Most Pitchers, Both Clubs, Game
14 Fla. (7) SF (7) NL Oct. 1, 2003
    Hou. (8) Atl. (6) NL Oct. 9, 2005 (18inn)
13 Tex. (8) NY (5) AL Oct. 5, 1996
    Extra-Inning AL Game:
14 Clev. (7) Bos. (7) AL Oct. 3, 1995 (13 inn)

Most Pitchers, Inning
4 Los Angeles, NL Oct. 6, 1995 (6th)
   Colorado, NL Oct. 6, 1995 (7th)
   Atlanta, NL Oct. 9, 1999 (8th)
   San Francisco, NL Oct. 5, 2002 (9th)
   Atlanta, NL Oct. 8, 2005 (7th)
   New York, AL Oct. 2, 1996 (12th)
   Boston, AL Oct. 10, 1999 (5th)
   Boston, AL Oct. 8, 2004 (7th)
   Boston, AL Oct. 7, 2005 (6th)

Most Left On Base, Series
49 Seattle, AL 1995
43 Atlanta, NL 2004

Most Left On Base, Game
14 San Diego, NL Oct. 7, 2006
12 Boston, AL Oct. 6, 1995
    New York, AL Oct. 7, 1995
    Oakland, AL Oct. 1, 2002
    Extra-Inning Game:
18 San Francisco, NL Oct. 3, 2003 (11 inn)
    Atlanta, NL Oct. 9, 2005 (18 inn)
13 Seattle, AL Oct. 8, 1995 (11 inn)
    Baltimore, AL Oct. 5, 1996 (12 inn)
    Boston, AL Oct. 1, 2003 (12 inn)

Most Left On Base, Both Clubs, Game
22 Bos. (12) Clev. (10) AL Oct. 6, 1995
    NY (12) Sea. (10) AL Oct. 7, 1995
    Atl. (11) StL. (11) NL Oct. 3, 2000
    LA (13) NY (9) NL Oct. 7, 2006
    Extra-Inning Game:
30 Fla. (12) SF (18) NL Oct. 3, 2003 (11 inn)
25 Oak. (12) Bos. (13) AL Oct. 1, 2003 (12 inn)

Longest Game, Innings
18 Atlanta at Houston, Oct. 9, 2005
15 Seattle at New York, AL Oct. 4, 1995

Longest Game, Time
4:13 New York at Oakland, AL Oct. 14, 2001
3:51 Los Angeles at New York, NL Oct. 7, 2006
      Extra-Inning Game:
5:50 Atlanta at Houston, NL Oct. 9, 2005 (18 inn)
5:12 Seattle at New York, AL Oct. 4, 1995 (15 inn)

Shortest Game, Time
2:00 Houston at Los Angeles, NL Oct. 10, 1981
2:19 Minnesota at Oakland, AL Oct. 3, 2006
      NL since 1995:
2:08 Atlanta at Los Angeles, NL Oct. 3, 1996

ALL-STAR GAME

No. 1 AL: Chicago July 6, 1933

NL	000	002	000	2	8	0
AL	012	001	00x	4	9	1

HALLAHAN, Warneke(3), Hubbell(7)
GOMEZ, Crowder(4), Grove(7)
A-47,595   T-2:05

No. 2 AL: New York July 10, 1934

AL	000	261	000	9	14	1
NL	103	030	000	7	8	1

Gomez, Ruffing(4), HARDER(5)
Hubbell, Warneke(4), MUNGO(5)
Dean(6), Frankhouse(9)
A-48,363   T-2:44

No. 3 AL: Cleveland July 8, 1935

NL	000	100	000	1	4	1
AL	210	010	00x	4	8	0

WALKER, Schumacher(3), Derringer(7), Dean(8)
GOMEZ, Harder(7)
A-69,831   T-2:06

No. 4 NL: Boston July 7, 1936

AL	000	000	300	3	7	1
NL	020	020	00x	4	9	0

GROVE, Rowe(4), Harder(7)
DEAN, Hubbell(4), Davis(7), Warneke(7)
A-25,556   T-2:00

No. 5 AL: Washington July 7, 1937

NL	000	111	000	3	13	0
AL	002	312	00x	8	13	2

DEAN, Hubbell(4), Blanton(4), Grissom(5), Mungo(6), Walters(8)
GOMEZ, Bridges(4), Harder(7)
A-31,391   T-2:30

No. 6 NL: Cincinnati July 6, 1938

AL	000	000	001	1	7	4
NL	100	100	20x	4	8	0

GOMEZ, Allen(4), Grove(7)
VANDER MEER, Lee(4), Brown(7)
A-27,067   T-1:58

No. 7 AL: New York July 11, 1939

NL	001	000	000	1	7	1
AL	000	210	00x	3	6	1

Derringer, LEE(4), Fette(7)
Ruffing, BRIDGES(4), Feller(6)
A-62,892   T-1:55

No. 8 NL: St. Louis July 9, 1940

AL	000	000	000	0	3	1
NL	300	000	01x	4	7	0

RUFFING, Newsom(4), Feller(7)
DERRINGER, Walters(3), Wyatt(5), French(7), Hubbell(9)
A-32,373   T-1:53

No. 9 AL: Detroit July 8, 1941

NL	000	001	220	5	10	2
AL	000	101	014	7	11	3

Wyatt, Derringer(3), Walters(5), PASSEAU(7)
Feller, Lee(4), Hudson(7), SMITH(8)
A-54,674   T-2:23

No. 10 NL: New York July 6n, 1942

AL	300	000	000	3	7	0
NL	000	000	010	1	6	1

CHANDLER, Benton(5)
COOPER, Vander Meer(4), Passeau(7), Walters(9)
A-33,694   T-2:07

No. 11 AL: Philadelphia July 13n, 1943

NL	100	000	101	3	10	3
AL	031	010	00x	5	8	1

COOPER, Vander Meer(3), Sewell(6), Javery(7)
LEONARD, Newhouser(4), Hughson(7)
A-31,938   T-2:07

No. 12 NL: Pittsburgh July 11n, 1944

AL	010	000	000	1	6	3
NL	000	040	21x	7	12	1

Borowy, HUGHSON(4), Muncrief(5), Newhouser(7), Newsom(8)
Walters, RAFFENSBERGER(4), Sewell(6), Tobin(9)
A-29,589   T-2:11

1945 No Game (World War II)

No. 13 AL: Boston July 9, 1946

NL	000	000	000	0	3	0
AL	200	130	24x	12	14	1

PASSEAU, Higbe(4), Blackwell (5), Sewell(8)
FELLER, Newhouser(4), Kramer(7)
A-34,906   T-2:19

No. 14 NL: Chicago July 8, 1947

AL	000	001	100	2	8	0
NL	000	100	000	1	5	1

Newhouser, SHEA(4), Masterson(7), Page(8)
Blackwell, Brecheen(4), SAIN(7), Spahn(8)
A-41,123   T-2:19

No. 15 AL: St. Louis July 13, 1948

NL	200	000	000	2	8	0
AL	011	300	00x	5	6	0

Branca, SCHMITZ(4), Sain(4), Blackwell(6)
Masterson, RASCHI(4), Coleman(7)
A-34,009   T-2:27

No. 16 NL: Brooklyn July 12, 1949

AL	400	202	300	11	13	1
NL	212	002	000	7	12	5

Parnell, TRUCKS(2), Brissie(4), Raschi(7)
Spahn, NEWCOMBE(2), Munger(5), Bickford(6), Pollet(7), Blackwell(8), Roe(9)
A-32,577   T-3:04

No. 17 AL: Chicago July 11, 1950

NL	020	000	001	000	01	4	10	0
AL	001	020	000	000	00	3	8	1

Roberts, Newcombe(4), Konstanty(6), Jansen(7), BLACKWELL(12)
Raschi, Lemon(4), Houtteman(7), Reynolds(10), GRAY(13), Feller(14)
A-46,127   T-3:19

No. 18 AL: Detroit July 10, 1951

NL	100	302	110	8	12	1
AL	010	110	000	3	10	2

Roberts, MAGLIE(3), Newcombe(6), Blackwell(9)
Garver, LOPAT(4), Hutchinson(5), Parnell(8), Lemon(9)
A-52,075   T-2:41

No. 19 NL: Philadelphia July 8, 1952 (rain)

AL	000	20	2	5	0
NL	100	20	3	3	0

Raschi, LEMON(3), Shantz(5)
Simmons, RUSH(4)
A-32,785   T-1:29

No. 20 NL: Cincinnati July 14, 1953

AL	000	000	001	1	5	0
NL	000	020	12x	5	10	0

Pierce, REYNOLDS(4), Garcia(6), Paige(8)
Roberts, SPAHN(4), Simmons(6), Dickson(8)
A-30,846   T-2:19

No. 21 AL: Cleveland July 13, 1954

NL	000	520	020	9	14	0
AL	004	121	03x	11	17	1

Roberts, Antonelli(4), Spahn(6), Grissom(6), CONLEY(8), Erskine(8)
Ford, Consuegra(4), Lemon(4), Porterfield(5), Keegan(8), STONE(8), Trucks(9)
A-68,751   T-3:10

No. 22 NL: Milwaukee July 12, 1955

AL	400	001	000	000	5	10	2
NL	000	000	230	001	6	13	1

Pierce, Wynn(4), Ford(7), SULLIVAN(8)
Roberts, Haddix(4), Newcombe(7), Jones(8), Nuxhall(8), CONLEY(12)
A-45,314   T-3:17

No. 23 AL: Washington July 10, 1956

NL	001	211	200	7	11	0
AL	000	003	000	3	11	0

FRIEND, Spahn(4), Antonelli(6), PIERCE, Ford(4), Wilson(5), Brewer(6), Score(8), Wynn(9)
A-28,843   T-2:45

No. 24 NL: St. Louis July 9, 1957

AL	020	001	003	6	10	0
NL	000	000	203	5	9	1

BUNNING, Loes(4), Wynn(7), Pierce(7), Mossi(9), Grim(9)
SIMMONS, Burdette(2), Sanford(6), Jackson(7), Labine(9)
A-30,693   T-2:43

No. 25 AL: Baltimore July 8, 1958

NL	210	000	000	3	4	2
AL	110	011	00x	4	9	2

Spahn, FRIEND(4), Jackson(6), Farrell(7)
Turley, Narleski(2), WYNN(6), O'Dell(7)
A-48,829   T-2:13

No. 26 NL: Pittsburgh July 7, 1959

AL	000	100	030	4	8	0
NL	100	000	22x	5	9	1

Wynn, Duren(4), Bunning(7), FORD(8), Daley(8)
Drysdale, Burdette(4), Face(7), ANTONELLI(8), Elston(9)
A-35,277   T-2:33

No. 27 NL: Los Angeles August 3, 1959

AL	012	000	110	5	6	0
NL	100	010	100	3	6	3

WALKER, Wynn(4), Wilhelm(6), O'Dell(7), McLish(8)
DRYSDALE, Conley(4), Jones(6), Face(8)
A-55,105   T-2:42

No. 28 AL: Kansas City July 11, 1960

NL	311	000	000	5	12	4
AL	000	001	020	3	6	1

FRIEND, McCormick(4), Face(6), Buhl(8), Law (9)
MONBOUQUETTE, Estrada(3), Coates(4), Bell(6), Lary(8), Daley(9)
A-30,619   T-2:39

No. 29 AL: New York July 13, 1960

NL	021	000	102	6	10	0
AL	000	000	000	0	8	0

LAW, Podres(3), Williams(5), Jackson(7), Henry (8), McDaniel (9)
FORD, Wynn(4), Staley(6), Lary(8), Bell(9)
A-38,362   T-2:42

No. 30 NL: San Francisco July 11, 1961

AL	000	001	002	1	4	4	2
NL	010	100	010	2	5	11	5

Ford, Lary(4), Donovan(4), Bunning(6), Fornieles(8), WILHELM(8)
Spahn, Purkey(4), McCormick(6), Face(9), Koufax(9), MILLER(9)
A-44,115   T-2:53

No. 31 AL: Boston July 31, 1961 (rain)

NL	000	001	000	1	5	1
AL	100	000	000	1	4	0

Purkey, Mahaffey(3), Koufax(5), Miller(7)
Bunning, Schwall(4), Pascual(7)
A-31,851   T-2:27

No. 32 AL: Washington July 10, 1962

NL	000	002	010	3	8	0
AL	000	001	000	1	4	0

Drysdale, MARICHAL(4), Purkey(6), Shaw(8)
Bunning, PASCUAL(4), Donovan(7), Pappas(9)
A-45,480   T-2:33

No. 33 NL: Chicago July 30, 1962

AL	001	201	302	9	10	0
NL	010	000	111	4	10	4

Stenhouse, HERBERT(3), Aguirre(6), Pappas(9)
Podres, MAHAFFEY(3), Gibson(5), Farrell(7), Marichal(8)
A-38,359   T-2:28

No. 34 AL: Cleveland July 9, 1963

NL	012	010	010	5	6	0
AL	012	000	000	3	11	1

O'Toole, JACKSON(3), Culp(5), Woodeshick(6), Drysdale(8)
McBride, BUNNING(4), Bouton(6), Pizarro(7), Radatz(8)
A-44,160   T-2:20

No. 35 NL: New York July 7, 1964

AL	100	002	100	4	9	1
NL	000	210	004	7	8	0

Chance, Wyatt(4), Pascual(5), RADATZ(7)
Drysdale, Bunning(4), Short(6), Farrell(7), MARICHAL(9)
A-50,844   T-2:27

No. 36 AL: Minnesota July 13, 1965

NL	320	000	100	6	11	0
AL	000	140	000	5	8	0

Marichal, Maloney(4), Drysdale(5), KOUFAX(6), Farrell(7), Gibson(8)
Pappas, Grant(2), Richert(4), McDOWELL(6), Fisher(8)
A-46,706   T-2:45

No. 37 NL: St. Louis July 12, 1966

AL	010	000	000	0	1	6	0
NL	000	100	000	1	2	6	0

McLain, Kaat(4), Stottlemyre(6), Siebert(8), RICHERT(10)
Koufax, Bunning(4), Marichal(6), PERRY(9)
A-49,936   T-2:19

No. 38 AL: California July 11, 1967

NL	010	000	000	000	001	2	9	0
AL	000	001	000	000	000	1	8	0

Marichal, Jenkins(4), Gibson(7), Short(9), Cuellar(11), DRYSDALE(13), Seaver(15)
Chance, McGlothlin(4), Peters(6), Downing(9), HUNTER(11)
A-46,309   T-3:41

No. 39 NL: Houston July 9n, 1968

```
AL      000   000   000       0    3    1
NL      100   000   00x       1    5    0
```
TIANT, Odom(3), McLain(5), McDowell(7),
  Stottlemyre(8), John(8)
DRYSDALE, Marichal(4), Carlton(6), Seaver(7), Reed
  (9), Koosman(9)
A-48,321   T-2:10

No. 40 AL: Washington July 23, 1969

```
NL      125   100   000       9   11    0
AL      011   100   000       3    6    2
```
CARLTON, Gibson(4), Singer(5), Koosman(7),
  Dierker(8), Niekro(9)
STOTTLEMYRE, Odom(3), Knowles(3), McLain(4),
  McNally(5), McDowell(7), Culp(9)
A-45,259   T-2:38

No. 41 NL: Cincinnati July 14n, 1970

```
AL      000   001   120  000   4   12    0
NL      000   000   103  001   5   10    0
```
Palmer, McDowell(4), J. Perry(7), Hunter(9),
  Peterson(9), Stottlemyre(9), WRIGHT(11)
Seaver, Merritt(4), G. Perry(6), Gibson(8), OSTEEN(10)
A-51,838   T-3:19

No. 42 AL: Detroit July 13n, 1971

```
NL      021   000   010       4    5    0
AL      004   002   00x       6    7    0
```
ELLIS, Marichal(4), Jenkins(6), Wilson(8)
BLUE, Palmer(4), Cuellar(6), Lolich(8)
A-53,559   T-2:05

No. 43 NL: Atlanta July 25n, 1972

```
AL      001   000   020   0    3    6    0
NL      000   002   001   1    4    8    0
```
Palmer, Lolich(4), G. Perry(6), Wood(8), McNALLY(10)
Gibson, Blass(3), Sutton(4), Carlton(6), Stoneman(7),
  McGRAW(9)
A-53,107   T-2:26

No. 44 AL: Kansas City July 24n, 1973

```
NL      002   122   000       7   10    0
AL      010   000   000       1    5    0
```
WISE, Osteen(3), Sutton(5), Twitchell(6), Giusti(7),
  Seaver(8), Brewer(9)
Hunter, Holtzman(2), BLYLEVEN(3), Singer(4), Ryan(6),
  Lyle(8), Fingers(9)
A-40,849   T-2:45

No. 45 NL: Pittsburgh July 23n, 1974

```
AL      002   000   000       2    4    1
NL      010   210   12x       7   10    1
```
G. Perry, TIANT(4), Hunter(6), Fingers(8)
Messersmith, BRETT(4), Matlack(6), McGlothen(7),
  Marshall(8)
A-50,706   T-2:37

No. 46 AL: Milwaukee July 15n, 1975

```
NL      021   000   003       6   13    1
AL      000   003   000       3   10    1
```
Reuss, Sutton(4), Seaver(6), MATLACK(7), R. Jones(9)
Blue, Busby(3), Kaat(5), HUNTER(7), Gossage(9)
A-51,480   T-2:35

No. 47 NL: Philadelphia July 13n, 1976

```
AL      000   100   000       1    5    0
NL      202   000   03x       7   10    0
```
FIDRYCH, Hunter(3), Tiant(5), Tanana(7)
R.JONES, Seaver(4), Montefusco(6), Rhoden(8),
  Forsch(9)
A-63,974   T-2:12

No. 48 AL: New York July 19n, 1977

```
NL      401   000   020       7    9    1
AL      000   002   102       5    8    0
```
SUTTON, Lavelle(4),Seaver (6), Reuschel(8),Gossage (9)
PALMER, Kern(3), Eckersley(4), LaRoche(6)
A-56,683   T-2:34

No. 49 NL: San Diego July 11n, 1978

```
AL      201   000   000       3    8    1
NL      003   000   04x       7   10    0
```
Palmer, Keough(3), Sorensen(4), Kern(7), Guidry(7),
  GOSSAGE(8)
Blue, Rogers(4), Fingers(6), SUTTER(8), P. Niekro(9)
A-51,549   T-2:37

No.50 AL: Seattle July 17n, 1979

```
NL      211   001   011       7   10    1
AL      302   001   000       6   10    0
```
Carlton, Andujar(2), Rogers(4), Perry(6) Sambito(6),
  LaCoss(6), SUTTER(7)
Ryan, Stanley(3), Clear(5), KERN(7) Guidry(9)
A-58,905   T-3:11

No. 51 NL: Los Angeles July 8n, 1980

```
AL      000   020   000       2    7    2
NL      000   012   10x       4    7    0
```
Stone, JOHN(4), Farmer(6), Stieb(7), Gossage(8)
Richard, Welch(3), REUSS(6), Bibby(7), Sutter(8)
A-58,088   T-2:33

No.52 AL: Cleveland August 9n, 1981

```
NL      000   011   120       5    9    1
AL      010   003   000       4   11    1
```
Valenzuela, Seaver(2), Knepper(3), Hooton(5),
  Ruthven(6), BLUE(7), Ryan(8), Sutter(9)
Morris, Barker(3), K.Forsch(5), Norris(6), Davis(7),
  FINGERS(8), Stieb(8)
A-72,086   T-2:59

No. 53 NL: Montreal July 13n, 1982

```
AL      100   000   000       1    8    2
NL      021   001   00x       4    8    1
```
ECKERSLEY, Clancy(4), Bannister(5), Quisenberry(6),
  Fingers(8)
ROGERS, Carlton(4), Soto(6),
  Valenzuela(8), Minton(8),
  Howe(9), Hume(9)
A-59,057   T-2:53

No. 54 AL: Chicago July 6n, 1983

```
NL      100   110   000       3    8    3
AL      117   000   22x      13   15    2
```
SOTO, Hammaker(3), Dawley(3), Dravecky(5), Perez(7),
  Orosco(7), L. Smith(8)
STIEB, Honeycutt(4), Stanley(6), Young(8),
  Quisenberry(9)
A-43,801   T-3:05

No. 55 NL: San Francisco July 10n, 1984

```
AL      010   000   000       1    7    2
NL      110   000   01x       3    8    0
```
STIEB, Morris(3), Dotson(5), Caudill(7), Hernandez(8)
LEA, Valenzuela(3), Gooden(5), Soto(7), Gossage(9)
A-57,756   T-2:29

No. 56 AL: Minnesota July 16n, 1985

```
NL      011   020   002       6    9    1
AL      100   000   000       1    5    0
```
HOYT, Ryan(4), Valenzuela(7), Reardon(8), Gossage(9)
MORRIS, Key(3), Blyleven(4), Stieb(6), Moore(7),
  Petry(9), Hernandez(9)
A-54,960   T-2:54

No. 57 NL: Houston July 15n, 1986

AL	020	000	100	3	5	0
NL	000	000	020	2	5	1

CLEMENS, Higuera(4), Hough(7), Righetti(8), Aase(9)
GOODEN, Valenzuela(4), Scott(7), Fernandez(8), Krukow(9)
A-45,774   T-2:28

No. 58 AL: Oakland July 14n, 1987

NL	000	000	000	000	2	2	8	2
AL	000	000	000	000	0	0	6	1

Scott, Sutcliffe(3), Hershiser(5), Reuschel(7), Franco(8), Bedrosian(9), L.SMITH (10),Fernandez(13)
Saberhagen, Morris(4), Langston(6), Plesac(8), Righetti(9), Henke(9), HOWELL(12)
A-44,671   T-3:39

o. 59 NL: Cincinnati July 12n, 1988

AL	001	100	000	2	6	2
NL	000	100	000	1	5	0

VIOLA, Clemens(3), Gubicza(4), Stieb(6)
Russell(7), D. Jones(8), Plesac(8), Eckersley(9)
GOODEN, Knepper(4), Cone(5), Gross(6), Davis(7), Walk(7), Hershiser(8), Worrell(9)
A-55,837   T-2:26

o. 60 AL: California July 11n, 1989

NL	200	000	010	3	9	1
AL	212	000	00x	5	12	0

Reuschel, SMOLTZ(2), Sutcliffe(3),Burke(4), M. Davis(6), Howell(7), M. Williams(8)
Stewart, RYAN(2), Gubicza(4), Moore(5), Swindell(6), Russell(7), Plesac(8), D. Jones(8)
A-64,036   T-2:48

o. 61 NL: Chicago July 10n, 1990

AL	000	000	200	2	7	0
NL	000	000	000	0	2	1

Welch, Stieb(3), SABERHAGEN(5), Thigpen(7), Finley(8), Eckersley(9)
Armstrong, R. Martinez(3), D. Martinez(4), Viola(5), D. Smith(6), BRANTLEY(6), Dibble(7), Myers(8), Franco(9)
A-39,071   T-2:53

lo. 62 AL: Toronto July 9n, 1991

NL	100	100	000	2	10	1
AL	003	000	10x	4	8	0

Glavine, D. MARTINEZ(3), Viola(5), Harnisch(6), Smiley(7), Dibble(7), Morgan(8)
Morris, KEY(3), Clemens(4), McDowell(5), Reardon(7), Aguilera(7), Eckersley(9)
A-52,313   T-3:04

lo. 63 NL: San Diego July 14n, 1992

AL	411	004	030	13	19	1
NL	000	001	032	6	12	1

BROWN, McDowell(2), Guzman(3), Clemens(4), Mussina(5), Langston(6), Nagy(7), Montgomery(8), Aguilera(8), Eckersley(9)
GLAVINE, Maddux(2), Cone(4), Tewksbury(5), Smoltz(6), D. Martinez(7), Jones(8), Charlton(9)
A-59,372   T-2:55

lo. 64 AL: Baltimore July 13n, 1993

NL	200	001	000	3	7	2
AL	011	033	10x	9	11	0

Mulholland, Benes(3), BURKETT(5), Avery(6), Smoltz(6), Beck(7), Harvey(8)
Langston, R. Johnson(3), McDOWELL(5), Key(6), Montgomery(7), Aguilera(8), Ward(9)
A-48,147   T-2:49

No. 65 NL: Pittsburgh July 12n, 1994

AL	100	003	300	0	7	15	0
NL	103	001	002	1	8	12	1

Key, Cone(3), Mussina(5), Johnson(6), Hentgen(7), Alvarez(8), L. Smith(9) BERE(10)
Maddux, Hill(4), Drabek(6), Hudek(6), Jackson(7), Beck(7), Myers(9), JONES(10)
A-59, 568   T-3:14

No. 66 AL: Texas July 11n, 1995

NL	000	001	110	3	3	0
AL	000	200	000	2	8	0

Nomo, Smiley(3), Green(5), Neagle(6), Perez(7), SLOCUMB(7), Henke(8), Myers(9)
Johnson, Appier(3), D.Martinez(5), Rogers(7), ONTIVEROS(8), Wells(8), Mesa(9)
A-50,920   T-2:40

No. 67 NL: Philadelphia July 9n, 1996

AL	000	000	000	0	7	0
NL	121	002	00x	6	12	1

NAGY, Finley(3), Pavlik(5), Percival(7), R. Hernandez(8)
SMOLTZ, Brown(3), Glavine(4), Bottalico(5), P. Martinez(6), Trachsel(7), Worrell(8), Wohlers(9), Leiter(9)
A-62,670   T-2:35

No. 68 AL: Cleveland July 8n, 1997

NL	000	000	100	1	3	0
AL	010	000	20x	3	7	0

Maddux, Schilling (3), Brown (5),P. Martinez (6), ESTES (7), B. Jones (8)
Johnson, Clemens (3), Cone (4), Thompson (5), Hentgen (6), ROSADO (7), Myers (8), Rivera (9)
A-44,916   T-2:36

No. 69 NL: Colorado July 7n, 1998

AL	000	413	113	13	19	2
NL	022	130	020	8	12	1

Wells, Clemens (3), Radke (4), COLON (5), Arrojo (6), Wetteland (7), Gordon (8), Percival (9)
Maddux, Glavine (3), Brown (4), Ashby (5), URBINA (6), Hoffman (7), Shaw (8), Nen (9)
A-51,267   T-3:38

No. 70 AL: Boston July 13n, 1999

NL	001	000	000	1	7	1
AL	200	200	00x	4	6	2

SCHILLING, Johnson (3), Bottenfield (4), Lima (5) Millwood (6), Ashby (7), Hampton (7), Hoffman (8), Wagner (8)
MARTINEZ, Cone (3), Mussina (5), Rosado (6), Zimmerman (7), Hernandez (8) Wetteland (9)
A-34,187   T-2:53

No. 71 NL: Atlanta July 11n, 2000

AL	001	200	003	6	10	2
NL	001	010	001	3	9	2

Wells, BALDWIN (3), Sele (4), Isringhausen (5), Lowe (6), Jones (7), Hudson (8), Rivera (9)
Johnson, Graves (2), Brown (3), LEITER (4), Glavine (5), Kile (6), Wickman (8), Hoffman (9)
A-51,323   T-2:56

No. 72 AL: Seattle July 10n, 2001

NL	000	001	000	1	3	1
AL	001	012	00x	4	8	0

Johnson, PARK (3), Burkett (4), Hampton (5), Lieber (6), Morris (7), Shaw (8), Wagner (8), Sheets (9)
Clemens, GARCIA (3), Pettitte (4), Mays (5), Quantrill (6), Stanton (6), Nelson (7), Percival (8), Sasaki (9)
A-47,364   T-2:48

No. 73 NL: Milwaukee July 9n, 2002 (called)

AL	000	110	410	00	7	12	0
NL	013	010	200	00	7	13	0

Lowe, Halladay (3), Buehrle (4), Zito (6), Guardado (6), Sasaki (7), Urbina (8), Rivera (9), Garcia (10)
Schilling, Williams (3), Perez (4), Gagne (5), Hoffman (6), Remlinger (7), Kim (7), Nen (8), Smoltz (9), Padilla (10)
A-41,871 T-3:29

No. 74 AL: Chicago July 15n, 2003

NL	000	050	100	6	11	1
AL	001	002	13x	7	9	0

Schmidt, Wolf (3), Wood (4), Ortiz (5), Williams (6), Wagner (7), GAGNE (8)
Loaiza, Clemens (3), Moyer (4), Hasegawa (5), Guardado (5), Mulder (6), DONNELLY (8), Foulke (9)
A-47,609 T-2:38

No. 75 NL: Houston July 13n, 2004

AL	600	102	000	9	14	0
NL	100	300	000	4	9	1

MULDER, Loaiza (3), Sabathia (4), Vazquez (5), Lilly (6), Nathan (7), Gordon (8), F. Rodriguez (8), Rivera (9)
CLEMENS, Kolb (2), Johnson (3), Zambrano (4), Pavano (5), Glavine (7), Sheets (8), Gagne (9)
A-41,886 T-2:59

No. 76 AL: Detroit July 12n, 2005

NL	000	000	212	5	11	0
AL	012	202	00x	7	11	1

Carpenter, SMOLTZ (2), Oswalt (3), Hernandez (4), Clemens (5), Willis (6), Lidge (7), Peavy (8), Cordero (8)
BUEHRLE, Colon (3), Santana (4), Clement (5), Garland (6), Rogers (7), Nathan (8), Wickman (9), Ryan (9), Rivera (9)
A-41,617 T-2:41

No. 77 NL: Pittsburgh July 11n, 2006

AL	010	000	002	3	7	1
NL	011	000	000	2	6	0

Rogers, Halladay (3), Zito (5), Kazmir (6), Santana (7), RYAN (8), Rivera (9)
Penny, Oswalt (3), Webb (4), Arroyo (5), Fuentes (6), Turnbow (7), Gordon (8), HOFFMAN (9)
A-38,904 T-2:33

ALL-STAR GAME CLUB BATTING

EAR	AB	R	ER	H	TB	1B	2B	3B	HR	RBI	SH	SF	BB	HP	SO	SB	CS	BAT	SLG
)33																			
NL	34	2	2	8	14	5	1	1	1	2	0	0	0	0	4	0	0	.235	.412
AL	31	4	4	9	12	8	0	0	1	4	1	0	6	0	4	1	0	.290	.387
)34																			
AL	39	9	9	14	23	7	5	2	0	9	0	0	9	0	12	2	0	.359	.590
NL	36	7	7	8	15	5	1	0	2	6	0	0	3	0	5	2	0	.222	.417
)35																			
NL	31	1	1	4	6	2	2	0	0	1	0	0	2	0	5	1	0	.129	.194
AL	32	4	4	8	15	4	2	1	1	4	0	0	3	0	9	0	0	.250	.469
)36																			
AL	32	3	3	7	11	5	1	0	1	3	0	0	7	0	7	0	1	.219	.344
NL	31	4	3	9	14	7	0	1	1	4	0	0	3	0	6	0	0	.290	.452
)37																			
NL	41	3	3	13	16	10	3	0	0	3	0	0	0	0	0	0	0	.317	.390
AL	35	8	8	13	21	8	3	1	1	8	0	0	4	0	7	0	0	.371	.600
)38																			
AL	34	1	1	7	9	5	2	0	0	1	0	0	2	0	5	1	0	.206	.265
NL	33	4	1	8	10	7	0	1	0	2	0	0	0	1	7	1	0	.242	.303
)39																			
NL	34	1	1	7	8	6	1	0	0	1	0	0	3	0	9	0	0	.206	.235
AL	31	3	2	6	9	5	0	0	1	2	0	0	4	0	6	0	0	.194	.290
)40																			
AL	29	0	0	3	4	2	1	0	0	0	0	0	2	0	7	0	0	.103	.138
NL	29	4	4	7	10	6	0	0	1	4	2	0	3	1	6	0	0	.241	.345
)41																			
NL	35	5	5	10	19	5	3	0	2	5	2	0	1	0	7	0	1	.286	.543
AL	36	7	7	11	17	7	3	0	1	7	0	0	4	0	6	0	0	.306	.472
)42																			
AL	35	3	3	7	14	4	1	0	2	3	0	0	0	0	8	0	0	.200	.400
NL	31	1	1	6	9	5	0	0	1	1	0	0	2	1	3	0	0	.194	.290
)43																			
NL	37	3	3	10	16	7	1	1	1	3	0	0	1	0	3	0	0	.270	.432
AL	29	5	4	8	13	5	2	0	1	4	2	0	3	1	10	0	0	.276	.448
)44																			
AL	32	1	1	6	6	6	0	0	0	1	0	0	1	0	5	0	0	.188	.188
NL	33	7	5	12	16	9	2	1	0	7	3	0	4	0	4	1	0	.364	.485
)45																			
No Game (World War II)																			
)46																			
NL	31	0	0	3	3	3	0	0	0	0	0	0	1	0	10	0	0	.097	.097
AL	36	12	12	14	25	9	2	0	3	12	0	0	4	0	3	0	0	.389	.694
)47																			
AL	34	2	2	8	10	6	2	0	0	1	0	0	1	0	8	1	0	.235	.294
NL	32	1	1	5	8	4	0	0	1	1	0	0	4	0	6	0	0	.156	.250
)48																			
NL	35	2	2	8	11	7	0	0	1	2	0	0	4	0	7	1	0	.229	.314
AL	29	5	5	6	9	5	0	0	1	5	1	0	7	0	7	3	0	.207	.310
)49																			
AL	41	11	7	13	18	8	5	0	0	10	0	0	5	0	5	1	0	.317	.439
NL	37	7	7	12	20	8	2	0	2	6	0	0	8	1	3	0	0	.324	.541
)50	**(14 innings)**																		
NL	52	4	4	10	19	6	1	1	2	4	0	0	3	0	7	0	0	.192	.365
AL	49	3	3	8	12	5	2	1	0	3	0	0	2	0	12	0	0	.163	.245
)51																			
NL	39	8	7	12	25	7	1	0	4	7	0	0	4	0	3	0	1	.308	.641
AL	35	3	3	10	21	5	1	2	2	3	1	0	3	0	7	0	1	.286	.600
)52	**(five innings, rain)**																		
AL	18	2	2	5	7	3	2	0	0	2	0	0	2	0	4	0	1	.278	.389
NL	18	3	3	3	10	0	1	0	2	3	0	0	2	1	6	0	0	.167	.556

ALL-STAR GAME CLUB BATTING

YEAR	AB	R	ER	H	TB	1B	2B	3B	HR	RBI	SH	SF	BB	HP	SO	SB	CS	BAT	SLG
1953																			
AL	31	1	1	5	5	5	0	0	0	1	0	0	3	0	5	0	1	.161	.161
NL	32	5	5	10	11	9	1	0	0	5	0	0	3	1	3	1	0	.313	.344
1954																			
NL	40	9	9	14	23	9	3	0	2	9	0	0	2	0	2	0	1	.350	.575
AL	39	11	11	17	29	13	0	0	4	11	0	1	4	0	10	0	0	.436	.744
1955 (12 innings)																			
AL	44	5	5	10	14	8	1	0	1	4	2	0	6	1	12	0	0	.227	.318
NL	45	6	4	13	17	11	1	0	1	4	0	0	2	0	8	0	0	.289	.378
1956																			
NL	36	7	7	11	19	7	2	0	2	6	1	0	4	0	12	1	1	.306	.528
AL	37	3	3	11	17	9	0	0	2	3	0	0	0	0	5	0	0	.297	.459
1957																			
AL	37	6	4	10	12	8	2	0	0	6	1	0	4	0	1	0	0	.270	.324
NL	34	5	5	9	13	6	2	1	0	4	0	0	2	0	6	0	0	.265	.382
1958																			
NL	30	3	3	4	4	4	0	0	0	2	0	1	3	1	2	1	0	.133	.133
AL	31	4	2	9	9	9	0	0	0	3	1	0	3	0	4	0	0	.290	.290
1959 #1																			
AL	36	4	4	8	12	6	1	0	1	4	0	0	3	0	9	0	0	.222	.333
NL	30	5	5	9	16	5	2	1	1	5	1	0	2	0	9	0	0	.300	.533
1959 #2																			
AL	33	5	4	6	15	3	0	0	3	5	0	0	6	0	12	1	1	.182	.455
NL	31	3	3	6	13	3	1	0	2	3	0	1	5	0	4	0	0	.194	.419
1960 #1																			
NL	38	5	5	12	23	6	3	1	2	5	0	0	1	1	6	1	0	.316	.605
AL	34	3	1	6	9	5	0	0	1	3	0	0	5	0	7	0	0	.176	.265
1960 #2																			
NL	34	6	6	10	22	6	0	0	4	6	1	0	3	0	3	1	1	.294	.647
AL	33	0	0	8	9	7	1	0	0	0	0	0	6	0	4	0	0	.242	.273
1961 #1 (10 innings)																			
AL	38	4	2	4	8	2	1	0	1	3	0	0	2	0	12	0	0	.105	.211
NL	37	5	4	11	18	7	2	1	1	5	0	2	1	1	6	1	0	.297	.486
1961 #2 (nine innings, rain)																			
NL	32	1	1	5	6	4	1	0	0	1	0	0	2	1	7	0	0	.156	.188
AL	30	1	1	4	7	3	0	0	1	1	0	0	3	0	8	1	0	.133	.233
1962 #1																			
NL	33	3	3	8	9	7	1	0	0	3	0	1	1	0	3	2	1	.242	.273
AL	29	1	1	4	6	3	0	1	0	1	0	1	3	2	5	0	0	.138	.207
1962 #2																			
AL	37	9	8	10	21	5	2	0	3	9	0	1	4	0	8	0	0	.270	.568
NL	35	4	4	10	17	6	2	1	1	4	0	0	2	1	3	0	0	.286	.486
1963																			
NL	34	5	4	6	6	6	0	0	0	5	0	0	3	0	6	3	0	.176	.176
AL	34	3	3	11	12	10	1	0	0	3	1	0	1	1	9	0	0	.324	.353
1964																			
AL	35	4	3	9	12	7	1	1	0	4	0	1	1	1	10	0	0	.257	.343
NL	34	7	7	8	18	4	1	0	3	6	0	0	2	0	8	1	0	.235	.529
1965																			
NL	36	6	6	11	20	8	0	0	3	6	1	0	3	0	7	0	0	.306	.556
AL	34	5	5	8	15	5	1	0	2	5	0	0	6	0	5	0	0	.235	.441
1966 (10 innings)																			
AL	35	1	1	6	8	5	0	1	0	0	0	0	1	0	6	0	0	.171	.229
NL	33	2	2	6	7	5	1	0	0	2	1	0	1	0	5	0	0	.182	.212
1967 (15 innings)																			
NL	51	2	2	9	16	6	1	0	2	2	1	0	0	0	13	1	0	.176	.314
AL	49	1	1	8	12	6	1	0	1	1	2	0	2	0	17	0	2	.163	.245
1968																			
AL	30	0	0	3	6	0	3	0	0	0	0	0	0	0	11	0	0	.100	.200
NL	27	1	0	5	6	4	1	0	0	0	0	0	6	0	9	1	0	.185	.231

ALL-STAR GAME CLUB BATTING

YEAR	AB	R	ER	H	TB	1B	2B	3B	HR	RBI	SH	SF	BB	HP	SO	SB	CS	BAT	SLG
1969																			
NL	40	9	7	11	22	6	2	0	3	8	0	0	3	0	10	0	0	.275	.550
AL	33	3	3	6	13	3	1	0	2	3	0	0	2	0	7	0	0	.182	.394
1970 (12 innings)																			
AL	44	4	4	12	16	9	2	1	0	4	1	1	3	0	7	0	1	.273	.364
NL	43	5	5	10	13	9	0	0	1	4	0	1	5	1	11	0	0	.233	.302
1971																			
NL	31	4	4	5	14	2	0	0	3	4	0	0	1	1	8	0	0	.161	.452
AL	29	6	6	7	16	4	0	0	3	6	0	0	3	0	5	0	0	.241	.552
1972 (10 innings)																			
AL	33	3	3	6	11	3	2	0	1	3	1	0	2	0	8	0	0	.182	.333
NL	33	4	4	8	11	7	0	0	1	4	1	0	3	0	5	1	0	.242	.333
1973																			
NL	34	7	7	10	21	5	2	0	3	7	1	0	5	0	6	0	0	.294	.618
AL	32	1	1	5	9	2	2	1	0	1	0	0	3	0	5	1	0	.156	.281
1974																			
AL	30	2	2	4	5	3	1	0	0	1	1	0	6	0	7	1	0	.133	.167
NL	33	7	6	10	18	5	3	1	1	6	0	1	3	0	7	1	0	.303	.545
1975																			
NL	37	6	6	13	20	10	1	0	2	6	0	1	0	1	3	1	1	.351	.541
AL	36	3	3	10	13	9	0	0	1	3	0	0	1	1	10	3	1	.278	.361
1976																			
AL	29	1	1	5	8	4	0	0	1	1	0	0	3	0	5	1	0	.172	.276
NL	33	7	7	10	20	6	0	2	2	7	0	0	1	0	5	0	0	.303	.606
1977																			
NL	33	7	7	9	21	3	3	0	3	7	1	0	3	1	9	0	1	.273	.636
AL	35	5	4	8	12	6	1	0	1	5	0	0	3	1	10	0	0	.229	.343
1978																			
AL	31	3	3	8	13	5	1	2	0	3	0	2	1	0	7	1	2	.258	.419
NL	32	7	7	10	13	8	1	1	0	6	0	0	6	0	6	1	1	.313	.406
1979																			
NL	35	7	7	10	18	5	3	1	1	7	0	1	6	0	5	0	0	.286	.514
AL	35	6	5	10	16	6	3	0	1	5	1	0	5	1	5	0	0	.286	.457
1980																			
AL	32	2	2	7	11	5	1	0	1	2	0	0	4	0	11	1	0	.219	.344
NL	31	4	3	7	10	6	0	0	1	2	0	0	2	0	4	2	0	.226	.323
1981																			
NL	35	5	5	9	23	3	2	0	4	5	0	0	4	0	6	2	0	.257	.657
AL	37	4	4	11	15	9	1	0	1	4	0	1	2	0	8	0	1	.297	.405
1982																			
AL	33	1	1	8	9	7	1	0	0	1	0	1	5	0	10	1	0	.242	.273
NL	29	4	4	8	14	5	1	1	1	4	0	1	2	0	2	2	3	.276	.483
1983																			
NL	35	3	2	8	9	7	1	0	0	2	0	0	1	0	6	2	0	.229	.257
AL	38	13	10	15	28	8	3	2	2	13	1	3	4	0	8	0	0	.395	.737
1984																			
AL	32	1	1	7	13	3	3	0	1	1	0	0	0	0	11	0	0	.219	.406
NL	32	3	2	8	15	5	1	0	2	2	0	0	2	0	10	4	0	.250	.469
1985																			
NL	35	6	6	9	13	5	4	0	0	6	0	0	7	1	8	2	0	.257	.371
AL	30	1	0	5	5	5	0	0	0	1	0	1	4	0	6	3	0	.167	.167
1986																			
AL	33	3	3	5	12	2	1	0	2	3	0	0	2	0	12	2	0	.152	.364
NL	32	2	1	5	6	4	1	0	0	1	0	0	1	0	7	1	0	.156	.188
1987 (13 innings)																			
NL	46	2	2	8	11	6	1	1	0	2	0	0	1	0	10	1	1	.174	.239
AL	42	0	0	6	7	5	1	0	0	0	3	0	5	0	7	0	0	.143	.167
1988																			
AL	31	2	2	6	11	3	2	0	1	2	0	1	2	0	3	0	0	.194	.355
NL	33	1	1	5	5	5	0	0	0	0	0	0	1	0	7	2	0	.152	.152

ALL-STAR GAME CLUB BATTING

YEAR	AB	R	ER	H	TB	1B	2B	3B	HR	RBI	SH	SF	BB	HP	SO	SB	CS	BAT	SLG
1989																			
NL	33	3	3	9	9	9	0	0	0	3	0	0	3	0	8	3	1	.273	.273
AL	35	5	5	12	20	8	2	0	2	5	0	0	1	0	5	1	0	.343	.571
1990																			
AL	32	2	2	7	8	6	1	0	0	2	0	0	7	0	5	4	0	.219	.250
NL	29	0	0	2	2	2	0	0	0	0	0	0	2	0	6	1	0	.069	.069
1991																			
NL	35	2	2	10	14	8	1	0	1	2	0	0	2	0	6	1	0	.286	.400
AL	30	4	3	8	11	7	0	0	1	4	1	1	3	0	6	0	0	.267	.367
1992																			
AL	44	13	13	19	29	13	4	0	2	13	0	0	1	0	7	2	0	.432	.659
NL	39	6	4	12	17	9	2	0	1	6	0	0	2	0	7	0	0	.308	.436
1993																			
NL	33	3	3	7	13	3	3	0	1	3	0	1	1	0	9	0	0	.212	.394
AL	35	9	6	11	21	5	4	0	2	7	0	0	4	1	7	1	0	.314	.600
1994 (10 innings)																			
AL	44	7	5	15	18	12	3	0	0	6	0	0	2	0	8	3	0	.341	.409
NL	36	8	8	12	21	7	3	0	2	8	0	1	1	1	5	0	0	.333	.583
1995																			
NL	29	3	3	3	12	0	0	0	3	3	0	0	3	0	1	0	1	.103	.414
AL	34	2	2	8	12	6	1	0	1	2	0	0	2	0	2	1	1	.235	.353
1996																			
AL	34	0	0	7	8	6	1	0	0	0	0	0	0	0	8	2	0	.206	.235
NL	35	6	6	12	23	6	3	1	2	6	0	0	0	0	8	1	2	.343	.657
1997																			
NL	29	1	1	3	6	0	0	0	1	1	0	0	4	0	7	1	0	.103	.207
AL	30	3	3	7	14	0	1	0	2	3	0	0	1	0	8	0	1	.233	.467
1998																			
AL	43	13	11	19	26	16	1	0	2	11	0	2	6	0	5	5	0	.442	.605
NL	36	8	7	12	17	10	0	1	1	8	1	0	5	1	8	0	0	.333	.472
1999																			
NL	32	1	1	7	9	5	2	0	0	1	0	0	4	0	12	0	2	.219	.281
AL	31	4	4	6	6	6	0	0	0	4	0	0	2	1	10	1	0	.194	.194
2000																			
AL	38	6	5	10	13	7	3	0	0	6	0	1	4	0	7	1	0	.263	.342
NL	36	3	2	9	12	8	0	0	1	3	0	0	1	0	4	0	0	.250	.333
2001																			
NL	29	1	1	3	4	2	1	0	0	1	0	1	2	0	5	1	0	.103	.138
AL	33	4	3	8	19	3	2	0	3	4	0	0	0	0	7	1	0	.242	.576
2002 (11 innings, called)																			
AL	45	7	6	12	20	7	3	1	1	7	0	0	2	0	12	3	0	.267	.489
NL	45	7	7	13	18	10	2	0	1	7	0	0	1	0	11	2	0	.289	.422
2003																			
NL	36	6	6	11	19	7	2	0	2	6	0	0	1	0	7	0	0	.306	.528
AL	33	7	7	9	20	4	2	0	3	7	0	0	2	1	11	0	0	.273	.606
2004																			
AL	41	9	6	14	28	8	1	2	3	9	0	0	2	0	8	0	0	.341	.683
NL	36	4	4	9	12	6	3	0	0	4	0	0	1	1	6	0	0	.250	.333
2005																			
NL	35	5	5	11	17	7	3	0	1	5	0	0	5	0	6	0	0	.314	.486
AL	32	7	7	11	19	7	2	0	2	7	0	0	3	0	6	0	0	.344	.594
2006																			
AL	33	3	3	7	13	4	1	1	1	3	0	0	0	0	7	0	0	.212	.393
NL	30	2	2	6	10	4	1	0	1	1	0	0	1	0	4	2	0	.200	.333

ALL-STAR GAME - INDIVIDUAL RECORDS

BATTING — GAME

Most At-Bats
5 By many players
Extra-Inning Game:
7 Willie Jones, NL:Phil. 1950 (14 inn)

Most Runs
4 Ted Williams, AL:Bos. 1946
3 Frankie Frisch, NL:StL. 1934
Jackie Robinson, NL:Brk. 1949

Most Hits
4 Joe Medwick, NL:StL. 1937
Ted Williams, AL:Bos.1946
Carl Yastrzemski, AL:Bos. 1970 (12 inn)

Most Total Bases
10 Ted Williams, AL:Bos. 1946
9 Arky Vaughan, NL:Pitt. 1941

Most Singles
3 By many players; Last:
Derek Jeter, AL:NY 2004
Ken Boyer, NL:StL. 1956

Most Doubles
2 Joe Medwick, NL:StL. 1937
Ted Kluszewski, NL:Cin. 1956
Ernie Banks, NL:Chi. 1959
Barry Bonds, NL:SF 1993
Damian Miller, NL:Ari. 2002
Albert Pujols, NL:StL. 2004
Al Simmons, AL:Chi. 1934
Paul Konerko, AL:Chi. 2002

Most Triples
2 Rod Carew, AL:Minn. 1978
1 By many NL players

Most Home Runs
2 Arky Vaughan, NL:Pitt. 1941 (cons)
Willie McCovey, NL:SF 1969 (cons)
Gary Carter, NL:Mtl. 1981 (cons)
Ted Williams, AL:Bos. 1946
Al Rosen, AL:Clev. 1954 (cons)

Most Runs Batted In
5 Ted Williams, AL:Bos. 1946
Al Rosen, AL:Clev. 1954
4 Arky Vaughan, NL:Pitt. 1941

Most Walks
3 Charlie Gehringer, AL:Det. 1934
Phil Cavarretta, NL:Chi. 1944

Most Strikeouts
3 Lou Gehrig, AL:NY 1934
Bob Johnson, AL:Phil. 1935
Joe Gordon, AL:NY 1942
Ken Keltner, AL:Clev. 1943
Jim Hegan, AL:Clev. 1950 (14 inn)
Mickey Mantle, AL:NY 1956
Tony Oliva, AL:Minn. 1967 (15 inn)
Kirby Puckett, AL:Minn. 1987 (12 inn)
Albert Belle, AL:Clev. 1996
Stan Hack, NL:Chi. 1939
John Roseboro, NL:LA 1961 (2g)
Willie McCovey, NL:SF 1968
Craig Biggio, NL:Hou. 1998
Extra-Inning Game:
4 Roberto Clemente, NL:Pitt. 1967 (15 inn)

Most Stolen Bases
2 Willie Mays, NL:SF 1963
Kelly Gruber, AL:Tor. 1990
Roberto Alomar, AL:Tor. 1992
Kenny Lofton, AL:Clev. 1996

Most Stolen Bases, Inning
2 Roberto Alomar, AL:Tor. 1992 (2nd)
1 By many NL players

Most Caught Stealing
2 Stan Musial, NL:StL. 1951
Tony Oliva, AL:Minn. 1967

Most Hit By Pitch
1 By many players

Most Grounded Into Double Plays
2 Bobby Richardson, AL:NY 1963
1 By many NL players

PITCHING — GAME

Most Innings
6 Lefty Gomez, AL:NY 1935
5 Larry Jansen, NL:NY 1950

Most Runs
7 Atlee Hammaker, NL:SF 1983
5 Sandy Consuegra, AL:Chi. 1954
Whitey Ford, AL:NY 1955 (12 inn)
Blue Moon Odom, AL:Oak. 1969
Jim Palmer, AL:Balt. 1977

Most Earned Runs
7 Atlee Hammaker, NL:S,F. 1983
5 Sandy Consuegra, AL:Chi. 1954
Jim Palmer, AL:Balt. 1977

Most Hits
9 Tom Glavine, NL:Atl. 1992
7 Tommy Bridges, AL:Det., 1937

Most Hits, Inning
7 Tom Glavine, NL:Atl. 1992 (1st)
5 Tex Hughson, AL:Bos. 1944 (5th)
Sandy Consuegra, AL:Chi. 1954 (4th)
Blue Moon Odom, AL:Oak. 1969 (3rd)

Most Walks
5 Bill Hallahan, NL:StL. 1933
4 Jim Palmer, AL:Balt. 1978

Most Walks, Inning
3 Early Wynn, AL:Chi. 1959 (5th)
Jim Palmer, AL:Balt. 1978 (3rd)
Jim Kern, AL:Tex. 1979 (9th)
Dan Petry, AL:Det. 1985 (9th)
Kevin Brown, NL:LA 2000 (3rd)

Most Strikeouts
6 Carl Hubbell, NL:NY 1934
Johnny Vander Meer, NL:Cin. 1943
Larry Jansen, NL:NY 1950 (14 inn)
Ferguson Jenkins, NL:Chi. 1967 (15 inn)
5 Billy Pierce, AL:Chi. 1956
Dick Radatz, AL:Bos. 1963-64
Pedro Martinez, AL:Bos. 1999

Most Strikeouts, Consecutive
5 Carl Hubbell, NL:NY 1934
Fernando Valenzuela, NL:LA 1986
4 Pedro Martinez, AL:Bos. 1999

Most Strikeouts, Consecutive Innings
6 Carl Hubbell, NL:NY 1934
5 Dick Radatz, AL:Bos. 1963
Pedro Martinez, AL:Bos. 1999

ALL-STAR GAME – INDIVIDUAL RECORDS

Most Strikeouts, Inning (only batters faced)
3   Johnny Sain, NL:Bos. 1948 (5th)
     Gene Conley, NL:Mil. 1955 (12th)
     Jerry Reuss, NL:LA 1980 (6th)
     Fernando Valenzuela, NL:LA 1984 (4th)
     Fernando Valenzuela, NL:LA 1986 (4th)
     Dwight Gooden, NL:NY 1984 (5th)
     Brad Lidge, NL:Hou. 2005 (7th)
     Brad Penny, NL:LA 2006 (1st)
     Bobby Shantz, AL:Phil. 1952 (5th)
     Bill Caudill, AL:Oak. 1984 (7th)
     Pedro Martinez, AL:Bos. 1999 (1st)

Most Home Runs Allowed
3   Jim Palmer, AL:Balt. 1977
2   By many NL players; Last:
     Roger Clemens, NL:Hou. 2004

Most Home Runs Allowed, Inning
2   By many players; Last:
     Roger Clemens, NL:Hou. 2004 (1st)
     Jim Palmer, AL:Balt. 1977 (1st)

Most Hit Batters
1   By many players

Most Wild Pitches
2   Tom Brewer, AL:Bos. 1956
     Dave Stieb, AL:Tor. 1980
     Juan Marichal, NL:SF 1962
     John Smoltz, NL:Atl. 1993

Most Balks
1   Bob Friend, NL:Pitt. 1960
     Stu Miller, NL:SF 1961
     Dwight Gooden, NL:NY 1986, 88
     Steve Busby, AL:KC 1975
     Jim Kern, AL:Tex. 1979
     Charlie Hough, AL:Tex. 1986
     Derek Lowe, AL:Bos. 2002

BATTING – LIFETIME

Most Games
24   Hank Aaron, NL:Mil./Atl; AL:Mil.
      Stan Musial, NL:StL.
      Willie Mays, NL:NY/SF-NY
18   Ted Williams, AL:Bos.
      Brooks Robinson, AL:Balt.
      Cal Ripken, AL:Balt.

Most Games, Consecutive
24   Stan Musial, NL:StL.
      Willie Mays, NL:NY/SF-NY
18   Brooks Robinson, AL:Balt.

Most Winning Teams
17   Willie Mays, NL:NY/SF-NY
      Hank Aaron, NL:Mil./Atl.
12   Cal Ripken, AL:Balt.

Most Losing Teams
15   Brooks Robinson, AL:Balt.
10   Stan Musial, NL:StL.

Highest Batting Avg. (Minimum: 20 at-bats)
.500   Charlie Gehringer, AL:Det. (20-10)
.433   Billy Herman, NL:Chi.-Brk. (30-13)

Highest Slugging Pct. (Minimum: 20 at-bats)
.900   Fred Lynn, AL:Bos.-Cal. (20-18)
.821   Steve Garvey, NL:LA-SD (28-23)

Most At-Bats
75   Willie Mays, NL:NY/SF-NY
49   Cal Ripken, AL:Balt.

Most Runs
20   Willie Mays, NL:NY/SF
10   Ted Williams, AL:Bos.

Most Hits
23   Willie Mays, NL:NY/SF
14   Ted Williams, AL:Bos.
      Nellie Fox, AL:Chi.

Most Extra Base Hits
8   Stan Musial, NL:StL.
     Willie Mays, NL:NY/SF
7   Ted Williams, AL:Bos.

Most Total Bases
40   Stan Musial, NL:StL.
      Willie Mays, NL:NY/SF
30   Ted Williams, AL:Bos.

Most Singles
15   Willie Mays, NL:NY/SF
14   Nellie Fox, AL:Chi.

Most Doubles
7   Dave Winfield, NL-SD AL:NY
5   Dave Winfield, AL:NY
3   Ted Kluszewski, NL:Cin.
     Ernie Banks, NL:Chi.
     Al Oliver, NL:Pitt.-Mtl.
     Barry Bonds, NL:Pitt.-SF

Most Triples
3   Willie Mays, NL:NY/SF
     Brooks Robinson, AL:Balt.

Most Home Runs
6   Stan Musial, NL:StL.
4   Ted Williams, AL:Bos
     Fred Lynn, AL:Bos.-Cal.

Most Runs Batted In
12   Ted Williams, AL:Bos.
10   Stan Musial, NL:StL.

Most Walks
11   Ted Williams, AL:Bos.
7   Stan Musial, NL:StL.
     Willie Mays, NL:NY/SF

Most Strikeouts
17   Mickey Mantle, AL:NY
14   Willie Mays, NL:NY/SF-NY

Most Stolen Bases
6   Willie Mays, NL:NY/SF
5   Roberto Alomar, AL:Tor.-Balt.
     Kenny Lofton, AL:Clev.

Most Hit By Pitch
1   By many players

PITCHING – LIFETIME

Most Games
10   Roger Clemens, AL:Bos.-Tor.-NY; NL:Hou.
8   Don Drysdale, NL:LA
     Juan Marichal, NL:SF
     Tom Seaver, NL:NY-Cin.
     Roger Clemens, AL:Bos.-Tor.-NY

Most Games, Consecutive
6   Ewell Blackwell, NL:Cin.
     Early Wynn, AL:Clev.-Chi.

Most Games Started
5   Lefty Gomez, AL:NY
     Robin Roberts, NL:Phil.
     Don Drysdale, NL:LA

ALL-STAR GAME – INDIVIDUAL RECORDS

Most Games Finished
6 Rich Gossage, NL:Pitt.-SD; AL:Chi.-NY
5 Mariano Rivera, AL:NY
3 Ewell Blackwell, NL:Cin.
   Bruce Sutter, NL:Chi.-StL.
   Rich Gossage, NL:Pitt.-SD

Most Saves (Since 1969)
3 Dennis Eckersley, AL:Oak.
   Mariano Rivera, AL:NY
2 Bruce Sutter, NL:Chi.-StL.

Most Games Won
3 Lefty Gomez, AL:NY
2 Bob Friend, NL:Pitt.
   Juan Marichal, NL:SF
   Don Drysdale, NL:LA
   Bruce Sutter, NL:Chi.

Most Games Lost
2 Mort Cooper, NL:StL.
   Claude Passeau, NL:Chi.
   Dwight Gooden, NL:NY
   John Smoltz, NL:Atl.
   Whitey Ford, AL:NY
   Luis Tiant, AL:Clev.-Bos.
   Catfish Hunter, AL:Oak.-NY

Lowest Earned Run Average (Minimum: 12 IP)
0.00 Mel Harder, AL:Clev. (13 inn)
0.50 Juan Marichal, NL:SF (18 inn)

Most Innings
19.1 Don Drysdale, NL:LA
18.0 Lefty Gomez, AL:NY

Most Runs
13 Whitey Ford, AL:NY
10 Robin Roberts, NL:Phil.
    Warren Spahn, NL:Bos./Mil.

Most Earned Runs
11 Whitey Ford, AL:NY
10 Robin Roberts, NL:Phil.

Most Hits
19 Whitey Ford, AL:NY
17 Robin Roberts, NL:Phil.
    Warren Spahn, NL:Bos.-Mil.

Most Home Runs
4 Vida Blue, AL:Oak.
   Catfish Hunter, AL:KC-Oak.-NY
3 Robin Roberts, NL:Phil.
   Mort Cooper, NL:StL.
   Tom Seaver, NL:NY-Cin.
   Steve Carlton, NL:StL.-Phil.

Most Walks
7 Jim Palmer, AL:Balt.
6 Lon Warneke, NL:Chi.
   Carl Hubbell, NL:NY
   Robin Roberts, NL:Phil.

Most Strikeouts
19 Don Drysdale, NL:LA
14 Jim Palmer, AL:Balt.

Most Hit Batters
1 By many players

Most Wild Pitches
2 Ewell Blackwell, NL:Cin.
   Robin Roberts, NL:Phil.
   Juan Marichal, NL:SF
   Steve Rogers, NL:Mtl.
   John Smoltz, NL:Atl.
   Tom Brewer, AL:Bos.
   Dave Stieb, AL:Tor.

Most Balks
2 Dwight Gooden, NL:NY
1 Steve Busby, AL:KC
   Jim Kern, AL:Tex.
   Charlie Hough, AL:Tex.
   Derek Lowe, AL:Bos.

ALL-STAR GAME – MOST VALUABLE PLAYER

1962 (1g)	Maury Wills, NL:LA	1985	LaMarr Hoyt, NL:SD
1962 (2g)	Leon Wagner, AL:LA	1986	Roger Clemens, AL:Bos.
1963	Willie Mays, NL:SF	1987	Tim Raines, NL:Mtl.
1964	Johnny Callison, NL:Phil.	1988	Terry Steinbach, AL:Oak.
1965	Juan Marichal, NL:SF	1989	Bo Jackson, AL:KC
1966	Brooks Robinson, AL:Balt.	1990	Julio Franco, AL:Tex.
1967	Tony Perez, NL:Cin.	1991	Cal Ripken, AL:Balt.
1968	Willie Mays, NL:SF	1992	Ken Griffey, Jr AL:Sea.
1969	Willie McCovey, NL:SF	1993	Kirby Puckett, AL:Minn.
1970	Carl Yastrzemski, AL:Bos.	1994	Fred McGriff, NL:Atl
1971	Frank Robinson, AL:Balt.	1995	Jeff Conine, NL:Fla.
1972	Joe Morgan, NL:Cin.	1996	Mike Piazza, NL:LA
1973	Bobby Bonds, NL:SF	1997	Sandy Alomar, Jr., AL:Clev.
1974	Steve Garvey NL:LA	1998	Roberto Alomar, AL:Balt.
1975	Bill Madlock, NL:Chi. &	1999	Pedro Martinez, AL:Bos.
	Jon Matlack, NL:NY	2000	Derek Jeter, AL:NY
1976	George Foster, NL:Cin.	2001	Cal Ripken, AL:Balt.
1977	Don Sutton, NL:LA	2002	no selection
1978	Steve Garvey, NL:LA	2003	Garrett Anderson, AL:Ana.
1979	Dave Parker, NL:Pitt.	2004	Alfonso Soriano, AL:Tex.
1980	Ken Griffey, Sr., NL:Cin.	2005	Miguel Tejada, AL:Balt.
1981	Gary Carter, NL:Mtl.	2006	Michael Young, AL:Tex.
1982	Dave Concepcion, NL:Cin.		
1983	Fred Lynn, AL:Cal.		
1984	Gary Carter, NL:Mtl.		

AMERICAN LEAGUE CLUB STANDINGS - 1901-1968

	BALT	BOS	CAL	CHI	CLEV	DET	KC	MIL	MINN	NY	OAK	PHIL	STL	WASH	WASH
1901	5	2	-	1	7	3	-	8	-	-	-	4	-	6	-
1902	8	3	-	4	5	7	-	-	-	-	-	1	2	6	-
1903	-	1	-	7	3	5	-	-	-	4	-	2	6	8	-
1904	-	1	-	3	4	7	-	-	-	2	-	5	6	8	-
1905	-	4	-	2	5	3	-	-	-	6	-	1	8	7	-
1906	-	8	-	1	3	6	-	-	-	2	-	4	5	7	-
1907	-	7	-	3	4	1	-	-	-	5	-	2	6	8	-
1908	-	5	-	3	2	1	-	-	-	8	-	6	4	7	-
1909	-	3	-	4	6	1	-	-	-	5	-	2	7	8	-
1910	-	4	-	6	5	3	-	-	-	2	-	1	8	7	-
1911	-	5	-	4	3	2	-	-	-	6	-	1	8	7	-
1912	-	1	-	4	5	6	-	-	-	8	-	3	7	2	-
1913	-	4	-	5	3	6	-	-	-	7	-	1	8	2	-
1914	-	2	-	6	8	4	-	-	-	6	-	1	5	3	-
1915	-	1	-	3	7	2	-	-	-	5	-	8	6	4	-
1916	-	1	-	2	6	3	-	-	-	4	-	8	5	7	-
1917	-	2	-	1	3	4	-	-	-	6	-	8	7	5	-
1918	-	1	-	6	2	7	-	-	-	4	-	8	5	3	-
1919	-	6	-	1	2	4	-	-	-	3	-	8	5	7	-
1920	-	5	-	2	1	7	-	-	-	3	-	8	4	6	-
1921	-	5	-	7	2	6	-	-	-	1	-	8	3	4	-
1922	-	8	-	5	4	3	-	-	-	1	-	7	2	6	-
1923	-	8	-	7	3	2	-	-	-	1	-	6	5	4	-
1924	-	7	-	8	6	3	-	-	-	2	-	5	4	1	-
1925	-	8	-	5	6	4	-	-	-	7	-	2	3	1	-
1926	-	8	-	5	2	6	-	-	-	1	-	3	7	4	-
1927	-	8	-	5	6	4	-	-	-	1	-	2	7	3	-
1928	-	8	-	5	7	6	-	-	-	1	-	2	3	4	-
1929	-	8	-	7	3	6	-	-	-	2	-	1	4	5	-
1930	-	8	-	7	4	5	-	-	-	3	-	1	6	2	-
1931	-	6	-	8	4	7	-	-	-	2	-	1	5	3	-
1932	-	8	-	7	4	5	-	-	-	1	-	2	6	3	-
1933	-	7	-	6	4	5	-	-	-	2	-	3	8	1	-
1934	-	4	-	8	3	1	-	-	-	2	-	5	6	7	-
1935	-	4	-	5	3	1	-	-	-	2	-	8	7	6	-
1936	-	6	-	3	5	2	-	-	-	1	-	8	7	4	-
1937	-	5	-	3	4	2	-	-	-	1	-	7	8	6	-
1938	-	2	-	6	3	4	-	-	-	1	-	8	7	5	-
1939	-	2	-	4	3	5	-	-	-	1	-	7	8	6	-
1940	-	4	-	4	2	1	-	-	-	3	-	8	6	7	-
1941	-	2	-	3	4	4	-	-	-	1	-	8	6	6	-
1942	-	2	-	6	4	5	-	-	-	1	-	8	3	7	-
1943	-	7	-	4	3	5	-	-	-	1	-	8	6	2	-
1944	-	4	-	7	5	2	-	-	-	3	-	5	1	8	-
1945	-	7	-	6	5	1	-	-	-	4	-	8	3	2	-
1946	-	1	-	5	6	2	-	-	-	3	-	8	7	4	-
1947	-	3	-	6	4	2	-	-	-	1	-	5	8	7	-
1948	-	2	-	8	1	5	-	-	-	3	-	4	6	7	-
1949	-	2	-	6	3	4	-	-	-	1	-	5	7	8	-
1950	-	3	-	6	4	2	-	-	-	1	-	8	7	5	-
1951	-	3	-	4	2	5	-	-	-	1	-	6	8	7	-
1952	-	6	-	3	2	8	-	-	-	1	-	4	7	5	-
1953	-	4	-	3	2	6	-	-	-	1	-	7	8	5	-
1954	7	4	-	3	1	5	-	-	-	2	-	8	-	6	-
1955	7	4	-	3	2	5	6	-	-	1	-	-	-	8	-
1956	6	4	-	3	2	5	8	-	-	1	-	-	-	7	-
1957	5	3	-	2	6	4	7	-	-	1	-	-	-	8	-
1958	6	3	-	2	4	5	7	-	-	1	-	-	-	8	-
1959	6	5	-	1	2	4	7	-	-	3	-	-	-	8	-
1960	2	7	-	3	4	6	8	-	-	1	-	-	-	5	-
1961	3	6	8	4	5	2	9	-	7	1	-	-	-	-	9
1962	7	8	3	5	6	4	9	-	2	1	-	-	-	-	10
1963	4	7	9	2	5	5	8	-	3	1	-	-	-	-	10
1964	3	8	5	2	6	4	10	-	6	1	-	-	-	-	9
1965	3	9	7	2	5	4	10	-	1	6	-	-	-	-	8
1966	1	9	6	4	5	3	7	-	2	10	-	-	-	-	8
1967	6	1	5	4	8	2	10	-	2	9	-	-	-	-	6
1968	2	4	8	8	3	1	-	-	7	5	6	-	-	-	10

AMERICAN LEAGUE CLUB STANDINGS 1969 –

| | EAST | | | | | | WEST | | | | | | |
	BALT	BOS	CLEV	DET	NY	WASH	CAL	CHI	KC	SEA MIL	MINN	OAK	
1969	1	3	6	2	5	4	3	5	4	6	1	2	
1970	1	3	5	4	2	6	3	6	4	4	1	2	
1971	1	3	6	2	4	5	4	3	2	6	5	1	

	BALT	BOS	CLEV	DET	MIL	NY	CAL	CHI	KC	MINN	OAK	TEX
1972	3	2	5	1	6	4	5	2	4	3	1	6
1973	1	2	6	3	5	4	4	5	2	3	1	6
1974	1	3	4	6	5	2	6	4	5	3	1	2
1975	2	1	4	6	5	3	6	5	2	4	1	3
1976	2	3	4	5	6	1	4	6	1	3	2	4

	BALT	BOS	CLEV	DET	MIL	NY	TOR	CAL	CHI	KC	MINN	OAK	TEX	SEA
1977	2	2	5	4	6	1	7	5	3	1	4	7	2	6
1978	4	2	6	5	3	1	7	2	5	1	4	6	2	7
1979	1	3	6	5	2	4	7	1	5	2	4	7	3	6
1980	2	4	6	5	3	1	7	6	5	1	3	2	4	7
1981 *Split Season*														
1st Half	2	5	6	4	3	1	7	4	3	5	7	1	2	6
2nd Half	4	2	5	2	1	6	7	7	6	1	4	2	3	5
1982	2	3	6	4	1	5	6	1	3	2	7	5	6	4
1983	1	6	7	2	5	3	4	5	1	2	5	4	3	7
1984	5	4	6	1	7	3	2	2	5	1	2	4	7	5
1985	4	5	7	3	6	2	1	2	3	1	4	4	7	6
1986	7	1	5	3	6	2	4	1	5	3	6	3	2	7
1987	6	5	7	1	3	4	2	6	5	2	1	3	6	4
1988	7	1	6	2	3	5	3	4	5	3	2	1	6	7
1989	2	3	6	7	4	5	1	3	7	2	5	1	4	6
1990	5	1	4	3	6	7	2	4	2	6	7	1	3	5
1991	6	2	7	2	4	5	1	7	2	6	1	4	3	5
1992	3	7	4	6	2	4	1	5	3	5	2	1	4	7
1993	3	5	6	3	7	2	1	5	1	3	5	7	2	4

| | EAST | | | | | CENTRAL | | | | | WEST | | | |
	BALT	BOS	DET	NY	TOR	CHI	CLEV	KC	MIL	MINN	ANA	OAK	SEA	TEX
1994	2	4	5	1	3	1	2	3	5	4	4	2	3	1
1995	3	1	4	2	5	3	1	2	4	5	2	4	1	3
1996	2	3	5	1	4	2	1	5	3	4	4	3	2	1
1997	1	4	3	2	5	2	1	5	3	4	2	4	1	3

	BALT	BOS	NY	TB	TOR	CHI	CLEV	DET	KC	MINN	ANA	OAK	SEA	TEX
1998	4	2	1	5	3	2	1	5	3	4	2	4	3	1
1999	4	2	1	5	3	2	1	3	4	5	4	2	3	1
2000	4	2	1	5	3	1	2	3	4	5	3	1	2	4
2001	4	2	1	5	3	3	1	4	5	2	3	2	1	4
2002	4	2	1	5	3	2	3	5	4	1	2	1	3	4
2003	4	2	1	5	3	2	4	5	3	1	3	1	2	4
2004	3	2	1	4	5	2	3	4	5	1	1	2	4	3

	BALT	BOS	NY	TB	TOR	CHI	CLEV	DET	KC	MINN	LA	OAK	SEA	TEX
2005	4	2	1	5	3	1	2	4	5	3	1	2	4	3
2006	4	3	1	5	2	3	4	2	5	1	2	1	4	3

NATIONAL LEAGUE CLUB STANDINGS 1876-1899

	BALT	BOS	BRK	BUFF	CHI	CIN	CLEV	DET	HART	IND	KC	LOU	MIL	NY	PHIL	PITT	PROV	STL	SYR	TROY	WASH	WOR
1876		4			1	8			2			5		6	7			3				
1877		1			5	6			3			2						4				
1878		1			4	2				5			6				3					
1879		2		3	4	5	6										1		8	7		
1880		6		7	1	8	3										2			4		5
1881		6		3	1		7	4									2			5		8
1882		3		4	1		5	6									2			7		8
1883		1		5	2		4	7						6	8		3					
1884		2		3	4		7	8						5	6		1					
1885		5		7	1			6						2	3		4	8				
1886		5			1			2			7			3	4			6			8	
1887		5			3			1		8				4	2	6					7	
1888		4			2			5		7				1	3	6					8	
1889		2			3		6			7				1	4	5					8	
1890		5	1		2	4	7							6	3	8						
1891		1	6		2	7	5							3	4	8						
1892-1st	12	1	2		7	4	5					9		8	3	6		11			10	
1892-2nd	10	2	3		6	4	1					12		9	7	5		8			11	
1893	8	1	7		9	6	3					11		5	4	2		10			12	
1894	1	3	5		8	10	6					12		2	4	7		9			11	
1895	1	6	5		4	8	2					12		9	3	7		11			10	
1896	1	4	9		5	3	2					12		7	8	6		11			10	
1897	2	1	6		9	4	5					11		3	10	8		12			7	
1898	2	1	10		4	3	5					9		7	6	8		12			11	
1899	4	2	1		8	6	12					9		10	3	7		5			11	

NOTE: 1892 split season. Boston defeated Cleveland, 5 games to 0 (1 tie) in best-of-nine playoff.

NATIONAL LEAGUE CHAMPIONS 1876-1899

	Club & Manager	W	L	PCT	GA
1876	Chicago (Al Spalding)	52	14	.788	6
1877	Boston (Harry Wright)	31	17	.646	7
1878	Boston (Harry Wright)	41	19	.683	4
1879	Providence (George Wright)	55	23	.705	5
1980	Chicago (Cap Anson)	67	17	.798	15
1881	Chicago (Cap Anson)	56	28	.667	9
1882	Chicago (Cap Anson)	55	29	.655	3
1883	Boston (John Morrill)	63	35	.643	4
1884	Providence (Frank Bancroft)	84	28	.750	10.5
1885	Chicago (Cap Anson)	87	25	.777	2
1886	Chicago (Cap Anson)	90	34	.726	21
1887	Detroit (Bill Watkins)	79	45	.637	31
1888	New York (Jim Mutrie)	84	47	.641	9
1889	New York (Jim Mutrie)	83	43	.659	1
1890	Brooklyn (Bill McGunnigle)	86	43	.667	6
1891	Boston (Frank Selee)	87	51	.630	3.5
1892	Boston (Frank Selee)	102	48	.680	8.5
1893	Boston (Frank Selee)	86	44	.662	5
1894	Baltimore (Ned Hanlon)	89	39	.695	3
1895	Baltimore (Ned Hanlon)	87	43	.669	3
1896	Baltimore (Ned Hanlon)	90	39	.698	9.5
1897	Boston (Frank Selee)	93	39	.705	2
1898	Boston (Frank Selee)	102	47	.685	6
1899	Brooklyn (Ned Hanlon)	89	41	.685	5

NATIONAL LEAGUE CLUB STANDINGS 1900-1968

	ATL	BOS	BRK	CHI	CIN	HOU	LA	MIL	NYG	NYM	PHIL	PITT	STL	SF
1900	-	4	1	5	7	-	-	-	8	-	3	2	5	-
1901	-	5	3	6	8	-	-	-	7	-	2	1	4	-
1902	-	3	2	5	4	-	-	-	8	-	7	1	6	-
1903	-	6	5	3	4	-	-	-	2	-	7	1	8	-
1904	-	7	6	2	3	-	-	-	1	-	8	4	5	-
1905	-	7	8	3	5	-	-	-	1	-	4	2	6	-
1906	-	8	5	1	6	-	-	-	2	-	4	3	7	-
1907	-	7	5	1	6	-	-	-	4	-	3	2	8	-
1908	-	6	7	1	5	-	-	-	2	-	4	2	8	-
1909	-	8	6	2	4	-	-	-	3	-	5	1	7	-
1910	-	8	6	1	5	-	-	-	2	-	4	3	7	-
1911	-	8	7	2	6	-	-	-	1	-	4	3	5	-
1912	-	8	7	3	4	-	-	-	1	-	5	2	6	-
1913	-	5	6	3	7	-	-	-	1	-	2	4	8	-
1914	-	1	5	4	8	-	-	-	2	-	6	7	3	-
1915	-	2	3	4	7	-	-	-	8	-	1	5	6	-
1916	-	3	1	5	7	-	-	-	4	-	2	6	7	-
1917	-	6	7	5	4	-	-	-	1	-	2	8	3	-
1918	-	7	5	1	3	-	-	-	2	-	6	4	8	-
1919	-	6	5	3	1	-	-	-	2	-	8	4	7	-
1920	-	7	1	5	3	-	-	-	2	-	8	4	5	-
1921	-	4	5	7	6	-	-	-	1	-	8	2	3	-
1922	-	8	6	5	2	-	-	-	1	-	7	3	3	-
1923	-	7	6	4	2	-	-	-	1	-	8	3	5	-
1924	-	8	2	5	4	-	-	-	1	-	7	3	6	-
1925	-	5	6	8	3	-	-	-	2	-	6	1	4	-
1926	-	7	6	4	2	-	-	-	5	-	8	3	1	-
1927	-	7	6	4	5	-	-	-	3	-	8	1	2	-
1928	-	7	6	3	5	-	-	-	2	-	8	4	1	-
1929	-	8	6	1	7	-	-	-	3	-	5	2	4	-
1930	-	6	4	2	7	-	-	-	3	-	8	5	1	-
1931	-	7	4	3	8	-	-	-	2	-	6	5	1	-
1932	-	5	3	1	8	-	-	-	6	-	4	2	6	-
1933	-	4	6	3	8	-	-	-	1	-	7	2	5	-
1934	-	4	6	3	8	-	-	-	2	-	7	5	1	-
1935	-	8	5	1	6	-	-	-	3	-	7	4	2	-
1936	-	6	7	2	5	-	-	-	1	-	8	4	2	-
1937	-	5	6	2	8	-	-	-	1	-	7	3	4	-
1938	-	5	7	1	4	-	-	-	3	-	8	2	6	-
1939	-	7	3	4	1	-	-	-	5	-	8	6	2	-
1940	-	7	2	5	1	-	-	-	6	-	8	4	3	-
1941	-	7	1	6	3	-	-	-	5	-	8	4	2	-
1942	-	7	2	6	4	-	-	-	3	-	8	5	1	-
1943	-	6	3	5	2	-	-	-	8	-	7	4	1	-
1944	-	6	7	4	3	-	-	-	5	-	8	2	1	-
1945	-	6	3	1	7	-	-	-	5	-	8	4	2	-
1946	-	4	2	3	6	-	-	-	8	-	5	7	1	-
1947	-	3	1	6	5	-	-	-	4	-	7	7	2	-
1948	-	1	3	8	7	-	-	-	5	-	6	4	2	-
1949	-	4	1	8	7	-	-	-	5	-	3	6	2	-
1950	-	4	2	7	6	-	-	-	3	-	1	8	5	-
1951	-	4	2	8	6	-	-	-	1	-	5	7	3	-
1952	-	7	1	5	6	-	-	-	2	-	4	8	3	-
1953	-	-	1	7	6	-	-	2	5	-	3	8	3	-
1954	-	-	2	7	5	-	-	3	1	-	4	8	6	-
1955	-	-	1	6	5	-	-	2	3	-	4	8	7	-
1956	-	-	1	8	3	-	-	2	6	-	5	7	4	-
1957	-	-	3	7	4	-	-	1	6	-	5	7	2	-
1958	-	-	-	5	4	-	7	1	-	-	8	2	5	3
1959	-	-	-	5	5	-	1	2	-	-	8	4	7	3
1960	-	-	-	7	6	-	4	2	-	-	8	1	3	5
1961	-	-	-	7	1	-	2	4	-	-	8	6	5	3
1962	-	-	-	9	3	8	2	5	-	10	7	4	6	1
1963	-	-	-	7	5	9	1	6	-	10	4	8	2	3
1964	-	-	-	8	2	9	6	5	-	10	2	6	1	4
1965	-	-	-	8	4	9	1	5	-	10	6	3	7	2
1966	5	-	-	10	7	8	1	-	-	9	4	3	6	2
1967	7	-	-	3	4	9	8	-	-	10	5	6	1	2
1968	5	-	-	3	4	10	7	-	-	9	7	6	1	2

NATIONAL LEAGUE CLUB STANDINGS 1969 –

| | EAST | | | | | | | WEST | | | | |
	CHI	MTL	NY	PHIL	PITT	STL		ATL	CIN	HOU	LA	SD	SF
1969	2	6	1	5	3	4		1	3	5	4	6	2
1970	2	6	3	5	1	4		5	1	4	2	6	3
1971	3	5	3	6	1	2		3	4	4	2	6	1
1972	2	5	3	6	1	4		4	1	2	3	6	5
1973	5	4	1	6	3	2		5	1	4	2	6	3
1974	6	4	5	3	1	2		3	2	4	1	6	5
1975	5	5	3	2	1	3		5	1	6	2	4	3
1976	4	6	3	1	2	5		6	1	3	2	5	4
1977	4	5	6	1	2	3		6	2	3	1	5	4
1978	3	4	6	1	2	5		6	2	5	1	4	3
1979	5	2	6	4	1	3		6	1	2	3	5	4
1980	6	2	5	1	3	4		4	3	1	2	6	5
1981 *Split Season*													
1st Half	6	3	5	1	4	2		4	2	3	1	6	5
2nd Half	5	1	4	3	6	2		5	2	1	4	6	3
1982	5	3	6	2	4	1		1	6	5	2	4	3
1983	5	3	6	1	2	4		2	6	3	1	4	5
1984	1	5	2	4	6	3		2	5	2	4	1	6
1985	4	3	2	5	6	1		5	2	3	1	3	6
1986	5	4	1	2	6	3		6	2	1	5	4	3
1987	6	3	2	4	4	1		5	2	3	4	6	1
1988	4	3	1	6	2	5		6	2	5	1	3	4
1989	1	4	2	6	5	3		6	5	3	4	2	1
1990	4	3	2	4	1	6		6	1	4	2	4	3
1991	4	6	5	3	1	2		1	5	6	2	3	4
1992	4	2	5	6	1	3		1	2	4	6	3	5

	CHI	FLA	MTL	NY	PHI	PITT	STL		ATL	CIN	COL	HOU	LA	SD	SF
1993	4	6	2	7	1	5	3		1	5	6	3	4	7	2

| | EAST | | | | | CENTRAL | | | | | WEST | | | |
	ATL	FLA	MTL	NY	PHI	CHI	CIN	HOU	PITT	STL	COL	LA	SD	SF
1994	2	5	1	3	4	5	1	2	3	3	3	1	4	2
1995	1	4	5	2	2	3	1	2	5	4	2	1	3	4
1996	1	3	2	4	5	4	3	2	5	1	3	2	1	4
1997	1	2	4	3	5	5	3	1	2	4	3	2	4	1

	ATL	FLA	MTL	NY	PHI	CHI	CIN	HOU	MIL	PITT	STL	ARI	COL	LA	SD	SF
1998	1	5	4	2	3	2	4	1	5	6	3	5	4	3	1	2
1999	1	5	4	2	3	6	2	1	5	3	4	1	5	3	4	2
2000	1	3	4	2	5	6	2	4	3	5	1	3	4	2	5	1
2001	1	4	5	3	2	3	5	1	4	6	2	1	5	3	4	2
2002	1	4	2	5	3	5	3	2	6	4	1	1	4	3	5	2
2003	1	2	4	5	3	1	5	2	6	4	3	3	4	2	5	1
2004	1	3	5	4	2	3	4	2	6	5	1	5	4	1	3	2

	ATL	FLA	WAS	NY	PHI	CHI	CIN	HOU	MIL	PITT	STL	ARI	COL	LA	SD	SF
2005	1	3	5	3	2	4	5	2	3	6	1	2	5	4	1	3
2006	3	4	5	1	2	6	3	2	4	5	1	4	4	1	2	3

AMERICAN LEAGUE CHAMPIONS (1901 to 1968)

* = mid-season replacement

YEAR	CLUB (MANAGER)	WON	LOST	PCT.	GA
1901	Chicago (Clark Griffith)	83	53	.610	4
1902	Philadelphia (Connie Mack)	83	53	.610	5
1903	Boston (Jimmy Collins)	91	47	.659	14.5
1904	Boston (Jimmy Collins)	95	59	.617	1.5
1905	Philadelphia (Connie Mack)	92	56	.622	2
1906	Chicago (Fielder Jones)	93	58	.616	3
1907	Detroit (Hughie Jennings)	92	58	.613	1.5
1908	Detroit (Hughie Jennings)	90	63	.588	0.5
1909	Detroit (Hughie Jennings)	98	54	.645	3.5
1910	Philadelphia (Connie Mack)	102	48	.680	14.5
1911	Philadelphia (Connie Mack)	101	50	.669	13.5
1912	Boston (Jake Stahl)	105	47	.691	14
1913	Philadelphia (Connie Mack)	96	57	.627	6.5
1914	Philadelphia (Connie Mack)	99	53	.651	8.5
1915	Boston (Bill Carrigan)	101	50	.669	2.5
1916	Boston (Bill Carrigan)	91	63	.591	2
1917	Chicago (Pants Rowland)	100	54	.649	9
1918	Boston (Ed Barrow)	75	51	.595	3.5
1919	Chicago (Kid Gleason)	88	52	.629	3.5
1920	Cleveland (Tris Speaker)	98	56	.636	2
1921	New York (Miller Huggins)	98	55	.641	4.5
1922	New York (Miller Huggins)	94	60	.610	1
1923	New York (Miller Huggins)	98	54	.645	16
1924	Washington (Bucky Harris)	92	62	.597	2
1925	Washington (Bucky Harris)	96	55	.636	8.5
1926	New York (Miller Huggins)	91	63	.591	3
1927	New York (Miller Huggins)	110	44	.714	19
1928	New York (Miller Huggins)	101	53	.656	2.5
1929	Philadelphia (Connie Mack)	104	46	.693	18
1930	Philadelphia (Connie Mack)	102	52	.662	8
1931	Philadelphia (Connie Mack)	107	45	.704	13.5
1932	New York (Joe McCarthy)	107	47	.695	13
1933	Washington (Joe Cronin)	99	53	.651	7
1934	Detroit (Mickey Cochrane)	101	53	.656	7
1935	Detroit (Mickey Cochrane)	93	58	.616	3
1936	New York (Joe McCarthy)	102	51	.667	19.5
1937	New York (Joe McCarthy)	102	52	.662	13
1938	New York (Joe McCarthy)	99	53	.651	9.5
1939	New York (Joe McCarthy)	106	45	.702	17
1940	Detroit (Del Baker)	90	64	.584	1
1941	New York (Joe McCarthy)	101	53	.656	17
1942	New York (Joe McCarthy)	103	51	.669	9
1943	New York (Joe McCarthy)	98	56	.636	13.5
1944	St. Louis (Luke Sewell)	89	65	.578	1
1945	Detroit (Steve O'Neill)	88	65	.575	1.5
1946	Boston (Joe Cronin)	104	50	.675	12
1947	New York (Bucky Harris)	97	57	.630	12
1948	Cleveland (Lou Boudreau)	97	58	.626	1
1949	New York (Casey Stengel)	97	57	.630	1
1950	New York (Casey Stengel)	98	56	.636	3
1951	New York (Casey Stengel)	98	56	.636	5
1952	New York (Casey Stengel)	95	59	.617	2
1953	New York (Casey Stengel)	99	52	.656	8.5
1954	Cleveland (Al Lopez)	111	43	.721	8
1955	New York (Casey Stengel)	96	58	.623	3
1956	New York (Casey Stengel)	97	57	.630	9
1957	New York (Casey Stengel)	98	56	.636	8
1958	New York (Casey Stengel)	92	62	.597	10
1959	Chicago (Al Lopez)	94	60	.610	5
1960	New York (Casey Stengel)	97	57	.630	8
1961	New York (Ralph Houk)	109	53	.673	8
1962	New York (Ralph Houk)	96	66	.593	5
1963	New York (Ralph Houk)	104	57	.646	10.5
1964	New York (Yogi Berra)	99	63	.611	1
1965	Minnesota (Sam Mele)	102	60	.630	7
1966	Baltimore (Hank Bauer)	97	63	.606	9
1967	Boston (Dick Williams)	92	70	.568	1
1968	Detroit (Mayo Smith)	103	59	.636	12

AMERICAN LEAGUE DIVISION CHAMPIONS (1969 to 1993)

(Championship Series Winner Capitalized)
(E = East; W = West)
(= mid-season replacement)*

YEAR	CLUB (MANAGER)	WON	LOST	PCT.	GA
1969	(E) BALTIMORE (Earl Weaver)	109	53	.673	19
	(W) Minnesota (Billy Martin)	97	65	.599	9
1970	(E) BALTIMORE (Earl Weaver)	108	54	.667	15
	(W) Minnesota (Bill Rigney)	98	64	.605	9
1971	(E) BALTIMORE (Earl Weaver)	101	57	.639	12
	(W) Oakland (Dick Williams)	101	60	.627	16
1972	(W) OAKLAND (Dick Williams)	93	62	.600	5.5
	(E) Detroit (Billy Martin)	86	70	.551	0.5
1973	(W) OAKLAND (Dick Williams)	94	68	.580	6
	(E) Baltimore (Earl Weaver)	97	65	.599	8
1974	(W) OAKLAND (Alvin Dark)	90	72	.556	5
	(E) Baltimore (Earl Weaver)	91	71	.562	2
1975	(E) BOSTON (Darrell Johnson)	95	65	.594	4.5
	(W) Oakland (Alvin Dark)	98	64	.605	7
1976	(E) NEW YORK (Billy Martin)	97	62	.610	10.5
	(W) Kansas City (Whitey Herzog)	90	72	.556	2.5
1977	(E) NEW YORK (Billy Martin)	100	62	.617	2.5
	(W) Kansas City (Whitey Herzog)	102	60	.630	8
1978	(E) NEW YORK (Bob Lemon*)	100	63	.613	1
	(W) Kansas City (Whitey Herzog)	92	70	.568	5
1979	(E) BALTIMORE (Earl Weaver)	102	57	.642	8
	(W) California (Jim Fregosi)	88	74	.543	3
1980	(W) KANSAS CITY (Jim Frey)	97	65	.599	14
	(E) New York (Dick Howser)	103	59	.636	3
1981	(E) NEW YORK (Bob Lemon*)	59	48	.551	--
	(W) Oakland (Billy Martin)	64	45	.587	--

Due to players' strike, 1981 season was divided into two halves. Leaders of each half met in a best-of-five series to determine the ALCS participants. East: New York 3, Milwaukee 2; West: Oakland 3, Kansas City 0.

YEAR	CLUB (MANAGER)	WON	LOST	PCT.	GA
1982	(E) MILWAUKEE (Harvey Kuenn*)	95	67	.586	1
	(W) California (Gene Mauch)	93	69	.574	3
1983	(E) BALTIMORE (Joe Altobelli)	98	64	.605	6
	(W) Chicago (Tony LaRussa)	99	63	.611	20
1984	(E) DETROIT (Sparky Anderson)	104	58	.642	15
	(W) Kansas City (Dick Howser)	84	78	.519	3
1985	(W) KANSAS CITY (Dick Howser)	91	71	.562	1
	(E) Toronto (Bobby Cox)	99	62	.615	2
1986	(E) BOSTON John (McNamara)	95	66	.590	5.5
	(W) California (Gene Mauch)	92	70	.568	5
1987	(W) MINNESOTA (Tom Kelly)	85	77	.525	2
	(E) Detroit (Sparky Anderson)	98	64	.605	2
1988	(W) OAKLAND (Tony LaRussa)	104	58	.642	13
	(E) Boston (Joe Morgan*)	89	73	.549	1
1989	(W) OAKLAND (Tony LaRussa)	99	63	.611	7
	(E) Toronto (Cito Gaston*)	89	73	.549	2.
1990	(W) OAKLAND (Tony LaRussa)	103	59	.636	9
	(E) Boston (Joe Morgan)	88	74	.543	2
1991	(W) MINNESOTA (Tom Kelly)	95	67	.586	8
	(E) Toronto (Cito Gaston)	91	71	.562	7
1992	(E) TORONTO (Cito Gaston)	96	66	.593	4
	(W) Oakland (Tony LaRussa)	96	66	.593	6
1993	(E) TORONTO (Cito Gaston)	95	67	.586	7
	(W) Chicago (Gene Lamont)	94	68	.580	8

AMERICAN LEAGUE POSTSEASON PARTICIPANTS (since 1995)

Championship Series Winner Capitalized)
E = East; C = Central; W = West; WC = Wild Card)
* = mid-season replacement)

YEAR	CLUB (MANAGER)	WON	LOST	PCT.	GA
1995	(C) CLEVELAND (Mike Hargrove)	100	44	.694	30
	(W) Seattle (Lou Piniella)	79	66	.545	1
	(E) Boston (Kevin Kennedy)	86	58	.597	7
	(WC) New York (Buck Showalter)	79	65	.549	--
1996	(E) NEW YORK (Joe Torre)	92	70	.568	4
	(WC) Baltimore (Davey Johnson)	88	74	.543	--
	(C) Cleveland (Mike Hargrove)	99	62	.615	14.5
	(W) Texas (Johnny Oates)	90	72	.556	4.5
1997	(C) CLEVELAND (Mike Hargrove)	86	75	.534	6
	(E) Baltimore (Davey Johnson)	98	64	.605	2
	(W) Seattle (Lou Piniella)	90	72	.556	6
	(WC) New York (Joe Torre)	96	66	.593	--
1998	(E) NEW YORK (Joe Torre)	114	48	.704	22
	(C) Cleveland (Mike Hargrove)	89	73	.549	9
	(W) Texas (Johnny Oates)	88	74	.543	3
	(WC) Boston (Jimy Williams)	92	70	.568	--
1999	(E) NEW YORK (Joe Torre)	98	64	.605	4
	(WC) Boston (Jimy Williams)	94	68	.580	--
	(C) Cleveland (Mike Hargrove)	97	65	.599	21.5
	(W) Texas (Johnny Oates)	95	67	.586	8
2000	(E) NEW YORK (Joe Torre)	87	74	.540	2.5
	(WC) Seattle (Lou Piniella)	91	71	.562	--
	(W) Oakland (Art Howe)	91	70	.565	0.5
	(C) Chicago (Jerry Manuel)	95	67	.586	5
2001	(E) NEW YORK (Joe Torre)	95	65	.594	13.5
	(W) Seattle (Lou Piniella)	116	46	.716	14
	(C) Cleveland (Charlie Manuel)	91	71	.562	6
	(WC) Oakland (Art Howe)	102	60	.630	--
2002	(WC) ANAHEIM (Mike Scioscia)	99	63	.611	--
	(W) Oakland (Art Howe)	103	59	.636	4
	(E) New York (Joe Torre)	103	58	.640	10.5
	(C) Minnesota (Ron Gardenhire)	94	67	.584	13.5
2003	(E) NEW YORK (Joe Torre)	101	61	.623	6
	(WC) Boston (Grady Little)	95	67	.586	--
	(W) Oakland (Ken Macha)	96	66	.593	3
	(C) Minnesota (Ron Gardenhire)	90	72	.556	4
2004	(WC) BOSTON (Terry Francona)	98	64	.605	--
	(E) New York (Joe Torre)	101	61	.623	3
	(C) Minnesota (Ron Gardenhire)	92	70	.568	9
	(W) Anaheim (Mike Scioscia)	92	70	.568	1
2005	(C) CHICAGO (Ozzie Guillen)	99	63	.611	6
	(W) Los Angeles (Mike Scioscia)	95	67	.586	7
	(E) New York (Joe Torre)	95	67	.586	--
	(WC) Boston (Terry Francona)	95	67	.586	--
2006	(WC) DETROIT (Jim Leyland)	95	67	.586	--
	(W) Oakland (Ken Macha)	93	69	.574	4
	(E) New York (Joe Torre)	97	65	.599	10
	(C) Minnesota (Ron Gardenhire)	96	66	.593	1

NATIONAL LEAGUE CHAMPIONS (1900 to 1968)

(= mid-season replacement)*

YEAR	CLUB (MANAGER)	WON	LOST	PCT.	GA
1900	Brooklyn (Ned Hanlon)	82	54	.603	4.5
1901	Pittsburgh (Fred Clarke)	90	49	.647	7.5
1902	Pittsburgh (Fred Clarke)	103	36	.741	27.5
1903	Pittsburgh (Fred Clarke)	91	49	.650	6.5
1904	New York (John McGraw)	106	47	.693	13
1905	New York (John McGraw)	105	48	.686	9
1906	Chicago (Frank Chance)	116	36	.763	20
1907	Chicago (Frank Chance)	107	45	.704	17
1908	Chicago (Frank Chance)	99	55	.643	1
1909	Pittsburgh (Fred Clarke)	110	42	.724	6.5
1910	Chicago (Frank Chance)	104	50	.675	13
1911	New York (John McGraw)	99	54	.647	7.5
1912	New York (John McGraw)	103	48	.682	10
1913	New York (John McGraw)	101	51	.664	12.5
1914	Boston (George Stallings)	94	59	.614	10.5
1915	Philadelphia (Pat Moran)	90	62	.592	7
1916	Brooklyn (Wilbert Robinson)	94	60	.610	2.5
1917	New York (John McGraw)	98	56	.636	10
1918	Chicago (Fred Mitchell)	84	45	.651	10.5
1919	Cincinnati (Pat Moran)	96	44	.686	9
1920	Brooklyn (Wilbert Robinson)	93	61	.604	7
1921	New York (John McGraw)	94	59	.614	4
1922	New York (John McGraw)	93	61	.604	7
1923	New York (John McGraw)	95	58	.621	4.5
1924	New York (John McGraw)	93	60	.608	1.5
1925	Pittsburgh (Bill McKechnie)	95	58	.621	8.5
1926	St. Louis (Rogers Hornsby)	89	65	.578	2
1927	Pittsburgh (Donie Bush)	94	60	.610	1.5
1928	St. Louis (Bill McKechnie)	95	59	.617	2
1929	Chicago (Joe McCarthy)	98	54	.645	10.5
1930	St. Louis (Gabby Street)	92	62	.597	2
1931	St. Louis (Gabby Street)	101	53	.656	13
1932	Chicago (Charlie Grimm*)	90	64	.584	4
1933	New York (Bill Terry)	91	61	.599	5
1934	St. Louis (Frankie Frisch)	95	58	.621	2
1935	Chicago (Charlie Grimm)	100	54	.649	4
1936	New York (Bill Terry)	92	62	.597	5
1937	New York (Bill Terry)	95	57	.625	3
1938	Chicago (Gabby Hartnett*)	89	63	.586	2
1939	Cincinnati (Bill McKechnie)	97	57	.630	4.5
1940	Cincinnati (Bill McKechnie)	100	53	.654	12
1941	Brooklyn (Leo Durocher)	100	54	.649	2.5
1942	St. Louis (Billy Southworth)	106	48	.688	2
1943	St. Louis (Billy Southworth)	105	49	.682	18
1944	St. Louis (Billy Southworth)	105	49	.682	14.5
1945	Chicago (Charlie Grimm)	98	56	.636	3
1946	St. Louis (Eddie Dyer)	98	58	.628	2
1947	Brooklyn (Burt Shotton*)	94	60	.610	5
1948	Boston (Billy Southworth)	91	62	.595	6.5
1949	Brooklyn (Burt Shotton)	97	57	.630	1
1950	Philadelphia (Eddie Sawyer)	91	63	.591	2
1951	New York (Leo Durocher)	98	59	.624	1
1952	Brooklyn (Chuck Dressen)	96	57	.627	4.5
1953	Brooklyn (Chuck Dressen)	105	49	.682	13
1954	New York (Leo Durocher)	97	57	.630	5
1955	Brooklyn (Walter Alston)	98	55	.641	13.5
1956	Brooklyn (Walter Alston)	93	61	.604	1
1957	Milwaukee (Fred Haney)	95	59	.617	8
1958	Milwaukee (Fred Haney)	92	62	.597	8
1959	Los Angeles (Walter Alston)	88	68	.564	2
1960	Pittsburgh (Danny Murtaugh)	95	59	.617	7
1961	Cincinnati (Fred Hutchinson)	93	61	.604	4
1962	San Francisco (Alvin Dark)	103	62	.624	1
1963	Los Angeles (Walter Alston)	99	63	.611	6
1964	St. Louis (Johnny Keane)	93	69	.574	1
1965	Los Angeles (Walter Alston)	97	65	.599	2
1966	Los Angeles (Walter Alston)	95	67	.586	1.5
1967	St. Louis (Red Schoendienst)	101	60	.627	10.5
1968	St. Louis (Red Schoendienst)	97	65	.599	9

NATIONAL LEAGUE DIVISION CHAMPIONS (1969 to 1993)

Championship Series Winner Capitalized)
E = East; W = West)
* = mid-season replacement)*

YEAR	CLUB (MANAGER)	WON	LOST	PCT.	GA
1969	(E) NEW YORK (Gil Hodges)	100	62	.617	8
	(W) Atlanta (Lum Harris)	93	69	.574	3
1970	(W) CINCINNATI (Sparky Anderson)	102	60	.630	14.5
	(E) Pittsburgh (Danny Murtaugh)	89	73	.549	5
1971	(E) PITTSBURGH (Danny Murtaugh)	97	65	.599	7
	(W) San Francisco (Charlie Fox)	90	72	.556	1
1972	(W) CINCINNATI (Sparky Anderson)	95	59	.617	10.5
	(E) Pittsburgh (Bill Virdon)	96	59	.619	11
1973	(E) NEW YORK (Yogi Berra)	82	79	.509	1.5
	(W) Cincinnati (Sparky Anderson)	99	63	.611	3.5
1974	(W) LOS ANGELES (Walter Alston)	102	60	.630	4
	(E) Pittsburgh (Danny Murtaugh)	88	74	.543	1.5
1975	(W) CINCINNATI (Sparky Anderson)	108	54	.667	20
	(E) Pittsburgh (Danny Murtaugh)	92	69	.571	6.5
1976	(W) CINCINNATI (Sparky Anderson)	102	60	.630	10
	(E) Philadelphia (Danny Ozark)	101	61	.623	9
1977	(W) LOS ANGELES (Tommy Lasorda)	98	64	.605	10
	(E) Philadelphia (Danny Ozark)	101	61	.623	5
1978	(W) LOS ANGELES (Tommy Lasorda)	95	67	.586	2.5
	(E) Philadelphia (Danny Ozark)	90	72	.556	1.5
1979	(E) PITTSBURGH (Chuck Tanner)	98	64	.605	2
	(W) Cincinnati (John McNamara)	90	71	.559	1.5
1980	(E) PHILADELPHIA (Dallas Green)	91	71	.562	1
	(W) Houston (Bill Virdon)	93	70	.571	1
1981	(W) LOS ANGELES (Tommy Lasorda)	63	47	.573	--
	(E) Montreal (Jim Fanning*)	60	48	.556	--

Due to players' strike, 1981 season was divided into two halves. Leaders of each half met in a best-of-five series to determine the NLCS participants. West: Los Angeles 3, Houston 2; East: Montreal 3, Philadelphia 2.

1982	(E) ST. LOUIS (Whitey Herzog)	92	70	.568	3
	(W) Atlanta (Joe Torre)	89	73	.549	1
1983	(E) PHILADELPHIA (Paul Owens*)	90	72	.556	6
	(W) Los Angeles (Tommy Lasorda)	91	71	.562	3
1984	(W) SAN DIEGO (Dick Williams)	92	70	.568	12
	(E) Chicago (Jimmy Frey)	96	65	.596	6.5
1985	(E) ST. LOUIS (Whitey Herzog)	101	61	.623	3
	(W) Los Angeles (Tommy Lasorda)	95	67	.586	5.5
1986	(E) NEW YORK (Davey Johnson)	108	54	.667	21.5
	(W) Houston (Hal Lanier)	96	66	.593	10
1987	(E) ST. LOUIS (Whitey Herzog)	95	67	.586	3
	(W) San Francisco (Roger Craig)	90	72	.556	6
1988	(W) LOS ANGELES (Tommy Lasorda)	94	67	.584	7
	(E) New York (Davey Johnson)	100	60	.625	15
1989	(W) SAN FRANCISCO (Roger Craig)	92	70	.568	3
	(E) Chicago (Don Zimmer)	93	69	.574	6
1990	(W) CINCINNATI (Lou Piniella)	91	71	.562	5
	(E) Pittsburgh (Jim Leyland)	95	67	.586	4
1991	(W) ATLANTA (Bobby Cox)	94	68	.580	1
	(E) Pittsburgh (Jim Leyland)	98	64	.605	14
1992	(W) ATLANTA (Bobby Cox)	98	64	.605	8
	(E) Pittsburgh (Jim Leyland)	96	66	.593	9
1993	(E) PHILADELPHIA (Jim Fregosi)	97	65	.599	3
	(W) Atlanta (Bobby Cox)	104	58	.642	1

NATIONAL LEAGUE POSTSEASON PARTICIPANTS (since 1995)

(Championship Series Winner Capitalized)
(E = East; C = Central; W = West; WC = Wild Card)
(* = mid-season replacement)

YEAR	CLUB (MANAGER)	WON	LOST	PCT.	GA
1995	(E) ATLANTA (Bobby Cox)	90	54	.625	21
	(C) Cincinnati (Davey Johnson)	85	59	.590	9
	(W) Los Angeles (Tommy Lasorda)	78	66	.542	1
	(WC) Colorado (Don Baylor)	77	67	.535	--
1996	(E) ATLANTA (Bobby Cox)	96	66	.593	8
	(C) St. Louis (Tony LaRussa)	88	74	.543	6
	(W) San Diego (Bruce Bochy)	91	71	.562	1
	(WC) Los Angeles (Bill Russell*)	90	72	.556	--
1997	(WC) FLORIDA (Jim Leyland)	92	70	.568	--
	(E) Atlanta (Bobby Cox)	101	61	.623	9
	(C) Houston (Larry Dierker)	84	78	.519	5
	(W) San Francisco (Dusty Baker)	90	72	.556	2
1998	(W) SAN DIEGO (Bruce Bochy)	98	64	.605	9.5
	(E) Atlanta (Bobby Cox)	106	56	.654	18
	(C) Houston (Larry Dierker)	102	60	.630	12.5
	(WC) Chicago (Jim Riggleman)	90	73	.552	--
1999	(E) ATLANTA (Bobby Cox)	103	59	.636	6.5
	(WC) New York (Bobby Valentine)	97	66	.595	--
	(C) Houston (Larry Dierker)	97	65	.599	1.5
	(W) Arizona (Buck Showalter)	100	62	.617	14
2000	(WC) NEW YORK (Bobby Valentine)	94	68	.580	--
	(C) St. Louis (Tony LaRussa)	95	67	.586	10
	(E) Atlanta (Bobby Cox)	95	67	.586	1
	(W) San Francisco (Dusty Baker)	97	65	.599	11
2001	(W) ARIZONA (Bob Brenly)	92	70	.568	2
	(E) Atlanta (Bobby Cox)	88	74	.543	2
	(C) Houston (Larry Dierker)	93	69	.574	--
	(WC) St. Louis (Tony LaRussa)	93	69	.574	--
2002	(WC) SAN FRANCISCO (Dusty Baker)	95	66	.590	--
	(C) St. Louis (Tony LaRussa)	97	65	.599	13
	(E) Atlanta (Bobby Cox)	101	59	.631	19
	(W) Arizona (Bob Brenly)	98	64	.605	2.5
2003	(WC) FLORIDA (Jack McKeon*)	91	71	.562	--
	(C) Chicago (Dusty Baker)	88	74	.543	1
	(E) Atlanta (Bobby Cox)	101	61	.623	10
	(W) San Francisco (Felipe Alou)	100	61	.621	15.5
2004	(C) ST. LOUIS (Tony LaRussa)	105	57	.648	13
	(WC) Houston (Phil Garner*)	92	70	.568	--
	(E) Atlanta (Bobby Cox)	96	66	.593	10
	(W) Los Angeles (Jim Tracy)	93	69	.574	2
2005	(WC) HOUSTON (Phil Garner)	89	73	.549	--
	(C) St. Louis (Tony LaRussa)	100	62	.617	11
	(E) Atlanta (Bobby Cox)	90	72	.556	2
	(W) San Diego (Bruce Bochy)	82	80	.506	5
2006	(C) ST. LOUIS (Tony LaRussa)	83	78	.516	1.5
	(E) New York (Willie Randolph)	97	65	.599	12
	(W) San Diego (Bruce Bochy)	88	74	.543	--
	(WC) Los Angeles (Grady Little)	88	74	.543	--

CONSECUTIVE VICTORIES
NATIONAL LEAGUE

No.	Club	H	A	Year
26	New York	26	0	1916
21	Chicago	11	10	1880
	Chicago	18	3	1935
20	Providence	16	4	1884
18	Chicago	14	4	1885
	Boston	16	2	1891
	Baltimore	13	5	1894
	New York	13	5	1904
17	Boston	16	1	1897
	New York	14	3	1907
	New York	0	17	1916
16	Philadelphia	5	11	1887
	Philadelphia	14	2	1890
	Philadelphia	11	5	1892
	Pittsburgh	12	4	1909
	New York	11	5	1912
	New York	13	3	1951
15	Detroit	12	3	1886
	Pittsburgh	11	4	1903
	Brooklyn	3	12	1924
	Chicago	11	4	1936
	New York	8	7	1936
	Atlanta	9	6	2000

AMERICAN LEAGUE

No.	Club	H	A	Year
20	Oakland	10	10	2002
19	Chicago	11	8	1906
	New York	6	13	1947
18	New York	3	15	1953
17	Washington	1	16	1912
	Philadelphia	5	12	1931
16	New York	12	4	1926
	Kansas City	9	7	1977
15	New York	12	3	1906
	Philadelphia	13	2	1913
	Boston	11	4	1946
	New York	9	6	1960
	Minnesota	8	7	1991
	Seattle	5	10	2001

AMERICAN ASSOCIATION

No.	Club	H	A	Year
15	St. Louis	15	0	1887

UNION ASSOCIATION

No.	Club	H	A	Year
20	St. Louis	16	4	1884

CONSECUTIVE LOSSES
NATIONAL LEAGUE

No.	Club	H	A	Year
24	Cleveland	5	19	1899
23	Pittsburgh	1	22	1890
	Philadelphia	6	17	1961
20	Louisville	0	20	1894
	Montreal	12	8	1969
19	Boston	3	16	1906
	Cincinnati	6	13	1914
18	Cincinnati	9	9	1876
	Louisville	0	18	1894
	St. Louis	4	14	1897
17	Washington	7	10	1894
	New York	7	10	1962
	Atlanta	8	9	1977
16	Troy	5	11	1882
	Buffalo	12	4	1885
	Cleveland	0	16	1899
	Boston	5	11	1907
	Boston	8	8	1911
	Brooklyn	0	16	1944
15	Louisville	10	5	1895
	St. Louis	11	4	1909
	Boston	0	15	1909
	Boston	0	15	1927
	Boston	0	15	1935
	New York	8	7	1963
	New York	6	9	1982

AMERICAN LEAGUE

No.	Club	H	A	Year
21	Baltimore	8	13	1988
20	Boston	19	1	1906
	Philadelphia	1	19	1916
	Philadelphia	3	17	1943
19	Detroit	9	10	1975
	Kansas City	8	11	2005
18	Philadelphia	0	18	1920
	Washington	8	10	1948
	Washington	3	15	1959
17	Boston	14	3	1926
16	Boston	9	7	1907
15	Boston	10	5	1927
	Philadelphia	10	5	1937
	Texas	5	10	1972
	Tampa Bay	9	6	2002

AMERICAN ASSOCIATION

No.	Club	H	A	Year
26	Louisville	5	21	1889
22	Philadelphia	6	16	1890
15	Baltimore	0	15	1882
	Washington	0	15	1884
	Louisville	0	15	1891

UNION ASSOCIATION

No.	Club	H	A	Year
15	Kansas City	3	12	1884

LONGEST GAMES, 18 OR MORE INNINGS

AMERICAN LEAGUE

25	Chi. 7 Mil. 6, May 8, 1984
24	Phil. 4 Bos. 1, Sept 1, 1906
	Det. 1 Phil. 1, July 21, 1945
22	NY 9 Det. 7, June 24, 1962
	Wash. 6 Chi. 5, June 12, 1967
	Mil. 4 Minn. 3, May 12, 1972
	Minn. 5 Clev. 4, Aug. 31, 1993
21	Det. 6 Chi. 5, May 24, 1929
	Oak. 5 Wash. 3, June 4, 1971
	Chi. 6 Clev. 3, May 26, 1973
20	Phil. 4 Bos. 2, July 4, 1905
	Wash. 9 Minn. 7, Aug. 9, 1967
	NY 4 Bos. 3, Aug. 29(2g), 1967
	Bos. 5 Sea. 3, July 27, 1969
	Oak. 1 Cal. 0, July 9, 1971
	Wash. 8 Clev. 6, Sept. 14(2g), 1971
	Sea. 8 Bos. 7, Sept 3, 1981
	Cal. 4 Sea. 3, Apr. 13, 1982
19	Wash. 5 Phil. 4, Sept. 27, 1912
	Chi. 5 Clev. 4, June 24, 1915
	Clev. 3 NY 2, May 24, 1918
	StL. 8 Wash. 6, Aug. 9, 1921
	Chi. 5 Bos. 4, July 13, 1951
	Clev. 4 StL. 3, July 1, 1952
	Clev. 3 Wash. 2, June 14(2g), 1963
	Balt. 7 Wash. 5, June 4, 1967
	KC 6 Det. 5, June 17(2g), 1967
	NY 3 Det. 3, Aug. 23(2g), 1968
	Oak. 5 Chi. 3, Aug. 10, 1972
	NY 5 Minn. 4, Aug. 25, 1976
	Clev. 8 Det. 4, Apr. 27, 1984
	Mil. 10 Chi. 9, May 1, 1991
	Bos. 7 Clev. 5, Apr. 11, 1992
	Sea. 5 Bos. 4, Aug. 1, 2000
	Chi. 6 Bos. 5, July 9, 2006
18	Chi. 6 NY 6, June 25, 1903
	Det. 0 Wash. 0, July 16, 1909
	Wash. 1 Chi. 0, May 15, 1918
	Det. 7 Wash. 6, Aug. 4(2g), 1918
	Bos. 12 NY 11, Sept 5(1g), 1927
	Phil. 18 Clev. 17, July 10, 1932
	NY 3 Chi. 3, Aug. 21, 1933
	Wash. 1 Chi. 0, June 8(1g), 1947
	Wash. 5 StL. 5, June 20, 1952
	Chi. 1 Balt. 1, Aug. 6, 1959
	NY 7 Bos. 6, Apr. 16, 1967
	Minn. 3 NY 2, July 26(2g), 1967
	Balt. 3 Bos. 2, Aug. 25, 1968
	Minn. 11 Sea. 7, July 19, 1969
	Oak. 9 Balt. 8, Aug. 24(2g), 1969
	Minn. 8 Oak. 6, Sept. 6, 1969
	Wash. 2 NY 1, Apr. 22, 1970
	Tex. 4 KC 3, May 17, 1972
	Det. 4 Clev. 3, June 9(2g), 1982
	NY 5 Det. 4, Sept. 11, 1988
	KC 4 Tex. 3, June 6, 1991
	Bos. 4 Det. 3, June 5, 2001
	Tex. 8 Bos. 7, Aug. 25, 2001
	Tex. 9 Sea. 7, June 24, 2004
	Oak. 6 Minn. 5, Aug. 8, 2004
	Tor. 2 LA 1, July 28, 2005

NATIONAL LEAGUE

26	Brk. 1 Bos. 1, May 1, 1920
25	StL. 4 NY 3, Sept. 11 1974
24	Hou. 1 NY 0, Apr. 15, 1968
23	Brk. 2 Bos. 2, June 27, 1939
	SF 8 NY 6, May 31(2g), 1964
22	Brk. 6 Pitt. 5, Aug. 22, 1917
	Chi. 4 Bos. 3, May 17 1927
	Hou. 5 LA 4, June 3, 1989
	LA 1 Mtl. 0, Aug. 23, 1989

21	NY 3 Pitt. 1, July 17, 1914
	Chi. 2 Phil. 1, July 17, 1918
	Pitt. 2 Bos. 0, Aug. 1, 1918
	SF 1 Cin. 0, Sept. 1, 1967
	Hou. 2 SD 1, Sept. 24(1g), 1971
	SD 11 Mtl. 8, May 21, 1977
	LA 2 Chi. 1, Aug. 17, 1982
20	Chi. 7 Cin. 7, June 30, 1892
	Chi. 2 Phil. 1, Aug. 24, 1905
	Brk. 9 Phil. 9, Apr. 30, 1919
	StL. 8 Chi. 7, Aug. 28, 1930
	Brk. 6 Bos. 2, July 5, 1940
	Phil. 5 Atl. 4, May 4, 1973
	Pitt. 5 Chi. 4, July 6, 1980
	Hou. 3 SD 1, Aug. 15, 1980
	Phil. 7 LA 6, July 7, 1993
	StL. 7 Fla. 6 Apr. 27, 2003
19	Chi. 3 Pitt. 2, June 22, 1902
	Pitt. 7 Bos. 6, July 31, 1912
	Chi. 4 Brk. 3, June 17, 1915
	StL. 8 Phil. 8, June 13, 1918
	Bos. 2 Brk. 1, May 3, 1920
	Chi. 3 Bos. 2, Aug. 17, 1932
	Brk. 9 Chi. 9, May 17, 1939
	Cin. 0 Brk. 0, Sept. 11, 1946
	Phil. 8 Cin. 7, Sept. 15(2g), 1950
	Pitt. 4 Mil. 3, July 19, 1955
	Cin. 2 LA 1, Aug. 8, 1972
	NY 7 LA 3, May 24, 1973
	Pitt. 4 SD 3, Aug. 25, 1979
	NY 16 Atl. 13, July 4, 1985
	Mtl. 6 Hou. 3, July 7, 1985
	Atl. 7 StL. 5, May 14, 1988
18	Prov. 1 Det. 0, Aug. 17, 1882
	Brk. 7 StL.7, Aug. 17, 1902
	Chi. 2 StL. 1, June 24, 1905
	Pitt. 3 Chi. 2, June 28(2g), 1916
	Phil. 10 Brk. 9, June 1, 1919
	NY 9 Pitt. 8, July 7, 1922
	Chi. 7 Bos. 2, May 14, 1927
	NY 1 StL. 0, July 2(1g), 1933
	StL. 8 Cin. 6, July 1(1g), 1934
	Chi. 10 Cin. 8, Aug. 9(1g), 1942
	Phil. 4 Pitt. 3, June 9, 1949
	Cin. 7 Chi. 6, Sept. 7, 1951
	NY 0 Phil. 0, Oct. 2(2g), 1965
	Cin. 3 Chi. 2, July 19, 1966
	Phil. 2 Cin. 1, May 21, 1967
	Pitt. 1 SD 0, June 7(2g), 1972
	NY 3 Phil. 2, Aug. 1(1g), 1972
	Mtl. 5 Chi. 4, June 27(2g), 1973
	Chi. 8 Mtl. 7, June 28(1g), 1974
	NY 4 Mtl. 3, Sept. 16, 1975
	Pitt. 2 Chi. 1, Aug. 10, 1977
	Chi. 9 Cin. 8, May 10, 1979
	Hou. 3 NY 2, June 18, 1979
	SD 8 NY 6, Aug. 26, 1980
	StL. 3 Hou. 1, May 27, 1983
	Pitt. 4 SF 3, July 13(2g), 1984
	Atl. 3 LA 2, Sept. 6, 1984
	NY 5 Pitt. 4, Apr. 28, 1985
	SF 5 Atl. 4, June 11, 1985
	Hou. 8 Chi. 7, Sept. 2, 1986
	Pitt. 5 Chi. 4, Aug. 6, 1989
	Atl. 5 LA 3, Aug. 3, 1996
	Ari. 1 SF 0, May 29, 2001
	Pitt. 8 Hou. 7, May 27, 2006
	Chi. 8 Hou. 6, Aug. 15, 2006
	Ari. 2 Col. 1, Aug. 15, 2006

AMERICAN LEAGUE CLUB HOME RUNS

*= Leader)

1901 Milwaukee total under StL.)

	BALT	BOS	CHI	CLEV	DET	KC	NY	PHIL	STL	WASH	TTAL
1901	24	*37	32	12	29	-	-	35	26	33	228
1902	33	42	14	33	22	-	-	38	29	*47	258
1903	-	*48	14	31	12	-	18	32	12	17	184
1904	-	26	14	27	11	-	27	*31	10	10	156
1905	-	*29	11	18	13	-	23	24	16	22	156
1906	-	13	7	12	10	-	17	*32	20	26	137
1907	-	18	5	11	11	-	15	*22	10	12	104
1908	-	14	3	18	19	-	13	*21	20	8	116
1909	-	20	4	10	19	-	16	*21	10	9	109
1910	-	*43	7	9	28	-	20	19	12	9	147
1911	-	*35	20	20	30	-	25	*35	17	16	198
1912	-	*29	17	11	19	-	18	22	19	20	155
1913	-	17	23	16	24	-	8	*33	18	19	158
1914	-	18	19	10	25	-	12	*29	17	18	148
1915	-	14	25	20	23	-	*31	16	19	12	160
1916	-	14	17	16	17	-	*35	19	14	12	144
1917	-	14	18	13	25	-	*27	17	15	4	133
1918	-	15	8	9	13	-	20	*22	5	4	96
1919	-	33	25	24	23	-	*45	35	31	24	240
1920	-	22	37	35	30	-	*115	44	50	36	369
1921	-	17	35	42	58	-	*134	82	67	42	477
1922	-	45	45	32	54	-	95	*111	98	45	525
1923	-	34	42	59	41	-	*105	53	82	26	442
1924	-	30	41	41	35	-	*98	63	67	22	397
1925	-	41	38	52	50	-	*110	76	*110	56	533
1926	-	32	32	27	36	-	*121	61	72	43	424
1927	-	28	36	26	51	-	*158	56	55	29	439
1928	-	38	24	34	62	-	*133	89	63	40	483
1929	-	28	37	62	110	-	*142	122	46	48	595
1930	-	47	63	72	82	-	*152	125	75	57	673
1931	-	37	27	71	43	-	*155	118	76	49	576
1932	-	53	36	78	80	-	160	*172	67	61	707
1933	-	50	43	50	57	-	*144	139	64	60	607
1934	-	51	71	100	74	-	135	*144	62	51	688
1935	-	69	74	93	106	-	104	*112	73	32	663
1936	-	86	60	123	94	-	*182	72	79	62	758
1937	-	100	67	103	150	-	*174	94	71	47	806
1938	-	98	67	113	137	-	*174	98	92	85	864
1939	-	124	64	85	124	-	*166	98	91	44	796
1940	-	145	73	101	134	-	*155	105	118	52	883
1941	-	124	47	103	81	-	*151	85	91	52	734
1942	-	103	25	50	76	-	*108	33	98	40	533
1943	-	57	33	55	77	-	*100	26	78	47	473
1944	-	69	23	70	60	-	*96	36	72	33	459
1945	-	50	22	65	77	-	*93	33	63	27	430
1946	-	109	37	79	108	-	*136	40	84	60	653
1947	-	103	53	112	103	-	*115	61	90	42	679
1948	-	121	55	*155	78	-	139	68	63	31	710
1949	-	*131	43	112	88	-	115	82	117	81	769
1950	-	161	93	*164	114	-	159	100	106	76	973
1951	-	127	86	*140	104	-	*140	102	86	54	839
1952	-	113	80	*148	103	-	129	89	82	50	794
1953	-	101	74	*160	108	-	139	116	112	69	879
1954	52	123	94	*156	90	-	133	94	-	81	823
1955	54	137	116	148	130	121	*175	-	-	80	961
1956	91	139	128	153	150	112	*190	-	-	112	1075
1957	87	153	106	140	116	*166	145	-	-	111	1024
1958	108	155	101	161	109	138	*164	-	-	121	1057
1959	109	125	97	*167	160	117	153	-	-	163	1091
1960	123	124	112	127	150	110	*193	-	-	147	1086

AMERICAN LEAGUE CLUB HOME RUNS

(* = Leader)

	ANA	BALT	BOS	CHI	CLEV	DET	KC	MIL	MINN	NY	OAK	SEA	TEX	TOR	WASH	TOTAL
1961	189	149	112	138	150	130	90	-	167	*240	-	-	-	-	119	1534
1962	137	156	146	92	180	*209	116	-	185	199	-	-	-	-	132	1552
1963	95	146	171	114	169	148	95	-	*225	188	-	-	-	-	138	1489
1964	102	162	186	106	164	157	166	-	*221	162	-	-	-	-	125	1551
1965	92	125	*165	125	156	162	110	-	150	149	-	-	-	-	136	1370
1966	122	175	145	87	155	*179	110	-	144	162	-	-	-	-	126	1365
1967	114	138	*158	89	131	152	69	-	131	100	-	-	-	-	115	1197
1968	83	133	125	71	75	*185	-	-	105	109	94	-	-	-	124	1104
1969	88	175	*197	112	119	182	98	-	163	94	148	125	-	-	148	1649
1970	114	179	*203	123	183	148	97	126	153	111	171	-	-	-	138	1746
1971	96	158	161	138	109	*179	80	124	116	97	160	-	-	-	86	1484
1972	78	100	124	108	91	122	78	88	93	103	*134	-	56	-	-	1175
1973	93	119	147	111	*158	157	114	145	120	131	147	-	110	-	-	1552
1974	95	116	109	*135	131	131	89	120	111	101	132	-	99	-	-	1369
1975	55	124	134	94	*153	125	118	146	124	110	151	-	134	-	-	1465
1976	63	119	*134	73	85	101	65	88	81	120	113	-	80	-	-	1122
1977	131	148	*213	192	100	166	146	125	123	184	117	133	135	100	-	2013
1978	108	154	172	106	106	129	98	*173	82	125	100	97	132	98	-	1680
1979	164	181	*194	127	138	164	116	185	112	150	108	132	140	95	-	2006
1980	106	156	162	91	89	143	115	*203	99	189	137	104	124	126	-	1844
1981	97	88	90	76	39	65	61	96	47	100	*104	89	49	61	-	1062
1982	186	179	136	136	109	177	132	*216	148	161	149	130	115	106	-	2080
1983	154	*168	142	157	86	156	109	132	141	153	121	111	106	167	-	1903
1984	150	160	181	172	123	*187	117	96	114	130	158	129	120	143	-	1980
1985	153	*214	162	146	116	202	154	101	141	176	155	171	129	158	-	2178
1986	167	169	144	121	157	*198	137	127	196	188	163	158	184	181	-	2290
1987	172	211	174	173	187	*225	168	163	196	196	199	161	194	215	-	2634
1988	124	137	124	132	134	143	121	113	151	148	156	148	112	*158	-	1901
1989	*145	129	108	94	127	116	101	126	117	130	127	134	122	142	-	1718
1990	147	132	106	106	110	*172	100	128	100	147	164	107	110	167	-	1796
1991	115	170	126	139	79	*209	117	116	140	147	159	126	177	133	-	1953
1992	88	148	84	110	127	*182	75	82	104	163	142	149	159	163	-	1776
1993	114	157	114	162	141	178	125	125	121	178	158	161	*181	159	-	2074
1994	120	139	120	121	*167	161	100	99	103	139	113	153	124	115	-	1774
1995	186	173	175	146	*207	159	119	128	120	122	169	182	138	140	-	2164
1996	192	*257	209	195	218	204	123	178	118	162	243	245	221	177	-	2742
1997	161	196	185	158	220	176	158	135	132	161	197	*264	187	147	-	2477

	ANA	BALT	BOS	CHI	CLEV	DET	KC	MINN	NY	OAK	SEA	TEX	TOR	TB	TOTAL
1998	147	214	205	198	198	165	134	115	207	149	*234	201	221	111	2499
1999	158	203	176	162	209	212	151	105	193	235	*244	230	212	145	2635
2000	236	184	167	216	221	177	150	116	205	239	198	173	*244	162	2688
2001	158	136	198	214	212	139	152	164	203	199	169	*246	195	121	2506
2002	152	165	177	217	192	124	140	167	223	205	152	*230	187	133	2464
2003	150	152	238	220	158	153	162	155	230	176	139	*239	190	137	2499
2004	162	169	222	*242	184	201	150	191	*242	189	136	227	145	145	2605

	LA	BALT	BOS	CHI	CLEV	DET	KC	MINN	NY	OAK	SEA	TEX	TOR	TB	TOTAL
2005	147	189	199	200	207	168	126	134	229	155	130	*260	136	157	2437
2006	159	164	192	*236	196	203	124	143	210	175	172	183	199	190	2456

NATIONAL LEAGUE CLUB HOME RUNS

* = Leader)

	BOS	BRK	CHI	CIN	LA	MIL	NY	PHIL	PITT	STL	SF	TOTAL
1900	*48	26	33	33	-	-	23	29	26	36	-	254
1901	28	32	18	38	-	-	19	24	28	*39	-	226
1902	14	*19	6	18	-	-	6	5	18	10	-	96
1903	25	15	9	28	-	-	20	12	*34	8	-	151
1904	24	15	22	21	-	-	*31	23	15	24	-	175
1905	17	29	12	27	-	-	*39	16	22	20	-	182
1906	16	*25	20	16	-	-	15	12	12	10	-	126
1907	22	18	13	15	-	-	*23	12	19	18	-	140
1908	17	*28	19	14	-	-	20	11	25	17	-	151
1909	14	16	20	22	-	-	*26	12	25	15	-	150
1910	31	25	*34	23	-	-	31	22	33	15	-	214
1911	37	28	54	21	-	-	41	*60	49	26	-	316
1912	35	32	42	21	-	-	*47	43	39	27	-	286
1913	32	39	59	27	-	-	31	*73	35	15	-	311
1914	35	31	42	16	-	-	30	*62	18	33	-	267
1915	17	14	53	15	-	-	24	*58	24	20	-	225
1916	22	28	*46	14	-	-	42	42	20	25	-	239
1917	22	25	17	26	-	-	*39	38	9	26	-	202
1918	13	10	21	15	-	-	13	25	15	*27	-	139
1919	24	25	21	20	-	-	40	*42	17	18	-	207
1920	23	28	34	18	-	-	46	*64	16	32	-	261
1921	61	59	37	20	-	-	75	*88	37	83	-	460
1922	32	56	42	45	-	-	80	*116	52	107	-	530
1923	32	62	90	45	-	-	85	*112	49	63	-	538
1924	25	72	66	36	-	-	*95	94	44	67	-	499
1925	41	64	86	44	-	-	*114	100	78	109	-	636
1926	16	40	66	35	-	-	73	75	44	*90	-	439
1927	37	39	74	29	-	-	*109	57	54	84	-	483
1928	52	66	92	32	-	-	*118	85	52	113	-	610
1929	33	99	139	34	-	-	136	*153	60	100	-	754
1930	66	122	*171	74	-	-	143	126	86	104	-	892
1931	34	71	84	21	-	-	*101	81	41	60	-	493
1932	63	110	69	47	-	-	116	*122	48	76	-	651
1933	54	62	72	34	-	-	*82	60	39	57	-	460
1934	83	79	101	55	-	-	*126	56	52	104	-	656
1935	75	59	88	73	-	-	*123	92	66	86	-	662
1936	67	33	76	82	-	-	97	*103	60	88	-	606
1937	63	37	96	73	-	-	*111	103	47	94	-	624
1938	54	61	65	110	-	-	*125	40	65	91	-	611
1939	56	78	91	98	-	-	*116	49	63	98	-	649
1940	59	93	86	89	-	-	91	75	76	*119	-	688
1941	48	*101	99	64	-	-	95	64	56	70	-	597
1942	68	62	75	66	-	-	*109	44	54	60	-	538
1943	39	39	52	43	-	-	*81	66	42	70	-	432
1944	79	56	71	51	-	-	93	55	70	*100	-	575
1945	101	57	57	56	-	-	*114	56	72	64	-	577
1946	44	55	56	65	-	-	*121	80	60	81	-	562
1947	85	83	71	95	-	-	*221	60	156	115	-	886
1948	95	91	87	104	-	-	*164	91	108	105	-	845
1949	103	*152	97	86	-	-	147	122	126	102	-	935
1950	148	*194	161	99	-	-	133	125	138	102	-	1100
1951	130	*184	103	88	-	-	151	108	137	95	-	1024
1952	110	*153	107	104	-	-	151	93	92	97	-	907
1953	-	*208	137	166	-	156	176	115	99	140	-	1197
1954	-	*186	159	147	-	139	*186	102	76	119	-	1114
1955	-	*201	164	181	-	182	169	132	91	143	-	1263
1956	-	179	142	*221	-	177	145	121	110	124	-	1219
1957	-	147	147	187	-	*199	157	117	92	132	-	1178
1958	-	-	*182	123	172	167	-	124	134	111	170	1183
1959	-	-	163	161	148	*177	-	113	112	118	167	1159
1960	-	-	119	140	126	*170	-	99	120	138	130	1042
1961	-	-	176	158	157	*188	-	103	128	103	183	1196

NATIONAL LEAGUE CLUB HOME RUNS

(* = Leader)

	ATL	CHI	CIN	HOU	LA	MIL	MTL	NY	PHIL	PITT	STL	SD	SF	TOTAL
1962	-	126	167	105	140	181	-	139	142	108	137	-	*204	1449
1963	-	127	122	62	110	139	-	96	126	108	128	-	*197	1215
1964	-	145	130	70	79	159	-	103	130	121	109	-	*165	1211
1965	-	134	183	97	78	*196	-	107	144	111	109	-	159	1318
1966	*207	140	149	112	108	-	-	98	117	158	108	-	181	1378
1967	*158	128	109	93	82	-	-	83	103	91	115	-	140	1102
1968	80	*130	106	66	67	-	-	81	100	80	73	-	108	891
1969	141	142	*171	104	97	-	125	109	137	119	90	99	136	1470
1970	160	179	*191	129	87	-	136	120	101	130	113	172	165	1683
1971	153	128	138	71	95	-	88	98	123	*154	95	96	104	1379
1972	144	133	124	134	98	-	91	105	98	110	70	102	*150	1359
1973	*206	117	137	134	110	-	125	85	134	154	75	112	161	1550
1974	120	110	135	110	*139	-	86	96	95	114	83	99	93	1280
1975	107	95	124	84	118	-	98	101	125	*138	81	78	84	1233
1976	82	105	*141	66	91	-	94	102	110	110	63	64	85	1113
1977	139	111	181	114	*191	-	138	88	186	133	96	120	134	1631
1978	123	72	136	70	*149	-	121	86	133	115	79	75	117	1276
1979	126	135	132	49	*183	-	143	74	119	148	100	93	125	1427
1980	144	107	113	75	*148	-	114	61	117	116	101	67	80	1243
1981	64	57	64	45	*82	-	81	57	69	55	50	32	63	719
1982	*146	102	82	74	138	-	133	97	112	134	67	81	133	1299
1983	130	140	107	97	*146	-	102	112	125	121	83	93	142	1398
1984	111	136	106	79	102	-	96	107	*147	98	75	109	112	1278
1985	126	*150	114	121	129	-	118	134	141	80	87	109	115	1424
1986	138	*155	144	125	130	-	110	148	154	111	58	136	114	1523
1987	152	*209	192	122	125	-	120	192	169	131	94	113	205	1824
1988	96	113	122	96	99	-	107	*152	106	110	71	94	113	1279
1989	128	124	128	97	89	-	100	*147	123	95	73	120	141	1365
1990	162	136	125	94	129	-	114	*172	103	138	73	123	152	1521
1991	141	159	*164	79	108	-	95	117	111	126	68	121	141	1430
1992	*138	104	99	96	72	-	102	93	118	106	94	135	105	1262

	ATL	CHI	CIN	COL	FLA	HOU	LA	MTL	NY	PHIL	PITT	STL	SD	SF	TOTAL
1993	*169	161	137	142	94	138	130	122	158	156	110	118	153	168	1956
1994	*137	109	124	125	94	120	115	108	117	80	80	108	92	123	1532
1995	168	158	161	*200	144	109	140	118	125	94	125	107	116	152	1917
1996	197	175	191	*221	150	129	150	148	147	132	138	142	147	153	2220
1997	174	127	142	*239	136	133	174	172	153	116	129	144	152	172	2163

	ARI	ATL	CHI	CIN	COL	FLA	HOU	LA	MIL	MTL	NY	PHIL	PITT	STL	SD	SF	TOTAL
1998	159	215	212	138	183	114	166	159	152	147	136	126	107	*223	167	161	2565
1999	216	197	189	209	*223	128	168	187	165	163	181	161	171	194	153	188	2893
2000	179	179	183	200	161	160	*249	211	177	178	198	144	168	235	157	226	3005
2001	208	174	194	176	213	166	208	206	209	131	147	164	161	199	161	*235	2952
2002	165	164	*200	169	152	146	167	155	139	162	160	165	142	175	136	198	2595
2003	152	*235	172	182	198	157	191	124	196	144	124	166	163	196	128	180	2708
2004	135	178	*235	194	202	148	187	203	135	151	185	215	142	214	139	183	2846

	ARI	ATL	CHI	CIN	COL	FLA	HOU	LA	MIL	WAS	NY	PHIL	PITT	STL	SD	SF	TOTAL
2005	191	184	194	*222	150	128	161	149	175	117	175	167	139	170	130	128	2580
2006	160	*222	166	217	157	182	174	153	180	164	200	216	141	184	161	163	2840

MANAGERS – AMERICAN LEAGUE
*also listed in NL)

Adcock, Joe Clev. 1967
*Altobelli, Joe Balt. 1983-85
*Anderson, Sparky Det. 1979-95
Appling, Luke KC 1967
Armour, Bill Clev. 1902-04
   Det. 1905-06
Aspromonte, Ken Clev. 1972-74
Austin, Jimmy StL. 1923
Baker, Del Det. 1933, 38-42
*Bamberger, George Mil. 1978-80; 85-86
Barrow, Ed Det. 1903-04
   Bos. 1918-20
Barry, Jack Bos. 1917
Bauer, Hank KC 1961-62
   Balt. 1964-68
   Oak. 1969
*Bell, Buddy Det. 1996-98
   KC 2005-
*Berra, Yogi NY 1964; 84-85
Bevington, Terry Chi. 1995-97
Birmingham, Joe Clev. 1912-15
Blackburne, Lena Chi. 1928-29
Bluege, Ossie Wash. 1943-47
*Boone, Bob KC 1995-97
*Boros, Steve Oak. 1983-84
Bottomley, Jim StL. 1937
*Boudreau, Lou Clev. 1942-50
   Bos. 1952-54
   KC 1955-57
*Bragan, Bobby Clev. 1958
*Bristol, Dave Mil. 1970-72
*Burke, Jimmy StL. 1918-20
*Bush, Donie Wash. 1923
   Chi. 1930-31
*Callahan, Nixey Chi. 1903-04; 12-14
Cantillon, Joe Wash. 1907-09
Carrigan, Bill Bos. 1913-16; 27-29
*Chance, Frank NY 1913-14
   Bos. 1923
Chase, Hal NY 1910-11
Cobb, Ty Det. 1921-26
Cochrane, Mickey Det. 1934-38
Collins, Eddie Chi. 1925-26
Collins, Jimmy Bos. 1901-06
Collins, Shano Bos. 1931-32
*Collins, Terry Ana. 1997-99
*Corrales, Pat Tex. 1978-80
   Clev. 1983-87
Corriden, Red Chi. 1950
Cottier, Chuck Sea. 1984-86
*Cox, Bobby Tor. 1982-85
*Craft, Harry KC 1957-59
Crandall, Del Mil. 1972-75
   Sea. 1983-84
Cronin, Joe Wash. 1933-34
   Bos. 1935-47
*Dark, Alvin KC /Oak. 1966-67; 74-75
   Clev. 1968-71
Davis, Harry Clev. 1912
Dent, Bucky NY 1989-90
Dickey, Bill NY 1946
Doby, Larry Chi. 1978
*Donovan, Patsy Wash. 1904
   Bos. 1910-11
*Donovan, Wild Bill NY 1915-17
*Dressen, Chuck Wash. 1955-57
   Det. 1963-66
*Duffy, Hugh Mil. 1901
   Chi. 1910-11
   Bos. 1921-22
Dwyer, Frank Det. 1902
*Dykes, Jimmy Chi. 1934-46
   Phil. 1951-53
   Balt. 1954
   Det. 1959-60
   Clev. 1960-61
Edwards, Doc Clev. 1987-89

Elberfeld, Kid NY 1908
Elliot, Bob KC 1960
Ermer, Cal Minn. 1967-68
*Evers, Johnny Chi. 1924
Farrell, Kerby Clev. 1957
Ferraro, Mike Clev. 1983
   KC 1986
*Fletcher, Art NY 1929
Fohl, Lee Clev. 1915-19
   StL. 1921-23
   Bos. 1924-26
*Fonseca, Lew Chi. 1932-34
*Francona, Terry Bos. 2004-
*Fregosi, Jim Cal. 1978-81
   Chi. 1986-88
   Tor. 1999-2000
*Frey, Jim KC 1980-81
Garcia, Dave Cal. 1977-78
   Clev. 1979-82
Gardenhire, Ron Minn. 2002-
Gardner, Billy Minn. 1981-85
   KC 1987
*Garner, Phil Mil. 1992-97
   Det. 2000-02
Gaston, Cito Tor. 1989-97
Gibbons, John Tor. 2004-
Gleason, Kid Chi. 1919-23
Gordon, Joe Clev. 1958-60
   Det. 1960
   KC 1961; 69
Goryl, John Minn. 1980-81
Grammas, Alex Mil. 1976-77
*Green, Dallas NY 1989
Griffith, Clark Chi. 1901-02
   NY 1903-08
   Wash. 1912-20
Guillen, Ozzie Chi. 2004-
Gutteridge, Don Chi. 1969-70
*Haney, Fred StL. 1939-41
Hargrove, Mike Clev. 1991-99
   Balt. 2000-03
   Sea. 2005-
Harrah, Toby Tex. 1992
*Harris, Lum Balt. 1961
*Harris, Bucky Wash. 1924-28; 35-42;
   50-54
   Det. 1929-33; 1955-56
   Bos. 1934
   NY 1947-48
Hart, John Clev. 1989
Hartsfield, Roy Tor. 1977-79
*Herman, Billy Bos. 1965-66
*Herzog, Whitey Tex. 1973
   KC 1975-79
Higgins, Pinky Bos. 1955-62
*Hitchcock, Billy Balt. 1962-63
Hobson, Butch Bos. 1992-1994
*Hodges, Gil Wash. 1963-67
*Hornsby, Rogers StL. 1933-37; 52
Houk, Ralph NY 1961-63; 66-73
   Det. 1974-78
   Bos. 1981-84
*Howe, Art Oak. 1996-2002
*Howley, Dan StL. 1927-29
Howser, Dick NY 1980
   KC 1981-86
Huff, George Bos. 1907
*Huggins, Miller NY 1918-29
Hunter, Billy Tex. 1977-78
*Hutchinson, Fred Det. 1952-54
Jennings, Hughie Det. 1907-20
Johnson, Darrell Bos. 1974-76
   Sea. 1977-80
   Tex. 1982
*Johnson, Davey Balt. 1996-97
Johnson, Tim Tor. 1998
Johnson, Walter Wash. 1929-32
   Clev. 1933-35

Jones, Fielder Chi. 1904-08
   StL. 1916-18
Joost, Eddie Phil. 1954
Jurges, Billy Bos. 1959-60
Kasko, Eddie Bos. 1970-73
*Keane, Johnny NY 1965-66
Kelly, Tom Minn. 1986-2001
*Kennedy, Bob Oak. 1968
Kennedy, Kevin Tex. 1993-1994
   Bos. 1995-96
Kerrigan, Joe Bos. 2001
Kessinger, Don Chi. 1979
*Killefer, Bill StL. 1930-33
*King, Clyde NY 1982
Kittredge, Malachi Wash. 1904
Kuenn, Harvey Mil. 1982-83
Kuhel, Joe Wash. 1948-49
Lachemann, Marcel Cal. 1994-96
*Lachemann, Rene Sea. 1981-83
   Mil. 1984
Lajoie, Nap Clev. 1905-09
*Lake, Fred Bos. 1908-09
*Lamont, Gene Chi. 1992-95
*LaRussa, Tony Chi. 1979-86
   Oak. 1986-95
Lavagetto, Cookie Wash./Minn.
   1957-61
*Lefebvre, Jim Sea. 1989-91
Lemon, Jim Wash. 1968
Lemon, Bob KC 1970-72
   Chi. 1977-78
   NY 1978-79; 81-82
*Leyland, Jim Det. 2006-
Lipon, Johnny Clev. 1971
*Little, Grady Bos. 2002-03
*Loftus, Tom Wash. 1902-03
Lopat, Ed KC 1963-64
Lopez, Al Clev. 1951-56
   Chi. 1957-65; 68-69
Lowe, Bobby Det. 1904
*Lucchesi, Frank Tex. 1975-77
Lyons, Ted Chi. 1946-48
Macha, Ken Oak. 2003-06
Mack, Connie Phil. 1901-50
Maddon, Joe Ana. 1999
   TB 2006-
Manning, Jimmy Wash. 1901
*Manuel, Charlie Clev. 2000-02
Manuel, Jerry Chi. 1998-2003
*Marion, Marty StL. 1952-53
   Chi. 1954-56
*Marshall Jim Oak. 1979
Martin, Billy Minn. 1969
   Det. 1971-73
   Tex. 1973-75
   NY 1975-78; 79; 83; 85; 88
   Oak. 1980-82
Martinez, Buck Tor. 2001-02
Mattick, Bobby Tor. 1980-81
*Mauch, Gene Minn. 1976-80
   Cal. 1981-82; 85-87
Mazzilli, Lee Balt. 2004-05
McAleer, Jimmy Clev. 1901
   StL. 1902-09
   Wash. 1910-11
McBride, George Wash. 1921
McCallister, Jack Clev. 1927
*McCarthy, Joe NY 1931-46
   Bos. 1948-50
McGaha, Mel Clev. 1962
   KC 1964-65
*McGraw, John Balt. 1901-02
McGuire, Deacon Bos. 1907-08
   Clev. 1909-11
*McKeon, Jack KC 1973-75
   Oak. 1977-78
McManus, Marty Bos. 1932-33

*McNamara, John Oak. 1969-70
  Cal. 1983-84; 96
  Bos. 1985-88
  Clev. 1990-91
McRae, Hal KC 1991-1994
  TB 2001-02
Mele, Sam Minn. 1961-67
*Melvin, Bob Sea. 2003-04
Merrill, Stump NY 1990-91
*Metro, Charlie KC 1970
*Michael, Gene NY 1981; 82
Milan, Clyde Wash. 1922
Miller, Ray Minn. 1985-86
  Balt. 1998-99
Mizerock, John KC 2002
Moore, Jackie, Oak. 1984-86
Morgan, Joe M. Bos. 1988-91
Moriarty, George Det. 1927-28
Moss, Les Det. 1979
Muser, Tony KC 1997-2002
*Narron, Jerry Tex. 2001-02
*Neun, Johnny NY 1946
Norman, Bill Det. 1958-59
Oates, Johnny Balt. 1991-1994
  Tex. 1995-2001
O'Connor, Jack StL. 1910
*O'Neill, Steve Clev. 1935-37
  Det. 1943-48
  Bos. 1950-51
Onslow, Jack Chi. 1949-50
Parrish, Larry Det. 1998-99
Peckinpaugh, Roger NY 1914
  Clev. 1928-33; 41
Pena, Tony KC 2002-05
Perlozzo, Sam Balt. 2005-
Pesky, Johnny Bos. 1963-64
Phillips, Lefty Cal. 1969-71
*Piniella, Lou NY 1986-87; 88
  Sea. 1993-2002
  TB 2003-05
Plummer, Bill Sea. 1992
Pujols, Luis Det. 2002
Queen, Mel Tor. 1997
Quilici, Frank Minn. 1972-75
Rader, Doug Tex. 1983-85
  Cal. 1989-91
Regan, Phil Balt. 1995
Rice, Del Cal. 1972
Richards, Paul Chi. 1951-54; 76
  Balt. 1955-61
*Rickey, Branch, StL. 1913-15
*Rigney, Bill Cal. 1961-69
  Minn. 1970-72
Ripken, Cal, Sr. Balt. 1987-88
*Robinson, Frank Clev. 1975-77
  Balt. 1988-91
*Robinson, Wilbert Balt. 1902
*Rodgers, Buck Mil. 1980-82
  Cal. 1991-1994
*Rojas, Cookie Cal. 1988
Rolfe, Red Det. 1949-52
Rothschild, Larry TB 1998-2001
Rowland, Pants Chi. 1915-18
Ruel, Muddy StL. 1947
Ryan, Connie Tex. 1977
Schaeffer, Bob KC 1991; 2005
Schalk, Ray Chi. 1927-28
*Scheffing, Bob Det. 1961-63
Schultz, Joe Sea. 1969
Scioscia, Mike Ana./LA 2000-
*Sewell, Luke StL. 1941-46
Shawkey, Bob NY 1930
Sherry, Norm Cal. 1976-77
*Showalter, Buck NY 1992-95
  Tex. 2003-06
Sisler, George StL. 1924-26
Skaff, Frank Det. 1966
Skinner, Joel Clev. 2002
*Smith, Mayo Det. 1967-70

Snyder, Jimmy Sea. 1988
Speaker, Tris Clev. 1919-26
Stahl, Jake Wash. 1905-06
  Bos. 1912-13
Stahl, Chick Bos. 1906
*Stallings, George Det. 1901
  NY 1909-10
*Stanky, Eddie Chi. 1966-68
  Tex. 1977
*Stengel, Casey NY 1949-60
Stovall, George Clev. 1911
  StL. 1912-13
*Street, Gabby StL. 1938
Strickland, George Clev. 1966
Stubing, Moose Cal. 1988
Sullivan, Haywood, KC 1965
Sullivan, Billy, Sr. Chi. 1909
Swift, Bob Det. 1965-66
*Tanner, Chuck Chi. 1970-75
  Oak. 1976
Taylor, Zack StL. 1948-51
*Tebbetts, Birdie Clev. 1963-66
Tighe, Jack Det. 1957-58
*Torborg, Jeff Clev. 1977-79
  Chi. 1989-1991
*Torre, Joe NY 1996-
Tosca, Carlos Tor. 2002-04
Trammell, Alan Det. 2003-05
*Trebelhorn, Tom Mil. 1986-91
Unglaub, Bob Bos. 1907
*Valentine, Bobby Tex. 1985-92
Vernon, Mickey Wash. 1961-63
*Virdon, Bill NY 1974-75
Vitt, Ossie Clev. 1938-40
Wagner, Heinie Bos. 1930
*Wallace, Bobby StL. 1911-12
Wathan, John KC 1987-1991
Weaver, Earl Balt. 1968-82; 85-86
Wedge, Eric Clev. 2003-
*Williams, Dick Bos. 1967-69
  Oak. 1971-73
  Cal. 1974-76
  Sea. 1986-88
*Williams, Jimy Tor. 1986-89
  Bos. 1997-2001
Williams, Ted Wash./Tex. 1969-72
Wills, Maury Sea. 1980-81
Winkles, Bobby Cal. 1973-74
  Oak. 1977-78
Wolverton, Harry NY 1912
*Zimmer, Don Bos. 1976-80
  Tex. 1981-82

MANAGERS – NATIONAL LEAGUE

Since 1901 (*also listed in AL)
Alou, Felipe Mtl. 1992-2001
  SF 2003-06
Alston, Walter Brk/LA 1954-76
*Altobelli, Joe SF 1977-79
Amalfitano, Joey Chi. 1980-81
*Anderson, Sparky Cin. 1970-78
Baker, Dusty SF 1993-2002
  Chi. 2003-06
*Bamberger, George NY 1982-83
Bancroft, Dave Bos. 1924-27
Bancroft, Frank Cin. 1902
Baylor, Don Col. 1993-98
  Chi. 2000-02
*Bell, Buddy Col. 2000-02
*Berra, Yogi NY 1972-75
Bezdek, Hugo Pitt. 1917-19
Bissonette, Del Bos. 1945
Blades, Ray StL. 1939-40
Bochy, Bruce SD 1995-06
Boles, John Fla. 1996, 99-2001
*Boone, Bob Cin. 2001-03
*Boros, Steve SD 1986
*Boudreau, Lou Chi. 1960

Bowa, Larry SD, 1987-88
  Phil. 2001-04
Bowerman, Frank Bos. 1909
Boyer, Ken StL. 1978-80
*Bragan, Bobby Pitt. 1956-57
  Mil./Atl. 1963-66
Brenly, Bob Ari. 2001-04
Bresnahan, Roger StL. 1909-12
  Chi. 1915
*Bristol, Dave Cin. 1966-69
  Atl. 1976-77
  SF 1979-80
Buckenberger, Al Bos. 1902-04
*Burke, Jimmy StL. 1905
*Bush, Donie Pitt. 1927-29
  Cin. 1933
*Callahan, Nixey Pitt. 1916-17
Carey, Max Brk. 1932-33
Cavarretta, Phil Chi. 1951-53
*Chance, Frank Chi. 1905-12
Chapman, Ben Phil. 1945-48
Clarke, Fred Pitt. 1900-15
Coleman, Bob Bos. 1944-45
Coleman, Jerry SD 1980
*Collins, Terry Hou. 1994-96
Coombs, Jack Phil. 1919
*Corrales, Pat Phil. 1982-83
*Cox, Bobby Atl. 1978-81; 90-
*Craft, Harry Chi. 1961
  Hou. 1962-64
Craig, Roger SD 1978-79
  SF 1985-92
Cravath, Gavvy Phil. 1919-20
Dahlen, Bill Brk. 1910-13
*Dark, Alvin SF 1961-64
  SD 1977
Davenport, Jim SF 1985
Davis, George NY 1901
Dierker, Larry Hou. 1997-2001
*Donovan, Patsy StL. 1901-03
  Brk. 1906-08
*Donovan, Wild Bill Phil. 1921
Dooin, Red Phil. 1910-14
*Dressen, Chuck Cin. 1934-37
  Brk. 1951-53
  Mil. 1960-61
*Duffy, Hugh Phil. 1904-06
Durocher, Leo Brk. 1939-46; 48
  NY 1948-55
  Chi. 1966-72
  Hou. 1972-73
Dyer, Eddie StL. 1946-50
*Dykes, Jimmy Cin. 1958
Elia, Lee Chi. 1982-83
  Phil. 1987-88
Ens, Jewel Pitt. 1929-31
Essian, Jim Chi. 1991
*Evers, Johnny Chi. 1913; 21
Fanning, Jim Mtl. 1981-82; 84
Felske, John Phil. 1985-87
Fitzsimmons, Freddie Phil. 1943-45
*Fletcher, Art Phil. 1923-26
Fogel, Horace NY 1902
Fox, Charlie SF 1970-74
  Mtl. 1976
  Chi. 1983
*Francona, Terry Phil. 1997-2000
Franks, Herman SF 1965-68
  Chi. 1977-79
Frazier, Joe NY 1976-77
*Fregosi, Jim Phil. 1991-96
*Frey, Jim Chi. 1984-86
Frisch, Frankie StL. 1933-38
  Pitt. 1940-46
  Chi. 1949-51
Fuchs, Judge Bos. 1929
Ganzel, John Cin. 1908
*Garner, Phil Mil. 1998-99
  Hou. 2004-

Gibson, George Pitt. 1920-22; 32-34
  Chi. 1925
Girardi, Joe Fla. 2006
Gomez, Preston SD 1969-72
  Hou. 1974-75
  Chi. 1980
Gonzales, Mike StL. 1938; 40
*Green, Dallas Phil. 1979-81
  NY 1993-96
*Griffith, Clark Cin. 1909-11
Grimes, Burleigh Brk. 1937-38
Grimm, Charlie Chi. 1932-38; 44-49; 60
  Bos./Mil. 1952-56
Haas, Eddie Atl. 1985
Hack, Stan Chi. 1954-56
  StL. 1958
*Haney, Fred Pitt. 1953-55
  Mil. 1956-59
Hanlon, Ned Brk. 1901-05
  Cin. 1906-07
Harrelson, Bud NY 1990-91
*Harris, Lum Hou. 1964-65
  Atl. 1968-72
*Harris, Bucky Phil. 1943
Hartnett, Gabby Chi. 1938-40
Hatton, Grady Hou. 1966-68
Heffner, Don Cin. 1966
Helms, Tommy Cin. 1989
Hemus, Solly StL. 1959-61
Hendricks, Jack StL. 1918
  Cin. 1924-29
*Herman, Billy Pitt. 1947
Herzog, Buck Cin. 1914-16
*Herzog, Whitey StL. 1980-90
Himsl, Vedie Cin. 1961
*Hitchcock, Billy Atl. 1966-67
*Hodges, Gil NY 1968-71
Hoffman, Glenn LA 1998
Holmes, Tommy Bos. 1951-52
*Hornsby, Rogers StL. 1925-26
  Bos. 1928
  Chi. 1930-32
  Cin. 1952-53
Howard, Frank SD 1981
  NY 1983
*Howe, Art Hou. 1989-93
  NY 2003-04
*Howley, Dan Cin. 1930-32
*Huggins, Miller StL. 1913-17
Hurdle, Clint Col. 2002-
*Hutchinson, Fred StL. 1956-58
  Cin. 1959-64
*Johnson, Davey NY 1984-90
  Cin. 1993-95
  LA 1999-2000
Jorgensen, Mike StL. 1995
*Keane, Johnny StL. 1961-64
Kelley, Joe Cin. 1902-05
  Bos. 1908
*Kennedy, Bob Chi. 1963-65
*Killefer, Bill Chi. 1921-25
Kimm, Bruce Chi. 2002
*King, Clyde SF 1969-70
  Atl. 1974-75
Klein, Lou Chi. 1961;62;65
Kling, Johnny Bos. 1912
Knight, Ray Cin. 1996-97
Krol, Jack StL. 1980
Kuehl, Karl Mtl. 1976
*Lachemann, Rene Fla. 1993-96
*Lake, Fred Bos. 1910
*Lamont, Gene Pitt. 1997-2000
Lanier, Hal Hou. 1986-88
*LaRussa, Tony StL. 1996-
Lasorda, Tommy LA 1977-96
*Lefebvre, Jim Chi. 1992-93
  Mil. 1999

*Leyland, Jim Pitt. 1986-96
  Fla. 1997-98
  Col. 1999
Leyva, Nick Phil. 1989-91
Lillis, Bob Hou. 1982-85
*Little, Grady LA 2006-
Lobert, Hans Phil. 1938; 42
Lockman, Whitey Chi. 1972-74
*Loftus, Tom Chi. 1901
Lopes, Davey Mil. 2000-02
*Lucchesi, Frank Phil. 1970-72
  Chi. 1987
Lumley, Harry Brk. 1909
Mackanin, Pete Pitt. 2005
*Manuel, Charlie, Phil. 2005-
Maranville, Rabbit Chi. 1925
*Marion, Marty StL. 1951
*Marshall, Jim Chi. 1974-76
Mathews, Eddie Atl. 1972-74
Mathewson, Christy Cin. 1916-18
*Mauch, Gene Phil. 1960-68
  Mtl. 1969-75
*McCarthy, Joe Chi. 1926-30
McClendon, Lloyd Pitt. 2001-05
McCloskey, John StL. 1906-08
*McGraw, John NY 1902-32
McInnis, Stuffy Phil. 1927
McKechnie, Bill Pitt. 1922-26
  StL. 1928-29
  Bos. 1930-37
  Cin. 1938-46
*McKeon, Jack SD 1988-90
  Cin. 1997-2000
  Fla. 2003-05
McMillan, Roy NY 1975
*McNamara, John SD 1974-77
  Cin. 1979-82
McPhee, Bid Cin. 1901-02
*Melvin, Bob Ari. 2005-
*Metro, Charlie Chi. 1962
Meyer, Billy Pitt. 1948-52
*Michael, Gene Chi. 1986-87
Miley, Dave Cin. 2003-05
Mitchell, Fred Chi. 1917-20
  Bos. 1921-23
Moore, Terry Phil. 1954
Moran, Pat Phil. 1915-18
  Cin. 1919-23
Murray, Billy Phil. 1907-09
Murtaugh, Danny Pitt.1957-64; 67,
  70-71; 73-76
Myatt, George Phil. 1969
*Narron, Jerry Cin. 2005-
*Neun, Johnny Cin. 1947-48
Nichols, Kid StL. 1904-05
Nixon, Russ Cin. 1982-83
  Atl. 1988-90
O'Day, Hank Cin. 1912
  Chi. 1914
O'Farrell, Bob StL. 1927
  Cin. 1934
*O'Neill, Steve Phil. 1952-54
Ott, Mel NY 1942-48
Owens, Paul Phil. 1972; 83-84
Ozark, Danny Phil. 1973-79
  SF 1984
Pedrique, Al Ari. 2004
Perez, Tony Cin. 1993
  Fla. 2001
*Piniella, Lou Cin. 1990-92
Prothro, Doc Phil. 1939-41
Randolph, Willie NY 2005-
Rapp, Vern StL. 1977-78
  Cin. 1984
*Rickey, Branch StL. 1919-25
Riddoch, Greg SD 1990-92
Riggleman, Jim SD 1992-1994
  Chi. 1995-99
*Rigney, Bill NY/SF 1956-60; 76

*Robinson, Frank SF 1981-84
  Mtl./Wash. 2002-06
*Robinson, Wilbert Brk. 1914-31
*Rodgers, Buck Mtl. 1985-91
*Rojas, Cookie Fla. 1996
Rose, Pete Cin. 1984-89
Royster, Jerry Mil. 2002
Runnells, Tom Mtl. 1991-92
Russell, Bill LA 1996-98
Ryan, Connie Atl. 1975
Sawyer, Eddie Phil. 1948-52; 58-60
*Scheffing, Bob Chi. 1957-59
Schoendienst, Red StL. 1965-76; 80; 90
Selee, Frank Bos. 1901
  Chi. 1902-05
*Sewell, Luke Cin. 1950-52
Sheehan, Tom SF 1960
Shepard, Larry Pitt. 1968-69
Shettsline, Bill Pitt. 1901-02
Shotton, Burt Phil. 1928-33
  Brk. 1947-50
*Showalter, Buck Ari. 1998-2000
Sisler, Dick Cin. 1964-65
Skinner, Bob Phil. 1968-69
Slattery, Jack Bos. 1928
Smith, Heinie NY 1902
Smith, Harry Bos. 1909
*Smith, Mayo Phil. 1955-58
  Cin. 1959
Southworth, Billy StL. 1929; 40-45
  Bos. 1946-51
*Stallings, George Bos. 1913-20
*Stanky, Eddie StL. 1952-55
*Stengel, Casey Brk. 1934-36
  Bos. 1938-43
  NY 1962-65
*Street, Gabby StL. 1930-33
*Tanner, Chuck Pitt. 1977-85
  Atl. 1986-88
Tappe, El Chi. 1961; 62
*Tebbetts, Birdie Cin. 1954-58
  Mil. 1961-62
Tenney, Fred Bos. 1905-07; 11
Terry, Bill NY 1932-41
Tinker, Joe Cin. 1913
  Chi. 1916
*Torborg, Jeff NY 1992-93
  Mtl. 2001
  Fla. 2002-03
*Torre, Joe NY 1977-81
  Atl. 1982-84
  StL. 1990-95
Tracy, Jim LA 2001-05
  Pitt. 2006-
Traynor, Pie Pitt. 1934-39
*Trebelhorn, Tom Chi. 1994
*Valentine, Bobby NY 1996-2002
*Virdon, Bill Pitt. 1972-73
  Hou. 1975-82
  Mtl. 1983-84
Wagner, Honus Pitt. 1917
Walker, Harry StL. 1955
  Pitt. 1965-67
  Hou. 1968-72
*Wallace, Bobby Cin. 1937
Walters, Bucky Cin. 1948-49
Westrum, Wes NY 1965-67
  SF 1974-75
Wilhelm, Kaiser Phil. 1921-22
*Williams, Dick Mtl. 1977-81
  SD 1982-85
*Williams, Jimy Hou. 2002-04
Wilson, Jimmie Phil.1934-38
  Chi. 1941-44
Wine, Bobby Atl. 1985
Yost, Ned Mil. 2003-
Zimmer, Chief Phil. 1903
*Zimmer, Don SD 1972-73
  Chi. 1988-91

HOME RUN
FIRST MAJOR LEAGUE AT-BAT

= Pinch-hitter
* = NOT first plate appearance

Alyea, Brant AL:Wash. Sept. 12, 1965#
Anderson, Marlon NL:Phil. Sept. 8, 1998#
Averill, Earl AL:Clev. Apr. 16, 1929
Ayala, Benny NL:NY Aug. 27, 1974
Bankhead, Dan NL:Brk. Aug. 26, 1947
Barragan, Cuno NL:Chi. Sept. 1, 1961
Bates, Johnny NL:Bos. Apr. 12, 1906
Bell, Jay AL:Clev. Sept. 29, 1986
Brown, Gates AL:Det. June 19, 1963#
Bullinger, Jim NL:Chi. June 8, 1992
Cabrera, Alex NL:Ari. June 26, 2000
Campaneris, Bert AL:KC July 23, 1964
Clark, Will NL:SF Apr. 8, 1986
David, Andre AL:Minn. June 29, 1984
Dobbs, Greg AL:Sea. Sept. 8, 2004#
Dudley, Clise NL:Brk. Apr. 27, 1929
Duggleby, Bill NL:Phil. Apr. 21, 1898
Dye, Jermaine NL:Atl. May 17, 1996
Eiland, Dave NL:SD Apr. 10, 1992
Ernaga, Frank NL:Chi. May 24, 1957
Felix, Junior AL:Tor. May 4, 1989
Fields, Josh AL:Chi. Sept. 18, 2006
Fitzgerald, Mike NL:NY Sept. 13, 1983
Fullmer, Brad NL:Mtl. Sept. 2, 1997#
Gaetti, Gary AL:Minn. Sept. 20, 1981
Gainer, Jay NL:Col. May 14, 1993
Gillespie, Paul NL:Chi. Sept. 11, 1942
Harrington, Joe NL:Bos. Sept. 10, 1895
Hasson, Gene AL:Phil. Sept. 9, 1937
Hermanson, Dustin NL:Mtl. Apr. 16, 1997
Hermida, Jeremy, NL:Fla. Aug. 31, 2005#
Ingram, Garey NL:LA May 19, 1994#
Jacobs, Mike NL:NY Aug. 21, 2005#
Jimerson, Charlton NL:Hou. Sept. 4, 2006
Jordan, Ricky NL:Phil. July 17, 1988*
Kennedy, John AL:Wash. Sept. 5, 1962#
Keough, Joe AL:Oak. Aug. 7 1968#
Kerr, Buddy NL:NY Sept. 8, 1943
Kouzmanoff, Kevin, AL:Clev. Sept. 2, 2006
Koy, Ernie NL:Brk. Apr. 19, 1938
Lamont, Gene AL:Det. Sept. 2, 1970
Layton, Les NL:NY May 21, 1948#
Lee, Carlos AL:Chi. May 7, 1999
LeFebvre, Bill AL:Bos. June 10, 1938
LeMaster, Johnnie NL:SF Sept. 2, 1975#
Leppert, Don NL:Pitt. June 18, 1961
Lockman, Whitey NL:NY July 5, 1945
Luna, Hector NL:StL. Apr. 8, 2004
Lyden, Mitch NL:Fla. June 16, 1993
Machemer, Dave AL:Cal. June 21, 1978
Martinez, Carmelo NL:Chi. Aug. 22, 1983*
Matranga, David NL:Hou. June 27, 2003*
Matsui, Kaz NL:NY Apr. 6, 2004
McDonald, Keith NL:StL. July 4, 2000#
McKay, Dave AL:Minn. July 22 1975#
Miller, John AL:NY Sept. 11, 1966
Miller, Hack AL:Det. Apr. 23, 1944
Montefusco, John NL:SF Sept. 3, 1974*
Moon, Wally NL:StL. Apr. 13, 1954
Morgan, Eddie NL:StL. Apr. 14, 1936#
Mota, Guillermo NL:Mtl. June 9, 1999

Mueller, Walter NL:Pitt. May 7, 1922
Mueller, Emmett NL:Phil. Apr. 19, 1938
Napoli, Mike AL:LA May 4, 2006
Narum, Buster AL:Balt. May 3, 1963
Nieman, Bob AL:StL. Sept. 14, 1951
Nunnally, Jon AL:KC Apr. 29, 1995
Offerman, Jose NL:LA Aug. 19, 1990
Olivo, Miguel AL:Chi. Sept. 15, 2002
Parker, Ace AL:Phil. Apr. 30, 1937#
Pellagrini, Eddie AL:Bos. Apr. 22, 1946
Phillips, Andy, AL:NY Sept. 26, 2004#
Renick, Rick AL:Minn. July 11, 1968
Richard, Chris NL:StL. July 17, 2000
Roman, Bill AL:Det. Sept. 30, 1964#
Rose, Don AL:Cal. May 24, 1972
Sanders, Reggie AL:Det. Sept. 1, 1974
Sanicki, Ed NL:Phil. Sept. 14, 1949
Slade, Gordon NL:Brk. May 24, 1930
Sosa, Jose NL:Hou. July 30, 1975#
Steinbach, Terry AL:Oak. Sept. 12, 1986
Stechschulte, Gene NL:StL. Apr. 17, 2001#
Stuart, Luke AL:StL. Aug. 8, 1921
Tanner, Chuck NL:Mil. Apr. 12, 1955#
Tappe, Ted NL:Cin. Sept 14, 1950#
Thames, Marcus AL:NY June 10, 2002
Tillman, Bob AL:Bos. May 19, 1962*
Vico, George AL:Det. Apr. 20, 1948
Vollmer, Clyde NL:Cin. May 31, 1942
Wainwright, Adam NL:StL. May 24, 2006
Wallach, Tim NL:Mtl. Sept. 6, 1980*
White, Bill NL:NY May 7, 1956
Wilhelm, Hoyt NL:NY Apr. 23, 1952
Woods, Al NL:Tor. Apr. 7, 1977#
Yan, Esteban, AL:TB June 4, 2000

TRIPLE CROWN WINNERS
(Led league in Batting Average, Home Runs & Runs Batted In)

Rogers Hornsby NL:StL. 1922
Rogers Hornsby NL:StL. 1925
Jimmie Foxx AL:Phil. 1933
Chuck Klein NL:Phil. 1933
Lou Gehrig AL:NY 1934
Joe Medwick NL:StL. 1937
Ted Williams AL:Bos. 1942
Ted Williams AL:Bos. 1947
Mickey Mantle AL:NY 1956
Frank Robinson AL:Balt. 1966
Carl Yastrzemski AL:Bos. 1967

50 OR MORE HOME RUNS, SEASON

73	Barry Bonds NL:SF 2001
70	Mark McGwire NL:StL. 1998
66	Sammy Sosa NL:Chi. 1998
65	Mark McGwire NL:StL. 1999
64	Sammy Sosa NL:Chi. 2001
63	Sammy Sosa NL:Chi. 1999
61	Roger Maris AL:NY 1961
60	Babe Ruth AL:NY 1927
59	Babe Ruth AL:NY 1921
58	Jimmie Foxx AL:Phil. 1932
	Hank Greenberg AL:Det. 1938
	Mark McGwire AL:Oak.-NL:StL. 1997
	Ryan Howard, NL:Phil. 2006
57	Luis Gonzalez NL:Ari. 2001
	Alex Rodriguez AL:Tex. 2002
56	Hack Wilson NL:Chi. 1930
	Ken Griffey, Jr. AL:Sea. 1997
	Ken Griffey, Jr. AL:Sea. 1998
54	Babe Ruth AL:NY 1920
	Babe Ruth AL:NY 1928
	Ralph Kiner NL:Pitt. 1949
	Mickey Mantle AL:NY 1961
	David Ortiz, AL:Bos. 2006
52	Mickey Mantle AL:NY 1956
	Willie Mays NL:SF 1965
	Mark McGwire AL:Oak. 1996
	George Foster NL:Cin. 1977
	Alex Rodriguez AL:Tex. 2001
	Jim Thome AL:Clev. 2002
51	Ralph Kiner NL:Pitt. 1947
	Johnny Mize NL:NY 1947
	Willie Mays NL:NY 1955
	Cecil Fielder AL:Det. 1990
	Andruw Jones, NL:Atl. 2005
50	Jimmie Foxx AL:Bos. 1938
	Albert Belle AL:Clev. 1995
	Brady Anderson AL:Balt. 1996
	Greg Vaughn NL:SD 1998
	Sosa, Sammy NL:Chi. 2000

MOST HRs, LIFETIME, BY POSITION

First Base
- 566 Mark McGwire, AL:Oak.(349); NL:StL.(217)
- 493 Lou Gehrig, AL:NY
- 446 Jeff Bagwell, NL:Hou.

Second Base
- 319 Jeff Kent, AL:Tor.-Clev.(2); NL:NY-SF-Hou.-LA(317)
- 317 Jeff Kent, NL:NY-SF-Hou.-LA
- 246 Joe Gordon, AL:NY-Clev.

Third Base
- 509 Mike Schmidt, NL:Phil.
- 319 Graig Nettles, AL:Clev.-NY

Shortstop
- 345 Cal Ripken, AL:Balt.
- 277 Ernie Banks, NL:Chi.

Outfield
- 721 Barry Bonds, NL:Pitt.-SF
- 686 Babe Ruth, AL:Bos.-NY

Catcher
- 396 Mike Piazza, NL:LA-NY-SD
- 351 Carlton Fisk, AL:Bos.-Chi.

Pitcher
- 37 Wes Ferrell, AL:Clev.-Bos.-Wash.(36); NL:Bos.(1)
- 36 Wes Ferrell, AL:Clev.-Bos.-Wash.
- 35 Warren Spahn, NL:Bos./Mil.

Designated Hitter
- 243 Edgar Martinez, AL:Sea.
- 10 Mike Piazza, NL:NY-SD

MOST HRs, SEASON, BY POSITION

National League

1B:	69	Mark McGwire, StL. 1998
2B:	42	Rogers Hornsby, StL. 1922
		Davey Johnson, Atl. 1973
3B:	48	Mike Schmidt, Phil. 1980
		Adrian Beltre, LA 2004
SS:	47	Ernie Banks, Chi. 1958
OF:	71	Barry Bonds, SF 2001
C:	42	Javy Lopez, Atl. 2003
P:	7	Don Newcombe, Brk. 1955
		Don Drysdale, LA 1958
		Don Drysdale, LA 1965
		Mike Hampton, Col. 2001
DH:	4	Jim Thome, Phil. 2004

American League

1B:	58	Hank Greenberg, Det. 1938
2B:	39	Alfonso Soriano, NY 2002
3B:	47	Alex Rodriguez, NY 2005
SS:	57	Alex Rodriguez, Tex. 2002
OF:	61	Roger Maris, NY 1961
C:	35	Ivan Rodriguez, Tex. 1999
P:	9	Wes Ferrell, Clev. 1931
DH:	47	David Ortiz, Bos. 2006

CLUB HOME RUN LEADERS, SEASON

National League

ARIZONA	57	Luis Gonzalez 2001
ATLANTA	51	Andruw Jones 2005
CHICAGO	66	Sammy Sosa 1998
CINCINNATI	52	George Foster 1977
COLORADO	49	Larry Walker 1997
		Todd Helton 2001
FLORIDA	42	Gary Sheffield 1996
HOUSTON	47	Jeff Bagwell 2000
LOS ANGELES	49	Shawn Green 2001
MILWAUKEE	45	Gorman Thomas (AL) 1979
		Richie Sexson 2001, 03
NEW YORK	41	Todd Hundley 1996
		Carlos Beltran 2006
PHILADELPHIA	58	Ryan Howard 2006
PITTSBURGH	54	Ralph Kiner 1949
ST. LOUIS	70	Mark McGwire 1998
SAN DIEGO	50	Greg Vaughn 1998
SAN FRANCISCO	73	Barry Bonds 2001
WASHINGTON	46	Alfonso Soriano 2006

American League

ANAHEIM	47	Troy Glaus 2000
BALTIMORE	50	Brady Anderson 1996
BOSTON	54	David Ortiz 2006
CHICAGO	49	Albert Belle 1998
CLEVELAND	52	Jim Thome 2002
DETROIT	58	Hank Greenberg 1938
KANSAS CITY	36	Steve Balboni 1985
MINNESOTA	49	Harmon Killebrew 1964
		Harmon Killebrew 1969
NEW YORK	61	Roger Maris 1961
OAKLAND	58	Jimmie Foxx (Phil.) 1932
SEATTLE	56	Ken Griffey, Jr. 1997-98
TAMPA BAY	34	Jose Canseco 1999
		Aubrey Huff 2003
TEXAS	57	Alex Rodriguez 2002
TORONTO	47	George Bell 1987

250 OR MORE HOMERS

(At-Bats per Home Run in parentheses; players active in 2006 in boldface)

755	Hank Aaron (16.38)	351	Dick Allen (18.04)	271	Tom Brunansky (23.21)
734	**Barry Bonds (12.95)**	350	Chili Davis (24.78)	271	Raul Mondesi (21.45)
714	Babe Ruth (11.76)	**350**	**Jim Edmonds (16.88)**	271	George Scott (27.43)
660	Willie Mays (16.49)	**350**	**Jason Giambi (16.06**)	268	Joe Morgan (34.62)
588	Sammy Sosa (14.29)	348	George Foster (20.18)	268	Brooks Robinson (39.75)
586	Frank Robinson (17.08)	**345**	**Jeff Kent (21.92)**	268	Gorman Thomas (17.45)
583	Mark McGwire (10.61)	**342**	**Andruw Jones (17.06)**	267	George Hendrick (26.70)
573	Harmon Killebrew (14.22)	342	Ron Santo (23.81)	266	Vic Wertz (22.93)
569	Rafael Palmeiro (18.40)	340	Jack Clark (20.14)	265	George Bell (23.11)
563	**Ken Griffey Jr. (14.74)**	339	Tino Martinez (20.98)	264	Bobby Thomson (23.88)
563	Reggie Jackson (17.52)	339	Dave Parker (27.60)	262	Danny Tartabull (19.13)
548	Mike Schmidt (15.24)	339	Boog Powell (19.71)	**260**	**Brian Giles (20.23)**
536	Mickey Mantle (15.12)	338	Don Baylor (24.25)	**260**	**Javy Lopez (20.46)**
534	Jimmie Foxx (15.23)	**338**	**Vladimir Guerrero (16.28)**	260	Tim Wallach (31.15)
521	Willie McCovey (15.73)	336	Joe Adcock (19.66)	**257**	**Troy Glaus (15.72)**
521	Ted Williams (14.79)	335	Darryl Strawberry (16.17)	256	Bob Allison (19.66)
512	Ernie Banks (18.40)	332	Bobby Bonds (21.21)	256	Larry Parrish (26.53)
512	Eddie Mathews (16.67)	**331**	**Luis Gonzalez (25.23)**	256	Vada Pinson (37.67)
511	Mel Ott (18.50)	331	Hank Greenberg (15.69)	255	Kirk Gibson (22.74)
504	Eddie Murray (22.49)	328	Mo Vaughn (16.87)	255	John Mayberry (21.36)
493	Lou Gehrig (16.23)	325	Willie Horton (22.46)	255	John Olerud (29.77)
493	Fred McGriff (17.76)	324	Gary Carter (24.60)	253	Larry Doby (21.14)
487	**Frank Thomas (15.24)**	324	Lance Parrish (21.81)	253	Joe Gordon (22.56)
475	Stan Musial (23.10)	321	Ron Gant (20.09)	**253**	**Scott Rolen (20.18)**
475	Willie Stargell (16.69)	**320**	**Vinny Castilla (21.32)**	253	Andre Thornton (20.91)
472	**Jim Thome (13.58)**	**319**	**Moises Alou (20.88)**	253	Todd Zeile (29.93)
470	**Manny Ramirez (13.99)**	319	Cecil Fielder (16.17)	252	Bret Boone (26.52)
465	Dave Winfield (23.66)	**318**	**Shawn Green (20.87)**	252	Bobby Murcer (26.71)
464	**Alex Rodriguez (14.58)**	318	Roy Sievers (20.08)	252	Joe Torre (31.25)
462	Jose Canseco (15.27)	317	George Brett (32.65)	251	Tony Armas (20.57)
455	**Gary Sheffield (17.66)**	316	Ron Cey (22.66)	251	Cy Williams (27.01)
452	Carl Yastrzemski (26.52)	**315**	**Jeromy Burnitz (18.13)**	251	Robin Yount (43.86)
449	Jeff Bagwell (17.37)	314	Reggie Smith (22.40)	**250**	**Albert Pujols (13.96)**
442	Dave Kingman (15.11)	310	Jay Buhner (16.17)		
438	Andre Dawson (22.66)	309	Edgar Martinez (23.34)		
434	Juan Gonzalez (15.11)	307	Greg Luzinski (21.19)		
431	Cal Ripken (26.80)	307	Al Simmons (28.53)		
426	Billy Williams (21.95)	306	Fred Lynn (22.63)		
419	**Mike Piazza (15.76)**	**306**	**Ruben Sierra (26.29)**		
414	Darrell Evans (21.67)	305	David Justice (18.44)		
407	**Carlos Delgado (14.87)**	**303**	**Steve Finley (30.70)**		
407	Duke Snider (17.59)	**303**	**Reggie Sanders (20.36)**		
399	Andres Galarraga (20.29)	301	Rogers Hornsby (27.15)		
399	Al Kaline (25.35)	300	Chuck Klein (21.62)		
398	Dale Murphy (20.00)	**299**	**Tim Salmon (19.85)**		
396	Joe Carter (21.27)	297	Rickey Henderson (36.91)		
390	Graig Nettles (23.04)	294	Robin Ventura (24.03)		
389	Johnny Bench (19.69)	293	Kent Hrbek (21.13)		
385	Dwight Evans (23.37)	292	Rusty Staub (33.29)		
384	Harold Baines (25.80)	291	Jimmy Wynn (22.86)		
383	Larry Walker (18.03)	288	Del Ennis (25.19)		
382	Frank Howard (16.98)	288	Bob Johnson (24.03)		
382	Jim Rice (21.53)	288	Hank Sauer (16.65)		
381	Albert Belle (15.36)	287	Bobby Bonilla (25.13)		
379	Orlando Cepeda (20.92)	**287**	**Bernie Williams (27.42)**		
379	Tony Perez (25.80)	**286**	**Todd Helton (17.85)**		
378	Matt Williams (18.52)	286	Frank J. Thomas (21.98)		
377	Norm Cash (17.79)	284	Will Clark (25.26)		
376	Carlton Fisk (23.29)	284	Eric Karros (22.68)		
374	Rocky Colavito (17.39)	282	Ken Boyer (26.44)		
370	Gil Hodges (19.00)	282	Eric Davis (18.87)		
369	Ralph Kiner (14.11)	282	Ryne Sandberg (29.73)		
361	Joe DiMaggio (18.89)	**281**	**Craig Biggio (36.86)**		
360	Gary Gaetti (24.86)	281	Paul O'Neill (26.04)		
359	Johnny Mize (17.95)	279	Ted Kluszewski (21.25)		
358	Yogi Berra (21.10)	**277**	**Ivan Rodriguez (27.96)**		
357	**Chipper Jones (17.89)**	277	Rudy York (21.27)		
355	Greg Vaughn (17.19)	275	Brian Downing (28.56)		
354	Lee May (21.49)	275	Roger Maris (18.55)		
352	Ellis Burks (20.55)	275	Dean Palmer (17.83)		
		274	Dante Bichette (23.29)		
		273	**Richie Sexson (15.44)**		
		272	Steve Garvey (32.48)		
		272	**Ryan Klesko (19.30)**		

3 OR MORE HOME RUNS, GAME
(4-HR Games in Boldface)

AMERICAN ASSOCIATION
Guy Hecker, Lou., Aug. 15(2g), 1886

AMERICAN LEAGUE
Bob Allison, Minn., May 17, 1963
Roberto Alomar, Balt., Apr. 26, 1997
Garret Anderson, Ana., June 4, 2003
Earl Averill, Clev., Sept. 17(1g), 1930
Bobby Avila, Clev., June 20, 1951
Carlos Baerga, Clev., June 17, 1993
Harold Baines, Chi., July 7, 1982
Harold Baines, Chi., Sept. 17, 1984 #2
Harold Baines, Oak., May 7, 1991 #3
Don Baylor, Balt., July 2, 1975
George Bell, Tor., Apr. 4, 1988
Albert Belle, Clev., Sept. 6, 1992 (12 inn)
Albert Belle, Clev., Sept. 19, 1995 #2
Albert Belle, Balt., July 25, 1999 (11 inn) #3
Juan Beniquez, Balt., June 12, 1986
Geronimo Berroa, Oak., May 22, 1996
Geronimo Berroa, Oak., Aug. 12, 1996 #2
Paul Blair, Balt., Apr. 29, 1970
Curt Blefary, Balt., June 6(1g), 1967
Steve Boros, Det., Aug. 6, 1962
Mickey Brantley, Sea., Sept. 14, 1987
George Brett, KC, July 22, 1979
George Brett, KC, Apr. 20, 1983 #2
Tom Brunansky, Bos., Sept. 29, 1990
Ellis Burks, Clev., June 19, 2001 (12 inn)
Jeff Burroughs, Sea., Aug. 14(2g), 1981
Mike Cameron, Sea., May 2, 2002
Jose Canseco, Oak., July 3, 1988 (16 inn)
Jose Canseco, Tex., June 13, 1994 #2
Joe Carter, Clev., Aug. 29, 1986
Joe Carter, Clev., May 28, 1987 #2
Joe Carter, Clev., June 24, 1989 #3
Joe Carter, Clev., July 19, 1989 #4
Joe Carter, Tor., Aug. 23, 1993 #5
Bob Cerv, KC, Aug. 20, 1959
Sam Chapman, Phil., Aug. 15, 1946
Ben Chapman, NY, July 9(2g), 1932
Tony Clark, NY, Aug. 28, 2004
Jack Clark, Bos., July 31, 1991 (14 inn)
Ty Cobb, Det., May 5, 1925
Mickey Cochrane, Phil., May 21, 1925
Rocky Colavito, Clev., June 10, 1959
Rocky Colavito, Det., Aug. 27(2g), 1961 #2
Rocky Colavito, Det., July 5, 1962 #3
Ed Coleman, Phil., Aug. 17(1g), 1934 (10 inn)
Darnell Coles, Tor., July 5, 1994 NL:1
Merv Connors, Chi., Sept. 17(2g), 1938
Cecil Cooper, Mil., July 27, 1979
Doug DeCinces, Cal., Aug. 3, 1982
Doug DeCinces, Cal., Aug. 8, 1982 #2
Carlos Delgado, Tor., Aug. 4, 1998
Carlos Delgado, Tor., Aug. 6, 1999 #2
Carlos Delgado, Tor., Apr. 4, 2001 #3
Carlos Delgado, Tor., Apr. 20, 2001 #4
Carlos Delgado, Tor., Sept. 25, 2003 #5
Bill Dickey, NY, July 26, 1939
Joe DiMaggio, NY, June 13(2g), 1937 (11 inn)
Joe DiMaggio, NY, May 23(1g), 1948 #2
Joe DiMaggio, NY, Sept. 10, 1950 #3
Larry Doby, Clev., Aug. 2, 1950
Bobby Doerr, Bos., June 8, 1950
Erubiel Durazo, Oak., Aug. 18, 2004 NL:1
Mike Epstein, Wash., May 16, 1969

Cecil Fielder, Det., May 6, 1990
Cecil Fielder, Det., June 6, 1990 #2
Cecil Fielder, Det., Apr. 16, 1996 #3
Darrin Fletcher, Tor., Aug. 27, 2000
Dan Ford, Balt., July 20, 1983
Jimmie Foxx, Phil., July 10, 1932 (18 inn)
Jimmie Foxx, Phil., June 8, 1933 #2
Bill Freehan, Det., Aug. 9, 1971
Nomar Garciaparra, Bos., May 10, 1999
Nomar Garciaparra, Bos., July 23(1g), 2002 #2
Lou Gehrig, NY, June 23, 1927
Lou Gehrig, NY, May 4, 1929 #2
Lou Gehrig, NY, May 22(2g), 1930 #3
Lou Gehrig, NY, June 3, 1932 #4
Troy Glaus, Ana., Sept. 15, 2002
Bill Glynn, Clev., July 5(1g), 1954
Jonny Gomes, TB, July 30, 2005
Juan Gonzalez, Tex., June 7, 1992
Juan Gonzalez, Tex., Aug. 28, 1993 #2
Juan Gonzalez, Tex., Sept. 24, 1999 #3
Goose Goslin, Wash., June 19, 1925 (12 inn)
Goose Goslin, StL., Aug. 19, 1930 #2
Goose Goslin, StL., June 23, 1932 #3
Bobby Grich, Balt., June 18, 1974
Ken Griffey Jr., Sea., May 24, 1996
Ken Griffey Jr., Sea., Apr. 25, 1997 #2
Travis Hafner, Clev., July 20, 2004
Ken Harrelson, Bos., June 14, 1968
Joe Hauser, Phil., Aug. 2, 1924
Dave Henderson, Oak., Aug. 3, 1991
George Hendrick, Clev., June 19, 1973
Larry Herndon, Det., May 18, 1982
Pinky Higgins, Phil., June 27, 1935
Pinky Higgins, Det., May 20, 1940 #2
Bobby Higginson, Det., June 30, 1997
Bobby Higginson, Det., June 24(2g), 2000 #2
Tony Horton, Clev., May 24(2g), 1970 (11 inn)
Willie Horton, Det., June 9, 1970
Willie Horton, Tex., May 15, 1977 #2
Reggie Jackson, Oak., July 2, 1969
Reggie Jackson, Cal., Sept. 18, 1986 #2
Bo Jackson, KC, July 17, 1990
Brook Jacoby, Clev., July 3, 1987
Manny Jimenez, KC, July 4, 1964
Cliff Johnson, NY, June 30, 1977
Wally Joyner, Cal., Oct. 3, 1987
Al Kaline, Det., Apr. 17, 1955
Charlie Keller, NY, July 28(1g), 1940
Ken Keltner, Clev., May 25, 1939
Harmon Killebrew, Minn., Sept. 21(1g), 1963
Jim King, Wash., June 8, 1964
Dave Kingman, Oak., Apr. 16, 1984 NL:4
Willie Kirkland, Clev., July 9(2g), 1961
Lee Lacy, Balt., June 8, 1986
Joe Lahoud, Bos., June 11, 1969
Carney Lansford, Cal., Sept. 1, 1979
Tony Lazzeri, NY, June 8, 1927 (11 inn)
Tony Lazzeri, NY, May 24, 1936 #2
Jim Lemon, Wash., Aug. 31, 1956
Don G. Leppert, Wash., Apr. 11, 1963
Hector Lopez, KC, June 26, 1958 (12 inn)
Fred Lynn, Bos., June 18, 1975
Bill Madlock, Det., June 28, 1987 (11 inn)
Mickey Mantle, NY, May 13, 1955
Nick Markakis, Balt., Aug. 22, 2006
Tino Martinez, NY, Apr. 2, 1997
Edgar Martinez, Sea., July 6, 1996
Edgar Martinez, Sea., May 18, 1999 #2
Victor Martinez, Clev., July 16, 2004
Charlie Maxwell, Det., May 3(2g), 1959

3 OR MORE HOME RUNS, GAME, A.L. (continued)
(4-HR Games in Boldface)
John Mayberry, KC, July 1, 1975
John Mayberry, KC, June 1, 1977 #2
Tom McCraw, Chi., May 24, 1967
Mark McGwire, Oak., June 27, 1987
Mark McGwire, Oak., June 11, 1995 #2 NL:3
Bill Melton, Chi., June 24(2g), 1969
Kevin Mench, Tex., June 30, 2005
Kevin Millar, Bos., July 23, 2004
Randy Milligan, Balt., June 9, 1990
Johnny Mize, NY, Sept. 15, 1950 NL:5
Paul Molitor, Mil., May 12, 1982
Bill Mueller, Bos., July 29, 2003
Pat Mullin, Det., June 26(2g), 1949
Bobby Murcer, NY, June 24(2g), 1970
Bobby Murcer, NY, July 13, 1973 #2
Eddie Murray, Balt., Aug. 29(2g), 1979
Eddie Murray, Balt., Sept. 14, 1980 (13 inn) #2
Eddie Murray, Balt., Aug. 26, 1985 #3
Trot Nixon, Bos., July 24, 1999
Ben Oglivie, Mil., July 8(1g), 1979
Ben Oglivie, Mil., June 20, 1982 #2
Ben Oglivie, Mil., May 14, 1983 (10 inn) #3
Tony Oliva, Minn., July 3, 1973
Al Oliver, Tex., May 23, 1979
Al Oliver, Tex., Aug. 17(2g), 1980 #2
Paul O'Neill, NY, Aug. 31, 1995
Larry Parrish, Tex., Apr. 29, 1985 NL:3
Freddie Patek, Cal., June 20, 1980
Carlos Pena, Det., May 19, 2003
Boog Powell, Balt., Aug. 10, 1963
Boog Powell, Balt., June 27, 1964 #2
Boog Powell, Balt., Aug. 15, 1966 (11 inn) #3
Jim Presley, Sea., Sept. 1, 1986
Tim Raines, Chi., Apr. 18, 1994
Manny Ramirez, Clev., Sept. 15, 1998
Manny Ramirez, Clev., Aug. 25, 1999 #2
Carl Reynolds, Chi., July 2(2g), 1930
Jim Rice, Bos., Aug. 29, 1977
Jim Rice, Bos., Aug. 29(2g), 1983 #2
Cal Ripken, Balt., May 28, 1996
Alex Rodriguez, Sea., Apr. 16, 2000
Alex Rodriguez, Tex., Aug. 17, 2002 #2
Alex Rodriguez, NY, Apr. 26, 2005 #3
Ivan Rodriguez, Tex., Sept. 11, 1997
Al Rosen, Clev., Apr. 29, 1952
Babe Ruth, NY, May 21(1g), 1930 NL:1
Pat Seerey, Clev., July 13, 1945
Pat Seerey, Chi., July 18(1g), 1948 (11 inn) #2
Al Simmons, Phil., July 15, 1932 (11 inn)
Cory Snyder, Clev., May 21, 1987 NL:1
Tony Solaita, KC, Sept. 7, 1975 (11 inn)
Moose Solters, StL., July 7, 1935
Mike Stanley, NY, Aug. 10(1g), 1995
Leroy Stanton, Cal., July 10, 1973 (10 inn)
Lee Stevens, Tex., Apr. 13, 1998
Darryl Strawberry, NY, Aug. 6, 1996 NL:1
Dale Sveum, Mil., July 17, 1987
Jim Tabor, Bos., July 4(2g), 1939
Danny Tartabull, KC, July 6, 1991
Mark Teixeira, Tex., July 13, 2006
Miguel Tejada, Oak., June 11, 1999
Miguel Tejada, Oak., June 30, 2001 #2
Frank Thomas, Chi., Sept. 15, 1996
Gorman Thomas, Sea., Apr. 11, 1985
Lee Thomas, LA, Sept. 5(2g), 1961
Jim Thome, Clev., July 22, 1994
Jim Thome, Clev., July 6, 2001 #2
Tom Tresh, NY, June 6(2g), 1965

Hal Trosky, Clev., May 30(2g), 1934
Hal Trosky, Clev., July 5(1g), 1937 #2
John Valentin, Bos., June 2, 1995 (10 inn)
Jose Valentin, Chi., July 30, 2003 NL:1
Jason Varitek, Bos., May 20, 2001
Mo Vaughn, Bos., Sept. 24, 1996
Mo Vaughn, Bos., May 30, 1997 #2
Otto Velez, Tor., May 4(1g), 1980 (10 inn)
Clyde Vollmer, Bos., July 26, 1951
Preston Ward, KC, Sept. 9, 1958
Claudell Washington, Chi., July 14, 1979 NL:1
Vernon Wells, Tor., May 30, 2006
Ernie Whitt, Tor., Sept. 14, 1987
Ken Williams, StL., Apr. 22, 1922
Matt Williams, Clev., Apr. 25, 1997
Ted Williams, Bos., July 14(1g), 1946
Ted Williams, Bos., May 8, 1957 #2
Ted Williams, Bos., June 13, 1957 #3
Dan Wilson, Sea., Apr. 11, 1996
Dave Winfield, Cal., Apr. 13, 1991
Chris Woodward, Tor., Aug. 7, 2002 (10 inn)
Carl Yastrzemski, Bos., May 19, 1976
Rudy York, Det., Sept. 1(1g), 1941
Dmitri Young, Det., Apr. 4, 2005
Ernie Young, Oak., May 10, 1996
Norm Zauchin, Bos., May 27, 1955
Gus Zernial, Chi., Oct. 1(2g), 1950

3 OR MORE HOME RUNS, GAME
(4-HR Games in Boldface)

NATIONAL LEAGUE
Hank Aaron, Mil., June 21, 1959
Joe Adcock, Mil., July 31, 1954
Edgardo Alfonzo, NY, Aug. 30, 1999
Dick Allen, Phil., Sept. 29, 1968
Moises Alou, Chi., July 4, 2003
Cap Anson, Chi., Aug. 6, 1884
Jeff Bagwell, Hou., June 24, 1994
Jeff Bagwell, Hou., Apr. 21, 1999 #2
Jeff Bagwell, Hou., June 9, 1999 #3
Ed Bailey, Cin., June 24(1g), 1956
Ernie Banks, Chi., Aug. 4, 1955
Ernie Banks, Chi., Sept. 14(2g), 1957 #2
Ernie Banks, Chi., May 29, 1962 #3
Ernie Banks, Chi., June 9, 1963 #4
Jake Beckley, Cin., Sept. 26(1g), 1897
Gus Bell, Cin., July 21, 1955
Gus Bell, Cin., May 29, 1956 #2
Les Bell, Bos., June 2, 1928
Johnny Bench, Cin., July 26, 1970
Johnny Bench, Cin., May 9, 1973 #2
Johnny Bench, Cin., May 29, 1980 #3
Lance Berkman, Hou., Apr. 16, 2002
Jeff Blauser, Atl., July 12, 1992 (10 inn)
Barry Bonds, SF, Aug. 2, 1994
Barry Bonds, SF, May 19, 2001 #2
Barry Bonds, SF, Sept. 9, 2001 (11 inn) #3
Barry Bonds, SF, Aug. 27, 2002 #4
Aaron Boone, Cin., Aug. 9, 2002
Aaron Boone, Cin., May 8, 2003 #2
Bret Boone, Cin., Sept. 20, 1998
Bret Boone, SD, June 23, 2000 (10 inn) #2
Russell Branyan, Cin., Aug. 4, 2002
Dan Brouthers, Det., Sept. 10, 1886
Brant Brown, Chi., June 18, 1998
Tommy Brown, Brk., Sept. 18, 1950
Smoky Burgess, Cin., July 29, 1955
Jeromy Burnitz, Mil., May 10, 2001
Jeromy Burnitz, Mil., Sept. 25, 2001 #2
Johnny Callison, Phil., Sept. 27, 1964
Johnny Callison, Phil., June 6(2g), 1965 #2
Ken Caminiti, SD, July 12, 1998
Roy Campanella, Brk., Aug. 26, 1950
Gary Carter, Mtl., Apr. 20, 1977
Gary Carter, NY, Sept. 3, 1985 #2
Rico Carty, Atl., May 31, 1970
Vinny Castilla, Col., June 5, 1999
Vinny Castilla, Hou., July 28(1g), 2001 #2
Orlando Cepeda, Atl., July 26(1g), 1970
Hee Seop Choi, LA, June 12, 2005
Jeff Cirillo, Col., June 28, 2000
Roberto Clemente, Pitt., May 15, 1967 (10 inn)
Roberto Clemente, Pitt., Aug. 13, 1969 #2
Nate Colbert, SD, Aug. 1(2g), 1972
Darnell Coles, Pitt., Sept. 30(2g), 1987 AL:1
Roger Connor, NY, May 9, 1888
Walker Cooper, Cin., July 6, 1949
Eric Davis, Cin., Sept. 10, 1986
Eric Davis, Cin., May 3, 1987 #2
Glenn Davis, Hou., Sept. 10, 1987
Glenn Davis, Hou., June 1, 1990 (11 inn) #2
Andre Dawson, Mtl., Sept. 24, 1985
Andre Dawson, Chi., Aug. 1, 1987 #2
Ed Delahanty, Phil., July 13, 1896
Don Demeter, LA, Apr. 21, 1959 (11 inn)
Don Demeter, Phil., Sept. 12, 1961 #2
Erubiel Durazo, Ari., May 17, 2002 AL:1
Damion Easley, Ari., June 3(2g), 2006

Bob Elliott, Bos., Sept. 24, 1949
Kevin Elster, LA, Apr. 11, 2000
Del Ennis, Phil., July 23, 1955
Morgan Ensberg, Hou., May 15, 2005
Bobby Estalella, Phil., Sept. 4, 1997
Darrell Evans, SF, June 15, 1983
Steve Finley, SD, May 19, 1997
Steve Finley, SD, June 23, 1997 #2
Steve Finley, Ari., Sept. 8, 1999 #3
Steve Finley, Ari., Apr. 28, 2004 #4
George Foster, Cin., July 14, 1977
Jack Fournier, Brk., July 13, 1926
Andres Galarraga, Col., June 25, 1995
Luis Gonzalez, Ari., June 8, 2001
Luis Gonzalez, Ari., May 10, 2004 #2
Shawn Green, LA, Aug. 15, 2001
Shawn Green, LA, May 23, 2002 #2
Willie Greene, Cin., Sept. 24, 1996
Ken Griffey Sr., Atl., July 22, 1986 (11 inn)
Jeffrey Hammonds, Cin., May 19, 1999
George W. Harper, StL., Sept. 20(1g), 1928
Von Hayes, Phil., Aug. 29, 1989
Todd Helton, Col., May 1, 2000
Todd Helton, Col., May 29, 2003 #2
Butch Henline, Phil., Sept. 15, 1922
Babe Herman, Chi., July 20, 1933
Gene Hermanski, Brk., Aug. 5, 1948
Jim Hickman, NY, Sept. 3, 1965
Richard Hidalgo, Hou., Sept. 16, 2003
Shea Hillenbrand, Ari., July 7, 2003
Gil Hodges, Brk., Aug. 31, 1950
Todd Hollandsworth, Col., Apr. 15, 2001 (10 inn)
Bob Horner, Atl., July 6, 1986
Rogers Hornsby, Chi., Apr. 24, 1931
Tyler Houston, Mil., July 9, 2000
Ryan Howard, Phil., Sept. 3(1g), 2006
Geoff Jenkins, Mil., Apr. 28, 2001
Geoff Jenkins, Mil., May 21, 2003 #2
Deron Johnson, Phil., July 11, 1971
Andruw Jones, Atl., Sept. 25, 2002
Chipper Jones, Atl., Aug. 14, 2006
Bill Joyce, Wash., Aug. 20, 1894
Alex Kampouris, Cin., May 9, 1937
George Kelly, NY, Sept. 17, 1923
George Kelly, NY, June 14, 1924 #2
Ralph Kiner, Pitt., Aug. 16, 1947
Ralph Kiner, Pitt., Sept. 11(2g), 1947 #2
Ralph Kiner, Pitt., July 5(1g), 1948 #3
Ralph Kiner, Pitt., July 18, 1951 #4
Dave Kingman, NY, June 4, 1976
Dave Kingman, Chi., May 14, 1978 (15 inn) #2
Dave Kingman, Chi., May 17, 1979 (10 inn) #3
Dave Kingman, Chi., July 28, 1979 #4 AL:1
Chuck Klein, Phil., July 10, 1936 (10 inn)
Ted Kluszewski, Cin., July 1(1g), 1956 (10 inn)
Mike Lansing, Col., Sept. 22, 1998
Barry Larkin, Cin., June 28, 1991
Hal Lee, Bos., July 6, 1934
Hank Leiber, Chi., July 4(1g), 1939
Mike Lieberthal, Phil., Aug. 10, 2002
Davey Lopes, LA, Aug. 20, 1974
Bobby Lowe, Bos., May 30(2g), 1894
Mike Lowell, Fla., Apr. 21, 2004 (12 inn)
Mike Lum, Atl., July 3(1g), 1970
Jack Manning, Phil., Oct. 9, 1884
Willard Marshall, NY, July 18, 1947
Eddie Mathews, Bos., Sept. 27, 1952
Gary Matthews Sr., SF, Sept. 25, 1976
Lee May, Hou., June 21, 1973

3 OR MORE HOME RUNS, GAME, N.L (continued)
(4-HR Games in Boldface)
Willie Mays, SF, Apr. 30, 1961
Willie Mays, SF, June 29(1g), 1961 (10 inn) #2
Willie Mays, SF, June 2, 1963 #3
Willie McCovey, SF, Sept. 22, 1963
Willie McCovey, SF, Apr. 22, 1964 #2
Willie McCovey, SF, Sept. 17, 1966 (10 inn) #3
Tom McCreery, Lou., July 12, 1897
Clyde McCullough, Chi., July 26(1g), 1942
Mark McGwire, StL., Apr. 14, 1998
Mark McGwire, StL., May 19, 1998 #2
Mark McGwire, StL., May 18, 2000 #3 AL:2
Roman Mejias, Pitt., May 4(1g), 1958
Kevin Mitchell, SF, May 25, 1990
George Mitterwald, Chi., Apr. 17, 1974
Johnny Mize, StL., July 13, 1938
Johnny Mize, StL., July 20(2g), 1938 #2
Johnny Mize, StL., May 13, 1940 (14 inn) #3
Johnny Mize, StL., Sept. 8(1g), 1940 #4
Johnny Mize, NY, Apr. 24, 1947 #5 AL:1
Rick Monday, Chi., May 16, 1972
Johnny Moore, Phil., July 22, 1936
Walt Moryn, Chi., May 30(2g), 1958
Don Mueller, NY, Sept. 1, 1951
Dale Murphy, Atl., May 18, 1979
Stan Musial, StL., May 2(1g), 1954
Stan Musial, StL., July 8, 1962 #2
Phil Nevin, SD, Oct. 6, 2001
Bill Nicholson, Chi., July 23(1g), 1944
Gene Oliver, Atl., July 30(2g), 1966
Jose Ortiz, Col., Aug. 17, 2001
Mel Ott, NY, Aug. 31(2g), 1930
Andy Pafko, Chi., Aug. 2(2g), 1950
Larry Parrish, Mtl., May 29, 1977
Larry Parrish, Mtl., July 30, 1978 #2
Larry Parrish, Mtl., Apr. 25, 1980 (11 inn) #3 AL:1
Jim Pendleton, Mil., Aug. 30(1g), 1953
Adolfo Phillips, Chi., June 11(2g), 1967
Mike Piazza, LA, June 29, 1996
Albert Pujols, StL., July 20, 2004
Albert Pujols, StL., Apr. 16, 2006 #2
Albert Pujols, StL., Sept. 3, 2006 #3
Aramis Ramirez, Pitt., Apr. 8, 2001
Aramis Ramirez, Chi., July 30, 2004 #2
Aramis Ramirez, Chi., Sept. 16, 2004 #3
Jose Reyes, NY, Aug. 15, 2006
Dusty Rhodes, NY, Aug. 26, 1953
Dusty Rhodes, NY, July 28, 1954 #2
Tuffy Rhodes, Chi., Apr. 4, 1994
Frank Robinson, Cin., Aug. 22, 1959
Bill Robinson, Pitt., June 5, 1976 (15 inn)
Pete Rose, Cin., Apr. 29, 1978
Cody Ross, Fla., Sept. 11, 2006
Babe Ruth, Bos., May 25, 1935 AL:1
Reggie Sanders, Cin., Aug. 15, 1995
Benito Santiago, Phil., Sept. 15, 1996
Hank Sauer, Chi., Aug. 28(1g), 1950
Hank Sauer, Chi., June 11, 1952 #2
Mike Schmidt, Phil., Apr. 17, 1976 (10 inn)
Mike Schmidt, Phil., July 7, 1979 #2
Mike Schmidt, Phil., June 14, 1987 #3
Andy Seminick, Phil., June 2, 1949
Richie Sexson, Mil., Sept. 25, 2001
Richie Sexson, Mil., Apr. 25, 2003 #2
Art Shamsky, Cin., Aug. 12, 1966 (13 inn)
Frank Shugart, StL., May 10, 1894
Reggie Smith, StL., May 22, 1976
Duke Snider, Brk., May 30(2g), 1950
Duke Snider, Brk., June 1, 1955 #2
J.T. Snow, SF, Aug. 13, 2004

Cory Snyder, LA, Apr. 17, 1994 AL:1
Alfonso Soriano, Wash., Apr. 21, 2006
Sammy Sosa, Chi., June 5, 1996
Sammy Sosa, Chi., June 15, 1998 #2
Sammy Sosa, Chi., Aug. 9, 2001 #3
Sammy Sosa, Chi., Aug. 22, 2001 #4
Sammy Sosa, Chi., Sept. 23, 2001 #5
Sammy Sosa, Chi., Aug. 10, 2002 #6
Willie Stargell, Pitt., June 24, 1965
Willie Stargell, Pitt., May 22, 1968 #2
Willie Stargell, Pitt., Apr. 10, 1971 (12 inn) #3
Willie Stargell, Pitt., Apr. 21, 1971 #4
Darryl Strawberry, NY, Aug. 5, 1985 AL:1
Dick Stuart, Pitt., June 30(2g), 1960
Bill Terry, NY, Aug. 13(1g), 1932
Frank J. Thomas, Pitt., Aug. 16, 1958
Hank Thompson, NY, June 3, 1954
Bob Thurman, Cin., Aug. 18, 1956
Bob Tillman, Atl., July 30(1g), 1969
Jim Tobin, Bos., May 13, 1942
Jeff Treadway, Atl., May 26, 1990
Jose Valentin, Mil., Apr. 3, 1998 AL:1
Greg Vaughn, Cin., Sept. 7(2g), 1999
Larry Walker, Col., Apr. 5, 1997
Larry Walker, Col., Apr. 28, 1999 #2
Larry Walker, Col., June 25, 2004 (10 inn) #3
Tim Wallach, Mtl., May 4, 1987
Lee Walls, Chi., Apr. 24, 1958
Claudell Washington, NY, June 22, 1980 AL:1
George Watkins, StL., June 24(2g), 1931
Wes Westrum, NY, June 24, 1950
Bill De. White, StL., July 5, 1961
Mark Whiten, StL., Sept. 7(2g), 1993
Del Wilber, Phil., Aug. 27(2g), 1951
Billy Williams, Chi., Sept. 10, 1968
Cy Williams, Phil., May 11, 1923
Ned Williamson, Chi., May 30(2g), 1884
Hack Wilson, Chi., July 26, 1930
Jimmy Wynn, Hou., June 15, 1967
Jimmy Wynn, LA, May 11, 1974 #2

GRAND SLAM HOME RUNS
Career Leaders
Players active in 2006 in Boldface)

23	Lou Gehrig
20	**Manny Ramirez**
19	Eddie Murray
18	Willie McCovey
	Robin Ventura
17	Jimmie Foxx
	Ted Williams
16	Hank Aaron
	Dave Kingman
	Babe Ruth
15	**Ken Griffey, Jr.**
14	Gil Hodges
	Mark McGwire
	Mike Piazza
	Richie Sexson
13	Harold Baines
	Albert Belle
	Joe DiMaggio
	George Foster
	Jeff Kent
	Ralph Kiner
	Alex Rodriguez
12	Ernie Banks
	Don Baylor
	Rogers Hornsby
	Rafael Palmeiro
	Joe Rudi
	Matt Williams
	Rudy York

3000 OR MORE HITS
Players active in 2006 in Boldface)

4256	Pete Rose
4191	Ty Cobb
3771	Hank Aaron
3630	Stan Musial
3515	Tris Speaker
3430	Honus Wagner
3419	Carl Yastrzemski
3319	Paul Molitor
3314	Eddie Collins
3283	Willie Mays
3255	Eddie Murray
3252	Nap Lajoie
3184	Cal Ripken
3154	George Brett
3152	Paul Waner
3142	Robin Yount
3141	Tony Gwynn
3110	Dave Winfield
3081	Cap Anson
3055	Rickey Henderson
3053	Rod Carew
3023	Lou Brock
3020	Rafael Palmeiro
3010	Wade Boggs
3007	Al Kaline
3000	Roberto Clemente

BATTERS' HITTING STREAKS, 30 OR MORE GAMES, SEASON

AMERICAN LEAGUE:

G	Year	Player & Club
56	1941	Joe DiMaggio, NY
41	1922	George Sisler, StL.
40	1911	Ty Cobb, Det.
39	1987	Paul Molitor, Mil.
35	1917	Ty Cobb, Det.
34	1925	George Sisler, StL.
	1938	George McQuinn, StL.
	1949	Dom DiMaggio, Bos.
33	1907	Hal Chase, NY
	1933	Heinie Manush, Wash.
31	1906	Nap Lajoie, Clev.
	1924	Sam Rice, Wash.
	1980	Ken Landreaux, Minn.
30	1912	Tris Speaker, Bos.
	1934	Goose Goslin, Det.
	1976	Ron LeFlore, Det.
	1980	George Brett, KC
	1997	Sandy Alomar, Jr., Clev.
	1997	Nomar Garciaparra, Bos.
	1998	Eric Davis, Balt.

NATIONAL LEAGUE:

G	Year	Player & Club
44	1897	Willie Keeler, Balt.
	1978	Pete Rose, Cin.
42	1894	Bill Dahlen, Chi.
37	1945	Tommy Holmes, Bos.
36	2005	Jimmy Rollins, Phil.
35	1895	Fred Clarke, Lou.
	2002	Luis Castillo, Fla.
	2006	Chase Utley, Phil.
34	1987	Benito Santiago, SD
33	1893	George Davis, NY
	1922	Rogers Hornsby, StL.
31	1899	Ed Delahanty, Phil.
	1969	Willie Davis, LA
	1970	Rico Carty, Atl.
	1999	Vladimir Guerrero, Mtl.
30	1876	Cal McVey, Chi.
	1898	Elmer Smith, Cin.
	1950	Stan Musial, StL.
	1989	Jerome Walton, Chi.
	1999	Luis Gonzalez, Ari.
	2003	Albert Pujols, StL.
	2006	Willie Taveras, Hou.

PITCHERS: GAMES WON, CONSECUTIVE, SEASON

19	Tim Keefe, NL:NY 1888
	Rube Marquard, NL:NY 1912
18	Hoss Radbourn, NL:Prov. 1884
17	Mickey Welch, NL:NY 1883
	John Luby, NL:Chi. 1890
	Roy Face, NL:Pitt. 1959
16	Jim McCormick, NL:Chi. 1886
	Smoky Joe Wood, AL:Bos. 1912
	Walter Johnson, AL:Wash. 1912
	Lefty Grove, AL:Phil. 1931
	Schoolboy Rowe, AL:Det. 1934
	Carl Hubbell, NL:NY 1936
	Ewell Blackwell, NL:Cin. 1947
	Jack Sanford, NL:SF 1962
	Roger Clemens, AL:NY 2001
15	Scott Stratton, AA:Lou. 1890
	Dazzy Vance, NL:Brk. 1924
	General Crowder, AL:Wash. 1932
	Johnny Allen, AL:Clev. 1937
	Bob Gibson, NL:StL. 1968
	Dave McNally, AL:Balt. 1969
	Steve Carlton, NL:Phil. 1972
	Gaylord Perry, AL:Clev. 1974
	Roger Clemens, AL:Tor. 1998
	Roy Halladay, AL:Tor. 2003
14	Jocko Flynn, NL:Chi. 1886
	Joe McGinnity, NL:NY 1904
	Jim McCormick, UA:Cin. 1884
	Jack Chesbro, AL:NY 1904
	Ed Reulbach, NL:Chi. 1909
	Walter Johnson, AL:Wash. 1913
	Chief Bender, AL:Phil. 1914
	Lefty Grove, AL:Phil. 1928
	Whitey Ford, AL:NY 1961
	Steve Stone, AL:Balt. 1980
	Rick Sutcliffe, NL:Chi. 1984
	Dwight Gooden, NL:NY 1985
	Roger Clemens, AL:Bos. 1986
	John Smoltz, NL:Atl. 1996
13	Larry Corcoran, NL:Chi. 1880
	Charlie Buffinton, NL:Bos. 1884
	Cy Young, NL:Clev. 1892
	Frank Killen, NL:Pitt. 1893
	Frank Dwyer, NL:Cin. 1896
	Fred Klobedanz, NL:Bos. 1897
	Ed Lewis, NL:Bos. 1898
	Christy Mathewson, NL:NY 1909
	Deacon Phillippe, NL:Pitt. 1910
	Walter Johnson, AL:Wash. 1924
	Stan Coveleski, AL:Wash. 1925
	Burleigh Grimes, NL:NY 1927
	Wes Ferrell, AL:Clev. 1930
	Bobo Newsom, AL:Det. 1940
	Ellis Kinder, AL:Bos. 1949
	Brooks Lawrence, NL:Cin. 1956
	Phil Regan, NL:LA 1966
	Dock Ellis, NL:Pitt. 1971
	Dave McNally, AL:Balt. 1971
	Catfish Hunter, AL:Oak. 1973
	Ron Guidry, AL:NY 1978
	Lamarr Hoyt, AL:Chi. 1983
	Tom Glavine, NL:Atl. 1992
	Johan Santana, AL:Minn. 2004
	Chris Carpenter, NL:StL. 2005

PITCHERS: GAMES LOST, CONSECUTIVE, SEASON

19	Jack Nabors, AL:Phil. 1916
18	Cliff Curtis, NL:Bos. 1910
	Roger Craig, NL:NY 1963
16	Dory Dean, NL:Cin. 1876
	Jim Hughey, NL:Clev. 1899
	Craig Anderson, NL:NY 1962
	Mike Parrott, AL:Sea. 1980
15	Bob Groom, AL:Wash. 1909
14	Frank Gilmore, NL:Wash. 1887
	Frank Bates, NL:Clev. 1899
	Joe Harris, AL:Bos. 1906
	Jim Pastorius, NL:Brk. 1908
	Buster Brown, NL:Bos. 1911
	Howie Judson, AL:Chi. 1949
	Paul Calvert, AL:Wash. 1949
	Matt Keough, AL:Oak. 1979
	Anthony Young, NL:NY 1992
13	Sam Moffett, NL:Clev. 1884
	Guy Morton, AL:Clev. 1914
	Burleigh Grimes, NL:Pitt. 1917
	Roy Moore, AL:Phil. 1920
	Joe Oeschger, NL:Bos. 1922
	Dutch Henry, AL:Chi. 1930
	Ben Cantwell, NL:Bos. 1935
	Lum Harris, AL:Phil. 1943
	Dutch McCall, NL:Chi. 1948
	Terry Felton, AL:Minn. 1982
	Rick Honeycutt, NL:LA (11)-AL:Oak. (2) 1987
	Anthony Young, NL:NY 1993
	Jose Lima, NL:Hou. 2000

WINNING TWO COMPLETE GAMES, ONE DAY

Joe McGinnity, (3) NL:NY Aug. 1, 8, 31, 1903
Grover Alexander, (2) NL:Phil. Sept. 23, 1916; Sept. 3, 1917
Mark Baldwin, (2) NL:Pitt. Sept. 12, 1891; May 30, 1892
Pud Galvin, (2) NL:Buff. July 12, 1879; July 4, 1882
Hi Bell, NL:StL. July 19, 1924
John Clarkson, NL:Bos. Sept. 12, 1889
Ray Collins, AL:Bos. Sept. 22, 1914
Cannonball Crane, PL:NY Sept. 27, 1890
Candy Cummings, NL:Hart. Sept. 9, 1876
Bert Cunningham, PL:Buff. Aug. 20, 1890
Dave Davenport, AL:StL. July 29, 1916
Al Demaree, NL:Phil. Sept. 20, 1916
Bill Doak, NL:StL. Sept. 18, 1917
Charlie Ferguson, NL:Phil. Oct. 9, 1886
Henry Gruber, PL:Clev. July 26, 1890
Guy Hecker, AA:Lou. July 4, 1884
Bill Hutchinson, NL:Chi. May 30, 1890
Tim Keefe, AA:NY July 4, 1883
Dutch Levsen, AL:Clev. Aug. 28, 1926
Carl Mays, AL:Bos. Aug. 30, 1918
Tony Mullane, AA:Cin. Sept. 20, 1888
George Mullin, AL:Det. Sept. 22, 1906
Frank Owen, AL:Chi. July 1, 1905
Pol Perritt, NL:NY Sept. 9, 1916
Hoss Radbourn, NL:Prov. May 30, 1884
Ed Reulbach, NL:Chi. Sept. 26, 1908
Amos Rusie, NL:NY Sept. 26, 1891
Doc Scanlon, NL:Brk. Oct. 3, 1905
Cy Seymour, NL:NY June 3, 1897
Urban Shocker, AL:StL. Sept. 6, 1924
Johnny Stuart, NL:StL. July 10, 1923
Ed Summers, AL:Det. Sept. 25, 1908
Fred Toney, NL:Cin. July 1, 1917
Ed Walsh, AL:Chi. Sept. 29, 1908
Monte Ward, NL:Prov. Aug. 8, 1878
Mule Watson, NL:Bos. Aug. 13, 1921
Mickey Welch, NL:Troy July 4, 1881
Jim Whitney, NL:Wash. Aug. 20, 1887
Cy Young, NL:Clev. Oct. 4, 1890

TWO OR MORE NO-HIT GAMES, LIFETIME

7	Nolan Ryan, AL:Cal. 1973(2)-75; NL:Hou.1981; AL:Tex. 90-91
4	Sandy Koufax, NL:LA 1962-65
3	Larry Corcoran, NL:Chi. 1880, 82, 84
	Bob Feller, AL:Clev. 1940, 46, 51
	Cy Young, NL:Clev. 1897; AL:Bos. 1904, 08
2	Al Atkinson, AA:Phil. 1884, 86
	Ted Breitenstein, AA:StL. 1891; NL:Cin. 1898
	Jim Bunning, AL:Det. 1958; NL:Phil. 1964
	Steve Busby, AL:KC 1973-74
	Carl Erskine, NL:Brk. 1952, 56
	Bob Forsch, NL:StL. 1978, 83
	Pud Galvin, NL:Buff. 1880, 84
	Ken Holtzman, NL:Chi. 1969, 71
	Randy Johnson, AL:Sea. 1990; NL:Ari. 2004
	Addie Joss, AL:Clev. 1908, 10
	Dutch Leonard, AL:Bos. 1916, 18
	Jim Maloney, NL:Cin. 1965, 69
	Christy Mathewson, NL:NY 1901, 05
	Hideo Nomo, NL:LA 1996; AL:Bos. 2001
	Allie Reynolds, AL:NY 1951(2)
	Frank Smith AL:Chi. 1905, 08
	Warren Spahn, NL:Mil. 1960-61
	Bill Stoneman, NL:Mtl. 1969, 72
	Adonis Terry, AA:Brk. 1886, 88
	Virgil Trucks, AL:Det. 1952 (2)
	Johnny Vander Meer, NL:Cin. 1938 (2)
	Don Wilson, NL:Hou. 1967, 69

NO-HIT GAMES — INACTIVE LEAGUES

9 OR MORE INNINGS

UNION ASSOCIATION (2)

1884

Dick Burns, Cin. Aug. 26 (at KC) 3-1
Ed Cushman, Mil. Sept. 28 (Wash.) 5-0

AMERICAN ASSOCIATION (15)

1882

Tony Mullane, Lou. Sept. 11 (at Cin.) 2-0
Guy Hecker, Lou. Sept. 19 (at Pitt.) 3-1

1884

Al Atkinson, Phil. May 24 (Pitt.) 10-1
Ed Morris, Colu. May 29 (at Pitt.) 5-0
Frank Mountain, Colu. June 5 (at Wash.) 12-0
Sam Kimber, Brk. Oct. 4 (Tol.) 0-0 (10 inn)

1886

Al Atkinson, Phil. May 1 (NY) 3-2
Adonis Terry, Brk. July 24 (StL.) 1-0
Matt Kilroy, Balt. Oct. 6 (at Pitt.) 6-0

1888

Adonis Terry, Brk. May 27 (Lou.) 4-0
Henry Porter, KC June 6 (at Balt.) 4-0
Ed Seward, Phil. July 26 (Cin.) 12-2
Gus Weyhing, Phil. July 31 (KC) 4-0

1890

Cannonball Titcomb, Roch. Sept. 15 (Syr.) 7-0

1891

Ted Breitenstein, StL. Oct. 4(1g) (Lou.) 8-0
(First major-league start)

NO-HIT GAMES — AMERICAN LEAGUE

*OR MORE INNINGS   * Denotes Perfect Game*

1902
Nixey Callahan, Chi. Sept. 20(1g) (Det.) 3-0

1904
*Cy Young, Bos. May 5 (Phil.) 3-0
Jesse Tannehill, Bos. Aug. 17 (at Chi.) 6-0

1905
Weldon Henley, Phil. July 22(1g) (at StL.) 6-0
Frank Smith, Chi. Sept. 6(2g) (at Det.) 15-0
Bill Dinneen, Bos. Sept. 27(1g) (Chi.) 2-0

1908
Cy Young, Bos. June 30 (at NY) 8-0
Bob Rhoads, Clev. Sept. 18 (Bos.) 2-1
Frank Smith, Chi. Sept. 20 (Phil.) 1-0
*Addie Joss, Clev. Oct. 2 (Chi.) 1-0

1910
Addie Joss, Clev. Apr. 20 (at Chi.) 1-0
Chief Bender, Phil. May 12 (Clev.) 4-0

1911
Smoky Joe Wood, Bos. July 29(1g) (StL.) 5-0
Ed Walsh, Chi. Aug. 27 (Bos.) 5-0

1912
George Mullin, Det. July 4(2g) (StL.) 7-0
Earl Hamilton, StL. Aug. 30 (at Det.) 5-1

1914
Joe Benz, Chi. May 31 (Clev.) 6-1

1916
Rube Foster, Bos. June 21 (NY) 2-0
Joe Bush, Phil. Aug. 26 (Clev.) 5-0
Dutch Leonard, Bos. Aug. 30 (StL.) 4-0

1917
Eddie Cicotte, Chi. Apr. 14 (at StL.) 11-0
George Mogridge, NY Apr. 24 (at Bos.) 2-1
Ernie Koob, StL. May 5 (Chi.) 1-0
Bob Groom, StL. May 6(2g) (Chi.) 3-0
Babe Ruth (0 inn) & Ernie Shore, (9 inn) Bos.
        June 23(1g) (Wash.) 4-0

1918
Dutch Leonard, Bos. June 3 (at Det.) 5-0

1919
Ray Caldwell, Clev. Sept. 10(1g) (at NY) 3-0

1920
Walter Johnson, Wash. July 1 (at Bos.) 1-0

1922
*Charlie Robertson, Chi. Apr. 30 (at Det.) 2-0

1923
Sam Jones, NY Sept. 4 (at Phil.) 2-0
Howard Ehmke, Bos. Sept. 7 (at Phil.) 4-0

1926
Ted Lyons, Chi. Aug. 21 (at Bos.) 6-0

1931
Wes Ferrell, Clev. Apr. 29 (StL.) 9-0
Bobby Burke, Wash. Aug. 8 (Bos.) 5-0

1935
Vern Kennedy, Chi. Aug. 31 (Clev.) 5-0

1937
Bill Dietrich, Chi. June 1 (StL.) 8-0

1938
Monte Pearson, NY Aug. 27(2g) (Clev.) 13-0

1940
Bob Feller, Clev. Apr. 16 (at Chi.) 1-0
(Opening Day)

1945
Dick Fowler, Phil. Sept. 9(2g) (StL.) 1-0

1946
Bob Feller, Clev. Apr. 30 (at NY) 1-0

1947
Don Black, Clev. July 10(1g) (Phil.) 3-0
Bill McCahan, Phil. Sept. 3 (Wash.) 3-0

1948
Bob Lemon, Clev. June 30 (at Det.) 2-0

1951
Bob Feller, Clev. July 1(1g) (Det.) 2-1
Allie Reynolds, NY July 12 (at Clev.) 1-0
Allie Reynolds, NY Sept. 28(1g) (Bos.) 8-0

1952
Virgil Trucks, Det. May 15 (Wash.) 1-0
Virgil Trucks, Det. Aug. 25 (at NY) 1-0

1953
Bobo Holloman, StL. May 6 (Phil.) 6-0
(First major-league start)

1956
Mel Parnell, Bos. July 14 (Chi.) 4-0

1957
Bob Keegan, Chi. Aug. 20(2g) (Wash.) 6-0

1958
Jim Bunning, Det. July. 20(1g) (at Bos.) 3-0
Hoyt Wilhelm, Balt. Sept. 20 (NY) 1-0

1962
Bo Belinsky, LA May 5 (Balt.) 2-0
Earl Wilson, Bos. June 26 (LA) 2-0
Bill Monbouquette, Bos. Aug. 1(at Chi.) 1-0
Jack Kralick, Minn. Aug. 26 (KC) 1-0

1965
Dave Morehead, Bos. Sept. 16 (Clev.) 2-0

1966
Sonny Siebert, Clev. June 10 (Wash.) 2-0

1967
Steve Barber (8.2 inn.) & Stu Miller (0.1 inn.), Balt.
        Apr. 30(1g) (Det.) 1-2 lost
Dean Chance, Minn. Aug. 25(2g) (at Clev.) 2-1
Joe Horlen, Chi. Sept. 10(1g) (Det.) 6-0

1968
Tom Phoebus, Balt. Apr. 27 (Bos.) 6-0
*Catfish Hunter, Oak. May 8 (Minn.) 4-0

1969
Jim Palmer, Balt. Aug. 13 (Oak.) 8-0

1970
Clyde Wright, Cal. July 3 (Oak.) 4-0
Vida Blue, Oak. Sept. 21 (Minn.) 6-0

1973
Steve Busby, KC Apr. 27 (at Det.) 3-0
Nolan Ryan, Cal. May 15 (at KC) 3-0
Nolan Ryan, Cal. July 15 (at Det.) 6-0
Jim Bibby, Tex. July 30 (at Oak.) 6-0

1974
Steve Busby, KC June 19 (at Mil.) 2-0
Dick Bosman, Clev. July 19 (Oak.) 4-0
Nolan Ryan, Cal. Sept. 28 (Minn.) 4-0

1975
Nolan Ryan, Cal. June 1 (Balt.) 1-0
Vida Blue (5 inn), Glenn Abbott, (1 inn), Paul Lindblad
        (1 inn) & Rollie Fingers, (2 inn), Oak. Sept. 28
        (Cal.) 5-0

NO-HIT GAMES — AMERICAN LEAGUE

*9 OR MORE INNINGS   * Denotes Perfect Game*
(continued)

1976
    Blue Moon Odom (5 inn) & Franciso Barrios (4 inn),
        Chi. July 28 (at Oak.) 2-1

1977
    Jim Colborn, KC May 14 (Tex.) 6-0
    Dennis Eckersley, Clev. May 30 (Cal.) 1-0
    Bert Blyleven, Tex. Sept. 22 (at Cal.) 6-0

1981
    *Len Barker, Clev. May 15 (Tor.) 3-0

1983
    Dave Righetti, NY July 4 (Bos.) 4-0
    Mike Warren, Oak. Sept. 29 (Chi.) 3-0

1984
    Jack Morris, Det. Apr. 7 (at Chi.) 4-0
    *Mike Witt, Cal. Sept. 30 (at Tex.) 1-0

1986
    Joe Cowley, Chi. Sept. 19 (at Cal.) 7-1

1987
    Juan Nieves, Mil. Apr. 15 (at Balt.) 7-0

1990
    Mark Langston (7 inn) & Mike Witt, (2 inn) Cal.
        Apr. 11 (Sea.) 1-0
    Randy Johnson, Sea. June 2 (Det.) 2-0
    Nolan Ryan, Tex. June 11 (at Oak.) 5-0
    Dave Stewart, Oak. June 29 (at Tor.) 5-0
    Dave Stieb, Tor. Sept. 2 (at Clev.) 3-0

1991
    Nolan Ryan, Tex. May 1 (Tor.) 3-0
    Bob Milacki (6 inn), Mike Flanagan (1 inn),
        Mark Williamson (1 inn) & Gregg Olson, (1 inn)
        Balt. July 13 (at Oak.) 2-0
    Wilson Alvarez, Chi. Aug. 11 (at Balt.) 7-0
    Bret Saberhagen, KC Aug. 26 (Chi.) 7-0

1993
    Chris Bosio, Sea. Apr. 22 (Bos.) 7-0
    Jim Abbott, NY Sept. 4 (Clev.) 4-0

1994
    Scott Erickson, Minn. Apr. 27 (Mil.) 6-0
    *Kenny Rogers, Tex. July 28 (Cal.) 4-0

1996
    Dwight Gooden, NY May 14 (Sea.) 2-0

1998
    *David Wells, NY May 17 (Minn.) 4-0

1999
    *David Cone, NY July 18 (Mtl.) 6-0
    Eric Milton, Minn. Sept. 11 (Ana.) 7-0

2001
    Hideo Nomo, Bos. Apr. 4 (at Balt.) 3-0

2002
    Derek Lowe, Bos. Apr. 27 (TB) 10-0

NO-HIT GAMES — NATIONAL LEAGUE

*OR MORE INNINGS * Denotes Perfect Game*

1876
George Bradley, StL. July 15 (Hart.) 2-0

1880
*Lee Richmond, Wor. June 12 (Clev.) 1-0
*Monte Ward, Prov. June 17 (Buff.) 5-0
Larry Corcoran, Chi. Aug. 19 (Bos.) 6-0
Pud Galvin, Buff. Aug. 20 (Wor.) 1-0

1882
Larry Corcoran, Chi. Sept. 20 (Wor.) 5-0

1883
Hoss Radbourn, Prov. July 25 (at Clev.) 8-0
Hugh Daily, Clev. Sept. 13 (at Phil.) 1-0

1884
Larry Corcoran, Chi. June 27 (Prov.) 6-0
Pud Galvin, Buff. Aug. 4 (at Det.) 18-0

1885
John Clarkson, Chi. July 27 (at Prov.) 4-0
Charlie Ferguson, Phil. Aug. 29 (Prov.) 1-0

1891
Tom Lovett, Brk. June 22 (NY) 4-0
Amos Rusie, NY July 31 (Brk.) 6-0

1892
Jack Stivetts, Bos. Aug. 6 (at Brk.) 11-0
Ben Sanders, Lou. Aug. 22 (Balt.) 6-2
Bumpus Jones, Cin. Oct. 15 (Pitt.) 7-1
(First major league game)

1893
Bill Hawke, Balt. Aug. 16 (at Wash.) 5-0

1897
Cy Young, Clev. Sept. 18(1g) (Cin.) 6-0

1898
Ted Breitenstein, Cin. Apr. 22 (Pitt.) 11-0
Jim Hughes, Balt. Apr. 22 (Bos.) 8-0
Red Donahue, Phil. July 8 (Bos.) 5-0
Walter Thornton, Chi. Aug. 21(2g) (Brk.) 2-0

1899
Deacon Phillippe, Lou. May 25 (NY) 7-0
Vic Willis, Bos. Aug. 7 (Wash.) 7-1

1900
Noodles Hahn, Cin. July 12 (Phil.) 4-0

1901
Christy Mathewson, NY July 15 (at StL.) 5-0

1903
Chick Fraser, Phil. Sept. 18(2g) (at Chi.) 10-0

1905
Christy Mathewson, NY June 13 (at Chi.) 1-0

1906
Johnny Lush, Phil. May 1 (at Brk.) 6-0
Mal Eason, Brk. July 20 (at StL.) 2-0

1907
Jeff Pfeffer, Bos. May 8 (Cin.) 6-0
Nick Maddox, Pitt. Sept. 20 (Brk.) 2-1

1908
Hooks Wiltse, NY July 4(1g) 10 inn. (Phil.) 1-0
Nap Rucker, Brk. Sept. 5(2g) (Bos.) 6-0

1912
Jeff Tesreau, NY Sept. 6(1g) (at Phil.) 3-0

1914
George Davis, Bos. Sept. 9(2g) (Phil.) 7-0

1915
Rube Marquard, NY Apr. 15 (Brk.) 2-0
Jimmy Lavender, Chi. Aug. 31(1g) (at NY) 2-0

1916
Tom Hughes, Bos. June 16 (Pitt.) 2-0

1917
Fred Toney, Cin. May 2 10 inn. (at Chi.) 1-0

1919
Hod Eller, Cin. May 11 (StL.) 6-0

1922
Jesse Barnes, NY May 7 (Phil.) 6-0

1924
Jesse Haines, StL. July 17 (Bos.) 5-0

1925
Dazzy Vance, Brk. Sept. 13(1g) (Phil.) 10-1

1929
Carl Hubbell, NY May 8 (Pitt.) 11-0

1934
Paul Dean, StL. Sept. 21(2g) (at Brk.) 3-0

1938
Johnny Vander Meer, Cin. June 11 (Bos.) 3-0
Johnny Vander Meer, Cin. June 15 (at Brk.) 6-0
(consecutive appearances)

1940
Tex Carleton, Brk. Apr. 30 (at Cin.) 3-0

1941
Lon Warneke, StL. Aug. 30 (at Cin.) 2-0

1944
Jim Tobin, Bos. Apr. 27 (Brk.) 2-0
Clyde Shoun, Cin. May 15 (Bos.) 1-0

1946
Ed Head, Brk. Apr. 23 (Bos.) 5-0

1947
Ewell Blackwell, Cin. June 18 (Bos.) 6-0

1948
Rex Barney, Brk. Sept. 9 (at NY) 2-0

1950
Vern Bickford, Bos. Aug. 11 (Brk.) 7-0

1951
Cliff Chambers, Pitt. May 6(2g) (at Bos.) 3-0

1952
Carl Erskine, Brk. June 19 (Chi.) 5-0

1954
Jim Wilson, Mil. June 12 (Phil.) 2-0

1955
Sam Jones, Chi. May 12 (Pitt.) 4-0

1956
Carl Erskine, Brk. May 12 (NY) 3-0
Sal Maglie, Brk. Sept. 25 (Phil.) 5-0

1960
Don Cardwell, Chi. May 15(2g) (StL.) 4-0
Lew Burdette, Mil. Aug. 18 (Phil.) 1-0
Warren Spahn, Mil. Sept. 16 (Phil.) 4-0

1961
Warren Spahn, Mil. Apr. 28 (SF) 1-0

1962
Sandy Koufax, LA June 30 (NY) 5-0

1963
Sandy Koufax, LA May 11 (SF) 8-0
Don Nottebart, Hou. May 17 (Phil.) 4-1
Juan Marichal, SF June 15 (Hou.) 1-0

NO-HIT GAMES — NATIONAL LEAGUE

*9 OR MORE INNINGS * Denotes Perfect Game*
(continued)

1964
Ken Johnson, Hou. Apr. 23 (Cin.) 0-1 lost
Sandy Koufax, LA June 4 (at Phil.) 3-0
*Jim Bunning, Phil. June 21(1g) (at NY) 6-0

1965
Jim Maloney, Cin. Aug. 19(1g) (10 inn.) (at Chi.) 1-0
*Sandy Koufax, LA Sept. 9 (Chi.) 1-0

1967
Don Wilson, Hou. June 18 (Atl.) 2-0

1968
George Culver, Cin. July 29(2g) (at Phil.) 6-1
Gaylord Perry, SF Sept. 17 (StL.) 1-0
Ray Washburn, StL. Sept. 18 (at SF) 2-0

1969
Bill Stoneman, Mtl. Apr. 17 (at Phil.) 7-0
Jim Maloney, Cin. Apr. 30 (Hou.) 10-0
Don Wilson, Hou. May 1 (at Cin.) 4-0
Ken Holtzman, Chi. Aug. 19 (Atl.) 3-0
Bob Moose, Pitt. Sept. 20 (at NY) 4-0

1970
Dock Ellis, Pitt. June 12(1g) (at SD) 2-0
Bill Singer, LA July 20 (Phil.) 5-0

1971
Ken Holtzman, Chi. June 3 (at Cin.) 1-0
Rick Wise, Phil. June 23 (at Cin.) 4-0
Bob Gibson, StL. Aug. 14 (at Pitt.) 11-0

1972
Burt Hooton, Chi. Apr. 16 (Phil.) 4-0
Milt Pappas, Chi. Sept. 2 (SD) 8-0
Bill Stoneman, Mtl. Oct. 2(1g) (NY) 7-0

1973
Phil Niekro, Atl. Aug. 5 (SD) 9-0

1975
Ed Halicki, SF Aug. 24(2g) (NY) 6-0

1976
Larry Dierker, Hou. July 9 (Mtl.) 6-0
John Candelaria, Pitt. Aug. 9 (LA) 2-0
John Montefusco, SF Sept. 29 (at Atl.) 9-0

1978
Bob Forsch, StL. Apr. 16 (Phil.) 5-0
Tom Seaver, Cin. June 16 (StL.) 4-0

1979
Ken Forsch, Hou. Apr. 7 (Atl.) 6-0

1980
Jerry Reuss, LA June 27 (at SF) 8-0

1981
Charlie Lea, Mtl. May 10(2g) (SF) 4-0
Nolan Ryan, Hou. Sept. 26 (LA) 5-0

1983
Bob Forsch, StL. Sept. 26 (Mtl.) 3-0

1986
Mike Scott, Hou. Sept. 25 (SF) 2-0

1988
*Tom Browning, Cin. Sept. 16 (LA) 1-0

1990
Fernando Valenzuela, LA June 29 (StL.) 6-0
Terry Mulholland, Phil. Aug. 15 (SF) 6-0

1991
Tommy Greene, Phil. May 23 (at Mtl.) 2-0
*Dennis Martinez, Mtl. July 28 (at LA) 2-0
Kent Mercker (6 inn), Mark Wohlers (2 inn) & Alejandro
Pena (1 inn) Atl. Sept. 11 (SD) 1-0

1992
Kevin Gross, LA Aug. 17 (SF) 2-0

1993
Darryl Kile, Hou. Sept. 8 (NY) 7-1

1994
Kent Mercker, Atl. Apr. 8 (at LA) 6-0

1995
Ramon Martinez, LA July 14 (Fla.) 7-0

1996
Al Leiter, Fla. May 11 (Col.) 11-0
Hideo Nomo, LA Sept. 17 (at Col.) 9-0

1997
Kevin Brown, Fla. June 10 (at SF) 9-0
Francisco Cordova (9 inn) & Ricardo Rincon (1 inn), Pitt.
July 12 (10 inn) (Hou.) 3-0

1999
Jose Jimenez, StL. June 25 (at Ari.) 1-0

2001
A.J. Burnett, Fla. May 12 (at SD) 3-0
Bud Smith, StL. Sept. 3 (at SD) 4-0

2003
Kevin Millwood, Phil. Apr. 27 (SF) 1-0
Roy Oswalt (1 inn), Peter Munro (2.2 inn), Kirk Saarloos
(1.1 inn), Brad Lidge (2 inn), Octavio Dotel (1 inn),
Billy Wagner (1 inn) Hou. June 11 (at AL:NY) 8-0

2004
*Randy Johnson, Ari. May 18 (at Atl.) 2-0

2006
Anibal Sanchez, Fla. Sept. 6 (Ari.) 2-0

⦁O-HIT GAMES

*WER THAN NINE INNINGS   * retired every batter faced*

⦁GHT INNINGS

Charlie Gagus, UA:Wash. Aug. 21, 1884 (Wil.) 2-1
Charles King, PL:Chi. June 21, 1890 (Brk.) lost 0-1
Henry Gastright, AA: Colu. Oct. 12, 1890 (Tol.) 6-0
Fred Frankhouse, NL:Brk. Aug. 27, 1937 (Cin.) 5-0
   (7.2 inn, rain)
Andy Hawkins, AL:NY July 1, 1990 (at Chi.) lost 0-4
Matt Young, AL:Bos. Apr. 12(1g), 1992 (at Clev.) lost 1-2

⦁EVEN INNINGS

Ed Crane, NL:NY Sept. 27, 1888 (Wash.) 3-0
Matt Kilroy, AA:Balt. July 29(2g), 1889 (StL.) 0-0
George Nicol, AA:StL. Sept 23, 1890 (Phil.) 21-2
(First major league game)
Elton Chamberlain, NL:Cin. Sept. 23(2g), 1893 (Bos.) 6-0
John Weimer, NL:Cin. Aug. 24(2g), 1906 (Brk.) 1-0
Grant McGlynn, NL:StL. Sept. 24(2g), 1906 (at Brk.) 1-1
*Ed Karger, NL:StL. Aug. 11(2g), 1907 (Bos.) 4-0
Len Cole, NL:Chi. July 31(2g), 1910 (at StL.) 4-0
Walter Johnson, AL:Wash. Aug. 25, 1924 (StL.) 2-0
Sam Jones, NL:SF Sept. 26, 1959 (at StL.) 4-0

⦁X INNINGS

Larry McKeon, AA:Ind. May 6, 1884 (at Cin.) 0-0
Charlie Getzien, NL:Det. Oct. 1, 1884 (Phil.) 1-0
George Van Haltren, NL:Chi. June 21, 1888 (Pitt.) 1-0
Ed Stein, NL:Brk. June 2, 1894 (Chi.) 1-0
Al Leifield, NL:Pitt. Sept. 26(2g), 1906 (at Phil.) 8-0
John Lush, NL:StL. Aug. 6, 1908 (at Brk.) 2-0
Carl Cashion, AL:Wash. Aug. 20(2g), 1912 (Clev.) 2-0
Johnny Whitehead, AL:StL. Aug. 5(2g), 1940 (Det.) 4-0
Melido Perez, AL:Chi. July 12, 1990 (at NY) 8-0

FIVE INNINGS

Charlie Sweeney, (2 inn) & Henry Boyle (3 inn) UA:StL. Oct. 5, 1884 (StP.) lost 0-1
Fred Shaw, NL:Prov. Oct. 7(1g), 1885 (at Buff.) 4-0
John Stivetts, NL:Bos. Oct. 15(2g), 1892 (at Wash.) 4-0
Leon Ames, NL:NY Sept. 14(2g), 1903 (at StL.) 5-0
(First major league game)
Rube Waddell, AL:Phil. Aug. 15, 1905 (StL.) 2-0
Jim Dygert (3 inn) & Rube Waddell (2 inn), AL:Phil. Aug. 29, 1906 (Chi.) 4-3
Ed Walsh, AL:Chi. May 26, 1907 (NY) 8-1
Howie Camnitz, NL:Pitt. Aug. 23(2g), 1907 (at NY) 1-0
*Harry Vickers, AL:Phil. Oct. 5(2g), 1907 (at Wash.) 4-0
Jim Tobin, NL:Bos. June 22(2g), 1944 (Phil.) 7-0
Mike McCormick, NL:SF June 12, 1959 (at Phil.) 3-0
   (*allowed hit in 6th inning before game was rained out and reverted to last full inning*)
*Dean Chance, AL:Minn. Aug. 6, 1967 (Bos.) 2-0
*David Palmer, NL:Mtl. Apr. 21(2g), 1984 (at StL.) 4-0
Pascual Perez, NL:Mtl. Sept 24, 1988 (at Phil.) 1-0
Devern Hansack, NL:Bos. Oct. 1, 2006 (Balt.) 9-0

NO HITS THROUGH NINE INNINGS, ALLOWED HIT IN EXTRA-INNING

Earl Moore, AL:Clev. (Chi.) May 9, 1901
   (*allowed hit in 10th, lost*)
Bob Wicker, NL:Chi. (NY) June 11, 1904
   (*allowed hit in 10th, won in 12th*)
Harry McIntyre, NL:Brk. (Pitt.) Aug. 1, 1906
   (*allowed hit in 11th, lost in 13th*)
Red Ames, NL:NY (Brk.) Apr. 15, 1909
   (*allowed hit in 10th, lost in 13th*)
Tom Hughes, AL:NY (Clev.) Aug. 30(2g), 1910
   (*allowed hit in 10th, lost in 11th*)
Jim Scott, AL:Chi. (at Wash.) May 14, 1914
   (*allowed hit in 10th, lost*)
Hippo Vaughn, NL:Chi. (Cin.) May 2, 1917
   (*allowed hit in 10th, lost*)
Bobo Newsom, AL:StL. (Bos.) Sept. 18, 1934
   (*allowed hit in 10th, lost*)
Johnny Klippstein (7 inn), Hersh Freeman (1 inn) & Joe Black (2.1 inn), NL:Cin. (at Mil.) May 26, 1956
   (*allowed hit in 10th, 2 hits in 11th, lost*)
Harvey Haddix, NL:Pitt. (at Mil.) May 26, 1959
   (*12 innings perfect; allowed hit in 13th, lost*)
Jim Maloney, NL:Cin. (NY) June 14, 1965
   (*allowed 2 hits in 11th, lost*)
Mark Gardner, NL:Mtl. (at LA) July 26, 1991
   (*allowed 2 hits in 10th, lost*)
Pedro Martinez, NL:Mtl. (at SD) June 3, 1995
   (*9 innings perfect, allowed hit in 10th, won*)

BATTING AVERAGE

1900:	.381	Honus Wagner, NL:Pitt.
1901:	.422	Nap Lajoie, AL:Phil.
	.382	Jesse Burkett, NL:StL.
1902:	.376	Ed Delahanty, AL:Wash.
	.357	Ginger Beaumont, NL:Pitt.
1903:	.355	Honus Wagner, NL:Pitt. (2)
	.355	Nap Lajoie, AL:Clev. (2)
1904:	.381	Nap Lajoie, AL:Clev. (3)
	.349	Honus Wagner, NL:Pitt. (3)
1905:	.377	Cy Seymour, NL:Cin.
	.308	Elmer Flick, AL:Clev.
1906:	.358	George Stone, AL:StL.
	.339	Honus Wagner, NL:Pitt. (4)
1907:	.350	Ty Cobb, AL:Det.
	.350	Honus Wagner, NL:Pitt. (5)
1908:	.354	Honus Wagner, NL:Pitt. (6)
	.324	Ty Cobb, AL:Det. (2)
1909:	.376	Ty Cobb, AL:Det. (3)
	.339	Honus Wagner, NL:Pitt. (7)
1910:	.385	Ty Cobb, AL:Det. (4)
	.331	Sherry Magee, NL:Phil.
1911:	.420	Ty Cobb, AL:Det. (5)
	.334	Honus Wagner, NL:Pitt. (8)
1912:	.410	Ty Cobb, AL:Det. (6)
	.372	Heinie Zimmerman, NL:Chi.
1913:	.390	Ty Cobb, AL:Det. (7)
	.350	Jake Daubert, NL:Brk.
1914:	.368	Ty Cobb, AL:Det. (8)
	.329	Jake Daubert, NL:Brk. (2)
1915:	.369	Ty Cobb, AL:Det. (9)
	.320	Larry Doyle, NL:NY
1916:	.386	Tris Speaker, AL:Clev.
	.339	Hal Chase, NL:Cin.
1917:	.383	Ty Cobb, AL:Det. (10)
	.341	Edd Roush, NL:Cin.
1918:	.382	Ty Cobb, AL:Det. (11)
	.335	Zack Wheat, NL:Brk.
1919:	.384	Ty Cobb, AL:Det. (12)
	.321	Edd Roush, NL:Cin. (2)
1920:	.407	George Sisler, AL:StL.
	.370	Rogers Hornsby, NL:StL.
1921:	.397	Rogers Hornsby, NL:StL. (2)
	.394	Harry Heilmann, AL:Det.
1922:	.418	George Sisler, AL:StL. (2)
	.401	Rogers Hornsby, NL:StL. (3)
1923:	.402	Harry Heilmann, AL:Det. (2)
	.384	Rogers Hornsby, NL:StL. (4)
1924:	.424	Rogers Hornsby, NL:StL. (5)
	.378	Babe Ruth, AL:NY
1925:	.403	Rogers Hornsby, NL:StL. (6)
	.392	Harry Heilmann, AL:Det. (3)
1926:	.378	Heinie Manush, AL:Det.
	.353	Bubbles Hargrave, NL:Cin.
1927:	.398	Harry Heilmann, AL:Det. (4)
	.380	Paul Waner, NL:Pitt.
1928:	.387	Rogers Hornsby, NL:Bos. (7)
	.379	Goose Goslin, AL:Wash.
1929:	.398	Lefty O'Doul, NL:Phil.
	.369	Lew Fonseca, AL:Clev.
1930:	.401	Bill Terry, NL:NY
	.381	Al Simmons, AL:Phil.
1931:	.390	Al Simmons, AL:Phil. (2)
	.349	Chick Hafey, NL:StL.

1932:	.368	Lefty O'Doul, NL:Brk. (2)
	.367	Dale Alexander, AL:Det.-Bos.
1933:	.368	Chuck Klein, NL:Phil.
	.356	Jimmie Foxx, AL:Phil.
1934:	.363	Lou Gehrig, AL:NY
	.362	Paul Waner, NL:Pitt. (2)
1935:	.385	Arky Vaughan, NL:Pitt.
	.349	Buddy Myer, AL:Wash.
1936:	.388	Luke Appling, AL:Chi.
	.373	Paul Waner, NL:Pitt. (3)
1937:	.374	Joe Medwick, NL:StL.
	.371	Charlie Gehringer, AL:Det.
1938:	.349	Jimmie Foxx, AL:Bos. (2)
	.342	Ernie Lombardi, NL:Cin.
1939:	.381	Joe DiMaggio, AL:NY
	.349	Johnny Mize, NL:StL.
1940:	.355	Debs Garms, NL:Pitt.
	.352	Joe DiMaggio, AL:NY (2)
1941:	.406	Ted Williams, AL:Bos.
	.343	Pete Reiser, NL:Brk.
1942:	.356	Ted Williams, AL:Bos. (2)
	.330	Ernie Lombardi, NL:Bos. (2)
1943:	.357	Stan Musial, NL:StL.
	.328	Luke Appling, AL:Chi. (2)
1944:	.357	Dixie Walker, NL:Brk.
	.327	Lou Boudreau, AL:Clev.
1945:	.355	Phil Cavarretta, NL:Chi.
	.309	Snuffy Stirnweiss, AL:NY
1946:	.365	Stan Musial, NL:StL. (2)
	.353	Mickey Vernon, AL:Wash.
1947:	.363	Harry Walker, NL:StL.-Phil.
	.343	Ted Williams, AL:Bos. (3)
1948:	.376	Stan Musial, NL:StL. (3)
	.369	Ted Williams, AL:Bos. (4)
1949:	.343	George Kell, AL:Det.
	.342	Jackie Robinson, NL:Brk.
1950:	.354	Billy Goodman, AL:Bos.
	.346	Stan Musial, NL:StL. (4)
1951:	.355	Stan Musial, NL:StL. (5)
	.344	Ferris Fain, AL:Phil.
1952:	.336	Stan Musial, NL:StL. (6)
	.327	Ferris Fain, AL:Phil. (2)
1953:	.344	Carl Furillo, NL:Brk.
	.337	Mickey Vernon, AL:Wash. (2)
1954:	.345	Willie Mays, NL:NY
	.341	Bobby Avila, AL:Clev.
1955:	.340	Al Kaline, AL:Det.
	.338	Richie Ashburn, NL:Phil.
1956:	.353	Mickey Mantle, AL:NY
	.328	Hank Aaron, NL:Mil.
1957:	.388	Ted Williams, AL:Bos. (5)
	.351	Stan Musial, NL:StL. (7)
1958:	.350	Richie Ashburn, NL:Phil. (2)
	.328	Ted Williams, AL:Bos. (6)
1959:	.355	Hank Aaron, NL:Mil. (2)
	.353	Harvey Kuenn, AL:Det.
1960:	.325	Dick Groat, NL:Pitt.
	.320	Pete Runnels, AL:Bos.
1961:	.361	Norm Cash, AL:Det.
	.351	Roberto Clemente, NL:Pitt.
1962:	.346	Tommy Davis, NL:LA
	.326	Pete Runnels, AL:Bos. (2)
1963:	.326	Tommy Davis, NL:LA (2)
	.321	Carl Yastrzemski, AL:Bos.
1964:	.339	Roberto Clemente, NL:Pitt. (2)
	.323	Tony Oliva, AL:Minn.

BATTING AVERAGE (CONTINUED)

1965:	.329	Roberto Clemente, NL:Pitt. (3)
	.321	Tony Oliva, AL:Minn. (2)
1966:	.342	Matty Alou, NL:Pitt.
	.316	Frank Robinson, AL:Balt.
1967:	.357	Roberto Clemente, NL:Pitt. (4)
	.326	Carl Yastrzemski, AL:Bos. (2)
1968:	.335	Pete Rose, NL:Cin.
	.301	Carl Yastrzemski, AL:Bos. (3)
1969:	.348	Pete Rose, NL:Cin. (2)
	.332	Rod Carew, AL:Minn.
1970:	.366	Rico Carty, NL:Atl.
	.329	Alex Johnson, AL:Cal.
1971:	.363	Joe Torre, NL:StL.
	.337	Tony Oliva, AL:Minn. (3)
1972:	.333	Billy Williams, NL:Chi.
	.318	Rod Carew, AL:Minn. (2)
1973:	.350	Rod Carew, AL:Minn. (3)
	.338	Pete Rose, NL:Cin. (3)
1974:	.364	Rod Carew, AL:Minn. (4)
	.353	Ralph Garr, NL:Atl.
1975:	.359	Rod Carew, AL:Minn. (5)
	.354	Bill Madlock, NL:Chi.
1976:	.339	Bill Madlock, NL:Chi. (2)
	.333	George Brett, AL:KC
1977:	.388	Rod Carew, AL:Minn. (6)
	.338	Dave Parker, NL:Pitt
1978:	.334	Dave Parker, NL:Pitt. (2)
	.333	Rod Carew, AL:Minn. (7)
1979:	.344	Keith Hernandez, NL:StL.
	.333	Fred Lynn, AL:Bos.
1980:	.390	George Brett, AL:KC (2)
	.324	Bill Buckner, NL:Chi.
1981:	.341	Bill Madlock, NL:Pitt. (3)
	.336	Carney Lansford, AL:Bos.
1982:	.332	Willie Wilson, AL:KC
	.331	Al Oliver, NL:Mtl.
1983:	.361	Wade Boggs, AL:Bos.
	.323	Bill Madlock, NL:Pitt. (4)
1984:	.351	Tony Gwynn, NL:SD
	.343	Don Mattingly, AL:NY
1985:	.368	Wade Boggs, AL:Bos. (2)
	.353	Willie McGee, NL:StL.
1986:	.357	Wade Boggs, AL:Bos. (3)
	.334	Tim Raines, NL:Mtl.
1987:	.370	Tony Gwynn, NL:SD (2)
	.363	Wade Boggs, AL:Bos. (4)
1988:	.366	Wade Boggs, AL:Bos. (5)
	.313	Tony Gwynn, NL:SD (3)
1989:	.339	Kirby Puckett, AL:Minn.
	.336	Tony Gwynn, NL:SD (4)
1990:	.335	Willie McGee, NL:StL. (2)
	.329	George Brett, AL:KC (3)
1991:	.341	Julio Franco, AL:Tex.
	.319	Terry Pendleton, NL:Atl.
1992:	.343	Edgar Martinez, AL:Sea.
	.330	Gary Sheffield, NL:SD
1993:	.370	Andres Galarraga, NL:Col.
	.363	John Olerud, AL:Tor.
1994:	.394	Tony Gwynn, NL:SD (5)
	.359	Paul O'Neill, AL:NY
1995:	.368	Tony Gwynn, NL:SD (6)
	.356	Edgar Martinez, AL:Sea. (2)
1996:	.358	Alex Rodriguez, AL:Sea.
	.353	Tony Gwynn, NL:SD (7)
1997:	.372	Tony Gwynn, NL:SD (8)
	.347	Frank Thomas, AL:Chi.
1998:	.363	Larry Walker, NL:Col.
	.339	Bernie Williams, AL:NY
1999:	.379	Larry Walker, NL:Col. (2)
	.357	Nomar Garciaparra, AL:Bos.
2000:	.372	Todd Helton, NL:Col.
	.372	Nomar Garciaparra, AL:Bos. (2)
2001:	.350	Larry Walker, NL:Col. (3)
	.350	Ichiro Suzuki, AL:Sea.
2002:	.370	Barry Bonds, NL:SF
	.349	Manny Ramirez, AL:Bos.
2003:	.359	Albert Pujols, NL:StL.
	.326	Bill Mueller, AL:Bos.
2004:	.372	Ichiro Suzuki, AL:Sea. (2)
	.362	Barry Bonds, NL:SF (2)
2005:	335	Derrek Lee, NL:Chi.
	.331	Michael Young, AL:Tex.
2006:	.347	Joe Mauer, AL:Minn.
	.344	Freddy Sanchez, NL:Pitt.

TOTAL BASES

1900:	305	Elmer Flick, NL:Phil.
1901:	345	Nap Lajoie, AL:Phil.
	314	Jesse Burkett, NL:StL.
1902:	289	Piano Legs Hickman, AL:Bos.-Clev.
	256	Sam Crawford, NL:Cin.
1903:	281	Buck Freeman, AL:Bos.
	272	Ginger Beaumont, NL:Pitt.
1904:	304	Nap Lajoie, AL:Clev. (2)
	255	Honus Wagner, NL:Pitt.
1905:	325	Cy Seymour, NL:Cin.
	259	George Stone, AL:StL.
1906:	291	George Stone, AL:StL. (2)
	237	Honus Wagner, NL:Pitt. (2)
1907:	286	Ty Cobb, AL:Det.
	264	Honus Wagner, NL:Pitt. (3)
1908:	308	Honus Wagner, NL:Pitt. (4)
	276	Ty Cobb, AL:Det. (2)
1909:	296	Ty Cobb, AL:Det. (3)
	242	Honus Wagner, NL:Pitt. (5)
1910:	308	Nap Lajoie, AL:Clev. (3)
	263	Sherry Magee, NL:Phil.
1911:	367	Ty Cobb, AL:Det. (4)
	308	Wildfire Schulte, NL:Chi.
1912:	331	Joe Jackson, AL:Clev.
	318	Heinie Zimmerman, NL:Chi.
1913:	298	Gavvy Cravath, NL:Phil.
	298	Sam Crawford, AL:Det.
1914:	287	Tris Speaker, AL:Bos.
	277	Sherry Magee, NL:Phil. (2)
1915:	274	Ty Cobb, AL:Det. (5)
	266	Gavvy Cravath, NL:Phil. (2)
1916:	293	Joe Jackson, AL:Chi. (2)
	262	Zack Wheat, NL:Brk.
1917:	335	Ty Cobb, AL:Det. (6)
	253	Rogers Hornsby, NL:StL.
1918:	236	George Burns, AL:Phil.
	202	Charlie Hollocher, NL:Chi.
1919:	284	Babe Ruth, AL:Bos.
	223	Hy Myers, NL:Brk.
1920:	399	George Sisler, AL:StL.
	329	Rogers Hornsby, NL:StL. (2)
1921:	457	Babe Ruth, AL:NY (2)
	378	Rogers Hornsby, NL:StL. (3)
1922:	450	Rogers Hornsby, NL:StL. (4)
	367	Ken Williams, AL:StL.
1923:	399	Babe Ruth, AL:NY (3)
	311	Frankie Frisch, NL:NY
1924:	391	Babe Ruth, AL:NY (4)
	373	Rogers Hornsby, NL:StL. (5)
1925:	392	Al Simmons, AL:Phil.
	381	Rogers Hornsby, NL:StL. (6)
1926:	365	Babe Ruth, AL:NY (5)
	305	Jim Bottomley, NL:StL.
1927:	447	Lou Gehrig, AL:NY
	342	Paul Waner, NL:Pitt.
1928:	380	Babe Ruth, AL:NY (6)
	362	Jim Bottomley, NL:StL. (2)
1929:	409	Rogers Hornsby, NL:Chi. (7)
	373	Al Simmons, AL:Phil. (2)
1930:	445	Chuck Klein, NL:Phil.
	419	Lou Gehrig, AL:NY (2)
1931:	410	Lou Gehrig, AL:NY (3)
	347	Chuck Klein, NL:Phil. (2)
1932:	438	Jimmie Foxx, AL:Phil.
	420	Chuck Klein, NL:Phil. (3)

1933:	403	Jimmie Foxx, AL:Phil. (2)
	365	Chuck Klein, NL:Phil. (4)
1934:	409	Lou Gehrig, AL:NY (4)
	369	Ripper Collins, NL:StL.
1935:	389	Hank Greenberg, AL:Det.
	365	Joe Medwick, NL:StL.
1936:	405	Hal Trosky, AL:Clev.
	367	Joe Medwick, NL:StL. (2)
1937:	418	Joe DiMaggio, AL:NY
	406	Joe Medwick, NL:StL. (3)
1938:	398	Jimmie Foxx, AL:Bos. (3)
	326	Johnny Mize, NL:StL.
1939:	353	Johnny Mize, NL:StL. (2)
	344	Ted Williams, AL:Bos.
1940:	384	Hank Greenberg, AL:Det. (2)
	368	Johnny Mize, NL:StL. (3)
1941:	348	Joe DiMaggio, AL:NY (2)
	299	Pete Reiser, NL:Brk.
1942:	338	Ted Williams, AL:Bos. (2)
	292	Enos Slaughter, NL:StL.
1943:	347	Stan Musial, NL:StL.
	301	Rudy York, AL:Det.
1944:	317	Bill Nicholson, NL:Chi.
	297	Johnny Lindell, AL:NY
1945:	367	Tommy Holmes, NL:Bos.
	301	Snuffy Stirnweiss, AL:NY
1946:	366	Stan Musial, NL:StL. (2)
	343	Ted Williams, AL:Bos. (3)
1947:	361	Ralph Kiner, NL:Pitt.
	335	Ted Williams, AL:Bos. (4)
1948:	429	Stan Musial, NL:StL. (3)
	355	Joe DiMaggio, AL:NY (3)
1949:	382	Stan Musial, NL:StL. (4)
	368	Ted Williams, AL:Bos. (5)
1950:	343	Duke Snider, NL:Brk.
	326	Walt Dropo, AL:Bos.
1951:	355	Stan Musial, NL:StL. (5)
	295	Ted Williams, AL:Bos. (6)
1952:	311	Stan Musial, NL:StL. (6)
	297	Al Rosen, AL:Clev.
1953:	370	Duke Snider, NL:Brk. (2)
	367	Al Rosen, AL:Clev. (2)
1954:	378	Duke Snider, NL:Brk. (3)
	304	Minnie Minoso, AL:Chi.
1955:	382	Willie Mays, NL:NY
	321	Al Kaline, AL:Det.
1956:	376	Mickey Mantle, AL:NY
	340	Hank Aaron, NL:Mil.
1957:	369	Hank Aaron, NL:Mil. (2)
	331	Roy Sievers, AL:Wash.
1958:	379	Ernie Banks, NL:Chi.
	307	Mickey Mantle, AL:NY (2)
1959:	400	Hank Aaron, NL:Mil. (3)
	301	Rocky Colavito, AL:Clev.
1960:	334	Hank Aaron, NL:Mil. (4)
	294	Mickey Mantle, AL:NY (3)
1961:	366	Roger Maris, AL:NY
	358	Hank Aaron, NL:Mil. (5)
1962:	382	Willie Mays, NL:SF (2)
	309	Rockey Colavito, AL:Det. (2)
1963:	370	Hank Aaron, NL:Mil. (6)
	319	Dick Stuart, AL:Bos.
1964:	374	Tony Oliva, AL:Minn.
	352	Dick Allen, NL:Phil.
1965:	360	Willie Mays, NL:SF (3)
	308	Zoilo Versalles, AL:Minn.

TOTAL BASES (CONTINUED)

966:	367	Frank Robinson, AL:Balt.
	355	Felipe Alou, NL:Atl.
967:	360	Carl Yastrzemski, AL:Bos.
	344	Hank Aaron, NL:Atl. (7)
968:	330	Frank Howard, AL:Wash.
	321	Billy Williams, NL:Chi.
969:	340	Frank Howard, AL:Wash. (2)
	332	Hank Aaron, NL:Atl. (8)
970:	373	Billy Williams, NL:Chi. (2)
	335	Carl Yastrzemski, AL:Bos. (2)
971:	352	Joe Torre, NL:StL.
	302	Reggie Smith, AL:Bos.
972:	348	Billy Williams, NL:Chi. (3)
	314	Bobby Murcer, AL:NY
973:	341	Bobby Bonds, NL:SF
	295	Sal Bando, AL:Oak.
	295	Dave May, AL:Mil.
	295	George Scott, AL:Mil.
974:	315	Johnny Bench, NL:Cin.
	287	Joe Rudi, AL:Oak.
975:	322	Greg Luzinski, NL:Phil.
	318	George Scott, AL:Mil. (2)
976:	306	Mike Schmidt, NL:Phil.
	298	George Brett, AL:KC
977:	388	George Foster, NL:Cin.
	382	Jim Rice, AL:Bos.
978:	406	Jim Rice, AL:Bos. (2)
	340	Dave Parker, NL:Pitt.
979:	369	Jim Rice, AL:Bos. (3)
	333	Dave Winfield, NL:SD
980:	342	Mike Schmidt, NL:Phil. (2)
	335	Cecil Cooper, AL:Mil.
981:	228	Mike Schmidt, NL:Phil. (3)
	215	Dwight Evans, AL:Bos.
982:	367	Robin Yount, AL:Mil.
	317	Al Oliver, NL:Mtl.
983:	344	Jim Rice, AL:Bos. (4)
	341	Andre Dawson, NL:Mtl.
984:	339	Tony Armas, AL:Bos.
	332	Dale Murphy, NL:Atl.
985:	370	Don Mattingly, AL:NY
	350	Dave Parker, NL:Cin. (2)
986:	388	Don Mattingly, AL:NY (2)
	304	Dave Parker, NL:Cin. (3)
987:	369	George Bell, AL:Tor.
	353	Andre Dawson, NL:Chi. (2)
988:	358	Kirby Puckett, AL:Minn.
	329	Andres Galarraga, NL:Mtl.
989:	345	Kevin Mitchell, NL:SF
	344	Ruben Sierra, AL:Tex.
990:	344	Ryne Sandberg, NL:Chi.
	339	Cecil Fielder, AL:Det.
991:	368	Cal Ripken, AL:Balt.
	303	Will Clark, NL:SF
	303	Terry Pendleton, NL:Atl.
992:	323	Gary Sheffield, NL:SD
	313	Kirby Puckett, AL:Minn. (2)
993:	365	Barry Bonds, NL:SF
	359	Ken Griffey, Jr. AL:Sea.
994:	300	Jeff Bagwell, NL:Hou.
	294	Albert Belle, AL:Clev.
995:	377	Albert Belle, AL:Clev. (2)
	359	Dante Bichette, NL:Col.

1996:	392	Ellis Burks, NL:Col.
	379	Alex Rodriguez, AL:Sea.
1997:	409	Larry Walker, NL:Col.
	393	Ken Griffey, Jr. AL:Sea. (2)
1998:	416	Sammy Sosa, NL:Chi.
	399	Albert Belle, AL:Chi. (3)
1999:	397	Sammy Sosa, NL:Chi. (2)
	361	Shawn Green, AL:Tor.
2000:	405	Todd Helton, NL:Col.
	378	Carlos Delgado, AL:Tor.
2001:	425	Sammy Sosa, NL:Chi. (3)
	393	Alex Rodriguez, AL:Tex. (2)
2002:	389	Alex Rodriguez, AL:Tex. (3)
	364	Vladimir Guerrero, NL:Mtl.
2003:	394	Albert Pujols, NL:StL.
	373	Vernon Wells, AL:Tor.
2004:	389	Albert Pujols, NL:StL. (2)
	366	Vladimir Guerrero, AL:Ana. (NL 1)
2005:	393	Derrek Lee, NL:Chi.
	370	Mark Teixeira, AL:Tex.
2006:	383	Ryan Howard, NL:Phil.
	355	David Ortiz, AL:Bos.

RUNS BATTED IN

Year	RBI	Player
1920:	137	Babe Ruth, AL:NY
	94	Rogers Hornsby, NL:StL.
	94	George Kelly, NL:NY
1921:	171	Babe Ruth, AL:NY (2)
	126	Rogers Hornsby, NL:StL. (2)
1922:	155	Ken Williams, AL:StL.
	152	Rogers Hornsby, NL:StL. (3)
1923:	131	Babe Ruth, AL:NY (3)
	125	Irish Meusel, NL:NY
1924:	136	George Kelly, NL:NY (2)
	129	Goose Goslin, AL:Wash.
1925:	143	Rogers Hornsby, NL:StL. (4)
	138	Bob Meusel, AL:NY
1926:	150	Babe Ruth, AL:NY (4)
	120	Jim Bottomley, NL:StL.
1927:	175	Lou Gehrig, AL:NY
	131	Paul Waner, NL:Pitt.
1928:	145	Lou Gehrig, AL:NY (2)
	136	Jim Bottomley, NL:StL. (2)
1929:	158	Hack Wilson, NL:Chi.
	157	Al Simmons, AL:Phil.
1930:	191	Hack Wilson, NL:Chi. (2)
	174	Lou Gehrig, AL:NY (3)
1931:	184	Lou Gehrig, AL:NY (4)
	121	Chuck Klein, NL:Phil.
1932:	169	Jimmie Foxx, AL:Phil.
	143	Don Hurst, NL:Phil.
1933:	163	Jimmie Foxx, AL:Phil. (2)
	120	Chuck Klein, NL:Phil. (2)
1934:	165	Lou Gehrig, AL:NY (5)
	135	Mel Ott, NL:NY
1935:	170	Hank Greenberg, AL:Det.
	130	Wally Berger, NL:Bos.
1936:	162	Hal Trosky, AL:Clev.
	138	Joe Medwick, NL:StL.
1937:	183	Hank Greenberg, AL:Det. (2)
	154	Joe Medwick, NL:StL. (2)
1938:	175	Jimmie Foxx, AL:Bos. (3)
	122	Joe Medwick, NL:StL. (3)
1939:	145	Ted Williams, AL:Bos.
	128	Frank McCormick, NL:Cin.
1940:	150	Hank Greenberg, AL:Det. (3)
	137	Johnny Mize, NL:StL.
1941:	125	Joe DiMaggio, AL:NY
	120	Dolph Camilli, NL:Brk.
1942:	137	Ted Williams, AL:Bos. (2)
	110	Johnny Mize, NL:NY (2)
1943:	128	Bill Nicholson, NL:Chi.
	118	Rudy York, AL:Det.
1944:	122	Bill Nicholson, NL:Chi. (2)
	109	Vern Stephens, AL:StL.
1945:	124	Dixie Walker, NL:Brk.
	111	Nick Etten, AL:NY
1946:	130	Enos Slaughter, NL:StL.
	127	Hank Greenberg, AL:Det. (4)
1947:	138	Johnny Mize, NL:NY (3)
	114	Ted Williams, AL:Bos. (3)
1948:	155	Joe DiMaggio, AL:NY (2)
	131	Stan Musial, NL:StL.
1949:	159	Tedd Williams, AL:Bos. (4)
	159	Vern Stephens, AL:Bos. (2)
	127	Ralph Kiner, NL:Pitt.
1950:	144	Walt Dropo, AL:Bos.
	144	Vern Stephens, AL:Bos. (3)
	126	Del Ennis, NL:Phil.
1951:	129	Gus Zernial, AL:Chi.-Phil.
	121	Monte Irvin, NL:NY
1952:	121	Hank Sauer, NL:Chi.
	105	Al Rosen, AL:Clev.
1953:	145	Al Rosen, AL:Clev. (2)
	142	Roy Campanella, NL:Brk.
1954:	141	Ted Kluszewski, NL:Cin.
	126	Larry Doby, AL:Clev.
1955:	136	Duke Snider, NL:Brk.
	116	Ray Boone, AL:Det.
	116	Jackie Jensen, AL:Bos.
1956:	130	Mickey Mantle, AL:NY
	109	Stan Musial, NL:StL. (2)
1957:	132	Hank Aaron, NL:Mil.
	114	Roy Sievers, AL:Wash.
1958:	129	Ernie Banks, NL:Chi.
	122	Jackie Jensen, AL:Bos. (2)
1959:	143	Ernie Banks, NL:Chi. (2)
	112	Jackie Jensen, AL:Bos. (3)
1960:	126	Hank Aaron, NL:Mil. (2)
	112	Roger Maris, AL:NY
1961:	142	Orlando Cepeda, NL:SF
	142	Roger Maris, AL:NY (2)
1962:	153	Tommy Davis, NL:LA
	126	Harmon Killebrew, AL:Minn.
1963:	130	Hank Aaron, NL:Mil. (3)
	118	Dick Stuart, AL:Bos.
1964:	119	Ken Boyer, NL:StL.
	118	Brooks Robinson, AL:Balt.
1965:	130	Deron Johnson, NL:Cin.
	108	Rocky Colavito, AL:Clev.
1966:	127	Hank Aaron, NL:Atl. (4)
	122	Frank Robinson, AL:Balt.
1967:	121	Carl Yastrzemski, AL:Bos.
	111	Orlando Cepeda, NL:StL. (2)
1968:	109	Ken Harrelson, AL:Bos.
	105	Willie McCovey, NL:SF
1969:	140	Harmon Killebrew, AL:Minn. (2)
	126	Willie McCovey, NL:SF (2)
1970:	148	Johnny Bench, NL:Cin.
	126	Frank Howard, AL:Wash.
1971:	137	Joe Torre, NL:StL.
	119	Harmon Killebrew, AL:Minn. (3)
1972:	125	Johnny Bench, NL:Cin. (2)
	113	Dick Allen, AL:Chi.
1973:	119	Willie Stargell, NL:Pitt.
	117	Reggie Jackson, AL:Oak
1974:	129	Johnny Bench, NL:Cin. (3)
	118	Jeff Burroughs, AL:Tex
1975:	120	Greg Luzinski, NL:Phil.
	109	George Scott, AL:Mil.
1976:	121	George Foster, NL:Cin.
	109	Lee May, AL:Balt.
1977:	149	George Foster, NL:Cin. (2)
	119	Larry Hisle, AL:Minn.
1978:	139	Jim Rice, AL:Bos.
	120	George Foster, NL:Cin. (3)
1979:	139	Don Baylor, AL:Cal.
	118	Dave Winfield, NL:SD
1980:	122	Cecil Cooper, AL:Mil.
	121	Mike Schmidt, NL:Phil.
1981:	91	Mike Schmidt, NL:Phil. (2)
	78	Eddie Murray, AL:Balt.

RUNS BATTED IN (CONTINUED)

1982:	133	Hal McRae, AL:KC
	109	Dale Murphy, NL:Atl.
	109	Al Oliver, NL:Mtl.
1983:	126	Cecil Cooper, AL:Mil. (2)
	126	Jim Rice, AL:Bos. (2)
	121	Dale Murphy, NL:Atl. (2)
1984:	123	Tony Armas, AL:Bos.
	106	Gary Carter, NL:Mtl.
	106	Mike Schmidt, NL:Phil. (3)
1985:	145	Don Mattingly, AL:NY
	125	Dave Parker, NL:Cin.
1986:	121	Joe Carter, AL:Clev.
	119	Mike Schmidt, NL:Phil. (4)
1987:	137	Andre Dawson, NL:Chi.
	134	George Bell, AL:Tor.
1988:	124	Jose Canseco, AL:Oak.
	109	Will Clark, NL:SF
1989:	125	Kevin Mitchell, NL:SF
	119	Ruben Sierra, AL:Tex.
1990:	132	Cecil Fielder, AL:Det.
	122	Matt Williams, NL:SF
1991:	133	Cecil Fielder, AL:Det. (2)
	117	Howard Johnson, NL:NY
1992:	124	Cecil Fielder, AL:Det. (3)
	109	Darren Daulton, NL:Phil.
1993:	129	Albert Belle, AL:Clev.
	123	Barry Bonds, NL:SF
1994:	116	Jeff Bagwell, NL:Hou.
	112	Kirby Puckett, AL:Minn.
1995:	128	Dante Bichette, NL:Col.
	126	Albert Belle, AL:Clev. (2)
	126	Mo Vaughn, AL:Bos.
1996:	150	Andres Galarraga, NL:Col.
	148	Albert Belle, AL:Clev. (3)
1997:	147	Ken Griffey, Jr. AL:Sea.
	140	Andres Galarraga, NL:Col.
1998:	158	Sammy Sosa, NL:Chi.
	157	Juan Gonzalez, AL:Tex.
1999:	165	Manny Ramirez, AL:Clev.
	147	Mark McGwire, NL:StL.
2000:	147	Todd Helton, NL:Col.
	145	Edgar Martinez, AL:Sea.
2001:	160	Sammy Sosa, NL:Chi. (2)
	141	Bret Boone, AL:Sea.
2002:	142	Alex Rodriguez, AL:Tex.
	128	Lance Berkman, NL:Hou.
2003:	145	Carlos Delgado, AL:Tor.
	141	Preston Wilson, NL:Col.
2004:	150	Miguel Tejada, AL:Balt.
	131	Vinny Castilla, NL:Col.
2005:	148	David Ortiz, AL:Bos.
	128	Andruw Jones, NL:Atl.
2006:	149	Ryan Howard, NL:Phil.
	137	David Ortiz, AL:Bos. (2)

RUNS SCORED

1900:	131	Roy Thomas, NL:Phil.
1901:	145	Nap Lajoie, AL:Phil.
	139	Jesse Burkett, NL:StL.
1902:	109	Dave Fultz, AL:Phil.
	109	Topsy Hartsel, AL:Phil.
	105	Honus Wagner, NL:Pitt.
1903:	137	Ginger Beaumont, NL:Pitt.
	108	Patsy Dougherty, AL:Bos.
1904:	113	Patsy Dougherty, AL:Bos.-NY (2)
	99	George Browne, NL:NY
1905:	124	Mike Donlin, NL:NY
	93	Harry Davis, AL:Phil.
1906:	103	Frank Chance, NL:Chi.
	103	Honus Wagner, NL:Pitt. (2)
	98	Elmer Flick, AL:Clev.
1907:	104	Spike Shannon, NL:NY
	102	Sam Crawford, AL:Det.
1908:	105	Matty McIntyre, AL:Det.
	101	Fred Tenney, NL:NY
1909:	126	Tommy Leach, NL:Pitt.
	115	Ty Cobb, AL:Det.
1910:	110	Sherry Magee, NL:Phil.
	106	Ty Cobb, AL:Det. (2)
1911:	148	Ty Cobb, AL:Det. (3)
	121	Jimmy Sheckard, NL:Chi.
1912:	137	Eddie Collins, AL:Phil.
	120	Bob Bescher, NL:Cin.
1913:	125	Eddie Collins, AL:Phil. (2)
	99	Max Carey, NL:Pitt.
	99	Tommy Leach, NL:Chi. (2)
1914:	122	Eddie Collins, AL:Phil. (3)
	100	George Burns, NL:NY
1915:	144	Ty Cobb, AL:Det. (4)
	89	Gavvy Cravath, NL:Phil.
1916:	113	Ty Cobb, AL:Det. (5)
	105	George Burns, NL:NY (2)
1917:	112	Donie Bush, AL:Det.
	103	George Burns, NL:NY (3)
1918:	88	Heinie Groh, NL:Cin.
	84	Ray Chapman, AL:Clev.
1919:	103	Babe Ruth, AL:Bos.
	86	George Burns, NL:NY (4)
1920:	158	Babe Ruth, AL:NY (2)
	115	George Burns, NL:NY (5)
1921:	177	Babe Ruth, AL:NY (3)
	131	Rogers Hornsby, NL:StL.
1922:	141	Rogers Hornsby, NL:StL. (2)
	134	George Sisler, AL:StL.
1923:	151	Babe Ruth, AL:NY (4)
	121	Ross Youngs, NL:NY
1924:	143	Babe Ruth, AL:NY (5)
	121	Frankie Frisch, NL:NY
	121	Rogers Hornsby, NL:StL. (3)
1925:	144	Kiki Cuyler, NL:Pitt.
	135	Johnny Mostil, AL:Chi.
1926:	139	Babe Ruth, AL:NY (6)
	113	Kiki Cuyler, NL:Pitt. (2)
1927:	158	Babe Ruth, AL:NY (7)
	133	Rogers Hornsby, NL:NY (4)
	133	Lloyd Waner, NL:Pitt.
1928:	163	Babe Ruth, AL:NY (8)
	142	Paul Waner, NL:Pitt.

1929:	156	Rogers Hornsby, NL:Chi. (5)
	131	Charlie Gehringer, AL:Det.
1930:	158	Chuck Klein, NL:Phil.
	152	Al Simmons, AL:Phil
1931:	163	Lou Gehrig, AL:NY
	121	Chuck Klein, NL:Phil. (2)
	121	Bill Terry, NL:NY
1932:	152	Chuck Klein, NL:Phil. (3)
	151	Jimmie Foxx, AL:Phil.
1933:	138	Lou Gehrig, AL:NY (2)
	122	Pepper Martin, NL:StL.
1934:	134	Charlie Gehringer, AL:Det. (2)
	122	Paul Waner, NL:Pitt. (2)
1935:	133	Augie Galan, NL:Chi.
	125	Lou Gehrig, AL:NY (3)
1936:	167	Lou Gehrig, AL:NY (4)
	122	Arky Vaughan, NL:Pitt.
1937:	151	Joe DiMaggio, AL:NY
	111	Joe Medwick, NL:StL.
1938:	144	Hank Greenberg, AL:Det.
	116	Mel Ott, NL:NY
1939:	139	Red Rolfe, AL:NY
	115	Bill Werber, NL:Cin.
1940:	134	Ted Williams, AL:Bos.
	113	Arky Vaughan, NL:Pitt. (2)
1941:	135	Ted Williams, AL:Bos. (2)
	117	Pete Reiser, NL:Brk.
1942:	141	Ted Williams, AL:Bos. (3)
	118	Mel Ott, NL:NY (2)
1943:	112	Arky Vaughan, NL:Brk. (3)
	102	George Case, AL:Wash.
1944:	125	Snuffy Stirnweiss, AL:NY
	116	Bill Nicholson, NL:Chi.
1945:	128	Eddie Stanky, NL:Brk.
	107	Snuffy Stirnweiss, AL:NY (2)
1946:	142	Ted Williams, AL:Bos. (4)
	124	Stan Musial, NL:StL.
1947:	137	Johnny Mize, NL:NY
	125	Ted Williams, AL:Bos. (5)
1948:	138	Tommy Henrich, AL:NY
	135	Stan Musial, NL:StL. (2)
1949:	150	Ted Williams, AL:Bos. (6)
	132	Pee Wee Reese, NL:Brk.
1950:	131	Dom DiMaggio, AL:Bos.
	120	Earl Torgeson, NL:Bos.
1951:	124	Ralph Kiner, NL:Pitt.
	124	Stan Musial, NL:StL. (3)
	113	Dom DiMaggio, AL:Bos. (2)
1952:	105	Solly Hemus, NL:StL.
	105	Stan Musial, NL:StL. (4)
	104	Larry Doby, AL:Clev.
1953:	132	Duke Snider, NL:Brk.
	115	Al Rosen, AL:Clev.
1954:	129	Mickey Mantle, AL:NY
	120	Stan Musial, NL:StL. (5)
	120	Duke Snider, NL:Brk. (2)
1955:	126	Duke Snider, NL:Brk. (3)
	123	Al Smith, AL:Clev.
1956:	132	Mickey Mantle, AL:NY (2)
	122	Frank Robinson, NL:Cin.
1957:	121	Mickey Mantle, AL:NY (3)
	118	Hank Aaron, NL:Mil.
1958:	127	Mickey Mantle, AL:NY (4)
	121	Willie Mays, NL:SF
1959:	131	Vada Pinson, NL:Cin.
	115	Eddie Yost, AL:Det.

RUNS SCORED (CONTINUED)

1960:	119	Mickey Mantle, AL:NY (5)	
	112	Bill Bruton, NL:Mil.	
1961:	132	Mickey Mantle, AL:NY (6)	
	132	Roger Maris, AL:NY	
	129	Willie Mays, NL:SF (2)	
1962:	134	Frank Robinson, NL:Cin. (2)	
	115	Albie Pearson, AL:LA	
1963:	121	Hank Aaron, NL:Mil. (2)	
	99	Bob Allison, AL:Minn.	
1964:	125	Dick Allen, NL:Phil.	
	109	Tony Oliva, AL:Minn.	
1965:	126	Tommy Harper, NL:Cin.	
	126	Zoilo Versalles, AL:Minn.	
1966:	122	Felipe Alou, NL:Atl.	
	122	Frank Robinson, AL:Balt.	
1967:	113	Hank Aaron, NL:Atl. (3)	
	113	Lou Brock, NL:StL.	
	112	Carl Yastrzemski, AL:Bos.	
1968:	98	Glenn Beckert, NL:Chi.	
	95	Dick McAuliffe, AL:Det.	
1969:	123	Reggie Jackson, AL:Oak.	
	120	Bobby Bonds, NL:SF	
	120	Pete Rose, NL:Cin.	
1970:	137	Billy Williams, NL:Chi.	
	125	Carl Yastrzemski, AL:Bos. (2)	
1971:	126	Lou Brock, NL:StL. (2)	
	99	Don Buford, AL:Balt.	
1972:	122	Joe Morgan, NL:Cin.	
	102	Bobby Murcer, AL:NY	
1973:	131	Bobby Bonds, NL:SF (2)	
	99	Reggie Jackson, AL:Oak. (2)	
1974:	110	Pete Rose, NL:Cin. (2)	
	93	Carl Yastrzemski, AL:Bos. (3)	
1975:	112	Pete Rose, NL:Cin. (3)	
	103	Fred Lynn, AL:Bos.	
1976:	130	Pete Rose, NL:Cin. (4)	
	104	Roy White, AL:NY	
1977:	128	Rod Carew, AL:Minn.	
	124	George Foster, NL:Cin.	
1978:	126	Ron LeFlore, AL:Det.	
	104	Ivan DeJesus, NL:Chi.	
1979:	120	Don Baylor, AL:Cal.	
	116	Keith Hernandez, NL:StL.	
1980:	133	Willie Wilson, AL:KC	
	111	Keith Hernandez, NL:StL. (2)	
1981:	89	Rickey Henderson, AL:Oak.	
	78	Mike Schmidt, NL:Phil.	
1982:	136	Paul Molitor, AL:Mil.	
	120	Lonnie Smith, NL:StL.	
1983:	133	Tim Raines, NL:Mtl.	
	121	Cal Ripken, AL:Balt.	
1984:	121	Dwight Evans, AL:Bos.	
	114	Ryne Sandberg, NL:Chi.	
1985:	146	Rickey Henderson, AL:NY (2)	
	118	Dale Murphy, NL:Atl.	
1986:	130	Rickey Henderson, AL:NY (3)	
	107	Tony Gwynn, NL:SD	
	107	Von Hayes, NL:Phil.	
1987:	123	Tim Raines, NL:Mtl. (2)	
	114	Paul Molitor, AL:Mil. (2)	
1988:	128	Wade Boggs, AL:Bos.	
	109	Brett Butler, NL:SF	

1989:	113	Wade Boggs, AL:Bos. (2)	
	113	Rickey Henderson, AL:NY-Oak. (4)	
	104	Will Clark, NL:SF	
	104	Howard Johnson, NL:NY	
	104	Ryne Sandberg, NL:Chi. (2)	
1990:	119	Rickey Henderson, AL:Oak. (5)	
	116	Ryne Sandberg, NL:Chi. (3)	
1991:	133	Paul Molitor, AL:Mil. (3)	
	112	Brett Butler, NL:LA (2)	
1992:	114	Tony Phillips, AL:Det.	
	109	Barry Bonds, NL:Pitt.	
1993:	143	Len Dykstra, NL:Phil.	
	124	Rafael Palmeiro, AL:Tex.	
1994:	106	Frank Thomas, AL:Chi.	
	104	Jeff Bagwell, NL:Hou.	
1995:	123	Craig Biggio, NL:Hou.	
	121	Albert Belle, AL:Clev.	
	121	Edgar Martinez, AL:Sea.	
1996:	142	Ellis Burks, NL:Col.	
	141	Alex Rodriguez, AL:Sea	
1997:	146	Craig Biggio, NL:Hou. (2)	
	125	Ken Griffey, Jr. AL:Sea.	
1998:	134	Sammy Sosa, NL:Chi.	
	127	Derek Jeter, AL:NY	
1999:	143	Jeff Bagwell, NL:Hou. (2)	
	138	Roberto Alomar, AL:Clev.	
2000:	152	Jeff Bagwell, NL:Hou. (3)	
	136	Johnny Damon, AL:KC	
2001:	146	Sammy Sosa, NL:Chi. (2)	
	133	Alex Rodriguez, AL:Tex. (2)	
2002:	128	Alfonso Soriano, AL:NY	
	122	Sammy Sosa, NL:Chi. (3)	
2003:	137	Albert Pujols, NL:StL.	
	124	Alex Rodriguez, AL:Tex. (3)	
2004:	133	Albert Pujols, NL:StL. (2)	
	124	Vladimir Guerrero, AL:Ana.	
2005:	129	Albert Pujols, NL:StL. (3)	
	124	Alex Rodriguez, AL:NY (4)	
2006:	134	Grady Sizemore, AL:Clev.	
	131	Chase Utley, NL:Phil.	

HITS

1900:	208	Willie Keeler, NL:Brk.
1901:	229	Nap Lajoie, AL:Phil.
	228	Jesse Burkett, NL:StL.
1902:	194	Ginger Beaumont, NL:Pitt.
	194	Piano Legs Hickman, AL:Bos.-Clev.
1903:	209	Ginger Beaumont, NL:Pitt. (2)
	195	Patsy Dougherty, AL:Bos.
1904:	211	Nap Lajoie, AL:Clev. (2)
	185	Ginger Beaumont, NL:Pitt. (3)
1905:	219	Cy Seymour, NL:Cin.
	187	George Stone, AL:StL.
1906:	214	Nap Lajoie, AL:Clev. (3)
	176	Harry Steinfeldt, NL:Chi.
1907:	212	Ty Cobb, AL:Det.
	187	Ginger Beaumont, NL:Bos. (4)
1908:	201	Honus Wagner, NL:Pitt.
	188	Ty Cobb, AL:Det. (2)
1909:	216	Ty Cobb, AL:Det. (3)
	172	Larry Doyle, NL:NY
1910:	227	Nap Lajoie, AL:Clev. (4)
	178	Bobby Byrne, NL:Pitt.
	178	Honus Wagner, NL:Pitt. (2)
1911:	248	Ty Cobb, AL:Det. (4)
	192	Doc Miller, NL:Bos.
1912:	227	Ty Cobb, AL:Det. (5)
	207	Heinie Zimmerman, NL:Chi.
1913:	197	Joe Jackson, AL:Clev.
	179	Gavvy Cravath, NL:Phil.
1914:	193	Tris Speaker, AL:Bos.
	171	Sherry Magee, NL:Phil.
1915:	208	Ty Cobb, AL:Det. (6)
	189	Larry Doyle, NL:NY (2)
1916:	211	Tris Speaker, AL:Clev. (2)
	184	Hal Chase, NL:Cin.
1917:	225	Ty Cobb, AL:Det. (7)
	182	Heinie Groh, NL:Cin.
1918:	178	George Burns, AL:Phil.
	161	Charlie Hollocher, NL:Chi.
1919:	191	Ty Cobb, AL:Det. (8)
	191	Bob Veach, AL:Det.
	164	Ivy Olson, NL:Brk.
1920:	257	George Sisler, AL:StL.
	218	Rogers Hornsby, NL:StL.
1921:	237	Harry Heilmann, AL:Det.
	235	Rogers Hornsby, NL:StL. (2)
1922:	250	Rogers Hornsby, NL:StL. (3)
	246	George Sisler, AL:StL. (2)
1923:	223	Frankie Frisch, NL:NY
	222	Charlie Jamieson, AL:Clev.
1924:	227	Rogers Hornsby, NL:StL. (4)
	216	Sam Rice, AL:Wash.
1925:	253	Al Simmons, AL:Phil.
	227	Jim Bottomley, NL:StL.
1926:	216	George Burns, AL:Clev. (2)
	216	Sam Rice, AL:Wash. (2)
	201	Eddie Brown, NL:Bos.
1927:	237	Paul Waner, NL:Pitt.
	231	Earle Combs, AL:NY
1928:	241	Heinie Manush, AL:StL.
	231	Freddie Lindstrom, NL:NY
1929:	254	Lefty O'Doul, NL:Phil.
	215	Dale Alexander, AL:Det.
	215	Charlie Gehringer, AL:Det.
1930:	254	Bill Terry, NL:NY
	225	Johnny Hodapp, AL:Clev.

1931:	214	Lloyd Waner, NL:Pitt.
	211	Lou Gehrig, AL:NY
1932:	226	Chuck Klein, NL:Phil.
	216	Al Simmons, AL:Phil. (2)
1933:	223	Chuck Klein, NL:Phil. (2)
	221	Heinie Manush, AL:Wash. (2)
1934:	217	Paul Waner, NL:Pitt. (2)
	214	Charlie Gehringer, AL:Det. (2)
1935:	227	Billy Herman, NL:Chi.
	216	Joe Vosmik, AL:Clev.
1936:	232	Earl Averill, AL:Clev.
	223	Joe Medwick, NL:StL.
1937:	237	Joe Medwick, NL:StL. (2)
	218	Beau Bell, AL:StL.
1938:	209	Frank McCormick, NL:Cin.
	201	Joe Vosmik, AL:Bos. (2)
1939:	213	Red Rolfe, AL:NY
	209	Frank McCormick, NL:Cin. (2)
1940:	200	Doc Cramer, AL:Bos.
	200	Barney McCosky, AL:Det.
	200	Rip Radcliff, AL:StL.
	191	Stan Hack, NL:Chi.
	191	Frank McCormick, NL:Cin. (3)
1941:	218	Cecil Travis, AL:Wash.
	186	Stan Hack, NL:Chi. (2)
1942:	205	Johnny Pesky, AL:Bos.
	188	Enos Slaughter, NL:StL.
1943:	220	Stan Musial, NL:StL.
	200	Dick Wakefield, AL:Det.
1944:	205	Snuffy Stirnweiss, AL:NY
	197	Phil Cavarretta, NL:Chi.
	197	Stan Musial, NL:StL. (2)
1945:	224	Tommy Holmes, NL:Bos.
	195	Snuffy Stirnweiss, AL:NY (2)
1946:	228	Stan Musial, NL:StL. (3)
	208	Johnny Pesky, AL:Bos. (2)
1947:	207	Johnny Pesky, AL:Bos. (3)
	191	Tommy Holmes, NL:Bos. (2)
1948:	230	Stan Musial, NL:StL. (4)
	207	Bob Dillinger, AL:StL.
1949:	207	Stan Musial, NL:StL. (5)
	203	Dale Mitchell, AL:Clev.
1950:	218	George Kell, AL:Det.
	199	Duke Snider, NL:Brk.
1951:	221	Richie Ashburn, NL:Phil.
	191	George Kell, AL:Det. (2)
1952:	194	Stan Musial, NL:StL. (6)
	192	Nellie Fox, AL:Chi.
1953:	209	Harvey Kuenn, AL:Det.
	205	Richie Ashburn, NL:Phil. (2)
1954:	212	Don Mueller, NL:NY
	201	Nellie Fox, AL:Chi. (2)
	201	Harvey Kuenn, AL:Det. (2)
1955:	200	Al Kaline, AL:Det.
	192	Ted Kluszewski, NL:Cin.
1956:	200	Hank Aaron, NL:Mil.
	196	Harvey Kuenn, AL:Det. (3)
1957:	200	Red Schoendienst, NL:NY-Mil.
	196	Nellie Fox, AL:Chi. (3)
1958:	215	Richie Ashburn, NL:Phil. (3)
	187	Nellie Fox, AL:Chi. (4)
1959:	223	Hank Aaron, NL:Mil. (2)
	198	Harvey Kuenn, AL:Det. (4)
1960:	190	Willie Mays, NL:SF
	184	Minnie Minoso, AL:Chi.

HITS (CONTINUED)

961:	208	Vada Pinson, NL:Cin.
	193	Norm Cash, AL:Det.
962:	230	Tommy Davis, NL:LA
	209	Bobby Richardson, AL:NY
963:	204	Vada Pinson, NL:Cin. (2)
	183	Carl Yastrzemski, AL:Bos.
964:	217	Tony Oliva, AL:Minn.
	211	Roberto Clemente, NL:Pitt.
	211	Curt Flood, NL:StL.
965:	209	Pete Rose, NL:Cin.
	185	Tony Oliva, AL:Minn. (2)
966:	218	Felipe Alou, NL:Atl.
	191	Tony Oliva, AL:Minn. (3)
967:	209	Roberto Clemente, NL:Pitt. (2)
	189	Carl Yastrzemski, AL:Bos. (2)
968:	210	Felipe Alou, NL:Atl. (2)
	210	Pete Rose, NL:Cin. (2)
	177	Bert Campaneris, AL:Oak.
969:	231	Matty Alou, NL:Pitt.
	197	Tony Oliva, AL:Minn. (4)
970:	205	Pete Rose NL:Cin. (3)
	205	Billy Williams, NL:Chi.
	204	Tony Oliva, AL:Minn. (5)
971:	230	Joe Torre, NL:StL.
	204	Cesar Tovar, AL:Minn.
972:	198	Pete Rose, NL:Cin. (4)
	181	Joe Rudi, AL:Oak.
973:	230	Pete Rose, NL:Cin. (5)
	203	Rod Carew, AL:Minn.
974:	218	Rod Carew, AL:Minn. (2)
	214	Ralph Garr, NL:Atl.
975:	213	Dave Cash, NL:Phil.
	195	George Brett, AL:KC
976:	215	Pete Rose, NL:Cin. (6)
	215	George Brett, AL:KC (2)
977:	239	Rod Carew, AL:Minn. (3)
	215	Dave Parker, NL:Pitt.
978:	213	Jim Rice, AL:Bos.
	202	Steve Garvey, NL:LA
979:	212	George Brett, AL:KC (3)
	211	Garry Templeton, NL:StL.
980:	230	Willie Wilson, AL:KC
	200	Steve Garvey, NL:LA (2)
981:	140	Pete Rose, NL:Phil. (7)
	135	Rickey Henderson, AL:Oak.
982:	210	Robin Yount, AL:Mil.
	204	Al Oliver, NL:Mtl.
983:	211	Cal Ripken, AL:Balt.
	189	Jose Cruz, NL:Hou.
	189	Andre Dawson, NL:Mtl.
984:	213	Tony Gwynn, NL:SD
	207	Don Mattingly, AL:NY
985:	240	Wade Boggs, AL:Bos.
	216	Willie McGee, NL:StL.
986:	238	Don Mattingly AL:NY (2)
	211	Tony Gwynn, NL:SD (2)
987:	218	Tony Gwynn, NL:SD (3)
	207	Kirby Puckett, AL:Minn.
	207	Kevin Seitzer, AL:KC
988:	234	Kirby Puckett, AL:Minn. (2)
	184	Andres Galarraga, NL:Mtl.
989:	215	Kirby Puckett, AL:Minn. (3)
	203	Tony Gwynn, NL:SD (4)

1990:	199	Willie McGee, NL:StL.-AL:Oak.
	192	Brett Butler, NL:SF
	192	Len Dykstra, NL:Phil.
	191	Rafael Palmeiro, AL:Tex.
1991:	216	Paul Molitor, AL:Mil.
	187	Terry Pendleton, NL:Atl.
1992:	210	Kirby Puckett, AL:Minn. (4)
	199	Terry Pendleton, NL:Atl. (2)
	199	Andy Van Slyke, NL:Pitt.
1993:	211	Paul Molitor, AL:Tor. (2)
	194	Len Dykstra, NL:Phil. (2)
1994:	165	Tony Gwynn, NL:SD (5)
	160	Kenny Lofton, AL:Clev.
1995:	197	Dante Bichette, NL:Col.
	197	Tony Gwynn, NL:SD (6)
	186	Lance Johnson, AL:Chi.
1996:	227	Lance Johnson, NL:NY (AL 1)
	225	Paul Molitor, AL:Minn. (3)
1997:	220	Tony Gwynn, NL:SD (7)
	209	Nomar Garciaparra, AL:Bos
1998:	219	Dante Bichette, NL:Col.(2)
	213	Alex Rodriguez, AL:Sea.
1999:	219	Derek Jeter, AL:NY
	206	Luis Gonzalez, NL:Ari.
2000:	240	Darin Erstad, AL:Ana.
	216	Todd Helton, NL:Col.
2001:	242	Ichiro Suzuki, AL:Sea.
	206	Rich Aurilia, NL:SF
2002:	209	Alfonso Soriano, AL:NY
	206	Vladimir Guerrero, NL:Mtl.
2003:	215	Vernon Wells, AL:Tor.
	212	Albert Pujols, NL:StL.
2004:	262	Ichiro Suzuki, AL:Sea. (2)
	221	Juan Pierre, NL:Fla.
2005:	221	Michael Young, AL:Tex.
	199	Derrek Lee, NL:Chi.
2006:	224	Ichiro Suzuki, AL:Sea. (3)
	204	Juan Pierre, NL:Chi. (2)

SINGLES

1900:	179	Willie Keeler, Brk.
1901:	180	Jesse Burkett, NL:StL.
	155	Irv Waldron, AL:Mil.-Wash.
1902:	167	Ginger Beaumont, NL:Pitt.
	150	Fielder Jones, AL:Chi.
1903:	166	Ginger Beaumont, NL:Pitt. (2)
	160	Parsy Dougherty, AL:Bos.
1904:	162	Willie Keeler, AL:NY (2)
	158	Ginger Beaumont, NL:Pitt. (3)
1905:	162	Mike Donlin, NL:NY
	147	Willie Keeler, AL:NY (3)
1906:	167	Willie Keeler, AL:NY (4)
	141	Miller Huggins, NL:Cin.
	141	Spike Shannon, NL:StL.-NY
1907:	163	Ty Cobb, AL:Det.
	163	George Stone, AL:StL.
	150	Ginger Beaumont, NL:Bos. (4)
1908:	153	Mike Donlin, NL:NY (2)
	131	Matty McIntyre, AL:Det.
	131	George Stone, AL:StL. (2)
1909:	164	Ty Cobb, AL:Det. (2)
	147	Eddie Grant, NL:Phil.
1910:	162	Nap Lajoie, AL:Clev.
	134	Eddie Grant, NL:Phil. (2)
1911:	169	Ty Cobb, AL:Det. (3)
	146	Jake Daubert, NL:Brk.
	146	Doc Miller, NL:Bos.
1912:	167	Ty Cobb, AL:Det. (4)
	159	Bill Sweeney, NL:Bos.
1913:	152	Jake Daubert, NL:Brk. (2)
	145	Eddie Collins, AL:Phil.
1914:	160	Stuffy McInnis, AL:Phil.
	128	Beals Becker, NL:Phil.
1915:	161	Ty Cobb, AL:Det. (5)
	135	Larry Doyle, NL:NY
1916:	160	Tris Speaker, AL:Clev.
	142	Dave Robertson, NL:NY
1917:	151	Ty Cobb, AL:Det. (6)
	151	Clyde Milan, AL:Wash.
	141	Benny Kauff, NL:NY
	141	Edd Roush, NL:Cin.
1918:	141	George Burns, AL:Phil.
	130	Charlie Hollocher, NL:Chi.
1919:	144	Sam Rice, AL:Wash.
	140	Ivy Olson, NL:Brk.
1920:	171	George Sisler, AL:StL.
	170	Milt Stock, NL:StL.
1921:	179	Jack Tobin, AL:StL.
	161	Carson Bigbee, NL:Pitt.
1922:	178	George Sisler, AL:StL. (2)
	166	Carson Bigbee, NL:Pitt. (2)
1923:	172	Charlie Jamieson, AL:Clev.
	169	Frankie Frisch, NL:NY
1924:	168	Charlie Jamieson, AL:Clev. (2)
	149	Zack Wheat, NL:Brk.
1925:	182	Sam Rice, AL:Wash. (2)
	164	Milt Stock, NL:Brk. (2)
1926:	167	Sam Rice, AL:Wash. (3)
	160	Eddie Brown, NL:Bos.
1927:	198	Lloyd Waner, NL:Pitt.
	166	Earle Combs, AL:NY
1928:	180	Lloyd Waner, NL:Pitt. (2)
	161	Heinie Manush, AL:StL.

1929:	181	Lefty O'Doul, NL:Phil.
	181	Lloyd Waner, NL:Pitt. (3)
	151	Earle Combs, AL:NY (2)
1930:	177	Bill Terry, NL:NY
	158	Sam Rice, AL:Wash. (4)
1931:	172	Lloyd Waner, NL:Pitt. (4)
	142	Oscar Melillo, AL:StL.
	142	John Stone, AL:Det.
1932:	158	Lefty O'Doul, NL:Brk. (2)
	145	Heinie Manush, AL:Wash. (2)
1933:	167	Heinie Manush, AL:Wash. (3)
	162	Chick Fullis, NL:Phil.
1934:	169	Bell Terry, NL:NY (2)
	157	Doc Cramer, AL:Phil.
1935:	170	Doc Cramer, AL:Phil. (2)
	160	Woody Jensen, NL:Pitt.
1936:	161	Rip Radcliff, AL:Chi.
	160	Joe Moore, NL:NY
1937:	178	Paul Waner, NL:Pitt.
	162	Buddy Lewis, AL:Wash.
1938:	160	Frank McCormick, NL:Cin.
	158	Mel Almada, AL:Wash.-StL.
1939:	162	Buddy Hassett, NL:Bos.
	147	Doc Cramer, AL:Bos. (3)
1940:	160	Doc Cramer, AL:Bos. (4)
	141	Burgess Whitehead, NL:NY
1941:	153	Cecil Travis, AL:Wash.
	141	Stan Hack, NL:Chi.
1942:	165	Johnny Pesky, AL:Bos.
	127	Enos Slaughter, NL:StL.
1943:	172	Mickey Witek, NL:NY
	159	Doc Cramer, AL:Det. (5)
1944:	146	Snuffy Stirnweiss, AL:NY
	142	Phil Cavarretta, NL:Chi.
1945:	155	Stan Hack, NL:Chi. (2)
	139	Irv Hall, AL:Phil.
1946:	159	Johnny Pesky, AL:Bos. (2)
	142	Stan Musial, NL:StL.
1947:	172	Johnny Pesky, AL:Bos. (3)
	146	Tommy Holmes, NL:Bos.
1948:	162	Dale Mitchell, AL:Clev.
	150	Stan Rojek, NL:Pitt.
1949:	161	Dale Mitchell, AL:Clev. (2)
	160	Red Schoendienst, NL:StL.
1950:	150	Phil Rizzuto, AL:NY
	143	Eddie Waitkus, NL:Phil.
1951:	181	Richie Ashburn, NL:Phil.
	150	George Kell, AL:Det.
1952:	157	Nellie Fox, AL:Chi.
	145	Bobby Adams, NL:Cin.
1953:	169	Richie Ashburn, NL:Phil. (2)
	167	Harvey Kuenn, AL:Det.
1954:	167	Nellie Fox, AL:Chi. (2)
	165	Don Mueller, NL:NY
1955:	157	Nellie Fox, AL:Chi. (3)
	152	Don Mueller, NL:NY (2)
1956:	158	Nellie Fox, AL:Chi. (4)
	157	Johnny Temple, NL:Cin.
1957:	155	Nellie Fox, AL:Chi. (5)
	152	Richie Ashburn, NL:Phil. (3)
1958:	176	Richie Ashburn, NL:Phil. (4)
	160	Nellie Fox, AL:Chi. (6)
1959:	149	Nellie Fox, AL:Chi. (7)
	144	Don Blasingame, NL:StL.
1960:	154	Dick Groat, NL:Pitt.
	139	Nellie Fox, AL:Chi. (8)

SINGLES (CONTINUED)

961:	150	Vada Pinson, NL:Cin.
	150	Maury Wills, NL:LA
	148	Bobby Richardson, AL:NY
962:	179	Maury Wills, NL:LA (2)
	158	Bobby Richardson, AL:NY (2)
963:	152	Curt Flood, NL:StL.
	139	Albie Pearson, AL:LA
964:	178	Curt Flood, NL:StL. (2)
	148	Bobby Richardson, AL:NY (3)
965:	165	Maury Wills, NL:LA (3)
	129	Don Buford, AL:Chi.
966:	160	Sonny Jackson, NL:Hou.
	143	Luis Aparicio, AL:Balt.
967:	162	Maury Wills, NL:Pitt. (4)
	140	Horace Clarke, AL:NY
968:	160	Curt Flood, NL:StL. (3)
	139	Bert Campaneris, AL:Oak.
969:	183	Matty Alou, NL:Pitt.
	147	Horace Clarke, AL:NY (2)
970:	171	Matty Alou, NL:Pitt. (2)
	156	Alex Johnson, AL:Cal.
971:	180	Ralph Garr, NL:Atl.
	171	Cesar Tovar, AL:Minn.
972:	156	Lou Brock, NL:StL.
	143	Rod Carew, AL:Minn.
973:	181	Pete Rose, NL:Cin.
	156	Rod Carew, AL:Minn. (2)
974:	180	Rod Carew, AL:Minn. (3)
	167	Dave Cash, NL:Phil.
975:	166	Dave Cash, NL:Phil. (2)
	151	Thurman Munson, AL:NY
976:	164	Willie Montanez, NL:SF-Atl.
	160	George Brett, AL:KC
977:	171	Rod Carew, AL:Minn. (4)
	155	Garry Templeton, NL:StL.
978:	153	Larry Bowa, NL:Phil.
	153	Ron LeFlore, AL:Det.
979:	159	Pete Rose, NL:Phil. (2)
	148	Willie Wilson, AL:KC
980:	184	Willie Wilson, AL:KC (2)
	155	Gene Richards, NL:SD
981:	117	Pete Rose, NL:Phil. (3)
	115	Willie Wilson, AL:KC (3)
982:	157	Willie Wilson, AL:KC (4)
	147	Bill Buckner, NL:Chi.
983:	160	Rafael Ramirez, NL:Atl.
	154	Wade Boggs, AL:Bos.
984:	177	Tony Gwynn, NL:SD
	162	Wade Boggs, AL:Bos. (2)
985:	187	Wade Boggs, AL:Bos. (3)
	162	Willie McGee, NL:StL.
986:	161	Tony Fernandez, AL:Tor.
	157	Tony Gwynn, NL:SD (2)
	157	Steve Sax, NL:LA
987:	162	Tony Gwynn, NL:SD (3)
	151	Kevin Seitzer, AL:KC
988:	163	Kirby Puckett, AL:Minn.
	147	Steve Sax, NL:LA (2)
989:	171	Steve Sax, NL:NY (NL 2)
	165	Tony Gwynn, NL:SD (4)
990:	160	Brett Butler, NL:SF
	136	Rafael Palmeiro, AL:Tex.
991:	162	Brett Butler, NL:LA (2)
	156	Julio Franco, AL:Tex.

1992:	152	Carlos Baerga, AL:Clev.
	143	Brett Butler, NL:LA (3)
1993:	149	Brett Butler, NL:LA (4)
	148	Kenny Lofton, AL:Clev.
1994:	117	Tony Gwynn, NL:SD (5)
	107	Kenny Lofton, AL:Clev. (2)
	107	Paul Molitor, AL:Tor.
1995:	154	Tony Gwynn, NL:SD (6)
	151	Otis Nixon, AL:Tex.
1996:	167	Paul Molitor, AL:Minn. (2)
	166	Lance Johnson, NL:NY
1997:	152	Tony Gwynn, NL:SD (7)
	142	Garret Anderson, AL:Ana.
	142	Derek Jeter, AL:NY
1998:	151	Derek Jeter, AL:NY (2)
	149	Tony Womack, NL:Pitt.
1999:	152	Randy Velarde, AL:Ana.-Oak.
	149	Doug Glanville, NL:Phil.
2000:	170	Darin Erstad, AL:Ana.
	158	Luis Castillo, NL:Fla.
2001:	192	Ichiro Suzuki, AL:Sea.
	163	Juan Pierre, NL:Col.
2002:	165	Ichiro Suzuki, AL:Sea. (2)
	160	Luis Castillo, NL:Fla. (2)
2003:	168	Juan Pierre, NL:Fla. (2)
	162	Ichiro Suzuki, AL:Sea. (3)
2004:	225	Ichiro Suzuki, AL:Sea. (4)
	184	Juan Pierre, NL:Fla. (3)
2005:	158	Ichiro Suzuki, AL:Sea. (5)
	152	Willy Taveras, NL:Hou.
2006:	186	Ichiro Suzuki, AL:Sea. (6)
	156	Juan Pierre, NL:Chi. (4)

DOUBLES

1900:	45	Honus Wagner, NL:Pitt.
1901:	48	Nap Lajoie, AL:Phil.
	39	Jake Beckley, NL:Cin.
	39	Honus Wagner, NL:Pitt. (2)
1902:	43	Harry Davis, AL:Phil.
	43	Ed Delahanty, AL:Wash.
	33	Honus Wagner, NL:Pitt. (3)
1903:	45	Socks Seybold, AL:Phil.
	32	Fred Clarke, NL:Pitt.
	32	Sam Mertes, NL:NY
	32	Harry Steinfeldt, NL:Cin.
1904:	50	Nap Lajoie, AL:Clev. (2)
	44	Honus Wagner, NL:Pitt. (4)
1905:	47	Harry Davis, AL:Phil. (2)
	40	Cy Seymour, NL:Cin.
1906:	49	Nap Lajoie, AL:Clev. (3)
	38	Honus Wagner, NL:Pitt. (5)
1907:	38	Honus Wagner, NL:Pitt. (6)
	35	Harry Davis, AL:Phil. (3)
1908:	39	Honus Wagner, NL:Pitt. (7)
	36	Ty Cobb, AL:Det.
1909:	39	Honus Wagner, NL:Pitt. (8)
	35	Sam Crawford, AL:Det.
1910:	53	Nap Lajoie, AL:Clev. (4)
	43	Bobby Byrne, NL:Pitt.
1911:	47	Ty Cobb, AL:Det. (2)
	38	Ed Konetchy, NL:StL.
1912:	53	Tris Speaker, AL:Bos.
	41	Heinie Zimmerman, NL:Chi.
1913:	40	Red Smith, NL:Brk.
	39	Joe Jackson, AL:Clev.
1914:	46	Tris Speaker, AL:Bos. (2)
	39	Sherry Magee, NL:Phil.
1915:	40	Larry Doyle, NL:NY
	40	Bobby Veach, AL:Det.
1916:	42	Bert Niehoff, NL:Phil.
	41	Jack Graney, AL:Clev.
	41	Tris Speaker, AL:Clev. (3)
1917:	44	Ty Cobb, AL:Det. (3)
	39	Heinie Groh, NL:Cin.
1918:	33	Tris Speaker, AL:Clev. (4)
	28	Heinie Groh, NL:Cin. (2)
1919:	45	Bobby Veach, AL:Det. (2)
	31	Ross Youngs, NL:NY
1920:	50	Tris Speaker, AL:Clev. (5)
	44	Rogers Hornsby, NL:StL.
1921:	52	Tris Speaker, AL:Clev. (6)
	44	Rogers Hornsby, NL:StL. (2)
1922:	48	Tris Speaker, AL:Clev. (7)
	46	Rogers Hornsby, NL:StL. (3)
1923:	59	Tris Speaker, AL:Clev. (8)
	41	Edd Roush, NL:Cin.
1924:	45	Harry Heilmann, AL:Det.
	45	Joe Sewell, AL:Clev.
	43	Rogers Hornsby, NL:StL. (4)
1925:	44	Jim Bottomley, NL:StL.
	44	Marty McManus, AL:StL.
1926:	64	George Burns, AL:Clev.
	40	Jim Bottomley, Jim NL:StL. (2)
1927:	52	Lou Gehrig, Lou AL:NY
	46	Riggs Stephenson, NL:Chi.
1928:	50	Paul Waner, NL:Pitt.
	47	Lou Gehrig, AL:NY (2)
	47	Heinie Manush, AL:StL.

1929:	52	Johnny Frederick, NL:Brk.
	45	Charlie Gehringer, AL:Det.
	45	Roy Johnson, AL:Det.
	45	Heinie Manush, AL:StL. (2)
1930:	59	Chuck Klein, NL:Phil.
	51	Johnny Hodapp, AL:Clev.
1931:	67	Earl Webb, AL:Bos.
	46	Sparky Adams, NL:StL.
1932:	63	Paul Waner, NL:Pitt. (2)
	47	Eric McNair, AL:Phil.
1933:	45	Joe Cronin, AL:Wash.
	44	Chuck Klein, NL:Phil. (2)
1934:	63	Hank Greenberg, AL:Det.
	42	Ethan Allen, NL:Phil.
	42	Kiki Cuyler, NL:Chi.
1935:	57	Billy Herman, NL:Chi.
	47	Joe Vosmik, AL:Clev.
1936:	64	Joe Medwick, NL:StL.
	60	Charlie Gehringer, AL:Det. (2)
1937:	56	Joe Medwick, NL:StL. (2)
	51	Beau Bell, AL:StL.
1938:	51	Joe Cronin, AL:Bos. (2)
	47	Joe Medwick, NL:StL. (3)
1939:	52	Enos Slaughter, NL:StL.
	46	Red Rolfe, AL:NY
1940:	50	Hank Greenberg, AL:Det. (2)
	44	Frank McCormick, NL:Cin.
1941:	45	Lou Boudreau, AL:Clev.
	39	Johnny Mize, NL:StL.
	39	Pete Reiser, NL:Brk.
1942:	40	Don Kolloway, AL:Chi.
	38	Marty Marion, NL:StL.
1943:	48	Stan Musial, NL:StL.
	38	Dick Wakefield, AL:Det.
1944:	51	Stan Musial, NL:StL. (2)
	45	Lou Boudreau, AL:Clev. (2)
1945:	47	Tommy Holmes, NL:Bos.
	35	Wally Moses, AL:Chi.
1946:	51	Mickey Vernon, AL:Wash.
	50	Stan Musial, NL:StL. (3)
1947:	45	Lou Boudreau, AL:Clev. (3)
	38	Eddie Miller, NL:Cin.
1948:	46	Stan Musial, NL:StL. (4)
	44	Ted Williams, AL:Bos.
1949:	41	Stan Musial, NL:StL. (5)
	39	Ted Williams, AL:Bos. (2)
1950:	56	George Kell, AL:Det.
	43	Red Schoendienst, NL:StL.
1951:	41	Alvin Dark, NL:NY
	36	George Kell, AL:Det. (2)
	36	Sam Mele, AL:Wash.
	36	Eddie Yost, AL:Wash.
1952:	43	Ferris Fain, AL:Phil.
	42	Stan Musial, NL:StL. (6)
1953:	53	Stan Musial, NL:StL. (7)
	43	Mickey Vernon, AL:Wash. (2)
1954:	41	Stan Musial, NL:StL. (8)
	33	Mickey Vernon, AL:Wash. (3)
1955:	38	Harvey Kuenn, AL:Det.
	37	Hank Aaron, NL:Mil.
	37	Johnny Logan, NL:Mil.
1956:	40	Jimmy Piersall, AL:Bos.
	34	Hank Aaron, NL:Mil. (2)
1957:	39	Don Hoak, NL:Cin.
	36	Billy Gardner, AL:Balt.
	36	Minnie Minoso, AL:Chi.

DOUBLES (CONTINUED)

)58:	39	Harvey Kuenn, AL:Det. (2)
	38	Orlando Cepeda, NL:SF
)59:	47	Vada Pinson, NL:Cin.
	42	Harvey Kuenn, AL:Det. (3)
)60:	37	Vada Pinson, NL:Cin. (2)
	36	Tito Francona, AL:Clev.
)61:	41	Al Kaline, AL:Det.
	39	Hank Aaron, NL:Mil. (3)
)62:	51	Frank Robinson, NL:Cin.
	45	Floyd Robinson, AL:Chi.
)63:	43	Dick Groat, NL:StL.
	40	Carl Yastrzemski, AL:Bos.
)64:	44	Lee Maye, NL:Mil.
	43	Tony Oliva, AL:Minn.
)65:	45	Zoilo Versalles, AL:Minn.
	45	Carl Yastrzemski, AL:Bos. (2)
	40	Hank Aaron, NL:Mil. (4)
)66:	40	Johnny Callison, NL:Phil.
	39	Carl Yastrzemski, AL:Bos. (3)
)67:	44	Rusty Staub, NL:Hou.
	34	Tony Oliva, AL:Minn. (2)
)68:	46	Lou Brock, NL:StL.
	37	Reggie Smith, AL:Bos.
)69:	41	Matty Alou, NL:Pitt.
	39	Tony Oliva, AL:Minn. (3)
)70:	47	Wes Parker, NL:LA
	36	Tony Oliva, AL:Minn. (4)
	36	Amos Otis, AL:KC
	36	Cesar Tovar, AL:Minn.
)71:	40	Cesar Cedeno, NL:Hou.
	33	Reggie Smith, AL:Bos. (2)
)72:	39	Cesar Cedeno, NL:Hou. (2)
	39	Willie Montanez, NL:Phil.
	33	Lou Piniella, AL:KC
)73:	43	Willie Stargell, NL:Pitt.
	32	Sal Bando, AL:Oak
	32	Pedro Garcia, AL:Mil.
)74:	45	Pete Rose, NL:Cin.
	39	Joe Rudi, AL:Oak.
)75:	47	Fred Lynn, AL:Bos.
	47	Pete Rose, NL:Cin. (2)
)76:	42	Pete Rose, NL:Cin. (3)
	40	Amos Otis, AL:KC (2)
)77:	54	Hal McRae, AL:KC
	44	Dave Parker, NL:Pitt.
)78:	51	Pete Rose, NL:Cin. (4)
	45	George Brett, AL:KC
)79:	48	Keith Hernandez, NL:StL.
	44	Cecil Cooper, AL:Mil.
	44	Chet Lemon, AL:Chi.
)80:	49	Robin Yount, AL:Mil.
	42	Pete Rose, NL:Phil. (5)
)81:	35	Bill Buckner, NL:Chi.
	35	Cecil Cooper, AL:Mil. (2)
)82:	46	Hal McRae, AL:KC (2)
	46	Robin Yount, AL:Mil. (2)
	43	Al Oliver, NL:Mtl.
)83:	47	Cal Ripken, AL:Balt.
	38	Bill Buckner, NL:Chi. (2)
	38	Al Oliver, NL:Mtl. (2)
	38	Johnny Ray, NL:Pitt.
)84:	44	Don Mattingly, AL:NY
	38	Tim Raines, NL:Mtl.
	38	Johnny Ray, NL:Pitt. (2)

1985:	48	Don Mattingly, AL:NY (2)
	42	Dave Parker, NL:Cin. (2)
1986:	53	Don Mattingly, AL:NY (3)
	46	Von Hayes, NL:Phil.
1987:	42	Tim Wallach, NL:Mtl.
	41	Paul Molitor, AL:Mil.
1988:	45	Wade Boggs, AL:Bos.
	42	Andres Galarraga, NL:Mtl.
1989:	51	Wade Boggs, AL:Bos. (2)
	42	Pedro Guerrero, NL:StL.
	42	Tim Wallach, NL:Mtl. (2)
1990:	45	George Brett, AL:KC (2)
	45	Jody Reed, AL:Bos.
	40	Gregg Jefferies, NL:NY
1991:	49	Rafael Palmeiro, AL:Tex.
	44	Bobby Bonilla, NL:Pitt.
1992:	46	Edgar Martinez, AL:Sea.
	46	Frank Thomas, AL:Chi.
	45	Andy Van Slyke, NL:Pitt.
1993:	54	John Olerud, AL:Tor.
	45	Charlie Hayes, NL:Col.
1994:	45	Chuck Knoblauch, AL:Minn.
	44	Craig Biggio, NL:Hou.
	44	Larry Walker, NL:Mtl.
1995:	52	Albert Belle, AL:Clev.
	52	Edgar Martinez, AL:Sea. (2)
	51	Mark Grace, NL:Chi.
1996:	54	Alex Rodriguez, AL:Sea.
	48	Jeff Bagwell, NL:Hou.
1997:	54	Mark Grudzielanek, NL:Mtl.
	47	John Valentin, AL:Bos.
1998:	51	Craig Biggio, NL:Hou. (2)
	50	John Gonzalez, AL:Tex.
1999:	56	Craig Biggio, NL:Hou. (3)
	45	Shawn Green, AL:Tor.
2000:	59	Todd Helton, NL:Col.
	57	Carlos Delgado, AL:Tor.
2001:	55	Lance Berkman, NL:Hou.
	47	Jason Giambi, AL:Oak.
2002:	56	Garret Anderson, AL:Ana.
	56	Nomar Garciaparra, AL:Bos.
	50	Bobby Abreu, NL:Phil.
2003:	51	Albert Pujols, NL:StL.
	49	Garret Anderson, AL:Ana. (2)
	49	Vernon Wells, AL:Tor.
2004:	53	Lyle Overbay, NL:Mil.
	50	Brian Roberts, AL:Balt.
2005:	50	Derrek Lee, NL:Chi.
	50	Miguel Tejada, AL:Balt.
2006:	53	Freddy Sanchez, NL:Pitt.
	53	Grady Sizemore, AL:Clev.

TRIPLES

1900:	22	Honus Wagner, NL:Pitt.
1901:	21	Bill Keister, AL:Balt.
	21	Jimmy Williams, AL:Balt.
	19	Jimmy Sheckard, NL:Brk.
1902:	23	Sam Crawford, NL:Cin.
	21	Jimmy Williams, AL:Balt.
1903:	25	Sam Crawford, AL:Det.
	19	Honus Wagner, NL:Pitt. (2)
1904:	19	Joe Cassidy, AL:Wash.
	19	Buck Freeman, AL:Bos.
	19	Chick Stahl, AL:Bos.
	18	Harry Lumley, NL:Brk.
1905:	21	Cy Seymour, NL:Cin.
	19	Elmer Flick, AL:Clev.
1906:	22	Elmer Flick, AL:Clev. (2)
	13	Fred Clarke, NL:Pitt.
	13	Wildfire Schulte, NL:Chi.
1907:	18	Elmer Flick, AL:Clev. (3)
	16	Whitey Alperman, NL:Brk.
	16	John Ganzel, NL:Cin.
1908:	20	Ty Cobb, AL:Det.
	19	Honus Wagner, NL:Pitt. (3)
1909:	19	Frank Baker, AL:Phil.
	17	Mike Mitchell, NL:Cin.
1910:	19	Sam Crawford, AL:Det. (2)
	18	Mike Mitchell, NL:Cin. (2)
1911:	25	Larry Doyle, NL:NY
	24	Ty Cobb, AL:Det. (2)
1912:	36	Owen Wilson, NL:Pitt.
	26	Joe Jackson, AL:Clev.
1913:	23	Sam Crawford, AL:Det. (3)
	21	Vic Saier, NL:Chi.
1914:	26	Sam Crawford, AL:Det. (4)
	17	Max Carey, NL:Pitt.
1915:	25	Tommy Long, NL:StL.
	19	Sam Crawford, AL:Det. (5)
1916:	21	Joe Jackson, AL:Chi. (2)
	16	Bill Hinchman, NL:Pitt.
1917:	24	Ty Cobb, AL:Det. (3)
	17	Rogers Hornsby, NL:StL.
1918:	15	Jake Daubert, NL:Brk.
	14	Ty Cobb, AL:Det. (4)
1919:	17	Bobby Veach, AL:Det.
	14	Hy Myers, NL:Brk.
	14	Billy Southworth, NL:Pitt.
1920:	22	Hy Myers, NL:Brk. (2)
	20	Joe Jackson, AL:Chi. (3)
1921:	18	George Sisler, AL:StL.
	18	Jack Tobin, AL:StL.
	18	Rogers Hornsby, NL:StL. (2)
	18	Ray Powell, NL:Bos.
1922:	22	Jake Daubert, NL:Cin. (2)
	18	George Sisler, AL:StL. (2)
1923:	19	Max Carey, NL:Pitt. (2)
	19	Pie Traynor, NL:Pitt.
	18	Goose Goslin, AL:Wash.
	18	Sam Rice, AL:Wash.
1924:	21	Edd Roush, NL:Cin.
	19	Wally Pipp, AL:NY
1925:	26	Kiki Cuyler, NL:Pitt.
	20	Goose Goslin, AL:Wash. (2)
1926:	22	Paul Waner, NL:Pitt.
	20	Lou Gehrig, AL:NY
1927:	23	Earle Combs, AL:NY
	18	Paul Waner, NL:Pitt. (2)
1928:	21	Earle Combs, AL:NY (2)
	20	Jim Bottomley, NL:StL.
1929:	20	Lloyd Waner, NL:Pitt.
	19	Charlie Gehringer, AL:Det.
1930:	23	Adam Comorosky, NL:Pitt.
	22	Earle Combs, AL:NY (3)
1931:	20	Bill Terry, NL:NY
	19	Roy Johnson, AL:Det.
1932:	19	Babe Herman, NL:Cin.
	18	Joe Cronin, AL:Wash.
1933:	19	Arky Vaughan, NL:Pitt.
	17	Heinie Manush, AL:Wash.
1934:	18	Joe Medwick, NL:StL.
	13	Ben Chapman, AL:NY
1935:	20	Joe Vosmik, AL:Clev.
	18	Ival Goodman, NL:Cin.
1936:	15	Earl Averill, AL:Clev.
	15	Joe DiMaggio, AL:NY
	15	Red Rolfe, AL:NY
	14	Ival Goodman, NL:Cin. (2)
1937:	17	Arky Vaughan, NL:Pitt. (2)
	16	Mike Kreevich, AL:Chi.
	16	Dixie Walker, AL:Chi.
1938:	18	Jeff Heath, AL:Clev.
	16	Johnny Mize, NL:StL.
1939:	18	Billy Herman, NL:Chi.
	16	Buddy Lewis, AL:Wash.
1940:	19	Barney McCosky, AL:Det.
	15	Arky Vaughan, NL:Pitt. (3)
1941:	20	Jeff Heath, AL:Clev. (2)
	17	Pete Reiser, NL:Brk.
1942:	17	Enos Slaughter, NL:StL.
	15	Stan Spence, AL:Wash.
1943:	20	Stan Musial, NL:StL.
	12	Johnny Lindell, AL:NY
	12	Wally Moses, AL:Chi.
1944:	19	Johnny Barrett, NL:Pitt.
	16	Johnny Lindell, AL:NY (2)
	16	Snuffy Stirnweiss, AL:NY
1945:	22	Snuffy Stirnweiss, AL:NY (2)
	13	Luis Olmo, NL:Brk.
1946:	20	Stan Musial, NL:StL. (2)
	16	Hank Edwards, AL:Clev.
1947:	16	Harry Walker, NL:StL.-Phil.
	13	Tommy Henrich, AL:NY
1948:	18	Stan Musial, NL:StL. (3)
	14	Tommy Henrich, AL:NY (2)
1949:	23	Dale Mitchell, AL:Clev.
	13	Stan Musial, NL:StL. (4)
	13	Enos Slaughter, NL:StL. (2)
1950:	14	Richie Ashburn, NL:Phil.
	11	Dom DiMaggio, AL:Bos.
	11	Bobby Doerr, AL:Bos.
	11	Hoot Evers, AL:Det.
1951:	14	Minnie Minoso, AL:Clev.-Chi.
	12	Gus Bell, NL:Pitt.
	12	Stan Musial, NL:StL. (5)
1952:	14	Bobby Thomson, NL:NY
	11	Bobby Avila, AL:Clev.
1953:	17	Jim Gilliam, NL:Brk.
	16	Jim Rivera, AL:Chi.
1954:	18	Minnie Minoso, AL:Chi. (2)
	13	Willie Mays, NL:NY

TRIPLES (CONTINUED)

955:	13	Dale Long, NL:Pitt.
	13	Willie Mays, NL:NY (2)
	11	Andy Carey, AL:NY
	11	Mickey Mantle, AL:NY
956:	15	Bill Bruton, NL:Mil.
	11	Jackie Jensen, AL:Bos.
	11	Jim Lemon, AL:Wash.
	11	Minnie Minoso, AL:Chi. (3)
	11	Harry Simpson, AL:KC
957:	20	Willie Mays, NL:NY (3)
	9	Hank Bauer, AL:NY
	9	Gil McDougald, AL:NY
	9	Harry Simpson, AL:KC-NY (2)
958:	13	Richie Ashburn, NL:Phil. (2)
	10	Vic Power, AL:KC-Clev.
959:	11	Wally Moon, NL:LA
	11	Charlie Neal, NL:LA
	9	Bob Allison, AL:Wash.
960:	13	Bill Bruton, NL:Mil. (2)
	10	Nellie Fox, AL:Chi.
961:	14	Jake Wood, AL:Det.
	12	George Altman, NL:Chi.
962:	15	Gino Cimoli, AL:KC
	10	Johnny Callison, NL:Phil.
	10	Willie Davis, NL:LA
	10	Bill Virdon, NL:Pitt.
	10	Maury Wills, NL:LA
963:	14	Vada Pinson, NL:Cin.
	13	Zoilo Versalles, AL:Minn.
964:	13	Dick Allen, NL:Phil.
	13	Ron Santo, NL:Chi.
	10	Rich Rollins, AL:Minn.
	10	Zoilo Versalles, AL:Minn. (2)
965:	16	Johnny Callison, NL:Phil. (2)
	12	Bert Campaneris, AL:KC
	12	Zoilo Versalles, AL:Minn. (3)
966:	13	Tim McCarver, NL:StL.
	11	Bobby Knoop, AL:Cal.
967:	13	Vada Pinson, NL:Cin. (2)
	12	Paul Blair, AL:Balt.
968:	14	Lou Brock, NL:StL.
	13	Jim Fregosi, AL:Cal.
969:	12	Roberto Clemente, NL:Pitt.
	8	Del Unser, AL:Wash.
970:	16	Willie Davis, NL:LA (2)
	13	Cesar Tovar, AL:Minn.
971:	11	Roger Metzger, NL:Hou.
	11	Joe Morgan, NL:Hou.
	11	Freddie Patek, AL:KC
972:	13	Larry Bowa, NL:Phil.
	9	Carton Fisk, AL:Bos.
	9	Joe Rudi, AL:Oak.
973:	14	Roger Metzger, NL:Hou. (2)
	11	Al Bumbry, AL:Balt.
	11	Rod Carew, AL:Minn.
974:	17	Ralph Garr, NL:Atl.
	11	Mickey Rivers, AL:Cal.
975:	13	George Brett, AL:KC
	13	Mickey Rivers, AL:Cal. (2)
	11	Ralph Garr, NL:Atl. (2)
976:	14	George Brett, AL:KC (2)
	12	Dave Cash, NL:Phil.
977:	18	Garry Templeton, NL:StL.
	16	Rod Carew, AL:Minn. (2)
978:	15	Jim Rice, AL:Bos.
	13	Garry Templeton, NL:StL. (2)

1979:	20	George Brett, AL:KC (3)
	19	Garry Templeton, NL:StL. (3)
1980:	15	Alfredo Griffin, AL:Tor.
	15	Willie Wilson, AL:KC
	13	Omar Moreno, NL:Pitt.
	13	Rodney Scott, NL:Mtl.
1981:	12	Craig Reynolds, NL:Hou.
	12	Gene Richards, NL:SD
	9	John Castino, AL:Minn.
1982:	15	Willie Wilson, AL:KC (2)
	10	Dickie Thon, NL:Hou.
1983:	13	Brett Butler, NL:Atl.
	10	Robin Yount, AL:Mil.
1984:	19	Juan Samuel, NL:Phil.
	19	Ryne Sandberg, NL:Chi.
	15	Dave Collins, AL:Tor.
	15	Lloyd Moseby, AL:Tor.
1985:	21	Willie Wilson, AL:KC (3)
	18	Willie McGee, NL:StL.
1986:	14	Brett Butler, AL:Clev. (NL 1)
	13	Mitch Webster, NL:Mtl.
1987:	15	Juan Samuel, NL:Phil. (2)
	15	Willie Wilson, AL:KC (4)
1988:	15	Andy Van Slyke, NL:Pitt.
	11	Harold Reynolds, AL:Sea.
	11	Willie Wilson, AL:KC (5)
	11	Robin Yount, AL:Mil. (2)
1989:	14	Ruben Sierra, AL:Tex.
	11	Robby Thompson, NL:SF
1990:	17	Tony Fernandez, AL:Tor.
	11	Mariano Duncan, NL:Cin.
1991:	15	Ray Lankford, NL:StL.
	13	Lance Johnson, AL:Chi.
	13	Paul Molitor, AL:Mil.
1992:	14	Deion Sanders, NL:Atl.
	12	Lance Johnson, AL:Chi. (2)
1993:	14	Lance Johnson, AL:Chi. (3)
	13	Steve Finley, NL:Hou.
1994:	14	Lance Johnson, AL:Chi. (4)
	9	Brett Butler, NL:LA (NL 2; AL 1)
	9	Darren Lewis, NL:SF
1995:	13	Kenny Lofton, AL:Clev.
	9	Brett Butler, NL:NY-LA (NL 3; AL 1)
	9	Eric Young, NL:Col.
1996:	21	Lance Johnson, NL:NY (AL 4)
	14	Chuck Knoblauch, AL:Minn.
1997:	14	Delino DeShields, NL:StL.
	11	Nomar Garciaparra, AL:Bos.
1998:	13	Jose Offerman, AL:KC
	12	David Dellucci, NL:Ari.
1999:	11	Bobby Abreu, NL:Phil.
	11	Neifi Perez, NL:Col.
	11	Jose Offerman, AL:Bos. (2)
2000:	20	Cristian Guzman, AL:Minn.
	14	Tony Womack, NL:Ari.
2001:	14	Cristian Guzman, AL:Minn. (2)
	12	Jimmy Rollins, NL:Phil.
2002:	11	Johnny Damon, AL:Bos.
	10	Jimmy Rollins, NL:Phil. (2)
2003:	14	Cristian Guzman, AL:Minn. (3)
	10	Steve Finley, Steve NL:Ari. (2)
	10	Rafael Furcal, Rafael NL:Atl.
2004:	19	Carl Crawford, AL:TB
	12	Juan Pierre, NL:Fla.
	12	Jimmy Rollins, NL:Phil. (3)
	12	Jack Wilson, NL:Pitt.
2005:	17	Jose Reyes, NL:NY
	15	Carl Crawford, AL:TB (2)
2006:	17	Jose Reyes, NL:NY (2)
	16	Carl Crawford, AL:TB (3)

HOME RUNS

1900:	12	Herman Long, NL:Bos.
1901:	16	Sam Crawford, NL:Cin.
	14	Nap Lajoie, AL:Phil.
1902:	16	Socks Seybold, AL:Phil.
	6	Tommy Leach, NL:Pitt.
1903:	13	Buck Freeman, AL:Bos.
	9	Jimmy Sheckard, NL:Brk.
1904:	10	Harry Davis, AL:Phil.
	9	Harry Lumley, NL:Brk.
1905:	9	Fred Odwell, NL:Cin.
	8	Harry Davis, AL:Phil. (2)
1906:	12	Harry Davis, AL:Phil. (3)
	12	Tim Jordan, NL:Brk.
1907:	10	Dave Brain, NL:Bos.
	8	Harry Davis, AL:Phil. (4)
1908:	12	Tim Jordan, NL:Brk. (2)
	7	Sam Crawford, AL:Det.
1909:	9	Ty Cobb, AL:Det.
	7	Red Murray, NL:NY
1910:	10	Fred Beck, NL:Bos.
	10	Wildfire Schulte, NL:Chi.
	10	Jake Stahl, AL:Bos.
1911:	21	Wildfire Schulte, NL:Chi. (2)
	11	Frank Baker, AL:Phil.
1912:	14	Heinie Zimmerman, NL:Chi.
	10	Frank Baker, AL:Phil. (2)
	10	Tris Speaker, AL:Bos.
1913:	19	Gavvy Cravath, NL:Phil.
	12	Frank Baker, AL:Phil. (3)
1914:	19	Gavvy Cravath, NL:Phil. (2)
	9	Frank Baker, AL:Phil. (4)
1915:	24	Gavvy Cravath, NL:Phil. (3)
	7	Braggo Roth, AL:Chi.-Clev.
1916:	12	Wally Pipp, AL:NY
	12	Dave Robertson, NL:NY
	12	Cy Williams, NL:Chi.
1917:	12	Gavvy Cravath, NL:Phil. (4)
	12	Dave Robertson, NL:NY (2)
	9	Wally Pipp, AL:NY (2)
1918:	11	Babe Ruth, AL:Bos.
	11	Tilly Walker, AL:Phil.
	8	Gavvy Cravath, NL:Phil. (5)
1919:	29	Babe Ruth, AL:Bos. (2)
	12	Gavvy Cravath, NL:Phil. (6)
1920:	54	Babe Ruth, e AL:NY (3)
	15	Cy Williams, NL:Phil. (2)
1921:	59	Babe Ruth, AL:NY (4)
	23	George Kelly, NL:NY
1922:	42	Rogers Hornsby, NL:StL.
	39	Ken Williams, AL:StL.
1923:	41	Babe Ruth, AL:NY (5)
	41	Cy Williams, NL:Phil. (3)
1924:	46	Babe Ruth, AL:NY (6)
	27	Jack Fournier, NL:Brk.
1925:	39	Rogers Hornsby, NL:StL. (2)
	33	Bob Meusel, AL:NY
1926:	47	Babe Ruth, AL:NY (7)
	21	Hack Wilson, NL:Chi.
1927:	60	Babe Ruth, AL:NY (8)
	30	Cy Williams, NL:Phil. (4)
	30	Hack Wilson, NL:Chi. (2)
1928:	54	Babe Ruth, AL:NY (9)
	31	Jim Bottomley, NL:StL.
	31	Hack Wilson, NL:Chi. (3)

1929:	46	Babe Ruth, AL:NY (10)
	43	Chuck Klein, NL:Phil.
1930:	56	Hack Wilson, NL:Chi. (4)
	49	Babe Ruth, AL:NY (11)
1931:	46	Lou Gehrig, AL:NY
	46	Babe Ruth, AL:NY (12)
	31	Chuck Klein, NL:Phil. (2)
1932:	58	Jimmie Foxx, AL:Phil.
	38	Chuck Klein, NL:Phil. (3)
	38	Mel Ott, NL:NY
1933:	48	Jimmie Foxx, AL:Phil. (2)
	28	Chuck Klein, NL:Phil. (4)
1934:	49	Lou Gehrig, AL:NY (2)
	35	Ripper Collins, NL:StL.
	35	Mel Ott, NL:NY (2)
1935:	36	Jimmie Foxx, AL:Phil. (3)
	36	Hank Greenberg, AL:Det.
	34	Wally Berger, NL:Bos.
1936:	49	Lou Gehrig, AL:NY (3)
	33	Mel Ott, NL:NY (3)
1937:	46	Joe DiMaggio, AL:NY
	31	Joe Medwick, NL:StL.
	31	Mel Ott, NL:NY (4)
1938:	58	Hank Greenberg, AL:Det. (2)
	36	Mel Ott, NL:NY (5)
1939:	35	Jimmie Foxx, AL:Bos. (4)
	28	Johnny Mize, NL:StL.
1940:	43	Johnny Mize, NL:StL. (2)
	41	Hank Greenberg, AL:Det. (3)
1941:	37	Ted Williams, AL:Bos.
	34	Dolph Camilli, NL:Brk.
1942:	36	Ted Williams, AL:Bos. (2)
	30	Mel Ott, NL:NY (6)
1943:	34	Rudy York, AL:Det.
	29	Bill Nicholson, NL:Chi.
1944:	33	Bill Nicholson, NL:Chi. (2)
	22	Nick Etten, AL:NY
1945:	28	Tommy Holmes, NL:Bos.
	24	Vern Stephens, AL:StL.
1946:	44	Hank Greenberg, AL:Det. (4)
	23	Ralph Kiner, NL:Pitt.
1947:	51	Ralph Kiner, NL:Pitt. (2)
	51	Johnny Mize, NL:NY (3)
	32	Ted Williams, AL:Bos. (3)
1948:	40	Ralph Kiner, NL:Pitt. (3)
	40	Johnny Mize, NL:NY (4)
	39	Joe DiMaggio, AL:NY (2)
1949:	54	Ralph Kiner, NL:Pitt. (4)
	43	Ted Williams, AL:Bos. (4)
1950:	47	Ralph Kiner, NL:Pitt. (5)
	37	Al Rosen, AL:Clev.
1951:	42	Ralph Kiner, NL:Pitt. (6)
	33	Gus Zernial, AL:Chi.-Phil.
1952:	37	Ralph Kiner, NL:Pitt. (7)
	37	Hank Sauer, NL:Chi.
	32	Larry Doby, AL:Clev.
1953:	47	Eddie Mathews, NL:Mil.
	43	Al Rosen, AL:Clev. (2)
1954:	49	Ted Kluszewski, NL:Cin.
	32	Larry Doby, AL:Clev. (2)
1955:	51	Willie Mays, NL:NY
	37	Mickey Mantle, AL:NY
1956:	52	Mickey Mantle, AL:NY (2)
	43	Duke Snider, NL:Brk.
1957:	44	Hank Aaron, NL:Mil.
	42	Roy Sievers, AL:Wash.

HOME RUNS (CONTINUED)

1958:	47	Ernie Banks, NL:Chi.
	42	Mickey Mantle, AL:NY (3)
1959:	46	Eddie Mathews, NL:Mil. (2)
	42	Rocky Colavito, AL:Clev.
	42	Harmon Killebrew, AL:Wash.
1960:	41	Ernie Banks, NL:Chi. (2)
	40	Mickey Mantle, AL:NY (4)
1961:	61	Roger Maris, AL:NY
	46	Orlando Cepeda, NL:SF
1962:	49	Willie Mays, NL:SF (2)
	48	Harmon Killebrew, AL:Minn. (2)
1963:	45	Harmon Killebrew, AL:Minn. (3)
	44	Hank Aaron, NL:Mil. (2)
	44	Willie McCovey, NL:SF
1964:	49	Harmon Killebrew, AL:Minn. (4)
	47	Willie Mays, NL:SF (3)
1965:	52	Willie Mays, NL:SF (4)
	32	Tony Conigliaro, AL:Bos.
1966:	49	Frank Robinson, AL:Balt.
	44	Hank Aaron, NL:Atl. (3)
1967:	44	Harmon Killebrew, AL:Minn. (5)
	44	Carl Yastrzemski, AL:Bos.
	39	Hank Aaron, NL:Atl. (4)
1968:	44	Frank Howard, AL:Wash.
	36	Willie McCovey, NL:SF (2)
1969:	49	Harmon Killebrew, AL:Minn. (6)
	45	Willie McCovey, NL:SF (3)
1970:	45	Johnny Bench, NL:Cin.
	44	Frank Howard, AL:Wash. (2)
1971:	48	Willie Stargell, NL:Pitt.
	33	Bill Melton, AL:Chi.
1972:	40	Johnny Bench, NL:Cin. (2)
	37	Dick Allen, AL:Chi.
1973:	44	Willie Stargell, NL:Pitt. (2)
	32	Reggie Jackson, AL:Oak.
1974:	36	Mike Schmidt, NL:Phil.
	32	Dick Allen, AL:Chi. (2)
1975:	38	Mike Schmidt, NL:Phil. (2)
	36	Reggie Jackson, AL:Oak. (2)
	36	George Scott, AL:Mil.
1976:	38	Mike Schmidt, NL:Phil. (3)
	32	Graig Nettles, AL:NY
1977:	52	George Foster, NL:Cin.
	39	Jim Rice, AL:Bos.
1978:	46	Jim Rice, AL:Bos. (2)
	40	George Foster, NL:Cin. (2)
1979:	48	Dave Kingman, NL:Chi.
	45	Gorman Thomas, AL:Mil.
1980:	48	Mike Schmidt, NL:Phil. (4)
	41	Reggie Jackson, AL:NY (3)
	41	Ben Oglivie, AL:Mil.
1981:	31	Mike Schmidt, NL:Phil. (5)
	22	Tony Armas, AL:Oak.
	22	Dwight Evans, AL:Bos.
	22	Bobby Grich, AL:Cal.
	22	Eddie Murray, AL:Balt.
1982:	39	Reggie Jackson, AL:Cal. (4)
	39	Gorman Thomas, AL:Mil. (2)
	37	Dave Kingman, NL:NY (2)
1983:	40	Mike Schmidt, NL:Phil. (6)
	39	Jim Rice, AL:Bos. (3)
1984:	43	Tony Armas, AL:Bos. (2)
	36	Dale Murphy, NL:Atl.
	36	Mike Schmidt, NL:Phil. (7)

1985:	40	Darrell Evans, AL:Det.
	37	Dale Murphy, NL:Atl. (2)
1986:	40	Jesse Barfield, AL:Tor.
	37	Mike Schmidt, NL:Phil. (8)
1987:	49	Andre Dawson, NL:Chi.
	49	Mark McGwire, AL:Oak.
1988:	42	Jose Canseco, AL:Oak.
	39	Darryl Strawberry, NL:NY
1989:	47	Kevin Mitchell, NL:SF
	36	Fred McGriff, AL:Tor.
1990:	51	Cecil Fielder, AL:Det.
	40	Ryne Sandberg, NL:Chi.
1991:	44	Jose Canseco, AL:Oak. (2)
	44	Cecil Fielder, AL:Det. (2)
	38	Howard Johnson, NL:NY
1992:	43	Juan Gonzalez, AL:Tex.
	35	Fred McGriff, NL:SD (AL 1)
1993:	46	Barry Bonds, NL:SF
	46	Juan Gonzalez, AL:Tex. (2)
1994:	43	Matt Williams, NL:SF
	40	Ken Griffey, Jr. AL:Sea.
1995:	50	Albert Belle, AL:Clev.
	40	Dante Bichette, NL:Col.
1996:	52	Mark McGwire, AL:Oak. (2)
	47	Andres Galarraga, NL:Col.
1997:	58	Mark McGwire, AL:Oak.-NL:StL. (ML 3)
	56	Ken Griffey, Jr. AL:Sea. (2)
	49	Larry Walker, NL:Col.
1998:	70	Mark McGwire, NL:StL. (ML 4)
	56	Ken Griffey, Jr. AL:Sea. (3)
1999:	65	Mark McGwire, NL:StL. (2, ML 5)
	48	Ken Griffey, Jr. AL:Sea. (4)
2000:	50	Sammy Sosa, NL:Chi.
	47	Troy Glaus, AL:Ana.
2001:	73	Barry Bonds, NL:SF (2)
	52	Alex Rodriguez, AL:Tex.
2002:	57	Alex Rodriguez, AL:Tex. (2)
	49	Sammy Sosa, NL:Chi. (2)
2003:	47	Alex Rodriguez, AL:Tex. (3)
	47	Jim Thome, NL:Phil.
2004:	48	Adrian Beltre, NL:LA
	43	Manny Ramirez, AL:Bos.
2005:	51	Andruw Jones, NL:Atl.
	48	Alex Rodriguez, AL:NY (4)
2006:	58	Ryan Howard, NL:Phil.
	54	David Ortiz, AL:Bos.

WALKS

1913:	99	Burt Shotton, AL:StL.
	94	Bob Bescher, NL:Cin.
1914:	112	Donie Bush, AL:Det.
	105	Miller Huggins, NL:StL.
1915:	119	Eddie Collins, AL:Chi.
	86	Gavvy Cravath, NL:Phil.
1916:	110	Burt Shotton, AL:StL. (2)
	84	Heinie Groh, NL:Cin.
1917:	94	Jack Graney, AL:Clev.
	75	George Burns, NL:NY
1918:	84	Ray Chapman, AL:Clev.
	62	Max Carey, NL:Pitt.
1919:	105	Jack Graney, AL:Clev. (2)
	82	George Burns, NL:NY (2)
1920:	150	Babe Ruth, AL:NY
	76	George Burns, NL:NY (3)
1921:	145	Babe Ruth, AL:NY (2)
	80	George Burns, NL:NY (4)
1922:	89	Whitey Witt, AL:NY
	80	Max Carey, NL:Pitt. (2)
1923:	170	Babe Ruth, AL:NY (3)
	101	George Burns, NL:NY (5)
1924:	142	Babe Ruth, AL:NY (4)
	89	Rogers Hornsby, NL:StL.
1925:	90	Max Bishop, AL:Phi.
	90	Willie Kamm, AL:Chi.
	90	Johnny Mostil, AL:Chi.
	86	Jack Fournier, NL:Brk.
1926:	144	Babe Ruth, AL:NY (5)
	69	Hack Wilson, NL:Chi.
1927:	137	Babe Ruth, AL:NY (6)
	86	Rogers Hornsby, NL:NY (2)
1928:	137	Babe Ruth, AL:NY (7)
	107	Rogers Hornsby, NL:Bos. (3)
1929:	128	Max Bishop, AL:Phil. (2)
	113	Mel Ott, NL:NY
1930:	136	Babe Ruth, AL:NY (8)
	105	Hack Wilson, NL:Chi. (2)
1931:	128	Babe Ruth, AL:NY (9)
	80	Mel Ott, NL:NY (2)
1932:	130	Babe Ruth, AL:NY (10)
	100	Mel Ott, NL:NY (3)
1933:	114	Babe Ruth, AL:NY (11)
	75	Mel Ott, NL:NY (4)
1934:	111	Jimmie Foxx, AL:Phil.
	94	Arky Vaughan, NL:Pitt.
1935:	132	Lou Gehrig, AL:NY
	97	Arky Vaughan, NL:Pitt. (2)
1936:	130	Lou Gehrig, AL:NY (2)
	118	Arky Vaughan, NL:Pitt. (3)
1937:	127	Lou Gehrig, AL:NY (3)
	102	Mel Ott, NL:NY (5)
1938:	119	Dolph Camilli, NL:Brk.
	119	Jimmie Foxx, AL:Bos. (2)
	119	Hank Greenberg, AL:Det.
1939:	111	Harlond Clift, AL:StL.
	110	Dolph Camilli, NL:Brk. (2)
1940:	119	Elbie Fletcher, NL:Pitt.
	106	Charlie Keller, AL:NY
1941:	147	Ted Williams, AL:Bos.
	118	Elbie Fletcher, NL:Pitt. (2)
1942:	145	Ted Williams, AL:Bos. (2)
	109	Mel Ott, NL:NY (6)
1943:	106	Charlie Keller, AL:NY (2)
	103	Augie Galan, NL:Brk.
1944:	101	Augie Galan, NL:Brk. (2)
	97	Nick Etten, AL:NY
1945:	148	Eddie Stanky, NL:Brk.
	112	Roy Cullenbine, AL:Clev.-Det.
1946:	156	Ted Williams, AL:Bos. (3)
	137	Eddie Stanky, NL:Brk. (2)
1947:	162	Ted Williams, AL:Bos. (4)
	104	Hank Greenberg, NL:Pitt.
	104	Pee Wee Reese, NL:Brk.
1948:	133	Bob Elliott, NL:Bos.
	126	Ted Williams, AL:Bos. (5)
1949:	162	Ted Williams, AL:Bos. (6)
	117	Ralph Kiner, NL:Pitt.
1950:	146	Eddie Stanky, NL:NY (3)
	141	Eddie Yost, AL:Wash.
1951:	144	Ted Williams, AL:Bos. (7)
	137	Ralph Kiner, NL:Pitt. (2)
1952:	129	Eddie Yost, AL:Wash. (2)
	110	Ralph Kiner, NL:Pitt. (3)
1953:	123	Eddie Yost, AL:Wash. (3)
	105	Stan Musial, NL:StL.
1954:	136	Ted Williams, AL:Bos. (8)
	125	Richie Ashburn, NL:Phil.
1955:	113	Mickey Mantle, AL:NY
	109	Eddie Mathews, NL:Mil.
1956:	151	Eddie Yost, AL:Wash. (4)
	99	Duke Snider, NL:Brk.
1957:	146	Mickey Mantle, AL:NY (2)
	94	Richie Ashburn, NL:Phil. (2)
	94	Johnny Temple, NL:Cin.
1958:	129	Mickey Mantle, AL:NY (3)
	97	Richie Ashburn, NL:Phil. (3)
1959:	135	Eddie Yost, AL:Det. (5)
	96	Jim Gilliam, NL:LA
1960:	125	Eddie Yost, AL:Det. (6)
	116	Richie Ashburn, NL:Phil. (4)
1961:	126	Mickey Mantle, AL:NY (4)
	93	Eddie Mathews, NL:Mil. (2)
1962:	122	Mickey Mantle, AL:NY (5)
	101	Eddie Mathews, NL:Mil. (3)
1963:	124	Eddie Mathews, NL:Mil. (4)
	95	Carl Yastrzemski, AL:Bos.
1964:	106	Norm Siebern, AL:Balt.
	86	Ron Santo, NL:Chi.
1965:	97	Joe Morgan, NL:Hou.
	93	Rocky Colavito, AL:Clev.
1966:	103	Harmon Killebrew, AL:Minn.
	95	Ron Santo, NL:Chi. (2)
1967:	131	Harmon Killebrew, AL:Minn. (2)
	96	Ron Santo, NL:Chi. (3)
1968:	119	Carl Yastrzemski, AL:Bos. (2)
	96	Ron Santo, NL:Chi. (4)
1969:	148	Jimmy Wynn, NL:Hou.
	145	Harmon Killebrew, AL:Minn. (3)
1970:	137	Willie McCovey, NL:SF
	132	Frank Howard, AL:Wash.
1971:	114	Harmon Killebrew, AL:Minn. (4)
	112	Willie Mays, NL:SF
1972:	115	Joe Morgan, NL:Cin. (2)
	99	Dick Allen, AL:Chi.
	99	Roy White, AL:NY
1973:	124	Darrell Evans, NL:Atl.
	122	John Mayberry, AL:KC
1974:	126	Darrell Evans, NL:Atl. (2)
	110	Gene Tenace, AL:Oak.

WALKS (CONTINUED)

1975:	132	Joe Morgan, NL:Cin. (3)
	119	John Mayberry, AL:KC (2)
1976:	127	Jimmy Wynn, NL:Atl. (2)
	97	Mike Hargrove, AL:Tex.
1977:	125	Gene Tenace, NL:SD
	109	Toby Harrah, AL:Tex.
1978:	117	Jeff Burroughs, NL:Atl.
	107	Mike Hargrove, AL:Tex. (2)
1979:	121	Darrell Porter, AL:KC
	120	Mike Schmidt, NL:Phil.
1980:	119	Willie Randolph, AL:NY
	93	Dan Driessen, NL:Cin.
	93	Joe Morgan, NL:Hou. (4)
1981:	85	Dwight Evans, AL:Bos.
	73	Mike Schmidt, NL:Phil. (2)
1982:	116	Rickey Henderson, AL:Oak.
	107	Mike Schmidt, NL:Phil. (3)
1983:	128	Mike Schmidt, NL:Phil. (4)
	103	Rickey Henderson, AL:Oak. (2)
1984:	107	Eddie Murray, AL:Balt.
	103	Gary Matthews, NL:Chi.
1985:	114	Dwight Evans, AL:Bos. (2)
	90	Dale Murphy, NL:Atl.
1986:	105	Wade Boggs, AL:Bos.
	94	Keith Hernandez, NL:NY
1987:	136	Jack Clark, NL:StL.
	106	Brian Downing, AL:Cal.
	106	Dwight Evans, AL:Bos. (3)
1988:	125	Wade Boggs, AL:Bos. (2)
	100	Will Clark, NL:SF
1989:	132	Jack Clark, NL:SD (2)
	126	Rickey Henderson, AL:NY-Oak. (3)
1990:	110	Mark McGwire, AL:Oak.
	104	Jack Clark, NL:SD (3)
1991:	138	Frank Thomas, AL:Chi.
	108	Brett Butler, NL:LA
1992:	127	Barry Bonds, NL:Pitt.
	122	Mickey Tettleton, AL:Det.
	122	Frank Thomas, AL:Chi. (2)
1993:	132	Tony Phillips, AL:Det.
	129	Len Dykstra, NL:Phil.
1994:	109	Frank Thomas, AL:Chi. (3)
	74	Barry Bonds, NL:SF (2)
1995:	136	Frank Thomas, AL:Chi. (4)
	120	Barry Bonds, NL:SF (3)
1996:	151	Barry Bonds, NL:SF (4)
	125	Tony Phillips, AL:Chi. (2)
1997:	145	Barry Bonds, NL:SF (5)
	120	Jim Thome, AL:Clev.
1998:	162	Mark McGwire, NL:StL. (AL 1)
	118	Rickey Henderson, AL:Oak. (4)
1999:	149	Jeff Bagwell, NL:Hou.
	127	Jim Thome, AL:Clev. (2)
2000:	137	Jason Giambi, AL:Oak.
	117	Barry Bonds, NL:SF (6)
2001:	177	Barry Bonds, NL:SF (7)
	129	Jason Giambi, AL:Oak. (2)
2002:	198	Barry Bonds, NL:SF (8)
	122	Jim Thome, AL:Clev. (3)
2003:	148	Barry Bonds, NL:SF (9)
	129	Jason Giambi, AL:NY (3)
2004:	232	Barry Bonds, NL:SF (10)
	95	Eric Chavez, AL:Oak.
2005:	119	Brian Giles, NL:SD
	108	Jason Giambi, AL:NY (4)
2006:	119	David Ortiz, AL:Bos.
	115	Barry Bonds, NL:SF (11)

STRIKEOUTS

1910:	81	John Hummel, NL:Brk.
1911:	78	Bob Bescher, NL:Cin.
	78	Bob Coulson, NL:Brk.
1912:	91	Ed McDonald, NL:Bos.
1913:	104	Danny Moeller, AL:Wash.
	74	George Burns, NL:NY
1914:	120	Gus Williams, AL:StL.
	80	Fred Merkle, NL:NY
1915:	88	Doug Baird, NL:Pitt.
	83	Doc Lavan, AL:StL.
1916:	89	Gavvy Cravath, NL:Phil.
	82	Wally Pipp, AL:NY
1917:	78	Cy Williams, NL:Chi
	73	Braggo Roth, AL:Clev.
1918:	58	Babe Ruth, AL:Bos.
	49	Dode Paskert, NL:Chi.
	49	Ross Youngs, NL:NY
1919:	79	Ray Powell, NL:Bos.
	70	Red Shannon, AL:Phil.-Bos.
1920:	92	George Kelly, NL:NY
	84	Aaron Ward, AL:NY
1921:	88	Bob Meusel, AL:NY
	85	Ray Powell, NL:Bos. (2)
1922:	98	Jimmy Dykes, AL:Phil.
	93	Frank Parkinson, NL:Phil.
1923:	94	Babe Ruth, AL:NY (2)
	92	George Grantham, NL:Chi.
1924:	81	Babe Ruth, AL:NY (3)
	63	George Grantham, NL:Chi. (2)
1925:	77	Gabby Hartnett, NL:Chi.
	70	Marty McManus, AL:StL.
1926:	97	Tony Lazzeri, AL:NY
	77	Barney Friberg, NL:Phil.
1927:	89	Babe Ruth, AL:NY (4)
	70	Hack Wilson, NL:Chi.
1928:	94	Hack Wilson, NL:Chi. (2)
	87	Babe Ruth, AL:NY (5)
1929:	83	Hack Wilson, NL:Chi. (3)
	71	Lou Gehrig, AL:NY
1930:	84	Hack Wilson, NL:Chi. (4)
	66	Jimmie Foxx, AL:Phil.
	66	Ed Morgan, AL:Clev.
1931:	86	Nick Cullop, NL:Cin.
	84	Jim Levey, AL:StL.
1932:	104	Bruce Campbell, AL:Chi.-StL.
	85	Hack Wilson. NL:Brk. (5)
1933:	93	Jimmie Foxx, AL:Phil. (2)
	77	Wally Berger, NL:Bos.
1934:	100	Harlond Clift, AL:StL.
	94	Dolph Camilli, NL:Chi.-Phil.
1935:	113	Dolph Camilli, NL:Phil. (2)
	99	Jimmie Foxx, AL:Phil. (3)
1936:	119	Jimmie Foxx, AL:Bos. (4)
	96	Bill Brubaker, NL:Pitt.
1937:	111	Vince DiMaggio, NL:Bos.
	107	Frankie Crosetti, AL:NY
1938:	134	Vince DiMaggio, NL:Bos. (2)
	97	Frankie Crosetti, AL:NY (2)
1939:	107	Dolph Camilli, NL:Brk. (3)
	95	Hank Greenberg, AL:Det.
1940:	127	Chet Ross, NL:Bos.
	96	Sam Chapman, AL:Phil.
1941:	115	Dolph Camilli, NL:Brk. (4)
	103	Jimmie Foxx, AL:Bos. (5)
1942:	95	Joe Gordon, AL:NY
	87	Vince DiMaggio, NL:Pitt. (3)
1943:	127	Vince DiMaggio, NL:Pitt. (4)
	105	Chet Laabs, AL:StL.
1944:	99	Pat Seerey, AL:Clev.
	83	Vince DiMaggio, NL:Pitt. (5)
1945:	97	Pat Seerey, AL:Clev. (2)
	91	Vince DiMaggio, NL:Phil. (6)
1946:	109	Ralph Kiner, NL:Pitt.
	101	Charlie Keller, AL:NY
	101	Pat Seerey, AL:Clev. (3)
1947:	110	Eddie Joost, AL:Phil.
	83	Bill Nicholson, NL:Chi.
1948:	102	Pat Seerey, AL:Clev.-Chi. (4)
	85	Hank Sauer, NL:Cin.
1949:	92	Duke Snider, NL:Brk.
	91	Dick Kokos, AL:StL.
1950:	114	Roy Smalley, NL:Chi.
	110	Gus Zernial, AL:Chi.
1951:	101	Gus Zernial, AL:Chi.-Phil. (2)
	99	Gil Hodges, NL:Brk.
1952:	117	Eddie Mathews, NL:Bos.
	111	Larry Doby, AL:Clev.
	111	Mickey Mantle, AL:NY
1953:	125	Steve Bilko, NL:StL.
	121	Larry Doby, AL:Clev. (2)
1954:	107	Mickey Mantle. AL:NY (2)
	96	Duke Snider, NL:Brk. (2)
1955:	106	Norm Zauchin, AL:Bos.
	102	Wally Post, NL:Cin.
1956:	138	Jim Lemon, AL:Wash.
	124	Wally Post, NL:Cin. (2)
1957:	104	Duke Snider, NL:Brk. (3)
	94	Jim Lemon, AL:Wash. (2)
1958:	123	Mickey Mantle, AL:NY (3)
	95	Harry Anderson, NL:Phil.
1959:	126	Mickey Mantle, AL:NY (4)
	103	Wally Post, NL:Phil. (3)
1960:	136	Pancho Herrera, NL:Phil.
	125	Mickey Mantle, AL:NY (5)
1961:	141	Jake Wood, AL:Det.
	121	Dick Stuart, NL:Pitt.
1962:	142	Harmon Killebrew, AL:Minn.
	129	Ken Hubbs, NL:Chi.
1963:	175	Dave Nicholson, AL:Chi.
	136	Donn Clendenon, NL:Pitt.
1964:	143	Nelson Mathews, AL:KC
	138	Dick Allen, NL:Phil.
1965:	150	Dick Allen, NL:Phil. (2)
	122	Zoilo Versalles, AL:Minn.
1966:	152	George Scott, AL:Bos.
	143	Byron Browne, NL:Chi.
1967:	155	Frank Howard, AL:Wash.
	137	Jimmy Wynn, NL:Hou.
1968:	171	Reggie Jackson, AL:Oak.
	163	Donn Clendenon, NL:Pitt. (2)
1969:	187	Bobby Bonds, NL:SF
	142	Reggie Jackson, AL:Oak. (2)
1970:	189	Bobby Bonds, NL:SF (2)
	134	Reggie Jackson, AL:Oak. (3)
1971:	161	Reggie Jackson, AL:Oak. (4)
	154	Willie Stargell, NL:Pitt.

STRIKEOUTS (CONTINUED)

1972:	145	Bobby Darwin, AL:Minn.
	145	Lee May, NL:Hou.
1973:	148	Bobby Bonds, NL:SF (3)
	137	Bobby Darwin, AL:Minn. (2)
1974:	138	Mike Schmidt, NL:Phil.
	127	Bobby Darwin, AL:Minn. (3)
1975:	180	Mike Schmidt, NL:Phil. (2)
	155	Jeff Burroughs, AL:Tex.
1976:	149	Mike Schmidt, NL:Phil. (3)
	123	Jim Rice, AL:Bos.
1977:	162	Butch Hobson, AL:Bos.
	140	Greg Luzinski, :NL:Phil.
1978:	166	Gary Alexander, AL:Oak.-Clev.
	145	Dale Murphy, NL:Atl.
1979:	175	Gorman Thomas, AL:Mil.
	131	Dave Kingman, NL:Chi.
1980:	170	Gorman Thomas, AL:Mil. (2)
	133	Dale Murphy, NL:Atl. (2)
1981:	115	Tony Armas, AL:Oak.
	105	Dave Kingman, NL:NY (2)
1982:	156	Reggie Jackson, AL:Cal. (5)
	156	Dave Kingman, NL:NY (3)
1983:	150	Ron Kittle, AL:Chi.
	148	Mike Schmidt, NL:Phil. (4)
1984:	168	Juan Samuel, NL:Phil.
	156	Tony Armas, AL:Bos. (2)
1985:	166	Steve Balboni, AL:KC
	141	Dale Murphy, NL:Atl. (3)
	141	Juan Samuel, NL:Phil. (2)
1986:	185	Pete Incaviglia, AL:Tex
	142	Juan Samuel, NL:Phil. (3)
1987:	186	Rob Deer, AL:Mil.
	162	Juan Samuel, NL:Phil. (4)
1988:	153	Andres Galarraga, NL:Mtl.
	153	Rob Deer, AL:Mil. (2)
	153	Pete Incaviglia, AL:Tex. (2)
1989:	172	Bo Jackson, AL:KC
	158	Andres Galarraga, NL:Mtl. (2)
1990:	182	Cecil Fielder, AL:Det.
	169	Andres Galarraga, NL:Mtl. (3)
1991:	175	Rob Deer, AL:Det. (3)
	151	Delino DeShields, NL:Mtl.
1992:	154	Dean Palmer, AL:Tex.
	147	Ray Lankford, NL:StL.
1993:	169	Rob Deer, AL:Det.-Bos. (4)
	147	Cory Snyder, NL:LA
1994:	128	Travis Fryman, AL:Det.
	114	Reggie Sanders, NL:Cin.
1995:	150	Mo Vaughn, AL:Bos.
	146	Andres Galarraga, NL:Col. (4)
1996:	160	Henry Rodriguez, NL:Mtl.
	159	Jay Buhner, AL:Sea.
1997:	175	Jay Buhner, AL:Sea.(2)
	174	Sammy Sosa, NL:Chi.
1998:	171	Sammy Sosa, NL:Chi. (2)
	159	Jose Canseco, AL:Tor.
1999:	171	Sammy Sosa, NL:Chi. (3)
	171	Jim Thome, AL:Clev.
2000:	187	Preston Wilson, NL:Fla.
	181	Mo Vaughn, AL:Ana. (2)
2001:	185	Jose Hernandez, NL:Mil.
	185	Jim Thome, AL:Clev. (2)
2002:	188	Jose Hernandez, NL:Mil. (2)
	176	Mike Cameron, AL:Sea.
2003:	182	Jim Thome, NL:Phil. (AL 2)
	140	Jason Giambi, AL:NY
2004:	195	Adam Dunn, NL:Cin.
	177	Mark Bellhorn, AL:Bos.
2005:	168	Adam Dunn, NL:Cin. (2)
	167	Richie Sexson, AL:Sea.
2006:	194	Adam Dunn, NL:Cin. (3)
	174	Curtis Granderson, AL:Det.

STOLEN BASES

1900:	45	Patsy Donovan, NL:StL.
	45	George Van Haltren, NL:NY
1901:	52	Frank Isbell, AL:Chi.
	49	Honus Wagner, NL:Pitt.
1902:	47	Topsy Hartsel, AL:Phil.
	42	Honus Wagner, NL:Pitt. (2)
1903:	67	Frank Chance, NL:Chi.
	67	Jimmy Sheckard, NL:Brk.
	45	Harry Bay, AL:Clev. (2)
1904:	53	Honus Wagner, NL:Pitt. (3)
	42	Elmer Flick, AL:Clev.
1905:	59	Art Devlin, NL:NY
	59	Billy Maloney, NL:Chi.
	46	Danny Hoffman, AL:Phil.
1906:	57	Frank Chance, NL:Chi. (2)
	39	John Anderson, AL:Wash.
	39	Elmer Flick, AL:Clev. (2)
1907:	61	Honus Wagner, NL:Pitt. (4)
	54	Ty Cobb, AL:Det.
1908:	53	Honus Wagner, NL:Pitt. (5)
	47	Patsy Dougherty, AL:Chi.
1909:	78	Ty Cobb, AL:Det. (2)
	54	Bob Bescher, NL:Cin.
1910:	81	Eddie Collins, AL:Phil.
	70	Bob Bescher, NL:Cin. (2)
1911:	83	Ty Cobb, AL:Det. (3)
	81	Bob Bescher, NL:Cin. (3)
1912:	88	Clyde Milan, AL:Wash.
	67	Bob Bescher, NL:Cin. (4)
1913:	75	Clyde Milan, AL:Wash. (2)
	61	Max Carey, NL:Pitt.
1914:	74	Fritz Maisel, AL:NY
	62	George Burns, NL:NY
1915:	96	Ty Cobb, AL:Det. (4)
	36	Max Carey, NL:Pitt. (2)
1916:	68	Ty Cobb, AL:Det. (5)
	63	Max Carey, NL:Pitt. (3)
1917:	55	Ty Cobb, AL:Det. (6)
	46	Max Carey, NL:Pitt. (4)
1918:	58	Max Carey, NL:Pitt. (5)
	45	George Sisler, AL:StL.
1919:	40	George Burns, NL:NY (2)
	33	Eddie Collins, AL:Chi. (2)
1920:	63	Sam Rice, AL:Wash. (6)
	52	Max Carey, NL:Pitt.
1921:	49	Frankie Frisch, NL:NY
	35	George Sisler, AL:StL. (2)
1922:	51	Max Carey, NL:Pitt. (7)
	51	George Sisler, AL:StL. (3)
1923:	51	Max Carey, NL:Pitt. (8)
	49	Eddie Collins, AL:Chi. (3)
1924:	49	Max Carey, NL:Pitt. (9)
	42	Eddie Collins, AL:Chi. (4)
1925:	46	Max Carey, NL:Pitt. (10)
	43	Johnny Mostil, AL:Chi.
1926:	35	Kiki Cuyler, NL:Pitt.
	35	Johnny Mostil, AL:Chi. (2)
1927:	48	Frankie Frisch, NL:StL. (2)
	27	George Sisler, AL:StL. (4)
1928:	37	Kiki Cuyler, NL:Chi. (2)
	30	Buddy Myer, AL:Bos.
1929:	43	Kiki Cuyler, NL:Chi. (3)
	28	Charlie Gehringer, AL:Det.
1930:	37	Kiki Cuyler, NL:Chi. (4)
	23	Marty McManus, AL:Det.

1931:	61	Ben Chapman, AL:NY
	28	Frankie Frisch, NL:StL. (3)
1932:	38	Ben Chapman, AL:NY (2)
	20	Chuck Klein, NL:Phil.
1933:	27	Ben Chapman, AL:NY (3)
	26	Pepper Martin, NL:StL.
1934:	40	Bill Werber, AL:Bos.
	23	Pepper Martin, NL:StL. (2)
1935:	29	Bill Werber, AL:Bos. (2)
	22	Augie Galan, NL:Chi.
1936:	37	Lyn Lary, AL:StL.
	23	Pepper Martin, NL:StL. (3)
1937:	35	Ben Chapman, AL:Wash.-Bos. (4)
	35	Bill Werber, AL:Phil. (3)
	23	Augie Galan, NL:Chi. (2)
1938:	27	Frankie Crosetti, AL:NY
	16	Stan Hack, NL:Chi.
1939:	51	George Case, AL:Wash.
	17	Stan Hack, NL:Chi. (2)
	17	Lee Handley, NL:Pitt.
1940:	35	George Case, AL:Wash. (2)
	22	Lonny Frey, NL:Cin.
1941:	33	George Case, AL:Wash. (3)
	18	Danny Murtaugh, NL:Phil.
1942:	44	George Case, AL:Wash. (4)
	20	Pete Reiser, NL:Brk.
1943:	61	George Case, AL:Wash. (5)
	20	Arky Vaughan, NL:Brk.
1944:	55	Snuffy Stirnweiss, AL:NY
	28	Johnny Barrett, NL:Pitt.
1945:	33	Snuffy Stirnweiss, AL:NY (2)
	26	Red Schoendienst, NL:StL.
1946:	34	Pete Reiser, NL:Brk. (2)
	28	George Case, AL:Clev. (6)
1947:	34	Bob Dillinger, AL:StL.
	29	Jackie Robinson, NL:Brk.
1948:	32	Richie Ashburn, NL:Phil.
	28	Bob Dillinger, AL:StL. (2)
1949:	37	Jackie Robinson, NL:Brk. (2)
	20	Bob Dillinger, AL:StL. (3)
1950:	35	Sam Jethroe, NL:Bos.
	15	Dom DiMaggio, AL:Bos.
1951:	35	Sam Jethroe, NL:Bos. (2)
	31	Minnie Minoso, AL:Clev.-Chi.
1952:	30	Pee Wee Reese, NL:Brk.
	22	Minnie Minoso, AL:Chi. (2)
1953:	26	Bill Bruton, NL:Mil.
	25	Minnie Minoso, AL:Chi. (3)
1954:	34	Bill Bruton, NL:Mil. (2)
	22	Jackie Jensen, AL:Bos.
1955:	25	Bill Bruton, NL:Mil. (3)
	25	Jim Rivera, AL:Chi.
1956:	40	Willie Mays, NL:NY
	21	Luis Aparicio, AL:Chi.
1957:	38	Willie Mays, NL:NY (2)
	28	Luis Aparicio, AL:Chi. (2)
1958:	31	Willie Mays, NL:SF (3)
	29	Luis Aparicio, AL:Chi. (3)
1959:	56	Luis Aparicio, AL:Chi. (4)
	27	Willie Mays, NL:SF (4)
1960:	51	Luis Aparicio, AL:Chi. (5)
	50	Maury Wills, NL:LA
1961:	53	Luis Aparicio, AL:Chi. (6)
	35	Maury Wills, NL:LA (2)
1962:	104	Maury Wills, NL:LA (3)
	31	Luis Aparicio, AL:Chi. (7)

STOLEN BASES (CONTINUED)

963:	40	Luis Aparicio, AL:Balt. (8)
	40	Maury Wills, NL:LA (4)
964:	57	Luis Aparicio, AL:Balt. (9)
	53	Maury Wills, NL:LA (5)
965:	94	Maury Wills, NL:LA (6)
	51	Bert Campaneris, AL:KC
966:	74	Lou Brock, NL:StL.
	52	Bert Campaneris, AL:KC (2)
967:	55	Bert Campaneris, AL:KC (3)
	52	Lou Brock, NL:StL. (2)
968:	62	Lou Brock, NL:StL. (3)
	62	Bert Campaneris. AL:Oak. (4)
969:	73	Tommy Harper, AL:Sea.
	53	Lou Brock, NL:StL. (4)
970:	57	Bobby Tolan, NL:Cin.
	42	Bert Campaneris, AL:Oak. (5)
971:	64	Lou Brock, NL:StL. (5)
	52	Amos Otis, AL:KC
972:	63	Lou Brock, NL:StL. (6)
	52	Bert Campaneris, AL:Oak. (6)
973:	70	Lou Brock, NL:StL. (7)
	54	Tommy Harper, AL:Bos. (2)
974:	118	Lou Brock, NL:StL. (8)
	54	Billy North, AL:Oak.
975:	77	Davey Lopes, NL:LA
	70	Mickey Rivers, AL:Cal.
976:	75	Billy North, AL:Oak. (2)
	63	Davey Lopes, NL:LA (2)
977:	70	Frank Taveras, NL:Pitt.
	53	Freddie Patek, AL:KC
978:	71	Omar Moreno, NL:Pitt.
	68	Ron LeFlore, AL:Det.
979:	83	Willie Wilson, AL:KC
	77	Omar Moreno, NL:Pitt. (2)
980:	100	Rickey Henderson, AL:Oak.
	97	Ron LeFlore, NL:Mtl.
981:	71	Tim Raines, NL:Mtl.
	56	Rickey Henderson, AL:Oak. (2)
982:	130	Rickey Henderson, AL:Oak. (3)
	78	Tim Raines, Tim NL:Mtl. (2)
983:	108	Rickey Henderson, AL:Oak. (4)
	90	Tim Raines, NL:Mtl. (3)
984:	75	Tim Raines, NL:Mtl. (4)
	66	Rickey Henderson, AL:Oak. (5)
985:	110	Vince Coleman, NL:StL.
	80	Rickey Henderson, AL:NY (6)
986:	107	Vince Coleman, NL:StL. (2)
	87	Rickey Henderson, AL:NY (7)
987:	109	Vince Coleman, NL:StL. (3)
	60	Harold Reynolds, AL:Sea.
988:	93	Rickey Henderson, AL:NY (8)
	81	Vince Coleman, NL:StL. (4)
989:	77	Rickey Henderson, AL:NY-Oak. (9)
	65	Vince Coleman, NL:StL. (5)
990:	77	Vince Coleman, NL:StL. (6)
	65	Rickey Henderson, AL:Oak. (10)
991:	76	Marquis Grissom, NL:Mtl.
	58	Rickey Henderson, AL:Oak. (11)
992:	78	Marquis Grissom, NL:Mtl. (2)
	66	Kenny Lofton, AL:Clev.
993:	70	Kenny Lofton, AL:Clev. (2)
	58	Chuck Carr, NL:Fla.
994:	60	Kenny Lofton, AL:Clev. (3)
	39	Craig Biggio, NL:Hou

1995:	56	Quilvio Veras, NL:Fla.
	54	Kenny Lofton, AL:Clev. (4)
1996:	75	Kenny Lofton, AL:Clev. (5)
	53	Eric Young, NL:Col.
1997:	74	Brian Hunter, AL:Det.
	60	Tony Womack, NL:Pitt.
1998:	66	Rickey Henderson, AL:Oak. (12)
	58	Tony Womack, NL:Pitt. (2)
1999:	72	Tony Womack, NL:Ari. (3)
	44	Brian Hunter, AL:Det.-Sea. (2)
2000:	62	Luis Castillo, NL:Fla.
	46	Johnny Damon, AL:KC
2001:	56	Ichiro Suzuki, AL:Sea.
	46	Juan Pierre, NL:Col.
	46	Jimmy Rollins, NL:Phil.
2002:	48	Luis Castillo, NL:Fla. (2)
	41	Alfonso Soriano, AL:NY
2003:	65	Juan Pierre, NL:Fla. (2)
	55	Carl Crawford, AL:TB
2004:	70	Scott Podsednik, NL:Mil.
	59	Carl Crawford, AL:TB (2)
2005:	62	Chone Figgins, AL:LA
	60	Jose Reyes, NL:NY
2006:	64	Jose Reyes, NL:NY (2)
	58	Carl Crawford, AL:TB (3)

EARNED RUN AVERAGE

Year	ERA	Pitcher
1912:	1.96	Jeff Tesreau, NL:NY
1913:	1.14	Walter Johnson, AL:Wash.
	2.06	Christy Mathewson, NL:NY
1914:	1.00	Dutch Leonard, AL:Bos.
	1.72	Bill Doak NL:StL.
1915:	1.22	Grover Alexander, NL:Phil.
	1.49	Smoky Joe Wood, AL:Bos.
1916:	1.55	Grover Alexander, NL:Phil. (2)
	1.75	Babe Ruth, AL:Bos.
1917:	1.54	Eddie Cicotte, AL:Chi.
	1.84	Grover Alexander, NL:Phil. (3)
1918:	1.27	Walter Johnson, AL:Wash. (2)
	1.74	Hippo Vaughn, NL:Chi.
1919:	1.48	Walter Johnson, AL:Wash. (3)
	1.72	Grover Alexander, NL:Chi. (4)
1920:	1.91	Grover Alexander, NL:Chi. (5)
	2.46	Bob Shawkey, AL:NY
1921:	2.46	Red Faber, AL:Chi.
	2.58	Bill Doak, NL:StL. (2)
1922:	2.81	Red Faber, AL:Chi. (2)
	3.00	Rosy Ryan, NL:NY
1923:	1.93	Dolf Luque, NL:Cin.
	2.76	Stan Coveleski, AL:Clev.
1924:	2.16	Dazzy Vance, NL:Brk.
	2.72	Walter Johnson, AL:Wash. (4)
1925:	2.66	Dolf Luque, NL:Cin. (2)
	2.84	Stan Coveleski, AL:Wash. (2)
1926:	2.52	Lefty Grove, AL:Phil.
	2.61	Ray Kremer, NL:Pitt.
1927:	2.28	Wilcy Moore, AL:NY
	2.47	Ray Kremer, NL:Pitt. (2)
1928:	2.08	Dazzy Vance, NL:Brk. (2)
	2.53	Garland Braxton, AL:Wash.
1929:	2.81	Lefty Grove, AL:Phil. (2)
	3.08	Bill Walker, NL:NY
1930:	2.54	Lefty Grove, AL:Phil. (3)
	2.61	Dazzy Vance, NL:Brk. (3)
1931:	2.06	Lefty Grove, AL:Phil. (4)
	2.26	Bill Walker, NL:NY (2)
1932:	2.37	Lon Warneke, NL:Chi.
	2.84	Lefty Grove, AL:Phil. (5)
1933:	1.66	Carl Hubbell, NL:NY (2)
	2.33	Monte Pearson, AL:Clev.
1934:	2.30	Carl Hubbell, NL:NY (3)
	2.33	Lefty Gomez, AL:NY
1935:	2.59	Cy Blanton, NL:Pitt.
	2.70	Lefty Grove, AL:Bos. (6)
1936:	2.31	Carl Hubbell, NL:NY (4)
	2.81	Lefty Grove, AL:Bos. (7)
1937:	2.33	Lefty Gomez, AL:NY (2)
	2.38	Jim Turner, NL:Bos.
1938:	2.66	Bill Lee, NL:Chi.
	3.07	Lefty Grove, AL:Bos. (8)
1939:	2.29	Bucky Walters, NL:Cin.
	2.54	Lefty Grove, AL:Bos. (9)
1940:	2.48	Bucky Walters, NL:Cin. (2)
	2.62	Bob Feller, AL:Clev.
1941:	2.20	Elmer Riddle, NL:Cin.
	2.37	Thornton Lee, AL:Chi.
1942:	1.77	Mort Cooper, NL:StL.
	2.10	Ted Lyons, AL:Chi.
1943:	1.64	Spud Chandler, AL:NY
	1.75	Howie Pollet, NL:StL.
1944:	2.12	Dizzy Trout, AL:Det.
	2.40	Bucky Walters, NL:Cin. (3)
1945:	1.81	Hal Newhouser, AL:Det.
	2.14	Hank Borowy, NL:Chi.
1946:	1.94	Hal Newhouser, AL:Det. (2)
	2.10	Howie Pollet, NL:StL. (2)
1947:	2.33	Warren Spahn, NL:Bos.
	2.46	Spud Chandler, AL:NY (2)
1948:	2.24	Harry Brecheen, NL:StL.
	2.47	Gene Bearden, AL:Clev.
1949:	2.50	Dave Koslo, NL:NY
	2.78	Mel Parnell, AL:Bos.
1950:	2.49	Jim Hearn, NL:StL.-NY
	3.20	Early Wynn, AL:Clev.
1951:	2.78	Saul Rogovin, AL:Det.-Chi.
	2.88	Chet Nichols, NL:Bos.
1952:	2.07	Allie Reynolds, AL:NY
	2.43	Hoyt Wilhelm, NL:NY
1953:	2.10	Warren Spahn, NL:Mil. (2)
	2.43	Ed Lopat, AL:NY
1954:	2.29	Johnny Antonelli, NL:NY
	2.64	Mike Garcia, AL:Clev.
1955	1.97	Billy Pierce, AL:Chi.
	2.84	Bob Friend, NL:Pitt.
1956:	2.47	Whitey Ford, AL:NY
	2.71	Lew Burdette, NL:Mil.
1957:	2.45	Bobby Shantz, AL:NY
	2.66	Johnny Podres, NL:Brk.
1958:	2.01	Whitey Ford, AL:NY (2)
	2.47	Stu Miller, NL:SF
1959:	2.19	Hoyt Wilhelm, AL:Balt. (NL 1)
	2.82	Sam Jones, NL:SF
1960:	2.68	Frank Baumann, AL:Chi.
	2.70	Mike McCormick, NL:SF
1961:	2.40	Dick Donovan, AL:Wash.
	3.01	Warren Spahn, NL:Mil. (3)
1962:	2.21	Hank Aguirre, AL:Det.
	2.54	Sandy Koufax, NL:LA
1963:	1.88	Sandy Koufax, NL:LA (2)
	2.33	Gary Peters, AL:Chi.
1964:	1.65	Dean Chance, AL:LA
	1.74	Sandy Koufax, NL:LA (3)
1965:	2.04	Sandy Koufax, NL:LA (4)
	2.18	Sam McDowell, AL:Clev.
1966:	1.73	Sandy Koufax, NL:LA (5)
	1.98	Gary Peters, AL:Chi. (2)
1967:	1.87	Phil Niekro, NL:Atl.
	2.06	Joel Horlen, AL:Chi.
1968:	1.12	Bob Gibson, NL:StL.
	1.60	Luis Tiant, AL:Clev.
1969:	2.10	Juan Marichal, NL:SF
	2.19	Dick Bosman, AL:Wash.
1970:	2.56	Diego Segui, AL:Oak.
	2.81	Tom Seaver, NL:NY
1971:	1.76	Tom Seaver, NL:NY (2)
	1.82	Vida Blue, AL:Oak.
1972:	1.91	Luis Tiant, AL:Bos. (2)
	1.98	Steve Carlton, NL:Phil.
1973:	2.08	Tom Seaver, NL:NY (3)
	2.40	Jim Palmer, AL:Balt.
1974:	2.28	Buzz Capra, NL:Atl.
	2.49	Catfish Hunter, AL:Oak.
1975:	2.09	Jim Palmer, AL:Balt. (2)
	2.24	Randy Jones, NL:SD
1976:	2.34	Mark Fidrych, AL:Det.
	2.52	John Denny, NL:StL.
1977:	2.34	John Candelaria, NL:Pitt.
	2.54	Frank Tanana, AL:Cal.

EARNED RUN AVERAGE (CONTINUED)

1978:	1.74	Ron Guidry, AL:NY
	2.43	Craig Swan, NL:NY
1979:	2.71	J.R. Richard, NL:Hou.
	2.78	Ron Guidry, AL:NY (2)
1980:	2.21	Don Sutton, NL:LA
	2.47	Rudy May, AL:NY
1981:	1.69	Nolan Ryan, NL:Hou.
	2.32	Steve McCatty, AL:Oak.
1982:	2.40	Steve Rogers, NL:Mtl.
	2.96	Rick Sutcliffe, AL:Clev.
1983:	2.25	Atlee Hammaker, NL:SF
	2.42	Rick Honeycutt, AL:Tex.
1984:	2.48	Alejandro Pena, NL:LA
	2.79	Mike Boddicker, AL:Balt.
1985:	1.53	Dwight Gooden, NL:NY
	2.48	Dave Stieb, AL:Tor.
1986:	2.22	Mike Scott, NL:Hou.
	2.48	Roger Clemens, AL:Bos.
1987:	2.76	Jimmy Key, AL:Tor.
	2.76	Nolan Ryan, NL:Hou. (2)
1988:	2.18	Joe Magrane, NL:StL.
	2.45	Allan Anderson, AL:Minn.
1989:	2.16	Bret Saberhagen, AL:KC
	2.28	Scott Garrelts, NL:SF
1990:	1.93	Roger Clemens, AL:Bos. (2)
	2.21	Danny Darwin, NL:Hou.
1991:	2.39	Dennis Martinez, NL:Mtl.
	2.62	Roger Clemens, AL:Bos. (3)
1992:	2.08	Bill Swift, NL:SF
	2.41	Roger Clemens, AL:Bos. (4)
1993:	2.36	Greg Maddux, NL:Atl.
	2.56	Kevin Appier, AL:KC
1994:	1.56	Greg Maddux, NL:Atl. (2)
	2.65	Steve Ontiveros, AL:Oak.
1995:	1.63	Greg Maddux, NL:Atl. (3)
	2.48	Randy Johnson, AL:Sea.
1996:	1.89	Kevin Brown, NL:Fla.
	2.93	Juan Guzman, AL:Tor.
1997:	1.90	Pedro Martinez, NL:Mtl.
	2.05	Roger Clemens, AL:Tor. (5)
1998:	2.22	Greg Maddux, NL:Atl. (4)
	2.65	Roger Clemens, AL:Tor. (6)
1999:	2.07	Pedro Martinez, AL:Bos. (NL 1)
	2.48	Randy Johnson, NL:Ari. (AL 1)
2000:	1.74	Pedro Martinez, AL:Bos. (AL 2; NL 1)
	2.58	Kevin Brown, NL:LA(2)
2001:	2.49	Randy Johnson, NL:Ari. (AL 1; NL 2)
	3.05	Freddy Garcia, AL:Sea.
2002:	2.26	Pedro Martinez, AL:Bos. (AL 3; NL 1)
	2.32	Randy Johnson, NL:Ari. (AL 1; NL 3)
2003:	2.22	Pedro Martinez, AL:Bos. (AL 4; NL 1)
	2.34	Jason Schmidt, NL:SF
2004:	2.27	Jake Peavy, NL:SD
	2.61	Johan Santana, AL:Minn.
2005:	1.87	Roger Clemens, NL:Hou. (AL 6)
	2.86	Kevin Millwood, AL:Clev.
2006:	2.77	Johan Santana, AL:Minn. (2)
	2.98	Roy Oswalt, NL:Hou.

WINNING PERCENTAGE

Minimum: 15 Decisions

1900	.778	28- 8	Joe McGinnity, NL:Brk.
1901:	.774	24- 7	Clark Griffith, AL:Chi.
	.737	14- 5	Sam Leever, NL:Pitt.
1902:	.824	28- 6	Jack Chesbro, NL:Pitt.
	.783	18- 5	Bill Bernhard, AL:Phil.-Clev.
1903:	.781	25- 7	Sam Leever, NL:Pitt. (2)
	.757	28- 9	Cy Young, AL:Bos.
1904:	.814	35- 8	Joe McGinnity, NL:NY (2)
	.774	41-12	Jack Chesbro, AL:NY
1905:	.800	20- 5	Sam Leever, NL:Pitt. (3)
	.730	27-10	Rube Waddell, AL:Phil.
1906:	.826	19- 4	Ed Reulbach, NL:Chi.
	.760	19- 6	Eddie Plank, AL:Phil.
1907:	.862	25- 4	Wild Bill Donovan, AL:Det.
	.810	17- 4	Ed Reulbach, NL:Chi. (2)
1908:	.774	24- 7	Ed Reulbach, NL:Chi. (3)
	.727	40-15	Ed Walsh, AL:Chi.
1909:	.806	25- 6	Howie Camnitz, NL:Pitt.
	.806	25- 6	Christy Mathewson, NL:NY
	.784	29- 8	George Mullin, AL:Det.
1910:	.875	14- 2	Deacon Phillippe, NL:Pitt.
	.821	23- 5	Chief Bender, AL:Phil.
1911:	.774	24- 7	Rube Marquard, NL:NY
	.773	17- 5	Chief Bender, AL:Phil. (2)
1912:	.872	34- 5	Smoky Joe Wood, AL:Bos.
	.727	24- 9	Claude Hendrix, NL:Pitt.
1913:	.837	36- 7	Walter Johnson, AL:Wash.
	.800	16- 4	Bert Humphries, NL:Chi.
1914:	.850	17- 3	Chief Bender, AL:Phil. (3)
	.788	26- 7	Bill James, NL:Bos.
1915:	.756	31-10	Grover Alexander, NL:Phil.
	.750	15- 5	Smoky Joe Wood, AL:Bos. (2)
1916:	.842	16- 3	Tom Hughes, NL:Bos.
	.684	13- 6	Nick Cullop, AL:NY
1917:	.778	14- 4	Ed Klepfer, AL:Clev.
	.750	21- 7	Ferdie Schupp, NL:NY
1918:	.762	16- 5	Sam Jones, AL:Bos.
	.741	20- 7	Claude Hendrix, NL:Pitt. (2)
1919:	.806	29- 7	Eddie Cicotte, AL:Chi.
	.760	19- 6	Dutch Ruether, NL:Cin.
1920:	.721	31-12	Jim Bagby, AL:Clev.
	.676	23-11	Burleigh Grimes, NL:Brk.
1921:	.750	27- 9	Carl Mays, AL:NY
	.737	14- 5	Babe Adams, NL:Pitt.
	.737	14- 5	Whitey Glazner, NL:Pitt.
1922:	.788	26- 7	Joe Bush, AL:NY
	.733	11- 4	Phil Douglas, NL:NY
1923:	.771	27- 8	Dolf Luque, NL:Cin.
	.760	19- 6	Herb Pennock, AL:NY
1924:	.842	16- 3	Emil Yde, NL:Pitt.
	.767	23- 7	Walter Johnson, AL:Wash. (2)
1925:	.800	20- 5	Stan Coveleski, AL:Wash.
	.714	15- 6	Bill Sherdel, NL:StL.
1926:	.769	20- 6	Ray Kremer, NL:Pitt.
	.711	27-11	George Uhle, AL:Clev.
1927:	.759	22- 7	Waite Hoyt, AL:NY
	.708	17- 7	Larry Benton, NL:Bos.-NY
1928:	.808	21- 5	General Crowder, AL:StL.
	.735	25- 9	Larry Benton, NL:NY (2)
1929:	.769	20- 6	Lefty Grove, AL:Phil.
	.760	19- 6	Charlie Root, NL:Chi.
1930:	.848	28- 5	Lefty Grove, AL:Phil. (2)
	.733	11- 4	Bud Teachout, NL:Chi.

1931:	.886	31- 4	Lefty Grove, AL:Phil. (3)
	.800	12- 3	Jesse Haines, NL:StL.
1932:	.810	17- 4	Johnny Allen, AL:NY
	.786	22- 6	Lon Warneke, NL:Chi.
1933:	.750	24- 8	Lefty Grove, AL:Phil. (4)
	.750	12- 4	Russ Van Atta, AL:NY
	.684	13- 6	Bud Tinning, NL:Chi.
1934:	.839	26- 5	Lefty Gomez, AL:NY
	.811	30- 7	Dizzy Dean, NL:StL.
1935:	.769	20- 6	Bill Lee, NL:Chi.
	.720	18- 7	Elden Auker, AL:Det.
1936:	.813	26- 6	Carl Hubbell, NL:NY
	.778	14- 4	Bump Hadley, AL:NY
1937:	.938	15- 1	Johnny Allen, AL:Clev. (2)
	.733	22- 8	Carl Hubbell, NL:NY (2)
1938:	.778	14- 4	Lefty Grove, AL:Bos. (5)
	.710	22- 9	Bill Lee, NL:Chi. (2)
1939:	.813	13- 3	Atley Donald, AL:NY
	.781	25- 7	Paul Derringer, NL:Cin.
1940:	.889	16- 2	Freddie Fitzsimmons, NL:Brk. (2)
	.842	16- 3	Schoolboy Rowe, AL:Det.
1941:	.826	19- 4	Elmer Riddle, NL:Cin.
	.750	15- 5	Lefty Gomez, AL:NY (2)
1942:	.813	13- 3	Howie Krist, NL:StL.
	.808	21- 5	Ernie Bonham, AL:NY
1943:	.833	20- 4	Spud Chandler, AL:NY
	.737	14- 5	Clyde Shoun, NL:Cin.
	.737	14- 5	Whitlow Wyatt, NL:Brk.
1944:	.810	17- 4	Ted Wilks, NL:StL.
	.783	18- 5	Tex Hughson, AL:Bos.
1945:	.789	15- 4	Harry Brecheen, NL:StL.
	.765	13- 4	Bob Muncrief, AL:StL.
1946:	.806	25- 6	Boo Ferriss, AL:Bos.
	.733	11- 4	Schoolboy Rowe, NL:Phil. (AL 1)
1947:	.808	21- 5	Larry Jansen, NL:NY
	.737	14- 5	Spec Shea, AL:NY
1948:	.813	13- 3	Rip Sewell, NL:Pitt.
	.783	18- 5	Jack Kramer, AL:Bos.
1949:	.793	23- 6	Ellis Kinder, AL:Bos.
	.722	13- 5	Ralph Branca, NL:Brk.
1950:	.818	18- 4	Sal Maglie, NL:NY
	.724	21- 8	Vic Raschi, AL:NY
1951:	.880	22- 3	Preacher Roe, NL:Brk.
	.733	22- 8	Bob Feller, AL:Clev.
	.733	11- 4	Morrie Martin, AL:Phil.
1952:	.833	15- 3	Hoyt Wilhelm, NL:NY
	.774	24- 7	Bobby Shantz, AL:Phil.
1953:	.800	16- 4	Ed Lopat, AL:NY
	.769	20- 6	Carl Erskine, NL:Brk.
1954:	.842	16- 3	Sandy Consuegra, AL:Chi.
	.750	21- 7	Johnny Antonelli, NL:NY
	.750	12- 4	Hoyt Wilhelm, NL:NY (2)
1955:	.800	20- 5	Don Newcombe, NL:Brk.
	.762	16- 5	Tommy Byrne, AL:NY
1956:	.794	27- 7	Don Newcombe, NL:Brk. (2)
	.760	19- 6	Whitey Ford, AL:NY
1957:	.727	16- 6	Dick Donovan, AL:Chi.
	.727	16- 6	Tom Sturdivant, AL:NY
	.720	18- 7	Bob Buhl, NL:Mil.
1958:	.750	21- 7	Bob Turley, AL:NY
	.667	22-11	Warren Spahn, NL:Mil.
	.667	20-10	Lew Burdette, NL:Mil.
1959:	.947	18- 1	Roy Face, NL:Pitt.
	.750	18- 6	Bob Shaw, AL:Chi.
1960:	.813	13- 3	Jim Coates, AL:NY
	.750	12- 4	Lindy McDaniel, NL:StL.

WINNING PERCENTAGE (CONTINUED)

1961:	.862 25- 4	Whitey Ford, AL:NY (2)
	.783 18- 5	Johnny Podres, NL:LA
1962	.821 23- 5	Bob Purkey, NL:Cin.
	.733 11- 4	Dave Wickersham, AL:KC
1963	.842 16- 3	Ron Perranoski, NL:LA
	.774 24- 7	Whitey Ford, AL:NY (3)
1964	.792 19- 5	Wally Bunker, AL:Balt.
	.792 19- 5	Sandy Koufax, NL:LA
1965:	.765 26- 8	Sandy Koufax, NL:LA (2)
	.750 21- 7	Mudcat Grant, AL:Minn.
1966:	.933 14- 1	Phil Regan, NL:LA
	.706 12- 5	Dave Boswell, AL:Minn.
1967:	.750 12- 4	Jose Santiago, AL:Bos.
	.737 14- 5	Neslon Briles NL:StL.
1968:	.838 31- 6	Denny McLain, AL:Det.
	.750 18- 6	Steve Blass, NL:Pitt.
1969:	.824 14- 3	Bob Moose, NL:Pitt.
	.800 16- 4	Jim Palmer, AL:Balt.
1970:	.824 14- 3	Wayne Simpson, NL:Cin.
	.750 24- 8	Mike Cuellar, AL:Balt.
1971:	.808 21- 5	Dave McNally, AL:Balt.
	.733 11- 4	Tug McGraw, NL:NY
1972:	.750 21- 7	Catfish Hunter, AL:Oak.
	.750 15- 5	Gary Nolan, NL:Cin.
1973:	.867 13- 2	Roger Moret, AL:Bos.
	.800 12- 3	George Stone, NL:NY
1974:	.813 13- 3	Tommy John, NL:LA
	.733 11- 4	Billy Champion, AL:Mil.
1975:	.824 14- 3	Roger Moret, AL:Bos. (2)
	.813 13- 3	Al Hrabosky, NL:StL.
1976:	.800 12- 3	Rick Rhoden, NL:LA
	.773 17- 5	Bill Campbell, AL:Minn.
1977:	.800 20- 5	John Candelaria, NL:Pitt.
	.778 14- 4	Don Gullett, AL:NY
1978:	.893 25- 3	Ron Guidry, AL:NY
	.778 21- 6	Gaylord Perry, NL:SD
1979:	.875 14- 2	Ron Davis, AL:NY
	.750 12- 4	Jim Bibby, NL:Pitt.
1980:	.781 25- 7	Steve Stone, AL:Balt.
	.760 19- 6	Jim Bibby, NL:Pitt. (2)
1981:	.875 14- 2	Tom Seaver, NL:Cin.
	.778 14- 4	Pete Vuckovich, AL:Mil.
1982:	.810 17- 4	Phil Niekro, NL:Atl.
	.750 15- 5	Jim Palmer, AL:Balt. (2)
	.750 18- 6	Pete Vuckovich, AL:Mil. (2)
1983:	.813 13- 3	Moose Haas, AL:Mil.
	.760 19- 6	John Denny, NL:Phil.
1984:	.941 16- 1	Rick Sutcliffe, NL:Chi.
	.739 17- 6	Doyle Alexander, AL:Tor.
1985:	.864 19- 3	Orel Hershiser, NL:LA
	.786 22- 6	Ron Guidry, AL:NY (2)
1986:	.857 24- 4	Roger Clemens, AL:Bos.
	.783 18- 5	Bob Ojeda, NL:NY
1987:	.733 11- 4	Dennis Martinez, NL:Mtl.
	.733 11- 4	John Cerutti, AL:Tor.
	.733 11- 4	Lee Guetterman, AL:Sea.
1988:	.870 20- 3	David Cone, NL:NY
	.774 24- 7	Frank Viola, AL:Minn.
1989:	.793 23- 6	Bret Saberhagen, AL:KC
	.737 14- 5	Sid Fernandez, NL:NY
	.737 14- 5	Scott Garrelts, NL:SF
1990:	.818 27- 6	Bob Welch, AL:Oak.
	.786 22- 6	Doug Drabek, NL:Pitt.

1991:	.750 12- 4	Joe Hesketh, AL:Bos.
	.714 20- 8	John Smiley, NL:Pitt.
	.714 15- 6	Jose Rijo, NL:Cin.
1992:	.783 18- 5	Mike Mussina, AL:Balt.
	.762 16- 5	Bob Tewksbury, NL:StL.
1993:	.824 14- 3	Juan Guzman, AL:Tor.
	.818 18- 4	Mark Portugal, NL:Hou.
1994:	.810 17- 4	Jimmy Key, AL:NY
	.778 14- 4	Bret Saberhagen, NL:NY (AL 1)
1995:	.905 19- 2	Greg Maddux, NL:Atl.
	.900 18- 2	Randy Johnson, AL:Sea.
1996:	.813 13- 3	Jamie Moyer, AL:Bos.-Sea.
	.750 24- 8	John Smoltz, NL:Atl.
1997:	.833 20- 4	Randy Johnson, AL:Sea. (2)
	.826 19- 4	Greg Maddux, NL:Atl. (2)
1998:	.850 17- 3	John Smoltz, NL:Atl. (2)
	.818 18- 4	David Wells, AL:NY
1999:	.852 23- 4	Pedro Martinez, AL:Bos.
	.846 22- 4	Mike Hampton, NL:Hou.
2000:	.769 20- 6	Tim Hudson, AL:Oak.
	.731 19- 7	Randy Johnson, NL:Ari. (AL 2)
2001:	.870 20- 3	Roger Clemens, AL:NY (2)
	.824 14- 3	Roy Oswalt, NL:Hou.
2002:	.833 20- 4	Pedro Martinez, AL:Bos. (2)
	.828 24- 5	Randy Johnson, NL:Ari. (AL 2; NL 2)
2003:	.800 12- 3	Johan Santana, AL:Minn.
	.773 17- 5	Jason Schmidt, NL:SF
2004:	.818 18- 4	Roger Clemens, NL:Hou. (AL 2)
	.778 21- 6	Curt Schilling, AL:Bos.
2005:	.813 13- 3	Jorge Sosa, NL:Atl.
	.783 18- 5	Cliff Lee, AL:Clev.
2006:	.800 12- 3	Francisco Liriano, AL:Minn.
	.733 11- 4	Chuck James, NL:Atl.

STRIKEOUTS

1900:	130	Rube Waddell, NL:Pitt.
1901:	239	Noodles Hahn, NL:Cin.
	158	Cy Young, AL:Bos.
1902:	225	Vid Willis, NL:Bos.
	210	Rube Waddell, AL:Phil.
1903:	302	Rube Waddell, AL:Phil. (2)
	267	Christy Mathewson, NL:NY
1904:	349	Rube Waddell, AL:Phil. (3)
	212	Christy Mathewson, NL:NY (2)
1905:	287	Rube Waddell, AL:Phil. (4)
	206	Christy Mathewson, NL:NY (3)
1906:	196	Rube Waddell, AL:Phil. (5)
	171	Fred Beebe, NL:Chi.-StL.
1907:	232	Rube Waddell, AL:Phil. (6)
	178	Christy Mathewson, NL:NY (4)
1908:	269	Ed Walsh, AL:Chi.
	259	Christy Mathewson, NL:NY (5)
1909:	205	Orval Overall, NL:Chi.
	177	Frank Smith, AL:Chi.
1910:	313	Walter Johnson, AL:Wash.
	190	Christy Mathewson, NL:NY (6)
1911:	255	Ed Walsh, AL:Chi. (2)
	237	Rube Marquard, NL:NY
1912:	303	Walter Johnson, AL:Wash. (2)
	195	Grover Alexander, NL:Phil.
1913:	243	Walter Johnson, AL:Wash. (3)
	168	Tom Seaton, NL:Phil.
1914:	225	Walter Johnson, AL:Wash. (4)
	214	Grover Alexander, NL:Phil. (2)
1915:	241	Grover Alexander, NL:Phil. (3)
	203	Walter Johnson, AL:Wash. (5)
1916:	228	Walter Johnson, AL:Wash. (6)
	169	Grover Alexander, NL:Phil. (4)
1917:	200	Grover Alexander, NL:Phil. (5)
	188	Walter Johnson, AL:Wash. (7)
1918:	163	Walter Johnson, AL:Wash. (8)
	148	Hippo Vaughn, NL:Chi.
1919:	147	Walter Johnson, AL:Wash. (9)
	141	Hippo Vaughn, NL:Chi. (2)
1920:	173	Grover Alexander, NL:Chi. (6)
	133	Stan Coveleski, AL:Clev.
1921:	149	Walter Johnson, AL:Wash. (10)
	136	Burleigh Grimes, NL:Brk.
1922:	149	Urban Shocker, AL:StL.
	134	Dazzy Vance, NL:Brk.
1923:	197	Dazzy Vance, NL:Brk. (2)
	132	Walter Johnson, AL:Wash. (11)
1924:	262	Dazzy Vance, NL:Brk. (3)
	158	Walter Johnson, AL:Wash. (12)
1925:	221	Dazzy Vance, NL:Brk. (4)
	116	Lefty Grove, AL:Phil.
1926:	197	Lefty Grove, AL:Phil. (2)
	140	Dazzy Vance, NL:Brk. (5)
1927:	184	Dazzy Vance, NL:Brk. (6)
	174	Lefty Grove, AL:Phil. (3)
1928:	200	Dazzy Vance, NL:Brk. (7)
	183	Lefty Grove, AL:Phil. (4)
1929:	170	Lefty Grove, AL:Phil. (5)
	166	Pat Malone, NL:Chi.
1930:	209	Lefty Grove, AL:Phil. (6)
	177	Bill Hallahan, NL:StL.
1931:	175	Lefty Grove, AL:Phil. (7)
	159	Bill Hallahan, NL:StL. (2)
1932:	191	Dizzy Dean, NL:StL.
	190	Red Ruffing, AL:NY1933

1933:	199	Dizzy Dean, NL:StL. (2)
	163	Lefty Gomez, AL:NY
1934:	195	Dizzy Dean, NL:StL. (3)
	158	Lefty Gomez, AL:NY (2)
1935:	190	Dizzy Dean, NL:StL. (4)
	163	Tommy Bridges, AL:Det.
1936:	238	Van Mungo, NL:Brk.
	175	Tommy Bridges, AL:Det. (2)
1937:	194	Lefty Gomez, AL:NY (3)
	159	Carl Hubbell, NL:NY
1938:	240	Bob Feller, AL:Clev.
	135	Clay Bryant, NL:Chi.
1939:	246	Bob Feller, AL:Clev. (2)
	139	Claude Passeau, NL:Phil.-Chi.
1940:	261	Bob Feller, AL:Clev. (3)
	137	Kirby Higbe, NL:Phil.
1941:	260	Bob Feller, AL:Clev. (4)
	202	Johnny Vander Meer, NL:Cin.
1942:	186	Johnny Vander Meer, NL:Cin. (2)
	113	Tex Hughson, AL:Bos.
	113	Bobo Newsom, AL:Wash.
1943:	174	Johnny Vander Meer, NL:Cin. (3)
	151	Allie Reynolds, AL:Clev.
1944:	187	Hal Newhouser, AL:Det.
	161	Bill Voiselle, NL:NY
1945:	212	Hal Newhouser, AL:Det. (2)
	148	Preacher Roe, NL:Pitt.
1946:	348	Bob Feller, AL:Clev. (5)
	135	Johnny Schmitz, NL:Chi.
1947:	196	Bob Feller, AL:Clev. (6)
	195	Ewell Blackwell, NL:Cin.
1948:	164	Bob Feller, AL:Clev. (7)
	149	Harry Brecheen, NL:StL.
1949:	153	Virgil Trucks, AL:Det.
	151	Warren Spahn, NL:Bos.
1950:	191	Warren Spahn, NL:Bos. (2)
	170	Bob Lemon, AL:Clev.
1951:	164	Don Newcombe, NL:Brk.
	164	Warren Spahn, NL:Bos. (3)
	164	Vic Raschi, AL:NY
1952:	183	Warren Spahn, NL:Bos. (4)
	160	Allie Reynolds AL:NY (2)
1953:	198	Robin Roberts, NL:Phil.
	186	Billy Pierce, AL:Chi.
1954:	185	Robin Roberts, NL:Phil. (2)
	185	Bob Turley, AL:Balt.
1955:	245	Herb Score, AL:Clev.
	198	Sam Jones, NL:Chi.
1956:	263	Herb Score, AL:Clev. (2)
	176	Sam Jones, NL:Chi. (2)
1957:	188	Jack Sanford, NL:Phil.
	184	Early Wynn, AL:Clev.
1958:	225	Sam Jones, NL:StL. (3)
	179	Early Wynn, AL:Chi. (2)
1959:	242	Don Drysdale, NL:LA
	201	Jim Bunning, AL:Det.
1960:	246	Don Drysdale, NL:LA (2)
	201	Jim Bunning, AL:Det. (2)
1961:	269	Sandy Koufax, NL:LA
	221	Camilo Pascual, AL:Minn.
1962:	232	Don Drysdale, NL:LA (3)
	206	Camilo Pascual, AL:Minn. (2)

STRIKEOUTS (CONTINUED)

1963:	306	Sandy Koufax, NL:LA (2)
	202	Camilo Pascual, AL:Minn. (3)
1964:	250	Bob Veale, NL:Pitt.
	217	Al Downing, AL:NY
1965:	382	Sandy Koufax, NL:LA (3)
	325	Sam McDowell, AL:Clev.
1966:	317	Sandy Koufax, NL:LA (4)
	225	Sam McDowell, AL:Clev. (2)
1967:	253	Jim Bunning, NL:Phil.
	246	Jim Lonborg, AL:Bos.
1968:	283	Sam McDowell, AL:Clev. (3)
	268	Bob Gibson, NL:StL.
1969:	279	Sam McDowell, AL:Clev. (4)
	273	Ferguson Jenkins, NL:Chi.
1970:	304	Sam McDowell, AL:Clev. (5)
	283	Tom Seaver, NL:NY
1971:	308	Mickey Lolich, AL:Det.
	289	Tom Seaver, NL:NY (2)
1972:	329	Nolan Ryan, AL:Cal.
	310	Steve Carlton, NL:Phil.
1973:	383	Nolan Ryan, AL:Cal. (2)
	251	Tom Seaver, NL:NY (3)
1974:	367	Nolan Ryan, AL:Cal. (3)
	240	Steve Carlton, NL:Phil. (2)
1975:	269	Frank Tanana, AL:Cal.
	243	Tom Seaver, NL:NY (4)
1976:	327	Nolan Ryan, AL:Cal. (4)
	235	Tom Seaver, NL:NY (5)
1977:	341	Nolan Ryan, AL:Cal. (5)
	262	Phil Niekro, NL:Atl.
1978:	303	J.R. Richard, NL:Hou.
	260	Nolan Ryan, AL:Cal. (6)
1979:	313	J.R. Richard, NL:Hou. (2)
	223	Nolan Ryan, AL:Cal. (7)
1980:	286	Steve Carlton, NL:Phil. (3)
	187	Len Barker, AL:Clev.
1981:	180	Fernando Valenzuela, NL:LA
	127	Len Barker, AL:Clev. (2)
1982:	286	Steve Carlton, NL:Phil. (4)
	209	Floyd Bannister, AL:Sea.
1983:	275	Steve Carlton, NL:Phil. (5)
	232	Jack Morris, AL:Det.
1984:	276	Dwight Gooden, NL:NY
	204	Mark Langston, AL:Sea.
1985:	268	Dwight Gooden, NL:NY (2)
	206	Bert Blyleven, AL:Clev.-Minn.
1986:	306	Mike Scott, NL:Hou.
	245	Mark Langston, AL:Sea. (2)
1987:	270	Nolan Ryan, NL:Hou.
	262	Mark Langston, AL:Sea. (3)
1988:	291	Roger Clemens, AL:Bos.
	228	Nolan Ryan, NL:Hou. (2)
1989:	301	Nolan Ryan, AL:Tex. (8)
	201	Jose DeLeon, NL:StL.
1990:	233	David Cone, NL:NY
	232	Nolan Ryan, AL:Tex. (9)
1991:	241	Roger Clemens, AL:Bos. (2)
	241	David Cone, NL:NY (2)
1992:	261	David Cone, NL:NY-AL:Tor. (ML 3)
	241	Randy Johnson, AL:Sea.
	215	John Smoltz, NL:Atl.
1993:	308	Randy Johnson, AL:Sea. (2)
	227	Jose Rijo, NL:Cin.
1994:	204	Randy Johnson, AL:Sea. (3)
	189	Andy Benes, NL:SD

1995:	294	Randy Johnson, AL:Sea. (4)
	236	Hideo Nomo, NL:LA
1996:	276	John Smoltz, NL:Atl. (2)
	257	Roger Clemens, AL:Bos. (3)
1997:	319	Curt Schilling, NL:Phil.
	292	Roger Clemens, AL:Tor. (4)
1998:	329	Randy Johnson, AL:Sea.-NL:Hou. (ML 4)
	300	Curt Schilling, NL:Phil. (2)
	271	Roger Clemens, AL:Tor. (5)
1999:	364	Randy Johnson, NL:Ari. (ML 5)
	313	Pedro Martinez, AL:Bos.
2000:	347	Randy Johnson, NL:Ari. (NL 2; ML 6)
	284	Pedro Martinez, AL:Bos. (2)
2001:	372	Randy Johnson, NL:Ari. (NL 3;ML 7)
	220	Hideo Nomo, AL:Bos. (NL 1)
2002:	334	Randy Johnson, NL:Ari. (NL 4; ML 8)
	239	Pedro Martinez, AL:Bos. (3)
2003:	266	Kerry Wood, NL:Chi.
	207	Esteban Loaiza, AL:Chi.
2004:	290	Randy Johnson, NL:Ari. (NL 5;ML 9)
	265	Johan Santana, AL:Minn.
2005:	238	Johan Santana, AL:Minn. (2)
	216	Jake Peavy, NL:SD
2006:	245	Johan Santana, AL:Minn. (3)
	216	Aaron Harang, NL:Cin.

MOST VALUABLE PLAYER

Baseball Writers Association of America *(Unanimous Selections Capitalized)*

AMERICAN LEAGUE	YEAR	NATIONAL LEAGUE
Lefty Grove, Phil. (p)	1931	Frankie Frisch, StL. (2b)
Jimmie Foxx, Phil. (1b)	1932	Chuck Klein, Phil. (of)
Jimmie Foxx, Phil. (1b)	1933	CARL HUBBELL, NY (p)
Mickey Cochrane Det. (c)	1934	Dizzy Dean, StL. (p)
HANK GREENBERG, Det. (1b)	1935	Gabby Hartnett, Chi. (c)
Lou Gehrig, NY (1b)	1936	Carl Hubbell, NY (p)
Charlie Gehringer, Det. (2b)	1937	Joe Medwick, StL. (of)
Jimmie Foxx, Bos. (1b)	1938	Ernie Lombardi, Cin. (c)
Joe DiMaggio, NY (of)	1939	Buck Walters, Cin. (p)
Hank Greenberg, Det. (of)	1940	Frank McCormick, Cin. (1b)
Joe DiMaggio, NY (of)	1941	Dolph Camilli, Brk. (1b)
Joe Gordon, NY (2b)	1942	Mort Cooper, StL. (p)
Spud Chandler, NY (p)	1943	Stan Musial, StL. (of)
Hal Newhouser, Det. (p)	1944	Marty Marion, StL. (ss)
Hal Newhouser, Det. (p)	1945	Phil Cavarretta, Chi. (1b)
Ted Williams, Bos. (of)	1946	Stan Musial, StL. (1b)
Joe DiMaggio, NY (of)	1947	Bob Elliott, Bos. (3b)
Lou Boudreau, Clev. (ss)	1948	Stan Musial, StL. (of)
Ted Williams, Bos. (of)	1949	Jackie Robinson, Brk. (2b)
Phil Rizzuto, NY (ss)	1950	Jim Konstanty, Phil. (p)
Yogi Berra, NY (c)	1951	Roy Campanella, Brk. (c)
Bobby Shantz, Phil. (p)	1952	Hank Sauer, Chi. (of)
AL ROSEN, Clev. (3b)	1953	Roy Campanella, Brk. (c)
Yogi Berra, NY (c)	1954	Willie Mays, NY (of)
Yogi Berra, NY (c)	1955	Roy Campanella, Brk. (c)
MICKEY MANTLE, NY (of)	1956	Don Newcombe, Brk. (p)
Mickey Mantle, NY (of)	1957	Hank Aaron, Mil. (of)
Jackie Jensen, Bos. (of)	1958	Ernie Banks, Chi. (ss)
Nellie Fox, Chi. (2b)	1959	Ernie Banks, Chi. (ss)
Roger Maris, NY (of)	1960	Dick Groat, Pitt. (ss)
Roger Maris, NY (of)	1961	Frank Robinson, Cin. (of)
Mickey Mantle, NY (of)	1962	Maury Wills, LA (ss)
Elston Howard, NY (c)	1963	Sandy Koufax, LA (p)
Brooks Robinson, Balt. (3b)	1964	Ken Boyer, StL. (3b)
Zoilo Versalles, Minn. (ss)	1965	Willie Mays, SF (of)
FRANK ROBINSON, Balt. (of)	1966	Roberto Clemente, Pitt. (of)
Carl Yastrzemski, Bos. (of)	1967	ORLANDO CEPEDA, StL. (1b)
DENNY McLAIN, Det. (p)	1968	Bob Gibson, StL. (p)
Harmon Killebrew, Minn. (3b)	1969	Willie McCovey, SF (1b)
Boog Powell, Balt. (1b)	1970	Johnny Bench, Cin. (c)
Vida Blue, Oak. (p)	1971	Joe Torre, StL. (3b)
Dick Allen, Chi. (1b)	1972	Johnny Bench, Cin. (c)
REGGIE JACKSON, Oak. (of)	1973	Pete Rose, Cin. (of)
Jeff Burroughs, Tex. (of)	1974	Steve Garvey, LA (1b)
Fred Lynn, Bos. (of)	1975	Joe Morgan, Cin. (2b)
Thurman Munson, NY (c)	1976	Joe Morgan, Cin. (2b)
Rod Carew, Minn. (1b)	1977	George Foster, Cin. (of)
Jim Rice, Bos. (of)	1978	Dave Parker, Pitt. (of)
Don Baylor, Cal. (of)	1979	Keith Hernandez, StL. (1b) & Willie Stargell, Pitt. (1b) (tied)
George Brett, KC (3b)	1980	MIKE SCHMIDT, Phil. (3b)
Rollie Fingers, Mil. (p)	1981	Mike Schmidt, Phil. (3b)
Robin Yount, in Mil. (ss)	1982	Dale Murphy, Atl. (of)
Cal Ripken, Balt. (ss)	1983	Dale Murphy, Atl. (of)
Willie Hernandez, Det. (p)	1984	Ryne Sandberg, Chi. (2b)
Don Mattingly, NY (1b)	1985	Willie McGee, StL. (of)
Roger Clemens, Roger Bos. (p)	1986	Mike Schmidt, Phil. (3b)
George Bell, Tor. (of)	1987	Andre Dawson, Chi. (of)
JOSE CANSECO, Oak. (of)	1988	Kirk Gibson, LA (of)
Robin Yount, Mil. (of)	1989	Kevin Mitchell, SF (of)
Rickey Henderson, Oak. (of)	1990	Barry Bonds, Pitt. (of)
Cal Ripken, Balt. (ss)	1991	Terry Pendleton, Atl. (3b)
Dennis Eckersley, Oak. (p)	1992	Barry Bonds, Pitt. (of)
FRANK THOMAS, Chi. (1b)	1993	Barry Bonds, SF (of)
Frank Thomas, Chi. (1b)	1994	JEFF BAGWELL, Hou. (1b)
Mo Vaughn, Bos. (1b)	1995	Barry Larkin, Cin. (ss)
Juan Gonzalez, Tex. (of)	1996	KEN CAMINITI, SD (3b)
KEN GRIFFEY, JR. Sea. (of)	1997	Larry Walker, Col. (of)
Juan Gonzalez, Tex. (of)	1998	Sammy Sosa, Chi. (of)
Ivan Rodriguez, Tex. (c)	1999	Chipper Jones, Atl. (3b)
Jason Giambi, Oak. (1b)	2000	Jeff Kent, SF (2b)
Ichiro Suzuki, Sea. (of)	2001	Barry Bonds, SF (of)
Miguel Tejada, Oak. (ss)	2002	BARRY BONDS, SF (of)
Alex Rodriguez, Tex. (ss)	2003	Barry Bonds, SF (of)
Vladimir Guerrero, Ana. (of)	2004	Barry Bonds, SF (of)
Alex Rodriguez, NY (3b)	2005	Albert Pujols, StL. (1b)
Juston Morneau, Minn. (1b)	2006	Ryan Howard, Phil. (1b)

CHALMERS AWARD

AMERICAN LEAGUE	YEAR	NATIONAL LEAGUE
TY COBB, Det. (of)	1911	Schulte, Wildfire Chi. (of)
Tris Speaker, Bos. (of)	1912	Doyle, Larry NY (2b)
Walter Johnson, Wash. (p)	1913	Daubert, Jake Brk. (1b)
Eddie Collins, Phil. (2b)	1914	Evers, Johnny Bos. (2b)

LEAGUE AWARD

AMERICAN LEAGUE	YEAR	NATIONAL LEAGUE
George Sisler, StL. (1b)	1922	No selection
BABE RUTH, NY (of)	1923	No selection
Walter Johnson, Wash. (p)	1924	Dazzy Vance, Brk. (p)
Roger Peckinpaugh, Wash. (ss)	1925	Roger Hornsby, StL. (2b)
George Burns, Clev. (1b)	1926	Bob O'Farrell, StL. (c)
Lou Gehrig, NY (1b)	1927	Paul Waner, Pitt. (of)
Mickey Cochrane, Phil. (c)	1928	Jim Bottomley, StL. (1b)
No selection	1929	Rogers Hornsby, Chi. (2b)

CY YOUNG AWARD

1956	Don Newcombe, NL:Brk.		1962	Don Drysdale, NL:LA
1957	Warren Spahn, NL:Mil.		1963	SANDY KOUFAX, NL:LA
1958	Bob Turley, AL:NY		1964	Dean Chance, AL:LA
1959	Early Wynn, AL:Chi.		1965	SANDY KOUFAX, NL:LA
1960	Vern Law, NL:Pitt.		1966	SANDY KOUFAX, NL:LA
1961	Whitey Ford, AL:NY			

AMERICAN LEAGUE	YEAR	NATIONAL LEAGUE
Jim Lonborg, Bos.	1967	Mike McCormick, SF
DENNY McLAIN, Det.	1968	BOB GIBSON, StL.
Mike Cuellar, Balt. (tied)	1969	Tom Seaver, NY
Denny McLain, Det.		
Jim Perry, Minn.	1970	Bob Gibson, StL.
Vida Blue, Oak.	1971	Ferguson Jenkins, Chi.
Gaylord Perry, Clev.	1972	STEVE CARLTON, Phil.
Jim Palmer, Balt.	1973	Tom Seaver, NY
Catfish Hunter, Oak.	1974	Mike Marshall, LA
Jim Palmer, Balt.	1975	Tom Seaver. NY
Jim Palmer, Balt.	1976	Randy Jones, SD
Sparky Lyle, NY	1977	Steve Carlton, Phil.
RON GUIDRY, NY	1978	Gaylord Perry, SD
Mike Flanagan, Balt.	1979	Bruce Sutter, Chi.
Steve Stone, Balt.	1980	Steve Carlton, Phil.
Rollie Fingers, Mil.	1981	Fernando Valenzuela, LA
Pete Vuckovich, Mil.	1982	Steve Carlton, Phil.
LaMarr Hoyt, Chi.	1983	John Denny, Phil.
Willie Hernandez, Det.	1984	RICK SUTCLIFFE, Chi.
Bret Saberhagen, KC	1985	DWIGHT GOODEN, NY
ROGER CLEMENS, Bos.	1986	Mike Scott, Hou.
Roger Clemens, Bos.	1987	Steve Bedrosian, Phil.
Frank Viola, Minn.	1988	OREL HERSHISER, LA
Bret Saberhagen, KC	1989	Mark Davis, SD
Bob Welch, Oak.	1990	Doug Drabek, Pitt.
Roger Clemens, Bos.	1991	Tom Glavine, Atl.
Dennis Eckersley, Oak.	1992	Greg Maddux, Chi.
Jack McDowell, Chi.	1993	Greg Maddux, Atl.
David Cone, KC	1994	GREG MADDUX, Atl.
Randy Johnson, Sea.	1995	GREG MADDUX, Atl.
Pat Hentgen, Tor.	1996	John Smoltz, Atl.
Roger Clemens, Tor.	1997	Pedro Martinez, Mtl.
ROGER CLEMENS, Tor.	1998	Tom Glavine, Atl.
PEDRO MARTINEZ, Bos.	1999	Randy Johnson, Ari.
PEDRO MARTINEZ, Bos.	2000	Randy Johnson, Ari.
Roger Clemens, NY	2001	Randy Johnson, Ari.
Barry Zito, Oak.	2002	RANDY JOHNSON, Ari.
Roy Halladay, Tor.	2003	Eric Gagne, LA
JOHAN SANTANA, Minn.	2004	Roger Clemens, Hou.
Bartolo Colon, LA	2005	Chris Carpenter, StL.
JOHAN SANTANA, Minn.	2006	Brandon Webb, Ari.

ROOKIE OF THE YEAR AWARD
(Unanimous Selections Capitalized)

AMERICAN LEAGUE	YEAR	NATIONAL LEAGUE
One selection	1947	Jackie Robinson, Brk. (1b)
One selection	1948	Alvin Dark, Bos. (ss)
Roy Sievers, StL. (of)	1949	Don Newcombe, Brk. (p)
Walt Dropo, Bos. (1b)	1950	Sam Jethroe, Bos. (of)
Gil McDougald, NY (3b)	1951	Willie Mays, NY (of)
Harry Byrd, Phil. (p)	1952	Joe Black, Brk. (p)
Harvey Kuenn, Det. (ss)	1953	Jim Gilliam, Brk. (2b)
Bob Grim, NY (p)	1954	Wally Moon, StL. (of)
Herb Score, Clev. (p)	1955	Bill Virdon, StL. (of)
Luis Aparicio, Chi. (ss)	1956	FRANK ROBINSON, Cin. (of)
Tony Kubek, NY (of)	1957	Jack Sanford, Phil. (p)
Albie Pearson, Wash. (of)	1958	ORLANDO CEPEDA, SF (1b)
Bob Allison, Wash. (of)	1959	WILLIE McCOVEY, SF (1b)
Ron Hansen, Balt. (ss)	1960	Frank Howard, LA (of)
Don Schwall, Bos. (p)	1961	Billy Williams, Chi. (of)
Tom Tresh, NY (ss)	1962	Ken Hubbs, Chi. (2b)
Gary Peters, Chi. (p)	1963	Pete Rose, Cin. (2b)
Tony Oliva, Minn. (of)	1964	Dick Allen, Phil. (3b)
Curt Blefary, Balt. (of)	1965	Jim Lefebvre, LA (2b)
Tommie Agee, Chi. (of)	1966	Tommy Helms, Cin. (3b)
Rod Carew, Minn. (2b)	1967	Tom Seaver, NY (p)
Stan Bahnsen, NY (p)	1968	Johnny Bench, Cin. (c)
Lou Piniella, KC (of)	1969	Ted Sizemore, LA (2b)
Thurman Munson, NY (c)	1970	Carl Morton, Mtl. (p)
Chris Chambliss, Clev. (1b)	1971	Earl Williams, Atl. (c)
CARLTON FISK, Bos. (c)	1972	Jon Matlack, NY (p)
Al Bumbry, Balt. (of)	1973	Gary Matthews, SF (of)
Mike Hargrove, Tex. (1b)	1974	Bake McBride, StL. (of)
Fred Lynn, Bos. (of)	1975	John Montefusco, SF (p)
Mike Fidrych, Det. (p)	1976	Butch Metzger, SD (p) (tied)
		Pat Zachry, Cin. (p)
Eddie Murray, Balt. (dh)	1977	Andre Dawson, Mtl. (of)
Lou Whitaker, Det. (2b)	1978	Bob Horner, Atl. (3b)
John Castino, Minn. (3b) (tied)	1979	Rick Sutcliffe, LA (p)
Alfredo Griffin, Tor. (ss)		
Joe Charboneau, Clev. (of)	1980	Steve Howe, LA (p)
Dave Righetti, NY (p)	1981	Fernando Valenzuela, LA (p)
Cal Ripken, Balt. (ss)	1982	Steve Sax, LA (2b)
Ron Kittle, Chi. (of)	1983	Darryl Strawberry, NY (of)
Alvin Davis, Sea. (1b)	1984	Dwight Gooden, NY (p)
Ozzie Guillen, Chi. (ss)	1985	VINCE COLEMAN, StL. (of)
Jose Canseco, Oak. (of)	1986	Todd Worrell, StL. (p)
MARK McGWIRE, Oak. (1b)	1987	BENITO SANTIAGO, SD (c)
Walt Weiss, Oak. (ss)	1988	Chris Sabo, Cin. (3b)
Gregg Olson, Balt. (p)	1989	Jerome Walton, Chi. (of)
SANDY ALOMAR, JR Clev. (c)	1990	David Justice, Atl. (of)
Chuck Knoblauch, Minn. (2b)	1991	Jeff Bagwell, Hou. (1b)
Pat Listach, Mil. (ss)	1992	Eric Karros, LA (1b)
TIM SALMON, Cal. (of)	1993	MIKE PIAZZA, LA (c)
Bob Hamelin, KC (dh)	1994	RAUL MONDESI, LA (of)
Marty Cordova, Minn. (of)	1995	Hideo Nomo, LA (p)
DEREK JETER, NY (ss)	1996	Todd Hollandsworth, LA (of)
NOMAR GARCIAPARRA, Bos. (ss)	1997	SCOTT ROLEN, Phil. (3b)
Ben Grieve, Oak. (of)	1998	Kerry Wood, Chi. (p)
Carlos Beltran, KC (of)	1999	Scott Williamson, Cin. (p)
Kazuhiro Sasaki, Sea. (p)	2000	Rafael Furcal, Atl. (ss)
Ichiro Suzuki, Ichiro Sea. (of)	2001	ALBERT PUJOLS, StL. (of)
Eric Hinske, Eric Tor. (3b)	2002	Jason Jennings, Col. (p)
Angel Berroa, KC (ss)	2003	Dontrelle Willis, Fla. (p)
Bobby Crosby, Oak. (ss)	2004	Jason Bay, Pitt. (of)
Huston Street, Oak. (p)	2005	Ryan Howard, Phil. (1b)
Justin Verlander, Det. (p)	2006	Hanley Ramirez, Fla. (ss)

OE DiMAGGIO, NEW YORK AL – 1941
6 CONSECUTIVE GAME BATTING STREAK

Date		Opp	Club and Pitcher	AB	R	H	2B	3B	HR	RBI
May	15	Chi	Edgar Smith.	4	0	1	0	0	0	1
	16	Chi	Thornton Lee	4	2	2	0	1	1	1
	17	Chi	Johnny Rigney	3	1	1	0	0	0	0
	18	StL	Bob Harris (2)							
			Johnny Niggeling (1)	3	3	3	1	0	0	1
	19	StL	Denny Galehouse	3	0	1	0	0	0	0
	20	StL	Elden Auker	5	1	1	0	0	0	1
	21	Det	Schoolboy Rowe (1)							
			Al Benton (1).	5	0	2	0	0	0	1
	22	Det	Archie McKain	4	0	1	0	0	0	1
	23	Bos	Dick Newsome	5	0	1	0	0	0	2
	24	Bos	Earl Johnson	4	2	1	0	0	0	2
	25	Bos	Lefty Grove	4	0	1	0	0	0	0
	27	Wash	Ken Chase (1)							
			Red Anderson (2)							
			Alex Carrasquel (1).	5	3	4	0	0	1	3
	28n	Wash	Sid Hudson	4	1	1	0	1	0	0
	29	Wash	Steve Sundra	3	1	1	0	0	0	0
	30	Bos	Earl Johnson	2	1	1	0	0	0	0
	30	Bos	Mickey Harris.	3	0	1	1	0	0	0
June	1	Clev	Al Milnar.	4	1	1	0	0	0	0
	1	Clev	Mel Harder.	4	0	1	0	0	0	0
	2	Clev	Bob Feller.	4	2	2	1	0	0	0
	3	Det	Dizzy Trout.	4	1	1	0	0	1	1
	5	Det	Hal Newhouser.	5	1	1	0	1	0	1
	7	StL	Bob Muncrief (1)							
			Johnny Allen (1)							
			George Caster(1)	5	2	3	0	0	0	1
	8	StL	Elden Auker	4	3	2	0	0	2	4
	8	StL	George Caster (1)							
			Jack Kramer (1)	4	1	2	1	0	1	3
	10	Chi	Johnny Rigney	5	1	1	0	0	0	0
	12n	Chi	Thornton Lee	4	1	2	0	0	1	1
	14	Clev	Bob Feller	2	0	1	1	0	0	1
	15	Clev	Jim Bagby	3	1	1	0	0	1	1
	16	Clev	Al Milnar.	5	0	1	1	0	0	0
	17	Chi	Johnny Rigney	4	1	1	0	0	0	0
	18	Chi	Thornton Lee	3	0	1	0	0	0	0
	19	Chi	Edgar Smith (1)							
			Buck Ross (2).	3	2	3	0	0	1	2
	20	Det	Bobo Newsom (2)							
			Archie McKain (2)	5	3	4	1	0	0	1
	21	Det	Dizzy Trout.	4	0	1	0	0	0	1
	22	Det	Hal Newhouser (1)							
			Bobo Newsom (1).	5	1	2	1	0	1	2
	24	StL	Bob Muncrief	4	1	1	0	0	0	0
	25	StL	Denny Galehouse	4	1	1	0	0	1	3
	26	StL	Elden Auker	4	0	1	1	0	0	1
	27	Phil	Chubby Dean.	3	1	2	0	0	1	2
	28	Phil	Johnny Babich (1)							
			Lum Harris(1).	5	1	2	1	0	0	0
	29	Wash	Dutch Leonard	4	1	1	1	0	0	0
	29	Wash	Red Anderson.	5	1	1	0	0	0	1
July	1	Bos	Mickey Harris (1)							
			Mike Ryba (1)	4	0	2	0	0	0	1
	1	Bos	Jack Wilson	3	1	1	0	0	0	1
	2	Bos	Dick Newsome	5	1	1	0	0	1	3
	5	Phil	Phil Marchildon	4	2	1	0	0	1	2
	6	Phil	Johnny Babich (1)							
			Bump Hadley (3).	5	2	4	1	0	0	2
	6	Phil	Jack Knott.	4	0	2	0	1	0	2
	10n	StL	Johnny Niggeling	2	0	1	0	0	0	0
	11	StL	Bob Harris (3)							
			Jack Kramer (1)	5	1	4	0	0	1	2
	12	StL	Elden Auker (1)							
			Bob Muncrief (1)	5	1	2	1	0	0	1
	13	Chi	Ted Lyons (2)							
			Jack Hallett (1)	4	2	3	0	0	0	0
	13	Chi	Thornton Lee	4	0	1	0	0	0	0
	14	Chi	Johnny Rigney	3	0	1	0	0	0	0
	15	Chi	Edgar Smith	4	1	2	1	0	0	2
	16	Clev	Al Milnar (2)							
			Joe Krakauskas (1)	4	3	3	1	0	0	0
	17n	Clev	Stopped in Cleveland (Al Smith and Jim Bagby)							

	PCT	AB	R	H	2B	3B	HR	RBI
TOTALS	.408	223	56	91	16	4	15	55

ROGER MARIS, NEW YORK AL — 1961   61 HOME RUNS

HR	Team Game	Ind. Game	Date	Inn	Opponent	Pitcher
1	11	11	Apr 26	5	at Detroit	Paul Foytack
2	17	17	May 3	7	at Minnesota	Pedro Ramos
3	20	20	May 6n	5	at Los Angeles	Eli Grba
4	29	29	May 17	8	Washington	Pete Burnside (L)
5	30	30	May 19n	1	at Cleveland	Jim Perry
6	31	31	May 20	3	at Cleveland	Gary Bell
7	32	32	May 21	1	Baltimore	Chuck Estrada
8	35	35	May 24	4	Boston	Gene Conley
9	38	38	May 28	2	Chicago	Cal McLish
10	40	40	May 30	6	at Boston	Gene Conley
11	40	40	May 30	8	at Boston	Mike Fornieles
12	41	41	May 31n	3	at Boston	Billy Muffett
13	43	43	June 2n	3	at Chicago	Cal McLish
14	44	44	June 3	8	at Chicago	Bob Shaw
15	45	45	June 4	3	at Chicago	Russ Kemmerer
16	48	48	June 6n	6	Minnesota	Ed Palmquist
17	49	49	June 7	3	Minnesota	Pedro Ramos
18	52	52	June 9n	7	Kansas City	Ray Herbert
19	55	55	June 11	3	Los Angeles	Eli Grba
20	55	55	June 11	7	Los Angeles	Johnny James
21	57	57	June 13n	6	at Cleveland	Jim Perry
22	58	58	June 14n	4	at Cleveland	Gary Bell
23	61	61	June 17n	4	at Detroit	Don Mossi (L)
24	62	62	June 18	8	at Detroit	Jerry Casale
25	63	63	June 19n	9	at Kansas City	Jim Archer (L)
26	64	64	June 20n	1	at Kansas City	Joe Nuxhall (L)
27	66	66	June 22n	2	at Kansas City	Norm Bass
28	74	74	July 1	9	Washington	Dave Sisler
29	75	75	July 2	3	Washington	Pete Burnside (L)
30	75	75	July 2	7	Washington	Johnny Klippstein
31	77	77	July 4	8	Detroit	Frank Lary
32	78	78	July 5	7	Cleveland	Frank Funk
33	82	82	July 9	7	Boston	Bill Monbouquette
34	84	84	July 13n	1	at Chicago	Early Wynn
35	86	86	July 15	3	at Chicago	Ray Herbert
36	92	92	July 21n	1	at Boston	Bill Monbouquette
37	95	95	July 25n	4	Chicago	Frank Baumann (L)
38	95	95	July 25n	8	Chicago	Don Larsen
39	96	96	July 25n	4	Chicago	Russ Kemmerer
40	96	96	July 25n	6	Chicago	Warren Hacker
41	106	105	Aug. 4n	1	Minnesota	Camilo Pascual
42	114	113	Aug. 11n	5	at Washington	Pete Burnside (L)
43	115	114	Aug. 12	4	at Washington	Dick Donovan
44	116	115	Aug. 13	4	at Washington	Bennie Daniels
45	117	116	Aug. 13	1	at Washington	Marty Kutyna
46	118	117	Aug. 15n	4	Chicago	Juan Pizarro (L)
47	119	118	Aug. 16	1	Chicago	Billy Pierce (L)
48	119	118	Aug. 16	3	Chicago	Billy Pierce (L)
49	123	122	Aug. 20	3	at Cleveland	Jim Perry
50	125	124	Aug. 22n	6	at Los Angeles	Ken McBride
51	129	128	Aug. 26	6	at Kansas City	Jerry Walker
52	135	134	Sept. 2	6	Detroit	Frank Lary
53	135	134	Sept. 2	8	Detroit	Hank Aguirre (L)
54	140	139	Sept. 6	4	Washington	Tom Cheney
55	141	140	Sept. 7n	3	Cleveland	Dick Stigman (L)
56	143	142	Sept. 9	7	Cleveland	Mudcat Grant
57	151	150	Sept. 16	3	at Detroit	Frank Lary
58	152	151	Sept. 17	12	at Detroit	Terry Fox
59	155	154	Sept. 20n	3	at Baltimore	Milt Pappas
60	159	158	Sept. 26n	3	Baltimore	Jack Fisher
61	163	161	Oct. 1	4	Boston	Tracy Stallard

Home—30   Road—31   Off RHP—49   Off LHP—12   Day-36   Night-25

BARRY BONDS, SAN FRANCISCO NL – 2001   73 HOME RUNS

HR	Team Game	Ind. Game	Date	Inn	Opponent	Pitcher
1	1	1	Apr. 2	5	San Diego	Woody Williams
2	9	8	Apr. 12	4	at San Diego	Adam Eaton
3	10	9	Apr. 13n	1	at Milwaukee	Jamey Wright
4	11	10	Apr. 14n	5	at Milwaukee	Jimmy Haynes
5	12	11	Apr. 15	8	at Milwaukee	David Weathers
6	13	12	Apr. 17n	8	Los Angeles	Terry Adams
7	14	13	Apr. 18n	7	Los Angeles	Chan Ho Park
8	16	15	Apr. 20n	4	Milwaukee	Jimmy Haynes
9	19	18	Apr. 24n	3	Cincinnati	Jim Brower
10	21	20	Apr. 26	8	Cincinnati	Scott Sullivan
11	24	22	Apr. 29	4	Chicago (NL)	Manny Aybar
12	26	24	May 2n	5	at Pittsburgh	Todd Ritchie
13	27	25	May 3n	1	at Pittsburgh	Jimmy Anderson (L)
14	28	26	May 4n	6	at Philadelphia	Bruce Chen (L)
15	35	32	May 11n	4	New York (NL)	Steve Trachsel
16	40	37	May 17n	3	at Florida	Chuck Smith
17	41	38	May 18n	8	at Atlanta	Mike Remlinger (L)
18	42	39	May 19n	3	at Atlanta	Odalis Perez (L)
19	42	39	May 19n	7	at Atlanta	Jose Cabrera
20	42	39	May 19n	8	at Atlanta	Jason Marquis
21	43	40	May 20	1	at Atlanta	John Burkett
22	43	40	May 20	7	at Atlanta	Mike Remlinger (L)
23	44	41	May 21n	4	at Arizona	Curt Schilling
24	45	42	May 22n	9	at Arizona	Russ Springer
25	47	44	May 24n	3	Colorado	John Thomson
26	50	46	May 27	1	Colorado	Denny Neagle (L)
27	53	49	May 30n	2	Arizona	Robert Ellis
28	53	49	May 30n	6	Arizona	Robert Ellis
29	54	50	June 1n	3	at Colorado	Shawn Chacon
30	57	53	June 4n	4	San Diego	Bobby J. Jones
31	58	54	June 5n	3	San Diego	Wascar Serrano
32	60	55	June 7	7	San Diego	Brian Lawrence
33	64	59	June 12n	1	Anaheim	Pat Rapp
34	66	61	June 14	6	Anaheim	Lou Pote
35	67	62	June 15n	1	Oakland	Mark Mulder (L)
36	67	62	June 15n	6	Oakland	Mark Mulder (L)
37	70	65	June 19n	5	at San Diego	Adam Eaton
38	71	66	June 20n	8	at San Diego	Rodney Myers
39	74	68	June 23n	1	at St. Louis	Darryl Kile
40	89	82	July 12n	1	at Seattle	Paul Abbott
41	95	88	July 18n	4	Colorado	Mike Hampton (L)
42	95	88	July 18n	5	Colorado	Mike Hampton (L)
43	103	96	July 26n	4	at Arizona	Curt Schilling
44	103	96	July 26n	5	at Arizona	Curt Schilling
45	104	97	July 27n	4	at Arizona	Brian Anderson (L)
46	108	101	Aug. 1n	1	Pittsburgh	Joe Beimel (L)
47	111	103	Aug. 4	6	Philadelphia	Nelson Figueroa
48	113	105	Aug. 7n	11	at Cincinnati	Danny Graves
49	115	107	Aug. 9n	3	at Cincinnati	Scott Winchester
50	117	108	Aug. 11	2	at Chicago (NL)	Joe Borowski
51	119	110	Aug. 14n	6	Florida	Ricky Bones
52	121	112	Aug. 16	4	Florida	A.J. Burnett
53	121	112	Aug. 16	8	Florida	Vic Darensbourg (L)
54	123	114	Aug. 18	8	Atlanta	Jason Marquis
55	127	118	Aug. 23n	9	at Montreal	Graeme Lloyd (L)
56	131	122	Aug. 27	5	at New York (NL)	Kevin Appier
57	135	126	Aug. 31n	8	Colorado	John Thomson
58	138	129	Sept. 3	4	Colorado	Jason Jennings
59	139	130	Sept. 4n	7	Arizona	Miguel Batista
60	141	132	Sept. 6	2	Arizona	Albie Lopez
61	144	135	Sept. 9	1	at Colorado	Scott Elarton
62	144	135	Sept. 9	5	at Colorado	Scott Elarton
63	144	135	Sept. 9	11	at Colorado	Todd Belitz (L)
64	147	138	Sept. 20	5	Houston	Wade Miller
65	150	141	Sept. 23	2	at San Diego	Jason Middlebrook
66	150	141	Sept. 23	4	at San Diego	Jason Middlebrook
67	151	142	Sept. 24n	7	at Los Angeles	James Baldwin
68	154	145	Sept. 28n	2	San Diego	Jason Middlebrook
69	155	146	Sept. 29	6	San Diego	Chuck McElroy (L)
70	159	150	Oct. 4n	9	at Houston	Wilfredo Rodriguez (L)
71	160	151	Oct. 5n	1	Los Angeles	Chan Ho Park
72	160	151	Oct. 5n	3	Los Angeles	Chan Ho Park
73	162	153	Oct. 7	1	Los Angeles	Dennis Springer

Home—37   Road—36   Off RHP—56   Off LHP—17   Day-26   Night-47

RICKEY HENDERSON, OAKLAND AL – 1982

130 STOLEN BASES *(* = 2nd Game)*

No.	Date	Game	Opp.
1	Apr. 8	3	Cal.
2	8	3	Cal.
3	9	4	Sea.
4	11	5	Sea.
5	11	5	Sea.
6	13	7	at Minn.
7	14	8	at Minn.
8	14	8	at Minn.
9	15	9	at Minn.
10	16	10	at Sea.
11	17	11	at Sea.
12	17	11	at Sea.
13	18	12	at Sea.
14	20	14	Minn.
15	21	15	Minn.
16	23	16	at Cal.
17	23	16	at Cal
18	28	19	at Balt.
19	28*	20	at Balt.
20	29	21	at Balt.
21	29	21	at Balt.
22	30	22	at Clev.
23	May 1	23	at Clev.
24	1	23	at Clev.
25	2	24	at Clev.
26	3	25	at NY
27	6	27	Clev.
28	6	27	Clev.
29	8	29	Clev.
30	8	29	Clev.
31	8	29	Clev.
32	9	30	Clev.
33	10	31	Balt.
34	11	32	Balt.
35	11	32	Balt.
36	15	36	NY
37	16	37	NY
38	16	37	NY
39	19	39	at Det.
40	22	42	at Bos.
41	22	42	at Bos.
42	23	43	at Bos.
43	26	45	at Mil.
44	26	45	at Mil.
45	26	45	at Mil.
46	30*	49	Det.
47	30*	49	Det.
48	30*	49	Det.
49	30*	49	Det.
50	June 1	51	Bos.
51	1	51	Bos.
52	4	53	Mil.
53	6	55	Mil.
54	6	55	Mil.
55	8	57	at Chi.
56	8	57	at Chi.
57	8	57	at Chi.
58	9	58	at Chi.
59	13	61	at Tor.
60	13	61	at Tor.
61	13	61	at Tor.
62	13	61	at Tor.
63	14	62	at Tor.
64	15	63	Chi.
65	18	66	Tor.
66	18	66	Tor.
67	22	70	KC
68	22	70	KC
69	25	73	at Tex.
70	25	73	at Tex.

No.	Date	Game	Opp.
71	26	74	at Tex.
72	29	77	at KC
73	30	78	at KC
74	July 2	79	Tex.
75	2	79	Tex.
76	3	80	Tex.
77	4	81	Tex.
78	6	83	Clev.
79	6	83	Clev.
80	8	85	NY
81	8	85	NY
82	9	86	Balt.
83	10	87	Balt.
84	11	88	Balt.
85	15	89	at NY
86	16	90	at NY
87	19	92	at Clev.
88	20	93	at Clev.
89	20	93	at Clev.
90	24	96	at Balt.
91	24	96	at Balt.
92	25	97	at Balt.
93	26	98	at Cal.
94	26	98	at Cal.
95	27	99	at Cal.
96	29	101	Minn.
97	30	102	Minn.
98	30	102	Minn.
99	30	102	Minn.
100	Aug. 2	105	Sea.
101	4	107	Sea.
102	4*	108	Sea.
103	4*	108	Sea.
104	6	109	at Minn.
105	8	111	at Minn.
106	11	113	at Sea.
107	11	113	at Sea.
108	14	115	Cal.
109	15	116	Cal.
110	17	118	Mil.
111	19	120	Mil.
112	21	122	Bos.
113	21	122	Bos.
114	21	122	Bos.
115	23	124	Det.
116	24	125	Det.
117	24	125	Det.
118	26	126	at Mil.
119	27	127	at Mil
120	27	127	at Mil.
121	27	127	at Mil.
122	27	127	at Mil.
123	30	128	at Bos.
124	Sept. 3	131	at Det.
125	25	142	KC
126	28	145	at Tex.
127	Oct. 1	148	at KC
128	2	149	at KC
129	2	149	at KC
130	2	149	at KC

CAUGHT STEALING: 42

STOLEN BASES BY OPPONENT

Opponent	Home	Away
Baltimore	6	7
Boston	5	4
California	4	5
Chicago	1	4
Cleveland	8	7
Detroit	7	2

Opponent	Home	Away
Kansas City	3	6
Milwaukee	5	8
Minnesota	6	6
New York	5	3
Seattle	7	6
Texas	4	4
Toronto	2	5
	63	67

HALL OF FAME

EXECUTIVES, MANAGERS, UMPIRES, NEGRO LEAGUES

Walter Alston (1983)	Manager
Sparky Anderson (2000)	Manager
Al Barlick (1989)	Umpire
Ed Barrow (1953)	Manager-Executive
Cool Papa Bell (1974)	Negro League Player
Ray Brown (2006)	Negro League Player
Willard Brown (2006)	Negro League Player
Morgan Bulkeley (1937)	Executive
Alexander Cartwright (1938)	Executive
Henry Chadwick (1938)	Writer-Statistician
Happy Chandler (1982)	Commissioner
Oscar Charleston (1976)	Negro League Player
Nestor Chylak (1999)	Umpire
Charles Comiskey (1939)	Player-Executive
Jocko Conlan (1974)	Umpire
Tom Connolly (1953)	Umpire
Andy Cooper (2006)	Negro League Player
Candy Cummings (1939)	Pioneer Pitcher
Ray Dandridge (1987)	Negro League Player
Leon Day (1995)	Negro League Player
Martin Dihigo (1977)	Negro League Player
Leo Durocher (1994)	Player-Manager
Billy Evans (1973)	Umpire-Executive
Bill Foster (1996)	Negro League Player
Rube Foster (1981)	Negro League Player
Ford Frick (1970)	Commissioner-Executive
Josh Gibson (1972)	Negro League Player
Warren Giles (1979)	Executive
Frank Grant (2006)	Pre-Negro League Player
Clark Griffith (1946)	Player-Manager-Executive
Ned Hanlon (1996)	Manager
Will Harridge (1972)	Executive
Bucky Harris (1975)	Player-Manager
Pete Hill (2006)	Pre-Negro League Player
Cal Hubbard (1976)	Umpire
Miller Huggins (1964)	Manager
William Hulbert (1995)	Executive
Monte Irvin (1973)	Negro League Player
Ban Johnson (1937)	Executive
Judy Johnson (1975)	Negro League Player
Bill Klem (1953)	Umpire
Kenesaw M. Landis (1944)	Commissioner
Tommy Lasorda (1997)	Manager
Buck Leonard (1972)	Negro League Player
Pop Lloyd (1977)	Negro League Player
Al Lopez (1977)	Player-Manager
Connie Mack (1937)	Manager-Executive
Biz Mackey (2006)	Negro League Player
Larry MacPhail (1978)	Executive
Lee MacPhail (1998)	Executive
Effa Manley (2006)	Negro League Executive
Joe McCarthy (1957)	Manager
Bill McGowan (1992)	Umpire
John McGraw (1937)	Player-Manager
Bill McKechnie (1962)	Manager
Jose Mendez (2006)	Pre-Negro League Player
Satchel Paige (1971)	Negro League Player
Alex Pompez (2006)	Negro League Executive
Cum Posey (2006)	Negro League Executive
Branch Rickey (1967)	Manager-Executive
Wilbert Robinson (1945)	Player-Manager
Joe Rogan (1998)	Negro League Player
Louis Santop (2006)	Pre-Negro League Player
Frank Selee (1999)	Manager
Hilton Smith (2001)	Negro League Player
Al Spalding (1939)	Player-Executive
Turkey Stearns (2000)	Negro League Player
Casey Stengel (1966)	Player-Manager
Mule Suttles (2006)	Negro League Player
Ben Taylor (2006)	Pre-Negro League Player
Cristobal Torriente (2006)	Negro League Player
Bill Veeck (1991)	Executive
Earl Weaver (1996)	Manager
George Weiss (1971)	Executive
Willie Wells (1997)	Negro League Player
Sol White (2006)	Pre-Negro League Executive
J.L. Wilkinson (2006)	Negro League Executive
Jud Wilson (2006)	Negro League Player
Smokey Joe Williams (1999)	Negro League Player
George Wright (1937)	Player-Manager
Harry Wright (1953)	Manager
Tom Yawkey (1980)	Executive

HALL OF FAME PITCHERS

*Special Committee Selection
(Capitalized pitchers were elected in their first year of eligibility.)

	Selected	Years	Years and Teams
Grover Alexander	1938	1911-1930	NL:Phil. 1911-17, 30; Chi. 18-26; StL. 26-29
*Chief Bender	1953	1903-1925	AL:Phil. 1903-14, 16-17; Chi. 25; FL:Balt. 15
*Mordecai Brown	1949	1903-1916	NL:StL. 1903; Chi. 04-12, 16; Cin. 1913; FL:StL. 14; Brk. 14; Chi. 15
*Jim Bunning	1996	1955-1971	AL:Det. 1955-63; NL:Phil. 64-67, 70-71; Pitt. 68-69; LA 69
STEVE CARLTON	1994	1965-1988	NL:StL. 1965-71; Phil. 72-86; SF 86; AL:Chi. 86; Clev. 87; Minn. 87-88
*Jack Chesbro	1946	1899-1909	NL:Pitt. 1899-1902; AL:NY 03-09; Bos. 09
*John Clarkson	1963	1882-1894	NL:Wor. 1882; Chi. 84-87; Bos. 88-92; Clev. 92-94
*Stan Coveleski	1969	1912-1928	AL:Phil. 1912; Clev. 16-24; Wash. 25-27; NY 28
Dizzy Dean	1953	1930-1947	NL:StL. 1930, 32-37; Chi. 38-41; AL:StL. 47
Don Drysdale	1984	1956-1969	NL:Brk./LA 1956-69
DENNIS ECKERSLEY	2004	1975-1998	AL:Clev. 1975-77; Bos. 78-84, 98; Oak. 87-95; NL:Chi. 84-86; StL. 96-97
*Red Faber	1964	1914-1933	AL:Chi. 1914-33
BOB FELLER	1962	1936-1956	AL:Clev. 1936-41, 45-56
Rollie Fingers	1992	1968-1985	AL:Oak. 1968-76; Mil. 81-82, 84-85; NL:SD 77-80
Whitey Ford	1974	1950-1967	AL:NY 1950, 53-67
*Pud Galvin	1965	1879-1892	NL:Buff. 1879-85; Pitt. 87-89, 91-92; StL. 1892; AA:Pitt. 85-86; PL:Pitt. 90
BOB GIBSON	1981	1959-1975	NL:StL. 1959-75
*Lefty Gomez	1972	1930-1943	AL:NY 1930-42; Wash. 43
*Burleigh Grimes	1964	1916-1934	NL:Pitt. 1916-17, 28-29, 34; Brk. 18-26; NY 27; Bos. 30; StL. 30-31, 33-34; Chi. 32-33; AL:NY 34
Lefty Grove	1947	1925-1941	AL:Phil. 1925-33; Bos. 34-41
*Jesse Haines	1970	1918-1937	NL:Cin. 1918; StL. 20-37
*Waite Hoyt	1969	1918-1938	NL:NY 1918, 32; Brk. 32, 37-38; Pitt. 33-37; AL:Bos. 19-20; NY 21-30; Det. 30-31; Phil. 31
Carl Hubbell	1947	1928-1943	NL:NY 1928-43
Catfish Hunter	1987	1965-1979	AL:KC/Oak. 1965-74; NY 75-79
Ferguson Jenkins	1991	1965-1983	NL:Phil. 1965-66; Chi. 66-73, 82-83; AL:Tex. 74-75, 78-81; Bos. 76-77
WALTER JOHNSON	1936	1907-1927	AL:Wash. 1907-27
*Addie Joss	1978	1902-1910	AL:Clev. 1902-10
*Tim Keefe	1964	1880-1893	NL:Troy 1880-82; NY 85-89, 91; Phil. 1891-93; AA:NY 83-84; PL:NY 90
SANDY KOUFAX	1972	1955-1966	NL:Brk./LA 1955-66
Bob Lemon	1976	1941-1958	AL:Clev. 1941-42, 46-58
Ted Lyons	1955	1923-1946	AL:Chi. 1923-42, 46
Juan Marichal	1983	1960-1975	NL:SF 1960-73; LA 75; AL:Bos. 74
*Rube Marquard	1971	1908-1925	NL:NY 1908-15; Brk. 15-20; Cin. 21; Bos. 22-25
CHRISTY MATHEWSON	1936	1900-1916	NL:NY 1900-16; Cin. 16
*Joe McGinnity	1946	1899-1908	NL:Balt 1899; Brk. 1900; NY 02-08; AL:Balt. 01-02
*Hal Newhouser	1992	1939-1955	AL:Det. 1939-53; Clev. 54-55
*Kid Nichols	1949	1890-1906	NL:Bos. 1890-1901; StL. 04-05; Phil. 05-06
Phil Niekro	1997	1964-1987	NL:Mil./Atl. 1964-83, 87; AL:NY 84-85; Clev. 86-87; Tor. 87
JIM PALMER	1990	1965-1984	AL:Balt. 1965-67, 69-84
Herb Pennock	1948	1912-1934	AL:Phil. 1912-15; Bos. 15-17, 19-22, 34; NY 23-33
Gaylord Perry	1991	1962-1983	NL:SF 1962-71; SD 78-79; Atl. 81; AL:Clev. 72-75; Tex. 75-77, 80; NY 80; Sea. 82-83; KC 83
*Eddie Plank	1946	1901-1917	AL:Phil. 1901-14; StL. 16-17; FL:StL. 15
*Hoss Radbourn	1939	1880-1891	NL:Buff. 1880; Prov. 81-85; Bos. 86-89; Cin. 91; PL:Bos. 90
*Eppa Rixey	1963	1912-1933	NL:Phil. 1912-17, 19-20; Cin. 21-33
Robin Roberts	1976	1948-1966	NL:Phil. 1948-61; Hou. 65-66; Chi. 66; AL:Balt. 62-65
Red Ruffing	1967	1924-1947	AL:Bos. 1924-30; NY 30-42, 45-46; Chi. 47
*Amos Rusie	1977	1889-1901	NL:Ind. 1889; NY 1890-95, 97-98; Cin. 1901
NOLAN RYAN	1999	1966-1993	NL:NY 1966, 68-71; Hou. 80-88; AL:Cal. 72-79; Tex. 89-93
TOM SEAVER	1992	1967-1986	NL:NY 1967-77, 83; Cin. 77-82; AL:Chi. 84-86; Bos. 86
WARREN SPAHN	1973	1942-1965	NL:Bos./Mil. 1942; 46-64; NY 65; SF 65
Bruce Sutter	2006	1976-1988	NL:Chi. 1976-80; StL. 81-84; Atl. 85-86, 88
Don Sutton	1998	1966-1988	NL:LA 1966-80, 88; Hou. 81-82; AL:Mil. 82-84; Oak. 85; Cal. 85-87
Dazzy Vance	1955	1915-1935	NL:Pitt. 1915; Brk. 22-32, 35; StL. 33-34; Cin. 34; AL:NY 15, 18
*Rube Waddell	1946	1897-1910	NL:Lou. 1897, 99; Pitt. 1900-01; Chi. 01; AL:Phil. 02-07; StL. 08-10
*Ed Walsh	1946	1904-1917	AL:Chi. 1904-16; NL:Bos. 17
*Mickey Welch	1973	1880-1892	NL:Troy 1880-82; NY 83-92
Hoyt Wilhelm	1985	1952-1972	NL:NY 1952-56; StL. 57; Atl. 69-71; Chi. 70; LA 71-72; AL:Clev. 57-58; Balt. 58-62; Chi. 63-68; Cal. 69
*Vic Willis	1995	1898-1910	NL:Bos. 1898-1905; Pitt. 06-09; StL. 10
Early Wynn	1972	1939-1963	AL:Wash. 1939, 41-44, 46-48; Clev. 49-57, 63; Chi. 58-62
Cy Young	1937	1890-1911	NL:Clev. 1890-98; StL. 99-1900; Bos. 11; AL:Bos. 01-08; Clev. 09-11

HALL OF FAME BATTERS

Special Committee Selection
Capitalized batters were elected in their first year of eligibility.)

	Selected	Years	Years and Team(s)
HANK AARON	1982	1954-1976	NL:Mil./Atl. 1954-74; AL:Mil. 75-76
*Cap Anson	1939	1876-1897	NL:Chi. 1876-97
Luis Aparicio	1984	1956-1973	AL:Chi. 1956-62, 68-70; Balt. 63-67; Bos. 71-73
Luke Appling	1964	1930-1950	AL:Chi. 1930-43, 45-50
*Richie Ashburn	1995	1948-1962	NL:Phil. 1948-59; Chi 60-61; NY 62
*Earl Averill	1975	1929-1941	AL:Clev. 1929-39; Det. 39-40; NL:Bos. 41
*Frank Baker	1955	1908-1922	AL:Phil. 1908-14; NY 16-19, 21-22
*Dave Bancroft	1971	1915-1930	NL:Phil. 1915-20; NY 20-23, 30; Bos. 24-27; Brk. 28-29
ERNIE BANKS	1977	1953-1971	NL:Chi 1953-71
*Jake Beckley	1971	1888-1907	NL:Pitt. 1888-89, 91-96; NY 96-97; Cin. 97-1903; StL. 04-07; PL:Pitt. 1890
JOHNNY BENCH	1989	1967-1983	NL:Cin. 1967-83
Yogi Berra	1972	1946-1965	AL:NY 1946-63; NL:NY 65
WADE BOGGS	2005	1982-1999	AL:Bos. 1982-92; NY 93-97; TB 98-99
*Jim Bottomley	1974	1922-1937	NL:StL. 1922-32; Cin. 33-35; AL:StL. 36-37
Lou Boudreau	1970	1938-1952	AL:Clev. 1938-50; Bos. 51-52
*Roger Bresnahan	1945	1897-1915	NL:Wash. 1897; Chi. 1900, 13-15; NY 02-08; StL. 09-12; AL:Balt. 01-02
GEORGE BRETT	1999	1973-1993	AL:KC 1973-93
LOU BROCK	1985	1961-1979	NL:Chi 1961-64; StL. 64-79
*Dan Brouthers	1945	1879-1904	NL:Troy 1879-80; Buff. 81-85; Det. 86-88; Bos. 89; Brk. 92-93; Balt. 94-95; Lou. 95; Phil. 96; NY 1904; PL:Bos. 1890; AA:Bos. 91
*Jesse Burkett	1946	1890-1905	NL:NY 1890; Clev. 91-98; StL. 99-1901; AL:StL. 02-04; Bos. 05
Roy Campanella	1969	1948-1957	NL:Brk. 1948-57
*ROD CAREW	1991	1967-1985	AL:Minn. 1967-78; Cal. 79-85
*Max Carey	1961	1910-1929	NL:Pitt. 1910-26; Brk. 26-29
Gary Carter	2003	1974-1992	NL:Mtl. 1974-84, 92; NY 85-89; SF 90; LA 91
*Orlando Cepeda	1999	1958-1974	NL:SF 1958-66; StL. 66-68; Atl. 69-72; AL:Oak. 72; Bos. 73; KC 74
*Frank Chance	1946	1898-1914	NL:Chi. 1898-1912; AL:NY 13-14
*Fred Clarke	1946	1894-1915	NL:Lou. 1894-99; Pitt. 1900-11, 13-15
ROBERTO CLEMENTE	1973	1955-1972	NL:Pitt. 1955-72
TY COBB	1936	1905-1928	AL:Det. 1905-26; Phil. 27-28
Mickey Cochrane	1947	1925-1937	AL:Phil. 1925-33; Det. 34-37
Eddie Collins	1939	1906-1930	AL:Phil. 1906-14, 27-30; Chi. 15-26;
*Jimmy Collins	1945	1895-1908	NL:Lou. 1895; Bos. 95-1900; AL:Bos. 01-07; Phil. 07-08
Earle Combs	1970	1924-1935	AL:NY 1924-35
*Roger Connor	1976	1880-1897	NL:Troy 1880-82; NY 83-89, 91, 93-94; Phil. 92; StL. 94-97; PL:NY 90
*Sam Crawford	1957	1899-1917	NL:Cin. 1899-1902; AL:Det. 03-17
Joe Cronin	1956	1926-1945	NL:Pitt. 1926-27; AL:Wash. 28-34; Bos. 35-45
*Kiki Cuyler	1968	1921-1938	NL:Pitt. 1921-27; Chi 28-35; Cin. 35-37; Brk. 38
*George Davis	1998	1890-1909	NL:Clev. 1890-92; NY 93-1901, 03; AL:Chi. 02, 04-09
*Ed Delahanty	1945	1888-1903	NL:Phil. 1888-91-1901; PL:Clev. 1890; AL:Wash. 1902-03
Bill Dickey	1954	1928-1946	AL:NY 1928-43, 46
Joe DiMaggio	1955	1936-1951	AL:NY 1936-42, 46-51
*Larry Doby	1998	1947-1959	AL:Clev. 1947-55, 58; Chi. 56-57, 59; Det. 59
*Bobby Doerr	1986	1937-1951	AL:Bos. 1937-44, 46-51
*Hugh Duffy	1945	1888-1906	NL:Chi. 1888-89; Bos. 92-1900; Phil. 04-06; PL:Chi. 1890; AA:Bos. 91; AL:Mil. 1901
*Johnny Evers	1946	1902-1929	NL:Chi 1902-13; Bos. 14-17, 29; Phil. 17; AL:Chi. 22
*Buck Ewing	1939	1880-1897	NL:Troy 1880-82; NY 83-89, 91-92; Clev. 93-94; Cin. 95-97; PL:NY 90
*Rick Ferrell	1984	1929-1947	AL:StL. 1929-33, 41-43; Bos. 33-37; Wash. 37-41, 44-45, 47
Carlton Fisk	2000	1969-1993	AL:Bos. 1969, 71-80; Chi. 81-93
*Elmer Flick	1963	1898-1910	NL:Phil. 1898-1902; AL:Clev. 02-10
*Nellie Fox	1997	1947-1965	AL:Phil. 1947-49; Chi. 50-63; NL:Hou. 64-65
Jimmie Foxx	1951	1925-1945	AL:Phil. 1925-35; Bos. 36-42; NL:Chi 42, 44; Phil. 45
Frankie Frisch	1947	1919-1937	NL:NY 1919-26; StL. 27-37
LOU GEHRIG	1939	1923-1939	AL:NY 1923-39
Charlie Gehringer	1949	1924-1942	AL:Det. 1924-42
*Goose Goslin	1968	1921-1938	AL:Wash. 1921-30, 33, 38; StL. 30-32; Det. 34-37
Hank Greenberg	1956	1930-1947	AL:Det. 1930, 33-41, 45-46; NL:Pitt. 47
TONY GWYNN	2007	1982-2001	NL:SD 1982-2001
*Chick Hafey	1971	1924-1937	NL:StL. 1924-31; Cin. 32-35, 37
*Billy Hamilton	1961	1888-1901	AA:KC 1888-89; NL:Phil. 90-95; Bos. 96-1901
Gabby Hartnett	1955	1922-1941	NL:Chi 1922-40; NY 41
Harry Heilmann	1952	1914-1932	AL:Det. 1914, 16-29; NL:Cin. 30, 32
*Billy Herman	1975	1931-1947	NL:Chi 1931-41; Brk. 41-43, 46; Bos. 46; Pitt. 47
*Harry Hooper	1971	1909-1925	AL:Bos. 1909-20; Chi. 21-25
Rogers Hornsby	1942	1915-1937	NL:StL. 1915-26, 33; NY 27; Bos. 28; Chi 29-32; AL:StL. 33-37
REGGIE JACKSON	1993	1967-1987	AL:KC/Oak. 1967-75, 87; Balt. 76; NY 77-81; Cal. 82-86
*Travis Jackson	1982	1922-1936	NL:NY 1922-36
*Hughie Jennings	1945	1891-1918	AA:Lou. 1891; NL:Lou. 92-93; Balt. 93-99; Brk. 99-1900, 03; Phil. 01-02; AL:Det. 07, 09, 12, 18
Al KALINE	1980	1953-1974	AL:Det. 1953-74
Willie Keeler	1939	1892-1910	NL:NY 1892-93, 1910; Brk. 1893, 99-1902; Balt. 94-98; AL:NY 1903-09
*George Kell	1983	1943-1957	AL:Phil. 1943-46; Det. 46-52; Bos. 52-54; Chi. 54-56; Balt. 56-57
*Joe Kelley	1971	1891-1908	NL:Bos. 1891, 1908; Pitt. 1891-92; Balt. 92-98; Brk. 99-1901; Cin. 02-06; AL:Balt. 02
*George Kelly	1973	1915-1932	NL:NY 1915-17, 19-26; Pitt. 17; Cin. 27-30; Chi 30; Brk. 32
*King Kelly	1945	1878-1893	NL:Cin. 1878-79; Chi. 80-86; Bos. 87-89, 91-92; NY 93; PL:Bos. 90; AA:Cin./Mil. 91; Bos. 91

HALL OF FAME BATTERS

*Special Committee Selection
(Capitalized batters were elected in their first year of eligibility.)

	Selected	Years	Years and Team(s)
Harmon Killebrew	1984	1954-1975	AL:Wash./Minn. 1954-74; KC 75
Ralph Kiner	1975	1946-1955	NL:Pitt. 1946-53; Chi 53-54; AL:Clev. 55
*Chuck Klein	1980	1928-1944	NL:Phil. 1928-33, 36-44; Chi 34-36; Pitt. 39
Nap Lajoie	1937	1896-1916	NL:Phil. 1896-1900; AL:Phil. 01-02, 15-16; Clev. 02-14
*Tony Lazzeri	1991	1926-1939	AL:NY 1926-37; NL:Chi 38; Brk. 39; NY 39
*Freddie Lindstrom	1976	1924-1936	NL:NY 1924-32; Pitt. 33-34; Chi 35; Brk. 36
*Ernie Lombardi	1986	1931-1947	NL:Brk. 1931; Cin. 32-41; Bos. 42; NY 43-47
MICKEY MANTLE	1974	1951-1968	AL:NY 1951-68
*Heinie Manush	1964	1923-1939	AL:Det. 1923-27; StL. 28-30; Wash. 30-35; Bos. 36; NL:Brk. 37-38; Pitt. 38-39
Rabbit Maranville	1954	1912-1935	NL:Bos. 1912-20, 29-33, 35; Pitt. 21-24; Chi 25; StL. 27-28
Eddie Mathews	1978	1952-1968	NL:Bos./Mil./Atl. 1952-66; Hou. 67; AL:Det. 67-68
WILLIE MAYS	1979	1951-1973	NL:NY/SF 1951-52, 54-72; NY 72-73
*Bill Mazeroski	2001	1956-1972	NL:Pitt. 1956-72
*Tommy McCarthy	1946	1884-1896	UA:Bos. 1884; NL:Bos. 85; 92-95; Phil. 86-87; Brk. 96; AA:StL. 88-91
WILLIE McCOVEY	1986	1959-1980	NL:SF 1959-73, 77-80; SD 74-76; AL:Oak. 76
*Bid McPhee	2000	1882-1899	AA:Cin. 1882-89; NL:Cin. 90-99
Joe Medwick	1968	1932-1948	NL:StL. 1932-40, 47-48; Brk. 40-43, 46; NY 43-45; Bos. 45
*Johnny Mize	1981	1936-1953	NL:StL. 1936-41; NY 42, 46-49; AL:NY 49-53
PAUL MOLITOR	2004	1978-1998	AL:Mil. 1978-92; Tor. 93-95; Minn. 96-98
JOE MORGAN	1990	1963-1984	NL:Hou. 1963-71, 80; Cin. 72-79; SF 81-82; Phil. 83; AL:Oak. 84
EDDIE MURRAY	2003	1977-1997	AL:Balt. 1977-88, 96; Clev. 94-96; Ana. 97; NL:LA 89-91, 97; NY 92-93
STAN MUSIAL	1969	1941-1963	NL:StL. 1941-44, 46-63
*Jim O'Rourke	1945	1876-1904	NL:Bos. 1876-78, 80; Prov. 79; Buff. 81-84; NY 85-89, 91-92, 1904; Wash. 1893; PL:NY 90
Mel Ott	1951	1926-1947	NL:NY 1926-47
Tony Perez	2000	1964-1986	NL:Cin. 1964-76, 84-86; Mtl. 77-79; Phil. 83; AL:Bos. 80-82
KIRBY PUCKETT	2001	1984-1995	AL:Minn. 1984-95
*Pee Wee Reese	1984	1940-1958	NL:Brk./LA 1940-42, 46-58
*Sam Rice	1963	1915-1934	AL:Wash. 1915-33; Clev. 34
CAL RIPKEN	2007	1981-2001	AL:Balt. 1981-2001
*Phil Rizzuto	1994	1941-1956	AL:NY 1941-42, 46-56
BROOKS ROBINSON	1983	1955-1977	AL:Balt. 1955-77
FRANK ROBINSON	1982	1956-1976	NL:Cin. 1956-65; LA 72; AL:Balt. 66-71; Cal. 73-74; Clev. 74-76
JACKIE ROBINSON	1962	1947-1956	NL:Brk. 1947-56
*Edd Roush	1962	1913-1931	AL:Chi. 1913; FL:Ind. 14; Nwk. 15; NL:NY 16, 27-29; Cin. 16-26, 31
BABE RUTH	1936	1914-1935	AL:Bos. 1914-19; NY 20-34; NL:Bos. 35
Ryne Sandberg	2005	1981-1997	NL:Phil. 1981; Chi. 82-94, 96-97
*Ray Schalk	1955	1912-1929	AL:Chi. 1912-28; NL:NY 29
MIKE SCHMIDT	1995	1972-1989	NL:Phil. 1972-89
*Red Schoendienst	1989	1945-1963	NL:StL. 1945-56, 61-63; NY 56-57; Mil. 57-60
*Joe Sewell	1977	1920-1933	AL:Clev. 1920-30; NY 31-33
Al Simmons	1953	1924-1944	AL:Phil. 1924-32. 40-41, 44; Chi. 33-35; Det. 36; Wash. 37-38; Bos. 43; NL:Bos. 39; Cin. 39
George Sisler	1939	1915-1930	AL:StL. 1915-22, 24-27; Wash. 28; NL:Bos. 28-30
*Enos Slaughter	1985	1938-1959	NL:StL. 1938-42, 46-53; Mil. 59; AL:NY 54-59; KC 55-56
OZZIE SMITH	2002	1978-1996	NL:SD 1978-81; StL. 82-96
Duke Snider	1980	1947-1964	NL:Brk./LA 1947-62; NY 63; SF 64
Tris Speaker	1937	1907-1928	AL:Bos. 1907-15; Clev. 16-26; Wash. 27; Phil. 28
WILLIE STARGELL	1988	1962-1982	NL:Pitt. 1962-82
Bill Terry	1954	1923-1936	NL:NY 1923-36
*Sam Thompson	1974	1885-1906	NL:Det. 1885-88; Phil. 89-98; AL:Det. 1906
*Joe Tinker	1946	1902-1916	NL:Chi 1902-12, 16; Cin. 13; FL:Chi. 14-15
Pie Traynor	1948	1920-1937	NL:Pitt. 1920-35, 37
*Arky Vaughan	1985	1932-1948	NL:Pitt. 1932-41; Brk. 42-44, 47-48
HONUS WAGNER	1936	1897-1917	NL:Lou. 1897-99; Pitt. 1900-17
*Bobby Wallace	1953	1894-1918	NL:Clev. 1894-98; StL. 99-1901, 17-18; AL:StL. 02-16
*Lloyd Waner	1967	1927-1945	NL:Pitt. 1927-41, 44-45; Bos. 41; Cin. 41; Phil. 42; Brk. 44
Paul Waner	1952	1926-1945	NL:Pitt. 1926-40; Brk. 41, 43-44; Bos. 41-42; AL:NY 44-45
*Monte Ward	1964	1878-1894	NL:Prov. 1878-82; NY 83-89, 93-94; Brk. 91-92; PL:NY 90
*Zack Wheat	1959	1909-1927	NL:Brk. 1909-26; AL:Phil. 27
Billy Williams	1987	1959-1976	NL:Chi 1959-74; AL:Oak. 75-76
TED WILLIAMS	1966	1939-1960	AL:Bos. 1939-42, 46-60
*Hack Wilson	1979	1923-1934	NL:NY 1923-25; Chi 26-31; Brk. 32-34 Phil. 34
DAVE WINFIELD	2001	1973-1995	NL:SD 1973-80; AL:NY 81-88, 90; Cal. 90-91; Tor. 92; Minn. 93-94; Clev. 95
CARL YASTRZEMSKI	1989	1961-1983	AL:Bos. 1961-83
*Ross Youngs	1972	1917-1926	NL:NY 1917-26
ROBIN YOUNT	1999	1974-1993	AL:Mil. 1974-93

BATTERS – 1,000 OR MORE GAMES - ACTIVE IN 2006

(OBA = On-Base Average   XBH = Extra-Base Hits)

PLAYER	YR	BA	SLG	OBA	G	AB	R	H	TB	XBH	1B	2B	3B	HR	RBI	BB	HBP	SO	SB	CS	GDP
Abreu, Bobby	11	.302	.507	.412	1485	5276	951	1595	2673	624	971	375	44	205	883	1003	25	1181	271	84	94
Alfonzo, Edgardo	12	.284	.425	.357	1506	5385	777	1532	2288	446	1086	282	18	146	744	596	41	617	53	17	110
Alomar, Sandy Jr.	19	.274	.407	.310	1369	4508	519	1233	1837	370	863	248	10	112	588	212	41	496	25	24	132
Alou, Moises	15	.301	.516	.368	1840	6660	1054	2005	3438	757	1248	400	38	319	1229	708	44	860	102	36	181
Anderson, Garret	13	.297	.470	.327	1760	7015	891	2081	3297	703	1378	431	31	241	1128	341	5	986	70	43	161
Aurilia, Rich	12	.278	.443	.332	1353	4863	662	1352	2156	447	905	259	19	169	655	390	19	736	22	17	116
Ausmus, Brad	14	.253	.347	.326	1716	5556	652	1408	1929	344	1064	240	31	73	547	560	58	883	95	50	182
Bagwell, Jeff	15	.297	.540	.408	2150	7797	1517	2314	4213	969	1345	488	32	449	1529	1401	128	1558	202	78	221
Batista, Tony	10	.251	.455	.298	1229	4467	615	1120	2034	459	661	223	17	219	702	275	44	776	47	26	105
Bell, David	12	.257	.396	.320	1403	4826	587	1239	1911	408	831	267	18	123	589	428	44	687	19	20	123
Belliard, Ronnie	9	.272	.411	.338	1049	3812	528	1036	1565	348	688	247	21	80	439	379	19	576	32	24	101
Beltran, Carlos	9	.281	.492	.355	1176	4559	826	1280	2244	503	777	245	55	203	763	522	29	836	227	32	81
Beltre, Adrian	9	.271	.457	.328	1278	4685	613	1269	2139	465	804	251	23	191	686	371	42	816	76	32	105
Berkman, Lance	8	.304	.567	.416	1059	3687	687	1120	2089	501	619	258	18	225	753	690	45	720	47	29	75
Biggio, Craig	19	.283	.436	.367	2709	10359	1776	2930	4514	970	1960	637	52	281	1125	1137	282	1641	410	121	145
Bonds, Barry	21	.299	.608	.443	2860	9507	2152	2841	5784	1398	1443	587	77	734	1930	2426	103	1485	509	141	152
Burnitz, Jeromy	14	.253	.481	.345	1694	5710	917	1447	2748	642	805	298	29	315	981	739	78	1376	74	58	99
Cabrera, Orlando	10	.269	.403	.317	1256	4663	605	1254	1881	422	832	306	27	89	541	333	20	429	145	35	115
Cairo, Miguel	11	.268	.361	.316	1010	2921	372	782	1054	193	589	141	25	27	280	175	45	336	113	32	61
Cameron, Mike	12	.252	.447	.342	1409	4881	778	1228	2181	515	713	272	48	195	708	629	66	1340	254	69	80
Casey, Sean	10	.302	.456	.368	1193	4414	636	1333	2011	415	918	278	11	126	664	421	58	510	15	6	141
Castilla, Vinny	16	.276	.476	.321	1854	6822	902	1884	3249	697	1187	349	28	320	1105	423	60	1069	33	43	224
Castillo, Luis	11	.293	.358	.369	1270	4931	759	1446	1763	223	1223	152	48	23	320	589	9	687	306	125	81
Cedeno, Roger	11	.273	.371	.340	1100	3174	478	865	1176	199	666	127	32	40	274	319	13	613	213	63	44
Chavez, Eric	9	.271	.489	.350	1166	4212	667	1143	2060	475	668	245	18	212	716	516	13	790	43	15	95
Cirillo, Jeff	13	.298	.432	.368	1539	5203	776	1550	2248	459	1091	330	19	110	700	544	66	675	61	37	143
Clark, Tony	12	.266	.490	.341	1302	4094	579	1087	2007	456	631	219	10	227	738	464	20	1071	6	9	114
Clayton, Royce	16	.258	.368	.313	2031	7184	911	1856	2642	513	1343	349	55	109	711	551	44	1362	229	99	208
Conine, Jeff	16	.286	.445	.348	1923	6701	845	1917	2983	615	1302	372	35	208	1034	644	41	1132	50	29	177
Counsell, Craig	11	.260	.350	.344	1053	3446	489	896	1205	219	677	160	28	31	283	419	36	470	90	40	53
Cruz, Jose Jr.	10	.249	.453	.339	1259	4419	670	1101	2000	470	631	239	33	198	602	616	5	1073	107	38	71
Damon, Johnny	12	.289	.436	.353	1704	6770	1188	1958	2951	600	1358	361	85	154	780	665	36	789	306	85	66
Delgado, Carlos	14	.282	.558	.390	1711	6053	1059	1709	3376	837	872	414	16	407	1287	973	149	1483	9	7	121
Durham, Ray	12	.281	.443	.354	1709	6574	1129	1846	2909	636	1210	384	77	175	759	714	68	1054	255	91	126
Dye, Jermaine	11	.277	.486	.339	1330	4886	742	1352	2373	527	825	269	22	236	817	444	48	989	41	21	134
Easley, Damion	15	.251	.404	.328	1517	4975	678	1247	2009	443	804	271	25	147	614	472	120	862	114	55	111
Edmonds, Jim	14	.289	.539	.382	1697	5907	1115	1709	3181	751	958	380	21	350	1068	878	46	1512	63	46	103
Encarnacion, Juan	10	.269	.441	.316	1181	4402	575	1184	1940	417	767	225	45	147	620	270	53	810	125	57	105

BATTERS – 1,000 OR MORE GAMES - ACTIVE IN 2006

(OBA = On-Base Average)
XBH = Extra-Base Hits

PLAYER	YR	BA	SLG	OBA	G	AB	R	H	TB	XBH	1B	2B	3B	HR	RBI	BB	HBP	SO	SB	CS	GDP
Erstad, Darin	11	.286	.416	.341	1320	5258	818	1505	2186	423	1082	279	30	114	625	419	35	796	170	51	78
Everett, Carl	14	.271	.462	.341	1405	4809	707	1304	2220	486	818	258	26	202	792	442	87	1021	107	54	83
Finley, Steve	18	.272	.444	.333	2540	9303	1434	2531	4134	873	1658	446	124	303	1165	836	53	1295	320	118	150
Floyd, Cliff	14	.279	.488	.359	1423	4775	752	1331	2331	552	779	317	22	213	781	537	81	952	147	43	75
Franco, Julio	22	.299	.419	.365	2472	8587	1277	2566	3594	630	1936	404	54	172	1178	903	38	1318	279	106	310
Garciaparra, Nomar	11	.318	.540	.367	1193	4832	847	1537	2610	599	938	336	52	211	833	349	58	474	89	29	107
Giambi, Jason	12	.292	.541	.413	1622	5620	1017	1639	3040	693	946	335	8	350	1144	1089	127	1131	15	10	132
Giles, Brian	12	.295	.525	.408	1518	5260	950	1552	2762	642	910	334	48	260	941	1006	44	691	102	37	128
Glaus, Troy	9	.253	.503	.357	1129	4040	706	1023	2031	486	537	221	8	257	716	640	34	1063	56	27	100
Gomez, Chris	14	.260	.360	.326	1333	4199	470	1090	1512	289	801	214	17	58	446	385	40	694	34	31	125
Gonzalez, Alex	9	.246	.392	.292	1007	3609	411	887	1414	322	565	207	25	90	425	192	56	739	24	17	79
Gonzalez, Alex	13	.243	.391	.302	1396	4977	623	1209	1948	438	771	274	27	137	536	392	45	1165	97	48	128
Gonzalez, Luis	17	.284	.484	.368	2316	8352	1312	2373	4043	943	1430	547	65	331	1324	1058	107	1119	121	83	191
Green, Shawn	14	.282	.499	.355	1821	6636	1067	1873	3310	767	1106	415	34	318	1024	707	75	1253	151	51	161
Griffey, Ken Jr.	18	.291	.557	.374	2234	8298	1467	2412	4622	1048	1364	449	36	563	1608	1077	76	1494	178	67	163
Grudzielanek, Mark	12	.288	.393	.330	1570	6158	830	1774	2418	449	1325	335	33	81	554	314	91	843	128	49	148
Guerrero, Vladimir	10	.325	.583	.390	1457	5502	952	1786	3206	705	1081	328	39	338	1052	544	70	674	166	80	173
Guillen, Jose	10	.272	.445	.321	1115	3892	513	1058	1732	368	690	205	6	143	574	203	95	716	22	24	112
Hatteberg, Scott	12	.271	.407	.360	1164	3813	485	1032	1551	321	711	219	0	96	473	506	39	461	3	7	109
Helton, Todd	10	.333	.593	.430	1424	5106	1018	1700	3029	728	972	413	29	286	996	864	46	686	36	25	121
Hernandez, Jose	15	.252	.418	.312	1587	4618	623	1166	1929	394	772	193	33	168	603	384	24	1391	41	38	125
Hollandsworth, Todd	12	.273	.439	.328	1118	3191	451	871	1401	312	559	192	22	98	401	262	9	701	75	43	44
Hunter, Torii	10	.269	.463	.323	1074	3892	578	1046	1802	403	643	214	25	164	604	279	44	769	108	51	117
Ibanez, Raul	11	.284	.469	.344	1073	3583	530	1017	1682	363	654	199	26	138	579	329	13	580	32	20	71
Jenkins, Geoff	9	.279	.499	.350	1102	3987	616	1114	1990	474	640	263	20	191	640	362	86	1002	29	11	98
Jeter, Derek	12	.317	.463	.388	1679	6790	1277	2150	3146	580	1570	347	50	183	860	705	115	1191	249	62	150
Jones, Andruw	11	.267	.505	.345	1607	5836	962	1556	2949	677	879	303	32	342	1023	647	75	1256	133	53	144
Jones, Jacque	8	.280	.461	.328	1125	4025	565	1126	1855	395	731	220	16	159	557	266	33	853	76	41	98
Jones, Chipper	13	.304	.542	.402	1761	6385	1188	1944	3458	770	1174	383	30	357	1197	1070	15	1006	129	42	170
Jordan, Brian	15	.282	.455	.333	1456	5160	755	1454	2347	488	966	267	37	184	821	353	74	842	119	48	118
Kendall, Jason	11	.301	.400	.381	1545	5759	852	1735	2306	405	1330	307	30	68	574	557	209	496	159	73	140
Kennedy, Adam	8	.280	.398	.332	1025	3436	447	961	1369	271	690	186	33	52	369	231	57	533	123	48	60
Kent, Jeff	15	.289	.504	.356	2041	7564	1200	2189	3815	891	1298	501	45	345	1380	719	113	1409	93	56	194
Klesko, Ryan	15	.280	.507	.372	1620	5249	823	1470	2662	618	852	316	30	272	943	771	28	1009	86	40	111
Konerko, Paul	10	.283	.496	.353	1275	4561	677	1292	2263	476	816	226	5	245	805	460	56	713	5	1	171
Kotsay, Mark	10	.285	.420	.340	1284	4811	644	1369	2022	408	961	265	41	102	540	411	12	569	88	50	112
Lawton, Matt	12	.267	.417	.368	1334	4763	756	1273	1988	422	851	267	17	138	631	681	94	613	165	66	113
Lee, Carlos	8	.286	.495	.340	1203	4570	720	1308	2263	502	806	270	11	221	782	370	30	653	96	32	108

BATTERS – 1,000 OR MORE GAMES - ACTIVE IN 2006

(OBA = On-Base Average) XBH = Extra-Base Hits

PLAYER	YR	BA	SLG	OBA	G	AB	R	H	TB	XBH	1B	2B	3B	HR	RBI	BB	HBP	SO	SB	CS	GDP
Lee, Derrek	10	.276	.500	.363	1235	4258	671	1177	2129	498	679	260	22	216	656	550	50	1036	86	37	108
Lee, Travis	9	.256	.408	.337	1099	3740	476	958	1526	322	636	191	16	115	488	457	9	704	59	20	92
Lieberthal, Mike	13	.275	.450	.338	1174	4141	528	1137	1862	415	722	255	10	150	609	331	88	560	8	7	112
Lofton, Kenny	16	.299	.423	.372	1967	7630	1442	2283	3230	591	1692	358	110	123	743	889	30	965	599	153	105
Lopez, Javy	15	.287	.491	.337	1503	5319	674	1527	2612	546	981	267	19	260	864	357	66	969	8	19	172
Loretta, Mark	12	.299	.402	.363	1385	4910	670	1466	1973	351	1115	263	20	68	525	462	65	513	45	32	127
Lowell, Mike	9	.273	.463	.339	1142	4142	557	1132	1917	455	677	288	4	163	658	401	43	590	23	9	104
Mabry, John	13	.265	.407	.323	1294	3375	378	894	1373	283	611	182	6	95	441	279	22	707	7	9	87
Matheny, Mike	13	.239	.344	.293	1305	3877	353	925	1334	266	659	190	9	67	443	266	45	795	8	14	97
Millar, Kevin	9	.287	.472	.366	1064	3430	483	983	1620	371	612	231	14	126	535	386	67	602	6	7	91
Mora, Melvin	8	.280	.441	.359	1015	3549	562	993	1565	323	670	193	11	119	483	369	88	663	76	40	49
Mueller, Bill	11	.291	.425	.373	1216	4223	663	1229	1793	372	857	265	22	85	493	543	35	571	20	18	105
Nevin, Phil	12	.270	.472	.343	1217	4188	584	1131	1976	423	708	209	6	208	743	449	30	1019	18	5	112
Ordonez, Magglio	10	.305	.513	.362	1238	4705	744	1436	2414	524	912	289	16	219	853	408	39	553	83	42	152
Ortiz, David	10	.283	.550	.374	1043	3666	622	1037	2015	505	532	263	11	231	763	540	19	796	6	2	81
Palmeiro, Orlando	12	.276	.354	.352	1105	2232	294	616	790	136	480	110	14	12	220	249	24	222	37	27	33
Perez, Neifi	11	.268	.376	.298	1370	5063	635	1359	1905	359	1000	235	61	63	483	227	7	495	57	45	90
Piazza, Mike	15	.309	.551	.379	1829	6602	1015	2042	3640	753	1289	327	7	419	1291	741	30	1052	17	20	220
Pierre, Juan	7	.303	.377	.350	1007	4110	607	1244	1551	222	1022	149	61	12	287	258	50	249	325	116	49
Polanco, Placido	9	.300	.409	.344	1029	3726	549	1117	1524	261	856	178	20	63	382	206	54	272	50	24	112
Posada, Jorge	12	.270	.472	.375	1288	4308	653	1163	2033	467	696	262	7	198	771	692	55	1041	14	18	125
Ramirez, Aramis	9	.279	.493	.332	1047	3897	517	1089	1923	431	658	224	11	196	669	279	53	596	11	11	114
Ramirez, Manny	14	.314	.600	.411	1817	6575	1258	2066	3946	924	1142	438	16	470	1516	1054	78	1451	34	31	192
Randa, Joe	12	.284	.426	.339	1522	5428	697	1543	2311	486	1057	327	36	123	739	432	55	738	42	26	139
Renteria, Edgar	11	.288	.402	.346	1598	6143	934	1770	2471	468	1302	340	23	105	705	551	28	864	263	99	176
Rodriguez, Alex	13	.305	.573	.386	1746	6767	1358	2067	3875	854	1213	364	26	464	1347	820	106	1404	241	60	158
Rodriguez, Ivan	16	.304	.483	.342	2023	7745	1159	2354	3742	792	1562	473	42	277	1119	437	51	1125	112	56	255
Rolen, Scott	11	.285	.515	.375	1393	5106	899	1454	2629	639	815	356	30	253	954	681	90	1041	99	39	100
Salmon, Tim	14	.282	.498	.385	1672	5934	986	1674	2958	662	1012	339	24	299	1016	970	67	1360	48	42	98
Sanders, Reggie	16	.266	.487	.342	1753	6168	1025	1643	3006	697	946	334	60	303	972	663	70	1599	304	114	119
Sexson, Richie	10	.269	.526	.350	1150	4214	661	1135	2218	520	615	230	17	273	844	494	47	1127	12	13	123
Sheffield, Gary	19	.297	.525	.398	2229	8037	1433	2390	4221	897	1493	418	24	455	1501	1293	119	971	220	96	196
Sierra, Ruben	20	.268	.450	.315	2186	8044	1084	2152	3616	793	1359	428	59	306	1322	610	7	1239	142	52	193
Snow, J.T.	15	.268	.427	.357	1715	5641	798	1509	2407	501	1008	293	19	189	877	760	64	1142	20	23	135
Spiezio, Scott	11	.255	.421	.327	1192	3676	486	936	1546	353	583	211	27	115	518	385	31	554	33	22	72
Stairs, Matt	14	.265	.483	.358	1416	4243	633	1125	2050	474	651	243	11	220	751	588	47	881	25	22	90
Stewart, Shannon	12	.299	.439	.364	1188	4823	760	1444	2115	429	1015	289	38	102	518	435	70	606	182	67	92
Sweeney, Mark	12	.260	.401	.352	1014	1615	198	420	647	138	282	89	9	40	232	230	9	368	14	9	35

BATTERS – 1,000 OR MORE GAMES - ACTIVE IN 2006

(OBA = On-Base Average)

XBH = Extra-Base Hits)

PLAYER	YR	BA	SLG	OBA	G	AB	R	H	TB	XBH	1B	2B	3B	HR	RBI	BB	HBP	SO	SB	CS	GDP
Sweeney, Mike	12	.302	.497	.373	1208	4404	674	1329	2189	476	853	282	4	190	799	467	61	526	50	25	121
Tejada, Miguel	10	.286	.480	.342	1422	5539	869	1584	2658	576	1008	318	18	240	952	421	80	777	64	24	162
Thomas, Frank	17	.305	.566	.424	2096	7422	1404	2262	4203	956	1306	458	11	487	1579	1547	77	1246	32	23	203
Thome, Jim	16	.282	.565	.409	1881	6409	1259	1806	3620	846	960	350	24	472	1302	1364	56	1909	18	19	110
Tucker, Michael	12	.256	.423	.339	1417	4083	625	1047	1728	382	665	208	49	125	528	490	39	960	114	56	67
Valentin, Jose	15	.243	.450	.322	1627	5373	854	1308	2417	577	731	291	40	246	798	615	29	1266	134	55	61
Varitek, Jason	10	.269	.450	.348	1068	3543	479	952	1596	372	580	231	10	131	543	406	40	780	24	15	97
Vidro, Jose	10	.301	.459	.363	1186	4257	614	1280	1953	431	849	304	12	115	550	397	36	463	21	15	119
Vizcaino, Jose	18	.270	.346	.318	1820	5379	633	1453	1859	287	1166	204	47	36	480	378	16	729	74	62	105
Vizquel, Omar	18	.276	.360	.342	2443	8966	1283	2472	3225	539	1933	398	68	73	818	897	46	903	366	146	174
Walker, Todd	11	.289	.437	.349	1270	4506	642	1303	1967	420	883	283	30	107	541	419	16	567	66	37	100
White, Rondell	14	.286	.465	.339	1436	5248	748	1500	2442	520	980	292	34	194	748	354	85	906	94	47	141
Williams, Bernie	16	.297	.477	.381	2076	7869	1366	2336	3756	791	1545	449	55	287	1257	1069	39	1212	147	87	223
Wilson, Preston	9	.264	.471	.330	1083	3939	567	1041	1855	422	619	218	16	188	663	346	51	1068	122	54	127
Winn, Randy	9	.284	.421	.343	1142	4252	618	1208	1792	375	833	246	49	80	457	355	44	707	153	77	69
Womack, Tony	13	.273	.356	.317	1303	4963	739	1353	1769	285	1068	190	59	36	368	308	28	649	363	74	53
Young, Dmitri	11	.289	.476	.346	1178	4152	576	1200	1975	439	761	257	28	154	599	335	43	769	25	22	129
Young, Eric	15	.283	.390	.359	1730	6119	996	1731	2387	452	1279	327	46	79	543	660	89	462	465	168	135

PITCHERS – 100 OR MORE WINS – ACTIVE IN 2006

PLAYER	YR	ERA	W	L	PCT	G	GS	GF	SV	SHO	INN	H	AB	BFP	R	ER	HR	BB	HBP	SO	WP	BK
Astacio, Pedro	15	4.67	129	124	.510	392	343	11	0	12	2196.2	2292	8470	9472	1213	1140	291	726	111	1664	59	18
Carpenter, Chris	9	4.09	100	68	.595	245	228	6	0	12	1516.0	1551	5832	6426	758	689	174	463	56	1161	44	2
Clemens, Roger	23	3.10	348	178	.662	691	690	0	0	46	4817.2	4086	17896	19820	1833	1661	354	1549	154	4604	136	20
Colon, Bartolo	10	3.98	140	87	.617	290	288	0	0	8	1876.0	1823	7129	7926	892	829	223	650	35	1466	37	5
Erickson, Scott	15	4.59	142	136	.511	389	364	10	0	17	2360.2	2586	9178	10284	1306	1203	228	865	103	1252	68	3
Fassero, Jeff	16	4.11	121	124	.494	752	242	146	25	2	2033.1	2083	7879	8810	1042	929	214	724	37	1643	86	8
Garcia, Freddy	8	4.01	116	71	.620	252	251	0	0	4	1643.2	1584	6292	6952	775	732	191	529	51	1202	69	7
Glavine, Tom	20	3.46	290	191	.603	635	635	0	0	24	4149.2	4012	15683	17468	1758	1596	322	1399	61	2481	63	5
Gordon, Tom	18	3.97	130	119	.522	809	203	328	150	4	2036.2	1815	7634	8739	972	885	166	944	36	1870	105	13
Hampton, Mike	13	3.97	138	101	.577	375	321	9	1	9	2074.0	2156	7958	8983	1041	916	177	826	46	1272	74	9
Hernandez, Livan	11	4.18	123	117	.513	318	317	0	0	7	2166.2	2302	8359	9347	1090	1007	237	751	59	1456	28	3
Hudson, Tim	8	3.53	119	60	.665	247	247	0	0	2	1651.0	1563	6244	6926	717	648	139	526	65	1155	50	3
Johnson, Randy	19	3.22	280	147	.656	556	546	5	2	37	3798.2	3013	13868	15644	1530	1357	361	1409	178	4544	101	31
Lieber, Jon	12	4.26	126	115	.523	361	314	10	1	4	2073.1	2238	8153	8754	1090	981	268	394	44	1472	29	12
Loaiza, Esteban	12	4.62	123	108	.532	360	323	11	0	6	2034.2	2289	8029	8826	1129	1044	245	579	73	1352	32	8
Lowe, Derek	10	3.81	100	82	.549	466	189	156	85	3	1530.0	1527	5886	6470	741	647	122	442	60	981	34	5
Maddux, Greg	21	3.07	333	203	.621	677	673	3	0	35	4616.1	4301	17363	18787	1784	1574	318	944	125	3169	63	26
Martinez, Pedro	15	2.81	206	92	.691	442	375	23	3	17	2645.2	2013	9631	10582	907	825	213	701	129	2998	59	5
Millwood, Kevin	10	3.85	123	87	.586	292	284	3	0	5	1774.1	1693	6773	7458	826	760	181	527	40	1437	39	2
Morris, Matt	9	3.79	111	77	.590	270	239	12	4	8	1585.0	1586	6044	6667	735	667	151	441	63	1103	24	9
Moyer, Jamie	20	4.17	216	166	.565	571	518	14	0	10	3351.0	3455	12970	14235	1678	1551	414	946	112	1992	51	11
Mulder, Mark	7	4.11	103	57	.644	199	199	0	0	10	1301.1	1326	4962	5491	638	594	137	403	48	829	46	1
Mulholland, Terry	20	4.41	124	142	.466	685	332	128	5	10	2575.2	2833	10092	11060	1396	1262	293	681	70	1325	64	3
Mussina, Mike	16	3.63	239	134	.641	475	475	0	0	23	3210.1	3058	12200	13118	1384	1296	345	719	48	2572	66	1
Ortiz, Russ	9	4.39	108	79	.578	270	245	8	0	3	1519.2	1456	5727	6671	807	741	167	787	35	1094	53	2
Park, Chan Ho	13	4.37	113	87	.565	323	274	9	0	3	1746.2	1620	6553	7642	914	848	202	820	126	1507	63	13
Pettitte, Andy	12	3.81	186	104	.641	367	359	3	0	4	2312.1	2398	8936	9820	1090	980	195	721	36	1703	48	10
Radke, Brad	12	4.22	148	139	.516	378	377	0	0	10	2451.0	2643	9592	10244	1233	1150	326	445	62	1467	28	3
Rogers, Kenny	18	4.19	207	139	.598	721	433	133	28	3	3066.0	3180	11860	13223	1585	1427	309	1079	117	1850	74	22
Schilling, Curt	19	3.44	207	138	.600	545	412	81	22	19	3110.0	2833	11719	12651	1250	1188	326	688	50	3015	72	8
Schmidt, Jason	12	3.91	127	90	.585	313	304	1	0	9	1953.0	1798	7375	8324	926	849	179	766	48	1728	91	11
Sele, Aaron	14	4.59	145	110	.569	370	352	5	0	16	2099.1	2335	8262	9284	1174	1070	220	777	110	1378	54	2
Smoltz, John	18	3.27	193	137	.585	670	429	204	154	16	3161.1	2029	11765	12957	1250	1150	257	937	50	2778	135	16
Suppan, Jeff	12	4.60	106	101	.512	317	301	6	0	5	1864.2	2029	7301	8103	1042	954	247	612	66	1048	63	5
Trachsel, Steve	14	4.28	134	143	.484	381	380	0	0	7	2303.1	2358	8839	9903	1197	1096	319	840	62	1519	55	13
Vazquez, Javier	9	4.34	100	105	.488	290	288	1	0	6	1845.2	1859	7141	7808	961	891	246	493	49	1602	50	4
Wakefield, Tim	14	4.30	151	134	.530	339	339	62	22	2	2432.0	2354	9308	10526	1329	1162	315	948	146	1680	82	6
Wells, David	20	4.07	230	148	.608	631	460	65	13	12	3281.2	3434	12784	13719	1605	1483	385	677	80	2219	100	17
Williams, Woody	14	4.09	124	101	.551	391	299	34	0	2	2028.1	2001	7784	8642	982	921	274	658	60	1379	57	4
Zito, Barry	7	3.55	102	63	.618	222	222	0	0	4	1430.1	1228	5289	5998	620	564	148	560	65	1096	26	5

GENERAL

INDIVIDUAL BATTING

INDIVIDUAL FIELDING

INDIVIDUAL PITCHING

CHAMPIONSHIP SERIES
Page

DIVISION SERIES
Page

ALL-STAR GAME
Page